Families and the Law

Cases and Commentary

Second Edition

Mary Jane Mossman
Osgoode Hall Law School

Natasha Bakht
University of Ottawa

Vanessa Gruben
University of Ottawa

Karen Pearlston
University of New Brunswick

Captus Press

Families and the Law: Cases and Commentary, Second edition

© 2015 Mary Jane Mossman, Natasha Bakht, Vanessa Gruben, Karen Pearlston, and Captus Press Inc.

Captus Press Inc.
Mail: Units 14 & 15
      1600 Steeles Avenue West
      Concord, Ontario
      Canada L4K 4M2
Telephone: (416) 736–5537
Fax: (416) 736–5793
Email: info@captus.com
Internet: http://www.captus.com

Library and Archives Canada Cataloguing in Publication
Mossman, Mary Jane, author
        Families and the law : cases and commentary / Mary Jane Mossman, Natasha Bakht, Vanessa Gruben, Karen Pearlston. -- Second edition.

First published under title: Families and the law in Canada. Toronto :
        Emond Montgomery Publications, 2004.

Includes bibliographical references and index.
ISBN 978-1-55322-333-7

        1. Domestic relations--Canada--Cases. 2. Domestic relations--Ontario--Cases. I. Bakht, Natasha, author II. Gruben, Vanessa, author III. Pearlston, Karen, author IV. Title.

KE539.M68 2015   346.7101'5   C2015-904722-6
KF505.ZA2M68 2015

Canadä

0 9 8 7 6 5 4 3 2 1
Printed in Canada

Contents (Abridged)

Contents

PART 1
LEGAL REGULATION OF FAMILY FORMATION

**PART 2
LEGAL REGULATION OF "INTACT" FAMILIES:
CARE AND PROTECTION**

Chapter 4   Families in the Shadow of the State:

PART 3
LEGAL REGULATION OF FAMILY DISSOLUTION

Preface to the Second Edition

We are all pleased to present this new Second Edition of *Families and the Law*.

As with the First Captus Edition, the book focuses on "families" and "law," and the connections, intersections and challenges created by this relationship. The organization of the book remains the same as in the First Captus Edition, exploring how "families" experience law in relation to family formation, interventions in intact families, and family dissolution. We have also tried to take account of the myriad issues of diversity among families and the impact of claims to legal equality by some families and family members in the law's evolution. As in earlier editions, the book continues to include references to critical and interdisciplinary literature and provides additional references and resources for instructors and students.

This Second Edition includes many updated cases, statutory provisions and other relevant family law material, generally as of 31 March 2015. In addition to updating, however, there are some significant revisions:

- **Chapter One** now provides updated statistics about families in Canada.
- **Chapter Two** includes an update on issues relating to forced marriage and new material about the legal recognition and regulation of transgender persons.
- **Chapter Three** has been reorganized and updated in relation to issues about biological parenthood and assisted reproduction.
- **Chapter Four** includes a new sub-section concerning child protection and Aboriginal children, and some expanded treatment of family violence, especially at family dissolution.
- **Chapter Five** has been updated with respect to issues about marriage contracts and separation agreements, including contracts negotiated in religious contexts.

- **Chapter Six** provides a substantial revision of SCC *Charter* challenges for cohabiting couples, as well as new developments in relation to pensions and other property for married couples, and the recent evolution of remedies for cohabiting couples at separation.
- **Chapter Seven** includes a reorganization of material regarding contracts and spousal support in relation to post-*Miglin* developments, as well as issues regarding post-separation changes pursuant to support in federal and provincial statutes.
- **Chapter Eight** includes new developments in relation to issues about custody and access, as well as more substantive treatment of child support issues.

With all the updated materials, as well as reorganization and additional substantive material, we are pleased to suggest that this book provides a highly comprehensive treatment of "families" and "law," as well as an informed and critical context for understanding both the history and the more contemporary and future challenges for these relationships.

ACKNOWLEDGEMENTS

First of all, Mary Jane Mossman acknowledges with warmest appreciation the willingness of her three co-authors, Natasha Bakht and Vanessa Gruben at the University of Ottawa and Karen Pearlston at the University of New Brunswick, to share responsibility for this Second Edition. It is no exaggeration to say that the new edition would not have been possible without their excellent and kind assistance, in particular:

- Natasha Bakht is responsible for Chapters Five and Eight.
- Vanessa Gruben is responsible for Chapters One and Three.
- Mary Jane Mossman is responsible for Chapters Four and Six.
- Karen Pearlston is responsible for Chapters Two and Seven.

We have all enjoyed this collaboration and cooperation and we will look forward to continuing this project in future.

We also want to thank our student research assistants:

- At Osgoode Hall Law School: Craig Mazerolle and Deanne Sowter, as well as Annie Chu and Michael Ashley
- At the University of Ottawa: Jordan Palmer and Michelle Thomarat
- At the University of New Brunswick: Leah Ferguson (With thanks also to Amber Carroll and the Fredericton Gender Minorities Group)

Updated materials are generally provided as of 31 March 2015, but with a few significant changes after this date.

Mary Jane Mossman, Natasha Bakht,
Vanessa Gruben, and Karen Pearlston
30 June 2015

Preface to First Captus Edition

"FAMILIES" AND "LAW": A NEW APPROACH

The title of this book, *Families and the Law*, reflects its focus on connections between "families" and "law."

To understand why this book uses this approach, a brief history of "family law" is necessary. Indeed, the idea of a subject called "family law" is quite recent, particularly in the common law world. Although civil law codes have often focused on family relationships (mainly in relation to marriage), the common law traditionally regarded the family as a "private" institution within society. For example, even marriage was not legally regulated by statute in England until the 18th century. Moreover, in other respects, the common law regarded legal regulation in the family as inappropriate except in the most egregious circumstances, leaving most decisions in the private and "patriarchal" family to the sole authority of the husband/father.

By the latter part of the 19th century, new statutory reforms about divorce, mothers' rights to physical (but not legal) custody of younger children, and state involvement in protecting children from harm revealed a growing societal acceptance of greater legal intervention in the family. In the early 20th century, however, this law appeared somewhat scattered among issues about "matrimonial causes" and "alimony," as well as child protection and child custody, and even newer statutory reforms regarding adoption. As divorce became more prevalent in the second half of the 20th century, eventually resulting in Canada's first federal *Divorce Act* in 1968, and new statutory provisions regarding property sharing, spousal support, and custody and access were enacted, a new conception of "family law" began to emerge, although it still tended to focus primarily on legal principles concerning either marriage or divorce and corollary relief.

However, these new legal developments prompted some law teachers in Canada and other common law jurisdictions in the 1960s to recognize the emergence of family law, even though this topic had long been recognized, at least to some extent, in the civil law of Québec. Moreover, law reformers in common law Canada in the 1970s consciously engaged in comparative studies in relation to Québec "family law" arrangements (for example, see Law Reform Commission of Canada, *Studies on Family Property Law* (Ottawa: Information Canada 1975); and Ontario Law Reform Commission, *Report on Family Law* (Toronto: Ministry of the Attorney General 1975); and others). And these reform projects and comparative studies have continued apace in relation to family law issues (for example, see Royal Commission on New Reproductive Technologies, *Proceed with Care* (Ottawa: Queen's Printer 1993); and Law Commission of Canada, *Beyond Conjugality: Recognizing and Supporting Close Personal Adult Relationships* (Ottawa: Law Commission of Canada 2001)).

In addition to these law reform efforts, however, a more important development has been an increasing social recognition of "families," whether or not they conform to traditional legal categories: for example, couples cohabiting with their children outside of marriage, same-sex couples and their children, mothers without adult partners who have biological or adopted children, etc. To some extent, these new "families" may reflect personal choices and new aspirations about family life, and some have been designed quite consciously "outside" the law. By contrast, however, some members of these "families" increasingly wanted to challenge their exclusion from legal recognition and its benefits in a variety of contexts, particularly as a result of the *Charter*'s equality guarantee. As a result, it now seems that there is a need to define this area of legal study as more than "family law," terminology that seems to privilege the law's definition of a "family."

Accordingly, this book's title reflects a new equality between "families" and "law" and the connections, intersections, and challenges created by this relationship. More specifically, the title of the book and its content reflect how it is organized around the lives and experiences of "families" and their members in different contexts: family formation, interventions in intact family units, and principles and processes for adjusting these relationships at family dissolution. In all these contexts, moreover, it is important to take account of how differences within and among families, in terms of class, gender, ethnicity, national origin, race, religion, sexual orientation, language, dis/ability, etc., may shape the experiences of families and family members in ways that necessitate the careful attention of legislators, judges, lawyers and others who are involved with these relationships between "families" and "law."

Thus, this book consciously focuses on these relationships between "families" and "law" in its presentation of issues and its attention to the goals of both families and law in their resolution. Remembering that this is a book about "families" and "law" is, therefore, important to its content, organization, and critiques.

ACKNOWLEDGMENTS

In my work as a family law teacher, I acknowledge the inspiration of colleagues and students at Osgoode and elsewhere who have shared materials and ideas with me. Osgoode Hall Law School has supported this project through assistance for research funding over a number of years, including the earlier edition published in 2004.

In relation to the work of revising and updating this book, I am especially grateful to Catherine Hayhow for longstanding support, and to recent research assistants at Osgoode: Alison Carr, Nathalie Kalina, Kalen Lumsden, Alison Pengelley, Claudia Schmeing, and Joshua Tong. I am also particularly appreciative of the excellent assistance of reference librarians Daniel Perlin and Sharon Wang, as well as Yemisi Dina, at Osgoode. Elizabeth Archampong, Ph.D. provided excellent help in creating the Table of Cases. Several good friends, especially Professor Karen Pearlston have been encouraging in relation to this revised and updated edition, and I also thank Emond-Montgomery Press for kind co-operation in the transition to this edition, the First Captus Edition. Finally, and especially in relation to this project about families and law, I thank Brian Bucknall and my families for their support.

Copyright Acknowledgment

This book contains extracts from various published materials. All extracts are referenced within the text so that students can easily locate the original source for further study. For extracts that exceed the "fair use" guideline, we have obtained permission from the copyright holders. The author and the publisher would like to thank the copyright holders for granting permission to include their materials in this publication. Below is a list of permission acknowledgment for these excerpts. (Note: Referenced pages may appear out of their original order in this text.)

Susan B Boyd, "Gendering Legal Parenthood: Bio-Genetic Ties, Intentionality and Responsibility" (2007) 25 *Windsor Yearbook of Access to Justice* 63 at 87 and 92. Reprinted with permission of author.

Angela Cameron, Vanessa Gruben, and Fiona Kelly, "De-Anonymising Sperm Donors in Canada: Some Doubts and Directions" (2010) 26:1 *Canadian Journal of Family Law* 95 at 96–97. Reprinted with permission of author and publisher.

Brenda Cossman, "Parenting beyond the Nuclear Family: *Doe v. Alberta*" (2007) 45 *Alberta Law Review* 501 at 504–505. Reprinted with permission of author and publisher.

Brenda Cossman and Bruce Ryder, "What is Marriage-Like Like? The Irrelevance of Conjugality" (2001) 18 *Canadian Family Law Journal* at 296–297, 326. Reprinted with permission of authors and publisher.

Developing Spousal Support Guidelines in Canada: Beginning the Discussion, page 65, <http://www.justice.gc.ca/eng/rp-pr/fl-lf/spousal-epoux/ss-pae/>. Department of Justice Canada, December 2002. Reproduced with the permission of the Department of Justice Canada, 2015.

John Dewar, "Family, Law and Theory" (1996) 16:4 *Oxford Journal of Legal Studies* at 725. By permission of Oxford University Press.

John Dewar, "Family Law and its Discontents" (2000) 14 *International Journal of Law, Policy and the Family* 59 at 59–61, 79, 80. (Footnotes omitted.) By permission of Oxford University Press.

John Eekelaar, "Uncovering Social Obligations: Family Law and the Responsible Citizen" in Mavis Maclean, ed, *Making Law for Families* (Oxford, UK: Hart Publishing, 2000) at 16. © Mavis Mclean, 2000. Reprinted with permission of Hart Publishing, an imprint of Bloomsbury Publishing Plc.

Margrit Eichler, "The Limits of Family Law Reform" (1990–91) 7 *Canadian Family Law Quarterly* 59 at 66–69 and 81–83. Reprinted with permission of author.

Philip Epstein and Lene Madsen, "Joint Custody with a Vengeance: The Emergence of Parallel Parenting Orders" (2004) 22 *Canadian Family Law Quarterly* 1 at 22–23, 27, 31–32. Reprinted with permission of authors.

Ronald S Foster, "*Moge v Moge*: What It Means to Family Law Lawyers" (1993) 43 RFL (3d) 465 at 465. Reprinted with permission of author.

Marie Gordon, " 'Making the Break': Support for Adult Children in 2006" in Martha Shaffer, ed, *Contemporary Issues in Family Law* (Toronto: Thomson Carswell, 2007) at 320. (Footnotes omitted.) Reproduced by permission of Carswell, a division of Thomson Reuters Canada Limited.

Peter Hogg, *Constitutional Law of Canada*, Fifth Edition Supplemented Vol. I (Toronto: Carswell, 2007) at s. 27.3(a). (Footnotes omitted.) Reproduced by permission of Carswell, a division of Thomson Reuters Canada Limited.

Winnifred Holland, "Intimate Relationships in the New Millennium: The Assimilation of Marriage and Cohabitation?" (2000) 17 *Canadian Journal of Family Law* 114 at 151–152, 158, 166, 167. Reprinted with permission of author and publisher.

Berend Hovius, "Property Rights for Common-Law Partners" in Martha Shaffer, ed, *Contemporary Issues in Family Law* (Toronto: Thomson Carswell, 2007) 115 at 116–117. (Footnotes omitted.) Reproduced by permission of Carswell, a division of Thomson Reuters Canada Limited.

Martha Shaffer, "Domestic Contracts, Part II: The Supreme Court's Decision in *Hartshorne v Hartshorne*" (2004) 20 *Canadian Journal of Family Law* at 261 (paras. 32–34). Reprinted with permission of author and publisher.

Martha Shaffer, "Joint Custody since *Kaplanis* and *Ladisa*: A Review of Recent Ontario Case Law" in Martha Shaffer, ed, *Contemporary Issues in Family Law* (Toronto: Thomson Carswell, 2007) 431 at 464–465, 470. (Footnotes omitted.) Reproduced by permission of Carswell, a division of Thomson Reuters Canada Limited.

Anthony F Sheppard, "*Rawluk v. Rawluk*: What Are the Limits of the Remedial Constructive Trust?" (1990) 9 *Canadian Journal of Family Law* 152 at 161–162, 164. Reprinted with permission of author and publisher.

Colleen Sheppard, "Uncomfortable Victories and Unanswered Questions: Lessons from *Moge*" (1995) 12 *Canadian Journal of Family Law* 283 at 328–329. Reprinted with permission of author and publisher.

Elizabeth B Silva and Carol Smart, "The 'New' Practices and Politics of Family Life" in Elizabeth B Silva and Carol Smart, ed, *The New Family?* (London: Sage Publications, 1999) 1 at 9. Reprinted with permission of authors and publisher.

Judge Murray Sinclair, Nicholas Bala, Heino Lilles, and Cindy Blackstock, "Aboriginal Child Welfare" in Nicholas Bala, Michael Zapf, James Williams, Robin Vogl, and Joseph Hornick, eds, *Canadian Child Welfare Law: Children, Families and the State*, 2nd ed (Scarborough, ON: Thompson Educational Publishing, 2004) at 213 and 243. Reprinted with permission of publisher.

Carol Smart, *The Ties That Bind: Law, Marriage, and the Reproduction of Patriarchal Relations* (London: Routledge & Kegan Paul, 1984) at 190–191. Copyright © 1984 and Routledge & Kegan Paul. Reproduced by permission of Taylor & Francis Books UK.

Carol Smart, "The 'New' Parenthood: Fathers and Mothers After Divorce" in Elizabeth B Silva and Carol Smart, eds, *The New Family?* (London: Sage Publications, 1999) at 113. Reprinted with permission of authors and publisher.

Carol Smart, "Stories of Family Life: Cohabitation, Marriage, and Social Change" (2000) 17 *Canadian Journal of Family Law* at 50. Reprinted with permission of author and publisher.

Carol Smart, Bren Neale, and Amanda Wade, *The Changing Experience of Childhood: Families and Divorce* (Cambridge: Polity Press, 2001) at 19, 37–38, 121–122, 167, 173. Reprinted with permission of publisher.

Special Joint Committee on Custody and Access, *For the Sake of the Children* (Ottawa: Parliament of Canada, 1998) at 31–33, 47–51. Reprinted with permission of House of Commons and Deputy Law Clerk of Senate of Canada.

Katherine Teghtsoonian, "Who Pays for Caring for Children? Public Policy and the Devaluation of Women's Work" in Susan B Boyd, ed, *Challenging the Public/Private Divide: Feminism, Law, and Public Policy* (Toronto: University of Toronto Press, 1997) at 132. Reprinted with permission of the publisher.

David Thompson, "A Consideration of the Mental Capacity Provisions of the Marriage Act in the View of the Charter of Rights and Freedoms and *Webb v. Webb*" (1986) 9 *Canadian Community Law Journal* 101 at 106. Reprinted with permission of author and Windsor Review of Legal and Social Issues.

DA Rollie Thompson, "Who Wants To Avoid the Guidelines? Contracting Out and Around" (2001) 19 *Canadian Family Law Quarterly* 1 at 2–3, 19, 20, 51. Reprinted with permission of author.

DA Rollie Thompson, "Annotation of *Walsh v Bona*" (2003) 32 RFL (5th) 87 at 90. Reprinted with permission of author.

DA Rollie Thompson, "Annotation of *Leonelli-Contino v Contino*" (2005) 19 RFL (6th) 272. Reprinted with permission of author.

DA Rollie Thompson, "Annotation: *Droit de la famille — 091889* and *Droit de la famille — 09668*" (2012) 6 RFL (7th) 1. Reprinted with permission of author.

DA Rollie Thompson, "Annotation: Droit de la famille — 091768" (2013) 21 RFL (7th) 325 at 325–326. Reprinted with permission of author.

George Thomson, "Judging Judiciously in Child Protection Cases" in Rosalie Abella and Claire L'Heureux-Dubé, ed, *Dimensions of Justice* (Toronto: Butterworths, 1983) 213 at 230, 231, 232. (Footnotes omitted.) Reprinted with permission of author.

Hon. Marguerite Trussler, "Managing High Conflict Family Law Cases for the Sake of the Children" (2007) 86 *Canadian Bar Review* 515 at 520–521. Reprinted with permission of author and publisher.

Vanier Institute of the Family, *Families Count: Profiling Canada's Families* (Ottawa: VIF, 2010) at xvi, xi–xiii, xix–xx, 2, 24–25, 42, 50, 64, 66, 68, 76, 80, 104, 106, 116, 139. Reprinted with permission of The Vanier Institute of the Family.

Bruce Ziff, "Recent Developments in Canadian Law: Marriage and Divorce" (1986) 18 *Ottawa Law Review* 121 at 135–136, 140. Reprinted with permission.

Families and Family Law:
An Introduction to This Book

THE CONTEXT FOR FAMILIES AND FAMILY LAW

Once upon a time, things were easy for family lawyers. Their object of study was clearly marked out (marriage, divorce and their consequences), while theoretical debate about the subject was rare or nonexistent. Although it is difficult to locate this Garden of Eden in real time, most family lawyers would share the perception that things have become more complex of late. For one thing, it is no longer obvious where the boundaries of the subject lie. Recent events have shown that marriage is only one of a number of legally significant concepts implicated in the legal regulation of family life, with parenthood and cohabitation increasingly presenting themselves as alternatives. There has been a move away from exploring exclusively the role of law when "things go wrong" (divorce, for example) towards an interest in how law regulates the ongoing family. In addition, and allied to this, there has been an explosion of theoretical interest in law and the family.... (John Dewar, "Family, Law and Theory" (1996) 16:4 Oxford J Leg Stud 725 at 725)

"Things have become more complex"

John Dewar's comment about families and the nature of family law identifies several important ideas for students who are beginning to study the principles of family law. As the comment suggests, many family lawyers agree that family law has become more complex in recent decades, particularly because of the following:

- The "boundaries" of family law, which used to be defined by "marriage," are becoming less clear, as "cohabitation" and "parenthood" increasingly define modern "families."

    Example: Consider the fact that many children are now born to parents who are not married. What is the role of family law for these "families"?

- The scope of family law, which used to focus primarily on legal intervention at divorce or separation, has been enlarged to include more legal regulation of intact families.

    Example: Consider recent developments relating to spousal violence or child sexual abuse. What is the role of family law in relation to these family issues?

- Family lawyers, who once emphasized mainly practical legal issues, have increasingly needed to take into account empirical and inter-disciplinary research and theoretical critiques of families and family law.

    Example: Consider to what extent family lawyers should be expected to take account of social science research relating to children's best interests in custody disputes? Or the impact of governmental policies of privatization in relation to economic issues for families?

In addition to these examples, Dewar's claim that family law has become more complex in recent decades may also reflect the following:

- An increase in social expectations about the use of law to resolve issues within families and among individual family members.

    Example: Consider the current debates about rights to access adoption records and data about sperm donors to determine biological parent–child relationships. What factors should be taken into account in enacting legislative guidelines for such access?

- Changing political views about the respective roles of families and the state to provide for vulnerable individuals, especially children.

    Example: Consider current debates about fathers' obligations to pay support for their children at family breakdown, and whether such payments should determine rights to custody or access. To what extent do these issues reflect current policies designed to reduce the social safety net, thereby increasing individual responsibility for economic security?

- The impact of *Charter* equality values in Canada.

    Example: Consider how ideas about equality for families strengthened claims about same-sex marriage. Are there problems in using equality claims in relation to families and family law? How should ideas about equality affect relationships among individuals who are family members: are they, or should they be, equal?

Family law *in context*

Questions such as those raised above all present challenges for the study of family law, and many of them remain unresolved or at least subject to ongoing debate. While the main focus of this book is family law, the materials explore legal issues about families within a broader social, political, and economic context. In this way, the book attempts to provide a study of family law within a socio-legal context.

As Susan Boyd argued some years ago, lawyers need to address the "larger questions around the impact of law, the role of law in social change ... to take responsibility for their actions, legal and otherwise, in the real world." As for students, they need

> ... to study the efficacy of legal change vis-à-vis the family in light of the wider social context ... [and to be reminded] that what legislation and judges say is not always an accurate description of reality, due to the sometimes false assumptions which our legal system contains about the family and family members. Students can learn to take a critical perspective on policy-oriented legal approaches which ignore the complex nature of social change, of which legal change is only one part. (Susan B Boyd, "Teaching Policy Issues in Family Law" (1989–90) 8 Can J Fam L 11 at 15)

FAMILIES AND FAMILY LAW: SOME INTRODUCTORY POINTS

> We all think we know what a family is, because we were all brought up in families. Even those who spent their childhoods in orphanages found surrogate families that became real to them. And how easily *is* becomes *ought*! We know what family ought to be, especially if ours was broken or conflicted or absent. Every individual's understanding of family is shaped by his or her past. (Eric Sager, "Family and Social Memory: Why History Matters" in Vanier Institute of the Family, *Families Count: Profiling Canada's Families* (Ottawa: VIF, 2010) xvi at xvi)

"Experiences" of family life and the study of family law

Unlike some areas of law, students bring a good deal of experience (even "expertise") to the study of family law because almost everyone has some experience of "family." This experience is often very helpful in thinking through family law problems. At the same time, it is very important to be able to understand that our own individual experiences as members of families are not universal — they are just our individual experience within our own families. More concretely, this suggestion means that we need to see how our experiences may have shaped our values, our aspirations, and our expectations about how families *should* live their lives. In doing so, we may then be able to appreciate how different experiences may shape different values, aspirations and expectations on the part of other individuals and their families. In this way, Tolstoy's famous comment in *Anna Karenina* — about how all happy families are much the same, while each unhappy family is quite distinctive — is particularly relevant to family law, since family law necessarily focuses much more often on unhappy families and their members. As a result, students need to bring their own experiences and "expertise" to the study of family law, but at the same time, to recognize that there are other experiences that may shape families and their legal needs. Sometimes, the need to take account of different experiences within families creates "hard questions" in family law.

"Facts" in the context of family law

In addition, facts are especially important in family law. Particularly because legal principles often require lawyers and judges to inquire into private matters and to make legal judgments about the character and/or capacity of individual family members and their needs, litigants in family law cases may have to disclose things in public that are highly embarrassing — for many different reasons. Thus, in reading the cases, it is always important to keep in mind three aspects of family law cases:

1. For some of these litigants, the issues were so important that they were willing to sacrifice their own privacy (and that of their families) in order to engage in litigation; and even when it seems difficult to believe their claims, or when their claims reflect different cultures or religious beliefs, there is a need for respect even if we disagree with them on the merits. Family law cases are not soap operas!

2. Family law, as law, must be selective with respect to facts, so that only facts that are relevant to legal principles are generally reported. Sometimes, it is useful to wonder about the stories that are *not* told in family law cases, either because some family members' voices are excluded from the cases or because lawyers did not hear what their clients (really) were trying to say. Sometimes, such questioning may result in family law reform.

3. Both "families" and families "in law" exist, although their definitions are not always congruent. This lack of congruence can appear problematic for people who form "families" that are not legally recognized, in terms of rights or responsibilities among "family" members; but it may also prove advantageous for people who wish to determine the rights and responsibilities of their private relationships without legal interference. In this way, the relationships between "Law's families" and "Life's families" may present both advantages and disadvantages for individuals within families, and notably, sometimes there are advantages for some and not for others within the same "family." Moreover, as will become apparent, this issue is complicated by the absence of a definition of "family"

in Canadian family law. That is, while the law defines a number of different kinds of status for individuals within families, such as "parent" or "child" or "spouse," there is no definition of "family."

FAMILIES AND FAMILY LAW: SOME INFORMATION ABOUT THIS BOOK

Organization

This book begins with an Introduction that provides some data about families and themes about family law as a foundation for the family law issues addressed in the book.

The book is then divided into three Parts, which focus on the following family law issues:

- the formation of families (marriage and cohabitation; and the creation of parent–child relationships by birth, adoption and assisted reproduction);
- legal regulation of intact families (with brief discussions of child care and protection, family violence, and elder abuse); and
- family dissolution (divorce and separation and forms of corollary relief, including issues about property, custody and access of children, and spousal and child support).

There is a brief Epilogue which emphasizes the need for *law* in achieving goals of family *justice*.

Scope

Most family law teachers in Canada focus primarily on one provincial jurisdiction, and this book's primary focus is Ontario. However, the book also aims to take account of interesting or useful developments in other parts of Canada in relation to family law, so that its scope includes both a primary focus as well as some attention to the larger family law picture in Canada and elsewhere.

There are three reasons for this approach:

1. Many students will study law in one jurisdiction and then decide to practise law in a different part of Canada. This book's effort to explore some different kinds of approaches to family law problems in different provincial and territorial jurisdictions may assist such students to become familiar with the regime of a new jurisdiction more readily.

2. Because parts of family law in Canada fall within the constitutional jurisdiction of the provinces, it is possible to explore how some provincial jurisdictions have embarked on "new" ways of dealing with "old" family law problems, and to compare the effectiveness of different kinds of legal solutions to similar problems in different parts

of Canada (including Québec), as well as in jurisdictions outside Canada with similar legal traditions.

3. The constitutional assignment of marriage and divorce to the federal jurisdiction in Canada means that there is also national legislation on some family law issues. Moreover, because the Supreme Court of Canada has been actively involved in recent years in defining "national" principles for some aspects of family law, it is possible to see the emergence of a national family law in Canada in relation to some issues.

The statutory framework

This casebook makes note of many statutory provisions, including both federal and provincial legislative regimes. Because of the rate of statutory change in family law across Canada, however, it will always be important to check and update statutory references in the book.

A problem-solving approach

This book tries to provide opportunities for student learning through problem solving in relation to issues in family law, and to support learning with examples from additional cases and references to comparative statutory provisions, critiques from family law and interdisciplinary scholars, reform suggestions and references to further reading.

Family law resources

- Case reports
  Family law cases in Canada (including those decided by the Supreme Court of Canada) are reported in a variety of law reports in Canada. A very good source is the *Reports of Family Law* (RFL), which sometimes includes case comments and short review articles, as well as reports of family law cases.

- Journals
  Developments in Canadian family law are discussed in articles and short notes, reviews and comments in two specialized family law journals: the *Canadian Journal of Family Law* (Can J Fam L) and the *Canadian Family Law Quarterly* (Can Fam LQ). There are family law journals in other jurisdictions as well: a useful resource is the *International Journal of Law, Policy and the Family* (Intl JL Pol'y & Fam).

- Family law services
  Services (often in loose leaf or digital format) are provided to practitioners by several law publishers, and may contain useful overviews and updates for family law developments across Canada.

- elaws from online jurisdictions, such as Department of Justice Canada <www.justice.gc.ca> and Justice Ontario <http://www.attorneygeneral. jus.gov.on.ca/english/justice-ont/default.asp> provide current family law resources.

Additional Resources

Alison Diduck, *Law's Families* (London: Lexis Nexis, 2003).

Alison Diduck & Felicity Kaganas, *Family Law, Gender and the State: Text, Cases and Materials*, 3rd ed (Oxford and Portland, OR: Hart Publishing, 2012).

Mary Ann Glendon, *The Transformation of Family Law: State, Law, and Family in the United States and Western Europe* (Chicago and London: University of Chicago Press, 1989).

Berend Hovius & Mary-Jo Maur, *Hovius on Family Law*, 8th ed (Toronto: Carswell, 2013).

James McLeod and Alfred Mamo, *Annual Review of Family Law* (Toronto: Carswell, 2009).

Katherine O'Donovan, *Family Law Matters* (London: Pluto Press, 1993).

Martha Shaffer, ed, *Contemporary Issues in Family Law* (Toronto: Thomson Carswell, 2007).

1

Families and Family Law:
Contexts and Themes

I.
INTRODUCING FAMILIES AND FAMILY LAW

Canada's liberal ideology may ... have placed limits on family law and policy. Our common law gave priority to property as the pre-eminent legal relationship, and to the individual as the primary legal entity. In contrast to [some European jurisdictions], the common law has given less emphasis to the family as a juridical entity with a collective interest that might take priority over the interests of individual family members. (Eric Sager, "Family and Social Memory: Why History Matters" in Vanier Institute of the Family, *Families Count: Profiling Canada's Families* (Ottawa: VIF, 2010) xvi at xix–xx)

This chapter explores the context for family law in Canada, a project that is complicated by the absence of legal definitions of "family" in family law. Unlike many other areas of law, "families" may exist without the need for law and legal definition: we all know what families are! However, the relationships between families and law are both empirically and theoretically complex and diverse. In this context, this chapter provides some basic data about families, explores some initial ideas about legal regulation of families, and introduces some of the themes in family law.

Organization of this chapter

The chapter begins with an overview of recent data about Canadian families, focusing particularly on current trends and recent changes in family forms and functions. This information is intended to provide a foundation for later discussions of family law and policy — and to ground legal principles in "real life."

The chapter then explores how law is involved in regulating families and family life. In particular, this section provides some examples of how law may sometimes fail to recognize some families; and on the other hand, how law may sometimes intervene to regulate "private" family decisions. These examples demonstrate some of the challenges and underlying values relating to the legal regulation of families.

Finally, the chapter examines some themes that are significant in the family law context:

- Equality: Ideas about equality within and among families, particularly as a result of the *Charter of Rights and Freedoms*;

- Autonomy and protection and the respective responsibilities of individuals, families and the state: Ideas about autonomy and the need for protection for vulnerable family members; and the role of individuals, families and the state in responding to need and dependency; and

- Access to justice: Ideas about access to justice in family law, including the constitutional context, the use of rules and discretion, and some family law process issues.

II.
"FAMILIES" IN CONTEXT

Based on detailed Census estimates for 2006, approximately 85% of Canadians (26.7 million people) lived in private households with someone to whom they are related. Of this group, the vast majority (87%) lived in "census families" (defined as husbands and wives or common-law partners with or without never-married children, and lone-parent families with their never-married children). The remaining 13% of those living in families (almost 3.4 million Canadians) lived with other relatives or in multi-family households. ("Canada's People, Canada's Families" in Vanier Institute of the Family, *Families Count* (Ottawa: VIF, 2010) 2 at 2)

DEFINING "FAMILIES": THE CENSUS DEFINITION AND "FUNCTIONAL" AND "FAMILIAL" APPROACHES

As noted in the Introduction, Canadian statute law tends to define family relationships, such as "spouse," "parent," or "child." Sometimes these definitions easily correspond to general notions of "families," but not always. Moreover, in the context of evolving ideas about families and family relationships, it is often important to be precise in using the term "families." In the legal context, three kinds of approaches may be important:

1. The census definition: This "official" census definition of "families" (noted in the quotation above) is important because census data is

used by policy makers to understand changing conditions in Canadian families and to design governmental programs, including specialized services or benefits for families, accordingly. The census definition is used more often by legislatures than by courts.

2. The functional definition: Another important way of thinking about families focuses on what families *do*, an approach which takes account of the *functions* of families (sometimes referred to as *functionalism*). This approach may be used by both legislatures and by courts.

3. The idea of "familialism": This concept, which has been subjected to a good deal of theoretical analysis and critique, generally refers to *ideals* about families, that is, how families *should* look or behave or work together. In practice, this concept may be used by courts to define some households as families, even when their members do not think of themselves as such — or it may be used to preclude some households from being regarded as families even when their members wish to be so defined. This approach may also be seen in legislative initiatives and in the decisions of courts.

In some ways, "familialism" and "functionalism" tend to reflect tensions between aspirational ideals and actual realities for families. For example, consider the following excerpt, in which the Vanier Institute of the Family focuses on how families provide meaning for individuals' lives, while also taking account of the functions that families may perform in our communities. In reading this excerpt, try to identify the "functional" and "familial" aspects of its assessment of families. Consider also how the Vanier Institute's approach differs from the census definition in Canada.

"Why Families Count"
Families Count (2010) xi

Vanier Institute of the Family

... We see around us men and women who are married to one another and we recognize them as a family whether or not they intend to have children. We see men and women raising children on their own without a partner. We see unmarried couples living together, with and without children, in committed and intimate relationships, sharing their lives, providing for and caring for one another. We see gay and lesbian couples caring for each other and raising children together. We see adult children living with parents or siblings. We see young couples just beginning their lives as families, parents with pre-schoolers and adolescents, and empty nesters whose children have gone on to establish their own households and families. We see families that draw upon a wide variety of ethnic, cultural, linguistic and religious traditions. And, we see families that go about the daily business of family living in different ways on farms and in cities, with one, two and sometimes three or more income earners.

The science of public opinion polling tells us that most Canadians today would agree there is no such thing as a "typical" family; these same

Canadians would also say that few things matter more to them than the well-being of their families.... Within families, we encounter the opportunity and responsibility to act not just as isolated individuals but as spouses and lovers, mothers and fathers, brothers and sisters, sons and daughters.

From a functional perspective, we also understand that "what families do" is of vital importance, both to the health and well-being of individual family members, but as importantly, to the vitality, security, and prosperity of the larger communities in which we live. Within families, individuals provide for and care for one another, they teach and discipline, they are financially, economically and psychologically inter-dependent and, last but not least, they express their love for one another. For many years, the Vanier Institute has been guided by an inclusive definition of the family that emphasizes what families do. As such it has employed a definition that directs attention toward the work and accomplishments of people who commit themselves to one another over time. Accordingly, the Vanier Institute has sought to acknowledge and respect family as:

... any combination of two or more persons who are bound together over time by ties of mutual consent, birth and/or adoption or placement and who, together, assume responsibilities for variant combinations of some of the following:

- Physical maintenance and care of group members
- Addition of new members through procreation or adoption
- Socialization of children
- Social control of members
- Production, consumptions, distribution of goods and services, and
- Affective nurturance — love.

[There are] many ways in which the structural, functional and affective dimensions of family life have changed. Today's families are smaller. Adults wait longer to marry if they do so at all. Common-law unions are no longer just a preliminary or trial stage before marriage but, for many, an alternative to marriage. On average, Canadians wait longer than did their parents or grandparents to have children. They are more likely to separate or divorce. In less than a lifetime, the dual-earner family has gone from an exception to the norm, and a growing number of women are primary income earners within their families. In contrast to the past when most children growing up with only one parent were living with a widow or widower, the children growing up today with a lone parent are most likely to have another living parent, albeit a mother or, as is most often the case, a father living elsewhere. All of these changes, and many others, can only be understood against the backdrop of wider social and economic trends: the evolution of a global economy, increasing respect for human rights, the emancipation of women, the migration of populations between and within countries, as well as from the country into cities, and the many technological innovations that have so profoundly changed the ways in which we work, play, communicate, and care.

The [statistical] profiles also reveal the many challenges and difficulties individuals face in carrying out their family responsibilities and obligations, and in realizing their aspirations, hopes and dreams. Two basic resources all families require are time and money, and for a growing number of families, these basics are in short supply. Family and child poverty remain persistent social problems, while enormous inequalities of wealth and income continue to separate rich and poor. Particularly vulnerable are Canada's Aboriginal families, new immigrants and families that rely on a single earner. Stress and illness associated with work-life conflict are common experiences, most notably among employed mothers with pre-school age children. With the expansion of the global economy, higher education has become a near-prerequisite to a reasonable wage, yet many families are unable to adequately save for their children's education. And in the wake of the baby boom years, the long-term decline in fertility rate has created, and will continue to create, enormous challenges in the caring capacity of families as parents age and fewer children, often separated by distance, are available for support.

How we choose to respond to these and other challenges, not just as individuals, but as a society, is vitally important.... What are the implications and challenges as you see them? Do current practices, policies and programs intended to support families do so fairly and equitably? What kinds of supports might be provided to better acknowledge and support the essential work of families? ... The capacity of families to make and respond to change is more than an innate characteristic of individual family members; it is something to be nurtured, strengthened and supported by society at large.

Notes and Questions

What statistics can tell us about families and family law issues

Taking account of the issues identified in the above excerpt, consider how the following statistics, mainly from the 2006 census, may affect policy making by legislatures about Canadian families. To what extent do such statistical profiles support the need for (more) legal intervention in families? How should these statistical profiles be used by legislatures? By courts?

1. **Marriage and cohabitation**

   - Marriage is on the decline. According to Statistics Canada, in 1961, married couples accounted for 91.6% of all census families but by 2011 this proportion had decreased to 67% (*Fifty years of families in Canada: 1961 to 2011* (Ottawa: Statistics Canada, 2012) at 1). By contrast, the number of cohabiting couples has increased: from 5.6% of all census families in 1981 (the first year this data was collected) to 16.7% in 2011 (*Fifty years* at 2). There are significant variations in different parts of Canada. In 2011, Ontario, Alberta and Prince Edward Island had the highest proportion of married couples (approximately 72%), while Québec and the territories had the highest proportion of cohabiting couples (ranging between 28–32%) (Statistics Canada, *Portrait of Families and Living Arrangements in Canada* (Ottawa: Statistics Canada, 2012) at 6).

   - Opposite sex marriage. The 2011 census reveals that opposite-sex marriage continues to be on the decline. In 2011, 80% of opposite-sex couples were married, a decrease of 2% from 2006 (*Portrait* at 7). This is consistent with the historical decline of opposite-sex marriage in Canada. In 1981, about 65% of both men and women could expect to marry at least once by the age of 50. By 2004, only 46% of women and 44% of men could expect to marry by age 50. However, as discussed above, there are significant variations in different parts of Canada: in Québec and the territories less than one half of men and women could expect to marry by age 50, while over 80% could expect to do so in Prince Edward Island (Vanier Institute of the Family, "Marriage rate continues to drop", *Fascinating Families* 40 (September 2011), online: <www.vanierinstitute.ca>). The rate of marriage dropped by 23% between 1981 and 2003, and the rate of first marriage showed an even greater decline at 28%. Another way of thinking about these figures is that about 88% of females born in 1948 were legally married by the age of 30; by contrast, for women born in 1970, only 55% were married by the age of 30. As the VIF stated, "Marriage and family, institutions once thought to be joined at the hip, are increasingly separate and distinct" (*Families Count* at 36).

- Same-sex couples: In Canada, the number of same-sex couples (both married and cohabiting partners) has continued to increase. In 2011, same-sex couples accounted for 0.8% of all couples in Canada, which is consistent with the data from Australia and the United Kingdom. As compared to opposite sex couples, same-sex married spouses and cohabiting partners were relatively young: approximately 25% were between the ages of 15 to 34 (*Portrait* at 8).

- Same-sex marriage: Statistics about same-sex marriage were collected for the first time in 2006. While marriage is on the decline overall, there has been a sharp increase in the number of same-sex couples who are married. In 2006, 16.5% of same-sex couples were married; by 2011, the proportion of same-sex couples who were married increased to 32.5% (*Portrait* at 7).

- Cohabiting couples: In 2011, cohabiting couples made up 16.7% of all census families (*Portrait* at 5). Young people often choose to cohabit: a 2009 survey of young persons aged 15 to 19 found that three quarters approved of cohabitation, and one-third stated explicitly that they planned to live with someone at some point. As mentioned, cohabitation is especially popular in Québec, where among women aged 30 to 39, barely 26% are expected to choose marriage, compared to 59% in other parts of Canada. Among older Canadians, cohabitation may occur after the dissolution of a first marriage. As the Vanier Institute of the Family suggested,

    The trends raise important questions for family law. Do couples who cohabit have the same obligations and responsibilities to each other as married couples? When [these] unions dissolve, should the same principles ... regarding division of property and assets apply? What if children are involved? (*Families Count* at 40)

Same-sex couples in cohabiting relationships were first counted in the 2001 census. The number of same-sex couples in cohabiting relationships has continued to increase since that time. Between 2006 and 2011, the number of same-sex cohabiting partners increased by 15% (*Portrait* at 7).

2. **Divorce and separation**
   • Divorce rates: The divorce rate is based on the proportion of couples that are expected to divorce before their 30th wedding anniversary. The divorce rate has remained relatively stable. The most recent national divorce rates are from 2008, the year that Statistics Canada stopped tracking divorce rates (discussed below). In 2008, the divorce rate was 41%, slightly higher than in 2004 and in the 1990s. Yet the 2008 rate is lower than the late 1980s when the *Divorce Act* was amended to make divorce available after one year of separation (previously, there was a three-year separation requirement). The province with the highest divorce rate in 2008 was Québec (47.4%) and the lowest was Newfoundland and Labrador (25%) (Vanier Institute of the Family, "Four in Ten Marriages End in Divorce", *Fascinating Families* 41 (26 October 2011), online: <www.vanierinstitute.ca>).

   In 2008, the average duration of a marriage that ended in divorce was 13.7 years; and the highest rate of divorce occurs in less than five years of marriage (Vanier Institute of the Family, "Separation and Divorce in Canada", *By the Numbers* (December 2013), online: <www.vanierinstitute.ca>). On average, men are 44.5 years old and women are 41.9 years old at the time of divorce ("Four in Ten"). Yet divorce is not just for the young. There has been a gradual increase in the divorce rate among men aged 50–54 from 7.2% in 1985 to 11.0% in 2005. For women, the rate grew from 5.4% to 8.9% over the same time period (Vanier Institute of the Family, "Grey divorce (silver separations)", *Fascinating Families* 51 (19 December 2012), online: <www.vanierinstitute.ca>).

   • Cohabitees and separation: According to the 2006 General Social Survey, the number of people that ended cohabiting relationships was similar to the number of people who divorced between 2001–2006. The Vanier Institute notes that "[g]iven that there are considerably more marriages, these data show that the risk of break-up of common-law unions is much higher than the risk of divorce" ("Four in Ten").

   • Repartnering: The majority of individuals who divorce or separate, repartner. As the Vanier Institute notes:

   In the aftermath of divorce or separation, the majority of Canadians repartner. About 26% of women and 37% of men enter into a new conjugal relationship within three years of marital dissolution. After five years, these proportions rise to 36% of women and 51% of men. After 20 years, 69% of women and 82% of men have formed new unions. (Vanier Institute of the Family, "Forming Unions — Again", *Fascinating Families* 30 (September 15, 2010), online: <www.vanierinstitute.ca>)

Many of those entering a second relationship choose cohabitation, especially those who are younger adults. In this context, the rate of remarriage has remained quite stable: "of those who were ever married, 10% had married twice and less than 1% had married three or four times" (*Families Count* at 46). According to 2006 data, about 48% used legal or alternative dispute resolution services and 29.8% used a social support service such as counselling.

> The dissolution of marriages and of [cohabiting] relationships is difficult for those directly involved, and for children, family members, and friends. Change in the relationship is more often than not accompanied by other changes in living arrangements, household income, social support, work status, residence and neighbourhood and in one's sense of self. The care and support that individuals have access to can make a significant difference in navigating these transitions and for the long term well-being of those involved. (*Families Count* at 50)

3. **Children**
   - Birth rates: The number of babies born in Canada has been rising since 2001. Between 2001 and 2011, the number of births increased by 13%. The rate was 1.61 children per woman in 2011. In addition, the age of first-time mothers increased to 28.5 years of age in 2011. The age for the highest fertility rate is also rising, with women between 30 to 34 now having the highest fertility rate ("Births, Fertility and Contraception in Canada", VIF *Transitions* 45:1 (2015) 16, online: <www.vanierinstitute.ca>).

     The birth rate among Aboriginal peoples is nearly six times faster than non-Aboriginal people in Canada, a situation which will result in a large influx of Aboriginal youth into the working population in the next decade. In addition, the 2006 census reported that almost 20% of Canadian residents were born outside Canada, the highest percentage since 1931 (and among the highest in the major industrial countries — only Australia was higher at 22%). These kinds of developments require us to rethink how we understand the idea of "Canadian families" (*Families Count* at 10, 12 and 52).

   - Birth rates and marriage/cohabitation and sole parenting: In 2007, most babies were born to married women (62%), but 26% of babies were born to women who were not and had never been married. There is considerable variation across Canada: "in Nunavut, over three quarters of babies were born to never married women, while only 12% of babies in Ontario had never married mothers. In Québec, nearly 60% of babies were born to unmarried women, an increase from 16% in 1981, and most of these babies were born to cohabiting couples. Between 1983 and 1997, the proportion of births to single mothers (who were not married or cohabiting) rose from 6% to 10%, with the highest proportions in British Columbia (9%) and in the Atlantic Provinces (11%)" (*Families Count* at 54).

The 2011 Census revealed that the proportion of children (aged 14 and under) living with cohabiting partners increased between 2001 and 2011 (from 12.8% to 16.3%), while the proportion of children living with married parents decreased between 2001 and 2011 (from 68.4% to 63.6%) (*Portrait* at 13–14).

- Lone-parent families: The proportion of lone-parent families doubled between 1961 and 2011 (from 8.4% to 16.3% of census families), yet the 4:1 ratio of female lone-parent families to male lone-parent families has remained constant (*Fifty years* at 2–3). In 2011, 50.8% of lone-parents were divorced or separated, 31.5% were never married and 17.7% were widowed (*Fifty years* at 4). Most separated or divorced parents (74%) are satisfied with the amount of time they spend with their children (Statistics Canada, "Study: Parenting and child support after separation or divorce, 2011" *The Daily* (February 12, 2014), online: <www.statcan.gc.ca>). More aboriginal children aged 14 and under (34%) live in lone-parent families than non-Aboriginal children aged 14 and under (17%) (Vanier Institute of the Family, "Aboriginal Families in Canada", *By the Numbers* (August 2013), online: <www.vanierinstitute.ca>).

- Same-sex families: The number of children raised by lesbian, gay, bisexual, transgender, two-spirit or queer (LGBTTQ) individuals increased between 2006 and 2011. In 2006, the proportion of same-sex couples raising children was 9.0% and increased to 9.4% in 2011; more female same-sex couples (16.5%) raise children than male same-sex couples (3.4%) (Vanier Institute of the Family, "Same-Sex Families Raising Children", *Fascinating Families* 51 (March 2013) at 1, online: <www.vanierinstitute.ca>).

- Assisted reproduction: There is limited data regarding the use of assisted reproductive technologies in Canada, which include assisted insemination, *in vitro* fertilization (IVF), and the use of donated eggs, sperm or embryos. As is discussed in Chapter Three, individuals suffering from medical infertility as well as same-sex couples and single women and men may use assisted reproduction to build their families. In 2012, the prevalence of medical infertility, which is defined as not achieving a pregnancy while being exposed to the possibility of conception over a 12-month period, ranged between 11.5% and 15.7% (Vanier Institute of the Family, "Trying to Conceive: Infertility in Canada", *Fascinating Families* 15 (March 2012), online: <www.vanierinstitute.ca>). According to the Canadian Fertility and Andrology Society's September 2014 media release, the rates of IVF indicate that the use of assisted reproduction is on the rise. In 2012, 16,062 cycles of IVF were undertaken in 32 of 33 IVF centers in Canada. The majority of these cycles were performed in Ontario (5336) and Québec (6761). The number of IVF cycles has almost doubled since 2005 (8,195 IVF cycles). Unfortunately, there is no available data regarding the use of assisted insemination or any data on who (e.g. heterosexual couples, lesbian couples, gay couples, single mothers or fathers by choice) is using assisted reproduction (Canadian Fertility and Andrology Society, Media Release, "Human Assisted Reproduction 2014 Live Birth Rates for Canada" (12 September 2014), online: <http://www.cfas.ca/index.php?option=com_content&view=article&id=260&Itemid=460>).

- Adoption: About 2600 adoptions — both public and private — take place in Canada each year; and there are also about 2000 international adoptions (with high rates of adoption from China, the United States, Ethiopia and Haiti). Aboriginal Canadians have more experiences with adoption, with 14% becoming foster parents (compared to 5% of the general public) and 12% of children being raised by a foster parent (compared to 3% of the general public). In 2007, there were 67,000 children in government care, many of whom were Aboriginal children (*Families Count* at 56 and 58).

  The Child Welfare League of Canada reported that in 2012, more than 50% of the children awaiting adoption were Aboriginal (Child Welfare League of Canada, "Policy Brief: Adoption and Foster Care in Canada", online: <http://www.cwlc.ca/sites/default/files/guidelines/Policy%20Brief_FosterCareAdoption_Mar2012.pdf>).

- Foster children: Foster children were counted for the first time in the 2011 Census. The majority of foster children are aged 14 and under. The majority of foster children (41%) are aged 10–14. Half of all foster children are Aboriginal children. Aboriginal children are much more likely to be foster children (4%) as compared to non-Aboriginal children (0.3%) (Statistics Canada, *Aboriginal People in Canada: First Nations People, Métis and Inuit* (Ottawa: Statistics Canada: 2013) at 5).

- Stepfamilies and blended families: The 2011 Census counted blended families or stepfamilies and stepchildren for the first time. In 2011, approximately 13% of couple families with children were stepfamilies (*Portrait* at 11). The majority (58.6%) of these stepfamilies were defined as *simple stepfamilies*, which is a couple family with children in which all children are the biological or adopted offspring of **one** of the married or cohabiting partners. By contrast, *complex stepfamilies*, which includes either a family in which there is at least one child of both parents and at least one child of only one parent, or a family in which there is at least one child of each parent, or a family in which there is at least one child of both parents and at least one child of each parent, make up 41.4% of stepfamilies. Blended families are much more prevalent among same-sex couples (50%) than among opposite sex couples (12.5%) (Vanier Institute of the Family, "Blended Families: New challenges and opportunities", *Fascinating Families* 49 (November 2012), online: <www.vanierinstitute.ca>.)

In 2011, one in 10 children lived in stepfamilies. Among these children, the majority (63%) were stepchildren. The Census defined a stepchild as a "child in a couple family who is the biological or adopted child of only one married spouse or common-law partner in the couple, and whose birth or adoption preceded the current relationship" (*Portrait* at 14).

- "Boomerang" children: This term refers to young adults who leave home and then later return to live with their parents again. In addition to these young adults, there are others who continue to live at home, a trend that was widespread in the 1990s when jobs were scarce. In 2006, about one-half of young adults in their 20s lived with their parents in Ontario and in Newfoundland and Labrador; by contrast, only one-third did so in Alberta and Saskatchewan (*Families Count* at 72).

4. Families and family economies

The capacity that each individual family, household or individual has to attain economic security is mediated by three primary determinants: labour market attachment, income distribution, and wealth accumulation. Each of these factors has profound impact on the extent to which families are able to fulfill their obligations of care and support, and to provide for the needs and opportunities of members. (*Families Count* at 76)

- Gender and labour force participation: Women's earnings are increasingly essential to the economic security of households. In 1976, 52% of women aged 25 to 54 years were in the paid labour force, but this figure had risen to 80% in 2011. Men's labour force participation fell in the same period, particularly during the 2008–09 recession, and there was also an erosion of wages for younger men, especially in manufacturing, natural resources, agriculture and transportation. "As a result of converging labour force participation rates [that is the rates of participation of men and women], the division of labour within families and the relationship between families and the economy continues to change" (*Families Count* at 78).

- Work and family life changes: Multiple income earners is now the norm for most families. Between 1994 and 2011, dual-income families increased. The proportion of husband-wife families that both earned income grew from 58% in 1994 to 64% in 2011 (Nathan Battams, Nora Spinks & Roger Sauvé, "The Current State of Canadian Family Finances: 2013–2014 Report" (Ottawa: VIF, 2014) at 8 ("Family Finances 2013–2014"), online: <www.vanierinstitute.ca>). Although mothers more than fathers tend to work part time, research shows that issues of work life balance are an important concern for dual earner families. Significantly, absences from work have increased in recent years, particularly absences relating to family responsibilities (*Families Count* at 80–88).

- Family incomes: Between 1976 and 1997, family incomes remained almost steady, in terms of average after-tax income. However, the period 1997 to 2007 was marked by a strong 27.5% advance in family after-tax income (*Families Count* at 96–104). Following the recession in 2008, family after-tax incomes have continued to increase, but at a much slower pace of approximately 2.8% (Roger Sauvé & Nathan Battams, "The Current State of Canadian Family Finances: 2012–2013 Report" (Ottawa: VIF, 2013) ("Family Finances 2012–2013"), online: <www.vanierinstitute.ca>). Female lone-parent families still earn significantly less than two-parent families and male lone-parent families in Canada. In 2009, female lone-parent families earned approximately one half of what two-parent families earned after tax. In 2008, the median net worth of female lone-parent families ($17,000) was approximately one quarter of that of male lone-parent families ($80,000) (Vanier Institute of the Family, "The Economic Well-Being of Women in Canada", *By the Numbers* (March 2013), online: <www.vanierinstitute.ca>).

- Income inequality: In real dollar terms, income inequality is growing in Canada. In 2011, the richest 20 percent of households took home 44% of all income in Canada (referred to as the "income pie") as compared to the poorest 20 percent of households, which took home less than 5% of the "income pie." Since 1999, this inequality has increased as only the richest 20 percent of households have taken home a larger share of the "income pie" ("Family Finances 2013–2014" at 12). Indeed, the incomes of middle-income earners shrunk between 2008 and 2011 ("Family Finances 2012–2013" at 7).

- The "poor" in Canada: There is no official poverty rate in Canada. Instead, poverty levels are measured using the LICO measure and are referred to as low-income rates. In 2011, the highest low-income rates were among non-senior couples with children and no earners (75.7%). Importantly, the low-income rate among female lone-parents in 2011 (21.2%) was less than half of what it was in 1990 (48.2%) ("Family Finances 2012–2013" at 9). Notably, in 2011, 13.3% of Canadian children under the age of 18 lived in low-income families, only slightly lower than 14% during the 2008 recession. Almost half of First Nations children living off reserve under the age of 6 live in low-income families (Carol Matusicky, "Wealth and Well-Being Among Canada's Children", VIF *Transitions* 43:4 (2014) at 15).

• Debt in Canada: Debt loads in Canada have been increasing since 2000. The total amount of debt per household increased by 75% between 2000 and 2013. Another way to measure debt is by examining the ratio of household debt to disposable income. A lower ratio indicates that the household has a greater capacity for managing debt. The ratio of household debt to disposable income also increased sharply, from 110% in 2000 to 165.5% in 2013. The biggest increase in debt has been for those aged 55–64 and those 65+ ("Family Finances 2013–2014" at 20–21).

• The cost of raising children: One study identified the cost of raising a child from birth to age 18 at about $167,000, including food, clothing, health care, personal care, recreation, transportation, child care, and shelter. The total figure is based on costs in Winnipeg in 2004 and may not be fully inclusive, and it does not include additional costs related to lost wages for parental caregivers, for example. Nor does this figure include governmental costs such as schools, playgrounds, hospitals and parks. All the same, it is a useful figure to keep in mind in relation to family law issues (*Families Count* at 130).

• Caring for children and others: Even though caregiving facilities have grown, "the family is still expected to shoulder a significant share of caring work, even for those living in care facilities" (*Families Count* at 146). Indeed, more mothers with young children are joining the paid labour force. The lowest employment rate was seen in mothers of children younger than three years and highest for mothers of children aged 6 to 15 ("Family Finances 2013–2014" at 8).

Further, many Canadians provide care to family members or friends with a long-term health condition, a disability or a person who is aging.

> Many of these caregivers incur direct or out-of-pocket expenses as a result of their responsibilities, while others incur indirect expenses, such as reducing their income (reducing hours at work, taking a leave from the labour force or early retirement) due to time required to provide care.... As the population continues to age and disability rates increase (among seniors *and* non-seniors), these caregiving expenditures are likely to become an increasingly important aspect of family finances. ("Family Finances 2013–2014" at 16)

5. **Sole person households**

The number of sole person households in Canada is increasing. In 2011, 27.6% of Canadian households included only one person, with Québec and Yukon having the largest numbers of "sole" person households. As the article indicated, however:

> Despite the image of the young urban hipster living alone, the incidence of solo dwelling among young adults aged 20–29 was significantly below the national average at 9.2%. *This could partially be explained by the fact that 42.3% of Canadians in this age group ... are living in the parental home, delaying marriage and home ownership.* ("House and Home", VIF *Transitions* 42:4 (2012) at 6, online: <www.vanierinstitute.ca>)

Research of the Vanier Institute reveals that 52% of Canadians aged 20–29 were part of a couple in 1981. In 2011, it was 31%. What is the explanation for this demographic phenomenon? Is this a legal or social policy issue? Or both?

6. **The "positive" and the "dark side" of family life**
   Recent Canadian data suggest that many families have strong social networks and support (including use of the Internet), and that many Canadians continue to be involved in volunteer work and activities. The data also report that Canadians have a strong sense of belonging to their communities, with the highest levels of such connections reported in Atlantic Canada. In this context, however, the Uniform Crime Reporting Survey indicated that spousal violence represented 53% of violent crime reported in Canada in 2009, with female victims in 83% of cases (the highest rate was for young women aged 25 to 34). In 2007, nearly 53,400 children were victims of assault, and 34% of all sexual assaults against children and youth were perpetrated by family members. Moreover, the rate of family violence against children and youth increased by 23% between 1998 and 2007; and in 57% of cases, the perpetrator was a parent. Seniors are also at risk of violence and abuse, including mistreatment and neglect as well as violence, and also financial or emotional abuse. Unfortunately as well, the data likely underestimate the problem of family violence since they represent only incidents reported to police (*Families Count* at 164).

   Child abuse and neglect also increased by 125% between 1998 and 2003. Neglect was the most common form of substantiated mistreatment at 30% of the cases (28% involved exposure to domestic violence, 24% involved physical abuse, 15% were emotional abuse and 3% were sexual abuse). Child abuse and neglect were more common among families experiencing high levels of stress (*Families Count* at 166).

Statistical profiles of "families" and family law

In examining the principles and processes of family law discussed in this book, these statistical profiles offer important data about "families" and family life in Canada.

To a significant extent, the statistics provide evidence of how families actually *function* as units and how individual family members may be affected by social, economic, or political events. In this way, the statistics offer some useful evidence for functional approaches to issues in family law.

By contrast, issues in family law and policy may be approached in terms of how families ought to function, a more *familialist* approach to family law decisions.

In this context, this brief overview of statistical profiles provides a useful basis for assessing legislative initiatives and judicial decisions in many family law issues: to what extent are these initiatives and decisions grounded in functional or familialist approaches to family law issues? On this basis, you may need to return to these statistical profiles in relation to the issues discussed in subsequent chapters in this book.

The cessation of statistics about annual rates of marriage and divorce in Canada

In 2011, Statistics Canada announced that it would cease to collect information about annual marriage and divorce rates. The agency has collected marriage data since 1921 and divorce data since 1972. Two reasons were cited for the decision to terminate collection of these data: one was the need to cut costs, but the other related to the changing nature of relationships in Canadian families and especially individual choices to create "families" outside marriage.

As some critics noted, this decision will make it difficult to assess the impact of the 2008 recession on rates of marriage and divorce because the data ends in 2008. In addition, policy makers have signalled how it will also be harder to determine whether, or to what extent, marriage breakdown affects child poverty, housing, education, and health care. According to the most recent data, 43.1 percent of marriages are expected to end in divorce before a couple's 50th anniversary, an increase from 39.3 percent a decade earlier. Although social scientists lamented this decision by Statistics Canada, the agency indicated that it will continue to examine trends in family composition through its census every five years (*The Globe and Mail*, 21 July 2011 at A3).

Additional Resources

Maureen Baker, ed, *Families: Changing Trends in Canada*, 6th ed (Toronto: McGraw-Hill Ryerson, 2009).

N Mandell & A Duffy, eds, *Canadian Families: Diversity, Conflict and Change*, 2nd ed (Toronto: Harcourt Canada, 2000).

A Milan, M Vézina & C Wells, *2006 Census: Family Portrait: Continuity and Change in Canadian Families and Households in 2006: Highlights* (Ottawa: Statistics Canada, 2006). Online: <http://www12. statcan.ca/census-recensement/2006/as-sa/97-553/p1-eng.cfm>.

National Council of Welfare, *Welfare Incomes 2009* (Winter 2010) 129 *National Council of Welfare Reports*.

Statistics Canada, *Earnings and Incomes of Canadians over the Past Quarter Century, 2006 Census* (Ottawa: Minister of Industry, 2008).

Vanier Institute of the Family, *The Current State of Canadian Family Finances — 2009 Report* (Ottawa, VIF, 2010).

III.
"FAMILIES," FAMILY RELATIONSHIPS, AND THE LAW

[There] exists within society a network of social norms which is formally independent of the legal system, but which is in constant interaction with it. Formal law sometimes seeks to strengthen the social norms. Sometimes it allows them to serve its purposes without the necessity of direct intervention; sometimes it tries to weaken or destroy them and sometimes it withdraws from enforcement, not in an attempt to subvert them, but because countervailing values make conflicts better resolved outside the legal arena. (John Eekelaar, "Uncovering Social Obligations: Family Law and the Responsible Citizen" in Mavis Maclean, ed, *Making Law for Families* (Oxford & Portland, OR: Hart Publishing, 2000) 9 at 16)

"FAMILIES" AND "LAW"

Eekelaar's comment explains how relationships between families and law may take a variety of different forms in different circumstances. This section provides some examples of contexts in which individuals defined their "families," and their rights and obligations as family members, in ways that were not always congruent with legal definitions.

As these examples illustrate, family law issues often intersect with other areas of law: practical issues about who is "family" regularly arise, for example, in defining who is a "spouse" for tax or pension purposes, or who are "family" members for purposes of residential tenancy, succession and immigration matters. In addition to these practical issues, members of families may want their relationships to be recognized for purposes of dignity and personal identity.

In examining each of the three cases that follow, consider these questions:

- To what extent did ideas about functionalism and/or familialism contribute to the outcome of the cases?

- To what extent did broader concerns about "public policy" influence the legal reasoning in these decisions?

- In assessing the consequences for individuals as a result of law's recognition of their "families" — or its failure to recognize them — consider whether, or to what extent, the claimants had options available to them other than decision making by courts?

Sefton Holdings v Cairns
[1988] 2 FLR 109 (HL (Eng))

LLOYD LJ:

This is an appeal from a decision of Her Honour Judge Downey sitting in the Liverpool County Court on 11th August 1987. It concerns a house at No 49, Cherry Avenue, Liverpool. The question is whether the defendant, Miss Florence Cairns, is entitled to protection under the Rent Acts, that is to say, whether she is a statutory tenant under section 2 of the Rent Act 1977. The answer depends on the meaning to be given to the word "family" in paragraph 7 of Part I of Schedule 1 of that Act.

The facts are that the plaintiffs, Sefton Holdings Limited, are the landlords of the premises in question. They let it to a Mr Richard Gamble some time between 1939 and 1941 when the house was built. Mr Gamble died in 1965. His daughter, Ada, then succeeded to the tenancy. Miss Ada Gamble died in 1986. The defendant came to live with Mr and Mrs Gamble and their daughter Ada in 1941. She was then 23 and single. Both her parents had died. Her boyfriend had just been killed in the war. Miss Ada Gamble asked her parents if they would take the defendant in, which they did. They treated her as their own daughter. She called them "Mom and Pop". She has lived in the same house ever since. She is now some 70 years of age.

On 6th June 1986, shortly after Miss Ada Gamble died, the plaintiffs served on the defendant a notice to quit. The defendant claims that she is entitled to remain on in the house as a statutory tenant under paragraph 7 of Part I of the first schedule, which provides as follows:

> "Where paragraph 6 above does not apply but a person who was a member of the first successor's family was residing with him at the time of and for the period of 6 months immediately before his death then, after his death, that person or if there is more than one such person such one of them as may be decided by agreement, or in default of agreement by the county court, shall be the statutory tenant if and so long as he occupies the dwelling-house as his residence."

Miss Ada Gamble was the first successor within the meaning of that paragraph. So what we have to decide in this case is whether the defendant is a member of her family who was residing with her at the time of, and for the period of six months immediately before, her death. The defendant was clearly residing with Miss Ada Gamble at the time of Miss Ada Gamble's death. But was she a member of Miss Ada Gamble's family? That is the question. The county court judge has decided that she was, and there is now an appeal to this court.

No court could help feeling sympathy for an elderly lady of 70 who is in danger of being turned out of the house in which she has lived for nearly 50 years. But it goes without saying that we have to put sympathy on one side and apply the law to the best of our ability. It has been held over and over again that, in deciding whether a person is a member of another person's family, we must give the word "family" its ordinary everyday meaning. We cannot extend that meaning in order to cover what might appear to be a hard case; we must not let affection press upon judgment.

If the judge has given the word too wide a meaning, then she has erred in law and we are obliged in this court to correct her, however much we might like to agree.

We have been referred to a number of cases as to what is meant by saying that a person is a member of another person's family. The cases go back at least 60 years. Not all the cases are, at first sight at any rate, easy to reconcile. That may be because, as has been suggested, the meaning of the word "family" has broadened over the years. But we do not have to go into that question now.

The most useful passage from among the decided cases is to be found in the judgment of Lord Justice Russell in the case of *Ross v. Collins* [1964] 1 WLR 425, 432. In that case Lord Justice Russell said this:

> "Granted that 'family' is not limited to cases of a strict legal familial nexus, I cannot agree that it extends to a case such as this. It still requires, it seems to me, at least a broadly recognisable de facto familial nexus. This may be capable of being found and recognised as such by the ordinary man — where the link would be strictly familial had there been a marriage, or where the link is through adoption of a minor, de jure or de facto, or where the link is 'step-', or where the link is 'in-law' or by marriage. But two strangers cannot, it seems to me, ever establish artificially for the purposes of this section a familial nexus by acting as brothers or as sisters, even if they call each other such and consider their relationship to be tantamount to that. Nor, in my view, can an adult man and woman who establish a platonic relationship establish a familial nexus by acting as a devoted brother and sister or father and daughter would act, even if they address each other as such and even if they refer to each other as such and regard their association as tantamount to such. Nor, in my view, would they indeed be recognised as familial links by the ordinary man."

That passage was expressly approved and adopted by Lord Diplock giving the leading speech in the House of Lords in *Joram Developments Ltd v. Sharratt* [1979] 1 WLR 928.

It seems to me that the facts of the present case are covered by the principle stated by Lord Justice Russell. I have no doubt that the defendant and Miss Ada Gamble did regard each other as sisters and may well have called each other such. There is evidence, to which I have already referred, that the defendant called Mr and Mrs Gamble "Mom and Pop". But the fact remains that when the defendant was taken in nearly 50 years ago she was taken in, to use the language of Lord Justice Russell, as a stranger; and however long she may have lived with the family and however kindly they may have treated her, and however close their friendship may have become, the defendant did not, and in my judgment could not, have become a member of Ada's family. As Miss Goodman put it in the course of the argument, length of residence cannot transform a resident into a member of the family.

Miss Pearce, in seeking to support the judge's judgment, argued that the defendant at any rate became a member of Mr and Mrs Gamble's family by adoption. If she had, then she would have been within the protection of the Act. For it has been held by this court in the case of *Brock v. Wollams* [1949] 2 KB 388, that de facto adoption is good enough to make a child a member of the family in question.

But there are two difficulties with that argument. In the first place, the section requires us to ask whether the defendant was a member of Miss Ada Gamble's family, not the family of her parents. Even if we could surmount that difficulty, there is a second difficulty. There is no case which has been drawn to our attention in which the courts have held that the protection of the Rent Acts covers the adoption of an adult (if such a concept is possible). It will be noted that in the passage I have read from Lord Justice Russell's judgment he refers to the adoption of a minor; and Lord Diplock (at page 929) refers to "adoption (de jure or de facto) during minority".

Miss Pearce sought to distinguish *Ross v. Collins* and *Joram Developments v. Sharratt* from the present case. She submits that in those cases a young person went to live with an older person and gradually took over the running of the house; here, by contrast, a young person, an orphan, was taken in by the family as a whole. It was not a case, says Miss Pearce, of one adult taking in another. The relationship therefore had, so she submits, the necessary quality to make it a familial relationship. Mr and Mrs Gamble should be treated as being *in loco parentis.*

I would, as I have said already, like to accept Miss Pearce's distinction if I could find a way of doing so. I agree that there are factual differences between the cases. There always are. But our approach should be the same as that laid down by Lord Justice Russell and adopted by Lord Diplock. No case has gone as far as Miss Pearce would like us to go in the present case. The defendant was 23 when she came to live with Mr and Mrs Gamble and their daughter. It cannot be said that she was brought up as an adopted child of the family. It may be that things were different in 1941 from what they are now. But, if I ask myself the question whether the defendant became a member of Mr and Mrs Gamble's family (if that be the right question) by adoption, whether de facto or de jure, I am in all honestly compelled to answer that question "No".

Various attempts have been made by the courts from time to time to define the word "family", by identifying various categories within which a person would be a member of another person's family. But Lord Diplock did not embark on that task in *Joram Developments v. Sharratt,* and I do not propose to embark on that task myself. All I would say is that, in approaching this case, I have found it useful to bear two matters in mind. First, there is the distinction drawn by Viscount Dilhorne in *Joram Developments v. Sharratt* between being a member of the family and being a member of the household. Secondly, there is the distinction between being a member of the family and living as a member of the family. There is no doubt that the defendant lived as a member of the family, and that may be why the judge decided this case in her favour. But the question we have to ask ourselves is not whether she lived as a member of the family, but whether she was a member of the family. I am clear that she was not, and that the man in the street would take the same view.

We should in this court be slow to reverse a county court judge on a matter of this kind. But, for the reasons which I have attempted to give, I for my part feel compelled to allow this appeal.

Appeal allowed; application for leave to appeal to the House of Lords refused.

Jane Doe v Alberta
2007 ABCA 50

BERGER JA:

[1] The issue in this appeal is whether an express written agreement entered into by the natural mother of a child and her co-habiting male partner (who did not father the child), which stipulates that the partner has neither parental rights nor any obligation to support the child, is effective in law. The Appellants question the constitutional validity of ss. 53, 85 and 86 of the *Family Law Act*, R.S.A. 2003, c. F-4.5, which permits a court to override agreements entered into with regard to parenting, including child support obligations.

THE FACTS

[2] The Appellants Jane Doe and John Doe are in an unmarried relationship. Jane Doe's child was born in August 2005 and resides in the same household as the Appellants.

[3] Jane Doe is a professional and has worked as such for more than ten years. She expressed her desire to have a child with John Doe. He did not wish to father a child, to stand in the place of a parent, act as a guardian, or support a child. Jane Doe became pregnant through an assisted conception by way of artificial insemination from an unknown sperm donor. Both Jane Doe and John Doe wish to continue their relationship. They have agreed to govern any rights or obligations with respect to the child of Jane Doe through an express written agreement which has yet to be executed. The agreement will stipulate that John Doe is not the father of the child and has neither parental rights nor any obligation of support towards Jane Doe's child.

[4] The Appellants brought an originating notice seeking a declaration that such an agreement would bind them and any third party, including any government authorities. They also sought a declaration that the *FLA*, if it does not allow such an agreement, breaches s. 7 of the *Charter*. They contend that to the extent that the Act breaches the *Charter*, agreements as contemplated by the Appellants should be read into the *FLA* or the Act should be read down to limit its scope.

[5] The Appellants argue that John Doe's settled intention not to be a father to the child is critical and dispositive and not merely a factor to determine if he is *in loco parentis*. They submit that where the intention is clear, the court should not look to other factors or circumstances to determine parentage. They say that s. 48 is in direct conflict with s. 13. They submit that s. 48 must be "interpreted to allow the intention expressed under s. 13(2) to operate as a conclusive expression of intention regarding all parental obligations, including child support" and that "[a]ny other interpretation would render the expressed intention pursuant to s. 13(2) largely meaningless." (Appellants' Factum, para. 29)

[6] The Appellants submit that s. 7 of the *Charter* provides that parental freedom to make personal life choices as a parent can only be interfered with when the child's life or health is threatened or when the parent is engaged in socially unacceptable conduct. Further, they argue that the *FLA* breaches principles of fundamental justice because the exercise of a *parens patriae* jurisdiction exceeds the mandate of the court, is over-broad in limiting s. 7 rights, is too vague in the determination of guardianship rights, and is arbitrary....

The court considered several provisions of Alberta's *Family Law Act*. A "father" is defined pursuant to section 13(2)(b); and a "parent" includes a "person standing in the place of a parent" pursuant to section 48. According to section 13(2)(b), a male person is a father if, although his sperm was not used in assisted conception, he consented in advance of conception to being a parent of the child. According to section 48(1), a person stands in the place of a parent if the person was in a relationship of interdependence of some permanence with the mother ... of the child, and has demonstrated a settled intention to treat the child as the person's own child. Section 48(2) includes a list of factors to determine whether the person has demonstrated a settled intention to treat the child as the person's own child. According to section 3 of the *Adult Interdependent Relationships Act*, a "relationship of interdependence" means a relationship outside marriage in which two persons share one another's lives, are emotionally committed to one another and function as an economic and domestic unit.

THE DECISION BELOW

[8] Although the Appellants have not yet executed a written agreement, and no proceedings have been brought to have John Doe declared a person standing in the place of a parent, the chambers judge found that there was a sufficient factual foundation to determine the legal issues before the court and that judicial economy favoured the determination of those issues on the present record. I agree.

[9] The chambers judge compared s. 13 and s. 48 of the *FLA* (the two ways in which a male person can be found to be a "parent"). Section 13(2)(b) addresses cases of assisted conception. A male person will not be considered the "father" of a child unless he consents in advance of conception to being the parent of the resulting child. Section 48 contemplates a situation where a person is not the "mother" or "father" of a child, but can still be adjudged a "parent" if he or she is "standing in the place of a parent". The chambers judge determined that s. 13 does not override s. 48. She held that the decision to withhold consent to be a "father" does not inevitably equate with a finding that an individual does not "stand in the place of a parent". She found that the latter requires a "contextual, holistic and [*ex post*] inquiry into the relationship between the child and a particular person which the Applicants cannot oust by even the most carefully drafted contract." She was of the view that an agreement cannot preclude the possibility that a court may sometime in the future find that John Doe stands in the place of a parent. She concluded that under s. 48(2) contractual intent may be relevant but it is not determinative. The chambers judge considered ss. 53, 85 and 86 of the *FLA*, noting that parties are at liberty to fashion their own arrangements but always subject to court supervision.

[10] The chambers judge found that the impugned provisions of the *FLA* did not breach s. 7 because they did not significantly or at all impair the parties' freedom to contract. They continued to enjoy the "essence of the desired freedom because they may enter into a contract on whatever terms they may consider advantageous." She held that the promises exchanged between the parties might ultimately not be upheld by a court in the exercise of its supervisory role, but that such a constraint on contractual freedom did not amount to an infringement of the Appellants' s. 7 right to life, liberty and security of the person otherwise than in accordance with the principles of fundamental justice.

ANALYSIS

[11] Section 13(2) says that a male is considered the father of a child from an assisted conception if he was either the spouse of or "in a relationship of interdependence of some permanence" with the mother and either his sperm was used in the conception, or if his sperm was not used in the conception, "he consented in advance of the conception" to being a parent of the child.

[12] It is clear that, in this case, John Doe is in a relationship of interdependence of some permanence with Jane Doe. It is equally clear that his sperm was not used in the conception, nor did he consent in advance of the conception to being a parent of the child. It follows that, pursuant to s. 13(2) of the Act, John Doe is not considered to be the father of the child.

[13] Is John Doe a person "standing in the place of the parent" such that he incurs "support obligations" pursuant to Part 3 of the Act? Section 48 of the Act says that a person is deemed to be standing in the place of a

parent if he is the spouse of the mother of the child or was in a relationship of interdependence of some permanence with the mother of the child
and has demonstrated a settled intention to treat the child as his own
child. In this case, there is no question that John Doe was and is in a
relationship of interdependence of some permanence with the mother of
the child. Can it be said that he has demonstrated a settled intention to
treat the child as his own?

[14] Section 48(2) of the *FLA* lists a number of factors that the Court
may consider in determining whether or not a person has "demonstrated
a settled intention". The Court is also entitled to consider any other relevant factor.

The court reviewed the decision of the chambers judge, which had
relied on a decision of the Supreme Court of Canada, *Chartier v Chartier*,
[1999] 1 SCR 242, a divorce case that concerned whether someone who is
already standing in the place of a parent and unilaterally withdraws from
that position upon the breakdown of the marriage is *in loco parentis* for child
support purposes. In *Chartier*, the Supreme Court had stated: "Whether a
person stands in the place of a parent must take into account all factors relevant to that determination, viewed objectively. What must be determined is
the nature of the relationship. ... The court must determine the nature of
the relationship by looking at a number of factors, among which is intention.
Intention will not only be expressed formally. The court must also infer
intention from actions, and take into consideration that even expressed
intentions may sometimes change. ... The relevant factors in defining the
parental relationship include, but are not limited to, whether the child participates in the extended family in the same way as would a biological child;
whether the person provides financially for the child (depending on ability to
pay); whether the person disciplines the child as a parent; whether the person represents to the child, the family, the world, either explicitly or implicitly, that he or she is responsible as a parent to the child; the nature or
existence of the child's relationship with the absent biological parent. ..."

[17] Intention was traditionally the main factor the Court considered in
determining whether a person stood in the place of a parent. *Chartier*
instead took a holistic approach by focussing on the "nature of the relationship".

[18] So while a person's "actual intention" is relevant, it is also not determinative....

[20] It emerges apparent that the analytical focus is the nature of the
relationship informed by an objective determination of intention premised
in large measure on the manner in which the person has "acted".

[21] The Appellants maintain that an express statement of intention not
to take on a parenting role is "the overriding factor". Mindful of s. 48
and the requirement for a "settled intention to treat the child as the person's own child", the Appellants submit that "settled" denotes having a
fixed, unchanging and established decision. The Appellants ask how can it
be said that a person has demonstrated a "settled intention" to take on a
parental obligation when there is a personal statement of intent from the
outset which is contrary to that?

[22] In my opinion, the answer is to be found in the context of the relationship between Jane and John Doe. The "settled intention" to remain in
a close, albeit unmarried, relationship thrust John Doe, from a practical

and realistic point of view, into the role of parent to this child. Can it seriously be contended that he will ignore the child when it cries? When it needs to be fed? When it stumbles? When the soother needs to be replaced? When the diaper needs to be changed?

[23] In my opinion, a relationship of interdependence with the mother of the child in the same household, of itself, will likely create a relationship of interdependence of some permanence, *vis-à-vis* the child. John Doe's subjective intent not to assume a parental role will inevitably yield to the needs (and not merely the physical needs) of the child in the same household. Were it otherwise, one can only imagine the emotional damage visited upon the child. One must keep in mind that, among the factors cited in s. 48(2) is the <u>child's</u> perception of the person as a parental figure.

[24] I would add only that I see no internal inconsistencies as alleged by the Appellants as between s. 48 and s. 13(2) of the *FLA*. Section 13(2) is not rendered meaningless. Section 48 merely provides a second legislative mechanism whereby a person may be found to be a parent. Nor am I of the view that the *FLA*'s recognition of the valid objective of agreements in the family law context (ss. 53, 85 and 86) is rendered meaningless in the face of s. 48(2). It is equally the case that the alteration or non-recognition by the court of such agreements does not, of itself, impact on the effect of s. 48(2) for parental obligations....

[27] As to the *Charter* argument, the liberty interest that is arguably engaged relates to the fundamental personal decision on whether or not to become a parent. Section 7 of the *Charter* does not apply to purely economic rights. The fact, however, that an economic aspect is engaged is, of course, not determinative. The question to be decided is whether a particular choice of an individual falls within the protection of s. 7 as being one of fundamental personal importance. The dividing line is whether the claimed right is inherently personal and of a fundamental nature.

[28] As I see it, John Doe was not deprived by the legislative scheme of the ability to order his life and his respective rights and obligations towards Jane Doe's child as he saw fit. In fact, he chose freely to enter into a relationship of interdependence of some permanence with the mother of a newborn child. Going back to the realities, support obligations flow from the choice made by John Doe. In the result, there was no unconstitutional state interference in the rights of Jane Doe or John Doe.

[29] There is yet another aspect to the appeal. The Appellants' posture invites the Court to take a snapshot of the relationship between John Doe and the child at a given point in time. That is not what the legislation contemplates. The nature of the child's relationship with John Doe is one that must be assessed over a period of time. Indeed, s. 48(2) requires the Court to consider the duration of the child's relationship with the person and the extent to which the person is involved in the child's care. It would be an error in law, in my opinion, for the Court to pronounce a week or two after the child's birth, relying exclusively on John Doe's declaration not to treat the child as his own. In this case, there is, in the result, a factual lacuna relative to the s. 48(2) factors, and, accordingly, the declaration sought must be refused.

[30] I would add only that the child's interests were not represented in the Court below nor on appeal. I question whether public policy would countenance a declaration of the sort sought by the Appellants without a careful assessment on an adequate factual foundation of the child's interests and benefits that might be adversely affected.

[31] The appeal is dismissed.

The following case was an appeal concerning interrelated immigration and family law proceedings.

_____

JH v FA
2009 ONCA 17

WEILER JA:

[3] The appellant is a citizen of St. Lucia. She moved with her daughter, Jewel, also a citizen of St. Lucia, to Ontario in the summer of 2003. Following their arrival, the appellant made a refugee claim on behalf of herself and Jewel in relation to threats by an abusive ex-boyfriend and the alleged failure of the state to protect her and her daughter from domestic violence. The claim was denied on November 14, 2003. The Refugee Protection Division member found the appellant credible and believed her history but concluded that she had failed to rebut the presumption of state protection.

[4] The appellant applied for leave to appeal and for judicial review of the decision. Her application was denied on March 24, 2004. The appellant says that she was then incorrectly advised to wait for a pre-removal risk assessment ("PRRA").

[5] In the meantime, the appellant became involved with the respondent F.A. The two had a child together named Fianna. The appellant and F.A. lived together in Ontario from approximately January 2004 to sometime in 2005 when they separated. F.A. is on good terms with the appellant and has seen Fianna on a weekly basis since the parties separated. He has married another woman and does not want custody of Fianna but wishes to continue to have frequent and regular access with her....

The court noted the involvement of the Children's Aid Society of Toronto, and that the PRRA assessment was negative. However, the removal order was also deferred, and the appellant applied for herself and Jewel to remain in Canada on humanitarian and compassionate grounds.

[10] The H&C application was based primarily on the best interests of the children. Specifically, the appellant argued that: (1) the children would be exposed to domestic violence or would witness violence against the appellant by her ex-boyfriend if they were sent back to St. Lucia; (2) Jewel needed to remain in Canada to get adequate treatment for a learning disability which is unavailable in St. Lucia; and, (3) Fianna is a Canadian citizen who has lived in Canada all her life; she would be deprived of a relationship with her father who is unable to care for her permanently and would suffer greatly from separation from her mother and sister....

In January 2007, the CAS supervision was terminated, and the deportation was scheduled for February 2007. When the appellant's counsel requested a deferral of the removal order pending a consideration of the children's best interests in the H&C application, the request was rejected.

[13] ... The enforcement officer noted that Jewel would be able to obtain whatever educational support there was available in St. Lucia, however inferior it would be according to Canadian standards. Furthermore, he observed that Jewel's learning disability was permanent and would likely require an indefinite deferral of removal which could only be granted in

very exceptional cases. The officer also noted that the matter had been deferred pending the child protection proceedings and that no further impediments to deportation existed.

[14] On February 23, 2007, the appellant brought an application before Scully J. in the Ontario Court of Justice for custody of her two children and a non-removal order. She admitted that the reason for the request was to obtain a court order that would trigger the statutory stay of the removal order under s. 50(a) of the *Immigration and Refugee Protection Act*, 2001, c. 27, I-2.5 ("*IRPA*"). That section provides:

A removal order is stayed:
(a) if a decision that was made in a judicial proceeding — at which the Minister shall be given the opportunity to make submissions — would be directly contravened by the enforcement of the removal order;

[15] The Ministers were given short notice and an opportunity to intervene.... [The motion judge granted the appellant's application for custody and the non-removal order....]

[17] The motion judge reasoned that while other courts may at times take the best interests of children into consideration, they are not mandated to do so. He observed that the only courts that must make such a decision are the Superior Court and the Court of Justice pursuant to the provisions of the *Children's Law Reform Act* ... ("*CLRA*").... He found that it would not be in Fianna's best interests to be separated from her mother and sister. He also accepted the appellant's contention that since Fianna's father would not be willing or able to take custody of her, she would be deprived of a relationship with her father in the absence of a non-removal order.

[19] With respect to Jewel, the motion judge expressed concern that if she were removed from Ontario she would be at risk of serious harm if exposed to domestic violence or if she witnessed violence committed against her mother. He accepted the appellant's contention that it would not be in Jewel's best interests to be removed from Canada prior to the H&C application given her learning disability which, based on the uncontradicted evidence, would not be adequately addressed by the St. Lucia school system....

The Ministers successfully appealed the motion judge's decision because there was no family law *lis* between the parties, and the non-removal order amounted to a circumvention of immigration law. The judge also reasoned that the interests of the children would be adequately considered on the motion for a stay of removal.

ANALYSIS

[22] While the custody order may have been appropriate, the non-removal order as an incident of custody was not.

[23] The purpose of non-removal orders under the *CLRA* is not to frustrate the deportation of persons who have been ordered removed from Canada pursuant to the relevant immigration legislation but to prevent parents from removing children from the jurisdiction in contested family law proceedings.... It is not open to applicants scheduled to be removed by federal immigration authorities to use the family courts to stay in Ontario "under the guise of determining [the] best interests of a child." ...

[24] In this case, there was no family law dispute with respect to incidents of custody between the parents. One child's father had not participated in

the proceedings at all. The other had no desire for custody. There was no suggestion that any of the parties had any interest in removing children from Ontario. The relevant paragraphs of the order were aimed not at the parents of the child but at the respondent Ministers pending the outcome of the H&C application. The *CLRA* should not be used to frustrate the *IRPA*. The *IRPA* and related legislation is the forum in which to address immigration and related claims.

[25] [The court also referred to *Idahosa v. The Minister of Public Safety and Emergency Preparedness* 2008 FCA 418, in which Evans JA held that a *CLRA* order would not affect a section 50(a) statutory stay of the removal order:]

> [p]aragraph 50(a) does not apply to a provincial court's order awarding custody to a parent of Canadian-born children for the purpose of delaying or preventing the enforcement of a removal order against the parent, when there is no *lis* respecting custody that is unrelated to the removal.
>
> ...

[27] I agree with and would apply this analysis to the consideration of whether the non-removal order should have been made in the circumstances of this case. The reasoning in *Idahosa* is consistent with the Ontario cases which indicate that non-removal orders under the *CLRA* should not be granted for the purpose of frustrating removal orders in immigration proceedings.

[28] Furthermore, as the appeal judge observed, it is open to the appellant to make an application in the Federal Court for a stay of removal pending the determination of her H&C application. This is the appropriate forum for consideration and weighing of the various competing interests....

Notes and Questions

Defining "families" according to "law"

Each of these cases tells a story about "families" and "law":

- In *Sefton*, the court held that, in spite of the plaintiff's claim that she had lived most of her life as a member of the Gamble family, she was not a "family" member for purposes of subsidized tenancy legislation in the United Kingdom.

- In *Doe*, a couple who wished to define their individual rights and responsibilities for a child born to the woman were nonetheless required to conform to the existing legal regime for "parents" in Alberta.

- In *JH v FA*, the court defined the rights of "family" members in ways that may have resulted in separating parents from their children.

To what extent do these cases reflect theories of functionalism or familialism? What "public policy" issues may have influenced the outcomes? Do these cases suggest that family law is a matter of "private" law or "public" law? To what extent do the outcomes suggest a need for legal reform? What principles should guide decisions about how law should intervene in families?

Models for legal intervention in families

In reflecting on these questions, consider the following suggestion made by Mavis Maclean about models for legal intervention in defining the relationships between families and law:

> My starting point is to set up a number of policy models for regulating the relationship between individual, family and the state, organised around the aim of the activity. These ideal types would include a residual model for family law, which would aim to keep law out of family life and do no more than protect personal safety. Such a function might be covered sufficiently by the criminal law, though even the strictest limits placed on legislative intervention within the family tend to favour a special role for child protection. The family is often conceptualised as a "Black Box," and in a residualist approach the walls of this box are both strong and opaque. The family is "trusted" by society with self-regulation — an approach that thrives in a cohesive and stable society with well understood norms and values, such as a traditional Catholic society, or where the state is committed to liberal non-intervention, as under the recent Thatcher administration in the UK. Such a model tends to favour the status quo and therefore to be unacceptable to reformers, including feminists, concerned to counter patriarchal hegemony. At the other extreme on the continuum lies the instrumentalist model of family law, where the walls of the Black Box are transparent and permeable. Here the state uses the law to direct family life in a particular direction — whether seeking to impose a religious regime as in Israel, or a political regime as in Central and Eastern Europe between the Second World War and 1990. Extreme communitarianism may lead to a similar approach, as, for example, in the close legal control over discipline for children in Scandinavia. A "third way" may be found in what I would describe as a facilitative rights-based model, which sits well with increasing experience of multiculturalism in a global society. Here the law aims to provide a framework within which individual choice is maximised, but within the constraints of protecting human rights. For example, different ways of raising children according to religious beliefs are acceptable only up to the point at which a child's health and safety might be put at risk. (Mavis Maclean, ed, "Introduction", *Making Law for Families* (Oxford & Portland, OR: Hart Publishing, 2000) at 1–2)

Although Maclean concluded that the third "facilitative rights-based model" was the most useful model for an increasingly multicultural and global society, she also cautioned (at 5) that it presented some fundamental conceptual problems:

> [The] conceptualisation of human rights comes from concern about the relationship between the individual and the state. In family law, on the other hand, the requirement is to balance the obligations and rights of individual, family and state, and of the individual as a member of a family, not only now but in the future.

To what extent does this analysis assist your assessment of the three cases above?

Legal intervention to protect children and vulnerability

Reflect on the concluding judicial comment in *Doe* about the absence of representation of the child in that case: does this comment "fit"

Maclean's concern to protect family privacy but only "up to the point at which a child's health and safety might be put at risk"?

Note also that in *JH v FA*, the court referred to a decision of the Supreme Court of Canada, *Baker v Canada (Minister of Citizenship and Immigration)* (1999), 174 DLR (4th) 193, in which L'Heureux-Dubé J described the balancing required in such cases, stating that "emphasis on the rights, interests, and needs of children and special attention to childhood are important values that should be considered in reasonably interpreting the 'humanitarian' and 'compassionate' considerations that guide the exercise of discretion."

Comparing *Doe* and *JH v FA*, why did these courts reach different conclusions about the need to intervene to protect a child? By contrast with *JH v FA*, see *Canabate v Ayala*, 2010 ONCJ 54 for an example of a case involving a *lis* between parents in relation to a custody dispute, in which the child's mother was subject to a possible deportation order. See also *AMRI v KER*, 2011 ONCA 417.

To what extent should the elderly woman in *Sefton* qualify for legal intervention on the basis of a need for protection for vulnerable "family" members. Do you agree that there is a difference between living *as* a member of the family and *being* a member of the family?

Using theories of familialism to critique *Doe*

The *Doe* case received criticism because it appeared to reflect familialist ideals about the heterosexual dual parent family. The case addressed the test defined in the Supreme Court's decision in *Chartier v Chartier*, [1999] 1 SCR 242, for determining when an adult (who is not the biological or adoptive parent) may nevertheless "stand in the place of a parent," based on a relationship with the child's parent — particularly for purposes of paying child support. Although *Chartier* will be considered more fully later in this book, it is important here to note how differing perspectives about parent–child relationships may influence decision making about families in law. Consider the following critique of the Alberta Court of Appeal judgment in *Doe*: to what extent is this view reflected in the three models proposed by Maclean? In *Sefton* or *JH*?

> There is virtually no interrogation of the actual relationship between John Doe and the child.... According to the Court of Appeal's decision, whether John Doe has a settled intention to remain in a relationship of some permanence with Jane Doe becomes the only question. This focus on the relationship between John and Jane Doe as determinative of his parenting status is unsustainable on the face of the legislation and the leading judicial approaches to determining whether a person stands in the place of a parent. The factors set out in s. 48(2) of the Family Law Act and by the Supreme Court ... are all directed towards the relationship between the person and the child, not the relationship between the person and the mother. Moreover, if this threshold were correct, Jane Doe — and any mother like her — would be at risk of losing her exclusive parental rights simply by virtue of beginning to cohabit with a man, regardless of the nature of the relationship between him and the child. It is an approach to standing in the place of a parent in which the parental liberty rights of single mothers would be undermined as soon as they

began an intimate relationship with a man.... (Brenda Cossman, "Parenting beyond the Nuclear Family: *Doe v. Alberta*" (2007) 45 Alta L Rev 501 at para 4)

"Families" and the public/private dichotomy

In the 19th century, there was a clear distinction between "public" and "private" spheres of life, with men generally engaged in public activities and women more often in the private sphere of the home, a place which was often seen as a sacrosanct space beyond the boundaries of legal regulation. In the 20th century, legal intervention in the private sphere of the family increased to provide protection for vulnerable family members, including children in need of protection, violence (particularly against women), and elder abuse. Yet, the traditional dichotomy between the "public" and "private" spheres continues to be important, particularly in relation to family law issues. Moreover, gender continues to be important in the construction of the public/private dichotomy.

In this context, however, it is important to understand how boundaries between "public" and "private" spheres are dynamic rather than static, and how legal intervention or non-intervention may be shaped by the state's interest in families. Consider the following comment in relation to the three case examples: is it helpful in explaining the outcomes?

> [The public and private spheres] exist not so much in opposition to one another, but rather *in reciprocal connection with* one another.... The ways in which the public sphere is organized ... *rely* on a particular way of organizing the private sphere. The ability of the unencumbered individual (man) to participate in the public sphere of work and politics assumes that someone, usually a woman, is preparing his food, cleaning his house, and raising the next generation of labourers through reproductive labour. The 'sexual contract' under which women purportedly voluntarily agree to do these things supports men's ability to succeed in the public sphere and to have greater power than women both there and in the private sphere.... Families that are not structured on this model have greater difficulty negotiating the demands of family and work.... Although many individual men do not dominate the market sphere *per se*, this model enhances profit making by corporate capitalists because of the subsidization it offers to business through women's unpaid labour.... Sometimes [this model makes assumptions about women that are contradictory], particularly in an economy that increasingly expects that women will work outside the home. For example, although socioeconomic structures reinforce women's primary responsibility for child care, gender-neutral family laws tend not to acknowledge the continuing gendered nature of caregiving.... Ideologies related to 'private lives' in families thus inform not only the private sphere, but also (public) laws and social policies.... (Susan B Boyd, "Challenging the Public/Private Divide: An Overview" in Boyd, ed, *Challenging the Public/Private Divide: Feminism, Law, and Public Policy* (Toronto: University of Toronto Press, 1997) 3 at 13 and 17–18)

"Families" and the history of legal intervention in Canada

Legal and public policies have sometimes resulted in significant legal intervention for reasons other than protection of vulnerability, often causing major disruption to families and family life. For example, what public policies fostered legal intervention in the lives of families in the following examples:

- Aboriginal families who were disrupted by the system of residential schools, which removed children from their families to educational institutions where they were often precluded from speaking their own languages or practising their own religions, and where many of them were subjected to physical and sexual abuse.

- Chinese immigrants to Canada who experienced family disruption because of the head tax imposed in 1885 (after Chinese workers had assisted in building the national railway); the head tax was prohibitively expensive so that many Chinese men who immigrated to Canada to work left their wives in China.

- Legislation enacted in 1910 that required South Asian immigrants to have $200, a sum that precluded many from immigrating to Canada. In addition, South Asian women were entirely prohibited from immigrating to Canada until 1919, and then only as wives, an issue that created problems because of the lack of systematic marriage registration in India in the early 20th century.

- After the bombing of Pearl Harbour during World War II, the mass evacuation of Japanese Canadians from the west coast of Canada, which resulted in men and older boys being removed to work camps in the interior, while women and children were relocated to different encampments, a breakdown of traditional Japanese family structures.

- Black Caribbean women and Filipina women who have been permitted to come to Canada for contractual domestic work, many of them leaving families in their home countries for many years.

- Until the late 20th century, the lack of recognition of gay and lesbian "family" relationships, as well as criminal punishment for some homosexual acts.

Some of these legal policies have been the subject of recent compensation claims based on their negative impact on families and individual family members. Moreover, gay and lesbian families have achieved recognition for most purposes, including marriage. However, even with compensation and recognition, the long-term impact on families may be quite significant. In this way, issues about legal intervention in families may be a matter of social and political policy, and not simply family policy. (For further details about these historical policies in practice, see Marlene Brant Castellano, *Aboriginal Family Trends: Extended Families, Nuclear Families, Families of the Heart* (Ottawa: VIF, 2002); Bettina Bradbury, ed, *Canadian Family History: Selected Readings* (Toronto: Irwin Publications 2000); Tania das Gupta, "Families of Native People, Immigrants, and People of Colour" in N Mandell & A Duffy, eds, *Canadian Families: Diversity, Conflict and Change* (Toronto: Harcourt Canada, 2000); and Shelley AM Gavigan, "Something Old, Something New? Re-Theorizing Patriarchal Relations and Privatization from the Outskirts of Family Law" (2012) 13 Theor Inq L 271.)

Additional Resources

Cindy L Baldassi, "DNA, Discrimination and the Definition of 'Family Class'" (2007) 21 JL & Soc Pol'y 5.

Hon P Boshier et al, "The Role of the State in Family Law" (2013) 51 Fam Ct Rev 184.

John Eekelaar & Thandabantu Nhlapo, eds, *The Changing Family: International Perspectives on the Family and Family Law* (Oxford: Hart Publishing, 1998).

Judy Fudge, "The Public/Private Distinction: The Possibilities of and the Limits to the Use of Charter Litigation to Further Feminist Struggles" (1987) 25:3 Osgoode Hall LJ 485.

Sarah de Leeuw, "State of Care: The Ontologies of Child Welfare in British Columbia" (2014) 21:1 Cultural Geographies 59.

Maleiha Malik, "Family Law in Diverse Societies" in John Eekelaar & Rob George, eds, *Routledge Handbook of Family Law and Policy* (Abingdon & New York: Routledge, 2014) 424.

Mavis Maclean & John Eekelaar, "Institutional Mechanisms: Courts, Lawyers and Others" in John Eekelaar & Rob George, eds, *Routledge Handbook of Family Law and Policy* (Abingdon & New York: Routledge, 2014) 372.

Katherine O'Donovan, *Family Law Matters* (London: Pluto Press, 1993).

Frances Olsen, "The Family and the Market: A Study of Ideology and Legal Reform" (1983) 96:7 Harvard L Rev 1497.

Nikolas Rose, "Beyond the Public/Private Division: Power and the Family" (1987) 14 JL & Soc'y 61.

Margaret Thornton, ed, *Public and Private: Feminist Legal Debates* (Melbourne: Oxford University Press, 1995).

E Jane Ursel, *Private Lives, Public Policy: 100 Years of State Intervention in the Family* (Toronto: Women's Press, 1992).

IV.
THEMES IN FAMILY LAW: AN INTRODUCTION

> The story of justice is central to our story of family. The family has been a primary site for questions of justice — a site where we have been able to focus some of our broader questions of cultural morality. To say that the family is a catalyst for justice is to suggest that the way we work out contentious questions in relation to family is indicative of our democratic character as a culture.... [In this way,] "Civil society must be built and rebuilt around the nation's kitchen tables." (Kerry Daly, "Reframed Family Portraits", VIF *Transition* (Spring 2005) 3 at 6)

This section explores some of the themes that are relevant to assessing issues in the family law context. Many of these themes are contested and some of them are highly contentious as matters of law and politics. However, if families are important as a catalyst for justice (as the comment suggests), it is likely that there will be different perspectives among families and among family members about how to achieve this goal. In briefly introducing these themes here, the following excerpts may help you to identify how family law cases often reflect differing perspectives about the meaning of justice for families in law.

PRINCIPLES OF EQUALITY AND THE *CHARTER*

Equality principles and family law

Principles of equality, both among families and among family members, have often been invoked to justify legislative or judicial intervention, a trend that accelerated after enactment of the equality guarantee in the *Charter of Rights and Freedoms* in the mid-1980s:

- The concept of equality resulted in the statutory abolition of "illegitimacy" in Ontario in the 1970s (before the *Charter*) so that there is now no legal distinction on the basis of the parents' marital status at the time of a child's birth. (Other provinces abolished illegitimacy after Ontario.)

- The concept of equality has been used by fathers' rights groups to argue that their rights to custody and access of children post-separation should be the same as for mothers. In this context, some mothers have claimed that law should focus on substantive, and not merely formal, equality concepts to take account of the fact that women continue to provide more caregiving than men — a distinction between "caring about" children and "caring for" children.

- The concept of equality has been used by same-sex partners of mothers to argue for automatic parental status in terms of entitlement to birth registration, just as fathers in opposite-sex relationships, with some recent success.

These examples are discussed more fully later in this book. At this point, however, they demonstrate how ideas about equality (perhaps more often formal than substantive) have promoted many law reform efforts. At the same time, there are differing perspectives on what equality means in particular circumstances. For example, the idea of equality was used by advocates of same-sex marriage to argue that their relationships were the same in all relevant respects to heterosexual marriages, a view strongly opposed by advocates who believed that procreation was a central feature of (heterosexual) marriage.

In an early case about whether a same-sex partner was entitled to "spousal" bereavement leave to attend the funeral of his partner's father (a case decided pursuant to the wording of a collective agreement), a majority in the Supreme Court of Canada denied the claim. However, L'Heureux-Dubé J's dissenting decision provides a good example of the use of equality arguments by same-sex advocates. In the following excerpt, consider the impact of ideas about functionalism and familialism in relation to equality ideas, and the relative impact of formal and substantive equality.

Canada (AG) v Mossop
[1993] 1 SCR 554

... To look beyond the specific forms a family might take is to ask what value one sees in the family and what lies at the base of society's desire to recognize and support families. In order to define "family status," it is no error to examine the underlying values of families so that, as Lisa R. Zimmer says in "Family, Marriage, and the Same-Sex Couple" (1990), 12 *Cardozo L Rev.* 681, at p. 699, "*actual* families, rather than theoretical stereotypes, may enjoy their protected status." ...

It was argued by the intervener Focus on the Family that one of the values of the family is its importance to society in fostering procreation, and that procreation requires families to be heterosexual. The argument is that procreation is somehow necessary to the concept of family, and that same-sex couples cannot be families as they are incapable of procreation. Though there is undeniable value in procreation, [it is not valid to suggest] that the capacity to procreate limits the boundaries of family. If this were so, childless couples and single parents would not constitute families. Further, this logic suggests that adoptive families are not as desirable as natural families. The flaws in this position must have been self-evident. Though procreation is an element in many families, placing the ability to procreate as the inalterable basis of family could result in an impoverished rather than enriched vision. ...

Given the range of human preferences and possibilities, it is not unreasonable to conclude that families may take many forms. It is important to recognize that there are differences which separate as well as commonalities which bind. The differences should not be ignored, but neither should they be used to de-legitimize those families that are thought to be different and as Audre Lorde puts it in "Age, Race, Class and Sex: Women Redefining Difference" in *Sister Outsider*, 114 at p. 122: "we must recognize differences among [people] who are our equals, neither inferior nor superior, and devise ways to use each other's differences to enrich our visions and our joint struggles." ...

Notes and Questions

Some additional examples of "family" equality claims

Consider the following examples in which equality principles were used to make claims about families and family relationships. What kinds of factors might have contributed to success or failure? Although some of these cases are considered later in this book, it is useful here to reflect on how equality concepts (formal or substantive) might be used as arguments in these contexts.

1. "Spousal" status pursuant to federal legislation or in the wording of an insurance contract?
   - A gay man who applied for a "spousal" allowance when his partner in a relationship of 45 years became eligible for a pension

under the *Old Age Security Act*. Claim denied. (See *Egan v Canada*, [1995] 2 SCR 513.)

- A man in a cohabiting opposite-sex relationship, who claimed entitlement to a "spousal" benefit under an insurance policy which defined "spouse" in terms of marriage. Claim succeeded. (See *Miron v Trudel*, [1995] 2 SCR 418.)

2. Spousal status in relation to "survivor" benefits?
   - A lesbian couple who claimed that the provisions of the Income Tax Act, which precluded registration of an employer pension plan that provided spousal survivor benefits for same-sex couples, infringed *Charter* equality principles. Claim succeeded. (See *Rosenberg v Canada* (1998), 158 DLR (4th) 664 (Ont CA).)
   - A gay man who claimed the rights of a surviving cohabiting spouse for purposes of entitlement to remain in a residential apartment after his partner's death. Claim succeeded. (See *Commission des Droits de la Personne et des Droits de la Jeunesse v Québec*, [1998] AQ No 3264 (QCTDP).)

3. Sharing property or conferring children's names?
   - A woman in a cohabiting relationship who separated from her male partner and claimed entitlement to share in the province's matrimonial property-sharing regime. Claim denied. (See *Nova Scotia (AG) v Walsh*, 2002 SCC 83.)
   - A man who claimed that provincial legislation, which permitted the mother to register the birth of her child without including him (a non-married and non-cohabiting father), was unconstitutional. Claim succeeded. (See *Trociuk v British Columbia (AG)*, 2003 SCC 34.)

4. Spousal support
   A woman in a cohabiting relationship who separated from her partner claimed that the exclusion of cohabiting partners from legal protections for support and property, which is provided for married couples, was unconstitutional. Claim denied. (See *Quebec (AG) v A*, 2013 SCC 5.)

In comparing these examples, consider the following comment, which suggests how ideas of equality are often based on the rights of individuals, so that these ideas may thus be less congruent with relationships within or among families:

> [There is] a deeply held view that there is something about family law, and familial relations, that makes application of the set of public values contained in the *Charter* more problematic than it might be, say, in criminal law. The rights paradigm — based as it tends to be on a liberal vision of "the citizen" (liberalism's unencumbered individual) — does not apply easily to the family law field, where individual family members are encumbered with complex interdependencies, needs, and relations of care. Legal arguments based on either individual or group rights do not always work

well in the context of the family, when the interests of parents, children, and government/community are often inter-related and/or all at stake in different ways. The powerful familial ideology that prevails in this field, with corresponding expectations that often differ for women and men, complicates the rights framework, which is premised on formal equality, due process, and liberty/autonomy. These values are not always seen as appropriate or workable in the familial context. (Susan B Boyd, "The Impact of the Charter of Rights and Freedoms on Canadian Law" (2000) 17 Can J Fam L 283 at 297–298)

Additional Resources

Nicholas Bala, "The Charter of Rights and Family Law in Canada: A New Era" (2001) 18 Can Fam LQ 373.

Nicholas Bala & Robert Leckey, "The Charter and Family Law — The First Three Decades: A Delayed but Profound Impact" (2013) 32 Can Fam LQ 21.

Brenda Cossman, "Lesbians, Gay Men, and the Canadian Charter of Rights and Freedoms" (2002) 40 Osgoode Hall LJ 223.

Hon Claire L'Heureux-Dubé, "What a Difference a Decade Makes: The Canadian Constitution and the Family Since 1991" (2001) 27 Queen's LJ 361.

Martha Minow, "All in the Family & in All Families: Membership, Loving and Owing" (1992–93) 95 W Va L Rev 275.

Mary Jane Mossman, "Individualism and Community: Family as a Mediating Concept" in Allan Hutchinson & Leslie Green, eds, *Law and the Community: the End of Individualism* (Toronto: Carswell, 1989) 205.

Susan Moller Okin, *Justice, Gender and the Family* (New York: Basic Books, 1989).

Bruce Ryder, "The Strange Double Life of Canadian Equality Rights" (2013) 63 2d SCLR 261.

AUTONOMY VERSUS PROTECTION: INDIVIDUALS, FAMILIES AND THE STATE AND THEIR RESPONSIBILITIES FOR ECONOMIC DEPENDENCY

[A]ny adequate family law must be based on principles that take account of two paradoxical characteristics of family life and the family's relationship to the state. First, the individual must be seen simultaneously as a distinct individual and as a person fundamentally involved in relationships of dependence, care, and responsibility.... Second, family law and political theory must take account of the additional paradox that family relationships are simultaneously outside of and yet shaped by the political order.... The creation of a just family law requires reform not only of family law itself but also of the larger political and legal processes by which family law is created and applied. (Martha Minow & Mary Lyndon Shanley, "Relational Rights and Responsibilities: Revisioning the Family in Liberal Political Theory and Law" (1996) 11 Hypatia 4 at 22–25)

Autonomy versus protection and legal intervention in families

As this comment suggests, political choices about relationships between individuals, families and the state have consequences for family law. These choices may be reflected in many areas of family law where it is necessary to determine the scope of individual and/or family autonomy on one hand, and the need to ensure legal protection for vulnerable family members on the other. As noted earlier, law's traditional non-interventionist role in the "private" family in the 19th century changed, at least to some extent, in the 20th century, with legislative interventions concerning children in need of protection and the protection of adult family members from violence (including both physical and sexual violence). In addition, legal regulation controls adoption processes and, at least to some extent, processes for assisted reproduction. Yet, while there is regulated child care in most provinces, few provide resources to ensure that all children are able to access this care. In this way, the form and extent of legal intervention affects individual autonomy to make "choices," while also reflecting the law's concern to ensure protection for vulnerable family members in some aspects of family life. The child care example also reveals how issues about economic responsibility for dependency are important in family law.

"Family" responsibility for economic dependency

Particularly in the context of higher rates of marriage breakdown and separation in the late 20th century, both legislatures and courts have been active in defining ongoing economic responsibilities for (former) families, a situation that has resulted in the creation of "post-separation families." Thus, even though adult partners may have divorced or separated, they may continue to be bound together by economic obligations. Recall the statistics about family incomes and family poverty at the beginning of this chapter. To what extent do these statistics suggest that families are generally positioned to meet these obligations — particularly if family members become involved in second or subsequent families? As will be evident later in this book, legislatures and courts have continued to grapple with these issues in the context of Canada's divorce reform, perhaps with only limited success.

Significantly, this issue is also connected to the recognition of "new families" as a result of litigation based on *Charter* equality principles. That is, if law increasingly recognizes the primary responsibility of "families" for dependency, the recognition of new families reduces the state's responsibility for individual dependency, transferring it to families instead. In this way, it is important to understand family law as grounded in economic relationships, as well as love and affection. Consider the following excerpt about some recent developments in Canada:

> ... In spite of law's acceptance of the ideas of autonomy and independence for individuals within classical liberalism, it is evident that [depend-

ence is a necessary part of the human condition]. Although age, infirmity, and other conditions may render an individual adult dependent, children are inevitably dependent when they are born, even though the extent of their continuing dependence into adulthood varies according to economic and other circumstances within their families. Economic dependence may also occur for adult caregivers, whose ability to continue to engage in paid work is compromised by their care-giving responsibilities, a situation which commonly affects custodial parents (usually mothers) at separation or divorce. More systemically, governmental economic policies that assume a level of national unemployment contribute to the economic dependency of workers and their families, as do levels of minimum wages that do not result in family incomes above the poverty line. Yet, recognizing that economic dependence is part of everyday life is much easier than determining who is responsible to support dependent individuals and their families....

In the context of governmental concerns about deficit reduction in recent decades, ... there has been a trend to replace universal programs with benefits that target the poor and disadvantaged, an approach which has arguably reinforced the stigma of poverty.... [In addition,] as sociologist Margrit Eichler argued, familial obligations to provide support may have both functional and normative aspects:

> As far as the support function of families is concerned, there is widespread consensus that families not only do support their own, but *should* do so. What is often overlooked is that there tends to be a direct opposition between the notion of the family as a support system and social security programmes: to the degree that the proper locus of support for an individual is seen to lie within that individual's family, the individual becomes *disentitled* from public support....

[Thus, in spite of permanent separation on the part of cohabiting spouses or a final divorce decree for married couples,] former spouses and their children have been categorized by the Supreme Court of Canada as a "post-divorce family unit," who *should* have continuing economic and other obligations to provide support for dependent family members....

[At the same time,] courts have responded positively to [equality] claims presented by opposite-sex cohabitees and by gay and lesbian activists for legal recognition of their "families," including entitlement to marry. However, such claims for judicial recognition of same-sex families have generally been designed to attain equal access to the *benefits* of "family status".... Yet, ... courts have *at the same time* been redefining responsibility for economic dependency within families, ... and shifting primary responsibility away from the state.... In this way, judicial decisions about "new families" and the evolving jurisprudence about "new family obligations" appear to have converged to expand not just the *rights*, but also the *obligations*, of Canadian families, including same-sex families.... (Mary Jane Mossman, "Conversations about Families in Canadian Courts and Legislatures: Are there 'Lessons' for the United States?" (2003) 32:1 Hofstra L Rev 171 at 183–185 and 190–191)

Notes and Questions

Economic dependency and autonomy
In *Moge v Moge*, [1992] 3 SCR 813, the Supreme Court of Canada took judicial notice of the phenomenon of the "feminization of poverty" for

post-separation women and children. As the statistics at the beginning of this chapter reveal, however, even intact Canadian families often have only marginal levels of income. As a result, divorce or separation — which frequently requires the establishment of two households — may result in economic challenges and distress for many families.

In this context, it is important to acknowledge that legal principles concerning the sharing of family resources at separation have most often been decided in cases where there was sufficient family wealth to make litigation possible, sometimes including an appeal to the Supreme Court of Canada. However, the same principles are generally applied in cases involving more "ordinary" families with much lower levels of wealth or income. In this way, concrete financial circumstances may need to be taken into account in assessing the relevance of theoretical ideas about autonomy and independence for family members, another aspect of the relationship between "families" and "law."

Additional Resources

Carlos A Ball, "This is Not Your Father's Autonomy: Lesbian and Gay Rights from a Feminist and Relational Perspective" in Jack Jackson, Martha Albertson Fineman & Adam P Romero, eds, *Feminist and Queer Legal Theory: Intimate Encounters, Uncomfortable Conversations* (Farnham & Burlington: Ashgate Publishing, 2013) 289.

Alison Diduck, *Law's Families* (London: LexisNexis, 2003).

Martha Fineman, "Equality, Autonomy, and the Vulnerable Subject in Law and Politics" in Martha Fineman & Anna Grear, eds, *Vulnerability: Reflections on a New Ethical Foundation for Law and Politics* (Farnham & Burlington: Ashgate Publishing, 2014).

Martha Fineman, "Masking Dependency: The Political Role of Family Rhetoric" (1995) 81 Va L Rev 2181.

Nancy Fraser, "A Genealogy of *Dependency*: Tracing a Keyword of the U.S. Welfare State" (Winter 1994) 19:2 Signs: Journal of Women in Culture and Society 309.

Jonathan Herring, *Relational Autonomy and Family Law* (Oxford: Springer, 2014).

Robert Leckey, *Contextual Subjects: Family, State and Relational Theory* (Toronto: University of Toronto Press, 2008).

Mary Jane Mossman, " 'Running Hard to Stand Still': The Paradox of Family Law Reform" (1994) 17:1 Dalhousie LJ 5.

Pamela Symes, "Property, Power and Dependence: Critical Family Law" (1987) 14 JL & Soc'y 199.

Lenore Weitzman & Mavis Maclean, eds, *Economic Consequences of Divorce: The International Perspective* (Oxford: Clarendon Press, 1992).

Margot Young, ed, *Poverty: Rights, Social Citizenship and Legal Activism* (Vancouver: UBC Press, 2007).

FAMILY LAW AND ITS PROCESSES: THE CONSTITUTION, LEGISLATORS AND JUDGES, AND CLIENTS

The Constitution and the division of legislative authority for family law

Later chapters in this book will review in more detail the impact of the division of legislative authority for specific family law matters in Canada, and their interpretation by the courts. At the outset, however, this section provides general information about family law and the Constitution.

Pursuant to section 91(26) of the Constitution, the federal Parliament has authority to legislate with respect to "marriage and divorce". In practice, only the federal government can legislate about divorce and, as a result of judicial interpretation of this power, the divorce power includes "corollary" matters such as support and child custody and access.

The federal Parliament's authority to legislate with respect to marriage is, however, limited by the Constitution's granting of provincial authority to legislate with respect to matters of solemnization or formalities relating to marriage. The federal Parliament's authority with respect to marriage pursuant to section 91(26), therefore, has been held to relate only to matters of inherent capacity to marry.

The provincial legislatures have two heads of power in relation to family law:

- Section 92(12) and the "solemnization of marriage": This power was interpreted early in the 20th century to include "formalities." As a result, provincial statutes may include requirements such as the need to obtain a licence, or the requisite language for a valid marriage ceremony.

- Section 92(13) and "property and civil rights": This power means that much of family law is found in provincial statutes. Moreover, because persons who cohabit without marrying are not able to divorce, provisions relating to the re-adjustment of financial matters at the end of a cohabiting relationship, including support and child custody and access, are also found in provincial statutes.

As will be clear, the constitutional division of powers in family law matters in Canada may be quite complex in some cases. The appendix at the end of this chapter offers a brief overview of statutes in Ontario relating to different kinds of family law issues discussed in this book. It is intended to provide a useful tool for further reference as you engage with these family law issues.

Access to justice: "Rules" or "discretion" in family law?

[Family law] becomes the context in which those contradictions or oppositions that cannot be resolved politically are worked through.... [I]n seeking legislatively to re-constitute a sense of organic or collective family values around the family and divorce, legislators have in fact created a set of inconsistent principles and commitments ... while at the same time using law to give the appearance of having created shared values; and then having off-loaded the detailed working out of those contradictions to the [family law] system. (John Dewar, "The Normal Chaos of Family Law" (1998) 61 Mod L Rev 467 at 484)

As Dewar's comment suggests, there is a tension in family law between legislative "rules" and judicial discretion. As he noted, family law statutes sometimes provide only general principles so that judges must exercise discretion in applying them to individual cases. For example, Dewar's comment focused on the legal principle concerning child custody, that is, that custody should be determined in accordance with "the best interests of the child." As he concluded, the general nature of this legislative principle may require the exercise of considerable judicial discretion in individual cases.

While some family law principles continue to be legislated in these general terms, recent legislative reforms have attempted to make some aspects of family law more certain. For example, child support guidelines now require judges to provide written reasons if they wish to deviate from the guidelines, and the property-sharing regime in Ontario has generally limited judicial discretion.

As will be evident in this book, family law frequently attempts to balance two different goals:

• Fairness in individual cases (generally achieved by the exercise of judicial "discretion" for individual families), and (at the same time)

• Certainty and finality (most often achieved by inflexible legislative "rules" that apply regardless of unfairness to some families in individual cases)

Obviously, these two goals may not be congruent. And, although these issues about rules and discretion often characterize other areas of law, the choice of individual fairness versus certainty and finality may be experienced particularly keenly by family law clients — people whose lives may be affected significantly, perhaps for a long time, by these choices of rules and/ or discretion.

As well, of course, most family law litigants can ill-afford to pay for legal services that include lengthy trials about matters that may seem to be only "minor" to lawyers and judges. In this way, legislative choices with respect to goals of fairness and certainty in family law matters must also balance the need for processes of access to justice that are inexpensive and uncomplicated. These issues — about fairness and certainty in relation to family law clients' expectations of justice, and the practical implementation of these goals in legal processes — will be much in evidence in the materials in this book.

Access to justice: Legal and other processes in family law matters

What are the stories told to us of family conflicts and disputes that go to law, and become the stuff of which the law is made? Do these stories represent what was told, or have they been transformed by lawyers, judges and others, by law's procedures and practices? And what of the stories untold in law because the silent cannot speak or lawyers cannot hear? (Katherine O'Donovan, *Family Law Matters* (London: Pluto Press, 1993) at 106)

"Facts" in Family Law Matters

As in other areas of law, judges and lawyers are generally interested in facts only if they are related to applicable legal principles. By contrast, family law clients all too often want to "tell their stories" to law, and they may experience a strong sense of injustice when the law provides no opportunity for them to do so. While this sense of injustice often occurs in courtroom litigation, some clients also become frustrated when even their own lawyers seem so uninterested in their "facts." Of course, lawyers' judgments about how to pursue clients' interests without excessive costs may also affect how lawyers hear their clients' stories, particularly if lawyers are committed to making family justice accessible. As a result, to understand the dynamics of some family law cases, it may be important to reflect on whether they present "untold" stories in family law, at least for some clients.

Although it may occur in a number of different family law contexts, this lack of "fit" between clients' stories and legally relevant facts is particularly evident in the context of no fault divorce, where no legal purpose is served by details of the reasons for marriage breakdown. In this context, clients who feel a need to "tell this story" may experience divorce as a legal process that fails to achieve justice for them. See Austin Sarat & William Felstiner, *Divorce Lawyers and their Clients: Power and Meaning in the Legal Process* (New York: Oxford University Press, 1995).

Courts and "Alternative" Processes for Resolving Family Law Disputes

In some cases, family law matters are complicated by jurisdictional requirements relating to courts: for example, in general terms, superior courts have exclusive jurisdiction in relation to some matters (such as divorce and property) and provincial courts have jurisdiction in other matters (such as adoption). Clearly, in the context of efforts to make family law courts and processes accessible to litigants, these jurisdictional complexities with respect to the appropriate court may represent significant barriers to effective reform. In parts of Ontario, and in some other provinces, the creation of Family Law Courts, with jurisdiction in all family law matters and frequently presided over by judges with special expertise in family law, may overcome some of these problems.

As will be explored later in this book, there are now a variety of alternatives to litigation for resolving family law disputes, particularly with respect to divorce and separation, and some of them require lawyers to use quite different skills from those that are employed in litigation. For many clients, the choice of process thus also becomes an important decision, so that information and advice is just as necessary with respect to legal procedures as in relation to substantive rights. Yet, in spite of these needs, increasing numbers of family law clients are self-represented for lack of financial resources, a situation that impedes access to justice in other ways. In this context, family law processes have been the subject of many studies and pilot projects designed to reduce barriers to access to justice. As many of these studies focus particularly on issues about divorce and separation, these issues are discussed more fully in this context later in this book.

The Use of Experts in Family Law Matters

Finally, like other civil law matters, family law disputes may raise issues about when and how to involve other professionals in such disputes. This issue about professional or expert evidence to determine facts in family law cases presents special challenges for the autonomy of individuals and families and their private lives, and another issue for determination by decision makers in family law cases. In addition, the use of experts may increase the cost of litigation for the parties, although cases involving children may sometimes permit courts to order assessments by social workers, psychologists or psychiatrists without cost to the parties. However, it also requires judges and other decision makers to assess evidence presented by family members and experts in determining family law "facts," a situation that sometimes has potential to create "untold stories."

Additional Resources

Rachel Birnbaum, Nicholas Bala & Lorne Bertrand, "The Rise of Self-representation in Canada's Family Courts: The Complex Picture Revealed in Surveys of Judges, Lawyers and Litigants" (2013) 91 Can Bar Rev 67.

Martha L Fineman & Anne Opie, "The Uses of Social Science Data in Legal Policy Making: Custody Determinations at Divorce" (1987) Wis L Rev 107.

Judge Nigel Fricker, "Family Law is Different" (1995) Fam Ct Rev 403 at 404.

Avner Levin & Asher Alkoby, "Is access to the profession access to justice? Lessons from Canada" (2012) 19.2–3 Intl J Leg Prof 283.

Julie Macfarlane, *The New Lawyer: How Settlement is Transforming the Practice of Law* (Vancouver: UBC Press, 2008).

Alfred Mamo, Peter Jaffe & Debbie Chiodo, *Recapturing and Renewing the Vision of the Family Court* (Toronto: Ministry of the Attorney General, 2007).

Carrie Menkel-Meadow, "Lawyer Negotiations: Theories and Realities — What We Learn from Mediation" (1993) 56 Mod L Rev 361.

Mary Jane Mossman, "Gender Equality, Family Law and Access to Justice" (1994) Intl JL & Fam 357.

Christine Piper, "How Do You Define a Family Lawyer?" (1999) 19 LS 93.

APPENDIX
A Brief Overview of Federal and Ontario statutes in Family Law Matters

Federal	Provincial
Section 91: Federal authority 91(26): "Marriage and divorce"	*Section 92: Provincial authority* 92(12): "Solemnization of marriage" 92(13): "Property and civil rights"
A. Marriage Inherent capacity: • Common law requirements • *Marriage (Prohibitive Degrees) Act* • *Civil Marriage Act*	*A. Marriage* Formalities: *Marriage Act*
B. Intact Families	*B. Intact Families* Adoption: • *Child and Family Services Act* Children in need of protection: • *Child and Family Services Act* Domestic Violence: • *Family Law Act*
C. Divorce and Corollary Relief Grounds: • *Divorce Act* Property: N/A Contracts: N/A Spousal support: • *Divorce Act* (for spouses seeking divorce) Custody/access: • *Divorce Act* (for spouses seeking divorce) Child support: • *Divorce Act* (for spouses seeking divorce)	*C. Divorce and Corollary Relief* Property: • *Family Law Act*, Parts I and II Contracts: • *Family Law Act*, Part IV Spousal support: • *Family Law Act*, Part III (for cohabitees; and for spouses not seeking divorce) Custody/access: • *Children's Law Reform Act* (for cohabitees; and for spouses not seeking divorce) Child support: • *Family Law Act*, Part III; and • *Children's Law Reform Act* (for cohabitees; and for spouses not seeking divorce)

PART 1

Legal Regulation of Family Formation

2

Forming Families:
Marriage in the Context of Cohabitation

I.
MARRIAGE: TRADITION VERSUS CHANGE?

Marriage has been well said to be something more than a contract, either religious or civil — to be an Institution. It creates mutual rights and obligations, as all contracts do, but beyond that it confers a status. (*Hyde v Hyde and Woodmansee* (1866), LR 1 P&D 130 at 133)

Marriage has been widely debated in recent years. Perhaps no single issue touches more people. Everyone — those who are married, those who have chosen not to marry or remarry and those who have not had the opportunity to choose — has an opinion. Their opinions are based on their own experiences and on the experiences of their parents, their children and families, friends and neighbours, as well as on their values and beliefs. (Department of Justice Canada, "Marriage and Legal Recognition of Same-Sex Unions: A Discussion Paper" (November 2002) at 1)

As these quotations suggest, ideas about marriage in Canada reflect both its traditional origins and a current state of flux:

• In the 19th century, "marriage" and "family" were historically linked and almost synonymous: that is, the law did not recognize families established without a legal marriage — the adult partners were not regarded as having any of the rights of marriage (including inheritance, etc.), and any children of the union were called "illegitimate." As the English court described the marriage relationship (above) in *Hyde* (just one year before Confederation in Canada), marriage was traditionally understood as both a contract and a legal status with its own prescribed rights and obligations. Yet, as rates of opposite-sex marriage increasingly declined in the latter part of the 20th century, many of these rights and obligations (but not all of them) have been increasingly extended to cohabiting couples.

* At the present time, ideas about marriage in Canada are in flux. As the Department of Justice's *Discussion Paper* in 2002 suggested, it is an issue that touches most people in Canada, particularly in the context of Canada's decision (among a number of other jurisdictions in the world) to legally recognize same-sex marriage in federal legislation in 2005. In the context of debates about same-sex marriage, there were a number of different reform proposals, some of which would have resulted in quite comprehensive changes. In the end, the 2005 legislation merely included same-sex couples in its requirement for "two persons" for a valid marriage (see *Civil Marriage Act*, SC 2005, c 33), a result that precludes recognition of plural unions (including polygamy) within the existing marriage regime. Some of these issues remain complex in relation to non-conjugal interdependent relationships and marriage for trans persons.

In this context, the law of marriage represents both traditional, sometimes rather ancient, notions about intimate adult relationships, and at the same time, new ideas about the meaning of marriage bonds in the 21st century. It also reveals how legal regulation has extended many of the rights and obligations of marriage to couples in cohabiting relationships. Thus, although many people form families without regard to the legal rights and obligations that result, their lack of attention to law does not make it irrelevant, nor does it make their legal obligations unenforceable. More importantly, the law of marriage may create norms and ideals about families that operate to create social expectations for families. In this way, an exploration of marriage provides an opportunity to examine the law's fundamental assumptions about intimate relationships, and the legal rights and obligations that flow from them, and to explore the impact of these assumptions on recent reforms.

Organization of this chapter

This chapter focuses on the formation of families by exploring the law relating to marriage, in the context of cohabitation.

It begins by examining the context for the law of marriage in relation to cohabitation, including some information about the extension of the legal rights and obligations of marriage to cohabiting couples.

The material then examines the historical context of marriage in relation to the traditional English law of annulment and the impact of the constitutional division of powers in Canada. This background is relevant to an examination of legal principles about the validity of marriage, including the historical requirements of English common law, some federal amendments, and provincial marriage statutes in Canada.

The chapter then explores law reform proposals and the law's underlying assumptions about marriage and conjugality by considering current challenges in the context of other interdependent relationships and marriage for trans persons.

II.
MARRIAGE IN THE CONTEXT OF COHABITATION

THE SOCIAL CONTEXT

> Cohabitation implies less commitment while offering many of the advantages of marriage. It allows the couple to live in a family environment, provides the couple with the scale of economy, and, at the same time, offers them benefits of the single state. More important, it allows them to try out the relationship and see whether the relationship will work.... (Zheng Wu, *Cohabitation: An Alternative Form of Family Living* (Toronto: Oxford University Press, 2000) at 154)

Data about marriage and cohabitation

Wu's comment reflects how people fashion their families to meet their own needs (often without regard to the law). As the data discussed in Chapter One reveals, the numbers of cohabiting couples are increasing: in 2011, they represented 16.7% of all census families, a proportion that had almost tripled in three decades (Statistics Canada, *Fifty Years of Families in Canada: 1961 to 2011* (Ottawa: Statistics Canada, 2012) at 1).

According to the Vanier Institute study (Vanier Institute of the Family, *Families Count: Profiling Canada's Families* (Ottawa: Vanier Institute of the Family 2010) at 32–42):

- Cohabitation is particularly prevalent among Canadians in their twenties and thirties, and many of these couples view cohabitation as a prelude to marriage (as Wu's comment suggested).

- A second group that increasingly favours cohabitation over marriage is older persons whose first marriage was dissolved by divorce.

- Cohabitation is especially widespread in Québec. About 70 percent of Québec women will start their conjugal life in a cohabiting relationship, compared with 34 percent elsewhere in Canada. Significantly, cohabiting couples in Québec have fewer legal rights and obligations than in other parts of Canada, thus making marriage and cohabitation quite distinctive choices in Québec.

- Among same-sex couples in Canada, about 16.5 percent were married, according to the 2006 census, with the highest percentage of such marriages in Ontario and British Columbia. Perhaps reflecting the preference for cohabitation rather than marriage there, Québec had the lowest percentage of married same-sex couples at 9.2 percent. By 2011, the proportion of married same-sex couples in Canada had nearly doubled, to 32.5%. (Statistics Canada, *Portrait of Families and Living Arrangements in Canada: Families, households and marital status, 2011 Census Population* (Ottawa: Statistics Canada, 2012) at 8.)

Both Wu's study and the details in the Vanier Institute's *Families Count* reflect how people are choosing to live in families — often without knowledge or concerns about legal consequences. Indeed, Wu suggested that cultural or ideological changes in ideas about "family," such as the increasing emphasis on individual interests, may encourage people to choose cohabitation rather than traditional marriage. Other sociological explanations focus on the rejection of traditional gender roles, women's increasing economic independence through labour force participation, and greater acceptance of sexual activity outside of marriage, all of which may contribute to weakening the attraction of marriage as a social institution (Wu at 154–156).

In a study published in 2003, Anne Millan examined data from the 2001 General Social Survey to determine the extent to which never married and previously married people, who had never lived in a cohabiting relationship, would be willing to do so in future. In her study, she has the following observations (Anne Millan, "Would You Live Common-Law?" *Canadian Social Trends*, Catalogue No. 11-008 (Ottawa: Statistics Canada, 2003) at 2):

- 62 percent of men, but only 36 percent of women, said they would consider cohabitation, although the willingness to do so declined with age for both sexes.

- Higher levels of education and labour force participation were factors more often associated with a willingness to consider cohabitation.

- People in Québec were more willing, by comparison with other parts of Canada, to cohabit. However, the proportion of people willing to consider cohabitation in Québec was higher for persons whose home language was French (63 percent) than for those whose home language was English (46 percent); and only 26 percent of those whose home language was other than English or French expressed a willingness to consider cohabitation. Similarly, the willingness to cohabit was higher for Canadian-born individuals than for those born outside Canada, and frequent attendance at religious services was associated with less willingness to cohabit and greater interest in marriage.

- Childhood experiences of family breakup were somewhat related to a willingness to cohabit; for men and women who lived with both parents up to the age of 15, there was less willingness to cohabit than among those whose parents had divorced, separated or become widowed.

THE LEGAL CONTEXT

In recognition of the changing patterns of non-marital cohabitation, the rights and responsibilities imposed on matrimonial couples should be extended to cohabiting couples in all provinces provided that some permanence of the relationship is established [by cohabiting continuously for one year, by becoming the natural or adoptive parents of a child, or by registering as partners pursuant to provincial legislation]. In short, cohabiting individuals should have the same rights and obligations as married persons (Wu at 167).

Marriage and cohabitation: Reform?

Wu's recommendation to extend the rights and obligations associated with marriage to cohabiting couples reflected his assessment that existing patterns of cohabitation in Canada reveal a high degree of functional similarity between marriage and cohabitation. Although he acknowledged arguments for distinguishing marriage and cohabitation, including the need to preserve choice for individuals to design their own families, or the need for the state to provide incentives to marry, Wu concluded that legal regulation of cohabitation was necessary for a number of reasons:

- To ensure protection for dependency when cohabitation ends (similar to marriage).
- To treat functionally similar relationships according to legal principles of equality.
- To avoid ongoing confusion about the (different) consequences of marriage and cohabitation.

Thus, after examining the nature of cohabiting relationships and the policy arguments about cohabitation and marriage, Wu recommended that they be treated in the same way (see Wu at 167).

This issue, about whether or not marriage and cohabitation should have the same treatment in family law, remains somewhat controversial. Recall the case in Chapter One, *Jane Doe v Alberta*, in which the court rejected the claim of adult partners who wished to structure their family life according to their own wishes. As this case revealed, an important reason for legal intervention in cohabiting relationships is the need to protect vulnerable family members. However, as the *Jane Doe* case revealed, there are other values that may be constrained by legal intervention in families. Some of these arguments are identified in the excerpt that follows: to what extent do you agree with the author's recommendations with respect to the rationale for legal intervention?

Intimate Relationships in the New Millennium:
The Assimilation of Marriage and Cohabitation
(2000) 17:1 Can J Fam L 114 at 151–167

Winnifred Holland

[The ascription] model is based on ascribing spousal status to cohabitants. It assumes that there is very little difference between marriage and cohabitation and that rights and obligations associated with marriage should be extended automatically to cohabitants who fit the criteria specified (unless there is a contract to the contrary).

The state has an interest in promoting long-lasting familial relationships, which embrace intimacy, sharing and interdependence. The state also has an interest in providing a scheme for the orderly, fair and equitable distribution of resources, once such relationships break down. It is recognized that spouses are entitled to share in the fruits of the relationship, which are the result of joint efforts during the relationship. Initially the focus was on marriage, but increasingly, it is being recognized that other relationships, particularly cohabitation relationships whether opposite or same-sex, are functionally similar.

Today, there is very little difference between marriage and cohabitation. Marriage encompasses a range of relationships, some characterized by various forms of dependency, while others involve spouses who are quite independent, financially and otherwise. Marriage may or may not involve procreation. Cohabitation relationships are found along a similar spectrum. There is no reason to differentiate between the two based on the notion that cohabitation is different from a traditional marriage. When we compare cohabitation and modern-day marriage there are few distinctions.

Those who focus on autonomy believe that it is important to maintain a distinction between marriage and cohabitation, based on the choice made by the cohabitants. However, it is not clear whether cohabitants have indeed chosen to avoid the obligations of matrimony. Undoubtedly there are some "free spirits" who choose to avoid matrimony, but in many other cases the couple may have drifted into cohabitation. In other cases, one party may have made the choice over the objections of the other who might have preferred to marry....

Most couples do not engage in "crystal-ball" gazing at the inception of the relationship and do not have a clear idea which obligations they are consciously choosing to avoid....

In any event, why is it appropriate to put so much emphasis on what occurs at the inception of the relationship? ... Whether the lives of cohabitants have subsequently become intertwined ("braided lives") and mutual sacrifices have been made are more important than original intentions in situations where those intentions were not embodied in any formal agreement....

If cohabitants were forced to resort to contract or register domestic partnerships, or the like, they would not enter into such agreements. There is no tradition in common law Canada of resorting to contract except in the use of separation agreements. Consequently, it is very important to determine the appropriate "default" position that would prevail in the absence of an agreement. It is preferable to put the onus on those who wish to avoid obligations rather than on those who wish to create them.... If one partner wishes to avoid such obligations the onus should be on that person to have a domestic contract drawn up so that they will not be going into the relationship with "eyes wide shut."

After considering the arguments in favour of continuing to distinguish between marriage and cohabitation, including the emphasis on choice for partners who are capable of deciding what is in their best interests, the author concluded:

There are compelling arguments on both sides but, on balance, the [ascription model] has more to commend it. On balance, it seems preferable to have inclusion rather than exclusion as the "default option," leaving it to those couples who want to avoid such consequences to opt out.... The gap between marriage and ... cohabitation has narrowed significantly to the point where there seems little justification for continuing to maintain any gap between the two.... We should at least attempt to ensure that both partners share similar views on the preservation of personal autonomy and requiring an opting-out contract goes some way towards that goal....

Notes and Questions

Empirical research and legal policies

Both the Vanier Institute's *Families Count* and the research study undertaken by Zheng Wu rely on data about cohabiting couples in Canada. Much of the data suggest that families of cohabiting couples fulfill the same functions as married couples, and Wu used this functional similarity to argue for equality of treatment in legal policies, thus "assimilating" cohabiting couples and married couples. To what extent should empirical data about families inform legal policies? Are there limitations to such data that should be considered? Is there a danger that functional similarity may also promote a view of "familialism," an ideology that privileges marriage as the primary relationship in law? This issue may be particularly important in the context of same-sex marriage and cohabitation, an issue that is addressed more fully later in this chapter.

Legislative and judicial approaches to marriage and cohabitation

In common law Canada, many of the rights and obligations of married partners have been extended, both in legislation and by the courts, to cohabiting couples. For example, obligations of spousal and child support currently apply to both married couples who divorce and cohabiting couples who separate. However, two important differences remain: only married persons are eligible to obtain a divorce. In addition, legislative entitlement to share in property at the end of a relationship is available to married persons in every Canadian jurisdiction, but not always to those in cohabiting relationships. However, the legal rights and obligations of married couples and cohabiting couples have been converging in recent decades in common law Canada with Nunavut, the Northwest Territories, Manitoba, Saskatchewan and British Columbia all passing legislation that extends property entitlements to cohabiting couples. (See Donalee Moulton, "Common law couples face changing reality", *The Lawyers Weekly* (6 April 2012) 10.) Interestingly, there are more significant differences in the legal rights and obligations of married partners and cohabiting couples under the Québec *Civil Code* (for details about property sharing at relationship dissolution, see Chapter Six).

The role of contracts: "Opting in" or "opting out"?

As the excerpt from Holland noted, one way of assessing the appropriateness of extending the rights and obligations of marriage to cohabiting couples is to define a "default" regime, and to permit parties to either "opt in" or "opt out" of the regime. Why did Holland consider that a default regime that treated married and cohabiting couples in the same way, with each group having the choice to "opt out" by contract, a better approach than one requiring cohabiting couples to "opt in" to the rights and responsibilities of marriage? To what extent does Holland's proposal continue to recognize a need for law to provide protection for vulnerable family members? A more recent proposal would permit a couple to enter into a "fixed-term" marriage that would dissolve after four years unless the parties took legal steps to renew it: see Sarah Boesveld & Tristan Hopper, "One Law Student Has a Radical Proposal for Fixing Marriage: Cut it Off After Four Years", *National Post* (8 August 8 2014). Would this proposal prove more or less workable than Holland's "opt out" model for cohabitants? What are the advantages and disadvantages of each model? In this context, of course, recall that courts may limit opportunities to contract "out" of some family responsibilities: see again *Jane Doe v Alberta*.

Reforming marriage and cohabitation

In the context of arguments about the extension of the rights and obligations of marriage to cohabiting couples, some scholars have suggested a need to reconsider the nature and indicia of marriage itself. Perhaps the most significant effort was the report of the Law Commission of Canada in 2001, *Beyond Conjugality: Recognizing and Supporting Close Personal Adult Relationships*. This document examined the underlying premises of marriage rights and responsibilities, assessed a number of proposals for redefining close personal adult relationships in law to include interdependent units other than married couples, and recommended expansion of law's concerns for dependency and vulnerability in such relationships. Some jurisdictions, such as New South Wales in Australia, now permit siblings and others who are not in intimate conjugal relationships to "opt in" to the legal rights and responsibilities traditionally associated with marriage. These issues are addressed briefly at the end of this chapter in terms of ongoing issues for law reform in Canada.

Additional Resources

Anne-Marie Ambert, "Cohabitation and Marriage: How are they Related?" (Ottawa: Vanier Institute of the Family, 2005).

Nicholas Bala, "The Controversy over Couples in Canada: The Evolution of Marriage and Other Adult Interdependent Relationships" (2003) 29 Queen's LJ 41.

Nicholas Bala & Marlène Cano, "Unmarried Cohabitants in Canada: Common Law and Civilian Approaches to Living Together" (1989) 4 Can Fam LQ 147.

Alain Bélanger & Pierre Turcotte, "L'Influence des caractéristiques sociodémographiques sur le début de la vie conjugale des Québécoises" (1999) 28 Cahiers québécois de démographie 173.

Ruth Deech, "The Case Against Legal Recognition of Cohabitation" in John Eekelaar & Sanford Katz, eds, *Marriage and Cohabitation in*

Contemporary Societies: Areas of Legal, Social and Ethical Change (Toronto: Butterworths, 1980) 300.

Alison Diduck, ed, *Marriage and Cohabitation* (Aldershot: Ashgate Publishing, 2008).

Évelyne LaPierre-Adamcyk, Céline Le Bourdais & Nicole Marcil-Gratton, "Vivre en couple pour la première fois: La signification du choix de l'union libre au Québec et en Ontario" (1999) 28 Cahiers québécois de démographie 199.

Robert Leckey, "Cohabitation and Comparative Method" (2009) 72:1 Mod L Rev 48.

Katherine O'Donovan, "Legal Marriage — Who Needs It?" (1984) 47 Mod L Rev 111.

Rebecca Probert, *The Legal Regulation of Cohabitation, 1600–2010: From Fornicators to Family* (Cambridge: Cambridge University Press, 2012).

Carol Smart, "Stories of Family Life: Cohabitation, Marriage and Social Change" (2000) 17:1 Can J Fam L 1.

III.
THE LEGAL CONTEXT FOR DEFINING THE VALIDITY OF MARRIAGE: THE LAW OF ANNULMENT AND THE CONSTITUTIONAL DIVISION OF POWERS

THE LAW OF ANNULMENT: A BRIEF HISTORY

An overview

The common law of marriage is complicated because marriage emerged first as a social and religious institution, and was not generally regulated in English law until the 18th century.

- **From private consent to public ceremony:** According to Martin Ingram, an indissoluble union could be created as early as the 12th century solely by the consent of the two parties expressed in words in the present tense (*per verba de praesenti*). Solemnization in church was not required, nor was the presence of witnesses. In this context, the emphasis was on individual freedom of consent by the parties. Eventually, concerns about evils arising from clandestine marriages, as well as confusion and uncertainty about marital status, resulted in the decree of the Council of Trent in 1563. The decree, which applied to Catholic Europe, invalidated marriages that were not performed in public before a parish priest. Although similar changes were adopted in some continental Protestant countries, it was not until 1753 that similar provisions were formally adopted by the English Parliament in *Lord Hardwicke's Act: An Act for the better preventing of clandestine marriages*, 26 Geo II, c 33. However, according to Ingram, social and legal pressures had encouraged public ceremonies of marriage even prior to 1753. (For details, see Martin Ingram, *Church Courts, Sex, and Marriage in England, 1570–1640* (Cambridge: Cambridge University Press, 1987) at 132–33 and 218.)

- **Marriage validity defined by ecclesiastical (church) courts:** In this context, it was early ecclesiastical courts that had responsibility for determining the validity of marriage, issuing decrees of nullity for marriages that failed to meet requirements based on social and religious practices, as well as a few established by Acts of Parliament. Some of these requirements remain in force still — for example, the consent of the parties remains an important requirement for a valid marriage, and affirmation of consent by the couple in a public setting is still part of the marriage ceremony. When the English *Matrimonial Causes Act* was enacted in 1857, however, it abolished the jurisdiction of ecclesiastical courts, assigning this jurisdiction to the regular system of courts in England.

- **The law of annulment in Canada:** Interestingly, for some years in the early 20th century, judges in Ontario asserted that Ontario courts did not have jurisdiction to grant decrees of nullity because no similar ecclesiastical court jurisdiction had ever existed in Ontario, and thus the nullity jurisdiction had never been transferred to Ontario courts. As a result, federal legislation was enacted in 1930 — the *Annulment of Marriages Act (Ontario)* — conferring on Ontario courts the jurisdiction to grant decrees of nullity: see RSC 1970, c A-14. This legislation introduced into Ontario the law of nullity in England as of 15 July 1870, so that Ontario's current law of nullity is derived from principles originally adopted by the English ecclesiastical courts. In the four western provinces of Canada, the 1857 English legislation remains the law of annulment, while some pre-1857 colonial statutes remain effective in the Maritimes; and because of their origin in canon law, these common law principles are similar to those in the Québec *Civil Code*. (For further details, see Christine Davies, *Family Law in Canada* (Scarborough, ON: Carswell Legal Publications, 1984) at 35–39.)

Distinguishing between annulment and divorce

Before the advent of accessible divorce actions in Canada, nullity actions represented the only way for married couples to end their relationships legally. However, after divorce reform in 1968 (as amended in the mid-1980s), grounds for divorce can now be readily established by proof of "marriage breakdown," most often by a period of separation for one year. In this context, actions for nullity are less common, although not unknown, particularly where one spouse wishes to avoid religious problems that may accompany divorce.

Yet, although annulment and divorce both result in the end of a marriage, it is the traditional law of annulment that continues to inform the principles concerning a valid marriage in Canada — in spite of their 19th century origins. Moreover, it is important to understand the significant conceptual difference between annulment and divorce.

An order to annul a marriage can be made only where the marriage is legally *invalid*: that is, one or more of the requisite elements of a valid marriage is not present. By contrast, a divorce can be granted only if the parties can prove that a *valid* marriage has existed.

"Void" and "voidable" marriage in the law of annulment: A brief note

The law of annulment traditionally distinguished between "void" and "voidable" marriages, although these distinctions are not discussed in detail in this book. Briefly, a void marriage is one that is non-existent in law, even if it has not been formally annulled by a court. By contrast, a voidable marriage is one that stands until it is annulled. In both cases, however, courts declare such marriages "void."

The issue of what makes a marriage void or voidable is a matter of some complexity in English common law. For example, bigamy usually renders a marriage absolutely void because there is a valid marriage in existence at the date of the second marriage; impotence renders a marriage voidable.

Rules also restrict applications for annulment to the parties to the marriage if the marriage is voidable, while permitting other interested parties to bring such actions if the marriage is void. In the civil law of Québec, the law of annulment also includes concepts of absolute and relative nullity. For further details, see HR Hahlo, *Nullity of Marriage in Canada* (Toronto: Butterworths, 1979).

CONSTITUTIONAL AUTHORITY FOR REGULATING MARRIAGE IN CANADA

Federal and provincial authority concerning marriage

Legislative authority with respect to marriage in Canada is shared by the federal Parliament and provincial legislatures in accordance with the Constitution.

Specifically, section 91(26) assigns authority to legislate with respect to "marriage and divorce" to the federal Parliament. This authority has been interpreted to mean that only the federal Parliament can enact legislation about "inherent capacity" to marry. A recent example is the *Civil Marriage Act* in 2005, in which the federal Parliament changed the definition of capacity to marry from requiring "a man and a woman" to "two persons," thus entitling same-sex couples to marry.

At the same time, section 92(12) provides that provincial legislatures may legislate with respect to "the solemnization of marriage in the province," a provision that clearly necessitates some division of responsibility in relation to marriage legislation. This provision, which focused on the process of "solemnization" was eventually interpreted to include the "formalities" of marriage, a term that may be somewhat broader than mere "solemnization." In addition, as will become evident later in this book, section 92(13), which accords responsibility to provincial legislatures for "property and civil rights," ensures that much of family law more generally falls within provincial jurisdiction. For details, see Peter Hogg, *Constitutional Law of Canada* (Toronto: Carswell, 2007).

Validity of marriage and sections 91(26) and 92(12)

The relationship between federal and provincial authority for legislating about marriage was considered in the early 20th century by the Privy Council in *Reference re Marriage Legislation in Canada*, [1912] App Cas 880 (PC). The Privy Council gave a large and liberal interpretation to the provincial authority; it specifically concluded (at 886–87) that provincial legislatures could enact "conditions as to solemnization which may affect the validity of the contract." This means that a marriage may be invalid, not only if the parties fail to meet the requirements of "capacity" pursuant to federal law, but also if the parties do not satisfy "solemnization" requirements, generally set out in provincial statutes. In either case, the marriage may be "void."

Enlarging the scope of provincial "solemnization" authority

Although the Privy Council decision thus confirmed that failure to comply with either federal or provincial requirements might result in the invalidity of a marriage, the precise scope of the provincial power to legislate with respect to "the solemnization of marriage" remained somewhat unclear. According to Hogg (at s 27.3(a)):

> Following the *Marriage Reference*, it is clear that a province has power to stipulate pre-ceremonial requirements such as, the issue of a licence or the publication of banns, and to stipulate the qualifications of the person performing the ceremony, even if breach of the stipulations renders the marriage a nullity. These are matters closely associated with the performance of the ceremony — the solemnization.

As Hogg also noted, however, two subsequent decisions of the Supreme Court of Canada concluded that provincial authority also extended to legislating a requirement of parental consent as a condition of validity of the marriage (*Kerr v Kerr*, [1934] SCR 72 at 82–83; and *Attorney General of Alberta v Underwood*, [1934] SCR 635). Hogg suggested that these cases were decided on "the dubious ground that parental consent was a 'formality' of marriage rather than a matter governing the capacity of the parties." As is evident, the court equated authority to legislate in relation to "solemnization" with the idea of "formalities," although "formalities" is arguably a broader category than ceremonial requirements. As a result, the scope of provincial authority with respect to marriage legislation was expanded.

The continuing significance of common law principles about "capacity" to marry

In addition to the complexities of federal and provincial constitutional authority for legislating with respect to marriage, the law of marriage in Canada is complicated by the fact that although the provinces have enacted statutes governing the requirements of solemnization/formalities, the federal Parliament has not enacted comprehensive marriage legislation.

With two recent exceptions, therefore, the federal law of marriage is based on common law requirements of capacity, frequently derived from 19th century English cases interpreting provisions of the 1857 *Divorce and Matrimonial Causes Act*, 20 and 21 Vict, c 85, cases that may not well reflect the needs of modern marriage law in Canada. At present, however, an understanding of the common law of marriage remains central to family law. For further details, see Christine Davies, *Family Law in Canada* (Scarborough, ON: Carswell Legal Publications, 1984) at chapters 2 and 3.

The need for reform?

In relation to the requirements for a valid marriage, illustrated in the sections that follow, consider the extent to which they appear to reflect matters of "capacity," or matters of "solemnization" or "formalities." In examining these principles, consider also whether there is a need for more comprehensive reform of the law of marriage in 21st century Canada.

Notes and Questions

"Common law" marriage and contemporary meanings
of "marriage"

Although the terminology of common law marriage is used colloquially and appears in sociological studies, it does not have much legal significance in Canada — common law marriage, that is a marriage that does not conform to statutory requirements, may be recognized in some U.S. states.

However, the concept of common law marriage was firmly rejected as a legal concept in *Dutch v Dutch* (1977), 1 RFL (2d) 177 (Ont Co Ct), a case about a couple who had married in 1954 and then divorced in 1971. Pursuant to their separation agreement, the former husband agreed to pay spousal support to his former wife "during her lifetime, and so long as she remains unmarried." The former wife commenced living with another man (G) after the divorce decree, but she did not marry him. Her former husband ceased paying spousal support to her, arguing that there was a "marriage at common law" between his former wife and G; and that his former wife had chosen not to marry G only to ensure continuation of the spousal support payments. In this context, the former husband argued that the "common law marriage" negated his obligation to pay support, and that this continuing obligation was contrary to public policy and inequitable. The court rejected both arguments, holding that the former husband had an obligation to continue to pay spousal support. The case also provides a review of the history of marriage in England and the reception of English marriage law in Canada at the time of Confederation.

"Common law marriage" may exist in limited situations in which Aboriginal peoples marry in accordance with their customary practices, but without complying with statutory requirements. For one example, see *Re Noah Estate* (1961), 32 DLR (2d) 185 (NWT Terr Ct), in which a marriage celebrated according to Inuit custom was recognized as a valid common law marriage. See also Bradford W Morse, "Indian and Inuit Family Law and the Canadian Legal System" (1980–81) 8–9 Am Indian L Rev 199. However, "customary" marriage practices in Australian Aboriginal communities have been the subject of a number of recent criminal prosecutions for statutory rape. See Heather Douglas " 'She Knew What was Expected of Her': The White Legal System's Encounter with Traditional Marriage" (2005) 13 Fem Leg Stud 181.

In a comment on the same-sex marriage case in British Columbia, Mark Walters noted that the reception of English law by the colonies of Nova Scotia, New Brunswick, and Upper Canada (Ontario) accommodated distinctive approaches to marriage for French Canadian and Aboriginal communities. See Mark D Walters, "Incorporating Common Law into the Constitution of Canada: *EGALE v. Canada* and the Status of Marriage" (2003) 41 Osgoode Hall LJ 75.

Additional Resources

Colin Chapman, *Ecclesiastical Courts, Their Officials, and Their Records* (Dursley, England: Lochin Publishing, 1992).

Stephanie Coontz, *Marriage, A History* (New York: Penguin, 2005).

Christine Davies, *Family Law in Canada* (Scarborough, ON: Carswell Legal Publications, 1984).

George Elliott Howard, *A History of Matrimonial Institutions*, 3 vols (Chicago: University of Chicago Press, 1904).

Leslie Katz, "The Scope of the Federal Legislative Authority in Relation to Marriage" (1975) 7 Ottawa L Rev 384.

Rebecca Probert, *Marriage Law and Practice in the Long Eighteenth Century: A Reassessment* (Cambridge: Cambridge University Press, 2009).

Carol Smart, *The Ties that Bind: Law, Marriage and the Reproduction of Patriarchal Relations* (London: Routledge & Kegan Paul, 1984).

Bruce Ziff, "Recent Developments in Canadian Law: Marriage and Divorce" (1986) 18 Ottawa L Rev 121.

IV.
PRINCIPLES OF THE VALIDITY OF MARRIAGE

THE CONTINUING INFLUENCE OF
PRINCIPLES OF NULLITY

> Nullity occupies a strange place within the sphere of family governance. It is in one sense the most law-like part of family law, for it is ostensibly concerned with technical questions of contract law and decisions about nullity of marriage are often made within the higher echelons of the legal system with all their attendant regalia. On the other hand nullity of marriage ... is both bizarre and rare [and there is something in the narratives of nullity that constitutes "the baroque"]. (Hilary Lim, "Messages from a Rarely Visited Island: Duress and Lack of Consent in Marriage" (1996) IV Fem Leg Stud 195 at 216–17)

This section examines the principles defining a valid marriage. As noted above, validity of marriage was defined historically in relation to the principles of annulment (or nullity) of marriage. That is, if a marriage was legally invalid, an order of annulment could be obtained. Because many of these principles about validity were derived from ecclesiastical law, and because current principles often reflect the context of 19th century cases interpreting them, this area of law often appears "ancient," if not entirely "baroque." In this brief exploration of the relevant principles, the materials also focus on the cases and critiques to reveal underlying assumptions about marriage in its historical context and to provide a foundation for assessing the need for legal reform.

"Capacity" to marry: Common law principles and federal legislation

In accordance with the constitutional authority discussed above, the federal Parliament has authority to legislate with respect to "marriage," authority which has been interpreted as relating to "capacity" to marry. With two exceptions (noted below), however, Parliament has not legislated about capacity to marry, leaving these requirements as defined in the common law.

According to these common law requirements (as amended by Parliament), a valid marriage requires that the parties meet the following six criteria:

1. The parties must be "two persons": this requirement was set out in the federal *Civil Marriage Act* in 2005, which repealed the long-standing common law requirement of "a man and a woman".

2. Both parties must have capacity to consent to the marriage — that is, have the capacity to understand, be free from duress, and without taking account of reservations about or limited purposes of marriage.

3. The parties must have capacity to consummate the marriage.

4. The parties must not be within the prohibited degrees of consanguinity and affinity (as now defined in the federal *Marriage (Prohibited Degrees) Act*).

5. The parties must not be a partner to an existing valid marriage.

6. The parties must have attained the age required for a valid marriage.

Formalities/solemnization of marriage and provincial legislation

In addition to the requirements relating to capacity, a valid marriage requires that the parties conform to the "formalities" set out in provincial statutes, such as Ontario's *Marriage Act*. These statutory requirements include ceremonial matters such as witnesses, the authority of the person celebrating the marriage, licences, etc.

CAPACITY TO MARRY: FEDERAL LEGISLATIVE AUTHORITY

1. Same-sex marriage: Parliamentary reform of the "opposite-sex" requirement

> What then, is the nature of [marriage] as understood in Christendom? ... [What] are its essential elements and invariable features? ... I conceive that marriage, as understood in Christendom, may ... be defined as the voluntary union for life of one man and one woman, to the exclusion of all others. (*Hyde v Hyde and Woodmansee* (1866), LR 1 P&D 130 at 133)

The Common Law Definition of Marriage in *Hyde v Hyde and Woodmansee*

This decision in an English court, one year before Canadian confederation, confirmed the opposite-sex requirement for a valid marriage: the requirement of "one man and one woman." *Hyde v Hyde and Woodmansee* thus became the precedent for excluding same-sex marriage, a precedent that was eventually challenged successfully in *Charter* litigation about same-sex marriage in British Columbia, Ontario and Québec; and following a reference to the Supreme Court of Canada, the opposite-sex requirement was repealed by the *Civil Marriage Act*, s 2: "Marriage, for civil purposes, is the lawful union of two persons to the exclusion of all others."

Although no longer a binding precedent, the *Hyde* case reveals how underlying ideas about the nature of marriage may have shaped its role as a legal precedent. The 1866 decision in *Hyde* focused primarily on the availability of divorce remedies in an English court in relation to a marriage entered into in a foreign jurisdiction in which polygamy was practised.

The parties had married in 1853 at Salt Lake City in Utah Territory, in a ceremony conducted by Brigham Young, president of the Mormon Church (both parties were Mormon) and also governor of the Territory. They cohabited and had children together. Three years later, the husband left Utah and renounced the Mormon faith, and a sentence of excommunication was pronounced against him in Utah; this sentence freed his wife to remarry. Although the parties communicated for a few years by letter, the wife elected to remain in Utah, and she remarried in 1859 or 1860 and had children with her second husband. The petitioner, English by birth, returned to England in 1857, and petitioned for divorce, based on his wife's adultery.

Although both parties were single at the time of the marriage in Utah in 1853, the court concluded that the jurisdiction of the English court was not available in relation to a marriage that took place in a jurisdiction that recognized polygamy. In giving judgment, it was Lord Penzance who made the statement about the nature of marriage, reproduced above, a statement that provides considerable evidence of the law's view of marriage in 19th century England. For example, note the use of Christianity in the definition of marriage, an indication of the significant relationship between Christian (Protestant) religious beliefs and legal views of marriage. And since adultery was clearly practised in the 19th century, the notion of marriage "to the exclusion of all others" seems more aspirational than factual.

Perhaps most striking is the fact that judicial divorce had become possible pursuant to the *Matrimonial Causes Act* of 1857, so that the concept of a union "for life" was no longer legally accurate.

Thus, it seems clear that the definition of marriage in *Hyde*, including the requirement of "a man and a woman," was not only obiter in terms of the facts of the case, but also legally inaccurate in several respects. At the same time, societal acceptance of the *Hyde* definition of marriage shows how law both reflected and reinforced ideas about marriage.

Challenges to the Opposite-Sex Requirement in Canadian Courts

Although early challenges to the opposite-sex requirement for marriage were unsuccessful in Canadian courts, based on *Hyde* (see *North v Matheson* (1974), 20 RFL 112 (Man Co Ct)), the equality guarantee in section 15 of the *Charter* became increasingly important for a variety of same-sex family issues in the late 20th century, particularly after the Ontario Court of Appeal decided that sexual orientation constituted an analogous ground for discrimination. See *Haig v Canada* (1992), 9 OR (3d) 495. In the early 1990s, a dissenting judgment in Ontario expressly argued that families take many forms, and that the law should evolve to recognize marriage in these different contexts:

> Surely the argument by the Attorney General that there is only one societal concept of marriage is flawed. One has only to examine how multiple marriages have become the norm in our North American society, how step-parents have become an integral part of children's lives in these marriages, how divorce has become widely recognized in society, and how "common law" relationships have become classified as marriages without

the sanction of a marriage certificate but with most of the benefits conferred by one. There was even a time in history when a woman became the property of her husband. That concept of marriage became no longer valid.... The common law and legislated law both change to meet a changing society. (*Re Layland and Beaulne and Ontario Ministry of Consumer and Commercial Relations* (1993), 14 OR (3d) 658 (Gen Div), dissenting judgment of Greer J at 680)

Although the challenge to the exclusion of same-sex marriage did not succeed in the *Layland* case, "spousal" status was increasingly recognized for same-sex couples in a number of different legal contexts: pensions, housing, spousal support at separation, and adoption and custody of children. Moreover, in relation to marriage, equality challenges were launched in 2001 in three provinces (British Columbia, Ontario, and Québec). In British Columbia, the trial judge held that the definition of marriage could not be amended at common law, but only by legislation; that the meaning of marriage in section 92(26) of the Constitution was defined at Confederation and was thus not amenable to *Charter* scrutiny; and that if it was subject to the *Charter*, it infringed section 15 equality but was saved by section 1. See *EGALE Canada Inc v Canada (AG)*, 2001 BCSC 1365.

Halpern v Canada (AG)
(2002), 60 OR (3d) 321 (Div Ct)

By contrast, the Ontario Divisional Court unanimously concluded in 2002 that the common law definition of marriage in *Hyde*, which excluded same-sex couples from marrying, contravened section 15 of the *Charter*, and was not saved by section 1. In doing so, the court commented on the need to understand marriage in the context of contemporary Canadian society:

[60] If the courts are to examine the common law definition of marriage through the prism of *Charter* rights and values, it seems to me they must recognize and appreciate the changes that have occurred over the centuries, and more rapidly in recent years, in the attitudes of society towards the family, marriage and relationships, as outlined above. To do otherwise is to abandon the purpose of section 15 — which is to promote equality and prevent discrimination arising from such ills as stereotyping, prejudice and historical wrongs — and to fail to consider the common law principle under review in a contextual fashion. ...

[61] Given this background of dramatically shifting attitudes towards marriage and the family, I have a great deal of difficulty accepting that heterosexual procreation is such a compelling and central aspect of marriage in 21st century post-*Charter* Canadian society that it — and it alone — gives marriage its defining characteristic and justifies the exclusion of same-sex couples from that institution. It is, of course, the only characteristic with which such couples are unable to conform (and even that inability is changing). ...

[64] If this understanding of marriage forms the starting point of the analysis, I agree [that] the argument that s. 15(1) is violated by the common law definition of marriage is harder to make. Viewed from this standpoint, same-sex couples are not excluded from the institution because of their sexual orientation; rather, they are simply ineligible

because they fall outside of the "definitional boundaries of marriage." They are incapacitated from entering the institution, not precluded from doing so on the basis of their personal characteristics.

[65] On the other hand, if marriage is viewed through a looking glass with a broader focus — and not conceived as a social, cultural, religious and legal edifice built upon heterosexual procreation as its fundamental infrastructure — the s. 15(1) analysis is directly engaged. In this approach to marriage, same-sex couples are not precluded from participating by reason of its innate characteristic. They are precluded simply because of their sexual orientation. The evidence is clear: same-sex couples can and do live in long-term, caring, loving and conjugal relationships — including those involving the rearing of children (and, in a modern context, even the birth of children). In short, their relationships are characterized by all the indicia of marriage, as traditionally understood, save for classic heterosexual intercourse, and they live in unions that are marriage-like in everything but name.

[66] The underlying question, then, is whether the law in Canada today is sufficiently open and adaptable to recognize a broader rationale as the defining characteristic of marriage than heterosexual procreation and its surrounding religious paraphernalia. In my view, it is....

[68] ... Cultural and religious diversity are defining features of the Canadian mosaic. Former "realities" are not necessarily any longer current "realities."

[69] "Procreation" — the production of offspring naturally — is amongst the concepts affected by the evolution wrought by these changes. Scientific advances have made it possible for children to be born to couples — heterosexual or homosexual — through artificial insemination, in vitro fertilization in its various forms, surrogate motherhood, et cetera. ...

[70] [Procreation is too] narrow, and too shaky, in my opinion, to be tenable as the legal base for such a foundational institution in society as marriage. To be sure, the production, care and raising of children is a principal purpose of marriage. But that purpose, as I have indicated, is presently attainable through means other than heterosexual intercourse. There is much more to marriage as a societal institution, in my view, than the act of heterosexual intercourse leading to the birth of children. Moreover, the authorities are clear that marriage is not dependent upon the presence of children; nor are incapacity or an unwillingness to have children a bar to marriage or a ground for divorce....

[71] Marriage has a physical sexual component to it, of course. Marriage is more fully characterized in my opinion, however, by its pivotal child-rearing role, and by a long-term conjugal relationship between two individuals — with its attendant obligations and offerings of mutual care and support, of companionship and shared social activities, of intellectual and moral and faith-based stimulation as a couple, and of shared shelter and economic and psychological interdependence — and by love. These are the indicia of the purpose of marriage in modern Canadian society. ...

The Aftermath of *Halpern* in Ontario, British Columbia, and Québec

In *Halpern*, a majority of the judges suspended the effect of their decision for a period of 24 months to permit Parliament to legislate on the issue. A few weeks later, the Superior Court of Québec adopted the reasoning and conclusions of the Ontario court. See *Hendricks v Québec (AG)*, [2002] JQ No 3816 (SC). Decisions from all three provinces were appealed. In May 2003, the B.C. Court of Appeal allowed the appeal, expressly agreeing with the reasoning in the Divisional Court in *Halpern* in Ontario and suspending the effect of its decision to correspond with the period of suspension in *Halpern*. See *EGALE Canada Inc v Canada (AG)*, 2003 BCCA 251.

However, on 10 June 2003, the Ontario Court of Appeal released its decision in *Halpern*, upholding the decision of the Divisional Court. The court focused on the principles of discrimination established in *Law v Canada (Minister of Employment and Immigration)*, [1999] 1 SCR 497, and held that the claimants were the subject of differential treatment because the common law definition of marriage "creates a formal distinction between opposite-sex and same-sex couples on the basis of their sexual orientation." Reiterating the multiple reasons why persons choose to marry, the court concluded that the common law requirement that marriage be between persons of the opposite sex does not accord with the needs, capacities and circumstances of same-sex couples. In addition, however, the Court of Appeal held that there was no reason to suspend its decision:

> [153] There is no evidence before this court that a declaration of invalidity without a period of suspension will pose any harm to the public, threaten the rule of law, or deny anyone the benefit of legal recognition of their marriage.... In our view, an immediate declaration will simply ensure that opposite-sex couples and same-sex couples immediately receive equal treatment in law in accordance with s. 15(1) of the *Charter*. (*Halpern v Canada (AG)* (2003), 65 OR (3d) 161 (CA))

Following this decision, the B.C. Court of Appeal lifted the order suspending its decision on 8 July 2003. See *EGALE Canada Inc v Canada (AG)*, 2003 BCCA 406; and in March 2004, the Québec Court of Appeal released its decision, unanimously upholding the lower court decision allowing gay marriages and confirming that Article 365 of the Québec *Civil Code* infringed the equality guarantee of the *Charter*. See *Hendricks v Québec (AG)*, [2004] JQ No. 2593 (QL). The federal government announced its decision not to appeal, and turned to Parliamentary action. In addition to marriages of same-sex couples in Ontario, British Columbia and Québec, same-sex marriages gradually became legal in other parts of Canada: by the time of the reference to the Supreme Court of Canada, five common law provinces, one territory and Québec all permitted same-sex marriage.

Parliament and the Reference Case in the Supreme Court of Canada

While the lower court decisions in Ontario, British Columbia, and Québec were being appealed, the federal government referred the issue to a Parliamentary committee. The issue remained politically controversial too, particularly after a coalition of conservative and religious groups vowed in

September 2003 to hold prayer protests and to target federal MPs who had expressed approval for same-sex marriage. See Tonda MacCharles, "Gay-Marriage Foes Plan Prayer Protests", *Toronto Star* (3 September 2003) A17. The House of Commons also voted on a motion proposed by the (then) Canadian Alliance, which called on Parliament to preserve the definition of marriage as "the union of one man and one woman, to the exclusion of all others"; the motion was narrowly defeated, 137–132. See Kim Lunman & Drew Fagan, "Marriage Divides the House", *The Globe and Mail* (17 September 2003) A1.

In this context, the federal government decided to refer a constitutional question to the Supreme Court of Canada and to request the Court to define the constitutionality of proposed federal legislation legalizing same-sex marriage. The constitutional reference requested the Court's opinion as to whether provisions respecting aspects of legal capacity for marriage for civil purposes were within the federal government's exclusive legislative authority; whether a provision extending capacity to marry to persons of the same sex was consistent with the *Charter*; and whether the *Charter*'s guarantee of freedom of religion would protect religious officials from being compelled to perform same-sex marriages, contrary to the officials' beliefs. (A fourth question, not answered by the Supreme Court, asked whether the opposite-sex requirement for marriage, established by common law principles, was consistent with the *Charter*, the question that had remained unanswered when the federal government had declined to appeal the decisions of the three appellate courts in Ontario, British Columbia, and Québec to the Supreme Court of Canada.)

The Supreme Court issued its unanimous decision in the reference on same-sex marriage in 2004, confirming that the issue was one of capacity and thus within the competence of the federal Parliament pursuant to section 91(26). In rejecting the argument that the concept of marriage was confined to its historical meaning in 1867, based on the common law principle set out in *Hyde*, the Court stated:

> [22] The reference to "Christendom" is telling. *Hyde* spoke to a society of shared social values where marriage and religion were thought to be inseparable. This is no longer the case. Canada is a pluralistic society. Marriage, from the perspective of the state, is a civil institution. The "frozen concepts" reasoning runs contrary to one of the most fundamental principles of Canadian constitutional interpretation: that our Constitution is a living tree which, by way of progressive interpretation, accommodates and addresses the realities of modern life....

The Court also held that same-sex marriage was consistent with the *Charter*, and that section 2(a) of the *Charter* provided protection for religious officials from being compelled to perform same-sex marriages, contrary to their beliefs. See *Re Same-Sex Marriage*, 2004 SCC 79; and Peter Hogg, "Canada: The Constitution and Same-Sex Marriage" (2006) 4:3 NYU Intl J Cont L 712.

In response to the reference, Parliament enacted the *Civil Marriage Act*, SC 2005, c 33, on 20 July 2005, legalizing same-sex marriage in Canada, the fourth country to do so after the Netherlands (2001), Belgium (2003) and

Spain (2005). Section 2 provides that "Marriage, for civil purposes, is the lawful union of two persons to the exclusion of all others."

Notes and Questions

Judicial reasoning and law reform

Does the reasoning in the Divisional Court in *Halpern* in 2002 reveal a shift in views about the fundamental nature of marriage? How would you characterize the arguments in the case about the importance of procreation in marriage? How should legal and policy arguments about the importance of reproduction for society as a whole be balanced with respect for individual choice about bearing and/or raising children? Should courts take account of increasing opportunities for non-biological reproduction among opposite-sex or same-sex couples? Do your answers to these questions suggest that legal intervention by courts should reflect social trends? Consider this critique of the Court of Appeal's decision to eliminate the two-year suspension of the Divisional Court order in *Halpern*:

> The critical question is who should make this decision. The fundamental question that the Court of Appeal did not even mention is whether courts have any role in changing fundamental social institutions like marriage where it is possible to remove any substantive legal discrimination without restructuring the fundamental social institution.... *Halpern* was all about social recognition and validation for same-sex relationships.... [The claimants] wanted the same social recognition and acceptance as married spouses in the eyes of the general public. With respect, if there is any distinction between judicial and legislative powers, this would appear to be where the line should be drawn. (James McLeod, "Annotation" (2003) 36 RFL (5th) 129)

Public officials' religious beliefs and same-sex marriage

Ontario enacted amendments in 2005, confirming that religious officials were not required to solemnize same-sex marriages or to permit a sacred place to be used for such marriages contrary to religious beliefs. See *Spousal Relationships Statute Law Amendment Act, 2005*, SO 2005, c 5.

In addition to marriages solemnized by religious officials, however, civil marriages are conducted by public officials, usually called "marriage commissioners." Can a marriage commissioner who does not wish to perform same-sex marriages on the basis of personal religious beliefs claim *Charter* protection in this situation?

Although the Ontario amendment does not address this issue directly, the issue of protection (accommodation) for public officials performing civil marriages (marriage commissioners) was litigated in Saskatchewan in a number of human rights complaints. As a result of ongoing controversy, the Saskatchewan government drafted two possible amendments to its *Marriage Act* in 2009, each of which would have released marriage commissioners from the duty to solemnize same-sex marriages on the basis of their religious beliefs (one amendment applied to all such commissioners, while the other protected only those appointed before 5 November 2004, the date when a Saskatchewan court struck down the common law requirement of "a man and a woman" for a valid marriage).

In January 2011, the Saskatchewan Court of Appeal released a unanimous decision, confirming that both proposed amendments infringed the *Charter*'s equality guarantee: see *Saskatchewan Marriage Reference*, 2011 SKCA 3. In addition, the court held that the amendments were not saved by section 1. In applying the proportionality test, Robertson JA concluded that the positive aspects of the objective sought by the proposed amendments did not outweigh their deleterious effects:

> [94] Both [proposed amendments} would perpetuate a brand of discrimination which our national community has only recently begun to successfully overcome. It would be a significant step backward if, having won the difficult fight for the right to same-sex civil marriages, gay and lesbian couples should be shunned by the very people charged by the Province with solemnizing such unions.

> [95] Second, and more concretely, allowing marriage commissioners to deny services to gay and lesbian couples would have genuinely harmful impacts.... Simply put, it is not just gay and lesbian couples themselves who would be hurt or offended by the notion that a governmental official can deny services to same-sex couples. Many members of the public would also be negatively affected by the idea.

> [97] The third, and in some ways most important deleterious effect of the [proposed amendments] is that both would undermine a deeply entrenched and fundamentally important aspect of our system of government. In our tradition, the apparatus of the state serves everyone equally without providing better, poorer or different services to one individual compared to another by making distinctions on the basis of factors like race, religion or gender.... Marriage commissioners do not act as private citizens when they discharge their official duties.... Accordingly, a system that would make marriage services available according to the personal religious beliefs of commissioners in highly problematic. It would undercut the basic principle that governmental services must be provided on an impartial and non-discriminatory basis.

In concurring reasons, Smith JA emphasized that a refusal by a marriage commissioner to solemnize a same-sex marriage could be devastating to the couple, and that there was no reason to believe that such refusals would be rare — citing the numbers of religious organizations which currently disapprove of same-sex marriage [paras 105 and 106], and then stating:

> [107] More important, however, is the affront to dignity, and the perpetuation of social and political prejudice and negative stereo-typing that such refusals would cause. Furthermore, even if the risk of actual refusal were minimal, knowing that legislation would legitimize such discrimination is itself an affront to the dignity and worth of homosexual individuals. History has established and jurisprudence has confirmed the extreme vulnerability of this group to discrimination and even hatred....

Most provinces have not permitted marriage commissioners to decline to perform same-sex marriages. For arguments about this issue, see Bruce MacDougall "Refusing to Officiate at Same-Sex Marriages" (2006) 69 Sask

L Rev 351; and Geoffrey Trotter "The Right to Decline Performance of Same-Sex Civil Marriages — a Response to Professor Bruce MacDougall" (2007) 70 Sask L Rev 365.

A similar issue has arisen as a result of the proposal to establish a law school at Trinity Western University, a private Christian institution in British Columbia. This proposal is controversial because Trinity Western requires its students to sign a Covenant in which they promise to abstain from sexual conduct outside of heterosexual marriage. Supporters of Trinity Western argue that this requirement is protected by the religious freedom guarantee in the *Charter*. Opponents argue that the requirement to sign the Covenant is discriminatory because it makes legal education less accessible for LGBTQ people. They also argue that although lawyers are not public officials, they have public duties and that provincial law societies should not license lawyers educated at Trinity Western until the requirement to sign the Covenant is removed. Three provincial law societies have agreed (Nova Scotia, Ontario, and British Columbia) and are defending law suits brought by Trinity Western. For arguments about these issues see Elaine Craig, "TWU Law: A Reply to Proponents of Approval" (2014) 37:2 Dal LJ 621; and Dwight Newman, "On the Trinity Western University Controversy: An Argument for a Christian Law School in Canada" (2012) 22 Const Forum 1.

"Conflicting" laws about same-sex marriage

Canada legalized same-sex marriage nationally pursuant to the *Civil Marriage Act* in 2005, and this statute permitted residents of other jurisdictions, as well as those resident in Canada, to marry here. However, many of the non-residents who have married in Canada have been denied recognition of their status as married persons in their own jurisdictions, based on principles of the conflict of laws. For example, because of the political controversy about same-sex marriage in the United States, many states have refused to recognize marriages solemnized in Canada, and a marriage of a same-sex couple from England was recognized as a civil partnership but not a marriage in the United Kingdom: see *Wilkinson v Kitzinger*, [2006] EWHC 2022).

In January 2012, the related issue of access to divorce for same-sex couples (who were married in Canada but resident in other jurisdictions) became controversial when a same-sex couple, resident respectively in Florida and England, applied for a divorce in an Ontario court. Since they had not been resident in a Canadian province for one year (see *Divorce Act*, s 3, discussed in Chapter Five), the lawyer acting in this divorce case launched a *Charter* challenge to this residency requirement. In response, a federal government lawyer filed pleadings claiming that the parties were not entitled to a divorce in Canada because they were not validly married in accordance with conflict of laws principles (which traditionally focus on the law of the parties' domicile to determine capacity to marry). The government then promised to resolve this problem and introduced Bill C-32 (amending the *Civil Marriage Act*) on 17 February 2012.

Before Bill C-32 reached second reading, the federal government intervened in an Ontario case involving two Canadian men who became civil partners under the U.K. *Civil Partnership Act* while living in the United Kingdom. Wayne Hincks and Gerardo Gallardo subsequently returned to Canada where they later separated. When Hincks applied for a divorce, Gallardo claimed that they had never been married. In response, Hincks sought a declaration that their civil partnership was a marriage within the meaning of Canada's *Civil Marriage Act*.

The Ontario Attorney General's argument supported Hincks's position, that is, that the civil partnership brought the couple within the definition of marriage under section 1 of the Ontario *Family Law Act*; and as same-sex marriage celebrated in Ontario had been recognized by courts in the United Kingdom as a civil partnership (see *Wilkinson v Kitzinger*, above), the reverse situation should hold and the U.K. civil partnership recognized as a marriage in Ontario. In contrast the federal government argued that the parties were not married. The Attorney General of Canada pointed to the conflicts of law rule that the validity of marriage is determined by the law of the place where the marriage was celebrated and argued that since the U.K. courts held that a civil partnership was not a marriage, Canada should not confer marital status on Hincks and Gallardo. Relief was available to them in England where the *Civil Partnership Act* provided remedies. Finally, section 15 of the *Charter* did not require the court to construe a U.K. civil partnership as a marriage. The judge held that a civil partnership in England constitutes a "marriage" in Canada and that it can be dissolved pursuant to the *Divorce Act* in Canada. In addition, she held that the parties are "spouses" for purposes of the *Family Law Act*. See *Hincks v Gallardo*, 2013 ONSC 129; and Christopher Guly, "Marriage by Any Other Name Is Still a Marriage in Canada", *The Lawyers Weekly* (1 February 2013) at 2.

Bill C-32, *An Act to Amend the Civil Marriage Act*, was given Royal Assent on 26 June 2013. The statute is designed to permit couples (mainly same-sex couples) who married in a Canadian province to obtain a divorce in that same province (based on the ground of living separate and apart in their home jurisdiction(s) for one year (s 7(1)). The new section 5 states:

> (1) A marriage that is performed in Canada and that would be valid in Canada if the spouses were domiciled in Canada is valid for the purposes of Canadian law even though either or both of the spouses do not, at the time of the marriage, have the capacity to enter into it under the law of their respective states.

Subsection (2) makes this law retroactive; and section 10 makes the divorce effective throughout Canada. However, the amending statute makes no provision for orders for corollary relief in relation to a divorce, leaving these issues to be negotiated in accordance with the jurisdiction of the parties' domicile. This situation has been criticized by family lawyers due to its lack of congruence with the law applicable to Canadian residents pursuant to the *Divorce Act* (discussed in Chapter Five):

- A non-resident couple's marriage can be dissolved in Canada if they have been separated for a year. Canadian residents may also apply for divorce after separation for one year, but the "marriage breakdown" ground in the *Divorce Act* includes not only separation for one year, but also adultery or cruelty.

- A non-resident couple's marriage can be dissolved if they have each been living for at least one year in a state that does not recognize the validity of their marriage. A married person in Canada must be resident in a Canadian province for one year before initiating divorce proceedings.

- Non-residents must usually apply jointly for divorce (with some exceptions), while Canadian residents may apply jointly or individually.

- Non-residents' divorce proceedings relate only to the dissolution of the marriage, and do not provide for corollary relief (property, support, and custody and access of children). These matters are left to the jurisdiction in which the parties are resident.

For critiques of the government's approach, see Tamara Baluja, "Same-Sex Marriage Bill said to be rife with 'Pretzel Logic'", *The Globe and Mail* (18 February 2012) A6; and Judy Van Rhijn, "Gay Divorce Litigation on hold pending Federal Bill", *Law Times* (12 March 2012) 9. For a detailed examination of the principles of conflict of laws, see Jean Castel & Janet Walker, *Canadian Conflict of Laws* (Toronto: LexisNexis Canada, looseleaf). For a critical examination of conflict of law principles in relation to the *Civil Marriage Act* amendments, see Jan Jacob Bornheim, "Same-Sex Marriages in Canadian Private International Law" (2013) 51 Alta L Rev 77.

Same-sex couples: Embracing marriage (or not)?

The availability of same-sex marriage was celebrated by many gay and lesbian couples. Between 10 June and 30 August 2003, a total of 590 gay and lesbian couples applied for marriage licences in Toronto, just over 10 percent of the 5,500 couples who received licences during that period. More than 100 of the gay couples were American. By contrast, others in the gay and lesbian community expressed concern about entering a relationship like marriage, fearing that it would undermine their unique sense of culture and the opportunity to foster social change for families; for these same-sex couples, marriage seemed likely to lead to "complacent ... gay and lesbian soccer moms." See Clifford Krauss, "Free To Marry, Canada's Gays Say, 'Do I'?" *New York Times* (31 August 2003); Mitchel Raphael, "Who Says All Gays Want To Marry?" *The Globe and Mail* (7 April 2004) A19; and Hugh Ryan, "We didn't queer the institution of marriage. It straightened us", *The Guardian* (29 June 2014).

In this context, Claire Young had earlier argued that it is necessary to pay attention to specific economic contexts in determining whether legal recognition of same-sex couples constitutes real advantages or disadvantages. Comparing the tax implications for three same-sex couples in different tax brackets, Young concluded that a couple in a relationship in which one partner is economically dependent on the other would benefit the most, and that gay men were more likely than lesbians to obtain tax benefits from marriage. See Claire Young, "Taxing Times for Lesbians and Gay Men: Equality at What Cost?" (1994) 17 Dal LJ 534 at 547 and 555.

Some scholars have also suggested that *Charter* equality arguments in the same-sex marriage cases, which necessarily focused on the functional similarity between gay and lesbian families and heterosexual families, undermined the more radical potential of the gay liberation movement. Thus, for gay and lesbian activists who wished to challenge the concept of marriage more fundamentally, the same-sex marriage cases seemed to narrow the options for those who did not wish to "conform" to the social and political norms of marriage. In addition, however, legal recognition of same-sex marriage (and thus, legal entitlement to other "family" benefits) enlarged opportunities for the privatization of economic support for dependent family members:

> [B]y including same-sex couples as spouses the government is further reducing its fiscal responsibilities to citizens by assigning that responsibility to the private same-sex family, with a significantly unequal impact on citizens. Thus, for example, if our relationships end, we may be required to provide spousal support to our partners, thereby alleviating the state's economic responsibility. Our incomes are aggregated for the purposes of many state benefits such as social assistance and student loans, thereby resulting in less access to state funding and placing more responsibility on the private sector. We can receive spousal survivor pensions provided by a deceased's spouse's employer, thereby lessening our reliance on (and entitlement to) the more universal public pensions. Moreover, trends that bolster privatization of economic responsibility tend to diminish general public support for publicly funded programs, especially among those who are already relatively economically privileged and can insulate themselves from the impact of cutbacks. (Susan B Boyd & Claire FL Young, "'From Same-Sex to No Sex'? Trends Towards Recognition of (Same-Sex) Relationships in Canada" (2002–2003) 1:3 Seattle Journal for Social Justice 757 at 776–777)

See also Susan B Boyd, "'Marriage is more than just a piece of paper': Feminist Critiques of Same Sex Marriage" (2013) 8 National Taiwan University Law Review 263; Miriam Smith, *Lesbian and Gay Rights in Canada: Social Movements & Equality Seeking, 1971–1995* (Toronto: University of Toronto Press, 1999); and Brenda Cossman, "Lesbians, Gay Men and the Canadian Charter of Rights and Freedoms" (2003) 40 Osgoode Hall LJ 223.

Legal benefits for same-sex families: Developments beyond marriage

At least to some extent, the same-sex marriage cases occurred in the context of significant developments concerning benefits for same-sex spouses. One important decision was *M v H* (discussed in Chapter Seven), in which the Supreme Court of Canada held that the opposite-sex requirement of Ontario's *Family Law Act*, in relation to entitlement to spousal support after separation, infringed the *Charter* equality guarantee and was not saved by section 1. The court suspended its declaration for six months, and the Ontario government then (apparently reluctantly) enacted *Amendments Because of the Supreme Court of Canada Decision in M v. H, 1999*, SO 1999, c 6, extending benefits and obligations pursuant to 67 provincial statutes to same-sex couples.

Earlier, the B.C. legislature had amended a number of statutes to extend spousal benefits to same-sex couples: *Family Relations Amendment Act, 1997*, SBC 1997, c 20; *Definition of Spouse Amendment Act, 1999*, SBC 1999, c 29; and *Definition of Spouse Amendment Act, 2000*, SBC 2000, c 24. Manitoba, New Brunswick, Newfoundland, and Saskatchewan also enacted legislation that extended some benefits to same-sex couples (see *An Act to Comply with the Supreme Court of Canada Decision in M v. H*, SM 2001, c 37; *An Act to Amend the Family Services Act*, SNB 2000, c 59; the *Family Law (Amendment) Act*, SN 2000, c 29; and *An Act to Amend Certain Statutes Respecting Domestic Relations*, SS 2000, c 47 and c 48, and SS 2001, c 50 and c 51).

Yet, the controversy about legal recognition of same-sex families was evident when the federal government enacted the *Modernization of Benefits and Obligations Act* in 2000, a statute that extended spousal benefits and obligations in many federal statutes to same-sex couples. This statute was amended to include a declaration (s 1.1) that the amendments did "not affect the meaning of the word 'marriage,' that is, the lawful union of one man and one woman to the exclusion of all others." Similarly, Alberta enacted the *Domestic Relations Amendment Act, 1999*, SA 1999, c 20, which defined "common law relationship" as an opposite-sex relationship, and then, in a direct challenge to the federal authority for defining capacity, by enacting the *Marriage Amendment Act, 2000*, SA 2000, c 3, which confirmed that "'marriage' means a marriage between a man and a woman."

Registered partnerships

In some provinces, legislation was enacted to permit opposite-sex and same-sex couples to register as "domestic partners" and thereby obtain most of the rights and obligations of married spouses. For example, Nova Scotia enacted domestic partnership legislation in 2000, and also amended other statutes to ensure that the definition of "common law partner" included both opposite-sex and same-sex couples who had cohabited for two years: see *Law Reform (2000) Act*, SNS 2000, c 29. In 2002, Québec enacted *An Act Instituting Civil Unions and Establishing New Rules of Filiation*, SQ 2002, c 6, a comprehensive set of amendments defining "civil union" relationships pursuant to the *Civil Code* and other statutes. While some gay and lesbian couples preferred this option since it permitted them to have all the benefits of marriage without having to accept the ideology of its traditional status, other couples criticized such a "separate but equal" approach. This "civil partnership" arrangement is further considered in relation to law reform options at the end of this chapter.

Same-sex marriage and developments outside Canada

As noted, Canada was the fourth jurisdiction to recognize same-sex marriage, after the Netherlands, Belgium, and Spain. Same-sex marriage has since been recognized in fifteen other countries on four continents and in many of the states in the United States: see "Freedom to Marry Internationally" at <http://www.freedomtomarry.org/landscape/entry/c/international consulted> (9 May 2015). Some jurisdictions that do not recognize same-sex marriage instead offer civil partnerships that extend some level of spousal recognition to same-sex couples. See Katharina Boele-Woelki, "The Legal Recognition of Same-Sex Relationships Within the European Union" (2008) 82 Tul L Rev 1949; and Geoffrey Lindell, "Constitutional Issues Regarding Same-Sex Marriage: A Comparative Survey — North America and Australasia" (2008) 30 Sydney L Rev 27.

The United Kingdom, which had provided a civil partnership regime for same-sex couples since 2004, passed the *Marriage (Same Sex Couples) Act* in 2013. Subsequent regulations, effective in December, 2014, have provided a procedure to convert civil partnerships to marriages. In addition, "married transgender people will be able to change their legal gender without ending their marriage, provided their partner agrees" (Rowena Mason, "Civil partnerships can be converted to marriages from December", *The Guardian* (26 June 2014)). Currently, people in same-sex relationships in the United Kingdom may either marry or enter into a civil partnership, but people in opposite-sex relationships are not permitted to enter into civil partnerships. This is an issue for some opposite-sex couples who wish to have their relationships recognized legally "without the social expectations, pressures and traditions surrounding marriage" (Charles Keidan & Rebecca Stanfield, "Civil Partnerships Should Be for Everyone, No Exceptions", *The Guardian* (3 December 2014)).

In the United States, a judge in California decided in August 2010 that Proposition 8 (a voter approved ban on same-sex marriage) violated due process and equal protection rights in the U.S. constitution. At the time of the trial decision, five states (Massachusetts, Connecticut, Iowa, Vermont, and New Hampshire, along with the District of Columbia) allowed same-sex marriages. In 2011, New York became the sixth state to recognize same-sex marriage, and a Gallup Poll in 2011 found for the first time that a majority (53%) of Americans supported same-sex marriage. See *The Globe and Mail* (2 July 2011) F1. In early 2012, the 9th U.S. Circuit Court of Appeals upheld the California trial court decision (2:1): see *Perry v Brown*, No 10-16696 and No 11-16577. However, legislatures in 39 states had explicitly prohibited such marriages, and the situation was also complicated by the enactment of the federal *Defense of Marriage Act* (*DOMA*), Pub L No 104-199, 110 Stat 2419 (1996), providing that states need not recognize same-sex marriages enacted in other states. In December 2012, the U.S. Supreme Court agreed to hear two appeals relating to same-sex marriage in the United States, including an appeal from the Proposition 8 case referred to above. The second case was initiated by Edith Windsor, a lesbian who had been legally married in Canada and who was claiming the benefit of estate tax provisions (available to heterosexual married couples) to avoid paying estate taxes on inheriting her deceased partner's estate. Windsor's appeal challenged the denial to gays and lesbians of inheritance rights, tax breaks, the ability to file joint tax returns, and health insurance coverage entitlements; and the constitutionality of *DOMA*. On 26 June 2013, the decisions for both cases were released. In the California Proposition 8 case (*Hollingsworth v Perry*, 133 S Ct 2652), the U.S. Supreme Court decided the case on a technical issue of procedure, holding 5–4 that the supporters of the ban on gay marriage did not have standing. As a result, same-sex marriages could again be conducted in California. In *US v Windsor* (133 S Ct 2675), the U.S. Supreme Court held, 5–4, that *DOMA* violated the U.S. constitutional guarantee of equal protection (the 5th Amendment). Ms. Windsor was therefore able to claim the estate tax deduction that was available to married opposite-sex couples at death, for a refund of $363,000. (For one assessment of these cases, see J Becker, *Forcing the Spring: Inside the Fight for Marriage Equality* (New York: Penguin Press, 2014.) In early August 2014, Secretary of State John Kerry announced that the United States would immediately start to treat visa applications for same-sex married couples in the same manner as opposite sex couples: see Michael Gordon, "US Gives Same-Sex Couples Equal Treatment for Visas", *The Globe and Mail* (3 August 2013) A13.

As a result of the U.S. Supreme Court decision in *Windsor*, litigants began to challenge state bans on same-sex marriage on the basis that the bans violated their federal constitutional rights, especially to equal protection. Most of those challenges have succeeded. Same-sex marriage is currently available in 37 states and the District of Columbia. In October 2014, the U.S. Supreme Court declined to hear any appeals from states that had eliminated restrictions on same-sex marriage. In November 2014, the Sixth Circuit Court of Appeals, serving Ohio, Michigan, Tennessee, and Kentucky, issued the only judgment from a federal appellate circuit court that upheld the ban on same-sex marriage. In January 2015, the U.S. Supreme Court announced that it would hear an appeal from that judgment. On June 26, 2015, that court found for the appellants, holding that all states are required to license and to recognize marriages between persons of the same sex (see *Obergefell v Hodges*, 2015 WL 213646). (The development of same-sex marriage law in the United States is too complex to be fully explained here. For a comprehensive account, see Richard Roane & Richard A Wilson, "Marriage Equality Update" (2014–2015) 27 Journal of the American Academy of Matrimonial Lawyers 123.)

The *Hyde* requirement of a union "to the exclusion of all others for life"

Although the *Hyde* definition of marriage has been cited frequently to deny same-sex marriage on the basis of its reference to "one man and one woman," it has seldom been invoked in relation to its requirement of a voluntary union "to the exclusion of all others for life." In the context of rising levels of divorce and remarriage, it is clear that marriage is not always enjoyed as "an exclusive union for life."

For example, in *Davis v Davis* (2002), 35 RFL (5th) 48 (Ont Sup Ct), the court considered the claim of an "uncontrolled philanderer" that his marriage became "an affair of simple carnal convenience" (at para 14) in 1985, so his wife's claim for a half share in his pension had become statute-barred. Although the parties lived together on weekends in Midland, he had a separate long-term relationship with another woman during his working week in Toronto. The court accepted evidence of neighbours in Midland and family members to conclude that there was an ongoing marriage: see Cristin Schmitz, "Marriage of 'Philanderer' Ruled Not a Mere 'Affair'", *The Lawyers Weekly* (24 January 2003) 3.

In the United States, the death of Douglas Cone's wife and his marriage to his mistress of 27 years, Hillary Carlson, created similar controversy. It appears that Mr. Cone had lived in a million-dollar home with his wife and their children on weekends, and with Ms. Carlson and their two children during the week: see Christine Boyd, "Two Names, Two Wives, Two Families, But One Man", *The Globe and Mail* (13 August 2003) S1. In the light of rates of divorce and remarriage in North America, where marriage is not always "for life," is it arguable that the *Hyde* definition is inappropriate for this reason as well?

Additional Resources

Elizabeth Abbott, *A History of Marriage* (Toronto: Penguin, 2010).

Nicholas Bala, "Alternatives for Extending Spousal Status in Canada" (2000) 17 Can J Fam L 169.

Nicola Barker, *Not the Marrying Kind: A Feminist Critique of Same-sex Marriage* (New York: Palgrave Macmillan, 2012).

Jennifer Gerarda Brown, "Competitive Federalism and the Legislative Incentives to Recognize Same-Sex Marriage" (1995) 68 S Cal L Rev 745.

Kathryn Chapman, "*Halpern v. Canada (AG)*, [2002] OJ No 2714 (Ont. Div. Ct.)" (2002) 19 Can J Fam L 423.

Barbara J Cox, "'The Little Project': From Alternative Families to Domestic Partnerships to Same-Sex Marriage" (2000) 15 Wis Women's LJ 77.

Philip Girard, "Marriage Laws have long Evolved to Respect Personal Choice", *Law Times* (21 July 2014).

Robert Leckey, "Profane Matrimony" (2006) 21:2 CJLS 1.

Claude Martin & Irène Théry, "The PACS and Marriage and Cohabitation in France" (2001) 15 Intl JL Pol'y & Fam 135.

Clare McGlynn, "Families, Partnerships and Law Reform in the European Union: Balancing Disciplinarity and Liberalisation" (2006) 69:1 Mod L Rev 92.

Esther Rothblum, "Same-Sex Marriage and Legalized Relationships: I Do, or Do I?" (2005) 1:1 Journal of GLBT Family Studies 21.

Miriam Smith, "The Politics of Same-Sex Marriage in Canada and the United States" (2005) 38:2 PS: Political Science and Politics 225.

Kristen Walker, "The Same-Sex Marriage Debate in Australia" (2007) 11: 1–2 Intl JHR 109.

2. Consent to marriage

> The essence of a marriage contract is an engagement between [two persons] to live together and to love one another as husband and wife to the exclusion of all others. It is a simple contract which does not require high intelligence to comprehend. It does not involve consideration of a large variety of circumstances required in other acts involving others, such as the making of a Will.... (*Lacey v Lacey (Public Trustee of)*, [1983] BCJ No 1016 (SC))

Issues about Capacity to Consent to Marriage

The requirement of consent for a valid marriage (historically, the only requirement) suggests a contractual agreement between the parties. Yet, as the court noted above, it is a "simple contract," requiring a minimal level of mental capacity. In the absence of federal legislation, the principles about consent to marriage continue to be derived from common law principles. In recent years, the requirement of consent has been considered in relation to three issues:

- Mental illness, or diminished mental capacity of a spouse, an issue often litigated in relation to marriages between an elderly spouse and a younger caregiver.

- Problems of duress, undue influence or fraud, sufficient to invalidate the contract, an issue that has arisen in marriages of older persons, as well as under age persons; it has also arisen in relation to "forced" marriages (to be distinguished from "arranged" marriages, to which the parties consent).

- The impact of marriage for a "limited purpose," especially the purpose of gaining immigration status in Canada.

Mental Capacity to Consent

The common law principle: *Durham v Durham*

In *Durham v Durham* (1885), 10 PD 80, the Earl of Durham sued for a declaration of nullity of marriage by reason that, at the time of the celebration of the marriage in 1882, Lady Durham was of unsound mind and incapable of contracting marriage. At the time of the hearing, Lady Durham was described by the court as "hopelessly insane." However, the court held that the burden of showing that she was insane at the time of the marriage rested with the party asserting it; that the test was whether she was capable of understanding the nature of the contract and the duties and responsibilities created by it; and that she was free from any "morbid delusions" about it. In this case, the court held that Lady Durham was able to give her consent at the time of the marriage. As Sir John Hannen stated (at 82):

> [It] appears to me that the contract of marriage is a very simple one, which does not require a high degree of intelligence to comprehend. It is an engagement between a man and a woman to live together, and love one another as husband and wife, to the exclusion of all others.

The relevance of mental illness: *Webb v Webb*

The requirement of consent focuses on whether a person has the mental capacity to give legal consent. In this context, the fact that a person has a mental illness is not, by itself, sufficient to invalidate a marriage — the issue is whether the person was able to give consent to the marriage.

The test was considered in *Webb v Webb* (1968), 3 RFL 129 (NS Div & Mat Causes Ct), a case in which two residents of a Nova Scotia psychiatric hospital married. The husband was 22 and had been diagnosed with chronic, progressive schizophrenia; the wife was a minor, also resident in the psychiatric hospital, and pregnant. Although four priests refused their request to marry, a judge agreed to perform the ceremony. Seven months later, the wife gave birth to a child, and less than a year after the child's birth, they separated permanently. The court held that the test for determining mental capacity was whether there was capacity to understand the nature of the contract and the duties and responsibilities it entailed. In this case, the court decided (at 144) that the (respondent) husband "was mentally capable of appreciating the nature of the contract of marriage and that it involved the responsibilities normally attached to marriage." The court rejected evidence about the limits of the respondent's ability to consent to marriage:

> The witnesses who gave it as their opinion that the respondent was not capable of understanding the nature of the contract he was entering into and the responsibilities normally flowing from that contract seemed to me to be having regard more to the capacity and ability of the respondent to discharge the responsibilities rather than his capacity to appreciate the responsibilities which normally flow from the marriage contract.

In the result, the application for a decree of nullity was dismissed. In commenting on the *Webb* case, David Thompson reviewed studies about marriages involving persons with mental disabilities and argued that such marriages should not be prohibited:

> There are studies that clearly indicate the success of mentally disabled individuals involved in marriages. In a 1973 study following forty marriages where one or both of the parties had been hospitalized: two had divorced, two separated and sixty percent indicated a satisfactory marriage. There were thirty-two children, two died, six had been removed from their parent's control and only three were retarded. A similar study conducted in 1975 of fifty-four couples showed only fifteen percent had divorced or separated, and only one case where the court had removed the child. The conclusion to the study indicated that at least fifty percent of the couples could sustain a marriage for at least several years with a reasonable degree of competence and that children did not, at least in the first few years, serve as a burden. Studies in 1975 and 1976 yielded the same type of results. It was obvious from these marriages that the major-

ity worked on a complementary basis with one partner taking up the slack of the other; as couples they were able to cope and appeared to be more highly motivated to make the marriage work. Finally they were realistic about the challenges that marriage presents. There was either little or no correlation between the degree of handicap and success of the partnership in either subjective or objective terms and in nearly every instance the marriage had brought a substantial enrichment to the lives of those people studied. (David Thompson, "A Consideration of the Mental Capacity Provisions of the Marriage Act in View of the Charter of Rights and Freedoms and *Webb v. Webb*" (1986) 9 Can Community LJ 101 at 106)

See also Kay Maxwell, "Family Law and the Intellectually Disabled in Australia" (1993) 7 Austl J Fam L 151.

Determining mental capacity: *Banton v Banton*

In *Banton v Banton* (1998), 164 DLR (4th) 176 (Ont Gen Div), five adult children of a deceased 88-year-old man, George Banton, challenged the validity of his marriage in 1994 to a young woman, Muna Banton aged 31, who was a waitress in the restaurant at the retirement home where George Banton lived. George Banton had undergone surgery for prostate cancer and was afflicted with deafness, incontinence, and mobility challenges. He had been declared financially incompetent under the *Mental Health Act*. The marriage ceremony took place without the knowledge of his children; indeed, when the marriage commissioner, Mr. Allen, arrived at Muna's apartment for the ceremony, it was necessary for him to arrange to have his wife attend as a witness, and the second witness was a person found in the apartment lobby. George Banton then signed two new wills, making Muna Banton his sole beneficiary.

The trial considered issues about testamentary capacity and undue influence, and Cullity J held that the wills executed by George Banton after his marriage to Muna were invalid because George Banton lacked testamentary capacity and that Muna Banton had exercised undue influence in relation to them. As a result of the invalidity of the wills, George Banton died intestate, and Muna Banton's entitlement to a significant portion of the estate thus depended on the validity of her marriage:

> [132] Mr. Allen testified that he was aware of the prohibition in the *Marriage Act* of marriages of persons who are "mentally ill". He stated that he had no concerns at all about George Banton's mental condition. He said he remembered George as being "quite a good conversationalist" and that there was nothing to indicate that he did not understand the purpose and nature of the ceremony. Mr. Allen also saw no signs of depression and nothing to suggest that George was afraid of, or being manipulated or controlled by, Muna. On the contrary, George's mood was convivial, he seemed affectionate towards Muna and, after the marriage was performed, he responded to the invitation to kiss her. Mr. Allen testified that he left immediately after the ceremony and did not participate in any reception or party. He did not see a walking frame or canes and he made no mention of any hearing disability or of hearing aids. His conclusion about George Banton's mental capacity appears to have been formed on the basis of George's general demeanour and his answers to the questions in the service rather than from any questions asked specifically for the purpose.

In relation to undue influence, the court followed the precedent of *S(A) v S(A)* (1988), 15 RFL (3d) 443 (Ont Unif Fam Ct), and concluded that the evidence did not warrant a conclusion that there was duress in this case. In addition, the court held that presumptions about undue influence in relation to inter vivos transactions have no application to the issue of validity of marriage.

[136] In late September and early October 1994 George Banton had tried to resist Muna's attempts to seduce him into marriage but, in November, he capitulated and consented to it. Although I have also found that marriage was part of Muna's carefully planned and tenaciously implemented scheme to obtain control and, ultimately, the ownership of his property, as far as the marriage was concerned he was, at the end, a willing victim. Shortly thereafter he told Victor that he had wanted "one last fling". ...

[139] ... George Banton wanted to marry Muna and the evidence of Ms. Yolanda Miranda, referred to below, indicates that he never regretted this. She may have misled him as to her motives but he was, as I have said, a willing victim who consented to the marriage. In these circumstances, I do not believe the marriage can be set aside if George Banton had the requisite capacity and, particularly, not by persons other than the parties to the marriage. My finding that there was undue influence sufficient to invalidate his testamentary dispositions does not require a similar conclusion with respect to the marriage from which he obtained benefits of care and companionship. ...

[142] It is well established that an individual will not have capacity to marry unless he or she is capable of understanding the nature of the relationship and the obligations and responsibilities it involves. The burden of proof on this question is on those attacking the validity of the marriage and, in my judgment, it has not been discharged in this case. There is virtually nothing in the evidence to suggest that George Banton's mental deterioration had progressed to the extent that he was no longer able to pass this not particularly rigorous test. The medical evidence indicates his acceptance of the marriage....

[156] The distinction between capacity with respect to the person and capacity with respect to property has been carried over into the *Substitute Decisions Act* with the line now drawn more sharply: each of the concepts being dealt with separately.

[157] While I believe that it may well be the case that a person who is incapable both with respect to personal care and with respect to property may be incapable of contracting marriage, I do not believe that incapacity of the latter kind should, by itself, have this effect. Marriage does, of course, have an effect on property rights and obligations, but to treat the ability to manage property as essential to the relationship would, I believe, be to attribute inordinate weight to the proprietary aspects of marriage and would be unfortunate. Elderly married couples whose property is administered for them under a continuing power of attorney, or by a statutory guardian, may continue to live comfortably together. They may have capacity to make wills and give powers of attorney. I see no reason why this state of affairs should be confined to those who married before incapacity to manage property supervened.

[158] George Banton was found by Dr. Chung to have capacity as far as personal care was concerned. Moreover, despite his physical problems, his weakened mental condition and his loss of memory, he was able to carry on more or less normal discourse on simple everyday matters.... Despite

these problems, I have no doubt that, with care and attention and avoidance of stress, he was capable of coping with the more mundane problems of everyday living and I do not see why the right to marry should be withheld from persons in his position.

[159] Accordingly, ... I find that, notwithstanding George Banton's incapacity to manage property ... he had capacity to marry and that his marriage to Muna was valid. In consequence, in view of my other findings, he died intestate.

Notes and Questions

Evidence and onus of proof in relation to capacity to consent to marriage

On what basis did the court conclude that George Banton had capacity to consent to the marriage? Compare the result in *Banton* to *Re Sung Estate* (2004), 9 RFL (6th) 229 (Ont CA), summarized below, in which the Ontario Court of Appeal upheld a lower court decision that a marriage was invalid.

The deceased married his caregiver in secret, without the knowledge of his children two months before his death, at a time when he was succumbing to lung cancer, needed a respirator to breathe and a wheelchair for transport, was taking a lot of medication and suffered from Parkinson's disease. His family doctor testified that he was then unable to think clearly and logically. When his children discovered the marriage a month before his death, the deceased reassured them that he and his "spouse" had prepared a prenuptial agreement protecting the children's interests. However, on inquiry, the children learned that the "spouse" had retrieved the retainer cheque from the lawyer, and that no agreement had been executed; in this situation, the deceased transferred property to the children. The evidence also showed that the "spouse" had withdrawn $26,500 from the deceased's bank account, immediately before and after his death, by visiting bank machines up to six times each day. In dismissing the caregiver's application for permanent support from the estate and her share of the estate as his wife, the court held that the marriage was invalid and the marriage certificate was to be set aside.

Why is the result in *Sung* different from the outcome in *Banton*? Who has the onus of proving the invalidity of a marriage? Why is the test for testamentary capacity different from the test to determine capacity to consent to marriage?

"Predatory" marriages

A recent article by Dorota Miler identifies a perceived problem with so-called "predatory marriages" in cases like *Banton* and *Re Sung Estate* and argues that Canadian law has yet to provide a workable solution:

... although a pattern characterizes such unions, there is no uniform approach to remedy predatory marriages in Canada's common law provinces. None of the courts acknowledged that the relevant cases bear significant similarities and tried to address the problem by providing a solution that could be applied to other cases rather than persist with a case-by-case approach.

The author argues that in a predatory marriage situation,

The victim spouse is denied the right to dispose his or her property according to his or her wish. Marriage, into which the victim spouse is manipulated, automatically revokes all previous testamentary dispositions regardless of the victim spouse's intent. If a new will is made under testamentary undue influence of the predatory spouse, the victim spouse is denied the right to express his or her testamentary intent and the will represents the wishes of the predatory spouse rather than of the testator. Further, if a person does not have testamentary capacity at the time he or she enters a marriage, he or she cannot decide the future division of his or her estate.

Further, the victim spouse's rights to enjoy his or her family are compromised. The predatory spouse alienates the victim spouse from his or her friends and family, and influences him or her, so they become delusional about his or her loved ones. As a result, he or she dies angry, unsatisfied, and disappointed in his or her family.

Theoretically, predatory marriage could be justified as a contract under which the parties agree to exchange care and companionship provided by the predatory spouse in exchange for the victim spouse's rights to his or her assets; however, a caregiver is usually compensated under an employment contract or an equivalent service contract. Using marriage for this purpose seems inappropriate, especially in Western society, wherein marriage is traditionally conceived of as a relationship between two people who wish to publicly manifest the love and commitment they share with each other. Marriage provides spouses with property rights to create a partnership based on respect and equality. In cases of predatory marriage, affection is supplanted by its illusion and the marriage is based on dependency, coercion, and a desire for financial benefit.

...

While only a few cases have been aired in court, there is a significant probability that most predatory marriages are not identified. Considerable costs prevent litigation in a majority of estate cases, while in many others there is no one interested in questioning the marriage or the will's validity. As lifespans increase in the elderly population, statistically, the predatory marriage problem will also increase. (Dorota Miler, "Elder Exploitation Through Predatory Marriage" (2012–13) 28 Can J Fam L 11 at 26–28)

Capacity to consent: Intoxication

Note the provisions in Ontario's *Marriage Act*, s 7, concerning procedures with respect to licences and ceremonies where there is a lack of capacity to consent: to what extent are these provisions within the legislative authority of the province?

Consider a case in which a Canadian couple met for the first time in Las Vegas and decided within hours to marry. When the wife later returned home to British Columbia and applied to annul the marriage, the evidence indicated that she had freely headed to the marriage chapel, followed instructions about obtaining the requisite marriage licence in a different location, and then returned to the marriage chapel and participated in the marriage ceremony. Later on, the wife recalled these events, but claimed that she was severely intoxicated at the time, and that she was thus unable to consent to the marriage. Is this marriage valid?

In *CMD v RRS*, 2005 BCSC 757, the B.C. Supreme Court held that the marriage was valid because the applicant "went through deliberate and time-consuming steps all rationally connected to entering into a marriage contract." Although her judgment and actions were compromised by her drunkenness, "the evidence [fell] far short of showing that she was incapable of understanding that she was entering a marriage." In the light of this case, how would you describe the legal test for consent? Is it a high test or a low one?

Duress and Undue Influence in Relation to Consent

Common law principles: *Scott v Sebright, Cooper v Crane*, and *Buckland v Buckland*

In *Scott v Sebright* (1886), 12 PD 21, a woman requested a declaration of nullity in relation to her marriage to the respondent a few months earlier. As a 22-year-old woman with a significant fortune, she had been persuaded to lend funds, which then fell into substantial arrears, to the respondent, causing her serious concerns for her reputation. The respondent persuaded her that the only way to avoid declaring bankruptcy was to marry him; he also threatened to shoot her if she suggested at the ceremony that she was not acting with free will. The parties separated after the ceremony, and the marriage was not consummated. Justice Butt granted a declaration of nullity, stating (at 23–24):

> The Courts of law have always refused to recognize as binding contracts to which the consent of either party has been obtained by fraud or duress, and the validity of a contract of marriage must be tested and determined in precisely the same manner as that of any other contract. True it is that in contracts of marriage there is an interest involved above and beyond that of the immediate parties. Public policy requires that marriage should not be lightly set aside, and there is in some cases the strongest temptation to the parties more immediately interested to act in collusion in obtaining a dissolution of the marriage tie.... It has sometimes been said that in order to avoid a contract entered into through fear, the fear must be such as would impel a person of ordinary courage and resolution to yield to it. I do not think that is an accurate statement of the law. Wherever from natural weakness of intellect or from fear — whether reasonably entertained or not — either party is actually in a state of mental incompetence to resist pressure improperly brought to bear, there is no more consent than in the case of a person of stronger intellect and more robust courage yielding to a more serious danger. The difficulty consists not in any uncertainty of the law on the subject, but in its application to the facts of each individual case.

Is the test in *Scott v Sebright* an objective or subjective test? *Scott v Sebright* was distinguished in *Cooper v Crane* (1891), P 369. In *Cooper* the action for annulment was brought three years after a marriage ceremony took place between cousins — the woman was 24 and the man not yet 21. Although she had previously rejected the man's proposal, the woman was persuaded to go through a ceremony of marriage at a church (previously arranged by the man) when he told her to come into the church and marry him or he would "blow [his] brains out and she would be responsible." After the ceremony, the parties returned to their own homes, and the woman did not mention the matter to her family or friends. The man subsequently discovered that the woman did not have money (as he had thought) and indicated that he was not interested in being married to her. However, the court refused to grant a declaration of annulment, stating that the facts were not sufficient to rebut the presumption of consent. Although there was evidence that the woman was of weak character, "without much power of resistance and easily overpowered by a stronger influence" (at 372), the court concluded (at 376–78) that the evidence did not demonstrate that she did not understand what she was doing, or that her powers of volition were paralyzed. Is this result consistent with *Scott v Sebright*?

Compare these two cases to *Buckland v Buckland*, [1967] 2 All ER 300 (PDA Div), involving a husband who claimed duress that vitiated his consent to a marriage. Justice Scarman granted a declaration of nullity at the request of the husband, a British police officer serving in Malta. The court concluded that the husband had agreed to marriage solely to avoid going to prison in relation to a charge of "corrupting a minor," a charge which Justice Scarman believed had been falsely laid against him by a Maltese family in relation to their pregnant daughter. In these circumstances, the court concluded (at 302) that the husband "agreed to his marriage because of his fears, and that his fears, which were reasonably entertained, arose from external circumstances for which he was in no way responsible." Is this test the same as the one applied in *Scott* and in *Cooper*? Do these precedents suggest that the test for duress is objective or subjective? Are the precedents consistent?

Duress in Canada: *S(A) v S(A)*

Consider the application of these precedents in *S(A) v S(A)* (1988), 15 RFL (3d) 443 (Ont Unif Fam Ct), a modern decision in Canada. Is the test for duress in Canada an objective or subjective test? To what extent do courts take account of factual circumstances in applying legal principles?

The applicant, a young woman, applied for annulment of her marriage to the respondent, or in the alternative, a divorce. The respondent did not file an answer or appear in the proceedings; the only evidence adduced was that of the applicant. In reviewing the facts, the judge explained:

> The applicant was born on 9th April 1969. On 28th February 1986 she went through a form of marriage with the respondent, who had recently arrived in Canada. The marriage was celebrated at the city hall, Hamilton, and the certificate of marriage was filed as Ex. 2. At this date, the applicant was 16 years of age. Her parents had separated, and she was living with her mother and her stepfather. The consent of the mother to the marriage was contained in a certificate of consent filed as Ex. 3.

Paragraph 8 of the application contains the grounds for relief and comprises subparas. (a) to (e). Subparagraphs (b), (c) and (d) read as follows:

> (b) The applicant married the respondent after considerable pressure being applied against her by her natural mother and stepfather. The applicant did not know the respondent but was told that he would be ordered to leave Canada unless he married a Canadian citizen.

> (c) The applicant's mother and step-father were to receive $500.00 for arranging to have the applicant marry the respondent. This was the motive for their participation. The applicant was particularly sensitive to the pressure because there was a history of sexual abuse by the step-father toward her. In fact, the applicant was removed from the home for a period of three years by the Children's Aid Society in Calgary, Alberta because of this abuse.

> (d) The applicant never lived with the Respondent and she has never had sexual intercourse with him.

The applicant stated that she was first approached by her mother and her stepfather, who applied pressure to her to marry the respondent. The applicant was told that the respondent wished to marry because he wanted to live in Canada. She testified that her mother and stepfather told her that there was $2,000 involved and that they said that "we can have all this nice stuff that we didn't have before with all this money." The applicant said that she told her mother that she did not want to marry the respondent, that her mother "was talking to my step-father and then there was more pressure." The applicant further testified that she did not want to marry the respondent, that she did not live with him after the ceremony, that the parties never engaged in sexual intercourse, and that the respondent subsequently left Canada. The applicant, in her evidence, stated that a few years ago she had been made a ward of the Children's Aid Society in Alberta because she had been sexually abused by her stepfather, and that she had remained in care until she turned 16 years....

[In relation to duress, the judge stated that:] It was submitted by Mr. Rogers that the applicant was pressured into marrying the respondent by her mother and stepfather and that, given the surrounding circumstances, she was not able to withstand that pressure. During argument, I questioned this submission.

The applicant made no allegation of the use of physical force, nor did she allege that the use of physical force had been threatened. Moreover, the conduct alleged as duress did not emanate from the respondent. The conduct contended by Mr. Rogers to constitute duress was pressure of a non-physical nature, which was directed at the applicant by the mother and stepfather, who sought to obtain financial benefit from the proposed marriage, be it $500, as stated in para. 8(b) of the application, or $2,000 as related by the applicant during her evidence....

Mendes da Costa J quoted the words of Butt J in *Scott v Sebright*, above, and continued:

> The principles expounded by Butt J. seem as sound today as they were when they were uttered in 1886. Public policy still requires that marriages "should not be lightly set aside." No doubt, also, there is in some cases the "strongest temptation to the parties more immediately interested to act in collusion." A court is, indeed, required to exercise care and circumspection to ensure that the ground alleged as duress has been established. However, since 1886 there has been a considerable change in the availability of divorce. Under the *Divorce Act, 1985*, S.C. 1986, c. 4, the

ground for divorce is breakdown of marriage. Leaving aside adultery and cruelty, relief is available where, in general terms, the spouses have lived separate and apart for at least one year. As a more or less parallel development, the status of illegitimacy has been eradicated from the law of the province and, to some extent, "spouse" has received an expanded definition in the *Family Law Act, 1986*, S.O. 1986, c. 4. At this point in time, there seems no need for parties to turn to the law of nullity simply to obtain relief denied them by divorce law. I believe, therefore, that the courts should approach a proceeding for nullity in a manner no different from that of any other matrimonial cause.

The above passage from *Scott v. Sebright* was referred to in *Thompson v. Thompson*, 4 RFL 376, [1971] 4 WWR 383, 19 DLR (3d) 608 (Sask. QB). In this case, the plaintiff sought the annulment of her marriage to the defendant. The court found that the plaintiff had agreed to marry the defendant as a result of his persistent urging, at a time when her resistance was reduced by her state of depression arising from her rejection by another man. Once the wedding plans were underway, the plaintiff was not able to muster sufficient courage to cancel them, because of the social consequences insofar as her family was concerned. She believed that, if she did cancel the marriage plans, there would be a rift between herself and her family. The plaintiff's mother, the court concluded, had exerted influence on the plaintiff to continue with the plans. The marriage was consummated, albeit reluctantly on the part of the plaintiff. The court held that the plaintiff had not established a case that would fall within the principles enunciated in the authorities and dismissed the action....

In *Pascuzzi v. Pascuzzi*, [1955] OWN 853 (HC), the plaintiff sought an annulment of her marriage. The claim was unopposed. At the time of the marriage she was 15 years of age and the defendant was 19 years of age. Prior to the marriage, during a visit to Toronto, the parties engaged in sexual intercourse. The plaintiff being a juvenile, complaints were made to the police and both the plaintiff and the defendant were taken into custody, the plaintiff being detained on a charge of juvenile delinquency and the defendant being faced with a criminal charge. According to the evidence, it was intimated to the plaintiff that if she and the defendant were married no criminal charges would be laid. It was necessary to secure the consent of the plaintiff's mother to the marriage and, at first, she refused but, finally, after she had been called upon by a solicitor representing the defendant, she gave her consent. The plaintiff was not only reluctant to go through a form of marriage but, on more than one occasion, protested that she would not do so. As stated by Aylen J. at p. 854:

> No doubt with the best intentions in the world, those to whom the plaintiff turned for advice all urged her so strongly to marry the defendant that it became practically an impossibility for a child of her age to continue to refuse, especially as her only home at the time was with the defendant's parents.

The ceremony was performed on 27th February 1954, and the plaintiff left the defendant on or about 31st December 1954. The court considered the delay in the plaintiff leaving the defendant understandable in the circumstances. Afer a reference to the law of duress, the court held that the marriage between the plaintiff and the defendant should be declared a nullity.... The last decision I will mention is *Marriage of S.* (1980), 42 FLR 94 (Aust. Fam. Ct.). In this case, the court pointed out that the emphasis on terror or fear in some judgments seemed unnecessarily limiting. In granting a decree of nullity, Watson J, at p. 102, stated that it was "the effect of the oppression on his mind that should be the operative factor, not the form of such oppression." I turn now to state my understanding of the authorities.

A valid marriage is grounded upon the consent of each party. Oppression may vitiate consent and, if there is no consent, there is no valid marriage. Different people may respond to oppression in different ways, and conduct that may overmaster the mind of one person may not have this impact upon the mind of another. It matters not, therefore, whether the will of a person of reasonable fortitude would — or would not — have been overborne; the issue is, rather, the state of mind of the applicant. To constitute duress, it must be established that the applicant's mind was so overcome by oppression that there was an absence of free choice. The point that falls for decision is whether the consent given at the time of the ceremony was a real, understanding and voluntary consent. Oppression can take various forms; it may be generated by fear, or by persuasion or pressure. Essentially, the matter is one of degree, and this raises a question of fact for the court. The determination involves a consideration of all relevant circumstances, including the age of the applicant, the maturity of the applicant, the applicant's emotional state and vulnerability, the lapse of time between the conduct alleged as duress and the marriage ceremony, whether the marriage was consummated, whether the parties resided together as man and wife and the lapse of time between the marriage ceremony and the institution of the annulment proceeding. As long as the oppression affects the mind of the applicant in the fashion stated, physical force is not required and, no more so, is the threat of such force a necessary ingredient. Nor is the source of the conduct material. Where duress is alleged, the onus of proof is upon the party seeking annulment, and it is an onus that is not lightly discharged.

The principles of law relating to duress seem to be relatively clear and certain. However, as pointed out by Butt J. in *Scott v. Sebright*, the difficulty consists in the application of the law to the facts of each individual case. I have given this matter my most anxious consideration and, upon reflection, I am satisfied that the applicant has discharged the onus of proof and is entitled to a declaration of nullity....

Mendes da Costa J granted a decree of annulment. In addition, he concluded that, if the applicant were not entitled to the decree of annulment, she would be able to establish grounds for divorce.

Notes and Questions

Evidence in relation to duress

Why were the claims of duress in *S(A) v S(A)* and *Pascuzzi* upheld, but a similar claim in *Thompson* rejected? Note again the onus of proving that a marriage is invalid, and the nature of evidence required to substantiate such a claim. Recall *Banton v Banton*, in which there was a similar onus to establish that the marriage was invalid. Is it appropriate to conclude that there is a legal presumption of validity for marriage?

Duress and claims about "forced" marriage

In recent cases, claims of duress have been made by petitioners whose parents have required them to enter into "forced" marriages. According to a 2007 report for the Department of Justice, Canada:

A forced marriage occurs when people are coerced into a marriage against their will and under duress, which can include both physical and emotional pressure. A forced marriage is very different from an arranged marriage in which the free and informed consent of both parties is present. Due to its confusion with the tradition of arranged marriage, forced marriage is often associated in developed states with South Asian immigrants, but it is important to remember that it occurs across many cultures and religions. Every major faith condemns the practice and requires freely given consent for marriage, as does the law in most states.

Forced marriage often affects young people, who may be taken abroad on false pretexts, or pressured to marry in order to sponsor their new spouse for immigration purposes. In many, if not all instances, it is the parents who are forcing the young person to marry because they see the forced marriage as protecting their child by controlling unwanted sexual interest or behaviour, preventing "unsuitable" relationships, protecting religious or cultural ideals, strengthening family links, or honouring long-standing family commitments. Yet forced marriage is an international human rights violation [prohibited under a number of United Nations conventions and state legislation and policies.] (Nadine Dostrovsky, Rebecca Cook & Michaël Gagnon, *Annotated Bibliography on Comparative and International Law relating to Forced Marriage* (Ottawa: Department of Justice Canada, 2007) at 1 [*Research Report*, 2007])

For a recent account of "forced" marriage in Canada, see Raveena Aulakh, "'They Think They're Doing What's Best for the Child'", *Toronto Star* (14 November 2009) A1 and A18–19.

Duress and "arranged" marriages

Legal debates about duress have often focused on "arranged marriages," even though it is now clear that there is a difference (at least in terms of legal principles) between a "forced marriage" on one hand (where there is no consent) and an "arranged marriage" (to which the individual parties consent). Thus, in a study in the 1980s, David Bradley reviewed two English decisions concerning "arranged" marriages and duress in relation to consent:

- In a decision in 1971, the English Court of Appeal distinguished economic, social, parental, or cultural pressures from the legal requirements of duress: "fear caused by threat of immediate danger ... to life, limb or liberty," and thus rejected the applicant's petition for annulment: see *Singh v Singh*, [1971] P 226; 2 All ER 828 (CA).

- In *Singh v Kaur* (1981), 11 FL 151 (Eng CA), the court rejected an application, where the petitioner gave in to his Sikh parents' request to accept an arranged marriage in order to avoid disgracing his family and losing the opportunity to work in the family business. Although the court recognized that the husband was in a sad position, the judgment indicated (at 152) that "he has to make up his mind, as an adult, whether to go through with the marriage or whether to withstand the pressure put upon him by his family."

In both these cases, it seems that the courts concluded that the marriages took place with the petitioners' consent, even though their marriages had been arranged for them.

By contrast, Bradley noted that in *Hirani v Hirani* (1982), 4 FLR 232, the English Court of Appeal granted a request for annulment to a young Hindu woman, aged 19. Although she wished to marry a Muslim man, her parents arranged for her to marry a Hindu man whom they had not previously met. The marriage was not consummated and the wife left her husband six weeks after the marriage. In granting the declaration of nullity in this case, the court concluded that

> [t]he crucial question in these cases, particularly where a marriage is involved, is whether the threats, pressure, or whatever it is, is such as to destroy the reality of consent and overbears the will of the individual. It seems to me that this case, on the facts, is a classic case of a young girl, wholly dependent on her parents, being forced into a marriage with a man she has never seen and whom her parents have never seen in order to prevent her (reasonably, from her parents' point of view) continuing in an association with a Muslim which they would regard with abhorrence. But it is as clear a case as one could want of the overbearing of the will of the petitioner and thus invalidating or vitiating her consent.

For further details, see David Bradley, "Duress and Arranged Marriages" (1983) 46 Mod L Rev 499.

Distinguishing "forced marriages" and "arranged marriages"

It may be difficult in practice to distinguish between a "forced" marriage (in which there is no consent) and one in which the parties are willing, if reluctant, participants in an "arranged" marriage (thus consenting to the marriage.) As the *Research Report*, 2007 (above) explained (at 2), "[P]arental pressure will not necessarily amount to duress in all situations because valid consent can be 'reluctant' or 'resentful.' What matters is whether the will of the individual has been overborne by the pressure."

Consider the following situation:

> A young Egyptian woman had glumly participated in an arranged marriage. She had done so solely out of love and respect for her parents and to avoid any prejudice to the future marital opportunities of her younger sisters. There were no other tangible or intangible repercussions that would have flowed from a refusal to marry.

When she petitioned for annulment, how should the court respond?

In this Australian case in 1980, Watson SJ held that duress creating a nullity should be broad enough to encompass non-violent, but controlling, parental coercion. In so holding, he emphasized the need to regard the coercive action from the subjective vantage point of the unwilling bride. See *In the Marriage of S*, [1980] FLC 90–820 (Fam Ct) (Austl).

By contrast, two Canadian courts rejected petitions for annulment in 1980 as well: see *Singh v Singh*, [1980] OJ No 2080 (Unif Fam Ct) (QL) and *Parihar v Bhatti* (1980), 17 RFL (2d) 289 (BCSC). In the latter case, the court noted that families often bring persuasion upon a person to marry, but that "duress sufficient to set aside the marriage must be of such a nature that her powers of volition were so affected that it really was no consent."

More recently, Hilary Lim argued that gender may create a distinction between a "forced" marriage and one that is "arranged." In a study focused on two cases in the United Kingdom, Lim suggested that when the applicant seeking annulment was a young woman, the court held that there was duress because she was dominated by a will stronger than her own (her parents) so that she was a "victim." However, when the applicant for annulment was a 30-year-old man, the court seemed to characterize duress in terms of the competing demands on his conscience from his girlfriend and from his family of origin. In this context, Lim suggested that the woman was "acted upon" passively by her family, while the man was involved in making an "active moral choice." See Hilary Lim, "Messages From a Rarely Visited Island: Duress and Lack of Consent in Marriage" (1996) 4 Fem Leg Stud 195. For details of the cases, see *Mahmood v Mahmood*, [1993] SLT 589; and *Mahmud v Mahmud*, [1994] SLT 599.

To what extent may gender define the difference between an "arranged" marriage and a "forced" one? What other factors may be relevant to this distinction?

Forced marriage: recent Canadian research

In a 2013 report, *Who/If/When to Marry: The Incidence of Forced Marriage in Ontario*, the South Asian Legal Clinic of Ontario (SALCO) provided data regarding 210 forced marriage cases in Ontario and Québec from 2010–2012. Of these, 92 percent involved women (there were also three cases involving trans people). Further, most people in forced marriage situations are young. Although it is disturbing to note that 10 percent of the cases involved people from 12 to 15 years of age, and another 25 percent between 16 and 18, the largest concentration of cases involved persons between the age of 19 to 24 (31%) with another 25 percent aged 25–34. As the Report explained,

> Bearing in mind that 19 to 24 is the age considered most eligible for marriage in many cultures, it stands to reason that young people in this age bracket face a greater risk of FM [forced marriage]. Basically the pressure to marry is heightened for this age bracket. Research also shows that a young person's vulnerability to being forced into a marriage can increase with intergenerational conflict (for example; between parent and child). In case studies, we have noted that intergenerational conflict seems to be heightened in this age bracket, thus compounding the vulnerability to FM. Another age-related factor that increases vulnerability for the 19 to 24 age group is that they are no longer minors. Child protection laws cannot protect them. This allows perpetrators of FM [to] engage in coercive activities without the repercussions entailing such treatment of a minor. (SALCO at 10)

There was also wide variation of educational level:

> The survey indicated that 33% of the individuals facing FM situations had not completed high school and 32% had a high school diploma. This statistic is consistent with the data that at least 30% of the reported cases involved individuals who were 18 or younger. Furthermore, 15% of the reported cases involved individuals with a college diploma and another 15% had a university degree. The variance in educational background reported confirms that FM does not correlate with lack of education. FM is a phenomenon that extends to victims with different levels of education. (SALCO at 14)

However, the survey results indicated that even where the individual's family had ample economic resources, the individual herself did not have access to an independent source of income. Further, "many of the women who did report a reliable source of income were often married and financially dependent on their partner (who they had been forced to marry). The data indicates that FM victims are often at a severe economic disadvantage." As a consequence, "Victims may feel powerless to leave a FM or attempt to stop an FM because of this lack of income. Furthermore, the idea of potential poverty as a result of leaving a FM could impact a victim's decision-making process on how to proceed" (SALCO at 15).

Legal policies about marriage in relation to individual and family values

While it is possible in principle to distinguish between "forced" marriages and "arranged" marriages, the factual contexts may continue to present challenges. As Bradley noted in relation to his discussion of arranged marriages (at 504):

> The diverse and sometimes conflicting interests involved in the arranged marriage system include those of the second and subsequent generations exposed to two cultures, the immediate family including siblings, the wider kinship network and the ethnic group as a whole. Inevitably these cannot all be accommodated in a family law in which the prevailing ethic is individualism.

To what extent do you agree with this assessment? To what extent should courts take account of "reluctant" or "resentful" consent in relation to duress? What factual circumstances may be most significant?

As explained by Máiréad Enright (in "Choice, Culture and the Politics of Belonging: The Emerging Law of Forced and Arranged Marriage" (2009) 72 Mod L Rev 331), the English law regarding forced marriage has developed considerably since the *Hirani* case in 1982 and was strengthened by the *Forced Marriage (Civil Protection) Act 2007*.

> The Act compliments the existing nullity jurisdiction with an armoury of judicial powers aimed at preventing rather than simply unpicking forced marriages. The preceding twenty years had seen the judicial liberalisation of duress as a ground for nullity.... This judicial activism was motivated by an appreciation of the means by which an individual may be forced into marriage. The courts had moved away both from the requirement that the petitioner show that her will was objectively overborne by an immediate threat to 'life, limb or liberty' to a subjective test of whether the actual pressure directed at her was enough to destroy her consent. (Enright at 343)

The liberalization process began in 1982 with *Hirani v Hirani*. The test from *Hirani*, discussed above, was followed in *NS v MI*, [2006] EWHC 1646 (Fam). In that case, "Munby J set out that very little pressure may be required where it was applied by a parent or other close and dominating relative using arguments based upon personal affection or duty, religious beliefs, powerful social or cultural conventions or asserted social, familial or domestic obligations" (Enright at 343).

The *Forced Marriage (Civil Protection) Act* empowers courts to go beyond their traditional nullity jurisdiction by giving them means to prevent forced marriages, including "power to grant a protection order to prevent an actual or apprehended act of forcing another into marriage" (Enright at 344). Significantly, "the Act provides that forcing another into marriage is a civil wrong rather than a crime." Although it was initially proposed that the act of forcing someone into a marriage should be criminalized, "this proposal was rejected ... primarily because it was felt that reluctance to prosecute family members arising from cultural pressures would discourage victims from engaging with the law at all" (Enright at 345).

Enright "disputes the easy ritual distinction so often drawn between forced and arranged marriage. While it is certainly possible to identify a forced or an arranged marriage in its individual context, the task of defining these concepts in more general terms is a complex one. In practice, substantial slippage occurs across the forced-arranged divide," especially when both forced and arranged marriages are widely associated with specific immigrant cultural groups (Enright at 332).

In the UK context, Enright notes that part of the problem is with a slippage between forced marriages and "transnational arranged marriages" which, while they ostensibly fall on the arranged marriage side of the divide, have nevertheless "come within the[ir] ambit" of anti-forced marriage "policy drives" (Enright at 332).

It is not clear that the same circumstance exists in Canada. According to the SALCO report, "a combined 85% of the cases reported in the survey involved Canadian citizens and permanent residents — A large number of FM victims had strong and significant connections to Canada either as their country of origin or what they consider their country of residence. FM cannot be painted as an issue impacting only new immigrants to Canada." The data reported by SALCO indicated that there was an almost even split between forced marriage cases that occurred within Canada and those where the victim was either taken out of Canada or brought to Canada for the marriage (SALCO at 12–14).

What policy should be adopted by Canadian courts in relation to issues of duress and "forced marriages"? As the Department of Justice *Research Report*, 2007 noted (at 2), other jurisdictions have adopted a variety of measures: for example, Norway and Belgium have criminalized forced marriages; France and some other jurisdictions have raised the minimum age for marriage; and Denmark has tightened its immigration laws. Finally, the United Kingdom recently criminalized forced marriage in the *Anti-Social Behaviour, Crime and Policing Act 2014*.

Which approach is most appropriate for reform, if any, in Canada? SALCO recommended against criminalization and suggested instead the expansion of social and economic supports for people avoiding or leaving forced marriages. These recommendations include classifying forced marriage as domestic violence so that victims can have access to shelters and housing programs and making possible for them to receive provincial social assistance from which many are currently barred "because they are considered to be dependent on the income of their families or husbands (the perpetrators of the FM)" (SALCO at 21).

In considering this issue, it is also useful to take account of the discussion below about "limited purpose marriage," particularly for marriages contracted to achieve immigration status in Canada.

Consent and Limited Purpose Marriage

The principle in Canada: *Iantsis v Papatheodorou*

In a number of cases, courts have been asked to grant decrees of nullity where a marriage has taken place solely in order for a non-citizen to acquire immigration status in Canada. Although there were some cases in which such requests were granted, the Ontario Court of Appeal held in 1971 that where "all that is alleged is a mental reservation on the part of the defendant, ... that is not sufficient to derogate from the effect to be given to the solemn declaration of the spouses made in the course of the marriage ceremony" (*Iantsis v Papatheodorou* (1970), 3 RFL 158 at 164 (Ont CA)).

The court in *S(A) v S(A)* (above) considered the judgment in *Iantsis* and explained the principle in that case:

> The mere fact ... that parties go through a form of marriage for a "limited" or "extraneous" purpose will not, of itself, render the marriage invalid. In this respect, no heed is paid to their mental reservations. Indeed, their motive would seem to support a finding of validity. Where parties seek, by marriage, to confer upon a respondent a right to reside in Canada, it would seem to follow that they do only what they intend: enter into a marriage relationship as the means of achieving the desired result.

Thus, if parties marry for the "limited purpose" of a non-citizen acquiring immigration status in Canada, they will be regarded as married for purposes of family law. In this context, they must seek a divorce to end the marriage, and they may be required to meet other obligations such as spousal support. At the same time, immigration laws in Canada permit the government to challenge a marriage or cohabiting relationship that is not genuine and "was entered into primarily for the purpose of acquiring [immigration] status" (Immigration and Refugee Protection Regulations, SOR 2002-227, s 4). In this way, the marriage may be valid for family law purposes, but subject to immigration sanctions (including deportation) because it was entered into only to obtain immigration status; from the immigration perspective (but not the family law perspective), it was not a genuine marriage.

More recently, an Ontario court declared a marriage void on the basis of fraud in relation to an "immigration marriage" in a case where the parties had married in Iran. The judge determined that the laws of Iran applied and that the facts would support a nullity declaration in that country. This decision was upheld (in a brief judgment) by the Ontario Court of Appeal: see *Torfehnejad v Salimi* (2006), 32 RFL (6th) 115 (Ont Sup Ct); and 2008 ONCA 583.

Torfehnejad was distinguished on a motion for summary judgment in *Grewal v Kaur* (2009), 75 RFL (6th) 443 (Ont Sup Ct). Sproat J held that the Court of Appeal's brief endorsement of the reasoning in *Torfehnejad* was confined to the facts in that case and could not be construed as a reversal of *Iantsis*. He went on to comment on the potential implications of permitting annulment on the ground of "immigration fraud," noting that "the federal government has already altered the definition of spouse for immigration purposes to exclude immigration fraudsters" (at para 20), and adding:

> [23] ... on a principled approach it may be difficult to differentiate immigration fraud from other types of fraud. In *Grewal v Sohal* (2004), 246 D.L.R. (3d) 743 (B.C. S.C.) the fraud consisted of the defendant fraudulently representing his marital intentions for immigration purposes and fraudulently representing that he did not have an alcohol or drug addiction. One can think of many other misrepresentations such as related to education, health or assets that might induce a decision to marry and which could be made fraudulently. If a fraud as to fundamental facts that ground the decision to marry is generally a ground for annulment, this certainly raises the spectre of an increase in the volume of costly litigation.

The trial judge affirmed this approach, refused the annulment, and granted a divorce. See *Grewal v Kaur*, 2011 ONSC 1812.

The principle established in *Iantsis v Papatheodorou* was criticized in a Nova Scotia decision, *Singla v Singla* (1985), 46 RFL (2d) 235 (NSSC (TD)), although the Nova Scotia court applied the *Iantsis* precedent (see also the Annotation by James McLeod, who argued (at 236)):

> The purpose ... of the validity rules should be to ensure that "marriage" only arises when people with the appropriate capacity enter into a relationship which has at least a chance of functioning as a social unit.

Do you agree? Or do you find the approach of the Ontario courts more persuasive. For more on these issues, see *Epstein's This Week in Family Law*, Fam L Nws 2011-26 (WLNext Can).

"Immigration" marriages and marriage fraud

The problem of fraudulent "immigration marriages" has received increased political attention in recent years.

According to recent news reports, there are about 55,000 spousal sponsorship applications annually, of which about 20 percent are rejected. An organization called Canadians Against Immigration Fraud, representing people who claim to have been duped by a "marriage fraud," has lobbied for changes to the arrangements for such sponsorships. See Nicholas Keung,

"Tories take 'ideas' on marriage fraud", *Toronto Star* (2 September 2010); Sarah Hampson, "With this fraud I thee wed", *The Globe and Mail* (22 May 2008); and Evan Wilson, "Your Cheatin' Heart", *Toronto Star* (17 July 2010).

Recently, the press reported on the results of research undertaken by a McMaster University professor who was granted site visits at 11 visa offices in Europe, the United States, the Middle East, South America, the Caribbean, Africa, and Asia to observe the processing of immigration applications and to conduct interviews with frontline officers with respect to decision making about the "validity" of marriages.

The research identified "flags" used to assess whether the marriage is a "real" marriage:

> Couples who don't have a common language of communication, have not met before marriage, do not know details in each others' personal histories and current lives, and are deemed not compatible in age, physical appearance and values.... An applicant facing deportation suddenly getting married often raises concerns.... Canadian officials [also] scrutinize photographic evidence — who and how many people attended the ceremony, the demeanor and if the guests smiled — to help assess credibility.... And an excessive confession of love in a couple's correspondence can backfire [because it is assumed that they are being written for the visa officer to read]. (Nicholas Keung, "A Rare Look Inside the 'Black Box' of Canada Immigration", *Toronto Star* (1 February 2014)).

In May 2015, it was reported that a Vancouver immigration lawyer had posted online a 3-page training guide for immigration officials, which he obtained using an access to information request. See Nicholas Keung, "Immigration Guide for Detecting Marriage Fraud Called 'Racist and Offensive'", *Toronto Star* (15 May 2015).

It seems that there are also some cases in which "immigration" marriages (that is, marriages entered into in order to obtain immigration status in Canada) may also be "forced" marriages (see Raveena Aulakh, "'They Think They're Doing What's Best for the Child'", *Toronto Star* (14 November 2009) 1).

In a 2006 decision in British Columbia, the court awarded tort damages for deceit to a Canadian woman whose Fijian husband lied about his intentions when he married her. Upon gaining entry to Canada, the husband commenced divorce proceedings and the court awarded the wife damages for her expenses in relation to the wedding and the sponsorship application, along with $10,000 in general damages for her "hurt feelings, humiliation, inconvenience and postponement of the opportunity to marry another man while she was still capable of bearing children" (*Raju v Kumar*, 2006 BCSC 439 at para 88; see also Cristin Schmitz, "Cheating Husband Pays for Lying to his Wife", *The Lawyers Weekly* (7 April 2006) 1).

Additional Resources

A Choice by Right: The Report of the Working Group on Forced Marriages (London: Home Office 2000).

David Bradley, "Duress, Family Law and the Coherent Legal System" (1994) 57 Mod L Rev 963.

Nadine Dostrovsky, Rebecca Cook & Michaël Gagnon, *Annotated Bibliography on Comparative and International Law relating to Forced Marriage* (Ottawa: Department of Justice 2007).

Michael Dunn, Isabel CH Claire & Anthony Holland, "To Empower or Protect? Constructing the 'Vulnerable Adult' in English Law and Public Policy" (2008) 28:2 LS 234.

RM Gordon, "Adult Protection Legislation in Canada: Models, Issues and Problems" (2001) 24 Intl J L & Psychiatry 117.

Anne Phillips & Moira Dunn, "UK Initiatives on Forced Marriage: Regulation, Dialogue and Exit" (2004) 52 Political Studies 531.

Edwige Rude-Antione, *Forced Marriages in Council of Europe Member States* (Strasbourg: Directorate General of Human Rights, 2005).

Prakash Shah, "Rituals of Recognition: Ethnic Minority Marriages in British Legal Systems" in Prakash Shah, ed, *Law and Ethnic Plurality: Socio-Legal Perspectives* (Leiden & Boston: Martinus Nijhoff Publishers, 2007) 177.

Amrit Wilson, "The Forced Marriage Debate and the British State" (2007) 49:1 Race & Class 25.

3. Capacity to consummate the marriage

A Principle in Need of Reform?

Like the need for consent for a valid marriage, the requirement of capacity to consummate derives from early marriage practices, and was recognized in the law of nullity by the ecclesiastical courts in England and then continued as a common law requirement after the 1857 legislation. Thus, it is still a requirement for a valid marriage in Canada that the parties have the capacity to consummate it — however, there is no requirement of proof that the marriage has been consummated. In the context of Canada's recognition of same-sex marriage, moreover, this requirement for the validity of a marriage may appear especially anachronistic. Interestingly, "capacity to consummate" has been abolished in some other jurisdictions, such as Australia. In contrast, U.K. legislation excludes non-consummation as a ground for nullity only in same-sex marriages. See *Marriage (Same Sex Couples) Act 2013* (UK), c 30, Schedule 4, s 4.

In addition, cases in which applicants seek an annulment on the grounds of incapacity to consummate inevitably require the presentation in public of evidence about the intimate relations of the parties. For this reason, the cases may appear to invade their privacy — the state is clearly intruding into "the bedrooms of the nation." Moreover, courts are often faced with conflicting accounts of the parties' efforts to consummate the marriage, so that issues of credibility must be determined. Thus, in choosing to accept the evidence of a husband or a wife (when their evidence conflicts), the decisions may sometimes reveal judges' ideas about what is "normal" or "reasonable" in heterosexual intimate relationships. In this context, it may also be important to consider why married spouses would ever seek an annulment on the grounds of incapacity to consummate. As Simon Fodden argued "citizens do not wish this form of state interference with respect to sexual practices within marriage." See Simon Fodden, *Family Law* (Toronto: Irwin Law, 1999) at 14–15.

Nonetheless, there continue to be litigated cases concerning "capacity to consummate" in Canada, evidence that suggests that some married spouses remain quite willing to assert this ground to obtain an annulment. As will become evident, moreover, a number of these decisions appear to involve "immigration" marriages. As you review the case excerpts concerning the requirement of capacity to consummate, try to assess why the claims were presented as applications for annulment? Why might the applicants have preferred annulment to other remedies available, including divorce? To what extent do these cases reflect the law's view of what constitutes a "real" marriage?

The test for capacity to consummate and its application in practice

The legal test was discussed in *Gajamugan v Gajamugan* (1979), 10 RFL (2d) 280 (Ont HC), where the court stated:

> A good overview of the essential ingredients to be proved in an action for nullity because of impotence was provided by Laidlaw JA in the Ontario Court of Appeal in 1944: *Rae v. Rae*, [1944] OR 266, [1944] 2 DLR 604; summarized in *Hardick (Fox) v. Fox* (1970), 3 RFL 153 (Ont.):
> (1) Impotence must exist at the time of marriage...;
> (2) the incapacity pleaded must be such as to render intercourse impractical...;
> (3) the incapacity may stem from "a physical or mental or moral disability...;" and
> (4) the impotence must be incurable....

Clearly, the test was derived from cases decided some decades in the past, a factor that has attracted some criticism from courts in attempting to apply it in contemporary circumstances. Examine the cases that follow in relation to this test.

Juretic v Ruiz
1999 BCCA 417

RYAN JA:

[1] This is an appeal and cross-appeal from a decision of Mr. Justice J.T. Edwards in the Supreme Court in Vancouver ordering the parties divorced, refusing Mr. Juretic's application for an order declaring the marriage to be null and void, and ordering spousal support and the division of family assets.

[2] Mr. Juretic appeals the order refusing him a decree of nullity. Both parties challenge the manner in which the family assets were divided and the amount of spousal support awarded.

[3] Following his retirement as a marine engineer, Mr. Juretic advertised for a bride in a Honduran newspaper. He was interested in finding a Spanish-speaking wife, a virgin, who wished to be a homemaker. Ms. Ruiz answered the advertisement.

[4] In 1995 Mr. Juretic travelled to Honduras where he met Ms. Ruiz and spent two weeks visiting her family. Ms. Ruiz agreed, with her parents' approval, to come to Vancouver and if things worked out, to marry Mr. Juretic.

[5] Ms. Ruiz arrived in Vancouver on July 28, 1996. Immediately on her arrival Ms. Ruiz moved into Mr. Juretic's apartment on West Broadway and began living with him.

[6] Mr. Juretic and Ms. Ruiz were married on October 5, 1996. At the time of the marriage Mr. Juretic was 66 years of age, and Ms. Ruiz was 23.

[7] Following the marriage ceremony and a reception at a local restaurant, the parties returned to Mr. Juretic's apartment where Mr. Juretic anticipated the consummation of the marriage. Ms. Ruiz rebuffed his affectionate embraces, she told him if he wanted sex she was his, but she did not want him to touch her. Mr. Juretic did not persist. Two days later when he made the same advances Ms. Ruiz told him again she would have sex with him, but that she did not wish to be touched. Mr. Juretic testified he never tried again. He told the trial judge that sex under those circumstances would be like rape. He gave up trying.

[8] Mr. Juretic and Ms. Ruiz continued to sleep in the same bed from the date of their marriage to the date of separation in March 1997. They ate together, lived together and represented themselves as a couple to others within the community. Ms. Ruiz left the matrimonial home on March 12, 1997. At the same time, or shortly afterward, she became romantically involved with another man.

The appeal court reviewed the test for capacity to consummate in law, an "invincible aversion" to the sexual act, and the conclusion of the trial judge that Mr. Juretic's inability to have an erection did not meet this test and continued:

[12] In this case Mr. Juretic was put off by the attitude of Ms. Ruiz. He was unable to pursue a cold sexual act which he found akin to rape. After two attempts at the beginning of his marriage he made no further attempts to have sexual relations with his wife. The trial judge was not persuaded that Mr. Juretic's response to his wife could be said to have reached the level of "invincible aversion." I cannot say he was wrong in his finding. Put another way, it could be said that Mr. Juretic's situation fell short of an "unconquerable repugnance." I would dismiss this ground of appeal.

The court also reviewed the division of property and spousal support ordered by the trial judge, confirming his order apportioning the interests in family assets to reflect a 90 percent interest for Juretic and a 10 percent interest for Ruiz, and awarding Ruiz spousal support of $1,250 per month for three years.

Sangha v Aujla
2002 BCSC 1472

McEWAN J:

[1] The plaintiff seeks a declaration of nullity of her marriage to the defendant.

[2] The parties were married February 16, 2002 in Vancouver, British Columbia. They ceased living together on April 4, 2002.

[3] The marriage was arranged by the parties' families. They first met in about March of 2001 through a go-between and discussions followed among the parties' parents and an uncle and aunt of the defendant. The discussions included whether or not the defendant had any kind of criminal record. I accept the plaintiff's evidence that there was a direct and repeated representation that the defendant had nothing of the kind in his past. The parties themselves had virtually no opportunity to get to know each other before the marriage, the suitability of which was assessed almost entirely on the basis of the representations that passed between more senior family members.

[4] Once the parties were married they lived in a basement suite in the home of the plaintiff's uncle and aunt. They were virtually never alone in that setting, and subsequently moved in with the plaintiff's parents.

[5] The plaintiff says the marriage was never consummated. In the first few weeks after the wedding this was because the plaintiff felt she had had no opportunity to get to know the defendant and wanted some time. The defendant respected her wishes.

[6] In the course of discussions during that time about who they were and what their experiences had been, the defendant had suggested that for a period of about four years he had "travelled." When he was more closely questioned, he acknowledged that this was untrue and that he had, in fact, been imprisoned in England for robbery.

[7] This was too much for the plaintiff and a short while later the parties separated.

[8] The defendant, by way of an improperly sworn but uncontroversial affidavit, agrees that the marriage was never consummated. He takes the position however, that the marriage should not be annulled, but that the plaintiff should simply ask for a divorce.

[9] The plaintiff's position is that an annulment is preferable in her circumstances because a divorce significantly diminishes her reputation and prospects of marriage within her culture.

[10] The plaintiff has offered two medical opinions to corroborate her evidence. The first, a letter from Dr. Arthur G. Willms, her family doctor, describes her condition as found on physical examination, and concludes as follows:

> I can state with a high degree of confidence that this woman has not had sexual intercourse with vaginal penetration. I would support her claim that she had not been sexually active in this marriage.

[11] The second is an opinion from a Dr. Douglas A. Steane, Registered Psychologist. His conclusions were as follows:

Sonia Sangha's marriage to Tarjinder Singh Aujla seems to have been a formal arrangement devoid of opportunities to develop a minimum amount of rapport or any psychological and emotional intimacy. While Tarjinder's point of view is not represented in this report, it is assumed that he is still motivated to make the marriage work and that he is more emotionally involved in the relationship than his wife, since it is believed that he will object to any attempt to annul the marriage, but may not necessarily object to a divorce. However, Sonia's discovery that Tarjinder was deceitful with respect to his criminal record, before getting emotionally involved with him, would naturally create an emotional barrier and repugnance to consummating the marriage. For these reasons, it is important to emphasize that Ms. Sangha is not refusing to consummate the marriage. She is a responsible, emotionally well-adjusted, young woman who is not psychologically capable of consummating the marriage because, from her perception of experiences with her husband, he has not succeeded in connecting with her cognitively and emotionally. Expecting a mature woman to consummate a marriage with a man with whom she has not developed a positive emotional connection is not that psychologically different from asking her to prostitute herself.

[12] I turn now to the law. ...

The court reviewed a number of authorities, including *Heil v Heil*, [1942] 1 DLR 657 (SCC), noting that the test for nullity on grounds of non-consummation was "rather high," and continued:

> [15] More recently, in *Deo v. Kumar*, [1993] BCJ No. 2051 (BCSC), Lander J. articulated the test in the following terms:
>
>> The test ... is a practical impossibility of consummation. It must be caused by physical or psychological defect. Wilful and persistent refusal amounting to caprice or obstinacy is not a ground for annulment. See *Heil v. Heil*, [1942] 1 DLR 657 (SCC).
>>
>> The words "invincible repugnance" are commonly used to describe such a psychological defect. It has been held that such repugnance may be toward the particular spouse, and not the act of sexual intercourse generally, see *Orr v. Orr* (1956), 2 DLR (2d) 627 (NS), and *Greenlees v. Greenlees*, [1959] OR 419–423, as well as *Koelman v. Lansdaal* (1953), 9 WWR 381 (NS). I find that, due to Ms. Deo's discovery of Mr. Kumar's pre-marital sexual activities, compounded by his contraction of a sexually transmitted disease, she has developed an overpowering psychological abhorrence for him, rendering her incapable of even the contemplation of consummation. She psychologically required no more of her prospective mate than she demanded of herself: a completely disciplined abstinence from pre-marital sexual relations.
>
> [16] Here, the plaintiff is in the position that a clear precondition or premise upon which the marriage was founded did not exist, and had, in fact, been actively misrepresented. I think it quite understandable that this, and the fact that in this particular arrangement, the parties remained effectively strangers until after they were married, renders consummation a practical impossibility for the plaintiff. I do not think it necessary for the court to describe her normal, predictable reaction to the situation in pathological terms in order to grant the declaration sought. There can be no basis in public policy for promoting marriage to the extent of denying this application.

[17] Accordingly, I declare the marriage of the plaintiff and defendant which took place February 16, 2002 and was registered in British Columbia under No. 2002-59-001294 (Certificate #66328767) annulled.

Notes and Questions

Judicial reasoning about consummation

What is the explanation for the decision to grant an annulment in *Sangha*, but to deny the decree of annulment in *Juretic*? To what extent do the judges in each situation rigorously apply the legal principles? Is gender relevant? To what extent is fault an issue? Is there a need for reform? Is there a need to abandon this requirement for a valid marriage altogether?

Consider the following example and the court's critique of this legal principle:

A young woman in British Columbia married a man who was a lawyer in India, an "arranged" marriage that followed discussions between their parents and one meeting between the couple prior to the marriage. The husband and his family asserted that he was vegetarian, in good health and not addicted to drugs or alcohol. According to the wife, her husband disclosed to her on their wedding night that he was addicted to drugs and that they would postpone consummation of the marriage until he was drug free — an assertion denied by the husband. The wife returned to British Columbia after the wedding, then visited India a few months later (without sexual relations), and completed a sponsorship application for her husband to immigrate to Canada.

When her husband arrived in Canada shortly afterwards, the wife concluded that he was addicted to drugs and refused to consummate the marriage. According to her affidavit, her husband "continued taking heavy doses of drugs, slept for up to 16 hours each day and threatened to go on welfare if he was evicted from her home [so that the wife would be obliged to repay the welfare costs as a result of her sponsorship of his entry to Canada]." She also asserted that the husband admitted that he had lied to her all along as this was "his only chance to immigrate to Canada," and that he had no intention of living with her after he received resident status.

In her application for annulment, the wife relied on *Sangha v Aujla* (above) to claim that the husband's misrepresentations concerning his health and character, and his fraudulent failure to disclose his intention to use the marriage to gain immigration status, created an obvious and understandable aversion to consummating the marriage. What result?

In *JG v SSS*, 2004 BCSC 1549, Davies J reviewed these facts in relation to the law concerning immigration marriages. In particular, he noted the approach of Learned Hand J, in *United States v Rubenstein* (1945), 151 F (3d) 915 at 918–19, that a marriage entered into without full consent is not a valid marriage: "a marriage in jest is not a marriage at all." According to this U.S. approach, the marriage in *JG* would not be valid because of the lack of consent to a "real" marriage, at least on the part of the husband.

However, the court also noted that the law in British Columbia was different from the principles applied in *Rubenstein* in the United States, and that the decision in *Iantsis* had been adopted as precedent by the B.C. Court of Appeal (see *Said v Said* (1986), 8 BCLR (2d) 323). In this context, however, Davies J criticized its application in modern law:

> [46] ... In my opinion, in circumstances where modern concepts of family law based upon evolving social mores have largely displaced the ecclesiastical approach to marriage as an institution, it is anachronistic at best to adhere to concepts of nullity that were developed in such a different age.

The court then considered and distinguished *Said* because this earlier case did not involve fraudulent inducement of marriage for immigration purposes. The court also engaged in an extensive review of legal precedents with respect to capacity to consummate in England and in Canada. On this basis, the court held (at para 60) that *Sangha* was not inconsistent with the traditional test for defining capacity to consummate, although it had been applied in the context of particular circumstances giving rise to the applicant's invincible aversion ("paralysis of the will") to consummation of the marriage. In granting an order of nullity, the court also rejected the husband's suggestion that divorce was a preferable remedy in the circumstances, concluding that if the wife was entitled to the order of nullity, it should be granted. Why might the husband have preferred to obtain a divorce?

Capacity to consummate and religious beliefs

In *Sahibalzubaidi v Bahjat*, 2011 ONSC 4075, a man and woman married in a civil ceremony in Malaysia, following investigations of the husband's family by the parents of the bride. However, the man and woman did not consummate the marriage at the time of the ceremony because the wife (a devout Muslim) believed that she required a religious blessing and then a public wedding feast (a *Walima*) before doing so. The woman, who was resident in Canada at the time of this marriage, sponsored her new husband to enter Canada, at which time her family discovered his true (abusive) character. In this context, she applied for an annulment on the basis of fraud and the fact that the marriage was "incomplete." In addition, she applied for annulment on the basis of non-consummation.

The case involved issues about the relevant law to be applied to the marriage ceremony in Malaysia. Although the court held that the husband's fraud did not vitiate the marriage, and that it was unclear whether or not the absence of a blessing and feast nullified the marriage in accordance with the law of Malaysia where the ceremony took place, the court granted the wife's application for annulment. According to the court, this result was justified on the basis of non-consummation by reason of the wife's strongly held religious beliefs which made consummation impossible.

To what extent does this reasoning suggest that the test for annulment, based on incapacity to consummate the marriage, has evolved from earlier cases such as *Gajamugan*? What are the reasons for this evolution? How should the policy issues about annulment in this context be addressed in law?

Evidence and credibility in establishing capacity to consummate

In *Falk v Falk*, 1999 ABQB 570, the court denied the husband's application for annulment based on his incapacity to consummate the marriage.

The parties had married in June 1998 and separated in November 1998, and the wife did not appear in the proceedings. The court denied the application because of the lack of evidence, stating (at para 33): "It would be far too convenient, based on my review of the case law to grant an annulment simply on the basis of one's refusal or self-described inability to consummate the marriage."

Are the reasons for denying the husband's application for annulment in *Falk* less persuasive than in *Juretic*? Taking account of the fact that the court awarded Ruiz an interest in Juretic's property, an entitlement generally available only to married spouses, were there other reasons for denying Juretic's application for annulment?

Cases about capacity to consummate often must be decided on the basis of issues of credibility. For example, in *Leung v Liang*, 2001 BCSC 1502; aff'd 2003 BCCA 313, a woman brought an action to annul her marriage. She gave evidence that she had never resided with her husband after their marriage, that he had rebuffed her suggestions of intimacy, and that he had claimed to be homosexual. Her husband, who had married her shortly after immigrating to Canada from China, testified that they had resided together and that they had engaged in sexual intercourse on 60 occasions, but there was no evidence corroborating his assertions, and he was unable to recall any distinguishing features of the woman's anatomy. The court granted the declaration of nullity, expressly accepting the woman's evidence rather than the man's.

Consider this situation:

> The parties married in India in 1996, but they did not consummate the marriage. The husband gave evidence that he wished to do so but that his wife had refused to engage in any kind of sexual activity and "steadfastly and cruelly resisted all his advances." The wife gave evidence that she was willing to engage in sexual intercourse and did everything she could to encourage him but that he was

never able to achieve penetration. According to her, the husband's frustration and embarrassment resulted in him becoming mean and cruel to her. Eventually she left and filed for divorce in British Columbia, but the parties agreed to stay the divorce application pending the outcome of the husband's action for annulment in Alberta. What result?

In granting the annulment in *SSC v GKC*, 1999 ABQB 822, the Alberta court stated (at paras 22–23):

> I understand there is no advantage to either party in ending this marriage by way of a divorce rather than an annulment. Indeed I was given to understand that in their culture an annulment is less problematic to them than a divorce. In all the circumstances I think it best that the parties be put out of their matrimonial misery as expeditiously as possible.
>
> I will therefore conclude the matter by accepting as fact the only relevant evidence the parties could agree on, namely that they at no time ever engaged in any sexual activity. I find that was either the result of the defendant's invincible repugnance toward the sex act with the plaintiff, or the result of his impotence. I accept that whichever is the case, the condition is permanent as between this couple. On that basis I will grant the annulment.

Is this an appropriate solution to the issue of credibility?

Annulment and ideology about marriage

In *Norman v Norman* (1979), 9 RFL (2d) 345 (Ont Unif Fam Ct), the court denied an action for annulment of a marriage between a 64-year-old widow and a 65-year-old widower. The wife gave evidence that, based on her husband's inability to consummate the marriage, she did not expect to have a sexual relationship but just "companionship" in the marriage. The court denied the wife's application for annulment, stating that it was not open to the woman, "having entered into what might be termed a platonic marriage, to complain of the absence of sexual intercourse." How should this case be characterized in relation to ideas about marriage as contract or status?

To what extent may courts' decisions be based on implicit ideas about the extent to which parties should be able to "consent" to end their marriage? For example, consider whether the following comments, expressed in *Rae v Rae*, [1944] OR 266 (CA) at 269, may have been relevant to the decision in *Norman*:

> A marriage ought not to be lightly interfered with, but on the contrary the Court ought to be fully satisfied that the grounds advanced by a petitioner are sufficient to justify the termination of the relationship of the parties. In my opinion it is not in the best interest of public morals and social welfare that the burden of proof necessary in law to end the solemn vows and undertakings of married persons should be discharged with any degree of ease.

Is the result in *Norman* consistent with the more recent analyses about capacity to consummate in *Juretic* and *Sangha*?

See also *M v M* (1984), 42 RFL (2d) 55 (PEISC (Fam Div)), an earlier decision in which a man obtained a declaration of annulment on the basis that his wife was psychologically unable to consummate the marriage, although no physical impediment existed. Compare this case to *W v W* (1987), 5 RFL (3d) 323 (PEISC (Fam Div)), decided a few years later, in which the court rejected a woman's application for nullity because there was no evidence of her "invincible repugnance" to sexual intercourse, but just an "inability to respond." Can these cases be reconciled? What underlying ideology about husbands and wives may be reflected in these decisions?

4. Prohibited degrees of consanguinity and affinity

Traditional Prohibitions

Persons related too closely by consanguinity (relationships of blood) and affinity (relationships by marriage) are prohibited from marrying.

- Traditionally, the prohibited degrees of consanguinity and affinity at common law were set out in Archbishop Parker's Table of 1563, as reproduced in the *Book of Common Prayer* of the Church of England.

- This list of prohibited degrees was incorporated into Ontario law through the *Annulment of Marriages Act (Ontario)*: see *Divorce Act (Ontario) 1930*, SC 1930, c 14, and *Annulment of Marriages Act*, RSC 1970, c A-14. This list was amended by the *Marriage Act*, RSC 1970, c M-5, ss 2–3, removing the following prohibitions: wife's sister, wife's niece, husband's brother, and husband's nephew.

The list of prohibited degrees was set out for convenience in Form 1 of Ontario's previous provincial *Marriage Act*.

Bruce Ziff discussed some of the rationales underlying the traditional prohibited degrees of consanguinity and affinity, in the context of Parliamentary amendments debated in the 1990s:

> [t]he traditional policies behind affinal restrictions, put succinctly, are the insulation of the nuclear or extended family from sexual meddling, the promotion of marriage outside of the family and the preservation of perceived societal norms or Judeo-Christian religious beliefs. Restrictions based on consanguinity have been supported on these grounds, but there is, as well, the additional concern that genetic and even eugenic defects are more common in the offspring of close blood relations. The amendments reflect an abandonment of the first cluster of reasons, presumably either because they no longer reflect public policy, or because marriage prohibitions are seen as ineffective vehicles with which to pursue these goals. A reduction in the restrictions based on consanguinity seems in accord with current scientific opinion that the physical dangers are not as significant as once was thought, particularly where the blood relationship between the parents is not close. (Bruce Ziff, "Recent Developments in Canadian Law: Marriage and Divorce" (1986) 18 Ottawa L Rev 121 at 135–36)

Parliamentary Reform Legislation

In 1990, the federal government enacted new principles concerning prohibited degrees of consanguinity and affinity, set out in the *Marriage (Prohibited Degrees) Act*, SC 1990, c 46, which came into force in 1991. The Hansard Report, 7 June 1990 (third reading in the Senate), provided the following statement about the intention of the new legislation:

> In the case of persons related by blood, Bill S-14 reaffirms the law that persons may not marry if they are related lineally or if they are brothers or sisters, but it otherwise relaxes the law to allow marriage between persons who are related as uncle and niece or as aunt and nephew. In the case of persons related by marriage, it clarifies the law by providing that a person whose marriage has been dissolved by divorce may marry the brother or sister, nephew or niece, or uncle or aunt of the divorced spouse; something that is not now permitted under the law. There would be no prohibition against marriages involving step-relationships.

An amendment to the Bill was included to treat the relationship of adopted persons within the family "as if they were natural relationships," an arrangement that is consistent with provincial adoption law and policy.

5. No prior subsisting marriage

Requiring Death or Divorce in Relation to a First Spouse

Although it is possible to marry more than once, it is necessary to end the first marriage — by a decree of divorce or nullity, or as a result of the death of the spouse — before marrying a second or subsequent time. Indeed, it is a criminal offence (bigamy) in Canada for a person who is married to go through a form of marriage with another person (see *Criminal Code*, s 290).

However, where a first marriage ends in divorce, problems may arise in relation to the recognition of foreign divorce decrees, as illustrated in *Knight v Knight* (1995), 16 RFL (4th) 48 (Ont Gen Div):

> A husband from Ontario obtained a divorce from his first wife in Mexico and then married his second wife in Pennsylvania. He gave evidence that he had decided to marry in Pennsylvania because Ontario did not recognize the validity of his Mexican divorce. When his second marriage ended, he argued that it was void because he was still validly married to his first wife at the time of the second marriage. However, the court decided (at 56) that it would be against public policy to permit the husband to succeed with this argument, and proceeded to determine issues of property and support in relation to the second marriage.

As James McLeod noted, the issues in such cases often require careful attention to conflict of laws principles. Indeed, he argued that the court's conclusion about the second marriage was not correct because the Mexican divorce would not have been recognized in Ontario (neither the husband nor his first wife was domiciled in Mexico), and thus the second marriage was void because of the prior subsisting marriage. See James McLeod, "Annotation of *Knight v. Knight*" (1995) 16 RFL (4th) 48 at 50. In this context, how should the court have resolved the issues concerning property sharing and support at the end of the second "marriage"? Note the definition of "spouse" in section 1 of Ontario's *Family Law Act*.

The "disappearance" of a first spouse

In addition to the death of a spouse, some persons may encounter difficulty with respect to the validity of a subsequent marriage when an earlier spouse "disappears." Section 9 of Ontario's *Marriage Act* permits a subsequent marriage to be solemnized in accordance with its procedures (and an order pursuant to the *Declarations of Death Act, 2002*, SO 2002, c 14), but it does not end the prior marriage. For examples of cases involving "disappearing" spouses, see *Meszaros v Meszaros*, [1969] 2 OR 336 (HC); and *Re Larsen* (1980), 18 RFL (2d) 14 (BCSC).

Polygamy and Plural Unions in Canadian Law

The "no prior marriage" requirement in the context of "plural unions"

Issues about polygamous marriages in Canadian law are both controversial and complicated, and it is important to distinguish the family law context from the criminal prohibition in section 293 of the *Criminal Code*:

- **The family law context:** Because the *Civil Marriage Act* in 2005 (re)defined marriage as a "union of two persons," it permitted same-sex marriage while continuing the *Hyde* principle about "the exclusion of all others." Thus, the *Civil Marriage Act* does not recognize marriages celebrated in Canada between more than two persons as valid.

    However, Ontario's *Family Law Act* (and legislation in Prince Edward Island) defines "spouse" (for purposes of property sharing and spousal support) to include marriages that are actually or potentially polygamous, but only if the marriage was celebrated in a jurisdiction in which such a marriage is valid. In this way, there is some limited economic protection for spouses in polygamous marriages who are in Canada, if their marriages are valid according to the law where the marriage was solemnized.

- **The criminal law context:** By contrast with these civil law principles, section 293 of the Canadian *Criminal Code* makes it a criminal offence for a person to have a marriage or a conjugal union with more than one person at the same time; and the offence is punishable by imprisonment for up to five years. In this context, it is important to note that section 293 proscribes both "marriage" and a "conjugal union" with two or more persons; as a result, it may be more accurate to characterize this prohibition as directed to "plural unions" (including non-marital unions) as well as polygamy (based on "marriage" to more than one person).

Criminal law proceedings in British Columbia

Recent controversy about polygamy has focused mainly on this *Criminal Code* provision in relation to a fundamentalist Mormon sect in the rural community of Bountiful, British Columbia (the Fundamentalist Church of Jesus Christ of Latter Day Saints, sometimes referred to as FLDS). Male members of this community practise polygyny, a form of polygamy in which men have more than one wife. (In the much less frequent practice of polyandry, women have more than one husband.)

Although investigated by police in the 1990s, the provincial government did not lay charges until recently, apparently because of concerns that such charges would not withstand a *Charter* challenge based on freedom of religion. When charges were eventually pursued in 2009 against Winston Blackmore and James Oler, leaders of two factions in the Bountiful community, the charges were stayed because the B.C. Attorney General had appointed a second prosecutor after his first appointee had submitted an opinion that charges should not be laid.

The B.C. reference case

Thus, in October 2009, the provincial government submitted a reference to the B.C. Supreme Court, requesting answers to two questions about the criminal prohibition against polygamy:

1. Is section 293 of the *Criminal Code of Canada* consistent with the *Canadian Charter of Rights and Freedoms*? If not, in what particular or particulars and to what extent?

2. What are the necessary elements of the offence in section 293 of the *Criminal Code of Canada*? Without limiting this question, does section 293 require that the polygamy or conjugal union in question involved a minor, or occurred in a context of dependence, exploitation, abuse of authority, a gross imbalance of power, or undue influence?

In the fall of 2010, the court began hearing witnesses, including experts who provided information about the harms of polygamy and plural unions. In early 2011, the court also heard evidence from women members of the Bountiful community (anonymously, using a video link in which their faces were hidden). Written arguments were filed by the federal and B.C. governments (defending the validity of section 293) and by several intervenors in the case. One intervenor, the B.C. Civil Liberties Association, filed written arguments suggesting that individuals should be permitted to make choices in their lives without state sanctions, unless their choices harm others or result from a lack of informed consent. See *Toronto Star* (18 March 2011) A12.

As this evidence (and the questions posed to the court) suggest, there were two issues in this case: whether freedom of religion is infringed by section 293; and whether the practice of polygyny (multiple wives) harms women and children. However, particularly in the context of arguments concerning section 1 of the *Charter*, these two questions are closely connected.

- **The *Charter* issue:** In relation to the constitutional issue, the focus has been mainly on the Bountiful community in British Columbia. In relation to this issue, Beverley Baines argued that a *Charter* challenge to section 293 might well succeed, and that the federal government should remove this prohibition from the *Criminal Code*. Baines also recognized that decriminalization might then lead to a challenge to the "two persons" requirement in the *Civil Marriage Act*, although she also argued that a court would likely conclude that monogamy could be justified pursuant to section 1 of the *Charter*. See Beverley Baines, "Equality's Nemesis?" (2006) 5 JL & Equality 57.

  Baines was also a co-author of one of four papers commissioned by Status of Women Canada in 2005. By contrast, in two of the other papers, the authors argued for the retention of section 293 of the *Criminal Code*, while suggesting that prosecutions should be conducted "with sensitivity to the vulnerabilities and equality concerns involved." See Status of Women Canada, *Polygamy in Canada: Legal and Social Implications for Women and Children — A Collection of Policy Research* (Ottawa: Status of Women Canada 2005); and Martha Bailey, "Should Polygamy be recognized in Canada? Ethical and Legal Considerations" (2007) 2:1 Les Ateliers de L'Éthique 18.

- **The "harms" issue:** In debates about the "harms" of polygamy or plural unions, some Canadian researchers have focused on the experiences of women in the Bountiful community. For example, Angela Campbell undertook field work interviews with members of the Bountiful community, concluding that it was a heterogeneous and dynamic community, in which monogamy was relatively common and some women enjoyed economic independence. See Campbell, "Bountiful Voices" (2009) 47:2 Osgoode Hall LJ 183.

  Both Campbell and others have also examined "harms" for women in other situations in Canada, particularly in relation to those who arrive in Canada after a polygamous marriage that was celebrated in a jurisdiction in which such marriages are legally valid. In a 2006 report for the Department of Justice, Rebecca Cook and Lisa Kelly noted that a UN committee with responsibility for the Convention on the Elimination of Discrimination against Women (CEDAW) concluded that "Polygamous marriage contravenes a woman's right to equality with men, and can have such serious emotional and financial consequences for her and her dependants that such marriages ought to be discouraged and prohibited" (General Recommendation 21, UN CEDAW OR, 13th Sess UN Doc A/47/38 (1994) at para 14).

This report also documented the "harms" of polygamy (including its non-exclusivity, competition between co-wives, mental health and sexual and reproductive issues, and economic harms), and concluded that polygamy violates women's international human rights. At the same time, citing the serious problems that occurred in France when polygamy was declared illegal, with immediate and retroactive effect on existing polygamous unions there, the report recommended measures of "transition" to alleviate these problems. See Rebecca Cook & Lisa Kelly, *Polygyny and Canada's Obligations under International Human Rights Law* (Ottawa: Department of Justice 2006).

Notes and Questions

The B.C. reference case

The decision in *Reference re Criminal Code of Canada (BC)*, 2011 BCSC 1588, was released on 23 November 2011. It was a lengthy judgment (1367 paragraphs and Appendices). The judge's decision included detailed analysis of the extensive evidence submitted in the case, including expert evidence about the practice of polygamy (and more specifically, polygyny). After assessing this evidence, Bauman CJSC concluded:

- Although section 293 of the *Criminal Code* infringes the guarantee of freedom of religion under the *Charter*, the provision is demonstrably justified in a free and democratic society (paras 1358–1360);

- However, children under the age of 18 at the time of entering a polygamous union were excluded from the application of section 293 (para 1361); and

- Section 293 does not require that the union involve a minor or occur in a "context of dependence, exploitation, abuse of authority, a gross imbalance of power or undue influence" (para 1364).

In formulating an approach to the issues in the case, the court noted that the Attorney General of British Columbia had argued that the constitutionality of section 293 was dependent on a determination of polygamy's "harm." Those who challenged the section's constitutionality argued that section 293 was an unacceptable intrusion by the State into the most basic of *Charter* rights, the freedom to practice one's religion and to associate in family units of one's choosing. At the outset, the court stated, in relation to these approaches:

> I have concluded that this case is essentially about harm; more specifically, Parliament's reasoned apprehension of harm arising out of the practice of polygamy. This includes harm to women, to children, to society and to the institution of monogamous marriage. (see para 5; and further details of these harms at paras 6–14).

From the perspective of "family law," are there other practices that may require discussion of such "harms"?

Values of personal autonomy and the need to protect vulnerable family members?

The evidence presented to the reference case by both experts and members of the Bountiful community was conflicting with respect to the existence of harms for women and children, whether women have "chosen" to live their lives in plural unions voluntarily in accordance with their own religious beliefs, and whether legal protection is required (see paras 749–751). For example, as the 2006 report to the Department of Justice argued, polygyny violates women's right to be free from discrimination:

> Where polygyny is permitted through religious or customary norms, it often relies on obedience, modesty, and chastity codes that preclude women from operating as full citizens and enjoying their civil and political rights. Within this framework, women can often be socialized into subservient roles that inhibit their full participation in family and public life. The physical, mental, sexual and reproductive, economic and citizenship harms associated with the practice violate many of the fundamental rights recognized in international law. (Cook & Kelly at 2)

However, Cook and Kelly also commented (at 7) on opposing arguments that the underlying problem is the patriarchal social context of polygyny rather than the practice itself: "Sexual stereotyping, male domination and the treatment of women as property ... are neither limited to polygyny nor inevitable within it." Moreover, a number of authors have pointed out that many people, in fact, practise alternatives to lifelong monogamy — including adultery, divorce, remarriage, and serial monogamy, and that it is therefore important to interrogate the law's interest in monogamy. See Elizabeth Emens, "Monogamy's Law: Compulsory Monogamy and Polyamorous Existence" (2004) 29 NYU Review of Law and Social Change 277. In addition, a small but increasingly visible number of people in Canada have chosen to live in plural unions that are referred to as "polyamorous" in order to differentiate them from the religious context and systemic gender inequality that is often associated with polygamy. See Leah McLaren, "What One Family Looks Like Today: Three Partners and Kids under One Roof", *The Globe and Mail* (6 March 2014).

Assuming that it is important to resolve these differing views about polygamous unions effectively, is the reference to the B.C. court the most appropriate forum? This is also a question about the process of law reform in relation to marriage and families in Canada, an issue that is addressed at the end of this chapter.

Additional Resources

Martha Bailey & Amy Kaufman, *Polygamy in the Monogamous World: Multicultural Challenges for Western Law and Policy* (Santa Barbara, CA: Praeger 2010).

Jessica Powell Barnett, "Polyamory and Criminalization of Plural Conjugal Unions in Canada: Competing Narratives in the s.293 Reference" (2014) 11 Sexuality Research and Social Policy 63.

Peter Bretschneider, *Polygyny: A Cross-Cultural Study* (Stockholm: Almqvist & Wiksell, 1995).

Gillian Calder, "Penguins and Polyamory: Using Law and Film to Explore the Essence of Marriage in Canadian Family Law" (2009) 21 CJWL 1.

Susan Drummond, "Polygamy's Inscrutable Criminal Mischief" (2009) 47:2 Osgoode Hall LJ 317.

Felicity Kaganas & Christina Murray, "Law, Women and the Family: The Question of Polygyny in a New South Africa" (1991) Acta Jur 116.

Amy Kaufman, "Polygamous Marriages in Canada" (2005) 21 Can J Fam L 315.

Lisa Kelly, "Bringing International Human Rights Law Home: An Evaluation of Canada's Family Law Treatment of Polygamy" (2007) 65 UT Fac L Rev 1.

BJ Wray, "How Same-Sex Marriage Helped Keep Polygamy a Criminal Offence" (2013) 32 NJCL 113.

6. Age and validity of marriage

Common Law Principles

The right to marry requires that the parties be "of age," a matter of "capacity" and thus within the federal government's authority to legislate.

However, as with other matters of capacity to marry, common law principles continue to apply since the federal government has not legislated with respect to age requirements. In *Legebokoff v Legebokoff* (1982), 28 RFL (2d) 212 (BCSC), a wife petitioned for an order declaring that her marriage was invalid because she was only 15 at the time of the ceremony, which was conducted in accordance with the rites of the Doukhobor faith. The parties lived together for 16 years, and they had three children. In this case, the court held (at 215) that the marriage was valid:

> The Parliament of Canada has exclusive legislative authority in regard to the capacity of persons to marry, and it is silent on the minimum age. At common law, derived from ecclesiastical law, the marriage of a child of less than seven years is void. The marriage of a male older than seven years but younger than 14 years, or a female older than seven but younger than 12 years is voidable at the instance of the infant upon his or her attaining the requisite minimum age. Further, a marriage where either or both parties were under age becomes validated if they continue to cohabit as husband and wife after reaching the age of capacity: *Kerr v Kerr.*

In rejecting the petitioner's request in *Legebokoff*, the court noted (at 215) the presumption of validity of a marriage, a presumption that reflected the law's "favourable attitude toward [marriage]."

In reaching its conclusion, the court may have taken into account the long period of cohabitation after the plaintiff was "of age." Are there reasons why a person might choose not to challenge the validity of marriage until 16 years after attaining the requisite age for entering into a valid marriage? If so, how should this issue be reflected in legal principles? Is there a need for legislative reform? How should the age requirement be reflected in reform legislation?

Provincial Statutes and the Age Requirement

As noted earlier in this chapter, courts in the early 20th century decided that issues of parental consent for underage marital partners were matters of formality (rather than matters of capacity) and thus within the authority of provincial legislatures. Moreover, although the issue seems quite close to a matter of capacity, provincial statutes in Canada generally provide that the issuance of a licence to marry is restricted to persons who are at least 18 (or at least 16 with parental consent). In practice, these provincial "formalities" tend to restrict access to marriage on the basis of age. For details, see Hahlo at 21–25.

SOLEMNIZATION AND FORMALITIES: PROVINCIAL LEGISLATIVE AUTHORITY

"Curing" defects of formality and solemnization

The provinces have jurisdiction to legislate in relation to the formal validity of marriage — for example, banns, licences, and permits; the authority of marriage officers; parental consent; witnesses; and the registration of marriages. Adherence to these formalities in provincial statutes, such as Ontario's *Marriage Act*, is a condition of a valid marriage.

Consider the significance of these requirements, and the role of section 31 (the "curative" provision) in Ontario's *Marriage Act*, in the following two cases.

Alspector v Alspector

In *Alspector v Alspector*, [1957] OR 454, the Ontario Court of Appeal considered the significance of section 33 (now section 31) of the Ontario *Marriage Act*. In this case, Mr. Alspector married Mrs. Noodleman in a marriage ceremony performed at the home of a cantor according to all of the requirements of the Jewish faith. However, the parties neglected to get a marriage licence. While Mr. Alspector had been told by his friends and by the cantor that a marriage licence was required, he did not believe that they needed one because they intended to live together in Israel. The couple lived together for seven years in Ontario. Then, Mr. Alspector had a stroke, and his family challenged the validity of the marriage in relation to succession issues. Mrs. Alspector brought an application for a declaration of the validity of the marriage (thereby entitling her to a major share of Mr. Alspector's estate). Mr. Alspector died before the trial.

The trial court took the view that the parties had intended to be married in accordance with both Jewish and Ontario law, and that section 33 (now section 31) of the *Marriage Act* applied. The Court of Appeal dismissed the appeal, stating (at 465–66):

Even if the cantor's evidence be accepted that he told Mr. Alspector that because no licence had been issued the marriage would not be a civil marriage there is no evidence that that opinion was conveyed to the plaintiff.... Even if it should be held that she knew as a fact that a licence had not been issued, I think it fair to conclude on her evidence that she did not know that the absence of a licence in the circumstances of this case could affect the validity of her marriage; and that she intended that the marriage be in compliance with the law of the Province. As for Mr. Alspector, it is not unreasonable to conclude that although he knew that a licence had not been issued he proceeded in good faith believing that a licence was not necessary because of his intention shortly thereafter to go with the plaintiff to reside in Israel.

To what extent is Mrs. Alspector's lack of knowledge about the licence significant to the outcome of this case?

Debora v Debora

In *Debora v Debora* (1999), 43 RFL (4th) 179 (Ont CA), the parties were married in a religious ceremony that they both knew did not comply with the *Marriage Act*. Seven years later, they were married in a valid ceremony. When they separated, the trial judge relied on *Reaney* [noted below] and held that equalization should be calculated from the date of the valid marriage. The Ontario Court of Appeal dismissed the appeal, stating (at 184–85):

> From a policy point of view, it is reasonable to argue for fairness in the interpretation of a statute such as the *Family Law Act*. However, it is my view that in this instance the stronger policy argument is for certainty of identification of the status of being married as the indicator for the distribution of assets. The appellant's reading of "good faith" [in section 1(1)], as referring to the state of mind of the applicant as to the legality of the marriage, which was knowingly not conducted pursuant to the laws of Ontario, creates unlimited scope for uncertainty and inevitable conflicts in the evidence presented by parties whose interests are at stake over what would be, in the last analysis, a subjective assumption as to a legal status....
>
> Thus, reading "marriage" as meaning marriage under the *Marriage Act* gives purpose to the definition of spouse consistent with the *Family Law Act* and does not introduce the myriad of uncertainties that would flow from a broader interpretation.

In this case, the wife alleged, and the husband disputed, that she had agreed to the absence of a marriage licence on the basis of representations from the husband that the effect of the marriage ceremony would be the same. Between the date of the religious ceremony and the *Marriage Act* ceremony, the husband acquired significant assets, and the court's decision that the first ceremony did not create a valid marriage meant that the husband did not have to include these assets as family property to be shared with his wife.

Notes and Questions

Policy issues and section 31 of the *Marriage Act*

How would you characterize the differences between *Debora* and *Alspector*? In relation to *Debora*, James McLeod criticized the Court of Appeal decision, suggesting that the fear of "floodgates" on such issues was unrealistic, and that it would be fairer to permit parties to access the property regime under the *Family Law Act* rather than rely on equitable principles. Contrasting judicial willingness to extend spousal rights to unmarried same-sex and opposite-sex couples, McLeod stated that this decision appeared inconsistent. See James McLeod, "Annotation of *Debora v. Debora*" (1999) 43 RFL (4th) 179 at 181. Do you agree?

In *Upadyhaha v Sehgal* (2000), 11 RFL (5th) 210, the parties went through a marriage ceremony according to the Hindu tradition, but did not obtain a licence pursuant to Ontario's *Marriage Act*. In a subsequent dispute about a "gift" from the man to the woman, the court held that there was no valid marriage because of the failure to comply with the statutory requirements, especially in relation to the licence. In addition, the "marriage" could not be cured by section 31 because the parties did not cohabit as man and wife following the ceremony.

"Good faith"

In *Reaney v Reaney* (1990), 28 RFL (3d) 52, the Ontario Supreme Court held that the term "spouse" under Part I of the *Family Law Act* included a party to a void marriage, only if the person claiming relief went through the marriage in good faith. In *Reaney*, the marriage was void due to the prior existing marriage of the plaintiff. Because the plaintiff knew he was already married at the time of the second marriage ceremony, he did not enter the second marriage "in good faith," and therefore, was not a "spouse" under the *Family Law Act*. Accordingly, he was not entitled to an equalization of net family property as set out in the Act. Was it appropriate for the court in *Debora* (above) to apply this case as a precedent? Can the cases be distinguished?

In *Guptill v Wilfred*, 2009 NSSC 44, Warner J rejected a claim by a husband for a share of matrimonial property at the end of a "marriage;" most of the property was held in the wife's name. The parties had married in Nova Scotia in 2001, and a month later, the wife discovered that the husband had been previously married in St Lucia in 1997, and that he had not obtained a divorce prior to his 2001 marriage. The court reviewed conflicting evidence from the parties and determined that some aspects of the husband's evidence lacked credibility. The court also rejected the husband's argument that so long as he had complied fully with Nova Scotia's statutory provisions regarding the solemnization of the marriage (including a licence and an authorized celebrant), he had acted in good faith. The court declared the "marriage" a nullity. This decision also provides an overview of statutory provisions concerning "good faith" in relation to void and voidable marriages in different provinces in Canada.

Solemnities in the context of community marriage traditions

Recognition of valid marriages, in terms of compliance with provincial requirements relating to "formalities," may be complicated in cases where parties marry in accordance with community traditions. For example, in *Keobounphan v Khamvongsa*, 1998 ABQB 143, the parties had participated in a traditional Chinese "tea ceremony" in 1989, cohabited and had two children, and then separated in 1996. When the woman applied for divorce, the court rejected her application because there was no valid marriage in accordance with the formalities required pursuant to the provincial *Marriage Act*. (Issues about custody, access and support were determined as if the parties were a cohabiting couple.)

In *Yangaeva v Kershtein* (2001), 21 RFL (6th) 234 (Ont Sup Ct), the court rejected a claim that the parties were married. The parties provided evidence of documents relating to negotiations in Tel Aviv, but there was no evidence of a marriage ceremony. The court concluded that there is a need for evidence of an "identifiable time and place" for a marriage to occur.

Similarly, in *Hassan v Hassan*, 2006 ABQB 544, the parties had participated in an Islamic marriage ceremony, performed in Alberta, in 1984. However, the man, a Pakistani citizen residing in Saudi Arabia, participated in the ceremony by telephone through an agent, and the woman, a Canadian citizen, was not present in the room where the ceremony took place. The parties were refused a marriage certificate in Alberta, but they later obtained a "marriage certificate" in Pakistan where they were then living in 1987; and the woman sponsored the man to immigrate to Canada (as her spouse). The parties separated in 2000, and the husband commenced an action for distribution of marital property in Alberta. The court held that the marriage ceremony in Alberta did not result in a valid marriage. (The court left open the possibility that the man could claim access to property on the basis of cohabitation and resulting or constructive trusts.)

Consider this situation:

> The parties met in North Vietnam in 1972 and began to live together in 1974. Although there was no marriage ceremony, the parties and their families considered them to be married, and a year later their marriage was officially registered in Hanoi on the basis of a certificate issued by their village confirming their cohabitation — the registered document was not signed by the parties and had no date or official identification. The parties fled Vietnam by boat and arrived in Canada as Convention refugees. By the late 1990s, the parties had become estranged but after the husband won a $10 million lottery, they reconciled. However, they later separated permanently, and the wife's application for divorce and property raised an issue of the validity of their marriage. What result?

In *Cao v Le*, 2007 BCSC 499, the court held that there was a valid marriage in accordance with the formal requirements of the place where the parties had married, Vietnam; and the marriage was so recognized by the parties, their families, village officials and governmental officials in Hanoi. Is this decision consistent with *Hassan*? For a recent decision to uphold a wedding conducted in accordance with religious beliefs but without a marriage licence, see *Isse v Said*, 2012 ONSC 1829.

Additional Resources

HR Hahlo, "Nullity of Marriage" in D Mendes da Costa, ed, *Studies in Canadian Family Law*, vol 2 (Toronto: Butterworths, 1972) 651; and *Supplement* 1977 at 250.

Leslie Katz, "The Scope of the Federal Legislative Authority in Relation to Marriage" (1975) 7 Ottawa L Rev 384.

Patrick Parkinson, "Taking Multiculturalism Seriously: Marriage Law and the Rights of Minorities" (1994) 16 Sydney L Rev 473.

Prakash Shah, "Rituals of Recognition: Ethnic Minority Marriages in British Legal Systems" in Prakash Shah, ed, *Law and Ethnic Plurality: Socio-Legal Perspectives* (Leiden & Boston: Martinus Nijhoff Publishers, 2007) 177.

V.
MARRIAGE AND THE NEED FOR LAW REFORM?

REFORMING "MARRIAGE"?

> With the slow, steady and (hopefully) relentless recognition of both the rights and obligations of same-sex relationships, we are all called upon to raise our eyes from the realm of conventional heterosexual families to look over a vista of other relationships which have always been present but have seldom been named.... Can we raise our eyes a little higher and see a whole range of relationships which the state should be fostering? (Brian Bucknall, "A New Model for State-Approved Familial Partnerships", *The Lawyers Weekly* (22 August 1997))

These comments were made shortly after the lower court's decision in *M v H*, a decision that recognized that same-sex partners had legal obligations of support at the end of their relationships. See (1996), 27 OR (3d) 593 (Gen Div). This case also raised broader issues about how to define families and familial rights and obligations. It was in this context that the same-sex marriage cases were initiated in 2001 in British Columbia, Ontario, and Québec — leading to Parliamentary reform in the *Civil Marriage Act*. However, it is important to take note of other reform initiatives occurring in the same period, some of which may have continuing significance.

The scope of Canada's marriage reform

As explained earlier in this chapter, Canadian courts concluded that the exclusion of same-sex marriage contravened the *Charter*, and after the reference to the Supreme Court of Canada, Parliament enacted the *Civil Marriage Act*. The statute contains a large number of "whereas" clauses, but its primary purpose is set out in section 2: removing the language of "one man and one woman" established by the common law principle in *Hyde* and replacing this phrase with the words "two persons."

Clearly, the reform process was successful in relation to the equality claims of same-sex couples who wished to marry. However, the reform achieved was relatively narrow, at least in relation to some of the options that were also available: separating church and state, codification of the common law requirements for validity, or establishing registration systems for non-conjugal couples. In its *Discussion Paper* (released a year after more comprehensive recommendations for reform in *Beyond Conjugality*, discussed below), the Department of Justice acknowledged the work of the Law Commission of Canada, but suggested that

> [f]ederal law currently includes family and other adult non-conjugal relationships only in some circumstances. But further study would be needed before Parliament can decide whether it is appropriate to treat non-conjugal relationships in the same way as spouses or common-law partners in all federal laws, and so these suggestions are beyond the scope of this paper. (Department of Justice, *Marriage and Legal Recognition of Same-sex Unions: A Discussion Paper* (Ottawa: Department of Justice 2002) at note 4)

What factors may have influenced the Department of Justice to conclude that reform should proceed only in relation to marriage and conjugality?

Separating church and state

In the context of debates about same-sex marriage, the Department of Justice's *Discussion Paper* canvassed a variety of views about marriage in Canada, and considered three possible approaches: one approach confirmed the status quo (maintaining marriage as an opposite-sex institution), while the second approach extended marriage to same-sex couples as well as opposite-sex couples.

Although the end result of the same-sex marriage litigation was recognition of same-sex marriage in the *Civil Marriage Act* in 2005 (the second option), it may be important to note the third proposed approach in this *Discussion Paper*, one that would have eliminated legal marriage and replaced it with a registration system. The Department's paper suggested (at 26) that marriage according to religious traditions would still be available, but such ceremonies would have no legal impact in the absence of registration:

> Parliament could choose to underscore the division of church and state in Canada by making a clearer distinction between the role of Parliament

and that of the religions in the area of marriage. To accomplish this goal, all legal effect could be removed from marriage, leaving marriage exclusively to the religions.... [All references to marriage law would be repealed and] replaced with a new registry for opposite-sex and same-sex couples using neutral language, for example registered partner.... Federal divorce laws would apply only to existing marriages, and the breakdown of registered partnerships would be governed by provincial and territorial law. A couple could choose to be married by a religious official, but that marriage would have no effect in law unless the couple also registered in the new system.

This third approach would have required the full co-operation of all provinces and territories, as the new register would replace provincial and territorial marriage registries as well as other registers creating analogous legal relationships. Divorce laws would apply only to existing marriages, and provincial and territorial law would apply to the breakdown of relationships in the new registry, including those where a religious marriage had taken place. In the end, the same-sex marriage litigation essentially precluded serious consideration of this third option. All the same, it offers some insights with respect to marriage law reform in relation to the separation of church and state — a return to the legal situation in England before 1753.

Is this approach to reform desirable? What factors might assist in broadening the scope of reform with respect to the separation of church and state? It is interesting that one reason why the lower court in *Halpern* decided to suspend the declaration of invalidity for two years was to permit Parliament to consider a variety of options and then legislate reforms. By contrast, the Ontario Court of Appeal concluded that there were no significant consequences to an immediate recognition of same-sex marriage. In the context of the *Civil Marriage Act* of 2005, is there need for further consideration about the separation of church and state in relation to marriage?

Statutory codification of common law principles

Another approach to marriage reform could involve a Parliamentary statute codifying the requirements for a valid marriage, and thus overcoming some of the challenges in the application of traditional common law principles. What criteria should be used to determine whether all the existing common law requirements should be included? In reflecting on these questions, consider the current federal law of Australia with respect to marriage: how does it differ from current requirements for a valid marriage in Canada? To what extent is such codification useful?

The *Family Law Act 1975* (Cth) states:

s. 51 An application under this Act for a decree of nullity of marriage shall be based on the ground that the marriage is void.

The *Marriage Act 1961* (Cth) provides that a marriage is void where:

s. 23 (1) ...
(a) either of the parties was, at the time of the marriage, lawfully married to some other person;

(b) the parties are within a prohibited relationship;

(c) [the formalities prescribed in s. 48 have not been met];

(d) the consent of either of the parties was not a real consent because:

    (i) it was obtained by duress or fraud;

    (ii) [the] party was mistaken as to the identity of the other party or as to the nature of the ceremony performed; or

    (iii) [the] party was mentally incapable of understanding the nature and effect of the marriage ceremony; or

(e) either of the parties was not of marriageable age. ...

[No other grounds are permitted]

    (2) Marriages of parties within a prohibited relationship are marriages —

(a) between a person and an ancestor or descendant of the person; or

(b) between a brother and a sister (whether of the whole blood or the half-blood).

    (3) Any relationship specified in sub-section (2) includes a relationship traced through, or to, a person who is or was an adopted child, and, for that purpose, the relationship between an adopted child and the adoptive parent, or each of his adoptive parents, of the child, shall be deemed to be or to have been the natural relationship of child and parent.

The *Marriage Amendment Act 1985* also provides detailed requirements about parental consent for the marriage of a minor.

Note that the requirement to consummate the marriage was not included in this statutory definition. In addition, as will be evident, the *Hyde* requirement was also omitted. However, when same-sex marriage became politically controversial in Australia, the federal Parliament passed amendments, which confirmed the Government's commitment to "protect the institution of marriage by ensuring that marriage means the union of a man and a woman and that same-sex relationships cannot be equated with marriage" (Explanatory Memorandum, *Marriage Amendment Bill*, 2004; and Australian House of Representatives *Hansard*, 24 June 2004 at 31).

What are the advantages of such a codification by the enactment of a federal statute? Are there other elements of the common law principles that should be revised or eliminated in such codification in Canada?

The role of civil unions and registered partnerships

The registration of partnerships for legal purposes was adopted in Denmark in 1989 and subsequently became available in a number of European jurisdictions. Although it was often initiated to provide legal recognition for same-sex couples, such partnerships have been available in some jurisdictions to opposite-sex couples as well.

In Canada, a number of provinces, including Québec, created arrangements for registered partnerships or civil unions, often available to both opposite-sex and same-sex couples. These registration schemes permitted individuals to choose to be included in legal rights and responsibilities that are often identical to those of marriage, but without the symbolic language of "marriage." While the absence of such language may have been desirable for some couples, the applicants in the same-sex marriage litigation in Canada obviously were unsatisfied with registered partnerships, seeking to have their relationships fully recognized as "marriage."

During the debates about same-sex marriage, the issue of marriage or civil unions for same-sex couples was quite controversial. For example, some commentators suggested that the existence of "civil union" legislation showed respect for gays and also for marriage, by legally recognizing same-sex partnerships while preserving marriage as a heterosexual institution involving the possibility of procreation. See Margaret Somerville, "Separate but Equal", *Ottawa Citizen* (3 September 2003) A13. By contrast, others recommended evolution of ideas about marriage. For example, the United Church Moderator suggested that faithfulness to marriage may require change, asserting that the United Church's decision to welcome all those "willing to give themselves to transformation by love in the honourable estate [of marriage]" was the appropriate response of religious faithfulness. See Right Rev Peter Short, "Let No One Be Turned Away", *The Globe and Mail* (31 January 2004) A21.

Registration schemes are often promoted because they offer autonomy and equality to couples. At the same time, they require couples to "opt in" to them. Recall Holland's discussion at the beginning of this chapter about cohabiting couples, and her concerns about "opt in" arrangements with respect to contracts. As she suggested, it was "preferable to put the onus on those who wish to avoid obligations rather than on those who wish to create them" (Holland at para 82). This concern again raises issues about balancing the role of law in providing protection for vulnerable family members and creating opportunities for individual autonomy. See also Nicholas Bala, "Controversy over Couples in Canada: The Evolution of Marriage and Other Adult Interdependent Relationships" (2003) 29 Queen's LJ 41.

As some registration schemes now recognize, there is no reason to restrict these schemes to persons in conjugal relationships. To the extent that other persons (such as siblings) may want to accept reciprocal legal rights and responsibilities for each other, it is possible to permit them to register as well. This issue was confronted in the Law Commission of Canada's report, *Beyond Conjugality*: to what extent do you agree with its analysis?

BEYOND CONJUGALITY: REFORMING LEGAL REGULATION OF ADULT RELATIONSHIPS

Beyond Conjugality: The LCC report (2001)

In its 2001 report, *Beyond Conjugality*, the Law Commission of Canada proposed (at ix) a "comprehensive and principled approach to the legal recognition and support of the full range of close personal relationships among adults." It defined three categories of these relationships:

- Conjugal relationships (including marriage and cohabitation, both opposite sex and same sex)
- Non-conjugal households and non-conjugal relationships ("economic families," such as adult siblings or non-relatives who live together)
- Persons with disabilities and their caregivers (paid and non-paid)

In this context, the report suggested (at xi) that "recognizing and supporting personal adult relationships that involve caring and inter-dependence is an important state objective." In the past, the report noted that governments have provided this recognition and support for married couples, and have gradually extended them to cohabiting couples. According to the report, however, it is now time to move away from conjugality as the marker for recognition and support for close personal relationships among adults. That is, rather than advocating that the law cover an ever broader range of relationships, the report argued (at xix) that "it is time for governments to re-evaluate the way in which they regulate personal adult relationships."

In the excerpt that follows, consider how the proposed values and relevant questions would affect current arrangements for marriage and cohabitation. (Note that some of these issues will also need to be addressed in relation to other aspects of family law later in this book.)

Beyond Conjugality
Beyond Conjugality (2001) at xi–xix

Law Commission of Canada

FUNDAMENTAL VALUES AND PRINCIPLES

Equality and autonomy are the two most important values that governments need to consider in framing policies that recognize and support personal adult relationships. State regulation of personal relationships should also seek to enhance other values: personal security, privacy and religious freedom, while pursuing legitimate government objectives in a coherent and efficient manner.

Governments must respect and promote two kinds of equality. *Relational equality* seeks to equalize the legal status among different types of relationships. Legislation like the federal government's *Modernization of Benefits and Obligations Act* largely eliminated distinctions between these two groups [married and cohabiting couples]. However, by focusing only on conjugal couples, it entrenches unequal legal treatment of conjugal and non-conjugal relationships which may share the functional characteristics of emotional and financial interdependence. The principle of relational equality requires more than equal treatment of conjugal couples.

The concept of *equality within relationships* seeks to overcome unequal distributions of income, wealth and power, much of it based on historic inequality between men and women, or the lack of state support for persons with disabilities.

The value of *autonomy* requires that governments put in place the conditions in which people can freely choose their personal relationships. While governments should discourage the formation of abusive relationships, they should not create financial or other kinds of pressure to discourage relationships without reference to their qualitative attributes. The state should therefore remain neutral with regard to the form or status of relationships and not accord one form of relationship more benefits or legal support than others.

Personal security — whether physical, psychological or economic — enhances the ability of individuals to make healthy choices about entering or remaining in relationships. The state has a role to play in ensuring physical security within a relationship as well as economic security outside the relationship.

Healthy personal relationships are founded on candour and trust; they can flourish only if we are confident that our intimate thoughts and acts will not be discovered by or revealed to others.... Privacy rights must be balanced, however, and in some circumstances must give way to compelling objectives such as the state interest in prosecuting and preventing crime, including the commission of crimes involving domestic violence and abuse.

Contemporary Canadian understandings of *religious freedom* and equality require that the state not take sides in religious matters. The history of marriage regulation in Canada has thus been characterized by a progressive uncoupling of religious and legal requirements, reflecting a growing emphasis on the separation of church and state in a secular and pluralistic political community. Our current understanding of religious freedom requires that laws and policies, including those that regulate personal adult relationships, pursue objectives that can be defended in secular rather than religious terms. *Coherence* requires that laws have clear objectives, and that their legislative design corresponds with the achievement of those objectives. This would avoid reliance on marital status in a law whose objectives do not necessarily relate to marriage.

The *efficiency* of a law, policy or program may be measured by how effective it is, for example, in reaching its intended beneficiaries and whether it can be administered without undue costs or delays. Perfect coherence may not be achievable if the costs of administering a specifically targeted law are prohibitive.

A comprehensive approach to the recognition and support of personal adult relationships should be guided, first and foremost, by the values of equality and autonomy. In addition, state policies should protect and advance personal security, privacy and religious freedom, and they should seek to accomplish legitimate state objectives in a coherent and efficient manner. Proposed laws and the operation of existing laws should be carefully scrutinized to eliminate any detrimental effects on these values and principles....

THE LEGAL ORGANIZATION OF PERSONAL RELATIONSHIPS

People want stability and certainty in their personal relationships, as in other aspects of their lives. The state must provide adequate legal structures to support the relationships that citizens develop, structures that respect the values of equality, autonomy and choice. Marriage has long been the main vehicle by which two people publicly expressed their commitment to each other and sought to ensure certainty and stability in their own and their family's relationship. But marriage is no longer a sufficient model, given the variety of relationships that exist in Canada today. What legal frameworks can the state offer to respond to the need of all its citizens for certainty and stability in their personal relationships?

Four legal modes can be used to regulate personal relationships: private law, ascription, registration and marriage. The *private law* model operates by default — when governments do not provide a legal framework, people are always at liberty to express their commitments through contracts. They can then turn to the courts when they feel that the other party has not fulfilled his or her contractual obligations. They may also rely on private law remedies, such as unjust enrichment or constructive trust. This mechanism is very burdensome. It can be costly, it favours the party with the greater resources or bargaining power and its after-the-fact remedies are uncertain.

Governments use *ascription* to prevent the risks of exploitation inherent in a contractual model by imposing (ascribing) a set of obligations on people in conjugal relationships that are presumed to correspond to the expectations of the majority of people involved in such relationships. While ascription may help to prevent exploitation, it is a blunt policy tool, treating all conjugal relationships alike. It infringes on autonomy, as people are not always aware they may opt out of certain provisions. While appropriate for conjugal relationships in some instances, it would be inappropriate for non-conjugal relationships.

Recently, there has been a move toward the creation of a new status, often called registered partnership. Its objective is to provide an alternative way for the state to recognize and support close personal relationships. When people register their relationships, a range of rights and responsibilities are then open to them. *Registrations* provide an orderly framework in which people can express their commitment to each other, receive public recognition and support, and voluntarily assume a range of legal rights and obligations. These regimes may also provide for an orderly and equitable resolution of the registrants' affairs if their relationship breaks down.

Registration schemes merit consideration because they provide a vehicle for recognizing a broader range of caring and supportive relationships, both conjugal and non-conjugal. They affirm the autonomy and choices of Canadians in their close personal relationships, offering the opportunity for public declarations of commitment that will be respected by government. Registration also does not compromise privacy within a relationship in the way that ascription often does....

CONCLUSION

In this Report, we argue that governments have tended to rely too heavily on conjugal relationships in accomplishing important state objectives. Rather than advocating simply that the law cover a broader range of relationships, the Law Commission is of the view that it is time for governments to re-evaluate the way in which they regulate personal adult relationships.

We are suggesting a new methodology for addressing the legal regulation of these relationships, consisting of four questions. Are the objectives of the legislation legitimate? If so, are relationships relevant to achieving them? If they are relevant, can individuals themselves choose which relationships should be subject to the law? Finally, if relationships are relevant and self-designation is not feasible, is there a better way for governments to include relationships?

Implementation of this methodology would greatly diminish government reliance on relationship status. However, the state would still have an important role to play with respect to personal relationships, providing the legal framework for the voluntary assumption of rights and obligations between the two parties. It should broaden the range of relationships that receive this kind of state recognition and support through the creation of a registration scheme and the legalization of same-sex marriage.

Legislative reform in Australia

As *Beyond Conjugality* suggested, there may be arguments to support the extension of rights and obligations of marriage and cohabitation to adults living in interdependent relationships (such as sisters who cohabit or two friends who wish to live interdependent lives — beyond conjugal relationships).

In Australia, for example, New South Wales enacted the *Property (Relationships) Legislation Amendment Act* in 1999, which extended existing protections for opposite-sex cohabitees to same-sex cohabiting couples, and also introduced a new concept of "domestic relationship," defined in section 5(1)(b) as follows:

> a close personal relationship (other than a marriage or de facto relationship) between two adult persons, whether or not related by family, who are living together, one or each of whom provides the other with domestic support and personal care.

Although the Law Commission of Canada's *Beyond Conjugality* may be more comprehensive in scope, the Australian legislation reveals that governments in other jurisdictions are also seeking to provide recognition and support for non-conjugal relationships. For further information, see Reg Graycar & Jenni Millbank, "The Bride Wore Pink ... to the *Property (Relationships) Legislation Amendment Act 1999*: Relationships Law Reform in New South Wales" (2000) 17 Can J Fam L 227 at 245–50; and Reg Graycar & Jenni Millbank, "From Functional Family to Spinster Sisters: Australia's Distinctive Path to Relationship Recognition" (2007) 24 Wash UJL & Pol'y 121.

Litigation challenges in the United Kingdom: *Burden v United Kingdom*

Two sisters, who had cohabited all their lives in the family home in Wiltshire (including as joint owners for a period of 31 years after the death of their parents), launched a claim in the European Court of Human Rights based on their entitlement to be treated in the same way as married and cohabiting couples with respect to the U.K.'s exemption for payment of inheritance taxes. Their concern was that following the death of the first sister, the survivor would be forced to sell the family home to pay the required tax in the absence of such an exemption. In a decision in 2006, the court denied their claim of discrimination under Article 14 of the European Convention on Human Rights by a vote of 4 to 3 (*Burden v United Kingdom*, [2006] ECHR 13378/05), and the sisters then appealed to the Grand Chamber.

The Grand Chamber (appeal court) upheld the 2006 decision by a vote of 15 to 2 (*Burden v United Kingdom*, [2008] ECHR 13378/05). According to the majority:

> [60] The court has established in its case law that in order for an issue to arise under art 14 there must be a difference in the treatment of persons

in relevantly similar situations.... The Contracting State [the UK] enjoys a margin of appreciation in assessing whether and to what extent differences in otherwise similar situations justify a different treatment, and this margin is usually wide when it comes to general measures of economic or social strategy....

[62] The Grand Chamber commences by remarking that the relationship between siblings is qualitatively of a different nature to that between married couples and homosexual civil partners under the United Kingdom's Civil Partnership Act. The very essence of the connection between siblings is consanguinity, whereas one of the defining characteristics of a marriage or Civil Partnership Act union is that it is forbidden to close family members.... The fact that the applicants have chosen to live together all their adult lives, as do many married and Civil Partnership Act couples, does not alter this essential difference between the two types of relationships....

[65] ... Rather than the length or the supportive nature of the relationship, what is determinative is the existence of a public undertaking, carrying with it a body of rights and obligations of a contractual nature.... [T]he absence of ... a legally binding agreement between the applicants renders their relationship of co-habitation, despite its long duration, fundamentally different to that of a married or civil partnership couple....

Compare this approach to the dissenting opinion of Judge Zupančič (at 22–25):

[T]ax policy is an economic policy but it is also a social policy in disguise, ... [and inheritance tax policy] is not a simple linear decision-making choice. Rather, it is an integral part of a complex web of economic decisions that heavily influence the distribution of wealth and thus the whole social structure....
[By contrast with some categories in Article 14, which call for strict scrutiny, the] mildest proportionality (reasonableness) test is applied to social and economic matters.... The question ... is whether not giving tax exemption to the two Burden sisters is rationally related to a legitimate government interest....
If the Government has decided not to tax married couples, this is the starting point for the suspicion of discrimination.... The Government may reasonably maintain that the close relationship of a couple provides sufficient reason for the tax exemption.... The cut-off criterion is clear.
However, when the Government decides to extend this privilege to other modes of association, this black and white distinction is broken and the door is open for re-consideration of the question whether the denial of the tax advantage to other modes of association is rationally related to a legitimate government interest....
I ask myself ... why would consanguinity be any less important than the relationship between married and civil partners? ... One could easily reverse the argument and say, for example, that the "consanguine" identical twins are far closer genetically and otherwise since in reality they are clones of one another, than anybody could ever be to anybody else. And yet if the Burden sisters were identical twins they would not be entitled to the same exemption, in counter distinction to even the most ephemeral and fleeting relationship. So, what does the qualitative difference referred to by the majority come to? Is it having sex with one another that provides the rational relationship to a legitimate government interest? ...
I believe making consanguinity an impediment is simply arbitrary.

Which reasoning is more compelling? Why? For critiques, see Brian Sloan, "The Benefits of Conjugality and the Burdens of Consanguinity" [2008] Cambridge LJ 484; and Rosemary Auchmuty, "Beyond Couples" (2009) 17 LS 205.

Additional Resources

Nicholas Bala, "The Controversy over Couples in Canada: The Evolution of Marriage and Other Adult Interdependent Relationships" (2003) 29 Queen's LJ 41.

Brian Bix, "The Public and Private Ordering of Marriage" (2004) U Chicago Legal F 295.

Brenda Cossman & Bruce Ryder, "What is 'Marriage-Like' Like? The Irrelevance of Conjugality" (2001) 18 Can J Fam L 269.

John Eekelaar & Mavis Maclean, "Marriage and the Moral Bases of Personal Relationships" (2004) 31 JL & Soc'y 4.

Caroline Forder, "European Models of Domestic Partnership Laws: The Field of Choice" (2000) 17 Can J Fam L 371.

Robert Leckey, *Contextual Subjects: Family, State and Relational Theory* (Toronto: University of Toronto Press, 2008).

Mary Ann Glendon, *The Transformation of Family Law: State, Law, and Family in the United States and Western Europe* (Chicago: University of Chicago Press, 1989).

Claude Martin & Irène Théry, "The PACS and Marriage and Cohabitation in France" (2001) 15 Intl JL Pol'y & Fam 135.

C Thomas, "The Roles of Registered Partnerships and Conjugality in Canadian Family Law" (2006) 22 Can J Fam L 223.

NEW CHALLENGES: TRANS PERSONS, MARRIAGE, AND SEX/GENDER IDENTITY

Until recently, trans persons were usually understood to be "transsexual": people who feel that they are the sex "opposite" from the one they were designated at birth and who have therefore sought to change their sex at a later point in their lives, usually by means of hormonal treatment and surgical intervention. This definition is based on the idea that gender is binary; that is, that "male" and "female" are self-evidently the only genders that exist and therefore every person must be either one or the other. However, many trans people reject the gender binary. Some do not (or do not consistently) identify as one sex or the other and may embrace a variety of gender expressions. Others may transition to a gender identity different from the one they were assigned at birth without ever seeking medical intervention or gender-confirming surgery. Further, the traditional approach relied on a medical model that defined trans identity as "Gender Identity Disorder" and required medical and psychiatric intervention as a precondition to legal recognition. As is explored below, there is increasing criticism of this approach. There is also criticism of the language used in the older cases, most of which refused to acknowledge the existence of non-binary gender categories and the people who inhabit them. In contrast, the commentary in this section will use language that is respectful of the chosen gender identities of the people in the cases.

From a legal perspective, Canada's recognition of same-sex marriage suggests that there is no barrier to marriage for trans persons. However, the issue of sex/gender identity remains central to the way that trans people wish to live their lives. In the past few decades there have been important developments concerning legal recognition of trans persons, and this section briefly reviews some of these issues.

Trans persons and marriage

Our law currently recognizes that persons who have undergone gender confirming surgery may be treated in all ways as a member of the sex to which they have transitioned. However, this is a recent development, as is illustrated in the marriage cases below.

Re Kevin in Australia

In this case, the court concluded that a "female to male" transsexual was validly married to a woman, an important conclusion in the context of Australia's lack of recognition for same-sex marriage:

> I do not agree ... that a decision in favour of the applicants is groundbreaking. ... It is true that this judgment canvasses some interesting new medical evidence, and that the discussion of legal principle has been wide-ranging. While I have made findings about the medical evidence and offered a view about the underlying basis for such decisions as Corbett, the end result does not depend on acceptance of either of these matters. Ultimately, the basis for this judgment is very simple and mundane. It is that no good reasons have been shown why the ordinary legal meaning of the word "man," which includes post-operative female to male transsexuals, should not also apply to marriage. Because the words "man" and "woman" have their ordinary contemporary meaning, there is no formulaic solution to determining the sex of an individual for the purpose of the law of marriage. (Chisholm J, in *Re Kevin: Validity of Marriage of Transsexual*, [2001] FamCA 1074 (Austl); upheld on appeal [2003] FamCA 94 (Austl))

In Australia, trans persons who fulfill the required pre-condition of gender-confirming surgery are permitted to obtain identity papers (for example, drivers' licences and passports) consistent with their gender identity. In this context, the court in *Re Kevin* concluded that there was no impediment to recognizing the male gender identity of the applicant. Thus, Kevin, who had been designated female at birth, was held to be validly married to a woman. In fact, Kevin and his wife had already been accepted as a heterosexual couple at an infertility clinic and, at the time of the court's decision, they were the parents of one child conceived using anonymous donor sperm; and Kevin's wife was pregnant with a second child.

The Attorney General for the Commonwealth appealed Chisholm J's decision, but the appellate court dismissed the appeal in a judgment that quoted from the report of the Law Commission of Canada, *Beyond Conjugality* (discussed earlier).

Corbett v Corbett and the impact of precedent

The lower court in *Re Kevin* declined to follow an earlier English decision, *Corbett v Corbett*, [1971] P 83. In *Corbett*, the court held that a marriage in which one partner had undergone gender-confirming surgery was void (at 1323):

> The biological sexual constitution of an individual is fixed at birth (at the latest), and cannot be changed, either by the natural development or organs of the opposite sex, or by medical and surgical means.

The court in *Corbett* held that each individual has a "true sex" that cannot be altered by surgery. In addition, the court stated (at 1324–25) that since marriage has an "essentially heterosexual character," the test for a person's sex must be biological because "even the most extreme degree of transsexualism in a male or the most severe hormonal imbalance" could not reproduce "a person who is naturally capable of performing the essential role of a woman in marriage."

Corbett was followed in South Africa in *W v W,* [1976] 2 SALR 308 (WLD). As well, most courts in the United States have reached a similar result. See *Anonymous v Weiner*, 270 NYS 2d 319 (NY Sup Ct 1966); *Anonymous v Anonymous*, 325 NYS 2d 499 (NY Sup Ct 1971); *In re Gardiner*, 42 P 2d 120 (Kan Sup Ct 2002)); and *Littleton v Prange*, 9 SW 3d 223 (Tex App Ct 1999). Note, however, that a New Jersey court recognized as valid a marriage in which one partner had undergone gender-confirming surgery. See *MT v JT*, 355 A 2d 204 (1976).

Overcoming *Corbett*: The European Court of Human Rights

Significantly, *Corbett* is no longer binding in the United Kingdom as a result of decisions of the European Court of Human Rights in *Goodwin v United Kingdom*, [2002] ECHR 28957/95, and *I v United Kingdom*, [2002] ECHR 25680/94, in which the ECHR confirmed violations by the United Kingdom of the applicants' rights to privacy and to marry pursuant to articles 8 and 12 of the European Convention on Human Rights.

As a result of these decisions, the U.K. Parliament introduced legislation permitting trans people who have undergone gender-confirming surgery to marry, the *Gender Recognition Act 2004*, c 7, which took effect in April 2005. A number of cases have considered the impact of *Goodwin* in relation to this legislation with respect to employment and pension discrimination (for example, see *A v Chief Constable of West Yorkshire Police*, [2004] UKHL 21). However, nothing in this statute changed the heterosexual requirement for a valid marriage.

Some scholars have criticized the statute's acceptance of gender dysphoria as a therapeutic diagnosis, thus rendering trans identity a medical issue:

> While the Gender Recognition Act regime is a step forward, it is merely a transformation of the *way* in which English Law pathologizes transsexuals, not an affirmation that gender transition may be a legitimate way of structuring one's personal identity. [The Act] does not read gender transition as giving effect to an individual's desire to challenge or move beyond stable gender categories, but as a therapeutic response to their misfortune in failing to fit the binary gender system. The result performs the neat hat trick of recognizing the reality of transsexual embodiment but strictly confining the significance of this recognition. Transsexuals are not seen as troubling gender outlaws, the natural allies of same sex couples in seeking to break down the essentialist links between sex, gender and marriage. Rather, they are seen as gender refugees, being offered an end to their exile from their true home in the heterosexual binary paradigm. (Lisa Fishbayn, "'Not Quite One Gender or the Other': Marriage Law and the Containment of Gender Trouble in the United Kingdom" (2007) 15 American University Journal of Gender, Social Policy and Law 413 at 441)

The statute has also been criticized because it provides grounds for annulment if a trans person fails to disclose his or her gender history to a prospective spouse prior to the marriage. See Alex Sharp, "Transgender Marriage and the Legal Obligation to Disclose Gender History" (2012) 75 Mod L Rev 33.

Trans persons, marriage and spousal status in Canada

The few cases in Canada concerning marriage and trans persons all occurred prior to recognition of same-sex marriage. See *M v M* (1984), 42 RFL (2d) 55 (PEI Sup Ct); *C(LA) v C(CC)*, [1986] BCJ No 2817 (SC); *C(L) v C(C)* (1992), 10 OR (3d) 254 (Gen Div). In *Canada v Owen* (1993), 70 FTR 308 (TD), the court denied widow's benefits under the *Old Age Security Act* to a trans person who had lived as a woman since 1951 but did not have gender confirming surgery. Her birth certificate designated her as male. She had been married to a man and was later widowed. The court held that she was a male person and therefore not a spouse because spouses had to be persons of the opposite sex.

Trans identity in relation to cohabitation and access to spousal support: *B v A*

In *B v A* (1990), 29 RFL (3d) 258 (Ont Sup Ct), a trans man brought an application for spousal support from a woman at the end of a cohabiting relationship that had lasted for about 20 years. The applicant had undergone gender confirming surgery and engaged in continuing hormonal therapy. He presented medical certificates supporting his application for a change in sex designation under the *Vital Statistics Act*. It seems that there were many people in the applicant's life who had always known him as a man.

Although the language concerning entitlement to spousal support in Ontario's *Family Law Act* now uses the language of "two persons," it required "a man and a woman" at the time of this case. Thus, when the cohabiting relationship broke down, the applicant's cohabiting partner resisted the claim for spousal support on the basis that the applicant was a woman, not a man, so that there was no entitlement to such support because their relationship did not involve "a man and a woman." This argument was accepted by the court. In the absence of any direct authority, the court focused on the provisions of the *Vital Statistics Act* and its requirements for gender confirming surgery as a precondition to changing a birth certificate. Contrary to the medical evidence presented by the applicant, the court interpreted these provisions as requiring "radical and irreversible surgical intervention with all the fundamental reproductive organs, more than their simple removal." In addition, the court seemed concerned that if the applicant ceased to continue hormonal therapy, the applicant's body would again become "female" (paras 20 and 23).

According to Diana Majury, it was not appropriate for the court to use the provisions of the *Vital Statistics Act*, regarding a change in birth registration, to interpret the meaning of "a man and a woman" for purposes of spousal support in a cohabiting relationship:

> While we may think that the categories of sex and gender are fairly fixed and certain, situations such as that of B should lead us to question our assumptions about the meaning and significance of gender in our society and to question our ability to define female and male, woman and man. In the absence of any "direct totally pertinent authority" on the matter at issue in this motion, Master Cork had the opportunity to apply a somewhat open-ended definition of "man" and "woman" that would take into consideration a person's self-identification and lived experience. Instead, he chose to apply a narrow and outdated biological definition of sex that many doctors and scientists would describe as inadequate. His choice to apply irrevocability as an essential criterion in the determination of one's sex is not justified either in terms of logic or legislative purpose. To reduce the issue of spousal support to this level of inquiry — is this person "really" a man or a woman — misses the point at a number of levels. Such a limited and limiting approach seems contrary to the intention of the expanded definition of spouse for the purposes of support under the *Family Law Act*.... (Diana Majury, "Annotation of *B v. A*" (1990) 29 RFL (3d) 258)

See also Mark Cardwell, "Litigious Transgender Lawyer Fights for Her and Others' Rights" (2010) 34:1 Can Lawyer 16; Ariel Levy, "Either/Or: Sports, Sex and the case of Caster Semenya", *The New Yorker* (30 November 2009); Matt Sedensky, "Grandpa Has Something to Tell You", *The Globe and Mail* (16 March 2010) L3; and J Wilson, "My Daughter, My Son", *The Globe and Mail* (13 March 2008) L8.

With the legalization of same-sex marriage, issues regarding whether trans people meet the requirements to be spouses have been rendered moot. However, as highlighted in the excerpt from Diana Majury's comment, the reasoning in the older cases focused on "irrevocability as an essential criterion in the determination of one's sex." When legal recognition began to be extended to trans persons, it was on a similar basis, as can be seen in *Re Kevin*. Can this approach be justified in a social context where transgender identity is increasingly understood as a movement away from the birth-assigned gender with no necessity for medical or surgical intervention and no requirement for identification with the "opposite" sex?

Trans persons, human rights, and vital statistics

In *XY v Ontario (Government and Consumer Services)*, 2012 HRTO 726 (11 April 2012), the Human Rights Tribunal considered an application by a trans woman which challenged s 36 of the Vital Statistics Act. That section required two doctors to certify that "transsexual surgery" had occurred as a precondition to changing the sex designation of the applicant on the VS Registry and issuing a new birth certificate. The applicant, XY, testified that she had identified as a girl since childhood but could not openly express her gender identity because of lack of familial support. When she left home in 1995 to go to university, she decided to live full-time as a woman and did so despite resistance from those around her. She legally changed her name to a "female name." She also inquired whether she could have the sex designation on her birth certificate changed from male to female and was informed that the change could not be made unless she had surgery. She faced many difficulties due to incongruence between her female name and gender expression and the male designation on her identification and was eventually forced to return to her parents' home:

> [50] ... The applicant testified that her mother was embarrassed of her and tried to hide her from the community because she did not want people to know that the applicant was transgendered. The applicant testified that she could not live like that, "cooped up like a chicken". She testified that she started working as a male "as a form of compromise" and because she needed to earn money to support herself and pay her bills. The applicant testified that she did not feel that she had any choice but to start working as a man, because she had no way, legally, to work as a woman as long as her identification indicated that she was male. The applicant testified that she only felt safe working as a man. She testified that she feared that if she were to try to live and work as a woman, her I.D. "might catch up" to her. She testified that she was "paranoid" about her I.D. and felt "hunted down".

> [51] In the fall of 1999, the applicant legally changed her name back to the one she had been given at birth. The applicant testified that she changed her name back because it was an ongoing discussion "if not battle" between her and her mother and because she could not think of any other way that she could be successfully employed without her history "haunting her". The applicant testified that although she presented herself publicly as a man, she continued to identify as female and to live as a woman in her private life....

XY eventually moved to Toronto and apprenticed to a skilled trade. She continued to present herself publicly as a man.

> [54] ... in or around December 2007, she was working as a tradesperson in Alberta when a very homophobic apprentice who had been harassing her and calling her "gay" poked her in the face with a tool and ripped some paperwork out of her hands. The applicant testified that she broke the tool defending herself and that both she and the apprentice were fired as a result of the incident.

After that incident, XY decided to obtain gender confirming surgery, which was performed in 2008, and she reverted back to her female name. Over the next several months she was able to complete the paperwork required in order to be issued with a birth certificate and other identification designating her as female. She testified that although she was "happy" to have had the surgery "because it allowed her to move on with her life as a woman, the decision to have surgery was not without trauma," and "she felt very angry that surgery had been required in order to obtain a change in sex designation on her birth registration." She also testified that "she felt angry about the respondent's certification process, and specifically, the fact that her family doctor was the person 'hovering over her' to determine if the applicant's gender was 'real' based on her genitals. The applicant testified that she felt insulted and degraded by the experience of having the validity of her gender judged based on her genitals" (paras 61 and 72).

The tribunal held that trans persons constitute an historically disadvantaged group who face stigma and prejudice, and that the requirement of surgery and certification perpetuates disadvantage for trans persons:

> Giving transgendered persons an official government document with a sex designation which is dissonant with their gender identity conveys the message that their gender identity in and of itself is not valid.... Section 36 of the VSA in particular perpetuates disadvantage and prejudice against transgendered persons because it gives force to the prejudicial notion that transgendered people are not entitled to have their gender recognized unless they surgically alter their bodies (paras 171–172).

The tribunal did not have jurisdiction to strike down the legislation, but directed the government not to follow the offending legislation with respect to the applicant and others similarly situated; and to take steps to eliminate the discriminatory effect of the VSA scheme up to the point of undue hardship within 180 days.

XY's application was based on section 1 of the Ontario *Human Rights Code* (discrimination with respect to a service on the grounds of sex and disability) and section 11 (adverse effect discrimination). The *Human Rights Code* has since been amended to specify that every person has a right to equal treatment without discrimination because of gender identity/gender expression with respect to: Services, goods and facilities; Accommodation; Contracting; Employment, and Membership in a trade union, trade, or self-governing profession. See *Toby's Act (Right to be Free from Discrimination and Harassment Because of Gender Identity or Gender Expression)*, 2012,

SO 2012, c 7. The Act also amends the *Human Rights Code* to provide for freedom from harassment because of sexual orientation, gender identity or gender expression: Robert Benzie, "Transgendered People win Human Rights Recognition", *Toronto Star* (14 June 2012) A12. Gender identity is also explicitly included as a protected ground in human rights legislation in the Northwest Territories, Manitoba, Nova Scotia, Prince Edward Island, Newfoundland and Labrador, and Saskatchewan.

The impact of *XY v Ontario*

The provincial government responded to the tribunal's decision by removing the requirement for surgery as a precondition to an application for a VSA Registry change of sex designation. Nova Scotia, Manitoba, British Columbia, Alberta, Québec, and Nunavut have also eliminated the requirement, and the federal government has announced that it will eliminate the surgery requirement for change of sex designation on citizenship papers: Lauren Strapagiel, "Transgender Canadians can now self-identify on citizenship documents without sex-reassignment surgery", *National Post* (28 April 2015). However, applicants must still provide a letter from a physician or psychologist confirming that he or she has treated or evaluated the applicant, that the applicant's gender identity does not conform with the current sex designation on his or her birth certificate, and that the requested change is "appropriate." Thus, while the decision in *XY v Ontario* removes the burden of surgery as a precondition to receiving identification indicating a trans persons' lived gender, it still requires medical certification, rather than allowing trans persons to define their own identity.

Jena McGill and Kyle Kirkup are critical of this continuing requirement for third-party verification. They are also critical of the tribunal's focus on a binary approach to gender that makes room only for those trans persons who identify as the gender "opposite" to the one they were assigned at birth:

> Mapping trans subjectivity in law according to this particular image of what it means to be a trans person casts the lines of inclusion and exclusion in troubling ways; by establishing a single model of the trans subject who properly falls within the law, legal discourse reinforces "the outlaw status" of those who continue to perform "bad" gender identities that do not neatly fit the mould established by the "good" trans subject. (Jena McGill & Kyle Kirkup, "Locating the Trans Legal Subject in Canadian Law: *XY v Ontario*" (2013) 33 Windsor Rev Legal Soc Issues 96 at 134)

The B.C. Human Rights Tribunal has agreed to hear the complaint of a group of trans and intersex persons who argue that gender should not be assigned at birth or recorded on official documents: Maria Caspani, "B.C. Human Rights Tribunal to review complaint over birth certificate gender markers", *The Globe and Mail* (28 May 2015). For more on this issue, see Graham Mayeda, "Who Do You Think You Are? When Should the Law Let You Be Who You Want to Be?" in Laurie J Shrage, ed, *"You've Changed": Sex Reassignment and Personal Identity* (Oxford: Oxford University Press, 2009) 194; and Dean Spade, "Documenting Gender" (2008) 59 Hastings LJ 731.

Should people have to be identified by sex on their official identification? How should the law respond to the needs of trans persons who do not identify as "male" or "female"?

Additional Resources

Helen G Berrigan, "Transsexual Marriage: A Trans-Atlantic Judicial Dialogue" (2003) 12 Law and Sexuality Review 87.

Anne Fausto-Sterling, "The Five Sexes: Why Male and Female are not Enough", *The Sciences* (March/April 1993) 20.

Taylor Flynn, "Protecting Transgender Families: Strategies for Advocates" (2003) 30:3 Human Rights 11.

Julie Greenberg, "Defining Male & Female: Intersexuality and the Collision Between Law and Biology" (1999) 41 Ariz L Rev 205.

Lori Johnson, "The Legal Status of Post-Operative Transsexuals" (1994) 2 Health LJ 159.

Celia Kitzinger & Sue Wilkinson, "Genders, Sexualities and Equal Marriage Rights" (2006) 7:2 Lesbian & Gay Psychology Review 174.

Graham Mayeda, "Re-imagining Feminist Theory: Transgender, Identity, Feminism, and the Law" (2005) 17:2 CJWL 423.

Laura Nixon, "The Right to (Trans)Parent: a Reproductive Justice Approach to Reproductive Rights, Fertility, and Family-building Issues Facing Transgender People" (2013–2014) 20 Wm & Mary J Women & L 73.

Kevin Tallant, "My 'Dude Looks Like a Lady': The Constitutional Void of Transsexual Marriage" (2002) 36 Ga L Rev 635.

3

Forming Families:
Parent–Child Relationships

I.
FAMILIES AND CHILDREN

Marriage is a relationship easily terminated. Parent–child ties, by contrast, tend to last — they are not as fragile in our contemporary society. (Martha Fineman, *The Neutered Mother, the Sexual Family and Other Twentieth Century Tragedies* (New York: Routledge, 1995) at 3)

Families and parent–child relationships

As this comment suggests, "families" are created by parent–child relationships, as well as by close relationships between two adults. Moreover, as Fineman also explains, ties between parents and their children tend to be more lasting than many adult relationships created by marriage or cohabitation. In addition, legal rights and responsibilities in parent–child relationships may be permanent or extend beyond the child's age of majority. In this way, while individuals may choose to bring a marriage or cohabiting relationship to an end, there may be less opportunity for individual choice about the scope and duration of parental responsibilities for children: at least in some circumstances, law considers that "parenthood is forever."

In this context, it is clear that the creation of parent–child relationships represents another way of forming families. Indeed, Fineman (an American family law scholar) argued some years ago that the mother–child relationship should replace marriage as the "core family unit" for purposes of legal policies. According to Fineman, the effort to fit more and more intimate and other unions into the category of marriage or "marriage like" relationships, as the basis for creating legal rights and responsibilities, is less useful than a focus on mother–child relationships: "a vertical rather than horizontal tie; a biological rather than a sexual affiliation, an intergenerational organization of intimacy":

> [In] defining a core family unit what has happened is the creation of a norm, a baseline. It does not mean that other adult family characters are excluded: fathers, or nonprimary caretakers who have sexual affiliation to the primary caretaker, are certainly free, under my model, to develop and maintain significant connections with their sexual partner and her children if she agrees to such affiliation. The mother may also wish to forge ties and relationships with nonsexual affiliates.
>
> Under my intimacy scheme, however, single mothers and their children, indeed all "extended" families transcending generations, would not be the "deviant" and forgotten or chastised forms that they are considered to be today because they do not include a male head of household. Family and sexuality would not be confluent; rather, the mother–child formation would be the "natural" or core family unit — it would be the base entity around which social policy and legal rules are fashioned. The intergenerational, nonsexual organization of intimacy is what would be protected and privileged in law and policy. (Fineman at 5–6)

Clearly, Fineman's proposal to define families for legal purposes in terms of mother–child relationships presents an alternative to the law reform proposals in Chapter Two (such as the Law Commission of Canada's study, *Beyond Conjugality)*, which focused on extending the rights and responsibilities usually related to marriage to other interdependent relationships. While Fineman's proposal seemed quite radical when it was first suggested in the mid-1990s, new developments in assisted reproduction and new issues about the roles of mothers and fathers have resulted in new kinds of legal challenges for the definition of "families." Particularly in examining some of these new developments in parent–child relationships, you may want to consider whether or to what extent Fineman's proposals may offer advantages for defining the formation of families in law.

Definitions of "parent" and "child"

In this chapter, it is important to pay close attention to definitions of "parent" and "child." First of all, the legal definitions do not always conform to everyday notions about parents and children. In addition, the definitions may vary according to the legal context: for example, the definition of "parent" for purposes of consenting to a child's adoption is found in Ontario's *Child and Family Services Act*; however, legal presumptions about who is a "mother" or "father" in law are found in Ontario's *Children's Law Reform Act*.

These definitions are not always exactly the same. As a result, the legal context in which families are formed by parent–child relationships requires careful attention to determine the rights and responsibilities involved.

Organization of this chapter

This chapter focuses on selected issues concerning the definition of parent–child relationships.

- **Biological mothers and fathers:** Although parent–child relationships are routinely formed as a result of biological reproduction, a number of recent claims have been litigated about the respective rights of mothers and fathers as parents, and the extent to which legal principles permit them to exercise choices about their parental status.

- **Adoption:** In addition to biological reproduction, processes for the adoption of children reflect important ideas about relationships between biological and social parents. Introduced in many common law jurisdictions in the late 19th and early 20th centuries, adoption laws were designed to create a new legal relationship between adoptive parents and an adoptee — and to erase forever the legal status of the adoptee's biological parents. The efficacy of these principles has been challenged in recent years by efforts to (re)open adoption records to permit biological parents and their adopted children to reconnect. New challenges have also arisen with respect to the recognition of customary adoption practices, interracial and international adoption arrangements, and legal rights to adopt by gay and lesbian couples. In these contexts, principles of adoption reveal important, sometimes hidden, assumptions about what families *should* look like and how their members should be defined.

- **Assisted reproduction:** Recent medical developments with respect to processes of assisted reproduction have also challenged legal norms about parent–child relationships. In the context of donated eggs and sperm and the use of gestational carriers, for example, it is now possible for intentional parents to have no genetic or biological connection to the child whose conception they planned. In this example, moreover, there are five potential parents, raising important questions about the appropriate legal principles for defining parent–child relationships in this new context. In these circumstances, definitions of who is a "parent" and who is a "child," pursuant to statutory provisions that reflect traditional biological reproduction, may need to be reformed to recognize family relationships.

Changing family relationships

This chapter provides an overview of some aspects of these issues in the context of socio-legal scholarship about changing family forms and new kinds of family relationships. For example, Elizabeth Silva and Carol Smart described how sociological researchers interested in issues about family relationships have typically asked their respondents to draw maps of their families. In this context, both the maps being drawn and the researchers' interpretation of them have changed in recent decades. For example, a child who drew more than one family in the past would likely have been regarded by sociologists as problematic. However, such drawings now elicit different responses, because the maps represent

> a reflection of how the subjective meaning of family is changing and how individuals may be shifting their locus of intimacy and support away from kin towards other people. In some instances the maps which are produced are a long way from the idealized picture of mother, father and two siblings, and even where the standard stock of kin appear within the circles, others now may find a place, disrupting the taken-for-grantedness of primacy of blood and marital relationships. (Elizabeth B Silva & Carol Smart, "The 'New' Practices and Politics of Family Life" in Elizabeth B Silva & Carol Smart, eds, *The New Family?* (London: Sage Publications, 1999) 1 at 9)

Recall the discussion in Chapter One about definitions of "family" in Canada. To what extent does this sociological comment reflect data about families in Canada generally? Or your family in particular? Is this view consistent with Fineman's proposal to eliminate marriage as the core unit, replacing it with the mother–child relationship? Why, or why not?

Additional Resources

Nicholas Bala & Christine Ashbourne, "The Widening Concept of Parent in Canada: Step-Parents, Same-Sex Partners, & Parents by ART" (2011–2012) 20 Am U J Gender Soc Pol'y & L 525.

Brenda Cossman, "Parenting beyond the Nuclear Family: *Jane Doe v. Alberta*" (2007) 45:2 Alta L Rev 501.

Rosalind Edwards, Val Gillies & Jane Ribbens McCarthy, "Biological Parents and Social Families: Legal Discourses and Everyday Understandings of the Position of Step-Parents" (1999) 13 Intl JL Pol'y & Fam 78.

Robert Leckey, ed, *After Legal Equality: Family, Sex, Kinship* (New York: Routledge, 2015).

Mavis Maclean & John Eekelaar, *Managing Family Justice in Diverse Societies* (Oxford: Hart Publishing Limited, 2013).

Nancy Mandell, "The Child Question: Links Between Women and Children in the Family" in Nancy Mandell & Ann Duffy, eds, *Reconstructing the Canadian Family: Feminist Perspectives* (Toronto: Butterworths, 1988) 49.

Ingeborg Schwenzer, *Tensions between Legal, Biological and Social Conceptions of Parentage*, European Family Law series 15 (Antwerpen: Intersentia, 2007).

Carol Smart, Bren Neale & Amanda Wade, *The Changing Experience of Childhood: Families and Divorce* (Cambridge: Polity Press, 2001).

Robert A Stebbins, "Men, Husbands, and Fathers: Beyond Patriarchal Relations" in Nancy Mandell & Ann Duffy, eds, *Reconstructing the Canadian Family: Feminist Perspectives* (Toronto: Butterworths, 1988) 27.

II.
BIOLOGICAL REPRODUCTION:
"MOTHERS" AND "FATHERS"

[In the background of the legal arguments is] a naturalized version of the traditional family, organized around a heterosexual conjugal unit which reflects the biological "truths" of human procreation. (Hester Lessard, "Mothers, Fathers, and Naming: Reflections on the *Law* Equality Framework and *Trociuk v. British Columbia (AG)*" (2004) 16:1 CJWL 165 at 189–190)

BIRTH REGISTRATION AND NAMING CHILDREN

Becoming mothers and fathers in "law"

Lessard's comment explains that legal arguments about parental status may reflect ideals about the traditional family, that is, familialist views about how families *should* appear. This comment may be particularly relevant to cases in this section, in which heterosexual relationships result in the birth of a child. In examining the cases that follow, consider the roles of mothers and fathers in a number of different factual circumstances, and the reasoning used by courts to define parental relationships. It will be necessary to reflect on these cases again in the context of similar legal challenges (birth registration, naming of children, and access by biological fathers) that occur for same-sex couples, discussed later in this chapter.

The above comment occurred in the context of Lessard's examination of statutory provisions in British Columbia about registration of a child's birth and the authority to determine a child's surname, and a successful legal challenge to these provisions in the Supreme Court of Canada.

Trociuk v British Columbia (AG)
2003 SCC 34; 2001 BCCA 368;
(1999), 47 RFL (4th) 79 (BCSC)

Darrell Wayne Trociuk and Reni Ernst were the parents of triplets born in 1996. The children's mother registered their birth on her own and marked the father as "unacknowledged by the mother"; she also chose and registered the children's surname as hers alone. Her actions were authorized pursuant to sections 3(1)(b) and 4(1)(a) of the B.C. *Vital Statistics Act*, RSBC 1996, c 479; and section 3(6)(b) precluded the father from altering the registration.

In particular, section 3(1)(b) provided that "the child's mother, if the father is incapable or is unacknowledged by or unknown to the mother" must register a child's birth within 30 days after birth. Section 4(1)(a) provided that, if only one parent completes the statement, the child's surname must be registered as the surname chosen by the parent registering the child.

The parents had cohabited for short periods, but they became estranged after the birth of the triplets. The father eventually obtained an order for court supervised access, while the mother was later granted an order for custody, child support, and paternity testing (which resulted in Trociuk being declared father of the children). In this context, Ernst explained in her affidavit the reasons for her decision to register the children's birth without including the name of the biological father, and her choice to give the children her surname:

> I felt there was no reason why the children should bear the last name of somebody that I was not married to and had no plans to set up a life with. I saw no important connection between Darrell's ability to be a good father, if that is what he wanted, and the children bearing his last name. My view was that the children were carried by me, raised by me, and that they should bear my last name. I am their primary caregiver, and, despite the Petitioner's protestations to the contrary, he has made very little effort outside of the litigation arena to be part of their lives. (2001 BCCA 368 at para 172)

Trociuk petitioned for an order of mandamus to compel the Director of Vital Statistics to register his name as father of the triplets on the forms concerning birth registration. He also asked the court to change the surname of the children to Ernst-Trociuk, relying on the court's inherent *parens patriae* jurisdiction. In addition, Trociuk also claimed a declaration that section 3(1) of the *Vital Statistics Act* infringed section 15 of the *Charter* on the grounds of sex discrimination. Trociuk's application was rejected by the trial judge, and this decision was upheld by the B.C. Court of Appeal, with one dissenting opinion.

The Supreme Court of Canada unanimously allowed the appeal from the judgment of the B.C. Court of Appeal. Applying the test for section 15 of the *Charter* set out in *Law v Canada (Minister of Employment and Immigration)*, [1999] 1 SCR 497, the court concluded that sections 3(1)(b) and 3(6)(b) were invalid because they infringed section 15 and were not saved by section 1:

> [9] Applications of s. 15(1) are now guided by the test set out in *Law v. Canada (Minister of Employment and Immigration)*.... In the present case, the first two elements of that test are clearly satisfied. The impugned provisions explicitly draw a distinction on an enumerated ground, and the claimant was subject to differential treatment on the basis of that ground....

> [10] Sections 3(1)(b) and 3(6)(b) of the Act distinguish between mothers and fathers. This distinction is drawn on the basis of sex as only women can be mothers and men fathers. The distinction gives rise to differential treatment as fathers are disadvantaged by comparison to mothers. When unacknowledged by the mother, fathers are disadvantaged with respect to their ability to have their particulars included on the birth registration and to participate in determining their children's surname.

> [11] First, taken together, the impugned provisions allow the permanent exclusion of a father's particulars from the birth registration if a mother,

for any or no reason, chooses to "unacknowledge" (list on the birth registration as "unacknowledged") him. If a mother under s. 3(1)(b) so chooses and registers the birth without his particulars, s. 3(6)(b) precludes the father from altering the registration.

[12] Second, ss. 3(1)(b) and 4(1)(a) of the Act permit a mother to unacknowledge a father for any or no reason and thereby to exclude him from the process of determining the surname of his children. After the initial decision to unacknowledge, neither the Act nor the *Name Act*, R.S.B.C. 1996, c. 328, provides the father any recourse. Under the latter legislation, even if he were the custodial parent, he would require the mother's consent to change the surname (s. 4(3) and (4)).

[13] The foregoing discussion leads to the conclusion that the impugned provisions draw an explicit distinction on the enumerated ground of sex and that this distinction gives rise to differential treatment. On the basis of his sex, these provisions expose the father to the possible arbitrary exclusion of his particulars from his children's birth registration and, consequently, of his participation in choosing their surname. Moreover, having been so exposed, the father is provided no recourse. The sole remaining question under the *Law* test is whether, from the perspective of the reasonable claimant, the present differential effects constitute a violation of dignity....

[15] Parents have a significant interest in meaningfully participating in the lives of their children....

[16] Including one's particulars on a birth registration is an important means of participating in the life of a child. A birth registration is not only an instrument of prompt recording. It evidences the biological ties between parent and child, and including one's particulars on the registration is a means of affirming these ties. Such ties do not exhaustively define the parent–child relationship. However, they are a significant feature of that relationship for many in our society, and affirming them is a significant means by which some parents participate in a child's life. The significance of this affirmation is not only subjectively perceived. The legislature of British Columbia has attached important consequences to the presence of a father's particulars on his child's birth registration. It has decided that where a father's particulars are included on the birth registration, his consent is always required for his child's adoption. However, where his particulars are not included, a father must fulfill at least one of an alternative set of conditions....

[17] Contribution to the process of determining a child's surname is another significant mode of participation in the life of a child. For many in our society, the act of naming a child holds great significance. As Prowse J.A. notes, naming is often the occasion for celebration and the surname itself symbolizes, for many, familial bonds across generations....

The court suspended its declaration of invalidity for one year to permit the provincial legislature to revise the statute in accordance with constitutional requirements. In doing so, the court directed the legislature to account for the variety of interests involved in registering and naming children, including the legitimate interests of the mother, the right of the father not to be discriminated against on the basis of sex, and the best interests of the child. The court's decision suggested that Trociuk could apply, pursuant to amendments enacted in October 2002, to have his particulars included on the birth registration: see *Health Planning Statutes Amendment Act*, SBC 2002, c 15. However, the court expressly declined to make an order with respect to the surname of the children. Since the children were already seven years old, the court indicated that their best interests would have to be considered in assessing this request.

Notes and Questions

The significance of biology/genetics in relation to parental status

In her comment on *Trociuk*, Hester Lessard questioned the Supreme Court's decision that recognized genetic relationship as a sole basis for establishing parental (fathers') rights with respect to the registration of children. As will be discussed later in this chapter, such a focus on biological relationships for defining parenthood is problematic in the context of developments in assisted reproduction. In thinking about the Supreme Court's decision in *Trociuk*, consider Lessard's examination of the facts in relation to legal definitions of "spouse" and "parent," and whether they should have been given more weight in the Supreme Court's reasoning:

> *Trociuk's* relationship to the triplets was something more than simply genetic although something less than what the case law would call parental. To begin with, Ernst's relationship with Trociuk itself does not fit easily into existing legal categories. It was not a casual short lived relationship. ... Trociuk and Ernst had lived together for a little more than a year at one time but then lived separately while maintaining a sexual relationship. However, the length of their cohabitation was too short for Ernst and Trociuk to meet the statutory criteria for imposing interspousal obligations on unmarried cohabitants. Furthermore, the triplets were conceived over a year after Trociuk and Ernst ceased cohabitation, with the result that legislative provisions that typically provide for a presumption of paternity based on cohabitation or marriage with the mother at time of conception or birth did not apply.... [Trociuk did, however, provide some emotional support during Ernst's risky pregnancy. Ernst was in hospital for a month after the birth; she then stayed with Trociuk for about six weeks before moving in with her foster daughter at the time when two of the triplets were first released from hospital. Although Trociuk sought and was granted access to the triplets, it seems that access was exercised infrequently.]
>
> Nothing in terms of Trociuk's interactions with Ernst and then with the triplets in the pre- and post-natal periods qualifies Trociuk as what the jurisprudence calls a "social parent." Thus, in law, Trociuk's claims are based solely on his contribution of genetic material for the conception of the children. The story of Ernst and Trociuk's relationship might support an argument that we need to complicate the legal discourse of fatherhood to recognize persons whose contributions to children's existence fall short of "social fatherhood" but are more than casual. Deschamps J's analysis goes in the opposite direction, reducing fatherhood to genetic paternity while at the same time according genetic fathers the full panoply of constitutionalized parental rights. (Lessard at 188–189)

As will be discussed later in the chapter, defining parenthood based on biological relationships is problematic in the context of developments in assisted reproduction.

Formal versus substantive equality

Lessard's comment is important for its questioning of underlying assumptions about what creates the parent–child bond, and its concern that constitutional equality principles should examine these relationships in *substance*, not just *form*. As she argued, *Trociuk* reveals an approach to section 15 that focuses primarily on formal equality. Indeed, one press report stated that this case was the first decision pursuant to section 15 of the *Charter* to recognize men as a "historically disadvantaged group". See *The Globe and Mail* (7 June 2003) A3.

In this context, it may be significant that the judgment of Deschamps J identified reforms to the Québec *Civil Code* in the 1970s, which extended to mothers the ability to transmit their surnames to their children, thus enhancing the legal status of mothers. In deciding that Trociuk's equality rights were infringed in this case, the Supreme Court accorded recognition based almost entirely on a biological relationship: the parents were not married, they did not cohabit long enough to be regarded as "spouses" in law, and Trociuk's participation in the children's lives was probably insufficient to create a "social parent" relationship in law. As a result of the Court's decision, however, Trociuk was entitled to exercise all the rights of a legal "father." Consider the implications of using a biological or genetic connection to determine the legal status of "mother" or "father," an issue that is addressed later in relation to assisted reproduction.

The emphasis on biological ties is also found in Canada's *Citizenship Act*. In *Canada (Citizenship and Immigration) v Kandola*, 2014 FCA 85, the Federal Court of Appeal concluded that a child conceived using donated sperm and ova and who was born to a Canadian father and Indian mother in India was not a Canadian. According to the Court, the *Citizenship Act* required that citizenship could only be granted to a child who has a genetic connection to a Canadian citizen, a connection which was absent in this case because the child was not genetically related to her father.

Purposes of vital statistics registers

Lessard also raised questions about the state's interest in registration and naming practices and the underlying assumptions of provincial vital statistics legislation. According to the UN *Handbook on Civil Registration and Vital Statistics*, vital statistics registers serve two related purposes:

> [First, as] legal records documenting the facts surrounding each registered vital event, ... civil registration records of birth supply legal proof of identity and civil status ... [affecting] a wide variety of rights to which an individual may be entitled, especially rights dependent on age, citizenship....
> [In addition, records of individual events serve administrative and governmental purposes.] Birth records facilitate public health activities, such as post-natal care of mother and infant, infant and child immunization, and infant feeding programmes.... [Birth records] may be used to provide documented data, such as birth weight or gestational age, for longitudinal studies of cohorts of infants.... [and the data may also be used in] the planning process for economic and social development ... and for public health and medical research.... Data about births, foetal deaths and infant deaths are essential for programmes and post-natal care of women,

and for infant survival and growth. (*Handbook on Civil Registration and Vital Statistics: Policies and Protocols for the Release and Archiving of Individual Records* (New York: United Nations, 1998) Studies in Methods Series F No. 70 at paras 6–12)

In reflecting on these purposes for vital statistics registers, consider whether, or to what extent, inclusion of the biological father's name on the register promotes the goals identified. As will be discussed below, it may be that Trociuk's primary reason for wanting to be named in the birth register was not the accuracy of the birth register, but rather the rights that would flow from his status as "father."

To what extent is there a need for legislative reform? How should it be drafted? Details of *Vital Statistics* statutes vary considerably across Canada, with some of them relying on traditional versions of reproduction and others reforming legislation to take account of complex relationships in the context of assisted reproduction. Some of these statutory provisions will be addressed in more detail later in this chapter.

Amendments to the B.C. legislation

The B.C. legislature enacted amendments to its *Vital Statistics Act* in 2002. The amended section 3(6) provided that if birth registration was completed by only one parent, the register must be altered on application by (among others)

> (d) the child's mother or father, if the application is accompanied by a copy of an order of the court declaring the child's paternity, unless the court orders that the father's particulars are not to be included on the child's registration of birth.

The amendments also indicated that section 3(6) was not applicable to court orders declaring paternity issued prior to 2002, but permitted a mother or father to apply in paternity proceedings for an order to register the father's particulars on the birth register. See *Health Planning Statutes Amendment Act, 2002*, SBC 2002, c 15; and *Vital Statistics Amendment Act*, SBC 2004, c 55. As is discussed below, Mr. Trociuk would not qualify as a presumptive "father" under the new parentage provisions of British Columbia's *Family Law Act*, SBC 2011, c 25, Part 3. The DNA tests would, however, confirm his biological fatherhood status. In this context, what is the (legal) significance of "biological" parenthood?

Birth registration and naming in Ontario:
Kreklewetz v Scopel

Immediately prior to the decision of the Supreme Court of Canada in *Trociuk*, the Ontario Court of Appeal had considered an application by a father to be named on the birth register and to give his surname to his son. The provisions of the Ontario *Vital Statistics Act* were the same as those analyzed in *Trociuk* in relation to B.C. legislation. In the Ontario case, both the lower court and the appeal court concluded that the unmarried mother was not required to acknowledge the biological father when she registered her child on her own, using her own surname, even though she was fully aware of the father's biological connection. The parents were no longer together at the time of the birth registration.

This different outcome was achieved on the basis of statutory interpretation because the father did not raise a section 15 equality claim, by contrast with the applicant in *Trociuk*. In reading the summary of *Kreklewetz v Scopel*, below, compare the reasoning in the two cases.

Kreklewetz v Scopel
(2002), 60 OR (3d) 187 (CA); (2001), 13 RFL (5th) 408 (Sup Ct);
(leave to appeal to SCC denied, (2003), 62 OR (3d))

The biological father of a child appealed from a lower court decision that had interpreted the Ontario *Vital Statistics Act* to deny an unmarried father's request to be named on the birth registration form and to give his surname to his son. The mother and father had engaged in an "on again off again" relationship that ended shortly after their son was born. The mother gave evidence that she had initially acceded to the father's request to register the child's birth, using both their surnames. However, she also stated that she had agreed to this arrangement as a result of being pressured by the father to do so, and on the understanding that the three of them would become a "family." Some months after the child's birth, however, the mother realized that the father had lied about his intentions, and that he had vacationed with other women on several occasions during the time that he and the mother were together. The father married another woman.

The Ontario Court of Appeal upheld the decision of Greer J, who had interpreted the statute so as to permit the child's mother to register the birth without acknowledging the father and to give the child her own surname. In interpreting sections 9(3)(b) and 10(3) of the Ontario statute, which provided authority for the mother to register the child's birth by herself and give the child her own surname if the father was "unacknowledged by or unknown to" her, the court held that the mother was not required to acknowledge the father for purposes of the birth registration and surname, even though she knew his identity and had acknowledged him as the child's father for purposes of access and child support. According to the appellate court (at 200–203):

> [35] If the Act is interpreted in the manner advocated by the appellant [father], having acknowledged the father for one purpose, the mother would be obliged to acknowledge him in her certifying statement. It would only be in circumstances where the mother has been able to successfully avoid identifying the father for any purpose, that she would also be able to avoid acknowledging him under the Act.

> [36] In my view, in structuring the provisions as it did, the legislature made a policy decision to allow the mother to have the ultimate ability to determine the surname of the child in recognition of the fact that there will be circumstances where a mother will have the ongoing responsibility

for the child, and should not be forced to have the child linked by name with the biological father....

[38] In the British Columbia Court of Appeal decision in *Trociuk*, all three judges agreed that the father could be unacknowledged by the mother even if he was not unknown to her. Having made that finding the majority concluded that the provisions did not contravene s. 15 of the *Charter*, while Prowse JA, in dissent, concluded that they did.

[39] In her reasons, Madam Justice Southin, one of the judges speaking for the majority, at para. 65 dismissed the argument of the father that "he had a right to complete the birth registration because he is not 'unacknowledged by or unknown to the mother' within s. 3(1)(b) of the Act." Although she found the submission attractive because it would preserve a right of husbands and give the same right to fathers of children born out of wedlock to have their names on the birth certificates of their children, she could not accept it. Her interpretation of the section as a whole, was that it gives the mother the choice of whether the father's name is on the birth certificate, and that the mother is under no obligation to either acknowledge paternity or give her child the father's surname....

[42] I agree with the conclusion reached by the British Columbia Court of Appeal. In my view, the only interpretation which gives an effective meaning to the phrase "unacknowledged by" as distinct from "unknown to" in s. 10(3) of the Act, is the one which allows the mother to know the identity of the father, to acknowledge him as the father for other purposes, but not to acknowledge him for the purpose of registration of the birth of a child under the Act. This is the only interpretation which gives effect to the plain meaning in the context of the section as a whole.

[43] I am satisfied that it is also the appropriate interpretation on the criteria endorsed in the *Teck* case [*Teck Corp. v. Ontario (Minister of Finance)* (1999), 124 OAC 58 (CA)]. It satisfies the requirements of plausibility, efficacy and acceptability as a legislative choice for accomplishing the purposes of the Act. Furthermore, for the appellant, as a father of a child born out of wedlock, the Act does not remove any right to be included in the register or to have the child bear his surname, as he never had such rights under prior legislation or at common law. There was no *Charter* challenge of the provision in this case. The issue of infringement of a father's rights will be dealt with by the Supreme Court of Canada in the *Trociuk* appeal.

Amendments to the *Vital Statistics Act* in Ontario

Recent amendments to the Regulations pursuant to the *Vital Statistics Act*, RSO 1990, c V.4, do not alter a mother's right to "not acknowledge" the biological father in registering a birth in Ontario (see O Reg 401/06).

Section 9 of the statute provides for the mother and father, or either of them, to register a child's birth in accordance with the Regulations. And, section 2(2) of the Regulations provides that in relation to section 9 of the Act, either "the mother and the father of the child" or "the mother and the other parent of the child" (the latter language captures same-sex families) are required to register the birth. However, section 2(2) is subject to section 2(3), which states that the duty does not apply to an incapable mother or other parent, nor does it apply to "the child's father, if he is incapable or is unacknowledged by, or unknown to, the mother." Clearly, this is the same provision at issue in both *Kreklewetz* and *Trociuk*.

However, these provisions must be read with section 9(6) of the Act, which creates authority for the Registrar General to amend a birth registration if an application is made in accordance with the Regulations. According to sections 2(15) and (16) of the Regulations:

> (15) If a statement completed by only one parent of the child ... is registered, any parent or both parents of the child may apply to ... amend the statement.
> (16) A parent who applies to amend the statement without the other person who is a parent shown on the statement ... may do so only if that other person is incapable [and a statutory declaration to that effect is attached].

In addition, provisions concerning naming continue to permit mothers to name children on their own: see *Vital Statistics Act*, s 10(3)4.

Do these provisions adequately reflect the interests of mothers and fathers in relation to birth registration? In *Kreklewetz*, the Court of Appeal noted that there may be circumstances, such as rape, in which mothers would wish not to include the name of the biological father in the register. However, as the court concluded (at para 36), "there is no provision in the Act for specific exceptions," so that the mother may exercise her volition freely in making this decision.

Trociuk and rights and responsibilities of mothers and fathers in "law": *Gallant v Lewis*

To what extent is the Supreme Court's decision in *Trociuk* binding in Ontario? In *Gallant v Lewis* (2008), 57 RFL (6th) 345 (Ont Sup Ct), the biological father applied for an order changing a child's surname to a hyphenated one after the mother registered the child in her own name. The parents began to date in April 2006, then cohabited in October 2006 and separated in December 2006 and the child was born in July 2007. At the time of the application, the parents were both 21 years old and the child was one year old; and the father had continued to exercise daily access to the child. The mother opposed the application on the basis that she was the primary caregiver and that the child lived with her.

In a decision granting the father's application, Quinn J noted that the Ontario Court of Appeal in *Kreklewetz* had relied on the decision of the B.C. Court of Appeal and that the B.C. appellate court's decision had been overruled by the Supreme Court of Canada in *Trociuk*, and he concluded:

> [24] In my opinion, it would bring the administration of justice into disrepute, be manifestly unfair to the father and not be in the best interests of the child, if I were to enforce the child-naming provisions of Ontario's *Vital Statistics Act* where British Columbia's virtually identical statute has been ruled unconstitutional as amounting to discrimination on the basis of sex.
>
> [25] The right of a mother to arbitrarily exclude the father in the naming of their child is a breathtaking example of sexual discrimination, leaving the father without recourse (short of the application launched) and ren-

dering him a second-class parent. It is not in the best interests of a child to have his or her parents differentiated in this fashion. There will be obvious instances where it will be entirely appropriate for a father to be unacknowledged and for a child to be given only the surname of the mother — but this is not one of them.

Significantly, the court also noted that there was no statutory authority for the court's order for a hyphenated surname for the child. In this context, the court granted the application using the *parens patriae* jurisdiction of the court and for the benefit of the child.

By contrast, in *SG v AS*, 2015 ONSC 752, the court refused to exercise its *parens patriae* jurisdiction to amend the child's maternal surname. After AKNS was born, her mother S registered her birth and name. S did not acknowledge the father, SG, on the record of birth because she did not see any future in the relationship. SG was incarcerated at the time of the birth and had a lengthy criminal record. SG sought to have his daughter's surname changed. He did not challenge the constitutionality of the child-naming provisions of Ontario's *VSA*. In considering whether to exercise the *parens patriae* jurisdiction, the court concluded that there was no gap in the legislation and that there was no a risk of harm or danger to the child.

[65] In my view, the court should determine whether there is a realistic prospect that the lack of a shared paternal surname will diminish the father–child relationship; or that it will negatively affect the child's sense of identity. Such determinations are specific to the child's individual circumstances, but must also be answered in contemplation of the societal norms in which the child will be raised.

[66] Such a test is consistent with decisions since Kreklewetz in which the court exercised its parens patriae jurisdiction to amend a child's surname. In each case the court looked to the child's best interests and specifically, to the risk to the child in not making an order to amend a surname, while acknowledging that there are proper reasons for excluding an unacknowledged father from the act of naming a child.

[67] In this case it cannot be said that the lack of a shared surname will diminish A.K.N.S.' relationship with her father. Nor does Mr. S.G. make any such suggestion. He did not initially pursue a relationship with his daughter, and to be fair, may not have been in a position to do so during early periods in A.K.N.S.' life when he was incarcerated, or A.K.N.S. was in care. Since August 2013 he has enjoyed more regular periods of access time with her. The supervision of his access is to be reviewed upon a determination of his present charges.

[68] Neither can it be said that the lack of a shared paternal surname will negatively affect A.K.N.S.' sense of identity. During her most formative years A.K.N.S. has developed her identity as A.K.N.S. All her records and documents are in her maternal surname, which she shares with two half siblings. Her name is an important element of stability in what has been a chaotic start to life.

[69] Mr. S.G. did not place A.K.N.S.' surname in issue until July of 2014, after the first calling of the matter for trial. By that time A.K.N.S. was over six years old. She is now approaching seven years of age. By not raising this issue earlier, and in a more fulsome manner, I find that it would be a change in name at this point in A.K.N.S.' life that would cause harm, rather than a continuation of her present maternal surname.

[70] I do not find that there is any risk of harm to A.K.N.S. should her maternal surname continue. I therefore decline to exercise my parens patriae jurisdiction. Absent any statutory mechanism per the VSA, Mr. S.G.'s claim to change A.K.N.S.' surname must be dismissed.

Additional Resources

Andrew Bainham, ed, *Parents and Children* (Aldershot, England and Burlington, VT: Ashgate, 2008).

Cindy Baldassi, "DNA, Discrimination and the Definition of Family Class: *MAO v. Canada (Minister of Citizenship and Immigration)*" (2007) 21 J L & Soc Pol'y 5.

Emily Carasco, "What's in a Name — Whose Name is it Anyway — a Comment on *Trociuk v. B.C.*" (2004) 37:1 UBC L Rev 259.

Richard Collier, *Men, Law and Gender: Essays on the "Man" of Law* (Oxford: Routledge, 2010).

Emily Jackson, "What is a Parent?" in Alison Diduck and Katherine O'Donovan, eds, *Feminist Perspectives on Family Law* (Oxford: Routledge-Cavendish, 2006) 59.

Carol Rogerson, "Developments in Family Law: The 2002–2003 Term" (2003) 22:2 SCLR 273.

Wanda Wiegers, "Fatherhood and Misattributed Genetic Paternity in Family Law" (2011) 36 Queen's LJ 623.

BIOLOGICAL/GENETIC FATHERS AND ACCESS RIGHTS

Fathers and access: *Johnson-Steeves v Lee*

In *Johnson-Steeves v Lee* (1997), 33 RFL (4th) 278 (Alta CA); (1997), 29 RFL (4th) 126 (Alta QB), the mother of Nigel, a child aged four and a half, initiated a claim seeking custody of the child, an order denying access to the biological father, and child support. The biological father claimed that access was in the child's best interests and indicated a willingness to continue to pay child support.

According to the facts in the case, the mother and Nigel's father had met some years prior to the mother's marriage and divorce (with another man), with whom she had two children. Following her divorce, the mother contacted the father to invite him to visit her and to travel with her to Las Vegas. During their stay in Las Vegas, the mother explained that she wished to have another child and that the father was a suitable partner for this project because of his small stature (to avoid difficulties with the pregnancy and birth), his financial resources (as a doctor in Toronto), the fact that the father was Chinese (so that the child would be mixed heritage), and that he was a friend and unmarried. After some discussion about the arrangement, the parties agreed that the father would not interfere with

respect to issues about the health and welfare of the child, but that he
would provide financial support and be allowed to see the child on visits to
Alberta. The parties had sexual intercourse and the mother became pregnant and gave birth to Nigel. The father provided financial support, but the
relationship between the mother and father deteriorated, and eventually,
the mother decided not to permit the father to see Nigel.

In this case, the trial court decided that no valid agreement existed
between the parties, and that the court was required to determine what was
in Nigel's best interests. Accordingly, the court held that it was in Nigel's
best interests to make an order for the father's access to him. The Alberta
Court of Appeal upheld the trial decision, rejecting the mother's claim that
the father's rights should be determined on the basis that he was merely a
sperm donor. Both courts also dismissed claims based on section 7 of the
Charter.

Consider the following passages from the trial decision:

> Ms. Johnson-Steeves asks this Court to redefine the term "family." She
> says the notion that a family consists of a mother, father and children, as
> long defined by our law, is antiquated and does not reflect current reali-
> ties. Ms. Johnson-Steeves says that Dr. Lee is only a sperm donor and not
> a father. It was her choice to create a family unit without a father and
> she did so. She argues that any access will create a family that was not
> intended and will violate Nigel's understanding of his family unit. This,
> she says, is not in Nigel's best interests.
>
> I am of the view ... that society and biology have not yet reached the
> point where we have dispensed with fathers or mothers completely. They
> form an integral part of each child's life whether or not they reside with
> their children.
>
> Nigel has a father and Ms. Johnson-Steeves' desire that it not be so,
> does not make it so. Ms. Johnson-Steeves' interest in arranging her world
> as she would like to see it does not mean that it is also in Nigel's best
> interest.... It is Nigel's right of access to his father and not his mother's
> right to bargain away. At this stage, it does not matter to Nigel whether he
> was conceived by artificial insemination, during a one night stand, or dur-
> ing a long-term relationship or marriage. What he does know is that he
> has a father and a mother. The fact that his father does not live with
> Nigel does not make Dr. Lee any less a father.... [The court also com-
> mented favourably on Dr. Lee's background and extended family.]

Notes and Questions

Reflecting again on *Jane Doe v Alberta*

Johnson-Steeves v Lee was decided some years before the application to
determine the validity of the contract between Jane Doe and her male partner was litigated in Alberta. Recall (Chapter One) that the contract in *Jane
Doe* was a formal written contract agreed to by both parties, by contrast
with the one that had been apparently discussed but not confirmed by writing in the *Johnson-Steeves* case. In addition, both parties in *Jane Doe* agreed
that the male partner would not have rights or responsibilities for the child
conceived using donor sperm, while the parties in *Johnson-Steeves* disagreed
about the relationship between Nigel's mother and the biological father

(who was not just a "sperm donor," according to the court). Yet, as in *Johnson-Steeves v Lee*, the Alberta Court of Appeal in *Jane Doe* upheld the trial decision that determined that the contract was not enforceable because it was not in the child's best interests, and that there was no constitutional infringement pursuant to the *Charter*. Thus, in spite of some differences between the two cases, the outcome was similar. Both the biological father in *Johnson-Steeves* and the non-biological father in *Jane Doe* were considered legal fathers with rights and responsibilities accordingly.

In this context, to what extent is there scope for contracts and the negotiation of parental rights and responsibilities? Note particularly the views expressed in the trial judgment (above) that it does not matter whether a child "was conceived by artificial insemination, during a one-night stand, or during a long-term relationship or marriage." In relation to access, should the method of conception be a relevant factor? You may also want to consider this case in relation to discussion about the legal status of sperm donors, discussed later in this chapter in relation to assisted reproduction.

The role of "fathers" in the creation of "families"

In *Trociuk* and in *Gallant*, the judges used similar language to describe the parties. In both cases, the mothers were characterized as "arbitrary" and in both cases, the courts concluded that the fathers were discriminated against ("breathtakingly" in *Gallant*). In thinking about this use of language, and the court's rejection of Johnson-Steeves' efforts to create a family on her own, consider whether these courts were resisting the creation of primary mother–child relationships, the proposal advocated by Fineman at the beginning of this chapter. For these judges, is a "father" necessary in order to create a "real" family?

In assessing *Trociuk*, Shelley Gavigan argued that the Supreme Court's decision reinforced patriarchy and failed to recognize the actual social relations between Trociuk and Ernst:

> It is almost impossible to imagine a more formal, less substantive, notion of "participation in a child's life." ... The construction of "disadvantaged" father and "arbitrary" mother could only be made by one who is indifferent to the actual social relations expressed in the facts of such a case, and for whom patriarchal relations have no relevance. It was an anathema to Mr. Trociuk ... and Deschamps J. that a single mother, with no ongoing relationship with the father, would have the temerity and legal authority to say to him, "You may be their father, but they will have my name." Only in a world where patriarchy is as invisible as it is present would such a mother be criticized as mean-spirited and arbitrary, and this man, the object of "discrimination." (Shelley Gavigan, "Equal Families, Equal Parents, Equal Spouses, Equal Marriage: The Case of the Missing Patriarch" (2006) 33 SCLR (2d) 317 at 324–325)

A number of other legal scholars have also focused on how courts invoke ideas about "fathers" in relation to "families." In the United Kingdom, Richard Collier suggested that there is a "gap between the rhetoric and reality of family life," at least with respect to the law's recognition of fathers' rights. In particular, he argued that even though issues about children are required to be determined in accordance with the legal principle of the "best interests of the child," the cases suggest that there is often almost a legal presumption in favour of contact with children's fathers that may be inconsistent with the children's wishes. As he explained:

> The question of what constitutes "good (enough) fathering" is one which has, throughout the 1990s, assumed a central importance within a range of conversations taking place around the legal regulation of family practices across western societies.... [A] concern with fatherhood can be seen to be central to contemporary cultural representations *of* and political debates *about* the parameters of "the family" and understandings of "family life." (Richard Collier, "In Search of the 'Good Father': Law, Family Practices and the Normative Reconstruction of Parenthood" (2001) 22 Studies in Law, Politics, and Society 133 at 133–134)

Did the court in *Johnson-Steeves* respond to Nigel's best interests or to Dr. Lee's? Were their interests the same or different? What factors might have altered the court's views with respect to Nigel's best interests in relation to Dr. Lee's request for access?

From a sociological perspective, Carol Smart examined the role of fathers in relation to families in the post-divorce context. While the context is different from the cases discussed above, her comments about the larger historical and policy issues may be relevant nonetheless:

> The focus on the welfare of the child and the concern to attach men to their children are both policies which have developed as correctives to what have been seen as past errors in family law policy. But because the scope of this policy is limited to the field of private law, this method of achieving "progress" may only exacerbate other problems which are outside the remit of family law.... The active pursuit — by family law — of equal, joint parenting *after* divorce combined with welfare and employment policies which make equal, joint parenting *during* marriage virtually impossible for the majority, gives rise to a form of disenfranchisement of motherhood rather than a new beginning for parenthood. Rather than increasing the quantum of care that children receive through the more active involvement of fathers *after* divorce, this policy may make it increasingly "rational" for mothers to behave more like fathers *during* marriage in order to ameliorate the future deficit to their status as citizens in the context of a modern welfare state which increasingly values paid work and independence over unpaid care and commensurate dependence. Under such a scenario the "new" parenthood may seem less desirable than once imagined. (Carol Smart, "The 'New' Parenthood: Fathers and Mothers After Divorce" in Elizabeth B Silva & Carol Smart, eds, *The New Family?* (London: Sage Publications, 1999) 100 at 113)

Do Smart's comments shed light on these cases about parenthood in relation to biological reproduction? Note, for example, that there was no evidence that any of the fathers in the above cases wished to have day-to-day custody and care of the children. Rather, they all appeared content to leave these responsibilities to the children's mothers. How should the rights and responsibilities of parents in relation to issues of recognition (registration, naming, and access) be balanced with issues about responsibility (caring for children on a daily basis)?

Finding fathers: *GES v DLC*
Consider this situation:

A man and a woman were involved in a non-sexual "special friendship" over a period of 12 years, during which they lived together on several occasions. At some point, the woman decided that she wanted to have a child and asked the man to be a sperm donor. Although the man refused this request, he supported the woman in the process of becoming pregnant using (anonymous) donor sperm, including paying for part of her treatment, attending prenatal classes with her, and being present when her twins were born. After their birth, the man visited the woman and her children often and, during a period when he was unemployed for several months, he babysat the twins while the mother was working full time. However, the mother of the twins eventually denied access to the man (perhaps because of his behaviour as a result of depression), and the man then applied to the court for custody and access. How should the man's claim be resolved?

In *GES v DLC*, 2005 SKQB 246, the trial judge accepted evidence from a psychologist that the man and woman and the twins constituted "a non-traditional family unit," and that there was an emotional benefit to the children in maintaining the relationship with the man. Thus, although he did not find the man to be a legal father, he awarded access. The Saskatchewan Court of Appeal allowed the mother's appeal, suggesting that while the man was "more than a babysitter," he was "much less than a parent" (see *GES v DLC*, 2006 SKCA 79; appeal to SCC dismissed, [2006] SCCA No 378). In relation to the trial judgment, Fiona Kelly argued that

> [the trial] decision in GES was the first of its kind in Canada. Never before had a court awarded access to a non-relative or non-step parent who had not at any time been in a conjugal relationship with the mother of the child. That the court would grant access in GES, where the man seeking access had expressly refused on several occasions to provide his own sperm to the mother of the children, seems unusual. It is possible that the court was trying to be progressive in recognizing "non-traditional family units" that extend beyond the boundaries of both biology and conjugality. However, a more likely reading of the case is that the access bestowed on GES was designed to provide the twins with a "father" and thus complete their "non-traditional" nuclear family unit. Either way, the effect of the decision was to undermine DLC's ability to parent autonomously in a family of her making. (Fiona Kelly, "Producing Paternity: The Role of Legal Fatherhood in Maintaining the Traditional Family" (2009) 21:2 CJWL 315 at 327)

Consider the outcome in these cases. Why did the male applicant succeed in *Gallant*, while the male applicant in *GES* was eventually denied access on appeal? How do these cases reveal the law's interest in biological connections? Were there other relevant factors?

The issue of "fathers" in families is also important in legal decisions about adoption and assisted reproduction, particularly in the context of same-sex family units. As discussed later in this chapter, it may be necessary to determine whether, or to what extent, the reasoning in cases about heterosexual families should be applied in other contexts.

Additional Resources

Chris Barton & Gillian Douglas, *Law and Parenthood* (London: Butterworths, 1995).

Susan B Boyd, "Autonomy for Mothers? Relational Theory and Parenting Apart" (2010) 18:2 Fem Leg Stud 137.

Susan B Boyd, *Child Custody, Law, and Women's Work* (Toronto: Oxford University Press, 2003).

Shelley AM Gavigan, "Something Old, Something New? Re-theorizing Patriarchal Relations and Privatization from the Outskirts of Family Law" (2012) 13 Theor Inq L 271.

Roxanne Mykitiuk, "Beyond Conception: Legal Determinations of Filiation in the Context of Assisted Reproductive Technologies" (2001) 39 Osgoode Hall LJ 771.

Carol Smart & Bren Neale, *Family Fragments?* (Malden, MA: Polity Press, 1999).

Alison Harvison Young, "Reconceiving the Family: Challenging the Paradigm of the Exclusive Family" (1998) 6 Am UJ Gender Soc Pol'y & L 505.

LEGAL REGULATION OF WOMEN'S SEXUALITY: A BRIEF OVERVIEW OF ABORTION AND STERILIZATION

The use of criminal law to regulate access to abortion ended when the Supreme Court of Canada struck down section 251 of the *Criminal Code*, RSC 1985, c C-46, in *R v Morgentaler*, [1988] 1 SCR 30. Chief Justice Dickson (Lamer J concurring) held that the law constituted state interference with bodily and psychological integrity, violating section 7 of the *Charter*. Further, the regulatory framework governing abortion was unconstitutional because its exculpatory provisions created unfair procedural irregularities. Beetz J (Estey J concurring) held that the procedural requirements of section 251(4) delayed legal procurement and unjustifiably risked a mother's health. Madam Justice Wilson alone found that the law violated a substantive liberty interest and that it also infringed upon freedom of conscience under section 2(a) of the *Charter*. Dissenting, McIntyre J (La Forest J concurring) held that section 7 did not protect a woman's right to procure an abortion.

Provincial reactions to the *Morgentaler* decision were varied, and some problems resulted in relation to access issues and funding. For example, although Nova Scotia initially obtained an injunction to prevent Dr. Morgentaler from conducting abortions outside a hospital, contrary to provincial legislation (see *Nova Scotia (AG) v Morgentaler* (1990), 96 NSR

(2d) 54 (SC (AD)); (1989), 93 NSR (2d) 202 (SC (TD)), he was acquitted of the charge because the legislation was, in pith and substance, criminal law and thus beyond the province's constitutional authority. See *R v Morgentaler*, [1993] 3 SCR 463; (1990), 99 NSR (2d) 293 (Prov Ct). Provincial funding varies significantly across the country. Certain provinces restrict abortion funding to public hospitals and others do not have non-hospital abortion facilities. Only six provinces cover the cost of clinic abortions (British Columbia, Alberta, Manitoba, Ontario, Quebec and Newfoundland and Labrador): Erin Nelson, *Law, Policy and Reproductive Autonomy* (Portland: Hart, 2013) at 138. Access to abortion remains elusive in Prince Edward Island, where abortions are not offered in the province. Rather, the legislature pays for the cost of an abortion outside the province where there is a medical referral and the procedure is done in hospital. The legislature does not cover the travel costs: Kevin Bissett, "Debate over access to abortion in Prince Edward Island intensifies", *The Globe and Mail* (27 May 2014), online: <www.globeandmail.com>.

Provincial legislatures have sought to impose additional barriers to access abortion services. In New Brunswick, women required the permission of two doctors who had to certify that the abortion was medically necessary and limited public funding for abortion services to those performed by a specialist in hospital: Regulation 84-20 of the *Medical Services Payment Act*, RSNB 1973, c M-7. This Regulation "deliberately recreated virtually the same barriers to women's health and safety that were held to be unconstitutional in *Morgentaler*": "Access to Abortion Fundamental Right for Women's Health" (28 April 2014), Impact Ethics (blog), online: <http://impactethics.ca/2014/04/28/access-to-abortion-fundamental-right-for-womens-health/>. The first two requirements, for a referral and performed by a specialist, were subsequently repealed.

By contrast, legislative action has been taken in British Columbia to improve access to abortion services. The provincial legislature has enacted "bubble zone" legislation designed to protect the staff and clients of abortion clinics, with ongoing legal and political challenges: *Access to Abortion Services Act*, RSBC 1996, c 1.

There was also reaction to the *Morgentaler* decision at the federal level. An effort in 1990 by the federal government to legislate Bill C-43, *An Act Respecting Abortion*, was defeated by a tie vote in the Senate. At the time, there were also a number of unsuccessful legal challenges by women's partners who wished to prevent their implementation of abortion decisions. See, for example *Murphy v Dodd* (1989), 63 DLR (4th) 515 (Ont HC); and *Tremblay v Daigle*, [1989] 2 SCR 530.

Courts have also reviewed applications for non-therapeutic operations, particularly with respect to reproductive capacity. For example, parents (usually mothers) have applied, often unsuccessfully, to obtain consent for hysterectomies for mentally disabled daughters. See *Re K* (1985), 19 DLR (4th) 255 (BCCA); and *Re Eve*, [1986] 2 SCR 388. Moreover, claims for compensation have been launched by "victims" of sterilization programs in previous decades. For example, Leilani Muir sued the Alberta government for sterilizing her under the province's *Sexual Sterilization Act*. She was one of 2,844 people sterilized in Alberta between 1928 and 1972 under this law, apparently created to prevent the "feeble minded" from having children who might inherit disabilities. In January 1996, Justice Joanne Veit of the Alberta Court of Queens Bench found the province's treatment of Muir "unlawful, offensive and outrageous," and ordered damages of $740,000: see *Toronto Star* (12 June 1995) and (30 June 1996). Although Alberta and British Columbia were the only Canadian provinces to pass sterilization laws, it is believed that operations may also have been carried out in other provinces, including Ontario.

Additional Resources

SI Bushnell, "The Welfare of Children and the Jurisdiction of the Court Under *Parens Patriae*" in Katherine Connell-Thouez & Bartha Knoppers, eds, *Contemporary Trends in Family Law: A National Perspective* (Scarborough, ON: Carswell, 1984) 223.

Rebecca J Cook, Joanna N Erdman & Bernard M Dickens, *Abortion Law in Transnational Perspective: Cases and Controversies* (Philadelphia: University of Pennsylvania Press, 2014).

BM Dickens, "Interactions of Law and Ethics affecting Reproductive Choice" (2005) 24:3 Med & L 549.

Claire Farid, "Access to Abortion in Ontario: From *Morgentaler* 1988 to the Savings and Restructuring Act" (1997) 5 Health LJ 119.

Bruce Feldthusen, "Suppressing Damages in Involuntary Parenthood Actions: Contorting Tort Law, Denying Reproductive Freedom, and Discriminating Against Mothers" (2014) 29:1 Can J Fam L 11.

Vijaya Krishnan & Kelly Martin, "Contraceptive Sterilization Among Canadians, 1984–1995" (2004) 31:1 Canadian Studies in Population 15.

Vanessa MacDonnell & Jula Hughes, "The German Abortion Decisions and the Protective Function in German and Canadian Constitutional Law" (2013) 50:4 Osgoode Hall LJ 999.

Patricia Peppin, "Justice and Care: Mental Disability and Sterilization Decisions" (1989/90) 6 Can Hum Rts YB 65.

Karen Stote, "The Coercive Sterilization of Aboriginal Women in Canada" (2012) 36:3 American Indian Culture and Research Journal 117, online: <http://aisc.metapress.com/content/7280728r6479j650/fulltext.pdf>.

III.
ADOPTION: BIOLOGICAL PARENTS, ADOPTIVE PARENTS, AND CHILDREN

[Are] the assumptions implicit in our adoption laws ... valid in our changing society? Do we still wish to continue premising our laws upon a concept of relinquishment? ... [By contrast, we might decide] that changing attitudes about family and the definition of a parent dictate an examination of other options different from our present one which envisages a permanent severing of the "old" family bond and a permanent new reconstituting. In any such examination, the customary attitudes of Native people towards adoption would be instructive. (Kerry J Daly & Michael P Sobol, *Adoption in Canada: Final Report* (Guelph, ON: National Adoption Study for Health and Welfare Canada, 1993) at 99)

THE CONTEXT FOR ADOPTION: HISTORICAL CONCEPTS AND NEW APPROACHES

The evolution of adoption legislation

In their study of adoption law and practices in Canada (above), Daly and Sobol reviewed the history of adoption in common law provinces. Although Indigenous peoples in North America often utilized customary practices of adoption, the common law did not recognize adoption at all, so that adoption became recognized in law only after the enactment of statutory regimes. In Canada, provincial adoption statutes now provide a complete framework for defining adoption practices, and litigation about adoption focuses primarily on principles of statutory interpretation.

Interestingly, although Britain did not enact adoption legislation until after World War I, New Brunswick passed an adoption statute as early as 1873, based on a model in existence in Massachusetts. Nova Scotia similarly enacted adoption legislation in 1896, and adoption statutes were passed in most other common law provinces in Canada between 1920 and 1930.

Early 20th century adoption legislation was enacted in a social context in which there were two concerns:

1. To avoid the stigma of "illegitimacy," pregnant unmarried women often needed to place their babies for adoption.
2. Childless couples often wanted to adopt children to avoid the problems of "incompleteness" in their families.

In the context of these twin goals, secrecy in the adoption process was necessary, so that the adoptive parents could be regarded "as if" they were the biological parents of a child.

To confirm that the adoptive parents and the adopted child were "family," there were often extensive efforts to match physical characteristics of the adoptive parents and the child. In addition, adoption statutes generally provided for the alteration of the child's birth certificate to show the adoptive parents as "birth parents," and the sealing up of the adoption file containing details about the birth parents. The statutes also provided for the complete elimination of the child's legal relationships to biological parents and their extended families, and the creation of new legal relationships with the adoptive parents and their families. As social views about children born "outside marriage" and single parenting changed in the latter part of the 20th century, there were a number of controversial adoption cases (see, for example, *Martin v Duffell*, [1950] SCR 737; and *Re Mugford*, [1970] SCR 261). In reflecting on these historical relationships between social and legal ideas about families, consider whether there is a need for further law reform.

Current approaches to adoption

According to statutory regimes in recent decades, adoption orders must meet the test of the "best interests of the child," a test which Daly and Sobol suggest has tended to promote more openness in adoption processes. Often, one result of greater openness in adoption is the continuing presence of a biological parent in the life of a child who, at the same time, has two legally recognized (adoptive) parents. In this way, a birth parent's ability to have a relationship with a child who is under the age of majority may depend on a contract with the adoptive parents, or their willingness to permit such a relationship — but the birth parent's legal status is usually eliminated after an order for adoption. Recent amendments in Ontario and other provinces now permit greater "openness" in adoption. In reflecting on these relationships in the context of the issues discussed in this section, consider whether there is a need for more legal recognition of the biological parent's relationship to the child in such cases? How should it be achieved?

Adoption statistics in relation to changing societal views

According to the Vanier Institute of the Family, support for adoption in Canada is high. The data indicates that there are about 2,600 domestic adoptions (including public and private adoptions) in Canada each year. (See Vanier Institute of the Family, *Families Count* (Ottawa: VIF, 2010) at 56.) Yet there are many children who are living in care, many of who were available for adoption. In a 2012 report, the Child Welfare League of Canada estimates that there were between 76,000 and 85,000 children in care, and over 22,000 children awaiting adoption. (See Jeff Denault, CWLC, "Policy Brief: Adoption and Foster Care in Canada" online: <http://www.cwlc.ca/sites/default/files/guidelines/Policy%20Brief_FosterCareAdoption_Mar2012.pdf>.) Significantly, in 2009, there were about 2,100 international adoptions. Approximately one-quarter of the adoptions came from China. Other countries included the United States (12%), Ethiopia (8%), Vietnam (8%), and Haiti (7%): Statistics Canada, "International adoptions" (Ottawa: Statistics Canada, 2012), online: <www.statcan.gc.ca>. For some parents, international adoption is more attractive than domestic adoption because it is less likely that birth parents might seek the return of the child (see Vanier Institute of the Family, *Families Count* (Ottawa: VIF, 2010) at 56).

Daly and Sobol reported that the number of children born in Canada and subsequently placed in adoptive homes has declined steadily, with 5,376 children adopted in 1981 but only 2,836 so placed in 1990, a drop of 47.3

percent. Both the numbers and proportions of public, by contrast with private (and international), adoptions also decreased. However, analysis of the data demonstrated that the decline in adoptions was not connected to increased access to abortion, but rather to a significant increase in the percentage of pregnancies that resulted in the birth mother or a non-adopting surrogate raising the infant. Thus, in 1981, 46.1 percent of single young women chose to raise their infant, but this figure had risen to 59.9 percent by 1989. At the same time, many young mothers viewed adoption as a good alternative to raising the child:

> Unlike abortion, adoption was believed to be a fairly good alternative, at least in theory. ... In general, it was seen as an altruistic act on the part of the mother because it would serve the best interests of the child. ... On the other hand, the physical commitment to carry the child to term and the ensuing emotional attachment to it were major barriers to choosing this option. (Daly & Sobel at 7–10 and 20)

In reviewing some of the materials about adoption that follow, consider the extent to which legal policies may affect individual decision making about adoption, as well as the ways in which social expectations about (good) parenting are reflected in legal principles.

The adoption process

Generally, there are two routes for adoption.

In involuntary adoption cases, a child may be removed from its family because a Children's Aid Society has obtained a court order that the child is "in need of protection" pursuant to Ontario's *Child and Family Services Act*. Such children are often placed in foster homes for a period of time, but if the child's parents are unable to make necessary changes to provide a home for the child, a court may order that the child become a permanent ward. In this situation, the parents' rights are terminated and the child becomes eligible for adoption. Many such children will no longer be babies, of course, and (as noted above by Daly and Sobel), large numbers of such children live "in care" in Canada. In 2011, the Ontario legislature enacted Bill 179, the *Building Families and Supporting Youth to be Successful Act* (Royal Assent 1 June 2011), which amended the *Child and Family Services Act* to permit Crown wards to be adopted by their foster parents, with some financial supports (see SO 2011, c 12; and O Reg 394/11). Ontario parents who assume legal custody for Crown wards over age 10, or for sibling groups of any age, became eligible on 15 June 2012 for financial support of $950 per month per child ($11,400 annually) where they had net family incomes below $85,000. Some parents who adopted siblings prior to the introduction of this program complained about their exclusion: see Laurie Monsebraaten, "Adoptive Parents feel Shut Out by New Rules", *Toronto Star* (15 June 2012) A10. Some additional issues about children in need of protection are considered in Chapter Four.

The other route to adoption, the voluntary route, is the one discussed here. In this situation, the mother, or the mother and father in some circumstances, must give consent in writing to the adoption of the child, and all their parental rights are usually terminated when the order for adoption is made. Because such a decision is an important one, there are a number of requirements to be met with respect to the giving of consent by birth parents, the process for placing the child with adoptive parents, arrangements for assessing their competence, and finalizing the adoption order in a court. This category of adoptions also includes adoptions by step-parents in relation to blended families.

In addition to focusing on some issues relating to the processes of voluntary adoption, this section explores issues involving customary adoption practices, as well as the challenges of racialized and international adoption. See also Theodore Giesbrecht, "Adoption" in Nicholas Bala et al, eds, *Canadian Child Welfare Law: Children, Families and the State*, 2nd ed (Toronto: Thompson Educational Publishing, 2004).

"PARENTAL" CONSENT FOR ADOPTION

> When a law alters the history and the dynamics of a relationship in such a fundamental way, there must be safeguards against misunderstanding or abuse. The most important of these is consent. (Daly & Sobol at 68)

Who is a "parent" for purposes of consent?

Provincial adoption statutes generally require parental consent before the placement of children or orders for adoption and the resulting change of the child's legal status. However, there are a variety of different provisions (designed to ensure that consent is voluntary and informed) with respect to the following:

- who is entitled to consent;
- whether there are any limits on giving consent immediately after a child's birth or only after a "cooling off" period;
- whether and how consents may be withdrawn;
- circumstances in which a court may "dispense" with the consent of a parent; and
- the extent to which informed consent is ensured by way of counselling or legal advice.

See Ontario's *Child and Family Services Act*, RSO 1990, c C-11, ss 137–139, and provincial comparisons in Daly & Sobol at 68–71 and appendix A.

Consent in relation to mothers and fathers

Significantly, Ontario's *Child and Family Services Act*, s 137, which lists a number of categories of persons whose consent may be required, expressly includes "the child's mother." However, the consent of the child's father is required only if he falls within one of the categories described in section 137, which refers to the presumptions in section 8(1) of the *Children's Law Reform Act*, RSO 1990, c C-12. For example, a man who is married to the child's mother at the time of birth is presumed to be the child's father, although this presumption can be rebutted with evidence, on the balance of probabilities, that he is not the father.

This differential treatment of mothers and fathers was challenged by the father of a child whose mother had consented to the child's adoption. Because the father did not qualify within any of the categories of section 8(1) of the *Children's Law Reform Act*, he claimed that the differential treatment of mothers and fathers under section 137 for purposes of consenting to a child's adoption contravened the provisions of section 15 of the *Charter* on the basis of sex discrimination. How should such a claim be resolved?

Re Attorney General of Ontario and Nevins
(1988), 64 OR (2d) 311 (HC)

Pursuant to adoption proceedings under the *Child and Family Services Act*, the biological mother had executed the required consent and sworn by affidavit that the biological father was a "non-parent" under the provisions of the *Child and Family Services Act*, now section 137(1). The trial judge raised a constitutional question about the validity of this section, which includes all biological mothers within the definition of "parent," but excludes biological fathers unless they have married or cohabited with the mother, or acknowledged parenthood or otherwise demonstrated responsibility for the child.

The trial judge held that the definition of parent violated section 15(1) of the *Charter* because it discriminated on the basis of sex. The Attorney General applied for judicial review of the decision, for a ruling on the constitutionality of section 137(1), and an order of mandamus requiring the trial judge to proceed with the adoption.

The Divisional Court held (at 316) that section 137 did not violate section 15 of the *Charter*. This case, which was decided prior to the Supreme Court of Canada decision in *Law Society of British Columbia v Andrews*, [1989] 1 SCR 143, adopted the "similarly situated" test for equality:

> [O]ur reading of the sections as a whole lead us to the view that the only natural father who is not by definition a "parent" whose consent is required by [s. 137(1)] of the Act, is a male person who by an act of casual sexual intercourse impregnates a woman and demonstrates no sense of responsibility for the natural consequences of the act of sexual intercourse. It is a man who shows no sense of responsibility to the woman he has made pregnant nor to the life that he has helped to procreate....

With regard to the differential treatment between biological mothers and biological fathers, the court held (at 316–317) that the two groups were not similarly situated:

> The mother because of physical necessity has shown responsibility to the child. She carried and gave birth to it. The casual fornicator who has not demonstrated any interest in whether he did cause a pregnancy or demonstrate even the minimum responsibility to the child required by [s 137] cannot be said to be similarly situated to the mother. The statute recognizes as a parent, a father who demonstrates the minimum interest in the consequences of his sexual activity. Most fathers are defined as parents. Only those who do not demonstrate some responsibility to the child are not.

Moreover, the court held (at 318–19) that the legislation was designed to promote early placement of such a child with adoptive parents. Noting that delay was not in the child's best interest, the court concluded that

> the legislative measure by which the consent of the irresponsible casual fornicator is dispensed with is obviously fair and cannot be said to be arbitrary.

The court further noted (at 319) that because "there is little realistic possibility that the right of the casual fornicator would be accepted and exercised by him," the court ought to be cautious "before letting the protection of that right obstruct the fulfilment of an important government objective." Thus, if section 137(1) violated the equality guarantee, it was nevertheless justified pursuant to section 1 of the *Charter.*

What was the "important government objective" in this situation? Did the court reach an appropriate balance in this case? Are there factual differences between this case and *Trociuk*? To what extent is the balance in the legislation appropriate? In considering this question, note the critique of these provisions in the context of *Re SS*.

Re SS
2010 ONCJ 235

In this case, a woman became pregnant as a result of a relationship with a co-worker over a period of about 18 months. The parties' relationship was not exclusive and there were gaps in their time together. They never cohabited and neither party regarded their relationship as one of "some permanence." The parties ceased contact prior to the child's birth.

After the birth of the child, the mother decided to place the child for adoption. In providing her consent, she identified the father's first name, and his place and date of birth, but no other information. She also decided not to advise the father of the child's birth, and he remained unaware of the child's existence for some time. In due course, the child was placed with an adoptive family and they filed an application for an adoption order. By the time of the court's decision, the child was two years old, and had bonded with the adoptive parents and was thriving in their care. In granting the application for an adoption order, however, Waldman J expressed concern about the current statutory provisions, as follows:

[3] The concern of the court is that, given the nature and duration of the relationship between the biological parents, it is more than casual. The mother knows the name of the father, has information about him and his family and it is likely that he can be located without significant difficulty. Mother chose not to tell him about the pregnancy and he is unaware of the existence of this child. The question then is, given the legislation, should the father be notified of the existence of the child and the adoption? ...

[5] The child was placed for adoption shortly after her birth. I am satisfied based on the information provided that the home is an excellent placement, that the potential adoptive parents have provided excellent care and that the child is doing well in their care. I am also satisfied that the child has bonded to her potential adoptive parents. The biological mother signed the consent to allow the adoption and did not withdraw her consent within the time period. She continues to support the adoption. Mother signed the affidavit of parentage and swore that, according to the criteria set out in the Child and Family Services Act, she is the only person who qualifies as a parent and whose consent is required for the adoption to proceed.

[6] It is the case that within the 300 days before the birth the biological mother was not cohabiting with another person in a relationship of some permanence. At the time of the birth, the mother was not married or cohabiting with another person. She remains unmarried. No man has certified that he is the father under the Vital Statistics Act. No man has been recognized by a Court as the father of the child. In the twelve months preceding the swearing of the affidavit, no person acknowledged to the mother that he was the father or filed a statutory declaration of paternity. There is no written agreement or court order requiring any person to pay support or giving any person custody of or access to the child. Having said this, the biological mother acknowledged that she chose not to advise the father of her pregnancy and the birth of the child. Therefore, the court cannot conclude that his failure to do any of the above is the result of his lack of interest or concern. Moreover, it is clear that the biological mother could locate the biological father if she wished to do so, In fact, I am satisfied that the father could be located now without difficulty....

[8] There is no requirement to give notice to the biological father even if he is known if he is not a parent as defined by section 137.

[9] The question then is whether the court ought to read into section 137(1) the requirement that the biological father must be notified of the birth of the child and given an opportunity to act in a manner that falls within the definition of parent where the relationship, although not one of permanence, is one that is more than casual; where the name of the father is known to the mother; where the father is easily located; and absent any special circumstances such as violence or fear.

[10] The purpose of the statutory requirements of Part VII is to create an adoption system that allows for the permanent placement of children in adoptive homes in a manner that ensures that the interests of the biological parents are protected and that the placements are appropriate for the child. These principles are, as always, balanced against the best interests of the child who is the subject of the adoption. Within this framework,

the definition of parent allows the biological mother to act unilaterally in determining whether to inform the father of the pregnancy and birth. The biological mother ought not to be put to the potentially onerous requirement of locating what has been traditionally called the "casual fornicator." Certainly, there are circumstances in which compelling the biological mother to locate the biological father would be too onerous or dangerous.

[11] Having said that, the requirement that she not be required to do so is based largely on the fact that success is highly unlikely and that making such a requirement would potentially cause great emotional stress to the mother. It arguably also remains in the statute from a time when being an "unwed mother" carried great social stigma. It is not rooted in the child's best interests except insofar as encouraging or at least failing to discourage adoption is arguably in the child's best interests.

[12] It is noteworthy that, in Part III of the Child and Family Services Act dealing with child protection, there has been the recognition of the importance of the biological connection and increased emphasis put on placement with biological parents, extended family (kin) and even community before adoption by strangers is considered. This is the case even in circumstances in which the child is apprehended at birth. In fact, in this case, if the baby had been apprehended at the hospital immediately after birth rather than placed for adoption, the appropriate Children's Aid Society would have been required by law to locate the father, and if he or his family wished to care for the child and was deemed able to do so, the child would be placed with that family member regardless of mother's wishes....

The court reviewed several cases, including *Re Attorney General and Nevins*, and continued:

[20] While there is no Charter issue in this case, the decision of the court presents a cogent statement of the policy and other considerations which form the underpinnings of the manner in which the courts have interpreted the legislation and arguably the very drafting of the legislation itself. I respectfully take issue with this argument as being outdated. Moreover, it is not consistent with the circumstances in this case.

[21] The relationship between the biological parents in this case, although not one of some permanence, was more than casual. The parents knew each other for a number of years and saw each other off and on for about 18 months. I assume that the lack of a sense of responsibility referenced above by the Divisional Court is caused by the so called casual fornicator not determining after the fact whether the sexual encounter resulted in pregnancy, not that he was informed and took no responsibility. In this case, there is no evidence that the biological father knew about the pregnancy. Given the dates provided, it is also unclear whether the biological mother knew she was pregnant before, according to her, they had their last contact. And given the biological mother's position about even advising him about the adoption, it is unclear whether she would have told him about the pregnancy even if asked.

[22] I would suggest that, given the general consensus that the single most significant factor governing the rules concerning adoption is the child's best interests, the legislature ought to reconsider allowing biological mothers not to inform the father of the child's birth and her plans to adopt, where the relationship is more than casual although not of some permanence, where the father is easily located and where there are no safety concerns, violence or otherwise. The growing understanding of the

importance of connection to biological roots, as reflected in the amendments to Part III of the CFSA, requires this reconsideration. Given the importance of early placement, the process needs to be done at the very front end of the adoption process.

CONSIDERATIONS IN THIS CASE

[23] I am satisfied that the relationship between the biological parents in this case was more than that of a "casual fornicator." I take no position about whether the biological father acted in an irresponsible manner. According to the evidence, he was not made aware of the pregnancy. The biological mother offers no reason other than her choice not to tell him because the relationship ended. There is evidence that the biological father was not honest and lost his job and faced criminal charges but no evidence that he was violent or posed any risk to the biological mother.

[24] I am satisfied, however, that, notwithstanding the above, the law does not require the biological mother to inform the biological father of the pregnancy, birth of the child or the adoption, even if he is known and easily found. Part VII is a complete code. It defines father for the purpose of adoption and I am satisfied that the biological father in this case does not fit within the definition. Moreover, this child was placed with her present potential adoptive family since birth. She is now almost two years old. These are the only parents that she knows. The evidence before this court is that she is bonded to these parents, considers them to be her parents and is thriving in their care. It would be virtually impossible to contemplate removing her from this family in order to place her with a stranger even if that stranger is her biological father.

[25] While I have expressed concerns about the legislation, I am satisfied for the reasons given that this adoption should be allowed and I will make the order requested.

Notes and Questions

Fathers and consent to adoption
Similar challenges have been raised in other provinces:

- In British Columbia, a constitutional challenge succeeded (in the context of a statute with somewhat different wording) in *Re FL; NM v Superintendent of Family and Child Services and Ministry of Human Resources*, [1987] 3 WWR 176 (BCSC). Some later decisions recognized the right to consent on the part of biological fathers if they had demonstrated an interest in the child. For example, see *M(CG) v W(C)* (1989), 63 DLR (4th) 216 (BCCA); and *Waddell v Halley* (1993), 48 RFL (3d) 203 (BCSC). See also the *Family Law Act*, SBC 2011, c 25, at Part 3.

- In Nova Scotia, a similar challenge by a biological father was initially upheld when the court invoked its *parens patriae* jurisdiction, but the trial court's decision was overturned on appeal. See *Re T and Children's Aid Society and Family Services of Colchester County* (1992), 91 DLR (4th) 230 (NSSC); (1992), 92 DLR (4th) 289 (NSCA).

More recently, courts have refused to extend parental rights to fathers unless they have made efforts to identify their parental status in accordance with applicable legislation. See *C v Y* (2003), 41 RFL (5th) 245 (Ont Ct J); and *Re British Columbia Birth Registration No 06-014023* (2007), 42 RFL (6th) 388 (BCSC). In the latter case, the court also concluded that *Trociuk* had no application to the adoption context, because the definition of "parent" was set out in the adoption statute.

In a comment on the legal definition of "father" in differing contexts, Navnit Duhra concluded that

> [e]mphasis in the law has been significantly placed on the genetic component of what it means to be a father, rather than on social and contextual factors. This is demonstrated by Deschamps J.'s decision in *Trociuk*, where she reduced fatherhood to genetic paternity and accorded genetic fathers the full panoply of constitutionalized paternal rights. [However, the list of factors to define "fathers" in the BC legislation include those related to contextual factors, and in this way, the legislation] is moving in the right direction. That is, there is more to be said for what constitutes a father than mere genetics, and the law should not blindly protect those men who engage in sexual relations and then do not attempt to determine if any child may have resulted.... (Navnit Duhra, "Fathers not Shortchanged by Current Adoption Legislation" (2008) 13 Appeal 22 at para 17)

Do you agree that there is more to fatherhood than genetics? How should "fathers" be defined in law in different contexts? To what extent is there a need for legislative reform in Ontario, as suggested in *Re SS*?

THE LEGAL STATUS OF AN ADOPTED CHILD

> [In adoption,] the woman who gave birth to [the child] is deemed to not have had a child and to not be the mother; a different woman is then deemed to have had the child and to be the mother. Leaving aside the issue of what exactly makes a mother ... why is the law so intent on erasing the motherhood of one of these women? (Katrysha Bracco, "Patriarchy and the Law of Adoption: Beneath the Best Interests of the Child" (1997) 35 Alta L Rev 1035 at 1044)

The traditional exclusion of birth parent access to a child after adoption

An order for adoption results in a child becoming in law the child of an adoptive parent and ceasing to be the child of a birth parent. For example, section 158(2) of Ontario's *Child and Family Services Act* states that, for all purposes of law, as of the date of the adoption order:

> (a) the adopted child becomes the child of the adoptive parent and the adoptive parent becomes the parent of the adopted child....

Section 158 also expressly eliminates the parent–child relationship with the birth parent, and section 143(1) provides that access orders are terminated when a child is placed for adoption by a Children's Aid Society. Courts have created a few exceptions to the application of section 143 in cases of family adoptions, subject to the child's best interests. See *Catholic Children's Aid Society v TS* (1989), 20 RFL (3d) 337 (Ont CA); and *R(S) v R(M)* (1998), 43 RFL (4th) 116 (Ont CA), and the case Annotation by James McLeod.

"Openness" orders and agreements: Recent developments

In this context, the concept of "open" adoption has steadily gained support. In 1998, the Canadian Bar Association — Ontario made recommendations for post-adoption "contact," distinguishing this concept from access after adoption. See Marvin Bernstein et al, "Adoption with Access or 'Open Adoption'" (1991–92) 8 Can Fam LQ 283. Daly and Sobel also recommended more openness in adoption (at 107).

In 2006, amendments were added to the *Child and Family Services Act* (SO 2006, c 5) to recognize "openness orders" (ss 145.1 and 145.2 and 153.1 to 153.5). In addition, section 153.6 recognized "openness agreements," which may be made at any time, before or after an adoption, and which may include a process for resolving disputes. The agreement is between the adoptive parent and any of the persons listed in section 153.6(1), including, for example, a birth parent, birth relative or birth sibling, or a member of the child's extended family or community with whom the child has a significant relationship; and if the child is a native person, the agreement may be made with the child's band or native community.

In *Re M(S)* (2007), 45 RFL (6th) 345 (Ont Sup Ct), the court reviewed the terms of an agreement between a birth father and two women, one of whom was the birth mother and the other her lesbian partner, and granted an adoption order, which permitted the lesbian partner to become a co-mother. In doing so, however, the court held that it was not possible to enforce portions of the agreement that provided residual custody rights to the birth father.

To what extent do recent amendments regarding "openness" in adoptions reflect a broader conception of "families" than in the past? Some scholars have argued, for example, that traditional arrangements for adoption masked ideologies about "natural" families and about mothering. In this context, the fact that birth mothers might relinquish their children tended to undermine ideas about the primacy of "natural" mother–child bonds. Similarly, an adoptive mother might not be seen as a "real" mother because of the lack of biological connection to an adopted child. For example, Katrysha Bracco argued that adoption practices in Canada perpetuate the nuclear family, a patriarchal family model. See Katrysha Bracco, "Patriarchy and the Law of Adoption: Beneath the Best Interests of the Child" (1997) 35 Alta L Rev 1035; and Josephine Reeves, "The Deviant Mother and Child: The Development of Adoption as an Instrument of Social Control" (1993) 20 JL & Soc'y 412.

Although these comments were made before the 2006 amendments regarding "openness" in adoption practices, is there a need for additional reforms to respond to these concerns?

Access after adoption: In the "best interests" of children

Most provincial statutes require that adoption orders be made in the best interest of children. See *Child and Family Services Act*, ss 136(2) and (3). In this context, however, it is important to have regard to the precise wording of provincial statutes. For example, some access for birth parents after adoption was confirmed in relation to New Brunswick's legislation in *Nouveau-Brunswick (Ministre de la Santé & des Services Communautaires) v L(M)*, [1998] 2 SCR 534.

However, a court in British Columbia held that although access by a birth father to his daughter was in the child's best interests, his claim for access was denied because the child's mother and her husband (who was seeking to adopt the child) found visits by the child's father emotionally difficult. Thus the court granted the adoption and denied the biological father's continuing access to the girl, aged three and a half. Although critical of the attitudes of the adoptive father and the child's mother, the court accepted that their emotions were understandable. See *Re British Columbia Birth Registration No. 86-09-038808* (1990), 26 RFL (3d) 203 (BCSC).

Issues about the best interests of the child test were also considered in a case involving a request for access by a young boy to his sister. Both had been permitted to immigrate to Canada to be adopted, but their adoptive mother later decided to raise only one child and placed the boy in foster care. See *P(MAR) v V(A)* (1997), 33 RFL (4th) 124 (Ont Prov Div); and (1998), 40 RFL (4th) 411 (Ont Gen Div). Although access was eventually arranged for the siblings, the adoptive mother thwarted the boy's access efforts and he was raised on his own in a series of foster homes. His tragic circumstances some years later, when he was facing deportation, were reported in the press. See Margaret Philp, "A One-Way Ticket Out of Only Nation He Knows", *The Globe and Mail* (15 July 2003) A1.

ADOPTION RECORDS AND DISCLOSURE

Traditional non-disclosure approaches

There can surely be no doubt but that any child, knowing he has been adopted, will be curious about his origins. ... [T]here is more than mere curiosity but a basic, if sometimes unexpressed, need for a child, who knows he has been adopted, to get in touch with his natural parents. This need becomes most apparent during early adolescence. To know who his *real parents* are gives a child a sense of identity, an assurance of belonging, and an awareness that he has not come from nowhere, but has his own place in history as the child of known parents....

On the other hand, the sense of security of the child in his new home ought not to be disturbed readily. He must continue to know that this is indeed his home, that he is entitled to demand the loyalty of his new parents and that he is obliged to give them his loyalty in return. That sense of security, and loyalty, would be diminished if the adopting parents felt that a natural parent could interfere with the affection of the child, or their authority over him. They might feel that they were *mere custodians* of the child, with less than *ordinary parental rights and responsibilities*. Another factor, of general public policy, which I think is almost conclusive with children's aid societies, is that prospective adopting parents would be more difficult to find if they were generally aware that natural parents might be permitted to regain contact with adopted children [emphasis added]. (*RJL v Children's Aid Society of Metropolitan Toronto*, [1976] OJ No 138 (HCJ) (QL) at paras 9–10)

This excerpt from a decision in the 1970s clearly reveals traditional views about the need to balance the interests of members of the "adoption triangle": the biological parent(s), the child and the adoptive parents. In many jurisdictions, including Ontario, adoption legislation responded to these views by providing for the release of only "non-identifying" information, such as medical records; by contrast, "identifying" information that might connect a birth parent and a child was subject to stringent controls, and generally released only for emergency purposes, if at all. Pursuant to Ontario's adoption regime, for example, courts denied applications by birth mothers for identifying information in relation to their adopted children. See *Ferguson v Director of Child Welfare* (1984), 36 RFL (2d) 405 (Ont CA); and *Tyler v District Court of Ontario* (1986), 1 RFL (3d) 139 (Ont Dist Ct).

This traditional approach of non-disclosure of adoption records was carefully reviewed in 1985 in a report that recommended greater openness with respect to these records. See Ralph Garber, *Disclosure of Adoption Information* (Toronto: Ministry of Community and Social Services, 1985). Following this report, an Adoption Disclosure Register was established, but identifying information could be exchanged only if both parties agreed. In 2006, an adult adoptee unsuccessfully challenged these provisions pursuant to section 7 of the *Charter*. See *Marchand v Ontario* (2006), 81 OR (3d) 172 (Sup Ct).

Recent disclosure amendments in Ontario legislation

However, in 2005, the Ontario legislature enacted the *Adoption Information Disclosure Act, 2005*, SO 2005, c 25, which amended sections of the *Vital Statistics Act*. According to these amendments, birth parents and adopted children (at the age of majority) could apply for identifying information, but if the other party had filed a "no contact" notice, their request for information would be subject to a written undertaking not to contact the other party — with a penalty of criminal prosecution and a fine of $50,000. The amendments also permitted parties to apply to a Review Board for a non-disclosure order. Significantly, these amendments applied to both past and future adoptions.

The legislation was challenged successfully in *Cheskes v Ontario (AG)* (2007), 87 OR (3d) 581 (Sup Ct), just two weeks after it was proclaimed in force. Four applicants (three adult adoptees and a birth parent) argued that the opening of confidential adoption records on a retroactive basis and the removal of the consent requirement violated their right to privacy under section 7 of the *Charter* and was not justified pursuant to section 1. As the court noted at para 70, Ontario's new legislation was unique — it was the only jurisdiction to give "a retroactive, unqualified right to obtain confidential identifying information of an adopted person or birth parent without the consent or even over the objections of the individual whose personal information is being disclosed." In the result, the court declared the amendments invalid as infringing the protection of privacy in section 7 of the *Charter.*

In June 2009, Ontario's *Access to Adoption Records Act*, a further effort to open adoption records, took effect. See *Access to Adoption Records Act (Vital Statistics Statute Law Amendment)*, SO 2008, c 5. This legislation included a disclosure veto to prevent release of identifying information for adoptions finalized before 1 September 2008. In addition, birth parents and adult adopted children may file no contact notices and if they are willing to be contacted, they may indicate contact preferences.

As of 15 June 2009, 2,737 persons had applied for adoption informa-tion, and there were 1,446 no contact requests, 1,827 requests regarding contact preferences and 5,905 requests for disclosure vetos. See Christopher Guly, "New Adoption Information Disclosure Law Protects Privacy", *The Lawyers Weekly* (3 July 2009). As Guly noted, Ontario was the fifth Canadian province, after British Columbia, Alberta, Manitoba, and New-foundland and Labrador, to open its adoption records — records that had been closed in Ontario since 1927.

Notes and Questions

Rethinking family secrets in the adoption context

In *Family Law and Personal Life*, John Eekelaar argued that there is a need to align legal and physical truth as a means of overcoming shame in relation to illegitimacy or adoption. According to Eekelaar, keeping secrets about paternity and parenthood denies "truth" and justice to children in a family. Instead, older family members seek to control the next generation by preserving their social order. See John Eekelaar, *Family Law and Personal Life* (Oxford: Oxford University Press, 2006).

In reflecting on Eekelaar's argument, Carol Smart analyzed the history of legal and social ideas about family secrets and suggested a need to assess how policies about truth may change personal and family relationships. For example, in the U.K. context, she argued that

[a]doptive parents are now encouraged to view adoption as a way of looking after someone else's child rather than as a way of acquiring their
"own" child. There is a clear policy preference for allowing an adopted
child to know about their bio-parent(s) and even to have contact if it is
suitable and feasible.... The drive towards genetic truth in familial relationships presumes that openness is good because it creates a level playing
field of knowledge. However, family members themselves may not be on
an equal footing and so this kind of openness may simply bring with it
different forms of vulnerability.... (Carol Smart, "Family Secrets: Law and
Understandings of Openness in Everyday Relationships" (2009) 38:4 Journal of Social Policy 551 at 564–565)

In the light of these approaches to "truth" in relation to families, consider whether the recent amendments concerning adoption disclosure in
Ontario achieve an appropriate balance. Are there family members who
may continue to be vulnerable? This issue is also relevant to assisted reproduction, particularly with respect to anonymity for sperm donors, an issue
addressed later in this chapter.

Additional Resources

Cindy L Baldassi, "The Quest to Access Closed Adoption Files in Canada:
    Understanding Social Context and Legal Resistance to Change"
    (2005) 21 Can J Fam L 211.
D Marianne Brower Blair, "The Impact of Family Paradigms, Domestic
    Constitutions and International Conventions on Disclosure of an
    Adopted Person's Identities and Heritage: A Comparative Examina-
    tion" (2001) 22 Mich J Intl L 587.
Naomi Cahn, "Birthing Relationships" (2002) 17 Wis Women's LJ 163.
Lori Chambers, "Newborn Adoption: Birth Mothers, Genetic Fathers, and
    Reproductive Autonomy" (2010) 26:2 Can J Fam L 339.
Alice Diver, *A Law of Blood-ties — The 'Right' to Access Genetic Ancestry*
    (New York: Springer, 2014).
Nancy E Dowd, "A Feminist Analysis of Adoption" (1994) 107 Harv L Rev
    913.
Jeannie House, "The Changing Face of Adoption: The Challenge of Open
    and Custom Adoption" (1997) 13 Can Fam LQ 333.
Office of the Information and Privacy Commissioner of Ontario, *A Review
    of the Literature on Adoption-Related Research: The Implications for
    Proposed Legislation* (2006).
Elizabeth J Samuels, "The Idea of Adoption: An Inquiry into the History of
    Adult Adoptee Access to Birth Records" (2001) 53 Rutgers L Rev
    367.
Shirley Senoff, "Open Adoptions in Ontario and the Need for Legislative
    Reform" (1998) 15 Can J Fam L 183.
Sarah Wilson, "Identity, Genealogy, and the Social Family: The Case of
    Donor Insemination" (1997) 11 Intl JL Pol'y & Fam 270.
SM Wolfgram, "Openness in Adoption: What we Know so Far — A Critical
    Review of the Literature" (2008) 53:2 Social Work 133.

ADOPTION IN CONTEXT: CUSTOMARY PRACTICES, INTERRACIAL AND INTERNATIONAL ADOPTION

Custom adoption

> For many Aboriginal people, customary Aboriginal adoption is preferable to statutory adoption schemes as it permits the natural parents to know where their child has been placed, and it emphasizes and recognizes the importance of maintaining the child's cultural ties. (Judge Murray Sinclair et al, "Aboriginal Child Welfare" in Nicholas Bala et al, eds, *Canadian Child Welfare Law: Children, Families and the State*, 2nd ed (Scarborough, ON: Thompson Educational Publishing, 2004) 199 at 213)

Custom Adoption, "Openness," and Legal Recognition

By contrast with statutory regimes for adoption in Canada, traditional arrangements among Indigenous people that allowed children to be raised by adults other than their biological parents were not secret, and the children's relationships with their biological parents often continued. However, although the term "custom adoption" is widely used, the actual arrangements for adoption vary among First Nations. See Jeannie House, "The Changing Face of Adoption: The Challenge of Open and Custom Adoption" (1997) 13 Can Fam LQ 333. Recent interest in "open" adoption and increasing access to adoption records also make some of these custom adoption practices more attractive.

In his memoirs, Justice Sissons described the problems created by the statutory requirements for adoption in the NWT. He explained that, because of these problems, when he went on circuit to the Eastern Arctic in 1965, he registered as many "custom adoptions" as possible; in Frobisher Bay (now Iqaluit), he issued more than 200 declarations. See J Sissons, *Judge of the Far North* (Toronto: McClelland & Stewart, 1968) at 142–145.

More recently, in *Casimel v Insurance Corp of BC* (1993), 106 DLR (4th) 720, the B.C. Court of Appeal legally recognized a custom adoption for members of the Stellaquo Band of the Carrier People, thereby entitling the adoptive parents to death benefits after their adopted son died in an accident.

In concluding that it was appropriate to recognize a custom adoption, the court cited a number of earlier cases in which Canadian courts had recognized custom adoption:

- In *Re Katie* (1961), 32 DLR (2d) 686 (NWT Terr Ct), Justice Sissons decided that an Inuit customary adoption conferred the status of parent and child on the respective parties to the adoption. In doing so, he concluded that the *Northwest Territories Act*, the *Adoption Ordinance* and the *Child Welfare Ordinance* did not end customary adoptions by Inuit custom.

- In *Re Beaulieu* (1969), 3 DLR (3d) 479 (NWT Terr Ct), Justice Morrow followed *Re Katie* and decided that a Dogrib Indian customary adoption should be recognized.

- In *Re Deborah E4-789* (1972), 27 DLR (3d) 225 (NWTSC) an Inuit customary adoption was challenged by the birth parents. Justice Morrow recognized the Inuit customary adoption and the status it conferred, and he rejected the claim of the birth parents. On appeal, this decision was upheld, and Justice Johnson confirmed that

> [c]ustom has always been recognized by the common law [on the basis of evidence extending] ... as far back as living memory goes, of a continuous, peaceable, and uninterrupted user of the custom ... (see (1972), 28 DLR (3d) 483 (NWT CA) at 488).

As a comment on *Casimel* concluded, by recognizing custom adoption, this case was also significant for Aboriginal self-government. See Caryl Silver, "Case Comment" (1995) 3 CNLR 8. In addition, the decision in *Re Tagornak*, [1984] 1 CNLR 185 (NWTSC), confirmed recognition of custom adoption for Aboriginal children pursuant to section 35 of the Constitution. In 1994, the NWT legislature enacted the *Aboriginal Custom Adoption Recognition Act*, SNWT 1994, c 26. For a case interpreting its application in relation to a request for child support against a biological father, see *SKK v JS*, [1999] NWTJ No 94 (SC).

Additional Resources

Cindy L Baldassi, "The Legal Status of Aboriginal Customary Adoption across Canada: Comparisons, Contrasts and Convergences" (2006) 39 UBC L Rev 63.

Bill Lomax, "Hlugwit'y, Hluuxw'y — My Family, My Child: The Survival of Customary Adoption in British Columbia" (1997) 14 Can J Fam L 197.

Maev O'Collins, "The Influence of Western Adoption Laws on Customary Adoption in the Third World" in Philip Bean, ed, *Adoption: Essays in Social Policy, Law, and Sociology* (London: Tavistock Publications, 1984) 288.

Report of the Aboriginal Justice Inquiry of Manitoba: The Justice System and Aboriginal People (Manitoba: Queen's Printer, 1991).

Norman Zlotkin, "Judicial Recognition of Aboriginal Customary Law in Canada: Selected Marriage and Adoption Cases" (1984) 4 CNLR 1.

Adoption and "best interests": Issues of race and culture

Aboriginal Children and Adoption Practices

[The decline in babies available for adoption in the 1960s and 1970s coincided with a rise in social consciousness, making transracial adoption attractive.] Some wanted a white child and settled for one of "mixed or other" race. Some were emotionally caught by agency advertising of available minority-race children. Others, moved by the so-called "rescue fantasy," adopted in order to "save" an imperilled child. A significant number found in transracial adoption a means of realizing their belief in racial integration, and viewed the child's racial and cultural heritage as a valuable contribution to the family.... The study of transracial adoption is a study of values in conflict. Adoption outside racial lines is an affirmation of ideals of racial integration; conversely, it is a blow to goals of racial autonomy. The two views are apparently irreconcilable. (Anne McGillivray, "Transracial Adoption and the Status Indian Child" (1985) 4 Can J Fam L 437 at 449–450)

To what extent is this critique applicable to the following case?

Racine v Woods
(1983), 36 RFL (2d) 1 (SCC)

WILSON J:

This appeal [from the Manitoba Court of Appeal (1983), 32 RFL (2d) 153] emphasizes once more, this time in an inter-racial context, that the law no longer treats children as the property of those who gave them birth but focuses on what is in their best interests.

L.G.W. ("L.") was born at Portage la Prairie, Manitoba, on 4th September 1976 to L.W., an Indian who was at the time the wife of L.W. L.W. was not the father of the child and divorce proceedings were underway when L. was born. There are two children of the W. marriage, J., aged 9, and L., aged 8. Mrs. W. on her own admission had a serious alcohol problem and was unable to care for L. First her brother and then her sister took the infant. The older children, J. and L., stayed with their father.

On 20th October 1976, when she was six weeks old, L. was apprehended by the Children's Aid Society of Central Manitoba pursuant to the protection sections of the *Child Welfare Act, 1974* (Man.), c. 30 (also CCSM, c. C80) ("the Act"), and placed in a foster home. In February 1977 Kimelman Prov. J., with her mother's consent, made her a ward of the society for a one-year period which was subsequently extended for a further six months. On 11th February 1977 L. was placed in the foster home of S.R. (later R.) and her husband L.R. The R.s separated in the summer of 1977 and in September of that year S. started to cohabit with A.R. whom she subsequently married. L. remained in their home with the sanction of the Children's Aid Society until the wardship order expired in March 1978. Arrangements were then made by the society to return her to her mother who was living in Brandon with her other two children. The R.s co-operated fully in this transfer which took place on 4th May 1978.

Mrs. W. had made no effort to contact L. during the period of the wardship but had suggested to the society early in 1978 that her sister might adopt her. The sister apparently had reservations about this and nothing came of it. The R.s by this time had, of course, developed an attachment to the child and were concerned as to whether she was being properly cared for. They therefore took up Mrs. W.'s invitation to pay her a visit. In fact they paid two visits to see L. and on the second visit in May 1978, with Mrs. W.'s consent, took L. home with them. The evidence as to Mrs. W.'s intention to [relinquish] custody of L. to the R.s is conflicting. She says they were to have L. "just for a while" until she came for her in a couple of weeks' time. The R.s believed that she had surrendered the child to them on a permanent basis. She had confided to them that she was having difficulties with L.W. with whom she was periodically cohabiting and she appeared to be aware herself that she was in a state of emotional instability. Consistent with the R.s' understanding that they were now to have L. on a permanent basis they got in touch with the Children's Aid Society about the possibility of adopting her. Mrs. W. by this time had returned to the reserve with L.W. The society advised the R.s that it no longer had responsibility for the child and that if they wished to adopt her they should retain legal counsel. They followed this advice and on 5th October 1978 filed a notice of receiving a child for private adoption under s. 102(1) [re-enacted 1979, c. 22, s. 72] of the Act.

The R.s heard nothing from Mrs. W. until October 1978 when she arrived at their home announcing that she had left L.W. because he was abusing her, that she was on her way to Regina and wanted her sister to have L. The R.s refused to give her up. They heard no further word from Mrs. W. until January 1982 when she launched an application for habeas corpus. On 24th February 1982 the R.s applied for an order of de facto adoption.

It is apparent from the evidence that Mrs. W. from January 1978 on was attempting with varying degrees of success to rehabilitate herself. She wanted to rid herself of her alcohol problem, to free herself of her association with L.W., and to engage in a program of self-improvement. However, none of this was easy and periods of achievement when she underwent treatment for alcoholism and attended classes to upgrade her education would be followed by periods of backsliding. It took her five years and the support of friends, relatives and her extended family on the reserve to accomplish her objective. By the time she did L. was 5 or 6 years old and an established part of the R. family. They had brought her up as if she were their own. The evidence discloses that they are a very fine couple, active and respected in their community, and excellent parents. They have two other children, M., aged 4 and 2-year-old J.

L. is apparently a well-adjusted child of average intelligence, attractive and healthy, does well in school, attends Sunday School and was baptized in the church the R. family attends. She knows that S.R. is not her natural mother, and Mrs. W. is her natural mother, and that she is a native Indian. She knows that A.R. is not her natural father and that he is a Métis. This has all been explained to her by the R.s who have encouraged her to be proud of her Indian culture and heritage. None of this seems to have presented any problem for her thus far. She is now 7 years old and the expert witnesses agree that the R.s are her "psychological parents."

An unfortunate incident occurred on 3rd February 1982. When the court proceedings brought by Mrs. W. in January 1982 were adjourned for the preparation of home study reports, she decided to take things into her own hands and with the assistance of friends attempted to abduct L. first from her school and then from the R. home. Fortunately, the child was not in the home at the time. The RCMP had to be called. The R.s obtained an ex parte order granting them interim custody and enjoining Mrs. W. from further attempts at abduction. Mrs. W. moved to vary the order and was granted supervised access. On her first exercise of access she arranged for a reporter and a photographer from the Winnipeg Free Press to be present. The story was given considerable prominence in the newspaper with a photograph of Mrs. W. and L. The child was upset by the notoriety.

The R.s' application for adoption and Mrs. W.'s application for custody were heard by Krindle Co. Ct. J. in a trial lasting eight days. The application for custody was dismissed and the adoption order granted. Mrs. W. appealed to the Manitoba Court of Appeal which overturned the adoption order, made L. a ward of the Court of Appeal, granted custody to the R.s and left it open to Mrs. W. to apply subsequently for access or custody. The Court of Appeal subsequently on a motion for directions referred Mrs. W.'s application for access to Huband JA. Huband JA, on being advised that an application was being made for leave to appeal to the Supreme Court of Canada, held the application for access in abeyance. This court gave the R.s leave to appeal on 17th May 1983 and ordered a stay of proceedings. L. continued to reside with the R.s and Mrs. W. has had no access since Krindle Co. Ct. J's order of adoption on 12th May 1982. Mrs. W. cross-appealed in this court on the ground that the Manitoba Court of Appeal erred in not restoring legal custody to her when they set aside the order of adoption in favour of the R.s.

The R.s' application for adoption was made under s. 103 [as amended 1982, c. 45, s. 22] of the Act, i.e., a de facto adoption based on the fact that L. had been cared for and maintained by them for a period of three consecutive years. Section 103(2) states that in the case of such an adoption the consent of the parents or guardian is not required. Krindle Co. Ct. J. found that the R.s had cared for and maintained L. for the required three-year period and indeed had rescued her as an infant from an intolerable situation, given her an excellent home, been devoted parents, were fully sensitive to the special problems of raising a native Indian child in a predominantly white environment and were coping with those problems in a mature and responsible fashion. She concluded that the R.s were well able to cope with any identity crisis L. might face as a teenager. Moreover, as a Métis A.R. was no stranger to the hurt racial prejudice could inflict on a sensitive soul and, in the view of the learned trial judge, was a model for L. of how to survive as a member of a much maligned minority. As to Mrs. W., Krindle Co. Ct. J. expressed respect and admiration for her courage and determination and the degree of success she had achieved in rehabilitating herself. At the same time, however, she expressed some concern as to whether she was going to be able to maintain her progress. She saw danger signals in "the venom of her anti-white feelings" and wondered what effect "her visible hatred for all things white" would have on her child. She also wondered whether Mrs. W.'s concern was for the child as a person or as a political issue. The media incident, in Krindle Co. Ct. J's view, manifested an incredible indifference to the effect such an incident might have on her child. It made L., a very private little girl, into a "cause célèbre" in her school and community. Krindle Co. Ct. J. concluded that it was in the child's best interests that she remain with the R.s.

In addition to finding that it was in L.'s best interests to remain with the R.s, Krindle Co. Ct. J. also made a finding that Mrs. W. had abandoned L. between October 1978 and January 1982. She made this finding because of her concern as to whether s. 103(2) had the effect of dispensing with parental rights in the case of a de facto adoption. If it did have that effect, then the sole issue was the best interests of the child. However, if it did not, then under the common law a natural mother could lose custody of her child to a stranger in blood only by abandoning it or so misconducting herself that in the opinion of the court it would be improper to leave the child with her: See *Martin v. Duffell*, [1950] SCR 737, 4 DLR 1; *Hepton v. Maat*, [1957] SCR 606, 10 DLR (2d) 1; *McNeilly v. Agar*, [1958] SCR 52, 11 DLR (2d) 721.

Having made her findings as to abandonment and the child's best interests, Krindle Co. Ct. J. made the adoption order in favour of the R.s and dismissed Mrs. W.'s application for custody.

As already mentioned, the Court of Appeal overturned the adoption order. Each of the panel of three judges gave separate reasons. Hall JA would have affirmed the adoption order but, because his two colleagues were for overturning it, he yielded to the majority and then went on to align himself with the alternate course advanced by O'Sullivan JA rather than that advanced by Matas JA.

O'Sullivan JA decided that the best course to follow was to make L. a ward of the court with custody in the R.s, leaving it open to Mrs. W. at some future time to apply for access. Matas JA, on the other hand, did not think making the child a ward of the court was a workable alternative. He favoured a new trial as to custody (as opposed to adoption) with interim custody in the R.s in the meantime and such access to Mrs. W. as might be agreed upon or as might be ordered by the court.

On what grounds then did the Court of Appeal upset the judgment of the learned trial judge? Hall JA identified the basis on which in his view it should have been affirmed. He pointed out that the trial judge had the tremendous advantage of seeing and hearing the parties and their witnesses and that she had accepted the evidence of some experts in preference to that of others. She had the benefit also of home study reports and reflected in her reasons the concern expressed in them about the consequences of moving the child from the only permanent home she had ever known and separating her from the de facto parents to whom she was now psychologically bonded. He referred to the strong statement made by the trial judge after a review of the whole of the evidence [32 RFL (2d), at 157]:

> I have absolutely no doubt whatsoever that the circumstances of this case demand the granting of an order of adoption of L. to the R.s.

He found that the findings and conclusions reached by the trial judge were fully supported by the evidence. He pointed out that the trial judge was well aware of the importance of L.'s cultural background and heritage and the potential difficulties involved in an inter-racial adoption. She gave particular attention to the evidence of the expert who suggested that L. could face a major identity crisis in her teenage years as a result of being reared in a predominantly white environment. She concluded that the R.s would be well able to deal with such a crisis if it arose.

Matas and O'Sullivan JJA had certain concerns in common about the judgment of the learned trial judge. ...

Wilson J reviewed these issues and concluded:

It is apparent that Matas and O'Sullivan JJA put an entirely different interpretation on the evidence from that put upon it by the learned trial judge and I agree with the appellant that it is not the function of an appellate court to re-interpret the evidence. ...

Accordingly, even if a finding of abandonment was a prerequisite for an adoption order under s. 103, I am of the view that the evidence was there to support Krindle Co. Ct. J's finding.

Nor do I accept the submission of counsel that the trial judge was precluded from finding abandonment by Mrs. W. on the basis of some kind of estoppel operating against the R.s. The R.s' refusal to return the child to Mrs. W. in October 1978 when she suddenly appeared at their home at a late hour in the evening and intimated that she had left L.W., was moving to Regina and wanted to pass L. on to her sister was in my view a perfectly responsible act on the part of the R.s. I do not think they were, as Matas JA suggests, setting themselves up as a court to decide the ultimate fate of the child. They had had the care of L. since she was an infant except for a brief period in May 1978 following the expiry of the wardship order and had become very attached to her. I believe their conduct was prompted by concern for the child. No doubt they were of the view that if Mrs. W.'s intention in taking L. from them was to pass her on to her sister rather than to look after her herself, she might well be better off with them — at least until a proper authority had looked into the kind of home she would have with the sister. It must be recalled that the R.s thought that Mrs. W. had given L. permanently into their care in May and were planning to adopt her. They had heard nothing from her from May until her sudden appearance in October and, indeed, heard nothing further from her until the writ of habeas corpus in January 1982. With all due respect to the majority of the Court of Appeal, I think it is quite inappropriate to characterize the conduct of the R.s as some kind of illegal assertion of title! We are dealing with a child who had been brought up in their home after being apprehended by the Children's Aid Society. It was for the court to decide whether the R.s' conduct in refusing to give up L. in October 1978 was reasonable in the circumstances and whether it really prevented Mrs. W. from pursuing her legal right to custody. The trial judge obviously concluded that it did not. She could have proceeded immediately with her habeas corpus application and not waited three years to do so. Matas JA, in holding the R.s estopped from alleging abandonment by their refusal to give up the child in October 1978, states [at 178–79]:

> In my view, Mr. and Mrs. R. cannot now rely on a claim that Mrs. W. abandoned her child when they deliberately refused to return the child to Mrs. W. in 1978 and embarked on a three-year waiting period to simplify the legal procedures to be followed in adopting L. And it is impossible for us to say now what may have been the result if an application for adoption had been made properly in 1978. At least the court would not have been faced with the argument of the particularly long lapse of time.

With respect, I see nothing "improper" about the R.s proceeding by way of de facto adoption. The statute contemplates it. Moreover, in my view the crucial question is not what a court would have done with an adoption application made in 1978 but what it would have done with a habeas corpus application. Mrs. W. might have succeeded on such an application in 1978 had she proceeded with it. Her failure to do so permitted her child to develop a dependency on the R.s as her psychological parents. It seems to me that Mrs. W. had a responsibility when her rights were challenged to pursue them in the court if necessary and not to wait until her child was bonded to the R.s with all the problems for the child that the disruption of that bond was likely to create.

I frankly cannot see this as a situation for the application of the doctrine of estoppel. I believe there was evidence before the learned trial judge on which she could make her finding of abandonment between October 1978 and January 1982 although I feel impelled to say that I myself would probably not have made that finding. I believe that the significance of a person's conduct must be assessed in the context of that person's circumstances. Acts performed by one may constitute abandonment when the same acts performed by another may not. I think I would have been disposed to take a more charitable view of Mrs. W.'s failure to contact her child given her circumstances than that taken by the learned trial judge.

Be that as it may, I do not think a finding of abandonment was necessary to the trial judge's decision. I think the statute is clear and that s. 103(2) dispenses with parental consent in the case of a de facto adoption. This does not mean, of course, that the child's tie with its natural parent is irrelevant in the making of an order under the section. It is obviously very relevant in a determination as to what is in the child's best interests. But it is the parental tie as a meaningful and positive force in the life of the child and not in the life of the parent that the court has to be concerned about. As has been emphasized many times in custody cases, a child is not a chattel in which its parents have a proprietary interest; it is a human being to whom they owe serious obligations. In giving the court power to dispense with the consent of the parent on a de facto adoption the legislature has recognized an aspect of the human condition — that our own self interest sometimes clouds our perception of what is best for those for whom we are responsible. It takes a very high degree of selflessness and maturity, for most of us probably an unattainable degree, for a parent to acknowledge that it might be better for his or her child to be brought up by someone else. The legislature in its wisdom has protected the child against this human frailty in a case where others have stepped into the breach and provided a happy and secure home for the child for a minimum period of three consecutive years. In effect, these persons have assumed the obligations of the natural parents and taken their place. The natural parents' consent in these circumstances is no longer required....

I turn now to the crucial issue on the appeal. Did the learned trial judge err in holding that L.'s best interests lay with the R.s? The majority of the Court of Appeal thought she did. They appear to share a concern about the finality of an adoption order in terms of cutting L. off both from her natural mother and from her Indian heritage and culture. Matas JA said [at 179–80]:

> As part of his submission, counsel for Mrs. W. argued that a transracial adoption results in the loss of contact by the child with his heritage and culture and that this would not be in the best interests of the child. I would reject this argument if counsel meant that no transracial adoption order should ever be granted by the courts in this province. The legislation is not restrictive. In an appropriate case, the court may grant a transracial order of adoption. However, I agree that a child's culture and heritage should be considered by the court as one of the factors to be weighed as part of the circumstances envisaged by s. 89 of the Act. Depending on the circumstances, it is a factor which could have greater or lesser influence in the court's final decision. In the case at bar, the evidence supports the view that the factor is an important one.

Hall JA did not underestimate the importance of the fact that the child was an Indian. However, he adopted the conclusion the trial judge drew from the expert evidence before her as to the R.s' sensitivity to the inter-racial aspect and their appreciation of the need to encourage and develop in L. a sense of her own worth and dignity and the worth and dignity of her people. The trial judge found that they had amply displayed their ability to guide L. through any identity crisis she might face in her teenage years. Hall JA also accepted the trial judge's finding based on the psychiatric evidence that to risk the removal of L. from the R.s' home at this stage could cause her permanent psychological damage. This was the only home she had ever known and she was securely bonded to the R.s. Hall JA concluded that, important a factor as her Indian heritage and culture might be, the duration and strength of her attachment to the R.s was more important.

The majority of the Court of Appeal obviously saw in their alternate courses a means of keeping the door open for access to the natural mother. If the child were a ward of the court the court could grant her access while maintaining custody in the R.s if this seemed appropriate. Similarly, if a new trial were ordered as to custody, access rights could be claimed in those proceedings. The majority were loath to close the door on access by the finality of an adoption order. With respect, I think this overlooks something — something adverted to by Hall JA when he said [at 156]:

In my opinion, it is quite unlikely that a solution to the problem will be found in either of the ways proposed by my colleagues. Rather, my forecast is lengthy, bitter and costly litigation which in itself would not serve the best interests of L. A difficult choice has to be made. Either the order of adoption should stand or she should be returned to Mrs. W. The record is as complete as it is ever likely to be.

I agree with Hall JA that this child should not be allowed to become a battleground, in the courts or in the media, and I believe that there is a very real risk of this if the court refuses to "bite the bullet." In my view, when the test to be met is the best interests of the child, the significance of cultural background and heritage as opposed to bonding abates over time. The closer the bond that develops with the prospective adoptive parents the less important the racial element becomes. As the witness, Dr. McCrae, expressed it [at 159–60]:

> I think this whole business of racial and Indian and whatever you want to call it all has to do with a parameter of time and if we had gone back to day one and L.W. is now being relinquished by her mother in terms of priorities at that time, we would have said — supported a hundred times over "let's place the child with its cultural background." That would be a very — would have been very reasonable. But if that is not done and time goes by, that priority drops down. The priority is no longer there, the priority of ethnic and cultural background. That drops and now must go way down because now it's the mother–child relationship. It doesn't matter if S.R. was Indian and the child was white and L.W. was white. This same argument would hold. It has nothing to do with race, absolutely nothing to do with culture, it has nothing to do with ethnic background. It's two women and a little girl, and one of them doesn't know her. It's as simple as that; all the rest of it is extra and of no consequence, except to the people involved, of course.

I think the learned trial judge recognized that reality, considered all the factors which were relevant to the determination of what was in the child's best interests including the fact that she was of Indian parentage, and weighed them in the balance. I cannot find that she erred in carrying out this rather difficult process.

Much was made in this case of the inter-racial aspect of the adoption. I believe that inter-racial adoption, like inter-racial marriage, is now an accepted phenomenon in our pluralist society. The implications of it may have been overly dramatized by the respondent in this case. The real issue is the cutting of the child's legal tie with her natural mother. This is always a serious step and clearly one which ought not to be taken lightly. However, adoption, given that the adoptive home is the right one and the trial judge has so found in this case, gives the child secure status as the child of two loving parents. While the court can feel great compassion for the respondent, and respect for her determined efforts to overcome her adversities, it has an obligation to ensure that any order it makes will promote the best interests of her child. This and this alone is our task.

I would allow the appeal and reinstate the order of adoption made by the trial judge. I would dismiss the cross-appeal. I would make no order as to costs.

Appeal allowed; adoption order reinstated

Notes and Questions

Reflecting on "best interests"

Identify the differing perspectives of Mrs. W and the Rs in relation to the facts in this case. Is it possible to argue that Mrs. W thought that she was arranging a custom adoption for her child? Why, or why not? By the time that the case reached the Supreme Court of Canada, was there anything that Mrs. W could have done to obtain a different outcome in this case? Is a child's bonding with adoptive parents always more important than other considerations — that is, is a significant degree of bonding always "in a child's best interest"? For another case that followed *ANR and SCR v LJW*, see *Sawan v Tearoe* (1993), 48 RFL (3d) 392; leave to appeal to the SCC refused. More recently, in *BL v Saskatchewan (Social Services)*, 2012 SKCA 38, the Court of Appeal upheld an order for permanent custody of two aboriginal children, EL and JL, who both had special needs in favour of CW, their foster mother. The Court of Appeal noted that CW, who was open to adopting the children, facilitated their special needs, was "sensitive to aboriginal and Metis cultural issues" and was concerned with the parenting abilities of the biological parents who had substance abuse problems and a history of domestic violence (at para 7).

In the decades since the Supreme Court decision in *ANR*, debate about the best way to resolve such issues has continued. Recognizing the harms to children and their Aboriginal communities by earlier policies of adoption by non-Aboriginal families, legislators and courts have struggled to resolve such cases in ways that contribute to children's best interests, an approach that now may include taking into account their Aboriginal heritage (see Ontario's *Child and Family Services Act*, s 136(3)).

Some scholars have argued, however, that the Supreme Court's decision failed to take account of the ways that "cultural concerns ebb and flow throughout lifetimes," and that the tools available to the court were insufficient:

> For the outcome of the ... decision to be just, it had to acknowledge that a determination of the task at hand was made impossible by the shortcomings of the conceptual tools available to the decision makers, including the best interests of the child test, law's commitment to carrying forward the past as an authoritative source of substantive norms, the tragic histories of Aboriginal child welfare in Canada, the dynamic, fluid, and contingent nature of culture, [the birth mother's] exclusion from the group of history's winners, who get to make law, and [the child] frozen before the Court as a seven-year-old child with only her immediate past and a thin description of her parents as a guide. (Gillian Calder, "'Finally I Know where I am going to be From': Culture, Context, and Time in a Look Back at *Racine v. Woods*" in Kim Brooks, ed, *Justice Bertha Wilson: One Woman's Difference* (Vancouver: UBC Press, 2009) 173 at 184)

Does this comment mean that issues about the best interests of Aboriginal children cannot be justly decided by the courts?

Consider this example:

> In *Jane Doe (Public Trustee of) v Awasis Agency of Northern Manitoba*, [1990] 4 CNLR 10 (Man CA), a thirteen-year-old girl was removed from her non-Aboriginal foster parents and returned to her remote reserve against her will. She was not accepted by the Aboriginal community, and was confined and sexually assaulted on a number of occasions before she was "rescued" by a fly-in doctor.

As Hadley Friedland argued, there may be different kinds of loss and suffering for Aboriginal children and their communities. See Hadley Friedland, "Tragic Choices and the Division of Sorrow: Speaking about Race, Culture and Community Traumatisation in the Lives of Children" (2009) 25 Can J Fam L 223.

How should these problems be resolved?

Rethinking race and "best interests" in the Supreme Court of Canada: *H v M*

In the context of these comments, consider another more recent case, *H v M*, [1999] 1 SCR 328.

In this case, an American couple had adopted two Native Canadian girls as children and raised them to adulthood. One of the girls had a child; apparently, the father was African American, but he did not acknowledge paternity and made no claim to the child. Shortly after her son's birth, the young mother discovered her biological parents (who were Aboriginal) in Vancouver. She went to visit her father, leaving her son in the care of her adoptive parents for eight months. After returning for a visit with her adoptive parents, she secretly travelled back to Vancouver, taking her son with her, and moved into the home occupied by her biological father and other members of his family. The family was poor and in receipt of social assistance. The child lived in this home for about two years.

After discovering the mother's whereabouts, the adoptive parents initiated action to obtain custody of the child. Although the child's mother did not wish to assert custody, she supported a claim launched by her biological father (the child's grandfather), who was awarded interim custody.

At the trial, however, the adoptive parents were awarded custody with reasonable access to the child's mother.

The B.C. Court of Appeal reversed this decision and granted custody to the mother's biological father, expressly acknowledging the legislative trend to keep Aboriginal children in Aboriginal families.

By the time that the case reached the Supreme Court of Canada, the child was nearly four years old and he had moved with his Aboriginal grandfather to the grandfather's reserve in Manitoba.

The Supreme Court of Canada allowed the appeal on the basis that there was no error in the decision of the trial judge.

What factors seem most significant in this case in relation to the best interests test? Does this case suggest that the Supreme Court's views about race and bonding have changed? Note that the court focused primarily on the principle that appellate courts should not interfere with trial decisions unless there is an error in the trial judgment, an approach also substantially followed in *ANR and SCR v LJW*. What is the rationale for this principle? Does this principle lead to more justice?

The role of First Nations communities in adoption proceedings

In *H v M*, the biological grandfather requested a rehearing to permit his First Nation to make arguments, but the Supreme Court dismissed his application on the ground that his counsel had already made arguments in support of the views of his First Nation (see [1999] 1 SCR 761). In a number of other cases, Aboriginal bands have participated in decisions about custody and adoption of Aboriginal children. For example, see *S(SM) v A(J)* (1992), 38 RFL (3d) 113 (BCCA); and *Sturgeon First Nations v Alberta* (1999), 47 RFL (4th) 199 (Alta CA).

In some recent cases, courts have criticized legislation in some provinces, which provides a veto to First Nations communities with respect to the adoption of children by non-Aboriginal families. In a Manitoba case, in which neither the provincial agency nor the Dakota Ojibway Child and Family Services could offer an Aboriginal placement for an Aboriginal child, the court held that the agency had established the child's need for protection, and that she had become eligible for adoption. In doing so, the court's decision began by critiquing the government's veto policy:

> This is a case about an aboriginal child who is being denied her right to a permanent, secure family because the aboriginal agency and the band's community committee have vetoed any such placement. The reason for the veto arises from a desire to stop the removal of aboriginal children from their cultural heritage. While a laudable goal, its dogmatic application is counterproductive and unfair. The tragedy in this case is that the best plan for the child, which would see her placed with a permanent family, has been rejected for historical and political reasons that have nothing to do with her case. The irony is that, in trying to make up for past wrongs to aboriginal children and past discrimination towards the aboriginal community, more wrongs are being committed and the discrimination against individual aboriginal children goes on in another form, this time perpetuated by the aboriginal agency and the band community committee. While non-aboriginal children are offered a permanent adoptive family, aboriginal children continue to be offered the lesser option of a foster family, which lacks the permanence and security that would come with an adoption. (*Winnipeg (Child and Family Services) v A(M)*, 2002 MBQB 209 at para 1)

In discussing options for the child, the court also noted (at para 25) the existence of "openness" agreements under section 33(1) of the *Adoption Act*, SM 1997, c 47. Is such an arrangement a better option for Aboriginal children?

Challenging the Aboriginal veto policy

In a similar case in Saskatchewan, five Aboriginal siblings were in the care of the Department of Community Resources and Employment, without permanent homes or parents. Although there were no extended family members or band members able or willing to assume care of the children, the Sturgeon Lake band invoked their veto pursuant to the province's adoption policy, refusing to allow the children to be placed for adoption. In this context, the trial judge considered the "best interests" test and appointed an independent legal advocate who successfully challenged the constitutionality of this policy pursuant to sections 7 and 15 of the *Charter*. While recognizing how the policy reflected a desire to keep First Nations children in their communities and the historical injustices suffered by Aboriginal people in the child welfare system, the court concluded that the practical effect of the policy was inappropriate:

> [It condemns] First Nations children who do not have suitable family or cultural resources to a lifetime of foster care, [making them] victims of a system meant to help and support them.... [and gives paramountcy to "culture" over other relevant factors.] (*Re RT* 2004 SKQB 112 at paras 21–22)

Recall that Ontario's *Child and Family Services Act*, s 136(3), requires a court to consider a child's native heritage in determining the child's best interests. Recognizing that this is not a veto, one court held that Native children do not have an absolute right to be placed with Native families See *Algonquins of Pikwokanagon First Nation v Children's Aid Society of Toronto*, [2004] 3 CNLR 1; and Joseph Brean, "Native Upbringing Not a Right, Judge Rules", *National Post* (1 May 2004).

Consider this situation:

> The applicants for an adoption order were non-Native foster parents of a five-year-old Native child for whom they sought guardianship; the child had been in their care for 22 months at the time of the trial. Although the child's biological parents were not involved in the trial, the Awasis Agency of Northern Manitoba intervened in the matter and sought that the child be transferred to their care by the Winnipeg CAS. What result?

In *C(JMN) v Winnipeg Child and Family Services* (1998), 33 RFL (4th) 175 (Man QB), the court ruled that it was in the best interests of the child to grant the applicants' request for guardianship of the child.

In response to the intervenor's arguments that cultural heritage is more important for Aboriginal children than constancy, the court noted that the child had not lived in a culturally appropriate residence for half of his life. The court also noted that the female applicant had the best guardianship qualifications it had ever encountered and was better qualified than the social worker in the case — she had specialized in early childhood education, qualified as a professional caregiver, and had done postgraduate work on emotional and mental health of children. The court also noted that the applicants were deeply committed to the child and his future, and that the experts who placed greater importance on culture and linguistic heritage than attachment and bonding had never observed or interviewed the child or the applicant parents.

How would you characterize the respective values of bonding and race in this case? See also *IW v Kaschkowew Child Wellness Society*, 2011 ABCA 160; and *Re KG* 2013 ABPC 237.

Aboriginal adoptions and "adoption breakdown"

Statistics on transracial adoption are not easily available, but it appears that children from some racial groups fare better than others, and that adoptions of First Nations children are especially susceptible to breakdown.

For example, a study of Native Canadian adoption breakdowns in the early 1990s reported that, by the age of 17, nearly half of these children had broken with their adoptive families. In this context, the study concluded that native children, as members of a cultural group, should not be adopted outside their communities.

A similar study in 1996 that examined Vietnamese, Korean, and Native Canadian adoptees found that a much smaller percentage of adoptees who were Native Canadians had developed successful attachments to their adoptive parents. One reason for this outcome is that Native adoptees have a double burden: they absorb the negative stereotypes of Native Canadians within Canadian society at the same time as they are isolated from all the positive aspects of Aboriginal culture and values. See Marie Adams, *Our Son, a Stranger: Adoption Breakdown and Its Effects on Parents* (Montreal & Kingston, ON: McGill-Queen's University Press, 2002; and see also EC Kimelman, *No Quiet Place: Review Committee on Indian and Métis Adoption and Placements* (Manitoba: Manitoba Community Services, 1985).

In the context of communities disabled by the residential school system and other policies of assimilation, moreover, Native Canadian children experience particular challenges in white society. As a brief from several native organizations to the Minister of Community and Social Services in Ontario stated in 1983:

> Even under the best of conditions, Native children do not, generally speaking, become successfully "integrated" or "acculturated" or "adjusted" within the dominant societal framework, as a result of being placed in non-Native settings, either family or institution. ... In simple words — it doesn't work. (Ontario Native Women's Association et al, quoted in Adams at 188–89)

In this context, a class action suit on behalf of 16,000 Aboriginal children taken from reserves in Ontario involved protracted and ongoing litigation. For some details, see the discussion in Chapter Four.

Additional Resources

Cindy L Baldassi, "The Legal Status of Aboriginal Customary Adoption Across Canada: Comparisons, Contrasts, and Convergences" (2006) 39 UBC L Rev 63.

Emily Grier, "Aboriginal Children in Limbo: A Comment on *RT*" (2005) 68 Sask L Rev 435.

Suzanne Hoelgaard, "Cultural Determinants of Adoption Policy: A Columbian Case Study" (1998) 12 Intl JL Pol'y & Fam 202.

Keri B Lazarus, "Adoption of Native American and First Nations Children: Are the United States and Canada Recognizing the Best Interests of the Children?" (1997) 14:1 Ariz J Intl & Comp L 255.

Angela T McCormick, "Transracial Adoption: A Critical View of the Courts' Present Standards" (1989–90) 28 J Fam L 303.

Tshepo L Mosikatsana, "*Sawan v. Tearoe*" (1994) 11 Can Fam LQ 89.

Tae Mee Park, "In the Best Interests of the Aboriginal Child" (2003) 16 Windsor Rev Legal Soc Issues 43.

Vandna Sinha & Anne Kozlowski "The Structure of Aboriginal Child Welfare in Canada" (2013) 4:2 The International Indigenous Policy Journal.

Shandra Spears, "Strong Spirit, Fractured Identity: An Ojibway Adoptee's Journey to Wholeness" in Martin J Cannon & Lina Sunseri, eds, *Racism, Colonialism, and Indigeneity in Canada* (Don Mills: Oxford University Press Canada, 2011).

"Best Interests" and race in non-aboriginal communities

Race and Culture Versus Bonding:
Re British Columbia Birth Registration No 030279

Race and culture have also been considered with respect to adoption applications involving other racialized children. In *Re British Columbia Birth Registration No 030279* (1990), 24 RFL (3d) 437 (BCSC), the application by a Korean birth mother to revoke her consent to the adoption of her child was refused. The adoptive mother was Chinese and father partly Chinese. At the time of her application, the mother was 29 years old and a Korean-born business woman. She had become pregnant during her engagement to a Korean diplomat, but the marriage was eventually called off. According to the court, the mother found herself in "an impossible position" because in the Korean culture, it was a matter of great shame to be pregnant without being married. At the same time, she did not want to have an abortion and could not imagine raising the child on her own. She had little or no support from close members of her family. Indeed, some of her family were estranged from her because of the shame and disgrace that she had brought to their family as a result of her pregnancy.

Although ambivalent about doing so, the mother eventually decided that the child would be better off in a two-parent family and signed the papers for the child to be adopted. She acknowledged that she had signed the consent forms voluntarily and with full knowledge of the contents. She signed the papers about two months after the child's birth, concerned about her ability to care for the child properly in the light of her need to work long hours in the family grocery store. The child was placed for adoption, but, about four months later, the mother decided that she had made a mistake and wanted to revoke her consent.

The court considered the birth mother's request to revoke her consent on the basis that both the mother and the adoptive parents were well-qualified to care for the child. The court decided to deny the mother's application, having regard to the best interests of the child, and stating that the scales were weighted in favour of the adoptive parents, totally apart from the burden of proof. Consider the court's assessment:

> In my view, the stability of the adoptive family, both in terms of their immediate family, and in terms of the family-oriented neighbourhood where they have lived for many years, is an important factor which weighs in the best interests of the child. The natural mother has stated that she wishes to move to another neighbourhood should this decision be in her favour, and, although I have no doubt that she would choose a proper home for the child, she is not in a settled arrangement at the present time. Although she has the ability to call upon her sister for support, she will have to set up a network of other supportive relationships in her new location. Again, that is not an insurmountable task, but it is a factor to consider.
>
> It is also a matter of some concern to me that both the natural mother and her sister allowed their pride to stand in the way of working out their problems in the past. Although I am satisfied that the natural mother has learned the folly of placing pride before more important concerns, it was not clear to me that her sister is flexible enough to offer her assistance unconditionally in the future. The natural mother would unquestionably need unconditional support in order to cope with the stresses of single parenthood.
>
> Another factor to consider is that the natural mother is embarking on a new job within the next month or so which will also place demands on her at precisely the time she would be attempting to settle into a relationship with her child. That job will involve her travelling to Los Angeles for a week in March 1990, and will also involve her travelling to Korea at least once a year, and to locations in the United States from time to time, depending on how well the business does. In other words, there are other changes taking place in the life of the natural mother at the present time, aside from the prospect of having to cope with motherhood for the first time.
>
> Of all of the factors which I have mentioned which weigh in favour of leaving the child with the adoptive parents, the most compelling is the fact that the child is safe, secure, happy and healthy in his present environment. He does not know the grief which his mother has suffered, for he has not suffered at all. Nor is there any evidence to suggest that he will suffer as a result of his adoptive status in the future. The adoptive parents impressed me as being well able to deal with any uncertainties which may arise in the future when the child comes to the realization that he is adopted.
>
> The question of how the factor of blood ties should be weighed in the balance in this case was present in my mind throughout the trial. I have given it serious consideration, bearing in mind the fact that some of the benefits that flow to a child from blood ties are intangible, and not readily put into words. Having struggled with the issue, I am drawn to the conclusion that the factor of the blood tie in this case, even when combined with the other factors favouring the natural mother, does not satisfy me that the consent of the natural mother to adoption should be set aside. The best interests of the child dictate otherwise.

In closing, I know that there are no words which I can say that will relieve the anguish which the natural mother will experience as a result of this decision. I trust that others will do their best to give her solace.

Notes and Questions

Race and culture versus bonding: A false dichotomy?

What factors were significant in the court's decision to deny the application to withdraw consent to the adoption? How would you characterize the relevance of race and bonding in this case? Is the case consistent with *ANR and SCR v LJW*?

Some scholars have argued that such cases create a false dichotomy, particularly for Aboriginal children. To what extent do these comments also reflect the concerns in *Re British Columbia Birth Registration No 030279*?

> The children [in such cases] cannot be separated from their cultural context, but neither can their needs be assessed without recognition that each child is an individual who requires, as any individual child in their situation would, continuity in relationships, a stable home, and someone to nurture them and look out for [their] physical, spiritual and emotional well-being. Children's culture is an integral part of their identity, is inseparable from their best interests and, by law, is required to be a primary consideration in determining their placement. Culture cannot be allowed to trump the children's individual rights, but neither can individual needs eclipse the importance of cultural identity. (Emily Grier, "Aboriginal Children in Limbo: A Comment on *RT*" (2005) 68 Sask L Rev 435 at para 32; see also Marlee Kline, "Child Welfare Law, 'Best Interests of the Child' Ideology and First Nations" (1992) 30 Osgoode Hall LJ 375)

Consider this situation:

> An Alberta court considered an application for adoption of a two-year-old child who was one-quarter Japanese. The natural parents had consented to adoption but the child's grandmother requested guardianship of the child. The expert evidence provided in the case was in conflict as to the effect of changing the primary caregivers, the importance of raising a child in the ethnic background of the natural parents, and the merits of inter familial and extra familial child-rearing. What result is in the child's best interests here?

In *C(DH) v S(R)* (1990), 26 RFL (3d) 301 (Alta QB), the court granted the adoption on the basis of the best interests of the child because of the risk of stress and development impairment if the child were moved from the adoptive home in Alberta to the grandmother in California. Do you agree that this decision was "in the best interests of the child"? Why, or why not?

Studies of interracial adoption

A 1993 study identified an "adoption breakdown" rate of about 10 percent for African American and mixed-race (Black-White and Asian-White) adoptions, a rate that is significantly lower than for Aboriginal adoptees (see Adams at xxiv–vii). However, in spite of this higher rate of integration in their adopted families, some Black adoptees have expressed concerns as adults about their adoption, revealing a personal sense of loss and sadness, even though their white parents were full of good intentions. See Bill Taylor, "Shades of Gray", *Toronto Star* (18 May 1995); and Ghislaine Routhier, "Black Children, White Parents" (1988) Intercultural Horizons 10.

Additional Resources

Karen Dubinsky, "A History of Racism? Canadians Imagine Interracial Adoption" in Mona Gleason et al, eds, *Lost Kids: Vulnerable Children and Youth in Twentieth-Century Canada and the United States* (Toronto: UBC Press, 2010) 15.

Jennifer Craven-Griffiths, "Race and Substitute Families" (1990) 134 Solicitors Journal 326.

Valerie Phillips Hermann, "Transracial Adoption: 'Child-saving' or 'Child-Snatching'?" (1993) 13 Nat'l Black LJ 147.

Twila L Perry, "Race, Color, and the Adoption of Biracial Children" (2014) 17 J Gender Race & Just 73.

Kerry O'Halloran, *The Politics of Adoption: International Perspectives on Law, Policy and Practice* (Dordrecht: Springer, 2006).

Twila Perry, "Race and Child Placement: The Best Interests Test and the Cost of Discretion" (1991) 29 J Fam L 51.

Melinda Smith, "What Makes a Home? Foster Care and Transracial Adoptions" (1993) 56 Tex BJ 492.

Jane Jeong Trenka, Julia Chinyere Oparah & Sun Yung Shin, eds, *'Outsiders Within': Writing on Transracial Adoption* (Cambridge, Mass: SouthEnd Press, 2006).

International adoption

New Challenges?

According to the Vanier Institute of the Family, about 22 percent of all international adoptions in 2008 were from the People's Republic of China, with 10 percent from the United States and Ethiopia, and about 8 percent from Haiti (see *Families Count* at 56).

However, the number of adoptions from China has been steadily decreasing. The proportion of adoptions from China peaked in 2005 (53%) and by 2009 had decreased to 22 percent. Between 1999 and 2009, approximately 8,000 children from China had been adopted in Canada ("International Adoptions"). The Adoption Council of Canada reported in 2003 that, although there were positive perceptions about these adoptions, research about the level of integration of these adoptees was not yet fully available. See Sue Ferguson, "A New Community Comes of Age", *Maclean's* (24 February 2003) 47. Some have argued that the decline in international adoption from countries such as Ethiopia and (especially) the PRC is good news for children in Canadian foster care. (See Jasmine Budak, "Canada's Most Unwanted", *The Walrus* (December 2012), online: <http://thewalrus.ca/canadas-most-unwanted/>.) According to a 2012 report, the average cost of international adoptions is about $35,000 to $40,000, including fees payable to a licensed international adoption agency, a social work study, travel, hotel, fees to foreign governments, and immigration papers in Canada. See Andrew Gorham, "The Painful New Realities of International Adoption", *The Globe and Mail*, 18 February 2012 at A8–A9.

In the context of declining rates of birth in the western nations of the world, international adoption practices raise issues about economic and political power more generally. For example, Gillian Pascall argued that for underdeveloped countries, the "export" of their children may in some cases impoverish and dislocate families of origin, even as their children find new and "better" homes. See Gillian Pascall, "Adoption: Perspectives in Social Policy" in Philip Bean, ed, *Adoption: Essays in Social Policy, Law, and Sociology* (London: Tavistock, 1984) at 19.

Some aspects of international adoption are now regulated by the *International Convention on Protection of Children and Co-operation in Respect of Intercountry Adoption* (29 May 1993), 32 ILM 1134. See William Duncan, "Regulating Intercountry Adoption — An International Perspective" in Andrew Bainham & David Pearl, eds, *Frontiers of Family Law* (London: Chancery Law Publishing, 1993) at 46.

Additional Resources

Karen Andrea Balcom, *The Traffic in Babies: Cross-border Adoption and Baby-selling Between the United States and Canada, 1930–1972* (Toronto: University of Toronto Press, 2011).

Cindy Baldassi, "DNA, Discrimination and the Definition of Family Class: *MAO v. Canada (Min of Citizenship and Immigration)*" (2007) 21 JL & Soc Pol'y 5.

Vaughan Black, "GATT for Kids: New Rules for Intercountry Adoption of Children" (1994) 11 Can Fam LQ 253.

Karen Dubinsky, "Babies without Borders: Kidnap, Rescue and Symbolic Child" (2007) 19:1 Journal of Women's History 147.

Marie A Failinger, "Moving Toward Human Rights Principles for Intercountry Adoption" (2014) 39:2 NCJ Intl L & Com Reg 523.

Madelyn Freundlich, *Adoption and Ethics: The Role of Race, Culture and National Origin in Adoption* (Washington: The Child Welfare League of America, 2000).

Jay W Rojewski & Jacy L Rojewski, *Intercountry Adoption from China: Examining Cultural Heritage and Other Postadoption Issues* (Westport, Conn: Bergin and Harvey, 2001).

Rita Simon & Howard Altstein, *Adoption across Borders: Serving the Children in Transracial and Intercountry Adoptions* (Lanham: Rowman and Littlefield Publishers, 2000).

Ann Laura Stoler, *Carnal Knowledge and Imperial Power: Race and the Intimate in Colonial Rule* (Berkeley and Los Angeles: University of California Press, 2002).

Zofia Sonia Worotynec, *Child Interrupted: International Adoption in the Context of Canadian Policy on Immigration, Multiculturalism, Citizenship, and Child Rights* (Toronto: CERIS, 2006).

ADOPTION AND SAME-SEX COUPLES

> Based on my academic and clinical work in this area of child psychiatry, it is my opinion that same sex couples should generally be treated in the same manner as are opposite sex common law couples with regard to the issue of adoption of children. Having regard to matters related to healthy child development, it is my view that sexual orientation of a person should not, in itself, be grounds for excluding a person from consideration as an adoptive parent. (Evidence of Dr. Susan Bradley in *Re K* (1995), 15 RFL (4th) 129 (Ont Prov Div))

Lesbian birth mothers and co-mother adoptions: *Re K*

The issue of adoption for gay and lesbian couples was litigated in the mid-1990s in Ontario, prior to the recognition of "spousal" status or same-sex marriage.

In *Re K*, the partners of four lesbian mothers (who had conceived using assisted reproduction measures) applied to be recognized as the adoptive parents of their partners' children. The *Child and Family Services Act*, s 146, permitted a "spouse" of a child's parent to apply for such an adoption order, but the relevant statutory definition of "spouse" at that time was limited to opposite-sex married and cohabiting couples. The application successfully challenged this limitation pursuant to section 15 of the *Charter*.

Although subsequent claims on the part of same-sex couples with respect to legal recognition of parent–child relationships have often been based on arguments that adoption is not the appropriate means to recognize their "family" relationships, *Re K* remains important for its recognition that adoption by a same-sex co-partner may be in a child's best interests. As the court stated (at paras 25, 32–46):

> In the course of the hearing on this constitutional issue, I have been presented with a considerable amount of evidence on the ability of homosexual persons to parent, individually or as couples, and the effects of homosexual parenting on children. This evidence was presented principally through the extensive affidavits from Dr. Margrit Eichler, Dr. Rosemary Barnes, and Dr. Susan Bradley. These documents and the research papers accompanying them as exhibits, reviewed in considerable detail the scien-

tific literature and research that has accumulated in this area over the last fifty years, and in particular since the mid-1970s. In addition to this affidavit evidence, I had the benefit of hearing viva voce evidence from Dr. Bradley.

...

Having considered the evidence received through these sources, I come to the following factual conclusions:

The traditional family model of two, middle class, heterosexual parents in which the woman is a full-time housewife and the man has full-time paid employment outside the home, which has long been assumed to be the structure most favourable to healthy child development, is now a minority and several varieties of non-traditional families appear in our society, including families in which gay fathers and lesbian mothers are the primary care-givers. The sexual orientation of the parents is considered along with race, ethnicity, household composition and maternal employment as one of a number of ways in which families vary from the traditional model....

During this century, families in highly industrialized countries have been undergoing drastic changes, not just in the nature of their composition but in gender roles within the family. These changes have precipitated research into the dimensions of family interactions and the result of this research indicates a wide variety in the nature and degree of interaction between family members. Moreover, studies by various researchers have convincingly demonstrated that the same internal variations exist between same-sex couples and opposite-sex couples and that both groups demonstrate the full range of dimensions indicative of family structure. As Dr. Eichler pointed out ...: "Overall, the differences among opposite-sex couples and among same-sex couples are greater than the differences *between* these two groups."

Recent studies on the effects of the non-traditional family structure on the development of children suggests that there is no reason to conclude that alteration of the family structure itself is detrimental to child development. The prevailing opinion of researchers in this area seems to be that the traditional family structure is no longer considered as the only framework within which adequate child care can be given. Rather, child development researchers have "highlighted the multiplicity of pathways through which healthy psychological development can take place and the diversity of home environments which can support such development" ...

Progressively more rigorous empirical research in the area of child development has produced the notion that *the most important element in the healthy development of a child is a stable, consistent, warm, and responsive relationship between a child and his or her care-giver.* Factors that appear to have a significant effect on the healthy emotional and psychological development of a child are more related to conflicts in spousal relations than family type or structure. A parent's capacity to support and be emotionally available to a child is enhanced in the context of a supportive relationship, especially if there is good communication, effective problem solving, and sharing of family responsibilities....

In concluding that section 136 of the *Child and Family Services Act* contravened section 15 of the *Charter* and was not saved by section 1, the court "read in" language to include same-sex couples. While *Re K* was an important decision, its significance has been overtaken by recognition of multiple mothers and fathers resulting from the use of assisted reproduction, discussed later in this chapter.

Notes and Questions

Gay and lesbian adoption: Families and ideology

Why was it necessary for the partners of same-sex mothers to be "spouses" in order to be parents? *Re K* was litigated in Ontario in the context of controversial debates in the 1990s about Bill 167 in the Ontario legislature, a Bill that would have redefined "spouse" to include persons in same-sex relationships in all provincial legislation. When it appeared destined for defeat, the Attorney General attempted to save it by introducing an amendment to restrict the definition of "spouse" in relation to adoption, an issue that was particularly controversial among opponents of the Bill. In the end, Bill 167 was defeated completely.

It was in this context that these four lesbian couples litigated the right to adopt the children they were parenting, and they were successful in achieving this goal. However, in doing so, the applicants were required to demonstrate that they "fit" the required legal form. As Shelley Gavigan argued:

> As profound as the challenge of the lesbian adoptions is, it is clear that striking down of the opposite sex requirement alone does not, cannot, address the constraints and assumptions that are embedded in the adoption legislation in Ontario. Under this legislation, it is not enough for the lesbian social parents to be "parents." In order to make a joint application, and thereby preserve the biological mother's tie to the child(ren), they must also be spouses in Ontario, and indeed in every province other than British Columbia. In order for the lesbian parents to be full parents, they have to be spouses, same-sex spouses to be sure, but spouses nonetheless. The spousal requirement for joint adoptions and preservation of children's ties to their biological parents is not amenable to constitutional challenge. The legal form of spouse coupled with its foundational place as a social form triumphs as it shapes and constrains the nature of the challenges that can succeed. (See Shelley AM Gavigan, "Legal Forms, Family Forms, Gendered Norms: What Is a Spouse?" (1999) 14:1 CJLS 127 at 156.)

Interestingly, lesbian co-mothers were subsequently involved in another test case when they claimed that co-mothers (non-biological parents) should be entitled to be registered as "parents" on the children's birth certificates, without the necessity of adoption. See *Rutherford v Ontario (Deputy Registrar General)* (2006), 81 OR (3d) 81 (Sup Ct), discussed later in relation to assisted reproduction. In spite of the limitations noted by Gavigan, is there a good reason why such couples might have chosen to litigate their claims on the basis of adoption prior to confronting the birth registration procedures directly?

Same-sex parents, adoption and assisted reproduction

In an early study of the bases for accepting applications for adoption, researchers reported that 84 percent of adoption agencies would reject an unmarried female applicant in a stable homosexual relationship. See Benjamin Freedman et al, "Criteria for Parenting in Canada: A Comparative Survey of Adoption and Artificial Insemination Practices" (1988) 3 Can Fam LQ 35 at 43 (table I). In this context, *Re K* may evidence changing views about gay and lesbian parenting.

The role of adoption in relation to same-sex couples must also take account of legal arrangements about assisted reproduction. As the next part of this Chapter reveals, assisted reproduction may challenge traditional ideas about biological parenthood and also about adoption policies, for both opposite-sex and same-sex couples.

Additional Resources

Malcolm Dort, "Unheard Voices: Adoption Narratives of Same-Sex Male Couples" (2010) 26:2 Can J Fam L 289.

J Ewall, "Sexual Orientation and Adoptive Matching" (1991) 25 Fam LQ 347.

John Fisher, "Outlaws or In-Laws? Successes and Challenges in the Struggle for LGBT Equality" (2004) 49:4 McGill LJ 1183.

Shelley Gavigan, "A Parent(ly) Knot: Can Heather Have Two Mommies?" in Julia J Bartkowiak & Uma Narayan, eds, *Having and Raising Children: Unconventional Families, Hard Choices and the Social Good* (Pittsburgh, PA: Pennsylvania State University Press, 1999) 87.

Margaret F Gibson, "Adopting Difference: Thinking through Adoption by Gay Men in Ontario, Canada" (2014) 39:2 Signs 407.

Fiona Kelly, "One of these Families is Not Like the Others: The Legal Response to Non-normative Queer Parenting in Canada" (2013) 51 Alta L Rev 1.

Nancy D Polikoff, "This Child Does Have Two Mothers: Redefining Parenthood To Meet the Needs of Children in Lesbian-Mother and Other Non-Traditional Families" (1990) 78 Geo LJ 459.

Joanna Radbord, "Same-sex Parents and the Law" (2013) 33 Windsor Rev of Legal Soc Issues 1.

Mary Lyndon Shanley, *Making Babies, Making Families* (Boston: Beacon Press, 2001).

Susan Ursel, "Bill 167 and Full Human Rights" in Katherine Arnup, ed, *Lesbian Parenting: Living with Pride and Prejudice* (Charlottetown, PEI: Gynergy, 1995) 341.

IV.
ASSISTED REPRODUCTION AND PARENTHOOD: NEW QUESTIONS FOR FAMILY LAW?

Family law has new questions to answer. Reproductive technologies have a wide range of consequences, with implications for family law that it has never been called on to deal with before. In some cases there may be no existing law which applies to the specific situation, while in other cases existing law may be based on assumptions which are no longer valid because of the use of assisted conception procedures. Therefore, there is a need to re-examine and to develop new legal principles to deal with some questions, and to rethink some underlying assumptions for others.... In the absence of legislation explicitly dealing with these situations, the courts are going to be in the position of having to determine the rights and obligations, if any, of each of these parties, so that the best interests of the child are protected.... It cannot possibly be in the best interests of a child to have issues such as these settled, case-by-case, in the courtrooms of our nation. Well thought out social policy goals are needed in this area, and the law needs to be amended in the attainment of these goals. (Patricia A Baird, "Reproductive Technology and the Evolution of Family Law" (1997–98) 15 Can Fam LQ 103 at 103 and 113)

THE CONTEXT FOR LEGAL POLICIES ABOUT ASSISTED REPRODUCTION IN CANADA

New principles for "new" family relationships?

As the above quotation explains, the availability of new forms of assisted reproduction necessitates reconsideration of existing assumptions underlying current principles, as well as the development of new legal principles, regarding parent–child relationships. In addition, Patricia Baird's comment emphasized a need for new social policy and new legislation, rather than the case-by-case enunciation of new legal principles defining the best interests of children. In this way, her comment identified both the need for new principles and a strong recommendation for legislative action rather than case-by-case development of these new principles in the courts.

Yet, as this section demonstrates, much recent activity concerning new legal principles in the context of assisted reproduction has occurred in courts rather than in legislatures. Although many of the decided cases reveal a deep concern to ensure the best interests of children in a variety of different situations, the case law is necessarily driven by the interests of individual litigants, and there remain significant gaps in the development of coherent legal and social policies concerning assisted reproduction. In this context, this section examines a number of recent efforts to create appropriate policies for parent–child relationships in this "new" family law context.

Comparing adoption and assisted reproduction

Perhaps because both adoption and assisted reproduction processes may create non-biological parent–child relationships, comparisons between them are quite frequent. Thus, it is useful at the outset to understand the processes involved in adoption and assisted reproduction.

As was explained earlier, the adoption process is most often defined by statute, and adoption is accomplished by a court order that redefines the child's legal relationship to birth parents (except in the contexts of custom adoption). Adoption processes are also subject to investigation, usually by social workers, to ensure that a proposed adoption is in a child's best interests in terms of bonding with the adoptive parents, an issue that is considered at the time of the court's order for adoption.

By contrast, assisted reproduction often takes place in a medical clinic where doctors are involved in a variety of procedures, including insemination of a woman with sperm from a known or anonymous donor, or more complex procedures such as the harvesting of eggs, fertilization with sperm and then the insertion of an embryo into a gestational carrier who gives birth to a child. In addition, it remains possible for a woman to become pregnant as a result of self-insemination with donor sperm.

In these differing contexts, it is important to understand adoption as a process for creating non-biological parental status for a child who has been born, while assisted reproduction involves processes for bringing a child into existence. To what extent is this distinction significant in terms of legal policies?

In a study some years ago that compared two groups of workers involved in these processes, researchers attempted to compare the significance of criteria that were in use for decision making about adoption and assisted reproduction. The researchers examined the criteria used by adoption agencies and Children's Aid Societies (who were involved in choosing adoptive parents) and by directors of infertility clinics (who were involved in selecting parents for artificial insemination by donor). The results of the study revealed a large amount of discretionary decision making in relation to both adoption and assisted reproduction, with different processes for determining "acceptable" parents and different degrees of reliance on factors deemed relevant to the decisions.

However, there were also some discernable differences between adoption agencies and fertility clinics.

Both groups agreed that adoption should be more restrictive than artificial insemination: adoption respondents pointed to the challenges of accepting a child that was not "biologically your own."

By contrast, physicians in fertility clinics appeared to be simply "aiding the natural reproductive process," and these decisions were generally characterized as medical rather than social.

In addition, the results suggested that adoption agencies were much more concerned with the probable stability of the relationship in the family unit, while fertility clinics proceeded on the basis that "our society does not require a person to satisfy some test to be licensed to parent." See Benjamin Freedman et al, "Criteria for Parenting in Canada: A Comparative Survey of Adoption and Artificial Insemination Practices" (1988) 3 Can Fam LQ 35 at 50.

In this context, should legal issues about assisted reproduction be framed as an analogy to adoption? Are there similarities or differences that need to be taken into account in designing legal principles with respect to assisted reproduction? For example, should the licensing regime that exists for adoptive parents apply to people using assisted reproduction to create their families? (See Carolyn McLeod & Andrew Botterell, "Not for the

Faint of Heart: Assessing the Status Quo on Adoption and Parental Licensing" in Françoise Baylis & Carolyn McLeod, ed, *Family-making: contemporary ethical challenges* (Oxford: Oxford University Press, 2014) 151.) Should the information disclosure provisions that exist in adoption legislation exist for individuals created using assisted reproduction? This is discussed in detail later in this chapter.

POLICIES ABOUT ASSISTED REPRODUCTION AND LEGISLATIVE HISTORY

The policy context prior to the *Assisted Human Reproduction Act* (2004)

The OLRC Report (1985)

The issue of assisted reproduction became a matter of public debate in the last decades of the 20th century as medical clinics and infertility procedures became more common. As early as 1985, the Ontario Law Reform Commission issued a *Report on Human Artificial Reproduction and Related Matters*. Its report was particularly controversial in relation to the issue of surrogacy, the process by which a woman becomes a gestational carrier for a child with the intention that the child will become part of the family of another woman and her partner. For the OLRC, the issue was framed in terms of the need to protect the gestational mother, the "surrogate," in relation to her contract with the intentional parent(s).

Thus, the OLRC recommended that any such contract should be in writing and enforceable only if it was approved by a judge of the Provincial Court prior to commencing a surrogacy procedure. As the *Report* stated, the court should ensure that the terms of the contract "adequately protect the child and the parties and are not inequitable or unconscionable." See Ontario Law Reform Commission, *Report on Human Artificial Reproduction and Related Matters* (Toronto: Ministry of the Attorney General, 1985) at 233–234.

In the Matter of Baby M (1988)

The surrogacy issue became especially controversial as a result of a well-publicized case in the United States, *In the Matter of Baby M*, 537 A 2d 1227 (NJ Sup Ct 1988).

In the *Baby M* case, Mary Beth Whitehead, a married woman with children, entered into a surrogacy contract with William Stern. Stern provided his own sperm to artificially inseminate Whitehead, who was to be paid $10,000 to become pregnant, give birth, deliver the child to the Sterns, and co-operate in the adoption of the child by Stern's wife. After the child was born, however, Whitehead changed her mind and fled with the child to preclude delivering it to the Sterns. The Sterns then sued to enforce the contract and the trial court upheld the validity of the contract, terminated

Whitehead's rights, granted custody to Stern and an order for adoption by his wife.

On appeal, however, the appellate court concluded that the contract was invalid as a matter of public policy and thus unenforceable. At the same time, using the test of the best interests of the child, the appellate court decided, in part based on expert evidence, that the Sterns should have custody of the child. In doing so, the court commented on Whitehead's motivation to keep the child, based on her love for the little girl, but also noted the lack of security in the Whitehead home and some personality characteristics that might interfere with the child's upbringing.

The Royal Commission on New Reproductive Technologies in Canada (1993)

In this context, the federal government established a Royal Commission on New Reproductive Technologies to provide advice about the regulation of assisted reproduction measures. Its report, *Proceed with Care* was released in 1993, and it recommended criminalizing commercial surrogacy arrangements and recognizing the gestational mother as the "mother" for legal purposes, an approach that would require adoption by an intentional, non-biological parent. See Royal Commission on New Reproductive Technologies, *Proceed with Care* (Ottawa: Queen's Printer, 1993).

The *Assisted Human Reproduction Act* 2004 and its impact

Although a number of Bills were introduced into Parliament after 1996, it was not until 2004 that Parliament enacted the *Assisted Human Reproduction Act*, SC 2004, c 2 ("*AHRA*"). However, this legislation has not been fully implemented, nor has it been effective. This has created considerable uncertainty in the practice of assisted human reproduction.

For example, it is unclear the extent to which the *AHRA* permits the payment of expenses for surrogacy and human eggs. Section 6 of the *AHRA* prohibits the payment of "consideration to a female person to be a surrogate mother" while section 7 prohibits the "purchase, offer to purchase, and advertising for purchase" of sperm or eggs. Section 12 of the *AHRA* provides that individuals may be "reimbursed" for "expenditures" incurred by the donor or surrogate mother. At the time of writing, the regulations detailing the authorized expenditures had not been drafted nor is section 12 in force. Notably a person committing this offence may be subject to a fine of up to $500,000 or 10 years' imprisonment. This legal uncertainty combined with significant penalties has caused many to operate "in the shadows of the law especially if any money changes hands". (See Karen Busby & Delaney Vun, "Revisiting *The Handmaid's Tale*: Feminist Theory Meets Empirical Research on Surrogate Mothers" (2010) 26:1 CJWL 13 at 28.)

There is strong evidence of Canadians importing human eggs from abroad and foreign nationals coming to Canada to provide human eggs for reproductive purposes. Does the *AHRA* apply to this conduct? There has been an important debate about the extent to which sections 7 and 12 apply to the transnational trade in human eggs. (See Jocelyn Downie & Francoise Baylis, "Transnational Trade in Human Eggs: Law, Policy and (In)Action in Canada" (2013) 41:1 J L Med Ethics 224; and Susan G Drummond & Sara R Cohen, "Eloquent (In)action: Enforcement and Prosecutorial Restraint in the Transnational Trade in Human Eggs as Deep Ambivalence about the Law" (2014) 26 CJWL 206.)

Charges have only been laid once pursuant to the *AHRA*. In 2013, Leia Picard plead guilty to violating sections 6 and 7 of the *AHRA*. She admitted to paying a flat fee to women who provided eggs ($15,000) and to women who acted as surrogates ($22,000). She was fined $60,000.00 (*R v Picard and Canadian Fertility Consulting Ltd.* (2013), Agreed Statement of Facts, online: <http://www.dal.ca/content/dam/dalhousie/pdf/sites/noveltechethics/AHRA_Facts.pdf>).

Challenging the Constitutionality of the *Assisted Human Reproduction Act*

To some extent, the failure to implement the *AHRA* successfully may be related to the constitutional challenge launched by Québec, which was eventually joined by Alberta, Saskatchewan and New Brunswick. In the Supreme Court of Canada, a majority of the court concluded that some sections of the *AHRA* were not within the federal authority to legislate with respect to criminal law, holding that Parliament had acted to establish national standards for assisted human reproduction, rather than legislating on the basis of an apprehension of harm. However, a number of sections were upheld, including section 8 concerning the donor's consent for the use of *in vitro* embryos. The surrogacy provisions were also held to be constitutional, including section 12 concerning payment of expenses (see *Reference re Assisted Human Reproduction Act*, 2010 SCC 61).

However, the *AHRA* as a whole may no longer be entirely coherent, and to the extent that the Supreme Court's decision now permits provincial governments to enact legislation concerning some aspects of assisted reproduction, it seems possible that there will be less national uniformity in the treatment of some of these issues. Ontario has not yet enacted legislation, and there is some uncertainty with respect to the precise arrangements now legally available to overcome problems of infertility, particularly with respect to surrogacy: see *Law Times* (22 August 2011) 12. In this context, some critics have recommended repeal of the *AHRA* because it is not consistent with current ideas and practices in relation to family formation. See André Picard, "Fertility Law Needs a Reset", *The Globe and Mail* (3 April 2012) L5.

How should the provinces respond to this challenge? For some general suggestions see Juliet Guichon, Ian Mitchell & Christopher Doig, "Assisted Human Reproduction in Common Law Canada after the Supreme Court of Canada Reference: Moving Beyond Regulation by Colleges of Physicians and Surgeons" (2013) 25:2 CJWL 315; for suggestions with respect to the regulation of egg donation see Vanessa Gruben, "Women as Patients, Not Spare Parts: Examining the Relationship between Physician and Egg Providers" (2013) 25:2 CJWL 249; and for suggestions regarding surrogacy, see Busby & Vun at 85–93.

Notes and Questions

Some "good news" stories about surrogacy

Newspaper accounts have confirmed *non-commercial surrogacy* arrangements in Canada, in which a friend or sister agrees to gestate and give birth to a child. For example, see Debra Black, "Surrogate Motherhood 'Expression of Love' ", *Toronto Star* (31 December 1999), providing an account of an agreement by a York Region police officer to gestate a child for her longtime friend living in California. In this case, the gestational mother was implanted with the intentional mother's egg and fertilized by the sperm of the intentional father. More recently, there was a similar news report about a woman who gestated a baby for her sister (see Megan Ogilvie, "Amazing Kindness: The Gift of a Son", *Toronto Star* (19 December 2009) A1).

Empirical studies of surrogacy practices in the United Kingdom, the United States, and Canada

In their review of empirical studies of surrogacy arrangements, a number of which have been conducted in the United Kingdom and the United States, Busby and Vun explained that there is a growing body of research that provides little support for concerns about contractual parenting and the potential for emotional damage for surrogate mothers, children or intended/social parents; and they argue that the *Baby M* case was thus an exception.

Surrogacy arrangements are now available pursuant to legislation that regulates the practice in a number of U.S. states, and some scholars have claimed that about 25,000 babies have been born to surrogates there. However, legislation in the United Kingdom prohibits commercial surrogacy arrangements and the use of for-profit agents, but permits payment of reasonable expenses, and there have been few litigated disputes (see *Surrogacy Arrangements Act 1985* and *Human Fertilization and Embryology Act 1990*).

In reviewing the literature (including feminist literature) that is critical of surrogacy, as well as a number of empirical investigations, Busby and Vun concluded overall that the empirical research does not support the views of many critics of surrogacy:

> The stories told by American and British women who have agreed to be surrogate mothers are quite different from the cautionary tale told by Atwood's handmaid and they indicate that the experience of Mary Beth Whitehead, the surrogate mother in the *Baby M* case, is the exception not the norm. The empirical research demonstrates that concerns that commercial surrogacy will lead to commodification and exploitation and that women cannot give meaningful consent to such arrangements, have not been realized in those countries. Because participation in surro-

gacy in Canada is a criminal offense, the stories of Canadian participants are, like the stories of Atwood's handmaids, only told in whispers of mediated forums or confidential conversations.... (Busby & Vun at 92)

In this context, how should legal policy makers proceed in the Canadian context? For one example of provincial legislation, see Québec statutes: *Act respecting clinical and research activities relating to assisted procreation*, CQLR c A-5.01; *Act respecting health services and social services*, CQLR c S-4.2; and *Act respecting medical laboratories, organ, tissue, gamete and embryo conservation, and the disposal of human bodies*, CQLR c L-O.2. British Columbia's *Family Law Act*, SBC 2011, c 25, also addresses some of these new issues of parentage (see Part 3).

New problems for family law?

- **The black market in eggs:** In spite of prohibitions on buying or selling eggs in Canada pursuant to the *AHRA*, press reports reveal want ads for eggs posted on free Internet classified sites such as Craigslist and Kijiji, as well as offers of eggs posted by potential donors, with prices of $3,000 to $9,500 (see Megan Ogilvie, "Hatching Babies: The Price of Eggs", *Toronto Star* (21 November 2009) A1; and Alison Motluk, "The Human Egg Trade", *The Walrus* (April 2010) 30). As described earlier in *Picard*, the sale of eggs for a flat fee resulted in one criminal conviction.

- **Mix-ups in fertility procedures:** Recently, there have also been some new problems with mix-ups of eggs or sperm in relation to surrogacy and other assisted reproduction measures. For example, a couple, who had used donor eggs fertilized by the husband's sperm and a gestational carrier in India that resulted in the birth of twins, were shocked to discover that DNA testing (required to obtain Canadian passports for the twins) indicated that there was no biological relationship between one of the twins and the father (see Reveena Aulakh, "Baby Quest Traps Couple in India", *Toronto Star* (21 December 2010) A1; and Raveena Aulakh, "Ottawa Urged to Bring Stranded Family Home", *Toronto Star* (22 December 2010) A4).

  A fertility doctor pleaded guilty to professional misconduct for inseminating three women with sperm that was not from their husband or the intended donor. As a result, the women later discovered that their children were not the biological children of their husband or intended donor. The College of Physicians and Surgeons ordered a public reprimand and a two-month suspension of Dr. Norman Barwin's medical licence: <http://www.cpso.on.ca/Whatsnew/News-Releases/2013/Discipline-Committee-Decisions-(13)>.

- **Disputes over frozen sperm:** The question of how to dispose of frozen sperm at the end of an intimate relationship was addressed in *JCM v ANA*, 2012 BCSC 584. A lesbian couple, JCM and ANA had purchased sperm together, which they had used to give birth to their two children. When they separated, the women signed a separation agreement dividing the assets equally between them. However, the women disagreed on the disposition of thirteen remaining sperm straws. JCM wished to give the sperm to her new partner to conceive a child who would be biologically related to the children from her relationship with ANA and argued that she was entitled to half of the sperm straws. ANA disagreed and argued that the sperm straws should be destroyed. The court concluded that the sperm straws should be divided in accordance with the property provisions of the separation agreement. For a case about reproductive materials as "property", see *Lam v University of British Columbia*, 2015 BCCA 2, in which sperm held in a freezer at the University of British Columbia was held to be "property" and that the *Warehouse Receipt Act* governed the contract between the donors and the University. This case is discussed more fully in Chapter Six.

- **Surplus embryos:** According to recent news reports, there may be tens of thousands of fertilized eggs abandoned in medical clinics by persons who succeeded in their efforts at in vitro fertilization and gave birth to children using one or more of a larger number of embryos. As a result, the remaining embryos constitute "leftovers." The report indicated that Beginnings Counselling & Adoption Services of Ontario Inc. was proposing to make these embryos available to infertile couples at a cost of $13,500, not including legal and medical fees. See Lisa Priest, "The Birth of Canada's First Embryo Donation Program", *The Globe and Mail* (3 April 2010) A1.

- **Disputes between the parties in relation to "frozen" embryos:** In *CC v AW*, 2005 ABQB 290, a woman had asked her male friend to assist her in becoming pregnant, using an in vitro fertilization process. The clinic used by the parties required them to sign a contract that prevented either of them from using the embryos without the consent of both parties. The procedure was successful and children were born, but the parties then disagreed about the remaining embryos. The father did not wish to have more children with the woman, but the court refused to enforce the contract and held that the embryos belonged to the woman, while giving the parents joint custody of the children. Importantly, section 8 of the *AHRA*, which came into force December 1, 2007, governs disputes over frozen embryos in Canada. Section 8 prohibits the use of an embryo unless the donor(s) consent in accordance with the regulations (*Assisted Human Reproduction (Section 8 Consent) Regulations*, SOR/2007-137).

    Section 8 is consistent with the approach taken in the United Kingdom. In *Evans v the United Kingdom*, the European Court of Human Rights upheld the U.K. legislation that prohibited Ms. Evans from using embryos fertilized by her former partner without his consent. The man did not wish to be a parent after they had separated (*Evans v United Kingdom*, (2008) 46 EHRR 34).

The role for contracts

In part because of the uncertainty surrounding parentage, intended parties often enter into agreements with surrogates and gamete donors.

These agreements may address a number of issues, such as parentage, reimbursement of expenses, and custody and access, among other things. To what extent are these contracts binding?

In most provinces, the law is silent on whether surrogacy and donor agreements are enforceable. In Quebec, surrogacy agreements are null and void (*Civil Code of Québec*, CQLR c C-1991, Art 541). In Alberta, the *Family Law Act* provides that surrogacy agreements are not enforceable. In addition, Alberta's *Family Law Act* and British Columbia's *Family Law Act*, state that an agreement cannot satisfy the consent requirement for purposes of the declaration of parentage (*Family Law Act*, SA 2003, c F-4.5, s 8.2(8); SBC 2011, c 25, s 29(6)).

To date, there have been very few cases of disputes arising from these agreements. Although both these reported cases are just interim decisions and were ultimately settled out of court, they illustrate legal issues that may arise in future cases.

- **Surrogacy agreements:** The terms of a surrogacy agreement was challenged in *HLW and THW v JST and JT*, 2005 BCSC 1679. A woman, HLW, agreed to act as a traditional surrogate for JCT and JT. HLW and her spouse, THW, entered into an agreement with JST and JT, the intended parents. The agreement provided that HLW would be artificially inseminated with semen from JCT, and that all expenses associated with the pregnancy would be paid to HLW. The child was released into the custody of JCT and JT following his birth. HLW and THW brought an application for access to AT. The parties disagreed about what the agreement provided in terms of ongoing contact with AT. The interim order for access was denied. Ultimately, the parties settled this dispute out of court.

  There have also been press reports about a British couple who had entered into a surrogacy contract with a woman in New Brunswick (using the Canadian woman's egg fertilized by the British husband's sperm). However, prior to the birth of baby twins, the British couple separated and advised the Canadian woman that they no longer wished to have the babies. Although the Canadian woman gave birth and then found adoptive parents for the twins, the case reveals the need for care in such contracts. (See Cynthia Vukets, "Surrogate mother's nightmare", *Toronto Star* (10 September 2011) A1 and 22.)

  Some scholars have argued that such contracts will best protect the interests of gestational and contracting mothers if they reflect the adoption context, in which the law recognizes the birth mother as the child's mother, subject to her decision to consent to the child's transfer to the contracting mother. According to Rosemarie Tong,

  > I oppose a ban on gestational motherhood. Although such a ban might have the welcome effect of protecting some gestational and contracting mothers from exploitation, these women (and their children) can be legally protected in less restrictive ways....
  >
  > Women as a *whole* will benefit from an approach that stresses their right, not their duty, to be mothers (and not simply baby machines). The adoption approach, with its change of heart clause,

replaces what strikes me as the *heartless* contract approach. A deal is not always a deal — at least not when one is trading in some of the deepest emotions human beings can ever feel. Any approach that *binds* women to reproductive decisions — as does the contract approach — must be regarded with deep suspicion. (Rosemarie Tong, "Feminist Perspectives and Gestational Motherhood: The Search for a Unified Legal Focus" in Joan C Callahan, ed, *Reproduction, Ethics, and the Law: Feminist Perspectives* (Bloomington and Indianapolis, IN: Indiana University Press, 1995) 55 at 75)

Recall that the *AHRA* prohibits commercial surrogacy in Canada (in *Picard*, above). In the United States, moreover, a surrogacy lawyer who was engaged in a lucrative baby-selling scheme was convicted of fraud and sentenced to a term in prison. See Julie Watson, "U.S. Surrogacy Lawyer Jailed after Babies sold for $150,000", *Toronto Star* (25 January 2012) A23.

- **Donor agreements:** In Ontario, there has been some litigation arising from an agreement executed between a lesbian couple and known sperm donor. The applicant, WW sought a declaration of parentage and access to the child, ZZ. XX gave birth to ZZ and was ZZ's genetic mother. YY was XX's spouse. WW had entered into a Donor Agreement with XX and YY prior to the birth of ZZ. In the Agreement, WW agreed to sign over any and all parental rights including custody or access, to any children created by his sperm. In January 2011, WW sought a declaration of parentage and access to ZZ.

  In the initial motion for interim access, the Court decided that it was in the best interests of the child to maintain the status quo and denied WW interim access to the child: 2012 ONSC 3949. Based on the evidence, the child was happy and properly cared for by XX and YY, and WW was not incapable of performing a parenting role. The judge noted that the donor would presumably have been selected due to his positive qualities. The Court explained:

  > **[10]** While it appears to be widely accepted by the Courts that it is important for children to maintain relationships with their biological parents, it has been stated judicially that this is simply one factor to be considered: see e.g. Law v. Siu, 2009 ONCA 61, [2009] O.J. No. 245.

  > **[12]** To that end, the child, who will not be two years of age until October 1, 2012, has never been introduced to his father. It was argued that by introducing the applicant into the child's life now, and should the respondent ultimately be successful on this application, the child may become confused and insecure. Despite the child's young age, it is impossible to know what disclosure of the applicant's status as his parent might mean. All circumstances considered, the risk of there being an adverse effect to the child is too great to ignore. I considered imposing limitations on the extent of the disclosure to the child, but attempting to enforce such limitations would be virtually impossible. In addition, it was also argued that by making an access order at this stage, I may indirectly influence the outcome of these proceedings. In light of the fact that the trial should take place very shortly, I find both of these arguments very convincing.

[13] Accordingly, I am satisfied that in this case, the usual rule maintaining the status quo pending trial should be adhered to, in the best interests of the child. Although seventeen months has already expired through no fault of the applicant, once we consider the age of the child, the possibility of the negative consequences referred to above, and the relativity short period remaining until the trial, there does not appear to exist adequate reason to disrupt the status quo. After trial, there will be sufficient opportunity for the applicant to develop a relationship with the child, should he be successful.

As this was the first case in Ontario that dealt with a disputed claim for parentage and access of a child conceived using donated gametes, the LGBTQ Parenting Network requested leave to intervene in the trial as a friend of the court: *WW v XX*, 2013 ONSC 1509. The Network's submissions illustrate the important legal questions concerning parentage that remain to be resolved:

[11] ... [the trial would] involve the consideration of a number of emerging socio-legal issues:

- How the recognition of diverse family forms and assisted reproduction issues interact with the best interests of the child.
- The legal security of lesbians and other non-biological parents who wish to create families through contracts dealing with assisted reproduction.
- The role and validity of such contracts in disputes on access and parentage.

[15] [The Network also] identified a number of public policy issues that the court may consider in reach a decision in this case including[:]

- LGBTQ experiences with assisted human reproduction services;
- methods of organizing families to avoid conflict; and
- LGBTQ adoption and children of LGBTQ parents.

Both parties consented to the Network as an intervenor.

In considering whether the Network would make a useful contribution to the resolution of the matter without causing injustice to the immediate parties, the Court explained:

[21] The parties in this case are solely interested in the resolution of the parentage and access dispute regarding child Z.Z. The respondents argue inter alia that the donor agreement is one but an important factor for the court to consider in making its determination. On the other hand, the Network seeks to ensure that the court has sufficient information to put donor agreements in a broader social context. They argue that in order for the court to fully appreciate the issues that arise in this proceeding, it is necessary and useful to be aware of the culture, customary practices and social organization of the LGBTQ community. An intended parental project, as they are called in the material filed by the proposed intervenor, refers [to] the creation of families by some means of assisted human reproduction, which are often governed by a contract such as a donor agreement. The context in which donor agreements are created, their meaning to those who are involved in intended parental projects, and their impact in the social and legal structure of intended families including children is the focus of the Network as intervenor in these proceed-

ings. This perspective, broadly defined, is distinct from the perspective of the parties.

[22] It is recognized that any decision in this case may have a much broader impact, particularly within LGBTQ-led families. The Network has the ability to present the perspective of a specific group whose interests may be affected by the outcome and who would not otherwise be heard. They have recognized expertise in the area of intentional parental projects through research, publications, community programming, workshops and the provision of guidance for those considering intentional parental projects.

[23] The Network submits and I accept that it is able to make submissions that consider the implications of this case for numerous family configurations and which include the experiences of children of LGBTQ parents, parents who choose to conceive using known sperm donors, non-biological co-parents and single parents.

The Court granted the Network intervenor status.

Ultimately, the parties settled this dispute out of court. Thus, the extent to which donor agreements may or may not be binding is still uncertain. What is certain is the urgent need for reform of Ontario's parentage laws to reflect the diversity of family configurations.

Additional Resources

Lori Andrews, *Between Strangers: Surrogate Mothers, Expectant Fathers, and Brave New Babies* (New York: Harper & Row, 1989).

Angela Campbell, "Law's Suppositions about Surrogacy against the Backdrop of Social Science" (2011–2012) 43:1 Ottawa L Rev 29.

Rachel Cook & Shelley Day Slater, with Felicity Kaganas, eds, *Surrogate Motherhood: International Perspectives* (Oxford & Portland, OR: Hart Publishing, 2003).

Martha Field, *Surrogate Motherhood: The Legal and Human Issues* (Cambridge, MA: Harvard University Press, 1990).

Caroline Forder, "Human Rights Aspects of Assisted Procreation: A European Perspective" (1999) 1 Journal of Women's Health and Law 69.

Vanessa Gruben & Angela Cameron, "Quebec's Constitutional Challenge to the Assisted Human Reproduction Act: Overlooking Women's Reproductive Autonomy?" in Stephanie Paterson, Francesca Scala & Marlene K Skolon, *Fertile Ground: Exploring Reproduction in Canada* (Montreal: McGill-Queen's University Press, 2014) 125.

Alison Harvison-Young & Angela Wasunna, "Wrestling with the Limits of Law: Regulating New Reproductive Technologies" (1998) 6 Health LJ 239.

Fiona Kelly, "(Re)forming Parenthood: The Assignment of Legal Parentage within Planned Lesbian Families" (2009) 40 Ottawa L Rev 185.

Pamela Laufer-Ukeles, "Approaching Surrogate Motherhood: Reconsidering Difference" (2002) 26 Vermont Law Review 407.

Diana Majury, "Is Care Enough?" (1994) 17 Dalhousie LJ 279.

Diana Majury, "Pre-Conception Contracts: Giving the Mother the Option" in Simon Rosenblum & Peter Findlay, eds, *Debating Canada's Future: Views from the Left* (Toronto: J. Lorimer, 1991) 197.

Adam Marshall, "Choices for a Child: An Ethical and Legal Analysis of a Failed Surrogate Birth Contract" (1996) 30 U Rich L Rev 275.

Christine Overall, "The Case Against Legalization of Contract Motherhood" in Simon Rosenblum & Peter Findlay, eds, *Debating Canada's Future: Views from the Left* (Toronto: J. Lorimer, 1991) 210.

Carl E Schneider, "Surrogate Motherhood from the Perspective of Family Law" (1990) 13 Harv JL & Pub Pol'y 125.

Barbara Stark, "Transnational Surrogacy and International Human Rights Law" (2012) 18:2 ILSA J Intl & Comp L.

Sarah Wilson, "Identity, Genealogy, and the Social Family: The Case of Donor Insemination" (1997) 11 Intl JL Pol'y & Fam 270.

ASSISTED REPRODUCTION: BIRTH REGISTRATION AND DECLARATIONS OF PARENTAGE

Registering children in assisted reproduction cases

Although there is one case reported in Canada about a dispute between a "surrogate" and the commissioning parents with respect to the terms of their agreement, the resolution in this case was not reported (see *HLW and THW v JST and JT*). In all the other cases, the dispute has focused on issues relating to the registration of the child's birth and/or entitlement on the part of an intentional parent to a declaration of parentage. Such cases have occurred in relation to both opposite-sex and same-sex intentional parents.

JR v LH
[2002] OJ No 3998 (Sup Ct)

KITELY J:

This is a good news case. It involves two families who shared a common goal. The applicants and respondents are not adverse. Indeed, they have collaborated in their gestational carriage agreement and this application is simply the legal outcome of a wonderful arrangement.

This is an application for a declaration that the applicants are the biological mother (J.R.) and father (J.K.) of twins; for an order awarding custody of the twins to the applicants; for a declaration that the respondent G.H. is not the father of the twins; and for an order directing the Registrar General to register a Statement of Birth consistent with the foregoing declaration.

The twins were born on February 9, 2002. This application was issued on March 1, 2002. The matter originally came on before me on March 5, 2002. There were difficulties with the affidavits and consequently the matter was adjourned to March 21, 2002. On that date, I received another application record and I heard further submissions from counsel.

Section 9 of the *Vital Statistics Act* requires the mother and father to make and certify a statement of the child's birth within thirty days of the birth. Section 9(12) provides that on receiving a certified copy of an order with respect to the child's parentage, the Registrar General shall amend the particulars of the child's parents shown on the registration. The Statement of Birth had not been contained in the affidavits. On March 21, 2002, I asked Ms. Blom to obtain it on the basis that I needed to see the existing Statement of Birth which had been filed to ascertain the amendments which the Registrar General should be required to make. Having heard submissions, I directed counsel to file supplementary evidence as to the Statement of Birth for each child.

Ms. Blom reported on April 8, 2002 that she was having difficulty obtaining the record due to the labour disruption. Ms. Blom filed a supplementary affidavit in early May. In that supplementary affidavit of a law clerk in Ms. Blom's office, I was given a copy of the "Proof and/or Time of Birth Statement" for each child. This appears to be the statement required to be provided pursuant to section 8 of the *Vital Statistics Act* by the medical practitioner who attends at the birth. In this supplementary affidavit, Ms. Deacon reported that the Statements of Birth required by section 9(2) had not been filed by the applicants. They had decided to await the outcome of this application before submitting the requisite form. Consequently, section 9(12) of the *Vital Statistics Act* does not apply because the Registrar General cannot be expected to amend a record which has not yet been filed. It may be that since May, a Statement of Birth has been filed. In view of the lengthy time between May 7th and the release of these reasons, I elected not to seek clarification from Ms. Blom. In the order below, I have tried to anticipate the procedural options.

The applicants are common law spouses. J.R. is unable to have children. J.R. and J.K. investigated the possibilities of gestational carriage. They were accepted as candidates for the in vitro fertilization program at a Toronto hospital. They signed the consent form required to participate in the program. The respondent L.H. is the woman who is the gestational carrier. She and her husband G.H. also signed the consent form. The applicants and respondents signed a gestational carriage agreement. On February 9th, 2002 the twins were born. On February 11th, J.R. and J.K. provided blood samples for the purpose of determining the biological parentage of the children. The results of the DNA testing established that J.R. and J.K. are the biological mother and father of the twins. The children have lived with the applicants since the birth.

The application was served on the respondents. In their affidavits filed by Ms. Blom, they support the application. They have signed a consent to a draft judgment which is consistent with the relief sought.

There is no issue as to the enforceability of the gestational carriage agreement.

DECLARATIONS WITH RESPECT TO PARENTAGE

Section 4 of the *Children's Law Reform Act* is as follows:

> (1) Any person having an interest may apply to a court for a declaration that a male person is recognized in law to be the father of a child or that a female person is the mother of a child.

> (2) Where the court finds that a presumption of paternity exists under section 8 and unless it is established, on the balance of probabilities, that the presumed father is not the father of the child, the

court shall make a declaratory order confirming that the paternity is recognized in law.

(3) Where the court finds on the balance of probabilities that the relationship of mother and child has been established, the court may make a declaratory order to that effect.

The court also referred to section 97 of the *Courts of Justice Act*, which provided for a superior court to make a binding declaration of right, whether or not any consequential relief could be claimed.

> I will first address the relief with respect to the applicants. The blood tests indicate that the probability that J.R. and J.K. are the mother and father respectively is greater than 99.99%. I find that on a balance of probabilities, they are the genetic parents of the twins. Pursuant to section 4(1), J.K. is entitled to be "recognized in law" as the father of the children and J.R. is entitled to be "recognized in law" to be the mother of the children.
>
> I turn next to the respondents. G.H. did not contribute genetic material. He is not the biological father. He is involved because he is the husband of the woman who is the gestational carrier and, pursuant to section 8(1) of the *Children's Law Reform Act*, he is presumed to be the father of the children. The presumption has been rebutted.
>
> Section 4(1) and (2) provide that the court may make positive declarations. But the *Children's Law Reform Act* is silent as to whether the court may make negative declarations. The *Courts of Justice Act* makes no such distinction. I agree with Potts J. that the right to know whether or not one is a parent of a child is of such significance that the issue may be the subject of a declaratory order pursuant to s. 97 of the *Courts of Justice Act*.... The applicants have established that a declaration that G.H. is not the father ought to be made.
>
> In the application there is no request for declaratory relief with respect to L.H. However, at paragraph 39 of the factum, there is a request for a declaration that L.H. is not the mother of the children. If the application had been opposed, the omission from the application may have been problematic. However, it has not been opposed. Furthermore, L.H. supports the requests contained in the application. In her affidavit, L.H. described the circumstances of the gestational carriage agreement and the birth of the children and she specifically deposed that she is not the "mother" of the children. In the draft judgment contained in the second application record, she has consented to a judgment in those terms.
>
> Even with the consent of all concerned, the issue with respect to L.H. has different dimensions from the others. In section 1 of the *Vital Statistics Act*, "birth" is defined as "the complete expulsion or extraction from its mother of a fetus that did any time after being completely expelled or extracted from the mother breathe or show any other sign of life...." L.H. is clearly the birth mother.
>
> In *Chapman and Linto v. Her Majesty the Queen in Right of the Province of Manitoba and the Department of Vital Statistics*, [2000] MJ No. 482 (October 20, 2000), the genetic parents, the birth mother and her spouse all applied before the birth of the child for a declaration compelling the Local Hospital Authority and staff attending the birth to complete documentation showing that the genetic parents were the natural and legal parents. The application was opposed. That case differs from this in that the application was brought before the birth. But it is similar to this case in that the potential parents were all in agreement. The court declined to grant a declaration primarily because the woman who was the gestational carrier would be giving "birth" within the meaning of

their legislation and accordingly, the "birth" had to be so recorded. But the court pointed out that a declaration of parentage could be made after that preliminary step.

In some cases, there is a conflict between the genetic parents and the woman who is the gestational carrier. For example, in *A.J. v. M.C.* (1992), 286 Cal. Rptr. 369, the woman who was the gestational carrier of an egg and sperm of the genetic parents sought to be declared the birth mother in addition to the genetic mother. The Court of Appeals agreed with the trial judge that the genetic parents were the "natural and legal parents of the child" and the woman who was the gestational carrier was not entitled to a declaration of her parenthood.

If such a conflict existed, I would have to consider whether s. 4(1) enables a declaration that there is more than one mother, as Benotto J. raised but did not determine in *Buist v. Greaves*, [1997] OJ No. 2646 (1997).... However, the disposition in this case is facilitated because the birth mother agrees with the genetic parents that she ought to be declared not to be a parent.

The *Children's Law Reform Act* does not apply. But it is appropriate to make the declaration pursuant to section 97 of the *Courts of Justice Act*.

In the few relevant cases, there is no suggestion that the "best interests of the children" ought to be considered in cases in which declaratory relief is sought. Whether or not it is a criterion which I must consider, I have no hesitation in finding that these declarations are in the best interests of the children. The affidavits describe thoughtful, responsible persons who entered into this arrangement with the sole objective of bringing children into the world who would be well-cared for. That objective has been achieved.

CUSTODY

Section 20 of the *Children's Law Reform Act* provides that the father and the mother are equally entitled to custody of the children. Pursuant to section 21, a parent may apply for an order respecting custody of the children. Any such order must be made in the best interests of the children.

Immediately after the birth, the twins began to live with J.R. and J.K. L.H. is not only content but enthusiastic about the care which the children will receive from the applicants. G.H. supports his wife in asserting that they believe that it will be in the best interests of the twins to remain in the care and custody of the applicants. The evidence amply supports such a finding.

AMENDMENT OF REGISTRATIONS

As indicated above, it appears that as of the end of April, 2002 the Statement of Birth had not been filed within the 30 days specified in section 9(2) of the *Vital Statistics Act*. If that is the case, then the Registrar General need not make any amendment to the records. It may be that the Statement has subsequently been submitted, in which case section 9(12) would apply. As the supplementary affidavit indicates, the physician did comply with section 8 by submitting the Proof and/or Time of Birth form for each child in which the mother was identified as L.H. It may be that the Registrar General has registered the birth of the twins based on the physician's form. Given the declaratory relief to be granted, it is logical that whatever order is required to enable the registrations consistent with the declarations ought to be made.

In response to a request to seal the court files, pursuant to section 137(2) of the *Courts of Justice Act*, the court concluded:

SEALING THE COURT FILE

In the absence of any evidence to justify the request, I am not prepared to speculate or infer what factors would be weighed on the part of the applicants. I have only the presumption of openness which I must apply.

The rules provide a less secretive remedy, namely the use of pseudonyms or initials [see rule 14.08]. This issue of gestational carriage agreements (and indeed traditional surrogacy agreements) is an emerging matter of public policy. Ms. Blom could not provide me with any cases in which orders such as this have been made. Undoubtedly there have been some, indeed many. A roadmap is necessary so that the genetic parents and the "birth mother" and her spouse if there is one, know what to expect in the conclusion of the legal process. It is in the public interest that the roadmap be available for those considering such a procedure. It is equally as important that the public have the opportunity to know and understand how these issues are resolved. But it does not mean that the identity of the members of the two families need to be publicized. Without evidence from any of the parties, the balance between those issues is found in the use of pseudonyms. I am prepared to find that these parties would consider it a significant intrusion on their privacy if their identities were made public. Their privacy can be protected while the fundamental value of openness is observed if the participants are identified with initials.

It will be necessary for Ms. Blom to prepare a copy of the order with the full names of the adults and the children in order that it be sent to the Registrar General. She may forward a copy of that order to me for signing.

ORDER TO GO AS FOLLOWS

1. Pursuant to s. 4(1) of the *Children's Law Reform Act*, I declare that J.K. is the father of the children J.N.K. and M.C.K., both born February 9, 2002 and that he shall be recognized in law to be their father.

2. Pursuant to s. 4(1) of the *Children's Law Reform Act*, I declare that J.R. is the mother of the children J.N.K. and M.C.K., both born February 9, 2002 and that she shall be recognized in law to be their mother.

3. Pursuant to section 97 of the *Courts of Justice Act*, I declare that G.H. is not the father of the children J.N.K. and M.C.K., both born February 9, 2002.

4. Pursuant to section 97 of the *Courts of Justice Act*, I declare that L.H. is not the mother of the children J.N.K. and M.C.K., both born February 9, 2002.

5. If a Statement of Birth has been filed pursuant to section 9(2) of the *Vital Statistics Act* for the children, or if the Registrar General has registered the parentage of the children based upon the "Proof and/or time of Birth Statement," on receiving a certified copy of an order consistent with the endorsement, the Registrar General shall amend the particulars of the parents of the children J.N.K. and M.C.K., both born February 9, 2002.

6. If a Statement of Birth has not been filed pursuant to section 9(2) of the *Vital Statistics Act* for the children, the applicants are authorized to submit a Statement of Birth for the children J.N.K. and M.C.K., both born February 9, 2002 which is consistent with the declarations contained above.

7. Pursuant to s. 21 of the *Children's Law Reform Act*, the applicants shall have custody of the children J.N.K. and M.C.K., both born February 9, 2002.

8. The request for an order pursuant to s. 137(2) of the *Courts of Justice Act* is refused.

9. The title of proceedings shall be changed for all purposes except item 6 above to reflect [this order]. ...

And the Registrar of the Superior Court of Justice is directed to amend the records accordingly.

Notes and Questions

Birth registration and genetic parents

- *Rypkema v* British Columbia, 2003 BCSC 1784: The genetic parents of a child born to a gestational mother were declared to be the child's parents for purposes of the birth registration process maintained by the provincial government. In *Rypkema*, the petitioners were opposite-sex genetic and social parents of the child, and the gestational mother supported their application for the child's birth registration in their names.

  In granting the application, the court cited the Supreme Court's decision in *Trociuk*, discussed earlier in this chapter, and its recognition of the significance of birth registration in establishing parent–child relationships. The court also criticized the vital statistics legislation because it had not kept pace with reproductive technologies. See Gary Oakes, "Genetic Parents in Surrogate Birth Win Registration Right", *The Lawyers Weekly* (16 January 2004) 7.

- *BAN v JH*, [2008] BCJ No 1169 (SC): The court granted a declaration of parentage to a wife and her husband, whose sperm had been combined using *in vitro* fertilization with a donor egg and implanted in a gestational carrier. Both the egg donor and the gestational mother consented to the application by the husband and wife, which was brought to avoid the expense, delay and potential uncertainty of an adoption application; in addition, affidavit evidence was provided in accordance with the requirements of the *Vital Statistics Act*. In this case, the court held that there was no jurisdiction to make the declaration of parentage pursuant to the *VSA* and there was no *parens patriae* jurisdiction, but that the declaration was available pursuant to the court's general power to grant equitable declaratory relief as to legal status under the Rules of Court. See now the *Family Law Act*, SBC 2011, c 25, s 29, regarding parentage in the context of surrogacy arrangements.

- *MD v LL* (2008), 52 RFL (6th) 122 (Ont Sup Ct): After considering the issues discussed in *JR v LH* above, and particularly in the light of the decision of the Ontario Court of Appeal in *AA v BB and CC* (a case that recognized three parents pursuant to the *parens patriae* jurisdiction, discussed later in this chapter), Nelson J held that there was a "gap" in the *Vital Statistics Act* because the definition of "mother" no longer accorded with recent developments in assisted reproduction:

> **[63]** ... In 1948 [when the current *VSA* definition of "birth" was first adopted], the notion that ova could be fertilized in a laboratory, and then implanted into a surrogate mother to gestate, would have been the stuff of science fiction. The current *VSA* has not changed with respect to its definition of "birth," and the consequent inference that the "mother" is the person who gave birth to the child. There is no recognition in the *VSA* that there can be two mothers: the birth mother and the genetic mother....

> **[65]** [The court then considered the "gap" that occurred because of this definition in the *VSA* and the need for an order to declare that the gestational mother was not the mother, pursuant to the *Courts of Justice Act*.] There is no gap that arises out of the *CJA*; rather, the gap stems from the effect of the *VSA* upon the ability of this court to issue a declaration of non-maternity. Therefore, the gap is indirect in nature. That said, it is no less of a gap, and I can think of no principled reason why the court's remedial *parens patriae* jurisdiction should not be available to rectify the situation by clarifying the legal status and rights of the parties.

> **[66]** The ruling does not affect in any way the legitimacy of the statutory and regulatory scheme of birth registration. This ruling simply pertains to the issue of whether the inferred definition of "mother" under the *VSA* prevents a declaration that the woman who gave birth to a child is <u>not</u> the mother of that same child after that child's birth has been registered in accordance with the law.

> **[67]** It is in the best interests of the child that this court issue a declaration that the child's surrogate mother, who is without a genetic link to the child, is not that child's mother.... In my opinion, there is no doubt that it is additionally in the best interests of the child to remove any ambiguity about who the child's mother is, where the circumstances of the child's birth and the operation of a statute combine to produce such ambiguity....

- *WJQM v AMA*, 2011 SKQB 317: WJQM and LJE, a same-sex couple, sought a declaration that Mary, the gestational carrier, was not the mother of their child. The child was conceived using an anonymous egg donor. WJQM was identified on the birth registration as the child's father, Mary was the mother and WJQM's same sex partner, LJE was identified as an "other parent." The court, after considering the decision in *MD v LL*, made a declaration of non-parentage that Mary was not the mother of the child.

JC v Manitoba: Birth registration prior to birth?

In *JR v LH*, the court referred to a Manitoba case, in which the gestational mother and her husband joined in an application, prior to the birth of a child, by the intentional parents for a declaration that the hospital documentation of the child's birth show the intentional parents as the "natural and legal parents" of the child to be delivered by the gestational mother. In this case, the intentional parents had supplied the egg and sperm that were placed in the womb of the man's sister, the gestational mother (see *JC v Manitoba*, 2000 MBQB 173).

The court considered the statutory provisions and concluded that only the person who gives birth may be recorded as the child's mother. The *Vital Statistics Act*, RSM 1987, c V60, s 1, defined "birth" as "the complete expulsion or extraction from its mother." Thus, no such declaration was possible, particularly in advance of the child's birth.

In denying the application, the court reviewed the policy issues, stating (at paras 9–10):

> Without going into any potential ramifications if the application were allowed, suffice it to say that the Department of Vital Statistics is set up to record just that, vital statistics, one of which is birth or the extraction from its mother of a product of conception. SJL is the individual who will be giving birth to this unborn child, and the records of the Department of Vital Statistics should reflect that fact. It is interesting to note that in the application the applicants themselves refer to SJL as the "birth mother." A declaration of parentage can follow the recording of this fact.
>
> I would be prepared to give a declaration of paternity in favour of JC at this point, but the applicants do not want JC named as father on the same birth registration that shows his sister as the birth mother. This is completely understandable. Therefore, rather than making that declaration of paternity, and not being prepared to make a declaration of maternity before a child is born and before the registration of birth shows the birth mother as SJL, the application for relief will be dismissed.

According to a subsequent newspaper account of this case, the result was that the intentional parents were required to "adopt their own child." See Mike McIntyre, "Parents Forced To Adopt Own Baby", *Winnipeg Free Press* (28 October 2000) A1. Recall the purposes of vital statistics legislation, discussed earlier in relation to the *Trociuk* case — does this decision reflect these goals?

Why was the birth mother's co-operation in *Rypkema, BAN, MD,* and *WJQM* so much more helpful than that of the birth mother in *JC v Manitoba*? Is there any danger that gestational mothers may be subjected to inappropriate pressures in such situations? In thinking about these cases, consider whether they suggest a need for further reform of vital statistics legislation?

Consider this situation:

> An anonymous embryo donation (both the egg donor and the sperm donor were anonymous) was implanted into a gestational surrogate, pursuant to a contract with the intentional parents. A month before the birth of the child, however, the intentional father petitioned to dissolve his marriage to the intentional mother, and in doing so, he indicated that he was accepting no responsibility for the child. The gestational mother disclaimed any parental rights or responsibility. And the intentional mother had no genetic or gestational link to the child. Who is/are the parent(s) of this child?

In *Re Marriage of Buzzanca*, 61 Cal App (4th) 1410 (App Ct 1998), the court held that the Buzzancas (the intentional parents) were the legal parents of the child. By the time of this court decision, the child was three years old. Does this situation suggest a need for urgent legislative action?

SAME-SEX PARENTS: CHALLENGING (HETEROSEXUAL) NORMS OF BIRTH REGISTRATION AND PARENTAGE

Human rights and birth registration for same-sex parents: *Gill v Murray*

In *Gill v Murray*, 2001 BCHRT 34, complaints were filed by two same-sex partners of birth mothers with the B.C. Human Rights Commission. The complainants alleged that their treatment by the Vital Statistics Agency constituted sex and sexual orientation discrimination because the agency refused to permit them to be registered as "parents" of children born to their partner "mothers." As a result, these same-sex partners had to obtain orders for adoption in order to be recognized as "parents."

In this context, the complainants demonstrated that the agency routinely permitted males in opposite-sex relationships to be registered as parents, without any inquiry as to whether the males were biologically related to the child whose birth was being registered. The Commission's decision confirmed that the agency was engaged in discrimination, stating in part (at paras 79–84):

> When the partner of the mother is not a biological parent of the child, Vital Statistics will only register that parent if an adoption order under the provisions of the *Adoption Act*, RSBC 1996, c. 5 has been obtained. Although this is theoretically the case whether the partner is the same or the opposite sex as the mother, in practice only same-sex partners of mothers are questioned as to their biological relationship with the child. Opposite sex partners of women giving birth are not similarly questioned.
>
> Furthermore, women who give birth to a child born using a donor egg are registered as mothers without question. Similarly, men who self-identify as fathers are able to register themselves as such on the Birth Registration forms. Neither parent is required to adopt, or resort to the Court, to establish the parent–child relationship.
>
> With the advent of various forms of reproductive technology, it is possible for a child to have legal social parents, biological parents, and a birth mother who is neither a legal, social or biological mother. It is evident that the Birth Registration regime established by Vital Statistics has not kept up with reproductive technologies. The same-sex partner of the biological mother of a child is denied the presumptive proof of her relationship to the child, including the right to register her child in school, to obtain airline tickets and passports for her child, as well as denying her the ability to assert her child's rights with respect to a myriad of other laws, from the *BC Benefits (Child Care) Act* to the *Young Offenders Act*, unless and until she resorts to the adoption process.
>
> In my view, Vital Statistics has denied same-sex couples the right to register a birth in the same way that opposite sex couples do, based on the Director's definition of "father," as well as its practice of allowing

males to register as fathers without any inquiry into a biological relationship with a child. The process of registering births, upon which birth certificates are based, is based solely on a heterosexual view of the family. Because the Complainants are women living in same sex relationships who have a child together, they can only establish families through the adoption process. This differential treatment to access to a process that confers a benefit offends the principles of equality on the bases of sexual orientation, family status and sex.

I conclude that Vital Statistics has denied the Complainants access to the benefit of verification and documentation of parent/child relationships available to others without the necessity of the adoption procedure, and has thus contravened s. 8 of the Code. I find that Vital Statistics has discriminated against Ms. Gill and Ms. Popoff on the basis of sex, sexual orientation and family status. I also find that Vital Statistics has discriminated against Ms. Maher and Ms. Murray on the basis of sex, sexual orientation and family status. Had Ms. Maher and Ms. Murray been male, they would not have been questioned as to their sex or biological connection to their child, nor would they have been directed to take steps to adopt their child.

Further, I find that Vital Statistics has discriminated against the infant children on the basis of sex, sexual orientation and their family status by denying them the right to have their parents named on the birth registration, and birth certificate, even though both parents acknowledge and fulfil the parental role. In that respect, the infant Complainants are treated differently than children of opposite sex parents.

The *Charter* and birth registration for same-sex parents: *Rutherford v Ontario (Deputy Registrar General)*

Gill v Murray succeeded in claims of discrimination pursuant to provincial human rights legislation in British Columbia.

A few years later, a similar challenge was launched in Ontario by applicants who were lesbian parents, whose children were conceived by anonymous donor insemination. They claimed that they were entitled to register accurate particulars of their children's parentage under the *Vital Statistics Act* and that they should be granted declarations of parentage pursuant to section 4 of the *Children's Law Reform Act*. The applicants asked the court to interpret these statutes to recognize modern methods of creating parent–child relationships, and in the alternative, to do so pursuant to the court's inherent *parens patriae* jurisdiction. Finally, the applicants submitted that if the relief sought could not otherwise be granted, the court should declare the *Vital Statistics Act* unconstitutional as a violation of sections 7 and 15 of the *Charter*.

In *Rutherford v Ontario (Deputy Registrar General)* (2006), 81 OR (3d) 81 (Sup Ct), the court rejected the arguments based on statutory interpretation and held that there was no "gap" which entitled the court to exercise its *parens patriae* jurisdiction. However, the court then decided that the provisions of the *Vital Statistics Act* infringed the equality guarantee in section 15 of the *Charter*:

[111] I have concluded that there is a breach of s. 15 of the *Charter* and that this breach cannot be saved by s. 1. In reaching this conclusion, I have focused on determining the appropriate comparator group in light of the purpose and effects of the VSA and the benefit sought.

[112] The purpose is as noted above. As to effect, it is reasonable to infer that heterosexual couples are successfully registering the names of non-biological fathers on the Statement of Live Birth. Conversely, lesbian co-mothers are not being registered. The benefit sought under the VSA is access to the benefit of being able to register both intended parents as of *right*, with the resulting presumption of parentage, or access to the social and symbolic institution of having their names on the birth record at first instance.

[113] Based on these factors, I have concluded that the claimants can be characterized as lesbian co-mothers who plan a pregnancy with a spouse using assistive reproductive technology and that the appropriate comparator group is heterosexual non-biological fathers who plan a pregnancy with a spouse using assistive reproductive technology. Equally, it is appropriate to compare the claimant children with children of heterosexual non-fathers who planned their pregnancy using reproductive technology. While I struggled with this issue, I have made the comparison groups very specific so as to only consider the particular situation of those before the court.

[114] On the basis of these comparator groups, I concluded that there is a distinction between the claimants and the comparator group on the basis of sex and the analogous ground of sexual orientation. This distinction is as a result of both the VSA itself and of state action. This distinction is discriminatory due to pre-existing disadvantage and stereotype, the lack of correspondence between the benefit and the needs of lesbian co-mothers who use reproductive technology and their children, and the engagement of core dignity interests.

[115] Section 1 is applicable in this case. Applying the Oakes test, I concluded that the government failed to offer evidence to establish that the objective of prompt and accurate registration of birth particulars and of the exclusion of lesbian co-mothers to further this purpose are pressing and substantial. Furthermore, the exclusion of lesbian co-mothers from the VSA is not rationally connected to that purpose, minimally impairing, or proportionate to the serious harm faced by lesbian co-mothers due to exclusion.

[116] It is my view that the respondent's submissions on the *Charter* remedy are substantially correct: it is appropriate to strike down the legislation but suspend. The key problem at the remedy stage is having rejected the argument that a child's parents at birth must be her biological parents, it becomes necessary to re-define who can be a parent under the VSA. Redefining the legal concept of parent under the VSA is a job for the legislature, not the court.

In *Rutherford*, the court held that the provisions of the *Vital Statistics Act* discriminated against non-biological partners of same-sex parents, by contrast with non-biological opposite-sex partners, and thus contravened section 15 of the *Charter*. As noted (at para 116), however, the court suspended its declaration of invalidity for a year to enable the legislature to amend the statute accordingly. Recall the provisions of the *Vital Statistics Act* which now permit "two parents" of a child to record the child's birth.

In addition, recall *Re K*, the case in which the court held that the definition of "spouse" in relation to adoption contravened the *Charter*, thereby enabling same-sex partners of birth mothers to adopt the mothers' children. Why did the same-sex partners in *Rutherford* wish to be named as "parents" on the birth certificates of their partners' biological children, rather than obtain orders for adoption, relying on *Re K*?

The Charter and declarations of parentage for same sex parents: *DWH v DJR*

A similar challenge was brought against Alberta's *Vital Statistics Act*, SA 2007, c V-4-1, and the birth registration provisions of the *Domestic Relations Act*, RSA 2000, c D-14. Although the claims regarding the birth registration provisions were not pursued, DWH sought a declaration that the parenting provisions in Alberta violated section 15 of the *Charter*. DWH and his former partner, DJR, had made arrangements with a lesbian couple, DD and her partner, to conceive a child. DD was impregnated with DJR's sperm through assisted reproduction. DWH and DJR were present for the birth and together cared for the child, S, for 3 years. At that time, DWH and DJR separated. DJR and DD executed a parenting agreement declaring themselves guardians of S and excluded DWH, who was HIV positive and whom they felt was making poor life choices. There were a series of court decisions regarding the custody and access of S: *DWH v DJR*, 2007 ABCA 57; and *DWH v DJR*, 2009 ABQB 438. In the course of the litigation, the court concluded that DD was the only legal parent of S. DJR applied for and was granted status as guardian of S. DWH did not have status as a parent or guardian.

DWH argued that the legislation's failure to include a presumption of paternity for gay male intended fathers violated section 15 of the *Charter*. The *Domestic Relations Act*, which was in force at the time of S's birth, deemed a male person in a spousal relationship of interdependence of some permanence with the female person who gave birth to the child to be the father of the resulting child by operation of law. The trial court concluded that the benefit of this presumption of paternity was restricted to heterosexual couples alone and could never arise in a same-sex relationship. Although this provision had been amended, the court concluded that the impugned provisions violated section 15 and were of no force and effect. Recognizing the gap in the legislation, the court exercised its *parens patriae* jurisdiction to declare DWH to be both a parent and guardian of S. The Court of Appeal upheld the trial judge's exercise of *parens patriae* jurisdiction: *DWH v DJR*, 2013 ABCA 240 at para 63.

Three parents in "law": *AA v BB and CC*

In *AA v BB and CC*, 2007 ONCA 2, the Ontario Court of Appeal recognized three legal parents.

M ROSENBERG JA:

[1] Five-year-old D.D. has three parents: his biological father and mother (B.B. and C.C., respectively) and C.C.'s partner, the appellant A.A. A.A. and C.C. have been in a stable same-sex union since 1990. In 1999, they decided to start a family with the assistance of their friend B.B. The two women would be the primary caregivers of the child, but they believed it would be in the child's best interests that B.B. remain involved in the child's life. D.D. was born in 2001. He refers to A.A. and C.C. as his mothers.

[2] In 2003, A.A. applied to Aston J. for a declaration that, like B.B. and C.C., she was D.D.'s parent, specifically his mother. Had he thought he had jurisdiction, Aston J. would have made that declaration. He found at para. 8 that:

> The child is a bright, healthy, happy individual who is obviously thriving in a loving family that meets his every need. The applicant has been a daily and consistent presence in his life. She is fully committed to a parental role. She has the support of the two biological parents who themselves recognize her equal status with them.

[3] However, the application judge found that he did not have jurisdiction to make the declaration sought, either under the *Children's Law Reform Act*, R.S.O. 1990, c. C.12 [the *CLRA*] or through exercise of the court's inherent *parens patriae* jurisdiction. He therefore dismissed the application. No constitutional argument was made before him.

[4] On appeal to this court, the appellant repeats the same arguments as those made before the application judge. For the first time, she also raises constitutional issues alleging violation of her rights to equality and fundamental justice under ss. 15 and 7 of the *Canadian Charter of Rights and Freedoms*. The appellant is supported by B.B., C.C. and various intervenors, including the Children's Lawyer acting on behalf of D.D., and the applicants from *M.D.R. v. Ontario (Deputy Registrar General)*, [2006] O.J. No. 2268 (S.C.J.), a case that raised related issues [*Rutherford*].

[5] The Alliance for Marriage and Family, a coalition of five public interest organizations, was permitted to intervene. The Alliance submits that the application judge properly dismissed the application, that the *CLRA* is not capable of being interpreted to permit a declaration that a child has two mothers, and that the *parens patriae* jurisdiction is not available. The Alliance also submits that this court should not entertain the *Charter* arguments and that, in any event, the *CLRA* is not unconstitutional.

[6] The Attorney General for Ontario has chosen not to intervene to support the legislation. In these circumstances, the court appointed Mr. Thomas G. Bastedo, Q.C. as *amicus curiae*. Mr. Bastedo submits that the application judge properly interpreted the *CLRA*. He submits, however, that the court should make the declaration sought under its *parens patriae* jurisdiction.

[7] For the following reasons, I would allow the appeal. While I agree with the application judge that the *CLRA* does not permit the making of the order sought, I am satisfied that the order can be made by exercising this court's *parens patriae* jurisdiction. Because they were not raised before the application judge, I would decline to deal with the *Charter* issues....

THE IMPORTANCE OF A DECLARATION OF PARENTAGE

[13] A.A. seeks a declaration that she is a mother of D.D. She and C.C. have not applied for an adoption order because, if they did so, B.B. would lose his status as D.D.'s parent by reason of s. 158(2) of the *Child and Family Services Act*, R.S.O. 1990, c. C.11. That section provides: "For all purposes of law, as of the date of the making of an adoption order ... (b) the adopted child ceases to be the child of the person who was his or her parent before the adoption order was made and that person ceases to be the parent of the adopted child, except where the person is the spouse of the adoptive parent".

[14] A.A., B.B. and C.C. seek to have A.A.'s motherhood recognized to give her all the rights and obligations of a custodial parent. Legal recognition of her relationship with her son would also determine other kindred relationships. In their very helpful factums, the *M.D.R.* Intervenors and the Children's Lawyer summarize the importance of a declaration of parentage from the point of view of the parent and the child: ...

the declaration of parentage is a lifelong immutable declaration of status;

it allows the parent to fully participate in the child's life;

the declared parent has to consent to any future adoption;

the declaration determines lineage;

the declaration ensures that the child will inherit on intestacy;

the declared parent may obtain an OHIP card, a social insurance number, airline tickets and passports for the child;

the child of a Canadian citizen is a Canadian citizen, even if born outside of Canada (*Citizenship Act*, R.S.C. 1985, c. C-29, s. 3(1)(b))2;

the declared parent may register the child in school; and,

the declared parent may assert her rights under various laws such as the *Health Care Consent Act, 1996*, S.O. 1996, c. 2, Sched. A., s. 20(1)5.

[15] Perhaps one of the greatest fears faced by lesbian mothers is the death of the birth mother. Without a declaration of parentage or some other order, the surviving partner would be unable to make decisions for their minor child, such as critical decisions about health care: see *M.D.R.* at para. 220. As the M.D.R. Intervenors say: "A declaration of parentage provides practical and symbolic recognition of the parent–child relationship." An excerpt from the *M.D.R.* record dramatically demonstrates the importance of the declaration from the child's point of view. I resort to this part of the *M.D.R.* record because D.D. is too young to provide this kind of information. The twelve-year old child of one of the applicants said this in her affidavit:

... I just want both my moms recognized as my moms. Most of my friends have not had to think about things like this — they take for granted that their parents are legally recognized as their parents. I would like my family recognized the same way as any other family, not treated differently because both my parents are women.

... It would help if the government and the law recognized that I have two moms. It would help more people to understand. It would make my life easier. I want my family to be accepted and included, just like everybody else's family.

[16] In *M.D.R.* at paras. 227 and 228, Rivard J. referred to some of the submissions discussed in the Victorian Law Reform Commission's position

paper entitled *Assisted Reproductive Technology & Adoption: Position Paper Two: Parentage* [which supported the claims of the applicants....]

THE CHILDREN'S LAW REFORM ACT

[17] The appellant applied for an order that she is the mother of D.D. under s. 4 in Part II of the *CLRA*. Section 4 provides as follows:

> Any person having an interest may apply to a court for a declaration that a male person is recognized in law to be the father of a child or that a female person is the mother of a child.

> 14. Where the court finds that a presumption of paternity exists under section 8 and unless it is established, on the balance of probabilities, that the presumed father is not the father of the child, the court shall make a declaratory order confirming that the paternity is recognized in law.
>
>> Where the court finds on the balance of probabilities that the relationship of mother and child has been established, the court may make a declaratory order to that effect.

> Subject to sections 6 and 7, an order made under this section shall be recognized for all purposes....

[18] The application judge accepted that the relationship of mother and child need not be biological or genetic, but after a careful consideration of the legislative scheme and the applicable rules of interpretation, he held that Part II of the *CLRA* contemplates only one mother of a child. He relied principally on the use of the words "the father" and "the mother" in s. 4(1), which connote a single father and a single mother. I do not find it necessary to repeat the same analysis. The application judge's reasons are reported at 225 D.L.R. (4th) 371 and 38 R.F.L. (5th) 1. I agree with his analysis of the statute. I would, however, elaborate on three points.

[19] As the application judge noted, the process of statutory interpretation favoured by the Supreme Court of Canada requires a court to consider the grammatical and ordinary meaning of the provisions in question, the legislative history and the intention of the Legislature, the scheme of the Act, and the legislative context. I wish to further elaborate on the legislative history and intention of the Legislature as well as on the scheme of the Act. Finally, I will comment on the use of the *Charter* as in interpretative aid.

LEGISLATIVE HISTORY AND INTENTION OF THE LEGISLATURE

[20] The *CLRA* was intended to remove disabilities suffered by children born outside of marriage. As the Ontario Law Reform Commission observed in its 1973 Report on Family Law at p. 1: "These disabilities arise at the moment of birth and may remain with the child throughout his lifetime." The Commission therefore "accorded high priority to finding a means by which the child born outside marriage may be allowed to enjoy the same rights and privileges as other children in our society". The Commission's central recommendation was that Ontario should abolish the concepts of legitimacy and illegitimacy and declare positively that all children have equal status in law. The Commission's recommendations were enacted into legislation in the form of Parts I and II of the *CLRA*. The Commission's central recommendation concerning equality of children is found in the Act's first section:

> 1.(1) Subject to subsection (2), for all purposes of the law of Ontario a person is the child of his or her natural parents and his or her status as their child is independent of whether the child is born within or outside marriage....

1.(4) Any distinction at common law between the status of children born in wedlock and born out of wedlock is abolished and the relationship of parent and child and kindred relationships flowing therefrom shall be determined for the purposes of the common law in accordance with this section.

[21] The *CLRA* was progressive legislation, but it was a product of its time. It was intended to deal with the specific problem of the incidents of illegitimacy — the need to "remove, as far as the law is capable of doing so, a stigma which has been cast on children who in the nature of things cannot be said to bear responsibility for it" (p. 11). The possibility of legally and socially recognized same-sex unions and the implications of advances in reproductive technology were not on the radar scheme. The Act does not deal with, nor contemplate, the disadvantages that a child born into a relationship of two mothers, two fathers or as in this case two mothers and one father might suffer. This is not surprising given that nothing in the Commission's report suggests that it contemplated that such relationships might even exist.

SCHEME OF THE ACT

[22] When the scheme of the *CLRA* is considered, especially the relationship between the various provisions in Parts I and II, it is apparent that the Act contemplates only one mother and one father. The application judge drew attention to many of these provisions. He referred in particular to s. 8, which deals with the presumption of paternity. He was of the view that this section contemplated only one father. This view of the legislation is also consistent with the adoption provisions in the Act whereby no more than two persons can apply for an adoption order and the order extinguishes other parental status. I agree with that interpretation of the legislation. [The court also noted section 12(2) of the Act] ...

[24] I agree with the application judge that the *CLRA*, and in particular s. 4(1), is unambiguous. The court has jurisdiction to make a declaration in favour of one male person as the father and one female person as the mother. Since D.D. already had one mother, the application judge had no jurisdiction under s. 4(1) to make an order in favour of A.A. that she too was the mother of D.D.

USE OF THE *CHARTER* AS AN INTERPRETATIVE AID

[25] A.A. and certain intervenors submit that the *CLRA* should be interpreted in a manner consistent with the *Charter*, and in particular the equality rights guaranteed in s. 15. However, the *Charter* may be used as an interpretive guide only in circumstances of genuine ambiguity. See *Bell ExpressVu Limited Partnership v. Rex*, [2002] 2 S.C.R. 559 at para. 62 where Iacobucci J. wrote: "[I]t must be stressed that, to the extent this Court has recognized a 'Charter values' interpretive principle, such principle can <u>only</u> receive application in circumstances of genuine ambiguity, i.e., where a statutory provision is subject to differing, but equally plausible, interpretations" [Emphasis in original]. Also see *Symes v. Canada*, [1993] 4 S.C.R. 695 at para. 105.

[26] Since I have found that there is no ambiguity, it is not open to this court to use *Charter* values to interpret the provision.

PARENS PATRIAE JURISDICTION

[27] The court's inherent *parens patriae* jurisdiction may be applied to rescue a child in danger or to bridge a legislative gap. This is not a case about a child being in danger. If the *parens patriae* authority were to be exercised it would have to be on the basis of a legislative gap.

[28] The application judge held that the court's *parens patriae* authority was not available to make the declaration in favour of A.A., although he appeared to accept that such an order would be in the best interests of the child. In his view, any gap was deliberate and the court was effectively being asked to legislate because of a perception that the legislation was under-inclusive. The application judge was also concerned about the potential impact on other children if other persons, such as stepparents or members of a child's extended family, came forward seeking declarations of parenthood.

[29] I take a different view of the exercise of the *parens patriae* jurisdiction. The Supreme Court of Canada has considered this jurisdiction on several occasions, in particular in *Beson v. Director of Child Welfare for Newfoundland*, [1982] 2 S.C.R. 716 and *E.(Mrs) v. Eve.*, [1986] 2 S.C.R. 388. La Forest J. reviewed the history of the *parens patriae* jurisdiction at length in *Eve*. He concluded at p. 426 with the following statement:

> As Lord MacDermott put it in *J. v. C.*, [1970] A.C. 668, at p. 703, the authorities are not consistent and there are many twists and turns, but they have inexorably "moved towards a broader discretion, under the impact of changing social conditions and the weight of opinion...." In other words, the categories under which the jurisdiction can be exercised are never closed. Thus I agree with Latey J. in Re X, supra, [1975] 1 All E.R. 697 at p. 699, that the jurisdiction is of a very broad nature, and that it can be invoked in such matters as custody, protection of property, health problems, religious upbringing and protection against harmful associations. This list, as he notes, is not exhaustive....

[30] The comments of La Forest J. about the broad nature of the *parens patriae* jurisdiction and the broader discretion under the impact of changing social conditions are particularly apt in this case. However, *Eve* concerned the court's jurisdiction to authorize a medical procedure. It was not principally concerned with the court's jurisdiction to fill a legislative gap. A case somewhat closer to the problem at hand is the Supreme Court's decision in *Beson*. In that case, the Director of Child Welfare for Newfoundland removed a child from an adoptive home shortly before the expiration of the probationary residence period required for an adoption. The legislation did not give the potential adoptive parents any right of appeal from the Director's action taken during the probationary period. Speaking for the court, Wilson J. found that there was accordingly a legislative gap that could be filled by the exercise of the *parens patriae* jurisdiction [adopting part of the reasons of Lord Wilberforce in *A. v. Liverpool City Council and another*, [1981] 2 All E.R. 385 (H.L.) at 388–89.] ...

[31] The determination of whether a legislative gap exists in this case requires a consideration of whether the *CLRA* was intended to be a complete code and, in particular, whether it was intended to confine declarations of parentage to biological or genetic relationships. If the *CLRA* was intended to be confined to declarations of parentage based on biology or genetics, it would be difficult to find that there is a legislative gap, at least as concerns persons with no genetic or biological link to the child.

[32] As discussed above, the application judge was of the view that the jurisdiction to make parentage declarations is not confined to biological or genetic relationships. The Alliance for Marriage and Family challenges that proposition. The Alliance points out that s. 1(1) of the *CLRA* refers to a person being the child of his or her "natural parents". I agree that

the Act favours biological parents. For example, s. 10 gives a court power to order blood tests or DNA tests where it is called upon to determine a child's parentage. However, the Act does not define parentage solely on the basis of biology. For example, s. 1(2) treats adopting parents as natural parents. Often one or both of the adopting parents will not be the biological parents of the child. Similarly, s. 8 enacts presumptions of paternity that do not all turn upon biology; the obvious example is the presumption of paternity flowing simply from the fact that the father was married to the child's mother at the time of birth. Further, as Ferrier J. pointed out in *T.D.L. v. L.R.L.*, [1994] O.J. No. 896 (S.C.J.) at para. 18, the declaration made under s. 4(1) is not that the applicant is a child's natural parent, but that he or she is recognized in law to be the father or mother of the child.

[33] Further, even if the *CLRA* was intended to limit declarations of paternity and maternity to biological parents, that would not answer the question of whether there is a gap. Advances in reproductive technology require re-examination of the most basic questions of who is a biological mother. For example, consider the facts of *M.D.R. v. Ontario (Deputy Registrar General)*. M.D.R. involved a case where one lesbian partner was the gestational or birth mother and the other partner was the biological mother, having been the donor of the egg.

[34] I return to the earlier discussion of the intention of the *CLRA*. The legislation was not about the status of natural parents but the status of children. The purpose of the legislation was to declare that all children should have equal status. At the time, equality of status meant recognizing the equality of children born inside and outside of marriage. The Legislature had in mind traditional unions between one mother and one father. It did not legislate in relation to other types of relationships because those relationships and the advent of reproductive technology were beyond the vision of the Law Reform Commission and the Legislature of the day. As MacKinnon A.C.J.O. said in *Re Bagaric v. Juric et al.* (1984), 44 O.R. (2d) 638 (C.A.) ...: "The Legislature recognized by this legislation present social conditions and attitudes as well as recognizing that such declarations have significance beyond material ones."

[35] Present social conditions and attitudes have changed. Advances in our appreciation of the value of other types of relationships and in the science of reproductive technology have created gaps in the *CLRA*'s legislative scheme. Because of these changes the parents of a child can be two women or two men. They are as much the child's parents as adopting parents or "natural" parents. The *CLRA*, however, does not recognize these forms of parenting and thus the children of these relationships are deprived of the equality of status that declarations of parentage provide.

[The court further considered and adopted the view of the "gap" in *Beson*.]

[37] It is contrary to D.D.'s best interests that he is deprived of the legal recognition of the parentage of one of his mothers. There is no other way to fill this deficiency except through the exercise of the *parens patriae* jurisdiction. As indicated, A.A. and C.C. cannot apply for an adoption order without depriving D.D. of the parentage of B.B., which would not be in D.D.'s best interests.

[38] I disagree with the application judge that the legislative gap in this case is deliberate. There is no doubt that the Legislature did not foresee for the possibility of declarations of parentage for two women, but that is a product of the social conditions and medical knowledge at the time.

The Legislature did not turn its mind to that possibility, so that over thirty years later the gap in the legislation has been revealed. In the result, the statute does not provide for the best interests of D.D. More-over, a finding that the legislative gap is deliberate requires assigning to the Legislature a discriminatory intent in a statute designed to treat all children equally. I am not prepared to do so. See the comments of Rivard J. in M.D.R. at paras. 93–103. There is nothing in the legislative history of the *CLRA* to suggest that the Legislature made a deliberate policy choice to exclude the children of lesbian mothers from the advantages of equality of status accorded to other children under the Act.

[39] This holding would, it seems, be consistent with the position of the government. As stated earlier, the Crown in Right of Ontario did not intervene in this case, but its position on this issue is known. In M.D.R., the Crown took the position that the *CLRA* in fact could be interpreted to allow for a declaration that two women were the mothers of a child. Since I have found otherwise, it does no violence to the government's position to make the declaration sought by the appellant in this case through exercise of the *parens patriae* jurisdiction.

[40] One final note. In *C.R. v. Children's Aid Society of Hamilton*, [2004] O.J. No. 3301 (S.C.J.) at para. 125, Czutrin J. held that the exercise of the *parens patriae* jurisdiction does not depend upon a legislative gap if the exercise of that jurisdiction is the only way to meet the paramount objective of legislation. I should not be taken as foreclosing that possibility. Since I have found a gap, I have not found it necessary to decide whether the same result could be achieved in the way suggested by Czutrin J.

DISPOSITION

[41] Accordingly, I would allow the appeal and issue a declaration that A.A. is a mother of D.D. I would order that there be no costs of the appeal or of the application. Finally, I would like to thank all counsel for their submissions, especially Mr. Bastedo who agreed to act as amicus curiae in this important and novel case.

Notes and Questions

Defining same-sex parents: Human rights statutes, the *Charter*, and *parens patriae*

In the three cases in this section, courts used different kinds of reasoning to define parental status in relation to same-sex couples and their use of assisted reproduction processes. In both *Gill v Murray* in British Columbia and *Rutherford* in Ontario, same-sex partners of biological mothers claimed parental status based on arguments about discrimination, either pursuant to human rights statutes or the *Charter*. However, in *AA v BB and CC*, the court rejected *Charter* claims because this argument had not been raised in the lower court decision. In addition to this procedural issue, were there other aspects of *AA v BB and CC* that differed from the two preceding cases?

To what extent do you agree with the court's conclusion in *AA v BB and CC* that there was a "gap" in the *Children's Law Reform Act* that mandated the use of the court's inherent *parens patriae* jurisdiction? In what circumstances should courts defer to legislatures for reform in cases such as this one? Is the court's reasoning about the need to fill the "gap" persuasive in this situation? To what extent does it depend on a conclusion that the legislation is now out of date with current arrangements for assisted reproduction? Do you agree that this decision might also have been supported by the argument that it was necessary to achieve the objective of the statute?

Recognition in law of three parents: The "new" family?

AA v BB and CC represented a significant new development in family law, an "intact" family with three parents. Although definitions of "parent" for purposes of child support, for example, routinely result in the creation of more than two parents, and "blended" families after separation and divorce may result in the recognition of both biological and social parents, *AA v BB and CC* established a new principle for recognition of three parents in intact families. In this context, the case raises a number of significant issues for family law.

One issue is the extent to which the problem in this case occurred because of the erasure of biological relationships in the context of adoption. That is, if the adoption statute were amended to permit not only "openness" but also continuing parental status for a biological parent after adoption, would such an approach overcome the problems in this case? Why might the parties have preferred the *parens patriae* approach here? In this context, it is important to reconsider the questions about the essential nature of legal adoption discussed earlier in this chapter. To what extent does *AA v BB and CC* represent a new way of thinking about parent–child relationships more generally, beyond the particular factual circumstances in this case?

A second issue relates to the elements of "parental" status. In a comment on this case, Robert Leckey argued that it was consistent with the law's recognition, after separation or divorce, of a number of different parents for different purposes. However, he also suggested that recognition of three parents for *all* purposes may create difficulties if these relationships break down. In this context, Leckey argued that law should recognize an "unbundling" of the rights and obligations of parenthood. For example, while recognizing full rights and responsibilities of some "parents," law should also recognize parents with intermediate rights and responsibilities, so that while such intermediate parents could visit a child in hospital and pick up a child from school, such a parent would not have an equal claim to custody and might enjoy a lesser obligation of child support. See Robert Leckey, "Lawmakers Should Create Intermediate Parenting Category", *The Lawyers Weekly* (9 November 2007). How might legislation be drafted to achieve such an objective?

Only one Canadian province has enacted legislation permitting a child to have three legal parents from birth. In 2013, section 30 of B.C.'s *Family Law Act* came into force. It provides that where there is a written agreement, three people may be declared parents of a child conceived through assisted reproduction (*Family Law Act*, SBC 2011, c 25). Thus, the Act would apply in situations akin to *AA*, where the birth mother, the person who is married to or in a marriage-like relationship with the birth mother and the donor are declared to be parents. In addition, the intended parents and a birth mother could also be declared to be parents where an agreement exists. While recognizing the potential of section 30, Fiona Kelly has argued that:

> ... it fails to challenge normative parenting in any meaningful way. While it permits a child to have more than two parents, the additional parent(s) must be biologically related to the child and, in the case of a same-sex family, will always include the biological parent of the opposite sex. There is no method by which to extend recognition to a nonbiologically related fourth parent, such as the partner of a sperm donor or surrogate. In addition, in order to enter into a section 30 agreement, the birth mother and her partner or the intended parents must be a conjugal couple in a married or marriage-like relationship. Non-conjugal co-parenting is not an option for the "primary" parents. Finally, section 30 agreements are only available to those who conceive via assisted reproduction, a disproportionate number of whom are same-sex couples. Those who conceive via intercourse — the majority of the heterosexual population — remain tethered to the traditional nuclear family, suggesting that nuclear families are still treated as the superior family form for the vast majority of the population. (Fiona Kelly, "Multiple-Parent Families Under British Columbia's New Family Law Act: A Challenge to the Supremacy of the Nuclear Family or a Method by which to Preserve Biological Ties and Opposite-Sex Parenting?" (2014) 47:2 UBC L Rev 565 at 594)

By contrast, section 9(7)(b) of Alberta's *Family Law Act*, SA 2003, c F-4.5, restricts declarations of parentage to two parents.

In two earlier cases, applications for recognition of a same-sex partner as a "parent" were denied: see *Re P(N)* (2000), 193 DLR (4th) 706 (Qc CA); and *PC v SL*, 2005 SKQB 502.

Rethinking "parental" status in relation to adoption: *C(MA) v K(M)*

In *C(MA) v K(M)*, 2009 ONCJ 18, a lesbian couple who wished to have a child approached a number of gay friends to find a man interested in providing donor sperm and being in a "family" relationship with the child to be born. Eventually, the couple selected MK to be the biological father and the couple and MK signed an elaborate written agreement in which they confirmed an intention to seek a declaration of triple parentage, as in *AA v BB and CC*. After the birth of the child, the three parents were all involved with her, but when she was about five years old, differences developed and the couple unilaterally restricted MK's access to the child. Although their written agreement provided for arbitration of disputes, MK applied to the court for interim access, which was granted, and the matter was then referred for further determination to arbitration. In this context, the lesbian couple submitted an application for adoption of the child by the non-biological co-mother, including an application to dispense with the consent of the biological father.

The court denied the application to dispense with the biological father's consent in accordance with the child's best interests. According to the court, the father's presence in the child's life posed no threat to security in the child's family; indeed it benefited her. After reviewing the evidence in detail and the strength and regularity of the relationship between the child and the biological father and his extended family, the court concluded that an adoption order (and the severing of the child's ties with the father) was not in the child's best interests:

> **[64]** I also believe that, if the adoption is granted and B.'s biological relationship with her father is legally severed, the effect would be to undermine B.'s sense of her place in the world, her confidence in her experience of the world and her understanding of who her family is. She is six years of age and she knows she has two mothers and a father. She knows where her primary home is and who her primary caregivers are. She also knows that she that she belongs to a second family. As the respondent testified, "B. recognizes herself as a child of the K. family as well". None of this is disputed. This is the world that B. knows and there is no evidence that she has any problems with it. It would be unfair not only to the respondent, but also to B., to now fundamentally change its character....

> **[66]** I believe this question of the difference between the respondent and a "mere sperm donor" goes to the heart of this proceeding, and I turn to it now in my concluding reasons. Criterion number six, "the child's relationships by blood or through an adoption order", deserves special comment in this case. Adoption is inescapably about biology, because adoption severs a child's biological link to a parent. Even in a society that has placed affectional ties at the centre of a child's best interests, the child's biological connections remain a fundamental value. Indeed the applicants seek the adoption order precisely so the respondent's biological connection to B. can be severed and so that Ms. C.A.D., the child's non-biological mother, and one of her primary caregivers, can assume the position that biology conferred on the respondent. However, in this case, the applicants also propose that the respondent will "continue to be a father" and continue to exercise access. Since the child's relationship by blood is only one of the factors in the "best interests" test, what weight should be attributed to the blood tie in these circumstances?

The court reviewed the definition of best interests in section 136(2), at para 6, the amendments concerning openness agreements, etc., and concluded:

> **[73]** The respondent has acted as a responsible parent. He has involved himself to the extent he was permitted in B.'s education and recreation. Whenever he was given the opportunity to care for B. by the applicants, he accepted the responsibility. The respondent's "parental rights" and his parental relationship with B. have arisen not only because he is her biological father, but because he has been actively and wholeheartedly involved with her as a father. It is relevant in this proceeding that the respondent's relationship with B. also developed because the applicants invited him to be a parent, initially agreed to, and encouraged, his relationship with B., and, whether willingly or not, allowed that relationship to grow.

> **[74]** The applicants in this case are intelligent, thoughtful and politically conscious of their positions as lesbians in a predominantly heterosexual society. Everything about who they are went into their decision to have this child. When they decided to have a child, they fully understood that, although engaging a sperm donor was a biological necessity, engaging a

known sperm donor was not. Thus, when they decided, even before they had chosen the respondent, that they wanted their child to have a known and involved father, they knew that, if they chose well, their child would develop a relationship with a parent who was not part of their immediate family. They knew that a parent-and-child relationship gives rise to rights and responsibilities. They anticipated that a third parent would be involved with their family and had to have anticipated that this parent might disagree with, or challenge, their parenting choices, just as they must do with one another. It is likely that they also knew, since Ms. M.A.C. is a lawyer and fraternizes with family lawyers, that some day, if their relations went badly with the biological father, a mediator or an arbitrator or a judge might interpret their child's best interests to include preserving her connection with that father. Now they want to turn back the clock and make a different choice. If this was ever possible, it is not possible after six years. Time and experience have proven that the respondent is not a "mere sperm donor" and B. is no longer a theoretical proposition, nor is her relationship with her father.

[75] I want to make two observations in closing. The first is that, despite the fact that this case involved gay and lesbian parties, many of the issues are common to those experienced by any couple who do not have complete control over the biological process of conception and by newly reconstituted families who must contend with a child's other parent. This case is not about protecting nuclear families to reduce their anxieties. The same imperative that compels us to reconsider our definition of parent in the modern context has equally compelled us to reconsider the concept of the nuclear family. In this case, I am considering the legal situation of a self-constructed, non-traditional family — the three-parent family created by these parties. However, even in this new context, this case is governed by the law of adoption and, having considered that law, I have concluded that the applicants are not entitled to an order dispensing with Mr. M.K.'s consent to their adoption of B. My second observation is that I appreciate how the applicants, as lesbians, might fear the loss of control over their own reproduction occasioned by the necessary involvement of a sperm donor in the creation of their family. I would remind them, using Ms. M.A.C.'s words, that the options for gay men "are in some ways much more bleaker than even ... ours." For the sake of B., and in their own best interests, these parties will have to learn to live with their choices.

To what extent is this case consistent with those discussed earlier in this chapter about fathers' rights to consent to adoption? Did the outcome in this case depend on the decision of the Ontario Court of Appeal in *AA v BB and CC*? Is this a case about adoption or about assisted reproduction — or both?

See also *Thomas S v Robin Y*, 599 NYS (2d) 377 (Fam Ct 1993); and 618 NYS (2d) 356 (Ct App 1994), where a gay male provided donor sperm to a lesbian couple pursuant to an oral agreement that he would have no parental rights or obligations. When he later changed his mind and sought an order of filiation, the Court of Appeal overturned the lower court's rejection of this claim, and held that such an order was appropriate and that the agreement was unenforceable. See also Katherine Arnup & Susan Boyd, "Familial Disputes? Sperm Donors, Lesbian Mothers, and Legal Parenthood" in Didi Herman & Carl Stychin, eds, *Legal Inversions* (Philadelphia: Temple University Press, 1995) at 77.

Additional Resources

Karen Busby, "Of Surrogate Mother Born: Parentage Determinations in Canada and Elsewhere" (2013) CJWL 284.

Joan C Callahan, ed, *Reproduction, Ethics and the Law: Feminist Perspectives* (Bloomington and Indianapolis: Indiana University Press, 1995).

Angela Cameron, "Regulating the Queer Family: The Assisted Human Reproduction Act" (2008) 24 CJWL 101.

Angela Cameron, "A Chip Off the Old (Ice) Block? Women-Led Families, Sperm Donors, and Family Law" in Jennifer Kilty, ed, *Within the Confines: Women and the Law in Canada* (Toronto: Canadian Scholars Press, 2014) 246.

Caroline Jones, "Parents in Law: Subjective Impacts and Status Implications around the Use of Licensed Donor Insemination" in Alison Diduck & Katherine O'Donovan, eds, *Feminist Perspectives on Family Law* (Abingdon, Oxford: Routledge-Cavendish, 2006) 75.

Fiona Kelly, "Equal Parents, Equal Children: Reforming Canada's Parentage Laws to Recognize the Completeness of Women-led Families" (2013) 64 UNBLJ 253.

Fiona Kelly, "Nuclear Norms or Fluid Families? Incorporating Lesbian and Gay Parents and their Children into Canadian Family Law" (2004) 21 Can J Fam L 133.

Robert Leckey, "The Practices of Lesbian Mothers and Québec's Reforms" (2011) 23:2 CJWL 579.

Jenni Millbank, "Unlikely Fissures and Uneasy Resonances: Lesbian Co-Mothers, Surrogate Parenthood and Fathers' Rights" (2008) 16:2 Fem Leg Stud 141.

Michael T Morley et al, "Developments in Law and Policy: Emerging Issues in Family Law" (2003) 21 Yale L & Pol'y Rev 169.

Erin Nelson, "Comparative Perspectives on the Regulation of Assisted Reproductive Technologies in the United Kingdom and Canada" (2006) 43 Alta L Rev 1023.

Jo Shaw, "The Right to Posthumous Use of Sperm and the Free Movement of Persons Under European Community Law" (1997) 19:4 J Soc Welfare & Fam L 507.

Richard Storrow, "Parenthood by Pure Intention: Assisted Reproduction and the Functional Approach to Parentage" (2002) 53 Hastings LJ 597.

Kristen Walker, "1950s Family Values vs. Human Rights: In Vitro Fertilization, Donor Insemination and Sexuality in Victoria" (2000) 11 Public Law Review 292.

Wanda Wiegers, "Assisted Conception and Equality of Familial Status in Parentage Law" (2012–2013) 28 Can J Fam L 147.

ASSISTED REPRODUCTION: ISSUES OF ACCESS AND DISCLOSURE

Access issues: Supply of Gametes

Provisions of the *AHRA* and other Regulations, which prohibited obtaining or transferring sperm or ova except in accordance with the Regulations, tended to make it difficult, if not impossible, for individual gay men to donate sperm, even though such a known donor arrangement was often preferred by lesbian couples who wished to have a child. These arrangements were unsuccessfully challenged pursuant to the *Charter* in *Susan Doe v Canada (AG)*, 2007 ONCA 11. (See Lisa Feldstein, "Access to Assisted Conception: A Call for Legislative Reform in Light of the Modern Family" (2010) 26:1 Can J Fam L 201, a comment on the *Susan Doe* case.)

In addition to these concerns, access issues to anonymous donor sperm may also be affected by changes to privacy issues. For example, there was an acute shortage of gamete donors following the abolition of donor anonymity in the United Kingdom in 2005. (See Ilke Turkmendag, Robert Dingwall & Therese Murphy, "The Removal of Donor Anonymity in the UK: The Silencing of Claims by Would-be-Parents" (2008) 22 Intl JL Pol'y & Fam 283.) However, recent reports indicate that a number of additional sperm donors have been recruited. (See Human Fertilisation and Embryology Authority, *Egg and Sperm Donation in the UK: 2012–2013*, at 10, online: <www.hfea.gov.uk>.)

Access issues: Public funding of assisted reproduction

Public funding significantly increases access to assisted reproductive technologies which range from artificial insemination to *in vitro* fertilization (IVF). Québec undertook a generous public assisted reproduction program in August 2010. The program covered all of the costs associated with artificial insemination and three cycles of IVF and six cycles of natural IVF. Notably, the program prohibited the transfer of more than one embryo per IVF cycle in most cases. Between 2010 and March 31, 2013, the province funded approximately 10,000 cycles of IVF. (See Le Commissaire à la santé et au bien-être — Recherche "Avis Synthèse sur les activités de procréation assistée au Québec" at 20, <http://www.csbe.gouv.qc.ca/fileadmin/www/2014/Procreation_assistee/CSBE_PA_Synthese_2014.pdf>.) Despite its popularity, the Québec government, in November 2014, announced that it would terminate the program. (See Geoffrey Vendeville, "Quebec cuts public funding for in vitro fertilization", *The Montreal Gazette* (28 November 2014), online: <http://montrealgazette.com/news/quebec/quebec-cuts-ivf-coverage-and-threatens-doctors-with-sanctions>.) On November 28, 2014, the Québec government has introduced Bill 20, *An Act to enact the Act to promote access to family medicine and specialized medicine services and to amend various legislative provisions relating to assisted procreation*, which would end IVF coverage but would introduce tax rebates for one to two cycles of IVF based on a woman's age and the family's income.

The New Brunswick government has created a fund to help alleviate the financial costs associated with infertility treatments by allowing individuals to claim up to 50 percent of the costs of IVF or artificial insemination. (See Department of Health, News Release, "Infertility treatment fund announced" (15 July 2014), online: <http://www2.gnb.ca/content/gnb/en/news/news_release.2014.07.0857.html>.) Finally, the Ontario government has also announced that it intends to fund one cycle of IVF. (See Ministry of Health and Long-Term Care, News Release, "Improving Access to Safe Fertility Treatments: Ontario Sharing Cost of IVF to Help People Who Cannot Conceive" (10 April 2014), online: <http://news.ontario.ca/mohltc/en/2014/04/improving-access-to-safe-fertility-treatments.html>.) The program has not yet been introduced. Any program that is introduced must reflect the diversity of people using assisted reproduction. (See Marie-France Bureau, "Opinion: Assisted reproductive technologies need regulation, for the sake of public health", *The Montreal Gazette* (7 November 2014), online: <http://montrealgazette.com/news/quebec/opinion-quebecs-policy-on-assisted-reproductive-technologies>.)

Disclosure (and privacy): Emerging policy issues

The Role of Children's "Rights" and "Openness" in Adoption

The UN Convention on the Rights of the Child requires registration of a child's birth (s 7), and asserts the child's right to know his or her parents. In addition, section 8 requires Canada to respect the right of the child to preserve his or her identity including family relations recognized by law. Cases such as *Trociuk* and *Rutherford* have identified the need to recognize both biological and social parents, but these cases may have tended to reflect the interests of the parents as well as their children. By contrast, the UN Convention focuses on the rights of children to know their parents. See Cheryl Milne, "What are the Rights of Children Conceived through Assisted Reproductive Technology?" *The Lawyers Weekly* (10 November 2006).

As noted earlier in this chapter, recent amendments to adoption statutes have tended to greater "openness" with respect to birth records, enabling birth parents and adult adoptees to locate one another more often. Similar issues have also become significant in relation to the disclosure of identity for "anonymous" sperm donors. See Paul McKeague, "Seeking the Mystery of Birth", *Ottawa Citizen* (27 September 1999); "I Just Want To Know Who My Father Is", *Ottawa Citizen* (28 September 1999); and Madeleine Bunting, "Donor Insemination Raises Big Questions About Children's Rights To Know Their Biological Fathers", *The Guardian* (2 July 2001). What kinds of legal issues arise in these situations? How should law respond?

Consider the current context:

> Whether sperm donor anonymity should remain the predominant law of Canada, or whether we should move to a system of compulsory identity release donors or even retroactive de-anonymisation, are questions Canadians have struggled with for many years. The issue has become more pressing recently for a number of reasons. First, more and more Canadians, whether they be heterosexual couples, same-sex couples, or single women, are using assisted reproduction technologies ... that require donated sperm to create their families. Second, there is a growing emphasis on the use of family and genetic history in the prevention and treatment of disease. This, in turn, is increasing the emphasis on biological connections and the desire to know one's biological progenitors. Third, a number of provinces have amended their adoption legislation to permit retroactive disclosure of adoption records once the adoptee has reached the age of majority. The shift towards retroactive identity disclosure in the adoption context has prompted Canadians to question ongoing anonymity in the context of sperm donation. Finally, a recent class action suit filed in British Columbia challenging the destruction of sperm donor records as well as donor anonymity more broadly, *Pratten v. Attorney General of BC and the College of Physicians and Surgeons of BC*, has brought significant public attention to the issue. Over the next few years, the *Pratten* litigation will force the Canadian courts to address the inappropriateness of donor anonymity.... (Angela Cameron, Vanessa Gruben & Fiona Kelly, "De-Anonymising Sperm Donors in Canada: Some Doubts and Directions" (2010) 26:1 Can J Fam L 95 at 96–97)

The authors canvass these issues in detail, recommending the enactment of new definitions of "parent" in provincial statutes and careful attention to the interests of children, donors and families (particularly women-led families). In this context, see the *Family Law Act*, SBC 2011, c 25, Part 3, regarding definitions of "parent" in different situations in which children are conceived.

Disclosure and Sperm Donors: The *Pratten* Litigation

Olivia Pratten was conceived in 1981 using sperm from an anonymous donor. In 2002, she requested information about the donor's identity from the B.C. doctor who had arranged the donation for insemination for Pratten's mother. However, pursuant to the rules of the College of Physicians and Surgeons in British Columbia, the doctor's obligation to retain files extended only six years after the last entry recorded in patient files, and thus, the doctor advised Pratten that all records relating to the insemination process that resulted in her conception and birth had been destroyed.

In October 2008, Pratten commenced an action on behalf of donor offspring against the B.C. Attorney General and the College of Physicians and Surgeons in British Columbia. Ms. Pratten claimed that, by enacting legislation that requires the collection and disclosure of information only for the benefits of adoptees, the legislature discriminated against donor offspring contrary to section 15(1) of the *Charter*. Further, Ms. Pratten claimed that the legislature's failure to enact this type of legislation for donor offspring violated the free-standing positive right to obtain information about one's biological origins contrary to section 7 of the *Charter*. Finally, Ms. Pratten claimed that the legislature deprived donor offspring of the rights to liberty and security of the person by not disallowing the rules and bylaws of the College of Physicians and Surgeons of British Columbia that authorize the destruction of patient records.

An application for an injunction was granted on 28 October 2008, prohibiting "the destruction, disposal, redaction or transfer out of British Columbia" of records created or maintained by persons who administered artificial insemination procedures, and which recorded information about donors, patients impregnated, and children conceived. In December 2008, this injunction was extended to the conclusion of the court proceedings.

In October 2010, the B.C. Attorney General was unsuccessful in an application to the court to dismiss the claim on the basis that it was moot, academic and/or futile, and that Pratten lacked standing to pursue the matter. These claims were rejected, along with the Attorney General's application for an adjournment until six months after the SCC decision regarding the *AHRA* (discussed earlier in this chapter). In September 2010, the court ordered a stay of proceedings against the College of Physicians and Surgeons.

The matter was heard in October and November 2010 and written arguments were submitted in March 2011. The B.C. Supreme Court issued a judgment in May 2011.

In a lengthy judgment of the summary trial on the merits, Adair J held that relevant provisions of the B.C. adoption legislation and regulations violated section 15(1) of the *Charter* and were not saved by section 1: *Pratten v British Columbia (AG)*, 2011 BCSC 656. She concluded:

> [268] ... that the appropriate comparison at step one of the analysis under s. 15(1) is between adoptees and donor offspring. I conclude further that excluding donor offspring from the benefits and protections of the Adoption Act and Adoption Regulation creates a distinction between adoptees and donor offspring, and that distinction is based on an analogous ground, namely manner of conception ... Section 15(2) has no application here because Ms. Pratten is not seeking to preclude the Province from enacting legislation to ameliorate the circumstances of adoptees. In context, the distinction made between adoptees and donor offspring creates a disadvantage to donor offspring by perpetuating stereotypes about donor offspring.

With respect to the section 7 claims, Adair J rejected Ms. Pratten's argument that section 7 confers a positive right to know one's origins (at para 291). She also rejected Ms. Pratten's negative rights claim on the basis that there was insufficient state action to support the claim (at para 315).

In considering Ms. Pratten's claim, Adair J reviewed approximately 50 affidavits, including some from experts. She made the following findings of fact:

> [111] ...
> (a) donor offspring fear that their health can be compromised, and may be seriously compromised, by the lack of information about their

donor. Based in particular on the evidence from Dr. Lauzon, these fears are justified. Even with the availability of genetic testing, a good old-fashioned family history is more predictive, and genetic testing is best interpreted in the context of a family history;

(b) because of a lack of information, donor offspring can face delayed medical treatment, and an inability to have conditions that are inherited or genetic diagnosed and treated. On the other hand, with information, donor offspring (for example, Barry Stevens) can and do modify their own behaviour;

(c) it is important, psychologically and medically, for donor offspring to have the ability to know identifying and non-identifying information about their donor, and their psychological and medical needs in that respect are substantially the same as adoptees;

(d) for donor offspring, having information — both identifying and non-identifying — matters deeply, both to complete their personal identities and to alleviate the stress, anxiety and frustration caused by not knowing. Donor offspring demonstrate a strong commitment to searching for information about the other half of their genetic make-up;

(e) donor offspring experience sadness, frustration, depression and anxiety — in other words, they suffer psychological and psychosocial difficulties — when they are unable to obtain information. They feel the effects both for themselves and, when they become parents, for their own children;

(f) donor offspring commonly, and legitimately, fear inadvertent consanguinity. Without further biological testing, many do not have the information required to determine if another individual is a biological half-sibling;

(g) the secrecy that often surrounds the process of conception, even when done with the best of intentions, can have devastating effects on donor offspring when the truth is revealed. Moreover, knowing the truth (that the other biological parent was a donor), but having no means to discover what the truth means for one's life, can be a significant source of anxiety, depression and frustration for donor offspring;

(h) while recognizing that parents have an important and legitimate interest in deciding what their child will know and when she or he will know it, anonymity and secrecy tips the balance heavily in favour of donors and parents, and away from the best interests of donor offspring; and

(i) donor offspring and adoptees experience similar struggles, and a similar sense of loss and incompleteness. However, donor offspring do not have the benefit of the kind of positive institutions and legislative support provided to and for adoptees in B.C.

Having concluded that the impugned provisions of B.C.'s adoption legislation and regulations violated section 15 and were not justified under section 1 of the *Charter*, Adair J declared the provisions to be of no force or effect and suspended the declaration of invalidity for 15 months (at para 335).

The B.C. Attorney General appealed the court's decision. The Attorney General did not challenge the factual findings and conclusions of the trial judge set out above. Rather, the Attorney General argued that the impugned provisions were valid by virtue of section 15(2) of the *Charter*. In addition, Ms. Pratten brought a cross-appeal against Adair J's rejection of her positive rights claim under section 7 of the *Charter*.

The Court of Appeal allowed the appeal and dismissed the cross-appeal: *Pratten v British Columbia (AG)*, 2012 BCCA 480. With respect to the appeal, the Court of Appeal concluded that the impugned provisions of British Columbia's adoption legislation and regulations qualify as an ameliorative program within the meaning of section 15(2) of the *Charter*.

> [41] The Legislature has made a decision to recognize and regulate adoption to provide adoptees with new and permanent family ties. That process involves changing the legal status of an adoptee. A consequence of that change is that adoptees are alienated from their biological origins and face barriers in accessing information about their origins. The purpose of impugned provisions is to reduce those barriers while maintaining the essentially socially beneficial stance of the legislation. Given that purpose, it cannot be said that excluding persons whose legal status has never changed goes "further than is justified by the object of the ameliorative program".

The Court of Appeal also rejected Ms. Pratten's cross appeal on the basis that she had not established that access to information about one's biological origins is so "fundamental" so as to warrant protection under the *Charter* (at para 49).

Ms. Pratten sought leave to appeal to the Supreme Court of Canada, which was refused on May 30, 2013: [2013] SCCA No 36.

Although British Columbia enacted a new *Family Law Act* in November 2011, which determines parentage in a variety of situations involving assisted reproduction, the Act does not address the issues of disclosure raised in the *Pratten* case.

Although Ms. Pratten's claim was not successful, the factual findings made by Adair J, which were not challenged on appeal, offer compelling grounds for legislative reform in this area. Indeed, there are a number of jurisdictions, such as the United Kingdom, that no longer permit anonymous gamete donation: Eric Blyth & Lucy Frith, "Donor-Conceived People's Access to Genetic and Biographical History: An Analysis of Provisions in Different Jurisdictions Permitting Disclosure of Donor Identity" (2009) 23 Int'l J L Pol'y and Fam 176.

A number of concerns have been raised about prohibiting donor anonymity in Canada. First, there is a concern that, in the absence of clear parentage legislation, donors might interfere and threaten the family unit's security. These concerns are particularly acute for women-led families (Cameron, Gruben & Kelly, above at 108; see also Lori Chambers & Heather Hillsburg, "Desperately Seeking Daddy: A Critique of *Pratten v British Columbia (AG)*" (2013) 28:2 CJLS 229). Second, some worry that, in the absence of anonymity, there will be less sperm and eggs available, as initially occurred in the United Kingdom (Turkmendag, Dingwall & Murphy, 2008). Finally, scholars have noted that claims like Ms. Pratten's overly emphasize genetic or biological connections. This overemphasis on biology may undermine bonds between parents and children, particularly in the diverse contexts in which families are created. See Angela Campbell & Robert Leckey, "Parentage is about more than DNA", *The Globe and Mail* (28 October 2010) A23.

Additional Resources

Angela Campbell, "Conceiving Parents Through Law" (2007) 21:2 Intl JL Pol'y & Fam 242.

Fiona Kelly, "An Alternative Conception: The Legality of Home Insemination Under Canada's *Assisted Human Reproduction Act*" (2010) 26:1 Can J Fam L 149.

Laura Shanner, "Viewpoint: Legal Challenges to Donor Anonymity" (2003) 11:3 Health Law Review 25.

Carol Smart, "Family Secrets: Law and Understandings of Openness in Everyday Relationships" (2009) 38:4 Journal of Social Policy 551.

PARENT–CHILD RELATIONSHIPS: THE NEED FOR REFORM?

Legislatures and courts: The role for empirical research

Consider this comment: to what extent do you agree with its conclusions?

> As the judge in [*Rutherford*] ... said, "[r]edefining the legal concept of parent ... is a job for the legislature, not the court." Given the current state of flux in the law, the moment is opportune to consider both the extent to which factors such as bio-genetic ties, intent to parent, and relationship with a biological parent should be weighted when determining legal parentage, and to what extent mothers and fathers can or should be treated the same in this determination. Empirical studies of "alternative families" are instructive, and point to the gap between the ways in which law defines parenthood or family and the lived realities of actual family practices. Alison Diduck has expressed this gap as the difference between the families we live *by* (e.g., the norms embedded within family law) and the families we live *with* (actual family practices). It is difficult to escape the conclusion that legal definitions of who constitutes a "parent" often do not accord with personal understandings of familial relations. Moreover, these definitions may actually "disable people legally from pursuing their own preferred options about where to draw their 'family' boundaries in everyday life."
> ... The legal system does not ... seem to have moved in the direction of distinguishing genetic ties from legal relationships as yet — in fact the trend may be in the opposite direction.... The problem is that the legal system still seems tempted to impose a father figure on families that are headed, and sometimes carefully designed, by women. Moreover, contractual arrangements are typically frowned upon or disallowed in relation to children in family law, in the name of their best interests.... (Susan B Boyd, "Gendering Legal Parenthood: Bio-Genetic Ties, Intentionality and Responsibility" (2007) 25 Windsor YB Access Just 63 at 87 and 92)

Additional Resources

Somer Brodribb, "Delivering Babies: Contracts and Contradictions" in Christine Overall, ed, *The Future of Human Reproduction* (Toronto: The Women's Press, 1989).

Naomi Cahn, "No Secrets: Openness and Donor-Conceived Half-Siblings" 39 (2011) Cap U L Rev 313.

Alison Diduck, *Law's Families* (London: LexisNexis Butterworths, 2003).

Vanessa Gruben & Daphne Gilbert, "Donor Unknown: Assessing the Section 15 Rights of Donor-Conceived Offspring" (2011) 27 Can J Fam L 247.

Fiona Kelly, *Transforming Law's Family: The Legal Recognition of Planned Lesbian Motherhood* (Vancouver: UBC Press, 2011).

Stu Marvel, ""Tony Danza Is My Sperm Donor?": Queer Kinship and the Impact of Canadian Regulations around Sperm Donation" (2013) 25:2 CJWL 221.

Nancy Polikoff, "The Deliberate Construction of Families without Fathers: Is it an Option for Lesbian and Heterosexual Mothers?" (1996) 36 Santa Clara L Rev 375.

Barbara Katz Rothman, *Recreating Motherhood* (New Brunswick, NJ: Rutgers University Press, 2000).

Alison Harvison Young, "Reconceiving the Family: Challenging the Paradigm of the Exclusive Family" (1998) 6 Am UJ Gender Soc Pol'y & L 505.

PART 2

Legal Regulation of "Intact" Families: Care and Protection

4

Families in the Shadow of the State: Responsibilities for Care and Protection

I.
"PRIVATE" FAMILIES AND LEGAL POLICIES OF CARE AND PROTECTION

> Designating [some matters] personal, private and subjective makes them appear to be outside the scope of the law as a fact of nature, whereas in fact non-intervention is a socially constructed, historically variable and inevitably political decision. The state defines as "private" those aspects of life into which it will not intervene, and then, paradoxically, uses this privacy as the justification for its non-intervention. (Nikolas Rose, "Beyond the Public/Private Division: Law, Power and the Family" (1987) 14 JL & Soc'y 61 at 64–65)

"PRIVATE" FAMILIES AND "PUBLIC" POLICIES

Rethinking issues about "private" and "public" in relation to families

Rose's comment captures the shifting boundary of "private" and "public" in the context of law's relationships to families and family life. It also suggests how issues about legal intervention in families may be constrained, on one hand, by ideas about needs for privacy and autonomy for "families" and, on the other, how vulnerable "family members" may require legal intervention to provide protection. Although some of these issues were addressed earlier in this book, this Chapter focuses briefly on some specific challenges for legal intervention or non-intervention in families: "families in the shadow of the state."

251

Issues about legal intervention or non-intervention in families arise in a number of different contexts:

- **Family formation:** As the material about the formation of families has revealed, legal policies carefully define the validity of marriage (and cohabitation, at least to some extent) and the legal status of parent–child relationships in a variety of different contexts. In this way, legal policies define the creation of families and family relationships.

- **Regulating "intact" families:** By contrast, law was not traditionally much involved in regulating the "intact" family after it was created in accordance with legal principles. Indeed, 19th century English law rendered women legally invisible on marriage, and the husband/father in a family had almost complete "ownership" and control of children (and servants), with little legal regulation of his actions. This model of family began to be eroded by child protection efforts, including legislative action, before the end of the 19th century, but legal efforts to protect women/wives from violence and abuse did not much exist until the second half of the 20th century, and it is only recently that the issue of "elder abuse" has attracted legal responses.

- **Family dissolution:** Significantly, these tensions between families as units of society that are entitled to autonomy, privacy and respect and the state's interest in ensuring protection for vulnerable family members may be relevant not only to "intact" families, but also for those involved in the dissolution of the family unit by separation or divorce. In this context, for example, issues about child custody may become intertwined with the state's concern about protecting vulnerable children; and issues about separation and divorce may become complicated by concerns about violence or abuse of individual family members.

Thus, this chapter provides a brief examination of some of the issues that reflect these tensions between "private" families and "public" legal policies designed to protect vulnerable family members. In addition to revealing how law intervenes in intact families, the materials provide important background information to the remaining chapters of this book concerning family dissolution. Although some of the issues discussed in this Chapter are not traditionally included in family law materials, they provide some important insights about the history of family law, the shifting boundaries of the private/public divide in relation to legal intervention, and an important backdrop to issues about family dissolution.

Legal regulation and non-regulation: Family law and beyond

At the outset, it is important to take note of the variety of contexts in which law intervenes in relation to families. Clearly, beyond what is generally regarded as "family law," law has been used to implement a range of governmental policies that affect the nature of rights and obligations for families and their individual family members. Thus, policy assumptions about families are frequently "hidden" within the interstices of many other areas of law: for example, tax law, property and inheritance law, criminal law and the rules of evidence, labour and employment law, and corporate and securities law. What examples can you think of in relation to any of these legal subject areas?

In addition, in thinking about issues of legal intervention, it is important to take into account not only positive state intervention but also the *absence* of legal regulation, and the ways in which the state may "privatize" responsibilities within families by failing to create or sustain policies that provide positive benefits to families and their members. In this context, private families may be required to assume responsibilities that were once provided publicly by the state. Moreover, to the extent that families fail to discharge their responsibilities according to legal standards, the state may be entitled to intervene. In this way, the state may delegate (its) responsibilities to families, but also hold them to account if they fail to meet state-defined standards of care and protection for family members. In this context, it has been argued that there is a "care deficit" in Canada:

> [P]ublic sector policies reflect an assumption that families can and should be responsible for providing care to family members. Community programs have experienced limited growth, even retrenchment, reducing resources allocated to the health and continuing care service sections, which is constraining the supply of formal care. *The net result of an escalating demand for care and a simultaneous shrinking supply of both family and formal care is a growing "care deficit."* (Janet Fast & Donna Lero, "Modern Caregiving in Canada" (2014) 44:2 VIF *Transition* 3 [emphasis added])

In assessing the materials in this chapter, reflect on the impact for families of this increasing "care deficit."

Organization of this chapter

This chapter provides a brief overview of issues relating to legal intervention and non-intervention with respect to issues that are particularly important to policies of care and protection for family members:

- **Child care:** This issue is an example of the general absence of legal intervention in families, so that caring for children is primarily a family responsibility. Although the significance of this issue has grown as the rate of participation by mothers in the paid workforce has increased in recent decades, there has been only limited state intervention to ensure adequate and affordable child care in Canada. Moreover, this issue not only creates problems for intact families, but it may result in a family crisis in the context of separation and divorce. Thus, this material forms an important backdrop to issues about family dissolution in the chapters that follow in this book.

- **Child protection:** Although issues about child protection are often discussed in more detail in courses about Children's Law, it is important to understand some basic connections between state intervention to protect vulnerable children and the broader contexts for both intact families and families involved in processes of dissolution. Children may become vulnerable for a variety of reasons, and although legislation often seeks to provide substantial safeguards, issues of resources may thwart the full implementation of legal policies. In this context, the material in this chapter provides some useful starting points for defining the "best interests" of children, in theory and practice.

- **Violence/abuse in intimate ("spousal") relationships:** Violence and abuse may occur in many intimate relationships, including marriage and cohabitation. Moreover, although women may be engaged in violent behaviour, the evidence indicates that male violence against women is far more prevalent. In addition, some data suggest that the rate of male violence often escalates at the time of separation, a factor that some women apparently take into account in choosing to remain in an abusive relationship with a man, especially if children are involved. This issue is particularly complex because it may involve both family law and criminal law issues that do not always intersect successfully to ensure family safety. The material in this chapter provides important contextual issues for the family dissolution material that follows in this book.

- **Elder abuse:** Issues about elder abuse have surfaced in recent decades, and there is some statistical data that suggest that such abuse often emanates from caregivers, who are frequently family members. In these cases, abuse takes a variety of forms, including physical and emotional abuse, but also inappropriate family interventions in the financial affairs of an elderly (dependant) family member. This issue may also exacerbate stress for family members involved in caregiving.

Overall, these issues provide an opportunity to examine the law's role in intervening (or not intervening) in intact families, and also provide some important contextual background to the discussion of issues of family dissolution in the remaining chapters of this book.

II.
FAMILIES AND THE STATE:
(FAMILY) RESPONSIBILITIES FOR CHILD CARE

Disagreements about Canadian child care policy have thus reflected far more than competing views about appropriate policy instruments. They have also engaged deeply held beliefs about motherhood, women's roles, and the nature of families and caregiving. Understanding the connections between public and private helps to illuminate the sources of resistance to redistributing the costs of caring for children away from individual women and into the public sphere. (Katherine Teghtsoonian, "Who Pays for Car-

ing for Children? Public Policy and the Devaluation of Women's Work" in
Susan B Boyd, ed, *Challenging the Public/Private Divide: Feminism, Law,
and Public Policy* (Toronto: University of Toronto Press, 1997) 113 at 132)

RETHINKING FAMILIES AND THE WORKPLACE: THE CONTEXT FOR MOTHERS

As this comment suggests, there have been significant changes in the rate
of women's participation in paid work in recent decades. Moreover, the
rate of participation of mothers of preschool children has also increased
sharply. According to recent statistics cited in *Families Count*,

> [t]hirty years ago, less than one half (48.1%) of married women aged 25
> to 54 years were in the paid labour force. By 2008, over eight in ten
> (81.5%) were employed or seeking paid work. There is now no statistically
> significant difference between the labour force participation of married
> women and single or divorced women.
>
> Motherhood is also much less likely to alter women's labour force
> participation. According to the 2006 Census, 73% of all women with chil-
> dren less than 16 years of age living at home were employed on a full
> time or part time basis, up from 39% in 1976.... [Moreover, by 2006], two
> thirds of women with children under age 3 years (64%) were employed,
> more than double the proportion in 1976 (at 28%)....
>
> [At the same time,] public supports for families such as child care
> and access to flexible hours vary widely across Canada resulting in tre-
> mendous inequities.... (Vanier Institute of the Family, *Families Count*
> (Ottawa: VIF, 2010) at 80)

Yet, in spite of a number of studies that have recommended the adoption of national standards and funding for child care, the care of young
children remains substantially a matter of (private) familial responsibility,
with only minimal state intervention. In reading the following excerpt, consider how Canada's policies of non-intervention compare to other jurisdictions, and the consequences for parents, particularly women, in the paid
workforce.

Citizen, Worker, Mother:
Canadian Women's Claims to Parental Leave and Childcare
(2002) 19 Can J Fam L 11 at 53ff

Lene Madsen

... Canadian law and policy makers have engaged, on paper at least, with
the issue of childcare for upwards of twenty years. Successive commission
and task forces have produced reports and recommendations, which,
although with variation in emphasis, agree in their findings that affordable
quality childcare would benefit Canadian children, support the Canadian
economy, reduce child poverty, and contribute to gender equality. In 1986,
the federally funded *Task Force on Child Care* appointed by the Liberals
in 1984 recommended the establishment of a fully funded childcare system; in 1987, the *Special Committee on Child Care* appointed by the Con-
servatives in 1985 recommended an expansion of tax measures, coupled
with a new federal spending program to address childcare needs; in 1987,

the Conservative government introduced the *National Strategy on Child Care*, followed in 1988 by the *Canada Child Care Bill* (sharply criticized at the time, but nevertheless an attempt to deal with childcare as a pressing social need), which died on the order paper, was not reintroduced after the election, and was formally abandoned in 1992; in 1993, the Liberals included a commitment to childcare in their "Red Book"; and in 1995 the report of the *Social Security Review* recognized the importance of childcare. Yet, in 2001, despite the thousands of pages written which document the need for and potential advantages of a comprehensive national childcare system, and despite clear evidence that most Canadian families consider childcare to be a pressing priority, childcare is presently poorly organized, haphazardly regulated, under-funded, of variable quality, and insufficiently available to the majority of families requiring services. As noted in a recent commentary in the *Globe and Mail*:

> [F]or all the political rhetoric about an agenda for children, for all the millions of dollars invested in research and pilot projects probing the precious first few years of life, most children are standing in the same spot they were a decade ago....

THE STATE OF CANADIAN CHILDCARE

At present, the available childcare mix includes a small number of regulated daycare centre spaces, a limited number of regulated family/home care spaces, and unregulated care, which may include care by relatives, care by friends and or neighbours, or paid-for but unlicensed care by others in the community. A very recent report estimated that while there are approximately 3.2 million Canadian children in need of childcare, a mere 360,000 regulated spaces are available to address this need. The vast majority of children are thus cared for in unregulated settings while their parents work outside the home. Given the consistent evidence that the quality of care in regulated settings is in general superior to that available in unregulated settings, assessments of the adequacy of Canadian childcare options focus on the former.

Childcare advocates and scholars typically assess regulated daycare options in Canada with respect to their accessibility, affordability, and quality, and have with alarming agreement found the situation on all three fronts to be sorely lacking. Assessing the state of *regulated* care, they have found that Canada's childcare provisions fall well behind those of European countries, and do not come close to meeting the needs of working parents. Says Maureen Baker, "Canada's child care system ranks well below those of most of the countries studied in terms of level of funding, availability of spaces, cost to parents, and quality of care."

Accessibility concerns the extent to which parents are able to find an age appropriate space for their child(ren); in a reasonably proximate location; with opening hours that match the needs of the parents; and which is sensitive to cultural, physical, social and developmental needs. Studies show and the numbers above indicate that only a fraction of the needed regulated spaces are available, thus compelling many parents to use unregulated care even when they would prefer a regulated setting. Opening hours are also a significant obstacle for many parents — while most care is provided on the basis of a "standard workweek," roughly corresponding to a 9–5 workday, many parents are in need of services during evenings, nights, and weekends. Indeed, over 40% of the Canadian workforce does not work a "standard" schedule. While home-based care is in general more flexible than centre-based care, there is still a serious shortage of care during "off-hours." Serious issues of accessibility also arise with respect to children with special needs. Most "regular" daycare centres are not open to children with disabilities, either due to physical barriers or staffing limitations. Although there is some funding to assist some parents, "a very significant number of children with special needs are not receiving childcare services." Maureen Baker summarizes the current situation with respect to accessibility:

> Parents with able-bodied children between three and five, who live in cities, and who can afford to pay higher fees, have the most options from which to choose.

Affordability concerns the extent to which parents who require care are able to purchase regulated spaces for their children. While there are important variations amongst the provinces, there is no question that childcare claims a significant portion of the after tax income of families requiring paid care. Indeed, one study indicated that childcare for *one* preschooler, for a family with an average income living in a medium-sized Ontario city, represented fully 15% of after-tax earnings. Maureen Baker has noted that the cost of daycare can "more than double the annual cost of raising young children and is usually the greatest single child-related expense the family incurs." Childcare is primarily funded through parent fees, which in some cases are reduced by subsidies. However, ... this mechanism is insufficient to alleviate the burden on many families requiring childcare. Studies consistently show that childcare is a significant financial burden for all but the wealthy, and that many parents who would prefer regulated care options for their children simply are not able to afford them....

CHILDCARE WITHOUT THE STATE

The sorry state of Canadian childcare can largely be attributed to the fact that at present, childcare in Canada is considered a private concern, to be addressed by individual families through the family or the market place.... [Childcare] in Canada ... is a state concern "only when the market or family fails, and this is presumed to apply to a small share or residual of the population." It is conceived of in many respects as an "anti-poverty program" for lower income groups, rather than as an entitlement *per se*....

Although subsidies could potentially be an important source of relief for parents paying for childcare, there are numerous limitations. First, they are available to a fraction of the many families who would require this assistance.... Second, the threshold to receive assistance is extremely low in most provinces, in general targeting only the very poorest working families.... Thirdly, due to the absence of any federal oversight, there is a great degree of variation across provinces, territories, and municipalities, both in terms of the level of subsidization available and priorities for eligibility. In some Ontario municipalities, for example, the priority may be teenaged parents who are returning to school after the birth of a child, while in another it may be the working poor. Finally, subsidies are currently jeopardized by restructuring, both in terms of size and coverage, due to the diminished transfer payments to the provinces under the CHST. Tyyskä reports that in Ontario, for example, between 1996 and 1998, allocations for daycare were reduced from $520 million to $432 million, with clear implications for the ability to maintain subsidy levels. With reference to childcare, she says, "The CHST opened a new door to a reduction in spending in an area particularly vulnerable to changes in economic or political climate."

Governments also engage in childcare policy through the regulation of some childcare spaces. This regulation is intended primarily to assure the basic safety of children, and to a much lesser degree, to ensure [that] certain minimum standards of quality are maintained. Provinces and in some cases municipalities will regulate daycare centres, for which standards are set regarding the training of staff and the staff–child ratio for example, as well as some home-based care providers.

There are two fundamental concerns with the current approach to regulation. The first is that there are simply not enough regulated spaces.... The second concern is that the level of regulation may simply not be high enough to ensure that children in these spaces are receiving a quality of care which would support their development....

Governmental engagement with childcare — through tax measures, subsidies, and regulations — thus essentially leaves the provision of childcare to the private realm of the family and the market. By choosing such a level of involvement, the federal government has effectively relinquished the opportunity to "shape the quality, availability, or afford-ability of childcare services." This approach also fails to recognize what has been identified as the critical link between childcare and other social issues, including the overall well-being of children, the need for a skilled and efficient workforce, and equality-based concerns. Further, the few chosen policy measures, while they may provide limited relief to some families and ensure a baseline level of care in some services, do not con-tribute in any way to increasing the supply of regulated care, nor do they contribute to improving the quality of childcare overall. According to the Childcare Resource and Research Unit (CRRU):

> Canada has not taken a pro-active or even facilitative approach to developing a system of high quality childcare services. Rather, childcare has developed in a haphazard manner driven by market forces.... The current childcare situation does not meet the needs of children, families, or women.

IMPACTS OF THE CHILDCARE DEFICIT ON WOMEN

... There are essentially three possible effects of the failure to provide ade-quate childcare options on the "choices" of women. First, some women may simply choose not to return to work after their children are born. As seen, this is a choice confined largely to women in two-parent families where the spouse or partner has a sufficiently large income to financially support the family. Where regulated care is unavailable, too expensive (as it will often be if the family has more than one child), or inaccessible due to scheduling constraints or the need for special needs care, women may decide to stay home rather than turn to unregulated care or other solu-tions. According to Judith Frankel, "many women are simply not able to work when such services (childcare) are not available."

Second, women may choose to work part time, in a position with more flexible hours, in order to be available when childcare is not. Doherty et al. indicate that due to the persistent wage gap, when families consider which parent should or could consider part time work in order to care for children, it will usually be the woman who reduces her labour market participation to accommodate family caregiving obligations. This echoes findings discussed above with respect to parental leave choices. Both of these solutions, as seen above, have serious and long-term impli-cations for women's economic independence and position. According to Freiler and Cerny, "[T]ime spent outside the labour force looking after young children is a major contributor to labour market poverty.... It is well documented that women continue to be at an economic disadvantage even after re-entry into the labour market." Meg Luxton similarly emphasizes that

> if women are out of the paid labour force for significant periods of time to provide caregiving for children and others, then those women are permanently disadvantaged, at risk of living in poverty for extended periods, and in need of a variety of protections, train-ing, and reentry assistance when they rejoin the labour force. Policy initiatives that facilitate women's labour force participation and

their work in social reproduction, such as a national, high quality, comprehensive daycare system, will in the long run be less disruptive and less costly.

Finally, women may "choose" either for professional or financial reasons to maintain full participation in the labour force despite the difficulties of securing care. Doing this may require the use of unregulated care, care by a relative, or sibling care if there are older children in the family. Where this approach is chosen in the current childcare milieu, it is likely to lead to a high degree of stress and anxiety, in addition to reduced work productivity for both parents, but particularly mothers, as they strive to meet the demands of both their full-time employment and family obligations. This is particularly so given the lack of parental leave in Canada for the purpose of tending to sick children or other family responsibilities. Again, this has implications for women's labour market status....

CONCLUSION: CONTEMPORARY LEAVE AND CHILDCARE ENTITLEMENTS — THE EROSION OF SOCIAL CITIZENSHIP

... The present state of parental leave policy and the childcare context can be understood within the context of economic and ideological restructuring underway in Canada at present, and illustrates the erosion of social citizenship which has accompanied the effective demise of the welfare state. From an economic perspective, ... the retrenchments in childcare testify to a continued and accelerating privatization of the care of children, and an aversion on the part of the state to viewing such care as a public investment.... The continued failure to act on childcare, and indeed the contraction of spending in this field in the wake of the CHST, reflect the current fiscal climate, focused as it is on spending reductions and a general withdrawal of the state from areas of formerly public provision. Present policy choices with respect to daycare, for example, are consistent with the approach of short-term cost-cutting rather than longer-term social investments and a market-based rather than public approach to social infrastructure....

From an ideological perspective, policy choices with respect to ... childcare are also quite consistent. As discussed above, the increased focus on "individual responsibility" and "self-reliance" has permeated contemporary political discourse, limiting the range of what can "legitimately" be claimed from the state. The care of children, whether in infancy or as they grow older has increasingly been defined as a "private responsibility." Parents are expected to identify private solutions to childcare needs, in line with their general obligation to "take care of themselves." ... Similarly, the failure to act on childcare issues, and the steady erosion of the already limited state involvement in this area confirms the ideological prioritization given to parents making private arrangements, whether through the market or through the family, for the care of their children.

Underpinning this renewed individualism has been the increased glorification of the family, and particularly of the "traditional" family.... As state supports are eroded and increasingly the provision of caring functions is downloaded onto the family, the "new moral order," as described by Janine Brodie, legitimates and justifies the increasing burdens on the family.... Similarly, the policy failures with respect to daycare are justified by a rhetoric that implies that family care of children is the best care.

Rendered invisible by the ideological veil are the very real consequences of ... daycare policy for women's caregiving responsibilities and capacity to engage in the paid labour force. The downloading of care is perceived as being onto the "family," not onto women *per se*, and families then "choose" how to share the increased burdens. The role of fiscal realities and gendered expectations is hidden as women "choose" to leave or reduce their participation in the paid workforce, or are compelled to reduce their labour market aspirations in order to accommodate family responsibilities.... This combination of fiscal and ideological restructuring illustrates ... that not only do gender relations underpin and shape social provision, but policy choices in turn shape gender relations. In the case of ... childcare, in downloading the responsibilities for childcare onto the family, policy-makers are acting, consciously or subconsciously, on assumptions that women will provide the care not offered by the state; and, in making this assumption, they are reinforcing and in fact continually recreating the household and market divisions of labour, which effectively consign women to continued inequality.

Notes and Questions

Public and private: Policy making about workplace equality and child care

As Madsen's comments suggest, the provision of child care is necessary to enable women to participate in paid work effectively, and on an equal basis with men. In a review of a 2001 publication about women's employment equality and child care policy in Canada, Judy Fudge commented on how these two policy issues have been characterized as separate matters, in part because of an underlying conception of "citizen workers" as male:

> ... In the period of reconstruction after the Second World War, the Canadian state, along with other welfare states, partially institutionalized social rights that were based on a specific conception of the worker-citizen — the prototypical male industrial worker. This conception of citizenship excluded women's caring labour from its terms at the same time as the demands for women's paid labour grew.... [Thus] "when questions about promoting equal opportunities for men and women began to emerge in the 1950s and 60s, they were framed in terms of women achieving the *same* opportunities as men."
>
> This policy inevitably resulted in a paradox. Owing to their caring responsibilities, especially for young children, women's experience and opportunities were (and remain) different from those of men.... Although the federal Women's Bureau, which was established in 1954 to provide the federal government with information specific to women's employment, explored the concept of "motherhood at work," federal bureaucrats resisted policies that focused on child care, which they considered to be the private and individual problem of married women employees. (Judy Fudge, "Review of Annis May Timpson, *Driven Apart: Women's Employment Equality and Child Care in Canadian Public Policy* (Vancouver: UBC Press, 2001)" (2001) 13 CJWL 371 at 373–374)

For another assessment, see Nora Spinks & Donna Lero, "Combining Caregiving and Work in Canada: Achievable or Not?" VIF *Transition* 4:1 (Winter 2011) 1–3.

Public and private responses: Models and approaches for child care policies

Debates about the need for national child care policies have continued to provoke a variety of different responses in Canada, although these responses have often been subjected to criticism. For example, in a detailed analysis of comparative family policy in eight countries, including Canada,

Kathy O'Hara concluded that Canadian policy incorporated values of self-reliance, individualism, and family privacy. Overall, O'Hara argued that Canadian policy exhibited ambivalence about the state's role in some family matters:

> This has meant that although the role of the state in the family has increased steadily in Canada, as in other countries, governments in Canada (with the exception of the provincial government in Quebec) have avoided major interventions and steering policies of the kind developed in some European countries. Canadian policy has instead taken a minimalist approach to the need to adapt to changing demographic and labour market realities. (Kathy O'Hara, *Comparative Family Policy: Eight Countries' Stories* (Ottawa: Canadian Policy Research Networks, 1998) at 7–8; and see also G Esping-Andersen, "The Three Political Economies of the Welfare State" (1989) 26:1 Canadian Review of Sociology and Anthropology 10)

As O'Hara's comment noted, Québec adopted a new child care policy, as part of its Early Childhood and Child Care Strategy, in 1997, a program designed to significantly increase the number of regulated child care spaces and to offer child care to parents for a fee of $5 per day. By contrast, the federal government introduced payments to families of $1,200 per year for each child under six years of age, arguing that care arrangements should be a matter of "choice" for families.

In examining these programs in practice, however, Angela Campbell concluded that both were based on implicit assumptions about "typical" families and their child care needs, and that they generally failed to respond to the needs of many families:

> [U]nderpinning these policy initiatives are quite specific assumptions relating to work and "the family." In particular, these initiatives are based on a model family characterized by particular economic resources, physical abilities, and work schedules and responsibilities. Yet, the reality of many families is incongruous with this ideal and, as a result, families that "don't fit the mold" are often excluded from state-supported benefits meant to support parents and children. (Angela Campbell, "Proceeding with 'Care': Lessons to be Learned from the Canadian Parental Leave and Quebec Daycare Initiatives in Developing a National Childcare Policy" (2005–2006) 22 Can J Fam L 171 at 177)

In addition to this critique, a 2004 report of the Organisation for Economic Co-operation and Development (OECD) criticized Canada's policy focus on the provision of care rather than on early learning programs for young children. The same report concluded that the Canadian child care system was adrift and underfunded, particularly by comparison with the United Kingdom and Scandinavia. See Margaret Philp, "Canada's Child Care is Failing, OECD Says", *The Globe and Mail* (25 October 2004). More recently, a 2008 study by the United Nations Children's Fund (UNICEF) ranked Canada last (with Ireland) in early learning and child care services among 25 developed countries. See Laurie Monsebraaten, "Child care is back on the public agenda", *Toronto Star* (5 February 2011); and see also Erin Anderssen, "Why Canada Needs to do Better at Helping Families", *The Globe and Mail* (15 November 2013) A4.

Why is the issue of providing child care a challenge for "public" policy? To what extent is this an issue that reflects a division between "private" families and "public" labour and employment policies?

In thinking about these issues, consider how problems about the provision of adequate child care may impact on women's ability to achieve financial independence or self-sufficiency, issues that may be especially significant at divorce or separation. In addition, reflect on how a lack of access to child care may affect the arrangements available to parents at divorce or separation.

To what extent do "public" policies about child care arrangements constrain "private" choices for parents?

"Family status" discrimination and childcare

In *Canada Border Services Agency v Johnstone*, 2014 FCA 110, the court held that protection from discrimination for childcare obligations flows from "family status," just as protection against discrimination on the basis of pregnancy flows from an individual's "sex." Ms Johnstone had asked her employer, the CBSA, for a "regular" shift at work so that she could arrange ongoing childcare for her two young children. Both Ms Johnstone and her spouse worked on rotating shifts at the CBSA, which interfered with her ability to make appropriate childcare arrangements. The CBSA denied her request on the basis that childcare arrangements were a matter of personal choice and that the solution was for her to move to part time work — resulting in a loss of both salary and benefits.

The Canadian Human Rights Tribunal held that the CBSA had discriminated against Ms Johnstone on the basis of family status, and that the employer was required to accommodate her (as it had done for other employees for medical and religious reasons) by providing a fixed shift. An appeal to the Federal Court was dismissed, as well as a further appeal to the Federal Court of Appeal.

The appeal court expressly rejected the employer's argument that employers should be required to accommodate parental obligations only if they were substantial and could not be delegated to a third party (an argument for a higher threshold re accommodation for "family status" claims of discrimination). The court stated that an employee must only demonstrate reasonable efforts to meet childcare obligations, an inability to reconcile competing family and work obligations, and that the interference is more than "trivial or insubstantial." Since Ms Johnstone had been working part time during this litigation, the court ordered the CBSA to pay her the difference in salary and benefits between part time and full time work; in addition, the court ordered $20,000 in special damages.

Although Ms Johnstone had a spouse, the childcare needs for lone-parent families is often especially challenging, a situation that needs to be taken into account by lawyers and judges in relation to human rights law:

> A lack of affordable and available childcare options is a symptom and cause of poverty in lone-parent families. This tension between childcare needs and precarious work schedules has led some parents and lawyers to view the issue through the lens of employment accommodation and

human rights law.... In recognizing the needs of lone-parent families to have their voices heard, ... it is important for lawyers and their clients to present a strong and explicit story of these struggles (for lone-parents). Judges and adjudicators must understand how Canada's 1.5 million lone-parent families live, struggle, and thrive in this country. (Craig Mazerolle, "Taking (Judicial) Notice of Workplace Precarity: Single Mothers and the Right to Childcare Accommodation" (2014) 1 Windsor Rev Legal Soc Issues — Digital Companion 19 at 22 and 28, online: <http://wrisi.ca/category/digital-companion/>)

See also Melody Jahanzadeh, "Family Status Accommodation: The Road to an Amalgamated Approach" (2012) 2:1 Western Journal of Legal Studies 1; and Laurie Monsebraaten, "Court Upholds Landmark Child-Care Ruling", *Toronto Star* (8 May 2014) A8.

Between public and private: Child care and domestic workers

Issues about the role of the state and families in relation to child care must also focus on the legal regulation of domestic workers, particularly foreign domestic workers, a complex intersection of issues in immigration and employment law in relation to families.

According to Sedef Arat-Koc, domestic workers are often regarded as "*in* the family, but not *of* it, ... involved in the work of a *house*, but not the pleasures and intimacies of a *home*." Neither a family member nor a worker with corresponding rights and privileges, domestic workers are "squeezed between the private and public spheres." Although some aspects of the work of domestic workers [have] been regulated, their situation is often precariously at the margins of regulation. (Sedef Arat-Koc, "In the Privacy of Our Own Home: Foreign Domestic Workers as Solution to the Crisis in the Domestic Sphere in Canada" (1989) 28 Studies in Political Economy 33 at 39; see also Davia Stasiulis & Abigail Bakan, "Negotiating the Citizenship Divide: Foreign Domestic Worker Policy and Legal Jurisprudence" in Radha Jhappen, ed, *Women's Legal Strategies in Canada* (Toronto: University of Toronto Press, 2002) at 239)

Legal challenges: Child care policies and women's equality in employment

In addition to issues about the provision of child care, there have been ongoing legal challenges in recent decades relating to issues about equality in employment for women who are mothers:

- **Challenges to the *Employment Insurance Act*, SC 1996:** Some challenges have focused on the impact of the Act's threshold for entitlement to benefits for part-time workers, many of whom are women who are working part time to provide child care. For example, see *Canada (AG) v Lesiuk* (2003), 299 NR 307 (FCA); leave to appeal dismissed, [2003] SCCA No 94. See also *Canada (AG) v Hunter*, 2013 FCA 12.

- **Challenges with respect to breast feeding in public:** In *Poirier v BC (Council of Human Rights)*, [1996] BCJ No 1795 (SC), the court reviewed a claim of sex discrimination when a woman was denied the opportunity to breast feed her child at work, on her own time, and in a private space. In concluding that there was discrimination, the court sent the case back to the human rights tribunal for determination.

• **Parental leave arrangements in employment insurance legislation:** There have also been a number of challenges to parental leave provisions, including *Schachter v Canada*, [1992] 2 SCR 679; and *Tomasson v Canada (AG)*, 2007 FCA 265.

These issues were addressed in a special issue of the *Canadian Journal of Women and the Law* in 2011. For a detailed overview, see Adelle Blackett, "Regulating Decent Work for Domestic Workers: Introduction" (2011) 23:1 CJWL 1. See also Elaine Jones, "Social Reality versus Family Law: The Experience of Mothers of Children with Long-Term Disabilities" (MA Thesis, University of New Brunswick, 2002).

A legal challenge to child care expenses and tax deduction policies: *Symes v Canada*

In this context, a major legal challenge was initiated concerning tax policies in *Symes v Canada*, [1993] 4 SCR 695, when a practising lawyer appealed from assessments of income tax in relation to payments to her full-time nanny who had cared for her two preschool children during the tax years 1982–1985. Symes claimed these payments as "business expense" deductions, ranging from about $10,000 to $13,300 in each of the four years. The Minister of National Revenue disallowed these amounts and permitted Symes to claim only the amounts allowed by section 63 of the *Income Tax Act* as deductions for child care ($1,000–$4,000 for each of the four years). In doing so, the Minister claimed that the amounts were not expended for the purpose of gaining or producing income from business, but were "personal or living expenses."

In the Federal Court Trial Division, Cullen J upheld Symes's claim, concluding that women workers' entry to the paid workforce required a modern interpretation of the idea of "business expenses," relying on expert evidence presented by Dr. Patricia Armstrong about changes in women's paid work. The Federal Court of Appeal overturned the lower court decision, and the case was further appealed to the Supreme Court of Canada.

In the Supreme Court of Canada, the majority dismissed the appeal, with L'Heureux-Dubé and McLachlin JJ dissenting. Although there was disagreement in the Supreme Court of Canada about the "discriminatory" nature of the provisions of the *Income Tax Act*, the majority concluded that Symes was not entitled to the deductions as "business expenses." The case was controversial because a successful outcome would have affected only women who, as self-employed women, were entitled to claim "business expenses," a result with some potential to undermine efforts to attain social equality:

> [A] successful challenge would have increased social inequality by making wealthier self-employed women relatively better off. In the long term,

unless the differential treatment of self-employed and employed persons could have been successfully challenged subsequently, a positive outcome in *Symes* could also have made employed women worse off in two possible ways. They could have been made worse off if governments reduced overall childcare funding as a result of increased tax expenditures. A major concern of critics was the potential fragmentation of the childcare lobby by reducing the involvement of middle-class self-employed women. Reduced support for childcare as a social responsibility would make it more difficult to advance the case for national daycare funding and could contribute to the privatization of childcare. (Wanda Wiegers, review of Rebecca Johnson, *Taxing Choices: The Intersection of Class, Gender, Parenthood and the Law* (Vancouver: UBC Press, 2002) in (2004) 16 CJWL 426 at 435)

To what extent does this critique concerning the broader issues of child care policy reflect different views about child care, about strategies for litigating equality claims, or about the respective roles of legislatures and courts? In this context, Lisa Philipps argued that, in relation to tax policy, the state redefines the boundary between public and private in ways that shift political and economic resources away from social reproduction. For other examples, see Lisa Philipps, "Tax Law and Social Reproduction: The Gender of Fiscal Policy in an Age of Privatization" in Brenda Cossman & Judy Fudge, eds, *Privatization, Law, and the Challenge to Feminism* (Toronto: University of Toronto, 2002) 41 at 45.

Consider this approach:

The mayor of the small town of Torredonjimeno in Spain announced in July 2003 that men would be fined by local police if they were found in bars in the town on Thursday evenings between 9 p.m. and 2 a.m. (the hours when men traditionally gathered in local bars in the town). The mayor explained that he expected men to remain at home on Thursdays (one night per week) to look after children and do the washing up so that women could have a night out, and that he hoped to turn the town into "an international reference point" for sex equality. Money collected from fines was to be directed to groups dealing with domestic violence and sex equality. (See Giles Tremlett, "Spanish Mayor Bans Men from Bars", *The Guardian* (21 July 2003).)

Is this example a solution in relation to child care policies and women's equality in employment? Does it reflect a "private" or "public" approach to the child care issue? See also Tim Harper, "Our Kids, Our Future and Two Competing Visions for Voters", *Toronto Star* (3 November 2014) A4.

Additional Resources

Erin Anderssen, "The Case for Publicly Funded Childcare", *The Globe and Mail* (21 October 2013) A6.

Canadian Human Rights Commission, *A Guide to Balancing Work and Caregiving Obligations* (Ottawa: Minister of Public Works and Government Services, 2014).

Patricia M Evans, "Divided Citizenship? Gender, Income Security, and the Welfare State" in PM Evans and G Wekerle, eds, *Women and the Canadian Welfare State: Challenges and Change* (Toronto: University of Toronto Press, 1997) 91.

Rebecca Johnson, *Taxing Choices: The Intersection of Class, Gender, Parenthood, and the Law* (Vancouver: UBC Press, 2002).

Audrey Macklin, "*Symes v. MNR*: Where Sex Meets Class" (1992) 5 CJWL 498.

Susan A McDaniel & Martha Friendly, "Child Care Policy in Canada: Putting the Pieces Together" (1996) 27 Journal of Comparative Family Studies 576.

Sheila Neysmith, *Restructuring Caring Labour: Discourse, State Practice, and Everyday Life* (Toronto: Oxford University Press, 2000).

"Policy Forum: Comments on *Taxing Choices: The Intersection of Class, Gender, Parenthood, and the Law*, by Rebecca Johnson" (2003) 51:5 Can Tax J 1918.

Davia Stasiulis & Abigail Bakan, eds, *Not One of the Family: Foreign Domestic Workers in Canada* (Toronto: University of Toronto Press, 1997).

Annis May Timpson, *Driven Apart: Women's Employment Equality and Child Care in Canadian Public Policy* (Vancouver: UBC Press, 2001).

Lorna Turnbull, *Double Jeopardy: Motherwork and the Law* (Toronto: Sumach Press, 2001).

Vanier Institute of the Family, *Families Count: Profiling Canada's Families IV* (Ottawa: VIF, 2010) 138 [Part III: *Care and Support*].

III.
CHILDREN "IN NEED OF PROTECTION": RESPONSIBILITIES FOR FAMILIES AND THE STATE

The suffering of children at the hands of the family is the hard case for law. The primacy of the family as the locus of childrearing and the foundational social unit is recognized in all societies. Respect may be expressed in protection of paternal or parental authority through doctrines of privacy which discourage scrutiny of parenting practices, confound development of coherent state-child relations and children's rights theory, render child abuse invisible and remove it from the ambit of "grown up" or principled law. (Anne McGillivray, "Reconstructing Child Abuse: Western Definition and Non-Western Experience" in Michael Freeman & Philip Veerman, eds, *The Ideologies of Children's Rights* (Dordrecht, Netherlands: Martinus Nijhoff Publishers, 1992) 213 at 230)

THE "HARD CASE" FOR LAW: CHILDREN'S INTERESTS AND FAMILY AUTONOMY

The context: Protecting children and/or preserving families?

As McGillivray concluded, state intervention in the family when a child is "in need of protection" directly confronts the boundary between the private family and the public state. Not surprisingly, legal regulation for the purpose of protecting children and, if necessary, even removing them from their families presents difficult and often highly contested issues for determination.

For example, the Gove Inquiry into Child Protection in British Columbia in the 1990s concluded that a child had died as a result of too little emphasis on the part of child protection workers on the needs of the *child* within the *family* context. (At the time of his death, Matthew Vaudreuil was severely underweight, his body revealed many bruises, and he had a fractured arm and 11 fractured ribs. According to the autopsy report, the injuries "show all the hallmarks of child abuse.")

> In spite of their mandate to make child safety and well-being their paramount concern, many social workers seem to consider family unity to be paramount, even to the detriment of the child. For example, one social worker testified that "the ministry's policy was families first and apprehension only as a last resort.... When dealing with Matthew, that was always my concern, ... to keep him in the home ... to ensure that the integrity of the family was maintained." (Gove Inquiry into Child Protection (BC), *Report of the Gove Inquiry into Child Protection in British Columbia*, vol 1 (Vancouver: Ministry of Social Services, 1995) at 136)

Even prior to the report's recommendations, British Columbia had enacted amending legislation that declared that "the safety and well-being of a child shall be the paramount consideration" in matters of child protection (see *Child, Family and Community Service Act*, SBC 1994, c 27, s 2). This principle means that children can be removed from their families and placed "in care," usually in a foster home, if their "best interests" warrant such intervention.

The child protection regime is thus a good example of legal regulation of an "intact" family, a context in which legal policies may breach family autonomy to protect vulnerable children to promote their "best interests." However, a decision to remove a child from the family may result in a series of temporary homes. As one study in the 1980s indicated, children removed from their families temporarily lived in an average of four foster homes before age 16, while children removed permanently lived in an average of eight homes before age 16. See Jeffery Wilson & Mary Tomlinson, *Children and the Law*, 2nd ed (Toronto: Butterworths, 1986) at 65. How might such data affect a social worker's decision about removing a child from the child's family? In this context, legislatures and courts continue to struggle to ensure the protection of children, and at the same time, to achieve the least possible disruption to family autonomy.

These tensions between family autonomy and protection of vulnerable family members are also evident in the law's responses to violence and abuse in intimate family relationships (spousal violence) and in relation to frail elderly persons (elder abuse). Significantly, however, child welfare legislation was enacted in many parts of Canada in the 19th century, and some features of common law and equity offered protection for children even earlier (see Kerry O'Halloran, *The Welfare of the Child: The Principle and the Law* (Aldershot, UK: Ashgate, 1999)). By contrast, legal intervention in relation to spousal violence and elder abuse represent more recent initiatives to protect vulnerable family members. However, in all these cases, tensions between "private" families and "public" legal regulation continue to provide challenges.

In examining the legislative framework and judicial reasoning in this chapter, consider how these tensions have been reconciled in these differing contexts.

Child protection in Ontario: The statutory framework

The paramount purpose is the "best interests" of a child. In Ontario, section 1(1) of the *Child and Family Services Act*, RSO 1990, c 11, identifies the Act's paramount purpose as promoting "the best interests, protection and well being of children." Section 1(2) then identifies a number of additional purposes of the Act, "so long as they are consistent with the best interests, protection and well being of children." For example, one of these additional purposes is

> To recognize that while parents may need help in caring for their children, that help should give support to the autonomy and integrity of the family unit and, wherever possible, be provided on the basis of mutual consent....

Clearly, while the legal principles are carefully defined in this statutory language, it may often be more difficult to apply them in the context of concrete factual circumstances.

Defining a "Child in Need of Protection"

Part III of the Act provides the framework for legal intervention to protect a child in need of protection. Part III includes definitions with respect to child protection.

Specifically, section 37(2) of the *CFSA* provides a list of the circumstances in which a child will be "in need of protection." The list includes physical, emotional, and mental harm — or a pattern of neglect — and includes conduct or neglect *in the past* as well as *risk of future harm*. In addition, the section includes sexual molestation or exploitation of a child, a child's need for medical treatment, and circumstances of abandonment, etc., in determining whether a child is "in need of protection." As Nicholas Bala concluded, however, a determination that a child is "in need of protection" requires "professional judgment and sometimes very difficult individualized decision-making." See Nicholas Bala, "Reforming Ontario's Child and Family Services Act: Is the Pendulum Swinging Back Too Far?" (1999) 17 Can Fam LQ 121.

These definitions were revised and strengthened following recommendations from a panel of experts that was convened to advise the government after several Ontario children died as a result of parental harm or neglect, even though these children were being supervised prior to their deaths by a child protection agency. See Panel of Experts on Child Protection (Ontario), *Protecting Vulnerable Children: Report of the Panel of Experts on Child Protection* (Toronto: Ministry of Community and Social Services, 1998).

More recently, as a result of the death of another child who was in the custody of her mother's friend, additional reforms were introduced with respect to custody and access orders (see *Family Statute Law Amendment Act, 2009*), which created new procedures for custody applications. See *Children's Law Reform Act*, ss 21–21.3, discussed in more detail in relation to custody and access later in this book.

Defining the "Best Interests" of a Child

According to Part III, decisions about children in need of protection must focus on the "best interests of the child."

Section 37(3) defines the factors to be taken into account when a decision maker must consider "the best interests of a child." Note, however, that the legislative framework does not identify any priority among these factors, one of which ("any other relevant circumstance") provides considerable scope for judicial discretion.

In addition, section 37(4) specifically requires that the importance of preserving a child's cultural identity must be taken into account where the child is an Aboriginal child, a provision that parallels the statutory direction in relation to adoption for Aboriginal children. In relation to both child protection and adoption, however, the statutory language makes this factor just one consideration, not determinative. Recall the cases and critiques of similar statutory language, examined earlier in relation to the adoption of Aboriginal children in Canada, and proposed reforms.

Procedures in Child Protection Matters

Part III of the Act also sets out in detail the procedures for apprehending a child in need of protection. Other parts of the statute define the roles and responsibilities of Children's Aid Societies in administering the child protection regime, including the provision of assistance to parents such as homemaking services or education about parenting skills. In this context, the administration of child protection involves not just the interpretation of statutory definitions but also the marshalling of (sometimes scarce) public resources to promote children's interests, a challenge that may sometimes be daunting for the professionals involved.

DECISION MAKING IN A CHILD PROTECTION CASE: A CASE STUDY

In *Winnipeg South Child and Family Services Agency v S(DD)*, the court heard evidence from a number of experts and others, as well as a father and mother, to determine whether the child was "in need of protection" and what disposition was in the child's "best interests." In examining this case study, consider whether, or to what extent, the court balanced the goals of family autonomy and of ensuring legal protection for a vulnerable child.

In this case, the child protection agency, which was requesting permanent guardianship of a child, had apprehended the child on a number of occasions since his birth. During the eight-day trial, a large number of professionals gave evidence about the assistance that had been provided to the father and mother in an effort to support the family together, and they also gave evidence about the (in)abilities of the parents to meet the needs of the child. In reviewing the decision, consider the factual evidence relied upon and the application of the statutory principles in Manitoba's legislation.

Winnipeg South Child and Family Services Agency v S(DD)
(1990), 24 RFL (3d) 290 (Man QB (Fam Div))

[6] The evidence is that, after giving birth to the child, the mother was anxious, upset and apprehensive about caring for the child and mentioned adoption. She was seen by a social worker, Susan Bugaliski, at the hospital and arrangements were made for a public health nurse to attend at the home, for a parent aide to help care for the child, and for a homemaker. She was also advised that she could obtain psychiatric care at the St. Boniface Hospital and should see the child's pediatrician.

[7] On 1st June, the social worker visited the mother at her home. The mother said she wanted to go away from the baby and her husband and be alone. The social worker was concerned about leaving her alone with the baby and stayed until her husband came home at 5:30 p.m. and talked to him until 5:45 p.m. She would normally have quit work at 4:30 p.m. The social worker subsequently contacted the agency and referred them to this family.

[8] On 1st June, the mother telephoned Margaret Dresler, an intake worker with the agency, and requested a live-in homemaker because she was having a terrible time with the baby. A homemaker was arranged for four hours on the next day. On 2nd June, Margaret Dresler was to see the mother in the afternoon, but the mother telephoned her in the morning, was very upset and said she wanted to be committed to the hospital. Margaret Dresler went right over to the home. The mother was very depressed and upset, said it was a mistake to have the baby and referred to the baby as "it". The worker was concerned with the comments of the mother that she did not really want the baby and that "it might be best if the Lord took the baby or herself". The mother said she wanted a live-in homemaker, but called the worker on 3rd June to cancel the homemaking service that had been arranged. The worker persuaded her to keep the service.

[9] On 6th June, the mother called Susan Bugaliski between 9:00 a.m. and 10:00 a.m. She was apprehensive, spoke quickly and told the worker that

caring for the child was a problem. The father was at home. The mother then phoned back and said she had taken all of the pills and was not sorry she did it. The worker asked her to go to the hospital by ambulance, but she refused. The mother said the father would not come to the hospital with her, that he was "tired of it". The worker went and picked up the mother in a cab and brought her to the hospital. The mother advised the worker later in the observation room that she needed help with the baby.

[10] On 7th June, Margaret Dresler attended at the parents' home to discuss medication, homemaking services and counselling. She saw the mother talking to the child and saying "Mommy doesn't like you, but will try". The worker referred the case to Mr. Scott MacDonald of the agency for long-term involvement because she was concerned about the parents' ability to care for the child and considered it a "volatile situation."

[11] Brenda Forgie gave evidence that she was placed in the home as a homemaker from June 1988 to early September 1988. She attended at the home twice per week, 1 1/2 to 3 hours each time. She was to help the parents and teach them how to take care of the child. In the beginning, the mother talked about not keeping the child and giving it up for adoption. She said the mother appeared to be uncomfortable and unsure of herself with the child.

[12] Chris Belanger, a public health nurse, made a home visit on 31st May 1988, after the child was at home for one day. She gave evidence that the mother appeared "stilted" with the baby and that there was "no real warmth". The mother said she did not feel she could cope with the baby by herself and made a lot of phone calls for help. She said she got pregnant because she just wanted to see what it was like, not because she wanted a baby. She said "babies are okay if you just have to feed them, but don't have to play with them or talk to them". She said it was cute when the baby cried because it sounded like a cat. Chris Belanger arrived at 3:00 p.m. that day and waited until the father arrived home at 5:30 p.m. to make sure the baby was safe. She talked to him about the care of the baby. The father expressed concern over the child being left alone with the mother. The nurse remained in contact with the family to make sure they had enough assistance and advised them on 4th August and 26th August 1988 of parenting groups they could go to. They advised on each occasion that they were not ready yet.

[13] Scott MacDonald is a social worker with the agency who has been involved with the family since 13th June 1988. He received reports from everyone involved in the case on a regular basis and had contact directly with the parents. He referred to the hospital records and, in particular, Ex. 5, which he says contained the same information he knew of. On 16th October 1988 the mother was hospitalized. She had visual and auditory hallucinations which were telling her to kill the baby because "she was no good". She tried to kill the baby by placing a pillow over his face, but he moved away. A few days later she was upset that the baby did not die so she filled the bathtub with water, placed the child in it, hoping he was going to die, and left the house. Later a male voice told her to kill herself and she put a knife against her forehead after taking half a bottle of ASA, but her own voice stopped her. The father said the baby should not be in the home. On 19th October 1988 the father phoned Mr. MacDonald and said that he and the mother had decided to give up the child for adoption. On 21st October 1988 the mother phoned Mr. MacDonald and said she had lied to the people at the hospital and had never tried to kill the child.

[14] Dr. Leslie Jocelyn is a pediatrician at the Child Development Clinic at Children's Hospital. She gave evidence with respect to her report, dated 2nd November 1988, which is contained in Ex. 6. She said that she

was concerned that the parents could not take care of the child and that it was a "high risk situation."

[15] Mr. MacDonald stated that the child was apprehended on 28th October 1988 in the pediatric ward of the St. Boniface Hospital. A plan was formulated, whereby supervised visits would be arranged with the parents to assess whether the child could be returned. The visits were increased by hours and the number of days until the child was returned on 13th March 1989. He noted that the mother was readmitted to the hospital on 6th December 1988 because her nerves were bad; she was depressed and hearing voices again.

[16] Pamela Ashton was a family support worker who was involved with the family and who was to supervise visits between the child and the parents, observe the interaction, and make sure the child was safe. She was placed with the family while the mother was in the hospital in late October 1988 until approximately mid-April 1989. The visits of the child with the parents were initially twice per week, on Tuesday and Thursday, two hours per visit and were increased by hours and days until they were actually full days and almost every day prior to the return of the child with the parents on 13th March 1989. She would pick the child up from the foster home, drive him to the parents' home, stay there during the visit and then return the child to the foster home.

[17] Pamela Ashton stated that sometimes the mother was rough with J., talked to too loudly in his face, would overpower him, smothering him and scare the child. She would often tell the mother when she scared the child, but the incidents would happen again.

[18] Roberta Goulet was an experienced counsellor who dealt with the family from 17th January 1989 to 13th April 1989. She was placed in the home on Tuesday and Thursday of each week. She was to assist the parents with parenting skills, how to handle, stimulate and nurture the baby. On 28th February 1989 she spoke to the mother, who was very upset and nervous about having J. in the home. The mother felt she wanted to give the child up for adoption because she was worried about her ability to parent and concerned he might be injured in light of what had happened before. She said she did not enjoy the visits with J. at her home because she felt "too nervous" and could not cope with crying and did not know how to deal with the child. She said she did not feel that her husband was good enough support for her. He was present and said nothing in response, although he continued to say he wanted J. returned home right away and everything would be fine.

[19] On 21st March 1989 Roberta Goulet went to the parents' home. The child was in bed and would apparently sleep from 7:00 p.m. to 7:00/7:30 a.m., then nap again from 9:00 a.m. to 11:30 a.m., and then would be put down again from 4:00 p.m. to 6:00 p.m. and then put down for the night at 7:00 p.m. The child was almost 10 months old at the time and Roberta Goulet told the parents that he was sleeping too much and needed time for play and stimulation. The mother was advised to speak to her pediatrician, but there were no changes made to the sleeping pattern. Roberta Goulet observed that the child never looked directly at his parents and never seemed to go to them on his own; there was no eye contact, no closeness, no embracing or hugging. The father advised Roberta Goulet on 28th March that they did not need her support because they knew how to handle parenting and they did not need to see their doctor.

[20] Roberta Goulet said that on 21st March 1989 she also observed the father bounce a six-inch round ball off J.'s forehead while he was sitting on the floor. The father was approximately three to four feet away from the child. The child cringed, was shocked and pulled back. Roberta Goulet

told the father of the danger of injuring the child's neck and head, then the father bounced the ball off the child's head four more times before he stopped. The child's neck jerked back when his head was hit with the ball. Roberta Goulet then explained again the dangers of such actions and other things that may be dangerous, like throwing the baby up in the air. Shortly thereafter, the mother threw the baby up in the air dangerously.

[21] Roberta Goulet also observed the mother playing too roughly with the child as she would attempt to tickle the baby, but actually choked him and he would start to cry. When warned, the mother stated she did not realize what she was doing.

[22] Roberta Goulet also observed that whenever the parents went toward the child, he would withdraw or pull back.

[23] On one occasion, the mother wanted the father to get up out of bed and look after the child, so she played the stereo at its highest level near J. in order to make him cry so that he would wake up his father and get him up. The child did cry and was scared and she warned the mother about such actions. On another occasion, the mother turned the playpen over J. and went down on her hands and knees and barked like a dog towards the baby and made him cry in another attempt to wake up his father.

[24] Roberta Goulet also observed that the mother was rough and rigid with the child and held him too tight, so much so that his face would turn red. She saw this happen on approximately five occasions and warned the mother.

[25] The mother would also not allow the baby to feed himself or eat cookies because it would make a mess, although Roberta Goulet tried to explain to her that this was not good for the child's development.

[26] When the mother told the stories of the playpen incident and stereo incident in front of the father, he laughed and said he knew what she was doing.

[27] The parents also told Roberta Goulet about how they had gone to the mother's aunt's place and left J. on a bed in a bedroom and when they went back to the room one hour later they could not find J. on top of the bed, but found him under the bed crying. Roberta Goulet also observed that the mother did not know how to play with J. and told her she did not know and as a result the child would simply be left sitting in the middle of the floor.

[28] On 28th March 1989 Roberta Goulet went to the parents' home. The child was in bed and the father had the stereo and television going on full blast. The mother was out and the father advised her that they did not need her help, or the doctor's help, or anyone else's help and that everything would be okay. He was very uncooperative.

[29] On 30th March 1989 Roberta Goulet inquired as to whether or not the mother would attend a group involved with victims of sexual abuse, but the mother said she did not want to deal with it at that time.

[30] Roberta Goulet said that when she first saw J. he appeared bright and content, but before long the child would just sit and stare; he would not play or do anything, would not go to the parents and appeared to be reduced to a "no activity level". She said that the mother did not appear to understand anything of what she was told and she had a high concern for the safety and well-being of the child and she recommended removal of the child from the parents' home.

[31] The foster mother, M., gave evidence with respect to her foster care of the child from 1st November 1988 to the date of the trial. In the initial

period, the child visited the parents once per week on Friday. After the visits, he changed from a happy, playful, affectionate child to a fussy, cranky child who had difficulty going to sleep, would wake up screaming and throw up, and seemed frightened and would not return to his normal self until the Sunday after the visit. During the period from 13th March 1989 to 10th April 1989, arrangements were made for M. to take care of the child every second weekend. She first saw the child on 24th March 1989 and was shocked because the child did not seem like the child she had sent back to the parents. He had been happy, playful, active and delighted with lots of energy and was then sullen, passive and tired with no energy. She said the difference was "like between night and day". She said it was sad because the child did not seem to be interested in toys or anything. The parents told M. that the child hated baths and fussed a lot when getting dressed or changed and did not like taking a bottle in their arms. However, M. said she bathed and dressed the child and held him to have his bottle and she had no problem. With respect to visits with the parents from 10th April 1989 to the date of the trial, when the child was returned, he was wakeful, fretful, crying and needed holding and cuddling. This behaviour would continue for two days after the visit, after which the child was normal and active. Although M. said that she and her husband were interested in adopting the child, if possible, she stated that she made the same observations to the agency's social worker prior to becoming interested in adoption of the child and stated that her observations were accurate and not coloured by her love for the child. I observed her carefully while she gave evidence, I was impressed with her demeanour and I believe her. Her evidence was confirmed by the social worker, Scott MacDonald.

[32] Linda Polz is a family support worker who supervised visits with the parents from 21st April 1989 to the date of the trial. She confirmed the change in demeanour of the child from the time she picked him up for a visit, during the visit and when she took the child back to the foster home. The child who had been happy and bubbly when picked up from the foster home became quiet and showed no response to the parents.

[33] Heather Carruthers is a social worker and was the supervisor for the agency in this matter. On 30th August 1989 the father told her they were not good parents, did not deserve the child and the child should have both a father and mother. In her evidence, she observed that the parents do not have the parenting skills to care for the child. She stated that there is no evidence of bonding with the parents and that the child needs a home. She said that she has equal concerns about "both" parents' ability to parent and that although the father had more skills than the mother, he chose not to use them. She was concerned that the father allowed the mother to take inappropriate care of the child. She said it was the totality of the evidence rather than one single event that caused the agency to apply for permanent guardianship. She said that the child could not thrive in the parents' home without the 24-hour presence of a third party, who would be the primary caregiver until the child is an adult, which would be very negative and confusing for the child. Such a plan has never been put in place by the agency to date. She stated that if a permanent order was granted, the agency would place the child for adoption and he had an "excellent" chance of being adopted. She also said the foster parents would be considered as adoptive parents.

[34] Scott MacDonald said the father always agreed with the agency, but did not do what he said he would do. He never took any initiative to intervene in the care of the child and did not do anything effective to counter the mother's care of the child.

[35] Dr. Jocelyn also gave evidence with respect to her letters contained in Ex. 4. She saw the child on 18th October 1989 and stated that there

was great urgency in making a permanent placement for infants and that each time children move they lose trust in people. She said that the child in this case went back and was adversely affected. She described the ball throwing incident, the playpen incident, the stereo incident, the feeding practices and the sleeping schedules as "inappropriate", which was equivalent to "inadequate" care. She further stated that the father was not sensitive to the child's needs by not interfering with the mother's care of the child.

[36] Dr. Linda Trigg, a clinical psychologist, gave evidence with respect to her report contained in Ex. 4. Dr. Trigg stated that the mother was child-like and dependent and had telephoned her 23 times, something she had never experienced before, although she deals with many very unsophisticated people. She said that the mother's childhood problem of sexual abuse by her father makes it very difficult for her to cope with caring for children and she requires therapy. She said that she would not recommend unification of the child with the parents and that she did not come to this conclusion lightly. She stated that the child appeared to have no connection or emotional attachment with the biological parents at 13 months of age. She stated that both parents were incapable of parenting. She stated that she had very significant concerns about the father's ability to parent alone because he had lied to her, he lacked impulse control or control of his temper and had been an active abuser of the mother. She also stated that it would take years for both parents to be capable of parenting and that the mother would always require a great deal of support and expressed doubt that she would ever become capable of parenting.

[37] Dr. A. de Rocquigny, a psychiatrist, gave evidence on behalf of the mother. His report, dated 24th November 1989, was filed as Ex. 10. He said that the mother has psychotic depression, but the ability to parent is a separate issue. He never observed the mother with the child or even saw the child. He said he is not an expert in child development. He said he thought there was some positive change in the mother because she was not telephoning him as much, but did not know whether she was telephoning others. The evidence is that she was telephoning other persons. He said that he had no evidence of hallucinations after 7th November 1988 and that his notes of 7th December say that the mother told him she was not hearing voices. He was not aware of her statements on admission to hospital on 6th December 1988. He said the mother told him she is a compulsive liar. He said she requires reparenting and intensive therapy and treatment would never take away her entire problem. He said that treatment would take a long time and she has not shown she is ready to take treatment. On cross-examination, with respect to the ball throwing incident, he said he would be concerned if the father did not listen to someone who was observing and thought the action was wrong.

[38] Dr. J.N. Joshi, a psychiatrist, gave evidence on behalf of the mother and the father. His report, dated 20th November 1989, was filed as Ex. 11. He said the mother would need prolonged supervision and training to be able to parent the child. He said his main involvement was with the parents, since 19th November 1988, for the purpose of marriage counselling and he felt that it was in the best interests of both to remain in the marriage. He has never seen the parents with the child and said he does not deal with infants, just adolescents. He also never received any reports from Dr. de Rocquigny nor did he read the hospital records. He just relied on what the father and mother told him. The mother never told him about her admission to the hospital on 6th December 1988 when she heard voices. He was not aware of what occurred when the child was in the parents' care from 13th March to 10th April. He said he was only "speculating" about the support the parents needed. When he said the

agency "acted in haste", he was devoid of any facts. He said the father told him he had not used marijuana for years, although the evidence is that he used marijuana after the child was born.

[39] The mother, who is 30 years of age, gave evidence and admitted that she is a compulsive liar, that she was wrong and made mistakes in caring for the child, but wants to start all over again. She said the father told her the previous night that all he wanted was to have them together with the child. With respect to the balance of her evidence, I observed her carefully while giving her evidence and regret that she is a sad, pathetic, simple woman whom I cannot believe. Without a doubt, she is not, and could not be, capable of caring for the child for a lengthy period, if ever. The risk of abuse would be extremely high.

[40] The father, who is 34 years of age, and who has been unemployed since shortly after the child's birth, also gave evidence. He admits to having lost his temper and pushed and slapped his wife to the extent that the police were called on four occasions, but no charges laid. He said that prior to the birth of the child, he was afraid the child would not be physically normal because of his problems with alcohol and drugs. He said he "wasn't sure what was what for the first two or three months", but his wife was not able to care for the child. He said he is guilty of not showing the child the love and support he should and he was blind to the way this emotionally affected the child. He said the child should not come home now because both he and the wife were not ready. If the child did, he would be gone in a month. He said the foster parents were the best thing for the child now. He said he has lost his bond with the child. He said that a child should not have to wait for him to get help to parent the child. He said he is leaving his wife and either getting a separation or a divorce. He also said he would like the child placed in his care. On cross-examination he said he agreed that he had absolutely no plans for care of the child and that he does not think he can give the child everything he needs. He said he is not sure what is best, that the only reason the child should be with him is because he is his biological father. He said he does not know if he can care for the child, that he may be selfish, and that he may not be ready to be a father. He said he does not want to make the decision and he thinks that the agency is more aware of the needs and wants of the child.

[41] This is a case that requires one to consider the totality of the evidence, including the hospital records. I find that the witnesses called on behalf of the agency were sincere, forthright and credible. I have not included the evidence given by certain witnesses called on behalf of the parents because I do not find their evidence credible. I find the evidence of Drs. de Rocquigny and Joshi to be very lacking in information and evidentiary support for the reasons I have noted and must attach little weight to any recommendations that they have made in support of the parents.

[42] Counsel for the father, during the course of the trial, pointed out that the court should not compare the foster home situation to the parents' home. I am mindful ... that permanent wardship is not to be ordered solely on the basis that the foster home is providing the child with better living conditions than those provided by the natural parents. The conditions in the foster home, although significantly better, were not a factor in my decision.

[43] I have also considered the decision in C.A.S., *Winnipeg v. M.* (1980), 15 R.F.L. (2d) 185 at 188 (Man. C.A.), wherein Freedman C.J.M. stated:

> The right of a natural parent to the care and control of a child is basic. It is a right not easily displaced. Nothing less than cogent evi-

dence of danger to the child's life or health is required before the court will deprive a parent of such care and control.

I am very mindful of the parents' rights to the care and control of the child.

[44] I have also considered the decision in *Re H. (R.M.)* (1985), 44 R.F.L. (2d) 196 at 197 (Alta. Q.B.), in which Quigley J. stated:

The power to extend temporary orders should only be used in those cases where the indications that the conduct, shortcomings, frailties or disabilities of the parent contributing to the child's neglect can be corrected and where concrete evidence manifests the parent's recognition of the cause of such deficiencies and a desire to pursue the means to eliminate them.

[45] I have also considered the ... proposition that the court should never be called upon to wait until physical injuries have been received and minds unhinged. It is sufficient if there be a reasonable apprehension that such things will happen, and the court should interfere before they have happened if that be possible.

[46] Finally, I have considered the decision in *C.A.S., Winnipeg v. Redwood* (1980), 19 R.F.L. (2d) 232 at 234 (Man. C.A.), in which Monnin J.A. (as he was then) stated as follows:

The test is: What is in the best interests of these children, and not whether the mother has merely seen the light and is now prepared to be a good mother, while in the past, on her own admission, she was not such. The test is whether the mother has in fact turned a new leaf and whether she is now able to give to the children the care which is in their best interests. Good intentions are not sufficient. As the chief justice of this court, speaking in a unanimous decision in another case, stated so ably: "to give this mother another chance is to give these children one less chance in life".

[47] I must, on the totality of the evidence before me, find that the child, J.D.S., born 25th May 1988, has been and is in need of protection as the parents have been and are obviously unable to provide adequate care, supervision or control of the child and are unlikely to be able to do so for a lengthy period of time, if ever.

[48] I must also find, based on the totality of the evidence before me and based on a balance of probabilities, that it is clearly in the child's best interests that the agency be appointed the permanent guardian of the child.

[49] I have considered s. 2 of the Child and Family Services Act and find that paras. (*a*), (*b*), (*c*), (*d*), (*e*) and (*g*) are applicable. The child is not bonded to the parents in any way and requires a secure, caring and nurturing home promoting healthy growth, development and education. He is approximately 18 months old and the agency advises that he has an excellent chance of being adopted, even if the present foster parents are not accepted. This is in contrast to the father who has absolutely no plans for the care of the child and the mother who is not capable of doing any proper planning or any proper care of the child.

[50] There has been no credible support for the father's position that the child should be returned to him alone. He has a history of abuse of his wife. He admits to misusing alcohol and drugs and has used marijuana up until recently. He admits to not giving proper care to the child and has stated that he is not ready to take care of the child. I believe the witnesses called on behalf of the agency, including Dr. Trigg, to the effect that he is unable to provide adequate care for the child. I observed him carefully when he gave evidence and believe that he is not able enough to parent the child and that it would, in fact, be dangerous to return the child to him. With respect to the mother, there is no basis whatsoever on which the court should even consider for a moment returning the child to her.

Application granted.

Notes and Questions

"In need of protection": Decision making in context

This case involved a number of different professionals and agencies, all of whom attempted to provide support to the parents over a period of time. Finally, however, a decision was made by the Winnipeg South Child and Family Services Agency (an agency similar to the Children's Aid Societies in Ontario) that the child should be removed from the parents' home permanently. In this context, the court hearing was necessary to obtain an order for the agency's permanent guardianship of the child, a prerequisite to the child being adopted. (Section 57 of the *Child and Family Services Act* permits a similar order of "Crown wardship" in Ontario.)

Consider the position of the professionals who testified about the parents' abilities and behaviours in the above case. How should parents in such cases relate to agency professionals who have responsibilities to provide assistance to parents and families, but who may subsequently be required to give evidence about their observations, including the parents' deficiencies in relation to their child? Although the parents in this case clearly lacked basic skills, and seemed unable to improve their abilities to meet the child's needs, were they entirely unrealistic in failing to trust agency personnel and others who were providing assistance to them? How should professionals respond to this dilemma? What were the most important factors in this case that resulted in the agency's application for permanent guardianship?

In this context, judicial determinations about whether a child is "in need of protection" in accordance with statutory definitions occur in situations that require difficult value judgments about parenting and community standards. Reflect again on *S(DD)* in the context of the following comments by a former family court judge about decision making in child protection cases: to what extent were any of these issues reflected in *S(DD)*?

> ... In most jurisdictions the issue of child abuse is not only receiving major attention generally, but is the subject of extensive media coverage. Further, the results of a decision not to intervene in a family tend to be much more visible than the results of one that brings the child into care. Or at least the causal connection between the decision and the results is more tenuous in the latter situation, given the fact that responsibility for decisions on behalf of the child is usually spread amongst a number of people. When these two factors are combined, it is easily recognized that the environment within which decisions are made is having a clear impact upon what is recommended. Appropriate risk-taking in this world of fallible decision-making becomes very difficult when one's whole career may be destroyed by a single decision to return a child to his or her home, if that child is then subjected to further abuse. This is particularly so when,

conversely, the decision to take the child out of the home normally passes responsibility on to someone else. As a judge, it can be very difficult to assess whether, at least subconsciously, possible proposals to the court are not being made because of the environment in which they would be carried out. And it is only logical to ask whether this also affects the judge, who must feel a sense of personal responsibility for the results when a child is returned to his or her home. This is perhaps less likely to be present when the child is removed and placed in the care of the state....

It is also possible to illustrate how the narrower environment of the court complicates decision-making. The easiest illustration is the artificial environment within which the hearing itself takes place, subject to rules and procedures that are often unintelligible to family and child, and in which one observes persons who, in the midst of the worst crisis of their lives, are functioning in ways that may only vaguely resemble their normal behaviour....

[In addition, matters] often come to court after those involved in the case have endured months of uncertainty about how to respond. Differing views and extensive debate may have characterized much of the time spent in case conferences and planning sessions. Once the decision to go to court is made, there is a natural tendency for expert opinion to coalesce around the decision that has been taken, the option that is about to be recommended....

A final point should be made, even though it is not strictly part of the discussion: what is presented to the judge may, of course, bear little relationship to what anyone might characterize as a full presentation of the information relevant to the issues at hand. The reasons for this may be both obvious and many in number: not all parties are represented; representation is inadequate on one or both sides; lawyers are demonstrating the role confusion that is the norm in these matters; much of the information ... is not known by those presenting the case to the court; much of it either is not seen as relevant, or is clearly inadmissible; only one expert is available and he or she has firm views on the issue of causation or risk of further abuse; insufficient time is available for the matter because of the pressure of court dockets; the factual data presented to the court are both imprecise and incomplete; and so on.... (George Thomson, "Judging Judiciously in Child Protection Cases" in Rosalie Abella & Claire L'Heureux-Dubé, eds, *Dimensions of Justice* (Toronto: Butterworths, 1983) 213 at 230–232)

After the court in *S(DD)* decided that the child was in need of protection, what factors did the court consider in determining the "best interests" of the child. Compare the list of factors for determining "best interests" in section 37(3) of Ontario's *Child and Family Services Act*. To what extent would the court in *S(DD)* have reached the same conclusion, using this list of factors?

Issues about decision making and (scarce) resources

The child welfare system in Canada is fraught with tensions and challenges. Children's Aid Societies of Ontario must balance their responsibility to protect children from abuse and neglect with supporting the capacity and abilities of families to take care of their children. The reality is that many families who come into contact with Children's Aid Societies lack the material and financial resources needed to adequately support their families. If the welfare state is unable to address the material and financial resource needs of families, then what is the role of the Children's Aid Societies other than to remove children at risk from individual families that falter? ... [Some argue] that, until the problem of child poverty is addressed, the child welfare system will continue to fail to recognise the social and economic problems that families face, especially disadvantaged racial minority families. (J Ying Lee, C Hackbusch & H Wong, "An Anti-Oppression Framework for Child Welfare in Ontario, Canada: Possibilities for Systemic Change" (2013) British Journal of Social Work Advance Access 1 at 2)

Decision making about child protection takes place within an overall context of community resources. Thus, while the scope of the legal definition of "child in need of protection" has been enlarged in Ontario, its implementation in relation to governmental policy goals depends on the availability of professional and financial resources. In his assessment of Ontario amendments in 1999 (which enlarged the definition of "child in need of protection" in the statute), Bala pointed out that, beyond legislative reforms, there is a need for "resources, training and morale in the child welfare and justice systems," suggesting that such resources may be more difficult to achieve than "inexpensive legislative reform" (see Bala at 172).

In an Annotation to *S(DD)*, James McLeod posed questions about resources even more bluntly:

In times of budgetary restraint, the hard question facing a court is: How much of a tight budget should the society be forced to devote to one family? Does there come a point where all concerned must "bite the bullet" and accept that the amount of money necessary to turn the parents/family into a marginally functioning unit does not justify the overall cost to the agency and other clients of the agency and permanent wardship or guardianship should be ordered? Should the court only look at the particular family in question or must it look to overall realities? (James McLeod, "Annotation of *Winnipeg South Child and Family Services Agency v S(DD)*" (1990) 24 RFL (3d) 290 at 290–91)

More recently, a family court judge identified how shrinking resources for implementing child protection legislation was occurring at the same time that the "child protection net" was widening, both legally and practically:

As the child protection net widens [a reference to the expanded definition of "child in need of protection"], and child protection resources shrink, child protection workers look more and more like frantic enforcement officers citing a litany of matters the parents have *not* attended to, such as acquiring adequate housing or arranging anger management counselling. The child protection workers so often seem to be working against the parent. I am sure much of this has to do with frustration at their own conditions of employment, which include limited resources and caseloads that seem too large.... (Justice Lynn King, "The Paucity of Resources" in Nicholas Bala et al, eds, *Canadian Child Welfare Law*, 2nd ed (Toronto: Thompson Educational Publishing, 2004) 421 at 422)

To what extent were resources a problem in *S(DD)*? How should current issues about resources be addressed?

The *Charter* and child protection

Resource issues are also complicated by statutory requirements regarding the process for apprehending a child who is believed to be "in need of protection," and the need to meet the constitutional protections of the

Charter. In *Winnipeg Child and Family Services (Central Area) v W(KL)*, [2000] 2 SCR 519, the Supreme Court of Canada dismissed the appeal of a woman whose child was apprehended without a warrant pursuant to section 21 of Manitoba's *Child and Family Services Act*, SM 1985-86, c 8. Although the court agreed that the apprehension of a child without a warrant created a grave risk of intervention in family life, a majority of the court held that the statute's requirement of an *ex post facto* hearing within a few days satisfied the principles of fundamental justice pursuant to section 7 of the *Charter*. For the majority, the balance between the state's responsibility for the well-being and safety of children on one hand, and parental rights and family autonomy on the other, was satisfied by the legislative requirement of a hearing soon after such a warrantless apprehension:

> The apprehension of children constitutes a significant state intrusion into the family. Less disruptive means of dealing with parenting issues are to be preferred as a matter of policy whenever possible.... [However,] provided that the threshold for apprehension is, at a minimum, that of a risk of serious harm to the child, the need for swift and preventive state action to protect a child's life or health in such situations dictates that a fair and prompt post-apprehension hearing is the minimum procedural protection mandated by the principles of fundamental justice in the child protection context (at para 131).

Two members of the court dissented, arguing that a warrantless apprehension in non-emergency situations did not meet the requirements of fundamental justice in the *Charter*. Indeed, several other provinces require warrants in such cases, usually on an *ex parte* basis. See, for example, Ontario's *Child and Family Services Act*, s 40. To what extent do these views reflect similarities or differences between family law and criminal law proceedings? Do these statutory arrangements reflect concerns about the effective use of scarce resources?

A different *Charter* challenge was launched with respect to section 43 of the *Criminal Code*, which provides an exception for the offence of assault for parents, teachers and those standing in the place of parents, who use "reasonable force" against a child for "corrective purposes." In *Canadian Foundation for Children, Youth and the Law v Canada (AG)*, 2004 SCC 4, the court concluded that section 43 did not contravene either section 7 or section 15 of the *Charter*. (For a critique of this decision, see Judith Mosoff & Isabel Grant, "Upholding Corporal Punishment: For Whose Benefit?" (2005) 31 Man LJ 177.)

To what extent do these cases suggest a need to strengthen children's rights?

Issues about legal representation for parents: Protecting family autonomy?

As *S(DD)* revealed, a state agency with responsibility for protecting children generally initiates the application to remove a child in need of protection from the family, that is, the child's parents. In doing so, they will often provide expert witnesses to prove that the child's circumstances fall within the statutory definition of "in need of protection."

In this context, the need for the child's parents to produce evidence to support their own position, perhaps including additional experts, represents a daunting challenge, and they may require legal representation to present their case effectively. Indeed, Joanne Wildgoose argued some years ago that parents may need to be represented at all stages of such proceedings, including negotiations about a child's welfare, because of the inherent power imbalance between parents and an agency such as the Children's Aid Society. As she noted, parents involved in child protection cases tend to be "the least educated, least articulate, poorest segments of our society" (Joanne Wildgoose, "Alternative Dispute Resolution of Child Protection Cases" (1987) 6 Can J Fam L 61 at 65).

Parents involved in child protection proceedings may often require legal aid assistance, and a decision of the Supreme Court of Canada in 1999 confirmed that such state-funded counsel was constitutionally mandated in certain child protection proceedings.

In *New Brunswick (Minister of Health and Community Services) v G(J)*, [1999] 3 SCR 46, the court held that state-funded legal counsel should have been provided for a mother in New Brunswick who faced the loss of her children in child protection proceedings. The court unanimously relied on section 7 of the *Charter*, concluding that the failure to provide state funded counsel constituted an infringement of the mother's "security of the person." As a result, the court held that state-funded counsel was required in child protection proceedings, having regard to the "seriousness of the interests at stake, the complexity of the proceedings, and the capacities of the [party]." See also Rollie Thompson, "Annotation" (1999) 50 RFL (4th) 74; and MJ Mossman, "*New Brunswick (Minister of Health and Community Services) v. G(J)*: Constitutional Requirements for Legal Representation in Child Protection Matters" (2000) 12 CJWL 490.

Prior to this Supreme Court decision, parents often faced significant challenges in relation to representation in child protection cases. For example, see *Child and Family Services of Western Manitoba v RAY and SDM* (1990), 29 RFL (3d) 330 (Man CA). Significantly, an Ontario court permitted an "unpaid, non-lawyer, agent friend" to appear on behalf of a parent in a child protection proceeding in *Children's Aid Society (Niagara Region) v P(D)* (2002), 62 OR (3d) 668 (Sup Ct), perhaps an indication that many parents continue to face challenges with respect to representation in such proceedings.

"In need of protection": Children's rights and representation

Children may be represented in child protection proceedings as well. Indeed, section 12 of the *United Nations Convention on the Rights of the Child*, adopted in 1989 and ratified by Canada in 1991, provides that a child's views can be presented in proceedings affecting the child. In this context, section 38 of Ontario's *Child and Family Services Act* provides for a court to order representation for a child where it is "desirable to protect a child's interests."

Representation is usually provided by the Office of the Children's Lawyer (part of the Ministry of the Attorney General), and its work has increased significantly in recent years. For example, there were 1471 court orders for representation in child protection proceedings in 1996–1997, but the number of such orders had increased to 3223 by 2002–2003, partly as a result of the increase in services following the amendments to the *Child and Family Services Act* in 1999 that made the "best interests, protection and well being of children" the paramount purpose of the legislation (see s 1(1)). The availability of legal representation for children in child protection proceedings in other provinces varies (see Dan Goldberg, "The Lawyer's Role" in Bala et al, eds, 245 at 256–259).

There continues to be some debate about the role of a children's lawyer: is the lawyer an *amicus curiae*, an advocate, or a guardian *ad litem*? However, the Ontario Court of Appeal stated, in the context of a custody and access case, that a child's lawyer should assume the role of advocate (*Strobridge v Strobridge* (1994), 4 RFL (4th) 169). The Office of the Children's Lawyer also issued a policy statement in 1995, identifying the lawyer's responsibility for advocating on behalf of the child and presenting evidence of the child's views and preferences, the surrounding circumstances of the views and preferences, and all relevant evidence with respect to the child's "best interests" (Office of the Children's Lawyer, *Policy Statement, Role of Child's Counsel* (3 April 1995; revised 18 January 2002) at 2; and Goldberg at 248–251).

What kinds of specialized skills may be required by lawyers who wish to represent children? In a recent initiative in Ontario, child protection lawyers and other professionals were involved in a four-day course to provide specialized training in relation to child protection. See Michael McKiernan, "Course Addresses Shortage of Child Protection Lawyers", *Law Times* (1 November 2010).

Child protection: Recent developments for Crown Wards

When a child is found to be "in need of protection," and parents are unable to provide care, a court may make an order for Crown wardship, transferring responsibility for the child to the state, if such an order is in the child's "best interests." Crown wards are often raised in foster homes with foster parents, but the court orders often provide that these children are not eligible for adoption because of their continuing contact with the birth parents. Indeed, it seems that among about 9000 Crown wards in Ontario, about two-thirds of them may be ineligible for adoption. See Laurie Monsebraaten, "Liberals Pass Adoption Law", *Toronto Star* (2 June 2011) A17.

Thus, acting on the recommendations of the 2009 Expert Panel on Infertility and Adoption, the Ontario legislature enacted Bill 179 in 2011, the *Building Families and Supporting Youth to be Successful Act*, SO 2011, c 12 (Royal Assent 1 June 2011).

This legislation permits orders for the adoption of Crown Wards, subject to "openness" arrangements in cases where it is in a child's "best interests" to continue to have contact with the child's birth parents.

The statute also provides for ongoing financial support for Crown Wards after age 16, including access to student loans to attend college and university.

In September 2011, the Ontario government also announced funding for subsidies to encourage adoption of siblings and children more than 10 years old. See O/Reg 394/11 and Laurie Monsebraaten, "$9.5 million to Help with Difficult Adoptions", *Toronto Star* (2 September 2011) A1; and "How One Town is Changing Adoption", *Toronto Star* (1 August 2011) A1 and A9. In addition, working parents in the "foster-to-adopt" program qualify for parental leave. See Laurie Monsebraaten, "New EI Rules for Adoptions", *Toronto Star* (4 January 2012) A3).

In May 2012, a team of young people in care (many of them Crown Wards) released a report of hearings they had organized to address problems with the current child welfare system. Supported by the Office of the Provincial Advocate for Children and Youth, they had organized the "Youth Leaving Care Hearings" at Queen's Park in late 2011 to examine the challenges they faced on turning 18. Their report made recommendations for fundamental changes, including raising the age for ongoing financial support from 21 to 25 for those in school; allowing them to stay in foster care until they are prepared for independence; and declaring a "Children and Youth in Care Day" to raise awareness of their challenges: see *My REAL Life Book: Report from the Youth Leaving Care Hearings*, online: <http://www.provincialadvocate.on.ca>; and see Ken Dryden, "Some Advice from Youth who Survived System", *Toronto Star* (14 May 2012) A15.

In response, the Ontario government established a panel of former Crown Wards and community representatives to make recommendations for change. The panel released its report, *Blueprint for Fundamental Change to Ontario's Child Welfare System* on 22 January 2013, and the government issued a press release two days later, announcing a number of new initiatives, including an increase in monthly financial support, an allowance for youth aged 21 to 25 in postsecondary education, and new mentorship opportunities, etc: see Laurie Monsebraaten, "Provincial Panel urges Boost for Ex-Crown Wards", *Toronto Star* (23 January 2013) A1 and A4; and Ministry of Children and Youth Services, News Release, "Help for Young People In and Leaving Care" (24 January 2013). The provincial government's *Children and Youth in Care Day Act*, SO 2014, c 2, received Royal Assent in March 2014.

However, a series of press reports in the *Toronto Star* in December 2014 revealed ongoing and significant problems in Ontario's child welfare system. According to these reports, Black children are being removed from their families and placed in foster care at much higher rates than white children; the report indicated that although only 8.2 percent of Toronto's population is under the age of 18, 41 percent of children and youth in care are Black. A related report identified a child in provincial care who had changed homes 88 times, although the child is under fifteen years old. In February 2015, the Children's Minister for the provincial government announced a proposal that all Children's Aid Societies in Ontario collect race-based data on children in care.

In this context, there were suggestions about the need for a new Children's Aid Society focused exclusively on Black children, and more information about systemic reasons for the breakdown of Black families, such as poverty and the lack of affordable housing. According to the press reports, lawyers, Black community leaders and child advocates blame cultural misunderstandings, stress, neglect caused by poverty, and systemic racism for the disproportionate numbers of Black children in care. See Sandro Contenta, Laurie Monsebraaten & Jim Rankin, "Just 8% of Toronto Kids are Black", *Toronto Star* (11 December 2014) A1 and A32–A33; "Ontario's Most Vulnerable Children Kept in the Shadows", *Toronto Star* (13 December 2013) at A1 and A34–A35. See also "Insight" *Toronto Star* (14 December 2014) IN1 and IN3; and "Province may seek CAS Racial Data", *Toronto Star* (17 February 2015) A1 and A4.

ABORIGINAL CHILDREN AND CHILD PROTECTION

The context: The impact of child protection law and policy

> Approximately 8,000 First Nations children are in the care of First Nation child welfare agencies, out of a total of 27,000 First Nations children in care. There are more First Nations children in child welfare care in Canada than at the height of residential schools. Available data suggest a range of 30%–40% of children in care are Aboriginal across Canada....
>
> Existing services have not kept up with the acute needs of these vulnerable children.... Given the overrepresentation of First Nations children in care, it is imperative to develop culturally sensitive policy and practice. Effecting change also calls for a much greater emphasis by child protection authorities on the structural factors contributing to child maltreatment such as poverty, poor housing, and parental mental health problems. (Vanier Institute of the Family, *Families Count: Profiling Canada's Families IV* (Ottawa: VIF, 2010) at 58)

As discussed in relation to adoption, the historical background concerning Aboriginal families in Canada, and particularly the residential school system, have resulted in ongoing challenges and dislocations for Aboriginal families and communities. In addition, Aboriginal cultures and philosophies about child care, which often reflect community responsibility for children, have not always been well-understood by child welfare agencies. In this context, cases involving child protection and Aboriginal children have often been based on issues of neglect, rather than harm.

Some court decisions have recognized a need to apply legal principles about parenting standards in ways that reflect the context of Aboriginal communities. For example, see *Re ECDM* (1980), 17 RFL (2d) 274 (Sask Prov Ct); and *Director of Child Welfare of Manitoba v BB* (1989), 2 SCR 291.

Recall the adoption case, *ANR and SCR v LJW*, in which an Aboriginal mother sought to prevent the adoption of her child by a couple in Manitoba. After the Supreme Court's decision, several provincial jurisdictions enacted child welfare provisions to take account of Aboriginal culture and heritage in decision making. Thus, section 1(2) of Ontario's *Child and Family Services Act* includes as one of its stated purposes:

> 5. To recognize that Indian and native people should be entitled to provide, wherever possible, their own child and family services, and that all services to Indian and native children and families should be provided in a manner that recognizes their culture, heritage and traditions and the concept of the extended family.

In a number of Canadian provinces, legislation now provides for Aboriginal child welfare services on reserves, in an effort to ensure that decision making reflects community values and the authority of Aboriginal communities with respect to their children. For example, see Ontario's *Child and Family Services Act*, Part X. For an overview of some early initiatives in other jurisdictions, see Anna Pellatt, *An International Review of Child Welfare Policy and Practice in Relation to Aboriginal People* (Calgary: Canadian Research Institute for Law and the Family, 1991).

Yet, in spite of a number of new initiatives, many challenges remain:

> The dominant non-Aboriginal society in Canada has not responded adequately to the problems of Aboriginal children and communities. Assimilationist and culturally insensitive policies have often harmed these children and their communities.... Poverty, alcoholism, spousal violence, fetal alcohol syndrome, neglect of children and child sexual abuse are very serious problems in many Aboriginal families and communities, and must be addressed by the communities themselves. Addressing these problems requires a significant investment in education, health and social services over an extended period of time.... [T]here are many parenting challenges in these communities. The problems of providing appropriate child welfare services for Aboriginal children will defy a single, quick solution.... (Judge Murray Sinclair et al, "Aboriginal Child Welfare" in Bala et al, eds, 199 at 243)

Recent reviews of child protection and Aboriginal children

In 2010, the Ontario government appointed John Beaucage (former Grand Council Chief of the Anishinabek Nation) as the Aboriginal Advisor to the Minister of Children and Youth Services. *Children First: The Aboriginal Advisor's Report on the status of Aboriginal Child Welfare in Ontario* was submitted to the Minister in July 2011. In preparing the Report, the Aboriginal Advisor met with Aboriginal leaders, as well as Political Territorial Organizations, First Nations communities and Aboriginal Children's Aid Societies; and co-hosted with the Minister a summit for 200 participants, *Together for a Better Tomorrow*, in 2011. The Aboriginal Advisor's *Report* included recommendations concerning best practices, capacity building, prevention, funding, governance and future challenges, and emphasized recognition of culture as the foundation for improved relationships with Aboriginal communities. The *Report* also recommended greater involvement of Aboriginal elders and others in child welfare agencies, and a parallel child welfare system: see Laurie Monsebraaten, "Reforms set for Child Welfare", *Toronto Star* (18 January 2013) at A6).

According to a press release, the Metis Nation of Ontario succeeded in efforts to include Metis youth in the review undertaken by the Aboriginal Advisor. According to the release, Metis peoples make up one-third of Aboriginal peoples in Ontario. See online: <http://www.metisnation.org/news—media/news/>.

In Saskatchewan, child welfare reviews also identified serious problems with placements of Aboriginal children in foster homes: see Caroline Tait, Robert Henry & Rachel Loewen Walker, "Child Welfare: A Social Determinant of Health for Canadian First Nations and Metis Children" (2013) 11:1 *Pimatisiwin: A Journal of Aboriginal and Indigenous Community Health* 39; and Caroline Tait & Doug Cuthand, *Child Welfare: The State as Parent*, a documentary film (Saskatoon: Blue Hills Production, 2011), online: <https://ethicaltoolkit.ca/content/documentaries>.

After the death of Tina Fontaine, a young Aboriginal woman, in Winnipeg in August 2014, the Manitoba government reviewed its use of hotels as foster care placements for children in care. According to a news report, nearly 90 percent of more than 10,000 children in care in the province are Aboriginal: see Kathryn Blaze Carlson, "Heartbreak Hotels", *The Globe and Mail* (1 November 2014) A3. In November 2014, the province announced that it would create 71 new emergency foster-home spaces, open a secure residential facility for at-risk girls and increase foster placements in rural areas; in addition, the government announced plans to hire an additional 210 child-care workers to reduce its reliance on third-party firms: see Kathryn Blaze Carlson, "Manitoba Revamps Child-Welfare Program", *The Globe and Mail* (19 November 2014) A1 and A18; and "Manitoba Promises Better Care for Foster Children", *The Globe and Mail* (19 December 2014) A5.

Recent litigation about Aboriginal children and child protection policies

Brown v Canada (AG): The "Sixties Scoop" Class Action

After several court actions in relation to a claim to have this class action certified, the claim was certified in 2013, and Canada's motion to strike the statement of claim as not disclosing a reasonable cause of action was dismissed: see 2013 ONSC 5637. In December 2014, Canada's appeal to the Divisional Court was dismissed: 2014 ONSC 6967. According to a news report, this case is the first in which Indigenous persons have claimed a loss of cultural identity: see Diana Mehta, "Lawsuit claiming Loss of Cultural Identity due to 60's Scoop to go Ahead", *Ottawa Citizen* (20 August 2013). There is also a website for this class action: <http://sixtiesscoopclaim.com/about-the-ontario-sixties-scoop-claim-registration-as-a-class-member/>. For an overview of the protracted litigation in relation to this class action suit, see the Divisional Court decision in December 2014 (2014 ONSC 6967 at paras 1–10).

First Nations Child and Family Caring Society of Canada v Canada (AG)

This case focuses on the funding formula used by the Government of Canada to fund First Nations child and family services on reserves, a formula that results in less funding than that provided by provincial child welfare services. The complaint was submitted to the federal Human Rights Commission on the basis that the under-funding constitutes discrimination in the provision of services customarily available to the public on the grounds of race and national origin. The Human Rights tribunal dismissed the complaint because there was no other group receiving child welfare services from the Government of Canada, and thus there was no "comparator group."

On judicial review, the Federal Court held that the tribunal had erred (citing *Withler v Canada (AG)*, 2011 SCC 12); Amnesty International was an intervenor in relation to Canada's international law obligations. The case was then remitted to a differently constituted human rights tribunal panel. An appeal by the Attorney General to the Federal Court of Appeal from this decision was dismissed: *Canada (AG) v Canadian Human Rights Commission*, 2013 FCA 75. The Federal Court of Appeal cited new developments in equality analysis in relation to comparator groups, including *Moore v BC (Education)*, 2012 SCC 61; and *Quebec (AG) v A*, 2013 SCC 5. A human rights tribunal began to hear evidence in this case on 25 February 2013, and the Commission's website reveals several procedural decisions but no final decision in the case: see online <www.chrc-ccdp.ca>. According to a press report, the federal government spent millions of dollars in its litigation opposing this complaint: see Gloria Galloway, "Ottawa's Aboriginal Child-Welfare Policies under Fire", *The Globe and Mail* (26 February 2013) A6.

Hamilton Health Sciences Corp v DH, 2015 ONCJ 229

This decision was an endorsement issued in April 2015 in relation to an earlier decision in November 2014 (see 2014 ONCJ 603). In his earlier decision in November 2014, Justice Edward denied an application (pursued by McMaster Children's Hospital) to compel Brant Child and Family Services to apprehend an 11-year-old Aboriginal girl in order to continue chemotherapy for leukemia. In this case, the girl's mother wished to treat the child with traditional Aboriginal medicine, and the court agreed that this was her "Aboriginal right" (pursuant to section 35 of the Constitution), one that was rooted in their culture from the beginnings: see Kelly Grant, "Ontario Judge Rules Hospital Can't Force Chemo on Native Girl" *The Globe and Mail* (15 November 2014) A20. Leaders of the Six Nations of the Grand River participated in the case.

The decision resulted in both support and critique from academic commentators and others: see Alyshah Hasham & Tim Alamenciak, "Aboriginal Medicine Ruling Ignites Debate on Children's Rights" *Toronto Star* (20 November 2014) GT1 and GT9, with supporters emphasizing that law must recognize Aboriginal culture and rights (as well as historical injustices) and critics focusing on the child's right to medical treatment for cancer: see also

Andre Picard, "Treating a Child's Cancer Does Not Constitute Abuse", *The Globe and Mail* (18 November 2014) A19. In this context, Justice Murray Sinclair, Chair of the Indian Residential Schools Truth and Reconciliation Commission, argued that Aboriginal people have good reasons to mistrust the medical system because of their experiences with the coercion experienced in the residential school system According to Sinclair, there is a need for the medical system to engage with Aboriginal parents more fully to (re)gain their trust: see Gloria Galloway, "Medical System Told to Examine Why Native Parents Distrust It", *The Globe and Mail* (21 November 2014) A8. In this context, a press report indicated that the parties in this case had agreed to permit an extension of time for the Ontario Attorney General to decide whether to appeal this decision: see *Toronto Star* (6 March 2015) GT1 and 7.

Thus, on a motion in April 2015 by the Attorney General of Ontario, accompanied by a joint submission signed by all the parties, Edward J held that, as he had not yet signed a formal order, the court was not *functus officio*. In relation to the reasons released in November 2014, the court emphasized the evidence that the child's mother had declared that she would not permit her child to die, and the comments of the SCC in *The Queen v Van der Peet*, [1996] 2 SCR 507 with respect to protection for Aboriginal rights in section 35 of the Constitution. The court also noted that children are considered gifts from the Creator among the Haudenosaunee, so that "it does no mischief to my decision to recognize that the best interests of the child remain paramount" (at para 4). Thus, the court concluded (at para 5) that:

> Written reasons given in a case seek to explain how a court has resolved an issue between parties who appear before it. Sometimes just reasons attract a wider audience. The Attorney General of Ontario was in that audience in this case. There were many calls for the Attorney General of Ontario to pursue litigation: however, the Attorney General chose to engage in a dialogue with the parties that ultimately led to an approach that spoke more to what joins us as opposed to what separates us. The joint submission, which has been read into the record, notes how the province and the family collaboratively worked to form a health care team to bring the best both had to offer to address JJ's ongoing treatment. This approach recognizes the province's acceptance of the family's right to practice traditional medicine and the family's acceptance western medicine will most certainly help their daughter. It is simply a recognition of what is in JJ's best interest. Such an approach bodes well for the future [and also reflects Article 24 of the *United Nations Declaration on the Rights of Indigenous Peoples*].

In the result, the court added two additional paragraphs to the decision released in November 2014 (at paras 83a and 83b).

The court reiterated that the child was not in need of protection pursuant to the *CFSA*, s 40(4), but also declared that, implicit in this decision is that "recognition and implementation of the right to use traditional medicines must remain consistent with the principles that the best interests of the child remain paramount" (at para 83a).

The court also confirmed that the Haudenosaunee have "an aboriginal right to use their own traditional medicines and health practices, and the same right as other people in Ontario to use the medicines and health practices available to those people" (at para 83b).

To what extent does the result in this case suggest an appropriate approach to issues about child protection for Aboriginal children? For a critique about the role of courts in such cases, see Andre Picard, "Court's No Place to Resolve Gut-Wrenching Medical Issues", *The Globe and Mail* (28 April 2015).

Additional Resources

Nicholas Bala et al, eds, *Canadian Child Welfare Law: Children, Families and the State*, 2nd ed (Toronto: Thompson Educational Publishing, 2004).

Xiaobei Chan, "Is it all Neo-Liberal? Some Reflections on Child Protection Policy and Neo-Conservatism in Ontario" (2000) 45–46 Canadian Review of Social Policy 237.

Brenda Cossman & Carol Rogerson, "Case Study in the Provision of Legal Aid: Family Law" in Ontario Legal Aid Review, *Report of the Ontario Legal Aid Review: A Blueprint for Publicly Funded Legal Services*, vol 3 (Toronto: Government of Ontario, 1996) 773.

James Felstiner, "Child Welfare Hearings from an Unfamiliar Perspective" in Nicholas Bala, Joseph Hornick & Robin Vogl, eds, *Canadian Child Welfare Law: Children, Families and the State* (Toronto: Thompson Educational Publishing, 1991) at 306.

Patrick Johnston, *Native Children and the Child Welfare System* (Toronto: Canadian Council on Social Development and James Lorimer & Company, 1983).

Anne McGillivray, "Child Physical Assault: Law, Equality and Intervention" (2004) 30 Man LJ 133.

Kerry O'Halloran, *The Welfare of the Child: The Principle and the Law* (Aldershot, UK: Ashgate, 1999).

Caroline Sawyer, "Conflicting Rights for Children: Implementing Welfare, Autonomy, and Justice within Family Proceedings" (1999) 21:2 J Soc Welfare & Fam L 99.

Karen Swift, "Contradictions in Child Welfare: Neglect and Responsibility" in Carol Baines, Patricia Evans & Sheila Neysmith, eds, *Women's Caring: Feminist Perspectives on Social Welfare* (Toronto: Oxford University Press, 1998) 160.

CHILD PROTECTION: SOME CHALLENGES AND CONTROVERSIES

The significance of the child protection context for family law

The brief discussion of the child protection context in relation to *S(DD)* examined the legal framework concerning the tensions between private families and public legal regulation to protect vulnerable children. In addition to these tensions, this discussion illustrated two aspects of child protection that are important as background to the discussion of family dissolution in later chapters:

- The legislative framework and judicial reasoning about child protection focus on the "best interests" of children. Although the legislative definitions of "best interests" concerning adoption (*Child and Family Services Act*, Part VII) and child protection (Part III) reveal some similarities, they are not exactly the same. In this way, this brief review of child protection serves to illustrate the contextual constraints of the "best interests" principle, a feature that will be addressed again in the context of custody and access decision making at family dissolution.

- A "private" dispute between parents at family dissolution may result in legal intervention if there is evidence that a child is "in need of protection"; therefore, it is possible for the state to intervene if a child is (or becomes) "in need of protection" in the context of family dissolution issues. In this way, the child protection context is also part of the background to issues at separation or divorce.

Before leaving child protection, this section briefly reviews three other examples of child protection issues, and cases in which legal regulation in the interests of vulnerable children has engaged with values relating to family autonomy. These issues involve definitions about who is a "child" and the circumstances in which a child is "in need of protection," and they provide a more expansive view about issues of child protection and children's "best interests" in families.

"In need of protection": Fetal apprehension

> Neither the majority nor the minority in *DFG* assess state interference in the reproductive lives of women in a manner fully compatible with women's equality and participation in Canadian life. Nor do they place this incidence of juridical intervention within a history of legal involvement with women's reproductive capacity, of which this is only the most recent example. (Sanda Rodgers, "*Winnipeg Child and Family Services v DFG*: Juridical Interference with Pregnant Women in the Alleged Interest of the Fetus" (1998) 36 Alta L Rev 711 at 720)

"In Need of Protection": Recognition of a Fetus?

Rodgers's comments focused on the 1997 decision of the Supreme Court of Canada, *Winnipeg Child & Family Services (Northwest Area) v G(DF)*, [1997] 3 SCR 925. In this case, a majority of the court concluded that there was no authority for the state to apprehend a fetus, either pursuant to tort law or on the basis of the court's inherent *parens patriae* jurisdiction. In reaching this conclusion, the majority recognized that it was not possible to apprehend the fetus without also apprehending a pregnant woman. By contrast, the dissenting judgment asserted a need to reconsider the "born alive" rule in tort law in the light of new medical developments, and to expand the court's *parens patriae* jurisdiction.

In reviewing this excerpt from the majority decision, identify the factors that were relevant to the court's conclusion that child protection legislation could not be extended to a fetus by means of the principle of *parens patriae*.

Winnipeg Child & Family Services (Northwest Area) v G(DF)
[1997] 3 SCR 925

The judgment was delivered by McLACHLIN J (Lamer CJC, La Forest, L'Heureux-Dubé, Gonthier, Cory, and Iacobucci JJ concurring). In the judgment, McLachlin J outlined the history of the proceedings and the agency's assertion that two of the respondent's three children had been injured by her glue-sniffing addiction, thereby justifying its decision to intervene. She noted as well that the respondent had sought treatment at an earlier point, but had been turned away because of a lack of facilities; the respondent had agreed to take treatment eventually; and she had remained at the hospital until she was discharged.

> ... This is not a story of heros and villains. It is the more prosaic but all too common story of people struggling to do their best in the face of inadequate facilities and the ravages of addiction. This said, the legal question remains: assuming evidence that a mother is acting in a way which may harm her unborn child, does a judge, at the behest of the state, have the power to order the mother to be taken into custody for the purpose of rectifying her conduct? It is on this footing that I approach the case....

McLachlin J reviewed the lower court decisions, including the decision of Schulman J to make an order for detention on two grounds: that the respondent was suffering from a mental disorder within the meaning of the Manitoba *Mental Health Act*, RSM 1987, c M110; and on the basis of the court's *parens patriae* jurisdiction — that is, "the power of the court to act in the stead of a parent for the protection of a child." As McLachlin J noted, Schulman J acknowledged that the courts have never exercised this power on behalf of an unborn child, but he saw no reason why the power should not be extended to the protection of the child before birth. The Court of Appeal held that the evidence did not establish incompetency under the *Mental Health Act*. Nor, in the view of the court, could the order be supported on the ground of an extension of the court's *parens patriae* jurisdiction to protect the child or as an injunction to restrain tortious conduct.

According to McLachlin J, the case raised two issues for the Supreme Court. One related to the scope of tort law; the other related to the scope of the *parens patriae* jurisdiction of the court. In a lengthy review of the tort law context, she reviewed existing legal principles concerning the lack of legal status of a fetus, and concluded that "there was no legal person in whose interests the agency could act or in whose interests a court order could be made." McLachlin J recognized that an action for injury to the fetus could be brought after the birth of the child, but the court had no power to entertain such an action prior to the child's birth. She also rejected arguments about extending the law of tort to cover such a situation, particularly in relation to a pregnant woman's duty not to engage in harmful "lifestyle" choices. She then addressed the *parens patriae* arguments:

> Alternatively, the appellant seeks to sustain the order for the detention of the respondent by an extension of the court's *parens patriae* jurisdiction to permit protection of unborn children. Courts have the power to step into the shoes of the parent and make orders in the best interests of the child; *E. (Mrs.) v. Eve*, [1986] 2 SCR 388. The agency argues that this power should be extended to orders on behalf of unborn children.
>
> I would reject this submission for reasons similar to those enunciated in connection with the submission that the law of tort should be extended to the unborn. The submission requires a major change to the law of *parens patriae*. The ramifications of the change would be significant and complex. The change involves conflicts of fundamental rights and interests and difficult policy issues. Not surprisingly these difficulties have led all appellate courts that have considered the extension to reject it. I share their view.
>
> The law as it stands is clear: the courts do not have *parens patriae* or wardship jurisdiction over unborn children. This is the law in the European Community, Great Britain and Canada. In Canada, all courts which have considered the issue, save for the trial judge in this case, appear to have rejected the proposition that the *parens patriae* jurisdiction of the court extends to unborn children. In *Re A.* (1990), 28 RFL (3d) 288 (Ont. UFC), the Children's Aid Society of Hamilton-Wentworth brought an action for a supervision order to ensure that a pregnant woman seek appropriate prenatal care deemed necessary for the welfare of the fetus. Steinberg UFCJ, having concluded that there was no jurisdiction to make the order under the *Child and Family Services Act*, S.O. 1984, c. 55, considered whether the *parens patriae* jurisdiction was broad enough to force the confinement of a pregnant woman to protect her fetus. He held it was not broad enough.... [The court also cited a decision of the English Court of Appeal, *Re F* [1988] 2 All ER 193, identifying four reasons given by the court for limiting the court's jurisdiction to born children.] First, a fetus does not attain legal personhood until birth and therefore, the order would be contrary to that principle.... Second, applying the principle that the interests of the child are to be predominant would create conflict between the existing legal interests of the mother and those of the unborn child. Third, there could be difficulties in enforcing against the mother any order in respect of an unborn child. And finally, he held that under the *Supreme Court Act 1981* only "minors" could be made wards of the court and that in light of the *Family Law Reform Act 1969*, a "minor" could only be a person, in the sense that he or she had been born....
>
> As the English Court of Appeal's reasons eloquently attest, the same problems encountered in relation to extending tort jurisdiction to the unborn, surface in relation to extending the *parens patriae* jurisdiction of the court. The law sees birth as the necessary condition of legal personhood. The pregnant woman and her unborn child are one. Finally, to make orders protecting fetuses would radically impinge on the fundamental liberties of the pregnant woman, both as to lifestyle choices and how and as to where she chooses to live and be.
>
> It is argued that the *parens patriae* jurisdiction over children necessarily involves overriding the liberty of parents, and that there is nothing new in this. This argument overlooks the fact that the invasion of liberty involved in making court orders affecting the unborn child, is of a differ-

ent order than the invasion of liberty involved in court orders relating to born children. The *parens patriae* power over born children permits the courts to override the liberty of the parents to make decisions on behalf of their children where a parental choice may result in harm to a child: *B.(R.) v. Children's Aid Society of Metropolitan Toronto* (1994), [1995] 1 SCR 315. The only liberty interest affected is the parent's interest in making decisions for *his or her child*. By contrast, extension of the *parens patriae* jurisdiction of the court to unborn children has the potential to affect a much broader range of liberty interests. The court cannot make decisions for the unborn child without inevitably making decisions for the mother herself. The intrusion is therefore far greater than simply limiting the mother's choices concerning her child. Any choice concerning her child inevitably affects her. For example, to sustain the order requested in the case at bar would interfere with the pregnant woman's ability to choose where to live and what medical treatment to undergo. The *parens patriae* jurisdiction has never been used to permit a court to make such decisions for competent women, whether pregnant or not. Such a change would not be an incremental change ... but a generic change of major impact and consequence. It would seriously intrude on the rights of women. If anything is to be done, the legislature is in a much better position to weigh the competing interests and arrive at a solution that is principled and minimally intrusive to pregnant women.

I conclude that the law of *parens patriae* does not support the order for the detention of the respondent....

Additional Resources

SI Bushnell, "The Welfare of Children and the Jurisdiction of the Court under *Parens Patriae*" in Katherine Connell-Thouez & Bartha Knoppers, eds, *Contemporary Trends in Family Law: A National Perspective* (Scarborough, ON: Carswell, 1984) 223.

Thelma McCormack, "Fetal Syndromes and the Charter: The Winnipeg Glue Sniffing Case" (1999) 14 CJLS 77.

Laura Shanner, "Pregnancy Intervention and Models of Maternal-Fetal Relationship: Philosophical Reflections in the Winnipeg CFS Dissent" (1998) 36:3 Alta L Rev 751.

"In need of protection": Children and medical treatment

The state always intervenes because it allocates power over the ... decision, whether it carves out a sphere of parental autonomy or instead permits strangers or state officials to challenge and supplant parental decisions. (Martha Minow, "Beyond State Intervention in the Family: For Baby Jane Doe" (1985) 18 U Mich JL Ref 933 at 951)

"Mature" Children and Decisions about Medical Treatment

Section 37(2)(e) of Ontario's *Child and Family Services Act* states that a child is "in need of protection" if the child requires medical treatment and the child's parent does not provide, or refuses to give consent for, available medical treatment. In an early appeal to the Supreme Court of Canada to determine whether a young child was "in need of protection" when doctors had determined that surgery was necessary and her parents refused to consent to blood transfusions because of their religious beliefs, the court upheld a lower court decision granting a short-term wardship to enable the transfusions and the surgery to take place. In doing so, the court also held that the *Charter* did not preclude this action, although there were a number of different reasons for this conclusion. See *B(R) v Children's Aid Society of Metropolitan Toronto*, [1995] 1 SCR 315; and DA Rollie Thompson, "Case Comment" (1995) 9 RFL (4th) 345.

This issue was again addressed by the Supreme Court of Canada in *AC v Manitoba (Director of Child and Family Services)*, [2009] SCJ No 30. In this case, the child was a girl aged nearly 15, who was admitted to hospital with intestinal bleeding as a result of Crohn's disease. Although doctors wished to provide blood transfusions, AC refused to consent on the basis of her religious beliefs as a Jehovah's Witness; and there was evidence that she had signed an advanced medical directive a few months earlier with instructions that she should not receive such transfusions under any circumstances. When her health deteriorated, however, she was apprehended by the Director of Child and Family Services as a child "in need of protection."

Pursuant to the provincial legislation, there was authority for a court to order medical treatment in a child's "best interests." But the legislation also provided that a court could not make such an order for a child over the age of 16 without the child's consent, unless the child was unable to understand information relevant to making the decision or unable to appreciate its consequences. The applications judge held that treatment should be ordered in the child's best interests and the Manitoba Court of Appeal upheld this decision. The Supreme Court of Canada dismissed the appeal (Binnie J dissenting), including arguments based on *Charter*, ss 7, 15 and 2(a).

In the following excerpts, examine the court's approach to the issue of "best interests" in relation to the personal autonomy of a "child" who is almost an adult. Identify the factors taken into account by the court in determining the child's best interests in this case.

AC v Manitoba (Director of Child and Family Services)
2009 SCC 30

ABELLA J:

[1] One of the most sensitive decisions a judge can make in family law is in connection with the authorization of medical treatment for children. It engages the most intensely complicated constellation of considerations and its consequences are inevitably profound....

[30] The question [in this case] is whether the statutory scheme strikes a constitutional balance between what the law has consistently seen as an individual's fundamental right to autonomous decision-making in connection with his or her body and the law's equally persistent attempts to pro-

tect vulnerable children from harm. This requires examining the legislative scheme, the common law of medical decision-making both for adults and minors, a comparative review of international jurisprudence, and relevant social scientific and legal literature. The observations that emerge from this review will inform the constitutional analysis....

COMMON LAW FOR MINORS

[46] The latitude accorded to adults at common law to decide their own medical treatment had historically narrowed dramatically when applied to children. However the common law has more recently abandoned the assumption that all minors lack decisional capacity and replaced it with a general recognition that children are entitled to a degree of decision-making autonomy that is reflective of their evolving intelligence and understanding. This is known as the common law "mature minor" doctrine. As the Manitoba Law Reform Commission noted, this doctrine is "a well-known, well-accepted and workable principle which ... raise[s] few difficulties on a day-to-day basis" (*Minors' Consent to Health Care* (1995), Report No. 91, at p. 33). The doctrine addresses the concern that young people should not automatically be deprived of the right to make decisions affecting their medical treatment. It provides instead that the right to make those decisions varies in accordance with the young person's level of maturity, with the degree to which maturity is scrutinized intensifying in accordance with the severity of the potential consequences of the treatment or of its refusal....

The court reviewed the common law principles in cases such as *Gillick v West Norfolk and Wisbech Area Health Authority*, [1985] 3 All ER 402 (HL), a case in which the issue was whether a doctor could prescribe contraception for a girl under the age of 16 without attracting liability in tort for proceeding without the consent of her parents.

... While accepting that assessing the sufficiency of a child's maturity created an uncertain standard, Lord Scarman, like Lord Fraser, was of the view that a level of uncertainty was worth the cost of keeping "the law in line with social experience"....

[52] *Gillick* was hailed as ushering in an era of judicial respect for children's rights to self-determination, and it clearly made great strides in that direction. Yet it is important to remember that the issue was a child's ability to authorize treatment that a medical professional considered to be in that child's best interests. Lord Fraser's conclusion that physicians could rely on the instructions of "mature" children rested at least partly on the assumption that "there may be circumstances in which a doctor is a better judge of the medical advice and treatment which will conduce to a [child's] welfare than her parents" (p. 412 (emphasis added)). The ultimate question was always "what is best in the interests of the ... [minor] patient" (p. 413)....

The court also reviewed cases in which a child's decisional capacity to refuse treatment was upheld, such as *Re LDK* (1985), 48 RFL (2d) 164 (Ont Prov Div), where the patient was a 12-year-old girl suffering from acute myeloid leukaemia. She and her parents were Jehovah's Witnesses, and refused to consent to chemotherapy that would necessitate blood transfusions. The Children's Aid Society apprehended the girl in order to compel the treatment, but two doctors testified that the odds of a favourable outcome after treatment were relatively low (around 30 percent) and that the side effects were severe. The trial judge accepted the girl's commitment to her religious beliefs and to fighting against any transfusion, and found that "the emotional trauma [the child] would experience" in forced treatment would outweigh the anticipated benefits.

[70] This reluctance to interpret the "mature minor" doctrine as demanding automatic judicial deference to the young person's medical treatment decisions where doing so will put the adolescent's life or health in grave danger seems to stem from the difficulty of determining with any certainty whether a given adolescent is, in fact, sufficiently mature to make a particular decision. As academic legal and social scientific literature in this area reveals, there is no simple and straightforward means of definitively evaluating — or discounting — the myriad of subtle factors that may affect an adolescent's ability to make mature, stable and independent choices in the medical treatment context.

[71] There is considerable support for the notion that while many adolescents may have the technical ability to make complex decisions, this does not always mean they will have the necessary maturity and independence of judgment to make truly autonomous choices. As Jane Fortin significantly observes: "... cognitive capacity to reach decisions does not necessarily correlate with 'mature' judgment" (*Children's Rights and the Developing Law* (2nd ed. 2003), at p. 73)....

INTERPRETING BEST INTERESTS

[80] These observations take us back to ... the *Child and Family Services Act*, and to an interpretive approach to "best interests" that is consistent with international standards, developments in the common law, and the reality of childhood and child protection.

[81] The general purpose of the "best interests" standard is to provide courts with a focus and perspective through which to act on behalf of those who are vulnerable. In contrast, competent adults are assumed to be "the best arbiter[s] of [their] own moral destiny", ... and so are entitled to independently assess and determine their own best interests, regardless of whether others would agree when evaluating the choice from an objective standpoint.

[82] The application of an objective "best interests" standard to infants and very young children is uncontroversial. Mature adolescents, on the other hand, have strong claims to autonomy, but these claims exist in tension with a protective duty on the part of the state that is also justified.

[83] The tension between autonomy and child protection is real, often dramatic, and always painful. It is described by Joan M. Gilmour as follows:

> While a mature minor can consent to medically recommended treatment, the extent to which he or she has the power to consent to a treatment that is not beneficial or therapeutic remains unclear. The argument that a minor can only consent to care that would be of benefit (or refuse that which is of little or no benefit) is sometimes referred to as "the welfare principle". It suggests that a mature minor can only make those decisions about medical care that others would consider to be in his or her interests; as such, it challenges the extent of the commitment in law to mature minors' interests in self-determination and autonomy....
>
> ... [The welfare principle] reflects an uneasiness with autonomy as the overriding value that the law advances in this context, rather than protection of the minor's life and health as one who is still vulnerable [quoting Gilmour "Death and Dying" in Mary Jane

> Dykeman et al., eds., *Canadian Health Law Practice Manual* (loose-leaf) 8.01 at paras. 8.52–8.54].

[84] In my view, any solution to this tension must be responsive to its complexity....

[92] The statutory factors reflect decades of careful study into children's needs and how the law can best meet them. We have come, with time, to understand the significance of so many relevant considerations which had been previously hidden behind formulaic solutions like "the tender years doctrine". With our evolving understanding has come the recognition that the quality of decision-making about a child is enhanced by input from that child. The extent to which that input affects the "best interests" assessment is as variable as the child's circumstances, but one thing that can be said with certainty is that the input becomes increasingly determinative as the child matures. This is true not only when considering the child's best interests in the placement context, but also when deciding whether to accede to a child's wishes in medical treatment situations.

[93] Such a robust conception of the "best interests of the child" standard is also consistent with international instruments to which Canada is a signatory [such as the *Convention on the Rights of the Child*....]

In the end, the court dismissed the appeal, rejecting as well the claims of *Charter* violation.

Additional Resources

Lori Beaman, *Defining Harm: Religious Freedom and the Limits of Law* (Vancouver: UBC Press, 2008).

Gerison Lansdown for Canadian International Development Agency, *Evolving Capacities and Participation* (Victoria: International Institute for Child Rights and Development, 2004).

MI Hall, "A Ministry for Children: Abandoning the Interventionist Debate in British Columbia" (1998) 12 Intl JL Pol'y & Fam 121.

Shauna Van Praagh, "Faith, Belonging, and the Protection of 'Our' Children" (1999) 17 Windsor YB Access Just 154.

"In need of protection" and sexual abuse

Reports made to authorities indicate that female children are sexually abused in greater numbers than male children, and that adult males are the majority of offenders. This picture is changing rapidly, however, as more First Nations adults who attended residential schools in Canada as children are speaking out. Also, there are increased reports from males [in church schools and other church settings, and in junior hockey clubs].... There remains considerable resistance from some professionals and the public to accept the prevalence of child sexual abuse. Moreover, individuals in authority positions who hold with a more conventional approach to the victimization of children have difficulty acknowledging that such abuse arises out of the social legitimation of unequal power relations within families. (Betty Joyce Carter, *Who's To Blame? Child Sexual Abuse and Non-Offending Mothers* (Toronto: University of Toronto Press, 1999) at 175)

Sexual Abuse and Child Protection

Section 37(2) of Ontario's *Child and Family Services Act* contains a number of provisions concerning sexual abuse and sexual exploitation of children which may render them "in need of protection." As this issue has gained increasing attention in recent decades, there have been a number of studies, governmental inquiries, and other reports:

• In 1984, the Badgley Report examined the prevalence of child sexual abuse, concluding that at some time during their lives, about one in two females and one in three males have been victims of one or more unwanted sexual acts. The report recommended a number of changes in the administration of justice, focusing primarily on the criminal law system: see Committee on Sexual Offences Against Children and Youths, *Sexual Offences Against Children: The Badgley Report* (Ottawa: Minister of Supply and Services Canada, 1984) at 175.

• In 1990, another report, *Reaching for Solutions*, identified the need for a broader range of actions to prevent child sexual abuse, including programs in university law schools concerning these issues and special interventions within Aboriginal communities: see Rix G. Rogers, *Reaching for Solutions: The Summary Report of the Special Advisor to the Minister of National Health and Welfare on Child Sexual Abuse in Canada* (Ottawa: Minister of Supply and Services, 1990).

Academic literature has also identified the need to examine sexual abuse of children by women, as well as by men. While men represent the vast majority of abusers, it is important to examine all types of abuse to gain an understanding of the complexity of this issue. See Myriam Denov, "A Culture of Denial: Exploring Professional Perspectives on Female Sex Offending" (2001) 43 Can J Crim 303.

In an effort to combat child sexual abuse, provincial statutes often create reporting requirements for professionals, including physicians and teachers, with penalties for failure to comply. Unfortunately, these provisions have not always been effective. See Ronda Bessner, "The Duty to Report Child Abuse" (2000) 17 Can Fam LQ 278.

Sexual Abuse and Fiduciary Obligations:
J(LA) v J(H)

In *J(LA) v J(H)* (1993), 102 DLR (4th) 177 (Ont Gen Div), a young woman brought a civil action against her mother and stepfather after her stepfather was convicted of sexually assaulting her and imprisoned. The successful civil action resulted in damages based in tort and for breach of fiduciary duty, based on tort principles. In relation to the mother's liability for breach of a fiduciary duty, the court held that the mother knew of the sexual assaults and failed to protect her daughter from harm. The evidence suggested that the mother had observed an assault on one occasion, but had (inappropriately) accepted her husband's promise that it would never happen again; that she was aware of lavish gifts to the daughter from her husband; and that she had discovered condoms under the daughter's bed. In addition, she had deflected inquiries from a social worker from the Children's Aid Society during a short period of time when she had fled to a shelter with her daughter; she had subsequently returned home.

In its decision, the court applied the principles concerning parental duties to care for and protect children, stating (at 185–86):

> ... In the circumstances of this case, recognizing that the defendant mother was of limited means and education, it was still well within her ability and, therefore, her discretion, to take her daughter away from the abusive situation which she was well aware of or report the situation to the authorities with the probable result of the abuser being removed from the situation. The defendant mother had relatives in the area who could have helped but she sought no help. There are social agencies which could have helped as well, but she sought no help and actively ensured that the Children's Aid Society was turned away from its legitimate inquiries. Instead of pursuing means that were open to her to protect her daughter from the injurious circumstances of which she was aware, the defendant mother put her own interests above those of her daughter. She wanted to keep her husband and her daughter with her but at the expense of her daughter's well-being.
>
> Some may think it harsh to hold a mother to a standard by which she must, in certain circumstances, choose to take action which is destructive to her family unit. However, where serious sexual abuse of a child within a family unit must be weighed against the destruction of that unit, there can be no doubt how the balance must tip. The consequences of serious child abuse are so clear, both for the immediate development of the victim as well as in terms of the sins of parents being repeated in subsequent generations, that the risks inherent in the fracturing of a family unit in order to separate a child from abuse are infinitely preferable to the risk of the consequences, both immediate and long-term, of leaving an abusive situation to continue to its natural conclusion.

What are the consequences of this approach to the problem of sexual abuse in families? Consider this critique:

> The propriety of imposing liability on mothers must be considered in light of the gender inequality that permeates our social, economic, and political structures (including families), as well as the lack of publicly-funded shelters and treatment facilities for victims of sexual and physical abuse.... It may be too late and, indeed, undesirable to turn back the clock on recent advances in the law pertaining to sexual assault that have imposed private law duties of care and fiduciary obligations on persons and institutions in positions of power and trust. However, there is a sad, if predictable, irony to these developments being used against one of the weakest links in the chain of child sexual abuse — namely, non-offending mothers. Unquestionably, mothers owe both a duty of care and a fiduciary duty to their children. The issue to be considered is whether, so long as they are denied viable choices and the power to prevent abuse, mothers should be held to have breached their legal obligations. (Elizabeth Grace & Susan Vella, "Vesting Mothers with Power They Do Not Have: The Non-Offending Parent in Civil Sexual Assault Cases: *J(LA) v. J(H) and J(J)*" (1994) 7 CJWL 184 at 186)

Lev Tahor and Sexual Abuse Claims

When child welfare authorities in Québec learned in late 2012 about the birth of children to underage girls, allegedly fathered by much older men in the Lev Tahor community, they were concerned about underage marriages and sexual misconduct in the community. Fearing intervention from these authorities, most of the members of the community fled across the Ontario–Québec border to new homes in Chatham–Kent in southern Ontario. Although the Québec court ordered some of the Lev Tahor children into foster care, there was no authority to implement the order in Ontario. A year later, when the Children's Aid Society of Chatham–Kent became actively involved, many members of the Lev Tahor fled to Guatemala.

According to the later litigation in Chatham–Kent, the Québec authorities raised concerns about forced marriage of children under 16, failure to provide adequate education for children in the community, inappropriate discipline in the use of force, and parental neglect in the physical care of the children: see *Chatham–Kent Children's Services v AH*, 2014 ONCJ 50. However, Ontario's *Child and Family Services Act* provides no authority for the enforcement of a child protection order from another province and an appeal decision confirmed this conclusion: see *Chatham–Kent Children's Services v JS*, 2014 ONSC 2352. In this context, Ontario refused to return the children to Québec, and Guatemala refused to return them to Ontario. Moreover, according to Martha Bailey, none of the existing international conventions offer a means of compelling the return of the children to Canada: see Martha Bailey, "Cross-Border Child Welfare: The Lev Tahor Case" (2014) 33 CFLQ 367. See also Tu Thanh Ha, "Jewish Sect Abused Teens, Court Applications Allege", *The Globe and Mail* (15 February 2014) A6; Arshy Mann, "Does Lev Tahor Case signal need for Legislative Change?" *Law Times* (16 June 2014) 11; and Allan Woods, "Authorities Knew of Sex-Abuse Claims before Lev Tahor Fled", *Toronto Star* (27 September 2014) A17.

Institutional Abuse and Fiduciary Obligations

Claims relating to institutional abuse have also made use of the concept of fiduciary obligation in actions for redress. For example, see *A v C* (1998), 42 RFL (4th) 427 (BCCA); and *Bonaparte v Canada (AG)* (2003), 64 OR (3d) 1 (CA).

In relation to such claims, the Law Commission of Canada reported in 2000 on the different kinds of needs of survivors of child abuse in institutions, including the need for a historical record and remembrance, acknowledgment, apology, accountability, access to therapy or counselling, access to education or training, financial compensation, and prevention/public awareness. See Law Commission of Canada, *Restoring Dignity — Responding to Child Abuse in Canadian Institutions* (Ottawa: Law Commission of Canada, 2000) at 74. These claims arose in a context in which children, particularly First Nations children, were removed from their families to live in institutional settings. Thus, in addition to the abuse they may have suffered, they also experienced the loss of family life. In *Bonaparte*, above, the claim included the loss of cultural traditions for the children of those institutionalized, since the latter were unable to pass on their heritage as a result of their removal as children. Should such losses be characterized as child abuse? Why, or why not?

Issues about institutional abuse have also been considered in other contexts. For example, in *KLB v British Columbia*, 2003 SCC 51, and *EDG v Hammer*, 2003 SCC 52, the abuse occurred in relation to foster parents and the plaintiffs were also suing the Crown with respect to the foster placements. In *MB v British Columbia*, 2003 SCC 53, the abuse related to an assault by a school janitor in which a school board was named defendant. See also Loretta P Merritt, "Trilogy of Abuse Cases Examined 6 Issues", *The Lawyers Weekly* (5 December 2003) 6. Although such issues are beyond the scope of discussion here, it is important to be aware of the many contexts in which child abuse may occur in families and communities.

Additional Resources

Kathy Au Coin, "Violence and Abuse Against Children and Youth by Family Members" in Canadian Centre for Justice Statistics, *Family Violence in Canada: A Statistical Profile 2003* (Ottawa: National Clearinghouse on Family Violence, Health Canada, 2003) 33.

Howard Davidson, "Child Abuse and Domestic Violence: Legal Connections and Controversies" (1995) 29:2 Fam LQ 357.

Margaret Hall, "'Intuitive Fiduciaries': The Equitable Structure of Family Life" (2002) 19 Can J Fam L 345.

Law Commission of Canada, *Restoring Dignity — Responding to Child Abuse in Canadian Institutions* (Ottawa: Law Commission of Canada, 2000).

Denise Réaume & Shauna Van Praagh, "Family Matters: Mothers as Secondary Defendants in Child Sexual Abuse Actions" (2002) 17 SCLR 179 at 211–12.

Rix Rogers, "The Anguish of Child Abuse — Is Prevention Possible?" VIF *Transition* (September 1995) 9.

B Wharf, *Rethinking Child Welfare in Canada* (Toronto: McClelland & Stewart, 1993).

CHILD PROTECTION PROCEEDINGS AND FAMILY DISSOLUTION

As the cases in this section reveal, section 37(2) of the *Child and Family Services Act* defines a wide range of circumstances in which children may be "in need of protection." Some of these same issues may also surface in the context of family dissolution. Thus, while the mother and father in *S(DD)* appeared unable to cooperate effectively in parenting their child, the judge's reasons also indicate that the father had decided to separate from the mother. Similarly, although the mother in *G(DF)* appeared to be a sole parent, it is important to take note of how issues of addiction may be a catalyst for family dissolution. And although the parents in the cases involving blood transfusions for their children seemed to be in intact families, serious family illnesses may also contribute to family breakdown. Moreover, as *J(LA) v J(H)* revealed, issues of child sexual abuse create complicated stresses for parents. In addition, since parents' decisions to separate may often extend over a period of weeks or months, parental inability to make appropriate decisions about their children may lead to the involvement of a child protection agency *in the process of family dissolution.*

In this context, issues about child protection may be connected to other issues at family breakdown, including especially decisions with respect to parental custody and access arrangements. However, there are some important differences between a custody and access dispute between parents, and a child protection proceeding between parents and the state:

> Child protection legislation has a different purpose than the statutes that govern disputes between parents. The function of child protection agencies is to protect children from harm, and to interfere in the lives of parents and children only when the standard of parental care falls below the minimum acceptable standard in the community. Accordingly, child protection agencies are usually permitted to intervene only if the child has, in fact, been harmed [or has been the subject of neglect], or if there is a ... risk that such harm is likely to result if the child remains in the home.
>
> The issues in a child protection case are, in theory, different from those that arise in disputes between parents. In a child protection case, the question is: Will this child be at serious risk of substantial harm if left in the care of the parent or parents? By contrast, in a contest between parents the question is: Where is it in the child's best interests to live? In child protection litigation, a court is largely restricted to choosing between a parent and the state with its appointed caregivers, though there may also be some flexibility to place a child in the care of another relative.... (Nicholas Bala, "Abuse and Neglect Allegations in the Context of Parental Separation" in Bala et al, eds, 291 at 299)

Is the issue of family autonomy likely to be less significant in a context in which a child protection proceeding occurs alongside an application by parents for custody or access? Should the "best interests" test be the same for these two legal processes? What kinds of social and economic factors may affect decision making in these differing contexts?

The issue of child protection is not the only basis for state intervention in the context of "intact" families, or those involved in the process of separation or divorce. Thus, the following sections briefly review issues about spousal violence and elder abuse in providing a context for discussion of issues about family dissolution.

IV.
ABUSE AND VIOLENCE IN INTIMATE RELATIONSHIPS: RESPONSIBILITIES FOR FAMILIES AND THE STATE

Over the past twenty years, the criminal justice system in Canada has come to recognize that spousal violence is not a "private matter," and there have been many changes that have resulted in the police and criminal justice system responding more effectively to spousal violence. The family justice system, however, has been slower to respond, even though spousal violence issues are present in roughly one quarter of all separations and divorces in Canada, and spousal violence is [the] fastest growing category of cases reported to child welfare agencies. Despite the slow pace of change in the family justice system, there is a growing awareness of the harmful effect of spousal violence, not only for direct victims, but also for children who live in families where there is spousal violence. There is also growing recognition that the types of non-adversarial dispute resolution approaches that are increasingly being used to help separated parents may not be appropriate if there are ongoing spousal abuse issues.

Cases involving spousal violence present complex, challenging issues for judges, lawyers, child welfare workers, assessors, mediators, police officers and other professionals in the family justice system.... (Nicholas Bala, Peter Jaffe & Claire Crooks, "Spousal Violence and Child-Related Cases: Challenging Cases requiring Differentiated Responses" (2009) 27 Can Fam LQ 1)

THE CONTEXT FOR ABUSE AND VIOLENCE IN INTIMATE RELATIONSHIPS

Statistics about family violence: Gender issues?

As the comment above suggests, there is growing awareness of the issue of spousal violence in families and its relationship to separation and divorce, as well as to child protection matters. Statistics and studies about violence in intimate relationships have proliferated in recent decades, as issues about violence and abuse have become more visible:

- In 1993, Statistics Canada reported that one-half of Canadian women reported violence by men known to them, one-quarter experienced violence by a stranger, and 15% reported violence by a current partner: see Statistics Canada, *The Violence Against Women Survey* (Ottawa: Statistics Canada, 1993), cited in *Families Count* at 164. See also Holly Johnson, *Dangerous Domains: Violence Against Women in Canada* (Toronto: Nelson Canada, 1996); Statistics Canada, *Family Violence in Canada: A Statistical Profile 2007* (Ottawa: Statistics Canada, Canadian Centre for Justice Statistics, 2007); and Maire Sinha, ed, *Measuring Violence Against Women: Statistical Trends* (Ottawa: Statistics Canada, Canadian Centre for Justice Statistics, 2013).

- In a 2006 study, Statistics Canada reported that female victims of intimate violence experience more severe (including lethal) and repeated forms of violence than do men. For example, women are 2.5 times as likely to report being beaten, choked, threatened with a gun or knife, and sexually assaulted; and they are also more likely to suffer serious physical and psychological injuries. And women are three times more likely to fear for their lives: see Statistics Canada, *Measuring Violence Against Women: Statistical Trends 2006*, Catalogue No 85-570-XIE (Ottawa: Statistics Canada, 2006) at 19 and 32–33, cited in *Families Count* at 164.

- According to the Uniform Crime Reporting Survey in 2009, more than one-half (53%) of violent crime targeting family members related to spousal violence. See also Vanier Institute of the Family, *Families Count* (Ottawa: VIF, 2010) at 164.

- According to former B.C. Justice Ted Hughes, there is a connection between the over-representation of Aboriginal children in the care system and the prevalence of violent outcomes for Aboriginal women and girls, citing factors of poverty, poor housing, intergenerational trauma, substance abuse and lack of educational and economic opportunities, and the relationship between these factors and colonization: see Mary Ellen Turpet-Lafond, "Put Native Women on the Agenda", *The Globe and Mail* (21 August 2014) A11.

- According to a press report in 2012, a major federal investigation into spousal violence concluded that it costs society at least $7.4 billion annually. The costs included policing and health care costs as well as funerals and lost wages. The study was based on 50,000 reports of spousal violence to the police, with more than 80% involving female victims: see Dean Beeby, "High Toll of Spousal Abuse means Everybody Pays", *The Globe and Mail* (24 December 2012) A7; and see also Leah Eichler, "The High Cost of Violence against Women", *The Globe and Mail* (20 July 2013) B17.

In this context, although the gender dimension of spousal violence has become quite controversial, it seems that most observers have concluded that women are more often victims of spousal violence and that their experiences involve more serious forms of violence, including homicide:

> Some fathers' rights advocates charge that "women's shelters have become bunkers in a war against men," but it is clear that some of the men's groups ... engage in hyperbolic, distorted advocacy [as do some women's advocates]. While false and exaggerated allegations of spousal abuse are a legitimate and important concern, ... it is clear that there are more cases of false denials of spousal violence by genuine abusers than cases of false allegations by [those] who are not genuine victims (see Bala, Jaffe & Crooks at 4–5).

Legal responses to spousal violence

State intervention in relation to spousal violence has increasingly emphasized that such violence constitutes criminal behaviour. In the early 1980s, federal and provincial police forces in Canada instituted a national charging policy, and the number of crisis intervention teams and the amount of specialized training increased quite significantly. In addition, systems for data collection were improved, sentencing patterns were monitored, and greater efforts were made to provide protection for victims. See Linda MacLeod, *Battered ... but not Beaten: Preventing Wife Battering in Canada* (Ottawa: Canadian Advisory Council on the Status of Women, 1987) at 81–85; and see also *Final Report of the Ad Hoc Federal–Provincial–Territorial Working Group Reviewing Spousal Abuse Policies and Legislation* (April 2003).

Across Canada, there have also been efforts to mandate prosecution (even against the victim's wishes), and to establish specialized domestic violence courts, computerized systems for coordinating data on offenders, specialized services for victims, and treatment for offenders. Such initiatives have been augmented by other measures, including ongoing training for judges, prosecutors, and police, and better coordination in relation to legal and other policies. In Ontario, the government announced an expansion of its domestic violence courts in May 2003, and arrangements to "stream" offenders into first-time and repeat offenders: first-time offenders must complete a counselling program, while specialized procedures for evidence and prosecution are provided for cases involving repeat offenders. The court program also provides additional assistance for victims.

In Ontario, the Ministry of Citizenship and Immigration released its "Domestic Violence Action Plan for Ontario" in 2005 (with subsequent updates). The Plan identified a series of principles including women's "right to safety;" equality between men and women in society; governmental leadership; shared responsibilities among groups and individuals; personal accountability on the part of abusers; recognition of the need to take account of diversity; a holistic response with an integrated continuum of supports; balanced efforts in relation to prevention, intervention, risk-assessment, and accountability; and monitoring and evaluation of strategies over time. In 2009, the *Family Statute Law Amendment Act, 2009*, SO 2009, c 11, added provisions to the *Family Law Act* that permit orders prohibiting contact or communication with another party "if the court determines that the order is necessary to ensure that an application [under Part I or Part II] is dealt with justly" (see ss 13.1 and 25.1). These provisions are in addition to existing provisions with respect to restraining orders (see s 46).

Moreover, in 2011, Ontario instituted a New York model for a court designed to integrate domestic violence cases (which are usually heard in criminal courts) and family law cases (which are heard in family courts). The Integrated Domestic Violence Court deals with cases that involve both family law matters and criminal charges relating to family violence in an effort to avoid the expense and time involved for two different court hearings, and to ensure that orders are better coordinated. The court, which operates at 311 Jarvis Street in Toronto, was initially a pilot project. See Allison Jones, "Court Integrates Domestic Violence and Family Cases", *The Globe and Mail* (11 June 2011) A15; and Robert Todd, "Domestic Violence Court Opens", *Law Times* 22:21 (20 June 2011). The IDV court has a dedicated Crown counsel, a community resource worker to connect families to community resources, and an officer who can provide victim and witness protection services. Although the court, which requires the consent of both parties to hear cases, experienced a slow start, a later news report indicated that it was beginning to hear cases more frequently. See Tamara Buluja, "A Bumpy Start for a New Type of Court", *The Globe and Mail* (2 August 2011) A7. The Ministry of the Attorney General reported that the IDV court was expanded to an additional Toronto location in April 2013: see Ministry of the Attorney General, "Results-Based Plan", 2013–2014.

British Columbia's *Family Law Act*, SBC 2011, c 25 (in force March 2013) defines "domestic violence" in Part 9 to include physical abuse of a family member; sexual abuse; psychological or emotional abuse; unreasonable restrictions of a family member's financial or personal autonomy; stalking; and intentional damage to property. The definition also includes, in the case of a child, direct or indirect exposure to family violence. In addition, Vancouver's Pivot Legal Society and Jane Doe Legal Network released a report, *Imagining Courts that Work for Women Survivors of Violence*. The report documented arrangements for justice-system responses to domestic violence in a number of different provinces in Canada, including the Winnipeg Family Violence Court, Calgary's HomeFront Domestic Violence Court and Edmonton's trial court, Regina's Domestic Violence Program, Ontario's Domestic Violence Court Program and the Integrated Domestic Violence Court, and Yukon's Domestic Violence Treatment Option (at 30–32). The report assessed the needs of victims of domestic violence and identified four essential factors for effective responses to domestic violence: political will (including strong commitments and resources); evidence-based program development for the court itself; victim service programs and programs targeting offenders; and judicial leadership along with collaborative multi-stakeholder engagement (at 56 ff). See also Jeremy Hainsworth, "BC takes Aim against Domestic Violence", *The Lawyers Weekly* (25 January 2013).

In addition to these reform proposals, the Ontario Law Commission released *Curriculum Modules in Ontario Law Schools: A Framework for Teaching about Violence against Women* in August 2012, a report that provided background information about domestic violence and curricular materials for a range of law school courses and programs, particularly Criminal Law, Family Law and Ethics and Professionalism.

Critiques of legal intervention in spousal violence cases: Systemic issues?

Although many judges and lawyers have welcomed the new domestic violence courts, some analyses of spousal violence have suggested that spousal violence needs to be addressed as a systemic issue, rather than focusing only on the individual circumstances of women who claim to have experienced violence. For example, see BC Task Force on Family Violence, *Is Anyone Listening?* (Victoria, BC: Minister of Women's Equality, 1992). Many researchers have argued that it is especially necessary to take account of gender in addressing the problem of spousal violence:

> A gender-neutral approach to violence assumes that men and women hold equal power within the family and society, and fails to acknowledge women's lower economic status or their unequal share of unpaid caring labour. The presence or absence of another income earner in the household is one of the key factors in determining whether women enter or exit poverty. Women attempting to leave violent relationships, therefore, face a much greater fear of poverty and homelessness than men. (METRAC & Woman Abuse Council of Toronto, *No Cherries Grow on our Trees*, A Social Policy Research Paper for the Take Action Project to Address Women's Poverty and Violence Against Women, funded by United Way Toronto (Toronto, 2008) at 27)

In addition, some researchers have argued that women's experiences of spousal violence, and their hopes for their families, need to be considered in designing responses that address family well-being. For example, Linda MacLeod argued:

> Even though different governments are attempting to make more effective use of peace bonds and restraining orders, which instruct batterers to stay away from their wives, battered women and shelter workers spoke of the fear of retribution many women experience if they report the battering to the police....
>
> Criminal justice services are only one part of a wide constellation of service options which should be available to battered women. Battered women share with all of us a human urge to hope.... As a result, some battered women may reject what they see as short-term solutions which may dash their long-term hopes. Therefore, the arrest option and reliance on the criminal justice system is, to *some* women, a very unpalatable solution because they perceive that the intervention of the law will increase the chances of the marriage ending. In addition, the law gives her no assurance that the violence will end. Most battered women want help which will give them long-term hope. (MacLeod, at 88–89)

See also "Stopping Family Violence: Steps along the Road" VIF *Transition* (September 1995) at 4–8.

In this context, moreover, Laureen Snider expressed concern about the extent to which some initiatives designed to combat spousal violence may have disparate impacts on members of disadvantaged communities:

> [T]here is no reason to conclude that arresting and charging more suspects is helpful to the women involved, or even that it represents the option she would have preferred. As always, the men arrested are not a representative sample of abusers — they are the abusers with the fewest resources and the least ability to resist. It is abundantly clear from self-report studies and other sources that poor men and natives are not the only, or even the most serious offenders against women. Mobilizing class bias (and probably racism as well) in the name of justice, *and of feminism*, is not a clever strategy. (Laureen Snider, "Feminism, Punishment, and the Potential of Empowerment" (1994) 9 CJLS 75 at 86–87)

How should governmental strategies respond to these criticisms? To what extent should legal intervention policies address individual or systemic aspects of this problem? To what extent does the Integrated Domestic Violence court respond to such critiques?

SPOUSAL VIOLENCE AND THE LEGAL SYSTEM: A CASE STUDY

Contextualizing spousal violence in relation to litigation at separation

The issue of spousal violence is particularly relevant for family law in the context of separation. It may be a catalyst that results in the separation of adult partners, or provide the impetus for one parent (usually a woman) to seek protection in a women's shelter for herself and her children. In this context, "fault" is generally irrelevant in determining entitlement to divorce or corollary relief.

However, there are a few situations in which issues of spousal violence may be considered. One of these is a spouse's application for exclusive possession of the matrimonial home, pursuant to section 24 of the *Family Law Act*. Regardless of the title to the matrimonial home, either spouse may bring an application for an order of exclusive possession, and section 24(3) defines the factors to be considered by a court in making any such order, including the following:

- the "best interests" of the children affected (further defined in s 4(4));
- the financial position of the spouses;
- the availability of other suitable and affordable accommodation; and
- "any violence committed by a spouse against the other spouse or the children."

Although these issues will be considered in more detail in Chapter Six, this section focuses on a case study of pleadings and affidavits in *Behrendt v Behrendt* (6 March 1990, Ottawa, unreported), a case decided two decades ago, in which a wife initiated an unsuccessful claim for interim exclusive possession of the family home, based in part on spousal violence and abuse. In reviewing this case, consider whether there were other legal strategies available to the wife. To what extent might her claim have succeeded in the Integrated Domestic Violence court?

Behrendt v Behrendt: A Case Study

In this case, the wife claimed that the husband's anti-social behaviour created psychological violence, and that there were also some incidents of physical violence on the part of the husband towards one of the two teenaged daughters living in the home. The husband had been on disability leave from his employment for about six years, and there was some evidence that he was suffering from depression and other unspecified psychiatric problems. Three months after the wife's application was rejected by the court, however, the husband murdered his wife and then took his own life, a major tragedy for the family involved.

In addition to being a tragedy, the evidence in this case, all provided by way of affidavits by the parties, provides a good opportunity to explore some of the underlying assumptions about the nature of violence, and the ways in which legal principles intersect with them in family law cases concerning spousal violence. As will be seen, some concerns about this case were later forwarded to the Attorney General by representatives of women's shelters in Ontario.

THE WIFE'S CLAIM

Pamella Behrendt filed an application for divorce, based on a period of separation, and also on the basis of her husband's cruelty, described as follows:

> The Respondent refuses to communicate and interact with the Petitioner.
> The Respondent locks himself into his son's bedroom which has two locks

on the door and avoids contact with the wife and the parties' two daughters. The Respondent remains in his pyjamas most of the day and does not maintain his personal [hygiene]. The respondent's behaviour has caused extreme tension in the household which affects the Petitioner and the parties' daughters.

At the time of this application, the wife's affidavit stated that the parties had been married for 21 years, and they had three children, including a son who was at university, and two daughters who were in Grades 12 and 13.

In addition to an application for divorce, the wife submitted an application for an order for interim exclusive possession, pursuant to section 24 of the *Family Law Act*, claiming the following:

(a) It is in the best interest of the children that the wife and children remain in the matrimonial home to allow the children to complete their schooling;

(b) The costs of maintaining the matrimonial home are minimal and there is no alternative accommodation available to the wife which she can afford in addition to supporting herself and the two daughters of the marriage; and

(c) The husband has acted violently towards one of the children. The father's behaviour towards the Petitioner and towards the children is adversely affecting the children. The children's performance at school is suffering and the children are ashamed to bring friends into their home because of their father's behaviour.

Both the wife and the husband filed affidavits in relation to this claim, and the wife filed a response to the husband's affidavit. In addition, the parties' son, who was no longer living at home, filed an affidavit generally supporting the husband's assertions.

THE WIFE'S AFFIDAVIT

The wife deposed that she was a registered nurse earning about $37,000 per year and was in her mid-50s. She stated that her husband was a few years older and that he was in receipt of a psychiatric disability pension of about $14,000 annually, which he had been receiving for six years after leaving his position as a university researcher (he held a Ph.D. degree). The wife also deposed that she had approached her husband's physician but that she had been advised that it was not possible to commit the respondent to a hospital. She also claimed that her husband had recently left the family home for five days, and that he took the family car with him and did not return with it, so that she had been required to rent a car in order to travel to work. She then stated:

> 16. When the Respondent left the matrimonial [home] in January he also took over $1000 from our joint account without telling me. He has not returned the monies to our bank account. The Respondent does not communicate with me except to be abusive to me or to criticize the girls. The Respondent's behaviour and my concern for my daughters' well-being is causing me extreme distress. I am not able to sleep well at night and I am reaching the point where I do not know whether I will be able to continue functioning in my employment as a registered nurse.

The wife's affidavit also explained that she had attempted to tolerate her husband's behaviour, although she had herself needed psychiatric help and she had also taken an overdose of sleeping pills three years earlier. She claimed that her husband had poisoned her son's mind with accusations, including accusations of adultery on her part, and that she had tolerated such behaviour in order to keep the family together. However, she indicated that her recent awareness of her daughters' suffering made her realize that the situation could not continue. And she indicated that her husband could use his pension income to relocate, as he did not contribute it to the household expenses. She also asserted that, as the matrimonial home did not have a mortgage, it was preferable for her to remain there with her daughters, where she would be able to provide adequate financial support for herself and the daughters on the basis of her own income. She also claimed that it would be disruptive for the girls to move at that stage of their high school studies. The wife also filed a detailed financial statement showing that her income was just sufficient to meet her expenses.

THE HUSBAND'S AFFIDAVIT

The husband filed an affidavit in response to the wife's motion, as well as a motion for interim support and interim occupation rent, in the event that the wife's motion for exclusive possession were to succeed. He identified his health problems as including coronary disease and hypertension, and indicated that he was unemployable. He confirmed his gross income (as the amount stated by the Petitioner), but also identified deductions so that his net annual income was only $11,440 — although he also claimed that the Petitioner could well afford other accommodation as her gross income was "almost 40,000" per year (at para 10). He indicated as well that a good portion of his income was used to pay for medications, that he purchased his own food, and that he also paid half of some of the household expenses as well as his son's rent and some recent credit card expenses for the Petitioner of more than $1000 (at para 7). He also stated:

> 8. If I am ordered to leave the matrimonial home, I have absolutely nowhere to go. In view of my income and expenses, I cannot afford to rent an apartment on my own without the financial support of the petitioner.

> 9. I categorically and absolutely deny ever having been in any way abusive to the children. This is a lie fabricated by the petitioner in order to evict me from the home since I have refused to leave voluntarily. [The respondent also claimed that the petitioner acted cruelly towards him, and attached a photocopy of a news clipping that he claimed that the petitioner had affixed to her bedroom door, which stated "What women want: if all else fails, a dead husband." He also indicated that he had slapped his younger daughter after she had called him vulgar and obscene names, that he referred to this daughter using a nickname that she disliked, that both daughters were excelling at school, and that the car had been sold to pay "family expenses" (at paras 12–17 and 20).]

> 19. I acknowledge that as the petitioner and I are separated, it is inevitable that the matrimonial home must be sold. I would consent that it be listed for sale immediately with a closing date following the end of the children's school year. If there are sufficient sale proceeds, this will assist

me in finding alternative accommodation. However, until the home is sold, I wish to remain there. The petitioner and I have separate rooms, and our involvement with one another is civil. We do not even quarrel. I do not have meals with her. In fact, we hardly see each other in the course of a day....

21. The petitioner and I have lived in the matrimonial home together for 18 years. I can see no reason why we cannot continue the status quo for the few months remaining before the home can be sold.

Other than the news clipping referred to in his affidavit, the Respondent did not file any financial information. The wife's financial statement indicated that the matrimonial home's value was $120,000.

THE SON'S AFFIDAVIT

The parties' son also filed an affidavit, in which he declared that although he did not wish to appear to be taking sides in this action, he wanted to clarify some inaccuracies in his mother's affidavit (at para 2). He indicated that he was a university student and in a co-op program, and that he had arranged to do a co-op term in Ottawa so that he could live at home. However, he stated that:

5. Contrary to my expectations, my mother forced me, through harassment, out of the home. She berated me almost continuously about trivial matters. She would scream at me incessantly. Her screaming was unprovoked. Eventually, she started telling me that she wished I would move out and that for her I no longer existed. I felt I had no alternative but to leave the home. My mother was making my life there intolerable. She obviously wanted me out of the house, so I left.

The son's affidavit indicated that he was living in a room at the YMCA, and that his father had paid the required rent in advance for this accommodation. He also deposed that he returned to the family home about once a week to collect his personal belongings and that his mother did not ask where he was living, but only commented on how long it was taking him to move out (at paras 4–7). He also deposed:

8. There is no hostility or aggression in the household. My father is a quiet man who spends most of his waking hours reading. From my own observations, if he tries to talk things over with my mother, she ignores him and stares at the television set.

The son also deposed that he had never observed any abusive behaviour on the part of his father in relation to his sisters, that he was never embarrassed to invite friends to the home when he lived there, and that the locks on the door to his bedroom related to a need to prevent his sister from destroying his computer there (at paras 9–11). Finally, he stated:

12. The level of stress claimed by my mother as existing in the household is greatly exaggerated. My sisters are functioning well in that home. The situation there has been about the same as it has always been.

THE WIFE'S AFFIDAVIT IN REPLY

The wife's reply affidavit challenged the husband's claims for expenses, stating that his medications were 80% covered by insurance at the university where he had worked (at para 3); that she did not refuse to allow him to share meals with the family; that he had not contributed to household expenses as he claimed for some months; and that if he had paid his son's rent, his son was working in the co-op program and could well afford to repay his father (at para 4). She also asserted that he must have had some-where to live when he left the home for five days, that he would likely have obtained about $6,000 on the sale of the car, and that he had gold bars and other monies available to him (at para 5). The wife also provided further details of physical violence to the daughters, including giving one a black eye, kicking her in the leg and twisting a wrist (at para 6) and verbal abuse and belittling (at para 7). She specifically rejected her husband's claim that she had posted the news clipping on her bedroom door, stating that it was her husband who had done so (at para 8); and she provided a lengthy explanation of her daughter's version of the events that resulted in her husband slapping the daughter as well as explaining the context of his nick-names that the daughter found insulting (at paras 9 and 10). After respond-ing to other claims on the part of her husband, the wife also indicated that she did not wish to sell the home, as suggested by the husband's affidavit, because she did not think that she would be able to rent other accommoda-tion for herself and her daughters as a sole support parent (at para 14). In addition, she alleged that he was probably planning to move because he was hoarding financial resources (at para 16). Finally, she responded to her son's affidavit, and in particular, asserted that he was unaware of circum-stances in the home as he had not lived there for some time, concluding:

> 22. I fail to see how [the son] can give an accurate statement about the stress in our household when he has not been present in the past sev-eral months when the stress and tension in our house has escalated to the point where it is intolerable.

> 23. I am disappointed to see that the Respondent has involved [our son] at all in this matter. Both of my daughters volunteered to give affidavit evidence to state that they want their father to leave the matrimonial home and that they find the situation in our home unbearable; however I do not want to involve them if it is at all possible.

Having regard to this affidavit evidence, what factors were likely to have been most significant for consideration by the motions judge in the context of the factors outlined in section 24 of the *Family Law Act*? How should the motions judge assess the inconsistency in the claims presented by the mother, and by the father and the son? Who has the onus of proof in such an application?

THE MOTION COURT'S DECISION
The decision of the motions judge, Justice Charron, was quite short:

> Undoubtedly it has become very difficult for the parties to live under the same roof. Nevertheless, the material presented on the motion does not, in my view, warrant granting exclusive possession of the matrimonial home to the applicant. The Court should only exercise its power to make such an Order with great care. The nature of the allegations, the contradictory view presented by one of the children and the age of the children living in the home all militate against the granting of such an order. The motion is

dismissed. In all the circumstances, each party should bear his or her own costs. [The husband's motion was also dismissed.]

A Critique of the Case

As noted, the case had a tragic end just three months later, when the husband murdered his wife with a chain saw and then took his own life with a hunting knife. See Charles Lewis & Mike Blanchfield, "Man Kills Wife, then Takes his own Life", *Ottawa Citizen* (12 June 1990). In this context, staff members from two women's shelters forwarded a letter to the Attorney General, criticizing the lack of protection for women in situations of violence. In examining these criticisms, consider the extent to which they can be refuted. Does this case reflect a failure of the justice system?

> This case is a tragedy.... However, we are not writing to lay blame at anyone's feet. There are no guarantees that the murder would not have been carried out and we assume that the affidavit evidence before Her Honour Judge Charron was not any more remarkable than in other similar cases.
>
> Nonetheless, ... [we] have several concerns with the assumptions underlying Judge Charron's decision to deny the Motion.
>
> First, she is not at all clear as to what she means by "the nature of the allegations." Presumably because there was little overt violence reported, the allegations were not viewed as being seriously disruptive [an assumption that is contrary to much medical and psychological evidence about the negative impact on security interests of other family members].
>
> Second, Judge Charron places weight on the contradictory view of one child.... We did not think that judges could place any weight on evidence of persons who have not been in a position to observe anything first hand.
>
> Third, she takes into account "the ages of the children living at home".... [The two daughters were 17 and 18, and] we can only assume that she feels that teenage children are not entitled to live in an environment that is free from violence, including psychological violence....
>
> We feel that these same assumptions are held by other members of the judiciary and are woven throughout the decisions that on a daily basis, deny families access to violence free homes....
>
> Clearly the judge felt that the situation was "very difficult" but that the balance of convenience lay in favour of keeping the seething negativity under one roof, rather than removing the source of the tension until such time as the home could be sold and the proceeds divided. Why does the potential harm (here fatal) weigh so little in comparison to the inconvenience of having one party move out of the house temporarily? ... Is this policy implicit in the legislation or it is a judicial creation? If the judge was concerned about the contradictory evidence why didn't she adjourn the matter and order the parties to conduct cross-examination on the affidavits?
>
> [In addition, the letter suggested concern about the absence of affidavits from the two daughters, and queried whether the wife's lawyer may have dissuaded her from preparing them because of judicial disdain for lawyers who involve children in such cases.] Should lawyers have to worry about judges dealing with their clients on a punitive basis?
>
> ... We write because the legal system failed that family and the assumptions that underly that failure continue to occur every day in court rooms throughout this province.... (Letter dated 18 November 1990 to Ontario's Attorney General, signed by representatives of two women's shelters. The letter was copied to the federal Minister of Justice, the Canadian Judicial Centre and to Professor Mossman.)

Notes and Questions

Decision making in relation to the "risk of violence"

In the context of affidavit evidence, which had not been subjected to cross-examination, were there any factors in this case that suggested that the situation was potentially more volatile than merely the difficulty for the parties living under the same roof? Would Justice Charron's conclusion have been the same without the son's affidavit? To what extent might affidavits from the daughters have been significant in achieving a different outcome? How should lawyers respond when clients wish to protect children from giving evidence against the other parent? Were there unstated reasons for concern for the husband's well-being in the event that the motion was granted?

In this context, some scholars argue that lawyers and judges (and other professionals) need to be alert to the "silencing" of victims of violence:

> Women who have been the targets of violence by their male partners in the home ... have many reasons for keeping silent about the violence. Violence against women involves actions on the part of the perpetrator that exert control over the target of the violence. Enforcing silence about the violence is a part of that control. The silence of the woman who has been a target of violence may be ensured by direct threats and warnings not to reveal the occurrence of the violence to others....
>
> [At the same time, women] are expected to be able to speak about the violence perpetrated against them when the main way in which our society deals with violence is by silence. Violence against women is something that is actively concealed, not only by the targets of that violence, but by its perpetrators, by family members, by agencies that deal with those individuals and by society as a whole.... (Hilary Astor, "The Weight of Silence: Talking about Violence in Family Mediation" in Margaret Thornton, ed, *Public and Private: Feminist Legal Debates* (Melbourne: Oxford University Press, 1995) 174 at 185–186)

Were there any suggestions in the *Behrendt* affidavits that the wife was concerned about breaking her silence with respect to the emotional and psychological abuse she experienced? How can lawyers and judges respond to "silences" in women's stories? As Astor noted, perpetrators of violence "write the script" for mediation (or litigation) by threats or beatings in the car park so that the "instruction not to tell the mediator about the violence is part of the violence."

Evidence in relation to spousal violence: The *Lavallee* case

In 1990, the same year in which the motion was heard in the *Behrendt* case, the Supreme Court of Canada reviewed the admissibility of evidence of the battered woman syndrome in relation to a woman charged with the murder of her cohabiting male partner. In *R v Lavallee*, [1990] 1 SCR 852, Wilson J concluded (at paras 871–73) that expert evidence of the syndrome was essential to assessing the woman's culpability in criminal law:

> Expert evidence on the psychological effect of battering on wives and common law partners must, it seems to me, be both relevant and necessary in

the context of the present case. How can the mental state of the appellant be appreciated without it? The average member of the public (or of the jury) can be forgiven for asking: Why would a woman put up with this kind of treatment? Why should she continue to live with such a man? How could she love a partner who beat her to the point of requiring hospitalization? We would expect the woman to pack her bags and go. Where is her self-respect? Why does she not cut loose and make a new life for herself? Such is the reaction of the average person confronted with the so-called "battered wife syndrome." We need help to understand it and help is available from trained professionals.

The gravity, indeed, the tragedy of domestic violence can hardly be overstated. Greater media attention to this phenomenon in recent years has revealed both its prevalence and its horrific impact on women from all walks of life. Far from protecting women from it the law historically sanctioned the abuse of women within marriage as an aspect of the husband's ownership of his wife and his "right" to chastise her. One need only recall the centuries old law that a man is entitled to beat his wife with a stick "no thicker than his thumb."

Laws do not spring out of a social vacuum. The notion that a man has a right to "discipline" his wife is deeply rooted in the history of our society. The woman's duty was to serve her husband and to stay in the marriage at all costs "till death do us part" and to accept as her due any "punishment" that was meted out for failing to please her husband. One consequence of this attitude was that "wife battering" was rarely spoken of, rarely reported, rarely prosecuted, and even more rarely punished. Long after society abandoned its formal approval of spousal abuse, tolerance of it continued and continues in some circles to this day.

Fortunately, there has been a growing awareness in recent years that no man has a right to abuse any woman under any circumstances. Legislative initiatives designed to educate police, judicial officers and the public, as well as more aggressive investigation and charging policies all signal a concerted effort by the criminal justice system to take spousal abuse seriously. However, a woman who comes before a judge or jury with the claim that she has been battered and suggests that this may be a relevant factor in evaluating her subsequent actions still faces the prospect of being condemned by popular mythology about domestic violence....

These comments occurred in the context of a challenge to a conviction for murder on the part of a woman who argued her position as a victim of violence in defending this charge. See also discussion in the Supreme Court of Canada in *R v Malott*, [1998] 1 SCR 123 and in *R v Ryan*, 2013 SCC 3. Although the context is clearly quite different from the *Behrendt* case, are there aspects of Justice Wilson's reasons that could have assisted the motions judge to better understand the context of the application for interim exclusive possession of the matrimonial home? How should evidence of family relationships, especially when they appear to be dysfunctional, be used in court proceedings about spousal violence? What is the relationship between family autonomy and state intervention in this context?

Statutory reforms about spousal violence in other Canadian provinces

In several Canadian provinces, legislation has been enacted to provide for civil actions to respond to problems of violence. For example, such reforms have been adopted in Saskatchewan, Prince Edward Island, Yukon,

Alberta, and Manitoba. See *Victims of Domestic Violence Act*, SS 1994, c V-6.02; *Victims of Family Violence Act*, SPEI 1996, c 47; *Family Violence Prevention Act*, SY 1997, c 12; *Protection Against Family Violence Act*, SA 1998, c P-19.2; and *Domestic Violence and Stalking Prevention, Protection and Compensation Act*, SM 1998, c 41.

Consider the following assessment of legislative reforms concerning civil actions in relation to spousal violence in Alberta and Saskatchewan: to what extent would such reforms have been useful in the *Behrendt* case?

> Across Canada, the most significant innovation introduced by civil domestic violence legislation has been the initial *ex parte* order. These orders, referred to as emergency intervention or protection orders..., may be issued where necessary by reason of seriousness or urgency for the immediate protection of the victim. The legislation in both [Saskatchewan and Alberta] provides that initial orders can be applied for without notice to the respondent at any time of day or night either in person or by telephone through designated agents [such as police.] In Saskatchewan, the majority of orders are issued outside court hours, and all are applied for by telephone, most often from the home of the claimant. In both provinces, applications are often made by police on behalf of victims to justices of the peace or provincial court judges having some specialized training in the dynamics of domestic violence.... Among other possibilities, emergency intervention or protection orders may grant exclusive possession of the family home and proscribe contact with the victim and children....
>
> The legislation has the potential to increase the options and material resources available to individual women, particularly in relation to the exclusive possession of the family residence, and to make such relief more accessible and immediate. The legislation can also reinforce the view that violence within the "private" familial context is unacceptable. However, there are limitations as well.... The legislation has the effect of privatizing the immediate costs of violence by allocating them to an individual respondent. As with a criminal response, the focus is on crisis intervention and on acts of violence between individuals, reinforcing a dominant norm of individual responsibility and obscuring the social norms and structures that must be addressed in order to end violence against women.... [The legislation also reinforces gender neutrality in relation to violence in families.] ...
>
> [Moreover, as a result of] the *ex parte* nature of the application and the possessory nature of the relief requested, reviewing courts have required a high threshold for meeting the criteria for emergency protection and intervention orders. JPs and judges have generally looked for a precipitating event that can be construed as creating a crisis or emergency, with an emphasis on the existence of discrete, isolated acts or threats of physical violence, rather than the cumulative impact of past violence or the ongoing coercive or controlling conduct that is typical of battering relationships.... (Jennifer Koshan & Wanda Wiegers, "Theorizing Civil Domestic Violence Legislation in the Context of Restructuring: A Tale of Two Provinces" (2007) 19 CJWL 145 at 146–148 and 174)

Despite the limitations of such statutes, are there reasons to consider adopting civil actions for spousal violence in provinces such as Ontario?

Tort actions in relation to spousal violence

Compare the civil actions for spousal violence to tort actions. For example, in January 2012, an Ottawa man was ordered to pay his ex-wife $65,000 in general and aggravated damages for fracturing her wrist during an altercation. In *Shaw v Brunelle*, 2012 ONSC 590, the court ordered $15,000 for aggravated damages in addition to general damages of $50,000 for pain and suffering, because the battery occurred in the context of a spousal relationship. Mr. Shaw had been acquitted in relation to a criminal charge of assault causing bodily harm to his wife in 2008, one year after the parties' marriage, but the family law court held that, on a balance of probabilities, the assault had occurred. In addition to ending the marriage, the assault permanently impaired the functioning of the wife's wrist, causing her chronic pain, and it also contributed to her anxiety and depression. The court also awarded additional costs, including future care costs.

According to one family lawyer quoted in the press, this decision reflects the views of newer judges appointed to the family law courts who have had significant judicial education about domestic violence. This press report also reviewed a number of recent cases in which violent spouses (all male in the survey) were subjected to such awards in the range of four figures to low five figures. For example, in *Tseng v Tseng*, [2007] OJ No 1918 (Sup Ct), the court awarded $275,000 to the wife (a jury award), which included general, aggravated and punitive damages for assault ($40,000), false imprisonment ($70,000), and intentional infliction of mental suffering ($165,000). The wife also was awarded $112,404 for her legal costs: see Cristin Schmitz, "Ex-Wife Awarded $65,000", *The Lawyers Weekly* (17 February 2012).

To what extent is it appropriate to join tort claims to family law matters? What are the advantages and disadvantages of joining such claims to family law proceedings?

Violence against women and the long-gun registry

In 2012, the federal government enacted *An Act to amend the Criminal Code and the Firearms Act*, SC 2012, c 6 (Royal Assent April 2012), which confirmed that the Government of Canada was entitled to eliminate the long-gun registry and to prevent future collection of data. Prior to this enactment, Québec had initiated legal proceedings to prevent destruction of data that was vital to the creation of a provincial long gun registry in Québec. In *Quebec (PG) v Canada*, 2012 JQ No 8319, the Québec Superior Court held that the data did not belong solely to the federal government because it had been established in partnership with the province. The court noted that evidence had been presented showing that, since the creation of the registry, there had been a drop in gun-related crime, homicides, and suicides in Québec. The court also held that the legislation constituted "an abusive act of criminal law jurisdiction to encroach on a domain of provincial jurisdiction." On 17 September 2012, the Public Safety Minister announced that it would appeal this decision.

In February 2013, the Québec government tabled gun control legislation to establish a firearm registry in the province, and the Bill was widely supported across party lines in the Québec legislature. There was also widespread public support, and it was estimated that the federal registry had cost Québec taxpayers $250 million: see *The Globe and Mail* (20 February 2013) A6. However, in June 2013, the Québec Court of Appeal allowed the federal government's appeal, concluding that the federal government had the power to create the registry and the power to destroy it unilaterally: [2013] JQ No 6676.

In Ontario, Toronto City Council passed a motion urging the provincial government to request Ottawa for its records on gun owners in the province, noting that there were more than 287,000 registered firearms in the GTA. In addition, the Barbra Schlifer Commemorative Clinic launched a *Charter* challenge, arguing that the federal *Act* contravened sections 7 and 15, and was not saved by section 1, because the legislation was likely to cause harm (especially physical harm) to women who are most often the victims of domestic violence. The City of Toronto obtained intervenor status to support this application (see *Barbra Schlifer Commemorative Clinic v HMQ Canada*, 2012 ONSC 4539), but the Clinic's application was eventually rejected: see *Barbra Schlifer Commemorative Clinic v Canada*, 2014 ONSC 5140.

In the context of other proposals for reforms to prevent domestic violence in Canada, how should this federal government action relating to the long-gun registry be interpreted? Although the courts in both Québec and Ontario confirmed that the issue was a matter of policy, and not a matter of constitutional law, what policy reasons supported the government's refusal to transfer data to the provinces?

Abused women and disadvantaged communities

> While violence cuts across all social classes and categories, women and girls from marginalized communities are more likely to experience violence.... Constructed as "others' who are not deserving of respect, not fully autonomous, and not full citizens, women marginalized by race or disability, by poverty, by immigration status, by age or Aboriginal identity experience higher rates of violence. (*No Cherries Grow on our Trees* at 27)

Recent literature on domestic violence reflects a need to examine different contexts in which women may experience violence in intimate relationships. For example, a national study of violence against women in Canada focused on differences for older women, women living in poverty, women with disabilities, rural women, lesbians, women of official language minorities, women of colour, young women, immigrant and refugee women, and domestic workers. In addition, the study looked at the situation of Inuit and Aboriginal women: see Canadian Panel on Violence Against Women, *Changing the Landscape: Ending Violence — Achieving Equality: Final Report* (Ottawa: Minister of Supply and Services, 1993).

Concerns about violence in relation to Aboriginal women have been documented in a number of studies, many of which link the issues of violence to broader community issues and Aboriginal conceptions of (extended) families:

- According to a 2007 report, the incidence of intimate violence in some northern Aboriginal communities may be as high as 75–90%: see Ontario Native Women's Association and Ontario Federation of Indian Friendship Centres, "A Strategic Framework to End Violence against Aboriginal Women" (2007).

- Statistics Canada reported that Aboriginal women experienced more severe forms of violence, including higher rates of lethal violence, greater physical injuries and higher rates of sexual assaults: see Statistics Canada, "Measuring Violence against Women: Statistical Trends 2006" at 64. See also "Aboriginal Women and Violence: Building Safe and Healthy Families and Communities" (report of a policy forum, Ottawa 2006); and Sharlene Frank, *Family Violence in Aboriginal Communities: A First Nations Report* (Victoria, BC: Minister of Women's Equality, 1992).

Studies have also documented the fears documented by immigrant women who have experienced violence in their homes, and particularly their worries about involvement with the police or with immigration authorities — and the possibility of deportation. As a result, researchers have concluded that the criminal justice system does not always serve these women victims of spousal violence at all well. See Dianne Martin & Janet Mosher, "Unkept Promises: Experiences of Immigrant Women with the Neo-Criminalization of Wife Abuse" (1995) 8 CJWL 3; and Susan McDonald with Pamela Cross, "Women's Voices Being Heard: Responsive Lawyering 1" (2001) 16 JL & Soc Pol'y 207.

How should legal policies concerning violence be formulated in relation to women in these differing situations?

A report in Ontario, for example, recommended that "government ministries may need to change their funding programs and structures to be more flexible, creative, and responsive in how support is provided to Northern communities [including Aboriginal communities]" (Joint Committee on Domestic Violence, *Working Toward a Seamless Community and Justice Response to Domestic Violence: A Five-Year Plan for Ontario* (Toronto: Ministry of the Attorney General, 1999) recommendation no 2).

The Joint Committee was formed to respond to recommendations arising from the inquest into the death of Arlene May by her estranged boyfriend, Randy Iles, who then killed himself. According to the report (at iv), the concept of "seamlessness" was central to the inquest recommendations — that is, "that individual domestic violence initiatives must be coordinated and integrated into a unified plan, and that each sector of the response system must work in concert with the others."

Additional Resources

Nicholas Bala, "Spousal Abuse and Children of Divorce: A Differentiated Approach?" (1996) 13 Can J Fam L 215.

Karen Busby, Jennifer Koshan & Wanda Wiegers, "Civil Domestic Violence Legislation in the Prairie Provinces: A Comparative Legal Analysis" in Jane Ursel, Leslie M Tutty & Janice Lemaistre, eds, *What's Law Got to Do With It? The Law, Specialized Courts and Domestic Violence in Canada* (Toronto: Cormorant Books, 2008).

Diane Dooley, "Constructing Nicole: Gender, Discourse and Victimization/ Criminalization in *R v. Ryan*" (MA Thesis, Saint Mary's University, 2013).

Susan Harris & Deborah Sinclair, "Holding the Big Picture: Working in the Best Interests of Children Exposed to Woman Abuse: Some Thoughts on Furthering Child Welfare and VAW Collaboration" (Winter 2002–3) 12:1&2 Education Wife Assault Newsletter 1.

Rosanna Langer, "Male Domestic Abuse: The Continuing Contrast Between Women's Experiences and Juridical Responses" (1995) 10:1 CJLS 65.

Lene Madsen, "A Fine Balance: Domestic Violence, Screening, and Family Mediation" (2012) 30:3 Can Fam LQ 343.

Anne McGillivray & Brenda Comaskey, *Black Eyes All of the Time: Intimate Violence, Aboriginal Women, and the Justice System* (Toronto: University of Toronto Press, 1999).

Ronagh McQuigg, "The Canadian Supreme Court and Domestic Violence: *R v Ryan*" (2013) 21 Fem Leg Stud 185.

Marina Morrow, Olena Hankivsky & Colleen Varcoe, "Women and Violence: The Effects of Dismantling the Welfare State" (2004) 24:3 Critical Social Policy 358.

Ruthann Robson, "Lavender Bruises: Intra-Lesbian Violence, Law, and Lesbian Legal Theory" (1990) 20 Golden Gate UL Rev 567.

Martha Shaffer, "The Battered-Woman Syndrome Revisited: Some Complicating Thoughts Five Years After *R v. Lavallee*" (1997) 47 UTLJ 1.

Elizabeth Sheehy, *Defending Battered Women on Trial: Lessons from the Transcripts* (Vancouver: UBC Press, 2013).

Leslie Tutty & Jennifer Koshan, "Calgary's Specialized Domestic Violence Court: An Evaluation of a Unique Model" (2012–2013) 50 Alta L Rev 731.

Roberta L Valente, "Addressing Domestic Violence: The Role of the Family Law Practitioner" (1995) 29:1 Fam LQ 187.

Wanda Wiegers, "Compensation for Wife Abuse: Empowering Victims?" (1994) 28 UBC L Rev 247.

Wanda Wiegers and Fiona Douglas, *Civil Domestic Violence Legislation in Saskatchewan* (Regina: Canadian Plains Research Centre, 2007).

V.
PROTECTION FOR VULNERABLE ELDERS: RESPONSIBILITIES OF FAMILIES AND THE STATE

That older adults may have special needs and special claims on society is undeniable. However, elder abuse legislation may reinforce social stereotypes of older persons as frail, vulnerable, and less worthy because of social, legal, physical, or cognitive incompetence. This mistaken view may invite predation and contribute to an environment conducive to abuse and exploitation. Negative stereotyping, in other words, creates disrespect and disrespect contributes to the dynamics of abuse and exploitation. (Manitoba Law Reform Commission, *Adult Protection and Elder Abuse* (Winnipeg: Manitoba Law Reform Commission, 1999) at 2)

ELDER ABUSE: AN EMERGING PROBLEM

Increasing numbers and diversity among older Canadians

Issues about elder abuse have become more prevalent as the proportion of the population over the age of 65 in Canada has increased. Although this proportion was about 8 percent in 1971, it had grown to 15.3 percent in 2013 and is projected to be close to 25 percent by 2050. This trend to increasing proportions of older persons is also occurring in Europe and in Japan and Korea, while the proportion of younger persons is declining. These trends have significant policy challenges with respect to caregiving by families and in care facilities, and they may also create more issues of abuse: see Donna Lero, "Intergenerational Relations and Societal Change" (2014) 44:4 VIF *Transition* 9.

From a policy perspective, however, it is important not to assume that all elderly persons are the same. In a study that involved focus group discussions with 87 participants of "cultural" minorities (Aboriginals, lesbians, refugees or immigrants from Latvia, China, and Farsi-speaking women and Punjabi-speaking men, elder abuse survivors, and older adults with mood disorders living in care communities, as well as family caregivers of seniors with dementia, and a seniors' peer support group), the authors discovered different kinds of concerns about elder abuse among these "marginalized" older adults. They concluded that there may be a diversity of perceptions of elder abuse within ethnic groups, as well as diversity between groups, so that it is necessary to take into account how:

> Older adults are a heterogeneous group with varying backgrounds, concerns, and vulnerabilities. It is important, therefore, to not only focus on commonly accepted types of abuse that all persons could experience, but to also take into account cultural and ethnic differences and explore in detail how an older person defines elder abuse. Understanding the various perspectives of elder abuse is necessary to design measures to accurately assess the prevalence and determinants of elder abuse and to inform strategies for assessment, intervention, and prevention of this major social problem. (Jenny Ploeg, Lynne Lohfeld & Christine Walsh, "What is 'Elder Abuse'? Voices from the Margin: The Views of Underrepresented Canadian Older Adults" (2013) 25:5 Journal of Elder Abuse & Neglect 396 at 420)

Legal intervention and vulnerable elderly persons

Legal intervention to protect vulnerable elderly persons is a relatively recent development. In part, this trend is related to Canada's aging population and the social impact it is creating: the need for adequate income programs for seniors, the availability of home care and supported housing, and the potential demand on the health care system. Significantly, since much of the care for elderly persons is provided by family members, vulnerable elderly persons are at risk of violence from spouses, children and other caregivers.

According to the report of the Manitoba Law Reform Commission, recognition of elder abuse emerged in the late 1970s, after the law's earlier recognition of child abuse and wife battering. The report identified the negative image of aging and older persons, and its entrenchment in societal values and institutions. It also described how elder abuse is connected with multiple factors on four levels of interaction: personal factors (including perceptions of dependency on the part of the elderly); interpersonal factors (including unresolved past conflicts and power struggles); situational factors (including the overburdening of middle-aged caregivers); and socio-cultural factors (including ideologies of the elderly as non-contributing members of society).

In a small-scale study in Winnipeg, the report identified 75 cases of psychological abuse, 50 of financial abuse, 47 of physical abuse, and 13 of neglect. Significantly, a majority of the perpetrators of abuse involved males, but there were a large number of daughters who were abusers. As the study concluded, there is a need for more assessment of this phenomenon: "Daughters abusing mothers may be doing so for very different reasons than husbands abusing wives, and sons abusing parents". See Manitoba Law Reform Commission, *Adult Protection and Elder Abuse* (Winnipeg: Manitoba Law Reform Commission, 1999) at 7–9 and 13; and RM Gordon & SN Verdun-Jones, *Adult Guardianship Law in Canada* (Scarborough, ON: Carswell, 1992) at 51–52.

In 1989, a national survey was conducted, which included over 2,000 older Canadians. Four percent of all seniors living in private dwellings indicated that they had recently experienced some form of mistreatment. The most prevalent form of abuse was material: victims were persuaded to give away their money, to sign over title to their homes or relinquish control over their finances, or were subjected to undue influence or threats in making their wills. Physical violence was less frequent (0.5%). Among those in the category of "high risk" were people over 75 years old, those who depended on someone else for daily care, seniors who were isolated, and those with behaviours that included aggression, wandering, or incontinence. See "Education the Key To Stop Elder Abuse", VIF *Transition* (September 1995) at 12–13.

A more recent study for the Public Health Agency of Canada (under the Federal Elder Abuse Initiative) focused on gender issues in its analysis of elder abuse. Using statistics from 2006, the study reported that gender differences in the prevalence of family-related elder abuse had remained steady over the previous five year period, with the rate of such violence for older women 22 percent higher than the rate for older men. The study also reported that family members accused of violence against seniors tended to be men (79%), even though women are more likely to be informal caregivers of seniors. Since 30 percent of males involved in family violence were over 65 years of age, it seems that a significant portion of violence among the elderly is spousal violence, and the report suggested, among other recommendations for further research, the need to examine how the paradigms of domestic violence and elder abuse are incorporated into practices and training: see Peggy Edwards, *Elder Abuse in Canada: A Gender-Based Analysis* (Ottawa: Public Health Agency of Canada, Division of Aging and Seniors, 2012) at 15 and 33.

In this context, consider the ways in which issues about elder abuse may reveal connections to other topics in this chapter, for example, issues about caregiving in families (discussed earlier in relation to children) or abuse of vulnerable family members (similar to the issues of spousal violence examined above). In this context, how might legal intervention measures differ, depending on whether these concerns are characterized as issues about family caregiving or as concerns to protect vulnerable family members?

The definition of elder abuse

Elder abuse has been defined by Judith Wahl as any harm done to an older person that is violent or abusive, and that is caused by a person who has control or influence over the older person. Elder abuse includes

- [p]hysical abuse (physical assault, sexual assault, forced confinement);
- [f]inancial abuse (forced sales, stealing possessions or money, fraud, forgery, extortion, and the wrongful use of a Power of Attorney);
- [n]eglect (abandonment or withholding of food or health services, failing to give a dependent person what they need); and
- [m]ental abuse (humiliation, insults, threats, or "treating an older person like a child").

According to Judith Wahl, most elder abuse is caused by a family member, but elderly people may also be abused by health care or social service providers, both in the community and in care facilities. See Judith A Wahl, *Elder Abuse: The Hidden Crime* (Toronto: Advocacy Centre for the Elderly and Community Legal Education Ontario, 1991) at 2–3 and 6–7.

In addition, elder abuse may occur in retirement and nursing homes. In 2011, the government announced protection measures for residents of retirement homes (pursuant to the *Retirement Homes Act*, SO 2012, c 11, and O/Reg 165/11). However, although the Retirement Homes Regulatory Authority began issuing licences, the number of inspectors in November 2012 was twelve; at that time, there were 677 retirement homes, and the inspectors investigated only if a resident complained: see "Seniors Need Real Oversight", *Toronto Star* (19 November 2012) A18; Judith Wahl, "Good Idea But ...", *ACE Newsletter* (Fall/Winter 2011) 8–9; and Carol Goar, "Elder Abuse Hotline Dangles by Fraying Thread", *Toronto Star* (27 January 2012) A15.

Reports have also documented abuse and rape in nursing homes. See Moira Welsh & Jesse McLean, "Abuse, Rape uncovered in Nursing Homes", *Toronto Star* (17 November 2011). According to this press report, there were at least 125 abusive incidents in Ontario in the previous year. Moreover, some incidents may not be reported in a timely way. For example, the City of Cornwall pleaded guilty in October 2011 to a charge of retaliating against a nurse, who was working as a Health and Safety Officer for the City, and who had reported a case of suspected abuse to the government Ministry. In this case, an investigation revealed that the supervisor of the home had not reported the alleged abuse for sixteen days: see *ACE Newsletter* (Fall/Winter 2011) 2.

In response to some of these concerns, the Ontario government created the Long-Term Care Task Force which issued its report in May 2012: see *Long-Term Care Task Force on Resident Care and Safety: An Action Plan to Address Abuse and Neglect in Long-Term Care Homes*, online: <http://longtermcaretaskforce.ca/images/uploads/LTCFTReportEnglish.pdf>. See also Moira Welsh & Jesse McLean, "Ontario Nursing Homes face Sweeping Change", *Toronto Star* (16 May 2012) A1. In June 2013, moreover, the Advocacy Centre for the Elderly successfully obtained a commitment from the provincial government to conduct annual inspections (Resident Quality Inspections) of long-term care facilities: see *ACE Newsletter* 2013 (www.acelaw.ca). However, a press report in March 2015 revealed that the owner of a retirement home in Toronto, who had earlier been fined $10,000 and had repeatedly flouted orders from the regulatory agency, received a jail term of fifteen days, a further fine of $2500 and two years' probation. This decision was the first conviction for operating without a licence since the legislative changes in 2012: see *Toronto Star* (12 March 2015) GT1 and GT7.

The Advocacy Centre for the Elderly has also reported receiving hundreds of complaints about financial abuse of older adults, and ACE recommends that seniors obtain legal advice before signing legal documents or giving away property or permitting a family member to use the seniors' pensions — since voluntary transfers may be characterized as gifts and thus be regarded as permanent transfers that cannot be recovered: see Graham Webb, "Restitution as a Remedy for Financial Abuse", *ACE Newsletter* 2009 (www.acelaw.ca). A press report also recommended that seniors should not guarantee loans if they cannot afford to make gifts, and that such transactions may sometimes qualify as financial abuse: see Rob Carrick, "Grandparents: Practise some Tough Love", *The Globe and Mail* (16 October 2012) B12.

Notes and Questions

Caring for and protecting elders
Although it is important to remember that not all elderly persons are vulnerable adults, increasing age is a factor. See also Report of the Review of Advocacy for Vulnerable Adults, *You've Got a Friend: A Review of Advocacy in Ontario* (Toronto: Queen's Printer, 1987) at 52–57.

Consider the list of factors (above) defining elder abuse: to what extent do they reflect the definition of "children in need of protection" in the *Child and Family Services Act*? Are there differences as well as similarities?

• Do these factors reflect a view that is primarily related to state intervention based on vulnerability, as in relation to child protection?

• Are there needs for elderly persons, particularly in relation to care, that are also reflected in this list? Do these factors reflect any similarities to caregiving in relation to children?

To what extent does the law need to provide similar levels of care for children and for the elderly? Similar levels of protection for children, spouses and the elderly? How might a more coherent set of legal and public policies be designed? To what extent is it necessary to take account of "private" families and "public" policies in such situations?

Mandatory reporting of elder abuse

In making recommendations, the Manitoba Law Reform Commission addressed the issue of mandatory reporting of elder abuse, recognizing this requirement as a significant factor in relation to issues of child abuse. However, rather than extending the general requirements for public reporting, the commission recommended "that professional and care-providing organizations develop mandatory reporting standards for members as a matter of professional organization" (Commission's report, recommendation 24).

Why might it be appropriate to have reporting requirements for elder abuse and child abuse, but not for wife abuse? Is it appropriate to have requirements of public reporting for child abuse, but not for elder abuse? Why, or why not? (For a review of some arguments, see Advocacy Centre for the Elderly, "Mandatory Reporting of Elder Abuse", *ACE Newsletter* (Fall 1989) 1 at 5–6.)

Additional Resources

Stephen G Coughlan et al, "Mandatory Reporting of Suspected Elder Abuse and Neglect: A Practical and Ethical Evaluation" (1996) 19 Dal LJ 45.

Brian K Payne, *Crime and Elder Abuse: An Integrated Perspective* (Springfield, Ill: Charles C. Thomas, 2000).

Special Senate Committee on Aging, *Special Senate Committee on Aging Final Report: Canada's Aging Population: Seizing the Opportunity* (Ottawa: The Senate, April 2009).

Martin Turcotte & Grant Schellenberg, *A Portrait of Seniors in Canada 2006*, Catalogue No 89-519-XIE (Ottawa: Statistics Canada, February 2007).

World Health Organization, *The Toronto Declaration on the Global Prevention of Elder Abuse* (Geneva: WHO, 2002).

VI.
A FINAL COMMENT:
FAMILIES AND LEGAL INTERVENTION

[F]amilies and their communities need our focused attention, deepest compassion and greatest support to end the cycle of violence, and to mitigate the devastating impact that violence has on a family's capacity to fulfill its obligations of care and support to all members — especially those that are most vulnerable.

These many and varied care giving experiences reinforce the importance of recognizing and supporting carers of all types — this includes valuing parents at all stages in the family lifecycle, understanding the unique needs of families caring for aging persons or persons with a disability, and engaging with families experiencing or recovering from family violence. Similarly, we need to better support those wanting to achieve a healthier balance between caring and working, and to address the constraints that limit people's care giving and receiving choices. (*Families Count* at 139)

PART 3

Legal Regulation of Family Dissolution

5

Family Dissolution:
Principles and Processes

The phenomenon of divorce is a far more complex issue than generally believed. Furthermore, statistics pertaining to divorce are difficult to understand and, as a result, are frequently misinterpreted. A little over a third of all marriages in Canada end in divorce; the rates are higher in some provinces and higher for remarriages. Rates of dissolution for cohabitations are not available but are much higher than those for marriages....

It is often said that the family has become an outdated institution: High rates of divorce, cohabitation, and births to solo mothers are often used to justify this statement. Is this true? No.... *[F]amilies fulfill more functions now than was the case 50 years ago*. What is also true is that conjugal dissolution (marriage + cohabitation) *complicates* and *burdens* family life but does not destroy it.... (Anne-Marie Ambert, *Divorce: Facts, Causes & Consequences*, 3rd ed (Ottawa: Vanier Institute of the Family, 2009) at 25)

I.
THE CONTEXT FOR FAMILY DISSOLUTION

THE LEGAL CONTEXT

Legal regulation of family dissolution: Creating the "post-dissolution" family unit

As this comment suggests, statistics about marriage breakdown and termination of cohabiting relationships indicate that more than one-third of Canadian families must confront issues of family dissolution. Moreover, because of the significant societal functions that families fulfill, family dissolution often creates major emotional challenges for family members. In addition, however, family dissolution may result in significant problems for family economies, and create needs to alter arrangements for household work and caregiving arrangements for children or other dependants. In this context, the potential for family dissolution to result in ongoing dependency of some family members has resulted in extensive legal regulation of divorce and separation. Indeed, as earlier material in this book indicated, the law regulates family dissolution much more carefully than family formation and much more extensively than it regulates "intact" families.

As a snapshot of the context of family dissolution, consider these developments:

- **"No fault" divorce:** As in other western jurisdictions, in which divorce became widely available in the second half of the 20th century, Canadian divorce law permits adult partners to sever a marriage on the basis of the no fault ground of "marriage breakdown."

- **Emergence of post-divorce/separation family unit:** At the same time, legal regulation of family dissolution provides for continuing contact between parents in relation to their children and, at least to some extent, by creating ongoing financial obligations for the former spouses. And, many of these same arrangements for contact with children, as well as financial obligations, are also legally applicable to cohabiting partners who separate.

    In this way, the legal dissolution of a family by divorce or separation may also provide for the legal emergence of a new "post-divorce" or "post-separation" family unit.

- **Challenges with the creation of blended families:** Moreover, since many spouses who divorce or separate will re-partner, and often create "blended" families with children from former family relationships, ongoing responsibilities for caregiving and economic well-being in relation to former families may sometimes be quite complicated.

As this snapshot summary reveals, legal regulation of family dissolution relates to both marriage and cohabitation, it may continue long after the adult partners have separated or divorced, and it may create complications in relation to the formation of new family relationships.

In addition, there is one further complexity for the law's regulation of family dissolution. As you will recall from the earlier discussion of legal regulation of marriage, the formation of a family through marriage may occur within religious traditions, some of which involve precepts about its inviolability except at death. Indeed, such views of marriage prevented legal recognition of divorce or separation in English law until the late 19th century (see below), and some remnants of these views remain in some aspects of current divorce law in Canada.

Thus, as numerous law reform studies have argued, law must seek a balance between fostering and supporting families on one hand, and providing access to fair and efficient processes for recognizing that adult relationships have ended, while protecting children, on the other.

As you review the material in this chapter, therefore, it is necessary to be aware of these competing tensions in the law of family dissolution, and the ways in which they are balanced in relation to different issues concerning "post-dissolution families."

The history and current context for the law of divorce and separation

The starting point for Canadian divorce law was the English *Divorce and Matrimonial Causes Act*, 20 and 21 Vict, c 85 in 1857. This legislation transferred jurisdiction for divorce in England from the ecclesiastical courts to the new Divorce and Matrimonial Causes Court, and introduced divorce into English law. In many provinces in Canada, this statute provided authority for judicial divorce (that is, divorce granted by a court order), but in some provinces, including Québec and Newfoundland, a spouse seeking a divorce was required to obtain a private act of the federal Parliament (that is, Parliamentary divorce). Divorce law in Canada was also complicated by the fact that grounds for divorce varied somewhat from province to province. Clearly, such arrangements were often cumbersome, time-consuming, and expensive. Moreover, there were increasing concerns about "manufactured" evidence to prove the ground of adultery and its negative impact on the integrity of legal proceedings for divorce. (For details, see Christine Davies, *Family Law in Canada* (Scarborough, ON: Carswell, 1984); and JG Snell, *In the Shadow of the Law: Divorce in Canada 1900–1939* (Toronto: University of Toronto Press, 1991). For further historical data on Canadian divorce, see: Constance Backhouse, *Petticoats and Prejudice: Women and Law in Nineteenth Century Canada* (Toronto: Women's Press for the Osgoode Society, 1991) c 6.)

In this context, the federal Parliament engaged in consultation with respect to divorce reform, and eventually enacted Canada's first federal divorce legislation in 1968, the *Divorce Act*, SC 1968, c 24. This legislation is now of only historic interest, but it is significant that it provided two sets of grounds for divorce: one group of grounds related to fault, including adultery and cruelty, for example. However, in addition to fault grounds, the 1968 *Divorce Act* also permitted a court to grant a divorce on no-fault grounds. For example, a divorce could be granted if one spouse had deserted the other: the deserted spouse was entitled to divorce after three years, while the deserting spouse was required to wait five years. As will be clear, this legislation reveals one example of the "balance" noted above between the law's interest in preserving families and in providing appropriate processes to end marriages that have broken down.

Almost two decades later, the federal Parliament again enacted divorce legislation, repealing and replacing the 1968 Act with the *Divorce Act*, RSC 1985, c 3, which was proclaimed in force as Canada's divorce law in 1986.

Pursuant to this legislation, a number of procedural changes were enacted to make divorce proceedings more efficient and accessible.

In addition, this Act introduced only one ground for divorce in Canada: "marriage breakdown," and it permitted either one or both parties together to apply for divorce (thus recognizing that parties may be in agreement with respect to their wish to divorce).

However, the ground of "marriage breakdown" does not mean that divorce is "on consent" in Canada, because it is necessary for the applicant(s) to prove "marriage breakdown" in one of three ways: a one-year period of separation, or either adultery or cruelty.

Note again how the law seems to "balance" its interest in preserving families with the need to provide appropriate means of regulating the end of a marriage relationship. As you review the materials in this chapter, keep in mind how these competing goals are reflected in different ways in the law's regulation of family dissolution.

A brief note on divorce, separation, and "corollary relief"

The legal arrangements with respect to family dissolution are somewhat different for married couples and cohabiting couples. In addition, because some married couples separate without actually divorcing, their circumstances must also be taken into account.

In summary,

- In the divorce context, arrangements for sharing property, spousal and child support, custody and access of children, and other post-divorce arrangements are referred to as "corollary relief."

- However, divorce is available only to married persons, who include same-sex as well as opposite-sex couples in Canada. Cohabiting couples who separate have no access to divorce.

- Cohabiting couples who separate may also be entitled to many of the same legal arrangements with respect to these "corollary relief" matters, with the exception of property sharing, but they are not usually referred to as corollary relief for cohabiting couples. And, because cohabiting couples may not be entitled to property sharing pursuant to provincial statutes, courts may make some forms of equitable relief available to cohabiting couples who separate (usually on the basis of equitable principles such as unjust enrichment).

- Note also that married couples who separate and who do not file for a divorce may have access to remedies that are available to cohabiting couples who separate, but as married couples, they may also be entitled to statutory property arrangements.

Thus, because only married couples are entitled to divorce, it is usually important to separate the legal authority defining rights and obligations for married couples from those available to cohabiting couples at family dissolution. Recall now the outline in Chapter One with respect to the division of powers in family law matters. As noted there,

- the federal Parliament has authority to legislate with respect to divorce and corollary relief; and
- the provincial legislatures have authority to legislate with respect to matters of property and civil rights.

In practice, this means that federal legislation governs the rights of married couples who initiate divorce proceedings, while provincial statutes govern the rights of cohabiting couples, as well as those married couples who separate and do not file for divorce. These issues of constitutional authority will be addressed again in more detail later in this chapter and then in relation to the chapters that follow with respect to issues of corollary relief (for divorce) and additional relief (for separations).

At this point, it is important to note that issues about family dissolution require a careful separation of those who are married and those who are cohabiting in terms of the legal authority governing their rights and obligations — even though many of their rights and obligations are very similar in practice.

Organization of this chapter

This chapter focuses first on the legal principles concerning the law of divorce in Canada and the provisions of the *Divorce Act*, taking account of the broader social issues and statistical data examined in this introductory section.

The chapter then examines briefly the consequences of divorce and separation in relation to family economies and responsibilities for dependency, comparing the obligations of families and the state for family members who become financially dependent as a result of family dissolution. As will be seen, many of these obligations continue to fall on families, albeit "post-dissolution" family units.

The chapter then provides an overview of the legal principles about processes for achieving separation and divorce. Although family law courses tend to focus on judicial decisions that interpret statutory language, such cases represent only a tiny proportion of family law matters, since most family dissolution matters are resolved by agreement, that is, a separation agreement. In concluding a separation agreement, family law clients may be involved in litigation, but they more often engage in processes of negotiation, collaborative law, mediation, or arbitration, contractual processes for achieving a separation agreement. In this context, the material considers how private separation agreements may be reviewed by courts to ensure fairness in private family agreements.

Because of this focus on contract in relation to separation agreements, this chapter also addresses some aspects of contract bargaining in relation to family law matters, specifically marriage contracts and cohabitation agreements. Such agreements may be negotiated many years prior to separation and divorce, although the statutory principles do not generally make distinctions between different forms of domestic contracts. Moreover, as earlier chapters revealed, while courts have tended to scrutinize some family law contracts very carefully (recall *Jane Doe v Alberta*), courts have tended to uphold these domestic contracts. The chapter concludes by examining family contracts negotiated in accordance with religious precepts, some of which have recently presented challenges to private ordering in the family law context.

Since subsequent chapters will focus on statutory provisions and their judicial interpretation in relation to corollary relief arrangements, it is important at the outset to note the significance of contracts, and how family bargaining in practice may occur "in the shadow of law."

THE SOCIAL CONTEXT OF DIVORCE AND SEPARATION

Current statistics about divorce and separation

Statistics about divorce and separation may be based on different kinds of measurements. According to Ambert, the most refined way of measuring divorce involves looking at couples who marry in a given year and then calculating the proportion expected to divorce before their 30th anniversary. For example, Canada's divorce rate of 37.9 divorces per 100 marriages means that 37.9% of marriages in 2004 will end before 2035, based on predictions of actual divorce patterns of the recent past (Ambert at 4).

However, there are many variations in divorce rates and a number of external influences must be taken into account. In examining these statistics about divorce, consider how legal regulation may need to take account of social and economic issues in families:

• The Canadian rate of 37.9% is a Canada-wide average, and there are some significant variations from province to province. For example, the rate for Newfoundland and Labrador is 21.6%, while the rate for Alberta is 41.9% (Ambert at 5). What kinds of factors may affect the divorce rate in different provinces?

• The Canada-wide divorce rate of 37.9 divorces per 100 marriages includes both first marriages, as well as subsequent ones. In fact, the rate of divorce for first marriages, Canada-wide, is about 33%, so that first marriages have an overall 67% chance of lasting for life (Ambert at 6). Are there explanations for the higher rate of breakdown of subsequent marriages, by contrast with first marriages?

• The divorce rate does not include the rate of breakdown of cohabiting couples. Since cohabitation is increasing, particularly in Québec, the divorce rate significantly underestimates the rate of family breakdown overall (Ambert at 6). To what extent would including the breakdown of cohabiting relationships in the rate of family breakdown provide a more accurate picture of family dissolution in Canada? Are all cohabiting couples the same? Are all cohabiting couples the same as married couples?

- In tracking rates of divorce since 1921, Statistics Canada reported as follows:

1921	588 divorces in Canada
1921 to 1986	Gradually increasing numbers to 1986
1986	78,304 divorces in Canada
1987	96,200 divorces in Canada
1990	80,998 divorces in Canada

The number of divorces fell in the 1990s, with a slight increase in 2005 to 71,269 (Ambert at 7). What factors may explain the substantial increase in the number of divorces in 1987? What factors may explain the decrease in the rate of divorce in the 1990s?

- Statistics concerning divorces for same-sex couples are only beginning to be available, because same-sex marriage became available only recently. There is some indication that many same-sex marriages in Canada have occurred between longstanding partners, so that the rate of marriage breakdown may be lower, at least initially (Ambert at 9). To what extent are the rates of same-sex divorces likely to reflect the rates for opposite-sex marriages?

- The highest number of divorces in Canada occurs after the 3rd and 4th anniversaries, however, decreasing each additional year thereafter (Ambert at 9). The average duration of marriages ending in divorce in 2005 was 14.5 years, and the average age for divorce was 44 for men and 41.4 for women. What kinds of financial and child care issues may arise for couples in their early 40s that may complicate legal arrangements for divorce at this stage of life?

In assessing the overall situation, Ambert concluded that

[w]hether divorce rates will increase or decrease in any substantial way in the future depends on the complex interplay between numerous socio-economic, political, cultural and demographic factors, as well as individual preferences and values ... [for example, pre-marriage cohabitation rates, the higher rate of "children of divorce" who marry because their marriages may be statistically at greater risk, a decline in the proportion of adults between ages 25 and 45 because this is the age range for most divorces, a rise in the rate of cohabitation without recognition of their family breakdowns in statistics].

To conclude, except for Québec, divorce rates have come down substantially since the 1990s. But, at the same time, marriage rates have come down — thus reducing divorce risk — while cohabitation rates have risen, especially in Québec. *Therefore, couple dissolution in general has certainly not decreased and may actually have increased.* (Ambert at 7–8, [emphasis added])

What are the consequences for legal regulation as a result of these conclusions?

As Ambert also noted, divorce rates increased in most European jurisdictions in the 1990s, and although U.S. rates of divorce have declined recently, they are still among the highest in the world, in part because of the high rate of sequential marriages in the United States (Ambert at 9).

What factors may have contributed to rising rates of divorce in the late 20th century? For example, one study suggested that the greater participation in the labour force by women made divorce more feasible economically, and that increasing secularization in Canadian society and the emphasis on philosophies of individualism and choice also contributed to social acceptance of divorce. See Department of Justice Canada, *Evaluation of the Divorce Act, Phase II: Monitoring and Evaluation* (Ottawa: Department of Justice Canada, 1990) at 36; see also R Phillips, *Putting Asunder: A History of Divorce in Western Society* (Cambridge, UK: Cambridge University Press, 1988), and Lawrence M Friedman, *Private Lives: Families, Individuals, and the Law* (Cambridge, MA: Harvard University Press, 2000).

Understanding the social context of divorce and separation for spouses

Family dissolution often takes place over time. That is, unlike marriage which occurs on a defined date, separation may be an ongoing process for both married and cohabiting couples, although a divorce order will eventually be issued for married couples on a specified date later in the process (usually after all the corollary issues have been settled). In practice, this process of separation and divorce may require spouses to seek or agree to interim arrangements as they finalize the details of their divorce or separation. In addition, the ongoing nature of separation for both cohabiting and married couples means that a legal process is proceeding at the same time as family members are adjusting to major changes in their family relationships.

Consider how the separation process may require insight and understanding on the part of family lawyers with respect to the experiences of spouses.

For example, Julien Payne argued that lawyers need to understand the complex relationship between legal processes of divorce and the social context in which they take place. According to Payne, there are three crises that may occur in the breakdown of a marriage (or cohabitation arrangement): an emotional crisis, an economic crisis, and a parenting crisis; and he concluded that these crises cannot be addressed in isolation from legal processes See Julien Payne, "The Dichotomy Between Family Law and Family Crises on Marriage Breakdown" (1989) 20 RGD 109.

From a slightly different perspective, Shelley Day Sclater identified the psychosocial nature of the breakdown process, suggesting that most people experience a sense of loss but they may also find new opportunities in the pursuit of autonomy. Like Payne, she also argued that lawyers need to take account of different kinds of survival strategies adopted by divorcing partners at different stages in the legal process. See Shelley Day Sclater, *Divorce: A Psychosocial Study* (Aldershot, UK: Ashgate, 1999).

Other scholars have traced societal views about divorce and separation historically, suggesting that although divorce was once characterized in terms of pathology and deviance, it is now more often understood as failure and loss. In addition, because marriage for some people represents status and identity, divorce may suggest bad judgment as well as personal loss. See Gay Kitson with William Holmes, *Portrait of Divorce: Adjustment to Marital Breakdown* (New York: Guilford Press, 1992).

Taking these comments into account, reflect on what kinds of decision-making arrangements and legal processes may be useful for spouses who separate or divorce. You may want to reconsider this question later in this chapter in assessing the processes available to assist decision making relating to family dissolution.

Understanding the social context of divorce and separation for children

In this context, it is also important to highlight some differing conceptions about the impact of separation and divorce on children. Their numbers are significant.

For example, in 2006, four in ten adults involved in family dissolution had dependent children, although children born to cohabiting couples were more likely to experience such change than those born to married parents (Ambert at 10).

For some of these children, divorce or separation of their parents resulted in escape from a violent or abusive home, while for other children, their parents' separation resulted in grief and loss. Thus, divorce and separation on the part of parents may be either positive or negative for children.

In this context, British researchers have suggested a need for caution in assessing the impact of separation and divorce for children, and an effort to avoid the tendency to see *only* harm for children whose parents separate. Characterizing this tendency as "harm-ism," these researchers concluded that it failed to capture the complexity of children's reactions to family dissolution:

> "Harm-ism" insists that the greatest harm to children is their parents' divorce; it pushes out or minimizes considerations of poverty, domestic violence, poor housing, inadequate financial provision and the possibility that an ongoing marriage might be worse for children than a divorce. [Harm-ism] has developed an independent existence and is resistant to any evidence which might modify the harm thesis. It has ... become a climate of opinion. (Carol Smart, Bren Neale & Amanda Wade, *The Changing Experience of Childhood: Families and Divorce* (Cambridge, UK: Polity Press, 2001) at 37–38)

In reflecting on the legal principles and processes involved in divorce and separation in this chapter and the ones that follow, consider how, and to what extent, current legal arrangements reflect how family dissolution involves more than a legal process. To what extent are legal principles and processes congruent with the social and economic realities of families at dissolution?

Additional Resources

Nancy F Cott, *Public Vows: A History of Marriage and the Nation* (Cambridge, MA: Harvard University Press, 2002).

Stephen Cretney, "Putting Asunder and Coming Together: Church, State and the 1969 Divorce Reforms"; and " 'Tell me the Old, Old Story': The Denning Report, Divorce and Reconciliation", *Law, Law Reform and the Family* (Oxford, UK: Clarendon Press, 1998) 33 and 137.

Law Reform Commission of Canada, *Report on Family Law* (Ottawa: Information Canada, 1976).

Jennifer E Macintosh et al, "Child-Focused and Child-Inclusive Divorce Mediation: Comparative Outcomes from a Prospective Study of Postseparation Adjustment" (2008) 46 Fam Ct Rev 105.

R Phillips, *Putting Asunder: A History of Divorce in Western Society* (Cambridge: Cambridge University Press, 1988).

Shelley Day Sclater, "Narratives of Divorce" (1997) 19:4 J Soc Welfare & Fam L 423.

Carol Smart & Bren Neale, *Family Fragments?* (Cambridge, UK: Polity Press, 1999).

JG Snell, *In the Shadow of the Law: Divorce in Canada 1900–1939* (Toronto: University of Toronto Press, 1991).

Bertha Wilson, "State Intervention in the Family" in Rosalie Abella & Melvin Rothman, eds, *Justice Beyond Orwell* (Montreal: Les Éditions Yvon Blais, 1985) 353.

Zheng Wu, *Cohabitation: An Alternative Form of Family Living* (Toronto: Oxford University Press, 2000).

II.
THE LEGAL REGIME FOR DIVORCE

[The 1986 *Divorce Act*] introduced the possibility of true no-fault divorce, and, together with the reduction of the waiting time, made something very like divorce on demand a reality. Moreover, where an application is uncontested, it is possible for parties to obtain a divorce simply by filing the necessary documents and affidavits; and, although it is still necessary for a court to judge that the grounds in fact exist, this can be done in chambers, and a personal appearance by the parties in an uncontested divorce is not required. ... [Yet, even] when the parties are in agreement as to what they want, a court must decide that the grounds for it exist. And the parties must provide the court with the evidence necessary for the making of that judgment. (Simon Fodden, *Family Law* (Toronto: Irwin Law, 1999) at 165)

AN OVERVIEW OF DIVORCE LEGISLATION AND THE CONSTITUTION

The requirements for divorce and the role of courts

As Simon Fodden explained, divorce is available in Canada virtually "on demand," but it continues to require a judicial decision, even when the parties are in agreement. In this way, divorce is not simply a private, consensual decision between two people who no longer wish to be married. The law is involved in effecting a divorce, just as law is involved in defining a valid marriage:

- **Section 3: the residency requirement**

  Section 3 of the *Divorce Act* establishes residency requirements for an application for divorce. Basically, a person must be "ordinarily resident" in a province in order to file an application for divorce (for example, see *Okmyansky v Okmyansky*, 2007 ONCA 427).

  Wang v Lin, 2013 ONCA 33, found that a wife who was living with her children and husband in China did not have ordinary residence in Ontario to begin a divorce action. The parties were Chinese and immigrated to Canada in 2005 with two children. The mother and the children acquired Canadian citizenship in 2010, but the father, whose business remained in China, lost his permanent resident status and remained a citizen of China. The mother and children returned to China in September 2010 where the children began school to become more proficient in Mandarin. The mother claimed that they planned to remain in China for only two years and then return to their home in Toronto. In April 2012, the mother travelled to Toronto and filed an application under the *Divorce Act*. The court held (at para 44) that "the fact that the parties maintained a home in Toronto while living in China is ... not sufficient to make the mother ordinarily resident in Ontario while she was living and carrying on her customary mode of life in China...."

  Recall that although a valid marriage requires the parties to obtain a licence to marry, there is no residency requirement. As noted in Chapter Two, a number of same-sex couples who married in Canada were not resident here. Thus, when a same-sex couple who had married in Canada but were resident in jurisdictions that did not recognize the validity of same-sex marriage applied for a divorce in Canada, their lawyer launched a *Charter* challenge in relation to the residency requirement in section 3 of the *Divorce Act*. As noted earlier, the federal government responded by introducing Bill C-32, amending the *Civil Marriage Act*, in February 2012. The Bill permits same-sex non-residents who were married in Canada to apply for divorce in Canada if they have lived separately for one year. However, these divorce proceedings relate only to dissolution of the marriage, leaving all corollary relief matters to be determined in the jurisdiction(s) where they are resident. For further details, and critiques of the Bill, see Chapter Two.

- **Section 8: the definition of "marriage breakdown"**
  Section 8 identifies "marriage breakdown" as the sole ground for divorce, although it may be proved either by a one-year period of separation or by adultery or cruelty. However, section 8 permits the spouses to make an application for divorce jointly if they are relying on separation to prove marriage breakdown.

  At the same time, section 8(2)(b)(ii) creates protection for the calculation of a period of living separate and apart, if the spouses resume cohabitation for a short period for purposes of reconciliation. In addition, note that sections 9 and 10 create specific obligations for lawyers and judges in relation to reconciliation.

Thus, taking into account the procedural arrangements noted by Fodden, if certain requirements are met, spouses may almost obtain divorce "on consent," but they still require approval of the court. Sections 12–14 of the Act provide for an order of divorce, with legal effect throughout Canada, which dissolves the spouses' marriage.

Why should divorce require a court order? To what extent are there reasons to require judicial oversight of divorce? Why does divorce, but not marriage, have a residency requirement? You may wish to reflect further on these questions after considering issues about corollary relief in the chapters that follow.

Legislative authority for divorce proceedings: The federal/provincial interface

Federal legislation concerning divorce was required because the authority for legislating with respect to divorce is set out in section 91(26) of the *Constitution Act, 1867*. Pursuant to this section, the federal government has authority to legislate with respect to "marriage and divorce." In this context, the constitutional validity of federal legislation relating to divorce is clear.

However, as Peter Hogg explained, provisions in federal divorce legislation that dealt with corollary relief were initially more controversial, because issues about support and child custody had been generally regarded as within the competence of provincial legislatures before the federal government's *Divorce Act* of 1968 (see Peter Hogg, "Constitutional Law of Canada" (Toronto: Thomson Carswell, looseleaf) at 27.5).

Corollary Relief in Relation to Divorce

So long as applications for corollary relief are connected to an application for divorce, the provisions of the Act are *intra vires* the federal Parliament:

- **Property:** Because issues concerning property at marriage breakdown appear to fall within provincial authority to legislate concerning "property and civil rights" (s 92(13)), it is difficult for federal divorce proceedings legislation to include provisions about spouses' entitlement to family property at divorce. As Hogg noted, although the federal Parliament probably could not enact a comprehensive regime of family property, corollary relief provisions authorizing the transfer of property from one spouse to another at divorce would probably be constitutional (Hogg at 27.7). In the absence of any federal legislation about property, however, it is provincial legislation that governs property entitlement for spouses at marriage breakdown, so that property rights at divorce (and sometimes separation) often vary across Canada.

• **Custody/access of children:** By contrast with these arrangements for property, authority with respect to issues of child custody has been held to be within federal jurisdiction if the issues relate to divorce. In *Papp v Papp* (1969), 1 OR 331, the Ontario Court of Appeal considered the validity of provisions of the 1968 *Divorce Act* concerning custody and concluded that they were valid because they had a "rational, functional connection" with divorce, and this decision has been followed in relation to interim and final orders and to applications for variation of these orders, so long as they are connected to divorce proceedings.

• **Support (spousal and child support):** Similarly, interim and final orders, and applications for variation, in relation to spousal and child support have been held to be within federal authority, so long as they are connected to divorce proceedings. Thus, the provisions of the federal *Divorce Act* relating to spousal and child support and to custody of children are valid in relation to divorce proceedings (Hogg at 27.5–27.6).

Property, Support, and Custody in the Absence of Divorce

Courts have held that provincial legislation governing spousal and child support and custody (as well as property) is valid in so far as it relates to applications that do not involve divorce. Such applications may involve cohabiting couples, or married couples who are not seeking to divorce:

• **Spousal and child support, custody and property for cohabiting couples:** Arrangements for support and custody at the end of a cohabiting relationship must be considered pursuant to provincial legislation, because no divorce application is possible in the absence of marriage. In Ontario, spousal and child support provisions are set out in the *Family Law Act*, while provisions concerning custody and access are found in the *Children's Law Reform Act*. And, although cohabiting couples are not entitled to the property-sharing provisions of the *Family Law Act* in Ontario, courts have sometimes used unjust enrichment principles as equitable remedies.

• **Spousal and child support, custody and property for married couples (no divorce):** Some spouses who are married may separate without making a decision about whether to divorce. In the absence of divorce proceedings, their claims to support and custody will also be considered pursuant to provincial legislation, and they may access provincial legislative arrangements concerning property.

In this way, issues about support (spousal and child) and custody (and access) may fall within either federal or provincial legislative authority, depending on the specific circumstances of the spouses. Property issues are within the provinces' legislative authority, and some provinces (not including Ontario) may extend their property provisions for married spouses to cohabiting couples. For those cohabiting couples without access to the legislative regime (as in Ontario), courts may provide equitable remedies such as constructive trusts, issues discussed in detail later in this book.

Federal/Provincial Authority to Legislate at Family Dissolution: Congruence and Conflicts

Fortunately, there appear to be few significant examples of differences in relation to the outcomes in family law cases in different provinces of Canada, even though the precise language of each provincial statute is often different, and also different from the corollary relief provisions of the *Divorce Act*.

- In part, this uniformity of outcomes has been created by decisions of the Supreme Court of Canada that have identified guiding principles on issues such as spousal and child support and child custody.

- In addition, the enactment of child support guidelines and spousal support advisory guidelines, by way of collective action on the part of the federal, provincial, and territorial governments, has tended to create expectations of greater uniformity, although a few differences remain in practice.

- Finally, the *Charter* has been used to define constitutional limits in relation to legislative action in some family law matters.

As a result of these legislative and judicial developments, it is arguable that a national system of family law is emerging in Canada. See also Rollie Thompson, "Rules and Rulelessness in Family Law: Recent Developments, Judicial and Legislative" (2000–2001) 18 Can Fam LQ 25; Robert Leckey, "Harmonizing Family Law's Identities" (2002) 28 Queen's LJ 221. To what extent is this "homogenization" of family law desirable? Are there issues relating to spousal and child support, custody and access, or property that should reflect provincial, rather than national, standards in Canada?

However, even though there may be increasing uniformity between federal and provincial family law regimes, the existence of two sets of legislative provisions may create conflicts for parties at separation. Hogg has suggested that the possibility of conflict between federal and provincial statutes in relation to family law orders should be determined according to the doctrine of paramountcy, while noting that family law courts have "often disregarded the doctrine of paramountcy and have produced a remarkably inconsistent patchwork of decisions." Sometimes, for example, courts have tended to decide disputes pursuant to conflict of laws rather than constitutional principles. For example, see *McKee v McKee*, [1951] 2 DLR 657 (PC). However, because an order of a divorce court in any province has effect throughout Canada (see *Divorce Act*, section 13) and is not an order of a foreign court but rather one pursuant to the federal divorce power, Hogg argued that it is the doctrine of paramountcy that should determine the priority between such an order and any order made according to provincial legislative authority (Hogg at 27.8). For a recent example of the interface between the federal *Divorce Act* and Ontario's *Courts of Justice Act*, see *Elgner v Elgner*, 2011 ONCA 483, leave to appeal to SCC refused, 34372 (17 November 2011).

Notes and Questions

Inconsistency between a federal and a provincial order in the family law context

Consider, for example, two orders made pursuant to a federal and a provincial statute respectively, where the orders are inconsistent.

- Custody: Using the express contradiction test, there is no doubt that there would be inconsistency between an order for custody and access made pursuant to the federal divorce power and a completely different order for custody and access made pursuant to a provincial statute.

- Spousal support: It may be more difficult to apply these principles in the case of spousal support. For example, Hogg suggested that a federal order to pay $500 per month and a provincial order to pay $600 per month in respect of spousal support are not necessarily inconsistent, because both can be honoured by paying $1,100 per month. Generally, however, courts have held that there is an express contradiction in such a case, although this result is not necessarily required by the test (Hogg at 27.8).

Provincial legislatures have attempted to foreclose the possibility of two courts reaching such inconsistent orders. In Ontario, statutes concerning custody and spousal support also include provisions to try to avoid inconsistency in family law matters in such cases (see *Children's Law Reform Act*, s 27; and *Family Law Act*, s 36).

Consider this situation:

A Manitoba court granted interim custody to the father in an application pursuant to the *Divorce Act*. However, there were also ongoing custody proceedings pursuant to provincial legislation in

Ontario, where a court granted custody to the mother. Clearly, these custody orders are inconsistent. How should this inconsistency be resolved?

Although the litigation was complicated by a number of additional factors, the Ontario Court of Appeal concluded in *Brooks v Brooks* (1998), 41 OR (3d) 191, that the *Divorce Act* proceedings in Manitoba superseded the Ontario order. In doing so, the court interpreted section 27 of the Ontario *Children's Law Reform Act*, requiring that a proceeding initiated pursuant to provincial legislation be stayed if an application for divorce is filed. Although the section is clearly designed to avoid the necessity of applying the paramountcy doctrine, by preventing the existence of two inconsistent orders, it was not entirely successful in this case until the intervention of the Court of Appeal.

For another example, see *Willenbrecht v Willenbrecht* (1999), 47 RFL (4th) 200 (Ont CA).

The scope of provincial legislation after an order for divorce

What happens when there is a divorce order and then a subsequent application relating to orders for corollary relief?

- **Where a divorce court has issued orders for both divorce and corollary relief:** In a case where a divorce court has issued an order for corollary relief at the time of a divorce order, the question is whether it is possible for a subsequent court to make a different (and inconsistent) order pursuant to provincial legislation at a later point in time. The early case law was somewhat inconsistent on this issue (see *Emerson v Emerson*, [1972] 3 OR 5 (HC); *Ramsay v Ramsay* (1976), 70 DLR (3d) 415 (Ont CA); and *Re Hall* (1976), 70 DLR (3d) 493 (BCCA)). According to *Hall*, there is no such authority in the later court, acting pursuant to provincial legislation, and Hogg concluded that this authority is probably the correct one (Hogg at 27.8).

- **Where a divorce order does not include an order for corollary relief:** If there has been no order for corollary relief at the time of the divorce order, Hogg suggested that the express contradiction test would validate any order pursuant to provincial legislation, made either before or after the divorce order. However, if an order for corollary relief is made by a divorce court after the divorce order, there will then be an express contradiction with an order pursuant to the provincial legislation, and the competing provincial order will be invalid.

- **Where there is an order pursuant to provincial legislation and then an order for divorce and corollary relief:** In a situation where there is a valid order pursuant to provincial law, and then an order for divorce is made, any order for corollary relief made by the divorce court that is inconsistent with the earlier order will be paramount to the provincial legislation (Hogg at 27.8).

Consider this situation:

The parties divorced and the mother was granted sole custody of the children in British Columbia. The divorce order referred to both the *Divorce Act* and the *Family Relations Act* of British Columbia, but did not specify under which *Act* the custody order was made. The father subsequently applied for an order for access in the Provincial Court, but the court refused to hear the application, holding that it had no jurisdiction following the previous ruling by the B.C. Supreme Court. The father petitioned for mandamus ordering the Provincial Court to hear the application, but the Supreme Court held that once an order for custody is made under the *Divorce Act*, the Provincial Court loses jurisdiction over the issue of access due to the doctrine of paramountcy.

As *Spiers v Spiers* (1995), 18 RFL (4th) 246 (BCSC), reveals, issues about legislative authority are intertwined with issues about jurisdiction for courts, an issue that is addressed later in this chapter. See also *Sun v Guilfoile*, 2011 ONSC 1685; and *Gavriluke v Mainard*, 2013 ONSC 2337.

Additional Resources

Canada, Parliament, Special Committee of the Senate and House of Commons, *Report of the Special Joint Committee of the Senate and the House of Commons on Divorce* (Ottawa: Queen's Printer, 1967).

Christine Davies, *Family Law in Canada* (Scarborough, ON: Carswell, 1984).

Frederick Jordan, "The Federal Divorce Act (1968) and the Constitution" (1968) 14 McGill LJ 209.

III.
"NO FAULT" GROUNDS FOR DIVORCE AND BARS TO DIVORCE

Successfully proving a ground will remain a necessary step in obtaining permanent corollary relief under the *Divorce Act* and the existence of such a ground provides the respective parties with bargaining endowments in the negotiation of corollary issues. Allegations of matrimonial misconduct in a petition may reduce settlement possibilities where the assertions offend the sensitivities of the respondent and precipitate the dropping of the gauntlet. Conversely, it is possible that the ability of the parties to vent their anger through such allegations serves a cathartic function and, absent this outlet, the tendency to use corollary relief proceedings as a vehicle for recrimination may be heightened. (Bruce Ziff, "Recent Developments in Canadian Law: Marriage and Divorce" (1986) 18 Ottawa L Rev 121 at 140)

FAULT AND "NO FAULT" IN DIVORCE PROCEEDINGS

As noted earlier, the 1968 *Divorce Act* included some grounds based on fault and others (such as the separation of the spouses) that did not require fault at all. In the current *Divorce Act*, "marriage breakdown" is the only ground for divorce pursuant to section 8. However, marriage breakdown can be proved by either a one-year period of separation or by an act of adultery or cruelty. In practice, applications for divorce are much more frequently filed based on separation, rather than claims of adultery or cruelty, as proof of "marriage breakdown."

As Ziff's comment (above) indicates, however, proving a ground for divorce pursuant to the Act may not always be free of constraints and emotions. That is, while living separate and apart for one year appears to be an easy ground to prove, some divorcing spouses may want to use the divorce application to "vent their anger" about fault in the marriage. And, as Ziff noted, the removal of fault grounds in relation to divorce may result in such issues being transferred to the parties' negotiation of matters of corollary relief. Does this comment suggest that lawyers need to take account of the "social divorce" as well as the legal arrangements? Does it affect arguments in favour of removing fault from divorce?

Some researchers in the United States, who conducted interviews with lawyers and with their divorce clients, identified contrasting approaches for the two groups. Quite often, the lawyers focused on the legal context of no fault, while their clients wanted to seek vindication by finding fault with their spouses. As a result, the researchers concluded that many clients were dissatisfied with their experiences in the family law system, at least in part because their lawyers prevented them from engaging with their need to find blame for the marriage breakdown. Ssee Austin Sarat & William Felstiner, "Law and Social Relations: Vocabularies of Motive in Lawyer/Client Interaction" (1988) 22:4 Law & Soc'y Rev 737.

Interestingly, a report in 2000 indicated that family law cases were the biggest source of complaints about judges to the Canadian Judicial Council, with family law disputes representing 84 out of 177 complaints (see Cristin Schmitz, "Family Law Cases Main Source of Complaints Against Judges", *The Lawyers Weekly* (17 November 2000) 20). How should these issues be addressed? Is legal reform needed or are there other measures that should be adopted?

PROVING THE GROUND FOR DIVORCE: "MARRIAGE BREAKDOWN"

Living "separate and apart" as "marriage breakdown"

The Definition of "Separate and Apart"

The language of section 8(2)(a) of the *Divorce Act* defines precisely how the one-year period must be calculated to meet the requirement of living separate and apart to prove marriage breakdown. Section 8(3) defines the circumstances of both physical separation and the intention (on the part of at least one spouse) to live separate and apart. Thus, spouses who live apart for purposes of work (for example, members of the armed forces deployed overseas) do not live separate and apart pursuant to this section.

Section 8(3)(b)(ii) also permits a court not to take into account a period or periods of cohabitation totalling not more than 90 days resumed for purposes of reconciliation. In this context, note how this section, as well as provisions in sections 9 and 10, contribute to the Act's support for maintaining family relationships.

However, the Act is silent as to whether spouses who continue to live in the same household may be able to meet the test of living separate and apart. In what circumstances might spouses who wish to separate and divorce continue to live under the same roof? As a matter of policy, how should courts respond to claims that the spouses live separate and apart in these circumstances?

Interpreting "Separate and Apart"

In the following two cases, the language of living "separate and apart" was included in the definition of grounds for divorce under the 1968 *Divorce Act*, although as noted, the previous legislation required a longer period of separation than the current *Divorce Act*. In this context, courts had to consider the issue of spouses living in the same household in relation to the requirement of living "separate and apart" and these decisions continue to be followed in relation to claims under the current statute.

Rushton v Rushton
(1968), 66 WWR 764 (BCSC)

McINTYRE J.: The parties were married in 1936. By 1960 they had come upon difficulties and had begun to live separate lives, although they continued to reside in the same suite in an apartment building. In February, 1965, and probably from an earlier date, sexual intercourse ceased entirely. The petitioner lived in one room of the suite, the respondent in another; there was almost no contact between them. The wife performed no domestic services for the husband. She shopped and cooked only for herself. He bought his own food, did his own cooking, his own laundry and received no services from his wife. He paid her a sum monthly for maintenance. While it is true that they lived in the same suite of rooms, they followed separate and individual lives.

The petitioner continued to live in the suite because she and her husband were the joint caretakers of the apartment building in which the suite was situate, and to keep the position it was necessary to be, or to appear to be, husband and wife and to reside in the caretaker's suite.

In August, 1968, they became responsible for another apartment building where no such requirement exists. They now maintain separate suites in the same building.

I am of the opinion that in the case at bar the parties have been living separate and apart for three years [the period required under the

Divorce Act, 1968] within the meaning of [the relevant section defining living "separate and apart]. The words "separate and apart" are disjunctive. They mean, in my view, that there must be a withdrawal from the matrimonial obligation with the intent of destroying the matrimonial consortium, as well as physical separation. The two conditions must be met. I hold that they are met here. The mere fact that the parties are under one roof does not mean that they are not living separate and apart within the meaning of the Act. There can be, and I hold that there has been, a physical separation within the one suite of rooms. To hold otherwise would be to deprive the petitioner here of any remedy under the new *Divorce Act* simply because she is precluded, or was for a period of time precluded, by economic circumstances from acquiring a different suite in which to live.

Dupere v Dupere
(1974), 19 RFL 270 (NB (QB))

STEVENSON J.: The petitioner by his petition dated 18th October 1973 and presented to the Court on 1st November 1973 sought a divorce on the alternative grounds of adultery or permanent marriage breakdown by reason of the spouses having lived separate and apart for a period of not less than three years.

By her answer the respondent disputes the grounds alleged by the petitioner and counter-petitions for a divorce alleging permanent marriage breakdown by reason that the spouses "have been living under the same roof but separate and apart for a period of almost five years." ... At the opening of the trial counsel for the petitioner abandoned the allegation of adultery.

Only the parties testified. In any case where the parties continue to live under the same roof the court must carefully consider the evidence in determining whether the spouses have been "living separate and apart" resulting in "a permanent breakdown of their marriage." ... Particular care is called for where, as here, both spouses seek a divorce on that ground alone.

The parties were married on 27th February 1960. The petitioner was 26 and the respondent 18. She had borne a child, Randle, of which the petitioner was the father, on 13th July 1958. There are two other children of the marriage — Heather, born 30th November 1960, and Jacqueline, born 9th February 1965.

Difficulties between the parties apparently developed in 1965 and they separated in 1966. A written separation agreement (Ex. R-1) was entered into on 12th July 1966. The respondent was to have custody of the children and the petitioner assumed financial obligations which were not clearly defined. The respondent took an apartment. When she was unable to pay the rent she rented a small house without toilet facilities for $30 per month. She and her two daughters resided there. Randle stayed with his maternal grandmother. The petitioner provided some financial support on a rather irregular basis.

In the fall of 1968, the petitioner moved in with the respondent and normal marital relations were resumed for about a month. However in December of that year the parties began to occupy separate bedrooms and both testify there has been no sexual intercourse between them since that time. They subsequently moved twice and had lived together at 72 Pauline Street in East Saint John from March 1970 until a week before the trial when the respondent moved to another address, taking the children with her.

The petitioner says he and the respondent stayed in the same house "for the sake of the kids." While I suspect the respondent may have stayed as a matter of economic necessity the evidence does not justify such a finding. The petitioner has supported the home, has clothed his wife and family and has given the respondent a $20 weekly allowance. The respondent says she was just a maid. It is not a situation where there was no communication between the parties and apparently where the children were concerned there was often mutual discussion and agreement. For instance the parties were able to jointly decide on how much should be spent on the children at Christmas and they "always made a big thing of Christmas." As between the parties discord continued and on only two occasions in the past five years did they go out together. The respondent has been friendly with another man with the knowledge and at least tacit consent of the petitioner.

The situation is not unlike that described by Holland J. in *Cooper v. Cooper* (1972), 10 RFL 184 (Ont.) [at 186]:

> The parties obviously cannot get along and clearly there is considerable bad feeling between them. At the same time there is clearly good feeling towards the children, the children are being well looked after and are receiving all necessary care and attention from their parents, in spite of the fact that the attitude of the parents toward each other must be upsetting for each of them.

The petitioner, though lacking in formal education, has been successful in his occupation as a crane operator and now earns about $16,000 annually. Occasionally his work takes him away for periods of several months but he anticipates his present work will keep him in Saint John for four or five years. He is presently working 12-hour shifts, alternating between day and night shifts every two weeks.

While the petitioner seeks a divorce it is not clear what he intended for the future with respect to his wife. In response to questioning by the Court he quite candidly admitted that he would have been content to have the same living conditions continue. At the date of the trial he had not finalized any plans for a new home or for the employment of a housekeeper.

The landlord of the parties had given them notice to quit at the end of February. The petitioner has entered into an agreement to purchase a home at South Bay but financing has not been finalized. The respondent, not being able to get satisfactory answers from the petitioner as to what accommodation and arrangements were to be provided after the end of February, rented an apartment on her own and, as already mentioned, moved there with the children a week prior to the date on which this action was to be tried.

The respondent has been employed since December 1973 and presently is earning a net of $66 weekly.

I have read most, if not all, of the decisions reported since the advent of the *Divorce Act* dealing with cases where marriage breakdown is alleged on the ground of separation even though the spouses continue to live under the same roof....

The cases of *Cooper v. Cooper*, supra, and *Lachman v. Lachman*, 2 RFL 207, [1970] 3 OR 29, 12 DLR (3d) 221 (CA), while not involving the particular issue, are also helpful.

I think the following general statements can be extracted as representing the weight of judicial opinion:

(1) Great care must be exercised in considering the evidence and each case determined on its own circumstances.

(2) There can be a physical separation within a single dwelling unit.

(3) A case is not taken out of the statute just because a spouse remains in the same house for reasons of economic necessity.

(4) To meet the statute there must be both (a) physical separation and (b) a withdrawal by one or both spouses from the matrimonial obligation with the intent of destroying the matrimonial consortium.

(5) Cessation of sexual intercourse is not conclusive but is only one factor to be considered in determining the issue.

(6) There may be an atmosphere of severe incompatibility but remain one household and one home — a distinction may be drawn between an unhappy household and a separated one.

The remarks of Denning L.J. (as he then was) in *Hopes v. Hopes*, [1949] P 227, [1948] 2 All ER 920, a desertion case, are also, I think, applicable by analogy. At pp. 235–36 he said:

> It is most important to draw a clear line between desertion, which is a ground for divorce, and gross neglect or chronic discord, which is not. That line is drawn at the point where the parties are living separate and apart. In cases where they are living under the same roof, that point is reached when they cease to be one household and become two households, or, in other words, when they are no longer residing with one another.

In *Cooper v. Cooper*, supra, Holland J. pointed out that generally a finding that spouses were living separate and apart was made where the following circumstances were present [at 187]:

(i) Spouses occupying separate bedrooms.

(ii) Absence of sexual relations.

(iii) Little, if any, communication between spouses.

(iv) Wife providing no domestic services for her husband.

(v) Eating meals separately.

(vi) No social activities together.

It is probably not necessary to establish all six elements in each case and each case must stand or fall on its own merits. I refrain from commenting on the wisdom of incompatible spouses remaining together "for the sake of the children" but I do not think it was the intention of Parliament that a spouse who does so, under the circumstances in this case, can at his or her option at any time after such circumstances have continued for three years or more elect to opt out of the marriage and claim a divorce on the ground of permanent marriage breakdown. A mutual opting out in such circumstances would be little more than divorce by consent, something Parliament has not yet provided for.

The evidence does not satisfy me that for three years or more prior to presentation of the petition in this action the parties were living separate and apart within the meaning of the Act or that there was an intention on the part of either spouse to destroy the matrimonial consortium. Accordingly both the petition and the counter-petition will be dismissed.

The decision was upheld on appeal where the appellate judge added a further condition: that the spouses not share the living room and recreational facilities together, such as the television. See (1975), 10 NBR (2d) 148 (CA).

Notes and Questions

The requirement to live "separate and apart"

How should courts deal with the criteria used in *Rushton* and *Dupere*? Should all the factors identified in *Cooper* be of equal weight in deciding whether the spouses are living separate and apart? To what extent do these factors reflect concepts of functionalism or familialism in relation to families?

Consider the following examples. How would the factors identified in *Rushton* and *Dupere* assist in deciding whether these spouses were living "separate and apart"?

- A husband regularly works away from home: see *Fotheringham v Fotheringham* (1999), 1 RFL (5th) 50 (Nfld CA).

- The spouses live in separate accommodation but they engage in "isolated or occasional" acts of sexual intercourse: see *Deslippe v Deslippe* (1974), 16 RFL 38 (Ont CA).

- The wife had remained in the home when her husband moved to live in a bottling plant that was on the same property. For several years thereafter, the husband supported the wife financially, continued to involve her in the business, occasionally had sexual relations with her, and claimed to be married for purposes of income tax: see *Severo v Severo*, 2007 BCSC 1542.

Do any of these examples suggest that courts are providing "divorce on demand"?

- A marriage can be "ongoing, yet at times stormy" as found in *Williams v Williams*, [1991] NWTR 53 at para 22 (decided November 1990). This was so even though prior to the petition being made, the parties had lived separate and apart for over 1 year, but were found not to be at the time of the petition.

- Parties cannot "separate in secret." In *Chan v Chan*, 2013 ONSC 7465, the husband claimed that living separate and apart had commenced three years before the wife left the home based on an argument the couple had had. The wife's separation date was upheld.

The requirement of intention in section 8(3)

Section 8(3) of the *Divorce Act* requires an intention, on the part of at least one spouse, to live separate and apart, in addition to physical separation. In a case in which there is some question about mental capacity to form such an intention, what standard of capacity is appropriate? Recall the test of capacity for marriage: should the test for an intention to live separate and apart be the same or different? Why?

Consider this example:

According to the evidence at trial, the wife had started to show some early signs of Alzheimer's in 1993. In early 1994, she went to visit her daughter in Calgary and never returned to Ontario. While in Calgary, she expressed the desire to divorce her husband and sought counsel from a family lawyer. The lawyer testified that he had no doubt that the wife had the capacity to give instructions to commence divorce proceedings. A medical doctor who examined the wife while she was in Calgary also testified that she had the capacity to separate from and divorce her husband. Should the wife's petition for divorce be granted some years later, when the wife's Alzheimer's disease rendered her incompetent?

In *Calvert v Calvert* (1997), 32 OR (3d) 281 (Gen Div), the court granted the wife's petition, stating that the wife, who was represented by a litigation guardian, had the capacity necessary to form an intent to separate from her husband and to seek a divorce. The court identified three levels of capacity relevant to the action — the capacity to separate; the capacity to divorce; and the capacity to instruct counsel. The court noted that separation is the simplest, requiring the lowest understanding; divorce, while simple, requires more understanding, because it is the undoing of the contract of marriage. Based on the evidence, the trial court found that the wife had all levels of capacity required to proceed.

When the husband appealed, the Ontario Court of Appeal rejected his argument that to support a finding of divorce, the court had to make a distinct finding with respect to the wife's mental capacity to intend to live separate and apart at the time of the petition for divorce and for the one-year period prior to the granting of the divorce. The court held that to require further proof or findings as to the wife's mental capacity and intention at each relevant point and for each relevant period would defeat the purpose of section 8(3)(b)(i) of the *Divorce Act*. The Court of Appeal also rejected the husband's argument that the trial judge erred in awarding equalization of property. See (1998), 36 RFL (4th) 169; leave to appeal to the SCC dismissed without reasons, [1998] SCCA No 161. (For additional litigation in this case, see (1998), 36 RFL (4th) 169 (Ont CA); and (1998), 42 RFL (4th) 313 (Ont CA).) *Calvert*'s reasoning on capacity to separate has been adopted by the B.C. Court of Appeal in *Wolfman-Stotland v Stotland*, 2011 BCCA 175.

Adultery and cruelty as proof of "marriage breakdown"

"Fault" in Relation to Adultery and Cruelty?

The definitions of adultery and cruelty pursuant to section 8(2)(b) of the *Divorce Act* are frequently derived from cases decided some years ago. Note that only the "innocent" spouse may apply for divorce on the basis of adultery or cruelty, even though adultery and cruelty are no longer grounds for divorce, but serve merely to prove "marriage breakdown."

Moreover, as noted, claims of adultery and cruelty are used much less frequently than proof of living "separate and apart" to establish marriage breakdown. According to Juristat, 95% of divorces now prove marriage breakdown by living separate and apart (*Divorce cases in civil court, 2010/ 2011* at 7, online: <http://www.statcan.gc.ca/pub/85-002-x/2012001/article/ 11634-eng.pdf>). Particularly because they are used only infrequently, why have these claims been retained in the current statute? To what extent has fault been preserved in divorce proceedings?

Adultery: Contexts for Adultery in Family Law

Adultery was once quite important in divorce law, as a husband who could establish that his wife had committed adultery had no legal obligation to pay for her continuing financial support (historically called "alimony"). The definition of adultery historically required an act of sexual intercourse, but it is arguable that there has been an evolution in law in identifying precisely what is at issue with respect to adultery.

In an early 20th century decision in Ontario, a wife responded to her husband's allegation that she had committed adultery by claiming that she had become pregnant as a result of donor insemination, without his knowledge or consent. The court dismissed her evidence with respect to the facts, concluding that she had committed adultery in the usual way. However, the court then considered whether the use of donor insemination could constitute adultery. In doing so, the court held that adultery by a woman "involves the possibility of introducing into the family of the husband a false strain of blood, ..." and concluded that, on the grounds of public policy, donor insemination constituted adultery in law (see *Orford v Orford* (1921), 58 DLR 251 (Ont HC)). A contrary view was expressed, however, in *MacLennan v MacLennan*, [1958] Sess Cas 105 (Scotland Ct Sess).

In more recent cases, what constitutes adultery has been defined in different ways.

P(SE) v P(DD)
2005 BCSC 1290

In this case, the wife applied for a divorce from her husband of 19 years on the basis that he had committed "adultery" with another man. The husband voluntarily admitted his sexual relationship with the man. Both the wife (and the Attorney General as intervenor) argued that adultery was not limited to sexual relationships with a member of the opposite sex. After considering submissions on this issue, the court noted that the 1968 *Divorce Act* had provided that a petitioner could file for divorce where the respondent has, since the celebration of the marriage "been guilty of sodomy, bestiality or rape, or has engaged in a homosexual act...." However, this provision was not included in the *Divorce Act*, and the court held that the definition of adultery should now reflect views consistent with the *Civil Marriage Act* and the *Charter*, stating in part:

> **[44]** I conclude that the definition of adultery used in our courts should reflect views that are consistent with the Civil Marriage Act and should be

harmonized with the values enunciated in the *Charter*. If necessary to achieve this result, an incremental change in the definition of adultery should be made....

[46] I turn next to the question of the definition of what sexual acts constitute adultery and whether this court should attempt to define adultery.

[47] The traditional definition of adultery included the requirement that the sexual activity be intercourse. Because sexual relations might involve no penetration at all, this requirement could serve to deny a divorce to a man or a woman whose partner is having a sexual affair with a person of the same sex. However, the uncertainty about precisely what would constitute adultery in a same-sex relationship is not a reasonable basis for denying spouses the ability to divorce on the basis of same-sex sexual activity.

[48] In the modern understanding of marriage, the wrong for which the petitioner seeks redress is something akin to violation of the marital bond. Viewed from this perspective, the heterosexual nature of the sexual acts is not determinative. Intimate sexual activity outside of marriage may represent a violation of the marital bond and be devastating to the spouse and the marital bond regardless of the specific nature of the sexual act performed.

[49] In this case, the evidence of an intimate sexual relationship outside of Mr. and Ms. P's marriage is sufficient to grant the divorce on the grounds of adultery, notwithstanding that the act alleged was a same-sex sexual act. Adultery may include same-sex sexual acts where as here the evidence supports a finding that such has occurred.

[50] In this case I do not consider it is necessary or desirable for me to define what type of intimate sexual activity constitutes adultery. Questions about the meaning of adultery in same-sex marriages should be clarified over time on a case-by-case basis, just as those questions have been resolved on a case-by-case basis in the context of heterosexual marriages.

Thebeau v Thebeau
2006 NBQB 154

In this similar case, the New Brunswick court followed the reasoning in *P(SE) v P(DD)*. Focusing on the amended definition of "spouse" in the *Divorce Act* (required by the changes to the *Civil Marriage Act*), which includes same-sex spouses, the court stated:

[8] ... To confine the statutory right to divorce on the basis of adultery only to spouses whose partners engage in heterosexual extra-marital activity would be discriminatory in more than one respect. Homosexual spouses should be bound by the same legal constraints as heterosexual spouses. Homosexual violation of marriage vows should have the same consequences under the *Divorce Act* as heterosexual violation....

[11] Equal treatment before the law endows rights. What is sometimes overlooked is that it also imposes responsibilities. Equal treatment means equal obligations, equal responsibilities, and the acceptance of equal consequences.

[12] The consequence of infidelity, at least in the context of the *Divorce Act*, should not be confined to heterosexual spouses. To do so grants

license to homosexual spouses to be sexually unfaithful and to violate vows, untrammeled by the prospect of a fault-based dissolution of their marriage. That is not equal treatment.

[13] The definition of adultery must be consistent with the governing legislation and the values enshrined in the *Charter*. The dynamic nature of the common law and the judicial recognition of the obligation to ensure that it keeps in step with both permit this court to apply a definition of adultery as a ground of divorce regardless of whether the sexual misconduct is homosexual or heterosexual....

In this context, is it appropriate to conclude that the concept of adultery has evolved? Are the approaches to this issue the same or different in British Columbia in *P(SE)* and in New Brunswick in *Thebeau*? If so, which approach is preferable? Why? Is there a need for an amendment to the *Divorce Act* to define "adultery" for the 21st century? Is kissing adultery? Electronic (phone or cyber) sex? Non-penetrative sex?

Proof of Adultery: *Burbage v Burbage*

In the cases above concerning adultery in same-sex relationships, the respondents admitted that they had engaged in sexual relations with a person outside marriage. However, respondents do not always admit adultery, so courts have had to fashion principles to determine whether adultery has taken place for purposes of divorce.

Consider the unique facts of *Burbage v Burbage* (1985), 46 RFL (2d) 22 (Ont HC):

A husband counter-petitioned for divorce on the ground of adultery. The evidence demonstrated that prior to separation, the wife had established a close relationship with a man, and had spent a lot of time with him. It was admitted that on two occasions, she had spent the night at this man's apartment, although both parties asserted that no sexual intercourse had taken place because the man was impotent. The man (the co-respondent) asserted that his impotence was due to back surgery some years earlier and to his own bad marriage, which had terminated the previous year. No evidence was called to confirm the back surgery because the surgeon had died. Do these facts constitute proof of adultery?

In *Burbage*, the court held that there was (1) evidence of opportunity and (2) evidence of inclination, and continued (at 37–38):

In the result the court is left on the one hand with at least a prima facie case of adultery because of the proven elements of opportunity and intimacy, and on the other hand with a bald-faced denial that any adultery occurred.

In my view, once opportunity and intimacy are established on a balance of probabilities, there is a burden on the alleged adulterers to call evidence in rebuttal sufficient to dislodge the preponderant evidence.

Despite the death of the back surgeon, the co-respondent could have submitted himself to a medical examination and either called the medical practitioner as a witness or submitted a medical report pursuant to the rules. This was not done and no sufficient explanation for the failure put forward. These facts may support an adverse inference. Furthermore, the testimony of the ex-wife could have been presented viva voce or by affidavit. Again, an adverse inference may be raised. I realize, of course, that psychic impotence may not be universal but may be directed or limited to a particular person, but the absence of evidence is not helpful in this case.

On a balance of probabilities, therefore, I find that the allegation of adultery has been established. There will be a decree nisi granted to the husband.

In *George v George and Logie*, [1951] 1 DLR 278 at para 32, the Ontario Court of Appeal held that the standard of proof for adultery is the typical civil burden of proof and "not that imposed on the Crown in a criminal prosecution ... The judicial mind must be 'satisfied' that the alleged act of adultery was in fact committed, but it need not be satisfied to the extent of a moral certainty as in a criminal case. Evidence that creates only suspicion, surmise or conjecture is, of course, insufficient."

Assuming that the wife in *Burbage* did commit adultery, why was she refusing to acknowledge it? Recall Ziff's comments about the continuing usefulness of "fault" issues in relation to negotiations between the spouses with respect to corollary relief. To what extent do such comments assist in understanding the wife's position in *Burbage*?

Cruelty in Marriage: Objective and Subjective Tests?

Mental or physical cruelty has also been retained as a basis for proving "marriage breakdown," and the same language appears in section 8(2)(b)(ii) that existed earlier in the *Divorce Act* of 1968. Thus, the principles applicable to defining cruelty were first established under the 1968 legislation, but they have continued to be applied pursuant to the *Divorce Act*.

... Over the years the Courts have steadfastly refrained from attempting to formulate a general definition of cruelty. As used in ordinary parlance "cruelty" signifies a disposition to inflict suffering; to delight in or exhibit indifference to the pain or misery of others; mercilessness or hard-heartedness as exhibited in action. If in the marriage relationship one spouse by his conduct causes wanton, malicious or unnecessary infliction of pain or suffering upon the body, the feelings or emotions of the other, his conduct may well constitute cruelty which will entitle a petitioner to dissolution of the marriage if, in the Court's opinion, it amounts to physical or mental cruelty "of such a kind as to render intolerable the continued cohabitation of the spouses."

Care must be exercised in applying the standard set forth in [s. 8(2)(b)(ii)] that conduct relied upon to establish cruelty is not a trivial act, but one of a "grave and weighty" nature, and not merely conduct which can be characterized as little more than a manifestation of incompatibility of temperament, between the spouses. The whole matrimonial relations must be considered, especially if the cruelty consists of reproaches, complaints, accusations or constant carping criticism. A question most relevant for consideration is the effect of the conduct complained of upon the mind of the affected spouses. The determination of what constitutes cruelty in a given case must, in the final analysis, depend upon the circumstances of the particular case having due regard to the physical and mental condition of the parties, their character and their attitude towards the marriage relationship.... (*Knoll v Knoll* (1970), 1 RFL 141 (Ont CA))

In *Knoll* and a number of other early cases, courts seemed to consider both objective and subjective tests to determine cruelty, although some later decisions appeared to emphasize the subjective impact on the petitioner. For example, see an Annotation to a 1981 case by James McLeod, "Annotation of *Mes v. Mes*" (1981) 24 RFL (2d) 257 (Ont HC).

More generally, courts have continued to assert that each case must be decided on its own facts.

In *Chouinard v Chouinard* (1969), 10 DLR (3d) 263, the New Brunswick Court of Appeal reiterated the approach in *Knoll*, indicating that "behaviour which may constitute cruelty in one case may not constitute cruelty in another" (at 264). However, the court also noted that there are both objective and subjective elements involved.

In *Barron v Bull* (1987), 5 RFL (3d) 427 (Alta QB), the court rejected a husband's petition for divorce on the basis of section 8(2)(b)(ii) because the alleged conduct of the wife, although displeasing to the petitioner, did not in fact cause him to suffer, stating:

> Realizing that the test for cruelty is largely subjective, I am unable to find that the petitioner has established the respondent's cruelty toward him could be characterized to be of such a kind as to render intolerable their continued cohabitation (at 432).

Similarly, in *Wright v Wright*, 2001 SKQB 301, the court concluded that the spouses were very different kinds of people but that their differences pointed more to incompatibility rather than cruelty. See also *JGS v WOJS*, 2004 BCSC 749, where the court dismissed the application for a divorce made solely on the basis of cruelty for vague and insufficient evidence; *IA v SD*, 2009 ABQB 513; and *Cernic v Cernic*, 2012 ONSC 922. These cases seem to further demonstrate that courts are giving little weight to cruelty actions and prefer to grant the divorce based on living separate and apart.

Notes and Questions

Fault and "marriage breakdown"

To what extent do the bases for finding "marriage breakdown" not only define the grounds for divorce, but also transform the nature of marriage? For example, Christine Davies argued that the introduction of no fault divorce has fundamentally altered the concept of marriage:

> Now it is a union dissoluble without misconduct at the will of one or both of the parties [if they have lived separate and apart]. Thus, it is said, it is in the public interest that a marriage which has irrevocably failed ought to be dissolved.

However, Davies also suggested that courts would continue to review the evidence with respect to the ground for divorce, carefully and thoroughly:

> It is submitted, however, that, although the grounds for divorce have been extended, the court will continue to guard against its own deception and will continue to insist that adultery [or cruelty] be proven to its satisfaction regardless of whether the parties themselves desire a divorce and the marriage has broken down. (Davies at 336)

Do you agree that the above cases about adultery and cruelty, in relation to proof of marriage breakdown, illustrate differing approaches to divorce applications based on "fault," by contrast with those that are proved by a one-year period of living separate and apart? To what extent should courts approach these applications differently? Might the availability of divorce after a one-year period of separation make courts reluctant to engage with fault issues such as adultery and cruelty? Is such an approach appropriate?

"Desktop" divorces, proof of cruelty and the role of courts: *B(Y) v B(J)*
Consider this situation:

In 1989, a wife applied for divorce on the grounds of adultery and mental cruelty. The petition was presented as a "desktop" divorce, with affidavit evidence and without the parties' appearance in court. In relation to "particulars of mental cruelty," the wife's affidavit stated that "the respondent has admitted to me and to my eldest daughter S. that he is a practising homosexual." Since same-sex intercourse was not yet identified as 'adultery' in Canada, this petition could not be presented on the basis of adultery.

In this case, the petition for divorce was refused on the basis that "something in addition to homosexual practices" must be submitted in evidence "as constituting the grave conduct necessary to ground a divorce judgment." As the court stated:

> Moreover, as our Court of Appeal has held in *Anderson v. Anderson*, [1972] 6 WWR 53, 8 RFL 299, 29 DLR (3d) 587, there is an element of wilfulness in mental cruelty; being a homosexual is not equivalent to treating your spouse with cruelty. Cruelty implies callousness or indifference as referred to in that judgment....
>
> The fact that Parliament has also authorized divorce judgments to be issued in the absence of appearances in court does not mean that the standards of cruelty have been relaxed. The fact that the husband does not contest his wife's petition does not relieve the wife from the test which Parliament has established.
>
> In addition, the conduct relied upon to establish cruelty must be intolerable to the petitioner. There are no particulars in the supplementary affidavit of the subjective aspect of the grounds invoked. (*B(Y) v B(J)* (1989), 20 RFL (3d) 154 (Alta QB) at 156)

Does this case suggest that the test for cruelty is both objective and subjective? Does such a case have any continuing relevance now, in the context of the *Civil Marriage Act*? What other remedies were available to the wife in this case?

Recall the discussion earlier in this chapter about how client wishes may not be congruent with their lawyers' views? How should a lawyer respond now to a client who wishes to petition for divorce because a spouse is gay or lesbian?

Bars to divorce

The Historical Background Relating to Some Current Bars to Divorce

Although most "bars to divorce" now have little practical impact, it is important to understand how such bars were developed historically to ensure the integrity of the legal process of divorce when the grounds for divorce were based on fault, especially adultery. In a context in which spouses were seeking divorce, and adultery was the main ground, spouses often "created" evidence of adultery with the use of a third party willing to be named as a co-respondent. Indeed, some practitioners in the period prior to the 1968 *Divorce Act* recognized how the same co-respondents appeared often in divorce proceedings. In such situations, the bars to divorce permitted a court to decide not to grant the divorce even though the grounds for divorce had been proven.

In the context of the current *Divorce Act*, three traditional bars have been retained, although they are now used primarily in cases that are based on proof of adultery or cruelty as marriage breakdown:

- **Collusion** (s 11(1)(a)) is an absolute bar to divorce, since a court is required to dismiss an application if collusion is found. "Collusion" is defined in section 11(4). In addition to cases based on adultery and cruelty, collusion is available as a bar in other cases. For example, collusion was used to bar a petition for divorce in which the court held that the marriage was an "immigration marriage" (see *Johnson v Ahmed* (1981), 22 RFL (2d) 141 (Alta QB)). Similarly in *Merchant v Dossani*, 2007 ABQB 487, the court set out that it would not give effect to dual-party "sham marriages." Single-party sham marriages can receive divorces such as in *Naseer v Latif*, 2002 ABQB 966, where a marriage was civilly entered into for immigration purposes, but the petitioner was not a knowing participant in the immigration marriage and divorce scheme. See also *Wei v Cao*, 2009 BCCA 268, in which the Court of Appeal upheld a trial judge's refusal to give effect to a divorce petition and marriage contract partially on the grounds that the parties had colluded by lying about their date of separation.

- **Condonation** and **connivance** (s 11(1)(c)) require a court to determine that there has been no condonation or connivance on the part of the petitioning spouse, and to dismiss any such petition, unless "the public interest would be better served by granting the petition," thus permitting a court to exercise some discretion. These bars are available only where a divorce petition is based on section 8(2)(b).

Condonation refers to the resumption of cohabitation of a "guilty" spouse after being forgiven by the innocent spouse in relation to an act of adultery (see *Leaderhouse v Leaderhouse*, [1971] 2 WWR 180 (Sask QB); and section 11(3), which promotes reconciliation of the spouses in this context).

Connivance may consist of any act done with corrupt intention of a husband or wife to promote or encourage either the initiation or the continuance of adultery of his or her spouse, or it may consist of passive acquiescence in such adultery: *Maddock v Maddock*, [1958] OR 810. In *Fleet v Fleet*, [1972] 2 OR 530 (CA), the court held that failure to prevent adultery does not necessarily meet the test for connivance. In that case, the petitioner arrived at the scene where her spouse's adultery was in progress. Similarly, *Davies v Davies* (1980), 17 RFL (2d) 130 at para 12, held that a frank discussion between the couple with reference to leading separate lives did not rise to the level of connivance.

"Reasonable Arrangements for Children": Section 11(1)(b) and Child Support Guidelines

In addition to these traditional bars, the *Divorce Act* requires a court to satisfy itself that there have been reasonable arrangements for the support of children of the marriage and, if necessary, to stay the granting of the divorce until such arrangements have been made (s 11(1)(b)).

Clearly, this bar was introduced to overcome problems of inadequate levels of child support. Prior to the enactment of legislative child support guidelines in 1997, section 11(1)(b) of the *Divorce Act* provided an important tool for judges to ensure adequate financial provision for children. For example, see *F(RD) v F(SL)* (1987), 6 RFL (3d) 413 (BCSC); and *Money v Money* (1987), 5 RFL (3d) 375 (Man CA).

In another case prior to the 1997 child support guidelines, an Ontario court reviewed these decisions, and identified a list of criteria for assessing the arrangements for the support of children in divorce proceedings, including the relationship between child support and social assistance payments, the extent to which any agreement between the parents should be respected; and the need to take account of income tax implications, indexing, and the availability of medical coverage. See *Harper v Harper* (1991), 78 DLR (4th) 548 (Ont Gen Div). *Harper v Harper* was followed by another hearing, [1991] OJ No 1214, in which the new partner and common law spouse of the petitioner mother demonstrated that he was voluntarily supporting the children and planned to marry the mother. While expressing that section 11(1)(b) still made the father's support inadequate to grant the divorce, Kurisko J granted the divorce based on the acceptability of the third party's support.

As is evident, courts were fashioning principles designed to implement section 11(1)(b) effectively.

With the introduction of the legislated child support guidelines across Canada in 1997, however, it was necessary for courts to reinterpret section 11(1)(b) in this new context. Although the guidelines will be discussed in greater detail later in this book, two features are important in the context of section 11(1)(b):

> First, the child support guidelines, which were adopted as a result of negotiated agreements on the part of the federal, provincial and territorial legislatures, are intended to be mandatory. That is, the guidelines mandate the amount of support payable by a payor parent. In this context, the issue of whether anything other than the guideline amount would be considered "reasonable" pursuant to section 11(1)(b) created some uncertainty for divorce courts.

> Consider this situation:

> A wife seeking a divorce from her husband (who had left Canada and then returned some years later but had failed to pay child support and did not exercise access to his two daughters) did not wish to pursue child support against her husband because she was engaged to marry another man who was acting as a father to, and who was willing to support, her daughters. In this case, the court exercised discretion to bar the divorce petition, stating that it was not open to the petitioner to fail to seek child support from the children's father, since he was in Canada, appeared to be employed, and had an outstanding order for payment of support. In this way, the failure to make appropriate arrangements for the support of children operated *independently* to prevent the granting of a divorce application..

In assessing *Orellana v Merino* (1998), 40 RFL (4th) 129 (Ont Gen Div), James McLeod argued that there were good reasons of policy to criticize the court's decision to stay the divorce:

> ... If a custodial parent is able to support the child and is prepared to do so, a court should grant the custodial parent's application for divorce regardless of whether the non-custodial parent is paying sufficient child support. The child's needs will be met and the State will not be called upon to support the family. No public interest justifies denying the custodial parent's application for a divorce.
> A custodial parent may be prepared to maintain a child because it is not worth his or her time and money to seek support from the other parent.... [There may be] good reason in a particular case not to pursue the issue of child support if a custodial parent has sufficient resources to maintain the child....
> By denying the wife a divorce, [the court] prevents her and her new partner from regularizing their relationship and marrying. The wife does not have sufficient information to bring a support application and should not have to spend money needed to support herself and the child to pursue the husband for child support if she has a reasonable alternative ... (James McLeod, "Annotation" (1998), 40 RFL (4th) 129)

As McLeod also pointed out, an application for child support could be filed later on, if the wife obtained information about the husband's financial resources. (However, McLeod agreed with the court in relation to criticism of the wife's lawyer for providing information about the client's situation by way of a letter from the lawyer to the court, rather than by way of a client affidavit.)

Should section 11(1)(b) be amended, so that a divorce would be stayed in a situation such as *Orellana* only where it is the payor parent who is petitioning for divorce? Why, or why not?

The second issue concerning section 11(1)(b) and the child support guidelines results from the fact that the amount of child support payable is based on the monthly income of the payor parent. In this context, if a payor parent has little or no income, is it appropriate for a court to refuse to grant a divorce? What if the recipient parent is in receipt of social assistance, so that receipt of child support may disentitle the recipient to social assistance, or reduce the amount of such entitlement? While these issues will be addressed in more detail later in this book, they are also relevant to some extent to the issue of "reasonableness" in section 11(1)(b).

Consider this situation:

> The husband, who earned about $15,000 per year had an informal arrangement with the wife to pay for some clothing for his daughter ($700 per year) and about $500 per year in access costs (so that the child could spend holidays at his home). Under the child support guidelines, however, his monthly payments would have been about $118. In this case, the judge granted the divorce because there were reasonable arrangements for child support, stating that courts should be loathe to interfere with private support arrangements.

See *McIllwraith v McIllwraith* (1999), 210 NBR (2d) 391 (QB); and a positive comment about the judge's approach in this case in Rollie Thompson "Who Wants to Avoid the Guidelines? Contracting Out and Around" (2001–2002) 19 Can Fam LQ 1; see also Thompson, "Getting Blood from a Stone: Or How to Find Ability to Pay when There Isn't Any" (1995) 12 Can Fam LQ 117.

Religious Bars to Divorce

Section 21.1 of the *Divorce Act* permits a court to take action in a context where one spouse refuses to remove religious barriers to the remarriage of the other spouse as part of their divorce negotiations. Specifically, pursuant to section 21.1(3)(c) and (d), the court may dismiss any application filed by the recalcitrant spouse and strike out their pleadings and affidavits. A number of provinces have enacted similar provisions (for example, see Ontario's *Family Law Act*, ss 56(5), (6) and (7)). Although these provisions in the *Divorce Act* and in provincial legislation do not refer to any religion in particular, they were adopted as a result of lobbying on the part of Jewish reformers with respect to Jewish divorce arrangements.

According to mainstream Jewish law, a marriage can be dissolved only if the husband delivers to the wife a religious bill of divorce or "get," and the wife accepts the get. Thus, even if the parties obtain a civil divorce pursuant to the *Divorce Act*, the parties remain married under Jewish law until there is delivery and acceptance of the get. Moreover, because the wife cannot remarry in religious form without the get, any children of new union that she may form are also disadvantaged. Because the husband does not face such major consequences, the husband's bargaining power in relation to the civil divorce and corollary relief may be substantially greater than the wife's:

> The plight of agunot (wives who have not received a get) has long been a concern for the global Jewish community, with divorcing spouses using the desire for a get to extract favourable maintenance or property settlements, to obtain enhanced custody rights or access to children of the marriage, or simply as a tool for spite or vengeance. (John Kleefeld & Amanda Kennedy, "'A Delicate Necessity': *Bruker v. Marcovitz* and the Problem of Jewish Divorce" (2008) 24 Can J Fam L 205 at 206)

The wording of section 21.1 was drafted carefully to avoid infringing the *Charter* guarantee of freedom of religion. In this context, section 21.1(4) permits the recalcitrant spouse to file an affidavit indicating "genuine grounds of a religious or conscientious nature" for refusing to remove barriers to remarriage. However, in the absence of such grounds, a court may dismiss or strike pleadings and affidavits filed by the recalcitrant spouse. For example, see *G v G* (7 August 1991), File No ND 155927/88 (Ont Gen Div); and *Tanny v Tanny* (2000), 8 RFL (5th) 427 (Ont Sup Ct), where the wife consented to receipt of the get and then claimed corollary relief. The husband argued that these claims had already been dismissed and that the matter was *res judicata*. The court held that striking pleadings under section 21.1 is a temporary bar to proceedings, not an ultimate one. Nonetheless, because the provisions of Jewish law also require that the get be delivered without coercion, it has been suggested that it may be prudent for lawyers to consult a rabbi or other expert on Jewish Law to ensure that divorce proceedings meet these religious requirements. See also John Syrtash, *Religion and Culture in Canadian Family Law* (Toronto: Butterworths, 1992).

As this brief overview suggests, issues about the Jewish get reveal relationships between family law, religion and values of multiculturalism in Canada. In this context, Shauna Van Praagh argued that it is important to acknowledge how Orthodox Jewish women are not simply waiting for courts to grant the relief they need:

> The complex interaction between the legal system of the state and that of a community within the state, in the form of carefully researched and worded legislation, will not resolve the problem of the *get* for Jewish women. It may provide a serious signal, however, *in addition to the women's voices themselves*, that substantive change is required in Jewish law. (Shauna Van Praagh, "Review" (1993) 38 McGill LJ 233 at 249 [emphasis added])

This comment may also need to be considered in relation to the discussion later in this chapter about private family contracts with respect to religious obligations, including the Supreme Court of Canada's decision in *Bruker v Marcovitz*, in which a woman was seeking damages for her husband's breach of a contractual obligation to deliver a get to her.

Duties to Promote Reconciliation

Judges and Lawyers: Obligations to Foster Reconciliation

In addition to the above bars to divorce, sections 9 and 10 of the *Divorce Act* require both lawyers and judges in divorce proceedings to discuss the possibility of reconciliation with the parties. In addition, lawyers must also explore possibilities for negotiation or mediation and certify compliance with this requirement before commencing a divorce proceeding. And judges are authorized to adjourn proceedings to permit reconciliation to take place.

Why are provisions about reconciliation included in legislation regarding divorce? How should lawyers and judges discharge these obligations in practice?

Additional Resources

Illana S Cristofar, "Blood, Water and the Impure Woman: Can Jewish Women Reconcile Between Ancient Law and Modern Feminism?" (2001) 10:2 S Cal Rev L & Women's Stud 451.

Alison Diduck, *Law's Families* (London: LexisNexis, 2003).

Lisa Fishbayn, "Gender, Multiculturalism and Dialogue: The Case of Jewish Divorce" (2008) 21 Can JL & Jur 71.

Pascale Fournier, "Calculating Claims: Jewish and Muslim Women Navigating Religion, Economics and Law in Canada" (2012) 8 International Journal of Law in Context 47.

James MacDonald & Ann Wilton, *The 1999 Annotated Divorce Act* (Scarborough, ON: Carswell, 2003).

D McKie, B Prentice & P Reed, *Divorce: Law and the Family in Canada* (Ottawa: Statistics Canada, 1983).

JD Payne, *Payne on Divorce*, 4th ed (Scarborough, ON: Carswell, 1996).

Austin Sarat & William F Felstiner, *Divorce Lawyers and Their Clients: Power and Meaning in the Legal Process* (New York: Oxford University Press, 1995).

Shelley Day Sclater & Christine Piper, *Undercurrents of Divorce* (Aldershot UK: Ashgate Dartmouth, 1999).

Carol Smart, *The Ties That Bind: Law, Marriage, and the Reproduction of Patriarchal Relations* (London: Routledge & Kegan Paul, 1984).

John Sopinka, "The Divorce Act, 1968: Collusion Defined" (1969) 47 Can Bar Rev 31.

Stephen Sugarman & Herma Hill Kay, eds, *Divorce Reform at the Crossroads* (New Haven and London: Yale University Press, 1990).

IV.
THE ECONOMIC CONSEQUENCES OF DIVORCE AND SEPARATION

> The economic vulnerability of lone-parent families — those headed by mothers, in particular — is well documented. Lone-mother families are significantly more likely than other family types to be poor, and more likely to receive social assistance.... Even with the important gains made by female lone parent households, on average, their incomes remain considerably lower than those of male lone-parent households, although this difference has narrowed over time. (Vanier Institute of the Family, *Families Count* (Ottawa: VIF, 2010) at 104)

DATA ABOUT THE ECONOMIC IMPACT OF FAMILY DISSOLUTION

Economic vulnerability and lone parents (including divorced and separated spouses)

Although family dissolution is only one path that may lead to lone-parent families, the economic vulnerability of such families includes many parents and children involved in separation or divorce. As the comment above indicates, lone-parent families are often economically vulnerable, particularly where they are headed by women.

The economic impact of family dissolution: Research studies in the United States and Canada

In addition to this data about lone-parent families generally, there have been some studies specifically focused on the economic impact of family dissolution. In the United States, for example, research conducted by Lenore Weitzman suggested significant disparities in post-separation economic security for women, by contrast with men.

According to Weitzman's U.S. research, women's households suffered a 73 percent drop in their standard of living post-separation, while men's households had a 42 percent rise.

However, Weitzman's figures were challenged in the 1990s by Richard Peterson, who re-analyzed Weitzman's original data and concluded that women's standard of living dropped by just 27 percent, and that men experienced a rise of only 10 percent.

According to a report in the *New York Times*, Weitzman accepted responsibility for the mistake in her computer calculations, but her original figures had already been cited in 348 social science articles, 250 law reviews, and 24 appellate cases in the United States. See RR Peterson, "A Re-Evaluation of the Economic Consequences of Divorce" (1996) 61 American Sociological Review 61; and LJ Weitzman, *The Divorce Revolution: The*

Unexpected Social and Economic Consequences for Women and Children in America (New York: Free Press, 1985).

The disparity in the economic circumstances of men and women after family dissolution has also been documented in Canada, although the research suggests some differences between Canadian and American data.

In the 1980s, Ross Finnie conducted a longitudinal study of the economic circumstances of Canadian men and women in marriages, based on their tax files at three points: in the years immediately prior to marriage breakdown, in the year of their separation, and in the few years immediately following separation. The results showed significant financial impact for both men and women.

However, the statistics demonstrated considerable disparity in the economic position of women, by contrast with men, both in the year of separation and in the years immediately after it. Finnie's findings indicated that women's family income dropped by one-half, and men's by one-quarter, in the first year of separation. Using calculations of income to needs ratios, Finnie also concluded that there was a small rise in men's economic well-being, while women experienced a 40 percent drop in theirs. (See Ross Finnie, "Women, Men, and the Economic Consequences of Divorce: Evidence from the Canadian Longitudinal Data" (1993) 30:2 Canadian Review of Sociology and Anthropology 205.)

According to Finnie, this data suggested that the neoclassical model of families, one that assumes that families remain intact throughout life, needs to be replaced by a model that takes into account the statistics about divorce rates. An economic model might well mean major changes in human capital investment, labour market participation, and earnings profiles for men and women.

In another study of Canadian married couples who separated between 1987 and 1993, researchers concluded that women experienced a decrease in adjusted family income after separation, while men showed a slight increase. To some extent, these differences reflected women's custodial responsibility for children after separation. (See Diane Galarneau & Jim Sturrock, "Family Income after Separation" (1997) 9:2 Perspectives on Labour and Income 18; and Galarneau, "Income after Separation — People without Children" (1998) 10:2 Perspectives on Labour and Income 32.)

Although these studies focused on married couples, it is likely that the end of cohabiting relationships may reflect some of these same concerns.

Notes and Questions

Factors affecting economic vulnerability at family dissolution

In general, there is consensus that divorce and separation have an economic impact on families, and also that there is likely to be some disparity in their impact on women, by contrast with men. And, although recent initiatives, such as the child support guidelines, may have alleviated some of this impact for some families, it is likely that many families will experience economic setbacks as a result of family dissolution.

Consider what kinds of factors may contribute to this economic worsening of families' economic situations:

- Recall the statistics at the beginning of this chapter about the average length of marriages that end in divorce, and the average ages of spouses at divorce: how might these factors affect the economic situation of men and women?

- Where children are involved, to what extent might child care issues (discussed earlier in this book) affect labour force participation for women and men? Note that a lone parent who is in receipt of social assistance received an average of $14,829 to $19,297 in 2009. (See National Council of Welfare, *Welfare Incomes 2009* (Ottawa: National Council of Welfare Reports, Winter 2010) at vii.)

- What additional expenses may attend separation or divorce? For example, what costs are involved in the divorce or separation process, such as legal and counselling expenses? What is the financial impact of creating two households rather than one?

Are there other factors that may affect a family's economic circumstances at family dissolution?

FAMILIES AND THE STATE: MODELS FOR RESPONDING TO ECONOMIC VULNERABILITY

> With increasing numbers of sequential marriages, solutions to the financial crisis of marriage breakdown must be sought not only within the parameters of family law but also in social and economic policies that promote the financial viability of all persons in need, including the economic victims of marriage breakdown. The war on the feminization of poverty must be won by innovative and coherent socioeconomic policies. (Julien Payne, "Family Law in Canada" in Maureen Baker, ed, *Canada's Changing Families: Challenges to Public Policy* (Ottawa: Vanier Institute of the Family, 1994) 13 at 27)

Family dissolution: "Unmasking" family support for dependency

As the brief examination of economic data reveals, family dissolution may have a significant economic impact for families, and there may be considerable disparity for women and children, at least by contrast with men, in some cases. What this means is that the "family economy" may be permanently shattered by separation or divorce. In other words, while some family members are often dependent in an intact family (including children, of course, but also adults who are ill, without workforce skills or experience, or who are unemployable by reason of disability or illness), the intact family "masked" their dependency. Separation or divorce thus "unmasks" the dependency for which intact families provide support.

The role of families in providing support and caregiving for individuals who are dependent is a significant responsibility in many contexts other than family dissolution. However, in the context of statistics about the rate of family dissolution (including both marriages and cohabiting relationships that end) and studies about the economic impact of family dissolution for vulnerable family members, there is considerable debate about whether, or to what extent, former family members should have significant ongoing responsibilities to alleviate vulnerability among some family members after separation or divorce.

This is a question about who has primary responsibility for economic dependency (especially after divorce or separation) in Canada: individuals, families or the state?

Although this chapter focuses on the context of divorce and separation, it is important to understand these issues in the family dissolution context in terms of broader societal concerns.

It is also important to note that legislation and judicial decisions in the family law context have tended to assign a high level of responsibility to the "post-dissolution" family unit to alleviate economic vulnerability for former family members after separation or divorce. That is, as will become evident in the chapters that follow (which focus on corollary relief, including property sharing, spousal and child support, and custody and access in relation to children), family law principles reinforce continuing obligations on the part of former family members to support the dependency of individuals that is "unmasked" by divorce or separation.

Thus, this section provides a brief examination of underlying policies about models to support dependency. In the excerpt that follows, Margrit Eichler assesses the problem of post-dissolution poverty for women and children, suggesting that even middle-class women are often "only one man away from welfare." In particular, note her analysis of the kind of legal reform that might respond to this problem most effectively.

"The Limits of Family Law Reform"
(1990–91) 7 Can Fam LQ 59 at 66–69 and 81–83

Margrit Eichler

... Models of the family that underlie policy analyses and proposals are rarely spelled out explicitly. If we wish to uncover underlying models, we therefore need to ask ourselves: What is the model of the family with which the policy under consideration would be consistent?

Elsewhere, I have argued that we are currently experiencing a shift from a patriarchal model of the family to the individual responsibility model of the family....

THE PATRIARCHAL MODEL OF THE FAMILY

The patriarchal model of the family is characterized by the following eight characteristics:

1. the household and family are treated as being identical;
2. as a consequence, a husband is equated with a father, and a wife is equated with a mother;
3. the family is treated, administratively, as a unit;
4. the father and/or husband is seen as responsible for the economic well-being of the family;
5. the wife-mother is seen as responsible for the household and personal care of family members, especially childcare;
6. conversely, the father and/or husband is *not* seen as responsible for the household and personal care of family members, especially childcare;
7. the wife and/or mother is *not* seen as responsible for the economic well-being of the family; and
8. society may give support to the man who supports his dependents (wife and/or children), but is not responsible for the economic well-being of the family where there is a husband (father) present, and is not responsible for the household and personal care of family members, especially childcare, where there is a wife (mother)....

THE INDIVIDUAL RESPONSIBILITY MODEL OF THE FAMILY
The individual responsibility model of the family shares the first three characteristics with the patriarchal family, but then diverges:
1. the household and family are treated as being identical;
2. as a consequence, a husband is equated with a father, and a wife is equated with a mother;
3. the family is treated, administratively, as a unit;
4. both husband and wife are seen as responsible for their own support as well as that of the other;
5. both father and mother are seen as responsible for the household and personal care of family members, especially children; and
6. society may give support to families, but, in principle, is not responsible for either the economic well-being of the family nor for the personal care of family members, especially childcare, when there is either a husband (father) or wife (mother) present.

Part of the attraction of the individual responsibility model is that it is ideologically premised on the notion of sex equality. However, the great problem with it is that it actually allows for a *decrease* in societal contributions to families. Where before the state would have replaced the financial contributions of the husband and/or father in case he cannot or does not make them, it will not do so if an individual responsibility model of the family is used, and likewise with the service contributions of the wife and/or mother. In such a case, the expectation on the lone-parent family will suddenly double — all in the name of equality.

This is clearly an absurd situation. It is intimately linked to Weitzman's [and others'] charge that to treat people equally when they are not equal will increase inequality rather than reduce it.

At this point then, there are theoretically two directions one can choose to go. Given that women, as a group, do not have the same economic power as men, and given that in the vast majority of cases women have the major (and often sole) responsibility for dependent children, we can, through judicial fiat, put some of the economic burden back on to the men who fathered the children and used to be married to the women.

Alternatively, we can redefine societal obligations towards the raising of children, try to move towards equalizing the economic position of women with that of men, or move towards a third model of the family, the social responsibility model of the family....

THE SOCIAL RESPONSIBILITY MODEL OF THE FAMILY

The social responsibility model of the family is characterized by only three assumptions:

1. Every adult is considered responsible for his or her own economic well-being. Where this is impossible, the support obligation shifts to the state, not to a family member.
2. For an adult in need of care, whether because of a permanent or temporary illness or handicap, it is the responsibility of the state (not of a family member) to pay for the cost of such care.
3. The cost of raising children is shared by the father, the mother, and the state, irrespective of the marital status of the parents.

Even if we were to move immediately towards the social responsibility model of the family, *in the absence of preceding economic changes* there would still be problems with respect to an equitable division of property between women and men, due to the weaker position of women in the economy. Nevertheless, such a move would go a far distance in solving some of the problems Weitzman has so well described.

In reality, it is a matter of how to place emphases, rather than what absolute choices to make at this moment in history. The problem I have with some (not all) of Weitzman's proposed solutions is that they point us towards the individual responsibility model of the family, which although ideologically premised on the notion of sex equality shares with the patriarchal model of the family the view that the economic status of wives and children is the individual responsibility of the spouses and parents (in fact, often of the man). Furthermore, these proposals are likely to be taken as a *substitute* for a move towards a social responsibility model of the family, rather than as a stop-gap measure.

Let us, then, consider into which direction the proposed solutions would lead us. At the heart of the proposals are three principles: first, to consider children as participants in their own merit when dividing property; second, to treat the family home as something more than property worth money, namely as a residence, a home, a means of providing social and emotional stability to its inhabitants; and third, to treat marriage under all circumstances as an economic union of equals, totally and unnegotiably.

Of these three principles, I full-heartedly endorse the first and second. It is the third principle with which I have problems.

Postulating an unnegotiable tight economic union between ex-husbands and ex-wives ties the economic status of the wife to that of the husband. To the degree that children are (in practice and in theory) rolled into that equation, we have reaffirmed the centrepiece of a patriarchal notion of the family — namely, that the economic status of the wife (and the children) is — and should be! — dependent on the economic status of the husband/father.

This approach can be characterized as neo-conservative, in so far as it points backwards rather than forwards, although in a different guise than we have had in the past....

THE LIMITATIONS OF THE INDIVIDUAL RESPONSIBILITY MODEL

As we have seen, even if we could solve all the problems that would come along with an even tighter economic union between ex-husbands and ex-wives and the compulsory sharing of the family home, and if we could somehow come up with an equitable formula for solving the competing claims of first and second families, we would only have addressed the problem of poverty for a small fraction of poor women and children.

Let us play this briefly through with the example of support. With the proclamation of the *Family Orders and Agreements Enforcement Assistance Act*, we will improve the enforcement of court-ordered support payments. That is a very important step forward.

However, the alternative to support payments for poor women and children is social assistance. Unfortunately, social assistance is likely to be cut exactly by the amount of the court-ordered support payment. Unless the support payment is higher than the amount paid by welfare (not likely in the majority of cases) the women and children are therefore *not* better off than they were on welfare. It is arguable whether it is harder to be dependent on support payments or social assistance payments. Better enforcement of support payments will therefore save the state money (we have seen this in Manitoba) but it will improve the situation of poor women and children only marginally, if at all.

In principle, family law is incapable of solving the problem of poverty of women and children. If, then, further reform of the family law is proposed as a solution to the problem of female and child poverty, we must ask ourselves what this *avoids* doing: namely asking for a comprehensive reform of the income security system, and of the overall economic structure such that poverty in general (whether subsequent to a divorce or not) is eradicated.

We need to break away from the idea that the economic status of wives and children is and should be a function of the economic status of the husband — a quintessentially patriarchal idea.

Arguing for a societal recognition of shared responsibility towards children between the father, mother and society, and for sex equality in the economy (which, of course, presupposes an excellent system of childcare, a wide network of services for families, etc., none of which are in place in Canada at the present time) does not mean that we should tolerate unfairness in the division of family property. It simply puts it into its proper place — something that is of social importance, that should be striven for, but that must not be burdened with expectations that it cannot, in principle, ever fulfil....

Notes and Questions

Problems of poverty and inequality for "post-dissolution" families: An issue of public policy?

Eichler's recommendations for reform focus on the problems of widespread economic inequality within and among families in Canada. In this context, she argued that "*[i]n principle, family law is incapable of solving the problem of poverty of women and children.*" This insight may provide a useful way of assessing the variety of legislative and judicial efforts (discussed in later chapters) that have been adopted to overcome vulnerability in post-dissolution families in Canada, and ongoing debates about their effectiveness in practice. Significantly, a recent report documented how divorce or separation may lead to poverty in retirement. See Talbot Boggs, "Coping with Divorce and Retirement", *The Globe and Mail* (16 February 2012).

Like Eichler, two American legal scholars also argued that family law may not be sufficient, by itself, to provide solutions to the economic problems of divorce:

Our central premise is that the legal issues surrounding divorce have been conceived too narrowly. Reform initiatives have too often treated divorce as a largely private dispute and have not adequately addressed its public dimensions.... In our view, the most pressing problems stem from the inadequacy of public commitments both to equality between the sexes and to the quality of life, especially for children, following divorce. Addressing those concerns will require more fundamental reforms, not just in divorce law but in the broader family, work, and welfare policies with which it intersects. (Deborah Rhode & Martha Minow, "Reforming the Questions: Questioning the Reforms" in SD Sugarman & HH Kay, eds, *Divorce Reform at the Crossroads* (New Haven, CT: Yale University Press, 1990) at 191)

Problems of poverty and inequality for "post-dissolution" families: Private (contract) remedies?

By contrast with these recommendations for broader societal reforms to overcome poverty and inequality in post-dissolution families, Douglas Allen focused on the need to equalize bargaining at family dissolution as a way of overcoming the problems of disparity in post-dissolution families. Thus he suggested changing "no fault" divorce to "mutual consent" divorce.

According to Allen, a "mutual consent" requirement for divorce would mean that neither partner could leave a marriage without the other spouse's written consent, a requirement that would restore the bargaining power of the unwilling party and ensure that benefits would flow to the couple's children. Specifically Allen argued that his proposal would prevent husbands from unilaterally deciding to leave the family and retaining the bulk of family assets (see Douglas W Allen, "No-Fault Divorce and the Divorce Rate: Its History, Effect, and Implications" in Douglas W Allen & John Richards, eds, *It Takes Two: The Family in Law and Finance* (Toronto: C.D. Howe Institute, 1999)).

Allen's proposal is also relevant to issues about family law bargaining, discussed later in this chapter. Are there limits to the usefulness of this focus on bargaining to overcome problems of inequality at divorce? For example, to what extent would Allen's proposal have assisted Mrs. Behrendt, discussed in the previous chapter? Could Allen's proposal exacerbate power imbalances by trapping an unhappy spouse in a marital relationship and allowing vindictive spouses to ensure that a divorce was never granted, significantly hampering an individual-centric model of divorce?

Rethinking responsibilities for dependency: Families and the state

As Eichler suggested, a "social responsibility" model of family assumes the active involvement of the state in supporting families and children. In this way, there is a link between the family as an economic unit and the wider social safety network.

- Thus, in the family law context, decisions that preclude dependants from receiving financial support may result in their entitlement to social assistance.

- Conversely, if a member of a post-dissolution family is required to provide financial support to other members of the family, it is likely that the recipients will be disentitled to social assistance.

In this way, there is a relationship between private family support on family dissolution and a dependent family member's entitlement to (public) social assistance. However, the principles of family law and social assistance are not always congruent. For example, see MJ Mossman & M MacLean, "Family Law and Social Assistance Programs: Rethinking Equality" in Patricia A Evans & Gerda R Wekerle, eds, *Women and the Canadian Welfare State: Challenges and Change* (Toronto: University of Toronto Press, 1997) 117.

For some recent examples of judicial decisions that assessed the roles of families and of the state (social assistance), see *Falkiner v Ontario* (2002), 59 OR (3d) 481 (CA); and *Gosselin v Quebec (AG)*, 2002 SCC 84, cases discussed later in this book. See also *Tanudjaja v Attorney General (Canada) (Application)*, 2013 ONSC 5410, where it was held that affordable housing provisions did not engage sections 7 or 15 of the *Charter*; 2014 ONCA 852, leave to appeal to SCC requested. To what extent should the availability of social assistance reduce or eliminate the obligation of a former family member to provide financial support post-family dissolution?

Additional Resources

Sarah Avellar & Pamela Smock, "The Economic Consequences of the Dissolution of Cohabiting Unions" (2005) 67 Journal of Marriage and the Family 315.

Arthur B Cornell, "When Two Become One, and Then Come Undone: An Organizational Approach to Marriage and Its Implications for Divorce Law" (1992) 26 Fam LQ 103.

M Fineman, "Masking Dependency: The Political Role of Family Rhetoric" (1995) 81 Va L Rev 2180.

Nancy Fraser, "Talking about Needs: Interpretive Contests as Political Conflicts in Welfare-State Societies" (1989) 99:2 Ethics 291.

Carolyne A Gorlick, "Divorce: Options Available, Constraints Forced, and Pathways Taken" in Nancy Mandell & Ann Duffy, eds, *Canadian Families, Diversity, Conflict, Change*, 2nd ed (Toronto: Harcourt Canada, 2000) 260.

M McCall, J Hornick & J Wallace, *The Process and Economic Consequences of Marriage Breakdown* (Calgary: Canadian Research Institute for Law and the Family, 1988).

Mary Morton, "Dividing the Wealth, Sharing the Poverty: The (Re)Formation of 'Family' in Law in Ontario" (1988) 25 Canadian Review of Sociology and Anthropology 254.

MJ Mossman, "'Running Hard To Stand Still': The Paradox of Family Law Reform" (1994) 17:1 Dal LJ 5.

Susan Moller Okin, *Justice, Gender, and the Family* (New York: Basic Books, 1989).

Pamela Symes, "Property, Power and Dependence: Critical Family Law" (1987) 14:2 JL & Soc'y 199.

Lenore Weitzman & Mavis Maclean, eds, *Economic Consequences of Divorce: The International Perspective* (Oxford: Clarendon Press, 1992).

Jay Zagorsky, "Marriage and Divorce's Impact on Wealth" (2005) 41:4 Journal of Sociology 406.

V.
FAMILY DISSOLUTION: LEGAL PROCESSES

Family law needs are complex, multidimensional, and extremely wide-spread. There is no way to finesse the fact that family law problems are legal problems and need legal assistance [but] there is no magical solution or blueprint to this complex set of social problems. (Brenda Cossman & Carol Rogerson, "Case Study in the Provision of Legal Aid: Family Law" in Ontario Legal Aid Review, *Report of the Ontario Legal Aid Review: A Blueprint for Publicly-Funded Legal Services*, vol 3 (Toronto: Ontario Legal Aid Review, 1997) 773 at 843–844)

DIVORCE PROCESSES AND FAMILY LAW BARGAINING

Divorce: Litigation and "alternative" processes

As noted earlier in this chapter, divorce in Canada requires an order of the court (see *Divorce Act*, s 14), even though spouses may jointly make a successful application for divorce on the ground of marriage breakdown, proved by a one-year period of living separate and apart. In this way, spouses who are in agreement may obtain a divorce after they have lived separately for one year.

Moreover, as also noted earlier, it is possible for spouses to obtain "desktop" divorces in uncontested cases where all corollary relief matters have been settled.

In this way, while it is necessary for a court to make an order of divorce, the spouses may achieve it efficiently if they are able to reach agreement with respect to their separation and corollary relief matters.

However, as Bruce Ziff noted, because no-fault divorce makes many matters irrelevant to the order for divorce, spouses sometimes transfer arguments about their marriage relationship to disagreements about issues of corollary relief. In this way, disagreements about property, spousal support, custody and access of children, and arrangements for child support may become "contested" issues even if the divorce itself is "uncontested."

In this context, some spouses become embroiled in lengthy, embittered and expensive litigation involving motions and counter motions and even a family court trial.

Other spouses may choose, or in some cases be required to engage in, other forms of dispute resolution, either with or without legal representation, including negotiation, collaborative law processes, mediation, or arbitration.

In general, these alternatives to litigation are designed to result in a settlement, usually a separation agreement, and this agreement may be formally adopted in a divorce order as corollary relief.

Traditionally, many non-litigation methods for reaching a settlement at separation or divorce have been referred to as "alternative dispute resolution" or ADR. However, since well over 90 percent of divorce cases are resolved without a trial, it is clear that these other methods of resolving disputes are, in fact, the primary means of reaching settlements in family law matters. Moreover, even in the context of litigation, few family law cases involve a full trial.

In this context, most of the processes for reaching settlement in family law matters involve bargaining on the part of spouses (whether or not they are represented by lawyers) and whether or not there is a third party involved (as in mediation and arbitration). *Thus, in practice, the divorce process is a process that depends on significant amounts of family law bargaining.*

As a result, issues about the respective roles of private family law bargaining on one hand, and the role of the state in ensuring fairness in settlements at separation and divorce on the other, remain contested and controversial. As you review the material in this section, assess the extent to which legislative and judicial guidelines appear to achieve an appropriate balance between these competing goals.

DIVORCE PROCESSES: LITIGATION AND THE COURTS

"Family law" courts

Recall the earlier discussion with respect to the legislative authority of the federal Parliament and the provincial legislatures in relation to divorce and separation. In addition to this complexity in terms of legislative authority, a further complication is the need to attend to the jurisdiction of courts with respect to family dissolution in Canada.

The Constitution requires that matters of divorce and property be heard only in "superior courts in the provinces," and matters of corollary relief in a divorce action are also heard by superior courts.

However, in the absence of divorce (for cohabiting couples, or in cases where married couples have separated but not filed a divorce application), issues of custody and support (often "interim" applications) are presented to provincial courts (see Hogg at 27.9).

Some of these jurisdictional issues have been alleviated by the creation of Unified Family Courts in a number of Canadian provinces, including Saskatchewan, Manitoba, New Brunswick and Newfoundland. Ontario has a mixture of courts hearing family law matters, with Unified Family Courts in some parts of the province presided over by judges who have expertise in family law matters. However, in a recent review of five sites of Family Courts in Ontario, the reviewers concluded that

> [t]he research team is cognizant that even after addressing the needs of the [Family Court], the province will still have a patchwork of provincially- and federally-appointed judges presiding over family law matters. The fragmented delivery of family court services creates inequity for families and children throughout the province. Therefore, we urge the Attorney General to undertake a comprehensive review of the family justice system. Ideally, this review must be conducted with full support and participation of the federal government.... (Alfred Mamo, Peter Jaffe & Debbie Chiodo, *Recapturing and Renewing the Vision of the Family Court* (Toronto: Ministry of the Attorney General, 2007) at 8)

Significantly, this report also advised the government about the need to expand non-litigation methods for resolving family law disputes at separation and divorce, and these latter recommendations seem to have garnered more attention than the recommendation to expand Unified Family Courts (see below).

In examining these materials about legal processes at family dissolution, consider the advantages of Unified Family Courts for these cases. In addition to overcoming jurisdictional issues for courts pursuant to the Constitution, are there other advantages to the creation of "family courts"? Are there any disadvantages of specialized "family courts"?

Litigation processes: The *Family Law Rules*

In Ontario, procedures concerning family dissolution issues are defined in the Family Law Rules, O Reg 114/99, which apply to proceedings in the courts.

After pleadings have been filed, it is mandatory for the parties to meet in a Case Conference, a process designed to encourage settlement by exploring options for the parties to reach agreement. In most cases, however, the parties cannot seek even interim relief unless they have participated in a Case Conference, and this requirement means that there may be a delay of several months if there is a shortage of judges to conduct Case Conferences.

After a Case Conference, the parties may bring motions for interim relief, that is a temporary order concerning custody or support, for example. Motions are generally decided on the basis of sworn affidavit evidence. Recall, for example, Mrs. Behrendt's application for possession of the matrimonial home (in Chapter Four), and the affidavit evidence filed by the spouses and their son.

There are also rules permitting requests for document disclosure and questioning by the parties, arrangements intended to ensure that relevant information is available.

The parties may also participate in a Settlement Conference, in which they are required to make an offer to settle, which may be relevant to the issue of costs if the case is not settled and a trial is conducted. The judge in a Settlement Conference is not the judge who sits at trial. If the parties proceed to trial, it is also likely that there may be a Trial Management Conference to organize arrangements for the trial, including information about witnesses, for example.

A trial is conducted in accordance with the rules for civil trials before a judge. If there is "divided success" in the trial, costs may not be awarded at all, but a party who behaves unreasonably may be denied costs or have costs awarded against him or her (for details, see *Family Law Rules*, O Reg 114/99).

The responsibilities of the parties at divorce: (Mandatory) information programs

In some provinces, spouses are required to attend mandatory educational programs about the divorce process. For example, procedural rules in Ontario have required (with a few exceptions) that all parties in divorce actions attend mandatory information programs within 45 days after commencing their proceedings, and any additional steps in their proceedings are precluded until both parties have filed certificates of (separate) attendance at the programs. Some family lawyers have expressed concern, however, that these information programs occur too late, and that access to information about options before initiating legal proceedings would be more beneficial. See Mark Brownlee, "Ontario Couples now have to Attend Information Session before Divorce", *The Globe and Mail* (18 July 2011).

Similar programs in the United States have focused particularly on improving parenting behaviour and stressed the need for divorcing parents to reduce the impact of conflict on their children. As Eileen Biondi reported in the mid-1990s, courts seeking to remedy the effect of divorce on children have benefited from state legislation mandating parental attendance at parent education programs prior to divorce (see Eileen D Biondi, "Legal Implementation of Parent Education Programs for Divorcing and Separating Parents" (1996) 34:1 Fam Ct Rev 82 at 90).

However, there are also criticisms of the content of some parental education programs. For example, some critics have noted that the programs tend to focus primarily on the needs of children and that issues about domestic violence have received only limited coverage. See Sanford L Braver et al, "The Content of Divorce Education Programs: Results of a Survey" (1996) 34:1 Fam Ct Rev 41 at 52–54.

Another study concluded that more intensive, skill-based programs (which focus on learning new skills and changing parental behaviours) may be more effective than short information-based programs. See Kevin M Kramer et al, "Effects of Skill-Based Versus Information-Based Divorce Education Programs on Domestic Violence and Parental Communication" (1998) 36:1 Fam Ct Rev 9.

In a national survey of mandatory parent education programs in the United States, two researchers noted concerns about requirements for attendance at such programs in the context of allegations of domestic violence, suggesting that encouraging communication and co-operation in these cases could lead to more abusive confrontations. See Susan Pollet & Melissa Lombreglia, "A Nationwide Survey of Mandatory Parent Education" (2008) 46:2 Fam Ct Rev 375.

What are the underlying assumptions about these educational programs for parents who are divorcing? Although the study by Kramer and others reported that parents who attended such programs litigated less than half as often as non-attending spouses in a two-year period following divorce, it may be important to question how such results should be interpreted. Is it always appropriate to create access barriers to family courts for clients in divorce actions? How should these issues be addressed in designing parent information programs?

The role of lawyers in family law matters

Particularly in a context of no fault divorce, some scholars have argued that lawyers remain essential to goals of efficiency and justice in family law matters. For example, two American scholars argued that a lawyer's role may often involve teaching clients about the limits of divorce law in terms of processing clients' feelings of anger or blame. See Austin Sarat & William LF Felstiner, *Divorce Lawyers and Their Clients: Power and Meaning in the Legal Process* (New York: Oxford University Press, 1995).

Similarly in the United Kingdom, Christine Piper suggested that family lawyers are engaged in an exercise of teaching values to "soon to be separated but continuing" family units. See Christine Piper, "How Do You Define a Family Lawyer?" (1999) 19 LS 93 at 106.

Moreover, some studies suggest that the need for lawyers to define client values may be especially significant in the context of children. See Carol Smart & Bren Neale, *Family Fragments?* (Cambridge: Polity Press, 1999).

Such comments reveal how the range of lawyers' interactions with their clients may be significant, particularly in defining what are, and just as importantly, what are not, legal issues for separating and divorcing clients.

Issues about legal representation for separating and divorcing clients in Canada

As Cossman and Rogerson noted in their study of access to legal aid in family law matters, issues in family law proceedings are often complex and multidimensional, and the need for legal advice and information is widespread. Yet family law has increasingly suffered from a lack of resources for legal representation, and it seems that significant numbers of family law litigants have been unrepresented. For example, see *Fowler v Fowler* (1997), 32 RFL (4th) 426 (Ont Gen Div). Julie Macfarlane explored the experiences of self-represented litigants in Alberta, British Columbia, and Ontario. Of the total number (283 interviews), 60% were family litigants and a majority of these litigants were involved in divorce courts. Among the findings, the study identified "[b]y far the most consistently cited reason for self-representation was the inability to afford to retain, or to continue to retain, legal counsel" (Julie Macfarlane, *The National Self-Represented Litigants Project: Identifying and Meeting the Needs of Self-Represented Litigants, Final Report* (May 2013) (Toronto: The Law Society of Upper Canada), online: <http://www.lsuc.on.ca/uploadedFiles/For_the_Public/About_the_Law_Society/Convocation_Decisions/2014/Self-represented_project.pdf>).

Family law clients unable to obtain representation because of financial problems ("unrepresented litigants") and those who have chosen to represent themselves ("self represented litigants") have created difficulties for lawyers representing the other side in family law disputes, and they also create challenges for judges. See DA Rollie Thompson, "A Practising Lawyer's Fieldguide to the Self-Represented" (2001–2) 19 Can Fam LQ 529; DA Rollie Thompson & Lynn Reierson, "No Lawyer: Institutional Coping with the Self-Represented" (in the same volume) at 455; and Hon Marguerite Trussler, "A Judicial View on Self-Represented Litigants" (in the same volume) at 547.

In *Cicciarella v Cicciarella*, [2009] OJ No 2906, a three-judge panel of the Ontario Divisional Court ordered a new trial, based on the wife's claim that the trial judge had interfered unreasonably and unfairly. She had been represented at trial, while her husband represented himself. In its decision, the court commented on the need to ensure judicial neutrality in spite of one party's lack of legal representation. Similar (advisory) directives were issued in 2006 by the Canadian Judicial Council (see "Statement of Principles on Self-Represented Litigants and Accused Persons"; and Steven Benmor, "Self-Represented Family Law Litigants pose Challenges", *The Lawyers Weekly* (23 September 2011) 9 and 13).

Cicciarella was applied in *Office of the Children's Lawyer v Family and Children Services of Renfrew County*, 2014 ONSC 4021, where with regard to an unrepresented party's submissions, the court stated:

> leeway is allowed for a self-represented part[y], especially as it relates to procedural matters. In the present case, I interpret this as meaning that the Court may look at the Appellant's documents and interpret what the Appellant is trying to say and how it relates to the legal issues. However, I must keep in mind that this must be done fairly while maintaining judicial neutrality. (at para 23)

A recent study concluded that costs increase because cases proceed more slowly where family law clients are unrepresented or self-represented, and that lawyers representing one party in a family law matter face significant problems where the other party is not represented or self-represented. See Nicholas Bala & Rachel Birnbaum, "Family Litigants without Lawyers: Study Documents Growing Challenges for the Justice System", *The Lawyers Weekly* (5 August 2011); see also *Law Times* (8 August 2011); and *Toronto Star* (2 August 2011).

In addition, the recent report of the Civil Legal Needs Project in Ontario, which surveyed legal needs in Ontario across all income ranges, concluded that family law issues were particularly important to resolve. Data from the Project's survey of needs indicated that 81 percent of those who had experienced a family problem had sought legal assistance, but 30 percent had experienced difficulty obtaining it. The report was clear about the need for new approaches to family law issues:

> Our Project consistently revealed that family relationship breakdown is the primary reason why most Ontarians enter the civil justice system. The breakdown of a family relationship is also often at the heart of people encountering multiple civil legal problems, and it is at the centre of clustering civil legal problems. Family relationship problems are also among the most difficult, complicated, and time consuming to resolve. This reality translates into making them most disruptive to people's daily lives and most draining on their resources. Our survey revealed that more than 4 in 10 people (44 per cent) with a family relationship problem had not resolved their problem within three years. Access to resources in family law in the form of information, legal and social assistance, and resolution of family law problems for low and middle-income Ontarians is a priority issue for the civil legal system. As identified in our Project results, addressing the gap in services and support in family law will require a range of services from all partners in our civil legal system. (Ontario Civil Legal Needs Project, *Listening to Ontarians: Report of the Ontario Civil Legal Needs Project* (Toronto: Ontario Civil Legal Needs Project Steering Committee, 2010) at 57)

However, as will be discussed shortly, although there have been numerous innovations in the legal arrangements for family law proceedings in the courts in recent years, most recent analyses tend to recommend measures that "divert" family law issues into other forums for dispute resolution. For example, see Kirk Makin & Erin Anderssen, "Divorce — the Canadian Way" and related comments, *The Globe and Mail* (26 March 2011) F6.

Yet, as Cossman and Rogerson noted, many of the systems recently introduced to promote settlement in family law, such as case management, are heavily reliant on the involvement of lawyers to encourage settlement between court appearances. Thus, some of these arrangements may *increase* the necessity for legal advice and representation, including assistance in preparing documents, obtaining interim relief, and in negotiations or other processes to achieve settlement at separation or divorce.

Significantly, the Interim Report of the Law Commission of Ontario recommended the creation of a comprehensive entry point to connect users to broader family services, a comprehensive website, and the expansion of Unified Family Courts in Ontario (see Law Commission of Ontario, *Towards a More Efficient and Responsive Family Law System, Interim Report* (Toronto: LCO, February 2012)). The Final Report of the Family Justice Working Group (*Meaningful Change for Family Justice: Beyond Wise Words* (Toronto: Canadian Forum on Civil Justice, 2013), online: <http://www.cfcj-fcjc.org>) explained the "implementation gap," that is, the problem that so many reports and recommendations have not resulted in significant change for family law litigants. The report suggested that there are two problems:

one is the "limited resources available to the family justice system;" and the second is the "culture of the justice system and its incomplete embrace of non-adversarial or consensual dispute resolution processes" (at 3). Echoing the report of the Civil Legal Needs Project, this report emphasized that:

> Family law has a very broad reach. There is perhaps no single area of law that touches as many people. The quality or adequacy of a family's encounter with the justice system can shape their lives and influence their wellbeing for the long term.... From a broader social perspective we see the risks associated with insufficient access to family justice. Access to justice is a corollary of the rule of law and is essential to the social and economic wellbeing of civil society. (at 4–5)

Access to legal aid and policies promoting non-litigation resolution of family law matters

The Report of the Ontario Civil Legal Needs Project also provided data about legal aid in the family law context. According to the data provided by Legal Aid Ontario (*Listening to Ontarians*, at 49):

- There was a 29 percent decrease in the number of lawyers accepting legal aid certificates in the period between 1999–2000 and 2006–2007.

- Lawyers became less willing to take such certificates as they become more established in their legal practices (855 "new" lawyers accepted certificates in 1999–2000 but only 392 of this group continued to do so in 2006–2007).

- Legal aid lawyers may generally be less experienced than lawyers providing family law services to paying clients.

Recall the discussion of *New Brunswick (Minister of Health and Community Services) v G(J)*, [1999] 3 SCR 46, in the context of child protection.

In *G(J)*, the Supreme Court of Canada unanimously concluded that the province was constitutionally obliged to provide state-funded counsel for an indigent mother in child protection proceedings. Some scholars have argued that this case may provide the basis for extending the right to legal aid services in family law and other proceedings. See Canadian Bar Association, *Report of the Canadian Bar Association, Making the Case: The Right to Publicly-Funded Legal Representation in Canada* (Ottawa: Canadian Bar Association, 2002); and Melina Buckley, *Moving Forward on Legal Aid* (Ottawa: Canadian Bar Association, 2010); Michael Trebilcock, Antony Duggan & Lorne Sossin, eds, *Middle Income Access to Justice* (Toronto: University of Toronto Press, 2012); and Laura Track, Shahnaz Rahman & Kasari Govender, *Putting Justice Back on the Map: The route to equal and accessible family justice* (Vancouver: West Coast LEAF (Women's Legal Action and Education Fund), 2014), online: <http://www.westcoastleaf.org/wp-content/uploads/2014/10/2014-REPORT-Putting-Justice-Back-on-the-Map.pdf>.

In July 2014, Legal Aid Ontario announced a "significant expansion" of legal aid services in family law matters. The program offers financially eligible couples free access to a family lawyer to negotiate a separation agreement (up to 10 hours) or to provide legal advice for mediation (up to 6 hours). A family client without dependants will qualify financially if the person has a gross income up to $18,000 per year (with increases for additional dependants); if one partner qualifies, the other will also be eligible so long as the other person's income is no more than $50,000. (See Rachel Mendleson, "Legal Aid hopes to discourage feuding couples from acting as own lawyers", *Toronto Star* (3 July 2014) A1 and A10.)

As Cossman and Rogerson pointed out in their earlier case study of legal aid services in family law, the lack of legal representation in litigation processes often resulted in governmental policies focusing on negotiation and other settlement processes as a way of deflecting family law matters away from litigation:

> [There] are ongoing efforts in family law to structure the process so as to promote settlement rather than litigation in recognition of both the inability of the majority of family law clients to bear the high costs of litigation and the higher levels of satisfaction that are likely with a negotiated outcome tailored to the parties' individual circumstances rather than one imposed by a court. The efforts to promote settlement include resort to alternative dispute resolution techniques, such as mediation, and the introduction of systems of case management, including settlement conferences and pre-trials, into family law litigation. (Cossman & Rogerson at 785)

In this context, consider whether there are some family law matters that should be determined only by courts? As will be discussed later in this chapter, the need for independent legal representation may not be avoided in processes for resolving family law matters that do not involve the courts. What criteria should be adopted to determine how to "stream" family law disputes?

Notes and Questions

Litigation and ADR: The state's interest?

In a study in the United Kingdom, Helen Reece examined the underlying messages of recent legislative changes, which abolished fault-based divorce in the United Kingdom, and required spouses to attend information sessions about divorce and consider reconciliation. In addition, the divorce proceedings were stayed for several months to permit spouses to "reflect" and to consider using mediation rather than litigation. However, in a subsequent evaluation of a pilot project, Reece reported that many divorcing couples resisted these policies completely, choosing to seek legal advice rather than marriage counselling and mediation. According to Reece, the government's policy was rejected because it was essentially coercive, directing rather than informing the parties' decision making. See Helen Reece, *Divorcing Responsibly* (Oxford and Portland, OR: Hart Publishing, 2003).

Consider Reece's analysis of these developments in the United Kingdom in relation to the processes for divorce in Ontario. Are the "costs of divorce" — for the parties and also for governments who provide court services — promoting greater use of alternative processes for dispute resolution in family law? What is the balance between information services for family law clients and adequate legal representation of family law clients? For an overview of the variety of current entry points to the family law system, see Law Commission of Ontario, *Voices from a Broken Family Justice System: Sharing Consultations Results* (Toronto: LCO, 2010).

Family law matters and privacy issues

In the litigation context, family law matters may reveal issues that are intensely private for the parties. As a result, the usual principle of openness of court proceedings has sometimes been qualified to protect family privacy:

- In *Edmonton Journal v Alberta (AG)*, [1989] 2 SCR 1326, the Supreme Court of Canada permitted the preservation of privacy with respect to some aspects of a family law proceeding.

- In British Columbia, the B.C. Supreme Court modified its practice of posting family law decisions on the court's website, opting to post only cases with precedential value and to "de-identify" personal factors not essential to the reasoning. See Gary Oakes, "BC Modifies Plan to Ban Family Law Decisions on Website", *The Lawyers Weekly* (19 July 2002) 9; and Cristin Schmitz, "Courts Struggle with Issue of Private Divorces in Public Courts", *The Lawyers Weekly* (7 March 2003) 9.

- In *MEH v Williams*, 2012 ONCA 35, the court allowed an appeal by media organizations from orders of non-publication and sealing of files in a divorce proceeding initiated by the spouse of a sexual predator and murderer. The appeal court held that the evidence did not support the trial judge's finding that such orders were necessary to prevent serious risk to the proper administration of justice. In granting the appeal, however, the Court of Appeal confirmed that the trial judge's order, which prevented publication of the wife's social insurance number, date of birth, bank account numbers and domestic contract, remained in effect, as well as medical information other than information included in the reasoning in both courts.

- In 2012, the issue of privacy with respect to divorce records was again raised, when details about the divorce of a federal Cabinet Minister were circulated on Twitter. Although some comments about this case suggested a need to reduce public access to such records, which may often contain personal details (such as social insurance numbers, tax returns, and investment details) as well as affidavits about the spouses' relationship and difficulties, other critics expressed concern about preserving the concept of an open legal system. See Jennifer Ditchburn, "Toews' Divorce sparks Debate", *Toronto Star* (12 March 2012) A7.

In reflecting on the competing policies of family privacy on one hand and the openness of family law courts on the other, consider this example:

In 2012, the Ontario Court of Appeal allowed an appeal of a claim for damages for invasion of privacy in *Jones v Tsige*, 2012 ONCA 32. In this case, the plaintiff and the defendant did not know one another, although they both worked at different branches of the same bank. Unbeknownst to the plaintiff, the defendant (who had formed a cohabiting relationship with the plaintiff's former husband) had used her right of access to the bank's computers to examine the plaintiff's personal accounts 174 times, although she did not publish or record this information. The trial judge had dismissed the plaintiff's motion for summary judgment on the basis that the tort of invasion of privacy does not form part of the common law in Ontario. By contrast, the appellate court held that technological change poses a novel threat to the right of privacy and that the defendant committed the tort of intrusion upon seclusion: it was intentional, it constituted an unlawful invasion of the plaintiff's private affairs, and it caused the plaintiff distress, humiliation or anguish. The appeal court awarded damages of $10,000.

Although it may not be possible for family law litigants to invoke this tort to prevent access to information about their divorce cases, it may be significant that some family law clients may choose to adopt non-litigation processes, at least in part, because ADR proceedings are generally conducted in private. How should this factor affect arguments about privacy claims in the courts?

PROCESSES FOR RESOLVING FAMILY DISPUTES: "PRIVATE ORDERING" AND FAMILY LAW BARGAINING

> In reviewing the evidence about the practice of family law in Canada, the Task Force found that the reality fell far short of our aspirations and our ideals. Lawyers struggling to provide justice to litigants in this area received little support despite verbal assurances from many levels of government. In the cynical words of one female lawyer, governments provide "all possible aid short of actual help." (Canadian Bar Association Task Force on Gender Equality in the Legal Profession, *Touchstones for Change: Equality, Diversity, and Accountability* (Ottawa: Canadian Bar Association, 1993) at 203)

The above comment suggests that family law matters lack adequate resources, including courts, judges and lawyers. In this context, arrangements for solving family disputes outside litigation processes have become increasingly prominent. There are a number of reasons for this development:

- Governmental policies (as noted above) often encourage non-litigation methods for resolving issues at family dissolution, particularly ADR, as a way of using scarce resources more effectively.

- The *Family Law Rules* provide a number of incentives to reach settlement, even within the litigation process, as a means of diverting family law clients from the use of court resources.

- Family law clients without legal representation may find some ADR processes less intimidating and more effective than litigation, although it seems that some clients also wish to have their "day in court."

In practice, however, both the encouragement to settle in the litigation process, as well as the increasing use of alternatives to litigation, result in an emphasis on family bargaining at divorce or separation. Indeed, it seems that family bargaining is central to the resolution of issues at family dissolution, and, at least in some cases, the scope of family law bargains may be wider than court orders. See Lorne Wolfson, "Eighteen Things You Can't Get in Court", *The Lawyers Weekly* (17 February 2012) 12.

Negotiation: Bargaining "in the shadow of the law"

As a number of scholars have argued, divorcing and separating spouses engage in family bargaining "in the shadow of the law" (see RH Mnookin & L Kornhauser, "Bargaining in the Shadow of the Law: The Case of Divorce" (1979) 88 Yale LJ 950). Of course, such an assertion assumes that the parties know their legal entitlements as they enter into family bargaining, a situation that may or may not exist in all cases, particularly if the spouses have inadequate access to legal advice.

In this context, it is important to understand the bargaining process in relation to issues at separation or divorce in order to assess its implications for family law clients. As Mnookin and Kornhauser suggested, negotiation (by contrast with litigation) is likely to be less expensive, the pain of an adversarial proceeding is avoided, there is likely to be less risk and delay, and a consensual solution may be more consistent with the parties' preferences (see Mnookin & Kornhauser at 956–957).

However, in a subsequent analysis, Mnookin also identified some of the limits of negotiation:

- **Issues about capacity:** Some spouses may lack capacity for such bargaining because they are not fully rational contracting parties at the time of separation and divorce. That is, although they may be competent, they lack "transactional capacity." Instead, because they are in the midst of great stress and psychological turmoil, they are unable to make deliberate and well-informed decisions.

- **Matters of bargaining power:** The bargaining power of each spouse may be affected by their individual preferences, their legal entitlements (the "shadow of the law"), the degree of uncertainty about a court's decision and the parties' ability to sustain risk, the ability to manage transaction costs, and strategic behaviour.

- **Issues about third parties:** The potential for the spouses' agreement to have negative consequences for third parties, particularly children, but also the state's fiscal interests.

As Mnookin concluded:

> This framework suggests] an important intellectual agenda for those concerned with dispute settlement and divorce. How do the rules and procedures used in court ... affect the bargaining process that occurs between divorcing couples *outside* the courtroom? How do various procedural requirements affect the parties' behavior during the time they are resolving various distributional issues, and thereafter? What rules and procedures facilitate dispute settlement, and how do alternatives affect the future relationship of the former spouses to each other and to their children in subsequent years? *In short, how do we best design rules and procedures that respect personal autonomy by facilitating private ordering, and ensure fairness by establishing appropriate safeguards against the risks that incapacity or third parties may lead to unjust results?* (Robert Mnookin, "Divorce Bargaining: The Limits on Private Ordering" (1985) 18:4 Mich JL Reform 1015 at 1036–1037 [emphasis added])

Mnookin's question (above) provides an important framework for assessing negotiation and other non-litigation methods of dispute resolution.

In this context, moreover, some scholars have suggested that gender may be an additional factor to be considered in relation to family law bargaining. For example, Marcia Neave examined the impact of gender on game theory in the work of Carol Rose to show why women may end up worse off than men in bargaining situations. Her assessment focused on two assumptions in Rose's game theory: first, that women tend to have a greater taste for co-operation than men; and second, that men believe that women have a greater taste for co-operation, whether or not this is true. Consider Neave's arguments in relation to family law bargaining (citing Carol Rose, "Women and Property: Gaining and Losing Ground" (1992) 78 Va L Rev 421):

> If the first assumption is correct Rose shows that in a zero-sum game a person with a greater taste for cooperation will inevitably end up worse off because he or she will be prepared to pay a higher price to induce the less cooperative party to enter into the agreement or to abide by its terms. For instance, suppose that wives, in general, tend to place a higher value on the maintenance of an amicable relationship with their former spouse and his relatives than husbands, in general, place on maintaining a continuing relationship with their wives. In this situation wives will be more likely than husbands to "trade off" matrimonial property or spouse maintenance in order to achieve this goal and will tend to do less well financially as a result....
>
> Even more interestingly, Rose argues that the same result may follow *even* if the propensity to behave cooperatively is equally distributed between men and women, *but* it is generally believed that women place a higher value than men on cooperative behaviour.... Suppose that most men assume that women will usually take a smaller share of matrimonial property in order to avoid conflict, or in return for retaining custody of the children. Wives who challenge this assumption will be perceived as acting unreasonably (in comparison with other women) by their husbands, who may take a tougher bargaining position as a result. They may also be

perceived as acting unreasonably by their own legal advisers, who will be influenced by their perception of the "normal" women's conduct.

Rather than singlehandedly challenging assumptions about the approach which women generally take in these situations, a particular woman may feel pressured to accept a smaller share of the matrimonial property, thus reinforcing the belief that all women are prepared to make such trade-offs. In other words, the effect of the assumption that women are more cooperative than men may be to make them behave more cooperatively....

Although it is not possible to obtain reliable figures on the extent of domestic violence, women are physically abused in a relatively high proportion of marriages. Violence sometimes continues even after separation and divorce. Women who fear violence from their husbands may bargain away their financial rights in order to protect themselves and their children. It is doubtful whether contractual doctrines dealing with duress can provide practical protection in these circumstances, for women in this situation are often too frightened and powerless to seek to have agreements set aside.... (Marcia Neave, "Resolving the Dilemma of Difference: A Critique of 'The Role of Private Ordering in Family Law'" (1994) 44 UTLJ 97 at 105 and 124–126)

In the context of these concerns, are there some family issues that should not be the subject of bargaining? To what extent might legal representation overcome some of the disadvantages identified by Mnookin and Neave?

Collaborative law

A "New" Approach to Family Law Bargaining

A collaborative law process, which is available in some other civil law proceedings as well, has gained considerable support in family law matters. Collaborative law is focused on a settlement model, with lawyers representing each party committed to creating an environment in which issues will be resolved in four-way meetings, without resorting to litigation. This process, in which lawyers act in supporting roles while the parties take primary roles in identifying their goals and agree to share all information fully among the participants, seeks to achieve both rights and interests for the parties. The parties sign a Collaborative Law contract, in which they agree to engage openly in the negotiations, and that, if they are unable to reach settlement, the contract requires that each client must seek another counsel to provide legal representation for litigation purposes.

According to Julie Macfarlane, the most important tool for a lawyer who uses collaborative law processes is

... a commitment to good outcomes that are not measured exclusively by the benchmark of adjudication. This means that the ... lawyer relies on a broader knowledge and understanding of the clients' goals and motivations, perhaps an established rapport with the other side and an insight into their goals and an acceptance of the potential significance of emotional factors for her clients.... (Julie Macfarlane, *The New Lawyer: How Settlement is Transforming the Practice of Law* (Vancouver: UBC Press, 2008) at 159–160)

Many family lawyers have embraced collaborative law practice as a less adversarial way to achieve good settlements for their clients (see Peter Bakogeorge, "Collaborative Law Gives 'Huge' Job Satisfaction", *Law Times* (17 March 2003) 12). In addition, Macfarlane and other scholars have assessed its potential for client satisfaction as much higher than traditional lawyer-assisted negotiation processes.

Limitations of Collaborative Law Processes?

Yet, as in other kinds of lawyer-assisted negotiation, lawyers are necessary in collaborative law processes, a problem for family law clients whose resources are inadequate to retain legal representation. Moreover, collaborative law involves family bargaining, even though it occurs in a different setting and in accordance with differing objectives.

In the context of its goals and procedures, to what extent might collaborative law offer greater opportunities in relation to dispute resolution in family law matters? Are there limitations to its effectiveness? In this context, consider this assessment from a small empirical study of collaborative law processes for family law clients:

> A number of different measures could assist CL lawyers in overcoming and avoiding many of the barriers to engagement identified by clients in this study. Perhaps of greatest importance would be an informed understanding of the impact of abusive relationships and inequalities on clients, an appreciation of both the possibilities and limits of the process and the skill set to ensure that such sensitivities are maintained throughout the process. Screening protocols could explore issues such as: incidence, severity and frequency of alleged past violence; long-term patterns of emotional abuse, controlling and manipulative behavior; alleged escalation of abuse; the parties' capacity to communicate; the likelihood of equal participation; and client needs for emotional healing.... Since the collaborative process will likely ... diminish the significance of abuse and other substantial inequalities (particularly where allegations are disputed) lawyers should also consider erring on the side of recommending against CL in favor of negotiation processes that use a more traditional lawyer-to-lawyer approach.... (Michaela Keet, Wanda Wiegers & Melanie Morrison, "Client Engagement inside Collaborative Law" (2008) 24:2 Can J Fam L 145 at 201–202)

Does this assessment assist you to determine whether, and in what kinds of cases, collaborative law may be useful as an alternative method of dispute resolution in family law?

Mediation

Statutory and Governmental Policies Encouraging Mediation

Unlike settlement negotiations or collaborative law, mediation involves a neutral third party who works with the parties to achieve agreement. Although the parties participating in mediation may also be represented by lawyers, the process often involves face-to-face discussions with only the mediator and the parties. Sometimes mediators are lawyers, but they may also be members of other professions, including social workers, psychologists and clergy.

Divorce legislation has increasingly emphasized the importance of achieving settlement for divorcing parents, particularly through the use of mediation. For example, section 9 of the *Divorce Act*, introduced a responsibility for lawyers to discuss with clients the appropriateness of mediation services. This provision raised expressly the possibility of alternatives to litigation and more traditional processes of negotiation in divorce matters.

In recent decades, mediation services have become more widely available, with a range of professionals, including lawyers, involved.

• In a survey of 500 family mediators in Canada, for example, Edward Kruk reported on practice issues, strategies, and models, and concluded that mediation services have become much more diversified in the past decade, moving beyond ideas about structured negotiation and neutrality. (See Edward Kruk, "Practice Issues, Strategies, and Models: The Current State of the Art of Family Mediation" (1998) 36:1 Fam Ct Rev 195 at 214–15.)

• In addition, the status of mediation has been enhanced by its express recognition in some statutory provisions. For example, Ontario statutes expressly authorize court-ordered mediation in some circumstances. (See Ontario's *Children's Law Reform Act*, s 31(1) and *Family Law Act*, s 3.)

• According to some experts, mediation offers four advantages to a divorcing couple: it ensures that the decision-making process remains within the clients' control; it avoids the trauma of the trial process; it produces settlements that work better for the parties than court ordered results; and it assists clients to achieve long-term working relationships, especially with respect to their children. (See B Landau, M Bartoletti & R Mesbur, *Family Mediation Handbook* (Toronto: Butterworths, 1997) at 20–22.)

By contrast with these positive claims about mediation, however, a number of scholars have expressed concern about the use of mediation processes, particularly in the context of family violence or abuse. For example, see Hilary Astor, *Mediation and Violence Against Women* (Canberra: National Committee on Violence Against Women, 1991); NZ Hilton, "Mediating Wife Assault: Battered Women and the 'New Family'" (1991) 9 Can J Fam L 29; Lene Madsen, "A Fine Balance: Domestic Violence, Screening and Family Mediation" (2012) 30 Can Fam LQ 343; and Lene Madsen, "More than 'Hanging Out a Shingle': Qualifications for Family Mediators in Ontario" (2012) Can Fam LQ 50.

In this context, some research in Canada has resulted in a protocol for assessing and managing the risk of domestic violence between partners during and following their participation in mediation. The protocol, Domestic Violence Evaluation (DOVE), was designed to examine links between pre-separation and post-separation violence against female ex-partners, and to identify safety plan interventions to prevent violence and abuse of female partners during and after participation in divorce mediation. Predictors of violence include harmful activities (such as assaults), relationship problems, conflict, control, anger and mental health problems. However, the research also indicated that these predictors did not apply to lethal violence. See Desmond Ellis & Noreen Stuckless, "Domestic Violence, Dove, and Divorce Mediation" (2006) 44:4 Fam Ct Rev 658; and "Separation, Domestic Violence, and Divorce Mediation" (2006) 23:4 Conflict Resolution Quarterly 461. To what extent might mediation using DOVE have assisted Mrs. Behrendt, discussed in the previous chapter?

Limitations of Mediation Processes?

Some critics of mediation in divorce proceedings have drawn attention to the propensity of mediation proponents to contrast mediation with litigation, even though litigation is used to resolve matters at family dissolution in only a small minority of such cases.

For these critics, the more appropriate comparison is between mediation and traditional negotiation, because the latter process has been used much more often to settle divorce cases.

In addition, these critics argue that traditional methods of negotiation might be preferable to mediation because negotiation processes ensure that bargaining occurs within "the shadow of the law," at least where clients have legal representation, and lawyers may assist clients in the bargaining process.

More specifically, critics also argue that there is a need for empirical investigation in relation to mediation before implementing proposals for mandatory mediation. See Sandra A Goundry, Yvonne Peters, Rosalind Currie & National Association of Women and the Law, *Family Mediation in Canada: Implications for Women's Equality* (Ottawa: Status of Women Canada, 1998) at 6 and 16–18.

Recent Developments in Ontario: Expanding Mediation in Family Law Matters

In spite of such concerns, mediation is gaining political support, perhaps in part as a way to reduce the costs of family law in the courts. For example, a recent report about family courts in Ontario suggested that

> [a]ll of the partners in the family justice system have to make a concentrated and deliberate effort to enhance the use of mediation services and to instil a solution-centred atmosphere in the family court. An automatic referral to mediation should be implemented in cases involving child custody/access, and motions to change and recalculate support.... (Alfred Mamo, Peter Jaffe & Debbie Chiodo, *Recapturing and Renewing the Vision of the Family Court* (Toronto: Ministry of the Attorney General, 2007) at 114–15)

As a result, the Attorney General in Ontario initiated a pilot project with Legal Aid Ontario in 2010, involving automatic referrals to mediation in several court locations in Ontario, particularly for family law clients who qualify for legal aid.

In June 2011, the Attorney General announced that this pilot project would be expanded to all family court sites in Ontario, as part of an initiative to resolve more family law disputes outside the court system (see *Law Times* (20 June 2011) 13). According to a press report in the fall of 2012 (see Lorna Yates, "Mediate393: New Family Mediation Program in Toronto", *The Lawyers Weekly* (23 September 2011) 11), the government's program, "Mediate393" has four components:

- the Family Law Information Centres staffed by a full-time Information and Referral Co-ordinator who is familiar with resources in the community to assist family law clients;

- the Mandatory Information Program for clients (discussed earlier in this chapter);

- a two-hour on-site mediation, available at family courts five days a week, with no income restrictions; however, cases are accepted on a first-come, first-served basis; and

- the availability of off-site mediation for cases that are more complex, a subsidized service with rates based on a sliding scale.

Even prior to this announcement, there were news reports about the need for increased mediator education programs. One report identified three organizations that provide mediator accreditation in Ontario, based on a 40-hour basic family mediation course, a 20-hour advanced course and a 14-hour domestic violence course. See Judy Van Rhijn, "Training Mediators to Meet New Demand", *Law Times* (4 April 2011).

However, Chief Justice Winkler suggested that the new reforms still were insufficient to ensure justice in family law cases, arguing that there is a need for free mediation at the heart of the system, with litigation reserved for those cases involving abuse, an imbalance of power or an unco-operative party. The Chief Justice also argued that these changes would be easier to implement if there were unified family courts in all parts of the province. See Michael McKiernan, "Family Law Reforms Fall Short, Winkler Says", *Law Times* (27 June 2011) 5.

In response to these comments, the Attorney General acknowledged a need for additional measures to improve the family justice system. However, he also pointed to the introduction of mandatory information systems, presented in court houses by volunteer lawyers, and the availability of limited on-site mediation, as well as off-site mediation available on a sliding scale based on the parties' incomes (see McKiernan).

Assessing Mediation: Scholarly Research in Canada and Elsewhere

These recent initiatives in Ontario are similar to developments in other jurisdictions, including the United Kingdom, some U.S. states, and Australia, where the mediation alternative has gained a good deal of support. However, this research suggests that mediation may not offer cost savings and that it may not result in family justice.

For example, research in the United Kingdom demonstrated that mediation saves costs in only a narrow band of cases: see Gwynn Davis et al,

Monitoring Publicly Funded Family Mediation: Summary Report to the Legal Services Commission (London: Legal Services Commission, 2000).

Similarly, empirical research in Australia demonstrated that referrals to mediation, *prior to receiving legal advice*, resulted in *higher costs*, rather than cost savings, because family law clients did not have enough legal information and assistance to conduct mediation successfully. (See Rosemary Hunter, "Adversarial Mythologies: Policy Assumptions and Research Evidence in Family Law" (2003) 30 JL & Soc'y 156.)

In addition, Colleen Hanycz expressed concern about studies that have tended to focus primarily on assessing mediation outcomes (that is, rates of settlement), rather than broader criteria reflecting the full context of mediation processes. In her study of mediator power in relation to mandatory mediation in non-family law cases in Ontario, Hanycz suggested the existence of a major conflict between the theory of mediation (which places priority on the interests of the parties) and the use of mediator power to achieve settlement (in accordance with mediation project goals, particularly where mediation is promoted by government):

> Recognizing the potential for such mediator self-interest begs the question: is the mediator a truly neutral and impartial agenda manager? Or does that mediator harness substantial power at the mediation table, power used to manipulate disputants through process management and interventions towards an outcome that corresponds with the mediator's settlement-orientation and perceptions of fairness? (Colleen Hanycz, "Through the Looking Glass: Mediator Conceptions of Philosophy, Process and Power" (2005) 42 Alta L Rev 819 at para 229)

To what extent do recent policy developments in Ontario respond to the issues in scholarly research about mediation in family law cases? Although this caution was issued a decade ago, it may be just as significant in the current context:

> [There] is a real danger that the current rush to embrace mediation as a panacea will result only in the entrenchment of the same problems that currently plague the court based family justice system. (Goundry et al at 67)

Arbitration

> In seeking the equality rights of all women (including religious women), we may need to acknowledge the seemingly contradictory position that the state cannot be viewed as the only actor capable of promoting equality, while insisting that the state play a role in ensuring that vulnerable individuals opting for alternative mechanisms of equality are also protected. (Natasha Bakht, "Religious Arbitration in Canada: Protecting Women by Protecting them from Religion" (2007) 19 CJWL 119 at 142)

Statutory Reforms Concerning Family Arbitration in Ontario

Bakht's comment captures the complex nuances embedded in recent debates in Ontario with respect to arbitration of family law matters, particularly religious arbitrations. Pursuant to the *Arbitration Act, 1991* in Ontario, parties were entitled to choose an arbitrator to resolve disputes, including family law disputes. However, after a Muslim group, the Islamic Institute of Civil Justice, announced its intention to create Islamic arbitration tribunals to decide cases of divorce, concerns were expressed about private ordering and its potential to promote inequality, particularly for women.

In response, the Ontario government appointed a former Attorney General, Marion Boyd, to investigate the issues. Her report, *Dispute Resolution in Family Law: Protecting Choice, Promoting Inclusion*, was submitted in 2004. The report recommended modifications to ensure free and informed consent by parties to arbitration, and measures to standardize the system by monitoring the qualifications of arbitrators and their awards. However, the government decided to reject these recommendations; instead, it announced its intention to "prohibit" religious arbitration in family law matters.

Thereafter, amendments to the *Family Law Act* were enacted in 2006 (see SO 2006, c 1, now included in Part IV, ss 59.1 to 59.8). In addition, the definition of "family arbitration" provides that it must be conducted exclusively in accordance with the law of Ontario or another jurisdiction in Canada (see s 51) in order to have legal effect (s 59.2(1)). Contracting out is prohibited (s 59.3) and there is no recognition of agreements entered into prior to the dispute arising (s 59.4), a section that prohibits agreements at the time of marriage from being legally enforced at separation. Section 59.6 also provides conditions of enforceability, including requirements that the agreement be in writing and signed, that the parties receive independent legal advice, and that the arbitrator comply with provisions of the *Arbitration Act, 1991*.

However, as Bakht noted, these amendments did not "forbid" religious arbitration altogether, and this situation may actually undermine feminist lobbying efforts about religious arbitrations in the interest of protecting vulnerable women:

> Firstly, people can always settle their differences on any basis that they please, so long as both parties consent. However, the new amendments mean that only arbitral decisions using the family law of a Canadian jurisdiction will have the power of the state behind them. Thus, Muslim women may still utilize religious arbitration (that is not binding in law) and the feminist concern regarding women's vulnerability to the conscious or unconscious patriarchal practices of arbitrators remains. Some commentators have noted that we lost an opportunity to prevent "back-alley arbitrations" through a regime of government regulation that could have ensured a measure of transparency, accountability and competence in adjudication.
>
> A second way in which the amendments do not actually ban religious arbitration is that religious arbitrators can simply conform to the regulations regarding training and record keeping and then perform religious arbitrations that are consistent with Canadian family law....
>
> Despite the government's description [of its intention to prohibit religious arbitrations], the new amendments appear to find a balance between religious freedom and equality by permitting family arbitration with religious principles, so long as such principles do not conflict with Ontario's family law.... (Natasha Bakht, "Were Muslim Barbarians Really Knocking on the Gates of Ontario? The Religious Arbitration Controversy — Another Perspective" (2006) Ottawa L Rev 67 at paras 26–28)

The religious arbitration controversy centred on the Islamic Institute of Civil Justice, but it also affected existing arrangements for religious tribunals, including the Jewish Beis Din, the Ismaili Muslim National Conciliation and Arbitration Board, and the El Noor Mosque in Toronto. As one writer commented, it "remains the case that at-risk women in minority communities will continue to feel the authority of faith-based tribunals, whether they are part of the province's arbitration regime or not." See Eli Walker, "Don't Throw out my Baby! Why Dalton McGuinty was Wrong to Reject Religious Arbitration" (2006) 11 Appeal 94 at para 27.

For other views on religious arbitration see: Farrah Ahmed & Senwung Luk, "How Religious Arbitration Could Enhance Personal Autonomy" (2012) 1:2 Oxford JL & Religion 424; Ayelet Shachar, "Privatizing Diversity: A Cautionary Tale from Religious Arbitration in Family Law" in Marie A Failinger, Elizabeth R Schiltz & Susan J Stabile, eds, *Gender in Law, Culture, and Society: Feminism, Law, and Religion* (Burlington, VT: Ashgate, 2013) 109; and Amanda M Baker, "A higher authority: Judicial review of religious arbitration" (2012) 37 Vermont L Rev 157.

Some recent cases suggest that courts will not generally interfere with arbitration decisions entered into by the parties:

- In *Rosenberg v Minster*, 2014 ONSC 845, the spouses engaged in two mediation sessions (both spouses were represented by counsel) and then entered into an agreement to arbitrate custody and parenting disputes, with the mediator acting as arbitrator. The arbitrator's decision was delayed until seven months after the arbitration, contrary to the agreement that it would be released within 60 days. Some months later, the arbitrator also released supplemental reasons. The mother issued a notice of appeal four months after the first award and just 8 days after the supplementary award; the father moved to incorporate the arbitrator's award into an order for purposes of enforcement. The court dismissed the mother's appeal and granted the father's motion.

- In *Kroupis-Yanovski v Yanovski*, 2012 ONSC 5312, the spouses submitted their claims for child and spousal support and equalization of net family property to arbitration, and agreed to a process of "final offer selection." After receiving their respective offers, the arbitrator suggested proceeding by way of each separate issue, but the husband indicated that he did not wish to alter the spouses' agreement to use a process of final offer selection. Thus, the arbitrator was required to choose one offer in its entirety, and he chose the wife's offer. The husband appealed on the basis of three issues: that final offer selection was not appropriate; there was no opportunity for sworn testimony or cross examination on the parties' affidavits; and the arbitrator's reasons were not sufficient. The court concluded that there was no requirement that the arbitration process "mirror" a court process, and that the arbitrator treated the parties equally and fairly and provided brief reasons that explained the arbitrator's decision. See also *Grosman v Cookson*, 2012 ONCA 551; and *Patton-Casse v Casse*, 2012 CarswellOnt 14417 (ONCA).

• *Collie v Collie*, 2013 ONSC 6213, held that the test for leave to appeal an arbitral award, despite appearing to be covered by Ontario's Rules of Civil Procedure, is actually set out in section 45(1) of the *Arbitration Act, 1991*.

Notes and Questions

Processes for dispute resolution at family dissolution and the role of precedents

As this overview of negotiation, collaborative law, mediation and arbitration processes demonstrates, many family law cases are settled in the absence of litigation and beyond the purview of courts. In divorce proceedings, judges do routinely review any agreement for corollary relief, although this review is often relatively superficial. For cohabiting couples who reach a settlement, the courts may not be involved at all unless one party seeks judicial assistance with respect to enforcement.

Nonetheless, this family law book and others like it use judicial decisions to explain the principles of family law, even though these cases represent only a tiny proportion of separation agreements and other forms of settlement at family dissolution. There are two main reasons for this focus:

• There is almost no access to privately negotiated separation agreements. Although there have been a few empirical studies of such agreements, it is the decisions of the courts that are more readily available. In the context of governmental initiatives to stream many family law cases to mediation and other forms of decision making, consider the impact on knowledge about family law principles and precedents.

• Lawyers assume that they must negotiate these agreements "in the shadow of the law," so most agreements with legal representation probably conform to basic family law principles. Note, however, in the context of increasing numbers of family law clients who are unrepresented or self-represented, and who may not have access to courts, it is less clear that their agreements will necessarily conform to these principles in future. Moreover, fundamental principles of collaborative law processes may tend to encourage departure from legal entitlements.

In addition to these two issues, it is also important to recognize how many cases that reach the courts involve families with relative wealth, which may contribute to their access to legal representation. In this context, should legal precedents, established in cases involving families that are atypical in terms of their economic circumstances, be routinely applied to other family law cases?

In reflecting on the processes and practices at family dissolution, you may need to keep these factors in mind as well. In particular, take note of the numbers of cases concerning issues of corollary relief in which the parties have considerable wealth.

Additional Resources

Becky Batagol & Thea Brown, *Bargaining in the Shadow of the Law? The Case of Family Mediation* (Sydney: Themis Press, 2011).

Melina Buckley et al, *What Do We Want? Canada's Future Legal Aid System* (Ottawa: Canadian Bar Association, 2015).

Rachel Birnbaum & Nicholas Bala, "Views of Ontario Lawyers on Family Litigants without Representation" (2012) 63 UNBLJ 99.

Melina Buckley, "The Challenge of Litigating the Rights of Poor People: The Right to Legal Aid as a Test Case" in Margot Young et al, eds, *Poverty: Rights, Social Citizenship, Legal Activism* (Vancouver, UBC Press, 2007) 337.

Desmond Ellis, *Family Mediation Pilot Project, Hamilton Unified Family Court* (Toronto: York University, 1995).

Trina Grillo, "The Mediation Alternative: Process Dangers for Women" (1991) 100 Yale LJ 217.

Carla Hotel & Joan Brockman, "The Conciliatory-Adversarial Continuum in Family Law Practice" (1994) 12 Can J Fam L 11.

Michaela Keet, "The Evolution of Lawyers' Roles in Mandatory Mediation: A Condition of Systemic Transformation" (2005) 68 Sask L Rev 313.

Joan B Kelly, "A Decade of Divorce Mediation Research" (1996) 34:3 Fam Ct Rev 373.

Shelley Kierstead, "Parent Education Programs in Family Courts: Balancing Autonomy and State Intervention" (2010) 49:1 Fam Ct Rev 140.

Anne-Marie Langan, "Threatening the Balance in the Scales of Justice: Unrepresented Litigants in the Family Courts of Ontario" (2005) 30 Queen's LJ 825.

Rosanna Langer, "The Juridification and Technicisation of Alternative Dispute Resolution Practices" (1998) 13 CJLS 169.

James McLeod, ed, *Family Dispute Resolution: Litigation and Its Alternatives* (Scarborough, ON: Carswell, 1987).

Carrie Menkel-Meadow, "Lawyer Negotiations: Theories and Realities — What We Learn from Mediation" (1993) 56 Mod L Rev 361.

MJ Mossman, "Gender, Equality, and Legal Aid Services" (1993) 15 Sydney L Rev 30.

Ruth Phegan, "The Family Mediation System: An Art of Distributions" (1995) 40 McGill LJ 365.

Austin Sarat & William F Felstiner, "Law and Strategy in the Divorce Lawyer's Office" (1986) 20 Law & Soc'y Rev 93.

Jaime Sarophim, "Access Barred: The Effects of the Cuts and Restructuring of Legal Aid in B.C. on Women Attempting to Navigate the Provincial Family Court System" (2010) 26:2 Can J Fam L 451.

Rick Shields, Judith Ryan & Victoria L Smith, *Collaborative Family Law: Another Way To Resolve Family Disputes* (Toronto: Carswell, 2003).

Pauline H Tesler, *Collaborative Law: Achieving Effective Resolution in Divorce Without Litigation* (Chicago: ABA Publications, 2001).

Wanda Wiegers & Michaela Keet, "Collaborative Family Law and Gender Inequalities: Balancing Risks and Opportunities" (2009) 46 Osgoode Hall LJ 733.

Caryn Litt Wolfe, "Faith-Based Arbitration: Friend or Foe? An Evaluation of Religious Arbitration Systems and their Interaction with Secular Courts" (2006–2007) 75 Fordham L Rev 427.

VI.
FAMILY BARGAINING AT SEPARATION OR DIVORCE: EXPLORING THE ISSUES

Students of negotiation seem to have begun to realize that negotiation processes were more complex than just mastering a number of simple strategies. The negotiator's objectives could be to "win" or to satisfy the underlying interests of the parties, or to achieve the most efficient or most just solution. And depending on what the objectives were, behaviour might have to be modified to achieve the outcome desired. (Carrie Menkel-Meadow, "Legal Negotiation: A Study of Strategies in Search of a Theory" (1983) American Bar Foundation Research Journal 905 at 936–937)

THE SIGNIFICANCE OF FAMILY BARGAINING AT SEPARATION AND DIVORCE

The legal process of separation and divorce occurs over a period of time, and may involve a variety of methods of dispute resolution. For example, spouses may engage in negotiation about some issues and then turn to mediation to resolve other issues, particularly those involving children. Some spouses may choose collaborative law, rather than traditional negotiation, and others may decide to use arbitration. Lawyers may be involved at some stages, but clients may choose to represent themselves at other times. For those who wish to divorce, the preparation of a divorce application is required, even if the parties opt for a desk top divorce without a court appearance. In this way, the range of procedures may be quite extensive over the course of the process of achieving divorce or final separation, including agreement with respect to matters of corollary relief.

Yet, in most methods of dispute resolution, some degree of family bargaining will be necessary. As noted above, even in divorce litigation, there are opportunities for the parties to negotiate about options for settlement, and bargaining will be involved in mediation and arbitration, as well as in relation to collaborative law and traditional negotiation. And, although lawyers and judges typically focus on the legal issues that must be resolved, family law clients involved in divorce and separation often have additional unresolved issues, some of which may be destabilizing in a family bargaining context.

This section provides an overview of the legal principles about family law bargaining, particularly in relation to separation agreements, one form of "domestic contracts" available in the family law context. In addition, this section focuses on issues about bargaining power in relation to contracts negotiated in a family context. Further issues that arise with respect to the scope for variation of these agreements are considered later in this book, because these issues have most often arisen in conjunction with claims about spousal support.

THE LEGAL CONTEXT FOR FAMILY CONTRACTS

The history of contracts in the family context

Although equitable settlements were often drafted by wealthy fathers in the 18th and 19th centuries, prior to the *Married Women's Property Acts*, equitable settlements were generally unenforceable at common law. Moreover, contracts between spouses respecting marriage breakdown were traditionally regarded as contrary to public policy and unenforceable. Thus, for example, when a wife in England in the early 20th century sought to enforce an agreement in which her husband had agreed to provide her with £30 per week in maintenance at separation, Lord Atkin stated:

> To my mind those agreements, or many of them, do not result in con-
> tracts at all.... [They] are not contracts because the parties did not intend
> that they should be attended by legal consequences.... [The] Courts of this
> country would have to be multiplied one-hundredfold if these arrange-
> ments were held to result in legal obligations. They are not sued upon,
> not because the parties are reluctant to enforce their legal rights when the
> agreement is broken, but because the parties, in the inception of the
> arrangements, never intended that they should be sued upon. Agreements
> such as these are outside the realm of contracts altogether. The common
> law does not regulate the form of agreements between spouses. (*Balfour v
> Balfour*, [1919] 2 KB 571 (Eng CA))

An overview of family contracts pursuant to Ontario's *Family Law Act*

In spite of such traditional legal views about family contracts, provincial family law reform statutes enacted after the *Divorce Act* of 1968 provided for the enforceability of "domestic contracts" between married and some opposite-sex spouses. And, after the Supreme Court of Canada's decision in *M v H*, [1999] 2 SCR 3, and the *Amendments Because of the Supreme Court of Canada Decision in M v. H Act*, SO 1999, c 6, these provisions about domestic contracts also became available to same-sex spouses. Thus, contracts can now be enforced for both same-sex and opposite-sex spouses, including married couples and cohabiting couples who meet the requisite statutory definition.

The Ontario *Family Law Act* includes a number of provisions concerning contracts:

• Section 2(10) of the Act provides that "a domestic contract dealing with a matter that is also dealt with in this Act prevails unless this Act provides otherwise." This section is significant because it permits spouses to make a domestic contract about any matters included in the *Family Law Act*, unless the Act prohibits inclusion of a matter specifically. In effect, this means that the *Family Law Act* provides a "default regime" for those who do not enter into "domestic contracts." In this way, the negotiated agreements of spouses, married or cohabiting, have been accorded substantial authority under provincial statutory regimes.

• Part IV of the Act now defines five kinds of "domestic contracts," including separation agreements and family arbitration agreements (which are usually negotiated at the end of a relationship), marriage contracts and cohabitation agreements (which may be entered into either before or during marriage or cohabitation), and paternity agreements (to provide generally for the support of a child). Part IV also defines formalities for domestic contracts (s 55) and the circumstances in which provisions of such contracts may be set aside by a court in certain situations (s 56).

• Section 33(4) also permits a court to set aside provisions of a domestic contract relating to support if the provision is unconscionable, if it results in a dependant qualifying for public support, or if there is default in payment of support pursuant to the contract.

Taken together, these provisions offer a good deal of scope for family contracts, an approach that emphasizes the role of private ordering for family members in regulating and adjusting their rights and obligations. However, as noted, there are some limitations on this "freedom of family contract" approach.

As you examine these statutory limits and their judicial interpretation concerning family contracts, reflect on the underlying rationale for legal intervention in private contracts. To what extent do the limits in Ontario's legislation strike an appropriate balance between contractual freedom on one hand and the need to protect vulnerable family members (and the public purse) on the other?

The legal scope for family contracts in Ontario

The definitions of "marriage contracts" (s 52), "cohabitation agreements" (s 53), and "separation agreements" (s 54) identify the rights and obligations about which the spouses may contract.

For example, note that marriage contracts may not include contractual provisions limiting a spouse's *possessory rights* in the matrimonial home; and neither marriage contracts nor cohabitation agreements may include provisions regarding the custody of or access to children, but this matter may be included in a separation agreement.

As noted above, there are also detailed provisions (ss 59.1 to 59.8) regarding the content (and procedures) for the negotiation of family arbitration awards.

Legal formalities for enforceable family contracts

Section 55 of the *Family Law Act* provides that an enforceable domestic contract must be in writing, signed by the parties and witnessed. However, in *Gallacher v Friesen*, 2014 ONCA 399, a separation agreement was upheld despite not being witnessed. The Court of Appeal discussed society's interest in having bargains upheld unless there were clear reasons not to do so. As noted above, there are additional procedural requirements for a valid family arbitration award.

However, Ontario does not require that parties to contracts, other than family arbitration awards, receive independent legal advice, prior to signing the contract. And, subject to provisions discussed below, a domestic contract may be valid in Ontario even if neither party received legal advice prior to signing it in accordance with section 55. By contrast, some other provinces, such as Alberta, require independent legal advice as one of the requirements of a valid family contract (see *Matrimonial Property Act*, RSA 1980, c M-9, s 38(2)).

In reviewing some of the cases discussed below, you may wish to consider whether Ontario should require independent legal representation for all family contracts, rather than only for family arbitration awards. What rationale supports the negotiation of family contracts without independent legal advice? What are the advantages and disadvantages of requiring independent legal advice for all domestic contracts in Ontario?

JUDICIAL REVIEW OF FAMILY CONTRACTS: AN OVERVIEW

Section 56 and the best interests of children

Section 56(1) of Ontario's *Family Law Act* provides that a court may disregard any provision of a domestic contract respecting the education, moral training, or custody of, or access to, a child where it is in the child's best interests to do so. Recall the earlier critiques about the discretionary nature of the "best interests" test in relation to adoption and child protection. What kinds of contractual provisions might contravene children's best interests in a separation agreement?

In addition, section 56(1.1) permits a court to disregard provisions in any domestic contract pertaining to the support of a child where it is unreasonable, having regard to the child support guidelines and other provisions in the contract.

Section 56 and circumstances surrounding the negotiation of the contract

Section 56(4) permits a court to set aside a contract or a provision in it because of a failure to disclose assets or debts, if a party failed to understand the nature and consequences of the contract, or on the basis of the law of contract.

Section 56(4)(a) and *Dochuk v Dochuk*

This disclosure provision was designed to ensure that parties negotiate separation agreements with full information. However, the cases suggest that parties must request information and that it must be significant in order to invoke this protection. For example, see *Butty v Butty*, 2009 ONCA 852; and *Quinn v Keiper*, 2007 ONCA 662.

In *Dochuk v Dochuk* (1999), 44 RFL (4th) 97 (Ont Gen Div), the court declined to set aside provisions in a contract where there was evidence that the husband had wilfully failed to disclose relevant information because it would not have affected the wife's decision to sign the contract. In doing so, the court identified a number of factors to be considered in exercising discretion pursuant to section 56(4):

> ... In *Demchuk* ... , Clarke LJSC observed that how the Court will exercise its discretion whether to set aside a separation agreement pivots on the facts of each case. His Honour set out the factors that he took into account. These included:
> (a) whether there had been concealment of the asset or material misrepresentation;
> (b) whether there had been duress, or unconscionable circumstances;
> (c) whether the petitioning party neglected to pursue full legal disclosures;
> (d) whether he/she moved expeditiously to have the agreement set aside;
> (e) whether he/she received substantial benefits under the agreement;
> (f) whether the other party had fulfilled his/her obligations under the agreement....
>
> In *Rosen...*, the Ontario Court of Appeal re-affirmed the approach that Courts should take, in general, toward the validity of separation agreements. It is desirable that parties should settle their own affairs if possible. In doing so parties should know that the terms of such settlement will be binding and will be recognized. The Court of Appeal was clear that this approach is not applicable to contracts that are unconscionable. I conclude that where there are vitiating factors and a Court is being asked to exercise its discretion, [this] approach must be taken into consideration. (*Dochuk v Dochuk* at paras 17–18)

A further qualification about the disclosure of deliberately misleading material information was added in the following case.

Virc v Blair
2014 ONCA 392

Although this case involved an appeal from a motion court's denial of an application to set aside a separation agreement, rather than a marriage contract, the Ontario Court of Appeal addressed the requirements of *FLA*, s 56(4), particularly in relation to the issue of non-disclosure (subsection (a)).

The appeal court identified the test in section 56(4) of the *FLA*, and adopted the two-stage analysis set out in *LeVan* (discussed later in this chapter):

> [51] Can the party seeking to set aside the agreement demonstrate that one or more of the s. 56(4) circumstances in engaged?
>
> If so, is it appropriate for the court to exercise its discretion to set aside the agreement?

The court held that the motion judge had erred in applying this test in *Virc v Blair*.

The spouses had married in 1994 and had three children; the wife was 26 at the time the parties met, and she was a lawyer in a Toronto firm. Her husband was 46 and the president and sole director of Renegade Capital Corporation. The wife was a stay at home mother for several years, and the evidence suggested that she became depressed when her husband began to discuss divorce. The separation agreement was signed in 2008, and an important issue was whether the husband had misstated the value of his property at the date of marriage. Because this value was overstated, the wife owed the husband an equalization payment at separation. The parties signed the separation agreement at their home and then the husband took it to the office, where a co-worker (who recognized both of their signatures) witnessed the agreement.

The Court acknowledged that the motion judge assumed that there had been a deliberate material misrepresentation by the husband with respect to the value of his property at the date of marriage:

> [58] Once the motion judge assumed that there had been deliberate material misrepresentations, she erred in shifting the onus to the appellant [wife] to inquire as to the veracity of the respondent's [husband's] financial disclosure. In the face of a deliberate material misrepresentation, the onus is not appropriately placed on the recipient spouse. Rather, the burden is on the party disclosing to establish actual knowledge of the falsehood by the recipient. The respondent could point to no authority for the proposition that the suggested duty of a spouse receiving financial disclosure in a matrimonial case, to investigate or test the veracity of the information provided, overtakes deliberate material non-disclosure by the other spouse.

> [68] It is one thing to disclose assets and liabilities and their values believing the disclosure to be true. It is quite another to deliberately misrepresent the values of assets and liabilities knowing them to be untrue. The law does not entitle a liar to succeed just because the recipient of falsehoods has not ferreted them out.

> [69] Furthermore, a clear finding of actual knowledge of the misrepresentation is required. While, as noted in *Cheshire and Fifoot*, actual knowledge of the falsehood may constitute a defence, a mere suspicion of lack of veracity does not absolve a fraudster of responsibility. In this case, there was insufficient evidence to conclude that the appellant had knowledge of the respondent's misrepresentations....

On the issue of section 55 and the need for a witness, the appeal court concluded that the motion judge had correctly determined that this was not an issue for trial because the wife admitted signing the agreement and accepting its benefits for two years and that she had not raised this issue for almost two years after signing the agreement (at para 81).

Section 56(4)(b) and *Rosen v Rosen*

Even though independent legal advice is not required in Ontario, provisions of the contract may be set aside if either of the parties did not understand the nature and consequences of the agreement. In this context, the absence of independent legal advice may be a significant factor in assessing whether a party understood the nature and consequences of the agreement. However, where parties have deliberately declined to seek legal advice, courts have refused to set aside provisions.

On 16 February 1994 (SCC Bulletin, 1995, at 340), for example, the Supreme Court of Canada dismissed an application for leave to appeal in relation to a decision of the Ontario Court of Appeal, *Rosen v Rosen* (1994), 18 OR (3d) 641, which concluded that the wife had acted voluntarily in deciding not to obtain legal advice before signing a separation agreement. In this case, the Court of Appeal had also determined that there was no inequality between the parties in terms of bargaining power.

Section 56(4)(c) and Claims about Duress and Unconscionability

As Nicholas Bala explained, this provision means that courts may consider unconscionability, duress, undue influence, fraud, misrepresentation, and mistake. See Nicholas Bala, "Domestic Contracts in Ontario and the Supreme Court Trilogy: A Deal Is a Deal" (1988) 13 Queen's LJ 1. The onus is on the person claiming remedial action to demonstrate that the circumstances surrounding the negotiation of the contract require that it be set aside, an onus that may be difficult to meet.

For example, Bala described the case of *Puopolo v Puopolo* (1986), 2 RFL (3d) 73 (Ont HC), in which a husband and wife signed a separation agreement relating to their family property, which included the matrimonial home (owned by the husband) and an apartment building (owned by the wife). During the negotiation of the separation agreement, the husband initially requested 100 percent of both properties and, after her husband physically threatened her with a knife, the wife agreed to sell the apartment building and divide the proceeds equally with her husband. The husband retained title to the matrimonial home. Before signing the agreement, the wife obtained legal advice, which included a suggestion that she might be able to set aside the agreement in future. The court expressed concern about such legal advice, and held that the wife was not under duress when she signed the agreement. According to the court, it was her wish to "buy peace" with her husband, and there was no basis for setting aside the contract.

Similarly, in *Saul v Himel* (1995), 9 RFL (4th) 419 (Ont Gen Div), the court upheld a separation agreement even though the husband claimed misrepresentation (as well as non-disclosure) in relation to provisions for supporting a child of whom he was not the biological father. However, the court decided that he had been aware, at the time of negotiating the agreement, that he might not be the biological father and that the wife had no duty to disclose these facts.

Consider this case:

A man and woman signed a cohabitation agreement. However, the man later wanted to set aside the agreement on several grounds including claims pursuant to section 56(4)(c). The man was suffering from depression and had sustained a physical injury at work, so that he was in receipt of workers' compensation payments. His cohabiting partner had recently received an inheritance of $2 million, and in return for making him a joint owner of a new home (to be paid for entirely by her), she requested that he sign a cohabitation agreement limiting his entitlement to a payment of $70,000 on separation.

In *Barton v Sauvé*, 2010 ONSC 1072, the court examined the cohabitation agreement in detail, rejecting all the grounds for setting it aside. In relation to section 56(4)(c), the court stated (at 781–782):

[A]lthough Mr. Sauvé was suffering from a debilitating physical injury and depression and anxiety, and was therefore in a vulnerable physical and mental state, I cannot find that there was an overwhelming imbalance in the power relationship between the parties nor can I find that Ms. Barton took advantage of Mr. Sauvé's vulnerability.... There must be evidence to warrant the court's finding that the agreement should not stand on the basis of a fundamental flaw in the negotiation process. The presence of vulnerabilities will not alone justify the court's intervention.

In this case Mr. Sauvé was a somewhat vulnerable party. However, he did receive independent legal advice, understood the nature and consequences of the agreement and signed it voluntarily. At that time, he was signing offers regarding the potential purchase of a new home, was discussing the cohabitation agreement with Ms. Barton and was indicating his desire to have the new [home] registered in both their names, although Ms. Barton would be paying the purchase price. He was, therefore, bargaining with Ms. Barton and negotiating with her. It is true that Ms. Barton was the one with the large inheritance, but she had paid off all the joint debts, resulting in a significant advantage to Mr. Sauvé. She was also offering him $70,000 in the event of a separation. I cannot find that she was in any way taking advantage of Mr. Sauvé to the extent contemplated by the law of contract. [The court also noted the evidence given by the lawyer for the man, who indicated that he had no concerns about Mr. Sauvé's understanding of the contract.]

Section 33(4) and support provisions

In an early case concerning section 33(4), *Salonen v Salonen* (1986), 2 RFL (3d) 273 (Ont Unif Fam Ct), the court declined to set aside the agreement, even though it meant that the wife and children would require social assistance. The husband and wife negotiated a separation agreement after the wife decided to live with another man, and the wife received legal advice before signing the agreement. The separation agreement required the husband to take responsibility for all of the couple's debts, a situation which left him unable to pay much child or spousal support. When her new relationship ended, the wife sought to set aside the contract in order to claim spousal and child support. In deciding to uphold the agreement, the court stated (at 286):

> [In] the case at bar, Mrs. Salonen not only had advice, but she retained her own lawyer who negotiated with Mr. Salonen's lawyer from September 1984 to December and he (on her behalf) drew the agreement and advised her away from the visible presence of her husband prior to signing. She had ample opportunity to consider its long- and short-term effects.... Agreements of this kind should be upheld as a matter of public policy, ... else parties will be less motivated to seriously bargain and conclude such contracts. Parties in circumstances of marital distress should be encouraged to settle by bargain rather than litigation....

Are there factors that may indicate that courts might approach the interpretation of section 33(4) differently now?

Section 56(5) and the removal of barriers to remarriage

This section is similar to section 21.1 in the *Divorce Act* with respect to the removal of barriers to remarriage. Although the provision in the *Family Law Act* is not as detailed as in the federal legislation, it offers the assistance of the court for parties who do not have access to the *Divorce Act*.

Notes and Questions

Policy issues in family contracts

To what extent do these provisions regarding family law bargaining achieve an appropriate balance between encouraging private ordering and ensuring fairness in the content and process of family negotiations? In relation to the *Salonen* case above (where the court declined to set aside the separation agreement), the court included an explicit statement of policy about family agreements:

> It is of great importance not only to the parties but to the community as a whole that contracts of this kind should not be lightly disturbed. Lawyers must be able to advise their clients in respect of their future rights and obligations with some degree of certainty. Clients must be able to rely on these agreements and know with some degree of assurance that once a separation agreement is executed their affairs have been settled on a permanent basis. The courts must encourage parties to settle their differences without recourse to litigation. The modern approach to family law is to mediate and conciliate so as to enable the parties to make a fresh start in life on a secure basis. If separation agreements can be varied at will, it will become much more difficult to persuade the parties to enter into such agreements. (*Dal Santo v Dal Santo* (1975), 21 RFL 117 at 120 (BCSC), cited in *Salonen*)

Does a policy of encouraging settlement of divorce proceedings meet the needs of public policies about the use of (scarce) judicial and other resources, as well as private interests in promoting family agreements? You may want to reconsider these issues in relation to cases discussed later in this chapter.

Reconsidering the role of independent legal advice
Consider this situation:

> The spouses separated after 23 years of marriage, having prepared and signed a separation agreement without legal assistance. Pursuant to the agreement, the wife received about $88,000 less than her entitlement in the equalization of the property. She later requested to have the agreement set aside by the court on the grounds of lack of independent legal advice, duress, and unconscionability.

In *Clayton v Clayton* (1998), 40 OR (3d) 24 (Gen Div), the court refused the wife's application, finding that she was quite capable of seeking legal advice, she had refused to do so, and there was no evidence of duress. Citing *Clayton* that a lack of independent legal advice is not determinative, the court in *Harnett v Harnett*, 2014 ONSC 359 held: "Parties are expected to use due diligence in ascertaining the facts underlying their agreements. A party cannot fail to ask the correct questions and then rely on a lack of disclosure" (para 89). The agreement was ultimately upheld.

Compare these cases to *Bossenberry v Bossenberry* (1994), 6 RFL (4th) 47 (Ont Gen Div), where a court refused a husband's request to set aside a separation agreement when he claimed to have signed the final agreement in a depressed and emotional state and without legal advice. The court held that the final agreement was not significantly different from a draft agreement for which he had received legal advice. Is it possible that the court placed too much reliance on independent legal advice in this case?

Do such cases suggest a need to require independent legal advice? Why, or why not?

FAMILY BARGAINING IN CONTEXT: TWO CASE STUDIES

Family bargaining and marriage contracts

Although it may seem ironic to discuss marriage contracts (or cohabitation agreements) in the context of divorce (or separation), it seems that the validity or enforceability of these domestic contracts is often tested in practice at the time of separation or divorce. Reflect on the contexts in which parties who are considering marriage or cohabitation may decide to negotiate a domestic contract governing their entitlement at divorce or separation.

To what extent should courts hold marriage contracts and cohabitation agreements to the same standards as separation agreements, as discussed in the above cases?

How, if at all, are these contractual contexts different?

What principles should apply in deciding whether to enforce the provisions of a marriage contract at the time of family dissolution?

This issue has been addressed in a number of recent cases, which are examined here.

LeVan v LeVan
2008 ONCA 388

In this case, the parties lived together for one year and then married in 1996. They had two children, and the wife (who was a teacher) did not work outside the home after the marriage, and she was the primary caregiver for the children. The husband and his family owned a group of major manufacturing companies. At the time of the marriage, he earned an annual salary of about $52,000 per year, but his interests in the companies and family trusts were valued at about $30 million.

The husband's family had negotiated arrangements to protect the family shares from outside influence by creating a model marriage contract to be signed by the prospective partners of the four children. The wife knew when she agreed to the marriage that she would be required to sign a contract to protect the family's control of the companies. In addition, however, the husband added provisions to the contract to exclude all the husband's business interests and severely restricted any claim to spousal support on the part of the wife at separation or divorce. The evidence indicated that the husband did not provide full financial information to his lawyer.

Prior to signing the contract, the wife had received advice from her own lawyer (her first lawyer) that the contract was unconscionable, and the lawyer had also been unsuccessful in obtaining financial disclosure from the lawyer acting for the husband. The husband's lawyer was a family lawyer working for the same firm that handled business matters for his family and their companies, and the evidence suggested that the firm was attempting to make as little disclosure as possible. As the wedding date approached, the husband requested assistance from his family lawyer, and the husband's lawyer then arranged for the wife to meet with another family lawyer (her second lawyer), advising that the meeting was urgent because the wedding was then about two days away. (The facts also indicated that the lawyer to whom the wife was referred had acted previously for the husband's lawyer in this lawyer's own divorce proceedings.)

The lawyer to whom the wife was referred had a meeting with the wife that lasted about an hour. Although this lawyer provided legal advice to the wife, she failed to request financial disclosure from the husband's lawyer. The wife gave evidence at trial that she believed that the marriage would not take place unless she signed an agreement to protect the family's interests from influence from outsiders, and she thus signed the agreement.

The parties separated in 2003, and the wife submitted that the contract should be set aside because the husband had failed to disclose significant assets and had misrepresented his net worth. The trial judge set aside the agreement, and awarded the wife an equalization payment of $5.3 million, as well as significant spousal and child support, and costs. The husband appealed this decision, and the Ontario Court of Appeal dismissed the appeal, stating in part:

> [32] The trial judge spent considerable time reviewing the testimony of the witnesses and making findings of credibility. Her [principal] finding of fact was that husband had breached his statutory obligation to provide financial disclosure to the wife. She found that he didn't make the required disclosure for two reasons. First, he did not want his wife to know his income or the value of his assets because he wanted to control their lifestyle during marriage. Second, he was afraid that full disclosure might lead to more aggressive demands and a less favourable contract. Thus, the trial judge concluded that the husband had deliberately breached s. 56(4)(a) of the *FLA* by choosing not to make complete financial disclosure to the wife of his income and his assets when entering into the contract.
>
> [33] It is now well established that a finding that a party has violated a provision of s. 56(4) of the *FLA* does not automatically render the contract a nullity. Rather, a trial judge must determine whether it is appropriate, in the circumstances, to order that the contract be set aside. This is a discretionary exercise. See *Dochuk v. Dochuk* (1999), 44 R.F.L. (4th) 97 (Ont. Gen. Div.). Here, the trial judge determined that it was appropriate to set aside the marriage contract. She recognized that it was appropriate to exercise that discretion not simply because of the failure to disclose, but also because of other factors relevant to s. 56(4), such as the wife's failure to understand the nature and consequences of the contract in accordance with s. 56(4)(b).
>
> [34] The trial judge relied upon the following findings to set aside the marriage contract apart from the husband's failure to disclose the value of his significant assets:
> 1. The husband failed to disclose his income tax returns.
> 2. The husband failed to disclose shares that he held ....
> 3. The footnote to Schedule A [of the contract] was inaccurate and did not contain sufficient information to be meaningful.
> 4. The disclosure provided was misleading [for example, the husband's lawyer stated his interest in the family trust as "minimal."]
> 5. The husband's lawyer failed to disclose that he had three siblings, and that [they were all treated equally under the trust].
> 6. The financial statements for [the companies and the trust] were not provided.
> 7. The husband's lawyer failed to disclose that [the husband was both a capital beneficiary and an income beneficiary of the trust].
>
> [35] The trial judge recognized each of these factors in support of her determination that the husband had failed to comply with his disclosure obligation under s. 56(4)(a) of the *FLA*. In exercising her discretion to set aside the marriage contract, the trial judge further identified the following factors:
> 1. The wife did not receive effective independent legal advice and some advice provided was wrong.
> 2. The wife did not understand the nature and consequence of the marriage contract.
> 3. The husband misrepresented the nature and terms of the marriage contract to the wife.

4. The husband's failure to disclose his entire assets to his wife was deliberate.

5. The husband interfered with the wife's receipt of legal assistance from her first lawyer....

[36] Virtually all of the trial judge's findings that I have outlined ... were material to the wife's decision to sign the marriage contract. [The court also agreed with the trial judge's decision to reject the husband's argument that the wife would have signed the contract anyway, quoting from the trial judgment:]

> ... The wife stated on cross-examination that no matter what number was in the husband's Schedule A, that she was going to sign the contract because she wanted to get married and "because she was signing this contract to protect [the husband's] interest in Wescast." I find that the wife was acknowledging that she understood that there would be no marriage without a marriage contract. I do not agree that she was acknowledging that she would sign any contract regardless of its terms and regardless of the extent of her future husband's income and assets.... [The wife misunderstood the scope of the contract] because of her future husband's misrepresentations.... I find that had he fully disclosed as required, it is likely that the marriage contract would have been more favourable to the wife, or that the wife, recognizing how unfair it was, would have refused to sign it.

...

[49] First, I will consider whether the trial judge erred in setting aside the marriage contract in accordance with s. 56(4)(a)....

[50] Section 56(4)(a) of the *FLA* was designed to address and codify prior concerns maintained by courts that both parties fully understood their rights under the law when contracting with their spouses. It has been characterized as the "judicial oversight" provision of marriage agreements [citing *Hartshorne* at para. 14]. The provision is of such significance that, in accordance with s. 5(7), it cannot be waived by the parties.

[51] The analysis undertaken under s. 56(4) is essentially comprised of a two-part process [citing *Demchuk*]. First, the court must consider whether the party seeking to set aside the agreement can demonstrate that one or more of the circumstances set out within the provision has been engaged. Once that hurdle has been overcome, the court must then consider whether it is appropriate to exercise discretion in favour of setting aside the agreement. This approach was adopted and applied by the trial judge....

[52] As discussed, the issue of focus at trial was whether the husband had complied with his financial disclosure obligation.... [The court referred to *Patrick v. Patrick* (2002), OJ No. 639, and the court's conclusion that parties are not permitted to contract out of the obligation to disclose. The court also referred to *Dubin v. Dubin* (2003), 34 RFL (5th) 227, which held that "knowing assets and liabilities at the date of the agreement is fundamental to an eventual calculation of net family property," and that financial disclosure is necessary for the parties to understand legal rights and obligations.]

[54] In this case, the disclosure provided by the husband was insufficient to enable the wife to have a clear understanding of exactly what rights she was giving up by entering into the contract. The husband failed to disclose that he held shares ... that were found to be of significant value. He failed to provide any financial statements.... No income tax returns were provided for the husband and there was no disclosure whatsoever of his income. Overall, the information provided by the husband made it impossible to calculate or determine his net worth.... The trial judge found that the husband's disclosure obligation required him to disclose the value of these significant assets.

[56] On appeal, the husband argued that the trial judge erred in importing the word "value" into section 56(4)(a), contrary to the plain wording of the section.... In addition, the husband submitted that it would be onerous and expensive to require valuations for marriage contracts and would often result in parties making estimates of values, thereby creating a risk of misrepresentation, which in itself could be a basis to set aside the agreement.

[57] [The court noted that the trial judge had relied on *Demchuk* to support her view that the disclosure obligation in the *FLA* encompassed an obligation to disclose the value of assets, and declined to engage in a statutory analysis of the use of the word "value" in the *FLA*.] Moreover, the trial judge's findings of fact which I have outlined in paras. 34 and 35 fully support her decision to set aside the marriage contract, essentially on the basis of the husband's reprehensible conduct leading to the signing of the marriage contract.

[58] In the circumstances of this case, it is my view that the husband's failure to disclose value for his interests in the LeVan Companies and the Family Trust is not critical to the disclosure analysis. As the trial judge indicated in her findings, there is an abundance of evidence indicating that the husband had failed to comply with his disclosure obligation apart from his failure to disclose value for these assets. As discussed, this failure was compounded by the serious misrepresentations respecting the extent and value of certain of the assets disclosed.

[59] In addition, the marriage contract itself was misleading.... These facts coupled with the wife's misunderstanding about the effect of the contract meant that the wife had no chance whatsoever of understanding what she was giving up when she signed the contract.

[60] [The trial judge exercised her discretion properly.] In deciding how to exercise discretion, the trial judge considered the "fairness" of the contract. The appellant emphasized that unfairness in a contract is not a proper basis for setting aside marriage contracts in Ontario. Although there is nothing in the governing legislation that suggests that fairness is a consideration in deciding whether or not to set aside a marriage contract, I do not see why fairness is not an appropriate consideration in the exercise of the court's discretion in the second stage of the s. 56(4)(a) analysis. In my view, once a judge has found one of the statutory preconditions to exist, he or she should be entitled to consider the fairness of the contract together with other factors in the exercise of his or her discretion. It seems to me that a judge would be more inclined to set aside a clearly unfair contract than one that treated the parties fairly. [The court also took into account the other reasons relied on by the trial judge for setting aside the contract, set out in para. 35.]

[62] These findings are reasonably supported by the evidence presented at trial. I therefore see no reason to interfere with them in this case. In essence, the trial judge found that the husband failed to make full disclosure of his significant assets, that his disclosure was incomplete and inadequate and that failure to make full disclosure was a deliberate attempt to mislead his wife. As such, the trial judge's decision to set aside the contract should be upheld....

The court also considered the issue of whether to take account of the decline in value of the husband's interests, an issue discussed in Chapter Six in relation to valuation of family property.

Notes and Questions

"Fairness" and statutory language

In *LeVan*, the court used the principles established in *Demchuk* to determine whether to set aside the contract, noting specifically that the Ontario *Family Law Act* provisions do not use a "fairness" test. Thus, section 56(4) defines the three grounds for setting aside a domestic contract, but (as noted in *Demchuk*), once the court makes a finding with respect to the breach of one of the requirements in section 56(4), a court must then address a second issue: whether to exercise discretion to set the agreement aside. In relation to this second issue, some courts have adopted a "fairness" test in the exercise of judicial discretion.

The Supreme Court of Canada released its decision in *Hartshorne*, with respect to marriage agreements, after an earlier consideration of the principles applicable to separation agreements in *Miglin v Miglin*, 2003 SCC 24 (reviewed in Chapter Seven in relation to spousal support and separation agreements). In both cases, the Court addressed the balancing of the parties' interests in finality and autonomy with the need to promote the goals of fairness for spouses at divorce or separation.

Hartshorne provides a good example of judicial reasoning about family law bargaining at the time of marriage and the principles applicable to contract enforcement at family dissolution.

Although, *Hartshorne* focused on the now repealed statute in British Columbia, which arguably had the most discretionary principles for judicial review of family law agreements, the case remains important for family law jurisprudence because it has not been explicitly overturned and it strongly emphasizes autonomy and choice in private bargaining. Later in this chapter, a comparison between B.C.'s repealed *Family Relations Act* and its current *Family Law Act* will be provided.

Hartshorne v Hartshorne
2004 SCC 22

The spouses began to live together in 1985, and their first child was born in July 1987. They married in March 1989, and their second child was born in November 1989. The marriage was a second marriage for both husband and wife, who had met when the wife became an articling student and later an associate in the law firm of which the husband was a partner. The husband later gave evidence that his willingness to marry a second time depended on the parties' agreeing to a contract because, in the event of marriage breakdown, he did not want to have to share his assets again (as he had been required to do in his earlier divorce proceedings).

In their discussions about the marriage contract, prior to marriage, the wife had obtained independent legal advice about the contract proposed by her husband to be. In part, the legal advice suggested that the agreement was "grossly unfair," and advised the wife not to sign it. Nonetheless, both parties signed the agreement, which included an acknowledgment that the wife was doing so at the insistence of the husband and not voluntarily. The agreement significantly limited the wife's entitlement to property sharing in the event that the marriage ended in separation.

At the time of the marriage, the husband had significant assets while the wife had few assets and some significant debts. The wife remained out of the workforce from 1987 to 1998 to care for the couple's two children, and the parties maintained separate financial accounts, with the husband providing a monthly amount to the wife to meet her needs. Based on the husband's income, the parties enjoyed a generous lifestyle. However, they separated in 1998 after nine years of marriage.

At separation, the wife applied for property and spousal support pursuant to British Columbia's *Family Relations Act*, RSBC 1996, c 128, contrary to the terms of the marriage agreement. The husband argued that the pre-nuptial agreement, signed by the parties on their wedding day and by which the wife's potential claims were expressly limited, prevented the application of the provincial legislative regime.

After reviewing the circumstances of the signing of the agreement, which occurred between the wedding ceremony at their home, and a celebratory dinner with their guests, the trial judge concluded that the evidence did not establish that the agreement was unconscionable or that it was entered into under duress, coercion, or undue influence, even though there was evidence that the wife was visibly upset at the time that she signed it (para 26). However, the trial judge concluded that the wife was entitled to share property owned by the husband because the pre-nuptial agreement was "unfair" in accordance with section 65 of British Columbia's *Family Relations Act* (see [1999] BCJ No 2861 (SC) (QL) and additional reasons at 2001 BCSC 325).

Section 65 expressly authorizes a court to reapportion property where a marriage agreement "would be unfair" having regard to a list of factors set out in the section. According to the trial judge, several factors were relevant, including the duration of the marriage, the fact that most of the husband's property had been acquired prior to this marriage, the needs of the wife to become economically independent and self sufficient, and the impact of her role in home and child care responsibilities in permitting the husband to concentrate on improving his law practice. Overall, the trial judge concluded that the agreement was unfair and thus exercised authority pursuant to section 65 to reapportion some assets.

(The result of the trial judge's reapportionment meant that the wife received 46 percent of the family assets. She would have received only 20 percent pursuant to the agreement (SCC decision, para 25).)

The husband appealed to the B.C. Court of Appeal, and a majority dismissed the appeal, Thackray JA dissenting (see 2002 BCCA 587).

BASTARACHE J wrote the majority decision, with three judges dissenting (LeBel, Deschamps, and Binnie JJ):

[1] Domestic contracts are explicitly permitted by the matrimonial property regime in British Columbia. They allow spouses to substitute a consensual regime for the statutory regime that would otherwise be imposed on them. Domestic contracts are, however, like the statutory regime itself, subject to judicial intervention when provisions for the division of property which they contain are found to be unfair at the time of distribution, after considering the various factors enumerated in s. 65 of the *Family Relations Act*....

[2] At issue in this appeal is whether a marriage agreement respecting the division of property, entered into after receiving independent legal advice, without duress, coercion or undue influence, can later be found to be unfair and set aside on the basis that it failed "to provide anything for the respondent's sacrifice in giving up her law practice and postponing her career development," notwithstanding that the parties' agreement preserved the right to spousal support. The parties in this appeal also raised the issues of whether an agreement entered into prior to or at the time of marriage should be subject to the same review on appeal as a separation agreement, and whether, where provisions for the division of property in a marriage agreement are found to be unfair at the time of distribution, the whole agreement should simply be ignored.

[9] The authorities generally agree that courts should respect private arrangements that spouses make for the division of their property on the breakdown of their relationship. This is particularly so where the agreement in question was negotiated with independent legal advice. The difficulty of course is in determining the proper approach to deciding, at the time of distribution, what is fair under the terms of s. 65 of the FRA. A domestic contract constituting a derogation from the statutory regime, it is obvious that its fairness cannot be determined simply on the basis of its consistency with the said regime. In fact, s. 65(1) also provides for judicial reapportionment on the basis of fairness in the case of the statutory regime in s. 56(2). The appellant in these proceedings argues that the majority of the Court of Appeal effectively found the Agreement to be unfair on the basis that it derogated from the statutory regime. After reviewing the provisions of the FRA as well as the Agreement, it is my opinion that said Agreement operated fairly at the time of distribution.

[14] Most of the provinces provide for judicial oversight of marriage agreements. For example, s. 56(4) of Ontario's *Family Law Act*, RSO 1990, c. F3, permits a court to set aside a domestic contract or a provision thereof if a party failed to disclose significant assets or liabilities, if a party did not understand the nature or consequences of the contract, or otherwise, in accordance with the law of contract. See also *Family Law Act*, RSNL 1990, c. F-2, s. 66(4); *Family Law Act*, SPEI 1995, c. 12, s. 55(4), for this language. The threshold in Nova Scotia is a finding that any term is "unconscionable, unduly harsh on one party or fraudulent": see *Matrimonial Property Act*, RSNS 1989, c. 275, s. 29. Saskatchewan allows a court to redistribute property where an interspousal contract was unconscionable or grossly unfair at the time it was entered into: see *Family Property Act*, SS 1997, c. F-6.3, s. 24(2). New Brunswick permits a court to disregard a provision of a domestic contract where a spouse did not receive independent legal advice and application of the provision would be inequitable: see *Marital Property Act*, SNB 1980, c. M-1.1, s. 41. By contrast, in British Columbia, as earlier noted, a court may reapportion assets upon finding that to divide the property as provided for in the

agreement or the FRA would be "unfair." Clearly, the statutory scheme in British Columbia sets a lower threshold for judicial intervention than do the schemes in other provinces.

Bastarache J reviewed the purpose of the *Family Relations Act*, concluding that the primary policy objective in relation to division of property was fairness, and continued:

> [36] To give effect to legislative intention, courts must encourage parties to enter into marriage agreements that are fair, and to respond to the changing circumstances of their marriage by reviewing and revising their own contracts for fairness when necessary. Conversely, in a framework within which private parties are permitted to take personal responsibility for their financial well-being upon the dissolution of marriage, courts should be reluctant to second-guess the arrangement on which they reasonably expected to rely. Individuals may choose to structure their affairs in a number of different ways, and it is their prerogative to do so: see generally *Nova Scotia (AG) v. Walsh*, [2002] 4 SCR 325, 2002 SCC 83.

> [38] Marital cases must reconcile respect for the parties' intent, on the one hand, and the assurance of an equitable result, on the other. The parties here adopted opposite views as to the degree of deference to be afforded marriage agreements; the appellant submitted that more and the respondent submitted that less deference should be paid to marriage agreements than to separation agreements.

> [39] This Court has not established, and in my opinion should not establish, a "hard and fast" rule regarding the deference to be afforded to marriage agreements as compared to separation agreements. In some cases, marriage agreements ought to be accorded a greater degree of deference than separation agreements. Marriage agreements define the parties' expectations from the outset, usually before any rights are vested and before any entitlement arises. Often, perhaps most often, a desire to protect pre-acquired assets or an anticipated inheritance for children of a previous marriage will be the impetus for such an agreement. Separation agreements, by contrast, purport to deal with existing or vested rights and obligations, with the aggrieved party claiming he or she had given up something to which he or she was already entitled with an unfair result. In other cases, however, marriage agreements may be accorded less deference than separation agreements. The reason for this is that marriage agreements are anticipatory and may not fairly take into account the financial means, needs or other circumstances of the parties at the time of marriage breakdown....

> [40] In addressing the issue of deference, this Court may apply *Miglin v. Miglin*, [2003] 1 SCR 303, 2003 SCC 24, for its general legal proposition that some weight should be given to marriage agreements....

Bastarache J reviewed the decision in *Miglin*, and the two-stage approach it adopted. He looked first to the circumstances of the negotiation to determine whether one party took advantage of the other's vulnerability or if the substance of the agreement failed to comply with the goals of the *Divorce Act*. He next sought to determine whether the agreement, viewed from the time of the application to review, still reflected the intentions of the parties and was still in compliance with the objectives of the Act. After reviewing the statutory framework and especially section 65, he concluded:

[44] Thus, the determination that a marriage agreement operates fairly or unfairly at the time of distribution cannot be made without regard to the parties' perspectives. A contract governing the distribution of property between spouses reflects what the parties believed to be fair at the time the contract was formed (presuming the absence of duress, coercion, and undue influence). The parties would usually not be expected to deal with their present situation without any consideration of how they expect their situation will evolve over time. If the parties' lives unfold in precisely the manner they had contemplated at the time of contract formation, then a finding that the contract operates unfairly at the time of distribution constitutes, in essence, a substitution of the parties' notion of fairness with the court's notion of fairness, providing that nothing else would suggest that the parties did not really consider the impact of their decision in a rational and comprehensive way. Thus, central to any analysis under s. 65(1) of the FRA is consideration of how accurately the parties predicted, at the time of contract formation, their actual circumstances at the time of distribution, whether they truly considered the impact of their decision and whether they adjusted their agreement during the marriage to meet the demands of a situation different from the one expected, either because the circumstances were different or simply because implications were inadequately addressed or proved to be unrealistic.

[45] ... At the time of the triggering event, both the financial and domestic arrangements between the appellant and the respondent were unfolding just as the parties had expected. With respect to their financial arrangement, they were living out their intention to "remain completely independent of the other with regard to their own property, both real and personal." There was no commingling of funds, there was no joint accounts of significant value, and the assets that the appellant brought into the marriage remained in his name. On a personal level, as planned, the appellant and respondent had a second child and, as decided by the respondent, she did not resume her position at the law firm but remained at home to raise their two children.

[46] Where, as in the present case, the parties have anticipated with accuracy their personal and financial circumstances at the time of distribution, and where they have truly considered the impact of their choices, then, without more, a finding that their Agreement operates unfairly should not be made lightly. This does not mean that no attention should be given to the possible deficit in the assets and future income of the spouse who chose to stay at home and facilitate the professional development of the other spouse, compared to what they would realistically have been otherwise. Section 65 mandates as much. A fair distribution of assets must of course take into account sacrifices made and their impact, the situation of the parties at the time of distribution, their age, education and true capacity to reintegrate into the work force and achieve economic independence in particular. But this must be done in light of the personal choices made and of the overall situation considering all property rights under the marriage agreement and other entitlements. In the present case, the main feature of the Agreement was the desire that each spouse retain the assets earned before the marriage, sharing equitably assets acquired afterwards being the rule. This will be fair on dissolution of the marriage if Mrs. Hartshorne is not left without means and facing true hardship in reclaiming her professional status and income, in light also of her parental obligations. Consideration must be given to the actual situation as it unfolded. ...

[47] The ultimate point then is this: in determining whether a marriage agreement operates unfairly, a court must first apply the agreement.

In particular, the court must assess and award those financial entitlements provided to each spouse under the agreement, and other entitlements from all other sources, including spousal and child support. The court must then, in consideration of those factors listed in s. 65(1) of the FRA, make a determination as to whether the contract operates unfairly. At this second stage, consideration must be given to the parties' personal and financial circumstances, and in particular to the manner in which these circumstances evolved over time. Where the current circumstances were within the contemplation of the parties at the time the Agreement was formed, and where their Agreement and circumstances surrounding it reflect consideration and response to these circumstances, then the plaintiff's burden to establish unfairness is heavier. Thus, consideration of the factors listed in s. 65(1) of the FRA, taken together, would have to reveal that the economic consequences of the marriage breakdown were not shared equitably in all of the circumstances. This approach, in my view, accords with the underlying principle of the FRA, striking an appropriate balance between deference to the parties' intentions, on the one hand, and assurance of an equitable result, on the other.

Bastarache J then considered the factors in section 65 of the *FRA* and the relationship between the wife's entitlement to spousal support pursuant to the agreement and its potential to enable her to become independent and self-sufficient. He concluded (at para 57) that spousal support was sufficient to meet these needs and that it would "continue the financial arrangement they lived out during the relationship." After examining the factors in section 65, he stated:

[58] It is highly significant that the Agreement explicitly preserves a right to spousal support and that ... the appellant has a healthy and continuous flow of income. In looking at the division of property under the Agreement, Beames J. [at trial] should have assessed fairness in light of the preservation of a right to spousal support. Only after determining that the factors of self-sufficiency and need could not be met through an order of spousal support, should the trial judge have concluded that the Agreement operated unfairly.

Bastarache J also examined the role of independent legal advice provided to the wife prior to her signing the agreement:

[60] Independent legal advice at the time of negotiation is an important means of ensuring an informed decision to enter an agreement. In the case at bar, the respondent's lawyer prepared a written legal opinion for her. In that opinion letter, the lawyer: (1) confirmed that the respondent was in agreement with the principle that the appellant would retain ownership of the assets which he acquired prior to the relationship, but that she wished that any agreement be fair to both parties and to any children born of the marriage; (2) concluded that the Agreement proposed by the appellant was "grossly unfair"; (3) advised the respondent that, in the event that the marriage broke down, under the FRA she would have a *prima facie* right to an undivided one-half interest in all family assets, which would include any matrimonial home, furnishings, vehicles, savings and pensions; (4) informed the respondent that the Agreement was such that she would not "earn" even close to a one-half interest in the matrimonial home unless the marriage continued for approximately 20 years; (5) advised the respondent that "a Court would easily find such provision to be unfair and would intervene to redistribute the property on a more

equitable basis"; (6) strongly recommended that the respondent not execute the Agreement "in its present form"; (7) recommended that in order
to achieve a more fair result and yet still satisfy the desires of the appellant to retain the majority of his property separately, that the following
assets remain the appellant's separate property — (a) bank deposits or
securities, (b) the apartment at Osoyoos, (c) the Oroville lot, (d) interest
in law firm and management company, (e) the 1969 Mercedes, (f) the
boat, and (g) the motorcycle; and (8) strongly recommended that any
agreement which the respondent executes makes it clear that there is
nothing to bar any claim for maintenance or support for herself or for
any children of the marriage.

[61] It is clear from the detail in this opinion letter that the respondent
was forewarned of the Agreement's "shortcomings." Indeed, the respondent made a few changes to the Agreement in response to her lawyer's
advice, including the inclusion of the preservation of spousal support
clause. The respondent was advised that the Agreement was "grossly
unfair" and that a court would "easily find" the provision relating to interest in the matrimonial home to be unfair and would redistribute the property on a more equitable basis. Despite this advice, or because of it, as
expressed by counsel for the respondent during the hearing before our
Court, the respondent signed the Agreement. The respondent cannot now
rely on her lawyer's opinion to support her allegation that because she
thought the Agreement was unfair from its inception, for all intents and
purposes, she never intended to live up to her end of the bargain. It is
trite that a party could never be allowed to avoid his or her contractual
obligations on the basis that he or she believed, from the moment of its
formation, that the contract was void or unenforceable.

Bastarache J reviewed the substantial assets brought into the marriage
by the husband and the debts of the wife at that time, and then decided
that the agreement was fair in accordance with section 65 of the *Family
Relations Act*:

[65] [By] signing the Agreement, the appellant and the respondent
entered their marriage with certain expectations on which they were reasonably entitled to rely. If the respondent truly believed that the Agreement was unacceptable at that time, she should not have signed it. In this
case, the intention of the parties, as expressed in the Agreement, was to
leave with each party that which he or she had before the marriage. The
question is not whether there is something fundamentally unfair about
that, but whether the operation of the Agreement will prove to be unfair
in the circumstances present at the time of distribution. In light of the
provisions of the FRA, and after examining all of the provisions of the
Agreement as well as the circumstances of the parties at the time of separation, it is my opinion that the Agreement was fair at the time of the
triggering event. The trial judge erred in finding otherwise. The Agreement should be left intact.

[67] ... [I]n a framework within which private parties are permitted to
take personal responsibility for their financial well-being upon the dissolution of marriage, courts should be reluctant to second-guess their initiative
and arrangement, particularly where independent legal advice has been
obtained. They should not conclude that unfairness is proven simply
by demonstrating that the marriage agreement deviates from the statutory
matrimonial property regime. Fairness must first take into account what
was within the realistic contemplation of the parties, what attention they
gave to changes in circumstances or unrealized implications, then what are

their true circumstances, and whether the discrepancy is such, given the s. 65 factors, that a different apportionment should be made....

DESCHAMPS J (dissenting):

[69] Contrary to what was argued before us by the appellant, this appeal is *not* about whether two people can enter into a prenuptial arrangement which will determine, or even influence, the division of family assets upon their separation. Rather, this case is about giving effect to the explicit legislative intention that only fair agreements be upheld. Furthermore, to construe the issue in the way suggested by the majority presupposes that even unfair agreements will be given weight. With respect, I have reached a different conclusion.

[70] The primary policy objective guiding the courts' role in division of assets on marital breakdown in British Columbia is fairness, regardless of whether the presumptive entitlement arises statutorily or through contract. The *Family Relations Act* ... does permit couples to sign marriage agreements on division of assets. However, to be enforceable, any such agreement must be fair; if it is not, it will be judicially reapportioned to achieve a fair division. To give effect to legislative intention, courts ought to encourage parties to enter into marriage agreements that are fair, and to respond to the changing circumstances of their marriage by reviewing and revising their own contracts for fairness over time. Telling parties that their unfair apportionment will nonetheless be given weight as a factor in reapportionment would defeat this objective.

Deschamps J reviewed the obligation of appellate courts to defer to the trier of fact. She also reviewed the extensive litigation involved in this case over a period of years. In the end, she concluded that the husband should not be required to share his interest in his law practice, even though it was a family asset, but that in other respects, the decisions of the lower courts were appropriate. She also reviewed *Miglin* and the legislation in other provinces to argue (at paras 74ff) that the B.C. statute recognized a lower threshold for judicial intervention and was therefore appropriate for the court to order reapportionment in this case pursuant to section 65.

Thus, according to Deschamps J:

[77] ... I believe that the deciding inquiry under s. 65(1) of the FRA is whether or not the agreement is *substantively fair at the time of application to the court* [emphasis in DLR]. ... Thus, under the FRA, the judge must review the fairness of the marriage agreement at the time of application to the court, considering the parties' rights, entitlements and obligations at that very moment, in light of the s. 65(1) factors. The legislation, both in its specific wording and taken as a whole, does not indicate otherwise. It is also clear from the nature of marriage agreements that their fairness only genuinely matters when they are invoked before a court. Finally, a judge can only review the fairness of such a prenuptial arrangement by considering it alongside the other conditions of separation covered by the FRA. These include custody as well as potential maintenance and support orders. This will only be feasible after an application has been made to the court.

[78] What does fairness at the time of application to the court entail? Although the statutory regime provides for equal sharing, it is only a starting point, just as it is for marriage agreements. Fairness will not always be synonymous with equal division. In some marriages, the contributions of

each spouse will not be equal. For example, one party may come into the marriage substantially wealthier, in an economic sense, than the other; the marriage may be very brief, indicating that an equal partnership never really came into being; or, a party may have transferred ownership of valuable personal assets. The various factors set out in s. 65(1) of the FRA reflect this reality. I believe the proper approach to determining whether a division of family assets under a marriage agreement is fair is for a judge to assess the division in light of the s. 65(1) factors. The original intention of the parties is relevant insofar as it points the court towards how the parties chose to address the requirements of fairness. If the parties fairly addressed the enumerated factors through other provisions in the agreement, that should be taken into account. That being said, the parties' original intention is not determinative at this stage. Fairness is a concept that is independent of any agreement. If a court establishes that a marriage agreement is fair in light of the s. 65(1) factors, it will stand. If it is not, the court will redress it. For greater certainty, a judge redressing the unfairness resulting from a marriage agreement may want to test the result of his or her s. 65(1) reapportionment by comparing it to the division the judge would have established had there been no agreement. Since the criteria are the same, the share apportioned to each spouse should be similar whether there is a contract or not.

[80] Unlike s. 15.2(4)(c) of the *Divorce Act*, which was in issue in *Miglin*, *supra*, which requires courts to take into consideration "any order, agreement or arrangement relating to support of either spouse," s. 65(1) makes no mention of the agreement in the list of factors for courts to consider when assessing the *substantive* fairness of a division of assets. Consideration of the marriage agreement is not even implicitly alluded to. This is not surprising given that what is under review is the agreement itself. It would be a useless exercise if the fairness test were to be based on an unfair agreement. Thus, in British Columbia, spouses may not seek to rely on unfair provisions for the division of assets on marital breakdown. Those are the bounds of meaningful choice for spouses in that province.

[81] Public policy supports this conclusion. The approach favoured by the majority would fail to encourage spouses to make genuine efforts to conclude fair agreements (and to update them for fairness as circumstances change), if a potentially intransigent party could tell himself or herself: "This may turn out to be unfair, but at least a court would still take it into account." In this case, the appellant testified that, on being informed that the respondent's lawyer considered the agreement "grossly unfair," he considered it "interesting," but refused to make substantive changes to render the agreement fair. Parties have many fair options about how to arrange their affairs and protect particular assets, and they need an incentive to consider them and take them seriously.

[89] ... The majority states that by choosing to execute the agreement despite having noticed that it might be unfair, the respondent signalled that she was not concerned. This analysis, in my view, is not acceptable and confuses fairness with unconscionability. While it is true that the agreement's shortcomings were apparent to some degree at the time of execution, foreseeability (or simply "signing" the agreement) does not cure its substantive unfairness. Although it may constitute a bar to setting the agreement aside on the ground of unconscionability, independent legal advice prior to execution does not render it fair nor does it leave the trial judge powerless....

[90] There are indications that the respondent was in a vulnerable position in negotiation — not enough for the agreement to be unconscionable,

but enough to suggest that the trial judge should be alive to the possibility that the agreement was unfair. The respondent had already been out of the workforce and dependent on the appellant for almost two years and had only ever worked as a lawyer (and before that, an articling student) in the appellant's firm. The agreement was concluded under pressure with the wedding fast approaching. The respondent sought changes to the agreement before execution but was unable to persuade the appellant to agree, except with respect to minor changes, such as the insertion of a clause to the effect that her signature was not voluntary and was at his insistence. These circumstances illustrate the appellant's position of power within the relationship, as well as the respondent's correlative dependence. That she remained at home for the rest of the marriage relationship to take care of the couple's children further illustrates the power dynamics at play. Taken as a whole, these circumstances justify reviewing the agreement with increased scrutiny.

[91] ... Marriage is a "joint endeavour," a socio-economic partnership.... On the one hand, married spouses are entitled to the full protection of their matrimonial regime. On the other, they must fully assume the responsibilities flowing from their decision to get married. By choosing to marry the respondent, to have children, and to support *and benefit* from his wife's work in the private sphere, Mr. Hartshorne agreed to bear all the consequences of the legislative regime regulating his decisions, including judicial review under s. 65 of the FRA. He cannot have his cake and eat it too.

In the end, the majority of the Supreme Court noted (at para 64) that any economic disadvantage could be compensated through a spousal support order and thus ordered (at para 65) that the marriage contract be enforced.

Private ordering and principles of fairness

Are the reasons in the majority and dissenting judgments in *Hartshorne* in agreement with respect to the principles that are relevant to determining the enforceability of marriage contracts? To what extent do the reasons of the majority and the dissent encourage parties to negotiate fair agreements? What is the distinction between "unconscionability" in contract law and "unfairness" in the B.C. statute?

What role did independent legal advice play in this case? Was it relevant that both spouses were lawyers? In the context of advice from her lawyer that the agreement was "grossly unfair," was Mrs. Hartshorne entitled to rely on this legal opinion when she signed the agreement under protest? How realistic was the majority's view that if the agreement was unacceptable, Mrs. Hartshorne should not have signed it?

Did the Supreme Court's majority decision in *Hartshorne* identify an appropriate balance between goals of autonomy and private ordering on one hand and fairness between the parties on the other? How did the majority define "fairness," by contrast with the definition promoted by the dissenting judges?

In reflecting on these questions, consider this assessment of the Supreme Court's decision:

... The majority's approach to "fairness" seems primarily motivated by a concern with the unfairness that would arise if people are unable to rely on freely negotiated contracts, rather than by a concern about the substantive fairness of the parties' arrangement in light of the structure of their marriage and their economic position at marriage breakdown.

[A] significant weakness of the majority's approach is its complete inability to address the emotionally laden nature of contracting within the marital and family contexts and the distinctive pressures within this context that may distort the fairness of the contracting process. In fact, one of the most disturbing aspects of the majority's analysis generally is its insensitivity to the emotional and personal context in which marriage contracts are negotiated and its corresponding tendency to view decisions as the product of unfettered and autonomous choice. The majority hardly mentions the circumstances leading up to the signing of the Hartshornes' agreement, including Mrs. Hartshorne's resistance to signing the contract and her extreme emotional distress when she did. It does not mention the clause Mrs. Hartshorne added to the contract stating that she was not signing voluntarily but at Mr. Hartshorne's insistence. Only in passing does it mention the fact that when Mrs. Hartshorne signed the agreement she already had a 20 month old child with Mr. Hartshorne and had been economically dependent on Mr. Hartshorne for almost two years. Instead of recognizing that these facts made Mrs. Hartshorne emotionally and economically dependent upon Mr. Hartshorne — and therefore less able to simply walk away from the negotiating table — the Court comes to the counter-intuitive conclusion that Mrs. Hartshorne's decision to sign away her claim to property was more informed since she was already economically dependent. Instead of seeing Mrs. Hartshorne's emotional and financial vulnerability when she agreed to Mr. Hartshorne's terms, the majority sees Mrs. Hartshorne as exercising a free and informed choice. Instead of seeing a woman pressured into signing a marriage contract that was against her best interests, the majority sees a woman choosing to enter into an agreement "after receiving independent legal advice, without duress, coercion or undue influence." Instead of seeing the contract as reflecting Mr. Hartshorne's wishes — not Mrs. Hartshorne's — the Court sees it as expressing the wishes of both parties to live separate as to property.

Under the majority's test, the power imbalances that existed in the Hartshorne's relationship, and that exist in many other relationships are simply not relevant in assessing fairness.... On the majority's test, the less Mr. Hartshorne shared with Mrs. Hartshorne during the marriage, the more likely the contract was to be viewed as fair. Had Mr. Hartshorne been more generous towards Mrs. Hartshorne by putting property in her name or by opening joint bank accounts, the more the Hartshornes would be seen to be departing from "their" original intentions, making it less likely that the contract would be viewed as fair. (Martha Shaffer, "Domestic Contracts, Part II: The Supreme Court's Decision in *Hartshorne v. Hartshorne*" (2004) 20 Can J Fam L 261 at paras 32–34)

The majority in *Hartshorne* held that "fairness" as defined in B.C.'s repealed *Family Relations Act* required a lower threshold for judicial review of domestic contracts than statutes in other Canadian provinces, including Ontario. Is it necessary to revise this conclusion, at least to some extent, after *LeVan*?

In *McCain v McCain*, 2012 ONSC 7344, the Ontario Superior Court took a different approach to "fairness" in setting aside a separation agreement between the McCains who had separated after 30 years of marriage and had five children together, two of whom were still dependants. Christine McCain did not work outside the home for the 26 years that she was raising their children, while Michael McCain was an extremely successful businessman, working in his family's business as President and CEO of Maple Leaf Foods. He was worth approximately $500 Million dollars. Michael's father, also an extremely wealthy businessman, required all of his children to enter into marriage contracts with their spouses in order to protect the assets he would eventually pass on to them or they would be disinherited. Christine concluded that if she did not sign the contract, their family lifestyle would suffer greatly. Both signed a marriage contract with independent legal advice in which Christine waived her entitlement to all property rights and spousal support in the event of separation. Christine also agreed not to pursue any claims for an interest in Michael's substantial investment properties, business, trusts and parents' estates. She was to receive title to their matrimonial home (which was mortgaged and in the midst of renovation), the sum of $7.3M, and she was permitted to retain any assets in her name (which included two mortgaged cottages).

Justice Greer held that Christine had very little choice but to sign the contract; she said: "How could the Wife have possibly refused to sign under those circumstances ... knowing that her Husband's father would cut her husband out of receiving his inheritance?" (at paras 65–66). Despite the independent legal advice, the contract was wholly inadequate in that the wife could not possibly know what her situation would be in the future without spousal support. Greer J also held that Christine was under subtle, psychological duress when she signed the marriage contract.

Greer J severed the waiver of spousal support, but upheld the rest of the contract. Michael was ordered to pay, *inter alia*, interim spousal support of $175,000 per month, and retroactive spousal support of $2.8M. The decision was not appealed, but ultimately settled in a confidential settlement.

Compare this case to *LeVan* and *Hartshorne*. Consider what you would regard as an appropriate settlement in this case.

A note on British Columbia's *Family Law Act* (2011)

In November 2011, British Columbia passed a new family law bill. The *Family Law Act*, SBC 2011, c 25, came fully into force on March 18, 2013, replacing the *Family Relations Act*. Part 5 of the new *Act* deals with issues about property division, and sections 92–97 relate specifically to agreements about property division and setting aside such agreements.

- For example, section 92 permits spouses to make agreements about the division of property and debt "equally or unequally." However, this section is subject to section 93, which requires a written agreement signed by each spouse and witnessed by another person (see also s. 93(6) with respect to unwitnessed agreements).

- In addition, section 93(3) authorizes a court to set aside an agreement if the court is satisfied that one of several circumstances existed when the parties entered into the agreement, including failure to disclose significant property or debts, evidence that a spouse took advantage of the other's vulnerability, failure to understand the nature or consequences of the agreement, or other circumstances that would cause a contract to be voidable at common law.

- More importantly, section 93(5) authorizes a court to set aside an agreement, even if none of the factors in section 93(3) existed at the time of the agreement, if the court is "satisfied ... that the agreement is significantly unfair," having regard to the time that has passed since the agreement was made, the intention of the spouses to achieve certainty in making the agreement, and the degree to which the parties relied on the agreement.

- In addition, section 95(1) authorizes the court to make an order for an unequal division of family property "if it would be significantly unfair" to divide family property or family debt equally.

Consider the extent to which these provisions would have changed the result in *Hartshorne*. Is the new legislation more or less deferential to private ordering? To what extent is *Hartshorne* relevant to the interpretation of "significantly unfair" in section 93(3)?

Independent legal advice in *Hartshorne* and *LeVan*
Consider also the role of independent legal advice in *Hartshorne* and *LeVan*.

Although the wife signed the agreement in *Hartshorne*, she did so on the basis of her lawyer's advice that it was grossly unfair, and she did so under pressure (although the court held that this pressure did not constitute duress, coercion or unconscionability).

In *LeVan*, the wife signed the contract in circumstances where the legal advice she received was incomplete and may not have been fully independent, but she signed the contract nonetheless — albeit without understanding its consequences.

To what extent did these courts (perhaps unconsciously) take account of differences in the level of legal knowledge on the part of Mrs. Hartshorne and Mrs. LeVan? To what extent should the standard in section 56(4)(b) vary according to a spouse's knowledge of the law? If the lawyer acting for Mrs. LeVan had been selected by her, without interference from her husband, would the court have reached the same conclusion? That is, did the court in *LeVan* focus on the inadequacy of the legal advice received, or on its lack of independence?

Marriage contracts and good faith
The statutory language in Part IV of the *Family Law Act* concerning domestic contracts does not make distinctions between marriage contracts and cohabitation agreements on one hand and separation agreements on the other.

In *Hartshorne*, the majority judgment considered and rejected any basis for making such a distinction in that case — although the issue seemed to be not entirely foreclosed for the future, at least in the majority judgment.

In *Dubin v Dubin* (2003), 34 RFL (5th) 227 (Ont Sup Ct), the court suggested that marriage contracts and cohabitation agreements are contracts of the utmost good faith, by contrast with separation agreements, a decision that was criticized, particularly with respect to obligations of disclosure: see James McLeod, "Annotation" (2003) 34 RFL (5th) 227. Should marriage contracts require good faith? If so, what factors fall within the scope of good faith? In reflecting on issues of good faith, consider the reasoning in *D'Andrade v Schrage*.

D'Andrade v Schrage
2011 ONSC 1174

In this case, a young woman aged 34 and an older man aged 61 married, and they entered into a series of contracts both before and during the marriage. At the time of the last marriage contract in 2007, the wife advised her lawyer that she was involved in an affair with another man and was considering a separation, but this information was not communicated to her husband. When the husband later discovered the affair and terminated the marriage, he sought to set aside the 2007 agreement on the basis that the wife had not signed it in "good faith." By doing so, the husband would have escaped significant obligations in the agreement. The parties disagreed about whether the wife's failure to disclose the possibility of a future separation constituted a breach of the good faith requirement.

The court noted that there was no precedent for this claim. Citing *Saul v Himel* and other cases, the court held that the contract should not be set aside on the basis that the wife failed to disclose her affair or that she was contemplating separation:

> [77] In the case at bar the evidence does not go so far as to support the conclusion that [the wife] had decided to separate from her husband when she signed the contract [in 2007]. She was definitely considering separation, but many partners go through times when they consider separation and do not, in fact, end up separating. It is also not infrequent that these thoughts occur when the partner in question is having an affair. Again, many marriages survive affairs, sometimes because the affair is never discovered by the other spouse.

> [78] To require spouses to disclose their thoughts about the likelihood of separation or their involvement in extra-marital sexual activity before signing a marriage contract could have serious implications for the survival of marital relationships [and the court also considered the evidentiary issues with respect to the seriousness of thoughts about separation, etc. However, the court concluded that if the public policy issues required consideration of thoughts of separation, then these issues would have to be determined.]

> [80] In this case, the public policy implications of requiring married couples to disclose their thoughts of separation or their involvement in extra-

marital relationships before executing a marriage contract are negative rather than positive. In recognition of the fact that marriages are complicated institutions, whose failure can rarely be attributed to one party or the other, the law has evolved in a fashion that by and large eliminates conduct from the analysis of financial entitlement. In essence, [the husband] is seeking to reintroduce conduct into the consideration of whether a marriage contract should be set aside. This is a road the law has been down before and, based on that experience, it is a road to be avoided unless justice demands it.

The court then held that justice in a marriage contract did not relate to personal obligations such as "the duty to remain faithful," etc. Instead, "domestic contracts are financial arrangements," so that couples have "an absolute obligation to disclose anything that would be relevant to the (financial) purpose of the contract":

> [82] ... Since the purpose of the contract is financial, that obligation demands the utmost good faith and fair dealing in disclosing their financial positions. The obligation does not extend to disclosing the existence of an extra-marital affair or the intention to separate.

By contrast, consider *Stevens v Stevens*, 2012 ONSC 706 (aff'd 2013 ONCA 267), which ruled that unlike the holding in *D'Andrade*, extramarital affairs should be disclosed in all circumstances. Justice Harper stated (at para 175):

> This is especially so when the Marriage Contract is being negotiated in circumstances of attempted reconciliation. In my view, the concept of *uberrimae fides* [utmost good faith] becomes very important when parties start their reconciliation process and negotiation of a Marriage Contract with the prerequisite condition that an affair that had been acknowledged is over. The potential continuance reflects on the *bona fides* of the spouse that may be relevant to the fairness of the negotiation process.

Which approach do you prefer?

In considering *D'Andrade*, note that the husband's claim to set aside the 2007 contract failed, so that the court did not need to exercise its discretion, including determining the "fairness" of the circumstances, as in *LeVan*. Are there other situations in which courts might have to take account of thoughts of separation? Do you agree that marriage contracts, like separation agreements, are intended to focus on financial arrangements, and not on pledges of faithfulness? Why, or why not?

Gender, bargaining inequality, and legal advice

As noted above, a number of scholars have suggested that there are gender issues in relation to family law bargaining. Particularly for women who have experienced violence or abuse within the family, inequality of bargaining power may be a significant problem even with lawyer assistance. In examining the comments of Diana Majury that follow, consider whether, or to what extent, this different approach might overcome some of these problems.

In exploring some of the features of lawyer-assisted negotiation for vulnerable women clients, focusing particularly on issues about unconscionability and the courts' authority to set aside an agreement on the basis of statutory provisions, Majury argued that courts must pay more attention to both the individual characteristics of the parties (which may affect their relative bargaining power), and also broader issues of systemic gender inequality. Focusing on issues of gender inequality in family law bargaining, Majury argued that even women who are strong and self-sufficient nonetheless operate "within a society in which women's agency is circumscribed by stereotypes, restricted opportunities, devaluation, violence (both overt and covert), hostility, and subordination."

As a result, in assessing contract unconscionability and the inequality of bargaining power, courts must examine these factors on an individual basis so that a party must demonstrate impaired judgment, infirmity, weakness, ignorance, gullibility, vulnerability, dire need, domination, and victimization in order to show contract unconscionability. In this way, the doctrine of unconscionability is paternalistic and does not accord well with ideas of equality in family law. Majury thus argued that family bargaining situations should be assessed as structural situations of inequality, as in other areas of law such as consumer or tenancy situations. As she suggested:

> [I]f the courts were willing to recognize systemic inequality of bargaining power, one would not, in the relevant situations, need to portray the individual as incompetent or inadequate in order to obtain relief. The two-fold unconscionability test would in these circumstances consist of an unfair bargain, coupled with a systemically induced inequality of bargaining power presumed to have given rise to that unfair bargain.... (Diana Majury, "Unconscionability in an Equality Context" (1991) 7 Can Fam LQ 123 at 134)

According to Majury, therefore, courts should adopt a gender-based approach to unconscionability by utilizing the usual requirements of an unfair bargain coupled with an inequality of bargaining power. Specifically, she argued that once an applicant has demonstrated an unfair bargain, this finding should result in a "presumption of inequality of bargaining position," flowing from a woman's systemically subordinated position in society (rather than a need to prove this inequality in relation to her individual circumstances). And the onus would then be on the man to prove that individualized factors existed which offset the systemic gender inequality. "Basically, he would be required to justify what, on the face of it, is an agreement that significantly advantages him at the expense of his former partner." See also Tess Wilkinson-Ryan & Deborah Small, "Negotiating Divorce: Gender and the Behavioral Economics of Divorce Bargaining" (2008) 26 Law & Ineq 109.

In addition to these recommendations, Majury also advocated some skepticism with respect to reliance on independent legal advice, arguing that the burden it places on lawyers is too onerous and unrealistic:

The assistance of a lawyer giving advice and negotiating on a client's behalf may, in most circumstances, mitigate inequality of bargaining power. However, a lawyer is limited by the information to which she or he has access, an issue which is particularly relevant in situations of violence or threatened violence. Ultimately, a lawyer must either take instructions from the client or refuse to act for the client. Lawyers do negotiate contracts, on the instructions of their client, that according to the lawyer is contrary to the client's interests. The fact that the female party to the contract was represented throughout by a lawyer should be given some weight in assessing the contract, but it should certainly not be considered determinative of either the question of the fairness of the agreement or of the equality of the bargaining power.

As distinct from a lawyer who negotiates for her or his client throughout the contract process, a lawyer who merely provides independent legal advice with respect to the ramifications of an agreement provides little in the way of protection against unconscionability. Accordingly, this lawyer's role should be accorded little weight in an unconscionability determination. While a lawyer may legitimately be able to attest to his or her belief that the client fully understands the consequences of the agreement, such a belief on the part of the lawyer in no way addresses issues relating to inequality of bargaining power or even necessarily the issue of fairness.... (Diana Majury, *ibid* at 147–148)

Reflect on Majury's suggestions with respect to issues of unconscionability. To what extent might her approach have assisted in *Hartshorne* or *LeVan*? Recognizing the challenges of finding unconscionability in cases of family bargaining, is this approach likely to have much impact in practice?

MARRIAGE CONTRACTS AND THE ENFORCEMENT OF RELIGIOUS OBLIGATIONS

Marriage contracts and religious obligations

Recall the requirements for establishing a valid marriage in Canada. As noted earlier, the federal Parliament has authority to legislate with respect to matters of capacity, while the provinces may legislate with respect to solemnization or formalities. However, while these requirements establish the necessary elements for a legally valid marriage in Canada, a number of religions have their own requirements for a valid marriage in accordance with their religious traditions.

Indeed, a number of religions regard the marriage ceremony as one of contract between the two spouses. For example, in the Muslim faith, part of the marriage contract involves the Mahr, a financial obligation with a variety of meanings during marriage and at marriage breakdown.

Moreover, while a rabbi may be present for a Jewish wedding, the marriage is effected by the parties' mutual consent, and the rabbi is an "officiant" only to ensure that the marriage is recognized as legal according to federal and provincial laws.

And, for fundamentalist Christian groups in the United States, states such as Louisiana have legislated for "covenant marriage," a contract by which the spouses promise not to seek divorce except in the most egregious circumstances.

As a result, divorce or separation and contracts relating to these processes may be complicated by the need to meet not only the requirements of Canadian law but also specific religious obligations. In this context, the issue of the enforceability of such contracts engages challenging issues about the relationship between religious precepts and Canadian family law.

Challenges relating to the Mahr in the Muslim faith

Religious Obligations and Civil Courts: *Kaddoura v Hammoud*

In a case that is probably now of historic interest only, an Ontario court was asked to enforce the payment of the Mahr, the traditional payment included in a Muslim marriage contract designed generally to protect the wife's interests at separation or divorce. In *Kaddoura v Hammoud* (1998), 44 RFL (4th) 228 (Ont Gen Div), the court held that the Mahr was an unenforceable obligation pursuant to Ontario law. The court cited *Hermann v Charlesworth*, [1905] 2 KB 123 (CA), in which a monetary element was regarded as an "unacceptable taint" in marriage, and continued (at paras 24–28):

> While there may be much to some if not all of the contract and marriage contract law arguments raised by Mr. Snipper, I have concluded that the obligation sought to be enforced here is one which should not be adjudicated in the civil courts.
>
> The Mahr and the extent to which it obligates a husband to make payment to his wife is essentially and fundamentally an Islamic religious matter. Because Mahr is a religious matter, the resolution of any dispute relating to it or the consequences of failing to honour the obligation are also religious in their content and context. While not, perhaps, an ideal comparison, I cannot help but think that the obligation of the Mahr is unsuitable for adjudication in the civil courts as is an obligation in a Christian religious marriage, such as to love, honour and cherish, or to remain faithful, or to maintain the marriage in sickness or other adversity so long as both parties live, or to raise children according to specified religious doctrine. Many such promises go well beyond the basic legal commitment to marriage required by our civil law, and are essentially matters of chosen religion and morality. They are derived from and are dependent upon doctrine and faith. They bind the conscience as a matter of religious principle but not necessarily as a matter of enforceable civil law....
>
> In my view, to determine what the rights and obligations of Sam and Manira are in relation to the undertaking of Mahr in their Islamic marriage ceremony would necessarily lead the Court into the "religious thicket," a place that the courts cannot safely and should not go.

Is there a difference between the arguments in *Kaddoura* and those of Lord Atkin in *Balfour*? Why, or why not? Is the comparison with the elements of the promises in the Christian marriage apt in this case? Or should the obligation of the Mahr be compared to financial obligations in marriage contracts more generally?

Enforcing the Mahr in Civil Courts: *Khan v Khan*

In some cases in British Columbia, the Mahr obligation has been held to be enforceable as a valid marriage contractual agreement (for example, see *NMM v NSM*, 2004 BCSC 346; *Nathoo v Nathoo*, [1996] BCJ No 2720 (SC) (QL); and *Amlani v Hiram*, 2000 BCSC 1653). In *Odatalla v Odatalla* (2002), 801 A2d 93, a New Jersey court also enforced a Mahr obligation.

In addition, an Ontario court upheld the enforceability of a *nika namma* or valid marriage contract in Pakistan as a domestic contract pursuant to Ontario's *Family Law Act*. In *Khan v Khan*, 2005 ONCJ 155, the court upheld the Muslim marriage contract, but concluded that the wife's waiver of spousal support under Hanafi Islamic jurisprudence was unconscionable, noting that

> deference should be given to religious and cultural laws and traditions of groups living in Canada ... [but] if cultural groups are given complete freedom to define family matters, they may tread on the rights of individuals within the group and discriminate in ways unacceptable to Canadian society (at para 52).

According to Natasha Bakht, this decision reveals a nuance that was missing from the religious arbitration debate in Ontario:

> This decision appears deceptively simple but was impressive in its nuance. A Muslim marriage contract was not summarily denied enforcement in Canada [as in *Kaddoura*] merely because of its religious origins. The beliefs of the religious participants were respected in this way. Yet a term of the contract, the waiver of spousal support, which clearly would have produced unconscionable results, was rejected for its inconsistency with Ontario's family law. [A similar logic could have informed the religious arbitration debate.] Rather than proposing a blanket prohibition on all religious arbitration, a more nuanced approach that showed consideration for the religious rights *and* the equality rights of women would have been more useful. (Natasha Bakht, "Religious Arbitration in Canada: Protecting Women by Protecting Them from Religion" (2007) 19 CJWL 119 at 129)

To what extent does *Khan* suggest that *Kaddoura* is now mainly of historic interest?

Legal Issues about Enforcement of Mahr Obligations in Canadian Courts

Some legal barriers to the enforcement of Mahr obligations in Canadian civil courts remain, in spite of the decision in *Khan*. For example, consider these two claims in British Columbia, both of which were rejected.

- In *Aziz v Al-Masri*, 2011 BCSC 985, the court concluded that the parties to the religious contract were the husband and the wife's uncle, not the wife herself, and declined to enforce the contract. The contract, written in Arabic, was entered into in Jordan, but no expert evidence about Jordanian law was called to explain the legal impact of the contract.

- In *Delvarani v Delvarani*, 2012 BCSC 162, the Court did not enforce the Mahr of 3000 Bahar Azadi coins, valued at approximately CAD $750,000 because the court did not accept that the husband would have agreed to such a large amount of money in addition to any other obligations he might have under the laws of British Columbia. The court noted "[e]ven if this is a valid marriage agreement under the *FRA*, it is clearly unfair" given the short duration of the marriage, the need of the wife and the ability of the husband to pay (para 209).

How should these legal issues be addressed by claimants who seek to enforce the Mahr in civil courts in Canada? Natasha Bakht argues that Mahr agreements should be treated as ordinary contracts rather than marriage contracts and may offer women one additional tool to combat poverty post relationship dissolution. The general contract approach to enforcing Mahr agreements is particularly useful for those Muslim women who may only marry religiously or according to Islamic law, but not civilly. For example, in *Rashid v Shaher*, 2010 ONSC 4351, because the couple went through a religious and not a civil marriage ceremony, their family law claims could not be addressed using the *Divorce Act*. The couple had also not lived together long enough to meet the definition of spouse in the *Family Law Act*. Thus, the Mahr of $40,000 was the only relief available to the woman. (See Natasha Bakht "The Incorporation of Sharia in North America: Enforcing the Mahr to Combat Women's Poverty Post-Relationship Dissolution" in Anver M Emon & Kristen Stilt, eds, *Oxford Handbook on Islamic Law* (New York: Oxford University Press, Forthcoming). See also Robert Matas, "Judge Rejects Woman's Claim for Sharia Divorce Settlement", *The Globe and Mail* (27 July 2011); Simon Schneiderman, "Husband's Atheism Leads Court to Nix Muslim Marriage Contract", *Law Times* (25 July 2011); Sheema Khan, "The evolving nature of Muslim marriage", *The Globe and Mail* (18 August 2012), online: <http://www.theglobeandmail.com>; and Elizabeth Raymer, "Separation of Church and State" (March 2013) 37:3 Can Lawyer 39.)

In thinking about these issues, consider also the reasoning in the Supreme Court of Canada with respect to the enforceability of a "religious obligation" in a separation agreement in *Marcovitz v Bruker*. Does this case suggest a method to ensure the enforceability of the Mahr obligation?

Civil Contracts and Religious Obligations: *Bruker v Marcovitz* and the Jewish Get

[A Jewish marriage] can only be dissolved by divorce or a spouse's death, and the only means of divorce is "by way of the husband delivering to his wife — and not vice versa — a bill of divorce [the "get"].... The husband's delivery of the get and its acceptance by the wife — these are considered discrete acts — are overseen by a Beth Din.... The touchstone here is consent, consistent with the Jewish notion that marriage is itself a highly consensual arrangement, with rabbis having a supervisory, rather than a sacramental, role in the marriage ceremony.... This is also the theory behind Jewish divorce.... The Beth Din does not divorce a couple by its decree; rather, it tells them of their obligation to divorce....

[T]he husband's refusal to grant a get, or the wife's refusal to accept one, means that the parties are still married under Jewish law, even after a civil divorce.... [and the consequences for the wife are severe as she cannot marry (even civilly) and her children are not fully included in the Jewish faith. By contrast, the husband is not similarly disadvantaged.] (John Kleefeld & Amanda Kennedy, "'A Delicate Necessity': *Bruker v. Marcovitz* and the Problem of Jewish Divorce" (2008) 24 Can J Fam L 205 at paras 3–7)

As was noted earlier in relation to section 21.1 of the *Divorce Act* and sections 56(5) to (7) of Ontario's *Family Law Act*, these statutory provisions may assist a wife to obtain a get from her husband, or at least prevent her husband from using the get as a bargaining tool in relation to corollary relief matters. However, what is the situation if a husband enters into a separation agreement that includes his promise to deliver a get to his wife? Is such a promise, a religious obligation included in a domestic contract, enforceable?

Bruker v Marcovitz
2007 SCC 54

In this case, the parties were married in 1969 and divorced in 1981. As part of their civil divorce, the parties negotiated an agreement with respect to corollary relief. One clause of this agreement stated that the parties "agree to appear before the Rabbinical authorities in the City and District of Montreal for the purpose of obtaining the traditional religious Get, immediately upon a Decree Nisi of Divorce being granted." In 1981, when the Decree Nisi was granted, the husband was 48 and the wife 31 years of age.

However, in spite of repeated requests on the part of the wife, the husband refused to grant a *get* over a period of 15 years, so that the wife was then nearly 47 years of age. She sought damages for breach of the agreement of 1981 and the trial judge held that the agreement was valid and binding. The Québec Court of Appeal allowed the husband's appeal, on the basis that the obligation was a moral one and not enforceable by the courts. The wife appealed to the Supreme Court of Canada, which upheld her claim (Deschamps and Charron JJ dissenting).

ABELLA J:

[1] Canada rightly prides itself on its evolutionary tolerance for diversity and pluralism. This journey has included a growing appreciation for multiculturalism, including the recognition that ethnic, religious or cultural differences will be acknowledged and respected. Endorsed in legal instruments ranging from the statutory protections found in human rights codes to their constitutional enshrinement in the *Canadian Charter of Rights and Freedoms* the right to integrate into Canada's mainstream based on and notwithstanding these differences has become a defining part of our national character.

[2] The right to have differences protected, however, does not mean that those differences are always hegemonic. Not all differences are compatible with Canada's fundamental values and, accordingly, not all barriers to their expression are arbitrary. Determining when the assertion of a right based on difference must yield to a more pressing public interest is a complex, nuanced, fact-specific exercise that defies bright-line application. It is, at the same time, a delicate necessity for protecting the evolutionary integrity of both multiculturalism and public confidence in its importance....

The court explained that there were two issues in this case. The first was whether the agreement to give a *get* constituted a valid and binding contractual obligation under Québec law; and the second involved consideration of the husband's right to freedom of religion to avoid the legal consequences of breaching the agreement. After considering the Québec *Charter*, the court held that an agreement between spouses to take the necessary steps to permit each of them to remarry in accordance with their religious beliefs constituted a valid and binding agreement that did not represent a harm to the husband's religious freedom by requiring the payment of damages for breach.

[18] This is not, as implied by the dissent, an unwarranted secular trespass into religious fields, nor does it amount to judicial sanction of the vagaries of an individual's religion. In deciding cases involving freedom of religion, the courts cannot ignore religion. To determine whether a particular claim to freedom of religion is entitled to protection, a court must take into account the particular religion, the particular religious right, and the particular personal and public consequences, including the religious consequences, of enforcing that right....

The court considered a number of precedents with respect to the justiciability of religious issues, especially *Re Morris v Morris* (1973), 42 DLR (3d) 550 (Man CA), and concluded that:

[47] ... the fact that Paragraph 12 of the Consent had religious elements does not thereby immunize it from judicial scrutiny. We are not dealing with judicial review of doctrinal religious principles, such as whether a particular *get* is valid. Nor are we required to speculate on what the rabbinical court would do. The promise by Mr. Marcovitz to remove the religious barriers to remarriage by providing a *get* was negotiated between two consenting adults, each represented by counsel, as part of a voluntary exchange of commitments intended to have legally enforceable consequences. This puts the obligation appropriately under a judicial microscope....

[51] I do not see the religious aspect of the obligation in Paragraph 12 of the Consent as a barrier to its civil validity. It is true that a party cannot be compelled to execute a moral duty, but there is nothing in the *Civil Code* preventing someone from transforming his or her moral obligations into legally valid and binding ones. ....

[62] I accept that there may well be agreements with religious aspects that would be against public order....

[63] There is no doubt in my mind, however, about Mr. Marcovitz's agreement to provide a *get*. It is consistent with, not contrary to, public order.... Moreover, as amplified later in these reasons, the enforceability of a promise by a husband to provide a *get* harmonizes with Canada's approach to religious freedom, to equality rights, to divorce and remarriage generally, and has been judicially recognized internationally....

The court further considered Mr. Marcovitz's arguments pursuant to the *Civil Code* and also canvassed the use of damages as compensation for someone whose spouse has refused to provide a *get* (citing *D v France*, Application No 10180/82 in the European Commission of Human Rights; *Brett v Brett*, [1969] 1 All ER 1007; Australian and American decisions; and decisions from Israel.

> [90] This international perspective reinforces the view that judicial enforcement of an agreement to provide a Jewish divorce is consistent with public policy values shared by other democracies.

> [91] Mr. Marcovitz cannot, therefore, rely on the Quebec *Charter* to avoid the consequences of failing to implement his legal commitment to provide the *get*.

> [92] The public interest in protecting equality rights, the dignity of Jewish women in their independent ability to divorce and remarry, as well as the public benefit in enforcing valid and binding contractual obligations, are among the interests and values that outweigh Mr. Marcovitz's claim that enforcing Paragraph 12 of the Consent would interfere with his religious freedom.

> [93] Despite the moribund state of her marriage, Ms. Bruker remained, between the ages of 31 and 46, Mr. Marcovitz's wife under Jewish law, and dramatically restricted in the options available to her in her personal life. This represented an unjustified and severe impairment of her ability to live her life in accordance with this country's values and her Jewish beliefs. Any infringement of Mr. Marcovitz's freedom of religion is inconsequential compared to the disproportionate disadvantaging effect on Ms. Bruker's ability to live her life fully as a Jewish woman in Canada.

The court concluded that the trial judge's assessment of damages was appropriate, having regard to Ms. Bruker's inability to marry or have children in accordance with her religious beliefs for a period of 15 years. Thus, the court upheld a damage award of $47,000.

"Covenant marriage" and access to divorce

The American state of Louisiana pioneered the concept of covenant marriage with legislation enacted in 1997. Particularly because of concerns on the part of fundamentalist Christian communities about no fault divorce and its impact on marriage, the state enacted covenant marriage legislation to permit an alternative to no fault divorce. The legislation permits spouses to choose to enter marriage as a permanent and binding obligation, one that requires the spouses to take all necessary steps, such as counselling, to preserve the marriage. In a covenant marriage, a spouse is not entitled to divorce except on the basis of serious fault on the part of the other spouse, and it relies on the support of communities, particularly Christian communities, to provide support for the institution of marriage and the family (see Katherine Shaw Spaht, "Louisiana's Covenant Marriage Law: Recapturing the Meaning of Marriage for the Sake of the Children" in Antony Dnes & Robert Rowthorn, eds, *The Law and Economics of Marriage and Divorce* (Cambridge, UK: Cambridge University Press, 2002) at 92).

Although covenant marriage legislation does not yet exist in Canadian jurisdictions, there may be issues for persons married in Louisiana, Arkansas, or Arizona (where covenant marriage is now available) who move to Canada and seek divorce here. For an analysis of the conflict of laws problems in such cases, see Lily Ng, "Covenant Marriage and the Conflict of Laws" (2006–2007) 44 Alta L Rev 815.

Notes and Questions

The impact of *Bruker v Marcovitz*

According to Kleefeld and Kennedy, *Bruker v Marcovitz* is significant because it may have applications beyond the context of Jewish divorces. As they note, the case was cited in a later decision concerning the Islamic Mahr in Alberta, *Nasin v Nasin*, 2008 ABQB 219.

Although the court in *Nasin* held that the prenuptial agreement was not enforceable in Alberta because it did not comply with the writing requirements in section 38 of the *Matrimonial Property Act*, RSA 2000, c M-8, the court indicated that if it had met the writing requirements, its religious elements would not have prevented a finding of contractual validity. Indeed the Mahr has been enforced, citing *Bruker v Marcovitz*, in *Khanis v Noormohamed*, [2009] OJ No 2245 (Sup Ct) (affirmed 2011 ONCA 127), giving effect to a "Maher" of $20,000 and in *Ghaznavi v Kashif-Ul-Haque*, 2011 ONSC 4062, in the amount of $25,000.

In this context, Kleefeld and Kennedy argued that

> *Bruker v. Markovitz* should remind us of the need for continued engagement in a discussion of the role between equality concerns ... and accommodations of multicultural or religious practices that tend to exacerbate such concerns.... [J]udicial and legislative solutions in this regard are neither total nor permanent, but they have helped to foster "transformative dialogue".... (Kleefeld & Kennedy at para 91, citing Lisa Fishbayn, "Gender, Multiculturalism and Dialogue: The Case of Jewish Divorce" (2008) 21 Can JL & Jur 71)

To what extent might these arguments be applicable also to covenant marriage?

Additional Resources

Barbara Bedont, "Gender Differences in Negotiations and the Doctrine of Unconscionability in Domestic Contracts" (1994–1995) 12 Can Fam LQ 21.

Anne Bottomley, "What Is Happening to Family Law? A Feminist Critique of Conciliation" in Julia Brophy & Carol Smart, ed, *Women in Law: Explorations in Law, Family, and Sexuality* (London: Routledge & Kegan Paul, 1985).

Rochelle Cade, "Covenant Marriage" (2010) 18 The Family Journal 230.

Lisa Fishbayn, "Gender, Multiculturalism and Dialogue: The Case of Jewish Divorce" (2008) 21 Can JL & Jur 71.

Pascale Fournier, "In the (Canadian) Shadow of Islamic Law: Translating Mahr as a Bargaining Endowment" (2006) 44 Osgoode Hall LJ 649.

Fareen L Jamal, "Enforcing Mahr in Canadian Courts" (2013) 32 Can Fam LQ 97.

Howard Kislowicz, "Freedom of Religion and Canada's Commitments to Multiculturalism" (2012) 31 NJCL 1.

Robert Leckey, "Contracting Claims and Family Law Feuds" (2007) 57 UTLJ 1.

Shelley McGill, "Family Arbitration: One Step Forward, Two Steps Back" (2007) 21 JL & Soc Pol'y 49.

Asifa Quraishi-Landes, "A Meditation on *Mahr*, Modernity, and Muslim Marriage Contract Law" in Marie A Failinger, Elizabeth R Schiltz & Susan J Stabile, eds, *Feminism, Law, and Religion* (Burlington, VT: Ashgate, 2013) 173.

Austin Sarat & William Felstiner, "Law and Social Relations: Vocabularies of Motive in Lawyer/Client Interaction" (1988) 22:4 Law & Soc'y Rev 737.

Marjorie Shulz, "Contractual Ordering of Marriage: A New Model for State Policy" (1982) 70 Cal L Rev 207.

FAMILY LAW AND FAMILY LAWYERS IN THE CONTEXT OF FAMILY DISSOLUTION

Challenges for lawyers in family bargaining: *Mantella v Mantella*

In *Mantella v Mantella* (2006), 80 OR (3d) 270 (Sup Ct), a lawyer acting for a wife in the negotiation of a separation agreement was later sued by her client's former husband in relation to the agreement and the lawyer's advice. The court granted the lawyer's motion to dismiss this claim on the basis that a lawyer has no duty to the opposite party in a family law dispute. In the course of the decision, Corbett J made the following comments about family law and the role of family lawyers in matters of family dissolution. Reflect on these comments in relation to this chapter and the ones that follow concerning corollary relief issues. To what extent do these comments suggest a need to move beyond litigation processes?

> Family law presents unique challenges. The household remains a core institution, and a domestic relationship is at once an emotional, social and financial partnership.... Although we have "no fault" divorce, deep emotional issues are never far from the surface in family law cases. Parties

often seek the catharsis of formal conflict over their personal issues, and family law litigation is but one of the canvasses upon which they limn their suffering.

The family lawyer must manage difficult conflict resolution processes in this context. The hurts done to the heart and soul may not be addressed at all in an accounting of family furniture and pensions. Although the division of property and the establishment of support may be relatively straight-forward, there is a timing and rhythm to negotiation that must account for the issues which, not properly before the court, may be in the minds of the parties.... Financially, family law presents an almost perfect "zero-sum" game: the parties have finite resources and income potential, and the longer their conflict subsists, the more of those resources are exhausted in the process of conflict....

The family lawyer faces the daunting challenge of supporting her client through the morass of issues, some legal and some otherwise. Cases still follow the classic model of "adversarial" litigation, although the destructive qualities of this system for personal relationships is well understood. Many cases are resolved through negotiation or mediation outside or parallel to the litigation process, and the justice system itself has fashioned a collaborative, arbitration-like process of case conferencing that has as its goal filtering issues and reducing conflict prior to resolution of outstanding issues through the classic adversarial motion or trial.

It is clearly in the interests of all parties, and society generally, that family law cases be resolved early, and without litigation, if possible.

And here the plot thickens for the family law practitioner, because family law conflict does not always end when a settlement agreement is signed. There are many reasons for this, including:

(a) family law is "dynamic," rather than "static," and settlements are subject to variation [in some cases];

(b) family law agreements may be set aside for the same reasons that other contracts may be set aside [and also on the basis of a failure to make adequate financial disclosure];

(c) post-settlement dissatisfaction may be amplified in a family law context, often by factors extraneous to the settlement itself, but central to the ongoing post-separation relationship of the parties; and

(d) inequality of bargaining power and emotional coercion are often present during the negotiation of separation agreements. These factors lie at the very heart of the parties' motivations in seeking settlement....

In view of these comments, reflect again on the competing goals of autonomy and finality in relation to family bargaining ("private ordering") on one hand, and the need for the family law system to ensure "fairness" in domestic contracts on the other.

6

Families, Property, and Family Property: Principles of Equality and Equity

There is a sense in which the law of matrimonial property is concerned, not with property at all, but with human relations and ideologies in respect of property.... The law regulating the spouses' property relations is fundamentally an index of social relations between the sexes, and ... affords a peculiar wealth of commentary on such matters as the prevailing ideology of marriage, the cultural definition of the marital roles, the social status of the married woman, and the role of the state *vis-à-vis* the family....

In terms of the model of matrimonial partnership, ... husband and wife are seen as equal partners in co-operative labour, both making ... an essential contribution towards the economic viability of the family unit, and hence, towards the accumulation of matrimonial property. Whatever property is acquired by them during marriage is therefore acquired by reason of the partnership effort. (Kevin J Gray, *Reallocation of Property on Divorce* (Oxford: Professional Books, 1977) 1 and 24)

I.
THE LEGAL AND SOCIAL CONTEXT OF FAMILY PROPERTY

PROPERTY LAW AND THE CONTEXT OF FAMILY DISSOLUTION

Accessible divorce and the reform of family property

Kevin Gray's comment occurred in his comparative study of matrimonial property regimes in 1977, at a time when a number of common law jurisdictions (including Canada) were just beginning to grapple with the *economic* consequences of more accessible divorce by designing new legal principles for sharing family property at marriage breakdown. In doing so, Gray acknowledged that a matrimonial partnership differed from commercial partnership, but he used the idea of partnership to recognize the unique community of life and purpose in a marriage relationship.

In the late 1970s, all the common law provinces in Canada enacted statutory reforms for property sharing at marriage breakdown. This reform process, which arguably represented the most significant changes for property law in many decades, became necessary as divorce rates escalated after the 1968 *Divorce Act* permitted no fault divorce. As discussed below, property-sharing reforms were initiated when some spouses who divorced after 1968 (particularly women) were denied any entitlement to "matrimonial" property because title to family property was in the names of their spouses (usually men). Although the cases reflected longstanding property law principles, reformers argued that accessible divorce laws created new social expectations and that legislation was required to create equality for men and women in the legal arrangements for sharing family property at divorce.

Murdoch v Murdoch: A reform catalyst

The history of this reform context is important to an understanding of the distinctive legal principles that now apply to married couples (now including same-sex married couples) at separation or divorce, by contrast with cohabiting couples (opposite sex and same sex) at separation. Interestingly, it was a claim by a married woman for a declaration of trust that eventually resulted in the current availability of trust doctrines in cases of cohabitation.

In *Murdoch v Murdoch* (1973), 41 DLR (3d) 367 (SCC), Mrs. Murdoch left her husband in 1968, after 25 years of marriage. At separation, she filed claims for (among other things) financial support, and a declaration that her husband was trustee for her of an undivided one-half interest in property owned by him and in relation to which she claimed that they were equal partners. During the years of their marriage, Mrs. Murdoch had worked extensively in maintaining their large rural properties in Alberta, and the couple had acquired a number of additional valuable properties as a result of their successful work. However, title to all the properties was in the name of Mr. Murdoch alone.

At trial, the judge concluded that there was no evidence of partnership and denied Mrs. Murdoch's claim to share in the property. He awarded her $200 per month by way of spousal support: (1971), 95 AR 119 (SC (TD)). The Alberta Court of Appeal dismissed her appeal: (1972), 95 AR 118 (SC (AD).

In the Supreme Court of Canada, Mrs. Murdoch argued that she was entitled to share in the property on the basis of the doctrine of resulting trust, an equitable doctrine then subject to numerous and sometimes conflicting judgments in Canada and in the United Kingdom. For example, in an earlier case before the Supreme Court of Canada in 1960 (*Thompson v Thompson* (1960), 26 DLR (2d) 1), the Court had stated its firm conclusion that, unless there was evidence to show that a wife had made a *financial* contribution to the acquisition of property held in her husband's name, she was not entitled to a declaration of resulting trust. That is, a wife's labour was not, by itself, sufficient to establish entitlement to a resulting trust. As the Court in *Thompson* stated:

> [No] case has yet held that, in the absence of some financial contribution, the wife is entitled to a proprietary interest from the mere fact of marriage and cohabitation and the fact the property in question is the matrimonial home (*Thompson* at 9).

The majority of the Supreme Court of Canada applied the reasoning in *Thompson* to Mrs. Murdoch's claim. As the Court noted, although Mrs. Murdoch had worked, along with her husband, on their large properties, she had made no financial contribution that would sustain a declaration of resulting trust. Indeed, the majority repeated the words of the trial judge who had concluded that the work done by Mrs. Murdoch during the 25 years of her marriage was merely "work done by any ranch wife" (*Murdoch* at 376). By contrast, in a dissenting judgment, Laskin J concluded that the facts justified a declaration of constructive trust, recognizing the wife's significant "contribution of physical labour beyond ordinary housekeeping duties" (at 379). In this way, the dissenting judgment introduced the equitable remedy of constructive trust to accomplish the goals of property sharing.

Ironically, however, it was the majority judgment, and particularly the judicial comment about work that was expected of "any ranch wife," that provided a significant catalyst for legal reform:

• Editorials in the press regularly referred back to the recommendation of the 1970 *Royal Commission on the Status of Women in Canada* that legislation recognizing equal partnership in marital property should be adopted. See Royal Commission on the Status of Women in Canada, *Report of the Royal Commission on the Status of Women in Canada* (Ottawa: Queen's Printer, 1970) at 246.

- In addition, provincial and federal law reform commissions recommended changes to protect the interests of wives like Mrs. Murdoch: for example, see Ontario Law Reform Commission, *Report on Family Property, Part IV* (Toronto: Ontario Law Reform Commission, 1974). Similarly, the federal report stated:

  > The need for some fundamental reorganization of the existing property laws ... regulating the rights and obligations of family members was underlined in the recent decision of the Supreme Court of Canada in *Murdoch v. Murdoch*. The public reaction to that decision clearly indicates that the existing laws discriminate to the prejudice of the married woman and are no longer acceptable in contemporary society. A property regime must be devised that will promote equality of the sexes before the law. (Law Reform Commission of Canada, *Studies on Family Property* Law (Ottawa: Information Canada, 1975) at 3)

- Significantly, moreover, Irene Murdoch's case became a *cause célèbre* when some women in Manitoba created a skit about the case, demonstrating wives' lack of legal entitlement to property. The skit was reproduced and circulated for performance by women's groups in many parts of Canada. The skit was called "The Balloon Lady," because it started with a puppet of a woman holding up balloons naming legal rights, and as the skit progressed to show that each of these rights did not exist, the balloons burst, one by one:

  > The exploding balloon represented both the illusion of the rights that women thought they had, as well as the explosive force of the revelation as reality hit them. By the end of the skit, the Balloon Lady was on the ground without any support and the women in the audience realized they were in the same position.... The success of the reform movement depended, in part, on the ability of women's organizations to generate a collective identity among its supporters, which they did by universalizing Irene Murdoch's plight and aligning her with wives. (Mysty Clapton, "*Murdoch v. Murdoch*: The Organizing Narrative of Matrimonial Property Law Reform" (2008) 20:2 CJWL 197 at 221–222 and 229–230)

In this way, the media, public opinion, and law reformers all agreed after *Murdoch* that reform was needed. As a result, statutes concerning property entitlement at marriage breakdown were enacted in all the common law provinces within a few years, beginning in 1978. In that year, the Supreme Court of Canada also decided *Rathwell v Rathwell*, [1978] 2 SCR 436, recognizing the appropriateness of the constructive trust remedy in the divorce context. However, with the enactment of statutory regimes for property sharing at marriage breakdown, the Supreme Court's constructive trust remedy did not have much impact for married couples.

Cohabiting couples, unjust enrichment and the constructive trust

Trust doctrines, particularly those relating to the constructive trust, were eventually extended to partners in cohabiting relationships at the time of separation. Because the provincial statutory reforms of the late 1970s applied only to couples who were married (and then separated or divorced), cohabiting couples were excluded from these legal arrangements. In this context, the constructive trust recognized in Laskin's dissenting judgment in *Murdoch* and then adopted by the Supreme Court in *Rathwell* was extended by the Court in 1980 to cohabiting couples in *Pettkus v Becker*, [1980] 2 SCR 834.

This legal categorization of differing claims for married and cohabiting couples was, however, later complicated by the decision of the Supreme Court of Canada in *Rawluk v Rawluk* (1990), 28 RFL (3d) 337, which held that married couples (at least in Ontario) were entitled to use trust doctrines, *in addition to* the statutory schemes, in resolving their property entitlements at marriage breakdown. *Rawluk* is included later in this chapter.

Moreover, a cohabiting woman in Nova Scotia eventually challenged the exclusion of such couples from the statutory regime applicable to married couples at breakdown in 2002, claiming an infringement of equality pursuant to the *Charter*. However, a majority of the Supreme Court of Canada upheld the distinction between married and cohabiting couples, for purposes of provincial statutes about marital property, in *Nova Scotia (AG) v Walsh*, 2002 SCC 83. More recently, the Supreme Court of Canada upheld the distinction in the Québec *Civil Code* between married and cohabiting couples — in relation to both property-sharing and spousal support at separation (see *Quebec (AG) v A*, 2013 SCC 5). Thus, although some provinces have enacted amendments to permit some cohabiting couples to utilize these provincial marital property statutes at separation, Ontario and other provinces continue to maintain this legal distinction. As a result, it is necessary in this chapter to discuss property sharing at separation (or divorce) in relation to *both* the statutory regimes for married couples and also equitable trust remedies for cohabiting couples.

Organization of this chapter

This chapter begins by providing some historical background and information about marital property as part of the corollary relief for married spouses and equitable relief for cohabiting couples who separate.

It then examines the Supreme Court's decisions in *Nova Scotia (AG) v Walsh* and *Quebec (AG) v A*, which confined the definition of "spouse" for purposes of provincial marital property statutes to married spouses. In doing so, this section re-examines the social context in Canada, in which rates of cohabitation are increasing, to explore whether there is a need for more provinces (including Ontario) to provide statutory property remedies at family dissolution.

The chapter then explores the details of Ontario's *Family Law Act* with respect to issues about equality goals and property sharing at separation or divorce, as well as special legal provisions concerning the matrimonial home. Although the focus is primarily directed to Ontario's statutory scheme, the material also provides useful comparative references to other provincial statutes in Canada. As with other areas of provincial constitutional authority, it is important to reflect on whether local differences or national uniformity are more appropriate goals for family law policies about property arrangements at separation or divorce.

Finally, this chapter examines the use of trust principles, which define equitable entitlements to property at separation for cohabiting couples, and provides some assessments of their significance and limitations.

THE SOCIAL CONTEXT FOR FAMILY PROPERTY

Property as part of economic adjustment at family dissolution

Family property constitutes just one aspect of economic re-adjustment at divorce. In addition to property sharing, there are other legal issues concerning spousal support, care arrangements for children, and child support (and additional issues such as possession of the matrimonial home.) These legal issues have emerged in different historical contexts, which sometimes influence their legal interpretation.

For example, spousal support was historically characterized as "alimony" or "maintenance" (pursuant to the English *Divorce and Matrimonial Causes Act* of 1857). Some legislation in Canada also used the language of "maintenance," but the current federal *Divorce Act*, and most provincial legislation now define this obligation as "spousal support" (see *Divorce Act*, s 15.2). Although the modern purposes of spousal support are identified in both federal and provincial statutes, these provisions (and their interpretation) sometimes engage a variety of objectives, including ideas that reflect the long traditions of this concept in family law.

By contrast, entitlement to family property at divorce is a much more recent development in common law provinces in Canada, all of which enacted legislation in the late 1970s in response to rising rates of divorce pursuant to the federal *Divorce Act* of 1968. And guidelines for child support are even more recent, having been negotiated by the federal, provincial, and territorial governments only in the late 1990s.

Yet, in spite of such different origins, these legal categories of corollary relief together create an overall economic re-adjustment package at marriage breakdown. Moreover, for many post-divorce families, the overall package may be more significant than individual legal categories. For post-divorce families, judicial concerns about characterization — that is, whether a source of family wealth should be regarded as property or support, or whether payment of a large sum for child support represents "hidden" spousal support — may appear quite unimportant.

Thus, while this book presents issues about corollary relief based on current legal categories, it is important to understand how they constitute an overall economic package for family members at divorce or separation. In this way, changes in one category may in practice result in adjustments in another category.

Property as a "final" arrangement

Moreover, relationships among different categories of corollary relief are sometimes important in achieving the goal of "finality" with respect to economic re-adjustment at family dissolution. In this context, there is a significant difference between property issues and support issues.

Provincial legislative regimes generally provide for a division of property, or its value, at one point in time, with no possibility of variation thereafter. In this way, property decisions are *final*.

By contrast, judicial views about whether, to what extent, and in what circumstances, it is appropriate to vary decisions about spousal support pursuant to federal and provincial legislation have sometimes appeared less concerned about finality, although the Supreme Court's decision in 2003 in *Miglin v Miglin*, 2003 SCC 24 (discussed in Chapter Seven), emphasized the need to respect spousal agreements about support. Nonetheless, there may be less concern about finality with respect to spousal support, by contrast with property. Similarly, child support awards are subject to variation and recalculation on the basis of changes in economic circumstances. In this way, the finality of property orders is quite different from orders for spousal or child support.

The significant point here is that if property decisions are not variable, while decisions about spousal and child support may be later revised in some circumstances, these differences may well influence the substance and process of negotiations about the economic adjustment package at family dissolution.

Property and the basis for entitlement at family dissolution

To some extent at least, there is a tension between traditional property principles and the impact of recent social changes in families. Family relationships and property principles have been linked historically, of course, but demands for recognition of women's roles in the accumulation of family property (including their contributions to household work and child care) in recent decades have challenged fundamental legal principles of property law in new ways. Thus, not only with respect to legislative reforms but also in judicial decisions concerning the law of trusts, the interpretation of legal principles about family property often reveals some tension between adherence to a traditional application of property principles and a need to recognize new understandings of property in the family law context.

In relation to equitable property interests for cohabiting couples, for example, Marcia Neave argued that it was essential to identify the *purpose* of reallocating family property at the dissolution of the relationship:

> Rather than discussing whether a claim by an unmarried partner can be fitted within an existing [legal] category or whether the [legal] category can be extended to achieve this result, we should first attempt to determine whether equitable intervention is justified. If we can pinpoint the *purpose* of that intervention it may assist in identifying a method of

analysis which is consistent with that purpose. (Marcia Neave, "Three Approaches to Family Property Disputes: Intention/Belief, Unjust Enrichment and Unconscionability" in TG Youdan, ed, *Equity, Fiduciaries and Trusts* (Scarborough, ON: Carswell, 1989) 247 at 251)

In the context of accessible divorce, legal arrangements for sharing family property require the application of traditional property principles to the new context and purpose of family law reform, a challenge that is significant for legislatures, lawyers and courts.

Notes and Questions

A brief history of property and marriage
The history of property in marriage provides important insights about social and legal relationships. Before 19th century statutory reforms, in accordance with the common law doctrine of coverture, married women were generally unable to hold interests in property. According to Blackstone's classic statement of this doctrine, "by marriage, the husband and wife are one person in law." As a result, on marriage, a woman's property (subject to a few exceptions for personal property) became her husband's.

In England, statutes to reform the legal rights to property for married women were enacted at several different times in the 19th century. In Canada, the provinces also began to enact such statutes early on.

The first legislation to reform married women's property was enacted in New Brunswick in 1851: see *An Act To Secure to Married Women Real and Personal Property Held in Their Own Right*, SNB 1851, c 24.

Several statutes were enacted in Ontario, beginning in 1859. See Lori Chambers, *Married Women and Property Law in Victorian Ontario* (Toronto: Osgoode Society for Canadian Legal History, 1997); and Karen Pearlston, "Book Review of Married Women and Property Law in Victorian Ontario by Lori Chambers" (2000) 12 CJWL 247.

In western provinces in Canada, issues about married women's property were concerned with dower interests. See Margaret McCallum, "Prairie Women and the Struggle for a Dower Law, 1905–1920" in Tina Loo & Lorna McLean, eds, *Historical Perspectives on Law and Society in Canada* (Toronto: Copp Clark Longman, 1994) 306.

Issues about the rationales for these historical developments about marriage and property continue to challenge legal scholars:

- In relation to the common law doctrine concerning married women's incapacity to hold property, a number of rationales have been suggested to justify it, but an American scholar has argued that none of them fully accounted for the common law principles: J Johnston, Jr, "Sex and Property: The Common Law Tradition, the Law School Curriculum, and Developments Toward Equality" (1972) 47 NYUL Rev 1033 at 1051.

- In relation to the 19th century reforms, other scholars have argued that married women's property legislation was often enacted to preserve husbands' property from seizure by creditors, not to enhance the property rights of married women. For examples, see Norma Basch, *In the Eyes of the Law: Women, Marriage and Property in Nineteenth-Century New York* (Ithaca, NY: Cornell University Press, 1982); and Lee Holcombe, *Wives and Property* (Toronto: University of Toronto Press, 1983).

Such studies seem to suggest that gender issues have always been present, perhaps invisibly so, in relationships between marriage and property. In examining the materials in this chapter, reflect on whether, or to what extent, some of these tensions may continue to exist.

Marriage, property, and the social context

Law reforms relating to marriage and property may often reflect problems of social conventions. For example, Mrs. Murdoch's problem at separation could have been easily resolved if, at the time of acquisition of each new ranch, she and her husband had agreed to place title in their joint names. What factors might have made this option unavailable in practice? Are there reasons why this problem needs to be addressed by legal reform? What factors might make legal reform, rather than social reform, more effective?

Rethinking *Murdoch*: Family property and the limits of law reform?

Although Mrs. Murdoch was left in a vulnerable position at separation and then by the decision in the Supreme Court of Canada, it is clear that the Murdochs were relatively secure, perhaps even wealthy, as landowners of valuable ranches during the course of their 25-year marriage. In this situation, many reformers seemed to conclude that law reform initiatives enabling women like Mrs. Murdoch to share in family property at separation or divorce was an obvious solution to this problem.

However, as the data about family economies and information about the timing of decisions to separate and divorce in earlier chapters demonstrated, many couples will have little or no property to share at family dissolution. Indeed, for some families, there will be more debts than assets at the time of spousal separation. In this way, the reform of family property laws in the 1970s may have reflected the interests of middle-class families, particularly middle-class women, much more than others. See Martha Fineman, "Implementing Equality: Ideology, Contradiction and Social Change: A Study in Rhetoric and Results in the Regulation of the Consequences of Divorce" [1983] Wis L Rev 789.

Murdoch was also a significant case because it related to family farm property. As Lori Chambers argued, this context is important, as farm women are engaged in productive labour along with men, so that the farm is both their home and their workplace, and their unrecognized labour results in subsidizing the cost of food in grocery stores:

> The reforms of the late 1970s and 1980s purport to consider the husband and wife as equal partners in marriage and quasi-marital relations [e.g.,

cohabitation]. Women's domestic labour, in theory, is validated and recognized through the equal division of the matrimonial home. But farm cases raise questions that legal theory and practice have yet to answer and starkly reveal the artificiality of the public/private divide that pervades property law and social thinking. If the farm business is only a home for the wife, despite her work, but is a business for the husband, then marriage in Canada is still not a partnership of equals. Instead, farm husbands are unjustly enriched at the expense of wives. (Lori Chambers, "Women's Labour, Relationship Breakdown and Ownership of the Family Farm" (2010) 25:1 CJLS 75 at 93; and see also *Farr v Farr*, [1984] 1 SCR 252)

In reviewing the materials in this chapter, consider the extent to which the reform of family property may not be the best strategy for achieving substantive equality.

Additional Resources

Constance Backhouse, "Married Women's Property Law in Nineteenth-Century Canada" (1988) 6 L & Hist Rev 211.

Maeve Doggett, *Marriage, Wife-Beating, and the Law in Victorian England* (London: Weidenfeld and Nicolson, 1992).

Judith Freedman et al, *Property and Marriage: An Integrated Approach* (London: Institute for Fiscal Studies, 1988).

Marsha Garrison, "The Economics of Divorce: Changing Rules, Changing Results" in Stephen Sugarman & Herma Hill Kay, eds, *Divorce Reform at the Crossroads* (New Haven & London: Yale University Press, 1990) 75.

Philip Girard & Rebecca Veinott, "Married Women's Property Law in Nova Scotia, 1850–1910" in Janet Guildford & Suzanne Morton, eds, *Separate Spheres: Women's Worlds in the 19th-Century Maritimes* (Fredericton NB: Acadiensis Press, 1994) 67.

Vanessa Gruben, Angela Cameron & Angela Chaisson, "'The Courts have turned Women into Slaves for the Men of this World': Irene Murdoch's Quest for Justice" in Eric Tucker, James Muir & Bruce Ziff, eds, *Property on Trial: Canadian Cases in Context* (Toronto: Irwin Law for the Osgoode Society for Canadian Legal History, 2012) 159.

Berend Hovius & Timothy Youdan, *The Law of Family Property* (Scarborough, ON: Carswell, 1991).

Nicholas Kasirer & Jean-Maurice Brisson, "The Married Woman in Ascendance, the Mother Country in Retreat: From Legal Colonialism to Legal Nationalism in Québec Matrimonial Property Reform (1866–1991)" in *University of Manitoba Canadian Legal History Project, Working Papers* (Winnipeg: University of Manitoba, 1993).

Margaret McCaughan, *The Legal Status of Women in Canada* (Scarborough, ON: Carswell, 1977).

Anne Morris & Susan Nott, *All My Worldly Goods: A Feminist Perspective on the Legal Regulation of Wealth* (Aldershot: Dartmouth, 1995).

II.
DEFINING A "SPOUSE" FOR FAMILY PROPERTY: THE SIGNIFICANCE OF MARRIAGE OR COHABITATION

Many relationships formed by unmarried heterosexual couples resemble marriages. Common-law spouses pool their resources and make joint economic plans, they provide each other financial and emotional support, and they raise children. Society values the performance of these functions. To the extent that [provincial legislation] provides an effective legal regime to deal with the economic consequences of marriage, it should apply equally to unmarried heterosexual couples in functionally similar relationships. (Ontario Law Reform Commission (OLRC), *Report on the Rights and Responsibilities of Cohabitants Under the Family Law Act* (Toronto: OLRC, 1993) at 27)

LAW REFORM RECOMMENDATIONS (OLRC)

This excerpt from the OLRC report in 1993, supporting the extension of the statutory property regime available to married couples at dissolution, argued that opposite-sex cohabiting couples lived in functionally similar relationships to married couples.

The Commission's recommendation, based on analysis of existing human rights and *Charter* equality jurisprudence, identified four policy rationales for its recommendation:

- functional similarities between married couples and opposite-sex cohabiting couples;
- reasonable expectations of family members;
- the need to compensate economic contributions to family well being; and
- relationships between family law and social assistance law.

Although cohabiting couples would be entitled, similar to married couples, to contract out of the provisions of the statutory regime, the OLRC concluded that the preferred approach was to extend the legislative regime to cohabiting couples, requiring those who wished to avoid the legislative regime to opt out. (In relation to same-sex cohabiting couples, the OLRC concluded in 1993 that it had insufficient information to recommend automatic spousal status for property sharing for these couples at separation, and thus recommended that only those same-sex couples who had registered their partnership in accordance with defined procedures [proposed by the OLRC] should be subject to the legislation.)

These recommendations are interesting for the ways in which they balance issues of individual choice and public policy. Recall the discussion in Chapter Two, where Holland considered these policy alternatives and recommended ascription, subject to contracting out (the "opting out" approach), as the basic policy for family law. That is, she argued that legal principles should apply to all those within marriage and cohabiting relationships, unless they have expressly contracted out of the obligations (as permitted). Like the OLRC, Holland specifically rejected the option of requiring people to "opt in" to a legal regime.

For another recommendation to extend property rights of married spouses to cohabiting couples, see Law Reform Commission of Nova Scotia, *Discussion Paper on Matrimonial Property in Nova Scotia: Suggestions for a New Family Law Act* (Halifax: Law Reform Commission of Nova Scotia, 1996).

COHABITING COUPLES AND PROPERTY IN THE SUPREME COURT OF CANADA

Charter Challenges about Cohabiting Couples and Property at Separation

Although the Law Reform Commissions in Ontario and Nova Scotia had both recommended the inclusion of cohabiting couples in their respective regimes for property sharing at separation, neither of these provincial legislatures amended their matrimonial property statutes to include cohabiting couples automatically — although both provinces permit cohabiting couples to "opt in" to these regimes. By contrast, legislatures in Manitoba, Saskatchewan, British Columbia, the Northwest Territories and Nunavut have all provided for property sharing between cohabiting couples at separation (which means that cohabiting couples are included unless they "opt out"). For example, British Columbia's *Family Law Act*, SBC 2011, c 25, defines "spouse" for purposes of its legislation to include cohabiting couples with two years of "continuous cohabitation" (s 3). (See also *Manitoba Family Property Act*, CCSM, c F-25; *The Family Property Act*, SS 1997, c F-6.3; *Family Law Act*, SNWT 1997, c 18; *Family Law Act (Nunavut)*, SNWT (Nu) 1997, c 18.)

Significantly, the Supreme Court of Canada had earlier held, in *Miron v Trudel*, [1995] 2 SCR 418, that an insurance policy that distinguished between married couples and those in cohabiting relationships infringed *Charter* equality in section 15 and was not saved by section 1. Moreover, in its subsequent decision in *M v H*, [1999] 2 SCR 3, the Supreme Court of Canada decided that the distinction in the definition of "spouse" in Ontario's *Family Law Act* between opposite-sex and same-sex cohabiting couples contravened *Charter* equality with respect to entitlement to spousal support.

In this context, when Catherine Walsh separated from her cohabiting partner, Wayne Bona, in Nova Scotia, she launched a constitutional challenge with respect to her exclusion from the property sharing regime for married couples pursuant to Nova Scotia's *Matrimonial Property Act*. Although her claim was denied by the trial judge, an appeal was allowed unanimously by the Nova Scotia Court of Appeal. Although it seems that Walsh and Bona then settled their property matters, the Attorney General in Nova Scotia decided to appeal to the Supreme Court of Canada, and a majority of eight judges allowed the appeal (L'Heureux-Dubé, J dissenting): see *Nova Scotia (AG) v Walsh*, 2002 SCC 83.

    Nova Scotia (AG) v Walsh was later reviewed by the Supreme Court of Canada in *Quebec (AG) v A*, 2013 SCC 5, and a majority of five justices concluded that the *Charter* equality analysis in *Nova Scotia (AG) v Walsh* was no longer appropriate, having regard to the Court's decisions after this case in *R v Kapp*, 2008 SCC 41, and *Withler v Canada (AG)*, 2011 SCC 12. Nonetheless, *Nova Scotia (AG) v Walsh* arguably remains important to family law jurisprudence in Canada for two reasons.

- One is the emphasis in the majority judgment of Bastarache, J on spousal "autonomy and choice" (an emphasis critiqued at length in the dissenting judgment). This emphasis was again reflected in the Court's majority judgments in two later cases concerning spousal agreements: *Miglin v Miglin*, 2003 SCC 24 and *Hartshorne v Hartshorne*, 2004 SCC 22.

- The other reason for continued interest in Walsh is the apparent preference among the majority judges for alternative remedies for cohabiting couples at separation, including remedies of contract and claims based on unjust enrichment ("opting in" arrangements that protect autonomy and choice and that may reflect ideas of "familialism"). By contrast with these views, the dissenting judgment was grounded in a "functional" approach to cohabiting couples and their families and the need to extend legislative regimes for married couples to those who cohabit ("opting out" arrangements that protect vulnerability in families). These issues were again reflected in *Quebec (AG) v A* in 2013, and they may remain significant for courts — or perhaps for legislatures.

Thus, it seems possible that *Nova Scotia (AG) v Walsh* may remain important for family law jurisprudence. In this context, consider the brief excerpts from the Supreme Court judgments in *Walsh* that follow here, before examining the more recent decision in *Quebec (AG) v A*.

Nova Scotia (AG) v Walsh
2002 SCC 83

On behalf of the majority judges, Bastarache J explained the factual background. The couple had lived together for ten years and had two children. At separation, Bona retained assets with a net value of $66,000, the property at issue in Walsh's equality claim.

    Bastarache J applied the principles in *Law v Canada (Minister of Employment and Immigration)*, [1999] 1 SCR 497, and noted that the Nova Scotia *Matrimonial Property Act* clearly provided differential treatment for married and cohabiting couples, and that *Miron v Trudel* had determined that marital status constituted an analogous ground pursuant to the *Charter*. However, Bastarache J rejected Walsh's argument that exclusion from the *Matrimonial Property Act* had the effect of demeaning personal dignity:

[39] As this Court has stated on numerous occasions, the equality guarantee is a comparative concept. It requires the location of an appropriate comparator group from which to assess the discrimination claim. The two comparator groups in this case are married heterosexual cohabitants, to which the MPA applies, and unmarried heterosexual cohabitants, to which the MPA does not apply. Although in some cases certain functional similarities between these two groups may be substantial, in this case it would be wrong to ignore the significant heterogeneity that exists within the claimant's comparator group. The contextual analysis of the respondent's claim reveals that reliance solely on certain "functional similarities" between the two groups does not adequately address the full range of traits, history, and circumstances of the comparator group of which the claimant is a member.

[40] It is indeed clear from the evidence that some cohabitants have specifically chosen not to marry and not to take on the obligations ascribed to persons who choose that status (see: Z. Wu, *Cohabitation: An Alternative Form of Family Living* (2000), at pp. 105–6, 116, 120–21; and University of Alberta Law Research and Reform Institute, *Survey of Adult Living Arrangements: A Technical Report* (1984), at pp. 64–72). In his study of alternative family forms, Professor Wu makes several conclusions, which include: (1) that common law relationships tend to be of much shorter duration than married relationships; (2) that cohabitation can be a "trial marriage"; (3) that cohabitation can be a deliberate substitute for legal marriage; (4) that persons who do not marry tend to have less conventional attitudes toward marriage and family and reject the institution of marriage on the basis of personal choice. These findings are indicative not only of the differences between married couples and cohabiting couples, but also of the many differences among unmarried cohabitants with regard to the manner in which people choose to structure their relationships....

[43] Where the legislation has the effect of dramatically altering the legal obligations of partners, as between themselves, choice must be paramount. The decision to marry or not is intensely personal and engages a complex interplay of social, political, religious, and financial considerations by the individual. While it remains true that unmarried spouses have suffered from historical disadvantage and stereotyping, it simultaneously cannot be ignored that many persons in circumstances similar to those of the parties, that is, opposite sex individuals in conjugal relationships of some permanence, have chosen to avoid the institution of marriage and the legal consequences that flow from it. As M. Eichler posited:

> Treating all common-law relationships like legal marriages in terms of support obligations and property division ignores the very different circumstances under which people may enter a common-law union. If they choose to marry, they make a positive choice to live under one type of regime. If they have chosen not to marry, is it the state's task to impose a marriage-like regime on them retroactively? (M. Eichler, *Family Shifts: Families, Policies, and Gender Equality* (1997), at p. 96.)

To ignore these differences among cohabiting couples presumes a commonality of intention and understanding that simply does not exist. This effectively nullifies the individual's freedom to choose alternative family forms and to have that choice respected and legitimated by the state....

In this context, Bastarache J distinguished *Miron v Trudel* because it involved the relationship between a cohabiting couple and a third party. By contrast, the Nova Scotia *Matrimonial Property Act* focuses on regulating the relationship between spouses themselves.

[55] In my view, people who marry can be said to freely accept mutual rights and obligations. A decision not to marry should be respected because it also stems from a conscious choice of the parties. It is true that the benefits that one can be deprived of under a s. 15(1) analysis must not be read restrictively and can encompass the benefit of a process or procedure, as recognized in *M. v. H.* ... [[1999] 2 SCR 3; (1999), 46 RFL (4th) 32]. It has not been established, however, that there is a discriminatory denial of a benefit in this case because those who do not marry are free to take steps to deal with their personal property in such a way as to create an equal partnership between them. If there is need for a uniform and universal protective regime independent of choice of matrimonial status, this is not a s. 15(1) issue. The MPA only protects persons who have demonstrated their intention to be bound by it and have exercised their right to choose.

[56] The respondent Walsh argues that the choice to marry, to enter into a domestic contract or to register a partnership under the LRA still does not address her situation, nor does it address the circumstances of those individuals whose unmarried partner either refuses to marry or to register their domestic partnership. For these persons, as Walsh argues, the decision is not entirely within their control. Similarly, she argues that maintaining the proprietary *status quo* in unmarried cohabiting relationships unduly disadvantages both the non-title holding partner, who have historically been women, as well as the children of the relationship. The respondent argues that protection of women and children from the potentially dire economic consequences of marriage breakdown is one of the main purposes of the MPA. Excluding unmarried cohabitants, then, constitutes a denial of equal protection of women in conjugal relationships and the children of those relationships, the persons whom the legislation was specifically designed to protect.

[57] On this basis, the respondent submits that the only constitutionally acceptable formula is to extend the ambit of the MPA to all unmarried cohabitants, while providing consenting couples the opportunity to opt out, as the current MPA does with regard to married couples. The problem with that proposition, in my view, is that it eliminates an individual's freedom to decide whether to make such a commitment in the first place. Even if the freedom to marry is sometimes illusory, does it warrant setting aside an individual's freedom of choice and imposing on her a regime that was designed for persons who have made an unequivocal commitment encompassing the equal partnership described in the MPA? While there is no denying that inequities may exist in certain unmarried cohabiting relationships and that those inequities may result in unfairness between the parties on relationship breakdown, there is no constitutional requirement that the state extend the protections of the MPA to those persons. The issue here is whether making a meaningful choice matters, and whether unmarried persons are prevented from taking advantage of the benefits of the MPA in an unconstitutional way.

[58] Persons unwilling or unable to marry have alternative choices and remedies available to them. The couple may choose to own property jointly and/or to enter into a domestic contract that may be enforced pursuant to the *Maintenance and Custody Act*, RSNS 1989, c. 160, s. 52(1) and the *Maintenance Enforcement Act*, SNS 1994-95, c. 6, s. 2(e). These couples are also capable of accessing all of the benefits of the *MPA* through the joint registration of a domestic partnership under the *LRA*.

[61] ... Those situations where the fact of economic interdependence of the couple arises over time are best addressed through the remedies like constructive trust as they are tailored to the parties' specific situation and grievances. In my view, where the multiplicity of benefits and protections are tailored to the particular needs and circumstances of the individuals, the essential human dignity of unmarried persons is not violated.

Overall, Bastarache J concluded that there was no infringement of section 15 of the *Charter*, and so he did not analyze section 1.

In a dissenting judgment, L'Heureux-Dubé J concluded that the *Matrimonial Property Act* constituted discrimination pursuant to section 15, and was not saved by section 1, of the *Charter*. In part, she addressed the remedial aspect of matrimonial property statutes, which provide for an equitable distribution at the end of a relationship.

[115] This remedial interpretation is further supported by reference to the fact that the presumption of equal sharing only arises when the relationship comes to an end....

[116] This need is further illustrated by the desire to avoid diverting funds from the public purse in order to support separated individuals. It is no secret that divorce increases the likelihood that one of the divorced spouses will fall below the poverty line. This problem is no different for heterosexual unmarried cohabitants who experience the end of their relationship. In a report released in 1992, one author noted that

> ... the end of a marriage or *common-law relationship* increased the likelihood of poverty substantially. For those who were married and had children, the risk of poverty rose from 3.1 percent to 37.6 percent after divorce or separation. ... In 1982–86, the family income of women (adjusted for changes in family size) dropped by an average of about 30 percent in the year after their marriage ended. [Emphasis added.] (T. Lemprière, "A New Look at Poverty" (1992), 16 *Perceptions* 18, at pp. 19–20, cited in M.J. Mossman, "'Running Hard To Stand Still': The Paradox of Family Law Reform" (1994), 17 *Dal. L.J.* 5, at p. 6.)

[117] The goal of matrimonial property regimes, and indeed the goal of family law generally, is a redistribution of economic resources on the breakdown of the family. While the relationship is a going concern, this redistribution is presumed to occur automatically. Family law only steps in on dissolution to distribute resources and alleviate economic burdens.... The preamble, this Court's previous statements concerning the goals of matrimonial property and similar legislation, the prevention of poverty, and the use of public funds all point to one purpose for the MPA, that of recognizing the problems that erupt at the end of the relationship and redistributing wealth to ensure that these problems are resolved. Infused in this interpretation is the notion that both parties have contributed to the relationship and that, in recognition of this contribution, wealth will be presumed to be distributed to each party equally.

The Needs of Heterosexual Unmarried Cohabitants

[118] This brings me to the central theme of this factor. I hold that heterosexual unmarried cohabitants experience similar needs as their married counterparts when the relationship comes to an end. In this sense, the relationships are functionally equivalent. Since the purpose of the MPA is to recognize this need and to alleviate it, limiting the recognition to married cohabitants implies that the needs of heterosexual unmarried cohabitants are not worthy of the same recognition solely because the people in need have not married. Further, the MPA equal presumption is based on the recognition of the contribution made by both spouses to the family. Functionally, spouses contribute to various types of families. Failing to recognize the contribution made by heterosexual unmarried cohabitants is a failure to accord them the respect they deserve. This failure diminishes their status in their own eyes and in those of society as a whole by suggesting that they are less worthy of respect and consideration. Their dignity is thereby assaulted: they are the victims of discrimination....

L'Heureux-Dubé J also focused on statistics about the rising numbers of unmarried cohabitants and how the equivalent functions of these cohabiting couples and married families give rise to "identical needs upon the breakdown of the family relationship" (para 133). As she concluded:

[140] It is no excuse to deny the benefit of equal sharing to all heterosexual unmarried cohabitants simply because some members of the group do not seem to deserve nor want this equal division. The legislature is in the best position to craft legislation that takes into account the difficulties associated with extending the benefit. It is clear, though, based on the purpose of the MPA and the functional equivalency of the two types of relationships relative to that purpose, that extending the benefit of the equal presumption solely to married cohabitants constitutes a serious attack upon the dignity of the claimant and all heterosexual unmarried cohabitants. It sends the message that, although the need for a simple means of dividing the assets on dissolution exists, only certain people are entitled to the benefit because of a status wholly unrelated to that need. In short, it demeans the dignity of an equal to treat him or her with less respect than his or her functional equals. Like the Court of Appeal, I agree that the MPA fails to recognize the contributions made by parties to a non-marital relationship and that such non-recognition has the effect of demeaning them as human beings....

In addition, L'Heureux-Dubé J examined the concept of choice in relation to marriage:

[143] I believe it to be highly problematic to conceive of marriage as a type of arrangement people enter into with the legal consequences of its demise taken into account. In the first place, most people are not lawyers. They are often not aware of the state of the law. Worse, many maintain positive misconceptions as to what obligations and rights exist in association with marriage and other relationships....

[148] If I am incorrect in concluding that the source of the obligations in the MPA is not based on the choice of marriage, it does not follow that heterosexual unmarried cohabitants enter into their relationships specifically to avoid those legal obligations. In other words, the choice argument fails from both sides: many unmarried partners do not choose to cohabit or remain unmarried so as to avoid the legal consequences of marriage.

[149] The reasons why people choose to cohabit are numerous. Some people have attempted to catalogue these potential reasons....

[150] It is impossible to pin any one of these reasons on all people who choose not to marry. In her study of heterosexual unmarried cohabitants living in Britain, C. Smart concluded that:

The majority of the men and women in our study did not cohabit because they were selfish and immoral, or because they rejected the ideological/patriarchal basis of marriage. Cohabitation was not necessarily a self-centred nor a progressive form of union. On the contrary, some of these cohabiting unions seemed be [*sic*] very similar to an ideal type of marriage with its emphasis on companionship, shared interests, commitment to children and shared economic resources. Other cohabiting unions however seemed to reproduce some of the worst aspects of traditional heterosexual marriage such as domestic violence, a rigid sexual division of labour and financial insecurity for mothers. Only about a quarter of those interviewed saw themselves as taking a stand against marriage as an institution or saw marriage as an irrelevance in the light of a superior form of private commitment. Many of the women we interviewed actually wanted to get married (albeit to a better person that they had yet to meet). Equally, some of the men went on to marry other women with whom they formed relationships later on. We cannot, therefore, simply describe these trends as "progressive" or "regressive" — the choices people make have different meanings in different contexts and we need to be constantly in tune with these complexities rather than oversimplifying and over-generalising. (C. Smart, "Stories of Family Life: Cohabitation, Marriage, and Social Change" (2000) 17 *Can. J. Fam. L.* 20, at p. 50.)....

[153] The argument that cohabitation is mainly the result of a considered choice was also rejected by the Court in *Miron, supra* [at para. 153]:

In theory, the individual is free to choose whether to marry or not to marry. In practice, however, the reality may be otherwise. The sanction of the union by the state through civil marriage cannot always be obtained. The law; the reluctance of one's partner to marry; financial, religious or social constraints — these factors and others commonly function to prevent partners who otherwise operate as a family unit from formally marrying. *In short, marital status often lies beyond the individual's effective control.* [Emphasis added.]

I made the same observations at paras. 95–97, concluding that "[i]t is small consolation, indeed, to be told that one has been denied equal protection under the *Charter* by virtue of the fact that one's partner had a choice." Nothing has changed since *Miron* was decided to indicate that these statements are incorrect. They apply with equal vigour to the *Charter* challenge in the present case.

In the result, L'Heureux-Dubé J concluded that the *Matrimonial Property Act* infringed section 15 and was not saved by section 1. Gonthier J also delivered separate reasons, concurring with the views of Bastarache J.

Notes and Questions

Legal rules for marriage and cohabitation: Recommendations of the American Law Institute

The contrasting views expressed in the majority and dissenting reasons in *Nova Scotia (AG) v Walsh* reveal fundamental differences in approaches to cohabitation and to the role of family law principles at the end of a cohabiting relationship.

In a comprehensive analysis of the law concerning domestic partners in the United States, the American Law Institute (ALI) suggested that the rising rate of cohabitation (which is lower in the United States than in Canada) meant that it was "increasingly implausible to attribute special significance to the parties' failure to marry." After identifying reasons for parties' failure to marry, the ALI concluded:

> In all of these cases, the absence of formal marriage may have little or no bearing on the intentions of the parties, the character of the parties' domestic relationship, or the equitable considerations that underlie claims between lawful spouses at the dissolution of a marriage. (American Law Institute, *Principles of the Law of Family Dissolution: Analysis and Recommendations* (St. Paul, MN: American Law Institute Publishers, 2002) at 36)

More significantly, the ALI suggested that the use of contract law to define the rights and obligations of non-marital cohabitants was unsatisfactory and that ordinary principles applicable to marriage dissolution should replace concepts of contract in defining the rights and obligations of cohabiting partners at the end of their relationships:

> American contractual treatment of nonmarital cohabitation is unusual in that no other country approaches cohabitation solely as a matter of contract law. Other countries primarily ask the question: Does this nonmarital family look like a marital family? If so, they apply some or all of their family law to the dissolution of the nonmarital family. In other words, other countries look to the character of the relationship as it developed over time, and not just to the statements the parties may have made, or not made, to one another at its inception. ... [In its recommendations, the Institute] draws inspiration from Canada, and also from Australia and New Zealand. (ALI at 37)

The ALI recommended use of the same principles for dividing marital and domestic partnership property (see recommendation no. 6.05). In doing so, it expressly noted the relative absence of social security for dependent individuals in the United States, by contrast with some other countries. As a result, principles that allocate more responsibility to family members, by contrast with the state, appeared particularly attractive in the United States.

In relation to the majority reasons in *Nova Scotia (AG) v Walsh* (which concluded that Walsh was not entitled to share in property at the dissolution of her cohabiting relationship with Bona), what is the practical result in terms of responsibilities of the family and the state to provide for dependency? To what extent did the majority and the dissenting opinions address the issues in *Nova Scotia (AG) v Walsh* from the perspective of state versus family support for post-separation economic dependency?

Evidence, empirical data, and the ideology of "choice"
What concepts of liberty and freedom of choice are reflected in the majority judgment, by contrast with the dissenting opinion? To what extent do these views rely on empirical evidence about cohabiting relationships generally or on the facts in this case? Should it make a difference whether cohabiting partners have discussed their intentions or not?

As Rollie Thompson explained in an Annotation of the decision, the issue about choice became significant only at a late stage in the litigation process. As a result, the case record contained no evidence about why Walsh and Bona had never married. Moreover, as Thompson noted, the use in the majority judgment of Zheng Wu's data about cohabitation patterns in Canada was ironic because (as explained in Chapter Two) Wu had recommended that married and cohabiting couples be treated the same in relation to economic issues at dissolution. see Zheng Wu, *Cohabitation: An Alternative Form of Family Living* (Oxford: Oxford University Press, 2000) at 161–167.

In the context of these issues about evidence and empirical data, Thompson argued:

> [I]t's not clear that data drive the analysis. The data are used to support a strong ideological view, that of not imposing property obligations upon partners "as between themselves." So long as "some" partners don't want to get married, either two at a time or one at a time, the Court is not willing to impose property consequences upon them.... [But] all of this misses the point. The question is not whether common-law couples are heterogeneous, but whether that heterogeneity makes their total exclusion from the MPA discriminatory. (DA Rollie Thompson, "Annotation of *Walsh v. Bona*" (2003) 32 RFL (5th) 87 at 90)

As Thompson also noted, one important result of the decision in *Nova Scotia (AG) v Walsh* is that "the vast majority of 'common-law couples' will just drift along, in blissful ignorance, believing that they have property rights, until they talk to a lawyer at the end of their relationship and learn the harsh truth" (Thompson at 87). Do you agree with the dissenting judgment that what is really at issue in *Walsh* is protection for vulnerability, not the parties' intentions?

Negotiating "in the shadow of the law"

According to Thompson, Walsh and Bona had settled Walsh's claim after the decision of the Nova Scotia Court of Appeal. As noted, the appellate court had held unanimously that Walsh was entitled to share equally in the property accumulated during the cohabiting relationship, based on an infringement of section 15 equality in the *Charter*. Arguably, the Court of Appeal's decision affected the balance of power between Walsh and Bona in relation to their negotiations. In addition, Walsh's entitlement to share in the accumulated property may have alleviated some of the economic impact of the dissolution of their relationship.

In this context, however, Thompson also argued that the majority judgment in the Supreme Court failed to take account of the interests of the two children in this family, and the "imbalances of power between partners, and other harsh realities of the breakdown of relationships" (see Thompson at 87 and 92). To what extent do these issues about the spouses' negotiations reflect some of the concerns about family law bargaining noted in Chapter Five?

The broader legal context of *Nova Scotia (AG) v Walsh*

Although there is no concrete evidence about why Bona and Walsh (and their legal advisors) decided to settle after the Court of Appeal decision, it is significant that it was the Nova Scotia government that pursued the appeal in the Supreme Court of Canada. What factors may have influenced the government's decision to argue that cohabiting couples should not be entitled to use the provincial statutory regime at separation?

Recall the discussion in Chapter Two about the incremental legal recognition of the rights and obligations of same-sex couples in Canada. Although it did not form a *ratio* for the Supreme Court's decision in *Nova Scotia (AG) v Walsh* in 2002, it may be relevant that the Nova Scotia government had enacted the *Law Reform (2000) Act*, SNS 2000, c 29, and SNS 2001 c 5 and c 45, legislation that permitted registration of domestic partner declarations in the province. Pursuant to this legislation, both same-sex and opposite-sex couples were permitted to register these declarations, thereby becoming entitled to rights and obligations as "spouses," including rights pursuant to the *Matrimonial Property Act*.

Recall that the same-sex marriage cases were also proceeding in British Columbia, Ontario, and Québec at this time, although same-sex marriage did not become legal until 2003. To what extent was this Nova Scotia legislation intended to provide similar rights and obligations for same-sex couples and for opposite-sex cohabiting couples, while preserving marriage as a special legal status? Is the Nova Scotia legislation an "opting in" or "opting out" arrangement? Does this arrangement reflect more or less concern with individual choice, emphasized in the majority judgment?

Marriage and cohabitation: Legal policies for "opting out" or "opting in"?

From a policy perspective, reconsider whether it is appropriate for married and cohabiting couples to have *exactly* the same rights and obligation. What are the fundamental issues for governments in making this legislative choice?

In considering this question, reflect on this assessment about cohabiting relationships:

> [Cohabiting unions] are not homogeneous. Some couples live together as a prelude to marriage and make a serious commitment to one another from the outset. Others, including a large proportion of young couples, begin to live together rather quickly after the onset of dating with little thought of permanency and least of all marriage. For them, cohabitation replaces long-term dating and a high dissolution rate is to be expected. For policy makers, it is also significant that people who cohabit outside of marriage are far less likely to pool their financial resources than are married couples. Older common law partners may well consider that cohabitation offers the advantage of economies of scale while still allowing them to maintain their respective children's inheritances intact.... The extent to which [cohabiting couples] are a heterogeneous group considerably complicates the question of whether they should be treated by the law as if they were married.... (Berend Hovius, "Property Rights for Common-Law Partners" in Martha Shaffer, ed, *Contemporary Issues in Family Law* (Toronto: Carswell, 2007) 115 at 116–117)

Recognizing that cohabitation may be somewhat different from marriage, recall the recommendations of both Wu and Holland with respect to the need to recognize rights and obligations for cohabiting couples that are the same as for married spouses. Does recognition that these two contexts are not the same require that they be treated completely differently in law?

Or, is the real issue in this policy debate between goals of individual choice and protection for vulnerable persons really a question about what is the appropriate default regime. That is, should the legislative "default regime" require couples to "opt in" or to "opt out"? Which arrangement assigns priority to choice or to protection of vulnerability? Are these goals equally important in all cases?

In this context, and in reviewing the material in this chapter about the statutory regimes and trust doctrines, try to assess why it was important to Walsh to gain access to the statutory regime in Nova Scotia. To what extent could Walsh succeed in a claim to share in Bona's property, based on principles of unjust enrichment?

Quebec (AG) v A
2013 SCC 5

A second *Charter* challenge focusing on cohabiting couples and property sharing, which began in Québec and focused on provisions of the Québec *Civil Code*, was decided by the Supreme Court of Canada in 2013. In this case, the spouses met and began to cohabit when the woman was 17 and the man in his early 30s. He was a successful business man and the woman left her home in Brazil to settle with him in Québec. They had three children and were together for seven years. The woman gave evidence that she had wanted to marry but that her partner had explained that he did not believe in marriage.

At separation, he agreed that she could remain in the matrimonial home until the children were all of the age of majority, and he also agreed to pay substantial monthly child support, based on his extensive wealth. By the time that the case was heard in the Supreme Court of Canada, the man had established a new cohabiting relationship, and there were some children in this relationship as well. LEAF intervened in the case, which was referred to in Québec as *Eric v Lola*. According to the *Civil Code* in Québec, only married spouses have entitlements at separation, including access to a variety of property (including the matrimonial home) and spousal support entitlements; and these rights are generally mandatory for married couples who separate. By contrast, cohabiting couples have no such entitlements to property, spousal support or any interests in the matrimonial home. Thus, the only option for cohabiting couples who separate in Québec is a contract ("opting in") or a civil partnership, a situation that is especially significant in the context of very high rates of cohabitation in Québec (see Chapter Two).

Like *Nova Scotia (AG) v Walsh*, this case also focused on the equality guarantee in the *Charter*, but it was necessary for the Supreme Court of

Canada to consider the impact of equality jurisprudence since the 2002 decision, particularly *R v Kapp* and *Withler v Canada (AG)*. As a result, the judges had to determine what test was appropriate with respect to discrimination pursuant to section 15, but they also had to decide whether the "Book of the Family" in the *Civil Code of Québec* constituted discrimination in its failure to recognize cohabiting couples in any of its provisions.

At trial, the court held that there was no discrimination in the *Civil Code* (2009 QCCS 3210). The Québec Court of Appeal allowed an appeal to the extent of an award of alimony (spousal support). The appeal court held that the distinction between married spouses and cohabiting couples in the *Civil Code* suggested that cohabiting spouses were less worthy of protection than married spouses or those who entered a civil union. By contrast, the trial judge had noted the high rate of cohabitation in Québec and concluded that the exclusion of cohabiting couples from the application of the *Civil Code*'s provisions for married persons created free choice for Quebecers about whether to marry or cohabit. In this case, A presented expert evidence at trial, suggesting that legal regimes did not play a role in most couples' decisions about whether or not to marry; and that most cohabiting couples assumed that family law principles applied to them just as they applied to married spouses. The appeal to the Supreme Court of Canada focused on A's entitlement to share in a number of remedies in the *Civil Code* available to married spouses at separation, including issues of property sharing and spousal support.

In the Supreme Court of Canada, the Court dismissed the appeal. However, the judges were quite divided in their views:

- Four judges (LeBel, Fish, Rothstein and Moldaver JJ) held that the *Civil Code*'s denial of entitlement to property and spousal support to a cohabiting spouse at separation did not contravene section 15 of the *Charter*; and these judges therefore did not consider section 1. These judges also held that the test for discrimination pursuant to the *Charter* had not changed since *Nova Scotia (AG) v Walsh* a decade earlier.

- Three judges (Deschamps, Cromwell, and Karakatsanis JJ) held that the *Civil Code*'s denial of entitlement to property and spousal support to a cohabiting spouse at separation contravened section 15, but that the property provisions were justified according to section 1. They held, however, that the *Civil Code*'s denial of entitlement to spousal support was not saved by section 1.

- One judge (Abella J) held that the *Civil Code*'s denial of entitlement to property and spousal support to a cohabiting spouse at separation contravened section 15 and was not saved by section 1.

- And one judge (McLachlin CJ) held that the denial of entitlement to property and spousal support to a cohabiting spouse at separation contravened section 15, but that all the relevant Code provisions were saved by section 1.

These latter five judges all suggested that the test for *Charter* discrimination had to take account of cases decided after *Nova Scotia (AG) v Walsh*. Moreover, Chief Justice McLachlin specifically held that the policy considerations about autonomy and choice should be considered in the section 1 analysis, rather than (as in *Nova Scotia (AG) v Walsh*) in relation to section 15. Thus, the result on the issue of the test for discrimination was a 5–4 decision, overruling the analysis of this test in *Walsh*.

In relation to the issue of discrimination in the *Civil Code* provisions, however, the provisions were all upheld because four judges held that there was no discrimination in the provisions of the *Civil Code*, and one judge held that although there was discrimination, all the provisions were justified according to section 1. Thus, this issue also resulted in a 5–4 decision.

However, the majority in each of these decisions was not the same. That is, on the issue about the appropriate test, McLachlin CJ, and Abella, Deschamps, Cromwell and Karakatsanis JJ represented the majority. By contrast, on the issue of whether the *Civil Code* provisions constituted a *Charter* equality infringement not justified by section 1, McLachlin CJ and LeBel, Fish, Rothstein, Moldaver JJ constituted the majority.

Consider these excerpts from three of the judgments. To what extent do the concerns expressed by the majority and the dissent in *Nova Scotia (AG) v Walsh* continue to be debated?

LeBEL J:

> [256] ... Like the Nova Scotia legislature in enacting the *MPA* at issue in *Walsh*, the Quebec National Assembly has not favoured one form of union over another. This conclusion can be inferred if the questions of freedom of choice and autonomy of the will of the parties are correctly considered. The legislature has merely defined the legal content of the different forms of conjugal relationships. It has made consent the key to changing the spouses' mutual patrimonial relationship. In this way, it has preserved the freedom of those who wish to organize their patrimonial relationships outside the mandatory statutory framework.

> [257] This makes it easier to understand the real purpose of these appeals. It concerns the mutual rights and obligations of spouses in the various forms of conjugal relationships available to them in Quebec law. In Quebec family law, these rights and obligations are always available to everyone, but imposed on no one. Their application depends on an express mutual will of the spouses to bind themselves. This express, and not deemed, consent is the source of the obligation of support and of that of partition of spouses' patrimonial interests. As we have seen, this consent is given in Quebec law by contracting marriage or a civil union, or entering into a cohabitation agreement. Participation in the protective regimes provided for by law depends necessarily on mutual consent....

> [261] In Quebec family law, ... choosing a *de facto* union permits spouses to opt out of the primary regime that is mandatory in the case of marriage or a civil union. By making this choice, they avoid entering into that regime and consequently assuming such obligations as that of support or the partition of the family patrimony. My colleague Abella J adopts a position that would require these spouses to perform positive acts to opt out of a regime they did not intend to adopt. She would thus require them to exercise a freedom of choice whose validity and relevance she

nonetheless denies in the context of opting for a particular form of conjugality.

McLACHLIN CJ:

McLachlin CJ agreed with Abella J that the *Civil Code* in Québec discriminated against *de facto* spouses pursuant to section 15 of the *Charter*. She also agreed that *Nova Scotia (AG) v Walsh* did not bind the court in the context of the evolution of s 15 analysis. However, the Chief Justice held that the infringement of section 15 was justified under section 1:

> [435] The objective of the distinction between *de facto* spouses and married or civil union couples made by the Quebec dual regime approach is to promote choice and autonomy for all Quebec spouses with respect to property division and support. Those who choose to marry choose the protections — but also the responsibilities — associated with that status. Those who choose not to marry avoid these state-imposed responsibilities and protections, and gain the opportunity to structure their relationship outside the confines of the mandatory regime applicable to married and civil union spouses.

> [436] The legislature pursued this objective in response to rapidly changing attitudes in Quebec with respect to marriage, namely a rejection of the gender inequalities associated with the tradition of marriage, a shift away from the influence of the Church and the assertion of values linked to individualism.... The legislator sought to accommodate the social rejection of the traditional control by the state and the Church over intimate relationships. When the family patrimony provisions were adopted in Quebec, the responsible Minister stated that a harmonization of the legislative treatment of marriage and *de facto* spousal relationships "would not be without consequences, for what then would be the meaning of marriage or the value in the civil context of religious marriage, and *what would be the form of union developed by those who do not want to be regulated?*" (emphasis in the judgment of McLachlin CJ, indicating the translation of the quoted material)

McLachlin CJ addressed the requirements of rational connection and minimum impairment, and then focused on proportionality:

> [449] The impact of the Quebec scheme on the exercise and enjoyment of the equality right is significant. However, the discriminatory effects of the exclusion of *de facto* spouses from the mandatory regime are attenuated in the modern era, as compared to earlier points in Quebec's history. The impugned provisions do not appear to perpetuate animus against *de facto* spouses. All parties to this appeal agreed that the *de facto* spousal relationship is a popular form of relationship in Quebec. There is no longer any stigma attached to *de facto* spousal relationships. Many spouses in Quebec appreciate and take advantage of the ability to structure their relationship outside the traditional strictures of marriage. The impugned provisions enhance the freedom of choice and autonomy of many spouses as well as their ability to give personal meaning to their relationships. Against this must be weighed the cost of infringing the equality right of people like A, who have not been able to make a meaningful choice. Critics can say and have said that the situation of women like A suggests that the legislation achieves only a formalistic autonomy and an illusory freedom. However, the question for this Court is whether the unfortunate dilemma faced by women such as A is disproportionate to the overall

benefits of the legislation, so as to make it unconstitutional. Having regard to the need to allow legislatures a margin of appreciation on difficult social issues and the need to be sensitive to the constitutional responsibility of each province to legislate for its population, the answer to this question is no.

(As noted, three judges concluded that the Québec *Civil Code*'s distinctions were justified in relation to property, but not with respect to spousal support. Part of the judgment of Deschamps J is reproduced in the Notes and Questions, below.)

ABELLA J:

Like McLachlin CJ, Deschamps, Cromwell, and Karakatsanis JJ, Abella J concluded that the provisions in the Québec *Civil Code*, which excluded *de facto* spouses from entitlements to spousal support and (in relation to McLachlin CJ) to property, constituted discrimination pursuant to section 15. Abella J then examined section 1, and accepted that the purpose of the exclusion was the preservation of freedom of choice for these spouses. In assessing the requirement of rational connection, however, she stated:

> [363] I concede that the exclusion of *de facto* spouses from spousal support and property regimes in Quebec was a carefully considered policy choice. As my colleague LeBel J points out, it was discussed and reaffirmed during successive family law reforms from 1980 onwards. But the degree of legislative time, consultation and effort cannot act as a justificatory shield to guard against constitutional scrutiny. What is of utmost relevance is the resulting legislative choice. Neither the deliberative policy route — nor the popularity of its outcome — is a sufficient answer to the requirement of constitutional compliance....

Abella J considered the alternative remedies for *de facto* spouses, including cohabitation agreements and claims of unjust enrichment, and suggested that they were inadequate:

> [372] The current opt in protections may well be adequate for some *de facto* spouses who enter their relationships with sufficient financial security, legal information, and the deliberate intent to avoid the consequences of a more formal union. But their ability to exercise freedom of choice can be equally protected under a protective regime with an opt out mechanism. The needs of the economically vulnerable, however, require presumptive protection no less in *de facto* unions than in more formal ones....

> [376] At the end of the day, the methodology for remedying the s 15 breach lies with the Quebec legislature. The Quebec scheme currently gives *de facto* spouses the choice of entering into a contract to enshrine certain protections, or marrying and receiving all the protections provided by law, or remaining unbound by any mutual rights or obligations. None of these choices is compromised by a presumptively protective scheme of some sort. It is entirely possible for Quebec to design a regime that retains all of these choices. Spouses who are aware of their legal rights, and choose not to marry so they can avoid Quebec's support and property regimes, would be free to choose to remove themselves from a presumptively protective regime. Changing the default situation of the couple,

however, so that spousal support and division of property protection of some kind applies to them, would protect those spouses for whom the choices are illusory and who are left economically vulnerable at the dissolution of their relationship....

Notes and Questions

The discrimination test and options for reform for cohabiting couples

In a comment about the Supreme Court's analysis in *Quebec (AG) v A*, Natasha Bakht suggested that although there have not been changes in the "day-to-day realities of married/registered partnerships versus *de facto* [cohabiting] relationships" since the decision in *Nova Scotia (AG) v Walsh*, equality jurisprudence had changed, and especially so as to encourage a more flexible, contextual inquiry, "one that actually furthered substantive equality." As she explained:

> The *Walsh* majority's decision was problematic following the *Kapp/Withler* evolutions for two reasons. First, in their analysis that common law couples are free to choose to marry, the *Walsh* majority effectively collapsed public interest considerations of the reasonableness of the legislation, a matter to be analyzed under section 1, into the section 15 analysis.... Second, the effect of combining respect for choice into the equality analysis negated the recognition of marital status as an analogous ground per *Miron v Trudel*.... Thus the arguments concerning freedom of choice and individual autonomy that were found to belie a section 15 infringement in *Walsh*, were relegated to section 1 in *Eric v Lola*....
>
> If a constitutional challenge like *Walsh* were to arise in Ontario or another province/territory where unmarried couples are excluded from the legislative property regime, it is likely that the Court would initially find that such a distinction is discriminatory and contrary to section 15. The discriminatory impact of the exclusion of cohabiting couples from the property-sharing regime in, for example, Ontario's *Family Law* Act, would be on the basis of marital status, but strong arguments could be made about the gendered effects of the differential treatment of married and unmarried spouses. As LEAF argued in *Eric v Lola*, an examination of the lived effects and systemic outcomes would show that the legislation perpetuates prejudice and disadvantage experienced by women in cohabiting relationships by disregarding need....
>
> A legislative scheme that is presumptively inclusive of cohabiting couples, but that nonetheless permits them to contract out of such a default scheme is beneficial because it automatically protects those most vulnerable who would not have the resources or knowledge to opt out, while still permitting those who wish to be independent as to property to retain individual autonomy. It would also rectify the ongoing confusion among many as to the different consequences of marriage and cohabitation.... (Natasha Bakht, "A v B and Attorney General of Quebec (Eric v Lola) — The Implications for Cohabiting Couples Outside Quebec" (2012–2013) 28:2 Can J Fam L 261 at 269–273)

Although Bakht suggested arguments that could be presented in another *Charter* challenge (one that focused especially on the section 1 "justification" for treating married and cohabiting couples differently at separation), it seems that legislative action may be necessary in practice. As Robert Leckey argued, the decision in *Quebec (AG) v A* disappointed some observers, but it also provides:

> [A] reminder of the limits of appellate litigation, in particular Charter litigation, in the field of family law. Often those cases that reach the Supreme Court of Canada, and even the appellate courts in the provinces, involve parties with significant wealth. Courts are called, then, to consider principles of family law in the context of factual situations of wealth. These principles are subsequently binding in the context of families whose financial circumstances are much more modest. (Robert Leckey, "Developments in Family Law: The 2012–2013 Term" (2014) 64 SCLR (2d) 241 at 264–265)

Do Leckey's comments suggest a further reason for seeking legislative action in relation to the recognition of property rights for cohabiting couples at separation?

As Leckey suggested, the man in this cohabiting couple was extremely wealthy. He had agreed to pay very generous child support as well as salaries for nannies and a cook, and to supply A with a car when she had custody of the children. In addition, A was allowed to remain in the matrimonial home. However, all these arrangements were to end when the children reach adulthood; at that time, according to Leckey, "A will have no capital assets and no income stream," a situation that seemed not to impress either the judges or the media (Leckey at 265).

Recall that some critics of *Nova Scotia (AG) v Walsh* suggested that the court failed to consider the needs of the children. Compare the factual context in *Walsh* with the generous child support that was provided in A's case. Does this comparison suggest that when children's needs are met (especially with generous levels of support), there is less need to take account of the needs of a former *de facto* spouse? How should this issue be addressed?

To what extent does A's situation affect your view about the need for reform of property rights for cohabiting couples in Québec? In common law provinces such as Ontario?

The impact of *Quebec (AG) v A* and family law in Canada

Consider this assessment of the impact of this case for Canadian family law:

> The practical effect of the decision is to leave the family law landscape just as it was. In Quebec, *de facto* [cohabiting] spouses have no matrimonial-like rights or obligations, still. In the rest of Canada, nothing changes either. The *Walsh* outcome is still valid, ie, no constitutional obligation to include [cohabiting] couples in matrimonial property laws. Where [cohabiting] couples are included, there is a legislative choice, as has been made in the Northwest Territories, Nunavut, Saskatchewan, Manitoba and British Columbia [the latter effective as of 18 March 2013]. Outside of Quebec, every legislature includes [cohabiting] partners under spousal support law, and this constitutional ruling will not change that legislative policy.
>
> At a theoretical level, the decision is important. Sadly, it marks the end of an era in family law and the *Charter*: the Court entirely abandons

a functional approach to the family, preferring a formalistic methodology. Its constitutional analysis is arid, divorced from social reality. It completely ignores the interests of children of [cohabiting] relationships. Its analysis of spousal support is thin and oddly-truncated....

For a family law lawyer, Justice Abella's position comes closest to our functional approach: if it walks, talks and behaves like a married family, then it should be treated in similar fashion and not be excluded from our family laws. What matters is not form, or consent, or choice, but what the relationship actually does and where the parents and children end up after separation. That was once the Canadian way, but no longer after this decision. (Rollie Thompson, "Annotation" (2013) 21 RFL (7th) 325 at 325–26)

How should provinces such as Ontario respond to this critique? In Québec, immediately following release of the Supreme Court's decision, the Attorney General announced that the government would examine its options. Should other provinces be encouraged to do so as well? Why or why not? (In a case that was filed prior to the new B.C. legislation, both the trial court and the B.C. Court of Appeal denied access to property to a cohabiting spouse, and the Supreme Court denied leave to appeal on 4 July 2013: see *Jackson v Zaruba*, 2013 BCCA 8, in which the appeal court applied *Quebec (AG) v A*.)

Distinguishing entitlements to "property" and to "spousal support"

Deschamps J (on behalf of Cromwell and Karakatsanis JJ) distinguished entitlement to property division from entitlement to spousal support:

[393] ... Whereas a plan to live together takes shape gradually and can result in the creation of a relationship of interdependence over which one of the parties has little or no control, property such as the family residence or pension plans can be acquired only as a result of a conscious act. The process that leads to the acquisition of a right of ownership is different from the one that causes a spouse to become economically dependent....

[396] The rationale for awarding support on a non-compensatory basis applies equally to persons who are married or in a civil union and to *de facto* spouses. If the legal justification for support is based on, among other things, the satisfaction of needs resulting from the breakdown of a relationship of interdependence created while the spouses lived together, it is difficult to see why a *de facto* spouse who may not have been free to choose to have the relationship with his or her spouse made official through marriage or a civil union, but who otherwise lives with the latter in a "family unit," would not be entitled to support. For someone in such a position, the possibility the parties have, according to the Attorney General, of choosing to marry or to enter into a civil union does not really exist....

[397] The Quebec government's decision to take care of persons in need by providing them with social assistance benefits is not likely to make up for the exclusion of *de facto* spouses from the protection of support. Minimalist assistance such as this is not an adequate response. Social assistance is intended to be a measure of last resort and is not a reasonable substitute for support from a spouse who can afford to pay it....

Although spousal support is considered in more detail in Chapter Seven, it may be helpful to consider whether, as a family law litigant, A was more interested in the "economic readjustment package" overall, rather than the legal distinctions between entitlements to either property or spousal support. Moreover, it is clear that, in the absence of spousal support (especially after the children have grown up), A may have to apply for social assistance, even though it may not be "a reasonable substitute for support from a spouse who can afford to pay it."

You may want to reconsider these arguments after reviewing issues about spousal support in the next chapter.

Additional Resources

Martha Bailey, "Regulation of Cohabitation and Marriage in Canada" (2004) 26 Law & Pol'y 153.

Nicholas Bala & Marlène Cano, "Unmarried Cohabitation in Canada: Common Law and Civilian Approaches to Living Together" (1989) 4 Can Fam LQ 147.

Helene Balleau & Pascale Cornut St Pierre, "Conjugal Independence in Quebec: From Legal Rules to Social Representations about Spousal Support and Property Division on Conjugal Breakdown" (2014) 29 CJLS 43.

Anne Barlow, *Cohabitation, Marriage and the Law: Social Change and Legal Reform in the 21st Century* (Oxford & Portland, OR: Hart Publishing, 2005).

June Carbone, "Morality, Public Policy and the Family: The Role of Marriage and the Public/Private Divide" (1996) 36 Santa Clara L Rev 267.

Colette Chelack & Joan MacPhail, "Sharing a Life: Manitoba Legislation Respecting Rights and Obligations of Common-Law Partners" (2005) 31 Man LJ 111.

Heather Conway & Philip Girard, "'No Place Like Home'" The Search for a Legal Framework for Cohabitants and the Family Home in Canada and Britain" (2005) 30 Queen's LJ 715.

Nicola Glover & Paul Todd, "The Myth of Common Intention" (1996) 16 LS 325.

Winnifred Holland, "Intimate Relationships in the New Millennium: The Assimilation of Marriage and Cohabitation" (2000) 17 Can J Fam L 169.

Robert Leckey, "Family Outside the Book of the Family" (2009) 88 Can Bar Rev 545.

Robert Leckey, "Self and Other: Cohabitation and Comparative Method" (2009) 72:1 Mod L Rev 48.

Robert Leckey, "Gimme Shelter" (2011) 34 Dal LJ 197.

Carol Rogerson, "Developments in Family Law: The 2002–2003 Term" (2003) 22 SCLR (2d) 273.

III.
LEGISLATIVE REGIMES FOR PROPERTY SHARING AT MARRIAGE BREAKDOWN: PRINCIPLES OF EQUALITY

People enter family relationships to satisfy many human needs: social, sexual, and economic. When two people enter into a relationship they make joint economic decisions for the benefit of the family unit. Their decisions about what contributions each partner makes to the economic relationship and how the assets of that relationship are divided may be made because of cultural assumptions about the proper role of each partner or because of economic advantages that they will enjoy together. If a relationship breaks down, family members face the difficult task of extricating themselves from the economic arrangements they have made together. ... Simply leaving family property in the name of the partner who had legal title to it during the relationship may be grossly unfair. (OLRC, *Report on Family Property Law* (Toronto: OLRC, 1993) at 1)

PRINCIPLES AND APPROACHES TO FAMILY PROPERTY ENTITLEMENT

Policy choices for property sharing at marriage breakdown

The principle that family property should be shared at the end of a marital partnership is relatively straightforward. However, its implementation in practice is more complex, and requires policy choices with respect to a number of legal principles:

- **The underlying rationale for property sharing:** What is the underlying rationale for sharing marital property at the dissolution of the relationship? Should it be based on a *presumption* of equal contributions by the partners to the acquisition and maintenance of family assets, or should it reflect *actual contributions* by the partners? If marriage itself provides the rationale, should there be any differences between long-term and short-term marriages? If equality of contribution is to be presumed, should such presumptions be rebuttable, and if so, who should bear the onus of proof? If contributions are to be assessed, what factors should be considered relevant?

- **The definition of "property" to be shared:** In terms of property owned by each spouse at the breakdown of their relationship, should they be permitted to exclude property that was a gift, or property that was acquired before the marriage? In other words, is it just property that was jointly accumulated that is to be shared, or should all property owned by each of them be shared, regardless of how or when title was acquired?

    Related to this question is the issue whether all "property" or just "family assets" should be shared. For example, if one spouse owns a business and the other spouse has contributed nothing to it, should it be shared at breakdown or excluded as a non-family asset?

In addition, there may be special issues about the matrimonial home. At breakdown, should the spouse who will provide primary care and custody for children have any right to stay in the home, even if it means postponing the division of family assets?

- **Equal (or unequal) shares:** What should be the basic unit of entitlement? Should there be a presumption that each spouse is entitled to one-half of the family property or its value? If so, what factors are relevant to rebutting this presumption of equal shares and who has the onus of proof? Or, should courts have discretion to allocate property or interests in property in accordance with legislative criteria designed to achieve equity and fairness (which may be different from equality) in certain circumstances?

  In other words, should there be fixed shares or discretionary decision making by courts? And how are these questions related to goals of certainty in terms of legal principles and efficacy in their implementation?

For an overview of these and related issues, see Law Reform Commission of British Columbia, *Working Paper on Property Rights on Marriage Breakdown* (Victoria: Ministry of the Attorney General, 1989); Discussion Paper, "Division of Family Property," *Family Relations Act Review* (Victoria: Ministry of the Attorney General, 2007); and OLRC *Report on Family Property* (Toronto: OLRC, 1993).

Marriage and equal shares: *FLA*, s 5(7)

Although provincial regimes in the common law provinces across Canada reveal differing approaches to some of the above questions, there appears to be general agreement with respect to the fundamental rationale for family property regimes:

> Marriage *per se* creates entitlement to a one-half share of family property for each spouse, subject to a limited number of exceptions (which may vary to some extent in different provinces in terms of specific factors).

This basic principle has often been defined in terms of a presumption that, in marriage, the contributions of the spouses are "deemed" to be equal (whether they are equal in practice or not). In this way, marriage provides the entitlement to an equal share of family property, or its value, on the basis of a *legal presumption* that spousal contributions were equal.

In Ontario, this legal presumption is stated in section 5(7) of the *Family Law Act*, RSO 1990, c F.3:

> **5(7)** The purpose of this section is to recognize that child care, household management and financial provision are the joint responsibilities of the

spouses and that inherent in the marital relationship there is equal contribution, whether financial or otherwise, by the spouses to the assumption of these responsibilities, entitling each spouse to the equalization of the net family properties, subject only to the equitable considerations set out in subsection (6).

Pursuant to this section, the spouses are presumed to have made equal contributions entitling them to equal shares in the value of family property. Although this presumption can be rebutted, it is necessary to show that the inequality of contributions was extreme. Indeed, the test is "unconscionability" (see s 5(6) and further discussion later in this chapter).

Legislative approaches to property: Sharing the *value* or sharing the "property"?

While there is general agreement among the common law provinces with respect to the fundamental basis for equal sharing of family property between the spouses at marriage breakdown, there are different approaches to the questions of what "property" is to be divided, the role and extent of judicial discretion to adjust basic entitlements, and whether a "property interest" or an "equalizing payment" is more appropriate.

That is, some provincial legislative schemes divide *property interests* between the spouses, while others require the *value* of the property owned by the spouses to be equalized by a money payment.

As a paper prepared for the B.C. Law Reform Commission explained, recognition of property interests for non-owning spouses may create problems for third party creditors that are, at least to some extent, avoided by a regime that provides for an equalizing payment but does not otherwise affect property interests. see Law Reform Commission of British Columbia (1989) at 110–113 and appendix E. However, although the 2007 "Discussion Paper" concerning family property noted that the B.C. *Family Relations Act* had been criticized because its flexibility resulted in a lack of predictability, the Paper concluded that lawyers preferred this flexibility because it allowed for consideration of each couple's individual circumstances in deciding what is fair.

In 2011, the British Columbia legislature enacted new family law legislation, the *Family Law Act*, SBC 2011, c 25 (in force 2013). The new statute preserves the province's approach to family property, although some of its property provisions may limit the scope of judicial discretion to some extent when the statute is in effect (see Part 5 of the statute and the discussion of these provisions in relation to *Hartshorne v Hartshorne* in Chapter Five).

As noted, the new B.C. family law statute applies to cohabiting spouses (see s 3) after a period of "continuous cohabitation" for two years, as well as to married spouses. In the context of this legislative action in British Columbia, as well as in a number of other Canadian provinces, to extend family property principles to cohabiting spouses, is there a need for reform in Ontario?

Family property at marriage breakdown in Ontario: The "equalization of value" approach

As will be evident in its *Family Law Act*, Ontario opted for a regime that is characterized by:

- A broad definition of "property" (see s 4(1));
- An adjustment (money payment) between the spouses based on the *value* of their property at the date of marriage breakdown (see s 5(1));
- Limited judicial discretion to ensure certainty and efficiency, using a test of "unconscionability" (see s 5(6));
- Deductions for pre-marriage property (s 4(1)), and exclusions for some property (including gifts and inheritances in some circumstances) pursuant to section 4(2); and
- Some special treatment of the matrimonial home (see "Deductions" and "Exclusions" and Part II of the *FLA*).

In this way, the Ontario legislation represents a "non-discretionary fixed shares" approach, by contrast with some other provincial property-sharing regimes in Canada. (Note also that the current statute uses a broad definition of "property" rather than the "family assets" approach, which had existed previously in the 1978 *Family Law Reform Act* in Ontario.)

Thus, the Ontario *Family Law Act* does not change the spouses' entitlement to property owned by each of them at the relevant date. Instead, the *value* of all property is calculated (defining each spouse's net family property (NFP)), and the spouse with the higher NFP value must make an *equalizing payment* to the other spouse.

The goal is that each spouse shares equally in the economic wealth of the marriage at breakdown, *without any change in property ownership*.

In this context, it is not technically appropriate to refer in Ontario to the "division of property," since only the *value* of property is divided between the spouses.

Consider the following excerpt from a case decided shortly after the adoption of this statutory scheme in Ontario, noting the court's process for determining the equalizing payment pursuant to Ontario's *Family Law Act*.

Skrlj v Skrlj
(1986), 2 RFL (3d) 305 (Ont HC)

In this case, one of the first to be decided under the *Family Law Act, 1986*, Galligan J explained the approach to be used in relation to the new legislation and then provided a step-by-step assessment of the value of the property owned by each spouse to determine the equalization amount required under section 5(1) and the overall interpretation of sections 4 and 5 (at 309).

> ... Before dealing with the property issues, I want to make a very brief observation about the new regime of family law in Ontario. As I read the

Family Law Act, 1986, it leaves the court with no discretion to decide spouses' affairs in accordance with a particular court's sense of fairness. Subject to a discretion if it finds unconscionability, under s. 5(6), the courts must decide the rights of separating spouses in strict compliance with the terms of the Act, even if, in an individual case, a judge may feel that the result does not appear fair according to that particular judge's sense of fairness. I think the legislature has clearly expressed its intent to remove judicial discretion from property disputes between separating spouses.

In this case certain suggestions were put to the court about how this dispute could be resolved by transferring assets to discharge corresponding liabilities. In my view, that is the stuff of settlement. Separating spouses can settle their differences as they see fit but if they do not settle them and decide to come to trial, they are entitled to, and should expect to get, adjudication, not mediation. I think that any remnants of "Palm Tree Justice" have now disappeared from Ontario.

I intend to decide this case, and other cases, strictly according to the *Family Law Act*, as I interpret it. The chips will fall where they may.

The scheme of the Act, insofar as it relates to property, is to determine the value of each spouse's net family property as at the valuation date as defined in the Act. (In this case it has been agreed that the valuation date is 18th June 1981.) Once the value of each spouse's net family property is determined, the spouse with the lesser value is entitled to one half of the difference, subject to any adjustment if unconscionability, as set out in s. 5(6) of the Act, is proved.

The first step is to determine what was owned by each spouse on the valuation date. The next is the deduction of debts and the value of assets owned by each spouse at the time of marriage. Property falling within s. 4(2) of the Act is of course excluded from a spouse's net family property.

In this case the assets are not extensive. I will discuss each of them briefly. The matrimonial home is owned jointly and has a present value of $75,000. There are no encumbrances. No estimate has been given of the value of the property on valuation day [V-day]. Since the property is owned jointly, in my opinion it is not necessary to be particularly concerned with its value on valuation day, because each spouse's property will have an identical amount attributed to it. I credit each spouse's property with one half of the appraised value, or $37,500....

Galligan J then identified a joint account at Canada Trust with a total value of $10,200. Thus, each spouse was credited with $5,100. There was also a Canada Trust account in the husband's name with a value of $23,300. Galligan J ignored accounts opened after valuation day, as well as an account held by the wife for the benefit of her children. The wife's account with a value of $758 was included in her NFP, along with an RRSP owned by the husband on V day (i.e., valuation day).

Once the value of the property owned by each spouse has been determined, there must be deducted from those amounts each spouse's debts or liabilities and the value of property owned by each at the date of marriage. I accept the wife's evidence that she had property at the time of marriage worth $1,000 and that her husband had a car with an equity worth approximately $300. I also accept her evidence that she had debts of $1,130 on valuation day. The husband had no debts or liabilities. The appropriate deductions will be made.

I have done a handwritten schedule and passed copies to counsel showing my calculations as follows:

	Wife	Husband
Property		
Matrimonial home	$37,500	$37,500
Canada Trust (Ex 3)	5,100	5,100
Canada Trust (Ex 4)		23,300
Canada Trust (Ex 16)	758	
RRSP		2,000
Total Property	$43,358	$67,900
Deductions		
Property at time of marriage	$1,000	$300
Debts or liabilities	1,130	
Net family property	$41,228	$67,900

The result is that on valuation day she had net family property valued at $41,228. He had net family property of $67,900. [It appears that the court made an arithmetical mistake. The judge failed to deduct Mr. Skrlj's pre-marriage property, so that the figure of $67,900 should have been $67,600.]

The difference is $26,672. She is *prima facie* entitled to payment of one half of that amount, of $13,336.

In the circumstances of this case, I think, however, that she is entitled to be awarded an amount greater than one half of the difference, because I find in this case that equalizing net family properties would be unconscionable. I do not intend to go into any lengthy discussion of the circumstances giving rise to the unconscionability. It will suffice to say that after valuation day each party took money out of the joint account Ex. 3 without permission of the other. The husband took $6,330 more than she did. In my opinion, it would have been unconscionable within s. 5(6)(h) of the Act for him to have that money and for her to have attributed to her property one half of the amount of the account on valuation day. One half of the amount of $6,330 ($3,165) will be added to her equalizing payment. She will therefore have an order for payment, that is, judgment against her husband, for $16,501....

Notes and Questions

The end of discretion?

Galligan J noted that the scope for judicial discretion in relation to Ontario's *Family Law Act* was very limited. His comments reflect the views of the Ontario Law Reform Commission's *Report on Family Property* in 1993, which suggested that the Act was designed to "operate as a mechanical scheme with little scope for judicial discretion" (OLRC, *Report on Family Property* (Toronto: OLRC, 1993) at 59). What goals are promoted by limiting judicial discretion and providing a mechanical scheme to determine the equalization payment? What goals may be compromised?

In the above case, did Galligan J exercise any discretion in determining the equalization payment?

Consider the following example:

On V day, the husband and wife owned a home (mortgage free) as joint tenants, valued at $800,000. The husband also owned a 2005 car valued at $6,000 and he had RRSP funds worth $10,000. The wife also had an RRSP, valued at $7,000 and jewellery worth $10,000. The husband and wife held a joint bank account with $6,000. On V day, the husband had debts of $100,000, and the wife had debts of $25,000. In addition, the husband is claiming property worth $2,000 at the date of marriage.

    Calculate the NFPs for each spouse and the equalization payment.

In this case, because the spouses are joint tenants, one-half the value of the home on V day is included in each of their NFPs. (Note that if the husband held title in his name alone, the full value of $800,000 would be included in his NFP.)

    The husband's other assets include his car and his RRSP. The wife's other assets include her RRSP and her jewellery.

    One-half the value of their joint bank account is included in each spouse's NFP.

    The husband's deductions include his debts at V day and the value of his pre-marriage property. The wife's only deduction is the value of her debts at V day.

    Thus, the NFPs are as follows:

	Husband	Wife
Property		
Home (JT)	$400,000	$400,000
Car	6,000	
RRSPs	10,000	7,000
Jewellery		10,000
Bank account (JT)	3,000	3,000
Totals	$419,000	$420,000
Deductions		
Debts at V day	100,000	25,000
Pre-marriage property	2,000	
Net Family Property	$317,000	$395,000

Equalization owed by Wife to Husband
= (½ the difference of $78,000)
= $39,000

Comparing the approach to "family property" in British Columbia

By comparison with the approach in Ontario, consider British Columbia's *Family Law Act*, SBC 2011, c 25. The new statute preserves the province's basic approach to sharing family *property* (rather than just its *value*, as in Ontario). Under this new B.C. legislation (in force 2013), the definition of "family property" in section 84 recognizes property owned by at least one spouse or in which one spouse has a beneficial interest, or property derived from such property after separation. Section 85 provides for some property to be excluded, and section 86 defines "family debt" which is also subject to sharing. Orders about property division may provide for an unequal division of property in some cases pursuant to section 95, although such orders may not generally set aside spousal agreements (s 94). Section 95(2) provides a list of factors to be considered in relation to an order for unequal division, including "any other factor ... that may lead to significant unfairness." As noted in Chapter Five, the *Family Law Act* also includes provisions about family contracts, and defines the circumstances in which a court order may set aside such agreements.

Thus, the *Family Law Act* in British Columbia continues to emphasize "fairness" in orders about family property. As you review the materials in this chapter, consider whether, or to what extent, Galligan J's views about the limits of judicial discretion to achieve fairness reveal a different approach to fairness in Ontario. For an overview of this statute, see R Treloar & Susan B Boyd, "Family Law Reform in (Neoliberal) Context: British Columbia's New Family Law Act" (2014) 28:1 Intl JL Pol'y & Fam 77.

Equality goals: Theory and practice

As noted, both law reform recommendations and statutory provisions about property seem to assume a goal of equality for the spouses at marriage breakdown. However, several scholars have challenged the idea of equality in family property regimes. For example, Jack Knetsch argued that spouses often make decisions, while the family unit is intact, that benefit the unit as a whole. As a result of this focus on the intact unit, however, some decisions may mean that one spouse, frequently the wife, may be less well-positioned at marriage breakdown in terms of future financial well-being. See Jack Knetsch, "Some Economic Implications of Matrimonial Property Rules" (1984) 34 UTLJ 263.

To what extent is it appropriate for marital property regimes to take account of broader, systemic economic inequalities for spouses post-divorce?

Martha Fineman also argued that the problem of presumptions of equality in family property statutes arises out of the statutory conception of equality as "formal" rather than "substantive":

> The ideal of equality between spouses is at the centre of our current views of marriage and therefore exerts a powerful and symbolic influence on our process of fashioning rules to govern distribution of marital assets. ... This approach of using equality as the organizational concept in assessing appropriate rules for property division creates dilemmas. In its simplest form, equality demands sameness of treatment, and differentiation in any sphere may be considered a concession of inferiority or "unequalness."
>
> The ramifications of symbolic adherence to equality may be significant. Contribution is an equalizing concept, while need demands an acknowledgment and evaluation of differences. As such, a commitment to equality initially encourages its proponents to minimize or deny differences between the individuals.... (Martha Fineman, *The Illusion of Equality* (Chicago: University of Chicago Press, 1991) at 46)

Fineman's argument is that a goal of equality in property allocations will not meet the *needs* of many women post-divorce.

At the same time, others have argued that there are limits on the role of property adjustment rules at divorce, and that they may not be able to address more fundamental, systemic problems of inequality in marriage. Thus, the American Law Institute concluded that a presumption of equality provides a "rough compromise" between competing claims of contribution and need, and that:

> [L]egislatures have resorted to the principle of equality as a basis for property division on divorce, not as an attempt to reflect "economic" values of the respective contributions [of the spouses], but as an ideological norm of the marriage partnership. (ALI at 833, citing John Eekelaar & Mavis Maclean, *Maintenance After Divorce* (Oxford: Clarendon Press, 1986) at 45)

Is this answer to Professor Fineman's argument entirely satisfactory? Is there a better solution available? In examining the materials in this chapter, you may wish to keep in mind these competing views about equality goals and marital property.

Empirical studies about marital property and equality

In an analysis of a small number of divorce files containing separation agreements of business couples in New Brunswick in the early 1990s, Donald Poirier and Lynne Castonguay concluded that married women frequently did not receive recognition for their contributions to business assets (assets excluded from sharing in the absence of proof of actual contribution by the non-owning spouse). According to their study, one third of the separation agreements did not respect the formal legal equality of New Brunswick's marital property law. (See Donald Poirier & Lynne Castonguay, "Formal Versus Real Equality in Property Division on Marriage Breakdown of Business Couples: An Empirical Study" (1994) 11 Can Fam LQ 71 at 85; see also D Poirier, "Les Femmes Collaboratrices et la Loi sur les Biens Matrimoniaux du Nouveau-Brunswick" (1990) 39 UNBLJ 23; and D Poirier & M Boudreau, "Formal Versus Real Equality in Separation Agreements in New Brunswick" (1992) 10 Can J Fam L 239.)

To what extent does this empirical research confirm concerns about family law bargaining (discussed in Chapter Five)? In the context of limits on judicial discretion in the NB statute, does this empirical research suggest that women should pursue litigation, rather than engage in bargaining separation agreements?

Property and the *FLA* definition of marriage

Section 1(1) of the *FLA* defines "spouse" in terms of marriage. This definition applies in relation to Parts I and II of the *FLA* relating to property equalization and the matrimonial home. However, Part III of the Act, relating to spousal support, provides for an extended definition of "spouse." And, of course, the Supreme Court decisions confirmed that provinces, such as Ontario, could limit access to the matrimonial property regime to married couples. Thus, this chapter now turns to the matrimonial property regime in the *Family Law Act* that is available only to married couples. Issues about equitable remedies for cohabiting couples are then discussed at the end of this chapter.

IV.
THE PROCESS OF EQUALIZATION IN ONTARIO

> Ontario legislation seems to provide a straightforward method of dividing entitlement to family property which, for the most part, does not depend upon judicial discretion or litigation. (Law Reform Commission of British Columbia, *Working Paper on Property Rights on Marriage Breakdown* (Victoria: Ministry of the Attorney General, 1989) at 109)

DEFINING THE EQUALIZATION AMOUNT: PRINCIPLES AND PROCESSES

An overview of steps in defining the equalization amount: *FLA*, ss 4 and 5

In this section, the material examines the principles and processes for defining "property" and determining its value, in order to compare one spouse's net family property with that of the other, so as to calculate the amount of an equalization payment. In reviewing these legal arrangements, it may be important to assess whether, or to what extent, these arrangements are "straightforward" in practice and thus require little "judicial discretion."

In determining the amount of an equalization payment pursuant to Part I (ss 4 and 5) of the *Family Law Act* in Ontario, the following steps are required:

Step 1   Determine the valuation date or V day (defined in s 4);

Step 2   Determine what property was owned by each spouse on V day (s 4);

Step 3   Determine whether any property constitutes excluded property (s 4(2)), and note tracing in section 4(2);

Step 4   Assign values to property;

Step 5   Determine the value of deductions (s 4):
  • Debts and liabilities at V day (including contingent tax liabilities); and
  • The value of property (other than the matrimonial home) owned at the date of marriage, after deducting debts and liabilities (other than those related directly to the acquisition or significant improvement of the matrimonial home) calculated at the date of marriage;

Step 6   Calculate each spouse's Net Family Property (NFP), and determine the amount that is one-half the difference between the greater and the lesser (s 5(1)). *Note that this amount represents a debt owing, not an entitlement to property*; and

Step 7   Assess any claim for entitlement to more than one-half the difference (s 5(6)).

Some basic principles concerning equalization in the *FLA*

- **Section 2(10) and the *FLA* as a default regime:** The equalization scheme in Part I of the *FLA* is a "default regime." That is, it is possible for spouses to contract out of this default arrangement.

  Section 2(10) of the *FLA* permits spouses to contract out of the default regime, unless the statute precludes such contracting out (for example, see *FLA*, section 52(2), regarding marriage contracts). In this way, married spouses who do not wish to be bound by the provisions regarding equalization of property values at separation or divorce may negotiate their own separation agreement, including most aspects of marital property. In addition, spouses may enter into a marriage contract, including provisions about marital property that will take effect on family dissolution. In this context, consider the extent to which the analysis in the Supreme Court's decision in *Hartshorne v Hartshorne*, discussed in Chapter Five, should apply to marriage contracts in Ontario?

- **The matrimonial home:** The matrimonial home is taken into account in some calculations to determine the equalization amount (see ss 4 and 5 of the *FLA*). However, there are additional matters relating to the matrimonial home, particularly issues relating to *possession* of the matrimonial home (*Family Law Act*, Part II), that receive special treatment. These issues are discussed later in this chapter.

- **Equalization at death and divorce:** The *Family Law Act* provides for equalization at death, as well as in relation to family dissolution. Although this book does not deal with the detailed arrangements with respect to the death of one spouse, it is important to understand how spousal rights with respect to marital property constitute enforceable legal obligations.

  For example, in *Stone v Stone* (1999), 46 OR (3d) 31 (Sup Ct), a wealthy husband who knew that he was fatally ill transferred business assets worth $1.3 million (more than half his net worth) to his children, in an effort to avoid equalization with his wife at his death. Following his death, however, his widow successfully challenged the transfers as contrary to the *Fraudulent Conveyances Act*, RSO 1990, c F.29. According to the court, the *FLA* created a "creditor–debtor relationship which takes the form of an open or running account which becomes a settled account on separation or death," and that this concept was consistent with the goal of spouses sharing their net accretion in wealth during the marriage. See also Maurice Cullity, "Ethical Issues in Estate Practice" in *Special Lectures of the Law Society of Upper Canada* (Scarborough, ON: Carswell, 1996) at 425.

STEP 1 DETERMINING THE VALUATION DATE (V DAY): *FLA*, s 4

The *FLA*'s "inflexible" V day: The limited role of judicial discretion

The valuation date is defined in section 4 of the *Family Law Act* as the earliest of five dates:

- the date the spouses separate and there is no reasonable prospect that they will resume cohabitation;
- the date of a divorce order;
- the date of an order of nullity;
- the date when one spouse commences an action for improvident depletion of assets (s 5(3)) that is subsequently granted; or
- the date prior to the date of death of one spouse, leaving the other a surviving spouse.

In most cases of separation and divorce, the valuation date is the date when the spouses permanently separate.

Examples of V day determinations: The relevance of discretion?

In spite of the clear wording of section 4 in the Ontario statutes, the dissolution of a marriage may not occur at one point in time. Some spouses do not separate on one, clearly defined date. Instead, the breakdown of their marriage may occur over a period of days, weeks, or even months. Thus, in determining the valuation date, the first step in calculating the equalization payment, courts may have to exercise some discretion.

In *Oswell v Oswell* (1992), 43 RFL (3d) 180 (Ont CA), where evidence showed that the marriage had been deteriorating between September 1987 and March 1988, the trial judge held that the valuation date should be January 1988, and the Ontario Court of Appeal declined to interfere with the trial judge's determination.

In *Caratun v Caratun* (1987), 9 RFL (3d) 337 (Ont HC), the court also had to determine whether the date of separation could be the date when just one of the spouses (and not the other) had decided to leave with no prospect of resuming cohabitation. The wife, who did not accept the separation, argued that the date of separation should be the point at which *both* parties accepted that there would be no reconciliation. Thus, although the husband had left his wife for another woman just as he obtained his qualifications in dentistry, the wife gave evidence that she had maintained a hope that he would return to the marriage. It was more advantageous, in relation to her claim for equalization, to have a valuation date that was three years after the date when her husband left their home. In determining that the date of separation was the date when the husband left the marriage, however, the trial judge held that the date of separation should be the date when there was no reasonable prospect of resumption of cohabitation, that is, when the husband left with no intention to return. The court also decided that the wife's continued expectation of reconciliation was not reasonable in the circumstances.

In the result, it appears that the valuation date is the date when one spouse separates with no prospect of resuming marital cohabitation. It is not necessary for both spouses to hold this view. (*Caratun* is considered in more detail later in this chapter.)

Although these cases reveal that courts may sometimes exercise limited discretion in defining the valuation date pursuant to the Ontario statute, particularly when the factual context is unclear, the *Family Law Act* does not permit a court to exercise discretion to change a valuation date to ensure fairness between the spouses.

In *Russell v Russell* (1999), 1 RFL (5th) 235, the Saskatchewan Court of Appeal provided a comprehensive review of provincial statutes and their differing approaches to the definition of valuation date. In this context, the court noted (at 251) that the Ontario statute "dictates an inflexible valuation date."

This lack of scope for discretion in the Ontario statute was confirmed by the Supreme Court of Canada in *Rawluk v Rawluk* (1990), 28 RFL (3d) 86. In *Rawluk*, the wife left the matrimonial home in 1984, and the value of the property owned by her husband increased dramatically in the next few years as a result of rezoning. Clearly, it was in the wife's interest to have the property valued at a later date than the date of separation. Although there were differing views in the Supreme Court about the availability of a remedy for the wife in these circumstances, all members of the court accepted that it was not open to the court to alter the valuation date pursuant to section 4 of the *Family Law Act*, but they did not express a view about whether such increases in value might constitute "unconscionability" pursuant to section 5(6). (*Rawluk* is also considered in more detail later in this chapter.)

Notes and Questions

Law reform proposals to amend the *FLA*'s V day

The OLRC *Report on Family Property Law* reviewed the fact that most provincial statutes provide for valuation of family property at the date of trial, or they permit courts to exercise discretion to ensure that spouses share post-separation changes in the value of family property (see OLRC *Report* at 51–59). In doing so, the report noted (at 56–57) the problems of an inflexible date in the Ontario statute, but also drew attention to the problems of uncertainty created by the exercise of judicial discretion pursuant to other provincial statutes:

> The different models for determining a valuation date adopted in common law provinces represent varied attempts to resolve the tension between the need to achieve consistency and predictability, and the desire to ensure that individuals receive fair treatment. In British Columbia, the great flexibility [under the statute] adopted by the courts has generated criticism of the inconsistencies that have resulted. In Ontario the rigidity

of the valuation date appears to have redirected litigation into the factual question of when separation occurs, or into trust claims. This has the disadvantage of embroiling the courts in complicated factual and legal issues which may bear little relation to the real problem faced by the parties — a substantial fluctuation in the value of assets accumulated during the relationship.

Responding to these problems, the OLRC reviewed a number of suggested solutions.

One solution might be to delay the date of valuation until the date of trial, but the *Report* concluded that this change might have an unwelcome impact on litigation tactics, with the spouse negatively affected by falling or rising markets seeking to delay the trial.

Another solution would permit courts to exercise discretion to choose an appropriate valuation date, taking into account whether the change in value reflected market valuations or efforts on the part of a spouse. However, the report rejected this option because it would require courts to determine, with some precision, the cause of changes in valuation.

In the end, the *Report* concluded (at 59) that none of these options was viable, and thus recommended no change to the definition of "valuation date" in section 4. Instead, the *Report* suggested (at 68–69) that these problems be addressed by other means, specifically by amendments to section 5(6) to extend the court's discretion to make unequal equalization payments. Do you agree that amendments to the statutory definition of valuation date are not appropriate? Why, or why not? You may wish to reconsider these issues in relation to section 5(6), discussed later in this chapter.

Approaches to defining the valuation date in other provinces

By contrast with the Ontario statute, legislation in other provinces and territories often expressly permits the use of judicial discretion in defining the date of separation.

For example, the trial judge in *Bartolozzi v Bartolozzi*, [1992] NWTR 347 (Terr Ct) exercised discretion pursuant to the statute to value the matrimonial home at the date of trial, rather than the date of separation, so that both parties would share in the increase in value between the date of separation and the date of trial. (For other similar examples, see *Pisiak v Pisiak* (2000), 1 RFL (5th) 419 (Sask QB); *Caldwell v Caldwell*, 1999 BCCA 389; *Thornett v Thornett*, 1999 BCCA 437; and *Reardon (Smith) v Smith*, 1999 NSCA 147.)

Balancing fairness and certainty in relation to V day: *Fleming v Fleming*

Consider this situation:

A husband argued that the date of separation would have occurred much earlier if he had known of his wife's extramarital affairs. He alleged that she had engaged in these affairs between 1986 and their separation in 1999. Do these facts suggest a need for the exercise of judicial discretion?

In *Fleming v Fleming* (2001), 19 RFL (5th) 274 (Ont Sup Ct), the court rejected the husband's argument, holding that there was no discretion pursuant to the Ontario *FLA* to alter the valuation date. In addition, the court held that the wife had no duty to disclose extramarital affairs during the marriage, and that her failure to do so was not tortious.

Does the court's approach achieve an appropriate balance between fairness and certainty?

To what extent may this lack of judicial discretion operate to the advantage of a spouse who knows details of the *FLA*, who has an intention to separate, and who then chooses the appropriate date for separation on the basis of rising or falling prices in the stock market or in real estate? You may wish to reconsider this example in the discussion later in this chapter about section 5(6) of the *Family Law Act*.

Additional Resources

Berend Hovius & Timothy Youdan, *The Law of Family Property* (Scarborough, ON: Carswell, 1991).

V Jennifer MacKinnon, "Property Valuation Issues in the Common Law Provinces: Common Law?" (1989) 17 RFL (3d) 255.

James McLeod, "Annotation of *Caratun v. Caratun*" (1987) 9 RFL (3d) 338.

STEP 2   DEFINING "PROPERTY": *FLA*, SECTION 4

> It seems to me ... that when the word appears in legislation defined in the broadest possible way, the limits are to be found through a consideration of the scope of that legislation, and the objects it seeks to accomplish. If the definition of the right or rights as property is consistent with the scheme of the legislation and advances its objects, then it should be so defined. If either of those attributes is absent, then, unless the right or rights under consideration fall with a category that has been legally recognized as property heretofore, it should not be so defined. (*Pallister v Pallister* (1990), 29 RFL (3d) 395 (Ont Gen Div) at 405)

"Property" in the *Family Law Act*: An overview of issues

The definition of "property" in section 4 of Ontario's *Family Law Act* encompasses a wide range of interests in real and personal property. In relation to this definition, it is important to note the following:

- By contrast with provinces where family dissolution requires the division of "family assets," the definition in Part I of the Ontario statute appears designed to capture much more than "family property" for purposes of equalization (subject to exclusions and deductions, as defined);

- The definition also "includes" some powers of appointment, property over which a person may revoke a disposition, and pension interests, but the wording of this section makes clear that other unnamed interests may also be "included" such as shares or the goodwill of a company; and

- According to Hovius and Youdan, the meaning of the term "property" must be derived from the context and purposes of Part I of the *Family Law Act* (see at 242). Recall section 5(7) as well as the Preamble of the *FLA* — to what extent do these provisions encourage the inclusion of most kinds of proprietary interests?

These factors mean that the definition of property in section 4 must be interpreted broadly. In this context, it is not surprising that spouses have engaged in litigation about the appropriateness of including "things of value" as property for purposes of equalization. Three kinds of "property" claims have generally been pursued:

- In the first years after enactment of the *Family Law Act* in 1986, there were a number of cases about professional degrees and whether they should be considered property and valued for equalization purposes. In 1992, however, the Ontario Court of Appeal confirmed in *Caratun* that a professional licence or a right to practise did not constitute "property" within section 4 of the *FLA*. In addition, however, there were a number of cases in which the issue was whether property capable of producing a "future stream of income" (such as income from trust funds) constituted "property";

- Second, an issue arose about whether the definition of "property" in section 4 included beneficial (equitable) ownership as well as legal title. This issue was resolved by the Supreme Court of Canada in *Rawluk* in 1990, when the Court held (with a strong dissenting judgment) that trust doctrines were available to married spouses in calculating equalization; and

- Although the definition of "property" in section 4 of the *FLA* specifically included some pension entitlement for purposes of an equalization claim, the statute provided no guidance about how such an entitlement should be valued, a matter that created controversy for family law clients and actuarial challenges for courts. This issue was addressed by the Law Commission of Ontario, and amendments were introduced to the *FLA* and the *Pension Benefits Act* in 2009 in Ontario in an attempt to resolve pension issues in the context of family dissolution.

These issues are briefly reviewed in this section. In examining them, it is important to take account of the broader context of economic adjustment at family dissolution in order to understand why some spouses pursued these claims about the definition of property in the *FLA*. You may also want to consider whether, or to what extent, the courts' decisions have fostered the goal of spousal equality in section 5(7).

1. "Property" and professional degrees

The Background to *Caratun v Caratun* in the Ontario Court of Appeal

For a few years between the enactment of the *Family Law Act* in 1986 and the Court of Appeal's decision in *Caratun* in 1992, there were a number of lower court decisions, one of which was also appealed to the Court of Appeal: *Linton v Linton*.

In *Corless v Corless* (1987), 5 RFL (3d) 256 (Ont Unif Fam Ct), the court held that the husband's law degree was property within the meaning of section 4. However, the court also decided that this property had no value for purposes of calculating the wife's NFP, because it could not be exchanged or transferred, being personal only to the holder. As a result, the court awarded spousal support to compensate the wife, taking into account that she had postponed her own career plans in order to assist her husband in his legal career.

By contrast, in the trial decision of *Caratun v Caratun* (1987), 9 RFL (3d) 337 (Ont HC), the court engaged in a detailed analysis of "new property," and thoroughly canvassed the Act's provisions to determine how best to reward the wife's contribution to the husband's acquisition of his professional dental qualifications. The facts in *Caratun* suggested that the husband had taken advantage of his wife's generosity and unquestioning commitment in order to immigrate to Canada and acquire a professional degree, and that he then abandoned her for a new relationship just a few days after obtaining his qualifications. In the result, the trial court held that the licence and right to practise were property. However, after canvassing possible approaches to implementing the Act, the judge decided to segregate this part of the property from the equalization accounting and assess it in terms of trust principles. On this basis, the wife was awarded a lump sum of $30,000 for her equitable interest relating to the acquisition of the husband's licence.

As will be discussed, however, the Ontario Court of Appeal held that the licence and right to practise did not constitute property under the *Family Law Act*. Instead, the court held that the wife's contribution should be compensated by an award of compensatory spousal support, using the support provisions of the *Divorce Act* (now s 15.2(6)) or similar provisions of the *Family Law Act* (particularly ss 33(9)(j) and (l)(ii)). Two other Ontario decisions had earlier adopted this support-based approach. See *Keast v Keast* (1986), 1 RFL (3d) 401 (Ont Dist Ct) [a medical degree]; and *Linton v Linton* (1988), 11 RFL (3d) 444 (Ont HC) and (1990), 30 RFL (3d) 1 (Ont CA) [a doctoral degree].

Policy Issues Concerning Professional Degrees as "Property"

What are the competing policy issues in these cases? Why did the claimants (all wives who had supported the acquisition of professional degrees by their husbands) argue that the degrees constituted "property" pursuant to section 4 of the *FLA*, thereby requiring that the value be included as part of the equalization? To what extent does this characterization of degrees as "property" foster the purposes of the *FLA* and particularly section 5(7)?

What concerns on the part of the courts resulted in decisions that these wives' contributions to their husbands' degrees should be recognized by orders for compensatory spousal support rather than property? In considering this question, note the following issues identified by the trial court in *Linton* (at 455):

> There is a larger and broader reason why professional licences or degrees should not be treated as property. If the courts hold that the lawyer's right to practise, or the doctor's or dentist's licence, is property, where are the limits for such a holding within the framework of the employment patterns of our community? These professional qualifications do nothing more nor less than enable their possessors to work in a particular occupation and earn an income. How, then, can the law draw any rational and logical dividing lines between occupations when deciding which kind of job qualification will attract property assessment under [the *Family Law Act*]? In other words, if the so-called professional person is to be caught..., why not any other person who is engaged in gainful employment? ... [W]here is the difference in substance between the position of the lawyer and that of an electrician or welder or plumber? All of these latter tradesmen are required to go through lengthy apprenticeship or training programs, with their spouses being required to make the same sacrifices as the professional's spouse along the way, and most of these tradesmen will remain as lucratively paid employees for the rest of their lives.
>
> If a right to practise as a professional person is property, then, logically, a right to work or, ultimately, any and every job must be considered as property. There is, I submit, no evidence in the [Act] that this was the intention of the legislature. To me, the legislature intended the courts, in interpreting and applying the [Act], to apply the existing common law criteria for property in identifying the net family properties of spouses....

What concerns influenced the courts' conclusion that an award of spousal support was more appropriate than a characterization of a degree as "property," in relation to the overall purposes of the *FLA*? How important is it to ensure that the *FLA* equalization process is simple and efficient? To what extent might differences between the finality of equalization, by contrast with the potential variability of spousal support awards, influence a court's conclusion about the meaning of "property" in section 4? As you review the appellate decision in *Caratun*, consider how it may affect family bargaining at separation or divorce:

Caratun v Caratun
(1992), 42 RFL (3d) 113 (Ont CA)

> ... The reasons of the trial judge make it quite clear that Dr. Caratun's primary objective in marrying Mrs. Caratun and fathering their child was to assist him in immigrating to North America to practise dentistry. Mrs. Caratun worked extremely hard over a number of years in Israel and in

Canada to assist Dr. Caratun in attaining his ultimate objective. Two days after attaining that objective, he rejected Mrs. Caratun as his wife, at a time when family assets were next to non-existent but his future income-earning ability was substantial.

Facts such as these raise difficult legal questions, given the purpose of the [*Family Law Act*], on the one hand, and its specific provisions, on the other. The combining of spousal efforts over a number of years to provide for the education and professional qualification of one spouse is not unusual in our society. The inevitable result, if there is a separation on attaining the joint objective, is that one family member is left with no assets and often very little in the way of educational or professional qualifications with which to sustain herself or himself in the future. The extreme unfairness of the situation is patent, but the possibility of a legal remedy is far from settled law.

DENTAL LICENCE AS PROPERTY

Mrs. Caratun's position at trial, which was accepted by the trial judge, was that Dr. Caratun's dental licence is property within the meaning of that word as defined in s. 4(1)....

That definition is broadly framed, and includes all conceivable types of property in the traditional common law sense. However, it does not, by its terms, extend the meaning of property beyond those limits. The contrary argument is that in construing that definition one must keep in mind the [Act's] policy of marriage partnership, which requires, on final separation, the equal division of wealth accumulated during the marriage; and that a licence to practise a particular profession constitutes wealth in the matrimonial context....

The court reviewed the lower court decisions on this issue in *Keast* and *Caratun*, as well as a number of American authorities, and stated (at 121):

In determining the issue of whether a professional licence constitutes "property," the cases and the numerous articles written on the subject concentrate primarily on two aspects of the problem: first, the nature or characterization of a licence, and, second, the difficulty of valuing a licence in the family property context.

CHARACTERIZATION OF LICENCE

The broad definition of property in the [Act] clearly encompasses many forms of intangibles — a classification into which a licence must fall if it is to be considered property. The common law has never had any difficulty in dealing with property evidenced by pieces of paper representing bundles of rights — such as a share certificate with its attendant rights to dividends, voting privileges, and distribution of assets on corporate dissolution. If a licence to practise a profession is property, what are its attendant rights? Apart from possible benefits, such as the right to join professional groups and clubs — which are not relevant in this context — the only real right conferred on the holder of the licence is a right to work in a particular profession. That right, assuming it is held at the time of separation, is a present right to work in the future, and it will continue for as long as the holder of the right is professionally and personally able to perform the activity involved. It is the nature of the right given by the licence which, in my view, causes insurmountable difficulties in treating such a licence as property for matrimonial purposes. Those difficulties arise, first, because it is not a right which is transferable; second, because it requires the personal efforts of the holder in order to be of any value in the future; and, third, because the only difference between such a licence and any other right to work is in its exclusivity....

The court considered each of these three difficulties. In relation to the issue of transferability, the court distinguished a licence from a professional practice created by the holder of a licence, stating (at 121) that "[t]he practice itself is clearly capable of transfer for value, although the market is limited to other licensees." On this basis, the court concluded that rights or things that are inherently non-transferable do not constitute property in any traditional sense. In examining the requirement of personal efforts of the licensee, the court suggested (at 122) that it was not possible to include in net family property "work to be performed by either spouse in the future". Instead, such efforts were to be compensated by support awards:

> The policy of the FLA emphasizes principles of partnership during marriage, and self-sufficiency following its termination. When the marriage ends, the partnership ends. Placing a value on future labours of either spouse for purposes of the equalization payment would frustrate those policy objectives.

The court also identified the problem that recognition of a licence as property would require the assessment of other kinds of work as well, concluding that it was not appropriate to consider these qualifications as property for purposes of equalization. The court then addressed (at 123) concerns about valuation of the licence:

> It is clear from the considerations referred to above that there are substantial difficulties, both practical and conceptual, in treating licences as "property." In addition, the valuation of such a right would be unfairly speculative in the matrimonial context. A myriad of contingencies, including inclination, probability of success in practice of the profession, length of physical and mental capability to perform the duties of the profession, competition within the profession, and many others, all render a fair valuation of the licence unusually difficult. But a further potential inequity arises: support orders may be varied if circumstances change, but no amendment of an equalization payment is possible regardless of changed circumstances....

After reviewing the trial judge's approach to valuing the licence and other possible methods of valuation in such cases, the court held (at 124):

> In the matrimonial context, the fallacy lies in treating a licence as property on valuation date, when most of its value depends on the personal labour of the licensed spouse after the termination of the relationship. That future labour does not constitute anything earned or existing at the valuation date.
> For all of the above reasons, it is my view that a professional licence does not constitute property within the meaning of [s. 4 of the *Family Law Act*].

The court reviewed the trial judge's conclusion that the appellant's dental licence was property, and then held that the licence was subject to a constructive trust in favour of the respondent in an amount of $30,000, an amount reflecting the value of the respondent's contribution to acquisition of the appellant's degree. The Court of Appeal concluded that it was not appropriate to segregate the value of the licence from the equalization process, and then reviewed the principles of constructive trust (including *Rathwell v Rathwell*, [1978] 2 SCR 436, and *Pettkus v Becker*, [1980] 2 SCR 834), distinguishing these and other cases from the facts in *Caratun* and the claim based on the licence to practise.

In the result, the appellate court concluded that if the licence was not "property," there was "nothing to which the constructive trust could attach." The court also considered section 5(6) and the possibility of awarding an unequal equalization payment. However, section 5(6) is also available only where there is property, and so it was not available to Mrs. Caratun. In the end, the court awarded compensatory support in the amount of $30,000, the sum initially determined by the trial judge to reflect Mrs. Caratun's contribution to the attaining of a dental licence on the part of her former husband.

Notes and Questions

The policy debate about *Caratun*

Although the Ontario Court of Appeal confirmed in 1992 that professional degrees (and other workplace qualifications) do not constitute "property" pursuant to section 4 of the *FLA*, the policy issues raised by this case continue to be reflected in spouses' claims, as they struggle for access to post-separation or post-divorce resources. As noted in Chapter Five, there are often significant and detrimental consequences of family dissolution. In this context, the issue of sharing the value of professional degrees (and the incomes flowing from them) is much more than a technical question. Moreover, it may be relevant that spousal support (in the late 1980s, at the time when these professional degree cases were being litigated) was relatively low in amount and short term in duration.

In this context, consider these two contrasting comments about professional degrees as "property":

> [Claims to treat professional degrees as property arise as "an argument for justice," and a spouse's earning capacity may be more valuable than any assets at marriage breakdown, an argument that suggests that professional degrees should be included as "property." By contrast, however, because section 4 refers to some forms of "non-traditional property" but without including professional degrees, it is not appropriate for courts to include such assets as "property." In addition, Ontario's rigid equalization process (by contrast with statutes permitting judges to exercise discretion) makes recognition of degrees difficult:]
>
>> It is one thing to characterize degrees, etc., as property so that they are included in the pool of assets over which a court may exercise a discretionary jurisdiction. It is another thing to include them as property in a system, like the *Family Law Act*, where the value of relevant property is put into a formula that produces an entitlement subject only to a very limited judicial discretion.
>
> (Berend Hovius & Timothy Youdan, *The Law of Family Property* (Scarborough, ON: Carswell, 1991) at 276–278 and 279)

[In *Linton v. Linton*, Justice Killeen concluded that] a limited reading of the meaning of the word property was appropriate given that the *Family Law Act* did not create a full economic partnership, but only a form of partnership, in which the equalization payment permitted "a narrow and deferred sharing of accretions in value to defined spousal properties." ...

An alternative approach would recognize that the meaning of property cannot be found in lists of the resources, tangible or intangible, that have been recognized as property in the past. Property is not things or rights, but relationships.... So the court, in deciding whether Mr. Caratun's career asset is property, could inquire about the appropriate relationship envisioned by the *Family Law Act* between him and his former wife with respect to sharing in the benefits of his right to practise dentistry, a right that he acquired with her help, although only he could exercise it....

Could the court in *Caratun* have found any guidance in the handling of similar problems when a business partnership ends? The *Partnerships Act* defines partnership property as "all property and rights and interests in property originally brought into the partnership stock or acquired, whether by purchase or otherwise, on account of the firm, or for the purposes and in the course of the partnership business." On dissolution of a business partnership, the Act provides for distribution of the partnership property, after payment of the firm's debts, in accordance with each partner's share in the partnership. In addition, where one partner pays a premium to another on entering the partnership and the partnership is dissolved before the expiration of its term, the court may order repayment of all or some of the premium, unless, *inter alia*, the dissolution is wholly or chiefly due to the misconduct of the partner who paid the premium....

It does not require much imagination to put Mrs. Caratun in the place of the wronged partner, who paid a premium to join the partnership, expecting to share in the future profits, but finds out that she had been the victim of fraud and misrepresentation.... [C]ourts could interpret the Act as giving one partner a lien on future profits of the other, given that its purpose is to provide a remedy for individuals whose investment plans go awry because they have chosen an untrustworthy partner....

Among the many meanings that one can draw from the result in *Caratun*, one stands out: a woman who sacrifices her own career opportunities in order to improve those of her husband is making a bad investment.... (Margaret McCallum, "*Caratun v. Caratun*: It Seems That We Are Not All Realists Yet" (1994) 7 CJWL 197 at 205–207)

Which of these assessments is more consistent with the concept of no fault divorce? Or the goals of equality in relation to property sharing? Are these two comments directed to the same issues? Is it important to separate ideas about the purposes of the *FLA* from the means used to achieve them?

Comparative approaches to property and professional degrees

In British Columbia, where courts have greater judicial discretion with respect to family property issues, judges nonetheless concluded that professional degrees do not constitute "property". See *Johnson v Johnson* (1988), 16 RFL (3d) 113 (BCCA). However, a trial court decided that a commercial fishing licence did constitute "property" because it was not linked to knowledge or ability unique to its holder. See *Seymour v Seymour* (1992), 71 BCLR (2d) 218 (SC). Do these decisions, which are similar to others in

Canadian provinces, suggest that the issue about whether to include professional degrees as property is not just based on the nature of the equalization process in Ontario? Are there more fundamental concerns?

In considering this question, it may be helpful to take account of cases about property and professional degrees that were litigated in a number of U.S. states in recent decades. For example, in *Morgan v Morgan* 366 NYS 2d 977 (Sup Ct 1975), a New York court ordered a husband (whose wife had supported him through college and law school) to support her attendance at medical school after their marriage ended, an approach later characterized as the "equivalent opportunity" approach. However, an appeal court later allowed the husband's appeal. See 383 NYS 2d 343 (Sup Ct App Div 1976).

Several cases in the state of New York have interpreted a legislative provision requiring "equitable distribution" of property to include professional degrees. See *O'Brien v O'Brien* 498 NYS 2d 743 (Ct App 1985); *McSparron v McSparron* 639 NYS 2d 265 (Ct App 1995); and *Grunfeld v Grunfeld* 709 NYS 2d 486 (Ct App 2000). In *McSparron*, the court recognized problems of valuation, but concluded that they did not preclude characterizing professional degrees as property (at 286):

> The existence of these complications ... is not a sound reason to introduce nettlesome legal fictions or to excise an asset to which the nontitled spouse has contributed from the marital estate. As we stated in *O'Brien*, the complexity of calculating the present value of a partially exploited professional license is no more difficult than the problem of computing wrongful death damages or the loss of earning potential that is occasioned by a particular injury.... Nor does it lead to significantly more speculation than is involved in the now-routine task of valuing a professional practice for the purpose of making a distributive award.

By contrast with New York, other American states have tended to exclude consideration of professional degrees as property, an approach recommended by the American Law Institute. According to the ALI, degrees should not be considered "property" but should instead be taken into account in assessing entitlement to spousal support:

> [Our] observations relate to a broader theme from which the differences between property and [spousal support] emerge. The law has treated [spousal support] as appropriate in only a subset of divorces in which there are circumstances ... that justify equitable adjustments in post-marriage income between former spouses. In contrast, marital property claims are normally viewed as property entitlements created by the marriage alone, even if subject to equitable adjustment. The principle underlying this difference is that marriage creates property entitlements to certain *things* acquired during it, but does not create property entitlements against the *person* of the other spouse.... [The recommendation that property should not include degrees] therefore reflects the longstanding distinction between claims on things and claims on another person's attributes.... (American Law Institute, *Principles of the Law of Family Dissolution* (St. Paul, MN: American Law Institute Publishers, 2002) at 776.)

Which of these U.S. approaches is most similar to the Ontario Court of Appeal's decision in *Caratun*? What are the advantages and disadvantages of these different approaches? Consider the ALI's distinction between entitlements to *things* and entitlements against the *person* in relation to McCallum's critique of *Caratun*. Does your assessment suggest that the goal of spousal equality in section 5(7) of the *FLA* might be better achieved by a principle of "equitable distribution," as exists in the New York statute? Why, or why not?

"Property" and "future income streams": *Brinkos v Brinkos* and *DaCosta v DaCosta*

As the professional degree cases reveal, there is some concern about including as "property" a qualification that may produce income in the future, particularly because of problems of valuation. Yet, in some other factual circumstances, courts have concluded that arrangements that result in future income streams may constitute "property." For example, in *Brinkos v Brinkos* (1989), 20 RFL (3d) 445, the Ontario Court of Appeal allowed a husband's appeal concerning whether to include in his wife's NFP the value of her entitlement to income for life from a trust fund. The trial judge had concluded that a future interest in income from property did not constitute "property" pursuant to section 4 of the *FLA*.

In *Brinkos*, the wife's father had established a bank account for his daughter when she was a child, and its value in 1965 (the date of marriage) was $224,475. A few years later, the father added contributions to the account in the amount of $71,750. In 1972, the wife settled a trust with her mother and brother as trustees, in which she was granted an inalienable life interest in the net income. The trust was then valued at $305,175, and in 1980, the father made a further gift to the trust of $100,000. In 1982, at the date of separation, the trust was worth $609,933.

The Court of Appeal held that the life interest in the trust constituted "property" for purposes of the *FLA*. However, the wife was allowed to deduct the value at marriage as pre-marriage property ($224,475), and she was permitted to exclude the gifts from her father (a third party) after the date of the marriage ($71,750 and $100,000), in calculating the present value of her right to the trust income.

Consider also *DaCosta v DaCosta* (1992), 40 RFL (3d) 216 (Ont CA), in which the Court of Appeal upheld the trial judge's decision that the husband's contingent interest in an estate constituted "property" under the *FLA*.

In *DaCosta*, the husband was an adopted great grandson of a man who died in Pennsylvania in 1923, leaving a substantial estate. After 1972, when the state of Pennsylvania first granted equal testamentary treatment to natural and adopted children, the husband was successful in his claim for recognition as a beneficiary of the estate. He was also entitled to share in the distribution of capital from the estate on the death of the only surviving grandchild, who was 87 years of age at the time of the husband's appeal to the Court of Appeal.

As noted, the Court of Appeal upheld the trial judge's decision that this contingent interest was property for purposes of calculating the husband's NFP, although the court permitted a modest discount of the value to recognize the possibility that the husband might die before the surviving grandchild. Thus, instead of valuing the contingent interest at $596,783, the court concluded that a value of $530,730 (and with a similar discount for the value of the pre-marriage deduction) was appropriate.

To what extent do these decisions suggest different approaches for trust interests and contingent testamentary interests, by contrast with professional degrees? Why were the courts able to value the interests in *Brinkos* and *DaCosta*, while holding that it was difficult to do so with respect to professional degrees? How would you characterize the differences between these two groups of cases?

"Property" in relation to disability benefits

In relation to issues about future income streams, consider the following decision.

Lowe v Lowe
(2006), 22 RFL (6th) 438 (Ont CA)

At the date of separation, a husband was receiving two monthly disability benefits under the *Workers Compensation Act*. One was based on the extent to which a workplace injury had impaired his ability to work (payable for life), while the other was a supplement for his low income which would end at age 65. Because the spouses could not agree on the treatment of these payments for equalization purposes, the wife applied to the court, and the applications judge held that the capitalized value of the husband's future benefits should be included in his NFP.

On appeal by the husband, the Ontario Court of Appeal reviewed a number of lower court decisions and held that disability benefits are more appropriately considered as income rather than "property," and that they are available for purposes of spousal support rather than being included as "property" in the equalization process. Relying in particular on *Pallister v Pallister* (1990), 29 RFL (3d) 395 (Ont Gen Div) and *Hamilton v Hamilton*, [2005] OJ No 3050 (Sup Ct), the Court of Appeal stated (at paras 15–24):

> **[15]** [According to *Pallister*, the] disability pension bore no relationship to the marriage partnership but rather arose because of a disability that impeded the recipient's capacity to earn a livelihood. It followed ... that the stream of benefits to be received post-separation should not be capitalized and included as family property for purposes of equalization. The benefits would be taken into consideration with respect to spousal support, but they fell outside the category of "property" and could be distinguished from a pension earned as part of a spouse's remuneration during the marriage....

The court also agreed with the result in *Hamilton* that disability benefits should not be considered family property for equalization purposes.

> **[17]** I agree with [the statement in *Hamilton*] that "the purpose of the disability payments is to replace in whole or in part the income that the person would have earned had he or she been able to work in the normal course." This makes disability benefits "more comparable to a future

income stream based on personal service" than to either a retirement pension plan [expressly included in section 4] or to a future stream of payments from a trust [as in *Brinkos*]. [The Court distinguished disability benefits that are part and parcel of an overall employee pension benefit plan totally funded by a company, and continued:] Ordinarily, however, disability benefits replace income during the working life of the employee and therefore are appropriately treated as income for purposes of equalization and spousal support. [In this way,] a disability pension is simply the flip side of employment or self-employment income....

[18] I also agree ... that disability benefits are distinguishable from other pensions in that they cannot realistically be valued if not in pay as of valuation day. It would be anomalous to include as property a disability benefit in pay the day before separation but to exclude a disability benefit not in pay until the day after separation. It seems to me that this serves to reinforce the point that disability benefits are, for purposes of family property and support, more readily dealt with as income rather than as property. They should be taken into account in relation to spousal support but excluded from consideration in relation to equalization of family property....

[24] [Finally, the Court rejected the inclusion of the lifetime disability benefit, even though it was a fixed entitlement:] It seems to me preferable from the perspective of clarity and predictability to treat all disability benefits the same whether they are calculated strictly in terms of lost income or as compensation for impairment to earning capacity.... In the end, the central point is that disability benefits represent income replacement and, from the perspective of family property and spousal support, are more appropriately treated on the same basis as income for employment.

Consider this situation also:

The husband became entitled at age 56 to a disability pension under the federal government's pension plan some years after he left the civil service. If he had not experienced the disability, he would have been required by the pension plan to wait until age 60 for an unreduced pension. Should this "disability pension" be considered "property"?

In *Maphangoh v Maphangoh*, 2007 ONCA 449, the trial judge's conclusion, that the husband's entitlement had the attributes of a retirement pension rather than a disability benefit, was upheld by the Court of Appeal. Distinguishing *Lowe*, the court stated that the disability pension was essentially an entitlement to take early retirement without penalty.

As these cases suggest, issues about disability benefits and retirement pensions must be carefully assessed. Pensions and related benefits are discussed in more detail later in this section.

Property in reproductive material

In *JCM v ANA*, 2012 BCSC 584, the B.C. Supreme Court considered a dispute between former lesbian partners, each of whom had conceived a child using the same anonymous donor sperm. In this way, their children were biologically related. When they separated, however, a dispute arose about whether 13 unused sperm straws constituted "property." The parties had negotiated a separation agreement that resolved all issues except with respect to these remaining sperm straws, held in a storage facility in British Columbia.

JCM had formed a new lesbian relationship with TL, and TL wished to have a child using the anonymous donor sperm, so that her child and the child of JCM would be biologically related. The anonymous sperm donor in the United States, from whom the sperm had originally been purchased by JCM and ANA, was no longer able to be identified, so that TL's wish required access to the 13 remaining sperm straws from the original purchase. In this context, JCM offered to purchase ANA's half interest in the sperm straws, but ANA refused, indicating that she wished to have the sperm straws destroyed. Thus, the court concluded that it was necessary to determine whether the sperm straws were "property."

The court cited an earlier Canadian decision, *CC v AW*, 2005 ABQB 290, in which a court had concluded that sperm, which had been donated by a known donor and which had resulted in fertilized embryos, were chattels that entitled the donee to use as she wished. The court also reviewed cases and academic literature in the United States and in the United Kingdom, and concluded that the court was "ill-equipped to handle moral and philosophical arguments" (at para 68), and that the "sperm is the property of the parties" (at para 69). As the court noted, JCM and ANA had treated the sperm as "property," as had the U.S. vendor (Xytex) and the B.C. storage facility (Genesis) (at para 69).

Although the court referred to section 7 of the *Assisted Human Reproduction Act*, which prohibits the purchase of sperm or ova from a donor in Canada, the court held that this provision did not dictate whether or not the gametes in this case constituted "property." Such purchases are legal in some U.S. states.

In the end, the court concluded (at para 75) that the gametes "should be treated as property for the purpose of dividing them upon the dissolution of the spousal relationship of the parties." The court also rejected a need to consider the best interests of the children in this case, and held that the issue in *Pratten* (the disclosure issue relating to donated sperm: see Chapter Three) was not relevant to this case. Thus, the court divided ownership of the sperm straws equally, which permitted ANA to destroy 6 sperm straws; however, the court ordered JCM to purchase the remaining one-half of the 13th sperm straw if it was not possible to divide it between JCM and ANA.

Is the outcome in *JCM v ANA* appropriate in relation to the need to define entitlement to "property" issues at separation? Should reproductive material be treated as "property" at separation just as other household goods and assets? Is there a need for legislative action in relation to such family law cases? For critiques, see J Wasylciw & S Romaniuk, "Commodifying Human Life: The *Numerus Clausus* Principle and Unconventional Property Rights" (2013) 2:1 International Law Research 102; and E Nelson, "Comparative Perspectives on the Regulation of Assisted Reproductive Technologies in the United Kingdom and Canada" (2006) 43 Alta L Rev 1023.

In *JCM v ANA*, the court also relied on a recent case in England, in which six male plaintiffs successfully sued a storage facility for damages for negligence when their sperm was destroyed after a malfunctioning in the storage facility. Each of these plaintiffs had provided sperm for storage after they had been diagnosed with cancer and were scheduled to undergo chemotherapy (a treatment which might render them infertile). In *Jonathan Yearworth & Ors v North Bristol NHS Trust*, [2009] 2 All ER 986, [2009] EWCA Civ 37 (Civil), the court departed from earlier precedents, which had held that a human body and substances generated by it are incapable of being owned. In this case, the court concluded that the common law must keep up with scientific advancements. The *Yearworth* decision was recently cited with approval in *Lam v University of British Columbia*, 2013 BCSC 2094; 2015 BCCA 2, a case in which these courts concluded that sperm in the university's super freezer was "property" and thus "goods" to which the *Warehouse Receipt Act* was applicable. (This statute held the university liable for the loss of sperm in its facility.)

Are there differences between claims for negligence in cases such as *Yearworth* and *Lam* on one hand, and issues about "property" at the breakdown of a conjugal relationship on the other? Is it appropriate to apply a definition of "property" in a torts action to a family law matter at separation? Why or why not?

Consider also the extent to which *JCM v ANA* may be used as a precedent with respect to "property" at separation in Ontario: how might the requirements of Ontario's *Family Law Act* affect the reasoning in this case? Does *Caratun* suggest a different outcome in Ontario? Is there a need for legislative action in Ontario, and if so, how should it be formulated? For some suggestions (especially about donor sperm), see Jessica Lee, "Sperm Donor Anonymity: A Call for Legislative Reform" (2014) 33:1 Can Fam LQ 1.

Additional Resources

Nicholas Bala, "Recognizing Spousal Contributions to the Acquisition of Degrees, Licenses, and Other Career Assets: Toward Compensatory Support" (1989) 8 Can J Fam L 23.

Heidi Foster, "Law and Ethics Meet: When Couples Fight over Their Frozen Embryos" (2000) 21:4 Journal of Andrology 512.

Alicia Brokars Kelly, "Sharing a Piece of the Future Post-Divorce: Toward a More Equitable Distribution of Professional Goodwill" (1998–1999) 51 Rutgers L Rev 569.

Joseph McKnight, "Defining Property Subject to Division at Divorce" (1989) 23:2 Fam LQ 193.

James McLeod, "Annotation of *Brinkos v. Brinkos*" (1989) 20 RFL (3d) 445.

James McLeod, "Annotation of *Caratun v. Caratun*" (1992) 42 RFL (3d) 113.

Bonnie Steinbock, "Sperm as Property" (1995) 6:2 Stan L & Pol'y Rev 57.

Lenore Weitzman, "Equity and Equality in Divorce Settlements: A Comparative Analysis of Property and Maintenance Awards in the United States and England" in John Eekelaar & Sanford Katz, eds, *The Resolution of Family Conflict: Comparative Legal Perspectives* (Toronto: Butterworths, 1984) 461.

Scott Willoughby, "Professional Licenses as Marital Property: Responses to Some of *O'Brien*'s Unanswered Questions" (1987) 73 Cornell L Rev 13.

2. "Property" and beneficial (equitable) ownership

... [A]s the development of the law ... has shown, the principles of unjust enrichment, coupled with the possible remedy of a constructive trust, provide a much less artificial, more comprehensive and more principled basis [than the resulting trust] to address the wide variety of circumstances that lead to claims arising out of domestic partnerships.... Claims for compensation as well as for property interests may be addressed. Contributions of all kinds and made at all times may be justly considered. The equities of the particular case are considered transparently and according to principle.... (*Kerr v Baranow*, 2011 SCC 10 at para 28)

Married Spouses and the Use of (Equitable) Unjust Enrichment Principles

As noted earlier in this chapter, it was the dissenting judgment in *Murdoch v Murdoch* that used the constructive trust to support an interest in family property for Mrs. Murdoch. Then, although a majority of the Supreme Court of Canada later adopted this approach in *Rathwell v Rathwell*, the concept of unjust enrichment and the remedy of constructive trust were not generally utilized by married spouses because of their access to marital property legislation enacted in the provinces in the late 1970s. However, as will be discussed in the last section of this chapter, the Supreme Court confirmed the use of the constructive trust to achieve "equity" for cohabiting couples in *Pettkus v Becker* in 1980. In this way, two separate property regimes initially seemed to be in place at family dissolution:

- Statutory marital property regimes for married spouses; and
- The use of equity and constructive trusts for cohabiting couples.

In this context, however, the Supreme Court considered a case in 1990, *Rawluk v Rawluk*, in which the wife claimed that the definition of "property" in section 4 of the *FLA* included equitable as well as legal proprietary interests. As a result, the wife claimed entitlement to an equitable interest in property in which her husband held legal title, and that this arrangement should be reflected in their respective NFPs. Consider the factual situation carefully to understand why the wife wanted to make such a claim.

Rawluk v Rawluk
[1990] 1 SCR 70

The Rawluks were married for 29 years until 1984. During the marriage, they worked together in two businesses, including a farm machinery (sales and service business) and a cash crop and livestock farming business. According to the Supreme Court of Canada, Mrs. Rawluk had devoted herself to the couple's children and to farm chores in the first few years of the marriage, but in the late 1960s, she began to play a large role in the farm machinery business by performing all the bookkeeping functions, including most of the invoicing and banking, and by operating the parts department. As well, she took a large role in the farm operation, with responsibility for the "birthings, needling and feeding of the animals, ... the employee payroll and bookkeeping, ... augering wheat and [helping] to transport employees and crops at harvest."

Over these years, the couple also acquired a number of other properties, and legal title to all of them was in the name of Harry Rawluk, except for a cottage property that was registered in Jacqueline Rawluk's name for tax purposes. The couple also conducted their financial affairs from a single bank account, virtually always maintained in the husband's name. For a period of one year, the account was a joint account when Mrs. Rawluk placed an inheritance from her mother ($7,000) in this account. However, for daily needs, the parties used cash stored in a teapot in a china cabinet in their home, both dipping into it as needed. This teapot was a source of some strife in the home, Mr. Rawluk claiming that his wife was a spendthrift and his wife claiming that he was miserly.

In the early 1970s, Mrs. Rawluk went to night school and qualified as a registered nursing assistant. In 1974, she worked full time in a Newmarket hospital. According to the court, she then changed her work arrangements because of complaints from her husband, and from 1975 to the date of separation, she worked part time, mostly evenings, so that she could also continue her previous work in the farming and farm machinery businesses. The parties initially separated when Mr. Rawluk left the matrimonial home in 1982, but they were reconciled, and then separated permanently as of 1 June 1984.

Although some proceedings had commenced under the former legislation, the *Family Law Act* was in effect by the time the parties came to trial in 1986. As of the valuation date (1 June 1984), the Newmarket farm and machinery lot had been valued at $400,000 and another property at $139,000. However, the value of the property had increased dramatically by the time of the trial in 1986. Thus, "in order to share in one-half of the increase in value, Mrs. Rawluk claimed by way of a remedial constructive trust a beneficial one-half interest in the home farm and machinery lot and the other property." The husband's lawyer agreed that Mrs. Rawluk's work entitled her to have her proprietary interests recognized, but claimed that the *Family Law Act* had abolished the remedy of constructive trust. Mrs. Rawluk's claim succeeded at trial and in the Ontario Court of Appeal. In the Supreme Court of Canada, four judges (Cory J, Dickson CJ, and Wilson and L'Heureux-Dubé JJ) upheld Mrs. Rawluk's claim (McLachlin, La Forest, and Sopinka JJ, dissenting).

CORY J:

> ... At trial [(1986) 3 RFL (3d) 113], Walsh J. held that a remedial constructive trust could be imposed by the court to determine the ownership of assets of married spouses under the *Family Law Act, 1986*. He determined that the *Family Law Act, 1986* requires a court to decide issues of ownership prior to equalizing net family property. He held that in determining ownership a court must look to both legal and beneficial interests, including an interest arising by means of constructive trust. He observed that it was unlikely that the Ontario legislature would deny married spouses a remedy that they would have had if unmarried. Having decided that the constructive trust doctrine survived the enactment of the *Family Law Act, 1986*, he found that the facts supported a declaration of constructive trust with regard to the Newmarket home farm and machinery lot and awarded Mrs. Rawluk a one-half interest in the contested property....
>
> The Court of Appeal [(1987) 10 RFL (3d) 113] affirmed Walsh J's decision. It decided that the provisions of the *Family Law Act, 1986*, far from superseding the constructive trust, appear to incorporate that doctrine into the process of determining ownership and equalizing net family property. The Act's provisions, it was said, clearly direct a court to determine ownership prior to ordering equalization. Accordingly, the constructive trust remedy should be applied as a part of the first step of ownership determination. The court reviewed several provisions of the Act in order to demonstrate that to deny the constructive trust remedy to married spouses in Ontario would create inconsistencies and inequalities. The court declined to decide whether a constructive trust can be forced upon a beneficiary to require that person to share in a decline in the value of property following valuation date. It simply noted that s. 5(6) of the Act might be used in such a situation to award an amount that differs from the standard equalization payment.

The Court noted the husband's argument that the equalization provisions of the *FLA* implicitly abolished the remedy of constructive trust in relation to property held by married persons, and then proceeded to examine the history of family property in Ontario:

> The issue presented by this appeal arises from a unique convergence of common law and statutory provisions, both of which are of relatively recent origin. The Canadian law of trusts with regard to matrimonial property was only in its infancy when the OLRC first proposed a matrimonial property regime of deferred equal sharing in its 1974 *Report on Family Law* (Ontario Law Reform Commission, *Report on Family Law*, Pt. IV (1974), p. 55). The Ontario legislature used that report as a model for the provisions of the *Family Law Act, 1986*, but declined to expressly clarify the relationship between the provisions of the Act and the doctrine of constructive trust, as it had evolved during the late 1970s and early 1980s.
>
> **THE DOCTRINE OF CONSTRUCTIVE TRUST AND ITS APPLICATION IN MATRIMONIAL CASES**
> The evolution of the remedial constructive trust doctrine in Canada and its application to the division of marital property can be traced through a series of well-known decisions of this court beginning with the dissenting

reasons of Laskin J. (as he then was) in *Murdoch v. Murdoch*, [1975] 1 SCR 423, 13 RFL 185, [1974] 1 WWR 361, 41 DLR (3d) 367 [Alta.], and culminating in Dickson CJC's decision for an unanimous court in *Sorochan v. Sorochan*, [1986] 2 SCR 38, 2 RFL (3d) 225, [1986] 5 WWR 289, 46 Alta. LR (2d) 97, 23 ETR 143, 29 DLR (4th) 1, [1986] RDI 448, [1986] RDF 501, 74 AR 67, 69 NR 81. The doctrine developed when it appeared that the traditional approach to resolving property disputes was inappropriate and inequitable when applied to situations of marital breakdown....

Cory J then reviewed the idea of "contribution" and "intent" and the Canadian and English decisions on the doctrine of constructive trust. He also considered the jurisprudence in the United States where "the constructive trust had long been recognized not as an institution, but as a broad restitutionary device that could be invoked in a wide variety of situations to compel the transfer of property to a claimant by the defendant in order to prevent unjust enrichment to the title holder." He then reviewed the Supreme Court's decisions in *Murdoch*, *Pettkus v Becker*, and *Sorochan* and concluded:

> These cases show that in Canada the doctrine of remedial constructive trust has been accepted for almost a decade as an important remedial device whose prime function is to remedy situations of unjust enrichment. It is clear that at the time that the *Family Law Act, 1986* was enacted, the constructive trust was widely recognized as the pre-eminent common law remedy for ensuring the equitable division of matrimonial property. The validity and importance of the remedy designed, as it is, to achieve a measure of fairness between married persons and those in a marital relationship, must have been well known to the framers of the legislation. It would seem unlikely that they would, without a precise and specific reference, deprive parties of access to such an equitable remedy....

Turning then to statutory reforms, Cory J reviewed the prior legislation in Ontario, the *Family Law Reform Act*, and relevant decisions pursuant to it. He then considered the *Family Law Act* provisions:

> In 1986, the *Family Law Reform Act* was replaced by the *Family Law Act, 1986*. In contrast to s. 8 of the *Family Law Reform Act*, the provisions of the *Family Law Act, 1986* did not attempt to duplicate the constructive trust remedy. Instead, the statute provided that all property should be equalized upon separation through the transfer of money from the title-holding or owning to the non-owning spouse.
>
> Prior to this case the trial courts in Ontario have followed one of two approaches in deciding whether these equalization provisions implicitly abolish the use of the constructive trust in the matrimonial property context. The majority of the decisions followed the reasoning of Walsh J. in the case at bar even before it was affirmed by the Ontario Court of Appeal: see *Seed v. Seed* (1986), 5 RFL (3d) 120, 25 ETR 315 (Ont. HC); *Leslie v. Leslie* (1987), 9 RFL (3d) 82, 27 ETR 247 (Ont. HC); *Cowan v. Cowan* (1987), 9 RFL (3d) 401 (Ont. HC); and *Corless v. Corless* (1987), 58 OR (2d) 19, 5 RFL (3d) 256, 34 DLR (4th) 594 (UFC). This approach was rejected, however, in two lower court decisions: *Benke v. Benke* (1986), 4 RFL (3d) 58, 25 ETR 124 (Ont. Dist. Ct.), and *Leonard v. Leonard*, [1987] OJ 1488 (unreported).

The reasoning set forth in the *Benke* decision was adopted by the appellant. In that case, the wife had claimed an interest in her husband's farm on resulting or constructive trust principles. The trial judge denied her claim, holding that the constructive trust could not be applied in the context of the *Family Law Act, 1986* and that the facts did not support a finding of resulting trust. In his opinion, the *Family Law Act, 1986* fully addressed the question of unjust enrichment between spouses by providing for monetary equalization based on the value of property at the time of separation. As he stated at p. 78:

> What Laskin J. (in *Murdoch*) declared to be "the better way" is now in place. The less adequate way was the doctrine of constructive trusts, and that less adequate way should no longer be available to, in effect, change the date of valuation whenever, either because of deflation or inflation, it suits the interests of one of the spouses to seek to advance it. If, in the total scheme of things, some injustice continues, it will be an injustice that arises from the application of an act of the legislature, and it will be for the legislature to correct it.

This position has been criticized. As Professor James McLeod comments in his annotation to *Benke v. Benke*, at p. 60:

> In the end, cases such as *Benke v. Benke* ... reflect an unwillingness on the part of the judiciary to investigate the realities of a relationship. It is easier to strictly apply an equal division in all cases than to determine whether such division is fair to the particular parties. It is easier, but is it fair?

I prefer the approach taken by Walsh J. and the Ontario Court of Appeal. In my view, far from abolishing the constructive trust doctrine, the *Family Law Act, 1986* incorporates the constructive trust remedy as an integral part of the process of ownership determination and equalization established by that Act.

Cory J then considered provisions of the *FLA* that confirm the continued application of the constructive trust doctrine:

> It is trite but true to state that as a general rule a legislature is presumed not to depart from prevailing law "without expressing its intentions to do so with irresistible clearness" (*Goodyear Tire & Rubber Co. v. T. Eaton Co.*, [1956] SCR 610 at 614, 56 DTC 1060, 4 DLR (2d) 1). But even aside from this presumption, when the structure of the *Family Law Act, 1986* is examined and the ramifications of a number of its provisions are studied, it becomes apparent that the Act recognizes and accommodates the remedial constructive trust.
>
> At the outset, the Act's preamble recognizes not only the need for the "orderly and equitable settlement of the affairs of the spouses," but also "the equal position of spouses as individuals within marriage" and the fact that marriage is a "form of partnership." These fundamental objectives are furthered by the use of the constructive trust remedy in appropriate circumstances. It provides a measure of individualized justice and fairness which is essential for the protection of marriage as a partnership of equals. Thus the preamble itself is sufficient to warrant the retention and application of this remedy.
>
> In addition, various provisions of the Act lead to the same conclusion.

SECTIONS 4 AND 5

Sections 4 and 5 of the *Family Law Act, 1986* create a two-step property division process that emphasizes the distinction between the determination of legal and equitable ownership and the equalization of net family property. These sections require a court first to determine individual "ownership piles" and then to equalize the spouses' assets by ordering the spouse with the larger ownership pile to pay money to the spouse with the smaller pile.

Before property can be equalized under s. 5 of the *Family Law Act, 1986*, a court is required by s. 4 to determine the "net family property" of each spouse. Under s. 4(1) this is defined as "the value of all property ... that a spouse owns on the valuation date." "Property" is defined in the same subsection as "any interest, present or future, vested or contingent, in real or personal property." This all-encompassing definition is wide enough to include not only legal but beneficial ownership. The appellant has conceded that "property" as defined under s. 4(1) includes a beneficial interest arising from an express or resulting trust. I see no reason why the remedial constructive trust should not be included in the list of equitable principles or remedies that may be used to calculate the beneficial ownership of net family property.

It is important in this respect to keep in mind that a property interest arising under a constructive trust can be recognized as having come into existence not when the trust is judicially declared but from the time when the unjust enrichment first arose. As Professors Oosterhoff and Gillese state, "the date at which a constructive trust arises ... is now generally accepted to be the date upon which a duty to make restitution occurs." ... It would seem that there is no foundation whatever for the notion that a constructive trust does not arise until it is decreed by a court. It arises when the duty to make restitution arises, not when that duty is subsequently enforced. ...

It must be emphasized that the constructive trust is remedial in nature. If the court is asked to grant such a remedy and determines that a declaration of constructive trust is warranted, then the proprietary interest awarded pursuant to that remedy will be deemed to have arisen at the time when the unjust enrichment first occurred. But, as Professor Scott makes clear, the fact that the proprietary interest is deemed to have arisen before the remedy was granted is not inconsistent with the remedial characteristics of the doctrine.

The distinction between a share in ownership and a share in property value through an equalizing transfer of money is more than an exercise in judicial formalism. This distinction not only follows the two-step structure of the *Family Law Act, 1986*, but reflects conceptual and practical differences between ownership and equalization. Ownership encompasses far more than a mere share in the value of property. It includes additional legal rights, elements of control and increased legal responsibilities. In addition, it may well provide psychological benefits derived from pride of ownership. Where the property at issue is one to which only one spouse has contributed, it is appropriate that the other spouse receive only an equalizing transfer of money. But where both spouses have contributed to the acquisition or maintenance of the property, the spouse who does not hold legal title should be able to claim an interest in that property by way of a constructive trust and realize the benefits that ownership may provide. The imposition of a constructive trust recognizes that the titled spouse is holding property that has been acquired, at least in part, through the money or effort of another. The non-titled spouse's constructive trust interest in this property is distinct from the right to an equalizing share of property value that is derived not from an independent property right but from the status as a married person.

SECTION 5(6)

Section 5(6) of the *Family Law Act, 1986* allows a court to "award a spouse an amount that is more or less than half the difference between the net family properties if the court is of the opinion that equalizing the net family properties would be unconscionable." The Court of Appeal observed that if a post-valuation date increase or decrease in property values is significant enough to render a simple equalization unconscionable, a court might utilize s. 5(6) to remedy the resultant inequities. I need not and do not express any opinion as to whether s. 5(6) could be used in that way or whether the Court of Appeal's observation is correct. I have assumed solely for the purposes of argument that s. 5(6) might be available in some cases as an alternative remedy for dealing with post-valuation date changes in value. Even so, the section does not have the effect of supplanting the constructive trust remedy. The constructive trust is used in the matrimonial property context to allocate proprietary interests, a function that is totally distinct from the process of determining how the value of matrimonial property should be distributed under the equalization process.

Under the Act a court is, as a first step, required to determine the ownership interests of the spouses. It is at that stage that the court must deal with and determine the constructive trust claims. The second step that must be taken is to perform the equalization calculations. Once this is done, a court must assess whether, given the facts of the particular case, equalization is unconscionable. The s. 5(6) analysis, even if it could be considered, would be a third step — a last avenue of judicial discretion which might be used in order to bring a measure of flexibility to the equalization process. This step in the process, if it could be used, would have to be kept distinct from the preliminary determinations of ownership....

Cory J also reviewed the impact of section 10, which permits a spouse to apply to the court to determine a question of ownership or possession prior to equalization, and stated:

> The creation under s. 10 of a proprietary remedy that can be commenced during cohabitation provides further evidence that the Ontario legislature could not have intended the provisions of the *Family Law Act, 1986* to completely supersede the remedial constructive trust. Section 10 enables non-titled spouses to assert control over matrimonial property during cohabitation to the extent that their beneficial interests entitle them to do so. Even if the appellant's argument that the *Family Law Act, 1986* equalization provisions replace the constructive trust remedy were to be accepted, this would not prevent a deserving spouse from obtaining a declaration of constructive trust in his or her spouse's property during cohabitation pursuant to s. 10. Certainly such an application will not necessarily be followed by separation and equalization of property.
>
> Since the spouse can thus obtain a constructive trust remedy prior to separation, it would be inconsistent to deny a spouse the same remedy when it is sought after a separation. To take such a position would encourage spouses to apply for a constructive trust interest early in a marriage, perhaps thereby creating unnecessary marital stress, fostering costly litigation and penalizing those spouses who waited until separation to enforce their common law rights. It is unlikely that the legislature intended a spouse's rights to depend on whether or not a constructive trust had been declared before or after the separation....

Cory J also examined section 14, which refers expressly to the resulting trust doctrine, and rejected the appellant's argument that this express reference to resulting trust meant that the doctrine of constructive trust had been abolished. He also considered section 64(2), which equalizes the legal rights of married men and married women, concluding that it would be inequitable and contravene section 64(2) if the remedial constructive trust were not available to married persons. In conclusion, Cory J stated:

> The review of the cases decided by this court from *Murdoch v. Murdoch, supra,* to *Sorochan v. Sorochan, supra,* demonstrates the importance that has been attached to the use of the remedy of constructive trust to achieve a division of property that is as just and equitable as possible. A marital relationship is founded on love and trust. It brings together two people who strive and sacrifice to attain common goals for the benefit of both partners. When it is terminated and acquired assets are to be divided, then in this of all relationships the concept of fairness should predominate in making decisions as to ownership. This was the fundamental equitable principle underlying the application of the constructive trust remedy to matrimonial cases. Where the application of the principle would achieve the goal of fairness it should not be discarded unless the pertinent legislation makes it clear that the principle is to be disregarded.
>
> The *Family Law Act, 1986* does not constitute an exclusive code for determining the ownership of matrimonial property. The legislators must have been aware of the existence and effect of the constructive trust remedy in matrimonial cases when the Act was proposed. Yet neither by direct reference nor by necessary implication does the Act prohibit the use of the constructive trust remedy. Indeed, the foregoing review of the provisions of the Act supports the view that the constructive trust remedy is to be maintained. The Act's two-step structure and its individual provisions indicate that the constructive trust remedy still has an important role to play in the determination of matrimonial property disputes in Ontario. The application of the remedy in the context of the *Family Law Act, 1986* can achieve a fair and just result. It enables the courts to bring that treasured and essential measure of individualized justice and fairness to the more generalized process of equalization provided by the Act. That vital fairness is achieved by means of a constructive trust remedy and recognition of ownership.
>
> In this case fairness requires that the dedication and hard work of Jacqueline Rawluk in acquiring and maintaining the properties in issue be recognized. The equitable remedy of constructive trust was properly applied.
>
> I would therefore dismiss the appeal with costs.

McLachlin J, dissenting, summarized at the outset two fundamental principles applicable to this case:

1. The doctrine of constructive trust, as it has developed in Canada, is not a property right but a proprietary remedy for unjust enrichment; as such, the availability of other remedies for the unjust enrichment must be considered before declaring a constructive trust.
2. The doctrine of constructive trust should not be applied in this case because the *Family Law Act, 1986* provides a remedy for the unjust enrichment of the husband to the detriment of the wife.

McLachlin J approached the issues in *Rawluk* by examining the history of principles concerning unjust enrichment and constructive trust. She suggested that there were two different views in English jurisprudence: a traditional view, which characterized the constructive trust as an obligation attaching to property in defined situations, and a new model, chiefly developed by Lord Denning, of the constructive trust as a general remedy for unjust enrichment. According to McLachlin J, Canada had tended to move toward the American view of the constructive trust as an equitable remedy for unjust enrichment. In this way, the constructive trust represents a discretionary remedy, dependent on the inadequacy of other remedies for unjust enrichment. McLachlin J summarized her view:

> These passages establish the fundamentals of the Canadian approach to constructive trust in relation to unjust enrichment. First, the doctrine has as its purpose the remedying of unjust enrichment. Second, it is remedial rather than substantive. Finally, the remedy of constructive trust is but one of many remedies that may be available to correct unjust enrichment. Before applying it, the court must consider whether, given other available remedies, the remedy of constructive trust remains necessary and appropriate in the case before it.
>
> This brings us to the issue raised in this case. Given that the doctrine of constructive trust, as it has developed in Canada, is remedial, what is the relationship of the remedy of constructive trust to other remedies for unjust enrichment? While Dickson CJC alludes to this issue in *Sorochan v. Sorochan*, little Canadian jurisprudence exists on the question. In these circumstances, it may be useful to have regard to the American experience....
>
> The American law on constructive trusts, as set out in the Restatement of Restitution, recognizes the panoply of remedies for unjust enrichment and the need for the court, in considering a claim for constructive trust, to select among them. As a general rule, the remedies which operate *in personam* must be brought first, for example, actions for money had and received, *quantum meruit* and account [citing Donovan Waters, *Law of Trusts in Canada*, 2d ed. (Scarborough, ON: Carswell, 1984) at 393]....
>
> Thus I arrive at this point. Without denying the importance of the remedy of constructive trust, it must be remembered that it may be only one of several remedies for unjust enrichment. It must also be remembered that as a proprietary remedy, its imposition may interfere with the operation of other doctrines and the exercise by others, including third parties, of the rights attendant on their interests in the property made subject to the trust. For these reasons, it may be wise to insist that a plaintiff has exhausted his or her personal remedies before imposing the remedy of constructive trust.

[QUESTION 1]

Against this background, I return to the first of the two questions I posed at the outset. Is the doctrine of constructive trust as it has developed in Canada a substantive doctrine of trust, automatically conferring a property interest where the basic criteria for the trust are made out? Or is it a remedy, to be applied where necessary to remedy unjust enrichment?

The answer must be that in Canada, constructive trust, at least in the context of unjust enrichment, is not a doctrine of substantive property law, but a remedy. It follows that a constructive trust cannot be regarded as arising automatically when the three conditions set out in *Pettkus v. Becker* are established. Rather, the court must go on to consider what other remedies are available to remedy the unjust enrichment in question and whether the proprietary remedy of constructive trust is appropriate.

Neither of the courts below approached the matter in this way. Both the trial judge and the Court of Appeal assumed that the doctrine of constructive trust gave the wife a beneficial half interest in the property, the only question then being whether the statute took that right away. My colleague Cory J. takes a similar approach, stating that the *Family Law Act, 1986* incorporates the constructive trust remedy "as an integral part of the process of ownership determination." ...

I cannot share this approach. In my opinion, the doctrine of constructive trust does not permit the court to retrospectively confer a property interest solely on the basis of contribution of one spouse and enrichment of the other. A further inquiry must be made, namely, whether, given the presence of another remedy, the remedy of constructive trust is necessary or appropriate. I now turn to that question....

[QUESTION 2]

This case poses the question of whether the doctrine of constructive trust should be applied where there exists a comprehensive statutory scheme providing a remedy for the situation where one spouse holds exclusive title to property to which the other spouse has contributed.

The *Family Law Act, 1986* sets up a comprehensive statutory scheme which recognizes the contributions of both spouses to the acquisition, preservation, maintenance or improvement of property during the marriage. It addresses the question of unjust enrichment between spouses by providing for a monetary equalization payment based on the value of the "net family property" at the valuation date, i.e., the time of separation (s. 5(1)).

The Act defines "property" broadly as including "any interest present or future, vested or contingent, in real or personal property ..." (s. 4). "Net family property" is defined as meaning "the value of all the property ... that a spouse owns on the valuation date" after deducting debts and the value of the property at the time of marriage (s. 4). The Act specifically requires the judge to apply the doctrine of resulting trust (s. 14), but makes no mention of constructive trust. The Act permits the judge to depart from the principle of equal distribution and adjust the award in a variety of circumstances, including "any other circumstance relating to the acquisition, disposition, preservation, maintenance or improvement of property" (s. 5(6)(h)).

The question may be put thus: given that there was an unjust enrichment arising from the fact that the property to which the wife contributed was in the husband's name, does the *Family Law Act, 1986* provide a remedy, which makes it unnecessary to resort to the doctrine of constructive trust? In my opinion, the answer to this question must be affirmative.

Both the statutory remedy and the remedy of constructive trust are, on the facts of this case, directed to the same end. The purpose of a constructive trust, as already discussed, is to permit a party without title to receive compensation for his or her contribution to the acquisition and maintenance of property standing in the other's name. The purpose of the *Family Law Act, 1986* is the same: it sets up a scheme to equalize the property holdings of each party to a marriage, regardless of who holds legal title. The only difference for the purposes of this case is that the *Family Law Act, 1986* provides for the equalization to be accomplished by a payment of money based on the value of the property at the time of the separation (a remedy *in personam*), while the doctrine of constructive trust would give a beneficial interest in the land which persists to the date of trial (a proprietary remedy).

If the doctrine of unjust enrichment is to be applied in this case, it is not for the purpose of rewarding the wife for her contribution to the property held in the husband's name, but for the purpose of permitting her to share in the increase in value of the property after separation. But this cannot support a claim for a constructive trust for two reasons.

First, the Act contemplates the problem that assets may increase or diminish in value between the date of separation and trial; s. 5(6)(h) permits the trial judge to vary the equal division of property as at separation, on the basis of circumstances relating to the disposition or improvement of the property. I agree with Cory J. that this step of the process is distinct from the preliminary determinations of ownership.

Second, it would appear that the elements necessary to establish a constructive trust are not present where the enrichment occurs as a result of appreciation of the market value of the land after separation. Under the statute, the wife already receives a payment sufficient to give her 50 per cent of the family property, valued at the date of separation. There is no unjust enrichment there. What then of the fact that because of delays in obtaining judgment, the value of the property held in the hands of the husband increases pending trial? True, this is an enrichment of the husband. But there is no corresponding deprivation to the wife giving rise to an injustice. The husband is not being enriched at her expense or because of her efforts. In these circumstances, the first two requirements of a constructive trust [in *Pettkus v. Becker*] — unjust enrichment of one party and corresponding deprivation of the other — are absent.

In the final analysis, the *Family Law Act, 1986* provides complete compensation for the wife's contribution to the date of separation. Any disproportionate enrichment must occur because of the increase in value due to changing market conditions after that date. But that does not constitute an unjust enrichment under the principles set forth in *Pettkus v. Becker*, given that the wife made no contribution after that date. As a matter of legal principle, the legislature having provided a remedy for the unjust enrichment which would otherwise have occurred in this case, it is not for this court to impose an additional equitable remedy aimed at correcting the same wrong.

McLachlin J then considered the practical problems that might arise if the remedy of constructive trust were added to the statutory scheme, including uncertainty and litigation because of the need to investigate the precise contributions of each party. She also took account of the rights of third parties, and continued:

One must also consider the converse situation to that of this case — the situation where instead of increasing in value after separation, the property loses value. Is the amount recoverable by the spouse lacking title to be diminished accordingly? One judge has said yes, imposing a beneficial constructive interest in the property on the wife as at separation, against her wishes and at the behest of the husband: *McDonald v. McDonald* (1988), 11 RFL (3d) 321, 28 ETR 81 (Ont. HC). So we arrive at the anomaly of the equitable remedy of constructive trust being applied against the wishes of the party found to have been unfairly treated, at the behest of the party who has been unjustly enriched. What does this leave of the maxim that he who seeks the aid of equity must come with clean hands? The fallacy at the root of such an approach is that of treating the *remedy* of constructive trust as though it were a *property interest*, which for the sake of consistency must be imposed regardless of the circumstances or of other remedies.

It is suggested that the position of the wife should not be worse than it would have been had the parties not married. The answer to this submission is that the legislature, acting within the proper scope of its authority, has chosen to confine the Act to married persons. Some Acts governing distribution of marital property apply to unmarried couples. While it may be a ground for criticism of the legislation, the fact that a person covered by legislation may be treated less generously than someone not under the statute cannot give rise to a claim for unjust enrichment; the doctrine of unjust enrichment does not go as far as that....

McLachlin J also rejected the views of Cory J in relation to section 10 of the Act, and continued:

I cannot leave this question without alluding to the quite different provisions found in Acts regulating the division of marital property in provinces other than Ontario. As Cory J. points out, the relationship between the constructive trust doctrine and its "statutory equivalents" has been variously treated in different jurisdictions. While it is interesting to consider dispositions in other jurisdictions, it should be noted that the legislative provisions from province to province are not truly equivalent. In particular, none of the provincial statutes governing the division of marital property, save that of Ontario, appears to have a statutorily fixed and inflexible valuation date, the feature of the Act which gives rise to the wife's grievance in this case. There can be no simple or universally applicable answer to the question of whether the doctrine of constructive trust will apply in a statutory context: in each case, the circumstances of the case and the efficacy of alternative remedies conferred by the applicable legislation must be examined to ascertain whether, in that situation, a declaration of constructive trust should be declared.

In this case, I conclude that the remedy of constructive trust is neither necessary nor appropriate, given the remedies available under the *Family Law Act, 1986*....

Appeal dismissed

Notes and Questions

Rawluk and the need for reform: The OLRC *Report*

The OLRC's *Report on Family Property Law* in 1993 reviewed the *Rawluk* decision in some detail. Conceding that a spouse might well prefer to have a property interest, by contrast with just a monetary amount, in relation to significant family assets, the *Report* noted the lack of precision in decisions about spousal contributions to property in the family context. In addition, it expressed concern about the impact of this remedy on third party creditors, and examined in detail the implications of using this remedy in the context of bankruptcy and tax law (see OLRC *Report* at 46–50).

Overall, the report concluded:

Without doubt, the remedial constructive trust continues to offer some benefits to spouses covered by Part I of the *Family Law Act*, but the problems in applying the common law to spousal relationships raise a question as to the advisability of preserving access to this remedy. The Ontario family property scheme, as conceived by this Commission and implemented by the Legislature, maintains separate ownership and creates a debt obligation. This approach balances the equitable sharing of spousal wealth with the need to preserve the ability of spouses to deal freely with their assets. Any apparent unfairness in restricting the ability of spouses to obtain an ownership interest must be considered in the light of this balance (see OLRC *Report* at 140).

The *Report* considered the advantages and disadvantages of either maintaining access to these remedies or abolishing such access entirely, particularly having regard to recommendations for reforming other sections of Part I of the *Family Law Act* more generally (a number of these recommendations are considered later in this section). Overall, the *Report* concluded that there should be limited access to the constructive trust and that access to the resulting trust should also be limited. Thus, recommendation no. 30 (at 150) stated:

> Part I of the *Family Law Act* should be amended to preclude a spouse from applying as follows:
> a) for a declaration of a remedial constructive trust with respect to property owned by his or her spouse, as restitution for his or her contribution, either direct or indirect, to the acquisition, preservation, or enhancement of that property.
> b) for a declaration of resulting trust with respect to property owned by his or her spouse, based on the common or presumed intention of the spouses regarding his or her contribution, either direct or indirect, to the acquisition, preservation, or enhancement of that property.

Instead, the OLRC *Report* recommended that a court have authority to vary an equalization payment if an asset fluctuates in value, if necessary, to prevent an inequitable result pursuant to section 5(6). (Note that these recommendations would apply to both married spouses and cohabiting couples, in accordance with other recommendations of the OLRC.)

To what extent do you agree that the goal of equality pursuant to the statutory scheme is preferable to the exercise of equitable jurisdiction of the courts? What goals are thereby enhanced? To what extent are these problems concerning trust remedies connected to the issue of an inflexible valuation date? In addition to the OLRC recommendations about trusts, recall its recommendations concerning the valuation date and the above recommendation to provide courts with discretion pursuant to section 5(6) to achieve an equitable result. Are these recommendations, taken together, more appropriate than the majority's approach in the Supreme Court of Canada?

Statutory and judicial reforms in other provinces

In assessing the need for reform in Ontario in this context, consider the arrangements in place in a number of other Canadian provinces:

- In Prince Edward Island, the *Family Law Act*, SPEI 1995, c 12, s 6(6), permits a court to award an amount that is more or less than half the difference between the spouses' NFPs, "if the court is of the opinion that equalizing the net family properties would be inequitable because of a substantial change after the valuation date in the value of any property" included in either spouse's NFP. For an example, see *Ballum v Ballum* (1999), 49 RFL (4th) 176 (PEISC (TD).

- A similar provision was recommended by the B.C. Law Reform Commission. See BC Law Reform Commission, *Working Paper on Property Rights on Marriage Breakdown* (Victoria: Ministry of the Attorney General, 1989) at 126.

- In Manitoba, the Court of Appeal concluded that the court had sufficient jurisdiction pursuant to its provincial *Marital Property Act* to re-adjust the spouses' entitlements after a decline in value of the husband's property post-separation. See *Gallant v Gallant* (1998), 42 RFL (4th) 353 (Man CA).

Do these arrangements in other provinces suggest a need for reform in Ontario? Why, or why not?

According to the empirical study undertaken by Poirier and Castonguay, cohabiting spouses appear to have obtained a better division of business assets in New Brunswick, by contrast with married spouses.

In this context, Poirier and Castonguay observed that the principles in *Rawluk* might assist married spouses by permitting them to obtain an equal division of family assets and a share of business assets pursuant to the principles of unjust enrichment and the remedial constructive trust. However, they also noted that lawyers and judges appeared not to recognize the application of the *Rawluk* decision in divorce negotiations in New Brunswick. See Donald Poirier & Lynne Castonguay, "Formal Versus Real Equality in Property Division on Marriage Breakdown of Business Couples: An Empirical Study" (1994) 11 Can Fam LQ 71.

Resolving the differences between judicial approaches in the Supreme Court?

The recommendations of the OLRC *Report* in relation to *Rawluk* and trust remedies have not been implemented in Ontario. In this context, consider another proposal about the relationship between the statutory remedy in the *FLA* and the equitable remedy of constructive trust:

> What is the effect of a statutory remedy on an equitable remedy? As the two judgments show, the question is a difficult one. Cory J. took the view that the enactment of the statutory regime for marital property did not affect the availability of the remedial constructive trust. He seemed to say that courts should grant a remedial constructive trust to any spouse who applies for and is entitled to it, because it is more just and equitable than the statutory scheme. On the other hand, McLachlin J. went to the opposite extreme; in her view, a court should never grant a remedial constructive trust over a family asset to a spouse who also has a remedy by way of an equalization payment under the Act. The courts should keep the remedial constructive trust only for a party who is not entitled to an equalization payment.
>
> Another approach may be worth considering, because it reconciles the two views, and is consistent with the result in *Rawluk v. Rawluk* and

with other authorities. According to this view, the statutory equalization payment is the rule of general application, and a claimant should be entitled to it as of right. The remedial constructive trust is an equitable remedy, which means that before granting it, the court should decide two questions: (1) Is the equalization payment an inadequate remedy in the circumstances? and (2) Since equitable remedies are discretionary, should the court exercise its discretion to grant the decree, after weighing the equitable considerations? If the answer to either question is negative, the court should refuse the declaration of constructive trust, leaving the claimant to the statutory equalization payment. It is respectfully suggested that this principle will eventually emerge as the ratio of *Rawluk v. Rawluk*. These two principles are fundamental to equity jurisdiction. They also meet the concerns expressed in the majority and dissenting reasons for judgment in the *Rawluk* case....

[In *Rawluk*, both Cory and McLachlin JJ. took extreme positions....] Instead of taking the view that either the remedial constructive trust or the statutory equalization payment must reign over the division of marital property, the courts should allow both remedies to co-exist and to flourish: peaceful co-existence between the remedies is preferable to domination by either. It is respectfully suggested that, before being awarded a declaration of trust, the claimant should be required to demonstrate to the court that the equalization payment is, or may be, inadequate. On the facts of *Rawluk v. Rawluk*, it was not established that an equalization payment would deprive Mrs. Rawluk of a share in the post-separation real estate boom. However, there is authority to support that view. A genuine doubt about the adequacy of the legal remedy is sufficient to allow the court of equity to intervene. The imposition of a constructive trust without any determination of the inadequacy of the equalization payment may have been an error in principle, but it did not lead to an erroneous result: Mrs. Rawluk could have shown that the equalization payment was only a partial remedy in the circumstances. (Anthony Sheppard, *"Rawluk v. Rawluk*: What Are the Limits of the Remedial Constructive Trust?" (1990–91) 9 Can J Fam L 152 at 161)

To what extent do you agree with this suggested resolution of the differing views in *Rawluk*? Does it accord with the underlying goals of family property legislation? Why or why not?

The impact of *Rawluk*

The issue about the relationship between a finding of unjust enrichment and the remedy of constructive trust was examined again by the Supreme Court of Canada in *Peter v Beblow* (1993), 44 RFL (3d) 329, a case concerning a cohabiting, rather than a married, couple. In *Peter v Beblow*, McLachlin and Cory JJ again wrote different judgments, but they were in agreement about the outcome in the case (see the section concerning cohabiting couples and trust remedies at the end of this chapter).

In a recent decision of the Ontario Court of Appeal, the court held that *Rawluk* confirmed the availability of a claim of unjust enrichment for a married spouse, although it was necessary for the court to order a new trial to determine whether the wife's claim could succeed in this case (see *McNamee v McNamee*, 2011 ONCA 533). This case is reviewed in more detail in the discussion of excluded property pursuant to *FLA*, s 4(2), later in this chapter.

Issues about these unjust enrichment claims have also been addressed in a number of other cases. See *Bigelow v Bigelow* (1995), 15 RFL (4th) 12 (Ont Gen Div); *Close v Close* (1997), 33 RFL (4th) 210 (Ont Gen Div); *Franken v Franken* (1997), 33 RFL (4th) 264 (Ont Gen Div); and *Roach v Roach* (1997), 33 RFL (4th) 157 (Ont CA).

Additional Resources

Rosemary Auchmuty, "Unfair Shares for Women: the Rhetoric of Equality and the Reality of Inequality" in Hilary Lim & Anne Bottomley, eds., *Feminist Perspectives on Land Law* (Abingdon, Oxford: Routledge-Cavendish, 2007) at 171.

Anne Bottomley, "Self and Subjectivities: Languages of Claim in Property Law" (1993) 20:1 JL & Soc'y 56.

Anthony Duggan, "Constructive Trusts from a Law and Economics Perspective" (2005) 55 UTLJ 217.

Berend Hovius & Timothy Youdan, *The Law of Family Property* (Scarborough, ON: Carswell, 1991) at 243–57.

Mitchell McInnes, "Unjust Enrichment and the Constructive Trusts in the Supreme Court of Canada" (1997–1998) 25 Man LJ 513.

James McLeod & Alfred Mamo, *Annual Review of Family Law 2009* (Toronto: Carswell, 2009) at 568–570.

Susan Scott-Hunt & Hilary Lim, eds, *Feminist Perspectives on Equity and Trusts* (London and Sydney: Cavendish Publishing Limited, 2001).

3. "Property" and Pensions

Virtually everyone agrees that the confusion around the division of pensions upon marriage breakdown should be addressed legislatively, but unfortunately there is no unanimity as to the choice of solution. (Law Commission of Ontario, *Division of Pensions Upon Marriage Breakdown: Final Report*, December 2008) at 1 [LCO, *Final Report*])

Pensions and Property at Marriage Breakdown

Most provincial legislation relating to property at marriage breakdown includes the value of a spouse's employment-based pension entitlement as "property."

For example, section 84(2)(e) of British Columbia's *Family Law Act* includes as "family property," "a spouse's entitlement under an annuity, a pension, a retirement savings plan or an income plan" (and see also Part 6 of the Act).

Even in circumstances where the legislation is silent, as in Nova Scotia, the Supreme Court of Canada concluded that a pension constituted matrimonial property: *Clarke v Clarke* (1990), 28 RFL (3d) 113 at 128–29, where the court asserted that "in the case of many Canadian families a pension is their only substantial asset".

Moreover, as the LCO study explained, occupational pensions form an important part of family economies for many families in Ontario:

> About 34 percent of employees in Ontario were members of an occupational pension plan in 2005, although it is important to note that 80 percent of public sector employees were members of such plans, compared to only 25 percent of private sector employees. Although the number of males who were members of such pension plans was slightly greater than the number of females (928,000 males and 832,000 females), the long-term rate of increase for male members of pension plans has been relatively steady while the number of females with pension plans has been increasing dramatically. Even so, because pension benefits are generally related to income from employment, and women generally earn less then men, the average pension income for women has tended to be substantially lower than for men. (See LCO, *Final Report* at 10–11, citing Richard Shillington, *Occupational Pension Plan Coverage in Ontario* (prepared for the Ontario Expert Committee on Pensions, Infometrica Limited, 2007); and Lynn MacDonald, "Gendered Retirement: The Welfare of Women and the 'New' Retirement" in Leroy Stone, ed, *New Frontiers of Research on Retirement* (Ottawa: Statistics Canada, 2006).)

Consider these statistics in relation to families and family dissolution. To what extent do statistics about family dissolution, discussed in Chapter Five, suggest that occupational pensions may be an important feature of family economies at dissolution? Why might the rate of occupational pensions be increasing for women, by contrast with men? To what extent are there issues about gender equality in pension arrangements at family dissolution?

Pensions and the Ontario *FLA*: A Brief History

In 1986, the definition of "property" in section 4 of the *FLA* included "a spouse's rights under a pension plan that have vested." However, the statute did not provide any further direction with respect to *how* these rights should be included in determining the NFP value. In 1993, the Ontario Law Reform Commission released its *Report on Pensions as Family Property: Valuation and Division* (Toronto: OLRC, 1993), with recommendations for amending the *FLA* to provide more direction about pensions and family property, but these recommendations were not implemented.

Thus, the LCO re-examined the issue of occupational pensions and family property and released its final report in December 2008, with recommendations for legislative amendments. The provincial government responded by enacting the *Family Statute Law Amendment Act, 2009*, which included amendments to the *FLA* (ss 22–26 and ss 37–40) and to the *Pension Benefits Act* (ss 41–50), and providing for additional Regulations. These changes, which became effective on 1 January 2012, now provide some direction with respect to including a pension in the equalization process. Although these amendments have also received some criticism, they offer much needed direction with respect to pensions in relation to equalization pursuant to the *FLA*.

This section reproduces some excerpts from the LCO *Final Report*, a brief overview of the 2009 amendments to the *FLA*, and some basic information about the changes in effect as of January 2012.

Pensions and Valuation: The LCO *Final Report*

In terms of the nature of the benefit provided, there are two main types of occupational pension plan, the defined benefit plan and the defined contribution plan. [In both types, employers are required to make contributions and both may also require contributions from employees.]

> Under a defined contribution plan, the contributions made by the employer and by the employee, if any, are set at a fixed amount or rate; those contributions are invested and the sum of accumulated contributions and returns on their investment is used to purchase an annuity when the employee retires [e.g., "money purchase" plans].
>
> In contrast, the amount of the pension benefit under a defined benefit plan has no immediate relation to the contributions and investment yield, but rather is determined according to a set formula [e.g., the annual pension amount is equal to the product obtained when the employee's number of years of service is multiplied by a specified percentage and then applied against the average salary earned by the employee for some specified number of years]....

Valuation of rights under a defined contribution plan generally poses few problems; the value for net family property purposes is simply the aggregate of the contributions made during the marriage and the returns on investment of those contributions as of the valuation date. With a defined benefit plan, however, this "contributions approach" plainly does not provide an appropriate value, because what the member is entitled to by way of a pension has no immediate relation to the accumulated contributions and investment yield.... Equating the value of [an employee's entitlement in a defined benefit plan] to the sum of contributions plus the return on their investment is likely to understate considerably its true worth....

In the ... context of marriage breakdown and defined benefit plans, the present value as of the valuation date is the amount that would have to have been invested on that date in order for the original investment and accumulated earnings to be just adequate to fund the monthly benefits when the pension comes into pay. Of course this figure is necessarily the product of conjecture:

> On the valuation date, the person performing the valuation does not know when the pension payments will begin [the date of the member's retirement is unknown], or even whether they ever will begin [the member may die before retirement];
>
> Or if they do begin, [the person performing the valuation does not know] how long they will last [the date of death is unknown];
>
> Nor does she know how much any given investment will ultimately earn [because future interest rates and inflation rates are unknown].

[L]acking omniscience concerning the future, the valuator must make speculative assumptions about all of these variables. As the Supreme Court of Canada has noted [in *Boston v. Boston*, [2001] 2 SCR 413 at para. 32], ascertaining a present value is "a matter of educated guesswork, undertaken by actuaries." (LCO, *Final Report* at 9 and 23)

The LCO *Final Report* reviewed two basic methods of valuing defined benefit pensions, and judicial decisions about valuation. See *Best v Best*, [1999] 2 SCR 868; and *Bascello v Bascello* (1995), 26 OR (3d) 342 (Gen Div). The *Final Report* also made recommendations about "settlement," that is, how a spouse may meet the obligation of equalization in the pension context.

Ontario's *Family Statute Law Amendment Act, 2009*

This legislation included a variety of amendments to family law in Ontario, including procedures for custody applications pursuant to the *Child and Family Services Act* and the *Children's Law Reform Act*; new provisions in the *FLA* regarding non-contact and restraining orders (see *FLA*, ss 13.1 and 25.1, and 46–47.1), and regarding arbitration awards (see *FLA*, Part IV) and recalculation of child support (s 39.1).

In addition, the statute also introduced provisions to amend the arrangements for pensions as family "property" in relation to equalization.

The following summary provides some information about the 2009 amendments to the *FLA* in relation to pensions:

- **The definition of "property":** The definition in section 4(1) includes

    "in the case of a spouse's rights under a pension plan, the imputed value, for family law purposes, of the spouse's interest in the plan, as determined in accordance with section 10.1, for the period beginning with the date of the marriage and ending on the valuation date".

- **CPP benefits as excluded property:** Section 4(2) excludes CPP benefits.

- **The valuation of a pension interest:** Section 10.1 provides for determining the imputed value, for family law purposes, of a spouse's interest in a pension plan in accordance with the *Pension Benefits Act* (see also Ont Reg 287/11, in force on 1 January 2012).

- **The settlement of a pension interest by equalization:** Section 10.1(3) provides for the immediate transfer of a lump sum out of a pension plan pursuant to *FLA*, ss 9 and 10, subject to considerations set out in section 10.1(4). Restrictions pursuant to the *Pension Benefits Act* continue to apply to pensions registered under it.

- **The pensions subject to these amendments:** Section 10.1(8) provides that these provisions apply "whether the valuation date is before, on or after the date on which this section comes into force," but section 10.1(9) restricts its application with respect to an order made before the section takes effect.

- **Domestic contracts and pensions:** Section 56.1 provides for application of the same rules with respect to pensions in relation to domestic contracts or arbitration awards. Section 56.1 defines "family law valuation date" as the valuation date under Part I that is applicable to the parties or "for parties to whom Part I does not apply, the date on which they separate and there is no reasonable prospect that they will resume cohabitation". Thus, cohabiting couples may now make separation agreements that include these provisions concerning pensions.

The amendments also include new provisions in the *Pension Benefits Act*, particularly with respect to determining the "imputed value, for family law purposes" and in relation to "settlement" of an equalization payment.

Pension Division on Marriage Breakdown
Presentation to the Ontario Bar Association, September 2011

Wendela Napier

The *Family Law Act* was enacted 25 years ago and it created our current system of property division. At that time, pensions were specifically defined as property and required to be included in an individual's net family property (NFP). Since then, lawyers practising in family law have struggled with the complexities of dealing with pensions. In part, this is because it was very difficult for lawyers and clients alike to determine accurately the value of an asset which cannot be converted to cash and which is to be received in the future for an undetermined period of time.

In addition, further difficulties arose at the stage of settlement of an equalization entitlement. Often, the payor spouse lacked the cash to make the equalization payment, especially if the payment was in large part due to an interest in a pension, when that pension was not convertible or exigible. Many spouses felt it was unfair to have to give up an interest in a home, or otherwise use up a cash asset to meet an obligation, when the obligation related to an asset they could not put their hands on.

With the passage of Bill 133 in 2009, which amended both the *Family Law Act* (FLA) and the *Pension Benefits Act* (PBA) and the recent promulgation of Regulations under the PBA, coming into force on January 1, 2012, [there is] a new regime ... with respect to how value is determined, [and] also with regard to how an equalization payment may be settled.

The new law applies to all spouses, regardless of the date of separation, unless there exists an agreement, order or arbitration award predating January 1, 2012 which resolves the issue of equalization. ...

WHAT HAS NOT CHANGED
- Pensions remain property to be included in a spouse's NFP.
- The manner of calculating an equalization payment will be the same.
- The valuation of Defined Contribution pensions will be largely unchanged (although Defined Benefit pensions will be valued differently than they are now).
- Spouses will, as they do now, assign a value for future income tax on pension income, and that value will be inserted as a deduction in the spouse's NFP calculation.

- Pension division will continue to be subject to a (revised) 50% rule under the PBA.
- The customary practice of excluding the value of an interest under the Canada Pension Plan in a spouse's NFP will continue, supported by a new provision specifically exempting these pensions from inclusion in NFP [see s. 4(2)]

WHAT HAS CHANGED

- The value of a Defined Benefit pension interest will now be calculated according to new rules.
- With certain exceptions, the value of the pension will be assigned by the pension plan administrator, at the request of a member or a spouse.
- The administrator may charge a fee for doing so.
- Except where a pension is already in pay at the date of separation, the manner of settlement of an equalization payment becomes governed by new discretionary rules. Therefore, the extent to which the equalization payment is funded by a cash payment or a transfer of funds out of the pension, will depend on an individual family's circumstances.
- With the consent of a pension plan only, and in the case of a pension not in pay, under the revised Acts a spouse could in theory become a member of a plan and share the pension income. ...
- A pension in pay prior to separation *may* be divided at source and the spouse will receive a share of the income stream directly from the pension plan. ...
- If the spouses consent, unmarried spouses will be able to effect a pension transfer or division, and married spouses may include a period of cohabitation prior to marriage in determining the pension's value.

DETERMINING PENSION VALUE UNDER THE NEW RULES

When reform was introduced, the Ontario government adopted the recommendation of the Law Commission of Ontario to standardize the determination of value. ... The new method of calculating value will lack the individual variations that we [have used], and which led to parties debating issues such as age of retirement, future indexation and (in some cases) shortened life expectancy.

In the new regime, the result will be more of a "one size fits all" approach which will certainly simplify matters and hopefully reduce areas of conflict between spouses. However, it may give rise to some concerns regarding fairness in an individual case. The solution, in my view, to perceived unfairness in value is to ensure that the equalization payment (or at least that part of it that is referable to the pension value) is made by using the pension itself. ...

New Terms:

Family Law Valuation Date: essentially the same as "Valuation Date" under the FLA

Preliminary Value: the calculation of pension value to be made by the pension plan administrator in accordance with the new Regulations

Imputed Value: that part of the Preliminary Value that accrued during the marriage (a pro-rata calculation)

The preliminary value of a Defined Contribution Pension is simply the total of all contributions plus interest. Thus the imputed value is easy to ascertain, since it is simply the increase in the balance in the member's account from the date of marriage to date of separation.

The preliminary value of a Defined Benefit Pension is determined by a new formula, which determines three separate commuted values (representing three possible dates of retirement). These are then combined but with a different weight assigned to each value, depending on the "T" factor. "T" is the number of years until the member of the pension plan can take early retirement with an unreduced pension. Therefore, the greater the years of service, the more the preliminary value will be weighted towards an early retirement (i.e. higher) value of the pension. ...

The mortality tables used will now be unisex, so account will no longer be taken of the different life expectancies of men and women.

The pension administrator will also place a value on the spouse's survivor benefit where the parties separate after retirement.

[The author noted that some pension values will not be included (for example, pensions which are not governed by the *Pension Benefits Act* in Ontario). In addition, she noted that the new provisions will limit taking into account a person's shortened life expectancy in relation to the value of the person's pension:]

One highly debated aspect of the Regulations is that only very limited account will be taken in determining the value of a pension of a person with health issues that affect normal life expectancy. Only when the Shortened Life Expectancy (SLE) provisions of the PBA are engaged will this affect value. SLE is only available where a pension member files medical proof that death will occur within two years. A plan member who qualifies can apply to withdraw the commuted value of the pension. ...

This is a significant departure from existing practice whereby any spouse with a life expectancy that is significantly reduced by a health issue can make an argument, based on medical evidence, to discount the value of a pension to reflect the fact that he or she will not live to collect the full value.

[The author also noted the rules concerning pension plan changes and deficiencies in funding. In addition:]

The new rules determining value do not take account of whether a pension plan is underfunded. Underfunding may be a factor for either or both spouses or a court in determining whether or not to settle the equalization payment by a transfer of a lump sum out of the pension plan. ...

PROCEDURE FOR OBTAINING ADMINISTRATOR'S STATEMENT

- Either spouse may apply for the statement.
- The Administrator may charge a fee of $600 for valuing a Defined Benefit Plan, $200 for a Defined Contribution Plan or $800 for a hybrid plan consisting of both types of plans *(some pension plans have indicated they will waive the fees, at least initially)*.
- The administrator must produce the statement within 60 days and it must be sent to both spouses.
- Where there is a dispute as to date of separation, the Administrator may send statements for two different dates, but may charge separate fees for each.

SETTLEMENT OF EQUALIZATION ENTITLEMENTS

With certain limitations, parties remain free to settle their equalization differences by means of domestic contract, or they may be resolved by court order or family arbitration award.

The equalization payment (EP) can be satisfied in one of the following ways:

1. a payment made in cash or by instalments of cash, or for other consideration (e.g. transfer of property) as is currently the case;
2. a transfer of a lump sum from the member's pension to a prescribed (retirement) investment in the name of the spouse;
3. a combination of part cash and part lump sum transfer from the pension plan (as in 1 & 2 above);
4. a division of a pension income stream.

Where a pension is in pay at the date of separation, options 2 & 3 are not available.

Option 4 is only available where the pension is in pay. ...

Discretion to Determine Method of Payment

The broadest area of discretion in the entire new regime lies in how to settle an equalization entitlement. This may be the area which generates the most uncertainty and hence conflict at least until some guidance is developed in the caselaw.

Section 10.1(4) of the FLA lays out the following five governing factors:

1. the nature of the assets available to each spouse at the time of the hearing;
2. the proportion of the spouse's net family property that consists of the imputed value, for family law purposes, of his or her interest in the pension plan;
3. the liquidity of the lump sum in the hands of the spouse to whom it would be transferred;
4. any contingent tax liabilities in respect of the lump sum that would be transferred;
5. the resources available to each spouse to meet his or her needs in retirement and the desirability of maintaining those resources.

This section allows much room for debate and delivers new tools to ensure certain policy considerations become a factor. For example, it is clear that a spouse does not have to be stripped of all liquid assets to make an EP, and that, where a pension's value makes up a significant share of a spouse's NFP, there should be a proportional funding of the EP out of the pension.

Furthermore, it can be used to ensure rational retirement planning for both spouses, which is a particularly important factor where there is a prospect of spousal support continuing beyond retirement. This may be a useful tool to avoid a future double dipping dispute.

If there is a concern that the value assigned to the pension is not fair, for any of the reasons mentioned earlier in this paper, there is ample support in the language of this section for an insistence on payment by lump sum transfer in proportion to the pension value as it relates to the total NFP.

Division of Pension Income for Pensions in Pay

Where spouses separate *after* the retirement of a spouse holding an interest in a pension, no payment out of the pension plan is available. Instead, the parties may divide the income stream into two pensions, subject to a

50% rule (similar to the old 50% rule). The pension will be paid, in two income streams to member and spouse of their respective interests, until the member dies. Thereafter, the spouse receives the survivor benefit. ...

Transfer of Lump Sum from the Pension

Pursuant to an order, domestic contract or arbitration agreement, a spouse may apply for a transfer of a lump sum out of a member's pension plan. The amount to be paid must be set out as a dollar amount or must be described as a proportion of the value of the pension interest.

Under s. 67.3(2) of the PBA and s. 27 of the Regulations, the lump sum must go into one of the following:

1. another pension plan;
2. a life income fund;
3. a locked-in retirement account (RSP).

The Act contemplated a further option, that the lump sum could in fact be retained in the pension plan to the credit of the spouse, if the administrator agreed and the circumstances were prescribed by regulation. Unfortunately, the Regulation has not yet prescribed such circumstances. It can only be hoped that a revised regulation does follow in the near future, as it is likely that spouses will be able to generate a higher retirement income from a well managed pension plan than options 2 & 3 above. ...

UNMARRIED SPOUSES

Where unmarried spouses consent by domestic contract, the spouse without a pension may apply for a lump sum transfer out of the member's pension or, if the pension is already in pay, for a division of the pension income.

The parties would, in their agreement, designate the dates for the commencement and end of their cohabitation. Only the member may apply for a statement of value.

Married spouses can also avail themselves of the PBA provisions to expand the period of marriage to include a period of cohabitation prior to marriage. ...

Notes and Questions

Pensions and family property: The definition of "spouse" and related issues

Although the 2009 amendments to the *Family Law Act* in relation to pensions as family property were designed to provide more direction to lawyers and clients, some issues have been litigated since January 2012 when these amendments became effective. (Recall that *FLA*, s 10.1(8), makes these amendments applicable whether the V Day is before, on or after this effective date.)

One important issue was the definition of "spouse." In *Carrigan v Carrigan Estate*, 2012 ONCA 736, the Ontario Court of Appeal held that the definition of "spouse" in section 48(3) of the *Pension Benefits Act* referred to the wife of a pension holder, even if the spouses had separated (but never divorced) many years prior to the pension holder's death. In *Carrigan*, the pension holder had remained on good terms with his (married) spouse, but he had lived with another woman in a cohabiting relationship for many years. This cohabiting spouse argued that she was entitled to the pension holder's survivor benefit according to the definition of "spouse" in section 29 of the *Family Law Act*. However, because section 48(3) of the *Pension Benefits Act* included a "spouse" who was "living separate and apart," the appeal court (LaForme JA dissenting) held that:

> [28] ... [I]t is apparent that the word "spouse" in s 48(3) must always refer to the legally married spouse. Under the *PBA*, it makes no sense to conceive of a common law spouse living separate and apart from the member. While a person may be a common law spouse in other contexts, only a legally married spouse can live separate and apart from the member and still be a "spouse" under the *PBA*.

An application for leave to appeal to the SCC was filed on 14 December 2012 and dismissed on 28 March 2013: see *Quinn v Carrigan*, 2012 SCCA No 532. In a subsequent application, the Ontario Court of Appeal remitted to the trial court the issue of entitlement to spousal support on the part of the cohabiting spouse, Ms Quinn: see *Carrigan v Carrigan Estate*, 2013 ONCA 96; and *Quinn v Carrigan*, 2014 ONSC 5682.

More significantly, the *Pension Benefits Act* was amended in 2014. See SO 2014, c 7, Schedule 26, s 4(1)) to create entitlement for a cohabiting "spouse" in the circumstances of the *Carrigan* case (see *PBA*, ss 48(3) and 48(3.1). For payments by pension administrators prior to this amendment, sections 10.1 and 10.2 provide protection from claims, so long as the administrators complied with all other aspects of the pension administration process.

To what extent do you agree that this legislative compromise is appropriate? Note also the need for lawyers for clients who are separating or divorcing to provide clear advice with respect to pension arrangements. (There are also provisions re "spouses" as designated beneficiaries: see *PBA*, ss 48(1) and (2)).

In addition to *Carrigan*, other cases have focused on pension splitting in terms of "linked" or "delinked" arrangements, issues that may affect entitlement for former spouses at the death of one of them: see *Kershaw v Kershaw*, 2012 CarswellOnt 1403 (Ont Sup Ct). There is some authority in Manitoba for a waiver of pension sharing in a marriage contract: see *Dundas v Schafer*, 2012 CarswellMan 158 (QB), and such a waiver might also be upheld in Ontario in a valid contract. There is also an issue about the payment of interest to a recipient spouse when funds are transferred from a former spouse's pension plan as part of an equalization settlement: see *Heringer v Heringer*, 2014 ONSC 7291, denying payment of interest in the absence of a specific term in a separation agreement to do so.

With the enactment of the federal *Pooled Registered Pension Plans Act*, SC 2012, c 16, for federal employees, and Ontario's plans for similar pooled pension arrangements, pension issues are likely to continue to create challenges at separation and divorce.

CPP benefits and credit splitting

There is legislative authority for splitting entitlement to pension credits pursuant to the Canada Pension Plan at divorce or separation, but it is necessary to make an application (see *Pension Benefits Division Act*, SC 1992, c 46, Schedule 11, ss 4(1) and 2(a)). In *Swan v Canada* (1998), 47 RFL (4th) 282 (Fed CA), the court reviewed the relationship between the federal *Pension Benefits Division Act* and the *Family Relations Act*. Both married spouses and some cohabiting couples may make applications for this credit splitting of CPP benefits. As noted, however, section 4(2) excludes CPP benefits from the *FLA* equalization regime.

In 2004, the CPP legislation was successfully challenged in a class action by surviving partners of same-sex contributors to the Plan in *Hislop v Canada (AG)* (2004), 73 OR (3d) 641 (CA).

Cohabiting couples and pensions

Although the LCO *Final Report* concluded that the issue of whether its recommendations about pensions should be extended to cohabiting couples was beyond the scope of its *Report*, leaving this matter to a more generic study of family law and property, the 2009 *Act* included provisions that would permit cohabiting couples to make a domestic agreement reflecting the amendments to the *FLA*: see *FLA*, s 56.1.

However, in *Symmons v Symmons*, 2012 ONCA 747, where there had been some years of cohabitation prior to marriage, the Ontario Court of Appeal rejected the wife's claim to share in the increased value of the husband's pension during the period of cohabitation prior to the spouses' marriage. As the court noted, any resulting "injustice" could be addressed in the process of equalization pursuant to the *FLA*. To what extent is this conclusion justified?

In the context of pensions as a significant part of family property arrangements at dissolution, is it appropriate for Ontario to revisit the overall issue of property arrangements for cohabiting couples, as has occurred in some other Canadian provinces?

A brief note on "double dipping"

In a number of cases, spouses have challenged "double dipping" with respect to the relationship between pensions and spousal support. That is, a spouse may have included the value of a pension for purposes of determining the NFP and an equalization payment, and then be faced after retirement with a claim for spousal support payable out of a pension benefit.

In *Boston v Boston*, 2001 SCC 43, the Supreme Court of Canada considered such a claim, and concluded that only the part of the husband's pension earned after separation should be considered in determining his support obligations. However, the court also recognized that if the spousal support is based on need and the recipient spouse has made efforts to achieve self-sufficiency but still suffers economic hardship, the payor spouse may have a more significant obligation.

In this context, the LCO *Final Report* suggested respectfully that the Supreme Court's analysis in *Boston* was flawed because the Court treated pensions as unique forms of "property" in the family law context. According to the LCO, however, there are other forms of "property" that may also be affected by these principles. Thus, the LCO concluded (at 34):

> So far as double-dipping is concerned, it is the LCO's view that there is no difference in principle between a member spouse giving cash to meet an equalization debt in hopes of keeping her pension income intact and a shareholder spouse giving cash to meet an equalization debt in hopes of keeping his dividend income intact. It follows that the issue of double dipping is not unique to pensions; it is relevant in the case of any income-producing asset that has been taken into account in the equalization process.

On this basis, the LCO suggested that the issue of double dipping required assessment in relation to a more generic family property law project, not one related only to pensions. You may want to reflect further on the *Boston* decision and the LCO *Final Report* in relation to discussion about spousal support in Chapter Seven.

Pensions and other employment benefits

In addition to pensions, workplaces may offer a number of other kinds of benefits, including sick leave benefits, severance pay, or similar kinds of entitlements to be included. Moreover, because these issues have to be addressed in the context of each provincial family property statute, there is little uniformity across the country:

- **Disability benefits:** The Ontario Court of Justice held that a disability pension, received after health problems rendered the husband unable to work, formed part of his net family property for purposes of calculating the equalization payment, because the pension was paid in respect of work done by the husband, not as compensation for disability which would have been exempt under section 4(2) of the *FLA*: *McTaggart v McTaggart* (1993), 50 RFL (3d) 110 (Ont Gen Div).

    Recall *Lowe v Lowe* and related cases, discussed earlier in relation to the definition of "property," in which the court held that disability payments, intended to replace employment income, did not constitute "property."

- **Sick leave:** In *Bremer v Bremer* (2004), 13 RFL (6th) 89, the Ontario Court of Appeal agreed that sick leave benefits were included in the spouse's NFP.

- **Severance packages:** In *Birce v Birce* (2001), 22 RFL (5th) 6, the Ontario Court of Appeal held that the portion of a severance package attributable to post-separation wages was not included in the husband's NFP. (Note, however, *Maber v Maber* (2007), 313 NBR (2d) 208, where the N.B. court held that a severance payment converted to an RRSP was "property.")

    In *Leckie v Leckie* (2003), 5 RFL (6th) 123, the Ontario Court of Appeal held that an employment severance package received after separation, and which was not proposed or even likely at the date of separation (V day) did not form part of the NFP, even though the package was based on years of service that occurred during marital cohabitation. See also *Dembeck v Wright*, 2012 ONCA 852.

- **Personal injury damages and section 4(2):** Although damages for personal injury constitute excluded property pursuant to *FLA*, s 4(2), any portion of the damages that relate to compensation for wages during cohabitation must be included in the spouse's NFP. See *Trendle v Trendle* (2003), 50 RFL (5th) 440 (Ont Sup Ct); and *Vanderaa v Vanderaa* (1999), 18 RFL (4th) 393 (Ont Gen Div).

Additional Resources

Afshan Ali, *"Boston v. Boston*: A Case Comment" (2004) 20 Can J Fam L 367.

G Edmond Burrows & Penny E Hebert, "The Supreme Court of Canada and *Best v. Best"* (2000) 17 Can Fam LQ 263.

Neil Campbell, "Division of Pensions Under the Ontario *Family Law Act*: A Comment on *Marsham v. Marsham* and *Humphreys v. Humphreys"* (1988) 7 Can J Fam L 79.

Georgina Carson & Vanessa Lam, "Payment Issues: How Equalization Will be Affected" (Toronto: Ontario Bar Association, October 2011).

Berend Hovius & Timothy G Youdan, *The Law of Family Property* (Toronto: Carswell, 1991).

Freya Kodai, "Pensions and Unpaid Work: A Reflection on Four Decades of Feminist Debate" (2012) 24 CJWL 180.

Law Commission of Ontario, *Division of Pensions Upon Marriage Breakdown: Pension Division Regimes in Canadian Jurisdictions other than Ontario*, February 2009.

Law Reform Commission of British Columbia, *Report on the Division of Pensions on Marriage Breakdown* (Victoria: Ministry of the Attorney General, 1992).

James McLeod & Alfred Mamo, *Annual Review of Family Law, 2009* (Toronto: Carswell, 2009).

Diane Pask & Cheryl Hass, "Division of Pensions: The Impact of Family Law on Pensions and Pension Plan Administrators" (1992–93) 9 Can Fam LQ 133.

Diane Pask, Cheryl Hass & Keith L McComb, *Division of Pensions* (Toronto: Carswell, 1990).

JB Patterson, "Confusion Created in Pension Valuation for Family Breakdown Case Law by the Use of Expressions 'Termination Method' and 'Retirement Method'" (1998–99) 16 Can Fam LQ 249.

Elizabeth Shilton, "Gender Risk and Employment Pension Plans in Canada" (2013) 17 CLELJ 101.

Monica Townson, "The Impact of Precarious Employment on Financial Security in Retirement" in Leroy Stone, ed, *New Frontiers of Research on Retirement* (Ottawa: Statistics Canada, 2006) 364.

Claire Young, "Pensions, Privatization, and Poverty: The Gendered Impact" (2011) 23:2 CJWL 661.

STEP 3   DETERMINING EXCLUDED PROPERTY:
FLA, s 4(2)

The definition of "excluded property"

Section 4(2) of the *FLA* permits a spouse to exclude certain defined property if it is owned on V day. Obviously, exclusion of any of the defined forms of property at V day will reduce a spouse's resulting NFP.

The defined properties for exclusion (if it is owned on V day) are as follows:

#1 and #2: Property acquired by gift or inheritance from a third party after the date of the marriage, *if it is not a matrimonial home*, and income from this property only if the donor has expressly stated that such income is to be excluded;

#3 and #4: Damages for personal injury and a right to proceeds of life insurance, as defined;

#5: Property into which property in #1–#4 can be "traced"; and

#6 and #7: Property excluded by a domestic contract, and pensionable earnings under CPP.

Silverberg v Silverberg
(1990), 25 RFL (3d) 141 (Ont Gen Div)

One of the issues in *Silverberg v Silverberg* was the characterization of some jewellery given to Mrs. Silverberg by her employer. Unbeknownst to her husband at the time of the gift, Mrs. Silverberg was involved in an affair with her employer with whom she subsequently decided to live. In discussing whether the jewellery was excluded property under the Act, the court stated (at 149):

> The parties agreed that the value of Mrs. Silverberg's jewellery on valuation date was $22,884. Mrs. Silverberg submits that jewellery having a value of $10,584 should be excluded from her net family property pursuant to s. 4(2) of the *Family Law Act* as such jewellery was a gift from Mr. Greenberg. While Mrs. Silverberg was working for Mr. Greenberg and living with her husband, Mr. Greenberg gave her a number of pieces of expensive jewellery. The jewellery was given to Mrs. Silverberg at Christmas and on her birthday. According to Mr. Silverberg, his wife told him that the jewellery was given to her in lieu of a monetary bonus. I am sure that Mrs. Silverberg made such statements to her former husband in order to wear the jewellery without Mr. Silverberg being suspicious that she was having an affair with Mr. Greenberg. If the jewellery was earned by Mrs. Silverberg, it must be included in her net family property.
>
> I am sure that part of the reason for Mr. Greenberg giving Mrs. Silverberg the jewellery resulted from their relationship and accordingly part of the value represents a gift. I am also sure that part of the value of the jewellery represents a bonus or payment for Mrs. Silverberg's work within Mr. Greenberg's law practice. Accordingly, part of the value of the jewellery should be excluded property but, as I am unable to determine

on the evidence which part is represented by a gift and therefore excluded, the plaintiff has failed to satisfy the onus of determining the property to be excluded as required by s. 4(3) of the FLA.

What evidence might have satisfied the court in *Silverberg* that part of the value of the jewellery represented a gift from Mr. Greenberg?

As will be discussed below, courts have often concluded that spouses may not change the characterization of property. That is, if a spouse has characterized a property interest in one way for tax purposes, for example, the spouse may not "re characterize" the interest for family law purposes. In this context, the court may not have been willing to permit Mrs. Silverberg, who had asserted during the marriage that the jewellery represented a bonus in relation to employment, to (re)characterize it at V day as a gift.

Section 4(2), the definition of "gift" and "family" transfers: *McNamee v McNamee*

In *McNamee v McNamee*, 2011 ONCA 533, the spouses separated in 2007 after more than 18 years of marriage. During the marriage, the parties shared their incomes and expenses, and held all their assets and liabilities in their joint names, as an "equal partnership" (at para 8). The husband was one of two sons of the founder of McNamee Concrete Ltd., and both sons worked in this business which had grown to 30 employees and annual sales worth $5 million.

In 2003, the father implemented a corporate estate freeze to protect the business from creditors and to limit the impact of taxation at his death. The business was folded into a holding company, fixing its value at $2 million for purposes of the freeze, which would accrue to the father. However, future growth in value would be reflected in common shares issued to his two sons (subject to controls retained by the father). In particular, the father's preference shares were voting shares, and these shares entitled him to take unlimited dividends from the company at any time (and which could fully eliminate retained earnings in the future).

The father executed a Declaration of Gift. This Declaration provided that "neither the shares, nor any increase in their value or income from them, were to form part of the net family property of the donee in the event of marital breakdown; and ... the shares were to remain the donee's separate property, free from the control of his spouse" (para 14). It seems that, although he signed documents in 2003, the husband did not fully understand them or the nature of this transaction, but he was aware that the shares were transferred to him as a gift. Moreover, he conveyed news of this transfer to his wife, and they both assumed that it would provide for their future security.

Significantly, however, the husband did not see the Declaration of Gift until after he and his wife had separated in 2007. At separation, the value of the husband's shares was $418,200.

The trial judge concluded that the transfer of shares to the husband did not constitute a "gift" for purposes of section 4(2). Instead, the trial judge concluded that this was a transfer for consideration, that the father did not intend to gift the shares to his sons, that the father did not divest himself of all power or control in relation to the shares, and that the husband did not accept the gift. Thus, the husband was required to include the value of the shares in his NFP for purposes of equalization.

In the Ontario Court of Appeal, however, the appeal was allowed. Although the court recognized that the father's motive in transferring the shares was to effect the estate freeze, the court held that motive was not the same as consideration, and that there was no consideration in this case (at para 31). Similarly, the court held that the trial judge had conflated "intention" with "motivation," and that the father's motivation to create the estate freeze did not negate his intention to gift the shares to give effect to his purpose (at para 34). The court also concluded that the husband had accepted the gift in accordance with the applicable legal principles (at para 49), and that there was effective delivery. Thus, having concluded that the transfer of shares from father to son constituted a "gift" in law, the court held that the value of the shares at V day constituted "excluded property" for the husband's NFP calculation.

The court then proceeded to consider an alternative claim submitted by the wife. At trial, she had argued that if the shares constituted excluded property for the husband's NFP, they were nonetheless subject to a claim of unjust enrichment. Because the trial judge had concluded that the shares did not constitute excluded property, he did not proceed with the analysis of this alternative claim.

In the appeal court, court reviewed the principles articulated in *Rawluk v Rawluk* me Court of Canada, and particularly the requirement ner of an asset before [a court] makes an invento... In other words, the consideration of construc an essential preliminary step before the determina and before equalization" (at para 59). Referring n the Supreme Court of Canada, the appeal cour cess of determining ownership and then proceed process. The court held that

[65] ... a c st apply trust principles to determine ownership before turnin e exclusions listed in s. 4(2). This is supported by the language of s. 4(2) which provides: "The value of the following property that a spouse *owns* on the valuation date does not form part of the spouse's net family property ..." (emphasis added). A spouse cannot exclude property that is beneficially owned by someone else.

[66] It must be stated that, in the vast majority of cases, any enrichment that arises as the result of a marriage will be fully addressed through the operation of the equalization provisions under the *Family Law Act*; the spouse who legally owns an asset will ordinarily share half its value with the other spouse as a result of the equalization provisions under the Act. However, a fair and contextual reading of the equalization and net family property provisions of the *Family Law Act* ensures that married spouses are not deprived of equitable remedies they would otherwise have avail-

able to them because, as noted above, ownership issues — equitable and otherwise — are to be determined before the net equalization payment exercise is undertaken....

[67] In our view, the conditions in the Declaration of Gift are of no force or effect. When the appellant's father gave the shares to the appellant, he did not disclose the conditions to the appellant, nor did he provide the appellant with a copy of the Declaration of Gift. The appellant accepted the gift of the shares believing that they were without conditions.... [When the appellant was shown the Declaration of Gift after he and his wife had separated,] if the shares were [already] impressed by a constructive trust, the conditions would not operate so as to invalidate such a trust or the gift. In the peculiar circumstances of this case, and where the conditions were not communicated to the appellant until well after the gift was accepted and it became impossible for the appellant to comply, the conditions could not operate so as to invalidate the gift or prevent the imposition of the constructive trust [citing *Yates v University College, London* (1875), KR 7 HL 438; and *In re Macklem and Niagara Falls Park Commissioners* (1887), 14 OAR 20 (CA)]....

Although there was some evidence in this case about the wife's contributions within the family, the trial judge had not engaged in a detailed factual analysis of the wife's claim based on unjust enrichment because he had concluded that the shares were not a gift pursuant to section 4(2). In this situation, the court ordered a new trial in relation to the wife's claims of unjust enrichment and constructive trust with respect to these shares.

As *McNamee* confirms, the analysis in *Rawluk* continues to impact the implementation of equalization pursuant to the *FLA*. In addition, this case may be significant for its analysis of section 4(2) and the definition of a "gift," particularly in a context in which the donee learns about restrictions on the gift only *after* separation. How should business owners in future deal with this issue to ensure that there is a valid gift, and that their "intentions" about its status as separate property will be enforced?

Notes and Questions

The problem of characterization re "transfers" and "gifts"

Courts often experience difficulty in determining, after the fact, how to characterize intra-family arrangements, especially between parents and children. For example, in *Buttar v Buttar*, 2013 ONCA 517, the court examined a couple's marriage of 36 years, during which time they were engaged in a dairy farming operation. At some point during the marriage, the husband's parents had transferred ownership and control of their farming business to the couple, and (as part of this transaction), they also transferred their dairy quota to the husband (their son) alone. Thirty years later, at the time of the separation of the husband and wife, the husband alleged that the dairy quota was a "gift" to him alone. However, the Ontario Court of Appeal affirmed the trial judge's decision that the transfer of the dairy quota was part of the larger transaction for consideration. After referring to *McNamee*, the appeal court held:

> [35] ... The application judge's findings as to the nature of the arrangement between [the spouses] and the [husband's] parents are supported by the evidence. The evidence shows that this [husband], unlike the husband in *McNamee*, was involved in the transaction. The milk quota was part of a much larger transaction for which there was consideration. The items identified by the application judge are capable of constituting consideration when the transfer of the milk quota transaction is placed within the context of the entire transaction and this family's history. [The appeal court also declined to give effect to the husband's arguments with respect to the tax treatment of the farm transfer on the basis that "the tax treatment of family farms is complex" (at para 36).]

In *Townshend v Townshend*, 2010 ONSC 6405, 2012 ONCA 868, there were also issues about intra-family gifts and the impact of *McNamee*. For example, the husband's mother had made a gift of money to him, and the husband had deposited it to the joint account of the husband and his wife. The court held that the husband could deduct one-half the value in his NFP list: see also *Cartier v Cartier* (2007), 47 RFL (6th) 436, discussed later in this chapter. In addition, however, the court also considered a transfer to the husband from his brother of a 1967 Buick Wildcat, for which the husband provided funds for new tires. According to the appeal court:

> [43] In these circumstances, ... it was unreasonable [for the trial judge] to conclude that the husband had not acquired the car by way of gift. To the extent that the value of the car exceeded the value of the new tires, this additional value was acquired by gift and should be excluded from the calculation of the husband's net family property. The husband paid for the new tires and it was only their value — $400 — that should have been included in the husband's net family property.

In reflecting on *McNamee, Buttar,* and *Townshend*, consider how these intra-family transactions may need to be more carefully structured in relation to the possibility of separation or divorce. Why might it be difficult to achieve a greater degree of certainty in practice? What is the role of lawyers (including lawyers other than family lawyers) in relation to such transactions? For another example of problems in relation to intra-family transactions (a family trust) and lawyers' obligations, see *Stevens v Stevens*, 2013 ONCA 267, 2012 ONSC 706.

The onus of proof: Section 4(3) and *Harrington v Harrington*

Section 4(3) provides that the onus of proof in relation to claims for exclusions and deductions is on the person asserting the claim. Moreover, as the cases suggest, there is a need for evidence to support proof of such claims, and any doubt is resolved by including the disputed item of property. For example, in *Flatters v Brown* (1999), 48 RFL (4th) 292 (Ont Sup Ct), the court reviewed a number of claims to exclude property from the calculation of a spouse's NFP, emphasizing (at 295) the onus of proof in section 4(3):

> Equal possibility does not meet the burden of proof. It must be found to be more likely than not to tip the balance of probability.

In *Harrington v Harrington*, 2009 ONCA 39, the wife appealed from the trial judge's decision to permit her husband to exclude from his NFP calculation the principal and interest of funds amounting to $640,000.

The husband held a power of attorney for his father, and had invested a principal of $500,000 to attain the V day amount. It was agreed that the principal amount belonged to the father (by way of resulting trust), but the husband's father had agreed that the husband could use the income for his own purposes. The husband had used interest income to pay for family vacations, to purchase a yacht, and to pay some credit card bills. He also regularly reported this interest income on his income tax returns.

The Ontario Court of Appeal concluded that the husband had not discharged the onus of proof in section 4(3) to prove an exclusion, so that the interest income fell within the definition of "property" in section 4(1). Thus, the husband was required to include the interest income on V day in his NFP.

Tracing

The concept of "tracing" is not defined in the *FLA*, and courts have fashioned this remedy, taking into account the common law and equitable principles relating to this concept.

Ho v Ho
(1993), 1 RFL (4th) 340 (Ont Gen Div)

In *Ho v Ho*, the husband and wife received cash gifts from the husband's parents during their marriage. The gifts were sometimes made to the husband, sometimes to the wife, and sometimes to both of them. In relation to the calculation of their NFPs at separation, the spouses agreed that these were gifts pursuant to section 4(2) #1, but the husband asserted that all of the gifts were really intended for him, and that some gifts were made to the wife because she was in a lower tax bracket than the husband.

In accepting that some of the gifts were made to the wife for tax purposes, the court held that the husband could not "have it both ways." That is, if he had been asked by the Canada Revenue Agency whether the funds belonged to his wife, he would have said yes. Thus, the court concluded that he could not change the facts for purposes of separation and the *FLA* and that the gifts of cash belonged to the wife.

The court then continued, in relation to a gift of $200,000 to the wife, to consider the impact of the wife having advanced $146,000 to the husband to invest in a property. The court concluded that this amount was a loan, and continued:

> The wife's counsel indicated that ... the situation ... is "a wash." In other words, the husband's net family property statement would show it as a lia-

bility and the wife's would show it as a receivable. To this extent, counsel for the wife is correct. However, because the funds were a gift from Mr. Ho, Sr., and because the wife is able to trace those funds to the receivable due from her husband, the value of the asset (the receivable) may be excluded under the *Family Law Act*. This is the correct treatment of the $146,000....

The court also held that the wife had succeeded in tracing $5,400 to a car and $10,000 to a Canada Savings Bond, so that these amounts were also excluded pursuant to section 4(2). However, the remainder of the funds from the $200,000 gift had been commingled with other funds so that they could not be traced. Thus, the wife succeeded in proving her entitlement to exclude $161,400. The husband was able to prove entitlement to exclude $20,000 which was in his bank account at separation, having been received as a gift from his father two weeks earlier.

Consider this situation:

A husband received a gift of valuable farmland from his mother, after the date of his marriage. He eventually sold the land and used the proceeds of about $1 million to acquire investment properties, title to which was held by the spouses jointly. When the parties separated, what value, if any, could the husband exclude from his NFP?

According to the court in *Cartier v Cartier* (2007), 47 RFL (6th) 436 (Ont Sup Ct) at para 3:

[W]hen a spouse transfers gifted or inherited property into joint names, thereby conferring an interest in the other spouse, the transferring spouse loses the exclusion *only* to the extent of the gift he or she made to the other spouse, provided that the result intended by the transfer is joint ownership....

As a result, the husband was entitled to trace the proceeds of the gift to the investment properties and to exclude the value of his one-half interest in these properties at V day.

For another example of tracing, see *Goodyer v Goodyer* (1999), 168 DLR (4th) 453 (Ont Gen Div).

As will be discussed later in relation to "deductions" for an NFP calculation, there is no similar tracing provision for "deductions."

Excluded property and the matrimonial home

Section 4(2) #1 permits a spouse to exclude property acquired as a gift or inheritance from a third party after the date of the marriage, *so long as it is property other than a matrimonial home*.

For example, in *Lefevre v Lefevre* (1992), 40 RFL (3d) 372 (Ont Gen Div), the court traced funds received by a husband from an inheritance and from a personal injury settlement to purchase of a home, which was the matrimonial home at V day. As a result, the husband was not entitled to exclude the value of the matrimonial home.

In this way, a spouse who uses gifts (otherwise entitled to be excluded under section 4(2) #1) to contribute to the purchase of a matrimonial home may result in the value of the home being *included* if the home is the matrimonial home on V day.

In understanding this result, consider the definition of "matrimonial home" in section 4(1) of the *FLA*, which refers to section 18 in Part II of the *FLA*:

> As this definition makes clear, a matrimonial home is "every property" in which a person has an interest and which was "ordinarily occupied" by the person and a spouse as "their family residence" at V day.

Thus, although gifts from third parties after the date of the marriage are ordinarily entitled to be excluded, if the gift (or funds that can be traced from it) is the "matrimonial home" at V day, the value of the matrimonial home must be included in a spouse's NFP.

DaCosta v DaCosta
(1990), 29 RFL (3d) 422 (Ont Gen Div)

In *DaCosta v DaCosta*, the husband claimed the right to exclude the value of a home, purchased with funds from an inheritance. He asserted that the home, a recreational property called Cedar Dee Farm, was not a matrimonial home pursuant to section 18 because it had not been "ordinarily occupied" by the husband and his wife as their family residence at the time of separation. In assessing the husband's claim, the court stated:

> There can be no doubt that [at] any given time spouses may have more than one matrimonial home, i.e., cottage, hobby farm or condominium. In this case it was the intention of the spouses to use Cedar Dee Farm as a weekend retreat. It had a beautiful house, swimming pool and stables for riding horses. The issue is whether it was ever "ordinarily occupied" by Mr. and Mrs. DaCosta as a matrimonial home....
>
> [The] evidence of Mrs. DaCosta is less than satisfactory. She claims to have cooked meals and moved furniture at Cedar Dee. I do not believe her on this aspect of the case. Prior to the closing of the purchase of Cedar Dee, Mrs. DaCosta attended at the farm on two occasions. After the closing she attended at the farm on no more than three occasions. They did not stay overnight at the farm nor did they do any cooking at the farm. Mrs. DaCosta did not attend at the farm after the end of October 1986. It was after this date that the furniture which would allow the farm to be used as a matrimonial home was delivered from the garage at 291 Oriole Parkway. After the furniture was delivered to the farm, Mr. DaCosta spent considerable time at the farm. I find it impossible to reconcile Mrs. DaCosta's position that Cedar Dee Farm was ordinarily used as a matrimonial home and her failure to attend at the farm between 1st November 1986 and 27th March 1987. Surely, if it was being used as a matrimonial home, she would have attended at the farm.

> In my view, because of the stress in the marriage, Mrs. DaCosta by
> her own choice never used Cedar Dee Farm as a matrimonial home. In
> order to be a matrimonial home, it must be ordinarily occupied by the
> spouses at the time of separation. In this case it was never occupied as a
> matrimonial home. They may have intended to occupy it as a matrimonial
> home but they never carried out their intention, notwithstanding that they
> had an opportunity to carry out such an intention. Accordingly, Mr.
> DaCosta is entitled to exclude from the value of Cedar Dee Farm as of
> valuation day the sum of $149,613 which he inherited from his mother,
> grandmother and great aunt after his marriage to Mrs. DaCosta: s. 4(2)
> and 5 of the FLA.

The Ontario Court of Appeal confirmed the trial decision. See (1992),
40 RFL (3d) 216; and see also *Kraft v Kraft* (1999), 48 RFL (4th) 132 (Ont
CA).

Notes and Questions

The matrimonial home exception in section 4(2) #1

The *FLA* treatment of the matrimonial home has attracted some
criticism. For example, the OLRC *Report on Family Property Law* examined
how special treatment of the matrimonial home in relation to excluded
property may create unfairness, permitting manipulation of the rules by a
knowledgeable spouse to disadvantage a spouse who is not aware of their
implications. In addition, the special treatment of the matrimonial home in
relation to exclusions may affect a spouse's decision making about the use
of funds received as a gift or inheritance:

> As an example, if a spouse chooses to pay off the mortgage on the matri-
> monial home using an inheritance, she may not exclude that sum from
> her net family property. If she invested her inheritance in a guaranteed
> investment certificate or another instrument held in her own name, she
> would be able to exclude this asset from her net family property. ...
> [T]hese rules will catch only the unwary. Their impact, for those who are
> aware of them, is to discourage a spouse from applying capital in what
> might otherwise be the most advantageous manner. (OLRC *Report on
> Family Property Law* (Toronto: Ministry of the Attorney General, 1993) at
> 80; and see also 79–81)

Similar problems may also arise with respect to the special treatment
of the matrimonial home in relation to deductions, discussed later in this
section. To some extent, these concerns raise fundamental issues about the
goals of the family property regime:

> A property regime such as that established by Part I of the *Family Law
> Act* is based on the premise that both spouses make an essential and
> basically equal contribution to the economic viability of the family unit
> and hence to the acquisition of wealth by the unit. The total financial
> product of the marriage as an economic partnership is, therefore, gener-
> ally shared equally when the relationship ends. It follows that the norm
> of equal sharing should be applied only to the net value of those prop-
> erty rights which constitute the economic product of the constructive col-
> laboration of husband and wife, not to the gross value of all property

held by the spouses at the end of the relationship. While this principle may be readily accepted, actual identification of the shareable financial product presents difficulty and may lead to reasonable differences of opinion.... [For example,] property may be acquired during the marriage ... by inheritance, [so] that its value does not originate in the joint efforts of the spouses. Should it, nevertheless, form part of the financial product of the marriage? If some credit is to be given for acquisition of property in this way, should it be for the value at the date of acquisition or its value at the end of the relationship? (Berend Hovius & Timothy G Youdan, *The Law of Family Property* (Scarborough, ON: Carswell, 1991) at 315–16)

Consider this assessment, in relation to special treatment of the matrimonial home, in relation to deductions as well as exclusions. Is reform needed with respect to this issue?

Trust property and the matrimonial home

In *Spencer v Riesberry*, 2012 ONCA 418, the appeal court upheld a trial judge's decision that the wife's beneficial interest in a trust (in which the couple's "matrimonial home" constituted part of the trust property) did not constitute a matrimonial home, pursuant to the *FLA*, s 18, and was therefore not part of the wife's net family property.

Sandra Spencer and Derek Riesberry were married in 1994 and lived together in a home with their two children. The home had been purchased by Sandra's mother the year prior to Sandra's marriage, and it was held in trust for Sandra's mother, Sandra and her three siblings. Originally, Sandra's mother was the trustee (with a life interest as beneficiary in the trust property) and Sandra and her siblings were the other beneficiaries. Later, the trust agreement was amended so that Sandra and one of her siblings became trustees in place of her mother. As a result, Sandra was both a trustee and a beneficiary of the trust, which held as trust property the home in which Sandra and her family resided.

According to the trust document, the trust property could be used by Sandra's mother during her lifetime, and on her death, the trust property was to be divided equally among the beneficiaries living at her death. Sandra and Derek and their children resided in one of the homes held as property of the trust (and there were similar arrangements with Sandra's siblings and their families). Sandra and Derek paid costs associated with the home. The trust agreement specifically stated that any distribution from the trust was not to be included in a spouse's NFP.

When Sandra and Derek separated, Sandra's mother gave notice to vacate the home, and Derek then claimed that the home was a "matrimonial home" pursuant to *FLA*, s 18. When the trial judge rejected this claim, Derek appealed.

The Court of Appeal dismissed the appeal, concluding that although Sandra held a "contingent beneficial interest in the ... trust property as a whole, ... the [wife] as a beneficiary [of the trust] has no property interest in any specific trust asset. Therefore she has no specific legal interest in the property within the meaning of s. 18(1) of the *FLA*." More specifically, the appeal court concluded:

[58] There are two conditions in s 18(1) that must be satisfied for a property to be a matrimonial home: (1) a person must have an interest in the property; and (2) at the time of separation, the property must be ordinarily occupied by the person and his or her spouse as their family residence. The trial judge recognizes that the second condition had been met.... However, ... he held that the first condition had not been met because [the wife's] interest is in the [trust], not the [home] property.

Thus, the value of the home was not included in the wife's net family property calculation.

Consider the broader impact of this decision. One comment about the case, for example, suggested that the decision "provides an appellate-level green light to move property outside of the purview of the *Family Law Act* by way of trusts, a shift that will allow families and spouses to create what are essentially "one-sided domestic contracts": see Amy Cull, "Family Trusts or One-Sided Domestic Contracts? The Ontario Court of Appeal Case of *Spencer v Riesberry*" (2013) 32 Est Tr & Pensions J 101 at 105–106.

Cull also recommended that courts should treat spousal interests in property held by family trusts in the same manner as interests held in corporately-owned property. To what extent do you agree that this issue can be resolved by courts, or is legislative action needed to implement these suggestions for reform?

The value of "excluded property" in section 4(2)

It is important to note that section 4(2) permits a spouse to exclude the value of property that a spouse owns on V day, so long as it meets the requirements of the section. This means that it is the value of the excluded property on V day that can be excluded, not the value of the gift, etc., when it was received.

Consider the following:

Assume that the wife's parents gifted her a valuable painting after her marriage. At the time of the gift, the painting was valued at $100,000, but its value increased to double that amount at V day. According to section 4(2), the painting is excluded property at V day, regardless of its value on that date.

Assume that the wife decided not to keep the painting, and sold it a few years after the gift was received for $150,000. When the wife seeks advice about whether to use these funds to pay off the mortgage of the matrimonial home, or invest them in the stock market, what legal advice is appropriate? To what extent does this example suggest that spouses need to consider the state of their marriage in relation to decisions about investments?

In this way, the "value" of excluded property is different from the valuing of deductions for pre-marriage property, discussed later in this section. The OLRC recommended amendments to ensure that married spouses shared the increase in capital value during the marriage (see OLRC *Report* at 75ff).

STEP 4   VALUING "PROPERTY" FOR THE *FLA*

Judicial principles about valuation of "property"

Even though Ontario's *FLA* depends fundamentally on establishing values for property in order to calculate the NFP, the statute originally contained no direction with respect to principles of valuation. As noted earlier in this chapter, the *FLA* amendments of 2009 now provide some guidance with respect to the valuation of pensions, but more general principles of valuation have not been included in the *FLA*.

As a result, the principles of valuation have been established by judicial decisions, often relying on expert evidence of accountants and others. For example, in *Rawluk v Rawluk*, the trial judge stated:

> While the Act speaks of value, it contains no definition of that term nor, indeed, guidelines of any kind to assist in the determination of its meaning other than the provision contained in section 4(4) that when value is required to be calculated as of a given date, it shall be calculated as of the close of business on that date. Absent any statutory direction, "value" must then be determined on the peculiar facts and circumstances as they are found and developed on the evidence in each individual case. While this approach does not lead to uniformity and predictability of result, it does recognize the individuality inherent in each marriage and case and permit the flexibility so often necessary to ensure an equitable result. (*Rawluk v Rawluk* (1986), 3 RFL (3d) 113 at 122 (Ont HC); aff'd (1990), 23 RFL (3d) 337 (SCC))

In general, courts have tended to accept "fair market value" as the appropriate measure of valuing property for the purposes of the *FLA*, while recognizing that other principles may be used if the property has no fair market value, or where it is an inappropriate measure of value for particular kinds of property. See *Menage v Hedges* (1987), 8 RFL (3d) 225 at 245 (Ont Unif Fam Ct). In addition, courts have concluded that valuations should take into account only facts known on V day. See *Heon v Heon* (1989), 69 OR (2d) 758 (HC).

Oswell v Oswell
(1990), 28 RFL (3d) 10 at 20–22 (Ont HC)

In this case, the court assessed the evidence of several experts with respect to Mrs. Oswell's "property" at V day, including some jewellery and furs. Is the judge using a fair market value, or some other approach? To what extent does the valuation process seem to require the exercise of judicial discretion?

> The expert evidence as to the value of Mrs. Oswell's jewellery and furs was not satisfactory from either party. Mr. Shore testified that he is a gemologist and that he had valued certain items of Mrs. Oswell's jewellery. Two diamonds were valued at $11,000 on the basis of being sold back to the trade. A higher return might be realized if the jewellery was sold at auction. Mr. Shore valued the gold jewellery he was shown by Mrs. Oswell as scrap jewellery and not on an estate basis, as he said that

many of the pieces were worn. He placed this value at $2,900. There was no list of the pieces which were brought to Mr. Shore to value. Mrs. Oswell's evidence is that all of the pieces with the exception of a watch were brought to him.

Mr. Robert Low, a consultant and evaluator with the firm of Campbell Valuation Partners, an expert in asset and business valuation with no personal expertise in valuing jewellery and furs, testified that the approach he had used for valuation was the appraised value of the item for insurance purposes less 50 per cent. The 50 per cent factor was reached after a conversation with a person he considered to be knowledgeable about such matters at Birks. The jewellery was not examined individually.

The valuations of Mr. Low are based on appraised value for insurance purposes, which was said to be replacement value as opposed to actual value. The 50 per cent reduction was an attempt to arrive at actual value, but it was admitted that the factor could vary. No account was taken of the price of gold when the jewellery was bought or the decline in the price of gold since 1977. Using this approach, Mrs. Oswell's jewellery was valued at $7,900 as at the date of marriage, $28,000 in 1984 and $32,400 in 1987 and 1988. Between 1977 and 1984 jewellery acquired by Mrs. Oswell cost $7,000. After that date Mr. Oswell did not purchase any other jewellery for his wife.

The parties would not agree to have the jewellery valued by a single independent appraiser whose values would be binding. In part this was because it was felt that, since Mr. Oswell had agreed to the method of valuation used by Campbell, the same method of valuation should be applied to Mrs. Oswell's assets. Despite the unsatisfactory evidence, the court must therefore do the best it can.

I am of the opinion that, with respect to the gold jewellery owned by Mrs. Oswell prior to marriage, any increase in value has been offset by the decline in the price of gold since 1977 and by normal wear. I find that Mrs. Oswell's net family property should show a net increase after marriage in the amount of $7,000 for jewellery. This figure assumes wear and tear is offset by any increase in the value of gem stones owned by Mrs. Oswell.

Mrs. Oswell testified that her father had been in the fur business and that she knew something about furs. A wild mink coat, which was purchased at a cost of $12,000, was indicated by her to be worth about $5,000 or $6,000 in 1984. I accept this value. According to a letter obtained by Mrs. Oswell from her furrier, this coat has a present value of $2,000. This is after a substantial decline in the price of furs in 1988. Given these parameters, I am of the opinion that the value to be assigned to this coat should be $4,000 in 1988. The value of the fox fur coat is also in dispute. It was purchased in late 1986 by Mr. Oswell for $7,500. It is indicated to have a value in 1990 of $1,500. In early 1988 I find that the value of this coat is $4,000.

According to Mrs. Oswell, the furs she owned at the date of marriage were worth $2,000 and are now practically worthless. I accept this. Mrs. Oswell's net family property statement should reflect her furs as a net increase of $6,000 after marriage.

The "time" for valuation

It is important to note that the valuation of net family property relates to all property owned by a spouse on V day, and that the value of property to be excluded similarly relates to property owned by a spouse on V day.

By contrast, the value of property for purpose of a pre-marriage deduction relates to the value of the property at marriage. This issue is further considered in the next section concerning Deductions.

Valuing property and costs of disposition

In many cases, the calculation of an equalization payment will necessitate the disposition of some assets to make the payment required. In a number of cases, courts have considered the issue of whether the costs of disposition should be used to discount the value of assets included in the spouses' NFP calculations.

For example, if it appears that it will be necessary for a spouse to cash an RRSP to make an equalization payment, should the spouse be permitted to deduct the tax liability that will result?

This issue is discussed later in the next section concerning Deductions.

Negative property values

In *Montague v Montague* (1997), 23 RFL (4th) 62, the Ontario Court of Appeal agreed with the trial judge that land owned by the husband had no value at all — because the land was extremely polluted, the cost of cleanup exceeded the value of the land. Thus, the trial judge had concluded that the land had no value for purposes of the *Family Law Act*. The Ontario Court of Appeal held that the value of land is the highest price obtainable in an open market between informed and prudent parties acting at arm's length. Because an informed and prudent purchaser would take into account the cleanup costs in determining the price to pay for the land, the court agreed that the trial judge's valuation was appropriate.

It is also important to distinguish between negative values and negative NFPs. The latter issue is addressed by section 4(5) and is considered in relation to equalization (Step 6).

STEP 5   DEDUCTIONS: *FLA*, s 4

Deductions and net family property: s 4(1)

The definition of "net family property" in section 4(1) includes all "property" except "excluded property," after two deductions have been taken into account:

- Debts and liabilities (including contingent tax liabilities) relating to property owned at V day; and

- The value of property that a spouse owned on the date of marriage, after deducting debts and liabilities (other than specified debts and liabilities), calculated at the date of marriage. That is, the value based on the date of marriage, see *Mittler v Mittler* (1988), 17 RFL (3d) 113 (Ont HC).

Significantly, however, the value of a "matrimonial home" owned at the date of marriage, and *still owned* at V day, *cannot* be deducted, and the debts and liabilities at marriage do not include those related to the acquisition or significant improvement of a matrimonial home.

Recall that section 4(3) creates an onus of proving a deduction on the spouse who is claiming it. As a result, there is a need to provide documentary evidence with respect to these deductions. In the case of pre-marriage property, this may sometimes prove difficult. As Stephen Grant suggested, this onus may mean that "Marriage, for the unwary, may turn out to be an exercise in bookkeeping, whatever else it is" (Stephen Grant, "Deductions Under the Family Law Act: The Sequel" (1990) 6 Can Fam LQ 257 at 258).

Debts and liabilities at V day: Disposition costs

As noted above, a number of cases considered the issue of deductions with respect to the costs of disposition, and there was initially some conflict in their conclusions.

In *McPherson v McPherson* (1988), 63 OR (2d) 641, the Ontario Court of Appeal reviewed provisions of the former *Family Law Reform Act*, and concluded that disposition costs were not deductible in the absence of evidence of a plan for disposition.

By contrast, in *Heon v Heon* (1989), 22 RFL (3d) 273 (Ont HC), the court recognized the validity of such deductions regardless of an intent to dispose of assets.

These conflicting views were resolved in *Starkman v Starkman* (1990), 28 RFL (3d) 208, when the Ontario Court of Appeal confirmed the views expressed in *McPherson*.

And in *Sengmuller v Sengmuller* (1993), 17 OR (3d) 208, the Court of Appeal again addressed this issue, concluding that:

> If the evidence satisfies the trial judge, on a balance of probabilities, that the disposition of any item of family property will take place at a particular time in the future, then the tax consequences (and other properly proven costs of disposition) are not speculative, and should be allowed either as a reduction in value or as a deductible liability....
>
> [Parties must] adduce evidence ... from which the trial judge could assess the likely time of disposition, the likely disposition costs at that time, and the present value of those costs as at the valuation date.... It is true that such calculations are not exact, but courts have never refused to make assessments merely because the evidence available is less than precise. [Thus, there are three rules to be applied:]
> 1) apply the overriding principle of fairness, i.e., that costs of disposition as well as benefits should be shared equally;
> 2) deal with each case on its own facts, considering the nature of the assets involved, evidence as to the probable timing of their disposition, and the probable tax and other costs of disposition at that time, discounted as of valuation day; and
> 3) deduct disposition costs before arriving at the equalization payment, except in the situation where 'it is not clear when, if ever,' there will be a realization of the property.

To what extent do these principles require the exercise of judicial discretion? Do these rules suggest that, at least in some cases, the courts' interpretation of the *Family Law Act* reflects goals of "fairness" rather than "certainty"? Recall the views expressed in 1986 by Galligan J in *Skrlj v Skrlj* that "the legislature has clearly expressed its intent to remove judicial discretion from property disputes."

The *FLA* was amended in 2009 to confirm specifically that "any contingent tax liabilities" may be included as "liabilities" in the definition of net family property: see s 4(1.1); and *Cosentino v Cosentino*, 2015 ONSC 271. Issues about the "fairness" of including such liabilities were considered by the Supreme Court of Canada in 2008 in relation to an appeal from British Columbia (pursuant to the earlier legislation, the *Family Relations Act*): see *Stein v Stein*, 2008 SCC 35; and Robert Leckey, "Developments in Family Law: The 2008–2009 Term — Just Divisions?" (2009) 48 SCLR 181.

In practice in Ontario, issues about disposition costs continue to require lawyers and judges to engage in discretionary decision-making: for an overview, see Stacie Glazman & Susan Blackwell, "New Developments in Disposition Costs and Why they Matter" (2014) 33:1 Can Fam LQ 49.

Deductions, Debts and "Fairness": *Zavarella v Zavarella*

A spouse's entitlement to "deduct" a debt or liability (including the value of pre-marriage property) results in a lower NFP for that spouse. This result may mean that the spouse entitled to make the deduction is required to make a *lower* equalization payment to the other spouse; or that the spouse entitled to the deduction receives a *higher* equalization payment from the other spouse. Thus, the calculation of net family property for each spouse may create disputes about whether particular deductions are appropriate.

This issue was addressed in *Zavarella v Zavarella*, 2013 ONCA 720. In this case, the wife made an assignment in bankruptcy in relation to debts of approximately $50,000. The assignment in bankruptcy occurred just prior to her marriage, and a few months after the marriage, she was discharged without an obligation to make any payments in relation to this pre-marriage debt. At trial, the judge included her debt of $50,000 as a debt at the time of the marriage because of the timing of the discharge after the marriage.

In the Court of Appeal, a majority concluded that the amount of the wife's debt at marriage should be revised to zero on the basis of the "reality" of the debt at V Day:

> [32] It will be readily apparent that the debt a spouse brings to the marriage will affect that spouse's entitlement in the equalization calculation. This makes sense because it can be assumed that the spouses paid off that debt during the course of the marriage and the family assets were diminished accordingly.

> [33] However, if the evidence does not support this assumption, the court cannot simply insert the face value of the debt into the NFP calculation. To do so could undermine the objective of equalization, which is to divide equally between the spouses the net wealth accumulated from the date of

marriage to the date of separation. Instead, in my view, the court must make a meaningful determination of the value to attribute to the date of marriage debt.

Although the court concluded that there were no cases directly on point, the majority analyzed cases about contingent liabilities to reach its result that the amount of the wife's marriage debt should be included in her NFP as zero.

By contrast with the majority's concern for "fairness," the dissenting opinion suggested a need to return to first principles in this case. Referring to *Skrlj v Skrlj* (and also to *Serra v Serra*, discussed later in this chapter), the dissenting opinion referred to the legislature's basic proposition in the *FLA* of a "formulaic" approach to equalization of family property — and an effort to minimize the exercise of judicial discretion (at para 75). Thus, the dissenting judgment concluded that:

> [84] In contrast to the *FLA* property rules, judicial discretion leads to trials. Its exercise requires detailed evidence about the unique circumstances, histories and expectations of the particular spouses. These finely tuned results come at a cost most often disproportionate to what is at stake....

To what extent do you agree with the result in *Zavarella* in the Court of Appeal? Does this result change your view about the balancing of goals of "certainty" (rules) and "fairness" (discretion) in the *FLA*? This issue is addressed again later in this chapter with respect to the 2009 amendment to the NFP definition of deductions relating to the matrimonial home.

Deductions and the matrimonial home: *Folga v Folga* and *Nahatchewitz v Nahatchewitz*

As with respect to issues about excluded property, the *FLA* in Ontario provides for special treatment of the matrimonial home in relation to deductions for property owned by a spouse at the date of the marriage.

To achieve the goal of ensuring that the spouses are required to share only the value of property accumulated during the marriage, section 4(1) permits a spouse to deduct the value of assets owned on the date of marriage. However, *if the asset is the matrimonial home at V day*, then its value at the date of marriage cannot be deducted as pre-marriage property. Although this approach ensures that a matrimonial home remains in the "joint" assets of the spouses at V day, it can create some hardship for a spouse who owns a home at marriage if the home remains the matrimonial home at V day. Consider these two examples:

1. The husband owned a home at marriage, which was valued at $100,000 at the date of marriage. The wife and husband resided in this home until V day, when the house is worth $300,000 and is still owned by the husband alone. What result?

According to the definition of "deductions" in the *FLA*, the husband must include in his NFP the value of the home at V day, that is $300,000, and because the home is the matrimonial home at V day (see *FLA*, s 18), he is not permitted to deduct its pre-marriage value of $100,000. Thus, in the absence of any other assets at V day for the husband and wife, the husband will have an NFP of $300,000, and the equalization payment to his wife will be $150,000 (assuming her NFP is 0).

> 2. Alternatively consider that the husband owned a home at marriage, valued at $100,000 at the date of marriage. He sold this home and used the proceeds to purchase a home for himself and his wife, which is in the husband's name alone, and this second home is the matrimonial home at V day (see *FLA*, s 18), valued at $300,000. What result?

According to the definition of "deductions" in the *FLA*, the husband must include in his NFP the value of the home at V day, that is $300,000. In this case, however, he will be able to deduct the value of first home, because it is no longer a matrimonial home at V day. Thus, in the absence of any other assets, his NFP will be reduced to $200,000 and he will owe an equalization payment to his wife of $100,000 (assuming her NFP is zero).

This result was confirmed in *Folga v Folga* (1986), 2 RFL (3d) 358 (Ont HC), where the court concluded that:

> The status of a matrimonial home is not immutable and a spouse may lose the protection [given] by the matrimonial home status and ... a spousal owner may regain the right to deduct under s. 4(1)(b).
>
> [In this case,] it appears that although [the property in issue] was once the matrimonial home it is no longer so under ss. 4(1) and 18 since the parties were not ordinarily resident in it at the date of separation. Not being a matrimonial home, it now qualifies for deduction under s. 4(1)(b).

To what extent does this treatment of the matrimonial home create problems for the unwary? For example, consider this situation:

> The husband married his wife and they moved into his home, owned by the husband at the date of marriage. However, the wife was required to live outside Canada for a period of time in order to complete the requirements for Canadian citizenship. While she was living outside Canada, her husband sold the home, and then, a few years later, the parties separated. Is the husband permitted to deduct the value of the home he owned at the date of marriage?

In *Nahatchewitz v Nahatchewitz* (1999), 1 RFL (5th) 395, the Ontario Court of Appeal concluded that the home was not "ordinarily occupied by the spouses as their family residence" at the time of separation (s 18), and thus, the husband was permitted to deduct the value of this house as pre-marriage property. The court expressly followed the decision in *Folga*. (For other examples, see *Mazzarello v Mazzarello* (1999), 44 RFL (4th) 142 (Ont CA); and *McDonald v McDonald* (1997), 33 RFL (4th) 3 (Ont CA).)

Moreover, unlike section 4(2) and the provision for "tracing" with respect to "excluded property," there is no similar provision relating to "deductions" in the definition of net family property. In what circumstances might this omission create unfairness?

Deductions for "matrimonial home expenses": The 2009 *FLA* amendment

The 2009 amendments to the *FLA* included an addition to the definition of deductions for pre-marriage property. As a result of this addition, "debts and liabilities related directly to the acquisition or significant improvement of a matrimonial home" are not included in the calculation of pre-marriage property.

This amendment substantially reflected the decision of the Ontario Court of Appeal in *Collier v Torbar* (2002), 27 RFL (5th) 304. To what extent do you agree that this amendment achieves fairness for the spouses?

Collier v Torbar

In this case, the wife purchased land in 1991 and built a house. The purchase of the land was financed by a loan from a company which the wife owned with a partner. The loan was not secured by a mortgage against the land, but by a housing loan under the *Income Tax Act*. The loan was later transferred to a holding company owned by the wife's mother, created to enable the wife to buy out her partner.

In 1994, the spouses began to cohabit and they were married in 1995. The wife's house became the matrimonial home. At the date of marriage, the wife owed $513,748 in relation to the loan. The spouses separated in 1997. At that time, the wife claimed a right to deduct the debt at marriage from the calculation of her NFP:

> [6] There is no dispute that in calculating the wife's net family property, the wife must include the valuation date value of the matrimonial home and may not deduct its marriage date value [pursuant to section 4(1)]....

> [7] The issue in this case is whether the amount of the housing loan must be deducted from the marriage date value of the property owned by the wife on the marriage date. Section 4(1)(b) provides that a spouse must deduct debts and other liabilities from the marriage date value of property owned on the marriage date. The result of deducting marriage date debts from the marriage date value of property owned on the marriage date is that a spouse's marriage date debts increase the spouse's net family property. Requiring the wife to deduct the amount of the housing loan from the marriage date value of the property she owned on the marriage date would increase her net family property by $513,748, the amount of the housing loan.

> [8] The wife submits that this result would be harsh and inequitable since she is already required to include the valuation date value of the matrimonial home and is not permitted to deduct the marriage date value of the home. She submits that this result could not have been intended by the Family Law Act. The husband concedes that if the loan on the matrimonial home had been secured by a mortgage, the amount of the loan would not be deducted from the marriage date value of the property owned by the wife on the marriage date. However, the husband submits that since the loan was not secured by a mortgage, the loan must be treated the same as any other debt not tied to the matrimonial home.

The court noted that the trial judge had accepted the wife's argument and held that the amount of the housing loan should not be deducted from the marriage date value of the property owned by the wife on the marriage date, and concluded that housing loans under the *Income Tax Act* are in the nature of an alternative mortgage.

In assessing the arguments, the court referred to *Menage v Hedges*, (1987), 8 RFL (3d) 225, where the Unified Family Court judge held that he had no option but to include the husband's debt, a loan of $35,000 from the husband's father, in calculating the husband's NFP. However, subsequent cases distinguished *Menage v Hedges* if the loan was in the form of a mortgage against the home. For example, see *DaCosta v DaCosta* (1990), 29 RFL (3d) 422 (Ont Gen Div); (1992), 7 OR (3d) 321 (CA); *Hulme v Hulme* (1989), 27 RFL (3d) 403 (Ont HC); and *Reeson v Kowalik* (1991), 36 RFL (3d) 396 (Ont Gen Div).

> [16] The decisions in DaCosta v. DaCosta, Hulme v. Hulme, Reeson v. Kowalik and Menage v. Hedges all recognize the unfairness of deducting the amount of a debt incurred to purchase a matrimonial home from the marriage date value of property owned on the marriage date. Section 4(1)(b) of the Family Law Act imposes a special burden on the spouse who brings a matrimonial home into the marriage by not permitting the spouse to deduct the marriage date value of the home in calculating his or her net family property. The legislature must have determined that the special character of a matrimonial home justified this special burden.

> [17] However, to require the spouse to deduct a debt incurred to purchase the matrimonial home from the marriage date value of property owned on the marriage date would impose a double burden. The spouse would receive no benefit for the marriage date value of the matrimonial home and would be further burdened by the marriage date amount of any debt attributable to the home. I agree with the reasoning in DaCosta v. DaCosta, Hulme v. Hulme and Reeson v. Kowalik that the Family Law Act should be interpreted so as to avoid this obvious unfairness....

In the result, the Court of Appeal held that the wife's housing loan was equivalent to a mortgage because it "must be documented to satisfy the *Income Tax Act*," and such constraints represented a "sufficient link between the debt and the matrimonial home" to bring this case within the principle of *DaCosta, Hulme,* and *Reeson*. The court then addressed the wife's alternative argument that no debts relating to the matrimonial home should be deducted from the marriage date value of property owned on the marriage date:

> [20] ... Although there is much to be said for treating all debts on the same basis regardless of the legal form they take, unsecured and undocumented family loans may require different treatment. In general terms, it seems to me that if the borrower can demonstrate that he or she is subject to some legal or financial constraint linking the debt to the matrimonial home, the debt should not be deducted from the marriage date value of other property owned by the borrower. While I do not wish to rue out the possibility of similar treatment for other debts incurred to purchase a matrimonial home, courts must closely scrutinize unsecured and undocu-

mented family loans to ensure the integrity of the equalization provisions of the Family Law Act.

To what extent does the 2009 *FLA* amendment to the definition of "deductions" create greater scope with respect to debts relating to the matrimonial home? Are there issues identified in *Collier* that may need to be resolved pursuant to this amendment in future?

As noted earlier, the special treatment of the matrimonial home in relation to "excluded property" and "deductions" can be a cause of some unfairness at separation or divorce. These issues are further discussed later in this chapter in relation to section 5(6).

Notes and Questions

The OLRC *Report* and "special treatment" of the matrimonial home (*FLA*, Part I)

At the time of enacting the *Family Law Act*, concerns were expressed about the need to preserve the matrimonial home for both spouses. Such concerns resulted in the exceptions in sections 4(1) and (2) of the *Family Law Act* with respect to deductions and exclusions. Because a matrimonial home, as defined in section 18, cannot be deducted or excluded, its value must always be included in the net family property of the title holder(s).

In this way, it is clear that a spouse with a valuable asset may be able to deduct it if it was pre-marriage property or exclude it if it was a gift from a third party during the marriage.

However, if the asset is the matrimonial home at V day, it cannot be either deducted or excluded.

Thus, as explained earlier, the different treatment of the matrimonial home may be experienced as unfair to a title holding spouse in some circumstances.

Clearly, the current legislative regime attempts to balance the interests of a title holder and a non-title holder at marriage breakdown. These arrangements were reviewed by the OLRC's *Report on Family Property Law*, which recommended abolition of this special treatment of the matrimonial home. Examine the reasoning of the OLRC *Report* which follows. To what extent do you agree with its statement of the problem and its proposals for reform? Is it sufficient to confine principles about the matrimonial home within Part II of the *Family Law Act*? Is the underlying purpose of equalization in Part I better achieved by treating all property, including the matrimonial home, in the same way?

The OLRC *Report* considered a number of possibilities for revising the treatment of the matrimonial home, and then continued (at 84–85):

> A more radical reform, but one in keeping with the central principle of Part I of the Act, would be to end special treatment of the matrimonial home under Part I. This would have the advantage of allowing owner spouses to take advantage of statutory deductions and exclusions. It would

also allow spouses to continue to allocate ownership of the matrimonial home to protect it from creditors, as they are able to do with other assets. If a spouse has debts and liabilities at the valuation date, these may be set off against the full equity in the house. The need to protect the interest of a non-owner spouse in the preservation of an asset which provides shelter and is often the family property of the greatest value, would continue to be guaranteed by the provisions in Part II of the Act. A spouse without title would continue to have possessory rights in the home and the rights of the titleholder to encumber or dispose of the home would remain severely restricted.

The disadvantage to this approach is that a non-owner spouse will not share in the benefits of ownership, both psychological and practical, although in many cases both spouses may regard the property as "our home" and each may have contributed to its acquisition and maintenance. In most of those cases, however, the value of the home will continue to be shared because it will be included in the net family property of the titleholder, although subject to any deductions, debts or liabilities of that spouse.

It would be inequitable in a long-term relationship in which the home is the sole or major asset to deny a non-owning spouse a share in the capital growth in the value of the home. This would occur under existing law which provides that capital growth in the value of an excluded asset is not included in the net family property of the owner. If the Legislature amends the statute to allow the inclusion of changes in capital value of an excluded asset in the net family property of an owner, however, as we recommend above, this problem will not arise. If the Legislature does not introduce this amendment, it should introduce a more limited amendment to ensure that all changes in capital value of a home are included in the net family property of the owner. This would recognize the special contribution to the preservation and maintenance of a shared family residence made by many non-titled spouses.

In our view, the potential disadvantages of ending special treatment of the home in Part I are outweighed by the advantages. This amendment would prevent disparities in the treatment of similarly situated parties and accord with the rationale that spouses should share only wealth generated by the marital partnership. At the same time the provisions in Part II of the Act will continue to recognize the special nature of the home.

The Commission recommends that paragraph (b) of the definition of "net family property" in section 4(1), and section 4(2) of the *Family Law Act* should be amended to delete the special treatment of the family home [matrimonial home] for the purposes of Part I of the Act.

Spouses should continue to share in any capital gains or losses in the value of a home during the relationship. If the Legislature implements the Commission's recommendation to include all capital gains and losses in the value of excluded assets in the net family property of an owner, all spouses will share in the change in value of a house during a relationship. If the Legislature does not implement that recommendation, the Commission recommends that it should implement this reform with respect to the family home [matrimonial home] alone.

Assess the extent to which these recommendations would solve the problems identified by the OLRC in relation to special treatment of the family home for purposes of equalization. What alternative reforms can you suggest? In this context, consider again the issues concerning discretion versus fixed shares in relation to family property. Is there a need for more discretion to achieve fairness in these situations?

Joint tenancy and the matrimonial home

As noted, if the matrimonial home is owned by the spouses as joint tenants at V Day, it is necessary to include one-half the total value in each spouse's NFP. Although this arrangement usually creates no problems, the death of one spouse while they are in the process of separating or divorcing may create some complexity.

For example, in *Hansen Estate v Hansen*, 2012 ONCA 112, the spouses held title to their matrimonial home as joint tenants, and they were in the process of separating and dealing with the matrimonial assets when the husband died. The wife claimed exclusive ownership of the matrimonial home as the surviving joint tenant (based on the right of survivorship). Shortly before his death, the husband had executed a new will that distributed his estate to his four daughters, and they claimed that the joint tenancy had been severed by a "course of dealing" prior to their father's death.

The trial judge dismissed the daughters' claim, but the Court of Appeal allowed their appeal. In the Court of Appeal, Winkler J identified an error in the test applied by the trial judge with respect to a "course of dealing" sufficient to sever a joint tenancy. According to the appeal court, the court must examine the totality of evidence to assess whether the parties intended to treat their interests as those of a tenancy in common — and that in this case, the spouses knew of each other's intentions to no longer treat their interests as a joint tenancy.

In relation to the facts in *Hansen*, the court noted that the wife had moved out of the matrimonial home, that the spouses were in the process of defining a division of their assets, that the wife had taken steps to value her interest in the home, and that the husband had rewritten his will in a way that was not consistent with a right of survivorship in his wife. According to the appeal court, these actions revealed that the spouses were treating their interests as a tenancy in common. As a result, the wife and the daughters held undivided one half interests in the matrimonial home.

What kinds of factors may need to be considered by spouses in relation to joint title to the matrimonial home?

What actions, if any, might have prevented the need for litigation in this context?

STEP 6   CALCULATING THE EQUALIZATION CLAIM: *FLA*, s 5

The equalization claim and the onus of proof

After calculating the value of each spouse's net family property, section 5(1) of the *FLA* requires that the spouse with the greater net family property pay to the other spouse one-half the difference between them. Recall that the onus of proving a claim for excluded property or for a deduction is on the person asserting it (s 4(3)).

Equalization and negative values: Section 4(5) and negative pre-marriage property values

In calculating an equalization claim, it is necessary to determine the NFP for both the husband and the wife in order to apply section 5(1). What if a spouse's NFP is a negative value?

Section 4(5) of the *FLA* provides that if a spouse's NFP results in a negative value, it will be deemed to be zero. To some extent, this provision may ensure that a spouse with extensive debts at V day is not thereby permitted to increase the equalization payment required from the other spouse. Instead the negative NFP is deemed to be zero, so that the other spouse's equalization payment is limited to one-half of that spouse's NFP.

However, the *FLA* is silent with respect to negative values in the calculation of deductions. For example, how should a spouse's pre-marriage property value be used in calculating the NFP if the pre-marriage property is a negative value? See example below:

Value of spouse's assets at V day		$100,000
Value of spouse's assets at marriage:		
Assets	$2,000	
Student loan	– $22,000	
Total value at marriage		– $20,000

In this context, a spouse who entered the marriage with $20,000 of indebtedness must increase the value of his or her assets by $120,000 in order to have V day assets of $100,000. In mathematical terms, the calculation involves the deduction of a negative value, so that the negative value is *added* to the spouse's assets at V day to show that the NFP is $120,000.

This result was approved in *Menage v Hedges* (1987), 8 RFL (3d) 225 (Ont Unif Fam Ct) at 229:

> Although s. 4(1)(b) of the Act refers to "the value of property ... after deducting the ... debts," I am satisfied that this language can encompass a negative balance. Section 4(5) specifically contemplates that net family property balances could be less than zero and provides a remedy where this occurs at the conclusion of the calculation. It would have been simple for the legislature to insert a similar provision with respect to "property owned on the date of marriage" had this been the intention. Since the intention of the Act is to provide for equal sharing of values, acquired after marriage, it seems logical that, where one spouse enters into the relationship with a negative balance, this negative balance be included in his or her "pile" for purposes of calculating the equalization claim.

See also Hovius & Youdan at 383–384.

STEP 7 UNEQUAL SHARES: *FLA*, s 5(6)

The requirements of section 5(6)

In the context of the limited role for discretion in the calculation of the equalization claim, pursuant to sections 4 and 5 of the *FLA*, section 5(6) provides some discretion to a trial judge. Pursuant to this section, a judge may award an amount that is more or less than half the difference between the net family properties in accordance with section 5(6).

However, the section is carefully drafted to limit the exercise of discretion to only the most egregious situations.

- First, section 5(6) provides that the judge may make an award that is unequal only if "the court is of the opinion that equalizing the net family properties would be unconscionable," a test that confirms a high threshold for intervention by the court;

- In addition, section 5(6) identifies a list of the specific circumstances or factors which permit the award of unequal sharing, including a failure to disclose assets or debts at marriage, the reckless incurring of debts, gifts between the spouses included in their NFPs, intentional or reckless depletion of NFP, a large equalization claim in relation to cohabitation that is less than five years, large debts incurred to support the family, or the provisions of an agreement that is not a domestic contract;

- Moreover, section 5(6)(h) also permits the court, after a finding that an equalization claim is "unconscionable," to make an award of unequal sharing on the basis of "any other circumstance relating to the acquisition, disposition, preservation, maintenance or improvement of property."

In the context of the wording of section 5(6), identify the potential for the exercise of judicial discretion in determining the equalization claim. Recall the judge's decision in *Skrlj v Skrlj* and the award of an unequal equalization payment to the wife. On what basis did the court make this award?

"Unconscionability" and section 5(6): Some early cases in Ontario

The underlying philosophy of Part I of the *FLA* and its approach to equalization was considered in *Waters v Waters* (29 December 1986), Doc 1024/86 (Ont Dist Ct), a case in which the wife claimed that she had taken care of all the household labour as well as the couple's financial affairs. Both spouses also worked outside the home and they had no children. The husband admitted that he did not share in household work because he was an alcoholic, but he also claimed that his wife was a workaholic. In assessing the wife's claim for an unequal share under section 5(6), the court focused carefully on section 5(7), stating in part:

> [Section 5(7)] does not say that inherent in the marital relationship there should be equal contribution; it says that inherent in the marital relationship "there is equal contribution." The rationale is hardly self-evident.... [Spouses usually make different and unequal contributions, so that to say that] it is inherent in the relationship that the contributions are equal is to say something that is patently untrue. [Thus] unless it is to be regarded as an affront to common sense [the section] must mean as a matter of public policy the contributions are deemed equal (even when they are not) and that this deemed equality of contribution is the rationale of the

equal division of family property provided for in section 5(1).... There are compelling public policy reasons which support the view that departures from equality should be uncommon....

In *Waters*, the court concluded that there was no basis for revising the equalization claim.

By contrast, in another early case, *Sullivan v Sullivan* (1986), 5 RFL (3d) 28 (Ont Unif Fam Ct), the court considered the wife's application for an unequal share. In *Sullivan*, the court determined that the wife had supported her husband and children financially with only small contributions from the husband, and that she had also performed the bulk of the household work and child care. In addition, the court noted that the wife's NFP was calculated taking account of one substantial asset, a business from which she derived most of her income. In this situation, the court concluded that the threshold of "unconscionability" had been met, and that it would be "patently and grossly unfair" to permit the husband to share in the equity in this business because his contribution had been "dismal." In making this decision, the court preserved the business as an asset for the wife and her future ability to support herself and her children.

Similarly, in *Hines v Hines* (1988), 23 RFL (3d) 261 (Ont HC), the court fashioned a remedy for a wife with few assets, whose husband left her 13 days after the *FLA* took effect, that combined an equalization award and spousal support. See James McLeod, "Annotation" (1988) 23 RFL (3d) 261 for a critique of this case. In *Leblanc v Leblanc*, [1988] 1 SCR 217, the Supreme Court of Canada reviewed the N.B. statute and concluded that the wife was entitled to an unequal share because of her extensive contributions and her husband's negligible ones.

In *Braaksma v Braaksma* (1992), 41 RFL (3d) 304 (Ont Unif Fam Ct) at para 17, the court held that the word "unconscionable" represents a higher threshold than "inequitable," although the court held that equal sharing in that case would have been "grossly unfair, unreasonable, and repugnant to anyone's sense of justice to the level of unconscionability."

Thus, a general consensus developed in Ontario that there was only very limited discretion in relation to section 5(6). As was suggested in a recent assessment:

> The creation of a high threshold for the variation of an equalization payment accords with the intent of the legislature when it enacted s. 5(6) of the FLA. It also has some practical benefits. It promotes certainty and predictability. As noted by various commentators, the high threshold helps to explain why there is less litigation concerning property rights following separation in Ontario than there is in a province such as British Columbia where courts have greater discretion. However, setting a high threshold means that individualized justice is restricted. General rules that produce a fair result in the vast majority of cases may cause injustice or unfairness in particular circumstances. In its 1993 *Report on Family Law*, the OLRC recognized that maintaining a high threshold carried a price, but recommended against lowering the standard for fear of "increased inconsistency and unpredictability of results." (Berend Hovius, "Unequal Sharing of Net Family Properties Under Ontario's *Family Law Act*" (2008) 27 Can Fam LQ 147 at 154)

Section 5(6) and length of cohabitation

Some earlier cases had concluded that "length of cohabitation" in section 5(6)(e) included only cohabitation during marriage. For example, see *Stewart v Stewart* (1991), 39 RFL (3d) 88 (Ont Gen Div). However, the Ontario Court of Appeal concluded in *MacNeill v Pope* (1999), 43 RFL (4th) 209 that "cohabitation" in section 5(6)(e) includes pre-marital as well as marital cohabitation. In this case, the parties had cohabited for many years before marriage, so that even though they lived together after marriage for less than five years, section 5(6)(e) did not apply. Is this decision consistent with the goals of the statute? Why, or why not?

An issue that may be significant in some cases is that the marriage is a short one because one spouse claims that the other was abusive or violent.

For example, in *Futia v Futia* (1990), 27 RFL (3d) 81 (Ont HC), the parties were married for less than two years and the wife alleged physical and mental cruelty in her petition for divorce. The petitioner and respondent were of different ages and religious persuasions (the petitioner was a Jehovah's Witness and the respondent a Roman Catholic). There was also friction in the marriage because the respondent's mother lived with the spouses, expressing hostility to the petitioner on many occasions.

The major family asset at the valuation date was the matrimonial home, purchased and owned by the respondent. It had substantially increased in value, and the court decided that an unequal share in favour of the respondent was appropriate pursuant to section 5(6)(e), even though the petitioner argued that the respondent's cruelty was the reason for the short duration of the marriage. In assessing the petitioner's claim, the court stated (at 85):

> ... While conduct may in some limited circumstances be relevant to the division of family property I am not persuaded that it is relevant to the issue in this case and accordingly I reject that argument. I reject the argument that the court should consider conduct of the respondent and disregard the shortness of cohabitation. In my view it would indeed be unconscionable for the petitioner to receive an equal division when she had contributed virtually nothing to the acquisition of the matrimonial home whose value increased substantially between the date of purchase and the date of separation.
>
> The question then becomes how much less than 50 per cent should the petitioner receive. The petitioner contends that if an amount less than 50 per cent is considered it should be not less than 40 per cent. The respondent proposes the division be fixed at 30 per cent.
>
> Having regard to the length of cohabitation which was one year and nine months and relating that period to the contemplated norm of five years, I accept the submission of counsel for the petitioner and find that she is entitled to receive 40 per cent of the net equity of the matrimonial home or $33,600. There is already $10,000 standing in court to the credit of this action. The petitioner is entitled to this amount and the amount payable to her by the respondent will be reduced to $23,600. The petitioner is also entitled to accrued interest on the funds in court.

In an Annotation to this case, James McLeod raised the question whether the *reasons* for a short-term marriage should ever be relevant to an inquiry under section 5(6):

The cases have made it clear that matrimonial misconduct, per se, is not relevant to proceedings for the distribution of matrimonial property. Accordingly, the wife should not be entitled to an increased share because her husband was abusive. However, this is not the same as saying the husband's conduct is irrelevant. Most courts have acknowledged that the economic effects of a spouse's conduct may be taken into account. No spouse should be expected to tolerate abusive behaviour. Thus, it does not seem unreasonable to adopt the *Firestone*, [(1979), 11 RFL (2d) 150 (Ont. H.C.)] analysis and refuse to allow a spouse to allege the short duration of cohabitation if the spouse has caused the separation by unreasonable or unacceptable behaviour. The problem is that this analysis introduces the law of desertion into property law. However, it is difficult to see how the court can assess the importance of the termination of cohabitation without examining the reason for the separation.... (James McLeod, "Annotation of *Futia v. Futia*" (1990) 27 RFL (3d) 81 at 81–82)

To what extent do you agree with McLeod's assessment? For an overview of the bases for exercising discretion pursuant to section 5(6), see Berend Hovius, "Unequal Sharing of the Economic Gain during Marriage in Ontario: An Update" (2012) 31 Can Fam LQ 155.

The OLRC *Report on Family Property* and section 5(6)

In its *Report on Family Property Law*, the OLRC reviewed the statutory language and judicial interpretation of section 5(6), noting (at 65) that the intent of section 5(6) was clear:

> Courts have acknowledged the policy of the Act to enforce an equal sharing of the value of assets at the end of a marriage, unless that equalization shocks the conscience of the court.

Thus, the high threshold for intervention required by the test of unconscionability in section 5(6) has generally restricted judicial discretion to award unequal equalization payments to spouses, although (as demonstrated in cases such as *Hines* above) some judges have exercised considerable ingenuity in order to achieve a fair result.

According to the OLRC, however, there was a demonstrated need to amend the statute to permit judicial discretion in a number of additional circumstances. For example, the OLRC recommended that courts should have discretion to vary an equalization payment "to recognize a substantial post-valuation date change in value of an asset if necessary to ensure an equitable result, having regard to the cause of the fluctuation" (see OLRC *Report* at 144, and the notes after *Serra v Serra*, the case that follows).

According to the OLRC, such an amendment would remove the incentive for spouses to seek a remedial constructive trust, and it would also offer more flexibility than altering the valuation date. Recognizing that this recommendation might increase the costs and complexity of litigation, the OLRC also suggested that

> [the amendment] should direct courts to consider both the cause of a change in value and the amount of that change. Such a provision will not

end litigation on this point but will redirect it to the real issue, rather than to the requirements for a common law remedy, which may not be relevant to the cause of a fluctuation in value or to the determination of who should bear it (see OLRC *Report* at 70).

Consider this proposal in relation to the facts in *Rawluk*, above. How would this proposal affect the outcome in that case? Is this outcome preferable? Why, or why not? In addition to this proposal, the OLRC Report also included recommendations to permit courts to consider post-separation events, including conduct that is relevant to the factors in section 5(6).

Section 5(6) and post-V day decreases in value

Although a number of courts considered the problem of a substantial change in value post-V day, it was only in 2009 that the Ontario Court of Appeal considered this issue in detail in *Serra v Serra*.

Serra v Serra
2009 ONCA 105

The spouses were married for 24 years. It was a third marriage for the husband who owned a successful textile operation. The wife entered the marriage as a young woman with few assets. She had been married briefly once before and had a child. After her marriage to Mr. Serra, she left the workforce to care for the couple's child, her child, and the husband's child from a previous marriage. The court found that the spouses had lived a lavish lifestyle with a nice home in Orillia, a condominium in Florida, several cars, and money for entertaining and vacations. By the time of the trial, the husband was 62 and had remarried and had a child aged 3. The wife at the time of the trial was 56 years old.

At separation, Mr. Serra's interest in his business (the principal asset) was valued at between $9.5 and $11.25 million. By the time of the trial, however, the value had decreased substantially to between $1.875 and $2.6 million. The decrease in value was not the fault of the husband, but rather the result of shifting market forces adversely affecting the Canadian textile industry generally. (However, the downturn predated the economic recession, and thus would not likely rebound.)

At trial, the husband argued that equalizing the net family properties would be unconscionable because his equalization payment of about $4 million exceeded his net worth and might even be twice his total net worth. However, the trial judge rejected the husband's claim on the basis that a market driven post-separation decline in value could not be taken into account pursuant to section 5(6).

The wife claimed periodic support, a trust interest in her husband's shares in the business, a restraining order prohibiting him from disposing of or dealing with his assets, and a preservation order with respect to his assets. The judge ordered that the husband pay interim spousal support of $12,500 per month, maintain the Florida condominium ($60,000 per year), and pay a further $7,500 per month, later characterized as an advance on the equalization claim. To fulfill these obligations, the husband depleted a $2 million loan account, borrowed $1 million, laid off employees, rolled back salaries, reduced shifts, closed some divisions and sold assets, mortgaged his home, cashed in RRSPs and life insurance policies, and injected all available cash into the business to keep it in operation. The orders sought by the wife to preserve property also affected the husband's ability to deal with the business effectively.

The Court of Appeal allowed the husband's appeal from the trial decision.

> [1] The important issue raised on this appeal is whether, and if so, in what circumstances, a market-driven post-valuation date change in value of a spouse's assets may be taken into account in determining whether an equalization of family property is unconscionable under s. 5(6) of the *Family Law Act*. This legal question has not previously been decided by this Court. A second issue is whether — if the decline in value of the appellant's principal asset may be taken into account — the equalization of family property would be unconscionable in the circumstances of this case....

The court noted that the husband relied on section 5(6)(h), arguing that the post-separation decline in value, coupled with the orders obtained by the respondent, were all circumstances relating to the disposition, preservation and maintenance of his business asset, so that it would be unconscionable to order equalization based on the separation date valuation.

> [39] The scope of the exception in s. 5(6) ... has been the subject of considerable controversy amongst family law professionals. This is perhaps because the exception appears to fly in the face of what is seen as the essential characteristic of present-day family law legislation in Ontario, namely, the promotion of certainty, predictability and finality in the determination of support obligations and property division and the removal of judicial discretion in those areas to the extent possible [and to avoid any suggestions that courts have power to deal with property on the basis of "discretionary fairness"].
>
> [40] In my opinion, however, the concern is overblown....

The court acknowledged different family property regimes in other provincial jurisdictions, but noted that Ontario chose a fixed valuation date approach. In this context, courts have no discretion to vary the V day, thus giving rise to the debate "about whether courts can vary an equalization payment if the value of the asset has changed significantly after the valuation date." The court also noted that judges have tended to limit the application of section 5(6) to circumstances arising from spousal misconduct.

> [46] In my opinion, a court may take into account a post-separation date change in the value of a spouse's assets, and the circumstances surrounding such a change, for purposes of determining under s. 5(6) of the *Family Law Act* whether equalizing net family properties would be unconsciona-

ble. An order for an unequal division of net family properties is exceptional, however, and may only be made on such a basis (i) where the circumstances giving rise to the change in value relate (directly or indirectly) to the acquisition, disposition, preservation, maintenance or improvement of property ... and (ii) where equalizing the net family property would be unconscionable, having regard to those circumstances (taken alone or in conjunction with the other factors mentioned in s. 5(6)).

The court acknowledged that the threshold of unconscionability is exceptionally high, and continued:

> [49] However, it does not follow that because the threshold is exceptionally high the factors to be taken into account in assessing whether that threshold has been crossed should not include post-separation changes in the value of a spouse's assets and the circumstances surrounding that change....

The court noted section 5(7) and its rationale for equalization, as well as themes in the cases that fault-based conduct was necessary to demonstrate unconscionability, but disagreed that such conduct was necessary, citing the provisions of section 5(6). As the court concluded, a number of these provisions did not concern fault, so that it was not necessary to interpret section 5(6)(h) as embodying fault-based conduct. On the basis of the legislation, the court concluded that "[j]udicial discretion with respect to equalization payments is ... severely restricted, by statutory design, but it is not eliminated altogether since there is discretion to order an unequal payment...."

> [58] There is no principled reason that I can see, given the language of the Act and its purpose or objects, to confine the word "unconscionable" in s. 5(6) only to circumstances arising from fault-based conduct on the part of one of the spouses. Although unconscionable conduct is obviously an appropriate consideration in determining whether equalizing the net family properties would be unconscionable, in my opinion the true target of the limited exception to the general rule is a situation that leads to an unconscionable result, whether that result flows from fault-based conduct or not....

The court then concluded that the downturn in the textile industry was a "circumstance relating to" the disposition, preservation and maintenance of the business owned by the husband. As the court noted, the orders obtained by Mrs. Serra also contributed to the problems faced by her husband, and that eight out of ten comparable businesses in Ontario had gone out of business in this period. This was not a temporary economic recession, and it was not possible for Mr. Serra to sell the business to preserve some of its value. On this basis, the court concluded that the trial judge should have taken into account this downward impact on the husband's assets in applying section 5(6).

> [64] It is worth emphasizing that the legal issue in question here is whether a market-driven decline in value of a spouse's assets post-separation may be considered as a factor in determining whether an equalization of net family property is unconscionable under s. 5(6). Concluding that it may be considered as a factor does not lead necessarily to

a finding on the facts that an equalization order would be unconscionable. This is an important distinction, in my view, and may sometimes be overlooked in the heat of the debate over finality and certainty versus discretionary fairness.

[65] Although a purely market-driven decline in the value of Mr. Serra's principal asset is at the heart of these proceedings, this case is not about whether a significant post-separation drop in the value of an individual's stock portfolio, precipitated by a deep but temporary recession, will amount to unconscionability. Such an occurrence may well be a factor for consideration under s. 5(6)(h), but whether it would be sufficient by itself to constitute "unconscionability" is quite another matter. Each case must be determined on its own facts. In the circumstances here, however, I am satisfied that an equalization of net family property would be unconscionable, given the dramatic downward turn in Mr. Serra's fortunes and the factors giving rise to, and surrounding, it.

The court distinguished cases in which other factors in section 5(6) need to be considered, particularly in relation to fault-based conduct or obligations to sell interests to preserve some value.

[67] In these circumstances, an equalization of net family property that requires Mr. Serra to pay more than his total net worth (and arguably as much as twice his net worth) because of a marked decline in the value of his major asset post-separation — over which he had absolutely no control and in spite of his best efforts to save the business in the face of Ms. Serra's trust claims, the preservation order and the need to comply with his support obligations — is, in my view, unconscionable. In so concluding, I have taken into account that Ms. Serra is not a woman without means. The trial judge found that she left the marriage "with assets worth a considerable amount." She has net family property of about $1 million in addition to her interest in the Florida property. She has lived, and continues to live, a life of relative luxury, 6 months in Canada and 6 months in Florida. The trial judge found she had been "very well compensated" for her contributions to the business during the course of the marriage....

The court then considered that, having concluded that equalization would be unconscionable, the court was required to exercise discretion by doing what was "just, fair and equitable" in the circumstances, having regard to sections 5(6) and 5(7) and the Preamble of the *FLA*. As a result, the court valued the business in accordance with the downturn and concluded that the net outstanding equalization payment should be $900,000. The court also made minor adjustments to the husband's obligation to pay spousal support.

Notes and Questions

Serra as a precedent for section 5(6): *Kean v Clausi*
To what extent does *Serra* represent a precedent in relation to claims for unequal equalization pursuant to section 5(6)? Although the Court of Appeal attempted to distinguish this case from the economic downturn in 2008–2009, why should it matter whether the downturn is short or long? To

what extent should spouses with obligations to pay equalization have been expected to sell their stocks to cut their losses?

Although it is clear that the Court of Appeal was attempting to distinguish the facts in *Serra* from the circumstances of the economic recession in 2008–2009, some commentators have concluded that there may now be three possible valuation dates in family law matters: the date of marriage, the date of separation and the date of trial (or a date that is between the latter two dates). In this situation, lawyers will need to turn their minds to the question of whether there are any factors sufficient to justify an attempt to assess post-V day values. In doing so, it will be necessary to focus on the factors identified by the court: the magnitude of decline for Mr. Serra and the nature of the decline. However, it is also clear that valuation will be a critical element in any such argument. See Stephen Grant & Andrew Freedman, "Case Comment on *Serra v. Serra* (2009), 61 RFL (6th) 39; and see also Andrew Freedman & Alison Thomas, *Money and Family Law* (February 2009) at 9.

In this context, consider this situation:

> The parties married in 1990 and had two children. They separated in 2006, and the wife sought an unequal division of property on the basis of a significant drop in the value of a TD investment account after the date of separation. Although the account was in the wife's name, it was created at the instigation of the husband. At separation, the account had a value of about $228,000 but it had dropped to $157,000 at the date of trial, and the entire decline was market-driven. In this case, the wife wished to use the decreased value at trial as the value of this investment account in calculating her NFP. What result?

In *Kean v Clausi*, 2010 ONSC 2583, the court quoted *Serra v Serra*, and stated:

> [11] It does not follow from the exceptional nature of an order of unequal division of property that post-separation declines in value cannot be taken into account. [In *Serra*, the Court] noted that while some of the factors in section 5(6) do relate to fault-based conduct on the part of a spouse who owns the asset, [other subsections] do not. The general factors contained in clause (h) at issue in *Serra* and relied on by a party may or may not involve misconduct....

> [13] The respondent argues that the reasoning in *Serra* should not be applied to the facts of this case, and argues that the facts ... do not rise to that threshold. I do not understand [the Court's reasons] to be limited to extreme cases involving only the very wealthy. Nor do I find that it should be limited to those cases in which the actual equalization payment would result in a figure greater than a party's net worth as was the case for Mr. Serra....

> [16] The asset in question was created at the instigation of the husband from the equity contained in the matrimonial home. It was created for the purpose of servicing the mortgage of the matrimonial home. It was largely managed by the husband, even after the parties separated.

[17] In the circumstances, I find it would be an unconscionable result for the wife to have to bear the entire burden of a decrease in value of an asset created at the instigation of the husband, for the purpose of maintaining the matrimonial home, out of the equity of the matrimonial home — and largely managed by the husband.... The nature of the account and the manner in which it was managed leads me to conclude that the account was an asset for the benefit and use of the whole family, and was in the wife's name only for credit-proofing reasons. The parties shall bear equally the decrease in its value by making an order that the parties' net family property be equalized in unequal shares....

Does *Kean v Clausi* influence your conclusion with respect to whether *Serra* constitutes a precedent? For cases in which courts concluded that the facts did not meet the high threshold of unconscionability, see *Czieslik v Ayuso* (2007), 86 OR (3d) 88 (CA); and *LeVan v LeVan* (2008), 51 RFL (6th) 237 (Ont CA). See also Berend Hovius, "Market Driven Changes in Property Values after the Valuation Date under Ontario's Family Law Act: The Story Continues" (2009) 28 Can Fam LQ 105.

Statutory reform and changes in value after V day?

As noted, the *Family Law Act*, SPEI 1995, c 12, includes a specific provision to take into account changes in valuation between separation and trial. Thus, in addition to the provisions similar to section 5(6) of the Ontario legislation, the statute contains an express provision as follows:

6(6) The court may award a spouse an amount that is more or less than half the difference between the net family properties if the court is of the opinion that equalizing the net family properties would be inequitable because of a substantial change after the valuation date in the value of any property included in either spouse's net family property.

Is this an appropriate solution to the problem of changes in value between V day and trial? Recall the Supreme Court's decision in *Rawluk* to permit the use of a trust when the value of property *increased* between V day and trial. Is *Serra* an appropriate method for permitting recognition of *decreases* in value between V day and trial?

Recall that the OLRC's *Report on Family Property* considered these problems (particularly *Rawluk*) and several options for responding to them. However, in the end, the OLRC concluded that it was not appropriate to change the basic arrangements with respect to V day. At the same time, the OLRC recommended that

Part I of the *Family Law Act* should be amended to grant courts the discretion to vary an equalization payment to recognize a substantial post-valuation date change in value of an asset if necessary to ensure an equitable result, having regard to the cause of the fluctuation. (OLRC *Report* at 71)

To what extent does *Serra* represent the implementation of this recommendation? Is there a need for further legislative reform? Why, or why not?

Excluded property, judicial discretion and section 5(6): *Ward v Ward*

In *Ward v Ward*, the Court of Appeal confirmed a trial decision (2011 ONSC 570) to award the wife an unequal equalization because she had used inheritance funds (at her husband's bidding) to repay the mortgage on the matrimonial home a few weeks before her husband separated.

The spouses had been married for eleven years and had two children. Although neither spouse came into the marriage with significant assets, both had good earnings, although the wife had left her career to raise the children; she returned to work after the separation.

In 2006, the wife's father gave her an inter vivos gift of $200,000; at that time, the marriage had already been in trouble for four years. The wife wanted to keep this money for retirement but her husband persuaded her to pay $180,000 of it against their line of credit which was secured by the family home. The wife acceded to this request, claiming that she did so in an effort to save the marriage and that she expected this money to be returned. The husband claimed that there was never any disagreement about how the money would be used and that he did not understand it to be loan.

Two months after the wife paid down their line of credit, the husband announced that he had purchased a condo and he left the marriage. The wife eventually purchased the husband's interest in the matrimonial home and remained there with the children. The couple agreed on spousal and child support, so that the only outstanding issue was the amount of the equalization payment. The wife sought an unequal equalization, amounting to $90,000, the amount by which the husband had benefitted by the wife's payment on the line of credit. The trial court held that it was reasonable to assume that the wife would not have advanced the inheritance funds to pay the line of credit if she had realized that the husband was planning to leave the marriage. As a result, the court used section 5(6) (paras c and h) to award an unequal equalization, so that the wife was entitled to an additional $90,000.

A majority of the Ontario Court of Appeal upheld the trial judgment: see *Ward v Ward*, 2012 ONCA 462. The appeal court reviewed *Serra v Serra*, and noted the need to limit the exercise of judicial discretion to achieve the goal of predictability and thereby discourage litigation. The majority concluded that the trial judge's approach to section 5(6) was appropriate in all the circumstances:

> [29] Applying this strict standard, the trial judge concluded that allowing the husband to reap a $90,000 benefit from the gift to the wife would be to countenance a result that was manifestly unjust and unconscionable. It would allow the husband to gain a windfall benefit because of the timing of the wife's father's gift to her. The marriage was crumbling, the husband persuaded the wife to put the gift money towards the house, the wife acceded in order to try to save the marriage but then the husband left the marriage. The wife had given up her career to raise the children. The husband had significant earning power while the wife's was limited. The gift from her father came from his savings and would not be repeated. Had the wife not given in to the husband's insistence that the gift be used to pay down the line of credit, she would have retained the full proceeds.

Taking all these circumstances into account, the trial judge was satisfied that a s. 5(6) order for unequal distribution of net family property was required to avoid an unconscionable result that would shock the conscience of the court....

[36] In my view, the trial judge made no error in law, nor in his factual findings. He fully understood that the test to be applied was not mere unfairness but a shock to the conscience. On the record before him, he was entitled to find "in the opinion of the court", that in the context of the history of this marriage, where the wife did not earn income but stayed home to raise the family while the husband earned a high salary, and where the husband's conduct pressured the wife to use her one-time gift from her father toward the matrimonial home knowing she was doing so to try to save the marriage, then leaving her soon thereafter, an equal division of the net family property would be unconscionable. There is no basis for this court to interfere, other than to substitute another view. It is not this court's role to conduct a de novo unconscionability analysis. As the Supreme Court of Canada has made clear in the context of the trial judge's discretion in making a support order, an appeal court is not entitled to intervene "simply because it would have made a different decision or balanced the factors differently": *Hickey v Hickey*, [1999] 2 SCR 518, at para 12.

The dissenting judgment disagreed with the trial judge's interpretation of the evidence about the differing views of the husband and wife with respect to the decision to use the inheritance funds to pay the line of credit. He also disagreed with the trial judge's specific focus on the inheritance funds in applying section 5(6), rather than the overall result of equalization, and particularly the need to respect the legislature's decision to create special treatment for funds related to the matrimonial home. In addition:

[100] Moreover, to use s. 5(6) to alleviate perceived unfairness arising from the application of the scheme set out in the Act would be to entirely undermine the goals of certainty and finality that the Act clearly aims to promote. Had the legislature desired a tailor-made equalization of property for each and every couple, this could have been easily achieved. The legislature clearly chose otherwise. ...

[110] To rely only on the fact that a matrimonial home was acquired by one spouse in whole or in part through gift or inheritance to find unconscionability is to effectively ignore the legislative choice that, following a marital breakdown, spouses should share the matrimonial home equally.

To what extent do these competing views in the appeal court in *Ward v Ward* continue to reveal the tension between goals of predictability and finality by contrast with discretion and fairness in Ontario's *Family Law Act*? Consider again the recommendations of the OLRC with respect to treatment of the matrimonial home and the extent to which implementing such reform proposals would alleviate the need to use section 5(6) in cases like *Ward*?

In reflecting on these differing views, consider an assessment of the *Family Law Act* in 2011 on the 25th anniversary of the enactment of this statute in Ontario:

[W]ith respect to fairness, the FLA fully implements the partnership view of marriage which sees spouses as equal partners, equally contributing to the marriage and equally entitled, at the relationship's termination, to an equal share of the profits of their joint efforts....

Ontario generates less matrimonial property litigation than other provinces, and this is the strength of the Act....

Despite the FLA's overwhelming success, it is also important to recognize that there was some truth in the comment that the FLA was a hastily patched together piece of legislation that had numerous defects ... Many of these early problems were identified by the OLRC in its series of three reports on reforming the FLA released in 1993, only 7 years after the Act had been brought into force.

Unfortunately, the history of the FLA ... is one of shocking legislative unwillingness and delay in responding to these problems. No significant reform took place for 16 years, until 2009, and even then, although pension valuation and division was finally dealt with, a range of other needed reforms remained unaddressed. In some cases, the Ontario Court of Appeal has eventually grappled with an issue and provided some much-needed resolution and guidance. However, in many cases these solutions have been constrained by the existing legislation and are no substitute for legislative amendment.... (Carol Rogerson, "The Life and Times of the FLA" (Law Society of Upper Canada, 25th anniversary conference of the FLA, Toronto, 1 March 2011) at 2–3)

In the context of a lack of legislative attention, to what extent is it appropriate for the Court of Appeal to provide resolution and guidance about problems with the *FLA*? Does this assessment change your views about the appropriateness of some of the appeal court's decisions? In this context, however, note that several decisions of the Ontario Court of Appeal have reflected ongoing tension among the judges between the goals of predictability and finality and those of fairness and discretion.

Equalization, excluded property, unjust enrichment, and section 5(6): A case study of *Roseneck v Gowling*

In *Roseneck v Gowling* (2002), 62 OR (3d) 789 (CA), the parties cohabited for approximately one year and then married. Their marriage lasted about four years. Both the husband and the wife had been married previously. At the time of trial, the husband was 40 years old and the wife 46 years old, and the husband had one daughter from his first marriage who was 24 years old. The wife made a number of claims with respect to property sharing pursuant to the *Family Law Act*.

The parties initially cohabited in 1994–95 in a home that Roseneck (the wife) had inherited from her mother. They separated briefly in 1995, during which time Gowling (the husband) purchased a home for $214,000, for which he made a small down payment and then secured a mortgage for $190,000. Gowling also undertook some renovations to this home, paying an additional $59,865.

In early 1996, Roseneck sold her home for $106,000 and moved into the home owned by Gowling. To assist with the renovation costs in relation to this home, Roseneck contributed about $89,000 from the proceeds of sale of her own home. The parties married in June 1996 and title to this home was transferred to Roseneck and Gowling as joint tenants in June

1997. The mortgage, however, remained in Gowling's name, and with the exception of the mortgage payment for one month, Gowling paid the monthly mortgage payments, as well as the taxes and utilities throughout the marriage. Roseneck, who ceased to work outside the home during the marriage, paid some hydro bills, did the painting and decorating as well as the landscaping and gardening, and she used some of her RRSP funds to pay for the installation of a deck. Following the parties' separation, the court fixed the value of the matrimonial home and Gowling purchased it for $282,000. The matrimonial home was the main asset of the marriage.

During the marriage, both parties had cashed in some RRSPs (Gowling cashed $80,000, while Roseneck cashed $28,600).

In February 2000, four months before the parties separated, Gowling received an inheritance from his mother in the amount of $165,000. He did not disclose this inheritance to Roseneck. After gifting some of these funds to his daughter, Gowling retained $133,000 of the inheritance funds at the time of the trial, and he was entitled to exclude these funds pursuant to section 4(2) of the *Family Law Act*. By contrast, Roseneck's inheritance funds (after selling the home she had inherited) had been substantially contributed to the renovations to the matrimonial home. Thus, her pre-marriage property value could not be deducted pursuant to section 4(1).

According to the appeal decision, the trial judge held that, as of the date of the marriage, Gowling was unjustly enriched by Roseneck's pre-marital contribution to the renovations of Gowling's home. Therefore, Wallace J ordered monetary compensation in the amount of $88,779.44 be paid to Roseneck and included in her pre-marriage property, thus enabling her to deduct this amount in calculating her net family property. Wallace J specifically concluded that a monetary amount was preferable to a constructive trust remedy. In addition, she included the total value of the matrimonial home in Gowling's net family property calculation on the basis that the marriage was a short one. On this basis, the trial judge rejected Roseneck's claim for an unequal division of matrimonial property pursuant to section 5(6), but she stated that, in the absence of a finding of unjust enrichment, she would have made such an unequal division by awarding an additional payment to Roseneck in the amount of $25,000. In the result, the equalization payment to Roseneck amounted to $31,130.68.

The Ontario Court of Appeal allowed Gowling's appeal. First, the court held that the matrimonial home was held, at the end of the marriage, in joint tenancy, thus creating an entitlement to an equal one-half value for each spouse. As a result, each spouse was entitled to a beneficial joint interest in the property in the absence of any finding that this presumption was rebutted. Moreover, as a result of Roseneck's one-half interest as a joint tenant, she had received an interest equal to Gowling's so that she did not suffer any deprivation at the end of the relationship. The appellate court also held that her expectation that she was contributing to the couple's future home was realized, with the result that there was an absence of juristic reason. Finally, the court concluded that, assuming that Roseneck had succeeded in establishing the basis for her claim of unjust enrichment, it was not appropriate to award monetary compensation in this case, stating (at 799):

> Roseneck's contribution to the matrimonial home was substantial and direct. She expected that the house would be "our home." No doubt she expected that the improvements made to the matrimonial home would be reflected in its value. A constructive trust with respect to one-half the property best accorded with the expectations of the parties.
>
> One of the reasons why the trial judge was moved to adopt the approach she did was undoubtedly the fact that Roseneck had in effect contributed her inheritance to the matrimonial home[(and thus it could not be excluded], whereas Gowling's inheritance, which had not been so contributed, was. No doubt the trial judge felt it was unfair for Roseneck to be substantially worse off at the end of the short relationship when, at the beginning of the relationship, she was in a slightly stronger financial position compared to Gowling. The fact that the trial judge was of the opinion that the result was unfair cannot ground recovery on the basis of unjust enrichment when the legal test for recovery is not met.

The trial judge had also reviewed the provisions of section 5(6), concluding that there was no basis for awarding an unequal division pursuant to any provisions, with the possible exception of sections 5(6)(e) and (h). As the appellate court stated (at 802):

> In relation to these two factors, the trial judge concluded that with the amount awarded for unjust enrichment, the result of equalizing the net family properties was not unconscionable. If, however, the amount awarded for unjust enrichment was excluded, the trial judge was of the opinion that, "... it would create an unconscionable situation that should be remedied." Her reasons reflect the fact that both parties received an inheritance but the wife "lost" hers because she contributed it to the matrimonial home. The trial judge also noted that the wife contributed work during the marriage that substantially improved the property. She observed that without an unequal division Roseneck would be leaving the marriage with far less assets than Gowling. Roseneck would have holdings of approximately $115,000 and Gowling $250,000.

By contrast, the Court of Appeal disallowed the alternative claim for unequal division of family property on the grounds that the parties were required to share the problem that the matrimonial home did not increase in value commensurate with the value of renovations and that the reason for Gowling's better position primarily reflected the fact that his inheritance was more valuable than Roseneck's. The appellate court also declined to interfere with the trial judge's conclusion that Roseneck was not entitled to receive spousal support. In the result, Roseneck's equalization payment was $2,356.43.

In assessing this case, consider the differing approaches identified at the beginning of this chapter. Do you think that a more discretionary approach, such as that provided by the B.C. *Family Law Act*, would achieve more fairness? To what extent would Ms. Roseneck have been better off if she had cohabited, rather than married, Mr. Gowling? Does this case suggest a need for legislative amendments, such as suggested by the OLRC?

V.
PART II OF THE *FLA* AND POSSESSORY RIGHTS IN THE MATRIMONIAL HOME

SPECIAL TREATMENT OF THE MATRIMONIAL HOME

Possessory rights and the matrimonial home

Recall that the current definitions of "excluded property" and "deductions" create special treatment for the matrimonial home, issues that have been addressed in the preceding section focused on Part I of the *FLA*.

By contrast, this section focuses on Part II of the *FLA*, and its creation of *possessory rights* for spouses (including non-titled spouses) in the matrimonial home.

In this context, note the definition of "matrimonial home" in section 18, and its application to condominium interests as well as family farms. Note that section 18 defined "matrimonial home" for purposes of Part I, and it is also the definition for possessory interests in Part II of the *FLA*.

The policy issues

Why should the matrimonial home receive special treatment? Consider this comment:

> [T]he matrimonial home is more than a valuable asset. It is the place around which family life revolves. As a result, the spouses often develop deep emotional attachment to it. This may be especially true for a spouse who has functioned as a full-time homemaker during the relationship. Moreover, the right to occupy the matrimonial home satisfies one of the basic needs of individuals in our society — namely, the need for accommodation. In her critical analysis of American law dealing with the economic consequences of divorce, Lenore Weitzman notes that an equal division of marital property, however defined, frequently results in the forced sale of the couple's family residence. This compounds the financial dislocation and impoverishment of women and children generated by divorce. Where the spouses' only significant tangible asset is the matrimonial home and it is sold on the breakdown of the relationship so that the proceeds can be shared equally, often the custodial parent's share will be insufficient to acquire suitable accommodation. While this problem might be remedied by more generous support payments, the loss of the matrimonial home will invariably necessitate a move to new accommodation. This may well disrupt a child's schooling or neighbourhood and friendship ties, thereby creating additional stress and dislocation at the very time when the child most needs continuity and stability. For these reasons, Part II of the *Family Law Act* recognizes that the right to occupy the matrimonial home is important and that it cannot be governed by reference to ownership alone. (Berend Hovius & Timothy Youdan, *The Law of Family Property* at 574–575)

As you review the cases and discussion concerning Part II of the *FLA*, consider whether, or to what extent, these emotional views about the family home are reflected in the claims for possession of the matrimonial home.

Possessory rights in the matrimonial home pursuant to *FLA*, Part II

Possessory rights in the matrimonial home are defined in Part II of the *Family Law Act*. More specifically, the provisions ensure that both spouses have rights to *possession* of the matrimonial home, regardless of the legal ownership arrangements. For example, whether title is in one spouse alone, or a joint tenancy, Part II creates a right to possession for each spouse. Since possessory rights in the law of property usually depend on title, these *FLA* provisions may create a right to possession of the matrimonial home that would not otherwise exist for a non-titled spouse.

In addition, in some cases, a non-titled spouse may be granted an order of exclusive possession of the matrimonial home, and thereby evict the titled spouse from possession. Section 24 provides statutory criteria to be considered by the court in determining whether or not to make an order for one spouse to have exclusive possession of the matrimonial home, generally for a time-limited period. Note that two of these criteria relate to children's best interests and evidence of violence or abuse. Recall, for example, Mrs. Behrendt's unsuccessful application for an order for exclusive possession of the family home. What specific factors were considered by the court in its decision to deny her application?

In examining the cases that follow, consider how courts have interpreted these possessory rights in different kinds of fact situations. Do these cases reflect an appropriate balance between the rights of the title holder and the non-titled spouse?

Applications for exclusive possession of the matrimonial home

Rosenthal v Rosenthal
(1986), 3 RFL (3d) 126 (Ont HC)

In this case, the court considered an application by the wife for exclusive possession of the matrimonial home, a claim that was denied, essentially for economic reasons. As the court stated (at 135):

> The matrimonial home is located as I have indicated at 1905 Labelle Street, in the city of Windsor. By agreement of counsel, its estimated value is $130,000 with a present mortgage of $85,000 to $86,000.
>
> The three sons are residing with the petitioner in this home. Michael is in attendance at St. Clair College, and pursuant to the minutes of settlement that were formulated into the decree nisi, the respondent is paying $300 a month toward the support and maintenance of Michael. Jeffrey and Mark, although not working, are in receipt of income, one through Unemployment Insurance, and the other as a result of a work related injury. Both of these young men are paying to their mother the sum of $30 per week; however, in her financial statement, the petitioner has indicated that the cost of groceries is $175 per week. It is quite clear that the

amount being paid for room and board does not even cover the individual cost of groceries to each of these young people.

They are accordingly being subsidized by their parents. The shelter costs, as indicated by the material filed, would include the monthly mortgage payment, the taxes, the utilities, the insurance, and annual repairs. On a monthly basis, this results in a cost of some $1,541.40. ...

The court reviewed section 24(3) and continued:

Certainly, Mark and Jeffrey cannot be considered to be children affected by this application. As I have indicated by agreement, the respondent is already paying the sum of $300 for the support of Michael so that he might continue his education.

Paragraphs (b), (d), (e) and (f) in my view have no application to support the claim for exclusive possession by the wife.

The respondent is presently residing in a one-bedroom apartment, paying rent in the amount of $600 per month.

There is no question that Mrs. Rosenthal finds herself to be the aggrieved party in this unfortunate situation. The evidence of her doctor, heard by the court as a result of an application for an adjournment, clearly identifies the emotional stress that the petitioner is suffering as a result of the marital breakdown. However, the court must be bound by the provisions of the statute.

Mrs. Rosenthal in her evidence stated quite clearly that in her view, her choice of living standards should not in any way be affected by her husband's situation. This, of course, is an entirely unrealistic view of the result of a marital breakdown.

It is axiomatic that two people can live cheaper together than they can apart and this is something that Mrs. Rosenthal unfortunately must face. Her attempts to maintain the standard at which she was living prior to the marital breakdown must be viewed in the light of the moneys that are available to maintain that standard. Even during cohabitation, it is apparent that these two parties were living beyond their means, despite the relatively large joint income enjoyed by them. When one considers the financial statements filed by both parties, it becomes readily apparent that there are not sufficient funds to continue the occupation of the marital home.

Pursuant to the provisions of the statute, each party is entitled to a one-half interest in the matrimonial home. In order to have the court set aside that statutory right of the respondent, Mrs. Rosenthal must establish on the balance of probabilities that she falls within the provisions of s. 24(3). On the totality of the evidence, she has failed to satisfy the court that she has met this requirement. Unfortunate as it may be, it is the view of the court that the present situation cannot continue and it is in the best interest of both parties that the matrimonial home be sold for the best available price and that the excess moneys would, in accordance with the statute, be divided between them and form a portion of each net family property.

This will, of course, require Mrs. Rosenthal to acquire other accommodations, be it an apartment or a less expensive dwelling, either by rental or ownership. It is, of course, laudable that Mrs. Rosenthal might wish to have the three sons continue to reside with her. If that is their choice, then of course the sons, who are in receipt of income, would be required to pay their fair share of maintaining such accommodation.

The court is cognizant of the adverse effect that this determination will have upon Mrs. Rosenthal; however, as I have indicated, the court is bound by the provisions of the statute. There is no legal obligation upon this respondent to maintain Mark and Jeffrey in a style to which they have been accustomed. It is, for example, noted that each of the three boys owns and operates their own motor vehicle, as does Mrs. Rosenthal. To require Mr. Rosenthal to pay for the continuing occupation of the family unit in the matrimonial home would in effect be requiring him to support and maintain both Mark and Jeffrey under the present circumstances. Even apart from that, I am satisfied after review of the financial statements filed by both parties, that Mr. Rosenthal is entirely incapable of paying the amount that would be required to continue their occupancy of the matrimonial home at the price that I have indicated.

The application for exclusive possession of the matrimonial home is therefore dismissed and it is ordered that the matrimonial home be sold, hopefully through the cooperation of both parties, which will be to the benefit of both parties.

Pifer v Pifer
(1986), 3 RFL (3d) 167 (Ont Dist Ct)

In this case, the court reviewed interim decisions regarding custody of children and exclusive possession of the matrimonial home. In considering the provisions of the *Family Law Act*, the court expressly noted the changes in the Act regarding entitlement to exclusive possession of the matrimonial home, by contrast with provisions in the *Family Law Reform Act*, the previous legislation. In particular, the court noted the reluctance of judges to remove a spouse from the matrimonial home, under the previous statute, unless there was serious and weighty evidence of physical and emotional harm to the children. By contrast, the court stated (at 170):

> The new legislation not only expands the criteria, it also is framed differently. It is significant to note that the question of violence committed by one spouse against the other spouse or children is a separate factor from the question of "the best interests of the children affected." Nor do I think that what constitutes "the best interests of a child" in subs. (4) is to be restricted solely to the two questions in that subsection, i.e., the disruptive effects of a move to other accommodation or the child's views and preferences. In my view, what amounts to the best interests of the child may include many other factors such as the psychological stresses and strains to a child arising out of the daily friction between parents.
>
> Turning now to the material before me, the parties were married on 11th December 1976 in Milwaukee, Wisconsin. They have two young daughters, Laura, aged 6, and Jennifer, aged 4. The plaintiff is a nurse and the defendant an accountant. Apparently, they enjoyed a relatively comfortable lifestyle until the defendant decided to go into business for himself and purchased a Go-Camping franchise which involved rental and sales of motor homes and travel trailers. Unfortunately, the business lasted only a few months and the defendant found himself unemployed. To assist in the family finances, the plaintiff decided to seek employment first in February 1984 in a doughnut shop and later in May 1984 as a nurse at the K-W Hospital where she remains today. The defendant sought and obtained work in the accounting department of a law office and later with a chartered accountant. Since February 1986 he has attempted to establish his own accounting business.
>
> The material indicates that until the plaintiff began to work, she assumed most of the responsibility for looking after the children. After she began work, the parties shared that responsibility with the defendant tak-

ing an active role particularly when the plaintiff was working shift work at the hospital. In April it was decided to hire a babysitter, Linda Gregoire, so that the defendant could devote more time to his new business.

The main allegation of the plaintiff is that the defendant has, over the last four months, started to drink heavily at home starting in the afternoon around 4:00 p.m. until he passes out around 10:00 p.m. There is also an allegation that he smokes heavily, leaving live cigarettes in the ashtrays, and leaves on a propane heater after he has gone to bed. She also says that the arguments between them have increased in frequency since he began to drink heavily and this affects the children and frightens the babysitter. The allegations of excessive drinking are supported by the babysitter in her affidavit. Although the defendant concedes drinking alcohol, he denies that it is to excess and also denies that he is endangering his family by the use of cigarettes or the propane heater.

The balance of all of the material indicates to me that there is a great deal of stress and strain in this household which is obviously affecting the children. There is no doubt in my mind that it would be in the best interests of the children if they were relieved of that stress by the separation of their parents. If it were not for the serious allegations of drinking and bizarre conduct by the defendant, as supported by the affidavit of Linda Gregoire, I might have considered granting him interim exclusive possession and custody because of the fact that he has more time to devote to looking after the children. However, because of those allegations, I am of the view that it would be in the best interests of the children that the plaintiff have custody of them and exclusive possession of the matrimonial home.

Insofar as access is concerned, the defendant will have liberal and generous access to his daughters subject to the condition that he not consume any alcohol while exercising access.

Hill v Hill
(1987), 10 RFL (3d) 225 (Ont Dist Ct)

FITZGERALD DCJ

The parties to this proceeding are the applicant wife and the respondent husband. Under the *Family Law Act* the wife, aged 69, seeks interim relief from her husband of the same age by way of exclusive possession of the matrimonial house, support and costs. There is no lack of money available in the short term to either party but it is apparent that the husband's business is the major asset and income producer in a marriage which lasted some 40 years. Within two years of marriage in August 1947, the wife gave up her employment as a clerk and has since devoted herself to running the matrimonial house and raising two sons born in 1951 and 1954.

The husband formed his own business firm in 1950. At first the wife assisted in that business but after the birth of the second child ceased to be active in the firm. The business has prospered. The parties enjoyed a generous lifestyle but their interests diverged. Mrs. Hill devoted her energies to the house while Mr. Hill devoted his to the business. Eventually Mrs. Hill indicated that she would seek a separation.

The response to this was delivery to Mrs. Hill by one of her sons of a handwritten statement of what would happen if she proceeded with her intention. These included:

We will evict you from house and cottage

You will have no money for 2 or 3 years until support awarded

You will die penniless and be buried in an indigent grave ...
You will be up against ... best lawyers — money no object — we are
going to drag this out
No more medical payments by G.O. Hill
We will take car away
How are you going to pay litigation costs?

It is apparent that "we" refers to Mr. Hill and at least one of his
sons. The effect of this document was intimidating in the extreme and
constitutes harassment of a particularly invidious character.

In addition on this application two affidavits were sworn by friends
of Mrs. Hill who, since the separation was contemplated, received anonymous notes identified by a handwriting expert as being written by Mr.
Hill. These vindictive missives are of some relevance in support of Mrs.
Hill's contention that her husband has undertaken a deliberate campaign
of what I regard as psychological warfare against her and her friends in
the hope of undermining her resolve to obtain a fair settlement on separation. Mr. Cyr sought to exclude these affidavits. While they must be
received with caution I deem them relevant to the evaluation of Mr. Hill's
conduct toward others as an indication of the veracity of Mrs. Hill's
allegation of his conduct toward her.

Giving further credence to her allegations of intimidating conduct on
his part is the actual conduct of the litigation to date.

The initial motion for interim relief in this matter resulted in an
interim order made on 25th June 1987. This order, in light of the threats
of legal and other consequences to arise from taking the application, led
to the issue of an order of mutual non-harassment. There was also an
order that neither party deplete assets and an order that Mrs. Hill be permitted to continue to use the Buick automobile she customarily used. The
application was adjourned *sine die* to be brought back on seven days'
notice by either party.

Delay now becomes apparent. Despite efforts to expedite the matter,
no financial statement was delivered by the husband. This forced the wife
to commence an action by delivery of a statement of claim dated 26th
July 1987, including the wife's financial statement and income tax return
[and] a notice to Mr. Hill to file a financial statement.

On 13th August 1987, not having received such statement, Mrs. Hill's
solicitors wrote advising that, if none was forthcoming by 19th August
1987, a motion to compel production would be brought. That motion was
brought returnable 20th August 1987. The statement of financial information was filed on the date the notice of motion was to be heard, 20th
August 1987.

This statement turned out to be inaccurate. It did not disclose certain assets and certain transfers of funds.

While there was an invitation subsequently to consult with Mr. Hill's
accountant, a revised statement was not received until 5th October 1987.
Mr. Hill has not been available for cross-examination thereon prior to
return of this motion on 8th October 1987.

Meanwhile the wife alleges that she continues to be harassed by the
husband and that his conduct and attitude have driven her to seek psychiatric help. This harassment has been subtle. It consisted of changing the
pattern of delivery of money for household and personal expenses as well
as the delay in coming to grips with the legal proceedings.

On the other hand Mr. Hill did pay all the usual household expenses
and did continue to supply Mrs. Hill with money. He spent only part of
his time in the matrimonial home preferring to spend his time at the family cottage. He did use the home for his noon hour siesta and slept there
some week nights. She reports that he frequently tells her such things as
"the judge and the lawyers say you are crazy to leave me" and "[t]he

judge is going to send you to an asylum [sic] where you will be locked up for several months and observed through a one-way mirror." As a result of such actions and his underhanded communications with her friends, the wife has begun to fear what her husband may do next and has begun absenting herself from home when he is there. Now that winter is approaching he will probably spend more time at home.

The report of Dr. Sheppard indicates that anxiety over the domestic situation, while not a cause of her neck pain, is a contributing factor. He says: "I believe that the continued co-habitation of Mrs. Hill and her husband is having a detrimental effect on her psychological state" and "since her decision to separate ... the symptoms have been worse."

While the doctor feels that emotionally she can handle a move out of the home he is far from enthusiastic. He puts it that "she would find some way of coping with moving out of the home" as she is "generally able to cope with a considerable amount of adversity."

As to the husband's effect on her he states:

> With regards to the issue of physical violence this does not seem to have been a feature of the marital relationship. ... [T]he symptoms to which Mrs. Hill is prone are symptoms of anxiety which are similar to symptoms of fear although the stimulus provoking these symptoms is different. I believe she finds the behaviour of her husband toward her to be of a "mentally abusive" nature. *It is this behaviour which in my opinion is largely responsible for the exacerbation of the severity of her anxiety symptoms.* [Emphasis added.]

Apart from filing a statement of defence and finally a corrected financial statement Mr. Hill has not responded to his wife's allegations. She has been extensively cross-examined on her affidavits. Mr. Hill has not yet made himself available for cross-examination on his financial statements.

On cross-examination, p. 52, Mrs. Hill admits that, if she had to, she could cope with leaving her home on the basis that anyone having any backbone "can manage to cope with anything." She reaffirms, however, the time and effort she has put into the home, the money of her own she had spent on it and that "the house is me" and "it would be more than traumatic" (to leave it). She goes on to say "I have given up the camp which was ... dreadful ... as I love the camp almost as much as I love the house."

From the wife's perspective the key issue is whether exclusive possession of the matrimonial home should be ordered.

The husband relies on statements made by the wife at pp. 40–42 which describe Mr. Hill on a typical day leaving the house at 8 a.m., coming home for lunch, lying down for a couple of hours and returning to work about 2 p.m. He would arrive home at 5 p.m. or later. He would spend Tuesday nights and weekends at the camp and would spend holidays there until Thanksgiving. I conclude that the husband uses the home primarily for his daily nap and, of course, resides there when he cannot be at the camp. There is no evidence that he has any emotional attachment to the home. The order for non-harassment of Mrs. Hill has been ignored.

In the short term both parties have the financial resources to find alternate accommodation. I find it is *not* feasible for the two of them to occupy the same dwelling having regard to the psychological warfare being waged by the husband against the wife and its effect upon her. Which of them should give up the house?

The *Family Law Act* provides in s. 24(3) that I shall consider:

c) the financial position of both spouses;

e) the availability of other suitable and affordable accommodation; and

f) any violence committed by a spouse against the other spouse or the children.

As to para. (c), the husband is worth at least $2 3/4 million and has available cash exceeding $150,000. The wife is worth $275,000 including cash of $39,000. If she is to maintain her lifestyle and finance an action involving the valuations necessary to a successful prosecution of her claim she can least afford to move.

As to para. (e) there is no evidence whatever from either party except that the respondent husband's two sons have physical room for his accommodation.

Paragraph (f) refers to "violence." In my view the violence in this context must be such that it makes continuation of joint cohabitation in the matrimonial dwelling impractical. Violence in my view includes psychological assault upon the sensibilities of the other spouse to a degree which renders continued sharing of the matrimonial dwelling impractical. Where, as here, the conduct of the husband in written and spoken communication to the wife is calculated to produce and does in fact produce an anxiety state which puts the wife in fear of her husband's behaviour and impinges on her mental and physical health, violence has been done to her emotional equilibrium as surely as if she had been struck by a physical blow.

Black's Law Dictionary includes in the definition of violence, "acting with or exerting great force on the mind."

Webster includes the definition, "the unjust use of force or power, as in a deprivation of rights" and "to do violence to ... to injure; as, he does violence to his own opinions."

In my view the sense and purpose of the *Family Law Act*, which is a remedial statute and hence to be liberally construed, must surely include in the meaning of violence that violence causing injury to a spouse which can be achieved by words and deeds and is not restricted to the violence which can be achieved solely by physical abuse.

I am required to consider the above criteria but I am not confined to these alone. As Nasmith Prov. J. so carefully decided in *Miller v. Miller* (1978), 2 RFL (2d) 239, at 144 (Ont. Prov. Ct.), there is a duty to exercise the power to order exclusive possession with great care. The court, however, as stated in *Steward v. Steward*, [[1948] 1 KB 507; [1947] 2 All ER 813 (CA)], adopted by Nasmith Prov. J. at pp. 143–44, "It must always be a question for the exercise of the discretion of the judge, on all the facts before him in all the circumstances."

In my view it is the conduct of Mr. Hill which has rendered the matrimonial home incapable of being shared. His is the lesser emotional attachment to the home. He will be the least inconvenienced by finding alternate accommodation. His are the greater resources to do so.

Mr. Cyr suggests that having to move from the home will prejudice the husband's ability to attend to his business and that he has not the time to look for alternatives. Having in mind the time he spent at his camp at leisure I reject this argument. His daily siesta can be taken anywhere quiet.

For all the foregoing reasons it is "an equitable settlement of the affairs of the spouses" (preamble to the Act) that Mrs. Hill have interim exclusive possession of the matrimonial home and contents and I so order.

The respondent shall have the weekend next following the date of this order to remove his personal effects. I suggest that this not be regarded an abandonment of title to anything not removed at that time, this being an interim disposition only....

Notes and Questions

Evidentiary requirements and the factors in section 24(3)

Although Mrs. Rosenthal was not successful in her application for exclusive possession of the matrimonial home, Mrs. Pifer succeeded in her claim for exclusive possession. Which factors in section 24(3) were most significant in these two cases? How important is the best interests of children? How significant is the availability of other accommodation?

Similarly, while Mrs. Behrendt was not successful in her application for exclusive possession of the matrimonial home, Mrs. Hill succeeded in her claim. Both claims involved aberrant behaviour on the part of their spouses. Moreover, in the context of issues with respect to psychological violence or abuse, why did Mrs. Hill succeed in providing evidence to support her claim while Mrs. Behrendt did not? What factors were most relevant in these two cases? Do these cases reflect different standards in relation to evidence and onus of proof, or are there other factors that are relevant?

Financial resources and section 24(3): *Wilson v Wilson*

In relation to issues of violence in families with fewer financial resources than the Hills, consider *Wilson v Wilson* (1989), 19 RFL (3d) 259 (Ont Dist Ct), in which the court found that the husband had a serious drinking problem and that he had committed acts of violence against his wife, resulting in criminal convictions. At the time of the wife's application for exclusive possession of the matrimonial home, the spouses were occupying separate households within the matrimonial home. According to the court (at 261):

> The husband is employed with Petro Canada Ltd. as a service station operator and earns an annual income of $17,034.80 which converts to approximately $1,400 per month. He shows actual expenses of approximately $1,600 which figure covers all household expenses including the expenses of himself, the wife and the three children, while residing in the home....
>
> The wife shows her monthly needs for herself and the three children while occupying the home as being approximately $1,000 per month, due mainly to the low monthly mortgage payment of $227 per month.
>
> It is acknowledged that there simply is not alternative affordable housing for the mother and the children. The wife who is unemployed receives approximately $100 per month by way of family assistance and is capable of supplementing this income by performing babysitting services.
>
> Maintaining two separate households on the basis of the husband's current income is a most difficult endeavour. The parties have sustained themselves financially by living together while apart. The wife should not have imposed upon her the continuation of such an arrangement because of the husband's limited means and realizes that she will have to accommodate her needs beyond the husband's ability to pay.
>
> It would be in the best interests of the children bearing in mind that the wife has been a full-time mother and will continue to be so if interim custody, care and control of the children were granted to the wife with generous access to the husband.
>
> The husband's behaviour including assault tendencies, and uncontrolled drinking, is a factor in granting interim exclusive possession of the

matrimonial home to the wife. Furthermore, this would also be in the best interests of the children who would remain in familiar surroundings. The economic circumstances and the lack of alternative affordable accommodations make exclusive possession of the home to the wife necessary.

The husband has the means to pay to the wife for interim spouse and child support the sum of $550 per month commencing 1st February 1989. The wife is expected to pay the household expenses including the mortgage payment.

In the context of limited resources in *Wilson*, what factors were significant to the court's decision to award exclusive possession? Are there similarities in this case and the *Behrendt* case? Do these cases suggest that courts exercise considerable discretion in assessing applications pursuant to section 24(3)?

Cohabitees and the family home

The definition of "spouse" in section 1(1) of the *Family Law Act* applies to both Part I and Part II of the statute. As a result, neither the equalization process nor possessory rights in the matrimonial home generally apply to cohabiting couples. A few courts have made orders for such possession for a cohabiting spouse pursuant to section 34 in Part III of the Act, where a cohabiting spouse has sought orders relating to spousal support (see *Young-Foong v Leong-Foong* (1980), 1 FLRAC 718 (Ont Master)). However, most courts have concluded that such orders are not available to cohabiting couples. For a critique and recommendations, see Alva Orlando, "Exclusive Possession of the Matrimonial Home: The Plight of Battered Cohabitees" (1987) 45 UT Fac L Rev 153.

Possessory rights in the matrimonial home were not expressly considered by the Supreme Court of Canada in *Nova Scotia (AG) v Walsh*, 2002 SCC 83, discussed at the beginning of this chapter. In this context, Robert Leckey argued persuasively that the majority judgment was focused primarily on asset division (see paragraph 4 in the judgment), an argument that suggests a need to narrow the scope of the court's decision as precedent (see Robert Leckey, "Gimme Shelter" (2011) 34 Dal LJ 197). In examining provincial legislative schemes, moreover, Leckey argued that while spouses are entitled (during the course of a marriage) to deal freely with property to which they have title, there are significant limitations on such dealings with the matrimonial home, a factor that also supports distinguishing asset-sharing on one hand and rights in the family home on the other. Thus, Leckey concluded that possessory rights in the matrimonial home were more appropriately characterized in terms of support, and thus not only distinct from the asset-sharing regime, but also subject to more discretionary decision-making than is often available for property-sharing.

Significantly, the 2009 amendments to the *FLA* included revised provisions relating to restraining orders, which are available to both married spouses and cohabiting couples (see s 46). Such orders may well affect access to the matrimonial home, another argument for limiting the *Nova Scotia (AG) v Walsh* decision to asset-sharing only. In addition, as noted earlier, the OLRC recommended an extension of Parts I and II of the *FLA* to cohabiting couples (see OLRC, *Report on the Rights and Responsibilities of Cohabitants under the Family Law Act*, 1993). In this context, it is clear that there have been many arguments supporting reform of family property arrangements for cohabiting couples, particularly with respect to possessory rights in the family home. Moreover, even if you support the current regime limiting access to Part I of the *FLA* to married couples, are there reasons that support the extension of Part II to cohabiting couples? In particular, consider a cohabiting spouse whose circumstances are similar to those of Mrs Behrendt? Should a cohabiting spouse be entitled to make a claim for exclusive possession of the family home in a case of violence or abuse?

Additional Resources

American Law Institute, *Principles of the Law of Family Dissolution* (St Paul, MN: American Law Institute Publishers, 2002).

Heather Conway & Philip Girard, "'No Place Like Home': The Search for a Legal Framework for Cohabitants and the Family Home in Canada and Britain" (2005) 30 Queen's LJ 715.

Berend Hovius & Timothy Youdan, *The Law of Family Property* (Toronto: Carswell, 1991).

Robert Leckey, "Gimme Shelter" (2011) 39 Dal LJ 197.

Ontario Bar Association Submission on Bill 133 (Toronto: OBA, 2009).

FAMILY PROPERTY AND THE RIGHTS OF THIRD PARTIES

The impact of Part II of the *FLA*: Section 21

Because Part II's provisions for possessory rights in the matrimonial home may grant rights to non-titled holders, these provisions clearly change the usual rules of property law by which possession follows title. In addition, Part II includes a number of provisions that affect arrangements for transfers and security interests in relation to property that constitutes a matrimonial home as defined in section 18.

For example, section 21(1) prohibits a spouse from disposing of or encumbering an interest in a matrimonial home unless one of several conditions has been met. This section required courts to determine what actions constituted "disposing of or encumbering" an interest in the matrimonial home. In *First City Trust Co v McDonough* (1993), 50 RFL (3d) 197 (Ont Gen Div), the court held that an unsecured loan from the trust company to the husband, without the wife's knowledge or consent, did not constitute such disposing of or encumbering the matrimonial home owned by the spouses as joint tenants.

Section 21(2) provides authority for a court to set aside a transaction that contravenes section 21(1), unless the person holding the interest or encumbrance at the time of a spouse's application acquired it "for value, in good faith and without notice" that the property was a matrimonial home. In *Shute v Premier Trust Co* (1993), 50 RFL (3d) 441 (Ont Gen Div), a wife forged her husband's signature to obtain a line of credit and later a mortgage on the matrimonial home, owned by the spouses as joint tenants. The trust company's lawyer never tried to contact the husband. The court reviewed the concept of notice and held that the mortgage should be set aside. In addition, the trust company was given judgment against the lawyer. See also James McLeod, "Annotation of *Shute v. Premier Trust Co*" (1993) 50 RFL (3d) 441, who suggested that the lawyer had violated rules of conduct as well as engaging in negligence.

In this context, it is important to note that section 20 permits spouses to "designate" which of a number of properties as the "matrimonial home," thus limiting the constraints on dealing with a number of different properties.

Applications pursuant to the *Partition Act*

In a number of cases after the enactment of the *FLA*, courts considered the relationship between this statute (providing for calculations of net family property at V day) and the right to partition for co-owners pursuant to the *Partition Act*, RSO 1990, c P4. In *Silva v Silva* (1991), 1 OR (3d) 436, the husband resisted his wife's application for partition and sale prior to determining the equalization claim. The Ontario Court of Appeal held that an application for partition must be determined in the light of the *FLA*, although the court decided that the wife's application for partition and sale on the facts in *Silva* should be permitted because it did not prejudice either spouse's claim with respect to the home under the *FLA*, and the wife needed the money immediately. See also *Martin v Martin* (1992), 39 RFL (3d) 360 (Ont CA).

Bankruptcy proceedings

The relationship between the *Family Law Act* and bankruptcy legislation has been particularly complex in some cases.

As the OLRC's *Report on Family Property Law* indicated (at 46–49), there are complicated issues concerning the relationship of bankruptcy procedures and the remedial constructive trust. For example, in *MacPherson v MacPherson* (1994), 4 RFL (4th) 214 (Ont Gen Div), the court held that a separation agreement entered into two weeks before the husband declared bankruptcy was void against the trustee in bankruptcy. For a comment on proposed amendments to bankruptcy legislation, in relation to family law, see Robert Klotz, "Comment on the Effect of the Federal Government's Bill C55 on the Intersection with Family Law", *The Lawyers Weekly* (18 November 2005).

In 2011, the Supreme Court of Canada reviewed and dismissed an appeal from a decision of the Manitoba Court of Appeal, concluding that the wife's equalization claim constituted a debt that was provable in the husband's application for bankruptcy. See *Schreyer v Schreyer*, 2011 SCC 35. However, the wife had been unable to pursue her claim because she learned of the husband's bankruptcy only after he (and his debts) had been discharged. The Supreme Court concluded that the appeal court in Manitoba had reached the appropriate conclusion because Manitoba (like Ontario) has matrimonial property legislation that creates an equalization claim (a debt owing); it does not alter the title to property owned by each spouse.

Perhaps as a result of concerns about the wife's situation, and the fact that the husband had not disclosed the existence of the family law issues in the bankruptcy proceedings initially, the wife brought a subsequent motion before the registrar to reopen the bankruptcy proceedings (after the SCC decision). The registrar held that the proceedings should be reopened: see *Re Schreyer*, 2013 MBQB 179. An appeal by the husband from this decision was later dismissed, particularly because there were no unsecured creditors other than the wife: see *Re Schreyer*, 2014 MBQB 44.

In addition, the relationship between bankruptcy proceedings and family law matters was addressed in a review by the Minister of Industry in 2014, which stated:

> Family law and insolvency proceedings often intersect. In recognition of the social importance of family-related obligations, the [*Bankruptcy and Insolvency Act*] provides that spousal and child support orders are not releasable in bankruptcy. In a recent case before the Supreme Court of Canada [*Re Schreyer*], a spousal claim for an equalization payment against property that was exempt from seizure under provincial law as against other creditors — but not as against a claim for equalization — was defeated. The Court suggested that as a matter of fairness insolvency law should ensure that such claims are protected in future.
>
> Stakeholders agreed with the Court's assessment that the *BIA* should expressly protect equalization claims against exempt property held by the bankrupt. (Industry Canada, *Fresh Start: A Review of Canada's Insolvency Laws* (2014) at 13; see also <http://www.ic.gc.ca/eic/site/cilp-pdci.nsf/eng/h_c100870.html>)

To date, no action has been taken with respect to this report. Moreover, a somewhat different view was expressed in a case in the Ontario Court of Appeal in 2011.

Thibodeau v Thibodeau
2011 ONCA 110

The spouses had settled their equalization matters by arbitration. The arbitrator had ordered the husband to pay an equalization amount to the wife out of his share of the sale proceeds of the matrimonial home. The wife applied by motion to incorporate the arbitration award into a court order just before the husband declared bankruptcy, in which proceedings the Bank of Nova Scotia was granted leave to stand in the place of the trustee to realize on the husband's net equity in the matrimonial home. The motions judge granted the wife's claim for equalization priority over the claims of the husband's unsecured creditors, holding that the arbitrator's award created an equitable trust in the wife's favour; and she also made additional orders to assist in implementing the wife's claim for costs.

Both the husband and the Bank appealed, and the Court of Appeal allowed the appeal. The court held that the arbitration award did not impose an equitable trust on the proceeds of sale of the matrimonial home, and commented on the relationship between the *Family Law Act* and the *Bankruptcy and Insolvency Act*:

> **[36]** [T]he Ontario family law regime with respect to equalization payments dovetails effectively with the federal distribution scheme dealing with the distribution of assets in the event of bankruptcy.... An equalization *payment* is the chosen legislative default position [under the *FLA*, not a division of property.] On the bankruptcy side, unsecured creditors are to be treated equally and the bankrupt's assets to be distributed amongst them equally.... Parliament has not accorded any preferred or secured position to a claim for an equalization payment. While it has recently chosen to amend the *BIA* to give certain debts or liabilities arising in relation to claims for support and/or alimony a preferred status, Parliament has made no such provision for equalization claims in relation to family property....

Thus, since the arbitrator's award did not effectively create property rights for the wife (see *FLA*, s 9), the wife's equalization claim did not achieve priority over the claims of other unsecured creditors. In reaching this conclusion, the court also noted the policy issues at play:

> **[44]** I recognize there are policy arguments at play here. On the one hand, spouses — often women — need protection to ensure that their just share of the value of the property accumulated during marriage will be paid by recalcitrant former spouses. These concerns are important, but can often be addressed without affecting the rights of other innocent third parties.... On the other hand, what is at issue in terms of enforcement and access to assets as between spouses, one-on-one, takes on a broader dimension in the insolvency context where third-party interests are involved. And this gives rise to the counter policy argument: equalization payee spouses are unsecured creditors and, like other unsecured creditors, should not receive higher protection one against the other....

In this case, the court indicated that the arbitrator, who had been granted full powers to make orders pursuant to section 9 of the *FLA*, could have issued an order to create a proprietary remedy for the wife, but he had not done so.

Notes and Questions

The need for reform?

Is the appeal court's resolution of this matter, and its assessment of the policy issues here, appropriate in all respects? As the appeal court noted, amendments to the *Bankruptcy and Insolvency Act*, RSC 1985, c B-3, granted a preferred status to a bankrupt's debts relating to spousal and child support (see ss 136(1)(d.1), 178(1)(b) and (c), and 121(4) and 2.1). However, the court then concluded that legislative action was required to grant a preferred status for family property. Submissions were made to the federal Minister of Justice by the Manitoba Bar Association (in response to the Supreme Court's decision in *Schreyer*), and it appears that the Ontario Ministry of the Attorney General supports legislative reform as well (see Press Release of the Federal/Provincial/Territorial Ministers Meeting, Charlottetown, 16 January 2012; and Cristin Schmitz, "Marital Property Law Change Urged", *The Lawyers Weekly* (30 January 2012)).

Consider this situation:

> In a situation where a husband and wife held joint title to the matrimonial home, the husband died, and the wife then acquired full title to the home by way of survivorship. At the time of his death, the husband was in debt to the Bank of Nova Scotia and about a year later, the husband's estate was adjudged bankrupt. In this situation, the bank moved for a ruling that the wife's acquisition was a "transfer at undervalue" that could be set aside under section 96 of the *Bankruptcy and Insolvency Act*; alternatively, the bank argued that the wife held the husband's former interest in trust for the bank. Significantly, if the husband had become bankrupt prior to his death, a bankruptcy order would have severed the joint tenancy. How should the bank's motion be decided?

In *Re Cameron*, 2011 ONSC 6471, the trial judge held that automatic vesting of title in relation to joint tenancy by way of survivorship was not a "transfer," and that section 96 of the *BIA* therefore had no application. Even if such vesting constituted a "transfer," however, it was not undervalued because, although the wife had not paid to acquire title to the matrimonial home following her husband's death, she had provided ample and adequate consideration for the right of survivorship. Furthermore, there was no enrichment and deprivation here, and if there were such enrichment and deprivation, there was no juristic reason for it because joint tenancy principles required this result. Thus, a constructive trust was not appropriate. In this case, the court concluded that the "equities" were in favour of the wife, not the bank:

> [53] The Bank, on behalf of the [bankrupt's] creditors, is entitled to the [bankrupt's] property to satisfy their claims. There is nothing inequitable in depriving the creditors of property which never vested in the trustee, was not owned by the [bankrupt's] estate ... at the date of death and to which s. 96 of the *BIA* does not apply. ...

Note that *Re Cameron* concerned a widow's entitlement to title by survivorship, while the wives in *Schreyer* and *Thibodeau* sought equalization at separation. In spite of these differences, does *Re Cameron* suggest a different approach to the "equities" with respect to family property and bankruptcy. For a comprehensive assessment of the relationship between family property and bankruptcy, and recommendations for legislative and judicial reforms, see Janis Sarra & Susan B Boyd, "Competing Notions of Fairness: A Principled Approach to the Intersection of Insolvency Law and Family Property Law in Canada" in J Sarra, ed, *Annual Review of Insolvency Law 2011* (Toronto: Thomson Reuters Canada Limited, 2012) 207.

Additional Resources

AF Goldwater, "Bankruptcy and Family Law" (1998) 15 Can Fam LQ 139.

Berend Hovius & Timothy Youdan, *The Law of Family Property* (Toronto: Carswell, 1991).

Robert A Klotz, "Bankruptcy and Family Law: Problems and Solutions" in Law Society of Upper Canada, *Special Lectures of the Law Society of Upper Canada, 1993 — Family Law: Roles, Fairness and Equality* (Scarborough, ON: Carswell, 1994) at 253.

Robert Leckey, "Developments in Family Law: The 2010–2011 Terms" (2012) 59 SCLR (2d) 193.

Robert Leckey, "Bankruptcy, Provincial Law, and the Family Farm" (2012) 91 Can Bar Rev 435.

A Merchant & J Vogel, "The Bankruptcy Dodge" (1992–93) 9 Can Fam LQ 161.

ZB Wiseman, "Women in Bankruptcy and Beyond" (1989) 65 Ind LJ 107.

A NOTE ON MATRIMONIAL PROPERTY AND ABORIGINAL RESERVES

The constitutional context

In 1986, the Supreme Court of Canada considered the application of provincial family law legislation to "family" homes on reserves.

- In *Derrickson v Derrickson*, [1986] 1 SCR 285, the court decided that the B.C. *Family Relations Act* was not applicable to lands on Indian reserves on the basis that "Indians and lands reserved for Indians" was a matter within federal legislative authority pursuant to the Constitution.

- In *Paul v Paul*, [1986] 1 SCR 306, the court similarly decided that the provisions of the B.C. legislation could not be used to grant occupancy rights in a matrimonial home located on a reserve to the wife. See MJ Mossman, "Developments in Property Law: The 1985–86 Term" (1987) 9 SCLR 419 at 430ff.

However, the Supreme Court of Canada decision in *Paul* was distinguished in *Wynn v Wynn* (1989), 14 ACWS (3d) 107 (Ont Dist Ct), where a wife sought interim exclusive possession of the matrimonial home, situated on an Indian reserve. Wright DCJ acknowledged that the court could not grant an order for exclusive possession of a matrimonial home that is located on a reserve. Instead, he made an *in personam* order, without reference to the property, restraining the husband from interfering with the wife's possession of the matrimonial home.

Similarly, in *George v George* (1997), 139 DLR (4th) 53, the B.C. Court of Appeal affirmed the trial judge's decision to award the wife a compensation order pursuant to section 52(2)(c) of the *Family Relations Act*, even though the appellate court confirmed the absence of any jurisdiction to grant the wife an interest in the matrimonial home located on reserve land. And in *Kwakseestahla v Kwakseestahla*, [1998] BCJ No 283 (SC), where the parties had agreed on a consent order granting the wife a life interest in the matrimonial home on reserve land, the court rejected the husband's claim that there was no jurisdiction to enforce the order. The court held that it was enforcing the parties' contract, not making an order pursuant to provincial legislation. See also Mary Ellen Turpel, "Home/Land" (1991) 10 Can J Fam L 17. As is evident, these issues have created ongoing challenges at separation for residents of reserve lands.

New family law arrangements in Aboriginal lands

In 1999, the federal government enacted the *First Nations Land Management Act*, SC 1999, c 24. According to this legislation, a First Nation may enter into a Framework Agreement on First Nation Land Management with the government and is then required to establish rules and procedures governing the use, occupation and possession of First Nation lands, and the division of interests in such lands, in cases of marriage breakdown. The legislation also requires community consultation in the development of general rules and procedures.

In Aboriginal communities where such Framework Agreements are negotiated, the agreements would overcome the problems encountered in *Derrickson* and *Paul* in relation to Aboriginal lands. For example, the Chippewas of Georgina Island adopted a *Matrimonial Real Property Law* in 2000, and it has been adopted as well by the Missisaugas of Scugog Island First Nation and Muskoday First Nation. However, not all Aboriginal communities have embraced this legislation. See Wendy Cornet & Allison Lendor, *Discussion Paper: Matrimonial Real Property on Reserve* (Ottawa: Indian and Northern Affairs Canada, 2002); and Assembly of First Nations, *Matrimonial Real Property on Reserves: Our Land, Our Families, Our Solutions* (Ottawa: Assembly of First Nations, 2007).

Beginning in 2008, the federal government introduced additional legislation; originally, it was Bill C-47, which died on the order paper in September 2008. It was reintroduced as Bill C-8, the *Family Homes on Reserves and Matrimonial Interests or Rights Act*, introduced in the House of Commons in February 2009, but it too died on the order paper when Parliament was prorogued in December 2009. When this Bill did not achieve support, a similar Bill was introduced in the Senate in July 2010 and it received third reading in spite of considerable controversy. In particular, Senator Sandra

Lovelace, a member of an Aboriginal community in New Brunswick, opposed it because of some inherent flaws but also because she asserted that there had been inadequate consultation with First Nations communities: see Bill Curry, "Senate Approves Bill to Help Divorced, Abused Female Natives", *The Globe and Mail* (7 July 2010). Following approval by the Senate, the Bill was re-introduced in the House of Commons and received first reading in September 2010, but died on the order paper when Parliament rose for the 2011 election.

In September 2011, Bill S-2 was introduced in the Senate. The Bill received third reading on 1 December 2011 and was given first reading in the House of Commons the following week. This Bill included some changes, particularly a 12-month transitional period after enactment, a provision designed to permit First Nations time to develop their own individual regimes for matrimonial property at separation or divorce. In this way, the new Bill provides the "default regime."

The *Family Homes on Reserves and Matrimonial Interests or Rights Act*, SC 2013, c 20, was finally enacted and received Royal Assent in June 2013. First Nations communities were required to create their own regimes prior to 14 December 2014; in the absence of such regimes, the provisions of the federal statute are applicable.

Unfortunately, the federal government did not provide resources to First Nations to assist in the development of their own matrimonial property regimes and, for some communities, the time period of twelve months was insufficient for them to do so; thus, for most reserves, the new statute now provides the default regime: see Sarah Morales, "Matrimonial Property Law on Reserve Lands" (Annual Inst of Fam Law, 8 May 2015).

For some information about developments in Ontario, see the Centre of Excellence for Matrimonial Real Property, an arms-length organization located in Curve Lake, created to assist communities to develop their own legal regimes with respect to matrimonial property on reserves: online at <http://www.coemrp.ca>.

Additional Resources

Christopher Alcantara, "Aboriginal Policy Reform and the Subsidiarity Principle: A Case Study of the Division of Matrimonial Real Property on Canadian Indian Reserves" (2008) 51 Canadian Public Administration 317.

Richard Bartlett, "Indian Self-Government, the Equality of the Sexes, and Application of Provincial Matrimonial Property Laws" (1986) 5 Can J Fam L 188.

Mary Eberts & Beverley Jacobs, "Matrimonial Property on Reserve" in Marylea MacDonald & Michelle Owen, eds, *On Building Equality Solutions for Women's Equality* (Ottawa: Canadian Research Institute for the Advancement of Women, 2004) 7.

Thomas Isaac, "First Nations Land Management Act and Third Party Interests" (2005) 42 Alta L Rev 1047.

Sharon McIvor, "Aboriginal Women Unmasked: Using Equality Litigation to Advance Women's Rights" (2004) 16 CJWL 106.

Martha Montour, "Iroquois Women's Rights with respect to Matrimonial Property on Indian Reserves" (1987) 4 CNLR 1.

Patricia Monture & Patricia McGuire, eds, *First Voices: An Aboriginal Women's Reader* (Toronto: Inanna Publications, 2009).

Jacinta Ruru, "Finding Solutions for the Legislative Gaps in Determining Rights to the Family Home on Colonially Defined Indigenous Lands" (2008) 41 UBC L Rev 315.

VI.
COHABITING COUPLES: EQUITY AND THE USE OF TRUST DOCTRINES

[T]he purpose of equitable intervention in disputes between unmarried partners would be to provide restitutionary relief for contributions made by one partner which enabled the other partner to accumulate property or increase its value.... In these circumstances, it is unjust for the other partner to retain the benefit of the contributions after the relationship has broken up. (Marcia Neave, "Three Approaches to Family Property Disputes — Intention/Belief, Unjust Enrichment and Unconscionability" in Timothy Youdan, ed, *Equity, Fiduciaries and Trusts* (Toronto: Carswell, 1989) 247 at 253)

COHABITING COUPLES AND EQUITABLE INTERVENTION IN FAMILY PROPERTY

From *Murdoch v Murdoch* to *Pettkus v Becker*

As noted at the beginning of this chapter, equitable intervention in family property began with the decision of the Supreme Court of Canada in *Murdoch v Murdoch*, [1975] 1 SCR 423. Although the majority held that Mrs. Murdoch had not established the elements necessary for a declaration of resulting trust, the dissenting judgment suggested that her contribution to the acquisition of land (title to which was in her husband's name) was sufficient to warrant a declaration of constructive trust, based on principles of unjust enrichment.

At the time when *Murdoch* was decided, there was an ongoing debate in English courts about the appropriateness of using constructive trusts in family matters. As the OLRC *Report* in 1993 pointed out (at 21–24), Lord Denning in the English Court of Appeal frequently used trust principles "as a tool to reallocate ownership rights between spouses to reflect their joint efforts and expectations regarding their matrimonial home." However, the House of Lords regularly rejected this approach, overturning some of the decisions of the Court of Appeal and emphasizing the need to apply legal principles in the same way in both commercial and family settings.

At least to some extent, the divergence between the majority and dissenting judgments in *Murdoch* reflected the differences between these two levels of courts in England. Nonetheless, it appeared that the Supreme Court of Canada had accepted the validity of the constructive trust in family law matters in its decision in *Rathwell v Rathwell*, [1978] 2 SCR 436. By that time, however, provincial statutes were creating entitlement for married spouses to equal sharing of marital property (or its value) at separation or divorce, and so the Supreme Court's decision in *Rathwell* had little practical impact on divorcing couples.

However, in 1980, the Supreme Court considered an appeal from the Ontario Court of Appeal, which involved the dissolution of a cohabiting opposite-sex relationship, in which Wilson JA had awarded the woman a one-half interest in land owned by her cohabiting partner. In examining the reasoning in the Supreme Court of Canada, consider the nature of the equitable principles for intervention in relation to property for cohabiting spouses, and the evidentiary basis for their application.

Pettkus v Becker
[1980] 2 SCR 834

The judgment was delivered by Dickson J (Laskin CJC and Estey, McIntyre, Chouinard, and Lamer JJ, concurring):

> The appellant, Lothar Pettkus, through toil and thrift, developed over the years a successful bee-keeping business. He now owns two rural Ontario properties, where the business is conducted, and he has the proceeds from the sale, in 1974, of a third property located in the province of Quebec. It is not to his efforts alone, however, that success can be attributed. The respondent, Rosa Becker, through her labour and earnings, contributed substantially to the good fortune of the common enterprise. She lived with Mr. Pettkus from 1955 to 1974, save for a separation in 1972. They were never married. When the relationship sundered in late 1974 Miss Becker commenced this action, in which she sought a declaration of entitlement to a one-half interest in the lands and a share in the bee-keeping business.

THE FACTS
Mr. Pettkus and Miss Becker came to Canada from central Europe separately, as immigrants, in 1954. He had $17 upon arrival. They met in Montreal in 1955. Shortly thereafter, Mr. Pettkus moved in with Miss Becker, on her invitation. She was 30 years old and he was 25. He was earning $75 per week; she was earning $25–28 per week, later increased to $67 per week.

A short time after they began living together, Miss Becker expressed the desire that they be married. Mr. Pettkus replied that he might consider marriage after they knew each other better. Thereafter, the question of marriage was not raised, though within a few years Mr. Pettkus began to introduce Miss Becker as his wife and to claim her as such for income tax purposes.

From 1955 to 1960 both parties worked for others. Mr. Pettkus supplemented his income by repairing and restoring motor vehicles. Throughout the period Miss Becker paid the rent. She bought the food and clothing and looked after other living expenses. This enabled Mr. Pettkus to save his entire income, which he regularly deposited in a bank account in his name. There was no agreement at any time to share either moneys or property placed in his name. The parties lived frugally. Due to their husbandry and parsimonious life-style, $12,000 had been saved by 1960 and deposited in Mr. Pettkus' bank account.

The two travelled to western Canada in June 1960. Expenses were shared. One of the reasons for the trip was to locate a suitable farm at which to start a bee-keeping business.

They returned to Montreal, however, in the early autumn of 1960. Miss Becker continued to pay the apartment rent out of her income until October 1960. From then until May 1961 Mr. Pettkus paid rent and household expenses, Miss Becker being jobless. In April 1961, she fell sick and required hospitalization.

In April 1961, they decided to buy a farm at Franklin Centre, Quebec for $5,000. The purchase money came out of the bank account of Mr. Pettkus. Title was taken in his name. The floor and roof of the farmhouse were in need of repair. Miss Becker used her money to purchase flooring materials and she assisted in laying the floor and installing a bathroom.

For about six months during 1961 Miss Becker received unemployment insurance cheques, the proceeds of which were used to defray household expenses. Through two successive winters she lived in Montreal and earned approximately $100 per month as a baby-sitter. These earnings also went toward household expenses.

After purchasing the farm at Franklin Centre the parties established a bee-keeping business. Both worked in the business, making frames for the hives, moving the bees to the orchards of neighbouring farmers in the spring, checking the hives during the summer, bringing in the frames for honey extraction during July and August and the bees for winter storage in autumn. Receipts from sales of honey were handled by Mr. Pettkus; payments for the purchases of beehives and equipment were made from his bank account.

The physical participation by Miss Becker in the bee operation continued over a period of about 14 years. She ran the extracting process. She also, for a time, raised a few chickens, pheasants and geese. In 1968, and later, the parties hired others to assist in moving the bees and bringing in the honey. Most of the honey was sold to wholesalers, though Miss Becker sold some door to door.

In August 1971, with a view to expanding the business, a vacant property was purchased in East Hawkesbury, Ontario at a price of $1,300. The purchase moneys were derived from the Franklin Centre honey operation. Funds to complete the purchase were withdrawn from the bank account of Mr. Pettkus. Title to the newly acquired property was taken into his name.

In 1973 a further property was purchased, in West Hawkesbury, Ontario, in the name of Mr. Pettkus. The price was $5,500. The purchase moneys came from the Franklin Centre operation, together with a $1,900 contribution made by Miss Becker, to which I will again later refer. 1973 was a prosperous year, yielding some 65,000 pounds of honey, producing net revenue in excess of $30,000.

In the early 1970s the relationship between the parties began to deteriorate. In 1972 Miss Becker left Mr. Pettkus, allegedly because of mistreatment. She was away for three months. At her departure Mr. Pettkus threw $3,000 on the floor; he told her to take the money, a 1966 Volkswagen, 40 beehives containing bees, and "get lost." The beehives represented less than ten per cent of the total number of hives then in the business.

Soon thereafter Mr. Pettkus asked Miss Becker to return. In January 1973, she agreed, on condition he see a marriage counselor, make a will in her favor and provide her with $500 per year so long as she stayed with him. It was also agreed that Mr. Pettkus would establish a joint bank account for household expenses, in which receipts from retail sales of honey would be deposited. Miss Becker returned; she brought back the car and $1,900 remaining out of the $3,000 she had earlier received. The $1,900 was deposited in Mr. Pettkus' account. She also brought the 40 beehives, but the bees had died in the interim.

In February 1974 the parties moved into a house on the West Hawkesbury property, built in part by them and in part by contractors. The money needed for construction came from the honey business, with minimal purchases of materials by Miss Becker.

The relationship continued to deteriorate and on 4th October 1974 Miss Becker again left, this time permanently, after an incident in which she alleged that she had been beaten and otherwise abused. She took the car and approximately $2,600 in cash from honey sales. Shortly thereafter the present action was launched.

At trial Miss Becker was awarded 40 beehives, without bees, together with $1,500, representing earnings from those hives for 1973 and 1974.

The Ontario Court of Appeal varied the judgment at trial by awarding Miss Becker a one-half interest in the lands owned by Mr. Pettkus and in the bee-keeping business.

Dickson J first considered the doctrine of resulting trust, suggesting that this case offered "an opportunity to clarify the equivocal state in which the law of matrimonial property was left, following *Rathwell*." After reviewing the cases in which these principles had been developed and some of the academic literature pointing out the artificiality of the idea of common intention (especially, express intention) in marriage-like relationships, Dickson J noted that the trial judge, somewhat ungallantly, had found as a fact that there had been no common intention between Mr. Pettkus and Ms. Becker because Mr. Pettkus so testified at the trial. He concluded:

> In the view of the Ontario Court of Appeal, speaking through Wilson JA, the trial judge vastly underrated the contribution made by Miss Becker over the years. She had made possible the acquisition of the Franklin Centre property and she had worked side by side with him for 14 years, building up the bee-keeping operation.
>
> The trial judge held there was no common intention, either express or implied. It is important to note that the Ontario Court of Appeal did not overrule that finding.
>
> I am not prepared to infer, or presume, common intention when the trial judge has made an explicit finding to the contrary and the appellate court has not disturbed the finding. Accordingly, I am of the view that Miss Becker's claim grounded upon resulting trust must fail. If she is to succeed at all, constructive trust emerges as the sole juridical foundation for her claim.

CONSTRUCTIVE TRUST

The principle of unjust enrichment lies at the heart of the constructive trust. "Unjust enrichment" has played a role in Anglo-American legal writing for centuries. Lord Mansfield, in the case of *Moses v. MacFerlan* (1760), 2 Burr. 1005, 97 ER 676, put the matter in these words: "[T]he gist of this kind of action is that the defendant, upon the circumstances of the case, is obliged by the ties of natural justice and equity to refund the money." It would be undesirable, and indeed impossible, to attempt to define all the circumstances in which an unjust enrichment might arise.

(See A.W. Scott, "Constructive Trusts" (1955), 71 LQR 39; Leonard Pollock, "Matrimonial Property and Trusts: The Situation from Murdoch to Rathwell" (1978), 16 *Alta. Law Rev.* 357.) The great advantage of ancient principles of equity is their flexibility: the judiciary is thus able to shape these malleable principles so as to accommodate the changing needs and mores of society, in order to achieve justice. The constructive trust has proven to be a useful tool in the judicial armoury. See *Babrociak v. Babrociak* (1978), 1 RFL (2d) 95 (Ont. C.A.); *Re Spears* (1975), 52 DLR (3d) 146 (NSCA); *Douglas v. Guar. Trust Co.* (1978), 8 RFL (2d) 98 (Ont. H.C.); *Armstrong v. Armstrong* (1978), 22 OR (2d) 223, 93 DLR (3d) 128 (Ont. HC).

How then does one approach the question of unjust enrichment in matrimonial causes? In *Rathwell* I ventured to suggest there are three requirements to be satisfied before an unjust enrichment can be said to exist: an enrichment, a corresponding deprivation and absence of any juristic reason for the enrichment. This approach, it seems to me, is supported by general principles of equity that have been fashioned by the courts for centuries, though, admittedly, not in the context of matrimonial property controversies.

The common law has never been willing to compensate a plaintiff on the sole basis that his actions have benefited another. Lord Halsbury scotched this heresy in the case of *Ruabon SS. Co. Ltd. v. London Assce.*, [1900] AC 6 (HL) with these words, at p. 10: "I cannot understand how it can be asserted that it is part of the common law that where one person gets some advantage from the act of another a right of contribution towards the expense from that act arises on behalf of the person who has done it." Lord Macnaughten, in the same case, put it this way, at p. 15: "There is no principle of law that a person should contribute to an outlay merely because he has derived a benefit from it." It is not enough for the court simply to determine that one spouse has benefited at the hands of another and then to require restitution. It must, in addition, be evident that the retention of the benefit would be "unjust" in the circumstances of the case.

Miss Becker supported Mr. Pettkus for five years. She then worked on the farm for about 14 years. The compelling inference from the facts is that she believed she had some interest in the farm and that that expectation was reasonable in the circumstances. Mr. Pettkus would seem to have recognized in Miss Becker some property interest, through the payment to her of compensation, however modest. There is no evidence to indicate that he ever informed her that all her work performed over the 19 years was being performed on a gratuitous basis. He freely accepted the benefits conferred upon him through her financial support and her labour.

On these facts, the first two requirements laid down in *Rathwell* have clearly been satisfied: Mr. Pettkus has had the benefit of 19 years of unpaid labour, while Miss Becker has received little or nothing in return. As for the third requirement, I hold that where one person in a relationship tantamount to spousal prejudices herself in the reasonable expectation of receiving an interest in property and the other person in the relationship freely accepts benefits conferred by the first person in circumstances where he knows or ought to have known of that reasonable expectation, it would be unjust to allow the recipient of the benefit to retain it.

I conclude, consonant with the judgment of the Court of Appeal, that this is a case for the application of constructive trust. As Wilson JA noted [at 5 RFL (2d) 344]: "The parties lived together as husband and wife, although unmarried, for almost 20 years, during which period she not only made possible the acquisition of their first property in Franklin Centre by supporting them both exclusively from her income during 'the lean years,' but worked side by side with him for 14 years building up the bee-keeping operation which was their main source of livelihood."

Wilson JA had no difficulty in finding that a constructive trust arose in favour of the respondent by virtue of "joint effort" and "team work," as a result of which Mr. Pettkus was able to acquire the Franklin Centre property, and subsequently the East Hawkesbury and West Hawkesbury properties. The Ontario Court of Appeal imposed the constructive trust in the interests of justice and, with respect, I would do the same.

THE COMMON LAW RELATIONSHIP

One question which must be addressed is whether a constructive trust can be established having regard to what is frequently, and euphemistically, referred to as a "common law" relationship. The purpose of constructive trust is to redress situations which would otherwise denote unjust enrichment. In principle, there is no reason not to apply the doctrine to common law relationships. It is worth noting that counsel for Mr. Pettkus, and I think correctly, did not, in this court, raise the common law relationship in defence of the claim of Miss Becker, otherwise than by reference to the *Family Law Reform Act, 1978* (Ont.), c. 2.

Courts in other jurisdictions have not regarded the absence of a marital bond as any problem. See *Cooke v. Head*, [1972] 1 WLR 518, [1972] All ER 38; *Eves v. Eves*, [1975] 1 WLR 1338, [1975] 3 All ER 768; *Re Spears*, *supra*; and, in the United States, *Marvin v. Marvin* (1976), 557 P. (2d) 106 and a comment thereon (1977), 90 Harv. LR 1708. In *Marvin* the Supreme Court of California stated that constructive trust was available to give effect to the reasonable expectations of the parties, and to the notion that unmarried cohabitants intend to deal fairly with each other.

I see no basis for any distinction, in dividing property and assets, between marital relationships and those more informal relationships which subsist for a lengthy period. This was not an economic partnership, nor a mere business relationship, nor a casual encounter. Mr. Pettkus and Miss Becker lived as man and wife for almost 20 years. Their lives and their economic well-being were fully integrated. The equitable principle on which the remedy of constructive trust rests is broad and general; its purpose is to prevent unjust enrichment in whatever circumstances it occurs.

In recent years, there has been much statutory reform in the area of family law and matrimonial property. Counsel for Mr. Pettkus correctly points out that the *Family Law Reform Act* of Ontario, enacted after the present litigation was initiated, does not extend the presumption of equal sharing, which now applies between married persons, to common law spouses. The argument is made that the courts should not develop equitable remedies that are "contrary to current legislative intent." The rejoinder is that legislation was unnecessary to cover these facts, for a remedy was always available in equity for property division between unmarried individuals contributing to the acquisition of assets. The effect of the legislation is to divide "family assets" equally, regardless of contribution, as a matter of course. The court is not here creating a presumption of equal shares. There is a great difference between directing that there be equal shares for common law spouses and awarding Miss Becker a share equivalent to the money or money's worth she contributed over some 19 years. The fact there is no statutory regime directing equal division of assets acquired by common law spouses is no bar to the availability of an equitable remedy in the present circumstances.

SETTLEMENT OR ESTOPPEL

Another question argued is whether acceptance by Miss Becker of $3,000, 40 beehives and a car, upon temporary separation, and the imposition of terms on her return, estopped further claim. The trial judge answered this question in the affirmative. With respect, I think that he was wrong in so holding. A person is not estopped by accepting a sum of money, the amount of which is not negotiated, thrown at one's feet. There was no agreement by Miss Becker as to her interest in what I would regard as joint assets, nor can the conditions exacted by Miss Becker upon resumption of cohabitation be any bar to her claim. The filing by Mrs. Rathwell in *Rathwell*, *supra*, of a caveat claiming a one-tenth interest was held to be no basis for rejecting her claim to share equally in assets accumulated by her and her husband.

CAUSAL CONNECTION

The matter of "causal connection" was also raised in defence of Miss Becker's claim, but does not present any great difficulty. There is a clear link between the contribution and the disputed assets. The contribution of Miss Becker was such as enabled, or assisted in enabling Mr. Pettkus to acquire the assets in contention. For the unjust enrichment principle to apply it is obvious that some connection must be shown between the acquisition of property and corresponding deprivation. On the facts of this case, that test was met. The indirect contribution of money and the direct contribution of labour is clearly linked to the acquisition of property, the beneficial ownership of which is in dispute. Miss Becker indirectly contributed to the acquisition of the Franklin Centre farm by making possible an accelerated rate of saving by Mr. Pettkus. The question is really an issue of fact: Was her contribution sufficiently substantial and direct as to entitle her to a portion of the profits realized upon sale of the Franklin Centre property and to an interest in the Hawkesbury properties and the bee-keeping business? The Ontario Court of Appeal answered this question in the affirmative, and I would agree.

RESPECTIVE PROPORTIONS

Although equity is said to favour equality, as stated in *Rathwell*, it is not every contribution which will entitle a spouse to a one-half interest in the property. The extent of the interest must be proportionate to the contribution, direct or indirect, of the claimant. Where the contributions are unequal, the shares will be unequal.

It could be argued that Mr. Pettkus contributed somewhat more to the material fortunes of the joint enterprise than Miss Becker but it must be recognized that each started with nothing: each worked continuously, unremittingly and sedulously in the joint effort. Physically, Miss Becker pulled her fair share of the load: weighing only 87 pounds, she assisted in moving hives weighing 80 pounds. Any difference in quality or quantum of contribution was small. The Ontario Court of Appeal in its discretion favoured an even division and I would not alter that disposition, other than to note that in any accounting regard should be had to the $2,600 and the car, which Miss Becker received on separation in 1974.

Dickson J also noted the conflict of laws question "lurking in the background" in this case. The parties were domiciled in Québec from 1955 to August 1971, so that it was arguable that laws of the province of Québec were applicable. However, this issue was not pleaded and the court concluded that it was appropriate to proceed without taking judicial notice of the statutory laws of another province that had been ignored in the pleadings. Thus, Dickson J concluded:

I would dismiss the appeal with costs to the respondent.

Notes and Questions

Resulting or constructive trust?

Ritchie, Maitland, and Beetz JJ agreed with the result in *Pettkus v Becker*, but for "substantially different" reasons. Ritchie J reviewed the cases concerning resulting trusts and the Court of Appeal's reasons and concluded that

> the advances made by [Becker] throughout the period of the relationship between the parties [were] such as to support the existence of a resulting trust which is governed by the legal principles adopted by the majority of this court in [*Murdoch* and *Rathwell*].

Thus, Ritchie J expressly held that Becker had made a financial contribution and that there was a common intention that it be used for the benefit of both parties.

Maitland J similarly concluded that the case could be resolved using the doctrine of resulting trust. After reviewing the idea of constructive trust in Anglo Canadian law, moreover, Maitland J concluded that

> the adoption of this concept [of constructive trust] involves an extension of the law as so far determined in this court. Such an extension is, in my view, undesirable. It would clothe judges with a very wide power to apply what has been described as "palm tree justice" without the benefit of any guidelines. By what test is a judge to determine what constitutes unjust enrichment? The only test would be his individual perception of what he considered to be unjust.

As is apparent, some judges in *Pettkus v Becker* were not comfortable with the discretionary decision making necessary to apply concepts of unjust enrichment in a family dissolution context. In reflecting on their differing views, consider which factors seemed to be most significant. For example, how important was it that the parties had been together for a lengthy period of time and they had both done a good deal of work in relation to the disputed property? How significant was it that the parties were both without assets at the outset or that the work done by Ms. Becker involved "more than just housework"?

In thinking about these questions, consider also what Ms. Becker would have been entitled to receive pursuant to the *FLA*. Did the court use "equitable" principles to achieve "equality" goals for cohabiting spouses in this case? (For an exploration of some of these principles, see Susan Westerberg Prager, "Shifting Perspectives on Marital Property Law" in Barrie Thorne with Marilyn Yalom, eds, *Rethinking the Family: Some Feminist Questions* (New York: Longman, 1982) at 111.)

Enforcing an equitable interest: Some constraints

In *Pettkus v Becker*, Ms. Becker "won." The court declared a constructive trust that entitled her to a one-half equitable interest in property owned by Mr. Pettkus. However, as subsequent news reports explained, Mr. Pettkus resisted legal efforts to realize Ms. Becker's entitlement.

- In November 1986, *The Globe and Mail* reported that Ms. Becker had committed suicide, leaving several letters in which she described her death as a protest against a legal system that prevented her from receiving a penny of the award, worth $150,000 at the time of the Supreme Court's decision. See Oakland Ross, "Ontario Fee System Cited in Woman's Legal Woe", *The Globe and Mail* (12 November 1986). Although the report indicated that Mr. Pettkus had been ordered to sell some property to comply with the court's decision, the sale had realized only $68,000, all of which was used to pay the legal fees of Ms. Becker's counsel.

- On 26 May 1989, *The Globe and Mail* reported that Ms. Becker's estate trustees had settled her financial claim with Mr. Pettkus for $13,000.

- In September 1996, *The Lawyers Weekly* reported on a libel suit launched by Mr. Pettkus against an artist living in Van Kleek Hill, Ontario, in relation to the artist's letter to a newspaper and a painting he had entitled "Homage to Rosa Becker." Rey J in the Divisional Court allowed the artist's appeal, holding that the artist's statements did not constitute libel (see *Cartwright v Pettkus*, unreported, 10 July 1996).

Although there are often problems of enforcing court orders in other legal contexts, is it possible that the problems are particularly acute in family law matters, especially in the context of an acrimonious end to a relationship? How should these problems be addressed? For example, should the Ontario legislature extend the *FLA* regime for sharing property at marriage breakdown to cohabiting couples? Does the outcome in *Pettkus v Becker* alter your view of the majority and dissenting opinions about cohabiting couples in *Nova Scotia (AG) v Walsh* and *Quebec (AG) v A*, discussed at the beginning of this chapter? Is it appropriate to make a recalcitrant former cohabiting partner a trustee for the other partner?

Extending the principles in *Sorochan v Sorochan*

In *Sorochan v Sorochan*, [1986] 2 SCR 38, a cohabiting opposite-sex relationship of more than 40 years ended, and the woman sought an interest in land owned by the man. However, the facts indicated that the man had owned almost all this land before the partners had begun to cohabit. Why was this fact a problem in the context of the test enunciated by Dickson J in *Pettkus v Becker*? Recognizing that the woman in *Sorochan* also contributed significant work over many years, how should such a claim have been resolved?

DICKSON, CJC:

Mary and Alex Sorochan lived together for 42 years, between 1940 and 1982, on a farm in the Two Hills district of Alberta. During this time, they jointly worked a mixed farming operation and had six children. They never married. Mary Sorochan did all of the domestic labour associated with running the household and caring for the children. In addition, she worked long hours on the farm. The family lived in modest circumstances.

At the time the parties began living together, Alex Sorochan was the owner, along with his brother, of six one-quarter sections of farmland. In

1951, the land was divided between the two brothers and the respondent became the registered owner of three one-quarter sections. From 1942 to 1945, and from 1968 to 1982, the respondent worked as a travelling salesperson. During these periods, Mary Sorochan often assumed responsibility for doing all of the farm chores on her own. In 1982, due to the failing health of the appellant and the deteriorating relationship between the couple, Mary Sorochan moved to a senior citizen's home. She subsequently commenced this legal action for an interest in the farm upon which she had worked for 42 years....

Dickson CJC reviewed the trial judge's application of the test in *Pettkus v Becker*. The trial judge had ordered the transfer of one of the three quarter sections of land into the name of Mary Sorochan upon her undertaking to transfer title forthwith to her six children. He also ordered Alex Sorochan to pay her $20,000 within one year (reduced to $15,000 if paid within six months). However, the Court of Appeal allowed an appeal, holding that there was "no link between the acquisition of the property in question and the plaintiff's labour," in accordance with the principles stated in *Pettkus v Becker*. On the facts in *Sorochan*, Mary Sorochan's contribution of labour was directed only to the *maintenance*, not the *acquisition*, of property to which Alex Sorochan held title.

In the Supreme Court of Canada, however, Dickson CJC held that the principles of *Pettkus v Becker* were applicable in that there had been (1) an enrichment, (2) a corresponding deprivation, and (3) the absence of any juristic reason for the enrichment. The court then reviewed the applicability of the constructive trust as a remedy for unjust enrichment in the context of the facts and a number of other cases, including *Murray v Roty* (1983), 34 RFL (2d) 404 (Ont CA), and held:

> These cases reveal the need to retain flexibility in applying the constructive trust. In my view, the constructive trust remedy should not be confined to cases involving property acquisition. While it is important to require that some nexus exist between the claimant's deprivation and the property in question, the link need not always take the form of a contribution to the actual acquisition of the property. A contribution relating to the preservation, maintenance or improvement of property may also suffice. What remains primary is whether or not the services rendered have a "clear proprietary relationship" [at 156], to use Professor McLeod's phrase. When such a connection is present, proprietary relief may be appropriate. Such an approach will help to ensure equitable and fair relief in the myriad of familial circumstances and situations where unjust enrichment occurs....
>
> In the present case, Mary Sorochan worked on the farm for 42 years. Her labour directly and substantially contributed to the maintenance and preservation of the farm, preventing asset deterioration or divestment. There is, therefore, a "clear link" between the contribution and the disputed assets....

After reviewing the order of the trial judge, Dickson CJC concluded that the monetary judgment was appropriate, but disagreed with the order concerning the land. In allowing the appeal, the court ordered a deletion of the requirement that Mary Sorochan transfer title of the quarter section to her children, stating:

Mary Sorochan is the one who suffered the deprivation and it is she who is entitled to the remedy — not her children. She may well decide to transfer title to the land to her children, but this will be her decision alone to make.

Although the court in *Sorochan* concluded that the test for unjust enrichment was met in this case, even though Mary Sorochan's work did not contribute to the *acquisition* of property, the court's decision made clear the requirement of a nexus, or connection, between the work done and the property itself. To what extent is the existence of a nexus between the property claimed and the work done capable of evidence? Does this factor limit the discretion to be exercised by a court in assessing such a claim?

The nexus requirement

In a number of cases, courts denied claims based on unjust enrichment because there was no sufficient nexus between the work and the property claimed.

For example, in *Everson v Rich* (1988), 16 RFL (3d) 337, the Saskatchewan Court of Appeal denied a declaration of constructive trust because there was no sufficient nexus between the provision of the woman's household services and the acquisition of the property. Why is this case different from the facts in *Pettkus v Becker* and in *Sorochan*? Note that in both the earlier cases, the claimant had performed *both* household services and "extraordinary work" outside the home.

By contrast, in *Kutt v Sam* (1990), 26 RFL (3d) 268, the Ontario High Court held that a woman applicant was entitled to a 25 percent interest in the matrimonial home because she had worked outside the home and also provided household services over many years, including entertaining her cohabitant's family for lengthy stays.

In some cases, courts denied claims because the traditional division of labour (with the woman doing household work and the man working at paid labour) meant that there was no enrichment or deprivation (for example, see *Stewart v Whitley* (1992), 41 RFL (3d) 362 (Ont Gen Div), where the court denied a constructive trust claim on the basis that neither party had been enriched or deprived as a result of their respective contributions).

Similarly, in *Stanish v Parasz* (1989), 23 RFL (3d) 207 (Man QB (Fam Div)), where the parties agreed that the woman would remain at home to perform household duties and care for a child, while the man worked in the labour force, the court concluded that:

> The evidence falls far short of proving a case of unjust enrichment.... The parties entered into a relationship which was mutually beneficial. Ms. Stanish clearly provided valuable services to Mr. Parasz, but he also provided valuable services to her. In looking at the three requirements for unjust enrichment, namely, (a) an enrichment, (b) a corresponding deprivation, and (c) the absence of a juristic reason for the enrichment, the court must look at the reasonableness of the bargain — the *quid pro quo*. Perhaps, to some degree, it can always be said that there is an enrichment to the person receiving the household services, and a deprivation to the person that remains out of the work force for a period of time to provide the services, but there is not the absence of a juristic reason, if the party

supplying the services is sufficiently compensated in return. The enrichment must be *unjust*. It must be against the conscience that the recipient should be allowed to retain the benefits without compensation. This requirement will be met where one party prejudices himself/herself with the reasonable expectation of receiving something in return, and the other person accepts that when he/she knows or ought to know of that expectation....

Recall the statistics in Chapter One about the financial circumstances of families in Canada and the analysis in the Chapter Five about the "feminization of poverty" at the breakdown of marriage and cohabiting relationships. To what extent do these statistics suggest that the principles of constructive trust may not be responsive to the needs of a majority of cohabiting couples at the dissolution of their relationships?

RETHINKING AN APPROPRIATE REMEDY FOR UNJUST ENRICHMENT

Alternatives to the remedy of constructive trust for unjust enrichment

In *Sorochan*, the Supreme Court of Canada explained that the principles of *Pettkus v Becker* required both a finding of unjust enrichment and also a determination that the appropriate remedy was a declaration of constructive trust. That is, the finding of unjust enrichment did not automatically lead to the declaration of constructive trust. Instead a trust would be imposed only if a monetary award was not sufficient. This principle seemed to be applied in an early case in Ontario

Georg v Hassanali
(1989), 18 RFL (3d) 225 (Ont HC)

A wealthy older man and a younger woman were involved in a cohabiting relationship of about 15 years. The woman provided extensive services to the tenants of a large apartment building owned by the man in Scarborough, as well as household and personal services to him. Although the man was not able to marry because he had never divorced his first wife, and although he had promised to marry the woman, he then married a different woman when his first wife died. According to the court, the facts clearly established unjust enrichment. However, in assessing an appropriate remedy, the court stated:

> It is urged on behalf of the plaintiff that this can best be accomplished by the imposition of a constructive trust.
> It is the defendant's submission, however, that the circumstances here do not justify the imposition of a constructive trust and the making of a proprietary award, as sought by the plaintiff. [Instead, the defendant suggested a monetary award on a *quantum meruit* basis, and the court

concluded that the nature of the property in this case, a 15 storey, 183 suite apartment building, required something other than a proprietary interest.]

An examination of the equities and circumstances of the parties reveals that he values this building at $8 million and derives rental income therefrom of over $363,000 per year and declares his net worth — after deducting a commitment of some $500,000 to charity — [at] almost $7 million.

By contrast, the plaintiff's financial statement discloses her only assets to be two fur coats given her by the defendant, furniture worth $500 and jewellery having a value of some $2,500. The only income she now receives are welfare payments.

After a most careful and anxious consideration of all the circumstances, I feel that an award of $725,000 is both a fair and realistic amount to require the defendant to pay to the plaintiff to redress her deprivation herein.

I impose a trust or proprietary interest to the extent necessary that such shall be and constitute a proprietary interest or charge against this building ... until such sum as I have awarded is paid in full. And, in addition, the plaintiff shall retain the exclusive right to occupy Suite 1412 therein, without payment of any kind, for a like period.

How should the award to the plaintiff in this case be characterized? If the court had declared a constructive trust, how would it have differed from the court's order here? To what extent is it possible that the court was mindful of the problems of enforcement in *Pettkus v Becker*?

Reconsidering remedies for unjust enrichment in the Supreme Court of Canada

Peter v Beblow
[1993] 1 SCR 980

Ms. Peter and Mr. Beblow lived in a cohabiting relationship for about 12 years. During their time together, Ms. Peter cared for the children (including her own and Mr. Beblow's from their previous relationships) and looked after their home and garden. Mr. Beblow owned the home and, prior to his relationship with Ms. Peter, he had paid a housekeeper to perform these tasks. Ms. Peter also worked on a part-time basis outside the home, while Mr. Beblow did seasonal work. At the end of their relationship, Mr. Beblow had paid off the mortgage on the home, and he also owned a car and a boat. Ms. Peter owned a vacation property that she had purchased during the relationship.

When their relationship ended, Ms. Peter brought an action claiming unjust enrichment, seeking a constructive trust in her favour respecting the home in which they lived or, alternatively, monetary damages as compensation for the labour and services she provided.

The B.C. Supreme Court allowed the action and awarded Ms. Peter the full interest in the home on the basis that there was an enrichment, a corresponding deprivation, and the lack of any juristic reason for the enrichment (see [1988] BCJ No 887 (SC)). The court also stated that there was a clear causal connection between the contribution founding the unjust enrichment and the property to be subject to the constructive trust.

The B.C. Court of Appeal allowed Mr. Beblow's appeal: (1990), 29 RFL (3d) 268 (BCCA).

In the Supreme Court of Canada, the court restored the order of the trial judge so that Ms. Peter received the entire interest in the home. However, the Court used this opportunity to review the concept of unjust enrichment in relation to the dissolution of cohabiting relationships and to identify principles for determining the appropriate remedy. In addition, although McLachlin J and Cory J concurred in their decisions, some aspects of their differing views in *Rawluk* remain apparent.

McLACHLIN J (for La Forest, Sopinka, and Iacobucci JJ):

[1] I have had the advantage of reading the reasons of Justice Cory. While I agree with his conclusion, and with much of his analysis, my reasons differ in some respects on two matters critical to this appeal: the issues raised by the requirement of the absence of juristic reason for an enrichment and the nature of application of the remedy of constructive trust....

[4] There is a tendency on the part of some to view the action for unjust enrichment as a device for doing whatever may seem fair between the parties. In the rush to substantive justice, the principles are sometimes forgotten. Policy issues often assume a large role, infusing such straightforward discussions as whether there was a "benefit" to the defendant or a "detriment" to the plaintiff. On the remedies side, the requirements of the special proprietary remedy of constructive trust are sometimes minimized. As Professor Palmer has said: "The constructive trust idea stirs the judicial imagination in ways that *assumpsit*, *quantum meruit* and other terms associated with quasi-contract have never quite succeeded in duplicating" (G.E. Palmer, *The Law of Restitution*, vol. 1, at p. 16). Occasionally the remedial notion of constructive trust is even conflated with unjust enrichment itself, as though where one is found the other must follow.

[5] Such difficulties have to some degree complicated the case at bar. At the doctrinal level, the simple questions of "benefit" and "detriment" became infused with moral and policy questions of when the provision of domestic services in a quasi-matrimonial situation can give rise to a legal obligation. At the stage of remedy, the trial judge proceeded as if he were making a monetary award, and then, without fully explaining how, awarded the appellant the entire interest in the matrimonial home on the basis of a constructive trust. It is only by a return to the fundamental principles laid out in cases like *Becker v. Pettkus* and *Lac Minerals* that one can cut through the conflicting findings and submissions on these issues and evaluate whether in fact the appellant has made out a claim for unjust enrichment, and if so what her remedy should be.

[THE APPELLANT'S CLAIM FOR UNJUST ENRICHMENT]

[6] I share the view of Cory J. that the three elements necessary to establish a claim for unjust enrichment — an enrichment, a corresponding deprivation, and the absence of any juristic reason for the enrichment — are made out in this case. The appellant's housekeeping and child-care services constituted a benefit to the respondent (1st element), in that he received household services without compensation, which in turn enhanced his ability to pay off his mortgage and other assets. These ser-

vices also constituted a corresponding detriment to the appellant (2nd element), in that she provided services without compensation. Finally, since there was no obligation existing between the parties which would justify the unjust enrichment and no other arguments under this broad heading were met, there is no juristic reason for the enrichment (3rd element). Having met the three criteria, the plaintiff has established an unjust enrichment giving rise to restitution.

[7] The main arguments on this appeal centred on whether the law should recognize the services which the appellant provided as being capable of founding an action for unjust enrichment. It was argued, for example, that the services cannot give rise to a remedy based on unjust enrichment because the appellant had voluntarily assumed the role of wife and stepmother. It was also said that the law of unjust enrichment should not recognize such services because they arise from natural love and affection. These arguments raise moral and policy questions and require the court to make value judgments.

[8] The first question is: where do these arguments belong? Are they part of the benefit–detriment analysis, or should they be considered under the third head — the absence of juristic reason for the unjust enrichment? The Court of Appeal, for example, held that there was no "detriment" on these grounds. I hold the view that these factors may most conveniently be considered under the third head of absence of juristic reason. This court has consistently taken a straightforward economic approach to the first two elements of the test for unjust enrichment: *Pettkus v. Becker*, *supra*; *Sorochan v. Sorochan*, [1986] 2 SCR 38; 69 NR 81; 74 AR 67; [1986] 5 WWR 289; 2 RFL (2d) 225; 46 Alta. LR (2d) 97; *Peel (Regional Municipality) v. Ontario*, [1992] 3 SCR 762; 144 NR 1, 59 OAC 81 (hereinafter "*Peel*"). It is in connection with the third element — absence of juristic reason for the enrichment — that such considerations may more properly find their place. It is at this stage that the court must consider whether the enrichment and detriment, morally neutral in themselves, are "unjust."

[9] What matters should be considered in determining whether there is an absence of juristic reason for the enrichment? The test is flexible, and the factors to be considered may vary with the situation before the court. For example, different factors may be more relevant in a case like *Peel*, *supra*, at p. 803, a claim for unjust enrichment between different levels of government, than in a family case.

[10] In every case, the fundamental concern is the legitimate expectation of the parties: *Becker v. Pettkus*, *supra*. In family cases, this concern may raise the following subsidiary questions:
(i) Did the plaintiff confer the benefit as a valid gift or in pursuance of a valid common law, equitable or statutory obligation which he or she owed to the defendant?
(ii) Did the plaintiff submit to, or compromise, the defendant's honest claim?
(iii) Does public policy support the enrichment?

[11] In the case at bar, the first and third of these factors were argued. It was argued first that the appellant's services were rendered pursuant to a common law or equitable obligation which she had assumed. Her services were part of the bargain she made when she came to live with the respondent, it was said. He would give her and her children a home and other husbandly services, and in turn she would look after the home and family.

[12] This court has held that a common law spouse generally owes no duty at common law, in equity or by statute to perform work or services for her partner. As Dickson CJ speaking for the court put it in *Sorochan v. Sorochan, supra,* at p. 46, the common law wife "was under no obligation, contractual or otherwise, to perform the work and services in the home or on the land." So there is no general duty presumed by the law on a common law spouse to perform work and services for her partner.

[13] Nor, in the case at bar was there any obligation arising from the circumstances of the parties. The trial judge held that the appellant was "under no obligation to perform the work and assist in the home without some reasonable expectation of receiving something in return other than the drunken physical abuse which she received at the hands of the respondent." This puts an end to the argument that the services in question were performed pursuant to obligation. It also puts an end to the argument that the appellant's services to her partner were a "gift" from her to him. The central element of a gift at law — intentional giving to another without expectation of remuneration — is simply not present.

[14] The third factor mentioned above raises directly the issue of public policy. While it may be stated in different ways, the argument at base is simply that some types of services in some types of relationships should not be recognized as supporting legal claims for policy reasons. More particularly, homemaking and childcare services should not, in a marital or quasi-marital relationship, be viewed as giving rise to equitable claims against the other spouse.

[15] I concede at the outset that there is some judicial precedent for this argument. Professor M. Neave has observed generally that "[a]nalysis of the principles applied in English, Australian and Canadian courts sometimes fails to confront this question directly ... Courts which deny or grant remedies usually conceal their value judgments within statements relating to doctrinal requirements." (M. Neave, "Three Approaches to Family Property Disputes: Intention/Belief, Unjust Enrichment, and Unconscionability," in T.G. Youdan, ed., *Equity, Fiduciaries and Trusts,* at p. 251.) More pointedly, Professor Farquhar has observed that many courts have strayed from the framework of *Sorochan* for public policy reasons: "the courts ... have, after *Sorochan,* put up warning signs that there are aspects of relationships that are not to be analyzed in the light of unjust enrichment and constructive trust." (Keith B. Farquhar, "Causal Connection in Constructive Trust After Sorochan v. Sorochan" (1989), 7 *Can. J. of Family Law* 337, at p. 343.) The public policy issue has been summed up as follows by Professor Neave, *supra,* at p. 251: "whether a remedy, either personal or proprietary, should be provided to a person who has made contributions to family resources." On the judicial side, the view of the respondent is pointedly stated in *Grant v. Edwards,* [1986] 2 All ER 426, at p. 439, per Browne-Wilkinson VC:

> Setting up house together, having a baby and making payments to general house-keeping expenses ... may all be referable to the mutual love and affection of the parties and not specifically referable to the claimant's belief that she has an interest in the house.

Proponents of this view, Professor Neave, *supra,* at p. 253 argues, "regard it as distasteful to put a price upon services provided out of a sense of love and commitment to the relationship. They suggest it is unfair for a recipient of indirect or nonfinancial contributions to be forced to provide recompense for those contributions." To support this position, the respondent cites several cases....

[16] It is my view that this argument is no longer tenable in Canada, either from the point of view of logic or authority. I share the view of Professors Hovius and Youdan that "there is no logical reason to distinguish domestic services from other contributions" (*supra*, at p. 146). The notion that household and childcare services are not worthy of recognition by the court fails to recognize the fact that these services are of great value, not only to the family, but to the other spouse. As Lord Simon observed nearly 30 years ago: "The cock-bird can feather his nest precisely because he is not required to spend most of his time sitting on it" (*With All My Worldly Goods*, Holdsworth Lecture, University of Birmingham, 20th March 1964, at p. 32). The notion, moreover, is a pernicious one that systematically devalues the contributions which women tend to make to the family economy. It has contributed to the phenomenon of the feminization of poverty which this court identified in *Moge v. Moge*, [1992] 3 SCR 813 ... per L'Heureux-Dubé J, at pp. 853–854.

[17] Moreover, the argument cannot stand with the jurisprudence which this and other courts have laid down. Today courts regularly recognize the value of domestic services. This becomes clear with the court's holding in *Sorochan*, leading one author to comment that "[t]he Canadian Supreme Court has finally recognized that domestic contribution is of equal value as financial contribution in trusts of property in the familial context" (Mary Welstead, "Domestic Contribution and Constructive Trusts: The Canadian Perspective," [1987] *Denning LJ* 151, at p. 161). If there could be any doubt about the need for the law to honestly recognize the value of domestic services, it must be considered to have been banished by *Moge v. Moge*, *supra*. While that case arose under the *Divorce Act*, RSC 1985 (2d Supp.), c. 3, the value of the services does not change with the legal remedy invoked.

[18] I cannot give credence to the argument that legal recognition of the value of domestic services will do violence to the law and social structure of our society. It has been recognized for some time that such services are entitled to recognition and compensation under the *Divorce Act* and the provincial Acts governing the distribution of matrimonial property. Yet society has not been visibly harmed. I do not think that similar recognition in the equitable doctrine of unjust enrichment will have any different effect.

[19] Finally, I come to the argument that, because the legislature has chosen to exclude unmarried couples from the right to claim an interest in the matrimonial assets on the basis of contribution to the relationship, the court should not use the equitable doctrine of unjust enrichment to remedy the situation. Again, the argument seems flawed. It is precisely where an injustice arises without a legal remedy that equity finds a role. This case is much stronger than *Rawluk v. Rawluk*, [1990] 1 SCR 70..., where I dissented on the ground that the statute expressly pronounced on the very matter with respect to which equity was invoked.

[20] Accordingly, I would agree with Cory J. that there are no juristic arguments which would justify the unjust enrichment, and the third element is made out. Like him, I conclude that the plaintiff was enriched, to the benefit of the defendant, and that no justification existed to vitiate the unjust enrichment claim. The claim for unjust enrichment is accordingly made out and it remains only to determine the appropriate remedy.

[THE REMEDY: MONETARY JUDGMENT OR CONSTRUCTIVE TRUST]

[21] The other difficult aspect of this case is the question of whether the remedy which the trial judge awarded — title to the matrimonial home —

is justified on the principles governing the action for unjust enrichment. Two remedies are possible: an award of money on the basis of the value of the services rendered, i.e. *quantum meruit*; and the one the trial judge awarded, title to the house based on a constructive trust.

[22] In Canada the concept of the constructive trust has been used as a vehicle for compensating for unjust enrichment in appropriate cases. The constructive trust, based on analogy to the formal trust of traditional equity, is a proprietary concept. The plaintiff is found to have an interest in the property. A finding that a plaintiff is entitled to a remedy for unjust enrichment does not imply that there is a constructive trust. As I wrote in *Rawluk, supra,* for a constructive trust to arise, the plaintiff must establish a direct link to the property which is the subject of the trust by reason of the plaintiff's contribution. This is the notion underlying the constructive trust in *Pettkus v. Becker, supra,* and *Sorochan v. Sorochan, supra,* as I understand those cases. It was also affirmed by La Forest J. in *LAC Minerals, supra.*

[23] My colleague Cory J. suggests that, while a link between the contribution and the property is essential in commercial cases for a constructive trust to arise, it may not be required in family cases....

[24] I doubt the wisdom of dividing unjust enrichment cases into two categories — commercial and family — for the purpose of determining whether a constructive trust lies. A special rule for family cases finds no support in the jurisprudence. Neither *Pettkus,* nor *Rathwell,* nor *Sorochan* suggest such a departure. Moreover, the notion that one can dispense with a link between the services rendered and the property which is claimed to be subject to the trust is inconsistent with the proprietary nature of the notion of constructive trust. Finally, the creation of special rules for special situations might have an adverse effect on the development of this emerging area of equity. The same general principles should apply for all contexts, subject only to the demonstrated need for alternation. Wilson J. in *Syncrude Canada Ltd. et al. v. Hunter Engineering Co. and Allis-Chamber Canada Ltd. et al.,* [1989] 1 SCR 426; 92 NR 1, at p. 519 (adopted by La Forest J. in *LAC Minerals, supra,* at p. 675), warns against confining constructive trust remedies ... stating that "to do so would be to impede the growth and impair the flexibility crucial to the development of equitable principles." The same result, I fear, may flow from developing special rules for finding constructive trusts in family cases. In short, the concern for clarity and doctrinal integrity with which this court has long been preoccupied in this area mandates that the basic principles governing the rights and remedies for unjust enrichment remain the same for all cases.

[25] Nor does the distinction between commercial cases and family cases on the remedy of constructive trust appear to be necessary. Where a monetary award is sufficient, there is no need for a constructive trust. Where a monetary award is insufficient in a family situation, this is usually related to the fact the claimant's efforts have given her a special link to the property, in which case a constructive trust arises.

[26] For these reasons, I hold the view that in order for a constructive trust to be found, in a family case as in other cases, monetary compensation must be inadequate and there must be a link between the services rendered and the property in which the trust is claimed. Having said this, I echo the comments of Cory J. at para. 99 that the courts should exercise flexibility and common sense when applying equitable principles to family law issues with due sensitivity to the special circumstances that can arise in such cases.

[27] The next question is the extent of the contribution required to give rise to a constructive trust. A minor or indirect contribution is insufficient. The question, to quote Dickson CJ in *Pettkus v. Becker, supra*, at p. 852, is whether "[the plaintiff's] contribution [was] sufficiently substantial and direct as to entitle her to a portion of the profits realized upon sale of the ... property." Once this threshold is met, the amount of the contribution governs the extent of the constructive trust. As Dickson CJ wrote in *Becker v. Pettkus, supra*, at pp. 852–853:

> Although equity is said to favour equality, as stated in *Rathwell*, it is not every contribution which will entitle a spouse to a one-half interest in the property. *The extent of the interest must be proportionate to the contribution, direct or indirect, of the claimant. Where the contributions are unequal, the shares will be unequal.* (Emphasis added.)

Cory J. advocates a flexible approach to determining whether a constructive trust is appropriate; an approach "based on common sense and a desire to achieve a fair result for both parties" (at para. 99). While agreeing that courts should avoid becoming overly technical on matters which may not be susceptible of precise monetary valuation, the principle remains that the extent of the trust must reflect the extent of the contribution.

[28] Before leaving the principles governing the remedy of constructive trust, I turn to the manner in which the extent of the trust is determined. The debate centres on whether it is sufficient to look at the value of the services which the claimant has rendered (the "value received" approach). Cory J. expresses a preference for a "value survived" approach. However, he also suggests, at para. 103, that "there is no reason why *quantum meruit* or the value received approach could not be utilized to quantify the value of the constructive trust." With respect, I cannot agree. It seems to me that there are very good reasons, both doctrinal and practical, for referring to the "value survived" when assessing the value of a constructive trust.

[29] From the point of view of doctrine, "[t]he extent of the interest must be proportionate to the contribution" to the property: *Pettkus v. Becker, supra*, at p. 852. How is the contribution to the property to be determined? One starts, of necessity, by defining the property. One goes on to determine what portion of that property is attributable to the claimant's efforts. This is the "value survived" approach. For a monetary award, the "value received" approach is appropriate; the value conferred on the property is irrelevant. But where the claim is for an interest in the property one must of necessity, it seems to me, determine what portion of the value of the property claimed is attributable to the claimant's services.

[30] I note, as does my colleague, that there may also be practical reasons for favouring a "value survived" approach. Cory J. alludes to the practical problems with balancing benefits and detriments as required by the "value received" approach, leading some to question whether it is the least attractive approach in most family property cases (see *Davidson v. Worthing* (1986), 9 BCLR (2d) 202; 6 RFL (3d) 113, McEachern CJSC; Hovius & Youdan, *supra*, at 136ff.). Moreover, a "value survived" approach arguably accords best with the expectations of most parties; it is more likely that a couple expects to share in the wealth generated from their partnership, rather than to receive compensation for the services performed during the relationship.

[31] To summarize, it seems to me that the first step in determining the proper remedy for unjust enrichment is to determine whether a monetary award is insufficient and whether the nexus between the contribution and the property described in *Becker v. Pettkus* has been made out. If these questions are answered in the affirmative the plaintiff is entitled to the proprietary remedy of constructive trust. In looking at whether a monetary award is insufficient the court may take into account the probability of the award's being paid as well as the special interest in the property acquired by the contributions: per La Forest J. in *LAC Minerals*. The value of that trust is to be determined on the basis of the actual value of the matrimonial property — the "value survived" approach. It reflects the court's best estimate of what is fair having regard to the contribution which the claimant's services have made to the value surviving, bearing in mind the practical difficulty of calculating with mathematical precision the value of particular contributions to the family property.

[32] I turn now to application of these principles to the case at bar. The trial judge began by assessing the value received by the respondent (the *quantum meruit*). He went on to conclude that a monetary judgment would be inadequate. The respondent had few assets other than his houseboat and van, and no income save for a War Veteran's Allowance. The judge concluded, as I understand his reasons, that there was a sufficiently direct connection between the services rendered and the property to support a constructive trust, stating that "[the appellant] has shown that there was a positive proprietary benefit conferred by her upon the Sicamous property." Accordingly, he held that the remedy of constructive trust was made out. This approach accords with principles discussed above. In effect, the trial judge found the monetary award to be inadequate on the grounds that it would not be paid and on the ground of a special contribution to the property. These findings support the remedy of constructive trust in the property.

[33] The remaining question is the quantification of the trust. The trial judge calculated the *quantum meruit* for her housekeeping for 12 years at $350 per month and reduced that figure by 50% "for the benefits she received." The final amount was $25,200. He then reasoned that, since the services rendered amounted to $25,200 after appropriate deductions, it follows that the appellant should receive title to the respondent's property, valued at $23,200. The missing step in this analysis is the failure to link the value received with the value surviving. As discussed above, a constructive trust cannot be quantified by simply adding up the services rendered; the court must determine the extent of the contribution which the services have made to the parties' property.

[34] Notwithstanding the trial judge's failure to make this link, his conclusion that the appellant has established a constructive trust entitling her to title to the family home can be maintained if a trust of this magnitude is supported on the evidence. This brings me to a departure from the methods used below. The parties and the Court of Appeal appear to have treated the house as a single asset rather than as part of a family enterprise. This led to the argument that the appellant could not be entitled to full ownership in the house because the respondent had contributed to its value as well. The approach I would take — and the approach I believe the trial judge implicitly to have taken — is to consider the appellant's proper share of all the family assets. This joint family venture, in effect, was no different from the farm which was the subject of the trust in *Becker v. Pettkus*.

[35] With this in mind, I turn to the evidence on the extent of the contribution. The appellant provided extensive household services, over a period of 12 years, including care for the children while they were living at the

house and maintenance of the property. The testimony of the plaintiff's son provides a general idea of her contribution to the family enterprise:

Q. What sort of things did she do?
A. She did all the motherly duties for all of us.
A. When [the defendant's] two sons and my brother and I were there still, even when my sisters were there, that was quite a long time ago, I was quite young, so there was nothing really bad then, but after the sisters left, she took care of all the duties, cooking and stuff like that, cleaning, laundry. She had her ringer washer, she would do the laundry, she'd worked in the garden, things like that. She took care of all things around the house, when he was gone especially. ...

Q. Do you remember what work your mother did in the yard outside?
A. M'hm, they both got together doing the garden, he would do the roto-tilling, they would both take care of the planting and stuff; when he was gone, she would do all the weeding and keeping up. They would share the watering of the garden. She put together three or four flower gardens all herself, except for the hard heavy work, like lifting rocks, when she first started, that was shared by all of us, including the kids.

Of all the chores performed around the property, the son states that the various siblings had minor chores, such as chopping wood and making beds. "Everything else, the major stuff, she would take care of." Other evidence, including testimony from Catherine Peter and William Beblow, supports this picture of the appellant's contribution. The trial judge held that while the respondent worked in the construction business,

> ... he would be away from home during the week and would return on the weekend whenever possible. While he was absent, the plaintiff would care for the property in the home and care for the children while he was away.

> In effect, the plaintiff by moving into the respondent's home became his housekeeper on a full-time basis without remuneration except for the food and shelter that she and the children received until the children left home.

[36] The respondent also contributed to the value of the family enterprise surviving at the time of breakup; he generated most of the family income and helped with the maintenance of the property.

[37] Clearly, the appellant's contribution — the "value received" by the respondent — was considerable. But what then of the "value surviving"? It seems clear that the maintenance of the family enterprise through work in cooking, cleaning, and landscaping helped preserve the property and saved the respondent large sums of money [with] which he was able to pay off his mortgage and to purchase a houseboat and a van. The appellant, for her part, had purchased a lot with her outside earnings. All these assets may be viewed as assets of the family enterprise to which the appellant contributed substantially.

[38] The question is whether, taking the parties' respective contributions to the family assets and the value of the assets into account, the trial judge erred in awarding the appellant a full interest in the house. In my view, the evidence is capable of supporting the conclusion that the house reflects a fair approximation of the value of the appellant's efforts as reflected in the family assets. Accordingly, I would not disturb the award.

[39] I would allow the appeal with costs.

CORY J (for L'Heureux-Dubé and Gonthier JJ):

[74] Business relationships concerned with commercial affairs may, as a result of the conduct of one of the corporations involved, result in a court's granting a constructive trust remedy. The constructive trust has been appropriately used to redress a gain made through a breach of trust in a commercial or business relationship (see for example: *Canadian Aero Service Ltd. v. O'Malley*, [1974] SCR 592; 40 DLR (3d) 371). Yet how much closer and trusting must be a long term common law relationship. In marriages or marriage-like relationships commercial matters and a great deal more will be involved. Clearly, parties to a family relationship will, in a commercial sense, share funds and financial goals. More importantly, couples such as the parties to this case will strive to make a home. By that I mean a place that provides safety, security and love and which is as well frequently the place where children may be cared for and nurtured. In a relationship that involves living and sleeping together, couples will share their worst fears and frustrations and their fondest dreams and aspirations. They will plan and work together to achieve their goals. Just as much as parties to a formal marriage, the partners in a long term common law relationship will base their actions on mutual love and trust. They too are entitled, in appropriate circumstances, to the relief provided by the remedy of constructive trust.

[75] This remedy should be granted despite the fact that [a] family will seldom keep the same careful financial records as business associates. Nonetheless, fairness requires that the constructive trust remedy be available to them and applied on an equitable basis without a minute scrutiny of their respective financial contributions. Indeed, in a situation such as the one presented in this case, it may be very difficult to assess the value of making a house a home and of sharing the struggle to raise children to become responsible adults.

[76] In the present case, although there was no formal marriage, the couple lived and worked together in the most intimate of relationships. They shared work and the monies which they earned. The amount of the contributions may have been varied and unequal. Yet the very fact that in addition to her household work the appellant contributed something of the income from her outside employment indicates that there was a real sharing of income. As a result of the relationship, the Sicamous property was looked after and maintained. None of this could have been achieved without the efforts of the appellant.

[77] Certainly, it cannot be said that the relationship was so short lived that it should not give rise to mutual rights and obligations. Twelve years is not an insignificant period of time to live in a relationship based on mutual trust and confidence. In those circumstances, there is a strong presumption that the services provided by one party will not be used solely to enrich the other. Both the reasonable expectations of the parties and equity will require that upon the termination of the relationship, the parties will receive an appropriate compensation based on the contribution each has made to the relationship.

[78] The respondent asserts that because the appellant loved him she could not have expected to receive compensation or an interest in the property in return for the contributions she made to the home and family. However, in today's society it is unreasonable to assume that the presence of love automatically implies a gift of one party's services to another. Nor is it unreasonable for the party providing the domestic labour required to create a home to expect to share in the property of the parties when the relationship is terminated. Women no longer are expected to work exclusively in the home. It must be recognized that when they do so, women forgo outside employment to provide domestic services and child care. The granting of relief in the form of a personal judgment or a property interest to the provider of domestic services should adequately reflect the fact that the income earning capacity and the ability to acquire assets by one party has been enhanced by the unpaid domestic services of the other. M. Neave in "Three Approaches to Family Property Disputes: Intention/Belief, Unjust Enrichment and Unconscionability," in T.G. Youdan (ed.), *Equity, Fiduciaries and Trusts* (1989), lucidly sets out the position in this way at p. 254:

> The characterization of domestic services as gifts reflects a view of family relationships which is now outdated and has a differential impact on women, since they are the main providers of such services. Women no longer work exclusively in the home. Those who do so sacrifice income that could otherwise be earned in paid work. Couples who decide that one partner, usually the woman, will forgo paid employment to provide domestic services and provide child care, presumably believe that this arrangement will maximize their economic resources. Grant of relief, whether personal or proprietary, to the provider of domestic services would recognize that the income-earning capacity of one partner and his ability to acquire assets have been enhanced by the unpaid services of the other and that those services were only provided free because it was believed that the relationship would continue.

[79] This same reasoning has been recently applied in the context of divorce in *Moge v. Moge*, [1992] 3 SCR 813. ... It is appropriate to recognize that the same principle be applied to long term common law relationships....

[98] I agree with my colleague that there is a need to limit the use of the constructive trust remedy in a commercial context. Yet I do not think the same proposition should be rigorously applied in a family relationship. In a marital or quasi-marital relationship, the expectations the parties will have regarding their contributions and interest in the assets acquired are, I expect, very different from the expectation of the parties engaged in a commercial transaction. As I have said, it is unlikely that couples will ever turn their minds to the issue of their expectations about their legal entitlement at the outset of their marriage or common law relationship. If they were specifically asked about their expectations, I would think that most couples would probably state that they did not expect to be compensated for their contribution. Rather, they would say, if the relationship were ever to be dissolved, then they would expect that both parties would share in the assets or wealth that they had helped to create. Thus, rather than expecting to receive a fee for their services based on their market value, they would expect to receive, on a dissolution of their relationship, a fair share of the property or wealth which their contributions had helped the parties to acquire, improve, or to maintain. The remedy provided by the constructive trust seems to best accord with the reasonable expectations of the parties in a marriage or quasi-marital relationship. Nevertheless, in situations where the rights of bona fide third parties would be affected as a result of granting the constructive trust remedy it may well be inappropriate to do so. (See: Berend Hovius and Timothy G. Youdan, *The Law of Family Property*, supra, at p. 146.)

[99] It follows that in a quasi-marital relationship in those situations where the rights of third parties are not involved, the choice between a monetary award and a constructive trust will be discretionary and should be exercised flexibly. Ordinarily both partners will have an interest in the property acquired, improved or maintained during the course of the relationship. The decision as to which property, if there is more than one, should be made the subject of a constructive trust is also a discretionary one. It too should be based on common sense and a desire to achieve a fair result for both parties.

Appeal allowed.

Notes and Questions

Rethinking family property and cohabitees: OLRC recommendations

After reviewing the decision in *Peter v Beblow*, the OLRC's *Report on Family Property Law* expressed the view (at 39) that there are inevitable problems with the application of the doctrine of unjust enrichment in domestic cases:

> The application of an analysis that rests on evidence of the expectation of the parties concerning property sharing or compensation, and of the respective economic contributions of spouses or others in intimate relationships, is bound to be difficult. Yet in spousal claims, courts experience tremendous pressure to ensure that each spouse receives a fair share of family property.

In this context, the report suggested that these problems may explain why the House of Lords in the United Kingdom adopted a restrictive approach to trust claims, leaving the matter to be addressed by Parliamentary reform. For example, see Law Commission, *Cohabitation: The Financial Consequences of Relationship Breakdown: A Consultation Paper* #179 (London: Law Commission, 2006).

After considering the cases in this section, reflect again on the extent to which trusts provide a remedy for cohabiting couples that is an effective alternative to a legislative matrimonial property regime (as was suggested by the majority in *Nova Scotia (AG) v Walsh*). Consider this assessment in the OLRC's *Report on Family Property Law* (at 39–40):

> The doctrine of unjust enrichment has serious limitations as a tool for the fair allocation of property between spouses, or others who have integrated their economic lives as part of an intimate relationship. The doctrine rests on a transfer of wealth, typically in the form of services, from one spouse to another, combined with an expectation of compensation, or an interest in an asset in return. In many cases, the expectation will not arise or the transfer of wealth may not be easily demonstrated on the evidence. Yet reasons of social policy may provide a sound basis for a sharing of property at the end of such a relationship.... The uncertainties that have appeared in the application of the doctrine of unjust enrichment may reflect a poor fit between its requirements and the realities of domestic relationships.

Recall that the OLRC recommendations included two related measures:

- First, the OLRC recommended the extension of the legislative regime to cohabiting couples, including both opposite-sex and consenting same-sex couples (see OLRC, *Report on the Rights and Responsibilities of Cohabitants Under the Family Law Act* (Toronto: OLRC, 1993), recommendation no 1).

- In addition, the OLRC concluded that all spouses (whether married or cohabiting) should be precluded from applying for resulting and constructive trusts (see *Report on Family Property Law*, recommendation no 30).

To what extent do you agree that these proposals are appropriate measures for achieving overall goals for a family property regime?

Fairness, cohabiting couples, and family property: *Matta v Smith* and *McLean v Danicic*

In assessing the contributions of a woman in a cohabiting relationship of 28 years in *Mattav Smith* (2002), 28 RFL (5th) 395 (Ont Sup Ct), the court referred to the unanimous decision of the Nova Scotia Court of Appeal in *Nova Scotia (AG) v Walsh*. Recall that the N.S. Court of Appeal had decided that the legislature's failure to extend the matrimonial property regime to cohabiting spouses constituted discrimination pursuant to section 15 of the *Charter*. *Matta v Smith* was decided in the period between the decision of the N.S. Court of Appeal and the release of the decision of the Supreme Court of Canada allowing the appeal. In this context, the court in *Matta v Smith* stated (at para 75):

> It seems so unfair that a wife in a married relationship, who hypothetically contributes fewer benefits to a marriage than Muriel did to her common-law relationship, results in the wife sharing equally in the family property while Muriel has no statutory right to share equally in the family assets.

Although the court indicated that the woman had made a strong case for an equal division of family property in this case, it seemed that the man had made a more substantial financial contribution. As a result, the court ordered an award of $400,000, and denied a claim for additional spousal support.

Do you agree that it would be more appropriate to apply the same legislative regime to married couples and cohabitees? To what extent does your assessment of these issues depend on issues about choice in forming such relationships? Or protection for vulnerable parties? Do you agree with the OLRC and others that the remedies available to cohabiting couples when their relationships end are not satisfactory?

Consider this situation:

> A man and woman cohabited for about five years, and the woman made significant contributions of money and labour in relation to renovations to properties owned by the man. She also made financial contributions to household expenses and assisted him with his business. Unfortunately, the woman became seriously ill and the

relationship then deteriorated. Because the man denied that she had any interest in the properties, the woman initiated legal proceedings and the man responded by making threats, engaging in harassment, and forwarding false reports to her disability insurer. He was charged with criminal harassment, extortion and attempting to obstruct justice, and then denied that there was any romantic involvement between the parties. He also claimed that a friend had a part interest in one property. Eventually, his pleadings were struck as he failed to comply with court orders. By the time of the trial, the woman claimed a declaration of trust in the man's properties, recovery on a *quantum meruit* basis, and damages for pain and suffering. What result?

In *McLean v Danicic* (2009), 95 OR (3d) 570 (Sup Ct), the court considered the evidence and concluded that the parties had cohabited in a spousal relationship. The court also noted evidence of the woman's financial contributions to the properties and to the expenses of the household, and that she also took responsibility for domestic duties as well as assisting the man in his photography business. In relation to her physical labour, the court found that she had been involved in painting, sanding, staining, taping drywall, helping to install vapour barriers, and with framing (at para 23). However, when the woman became ill, the man became verbally abusive to her and the relationship ended.

In assessing the claim for equitable intervention, the court considered *Pettkus v Becker* and *Peter v Beblow*, and held that the claim of unjust enrichment was established. In assessing whether to award a constructive trust or a monetary remedy, the court considered the presumption of monetary relief in *Peter v Beblow*, the strong link between the woman's contributions and the properties, and the relative short duration of the relationship, and concluded:

> [66] I conclude that this is a case in which a monetary award would be sufficient. Although the imposition of a constructive trust representing an interest in property or properties is generally a stronger remedy than an *in personam* monetary award, that may not be true in the present case. The reason for this is the fact that there is some evidence that Mr. Danicic has, through his actions, depreciated the value of the assets since the date of separation [and a mortgagee was in the process of exercising its power of sale rights in relation to one property.] The applicant is also concerned that both properties have been neglected and/or mistreated since the separation with a view to defeating her claims.... The point is that there is no way of assessing what the present value of any interest in the property or properties would amount to.... [In addition,] an *in rem* remedy may prejudice third-party creditors.

In the result, the court concluded that a monetary payment was more appropriate here and ordered a *quantum meruit* award of $76,124.63. The court also awarded lump sum support of $15,000, damages for intentional infliction of mental distress in the amount of $15,000, a restraining order against the man, and costs in the amount of $200,000.

There are similar cases in other provinces. For example, see *Thomas v Fenton*, 2006 BCCA 299; and *Pegler v Avio*, 2008 BCSC 128.

In New Brunswick, a woman who entered a cohabiting relationship and agreed at the outset to limit her claim if the parties later separated, changed her mind when the parties separated after 8 years. In *MacFarlane v Smith*, 2003 NBCA 6, the court awarded her a monetary payment of $65,100.

To what extent do these cases reveal the discretionary nature of results relating to claims by cohabiting spouses? Does this factor suggest a reason for extending the matrimonial property regime to cohabiting couples? Why, or why not?

"Quasi-spousal" relationships: *Nowell v Town Estate*

In assessing appropriate legislative responses to property-sharing regimes for cohabitees, consider *Nowell v Town Estate* (1997), 30 RFL (4th) 107 (Ont CA) (leave to appeal to the Supreme Court of Canada granted, (1998), 35 OR (3d) 415, and discontinued 8 September 1998):

> In this case, a woman (Nowell) had a relationship with a married man (Town) for 24 years. During these years, Town was married and both his marriage and his family responsibilities continued. Throughout their relationship, Town and Nowell never cohabited, although Town bought a farm 13 years after the relationship began, and the two spent most weekends there. Nowell made various contributions to the farm, including cooking, cleaning, gardening, and organizing social events that the two attended or hosted together. During the course of their relationship, Town became a famous artist and gave Nowell many works of art as gifts, some of which she later sold for over $120,000.
>
> After the relationship ended, Nowell demanded a settlement of $100,000 from Town on the basis of his previous assurances that he "would look after her." Town delivered certain works of art to Nowell, which she sold. At the time of Town's death, he had assets worth between $20 and $50 million. Nowell brought an action for a declaration that he had been unjustly enriched as a result of the services that she had performed during their relationship. Nowell sought a constructive trust remedy in relation to Town's estate, or damages in the alternative.

The trial judge dismissed the action, finding that although Nowell had made many contributions to Town's life, Town, in turn, had enriched her. The court held that Nowell had received gifts of substantial value from Town and had benefited both personally and professionally from having had the opportunity to participate in Town's social and artistic life. Finally, the court also ruled that there was no basis for a finding that Nowell and Town's relationship had been quasi-marital.

Nowell appealed the decision to the Ontario Court of Appeal, claiming a 20 percent entitlement to Town's estate. The appellate court revised the trial decision, and held that although Nowell was not entitled to 20 percent of the estate, she was entitled to a money payment of $300,000. In reaching its decision, the court ruled that the relationship had not been a casual one and that, at least for the last 13 years, it had resembled a quasi-spousal relationship. The court also took note of the many verbal assurances Town had made to Nowell to "look after her," demonstrated in part by his gifts of art to her. With respect to whether Town had been unjustly enriched by Nowell, the court held that Nowell had so demonstrated, noting that Nowell made Town the focal point of her life, and that there was clear evidence of an enrichment to him and a corresponding financial deprivation to her.

It appears that the Court of Appeal viewed the relationship between Nowell and Town as similar to that of cohabitees, although the existence of Town's wife complicated the legal situation for Nowell. Moreover, although the relationship ended before Town's death, Nowell's claim was pursued against his estate — that is, against his widow. Do the principles of *Peter v Beblow* apply to these facts?

In reflecting on this question, consider the comments of James McLeod, "Annotation of *Nowell v. Town Estate*" (1997), 30 RFL (4th) 107 at 109:

> While Nowell and Town may have been a "couple," they did not cohabit in any traditional sense of the word. Town made clear to Nowell that he would not marry her or leave his wife. The couple maintained separate bank accounts and separate residences. There is no case law to support the conclusion that people who spend weekends together while one is married and living with his or her spouse are "cohabiting." ... The trial judge held that the case was not like *Peter v. Beblow*. By this he meant that there was no merging of the parties' economic, social and emotional lives.... The couple formed a symbiotic relationship which met each of their needs and interests. Nowell received an entry to a world and lifestyle that she might not have been able to achieve on her own. She also received valuable gifts throughout the relationship. The legislators created matrimonial property rights for married couples. The Supreme Court of Canada extended similar rights to unmarried couples. The reasons in *Nowell v. Town Estate* come close to asserting an almost automatic right to relief to long-time lovers.

Consider the following situation:

The petitioner and deceased had a relationship for 17 years. The deceased had purchased a house for the petitioner to live in, but he charged her rent and he lived in his own residence. The petitioner cooked dinner for the deceased regularly at her house and cleaned and maintained the deceased's house. The petitioner claimed that the deceased had stated that she "would never have to worry" about the house in which she lived. When he died, however, his will left all his property to his nephews and nieces. (The will had been prepared with the help of the family of the deceased's wife, who had died before him, and these family members asserted that the relationship between the deceased and the petitioner was that they were just dating.) What result?

In *Pelechaty v Martyniuk Estate* (1999), 48 RFL (4th) 193 (Sask QB), the court held that the elements of unjust enrichment had been satisfied and that a monetary award was insufficient. The court calculated the petitioner's interest at 20 percent, and awarded her the home in which she lived (which corresponded to the 20 percent value). Is this case consistent with *Nowell v Town Estate*? Does *Pelechaty* suggest that unjust enrichment and constructive trust remedies may be applicable to couples who are not "cohabiting"?

Compare *Pelechaty* to *Knoll v Knoll Estate*, [2001] 5 WWR 374 (Sask QB), where a wife claimed unjust enrichment against her husband's estate in relation to her increased financial and caregiving services after her husband fell ill. Before their marriage, the parties had made a prenuptial agreement in which the wife had agreed not to make a claim against her husband's estate (both had grown children from their first marriages when they decided to marry). In denying her claim, the court relied on the agreement between the parties, but also stated (at 379) that "the extra responsibility that goes along with an ill spouse goes hand in hand with marriage," and that the wife had not provided her services for reward, but "out of love and affection for her husband." Does this reasoning suggest that married spouses may be disadvantaged in claims for equitable remedies? Is this reasoning consistent with *Peter v Beblow*? (For other examples, see *Tracey v Tracey* (1998), 41 RFL (4th) 278 (Ont Gen Div); and *Ferrera v Ouellet* (1999), 48 RFL (4th) 75 (BCSC).)

Unjust enrichment claims and same-sex relationships

Issues about unjust enrichment and the availability of constructive trusts have also been considered in a number of cases involving same-sex relationships at separation (particularly prior to Canada's recognition of same-sex marriage). For example, in *Forrest v Price* (1992), 48 ETR 72 (BCSC), the court assessed the relationship between cohabiting same-sex partners and stated (at para 37):

> [T]his was by all accounts a spousal relationship. The parties lived in a lengthy, sexually faithful relationship for 13 years. They fulfilled their traditional roles as homemaker and breadwinner. They intermingled their possessions and finances, with no attempt to keep any track of their respective contributions or the benefits received by either. They impressed all those around them as a couple and discussed "their" homes and projects. They instructed solicitors on two different occasions to prepare mutual wills — that is wills in which each designated the other as beneficiary.... In light of these facts, I do not accept the defendant's evidence that he repeatedly told the plaintiff he had no proprietary interest in the successive properties.... Accordingly, I find that, given the history of this relationship and the defendant's assurances throughout, the plaintiff reasonably expected to receive an actual interest in the various properties and that the defendant either was or ought to have been cognizant of that expectation.

In assessing the plaintiff's entitlement to a remedial constructive trust, the court took into account (at 82–85) the defendant's debts, the increase in the value of the property since separation, and a process for selling the contents of the property. Other courts have similarly held that unjust enrichment has occurred and ordered *quantum meruit* awards or a declaration of constructive trust in same-sex cohabiting relationships. See *Anderson v Luoma* (1984), 14 DLR (4th) 749 (BCSC).

However, not all such claims are successful for same-sex applicants. For example, in *Buist v Greaves*, [1997] OJ No 2646 (Gen Div), the court concluded that there was no unjust enrichment when a lesbian couple separated after a 10-year relationship. At trial Buist claimed that her contributions to the relationship unjustly enriched Greaves and that she was, therefore, entitled to restitution. Buist substantiated her claim by filing volumes of documentation itemizing expenses that she paid for during their relationship and cohabitation. These expenses included living expenses, purchase of assets, and renovations done to Greaves' property (the home where the parties had lived together). She also sought compensation for the domestic services she performed, such as cutting the grass, helping to build the deck, and doing the gardening. In rejecting this claim, the court held that no unjust enrichment had occurred — there was no evidence that Buist's contributions contributed to the increase in value of any of the assets; Buist did not enhance the earning potential of Greaves; the parties shared equally in the division of household duties; and there was no evidence that Buist was financially worse off personally or professionally because of the relationship.

Similarly, the plaintiff in *Chowdhury v Argenti Estate*, 2007 BCSC 1207, did not succeed in a claim for constructive trust. The court held that the plaintiff had made no contribution of value to the defendant's home, either in money or services and that the claim that the plaintiff had "contributed to Mr. Argenti's happiness and made him joyful" was not relevant.

Do these cases suggest that opposite-sex and same-sex cohabiting couples must meet the same test to establish unjust enrichment?

NEW DIRECTIONS IN UNJUST ENRICHMENT CLAIMS FOR COHABITING SPOUSES? THE "JOINT FAMILY VENTURE"

The "joint family venture" principle: *Kerr v Baranow; Vanasse v Seguin*

In *Kerr v Baranow; Vanasse v Seguin*, 2011 SCC 10, the Supreme Court of Canada considered two appeals concerning property entitlement at the end of cohabiting relationships:

- *Kerr v Baranow* was an appeal from British Columbia: 2009 BCCA 111; and 2007 BCSC 1863)

  In *Kerr v Baranow*, a couple, both in their late 60s, separated after cohabiting for more than 25 years. Both had worked and contributed to their mutual well-being. Kerr claimed a share of property held in Baranow's name on the basis of resulting trust and unjust enrichment.

Baranow counterclaimed in relation to his housekeeping and personal assistance to Kerr after she suffered a stroke. The trial court had awarded Kerr a one-third value of the home in Baranow's name, but the B.C. Court of Appeal held that Kerr had made no financial contribution relating to the acquisition or improvement of the property, and dismissed her claims based on resulting trust and on unjust enrichment. Since the trial judge had not decided Baranow's counterclaim, the appeal court in British Columbia had ordered a new trial for this claim.

In the Supreme Court of Canada, Cromwell J identified a number of problems and omissions with the evidence at trial, and ordered a new trial for both Kerr's claim and Baranow's counterclaim.

- *Vanasse v Seguin* was an appeal from Ontario: 2009 ONCA 595; and [2008] OJ No 2832 (Sup Ct) (QL)

  In *Vanasse v Seguin*, the parties enjoyed a relationship for 12 years. For the first four years, they had each pursued independent careers, but when Seguin was afforded an important opportunity for his business, the couple moved from Ottawa to Halifax, and Vanasse took a leave from her position with CSIS. During the period in Halifax, the couple had two children, and Vanasse provided child care and domestic labour while Seguin worked long hours and travelled extensively in relation to his business. Eventually, Seguin stepped down as CEO of the business, and the couple moved back to Ottawa and bought a house in their joint names. In 2000, Seguin sold his shares in the business for about $11 million, and he then participated more in the family's domestic chores. The trial judge found no unjust enrichment for the first and last period of cohabitation, but held that Seguin had been unjustly enriched during the period in Halifax. Thus, he held that Vanasse was entitled to half the value of the wealth accumulated by Seguin in that period, less her interest in the home and an RRSP. The Ontario Court of Appeal set aside this award and directed a new valuation on the basis of *quantum meruit*, in which the value each party received from the other was assessed and set off.

  In the Supreme Court of Canada, the Court allowed the appeal and restored the order of the trial judge.

The reasons for judgment of Cromwell J were unanimous, and in addition to deciding the appeals, the reasoning reviewed the cases and principles applicable to property interests for cohabiting couples over the past 30 years, and set out some guiding principles for future claims.

In its reasoning, the Supreme Court of Canada addressed several issues relating to these cases:

CROMWELL J:

[6] These appeals require us to resolve five main issues. The first concerns the role of the common intention resulting trust in claims by domestic partners. In my view, it is time to recognize that the common intention approach to resulting trust has no further role to play in the resolution of property claims by domestic partners on the breakdown of their relationship.

[7] The second issue concerns the nature of the money remedy for a successful unjust enrichment claim. Some courts take the view that if the claimant's contribution cannot be linked to specific property, a money remedy must always be assessed on a fee-for-services basis. Other courts have taken a more flexible approach. In my view, where both parties have worked together for the common good, with each making extensive, but different, contributions to the welfare of the other and, as a result, have accumulated assets, the money remedy for unjust enrichment should reflect that reality. The money remedy in those circumstances should not be based on a minute totting up of the give and take of daily domestic life, but rather should treat the claimant as a co-venturer, not as the hired help.

[8] The third area requiring clarification relates to mutual benefit conferral. Many domestic relationships involve the mutual conferral of benefits, in the sense that each contributes in various ways to the welfare of the other. The question is how and at what point in the unjust enrichment analysis should this mutual conferral of benefits be taken into account? For reasons I will develop below, this issue should, with a small exception, be addressed at the defence and remedy stage.

[9] Fourth, there is the question of what role the parties' reasonable or legitimate expectations play in the unjust enrichment analysis. My view is that they have a limited role, and must be considered in relation to whether there is a juristic reason for the enrichment....

[As the court noted, there was also an issue with respect to the appropriate date for commencement of an award of spousal support.]

ISSUE #1 THE RESULTING TRUST

The Court first addressed the role of the "common intention" resulting trust in Canadian law, a construction based on the idea that the parties had a common intention that the partner with title would hold it by way of resulting trust for the other. As the Court noted, the resulting trust had been eclipsed by principles of unjust enrichment in *Pettkus v Becker*, but the common intention resulting trust remained in place (for example, in the trial and appeal judgments in *Kerr v Baranow*).

The Court reviewed resulting trusts arising from gratuitous transfers (such as *Pecore v Pecore*, 2007 SCC 17), and as a result of joint contributions to the acquisition of property, where title is in one party alone (as evidenced in *Murdoch* and then in *Rathwell*). As the Court noted, Dickson J in *Pettkus v Becker* had recognized problems with this common intention resulting trust, and clearly rejected the idea that it could be attributed to the parties where the evidence negated such an intent. Thus, the Court concluded (at para 24) that "the time has come to say that the common intention resulting trust has no further role to play in the resolution of domestic cases" for four reasons:

1. The common intention resulting trust is doctrinally unsound and inconsistent with the underlying principles of resulting trust law;
2. The notion of common intention may be highly artificial, particularly in domestic cases;

3. The common intention resulting trust (which exists mainly in Canada) came about as a result of a misreading of some English authorities; and

4. The principles of unjust enrichment, with the possible remedy of constructive trust, provide "a much less artificial, more comprehensive and more principled basis to address the wide variety of circumstances that lead to claims arising out of domestic partnerships" (at para 28).

In conclusion, the Court stated:

> **[29]** I would hold that the resulting trust arising solely from the common intention of the parties, as described by the Court in *Murdoch* and *Rathwell*, no longer has a useful role to play in resolving property and financial disputes in domestic cases. I emphasize that I am speaking here only of the common intention resulting trust. I am not addressing other aspects of the law relating to resulting trusts, nor am I suggesting that a resulting trust that would otherwise validly arise is defeated by the existence in fact of common intention....

ISSUE #2 UNJUST ENRICHMENT AND THE JOINT FAMILY VENTURE

The Court's reasons outlined the existing framework, articulated issues requiring clarification, and proposed solutions to address these issues.

At the outset, the Court reviewed the legal framework for unjust enrichment claims, noting that the application of such claims in domestic cases was resisted until the decision in *Pettkus v Becker*. In addition, the Court noted that the basic principles of unjust enrichment "remain the same for all cases," although their application must take account of the particular factual and social context (citing *Peter v Beblow*). The Court then reviewed the elements of an unjust enrichment claim: the enrichment and corresponding deprivation, and the absence of a juristic reason, and the cases (including *Peter*) in which courts have recognized the provision of domestic services as founding a claim for unjust enrichment. The Court cited *Garland v Consumers' Gas Co*, 2004 SCC 25, for its two-step analysis for the absence of juristic reasons: The first step requires consideration of established categories of juristic reasons (such as contract or donative intent). In their absence, the plaintiff has established a *prima facie* case, but one that is rebuttable by evidence on the part of the defendant to show why the enrichment should be retained. In this context, "courts should have regard to two factors: the reasonable expectations of the parties, and public policy considerations" (at para 43).

> **[44]** Thus, at the juristic reason stage of the analysis, if the case falls outside the existing categories, the court may take into account the legitimate expectations of the parties (*Pettkus* ...) and moral and policy-based arguments about whether particular enrichments are unjust (*Peter* ...).

The Court expressly confirmed that legislative decisions not to extend marital property regimes to unmarried cohabiting couples resulted in the need to apply unjust enrichment principles in relation to property entitlement at the end of these relationships (citing both *Peter v Beblow* and *Nova Scotia (AG) v Walsh*).

Remedy ...

The Court noted that the remedy for a claim of unjust enrichment can be either monetary or proprietary, and that the first remedy to consider is the monetary award.

However, the Court noted ongoing issues with respect to both monetary and proprietary awards:

- Monetary award
  Where there has been mutual conferral of benefits, what constitutes adequate compensation? This is the problem characterized by John McCamus as "duelling *quantum meruits.*"

  Second, how should a monetary award be calculated? That is, must it be calculated on the basis of monetary value of unpaid services, the "value received" or "fee-for-services" approach (adopted in several cases), or should it be assessed more flexibly on a "value survived" basis, taking account of the overall increase in the couple's wealth during the relationship (as suggested by other cases)?

- Proprietary award
  The Court also noted issues with respect to the link required between the contribution and the property (the nexus), and with respect to assessing whether a monetary award would be insufficient (including issues with respect to the probability of recovery). In addition, the Court noted that the extent of the constructive trust interest should reflect the proportion of the claimant's contributions.

The Court then identified three issues requiring clarification (see paras 7, 8 and 9, above): how to assess a monetary claim, how and where to address the mutual benefit problem, and the role of the parties' reasonable or legitimate expectations.

Calculating a Monetary Award

[55] ... If, as some courts have held, a monetary remedy must invariably be quantified on a *quantum meruit* basis, the remedial choice in unjust enrichment cases becomes whether to impose a constructive trust or order a monetary remedy calculated on a *quantum meruit* basis. One scholar [J.D. McCamus] has referred to this approach as the false dichotomy between constructive trust and *quantum meruit*. Scholars have also noted this area of uncertainty in the case law, and have suggested that an *in personam* remedy using the value survived measure is a plausible alternative to the constructive trust. [Identifying *Peter v Beblow* as having created this dichotomy, the Court noted that the focus in that case was on the availability of the constructive trust remedy, and that its conclusions should not limit the calculation of the monetary award.] In appropriate circumstances, monetary relief may be assessed on a value survived basis....

The Court then addressed the remedial dichotomy, noting that the monetary remedy was assessed on a fee-for-services basis, while the constructive trust required a nexus between the contribution and the property. In this context, for example, the Court explained how the Ontario Court of

Appeal had rejected Vanasse's claim because she could not show a direct link between her contributions and specific property. As the Court then explained, this remedial dichotomy should be rejected:

[58] In my view, restricting the money remedy to a fee-for-services calculation is inappropriate for four reasons. First, it fails to reflect the reality of the lives of many domestic partners. Second, it is inconsistent with the inherent flexibility of unjust enrichment. Third, it ignores the historical basis of *quantum meruit* claims. Finally, it is not mandated by the Court's judgment in *Peter*. For those reasons, this remedial dichotomy should be rejected. [The Court also noted that its reasons concerned only the monetary remedy, as "the law relating to when a proprietary remedy should be granted" was well established and remained unchanged.]

Life Experience: the "Joint Family Venture"

[59] The remedial dichotomy would be appropriate if, in fact, the bases of all domestic unjust enrichment claims fit into only two categories — those where the enrichment consists of the provision of unpaid services, and those where it consists of an unrecognized contribution to the acquisition, improvement, maintenance or preservation of specific property. To be sure, those two bases for unjust enrichment claims exist. However, all unjust enrichment cases cannot be neatly divided into these two categories.

[60] At least one other basis for an unjust enrichment claim is easy to identify. It consists of cases in which the contributions of both parties over time have resulted in an accumulation of wealth. The unjust enrichment occurs following the breakdown of their relationship when one party retains a disproportionate share of the assets which are the product of their joint efforts. The required link between the contributions and a specific property may not exist, making it inappropriate to confer a proprietary remedy. However, there may clearly be a link between the joint efforts of the parties and the accumulation of wealth; in other words, a link between the "value received" and the "value surviving," as McLachlin J. put it in *Peter*.... Thus, where there is a relationship that can be described as a "joint family venture," and the joint efforts of the parties are linked to the accumulation of wealth, the unjust enrichment should be thought of as leaving one party with a disproportionate share of the jointly earned assets.

[61] There is nothing new about the notion of a joint family venture in which both parties contribute to their overall accumulation of wealth. It was recognition of this reality that contributed to comprehensive matrimonial property legislative reform in the late 1970s and early 1980s. As the Court put it in *Clarke v. Clarke*, [1990] 2 S.C.R. 795 ... (in relation to Nova Scotia's *Matrimonial Property Act*), "... the Act supports the equality of both parties to a marriage and recognized the joint contribution of the spouses, be it financial or otherwise, to that enterprise.... The Act is accordingly remedial in nature. It was designed to alleviate the inequities of the past when the contribution made by women to the economic survival and growth of the family was not recognized" (emphasis added).

[62] Unlike much matrimonial property legislation, the law of unjust enrichment does not mandate a presumption of equal sharing. However, the law of unjust enrichment can and should respond to the social reality identified by the legislature that many domestic relationships are more realistically viewed as a joint venture to which the parties jointly contribute....

The Court then reviewed *Murdoch, Rathwell*, and *Pettkus v Becker* to show how these cases recognized joint efforts of the spouses in both married and cohabiting relationships. In relation to *Pettkus*, the Court concluded that Mr. Pettkus was unjustly enriched because he and Ms. Becker "were in reality partners in a common venture" (para 66). In addition, the Court identified a number of places in *Peter v Beblow* where the Court recognized the "joint family venture." Thus, the Court concluded:

> **[69]** Relationships of this nature are common in our life experience. For many domestic relationships, the couple's venture may only sensibly be viewed as a joint one, making it highly artificial in theory and extremely difficult in practice to do a detailed accounting of the contributions made and benefits received on a fee-for-services basis. Of course, this is a relationship-specific issue; there can be no presumption one way or the other. However, the legal consequences of the breakdown of a domestic relationship should reflect realistically the way people live their lives. It should not impose on them the need to engage in an artificial balance sheet approach which does not reflect the true nature of their relationship....

Flexibility

The Court emphasized the need for flexibility for equitable remedies and particularly in relation to unjust enrichment, referring to a number of cases involving contexts other than domestic relationships. As the Court stated, a "monetary remedy must match, as best it can, the extent of the enrichment unjustly retained by the defendant" (at para 73).

History

The Court also reviewed the history of the unjust enrichment principle, and the role of *quantum meruit* as a remedy, noting that it expanded over time and was flexible, concluding that "There is no reason in principle why one of the traditional categories of unjust enrichment should be used to force the monetary remedy for all present domestic unjust enrichment cases into a remedial straitjacket" (at para 74).

> **[75]** *Peter* does not mandate strict adherence to a *quantum meruit* approach to money remedies for unjust enrichment. One must remember that the focus of *Peter* was on whether the plaintiff's contributions entitled her to a constructive trust over the former family home. While it was assumed by both McLachlin J. and Cory J., who wrote concurring reasons in the case, that a money award would be fashioned on the basis of *quantum meruit*, that was not an issue, let alone a holding, in the case.

The Court then considered the judgment in *Peter* in detail and concluded that a restrictive reading of the *quantum meruit* remedy was not consistent with the underlying principles in *Pettkus* which were based on "a claimant's right to share surplus wealth created by joint effort and teamwork" (at para 78). The Court thus held that:

> **[78]** ... [T]his reasoning is persuasive whether the joint effort has led to the accumulation of specific property, in which case a remedial constructive trust may be appropriate according to the well-settled principles in that area of trust law, or where the joint effort has led to an accumulation of assets generally. In the latter instance, when appropriate, there is

no reason in principle why a monetary remedy cannot be fashioned to reflect this basis of the enrichment and corresponding deprivation. What is essential, in my view, is that, in either type of case, there must be a link between the contribution and the accumulation of wealth.... Where that link exists, and a proprietary remedy is either inappropriate or unnecessary, the monetary award should be fashioned to reflect the true nature of the enrichment and the corresponding deprivation....

[80] The next step in the legal development of this area should be to move away from the false remedial dichotomy between *quantum meruit* and constructive trust, and to return to the underlying principles governing the law of unjust enrichment. These underlying principles focus on properly characterizing the nature of the unjust enrichment giving rise to the claim.... [N]ot all unjust enrichments arising between domestic partners fit comfortably into either a "fee-for-services" or "a share of specific property" mold. Where the unjust enrichment is best characterized as an unjust retention of a disproportionate share of assets accumulated during ... a "joint family venture" to which both partners have contributed, the monetary remedy should reflect that fact.

[81] In such cases, the basis of the unjust enrichment is the retention of an inappropriately disproportionate amount of wealth by one party when the parties have been engaged in a joint family venture and there is a clear link between the claimant's contributions to the joint venture and the accumulation of wealth. Irrespective of the status of legal title to particular assets, the parties in those circumstances are realistically viewed as "creating wealth in a common enterprise that will assist in sustaining their relationship, their well-being and their family life" (*McCamus*...). The wealth created during the period of cohabitation will be treated as the fruit of their domestic and financial relationship, though not necessarily by the parties in equal measure. Since the spouses are domestic and financial partners, there is no need for "duelling *quantum meruits*." In such cases, the unjust enrichment is understood to arise because the party who leaves the relationship with a disproportionate share of the wealth is denying to the claimant a reasonable share of the wealth accumulated in the course of the relationship through their joint efforts. The monetary award for unjust enrichment should be assessed by determining the proportionate contribution of the claimant to the accumulation of the wealth.

The Court indicated that this joint family venture approach was consistent with the treatment of unjust enrichment claims as flexible in *Nova Scotia (AG) v Walsh* and in *Peter v Beblow*. Thus the Court concluded that:

[84] It is not the purpose of the law of unjust enrichment to replicate for unmarried partners the legislative presumption that married partners are engaged in a joint family venture. However, there is no reason in principle why remedies for unjust enrichment should fail to reflect that reality in the lives and relationships of unmarried partners.

[85] I conclude, therefore, that the common law of unjust enrichment should recognize and respond to the reality that there are unmarried domestic arrangements that are partnerships; the remedy in such cases should address the disproportionate retention of assets acquired through joint efforts with another person. This sort of sharing, of course, should not be presumed, nor will it be presumed that wealth acquired by mutual effort will be shared equally. Cohabitation does not, in itself, under the common law of unjust enrichment, entitle one party to a share of the

other's property or any other relief. However, where wealth is accumulated as a result of joint effort, as evidenced by the nature of the parties' relationship and their dealings with each other, the law of unjust enrichment should reflect that reality.

[86] Thus the rejection of the remedial dichotomy leads us to consider in what circumstances an unjust enrichment may be appropriately characterized as a failure to share equitably assets acquired through the parties' joint efforts. While this approach will need further refinement in future cases, I offer the following as a broad outline of when this characterization of an unjust enrichment will be appropriate.

Identifying Unjust Enrichment Arising from a Joint Family Venture

[87] My view is that when the parties have been engaged in a joint family venture, and the claimant's contributions to it are linked to the generation of wealth, a monetary award for unjust enrichment should be calculated according to the share of the accumulated wealth proportionate to the claimant's contributions. In order to apply this approach, it is first necessary to identify whether the parties have, in fact, been engaged in a joint family venture. In the preceding section, I reviewed the many occasions on which the existence of a joint family venture has been recognized. From this rich set of factual circumstances, what emerge as the hallmarks of such a relationship?

[88] It is critical to note that cohabiting couples are not a homogeneous group. It follows that the analysis must take into account the particular circumstances of each particular relationship. Furthermore, as previously stated, there can be no presumption of a joint family venture. The goal is for the law of unjust enrichment to attach just consequences to the way the parties have lived their lives, not to treat them as if they ought to have lived some other way or conducted their relationship on some different basis. A joint family venture can only be identified by the court when its existence, in fact, is well-grounded in the evidence. The emphasis should be on how the parties actually lived their lives, not on their *ex post facto* assertions or the court's view of how they ought to have done so.

[89] In undertaking this analysis, it may be helpful to consider the evidence under four main headings: mutual effort, economic integration, actual intent and priority of the family. There is, of course, overlap among factors that may be relevant under these headings and there is no closed list of relevant factors. What follows is not a checklist of conditions for finding (or not finding) that the parties were engaged in a joint family venture. These headings, and the factors grouped under them, simply provide a useful way to approach a global analysis of the evidence and some examples of the relevant factors that may be taken into account in deciding whether or not the parties were engaged in a joint family venture. The absence of the factors I have set out, and many other relevant considerations, may well negate that conclusion.

In assessing the "joint family venture," the Court outlined these factors:

- In relation to mutual effort, the Court suggested a need to examine indicators such as the pooling of effort and team work, the decision to have and raise children together, and the length of the relationship, to assess whether "the parties have formed a true partnership and jointly worked towards important mutual goals" (at para 90).

- In relation to economic integration, the Court suggested that "the more extensive the integration of the couple's finances, economic interests and economic well-being, the more likely it is that they should be considered as having been engaged in a joint family venture" (at para 92).

- In relation to "actual intent," the Court cautioned that it is necessary to examine actual intent as expressed or inferred, not what in the court's view "reasonable" parties *ought* to have intended in the same circumstances. Courts must be vigilant not to impose their own views, under the guise of inferred intent, in order to reach a certain result" (at para 94). According to the court, the parties' conduct, whether they held themselves out as married, and whether they held title to property jointly, may evidence a "joint family venture" (at paras 95 and 96). In addition, "The parties' actual intent may also negate the existence of a joint family venture ..." (at para 97).

- Finally, the extent to which the parties have given priority to the family is also relevant to determining whether a "joint family venture" existed. In this context, the Court quoted John McCamus, who suggested that the question is whether the parties have been "[p]roceeding on the basis of understandings or assumptions about a shared future which may or may not be articulated" (at para 98). In this context, leaving the workforce for a period of time to raise children, relocating to benefit a partner's career, foregoing career or educational advancement for the benefit of the family, and accepting underemployment to balance domestic and financial needs, might all indicate a "joint family venture" (at para 98).

At para 100, the Court summarized its views about *quantum meruit* and constructive trust:

> **[100]** I conclude:
>
> 1. The monetary remedy for unjust enrichment is not restricted to an award based on a fee-for-services approach.
> 2. Where the unjust enrichment is most realistically characterized as one party retaining a disproportionate share of assets resulting from a joint family venture, and a monetary award is appropriate, it should be calculated on the basis of the share of those assets proportionate to the claimant's contributions.
> 3. To be entitled to a monetary remedy of this nature, the claimant must show both (a) that there was, in fact, a joint family venture, and (b) that there is a link between his or her contributions to it and the accumulation of assets and/or wealth.
> 4. Whether there was a joint family venture is a question of fact and may be assessed by having regard to all of the relevant circumstances, including factors relating to (a) mutual effort, (b) economic integration, (c) actual intent and (d) priority of the family.

ISSUE #3 MUTUAL BENEFIT CONFERRAL

The Court then considered issues relating to its third concern (identified in para 8 above), the conferral of mutual benefits by the partners in a domestic situation. In the context of the "joint family venture," the remedy is a share of wealth proportionate to the claimant's contributions:

> [102] ... Once the claimant has established his or her contribution to the joint family venture, and a link between that contribution and the accumulation of wealth, the respective contributions of the parties are taken into account in determining the claimant's proportionate share. While determining the proportionate contributions of the parties is not an exact science, it generally does not call for a minute examination of the give and take of daily life. It calls, rather, for the exercise of judgment in light of all the evidence....

The problem, however, arises where the appropriate remedy is a money award based on a fee-for-services approach. After reviewing the treatment of mutual benefits by different courts, the Court suggested that "mutual enrichments should mainly be considered at the defence and remedy stages, but that they may be considered at the juristic reason stage to the extent that the provision of reciprocal benefits constitutes relevant evidence of the existence (or non-existence) of juristic reason for the enrichment" (at para 104). The Court then considered the reasoning in *Peter v Beblow*, where the Supreme Court approved the trial judge's approach of taking account of the benefits to Ms. Peter at the remedy stage of his decision.

The Court then proceeded to identify the correct approach, explaining that mutual benefits should not be addressed at the benefit/detriment stage of analysis in accordance with *quantum meruit* principles and the economic approach adopted by the Supreme Court in such cases. In addition, the Court held that mutual benefits should have only a limited role at the juristic reason stage of analysis, that is, only with respect to the issue of whether the enrichment was just, not its extent.

ISSUE #4 PARTIES' EXPECTATIONS

The Court then considered the parties' expectations, the fourth issue (identified in para 9 above), stating:

> [117] ... My conclusion is that, while in the early domestic unjust enrichment cases the parties' reasonable expectations played an important role in the juristic reason analysis, the development of the law, and particularly the Court's judgment in *Garland*, has led to a more limited and clearly circumscribed role for those expectations.

The Court examined the development of these principles in relation to restitutionary claims more generally, and especially with respect to the two-step analysis in *Garland*. As the Court noted, the conferral of benefits and parties' reasonable expectations have little role in the first step (relating to existing categories of juristic reasons). However, in the second step, there is a category of residual situations, in which courts can examine all the circumstances to determine whether there is reason to deny recovery. "[I]t is here that the court should consider the parties' reasonable expectations and questions of policy" (at para 122). Thus, the Court suggested that:

[123] ... It seems to me that, in light of *Garland*, where a "bargain" which does not constitute a binding contract is alleged, the issue will be considered at the stage when the defendant seeks to show that there is a juristic reason for the enrichment that does not fall within any of the existing categories; the claim is that the "bargain" represents the parties' reasonable expectations, and evidence about their reasonable expectations would be relevant evidence of the existence (or not) of such a bargain....

Vanasse v Seguin

The Court then turned to examine the two cases on appeal, beginning with *Vanasse v Seguin*. As the Court noted, the appeal raised two issues:

- Did the Court of Appeal err by insisting on a strict *quantum meruit* (i.e., "value received") approach to quantify the monetary award for unjust enrichment?
- Did the Court of Appeal err in finding that the trial judge had failed to consider relevant evidence of Mr. Seguin's contributions?

As the Court concluded, the appeal was allowed and the trial judge's order restored:

[128] ... For the reasons I have developed above, my view is that money compensation for unjust enrichment need not always, as a matter of principle, be calculated on a *quantum meruit* basis. The trial judge here, although not labelling it as such, found that there was a joint family venture and that there was a link between Mrs. Vanasse's contribution to it and the substantial accumulation of wealth which the family achieved. In my view, the trial judge made a reasonable assessment of the monetary award appropriate to reverse this unjust enrichment, taking due account of Mr. Seguin's undoubted and substantial contributions.

Thus, although Mr. Seguin argued that he had been enriched during the three years when he worked in his business while Ms. Vanasse provided household labour and child care, he also argued that there was no corresponding deprivation because he had given her a one-half interest in the home as well as $44,000 in RRSPs. As noted, the trial judge rejected this argument, holding that Ms. Vanasse had been "an equal contributor to the family enterprise" (at para 137), and concluded that a monetary judgment was appropriate, based on Mr. Seguin's ability to pay and the lack of a direct link between Ms. Vanasse's contribution and the company (making a constructive trust remedy inapplicable). In the result, the trial judge had awarded Ms. Vanasse a one-half interest in the prorated increase in Mr. Seguin's net worth during the period of unjust enrichment, less the value of her interest in the family home and the RRSPs. The award was just under $1 million. The Court then analyzed the issues on appeal:

[142] I agree with the appellant that a monetary award for unjust enrichment need not, as a matter of principle, always be calculated on a fee-for-service basis. As I have set out earlier, an unjust enrichment is best characterized as one party leaving the relationship with a disproportionate share of wealth that accumulated as a result of the parties' joint efforts. This will be so when the parties were engaged in a joint family venture and where there is a link between the contributions of the claimant and the accumulation of wealth. When this is the case, the amount of the

enrichment should be assessed by determining the claimant's proportionate contribution to that accumulated wealth. As the trial judge saw it, this was exactly the situation of Ms. Vanasse and Mr. Seguin....

The Court noted that the trial judge did not analyze the issues in terms of the factors identified by the Court: mutual effort, economic integration, actual intent, and priority of the family. However, in reviewing the judge's findings, the Court held that they fit under these headings all the same. Thus, the Court held that these cohabiting partners were engaged in a joint family venture (at para 154). In addition, the Court reviewed the trial judge's conclusions with respect to the link between Ms. Vanasse's contribution during the three-year period of unjust enrichment, and held that there was a clear link between her contribution and the accumulation of wealth (at para 157). However, the Court concluded that there was little argument about the way the trial judge approached the calculation of the proportionate shares of the parties' accumulated wealth. In this situation, the Court suggested that it should not necessarily provide a template for the future, and indicated its preference not to make general statements about the quantification process, except to affirm the principle of deference to a trial judge's assessment of damages. Finally, the Court noted that the trial judge had taken account of Mr. Seguin's contributions to household work, by excluding the third period of the relationship from her assessment of unjust enrichment (para 160). In allowing the appeal, the Court awarded costs to Ms. Vanasse throughout.

Kerr v Baranow

At the end of this 25-year relationship, the trial court in British Columbia awarded Ms. Kerr $315,000 on the basis of both resulting trust (reflecting her contribution to the acquisition of property) and as a remedy for unjust enrichment on the part of Mr. Baranow. (There was also an award of spousal support, effective on the date that Ms. Kerr had commenced her proceedings.) The B.C. Court of Appeal allowed Mr. Baranow's appeal, concluding that there was no basis for a resulting trust or unjust enrichment, and that the trial court had failed to deal with Mr. Baranow's claim for unjust enrichment during the period of Ms. Kerr's disability. (The Court of Appeal also ordered spousal support as of the first day of trial.) In this context, Cromwell J concluded that:

> [165] In my view, the Court of Appeal was right to set aside the trial judge's findings of resulting trust and unjust enrichment. It also did not err in directing that Mr. Baranow's counterclaim be returned to the Supreme Court of British Columbia for hearing. However, my view is that Ms. Kerr's unjust enrichment claim should not have been dismissed, but rather a new trial ordered. While the trial judge's errors certainly were not harmless, it is not possible to say on this record, which includes findings of fact tainted by clear error, that her unjust enrichment claim would inevitably fail if analyzed using the clarified legal framework set out above.... [The Court also set aside the Court of Appeal's order with respect to spousal support, and restored the order of the trial judge.]

The Court then proceeded to examine the facts in this case in detail, noting that the trial judge had focused only on monetary contributions, but had failed to make findings of fact with respect to the parties' non-monetary contributions (at para 166).

With respect to the resulting trust issue, the Court held that Ms. Kerr did not make a gratuitous transfer to Mr. Baranow, since he had injected considerable cash into her initial home to enable her to keep it (at paras 176–180). The Court also held that Ms. Kerr did not make contributions to the acquisition of the new home acquired by the parties (at paras 181–183). In addition, the Court rejected the trial judge's conclusion that the parties had a common intention to share in the new property they acquired:

> [184] ... For the reasons I have given earlier, the "common intention" resulting trust has no further role to play in the resolution of disputes such as this one. I would hold that a resulting trust should not have been imposed on the Wall Street property on the basis of a finding of common intention between these parties....

Turning to the issue of unjust enrichment, the Court reviewed the trial judge's findings with respect to benefit and corresponding deprivation, and concluded that the Court of Appeal was correct to reject the trial judge's analysis, because Mr. Baranow had made direct and indirect contributions by which Ms. Kerr was enriched and for which he was not compensated. Thus, the Court of Appeal concluded that there was a juristic reason for any enrichment he experienced.

The appellant argued that the mutual benefit analysis should take place in relation to the assessment of enrichment and corresponding deprivation, and secondly, that the Court should adopt a "family property approach" to unjust enrichment, one that reflected reasonable expectations with respect to the share of assets accumulated during the relationship.

According to Cromwell J, both the trial judge and the Court of Appeal were in error, because the trial judge had completely ignored Mr. Baranow's contributions, and the Court of Appeal had assessed his contributions as part of the juristic reason analysis. Thus, the Court ordered a new trial of Ms Kerr's unjust enrichment claim and of Mr. Baranow's counterclaim, concluding that "The principles set out above must accordingly be applied at the new trial of these issues" (at para 193). In addition, the Court rejected the appellant's argument about a "family property approach":

> [194] ... As set out earlier in my reasons, for Ms. Kerr to show an entitlement to a proportionate share of the wealth accumulated during the relationship, she must establish that Mr. Baranow has been unjustly enriched at her expense, that their relationship constituted a joint family venture, and that her contributions are linked to the generation of wealth during the relationship. She would then have to show what proportion of the jointly accumulated wealth reflects her contributions.... [T]hese requirements are quite different than those advanced by the appellant and accordingly her "family property approach" must be rejected....

The Court then considered whether to dismiss Ms. Kerr's claim or order a new trial, and reluctantly concluded that a new trial was the more just option, in order to give the parties an opportunity to present evidence to support their claims in accordance with the Court's analysis of unjust enrichment claims (at para 198). In the result, the Court ordered a new trial to consider the claims of both Ms. Kerr and Mr. Baranow with respect to unjust enrichment. The Court affirmed the trial judge's order with respect to spousal support, and awarded Ms. Kerr costs throughout.

Notes and Questions

Cohabiting relationships: Differences and dichotomies

In *Vanasse v Seguin*, the parties cohabited for just 12 years, while in *Kerr v Baranow*, the couple had lived together for more than 25 years. Yet, the result of these two cases suggests that the context of cohabiting relationships may be significant to a determination of whether the parties meet the test of a "joint family venture." What factors were significant in the Supreme Court's assessment that Vanasse and Seguin were engaged in a joint family venture? Consider these factors in relation to Kerr and Baranow. What additional evidence will these parties need to supply to meet the "joint family venture" test? If Kerr and Baranow are unable to demonstrate a joint family venture, does this suggest that it is the nature of the relationship, rather than its length, that is important? Why, or why not?

If Kerr and Baranow had decided to enter into a cohabitation agreement at the outset of their relationship, is it likely that they would have agreed to share their economic assets and liabilities equally? Does your answer to this question suggest that people may have different views when they enter a cohabiting relationship than when they decide to separate? Do you agree that there is a significant dichotomy between a long-term cohabiting relationship and marriage?

Cohabiting relationships, unjust enrichment, and options for reform

Consider the features of the "joint family venture" identified in the Supreme Court's consideration of these two cases. To what extent does it structure or limit the role of judicial discretion in unjust enrichment claims in domestic relationships?

Although the Supreme Court's decision was intended to clarify the principles applicable in claims of unjust enrichment in domestic relationships, did it simplify the requirements to be proved to succeed in such claims?

For example, would Ms. Walsh in *Nova Scotia (AG) v Walsh* have succeeded in establishing a "joint family venture"? Does your answer suggest that the concept of "joint family venture" may be more easily established in cases involving significant family wealth? Does your answer suggest some limitations in the views of the majority in *Nova Scotia (AG) v Walsh* that there is no need for cohabiting couples to have access to marital property regimes because they can make claims in unjust enrichment?

Does your answer change your view about the appropriateness of extending the *FLA* arrangements to cohabiting couples who have lived together for a defined period of time? Or is it more appropriate to continue to permit such couples to "opt in" to the *FLA* regime by contract?

In a comprehensive review of *Kerr v Baranow; Vanasse v Seguin*, Berend Hovius assessed this decision of the Supreme Court in relation to lower court decisions, identifying how the decision resolved some issues but left others to be decided in future. Noting that determining whether a cohabiting couple had a Joint Family Venture is likely to be a complex exercise in a variety of different factual contexts, he also suggested that there may be challenges in identifying the wealth attributable to the joint efforts of the partners. He concluded that whether the remedy is a monetary award rather than a proprietary constructive trust may not be as significant for the future. Significantly, Hovius also suggested that the new *Family Law Act* in British Columbia, which extended the matrimonial property rules to cohabiting spouses, may provide a better remedy than unjust enrichment claims that are "hard-to-settle, complex, and expensive to pursue." See *Family Law Act*, SBC 2011, c 25; and Berend Hovius, "Property Disputes between Common-Law Partners: The Supreme Court of Canada's Decisions in *Vanasse v Seguin* and *Kerr v Baranow* (2011) 30 Can Fam LQ 129 at 163.

Similarly, Robert Leckey concluded that:

> If [*Kerr v Baranow; Vanasse v Seguin*] has left many cheering, it is no substitute for a comprehensive, legislated treatment of the property relations of unmarried couples, to the extent that one is appropriate. A robust approach to unjust enrichment may allocate the value of assets. It does nothing, however, to palliate the difficulties arising from the fact that, in a majority of provinces, legislated protections of the family home as shelter do not apply to the dwellings of unmarried cohabitants and their children. (Robert Leckey, "Developments in Family Law: The 2010–2012 Terms" (2012) SCLR (2d) 193 at para 23)

Nonetheless, Leckey approved the approach of the Supreme Court of Canada in this case, particularly by contrast with the Court's later decision in *Quebec (AG) v A*:

> Although invited to do so, the justices who rejected A's claim espied no hint of undertaking in the conduct of a shared life. A had suggested that her former partner, B, while having made no public gesture of consent to spousal obligations, "had doubtless made thousands in private, daily life"....
>
> The "formalistic methodology" of the reasons supporting the outcome in *Quebec v A* contrasts with the Court's recent unanimous opinion on unjust enrichment. In [*Kerr v Baranow; Vanasse v Seguin*], Cromwell J for the Court had elaborated factors indicative of a "joint family venture" so as to attach legal consequences to familial conduct. He nodded to the parties' autonomy as an "appropriate concern" in connection with consideration for the parties' actual intent. But he set out three other potentially countervailing factors for making sense of "how the parties actually lived their lives": mutual effort, economic integration and priority of the family....

> [S]ome readers will sense tension between the depictions of family
> life in the two judgments, detecting a much greater measure of judicial
> creativity and intervention in *Kerr*.... The justices who rejected [A's claim
> in *Quebec (AG) v A*] did not explore A's proposition that autonomy might
> call for honouring relationships and the responsibilities that take root
> through them.... (Robert Leckey, "Developments in Family Law: The
> 2012–2013 Term" (2014) SCLR (2d) 241 at 256–258)

In the context of these academic critiques, do you agree that legislative
reform to extend Parts I and II of the *FLA* in Ontario to cohabiting
spouses is preferable to continued use of principles of unjust enrichment?
What are the competing policy issues? Is it appropriate to create the same
obligations of "opting out" for cohabiting spouses as for married spouses,
or is it still preferable to require cohabiting spouses to enter into cohabitation contracts, pursuant to Part IV of the *FLA* (the "opting in" solution)?
See also Jennifer Flood, "Share the Wealth? *Kerr v Baranow* and the 'Joint
Family Venture'" (2011) 27 Can J Fam L 361.

Unjust enrichment, the "joint family venture": Critiques and concerns

Academic critiques of the decision in *Kerr v Baranow; Vanasse v Seguin*
have also identified some of the broader issues with respect to the princi-
ples of unjust enrichment and appropriate remedies. For example, see
Mitchell McInnes, "A Return to First Principles in Unjust Enrichment:
Kerr v Baranow" (2012) 51 Can Bus LJ 275; and John McCamus, "Unjust
Enrichment, 'Existing Categories' and *Kerr v Baranow*: A Reply to Professor
McInnes" (2012) 52 Can Bus LJ 390.

For an international assessment of some of these issues, see Anne
Saunders, "Cohabitation in Private Law: Trust, Frustration and Unjust
Enrichment in England, Germany and Canada" (2013) ICLQ 629.

Unjust enrichment and marriage: *Martin v Sansome*

In *Martin v Sansome*, 2014 ONCA 14, the court considered interests
in farm property for a husband and wife who had cohabited for about
10 years, then were married for 8 years and then separated. The spouses
had signed a domestic contract at separation which had been set aside by
the trial judge because the wife failed to understand its nature and consequences: *FLA*, s 56(4)(b).

The wife claimed an interest in the farm property (title was in the
husband's name) based on unjust enrichment. The court relied on *Rawluk v
Rawluk* to confirm that questions of title must be determined prior to
calculating the spouses' NFPs. The court also reviewed the remedial options
in *Kerr v Baranow; Vanasse v Seguin*. In addition, although the court agreed
with the husband that the trial judge had failed to consider whether the
husband had been unjustly enriched, the appeal court concluded that the
trial judge had sufficient evidence to support a conclusion that the test for
unjust enrichment had been met.

However, the appeal court concluded that the trial judge had erred,
after finding unjust enrichment, in failing to consider a monetary award

prior to examining the availability of a remedy of constructive trust. The appeal court also noted that the wife had not provided evidence with respect to the issue of whether a monetary remedy would suffice. After reviewing the circumstances, the court concluded:

> [66] In my view, if unjust enrichment as the result of a marriage has been found, and it has been determined that monetary damages can suffice, the aggrieved party's entitlement under the equalization provisions of the *FLA* should first be calculated. Where appropriate, s 5(6) of the *FLA* ... should be invoked.

In this context, the appeal court examined the evidence and ordered an equalization payment to the wife, with interest, and placed a charge on the farm as security for payment.

Does the result in *Martin v Sansome* suggest that the remedy for unjust enrichment in *Kerr v Baranow; Vanasse v Seguin*, based on the joint family venture, is most often confined to cohabiting couples? Recall the factual circumstances in *Rawluk* and in *McNamee*, which involved claims of unjust enrichment in the context of married spouses: why was it possible to pursue claims of unjust enrichment in those cases, while the claim of unjust enrichment by the wife in *Martin v Sansome* was held to be remedied by *FLA* equalization? Does this result suggest that there is a strong parallel between equalization for married couples pursuant to the *FLA* and the "joint family venture" for cohabiting couples at separation — at least in the absence of special factors such as changes in value between V Day and the date of trial (*Rawluk*), or the impact of "intra-family" transactions (*McNamee*)? See also *Kramer v Kramer*, 2014 ONSC 5952.

In an assessment of *Martin v Sansome*, Berend Hovius suggested that the appeal court's decision left some issues uncertain, including how parties should integrate a monetary award for unjust enrichment into the equalization process in the "extraordinary" situations where equalization does not address the unjust enrichment claim. As Hovius noted, the appeal court also did not identify the factors that would create such an "extraordinary" situation, but he proceeded to suggest some circumstances, including a change in property values after V Day, a spouse's contribution to excluded assets owned by the other spouse, the need to establish priority over other creditors, the accumulation of assets during a period of cohabitation that precedes marriage, and the possibility of a negative NFP. (See Berend Hovius, "Unjust Enrichment Claims by Spouses upon Marriage Breakdown: Achieving a Measure of Fairness or Causing Uncertainty and Complexity?" (2014) 33 Can Fam LQ 141.)

The limitation period for unjust enrichment claims: *McConnell v Huxtable*

In *McConnell v Huxtable*, 2014 ONCA 86, the court affirmed a lower court decision that the applicable limitation period for a claim of unjust enrichment is the 10-year period in the *Real Property Limitations Act* (and not the 2-year limitation period in the *Limitations Act*).

The couple had cohabited for more than a decade and separated in 2007. At that time, McConnell engaged a lawyer who wrote to Huxtable about negotiating a settlement, but no action was taken at that time. In 2012, however, McConnell became aware that Huxtable was planning to sell the home that was potentially subject to her claim of unjust enrichment, and she initiated the claim. Huxtable then brought a motion to dismiss the claim on the basis of the *Limitations Act*.

The motions judge concluded that section 4 of the *Real Property Limitations Act*, which refers to an "action to recover any land," was applicable, so that McConnell's claim was not barred in 2012. In the alternative, the motions judge concluded that there was a legislative gap, and that the court was required to devise a time limit pursuant to its equitable jurisdiction: see 2013 ONSC 948.

In Huxtable's appeal to the Court of Appeal, the court unanimously agreed that the limitation period in the *Real Property Limitations Act* was applicable so that McConnell's claim could proceed. The court specifically confirmed the motion judge's conclusions that a claim for unjust enrichment was a claim relating to the recovery of land. Quoting the motions judge, the court stated:

> [23] The motion judge held that the plain meaning of recover any land includes seeking an equitable interest in land through imposition of a constructive trust. As he said at para 59, "a case in which someone asks the court to award them ownership of part or all of a piece of land held by somebody else is an action to recover land...." [And quoting the motions judge:]
>
> > [77] A party seeing an ownership interest by way of constructive trust must plead and then prove facts establishing entitlement to it. The fact that a claimant must prove enrichment of the other party and a corresponding deprivation of the claimant, with no juristic reason for the enrichment in order to show that damages alone are insufficient and only a proprietary remedy is adequate, does not alter the fact that the claimant has asked the court from the beginning to award an interest in land....

After reviewing the decision of the Supreme Court of Canada in *Kerr v Baranow; Vanasse v Seguin*, the Court of Appeal returned to consideration of:

> [38] ... the interpretive issues and specifically to the question of whether an application for the equitable remedy of a constructive trust in real property is an application for recovery of any land. In my view, [McConnell] is making a claim for recovery of land in the sense that she seeks to obtain land by judgment of the Court. That the court might provide her with the alternative remedy of a monetary award does not take away from the fact that her claim is for a share of the property....

In reflecting on this decision, consider whether there are good policy reasons to permit claimants seeking a remedy for unjust enrichment to have a 10-year limitation period. Note the *Family Law Act* provisions regarding limitation periods for equalization claims in section 7 (the earliest of two years after a decree of divorce or nullity, or six years after the spouses' separation with no prospect of resumption of cohabitation). Is there a need for legislative action in relation to the limitation period for claims of unjust enrichment? For another case discussing the equitable claim in *McConnell v Huxtable*, see *Cork v Cork*, 2014 ONSC 2488.

Quantum meruit, constructive trusts and non-spousal relationships

Although claims about unjust enrichment and appropriate remedies are less frequent in non-spousal "family" relationships, some recent cases suggest a need to consider such claims and remedies in other kinds of "family" circumstances. For example, claims have been presented by children, relatives, extended family members or "friends of the family" in relation to the provision of physical, emotional or economic care for family members.

In *Lineham v Forfert Estate*, 2003 BCSC 1324, for example, a realtor who had acted as a "son" to the deceased succeeded in a claim against the estate, while in *Wiffen v Wiffen*, 2001 BCSC 1716, a daughter-in-law was successful in a claim concerning a family farming operation. However, not all such claims have succeeded: for example, see *Russo v Russo*, 2002 BCSC 554.

To what extent are "spousal" claims about unjust enrichment useful in assessing such claims by other family members?

Additional Resources

Anne Bottomley, "Women and Trust(s): Portraying the Family in the Gallery of Law" in Susan Bright & John Dewar, eds, *Land Law: Themes and Perspectives* (Oxford: Oxford University Press, 1998) 206.

Anne Bottomley & Simone Wong, eds, *Changing Contours of Domestic Life, Family and Law: Caring and Sharing* (Oxford & Portland, OR: Hart Publishing, 2009).

Gillian Douglas, Julia Pearce & Hilary Woodward, *A Failure of Trust: Resolving Property Disputes on Cohabitation Breakdown* (Cardiff University and University of Bristol, Cardiff Law School Research Papers No. 1, 2007).

David Frenkel, "Joint Family Venture: A Synthesis of the Post-Kerr Case Law" (2014) 34 Can Fam LQ 35.

Simon Gardner, "Rethinking Family Property" (1993) 109 Law Q Rev 263.

Berend Hovius, "Property Division for Unmarried Cohabitees in the Common Law Provinces" (2003–2004) 21 Can Fam LQ 175.

Berend Hovius, "Property Disputes between Common-Law Partners: The Supreme Court of Canada's Decisions in *Vanasse v. Seguin* and *Kerr v. Baranow*" (2011) 30 Can Fam LQ 129.

Robert Leckey, "Unjust Enrichment and De Facto Spouses" (2012) 114 R du N 475.

JD McCamus, "Restitution on Dissolution of Marital and Other Intimate Relationships: Constructive Trust or Quantum Meruit" in JW Neyers,

M McInnes & SGA Pitel, eds, *Understanding Unjust Enrichment* (Oxford & Portland, OR: Hart Publishing, 2004) 359.

MJ Mossman, "Equity and 'Family' Relationships: Cohabitation and Constructive Trusts" in Mark Gillen & Faye Woodman, eds, *The Law of Trusts: A Contextual Approach*, 3rd ed (Toronto: Emond Montgomery Publications, 2015).

Donnalee Moulton, "Common Law Couples — Til Death Do They Part" (October 2011) 35:10 Can Lawyer 49.

Marcia Neave, "Living Together — the Legal Effects of the Sexual Division of Labour in Four Common Law Countries" (1991) 17 Monash UL Rev 14.

Anne Saunders, "Cohabitants in Private Law: Trust, Frustrations and Unjust Enrichment in England, Germany and Canada" (2013) ICLQ 629.

RE Scane, "Relationships 'Tantamount to Spousal,' Unjust Enrichment, and Constructive Trusts" (1991) 70 Can Bar Rev 260.

Simone Wong, "Property Rights for Home-Sharers: Equity Versus a Legislative Framework?" in Susan Scott-Hunt & Hilary Lim, eds, *Feminist Perspectives on Equity and Trusts* (London: Cavendish Publishing Ltd, 2001) 133.

7

Spousal Support, Compensation and Dependency: Legislative Goals, Court Orders and Private Agreements

Spousal support rights and obligations ... do not exist in a social or economic vacuum. Statutory support provisions and their judicial interpretation reflect fundamental aspects of social policy, such as the respective obligations of the individual and the State to provide financial security for economic victims of family breakdown and divorce. (Julien D Payne, "An Overview of Theory and Reality in the Judicial Disposition of Spousal Support Claims Under the Canadian Divorce Act" (2000) 63 Sask L Rev 403 at 404)

I.
ECONOMIC ADJUSTMENT POST-SEPARATION: CONTEXTS AND RESPONSIBILITIES

FAMILY POLICIES AND FAMILY LAW

The policy context for "family" responsibility for dependency post-separation

By contrast with a final order for property sharing, which results in a "clean break" for spouses who separate, ongoing financial support for a dependent spouse ("spousal support") means that former spouses must continue to interact with each other with respect to financial matters. This aspect of economic adjustment post-separation is significant in two ways:

• First, assigning responsibility to provide financial support for a former spouse's post-separation dependency (along with issues relating to children and their support) to a former family member contributes to the creation of a new "post-separation family unit." In this way, divorce or separation does not provide a "clean break" for family members, since their lives remain entwined in financial relationships, sometimes long after separation. Thus, to the extent that family law policies are intended to foster a "clean break," the legal arrangements for spousal support may sometimes undermine this policy goal.

• Second, assigning responsibility to provide financial support for post-separation dependency to a former family member suggests that, in spite of governmental policies creating accessible no fault divorce, obligations to alleviate ongoing dependency for former spouses who separate or divorce are "private" rather than "public" responsibilities. In this context, the shrinking of state support for dependency (including dependency that occurs post-separation or divorce) means that Canadian courts have increasingly recognized a primary obligation on the part of former family members to respond to financial dependency. In this way, issues about spousal support also engage broader issues of public policy with respect to economic welfare for individuals who remain dependent post-separation.

In this context, the American Law Institute's assessment of ongoing responsibilities for spousal support post-separation concluded that

> [t]here is ... [a] failure to provide any satisfactory explanation for placing the obligation to support needy individuals on their former spouses rather than on their parents, their children, their friends or society in general. The absence of any explanation for requiring an individual to meet the needs of a former spouse leads to ... the law's historic inability to provide any consistent principle for determining when, and to what extent, a former spouse is "in need". (American Law Institute, *Principles of the Law of Family Dissolution: Analysis and Recommendations* (St. Paul, MN: American Law Institute Publishers, 2002) at 878)

In the Canadian context, moreover, courts have sometimes focused on the relationship between income security programs provided by government on one hand, and the availability of family-based obligations on the other, with respect to relieving dependency.

For example, in *Bracklow v Bracklow*, discussed later in this chapter, the Supreme Court held that it was preferable for a needy former spouse to continue to receive support from her former husband, "recognizing the potential injustice of foisting a helpless former partner onto the public assistance role" ([1999] 1 SCR 420 at para 31).

Thus, it appears that policy choices to assign responsibility for ongoing dependency to former family members, even without any underlying rationale, have fundamentally shaped the legal principles concerning spousal support. At the same time, since these choices are not congruent with other goals of family dissolution, particularly the "clean break," issues about spousal support often reflect a variety of different approaches.

Indeed, as the cases in this chapter reveal, courts have often shifted their approaches to spousal support, as they attempt to determine entitlement according to legislative requirements which may not always be consistent.

And, although the recent Spousal Support Advisory Guidelines (using computerized calculations) have created greater consistency with respect to issues about *quantum* and *duration* of support, they do not alter basic issues of *entitlement*.

In considering the material in this chapter, therefore, it is important to keep in mind how the choice to "privatize" responsibility for spousal support has created challenges for legislatures and courts, as well as for families.

The economic re-adjustment package and spousal support

As explained in Chapter Six, the economic re-adjustment package at separation or divorce may include both property sharing and entitlement to spousal and child support.

For example, recall the cases in Chapter Six, in which courts were required to decide whether professional degrees should be characterized as property. In the end, the Ontario Court of Appeal held that professional degrees were not "property," but that the former wife in *Caratun v Caratun* was entitled to a lump sum amount of spousal support. In this way, the former spouse received compensation for her contribution to the marriage in the form of "spousal support," even as the court declined to recognize that she had a "property" interest in her former husband's professional degree.

Yet, it is not appropriate to regard property sharing and spousal (or child) support as just similar or interchangeable methods of achieving post-separation economic adjustment for all former spouses.

- First, because only married spouses have access to property-sharing principles in most provincial regimes (see *Nova Scotia (AG) v Walsh*, discussed in Chapter Six), principles about spousal support must not only interact with legislative regimes applicable to married spouses, but also to trust doctrines for cohabiting spouses. Since the requirements for each of these property entitlement arrangements differ, their relationship to issues of spousal support may also require differential treatment.

- Second, property-sharing principles in provincial statutes usually provide for a determination of entitlement at one point in time, a "once and for all" decision. That is, once the property settlement has been defined in a negotiated agreement or court order, there is generally no opportunity for recalculation of issues about entitlement or quantum at a later date (there is a "clean break" with respect to issues about property). By contrast, spousal support may often (although not in all circumstances) be varied at a later date, having regard to changes, either positive or negative, in the economic circumstances of the former spouses.

As a result, spousal support may appear to encourage ongoing connections between former spouses and thus deflect clean break objectives. Although the circumstances in which such variations of spousal support are legally available remains a frequently contested issue, the basic difference between the finality of property decisions and the potential for variation of spousal support agreements or orders remains intact.

- Third, because some property regimes, such as Ontario's *Family Law Act*, are based on fixed rules (particularly with respect to the elimination of some pre-marriage property from the calculation), it is possible that some assets will not be taken into account in property sharing. As a result, courts may conclude that there are reasons to exercise discretion to achieve a fair economic adjustment by means of orders for lump sum or ongoing spousal support. In this way, spousal support may appear to be based on more discretionary decision making than determinations about property.

- Finally, spousal support orders are dependent on the existence of financial resources in relation to both child support and property. For example, entitlement to spousal support may be linked to child support (to be discussed in Chapter Eight), and section 15.3 of the *Divorce Act* expressly provides that courts must give priority to orders for child support before awarding spousal support. In addition, for families that have few, if any, assets at the end of marriage or cohabitation, the property-sharing principles will not apply in practice, while financial resources may not be available to support an order for spousal support either. In such cases, while there may be a need for ongoing spousal support, there may be few, if any, resources available to meet this ongoing financial need. Recall the situation of Mrs. Caratun, whose husband had no assets at V day, but an expectation of substantial income from his dental practice in the future. Thus, spousal support decisions must take into account the overall economic circumstances of families at separation, and the availability of resources to meet these claims.

In a context of limited financial resources, it is possible that there may be neither property sharing nor a spousal support award because all available family resources on separation are directed to child support. In this way, economic circumstances in a particular family may influence the way that principles concerning support entitlement at separation or divorce are applied in practice.

The definition of "spouse" for purposes of spousal support

Although the relevant definitions of "spouse" for purposes of divorce and separation will be considered in detail in the next section of this chapter, it is necessary at the outset to identify how the definition of "spouse" differs for support, by contrast with property.

As noted, the Ontario *FLA* confines its legislative regime for property in Parts I and II to married spouses (see s 1(1)), including opposite-sex and same-sex spouses. In this context, cohabiting couples who separate must engage with principles of unjust enrichment to obtain property entitlements at separation.

However, the Ontario *FLA*, Part III, includes an "expanded" definition of "spouse" for purposes of spousal support (see s 29). This means that the *FLA* provisions with respect to spousal support apply to both married spouses and cohabiting spouses who meet the requirements of section 29 (including both opposite sex and same sex).

Most provincial legislation in Canada includes such "expanded" definitions of "spouse" for purposes of spousal support, even though only a few provinces have extended their property-sharing regimes to cohabiting couples, as noted in Chapter Six. In addition, the definition of "spouse" in the *Divorce Act* is limited to married spouses (opposite sex and same sex).

In practice in Ontario, the legislative arrangements mean that the definition of "spouse" may be quite different for property sharing, by contrast with entitlement to spousal support. Thus, attention to legislative definitions in relation to different aspects of the economic re-adjustment package is essential.

Organization of this chapter

This chapter begins with an examination of the definition of "spouse" in the *Divorce Act* and the *Family Law Act*, and particularly the judicial interpretation of the *FLA*'s expanded definition of "spouse" for purposes of spousal support. This section also examines the cases and legislation that resulted in the inclusion of same-sex couples as "spouses" in relation to spousal support entitlement.

The chapter then examines the evolution of principles of spousal support in the legislation and in significant judicial decisions. To some extent, these principles developed differently for spousal support ordered by courts, by contrast with spousal support agreed to by the parties in a domestic contract (a separation agreement). Thus, this section first explores the early cases about spousal support under the 1968 *Divorce Act*, and then the Supreme Court's decisions in *Moge v Moge* and *Bracklow v Bracklow*, which defined principles for spousal support orders. In this context, this section also examines issues about "compensation," "need," and "fault" in judicial decisions.

The chapter then turns to *Miglin v Miglin*, in which the Supreme Court of Canada re-examined the issue of a spouse's application for spousal support after signing a final agreement limiting or waiving such support. This section then examines the impact of *Miglin*, connecting it to the issues about individual "choice" and the discussion of private bargaining in Chapter Five, especially in relation to marriage contracts and *Hartshorne v Hartshorne*.

In addition, the chapter briefly examines the role of the Spousal Support Advisory Guidelines (SSAGs), adopted in an effort to create more certainty with respect to the quantum and duration of spousal support awards. Since the SSAGs are intended to operate within the existing legal principles with respect to entitlement, it is appropriate to consider their impact following discussion of the basic principles of spousal support. In the context of this reform initiative, the chapter also addresses briefly the limits of reforms relating to spousal support in the broader context of economic restructuring for post-separation family units.

Additional Resources

John Eekelaar, "Uncovering Social Obligations: Family Law and the Responsible Citizen" in Mavis Maclean, ed, *Making Law for Families* (Oxford and Portland, OR: Hart Publishing, 2000) 9.

Faith Elliott, "The Family: Private Arena or Adjunct of the State?" (1989) 16:4 JL & Soc'y 443.

Mavis Maclean & John Eekelaar, "Child Support, Wife Support, or Family Support" in Lenore Weitzman & Mavis Maclean, eds, *The Economic Consequences of Divorce: The International Perspective* (Oxford: Clarendon Press, 1992) 239.

Mary Morton, "Dividing the Wealth, Sharing the Poverty: The (Re)Formation of 'Family' in Law in Ontario" (1988) 25 Canadian Review of Sociology and Anthropology 254.

Janet Mosher, "The Harms of Dichotomy: Access to Welfare Benefits as a Case on Point" (1991) 9 Can J Fam L 97.

MJ Mossman, "'Running Hard to Stand Still': The Paradox of Family Law Reform" (1994) 17 Dal LJ 5.

II.
DEFINING A "SPOUSE" FOR PURPOSES OF SPOUSAL SUPPORT

CONSTITUTIONAL POWERS TO LEGISLATE ABOUT SPOUSAL SUPPORT

As explained earlier in Chapter Five, spousal support is available pursuant to the federal *Divorce Act* (for married spouses who divorce) or pursuant to provincial statutes (for married spouses who separate without filing for divorce and for cohabiting couples who meet the statutory definition for eligibility).

- The federal Parliament has authority to legislate with respect to marriage and divorce under section 91(26) of the constitution. And, its authority to legislate *corollary relief in relation to a divorce decree* was recognized in a number of cases after the enactment of divorce legislation in 1968. For example, see *Zacks v Zacks* (1973), 10 RFL 53 (SCC).

- Provincial legislatures have enacted statutes providing for spousal support based on provincial authority for property and civil rights under section 92(13) of the constitution.

As was noted earlier, however, there are some situations in which jurisdictional arguments may complicate or delay family law proceedings.

For example, if one spouse has commenced an action for spousal support pursuant to provincial legislation, and the other spouse then applies for divorce, the provisions of the federal statute with respect to spousal support will apply, in accordance with the doctrine of paramountcy.

In addition, after the granting of a divorce in which no claim for support was presented, it seems that any subsequent application for spousal support must be made pursuant to the federal statute. For example, see *Richards v Richards* (1972), 7 RFL 101 (Ont CA).

There are also provisions in some provincial statutes that provide for the staying of an action pursuant to provincial authority, when another action pursuant to the federal authority is commenced. For example, see Ontario's *Family Law Act*, s 36. These provisions attempt to avoid the necessity of applying the doctrine of paramountcy in relation to two inconsistent orders.

For further information, see Peter Hogg, *Constitutional Law of Canada* (Toronto: Carswell) (looseleaf) at chapter 27, and the earlier discussion in Chapter Five.

LEGISLATIVE DEFINITIONS AND "SPOUSAL" STATUS

Spouses and support pursuant to the *Divorce Act*

Section 2(1) of the federal *Divorce Act* provides that "spouse" means "either of two persons who are married to each other." This definition now includes both opposite-sex and same-sex couples who are married, as this definition was amended by the *Civil Marriage Act* in 2005.

Section 15.2(1) of the *Divorce Act* provides that either or both spouses may make an application for an order for spousal support. Support may be either a lump sum or a periodic payment, and a court may also make an order to secure payment of support. Section 15.2 also permits courts to impose terms and conditions, but "misconduct in relation to the marriage" is not to be considered in ordering support (see s 15.2(5)).

Finally, section 15.2(4) includes a list of factors to be considered, and section 15.2(6) provides a list of objectives to be promoted by spousal support orders, in relation to court orders. These sections will be considered in more detail in relation to the principles of spousal support, discussed later in this chapter.

In this context, recall that section 15.3 provides for priority for child support if there are insufficient resources to meet claims of both child and spousal support.

"Spouses" in provincial legislation in relation to support

As noted above, provincial legislatures have tended to expand the definition of "spouse" for purposes of support to include some cohabiting couples. These provisions generally include as "spouses" persons who have cohabited for a defined period and persons who have become the parents of a child if they have cohabited even for a short period. These definitions now apply to both opposite-sex and same-sex couples, as follows:

- **Length of cohabitation:** Provincial statutes define cohabiting couples as spouses for purposes of spousal support if they have cohabited for a defined period of time. However, the length of time may vary from province to province. For example, the required period of cohabitation is three years in Ontario, New Brunswick and Manitoba, two years in British Columbia, Nova Scotia, Newfoundland, and the Northwest Territories, and one year in Yukon. See *Family Law Act*, RSO 1990, c F3; *Family Services Act*, SNB 1980, c F-2.2; *Family Maintenance Act*, RSM 1987, c F20; *Family Law Act*, SBC 2011, c 25; *Maintenance and Custody Act*, RSNS 1989, c 160; *Family Law Act*, RSNL 1990, c F-2; *Family Law Act*, SNWT 1997, c 18; and *Family Property and Support Act*, RSY 2002, c 83).

  In addition, some provincial statutes define cohabitation as a "conjugal relationship", For example, see Ontario's *Family Law Act*, s 1(1). This requirement has been the subject of criticism, examined below.

- **Cohabitation and parenthood:** Most provincial statutes include in the definition of "spouse" those persons in cohabiting relationships who are the biological or adoptive parents of a child. For example, Ontario's *Family Law Act*, s 29(b) defines as a "spouse" a person who cohabits with another person "in a relationship of some permanence" where they are the natural or adoptive parents of a child. Similarly, Newfoundland's *Family Law Act*, RSNL 1990, c F2 defines as a "spouse" a person who has cohabited with another person for at least one year where they are the biological or adoptive parents of a child.

- **Same-sex couples are also "spouses":** Although these provincial definitions were originally adopted for opposite-sex cohabiting couples, they have generally been extended to include same-sex couples who cohabit, as discussed later in this section.

In examining these definitions, this chapter first explores some interpretive issues arising from the expanded definition of spouse in the context of opposite-sex spouses, and then reviews developments in courts and legislatures with respect to spousal status for same-sex cohabiting couples at separation. In addition, the section includes recent criticisms of legislative and judicial approaches to the definition of "spouse" for purposes of support.

JUDICIAL INTERPRETATION: DEFINING (OPPOSITE-SEX) "SPOUSES"

Interpreting section 29: "Continuous" cohabitation and "conjugality"

Because the wording of the expanded definition of spouse differs from province to province, this review of cases interpreting legislative definitions focuses on Ontario's *Family Law Act*, s 29.

One part of the expanded definition of spouse in section 29 requires cohabitation "continuously for a period of not less than three years." This same language was used in the former Ontario statute, the *Family Law Reform Act*, s 14, even though the requisite period of cohabitation under the *FLRA* was five years.

In addition, note that the definition of "cohabit" in section 1(1) of the *FLA* means "to live together in a conjugal relationship whether within or outside marriage."

In the context of this definition, courts have had to interpret the meaning of cohabitation in terms of the requirement of "continuous" cohabitation, as well as the meaning of "conjugality." In examining the reasoning in the cases that follow, consider the factors identified by the courts to demonstrate that persons in a cohabiting relationship meet the definition of "spouse" in section 29 of the FLA. Do the cases suggest that courts use a narrow or a broad approach? What are the consequences of these differing approaches for former family members and the state with respect to responsibilities for economic dependency post-separation?

Molodowich v Penttinen
(1980), 17 RFL (2d) 376 (Ont Dist Ct)

In *Molodowich v Penttinen*, a case decided pursuant to the former *Family Law Reform Act*, the court held that there were seven components involved in cohabitation: arrangements for shelter; arrangements for sexual and personal behaviour; arrangements for domestic services; social activities; the attitude and conduct of the community toward the couple; financial arrangements; and the attitude and conduct of the couple toward children.

Kurisko DCJ formulated (at 381) a series of questions for determining whether a couple was cohabiting within a conjugal relationship. Consider whether, or to what extent, the following factors should determine whether a person is a "spouse" for purposes of spousal support:

1. Shelter
    a. Did the parties live under the same roof?
    b. What were the sleeping arrangements?
    c. Did anyone else occupy or share the available accommodations?

2. Sexual and Personal Behaviour
   a. Did the parties have sexual relations? If not, why not?
   b. Did they maintain an attitude of fidelity to each other?
   c. What were their feelings toward each other?
   d. Did they communicate on a personal level?
   e. Did they eat their meals together?
   f. What, if anything, did they do to assist each other with problems or during illness?
   g. Did they buy gifts for each other on special occasions?

3. Services
   What was the conduct and habit of the parties in relation to
   a. preparation of meals;
   b. washing and mending clothes;
   c. shopping;
   d. household maintenance; and
   e. any other domestic services?

4. Social
   a. Did the parties participate together or separately in neighbourhood and community activities?
   b. What was the relationship and conduct of each of them toward members of their respective families and how did such families behave toward the parties?

5. Societal
   What was the attitude and conduct of the community toward each of them and as a couple?

6. Support (economic)
   a. What were the financial arrangements between the parties regarding the provision of or contribution toward the necessaries of life—for example, food, clothing, shelter, and recreation?
   b. What were the arrangements concerning the acquisition of ownership of property?
   c. Was there any special financial arrangement between them that both agreed would be determinant of their overall relationship?

7. Children
   What was the attitude and conduct of the parties concerning children?

Sullivan v Letnik
(1994), 5 RFL (4th) 313 (Ont Unif Fam Ct)

BECKETT J:

This was the trial of an issue, i.e., whether the applicant is a spouse of the respondent within the meaning of section 29 of the *Family Law Act, 1986*. The applicant claims support and an interest in the respondent's property. The parties are not married, and if the applicant is found not to be a spouse within the meaning of the Act, the Unified Family Court has no jurisdiction in this case. The applicant says that she and the respondent have had both a business and an intimate personal relationship for almost 22 years, of which at least 7 years were as common law spouses. The respondent's position is that, although they had a business relationship as well as an intimate personal relationship, they did not live together continuously so that they could be defined as spouses either under the *Family Law Act, 1986* or its predecessor, the *Family Law Reform Act*....

The applicant's evidence is quite different from that of the respondent. Accordingly, I shall review the evidence in some detail, as the credibility of the parties becomes the main issue before me.

The respondent is the owner of a company called Captain Normac's Riverboat Inn Ltd., which operated the vessel "Normac" converted to a restaurant called "Captain John's." The "Normac" was moored at Queen's Quay in Toronto. He had opened this business some time around 1971. With her background in accounting in the hotel industry, the applicant was hired by the respondent in August of 1971. At that time, both parties were married to others. On October 29th, 1972, the business relationship between the parties became intimate, and that date was subsequently remembered by both parties as "their anniversary." There was a period of time in 1972 and 1973 that the applicant was employed elsewhere but continued as a consultant to Mr. Letnik and continued their personal relationship. About 1975, Mr. Letnik found another ship, the "Jadrin," and brought it to Toronto to operate alongside the "Normac." In 1976, the applicant entered into a five-year employment contract with the respondent's company.

On the 2nd of June 1981, the "Normac" was struck at its mooring by the Toronto ferry "Trillium," causing extensive damage, as a result of which the "Normac" sank several days later. On hearing of the accident, Mrs. Sullivan drove to the ship, accompanied by her husband and her daughter.

At this point, I should say something about the relationship between Mrs. Sullivan and her husband. They had married in 1966, but after about 1967, there was no further intimacy between them, and from the evidence, it appears that they had accommodated themselves to a lifestyle that allowed Mrs. Sullivan a great deal of freedom. They have a daughter, who was born in 1971, but she is not the biological child of Mr. Sullivan.

On June 21, 1981, Mrs. Sullivan did not return to her home in Unionville with her husband and child. Instead, she remained on the ship to carry out her administrative duties. At first she slept on the couch in her office but soon after, Mr. Letnik asked her to move into his personal quarters and from that time on, she not only worked for Mr. Letnik but lived with him in a conjugal relationship.

The following spring, on April 29th, 1982, Mr. Letnik asked Mrs. Sullivan to marry him and marked the occasion by giving her an engagement ring, which she displayed in court. He had divorced in 1977, but Mrs. Sullivan was still married. However, they were both Catholics and apparently felt that it was necessary to go through annulment proceedings with the church, which they ultimately did, to which I will refer later.

Up to June 2nd, 1981, Mrs. Sullivan and her husband and daughter had resided at 21 Cullen Street in Carlisle, Ontario, but after that date, she says she spent 85% to 90% of her time on the vessel with Mr. Letnik, and the balance of her time visiting with her daughter at the home in Carlisle, which she owned.

In 1984, the respondent refurbished the "Jadrin" and created a large apartment for himself and for Mrs. Sullivan. She testified that she was responsible for the decorating of this apartment. On completion, they both moved into it and continued to share the apartment, to all intents and purposes as husband and wife.

On January 2nd, 1985, Mr. and Mrs. Sullivan had a conversation in which they decided that the time had come to formally part, and in May of 1985, Mr. Sullivan moved out of the Carlisle house with their daughter.

As it was owned by Mrs. Sullivan, she "took over" the house and brought in a housekeeper to look after it. She continued to live on the vessel with the respondent full time from and after January 1985.

In about 1989, the "Normac" was towed to Cleveland, Ohio and, in June of that year, Mr. Letnik opened a "Captain John's" in Cleveland's harbour. Mrs. Sullivan was an important element in Mr. Letnik's business, which required both of them to be in Cleveland a considerable amount of time. As a result, they bought a house in their joint names in a suburb of Cleveland. At this time, the parties were either living on the "Jadrin" or in the Cleveland house or, from time to time, at the house she owned in Carlisle. In 1987, they purchased two farms; in 1988, a building in Strathroy; and in 1989, a third farm. One of the farms was in the corporate name of a company owned by the applicant, another farm in the names of the applicant and respondent, and the third farm in the names of the applicant's company and a company owned by Mr. Letnik's sister and brother.

After the start-up of the Cleveland business, Mrs. Sullivan spent some time there, but mostly spent her time looking after the Toronto operation while Mr. Letnik continued to look after the Cleveland operation. She testified that on weekends, he would return and they would stay together, mostly on the "Jadrin."

Mrs. Sullivan's annulment proceeding in the church was final on the 20th of December 1990 and Mr. Letnik's in 1990 or 1991. It appears to me that the parties had gone through the church annulment procedure in order to marry within the church.

In 1990, trouble developed in the working relationship between Mrs. Sullivan and Mr. Letnik. In January of that year, they had serious arguments about business, as a result of which she claims he physically abused her in Cleveland. She later had Mr. Letnik's corporate lawyer write to him on her behalf to the effect that their working relationship would terminate on May 1st, 1990. Although this saw the end of their working relationship at that time, her testimony, which I accept, was that their personal relationship continued. She went away for a couple of weeks in May and did some work in Cleveland, but did not sleep on the "Jadrin" between May of 1990 and the end of the year for fear of his violence. However, their personal relationship continued off the ship, including at her home in Carlisle.

At the urging of the company's auditor, she agreed to go back to work in January of 1991, and she thereupon committed to stay on the ship full time. Mr. Letnik continued to spend most of the time in Cleveland looking after the business there until that business closed near the end of 1991. They continued, throughout this period, however, to be with each other when he was in Toronto or she was in Cleveland. By January of 1992 and after the Cleveland business had closed, both were on the "Jadrin" living together, and continued to do so until the 1st of March 1992.

The story told by Mr. Letnik varies from that of Mrs. Sullivan: he claims that at no time did they have a "common law" relationship. He maintains that she only stayed from time to time on the "Jadrin" or in the Cleveland house. He painted a picture of an intimate relationship but one that had no degree of continuity or commitment, falling short of what we would understand to be a common law relationship. He denied that he had ever promised to marry her. He denied that she had stayed *most* of the time on the vessel after June of 1981. In his examination and cross-examination, he attempted to paint their relationship as being a business relationship with a personal relationship that was only slightly above casual. His version of the relationship cannot be resolved with hers by allowing for differences only in minor details. I have no hesitation in concluding that the applicant's description of the relationship is credible, while Mr. Letnik's is not.

Mrs. Sullivan is one of those people who rarely throws away a greeting card; she put into evidence over 60 such cards (of which 29 were undated) sent or given to her during the course of their relationship by Mr. Letnik. The majority were sentimental cards with messages of love and affection. Most significantly, many were "To My Wife" or "What is Marriage?," "To my Wonderful Wife on her Birthday" or "My Wonderful Wife on Mother's Day." There were cards for Easter, cards for her birthday, cards for no reason at all, and many for their "anniversary" on the 29th of October. The last dated card was "To my Wife" at Christmas 1991. In cross-examination, Mr. Letnik claimed that he had never referred to Mrs. Sullivan as his wife, but when confronted with the cards, was unable to give any rational explanation. When asked about the anniversary cards, all he had to say was that she had "all kinds of anniversaries." He said he sent her the cards to keep her "cool." He denied that he had promised to marry the applicant. Mrs. Sullivan testified that her parents treated him like their son-in-law, and, in fact, she produced two birthday cards from her parents to Mr. Letnik, referring to him as "son." He seemed to shrug that off. He admitted that he referred to them as "Daddy" and "Mom," but said that this was simply the custom in his culture.

Mr. Letnik and Mrs. Sullivan appeared to hold themselves out to others as husband and wife; as an example, a photograph in the *Cleveland News Herald* showed the parties beside their ship, and referred to Jeannine Sullivan and "her husband," John Letnik. There were portraits of the applicant and the respondent, and pictures at her family Christmas parties and in her garden at Carlisle. Mrs. Sullivan produced a plaque that had hung in their suite on the "Jadrin," "The Marriage Prayer."

Tracey Ostapa, who had worked as a bookkeeper on the ship from November of 1981 to April of 1992, testified that the parties lived together on the boat. She confirmed that it was Mrs. Sullivan who did the interior decorating on the suite that he had constructed on the ship, although Mr. Letnik denies this. She said they were always together, either on the boat or in Carlisle or in Cleveland. Another witness, David Clegg, who knew them both as a friend, testified that, as far as he was concerned, they were engaged and after learning that she had her annulment, expected them to get married. He worked for the company for awhile, and lived in the house in Cleveland. He confirmed that the parties, when they were there, stayed in the master bedroom. Mr. Clegg also testified that at a Christmas staff party in 1989 when Mrs. Sullivan was not present, Mr. Letnik apologized to the assembled guests for "his wife not being there."

Mr. Letnik called, in support of his position, one witness, his friend, William Meleta, a retired fireman. He was a frequent visitor on the "Jadrin." Although he attempted to support Mr. Letnik's evidence that the parties did not live together, I found nothing essentially inconsistent between his evidence and that of Mrs. Sullivan. Although he tried to help Mr. Letnik, I do not accept his evidence when it conflicts with that of the applicant.

In summary, Mr. Letnik and Mrs. Sullivan had an intimate relationship starting in 1972 that continued until she moved on to the "Jadrin" with Mr. Letnik almost full time, in June of 1981. She had an estranged husband and a daughter whom she continued to visit from time to time. By 1984, she was living full time on the "Jadrin" with Mr. Letnik in an open conjugal relationship, apparent to friends and relatives alike. They behaved like any other married couple and times that they were away from each other were times necessitated by business in Cleveland, or the occasional overnights when she returned to her home, or during a period in 1990 when she did not go on the ship for fear of his violence. But even during that period of time in 1990, their personal relationship continued off the ship.

I found Mr. Letnik to be less than frank. He was evasive, hesitant, and his testimony was totally inconsistent with their documented behaviour over the course of their relationship. On the other hand, I found Mrs. Sullivan to be credible, straightforward, and believable. I prefer and accept her evidence over that of Mr. Letnik.

I am of the opinion that the parties cohabited in a conjugal relationship after June 2nd, 1981, and certainly since January 2nd of 1985, when the applicant and her husband formally separated. The relationship was continuous from that time until March of 1992. There was a time when she would not go on the "Jadrin" in 1990 but that was because of the business turmoil between them and her fear of violence, but that did not mean that the relationship had terminated.

It was argued on behalf of the respondent that the cohabitation, if it existed, was not continuous, that the very brief stays at the Carlisle house from time to time interrupted the continuity of the cohabitation. He also argued that the period when she was off the ship from May until December 1990 broke the continuity. With respect, I cannot accept those arguments. Whether couples are separated is a question of intent, not geography; at least one of the parties must intend to permanently sever the relationship....

Section 29 of the *Family Law Act, 1986* defines "spouse" as follows:

29. In this Part...

"spouse" means a spouse as defined in subsection 1(1), and in addition includes either of a man and woman who are not married to each other and have cohabited,

(a)   continuously for a period of not less than three years....

In *Harris v Godkewitsch* (1983), 41 OR (2d) 779 (Fam. Ct.), Nasmith Prof. J., in addressing the requirement of continuous cohabitation under the *Family Law Reform Act*, gives a good review of the case law. He pointed out that there may be interruptions by temporary separations. Their effect depends upon the intentions of the parties.

He relied on *Feehan v. Attwells* (1979), 24 OR (2d) 248 (Co. Ct.), as authority for the proposition that temporary separations do not preclude a finding that the parties have cohabited continuously. In that case, there had been some short periods of separation which the trial judge had considered to be periods of reflection or reassessment, but found no withdrawal from the relationship — no termination of the consortium.

In *Sanderson v. Russell* (1979), 24 OR (2d) 429, 99 DLR (3d) 713, 9 RFL (2d) 81 (CA), Morden J.A. stated at pp. 87–88 RFL:

Without in any way attempting to be detailed or comprehensive, it could be said that such a relationship has come to an end when either party regards it as being at an end and, by his or her conduct, has demonstrated in a convincing manner that this particular state of mind is a settled one. While the physical separation of parties following "a fight" might, in some cases, appear to amount to an ending of cohabitation, the test should be realistic and flexible enough to recognize that a brief cooling off period does not bring the relationship to an end. Such conduct does not convincingly demonstrate a settled state of mind that the relationship is at an end.

For the above reasons, I find as a fact that the parties lived continuously in a conjugal relationship, probably from the 2nd of June 1981 but certainly from the 2nd of January 1985 until March 1st, 1992.

The parties are therefore found to be spouses within the meaning of the *Family Law Act, 1986*. The result of this finding is that a trial must now be scheduled in the Unified Family Court for the balance of the issues. Counsel may speak to me concerning this and the question of costs for this portion of the trial.

Order accordingly.

An appeal from this decision was dismissed. See (1997), 27 RFL (4th) 79 (Ont CA).

Interpreting section 29: Parenthood and a "relationship of some permanence"

Hazlewood v Kent
[2000] OJ No 5263 (Sup Ct)

In *Hazlewood v Kent*, a man and a woman had a relationship for about seven years, and two children were born. Their relationship with each other was exclusive, although they lived in separate homes. The man visited the woman and the children on most weekends, and they had a sexual relationship, even though the man also had his own room in her home. On these weekend visits, the man cared for the children as a father and the couple spent time together with the children in shared family activities. The man also named the woman as his spouse for purposes of health benefits for her and the children, and they had discussed marriage in the future and the sale of one of the two homes. Is this a "relationship of some permanence"?

In *Hazlewood v Kent*, the court stated in part:

[10] It is clear that a finding of cohabitation does not turn exclusively on the amount of time that the parties spent living under the same roof. There are cases where parties live under one roof but are not found to be cohabiting. There are also cases where parties maintain separate residences but are found to be cohabiting. Where there is any suggestion of a common residence at some point in the relationship, it is necessary to look at the particular circumstances of each case to determine whether or not the time spent sharing living quarters is sufficient to constitute "cohabitation" in the legal sense....

[38] One of the strongest indicia of an intention to be treated as a family is the existence of children born to the couple. When this is combined with an element of financial support by one party to the other, an altering of the roles in the relationship as a result of the birth of the children and some time spent together on a regular basis, this relationship should be considered to be "cohabitation in a relationship of some permanence" within the meaning of the *Family Law Act*. The amount of residence shar-

ing which is necessary to support a spousal finding where there are children and ongoing financial support is probably less than would be required if either of these important factors were absent. Although these two criteria are not determinative of the question for all cases, their existence is very persuasive to the Court in assessing whether or not a family unit has been established....

In this case, the court held that the couple had cohabited pursuant to section 29 and ordered the man to pay interim spousal support to the woman.

Notes and Questions

Defining "spouse": Intention and credibility

Examine the factors identified in *Molodowich v Penttinen*. To what extent are these factors objective or subjective? Are they all equally relevant? To what extent does *Sullivan v Letnik* rely on similar factors?

In a context in which a cohabiting couple has separated, how should courts determine the facts of their relationship while it was intact? Is it possible that Mr. Letnik had a different intention that Mrs. Sullivan during their relationship? What factors were significant to the court's conclusion?

Why did the court in *Sullivan v Letnik* conclude that Mrs. Sullivan's evidence was more credible than Mr. Letnik's? To what extent is it likely that most cases about spousal status in relation to cohabiting couples will necessitate an assessment of credibility?

Consider this situation:

A woman filed an application for interim spousal support at the end of a 5- or 6-year intimate relationship with a man. The man was married to another woman, with whom he lived, and the applicant maintained her own separate residence. Can this woman meet the test of cohabitation for purposes of spousal support?

In *Mahoney v King* (1998), 39 RFL (4th) 361 (Ont Gen Div), the court did not award interim support, but nonetheless stated that it was possible for a woman in these circumstances to be a "spouse," even though she maintained a separate residence and even though the man was married to and lived with a different woman.

Recall *Nowell v Town Estate*, discussed in Chapter Six, in which a woman claimed unjust enrichment in relation to a man with whom she spent weekends for many years, although he was married to and lived with his wife during the week. In that case, the court awarded a monetary remedy on the basis that the parties had a "quasi-spousal" relationship. James McLeod criticized *Mahoney v King* on the basis that it would mean that many dating couples and engaged couples are cohabiting "spouses". See James McLeod, "Annotation of *Mahoney v. King*" (1998) 39 RFL (4th) 361. Do you agree with McLeod? Why, or why not?

Reconsidering intention: The *Charter* and *Brebric v Niksic*

In *Brebric v Niksic* (2002), 60 OR (3d) 630 (CA), the plaintiff cohabited with a man for about 18 months and they bought a home together. The parties shared expenses, including expenses for the plaintiff's two sons from an earlier relationship, and planned to marry in February 1994. Unfortunately, the man was killed in December 1993 in a collision between the vehicle in which he was riding and a train.

The plaintiff wished to sue the driver of the vehicle for damages, but her right to do so depended on whether she could demonstrate that she was a "spouse" pursuant to the *Family Law Act*. What result?

Because the plaintiff had not cohabited for the requisite three-year period and the parties had not had a child together, she could not meet the requirements of section 29. Thus, she challenged the constitutionality of the three-year cohabitation requirement. The Ontario Court of Appeal held that there was no infringement of section 15, commenting (at 640):

> Although the three-year minimum period of cohabitation may not correspond precisely with the characteristics of all common law relationships, any deleterious effects of the definition of spouse are outweighed by the advantages of having an objective standard by which individuals and the courts can determine when state-imposed support obligations and rights of action arise.

Do you agree that it is always appropriate to use the requirement of three years' cohabitation as an "objective" standard? Does this approach take into account cohabiting relationships that might meet all the tests of *Molodowich v Penttinen* before the parties have lived together for three years? If section 29 uses the length of cohabitation (three years) as a general way of establishing commitment to the relationship, should the legislation be amended to permit cohabiting couples who can prove their committed intentions according to the *Molodowich v Penttinen* tests, even though they have not lived together for three years? Why, or why not? Is the rigid legislative requirement in section 29 contrary to the views expressed by the majority in *Nova Scotia (AG) v Walsh*, particularly in relation to the need to respect the choices made by cohabiting couples?

Parenthood and section 29

Courts seem to hold that parents of a child are "spouses" for purposes of payment of spousal support at separation, and they may, of course, also have obligations of child support:

- In *DeSouza v DeSouza* (1999), 48 RFL (4th) 63 (Ont Prov Div), the parties were married and had two children, and then divorced. However, they subsequently reconciled and cohabited for about six months, and then separated permanently. When the woman sought spousal support, the court held that the six-month period of cohabitation after divorce constituted "some permanence." The court also considered the children and held that it was not relevant that they had been born prior to the period of cohabitation.

- In *Labbe v McCullough* (1979), 23 OR (2d) 536 (Prov Ct (Fam Div)), a young woman lived with a man for 6 weeks (4 weeks in Toronto and later 2 weeks in North Bay) over a period of 19 months. When she announced her pregnancy, the young man ended their relationship. Was this a "relationship of some permanence"? According to the court, the fact that the evidence showed that the parties had discussed marriage some day gave the relationship "a touch of permanence." However, in view of the shortness of their time together, the court ordered spousal support of $150 per month for 12 months.

To what extent do these cases suggest that courts exercise their discretion to ensure that cohabiting couples will often meet the requirements of section 29? What policies are enhanced by a generous interpretation of section 29 and obligations of spousal support?

Rethinking "spouses": Focusing on economic relationships?

As the factors set out in *Molodowich v Penttinen* indicate, courts are required to examine the nature of the "spousal" relationship overall. To what extent do these factors reflect functional or familialist notions about family relationships?

In a context in which the result is a determination that the parties are "spouses" for purposes of support at the end of the relationship, should the legislation give greater priority to the spouses' economic relationships during their cohabitation?

For example, in an early case in 1978 under the *Family Law Reform Act*, a court held that a man and woman were not cohabiting as spouses although they were involved in an intimate relationship. The woman, who was in receipt of social assistance, shared an apartment with the man and provided him with some services, including cooking and washing his clothes. She also contributed her share of the rent each month.

In *Stoikiewicz v Filas* (1978), 7 RFL (2d) 366 (Ont Unif Fam Ct), the court held that unmarried persons could not be found to be cohabiting pursuant to [*FLA*, s 29] unless their relationship is such that they have assumed obligations to support and provide for each other as married spouses are obliged to do.

Why might the court have concluded in this case that the parties were not "spouses"?

As noted earlier, the current allocation of primary responsibility to former family members, rather than the social assistance regime, with respect to post-separation dependency means that this case would not likely be followed today. For example, see the rejection of emphasis on the parties' economic relationship in *Armstrong v Thompson* (1979), 23 OR (2d) 421 (SC).

In this context, consider also *Brunette v Québec*, [2000] RJQ 2664 (CS):

In this case, a woman, aged 64, invited a man, aged, 54 to share accommodation. The woman was permanently disabled and the man was mentally disabled, and they provided each other with care and support. They were in a relationship of interdependency but they did not have an intimate relationship.

The welfare authorities eventually ceased to provide benefits to the woman, on the basis that the parties' relationship was like a marriage, and this decision was confirmed by the welfare tribunal in Québec. However, on appeal, the superior court held that the relationship was not "spousal" because it was not sexual.

Does this case suggest that courts are more concerned with sexual, than with economic, relationships in defining who is a "spouse"? Should the Ontario *Family Law Act* be amended so that the definition of "spouse" no longer refers to cohabitation in a "conjugal" relationship?

For one example of such an approach, see Alberta's *Adult Interdependent Relationships Act*, SA 2002, c A-4.5, which permits two persons who live together in an interdependent relationship (including both conjugal and non-conjugal relationships) to be held responsible for support at the end of a relationship.

JUDICIAL INTERPRETATION: THE INCLUSION OF SAME-SEX "SPOUSES"

The historic exclusion of same-sex spouses and *M v H*

Prior to the 1999 decision in *M v H*, provincial statutes that expanded the definition of spouse excluded same-sex couples from making applications for support.

For example, Ontario's *Family Law Act*, s 29, provided that the expanded definition applied to "a man and a woman" who cohabited continuously or were the parents of a child.

In *M v H*, the plaintiff, a woman who was separated from her same-sex partner, successfully challenged the constitutionality of this opposite-sex requirement.

M v H
[1999] 2 SCR 3

In this case, two women, M and H, cohabited in a same-sex relationship from 1982 until they separated in 1992. They lived in H's home, started a successful advertising business, and jointly bought business property and a vacation property. H was more involved in the business.

In 1992, M left the home and applied for support under the *Family Law Act*. She sought a declaration that the opposite-sex definition of spouse in section 29 of the *Family Law Act* was invalid because it violated section 15 of the *Charter*, and was not saved by section 1. The motions judge granted the declaration and read in words inclusive of same-sex relationships. On appeal by H and the Ontario Attorney General, the Ontario Court of Appeal upheld the decision of the motions judge, but suspended the decision for one year to allow the legislature in Ontario time to amend the *Family Law Act*. The Attorney General appealed to the Supreme Court of Canada.

In the Supreme Court of Canada, the appeal was dismissed, Gonthier J dissenting. Both Major and Bastarache JJ wrote opinions concurring with the majority judgment of Cory and Iacobucci JJ (on behalf of Lamer CJ and L'Heureux-Dubé, McLachlin, and Binnie JJ). All the judges stated that they were following the decision in *Law v Canada (Minister of Employment and Immigration)*, [1999] 1 SCR 497, in which the court reviewed its approach to section 15 of the *Charter* in relation to a claim of age discrimination for a surviving spouse pursuant to the *Canada Pension Plan*. In *Law*, the court held that there was no infringement of section 15 in that case.

M v H represented a significant legal development with respect to recognition of same-sex relationships and its reasoning contributed to the recognition of same-sex marriage by the Ontario Court of Appeal in 2003. It also provided the catalyst for reform of section 29 of the *Family Law Act* by the Ontario legislature, discussed later in this section.

In examining this brief excerpt from the decision of the Supreme Court of Canada, consider the reasoning adopted. Significantly, the Court noted expressly that the case was not concerned with same-sex marriage issues, but was confined to issues about spousal support.

CORY and IACOBUCCI JJ:

... The principal issue raised in this appeal is whether the definition of "spouse" in s. 29 of the *Family Law Act*, RSO 1990, c. F3 (*FLA*) infringes s. 15(1) of the *Canadian Charter of Rights and Freedoms*, and, if so, whether the legislation is nevertheless saved by s. 1 of the *Charter*. In addition, M. was granted leave to cross-appeal on the issue of the appropriate remedy to be granted and also as to costs.

Our view on this principal issue may be summarized as follows. Section 15(1) of the *Charter* is infringed by the definition of "spouse" in s. 29 of the *FLA*. This definition, which only applies to Part III of the *FLA*, draws a distinction between individuals in conjugal, opposite-sex relationships of a specific degree of duration and individuals in conjugal, same-sex relationships of a specific degree of duration. We emphasize that the definition of "spouse" found in s. 1(1) of the *FLA*, and which applies to other parts of the *FLA*, includes only married persons and is not at issue in this appeal. Essentially, the definition of "spouse" in s. 29 of the *FLA* extends the obligation to provide spousal support, found in Part III of the *FLA*, beyond married persons to include individuals in conjugal opposite-sex relationships of some permanence. Same-sex relationships are capable of being both conjugal and lengthy, but individuals in such relationships are nonetheless denied access to the court-enforced system of support provided by the *FLA*. This differential treatment is on the basis of a personal characteristic, namely sexual orientation, that, in previous jurisprudence, has been found to be analogous to those characteristics specifically enumerated in s. 15(1).

The crux of the issue is that this differential treatment discriminates in a substantive sense by violating the human dignity of individuals in same-sex relationships. As *Law v. Canada (Minister of Employment and Immigration)*, [1999] SCJ No. 12 (QL) established, the inquiry into substantive discrimination is to be undertaken in a purposive and contextual manner. In the present appeal, several factors are important to consider. First, individuals in same-sex relationships face significant pre-existing disadvantage and vulnerability, which is exacerbated by the impugned legislation. Second, the legislation at issue fails to take into account the claimant's actual situation. Third, there is no compelling argument that the ameliorative purpose of the legislation does anything to lessen the charge of discrimination in this case. Fourth, the nature of the interest affected is fundamental, namely the ability to meet basic financial needs following the breakdown of a relationship characterized by intimacy and economic dependence. The exclusion of same-sex partners from the benefits of the spousal support scheme implies that they are judged to be incapable of forming intimate relationships of economic interdependence, without regard to their actual circumstances. Taking these factors into account, it is clear that the human dignity of individuals in same-sex relationships is violated by the definition of "spouse" in s. 29 of the *FLA*.

This infringement is not justified under s. 1 of the *Charter* because there is no rational connection between the objectives of the spousal support provisions and the means chosen to further this objective. The objectives were accurately identified by Charron J.A., in the court below, as providing for the equitable resolution of economic disputes when intimate relationships between financially interdependent individuals break down, and alleviating the burden on the public purse to provide for dependent spouses. Neither of these objectives is furthered by the exclusion of individuals in same-sex couples from the spousal support regime. If anything, these goals are undermined by this exclusion.

In this case, the remedy of reading in is inappropriate, as it would unduly recast the legislation, and striking down the *FLA* as a whole is excessive. Therefore the appropriate remedy is to declare s. 29 of no force and effect and to suspend the application of the declaration for a period of six months....

Cory J set out the factual background and the provisions of the *Family Law Act* and the *Divorce Act*, as well as a resumé of the decisions of the motions judge and the Ontario Court of Appeal. The court decided that the issue was not moot because even though M and H had settled their dispute, "the social cost of leaving this matter undecided would be significant." Cory J then considered the application of *Law* to the interpretation of section 15 and reviewed the structure of the *Family Law Act* in terms of differential treatment. He then examined section 29:

The definition [in s. 29] clearly indicates that the legislature decided to extend the obligation to provide spousal support *beyond* married persons. Obligations to provide support were no longer dependent upon marriage. The obligation was extended to include those relationships which:
 (i) exist between a man and a woman;
 (ii) have a specific degree of permanence;
 (iii) are conjugal.

Only individuals in relationships which meet these minimum criteria may apply for a support order under Part III of the *FLA*.

Same-sex relationships are capable of meeting the last two requirements. Certainly same-sex couples will often form long, lasting, loving and intimate relationships. The choices they make in the context of those relationships may give rise to the financial dependence of one partner on the other. Though it might be argued that same-sex couples do not live together in "conjugal" relationships, in the sense that they cannot "hold

themselves out" as husband and wife, on this issue I am in agreement with
the reasoning and conclusions of the majority of the Court of Appeal.

Molodowich v. Penttinen (1980), 17 RFL (2d) 376 (Ont. Dist. Ct.) sets
out the generally accepted characteristics of a conjugal relationship. They
include shared shelter, sexual and personal behaviour, services, social
activities, economic support and children, as well as the societal perception of the couple. However, it was recognized that these elements may
be present in varying degrees and not all are necessary for the relationship to be found to be conjugal. While it is true that there may not be
any consensus as to the societal perception of same-sex couples, there is
agreement that same-sex couples share many other "conjugal" characteristics. In order to come within the definition, neither opposite-sex couples
nor same-sex couples are required to fit precisely the traditional marital
model to demonstrate that the relationship is "conjugal."

Certainly an opposite-sex couple may, after many years together, be
considered to be in a conjugal relationship although they have neither
children nor sexual relations. Obviously the weight to be accorded the
various elements or factors to be considered in determining whether an
opposite-sex couple is in a conjugal relationship will vary widely and
almost infinitely. The same must hold true of same-sex couples. Courts
have wisely determined that the approach to determining whether a relationship is conjugal must be flexible. This must be so, for the relationships
of all couples will vary widely. In these circumstances, the Court of
Appeal correctly concluded that there is nothing to suggest that same-sex
couples do not meet the legal definition of "conjugal."

Since gay and lesbian individuals are capable of being involved
in conjugal relationships, and since their relationships are capable of
meeting the *FLA*'s temporal requirements, the distinction of relevance to
this appeal is between persons in an opposite-sex, conjugal relationship of
some permanence and persons in the same-sex, conjugal relationship of
some permanence. In this regard, I must disagree with the dissenting
opinion in the court below, which characterized the distinction arising in
s. 29 as being between opposite-sex and same-sex *couples*. This conclusion
would require that the section be scrutinized for any discriminatory
impact it may have on same-sex couples, and not on the individual members of that couple. Section 29 defines "spouse" as "*either* of a man and a
woman" who meet the other requirements of the section. It follows that
the definition could not have been meant to define a couple. Rather it
explicitly refers to the *individual* members of the couple. Thus the distinction of relevance must be between individual persons in a same-sex, conjugal relationship of some permanence and individual persons in an
opposite-sex, conjugal relationship of some permanence....

Cory J determined that sexual orientation was an analogous ground for
section 15 and then considered how there was discrimination here "in a
purposive sense." In particular, he focused on the dignity impugned by pre-
existing disadvantage, stereotyping, prejudice, or vulnerability:

... In this case, there is significant pre-existing disadvantage and
vulnerability, and these circumstances are exacerbated by the impugned
legislation. The legislative provision in question draws a distinction that
prevents persons in a same-sex relationship from gaining access to the
court-enforced and -protected support system. This system clearly provides
a benefit to unmarried heterosexual persons who come within the definition set out in s. 29, and thereby provides a measure of protection for
their economic interests. This protection is denied to persons in a same-sex
relationship who would otherwise meet the statute's requirements, and as a

result, a person in the position of the claimant is denied a benefit regarding an important aspect of life in today's society. Neither common law nor equity provides the remedy of maintenance that is made available by the *FLA*. The denial of that potential benefit, which may impose a financial burden on persons in the position of the claimant, contributes to the general vulnerability experienced by individuals in same-sex relationships....

Cory J also examined the other contextual factors — the correspondence (or lack of it) between the ground of the claim and the actual need, capacity, or circumstances of the claimant; whether the impugned legislation has an ameliorative purpose or effect for a group historically disadvantaged in the context of the legislation; and the nature of the interest affected by the impugned legislation; whether the distinction restricts access to a fundamental social institution, affects a basic aspect of full membership in Canadian society, or constitutes a complete non-recognition of a particular group. He continued:

> The societal significance of the benefit conferred by the statute cannot be overemphasized. The exclusion of same-sex partners from the benefits of s. 29 of the *FLA* promotes the view that M., and individuals in same-sex relationships generally, are less worthy of recognition and protection. It implies that they are judged to be incapable of forming intimate relationships of economic interdependence as compared to opposite-sex couples, without regard to their actual circumstances. As the intervener EGALE submitted, such exclusion perpetuates the disadvantages suffered by individuals in same-sex relationships and contributes to the erasure of their existence....

Accordingly, Cory J concluded that the definition of spouse in section 29 violated section 15(1) of the *Charter*. In reviewing the application of section 1, Iacobucci J then identified the "redefinition of our democracy" brought about by the *Charter* (as stated in *Vriend*) and considered the "pressing and substantial objective" test in the context of the Preamble of the *Family Law Act*, reports of the Ontario Law Reform Commission (OLRC), and cases such as *Moge v Moge*, concluding that the differential treatment was not saved by section 1.

Notes and Questions

The dissenting opinion in *M v H*

Gonthier J dissented in *M v H*. In examining this brief excerpt from his opinion in the Supreme Court of Canada, identify whether he considered the same, or different, factors in analyzing the context for same-sex spouses. To what extent do his comments refute the argument in the majority judgment based on functionalism in opposite-sex and same-sex families? In this context, could his concerns be applicable in *M v H* because the spouses were women?

> ... In my opinion, this legislation seeks to recognize the specific social function of opposite-sex couples in society, and to address a *dynamic* of dependence unique to both men and women in opposite-sex couples that

flows from three basic realities. First, this dynamic of dependence relates to the biological reality of the opposite-sex relationship and its unique potential for giving birth to children and its being the primary forum for raising them. Second, this dynamic relates to a unique form of dependence that is unrelated to children but is specific to heterosexual relationships. And third, this dynamic of dependence is particularly acute for women in opposite-sex relationships, who suffer from pre-existing economic disadvantage as compared with men. Providing a benefit (and concomitantly imposing a burden) on a group that uniquely possesses this social function, biological reality and economic disadvantage, in my opinion, is not discriminatory. Although the legislature is free to extend this benefit to others who do not possess these characteristics, the Constitution does not impose such a duty on that sovereign body....

In reflecting on the majority and dissenting opinions in *M v H*, consider whether it is appropriate to use the factors set out in *Molodowich v Penttinen* with respect to opposite-sex spouses to determine whether two women are "spouses"?

Legislative responses to *M v H*

- **The Ontario legislature:** Following the Supreme Court's decision in *M v H*, the Ontario legislature enacted amending legislation in October 1999, just within the six-month timeframe of the Court's remedy. Perhaps significantly, the amending legislation was called the *Amendments Because of the Supreme Court of Canada Decision in M v. H Act*, SO 1999, c 6. The amendments affected 67 Ontario statutes, including section 29 of the *Family Law Act*.

  However, the amendments to the *Family Law Act* provided a definition of "same-sex partner" (making this definition analogous to the definition of "spouse"), and extended "spousal" entitlements to "same-sex partners." Counsel for M in *M v H* suggested that the provincial legislation did not comply with the Supreme Court's decision, and that this legislative amendment created a separate but equal status for gays and lesbians, one that was inferior to opposite-sex spouses. See EGALE Canada, Press Release, "Ontario's 'Separate and Unequal' Regime To Be Challenged in Supreme Court of Canada" online, 25 November 1999.

  In 2005, the language of section 29 was again amended so that the definition of "spouse" now refers to "either of two persons" in a cohabiting relationship who otherwise meet the requirements in the section.

- **The federal Parliament:** In April 2000, the federal House of Commons enacted the *Modernization of Benefits and Obligations Act*, SC 2000, c 12. This statute altered the definition of spouse in federal statutes to confer the same benefits available to opposite-sex couples to same-sex couples. Significantly, however, the interpretation section of the statute expressly declared (in section 1.1):

  > For greater certainty, the amendments made by this Act do not affect the meaning of the word "marriage," that is, the lawful union of one man and one woman to the exclusion of all others.

Why was this interpretation section added to this legislation in 2000? Recall the discussion in *Halpern v Canada* in relation to the issue of same-sex marriage, discussed in Chapter Two. Why did the court in Ontario conclude that this section of the federal statute did not constitute federal legislation with respect to marriage?

Rationales for legal recognition of spousal relationships

As was evident in the judgments in *M v H*, there was some disagreement about the underlying rationale for ascribing spousal status, particularly in relation to the meaning of a conjugal relationship. Consider the following critique:

> In *M. v. H.*, the Supreme Court has once again simply set out a wide-ranging list of factors that will have to be balanced by trial courts. The Court has given very little guidance on the question of what, if anything, makes a spousal relationship unique. Many of the seven *Molodowich* factors will be met to varying degrees by most adult domestic relationships. If none is essential, what makes a spouse a spouse? What distinguishes spouses from other interdependent domestic relationships between adults? How many of the factors must co-residents meet before they are considered spouses? Are any of the seven *Molodowich* factors more important than others? The Court gives little guidance, other than to emphasize discretion, flexibility and diversity. (Brenda Cossman & Bruce Ryder, "What Is Marriage-Like Like? The Irrelevance of Conjugality" (2001) 18 Can J Fam L 269 at 296–297)

In this context, the authors argued that conjugality was no longer a relevant factor for defining spousal status for purposes of provincial family law statutes. Recall the recommendations of the Law Commission of Canada, *Beyond Conjugality*, discussed in Chapter Two, which suggested a need to examine adult personal relationships in terms of specific legal purposes.

To what extent do you agree with the conclusions of Cossman and Ryder (at 326):

> We have argued that the question of whether a relationship has a sexual component bears no connection to legitimate state objectives. Once this is recognized, and sex is removed from the scope of relational inquiries, the distinction between conjugal and non-conjugal relationships collapses. And then we need to develop better ways to determine when and how the existence of an adult personal relationship is relevant and should be recognized in law.... To redirect inquiries to the right questions, it is necessary to reformulate relational definitions to focus more precisely on the facts relevant to the objectives of particular legislative schemes.

Reforming the law's recognition of "spouses"?

In 1993, the OLRC's *Report on the Rights and Responsibilities of Cohabitees* (Toronto: Ministry of the Attorney General, 1993) recommended the extension of the definition of spouse in section 1(1) to include all heterosexual cohabitees and those same-sex couples who chose to register as domestic partners. Pursuant to these recommendations, all such spouses would be entitled to the benefits and obligations of Parts I and II of the *FLA*.

In this context, the OLRC recommendations included (at 68–69) a revised preamble to the *Family Law Act*:

> Whereas it is desirable to *recognize and accommodate the diversity of family forms*; and whereas for that purpose it is necessary to recognize the equal position of spouses as individuals within *family relationships* and to recognize *family relationships as equal partnerships*; and whereas in support of such recognition it is necessary to provide in law for the orderly and equitable settlement of the affairs of the spouses upon the breakdown of the partnership and to provide for other mutual obligations in family relationships, including the equitable sharing by parents of responsibility for their children.

To what extent does this revised Preamble suggest a need for more comprehensive reform of Ontario's *FLA*? In this context, consider these legislative arrangements from other Canadian provinces. Should these approaches to "spouses" be adopted in Ontario? Why, or why not?

- In New Brunswick, legislation provides for spousal support obligations when two persons have lived together "in a family relationship in which one person has been substantially dependent upon the other for support," thus extending financial entitlement and responsibility beyond conjugal relationships. See *Family Services Act*, SNB 1983, c 16, s 112(3), as amended by SNB 2000, c 59.

- In Nova Scotia, two individuals who are cohabiting or intending to cohabit in a conjugal relationship may register as domestic partners. By doing so, the partners attain access to the rights and obligations of married couples. This provision also requires unmarried cohabitants to prove that they were "substantially dependent" on their former partner during the relationship as a precondition for accessing spousal support, a condition that does not have to be met by married spouses. See *Family Services Act*, SNB 1983, c 16, s 112(3), as amended by SNB 2000, c 59; *MacFarlane v Smith* (2003), 35 RFL (5th) 112 (CA); *Tays v Bastiaens* (2011), 338 D.L.R. (4th) 168 (QB).

In this context, recall that cohabiting partners in Québec ("unions de fait") have no access to spousal support available to married couples pursuant to the *Civil Code*. See *Quebec (AG) v A*, 2013 SCC 5, discussed in Chapter Six.

Additional Resources

N Bala & R Jaremko Bromwich, "Context and Inclusivity in Canada's Evolving Definition of the Family" (2002) 16 Intl JL Pol'y & Fam 145.
Susan B Boyd & Claire Young, "Feminism, Law and Public Policy: Family Feuds and Taxing Times" (2004) 42 Osgoode Hall LJ 545.
Brenda Cossman, "Family Feuds: Neo-Liberal and Neo-Conservative Visions of the Reprivatization Project" in B Cossman & J Fudge,

eds, *Privatization, Law, and the Challenge to Feminism* (Toronto: University of Toronto Press, 2002) 169.

John Eekelaar & Mavis Maclean, *Maintenance after Divorce* (Oxford: Clarendon Press, 1986).

Martha Fineman, *The Neutered Mother, the Sexual Family, and Other Twentieth Century Tragedies* (New York: Routledge, 1995).

Shelley Gavigan, "Legal Forms, Family Forms, Gendered Norms: What is a Spouse?" (1991) 14:1 CJLS 127.

Law Commission of Canada, *Beyond Conjugality: Recognizing and Supporting Close Personal Adult Relationships* (Ottawa: LCO, 2001).

Patricia Lefebour, "Same-sex Spousal Recognition in Ontario: Declarations and Denials — A Class Perspective" (1993) 9 JL & Soc Pol'y 272.

Noel Semple, "In Sickness and Health? Spousal Support and Unmarried Cohabitants" (2008) 24 Can J Fam L 317.

III.
PRINCIPLES OF SPOUSAL SUPPORT: THE LEGISLATIVE CONTEXT

Social forces have brought about significant change in family law in Canada since 1968. The law of support consequently faces two very challenging and potentially irreconcilable tasks. First and foremost, it must strive to do justice between individual parties before it in a way that is responsive to the dynamic underlying each unique relationship. To this end, it must demonstrate sensitivity to context. Second, it must prove itself capable of evolving with, yet imparting stability to, the very institution it professes to regulate. In this sense, it must be responsive to greater social change, while nonetheless adhering to a reasonably identifiable underlying philosophy. These two divergent mandates, sensitivity to context versus consistency of principle, pose a considerable challenge to lawmakers and judges. (Hon Claire L'Heureux-Dubé, "Equality and the Economic Consequences of Spousal Support: A Canadian Perspective" (1994) 7 U Fla JL & Pub Pol'y 1 at 38)

THE CONTEXT FOR SPOUSAL SUPPORT

The history of spousal support

Traditionally, spousal support was called "alimony." Alimony was a remedy available in the ecclesiastical courts at a time when divorce was relatively rare, and when gender roles in families were often quite rigid. Because a husband had a duty to provide economic support for his (innocent) wife, his duty continued even after the parties separated.

When judicial divorce became available, alimony was retained as a remedy on the basis that the husband's duty to support his wife could not be terminated by his own misconduct. This view was the basis for the development of the principle that alimony was available to an "innocent" wife, although courts eventually extended alimony to wives more generally because of their economic vulnerability post-separation or divorce.

These traditional rationales for alimony were undermined, of course, by modern reforms that removed fault from divorce and that promoted gender neutrality. Yet, as one commentator noted:

> [S]pousal support has persisted as a remedy in the no-fault era, despite the eradication of its theoretical underpinnings — a remedy without a rationale. The theoretical challenge has been to come up with new justifications for the imposition of a continuing spousal support obligation after divorce to replace explanations based on status [marriage] and fault. (Carol Rogerson, "The Canadian Law of Spousal Support" (2004) 38:1 Fam LQ 69 at 72)

Moreover, as the comment at the beginning of this section explained, spousal support now must meet a number of different goals, including doing justice in individual cases while providing certainty and predictability in family law principles.

"Ways of thinking about and justifying" spousal support: Three models

Before examining the legislative provisions and cases concerning entitlement to spousal support, it may be helpful to examine some conceptions about the basis for modern awards of spousal support, in a context of accessible no fault divorce and aspirations about gender equality in families.

As Rogerson suggested in the early 1990s, there was no clear consensus as to what should be the basis for spousal support. There were a number of reasons for this lack of consensus:

- There are many different kinds of marriages and differing views (both traditional and modern) about the nature of a marriage relationship.

- The lack of consensus was reflected in the provisions concerning spousal support in both provincial statutes and in the *Divorce Act*, where a number of different objectives and factors are included, not all of which are complementary and consistent with each other. In this way, the statutes provide a range of rationales for the awarding of support.

- Courts often responded to this situation by using those aspects that seem appropriate in a particular fact situation. Thus, as Rogerson then concluded, the result was highly discretionary, with differing views among judges in different courts about how to approach such applications.

In examining this context, Rogerson identified three models or "ways of thinking about and justifying" modern spousal support, although she also noted that they are not "pure models" and that they all interact and modify each other. See Carol Rogerson, "The Causal Connection Test in Spousal Support Law" (1989) 8 Can J Fam L 95 at 106–118.

Consider these three models for spousal support: are they likely to produce consistency in decision making about entitlement to such support?

"Needs and Means": Spousal Support as an "Income Security Scheme"

According to this model, the basic rationale for spousal support is economic need: "It is the fact of being married, combined with the existence of an economic need, which gives one an entitlement to draw on the resources of the other spouse." In this model, it is irrelevant whether or not the marriage caused the financial need. This model also assumes that it is "the primary responsibility of the family to provide a cushion of income security to those citizens who are unable to meet their own needs and this is one of the obligations which is undertaken in marriage."

Although the needs and means approach does not require any particular level of support, there is some statutory authority to support the idea of spousal support being available in this model at the level of the standard of living during the marriage. Although this model is most similar to the traditional model of marriage and support, it requires an element of financial need, in addition to marriage, to bring it into consideration.

"Economic Advantages and Disadvantages of Marriage": The "Compensatory/Loss of Opportunity Model" of Spousal Support

The compensatory model of spousal support is based on the idea of compensating a spouse for "economic disadvantages which they have suffered as a result of the marriage and the economic advantages which they have conferred on the other spouse during the course of the marriage." In this model, the marriage and economic need *per se* do not justify spousal support, but rather the economic consequences that flow from the particular relationship between the spouses. As Rogerson stated: "Spousal support does not redress all needs — it only redresses needs created as a result of the marriage."

Under this model of "compensatory support," claims for spousal support are often based on the need to compensate a spouse (usually the wife) who has "sacrificed labour force participation in order to perform family responsibilities" for the loss of economic opportunity suffered. This model may also be used to compensate for economic disadvantage flowing from primary child care responsibilities after divorce. As Rogerson also suggested, this model may also need to take account of the length of a marriage in quantifying the disadvantages experienced.

Self-sufficiency and Spousal Independence: The "Clean Break" Model

The basic idea of this model is that the law of spousal support should recognize that the marriage has ended and should encourage economic disengagement of the parties and the assumption of responsibility by spouses for their own support. This model of support may be joined with either of the other two models, but it may also exist on its own.

According to Rogerson, where it exists alone, this model encourages the termination of economic ties between the spouses as quickly as possible. In this way, spousal support is seen to be for only a limited time period, as a matter of principle, and spouses are held accountable for their own support regardless of, for example, any negative consequences flowing from the marriage. As Rogerson noted, this model of spousal support (self-sufficiency) was least evident in the legislative provisions, but quite frequently adopted in the cases.

Consider what kinds of fact patterns might attract each of these models of spousal support. To what extent do they overlap with each other? As you analyze the statutory provisions and judicial decisions about spousal support in this chapter, consider whether, or to what extent, these models provide a useful "way of thinking about and justifying" spousal support principles in Canada.

THE EVOLUTION OF LEGISLATIVE PRINCIPLES ABOUT SPOUSAL SUPPORT

The *Divorce Act*, 1968 and judicial discretion in the 1980s

As noted in Chapter Five, the first federal *Divorce Act* in 1968 included grounds for divorce that were based on both fault and no fault. In this context, section 11(1) provided authority for a court to order spousal support (lump sum or periodic amounts):

> 11(1) ... if it thinks it fit and just to do so having regard to the conduct of the parties and the condition, means and other circumstances of [the parties].

In addition, section 11(2) permitted a court to make an order for variation of a spousal support award, using the same principles set out in section 11(1).

Clearly, this statutory language permitted the exercise of considerable judicial discretion in determining an award of spousal support. In addition, note that conduct remained an explicit consideration for awarding spousal support.

These provisions in the 1968 *Divorce Act* became the focus of attention in the Supreme Court of Canada in the 1980s in two contexts.

- In one case, the Court divided quite sharply on the issue of the extent of a former husband's duty to continue providing financial support to his former wife some years after their divorce. For those judges who believed that the obligations of a former spouse were limited, it was the obligation of the state to meet the needs of a dependent family member.

- In the second case (in fact, a trilogy of cases), the Court attempted to define principles to limit a former spouse's duty to provide continuing support (on the assumption that this responsibility belonged to the state) in the context of a separation agreement negotiated by the parties that provided for support for only a limited period.

In examining these two cases, consider the scope of judicial discretion involved in defining spousal support awards. As will be apparent, the issues in these cases appear to have some continuing relevance for more recent cases pursuant to the *Divorce Act*.

Messier v Delage
[1983] 2 SCR 401

In *Messier v Delage*, the parties had married in 1962, and they separated in 1974. The wife was awarded custody of the three children, as well as child and spousal support. At that time, the wife, who had not worked outside the home during the marriage, was enrolled in a master's degree program. Five years later in 1979, the husband applied to vary the spousal support order on the ground that, although she had not yet secured employment, the wife had completed her studies and had had five years to become self-sufficient.

At trial, the amount of spousal support was reduced and a termination date was provided for payment of spousal support.

However, the Québec Court of Appeal reversed the decision with respect to the termination date, thus requiring the former husband to continue to pay the reduced amount of support indefinitely.

In the Supreme Court of Canada, Chouinard J, writing for the majority, held that the trial court had erred in disregarding the actual circumstances of the parties and that the Court of Appeal had intervened appropriately. Thus, the former wife continued to be entitled to spousal support indefinitely.

However, Lamer J (as he then was, with MacIntyre and Wilson JJ concurring) wrote a dissenting opinion, stating (at 419–21):

> In my opinion, the purpose of maintenance is to reduce in material terms the consequences resulting from breaking the marriage bond. Maintenance will be awarded to a spouse who cannot provide for her own needs. The division of functions in traditional society has meant that it is nearly always the wife who is in this position. It was almost impossible for her, without proper training after several years of not earning her living, to find employment and so be able to provide for her own needs.
>
> The evolution of society and the status of women both require us to re-examine what the nature of maintenance should be....

Justice Lamer's dissenting opinion emphasized that support ought to be rehabilitative in nature, and that each spouse had a mutual obligation to become self-sufficient. He then considered the facts of this case, and particularly the wife's ability to work even though she had not secured employment. He concluded (at 426):

> In my view the evolution of society requires that one more step be taken in favour of the final emancipation of former spouses. To me, aside from

rare exceptions the ability to work leads to "the end of the divorce" and the beginning of truly single status for each of the former spouses. I also consider that the "ability" to work should be determined intrinsically and should not in any way be determined in light of factors extrinsic to the individual, such as the labour market and the economic situation.

As maintenance is only granted for so long as it takes to acquire sufficient independence, once that independence has been acquired it follows that maintenance ceases to be necessary. *A divorced spouse who is "employable" but unemployed is in the same position as other citizens, men or women, who are unemployed. The problem is a social one and it is therefore the responsibility of the government rather than the former husband.* Once the spouse has been retrained, I do not see why the fact of having been married should give the now single individual any special status by comparison with any other unemployed single person. In my view, the duty of a former spouse is limited in the case of retrainable persons to the retraining period.... [Emphasis added]

The *Pelech* trilogy: *Pelech*, *Richardson*, and *Caron*
[1987] 1 SCR 801 at 857 and 892

In the *Pelech* trilogy of cases, the views expressed by the dissenting judges in *Messier v Delage* were adopted by majority judgment of Wilson J:

In all three of these cases, the parties had signed separation agreements (or consent orders), which limited the duration of spousal support. However, in each case, the former wife eventually became economically vulnerable and needed additional financial support.

Pelech was on appeal from the B.C. Court of Appeal, while *Richardson* was on appeal from Ontario and *Caron* was appealed from Yukon. Because all of these cases had commenced prior to the *Divorce Act*, the Supreme Court focused on section 11 of the 1968 statute.

In *Pelech*, the spouses were married for 15 years and had two children. During the marriage, Mr. Pelech ran a general contracting business (which expanded during the course of the marriage), while Mrs. Pelech worked as a bookkeeper and receptionist for the first 10 years or so of the couple's marriage. At the time of separation, the parties, having each obtained independent legal advice, signed a settlement agreement. Under the agreement, Mrs. Pelech received a lump sum, payable over 13 months, in full satisfaction of her maintenance. She also transferred to Mr. Pelech one share that she held in his business. The settlement agreement was incorporated into the divorce decree and the husband paid the money as agreed. At the time of the divorce, Mrs. Pelech was 37 years old and Mr. Pelech was 44.

During the years following the divorce, Mrs. Pelech's physical and mental state deteriorated to the point that she was unable to work full time and she was forced to draw on her settlement fund in order to survive. By 1982, the fund was completely depleted and Mrs. Pelech was on welfare. Mr.

Pelech's position, on the other hand, had improved significantly — at the time of the divorce, his net worth was $128,000, but in the 15 years after the divorce, his net worth had grown to $1,800,000. Mrs. Pelech applied under section 11 of the *Divorce Act* of 1968 to vary the terms of the parties' separation agreement by awarding additional spousal support.

At trial, the judge allowed the application and ordered Mr. Pelech to pay $2,000 per month to Mrs. Pelech, having regard to Mr. Pelech's resources and the need to avoid having Mrs. Pelech become a burden on the "public purse." Mr. Pelech appealed the decision to the B.C. Court of Appeal, which overturned the trial decision and held that the parties should be bound by their agreement.

Mrs. Pelech then appealed to the Supreme Court of Canada, which dismissed her appeal, confirming the decision of the Court of Appeal. There were a number of significant developments about spousal support entitlement in the reasoning in the *Pelech* trilogy:

- First, the judgment of Wilson J reflected a view that spousal support should not continue indefinitely, and that a former spouse's obligation to provide support should be shared with the resources of the state in social assistance entitlements.

    According to Wilson J:

    > I believe that the courts must recognize the right of the individual to end a relationship as well as to begin one and should not, when all other aspects of the relationship have long since ceased, treat the financial responsibility as continuing indefinitely into the future....

- Second, the Supreme Court's decision also confirmed that separation agreements signed by the parties should be given considerable deference in the context of subsequent requests for spousal support orders pursuant to section 11 of the 1968 *Divorce Act*. Indeed, the Court concluded that the terms of separation agreements should not be revised except in very specific circumstances. Wilson J formulated a test designed to promote a "clean break," a test often described as the "causal connection" test:

    > Absent some causal connection between the changed circumstances and the marriage, it seems to me that parties who have declared their relationship at an end should be taken at their word. They made the decision to marry and they made the decision to terminate their marriage. Their decisions should be respected.... *[Only] where an applicant seeking maintenance or an increase in the existing level of maintenance establishes that he or she has suffered a radical change in circumstances flowing from an economic pattern of dependency engendered by the marriage, [should] the court ... exercise its relieving power.* Otherwise, the obligation to support the former spouse should be, as in the case of any other citizen, the communal responsibility of the state.... [Emphasis added]

- Finally, the Court focused on section 11 of the 1968 *Act*, and concluded that the rationale for both sub sections was the same. In this way, it seemed that the same principles were relevant to an initial order and to an application to vary such an order. In both cases, the Court wished to defer to the parties and their agreement, and to limit the scope for continuing support from a former spouse.

Notes and Questions

The impact of *Pelech*'s "clean break" on separating spouses

Although it is clear that the reasoning in the trilogy limited the extent of a former spouse's obligation for ongoing financial support because the Court believed that it was an obligation of the state, the reasoning was criticized for failing to acknowledge substantive inequality between former wives and their former husbands, and the extent to which this inequality was likely to be exacerbated by a clean break philosophy. For example, Martha Bailey argued that:

> [t]he clean break philosophy relieves men, who are almost always the payors, from continuing support obligations, and enables them to form (and abandon) new relationships without on-going financial burdens. Women are disadvantaged by the emphasis on self-sufficiency and a clean break insofar as their true condition of continuing economic inequality is not addressed. (Martha Bailey, *"Pelech, Caron, and Richardson"* (1989–90) 3 CJWL 615 at 626; see also MJ Mossman, "'Running Hard To Stand Still': The Paradox of Family Law Reform" (1994) 17 Dal LJ 5)

In addition to such criticism, an empirical study demonstrated how the clean break philosophy contributed to lower levels and fewer awards of spousal support. In 1990, the Department of Justice published an analysis of divorce files during a five-year period. According to its data:

> ... women requested support in only 16 per cent of applications for divorce, and they received an award of support in only 6 percent of cases in 1988, in spite of figures that showed that women earned 60 percent of men's earnings in 1988. (Department of Justice, *Evaluation of the Divorce Act, Phase II: Monitoring and Evaluation* (Ottawa: Department of Justice, 1990) at 74–76)

The impact of *Pelech*'s "clean break": The absence of consensus

In addition to the impact on separating spouses (especially women), Carol Rogerson, who conducted a review of cases concerning spousal support after the trilogy cases in the Supreme Court of Canada, reported a high level of diversity among lower court decisions, both in relation to the principles applied and with respect to the levels of support awarded. According to Rogerson, the level of diversity reflected "the absence of clear normative standards in the legislation," a problem also reflected in "the absence of a strong social consensus on the appropriate principles of support after marriage breakdown." As Rogerson suggested:

> Principles of support are ultimately rooted in social understandings of the meaning of marriage and parenthood. Those understandings are currently in a state of confusion as a result of significant social changes during the past two decades, in particular the increasing acceptance of divorce and

the changing social roles of women. (Carol Rogerson, "Judicial Interpretation of the Spousal and Child Support Provisions of the Divorce Act, 1985 (Part I)" (1992) 7 Can Fam LQ 155 at 161–162).

As well, Rogerson reported (at 162) that her review of the cases suggested that "courts now operate under a model of support which sees the primary goal of support law as promoting the self-sufficiency of the spouses after divorce.... This is the [objective] most frequently discussed in the reported cases." According to her analysis, older women leaving long marriages were not expected to become self-sufficient, but the situation was entirely different for younger women or those in shorter marriages:

> It would appear that those suffering even more under the legislation, however, are younger women whose marriages break down when they are in their 30s and 40s, who had reduced or ceased their participation in the labour force during the marriage, and who are often left with the post-divorce responsibility for the care of the children. In these cases concepts of self-sufficiency are being given more weight, resulting in either time-limited orders or, as is more often the case, an eventual variation application by the husband to terminate what was originally an indefinite order for support. In these cases it is generally accepted that the support obligation must be brought to an end....
>
> The real problem in these cases is the level at which self-sufficiency is being set. One court stated it quite explicitly: self-sufficiency means full-time employment or earning $20,000 per year. A striking aspect of the case law in this area is the relatively low income levels women have achieved at the point at which they are deemed to be self-sufficient and the disparity between their income-earning positions and those of their former husbands. Courts on the whole fail to understand that while the attainment of such income levels may be understood, for social security purposes, as the achievement of self-sufficiency, it does not constitute adequate compensation for the economic losses suffered by these women who have spent the first half of their adult lives giving priority to marriage and children rather than paid employment. Furthermore, in those cases where children remain in the mother's custody, the termination of spousal support results in the indirect deprivation of children, thus undermining the objectives of child support.
>
> A final problem with respect to spousal support concerns the role of contracts. Courts have generally adopted a position of strict enforcement of contractual provisions dealing with spousal support. Admittedly in some cases women receive more generous spousal support in a negotiated settlement than they would if support had been court-ordered. However, with respect to those contracts which are the subject of subsequent dispute and which thus find their way into the law reports, there are indications of a disturbing pattern of contracts in which women have agreed to support much less generous than that which they would have been awarded by the courts. In particular, some women contractually agree to time-limited support, which, as indicated above, many courts are unwilling to impose. This suggests that lawyers negotiating contracts on behalf of wives may assume a model of spousal support in which spousal self-sufficiency plays an even greater role than is actually accepted by the courts. (Rogerson at 163–165)

As Rogerson's analysis of cases after the *Pelech* trilogy suggested, the clean break approach, as set out in the test for judicial intervention in privately negotiated agreements in *Pelech*, had become the overriding goal in cases about spousal support. Thus, after the *Pelech* trilogy, courts generally limited a former spouse's obligation to pay spousal support, including its quantum and duration.

Pelech and the limits of state support for dependency

However, at the same time in the 1990s, there were significant reductions in income security programs in many parts of Canada. In this context, former wives and their children often had little access to economic support, either from their former spouses or from the state. Not surprisingly, many of these families experienced a good deal of economic disadvantage and poverty.

For example, as a 1992 report indicated, the breakdown of a marriage or cohabiting relationship increased substantially the risk of poverty — for those who were married and had children, the risk of poverty rose from 3.1 percent to 37.6 percent after divorce or separation. See T. Lemprière, "A New Look at Poverty" (1992) 16 *Perceptions* 18 at 19–20.

Thus, the combination of limitations on private family support post-*Pelech* and the shrinking of state support in relation to social assistance programs resulted in a social context in Canada in which many post-separation women and children experienced the "feminization of poverty." In reflecting on these concerns, consider the options available to legislatures and courts to respond to these problems. Significantly, divorce reforms were occurring in the 1980s when these cases were before the courts. And, as will be apparent in the next section, both legislatures and courts attempted to respond to these issues about responsibility for dependency post-separation.

THE 1985 *DIVORCE ACT* AND NEW LEGISLATIVE GOALS FOR SPOUSAL SUPPORT

Spousal support in a context of no-fault divorce

By contrast with the 1968 *Divorce Act*, the 1985 *Divorce Act* was based entirely on the no fault ground of divorce, "marriage breakdown." In such a context, any lingering interest in fault as a basis for spousal support was explicitly abandoned in the new Act. As noted earlier, section 15.2(5) expressly precludes a court from considering "misconduct ... in relation to the marriage" in making an order for spousal support, an issue discussed more fully later in this chapter.

However, section 15.2 in the 1985 Act provides for the exercise of discretion in determining entitlement to spousal support. For example, section 15.2(1) authorizes a court to make an order for spousal support "as the court thinks reasonable," and section 15.2(3) authorizes a court to impose terms, conditions or restrictions in the order "as [the court] thinks fit and just."

In addition, section 15.2(4) provides that a court "shall take into consideration the condition, means, needs and other circumstances of each spouse," including three specific factors: the length of cohabitation, the functions performed by each spouse, and "any order, agreement or arrangement relating to support" for either spouse. The language of this section clearly suggests that additional factors may also be considered, thus expanding the scope for discretionary decision making.

Finally, section 15.2(6) identifies four goals to be promoted by orders for spousal support:

- Recognize economic advantages or disadvantages arising from the marriage or its breakdown;
- Apportion financial consequences arising from child care (over and above child support obligations);
- Relieve economic hardship arising from marriage breakdown; and
- "In so far as practicable," promote economic self-sufficiency within a reasonable period of time.

As a careful examination of these objectives reveals, they reflect the three models of spousal support identified earlier by Rogerson: recognition of "needs," "compensation," and "self sufficiency/clean break." What is also evident is that the goals in section 15.2(6), like those identified by Rogerson, are not entirely consistent.

For example, how should a court take account of the need to recognize the economic disadvantages arising from marriage breakdown, as well as promote a spouse's duty to achieve self-sufficiency? Which objective should have priority? How can these goals be balanced effectively?

In such a legislative context, there is significant scope for judicial discretion. Moreover, although the introduction of Spousal Support Advisory Guidelines have recently encouraged more uniformity with respect to issues about *quantum* and *duration*, the fundamental issue of *entitlement* must be determined by courts, having regard to these legislative provisions. These provisions were systematically examined by the Supreme Court of Canada in cases to be discussed in the next section.

Provincial statutes and spousal support principles

Recall that cohabiting spouses, as well as married spouses who are not seeking divorce, must apply for spousal support pursuant to provincial statutes. In Ontario, Part III of the *FLA* is concerned with spousal support:

- Section 30 provides that a spouse has an obligation to support himself or herself, and the other spouse, according to a means and needs assessment.

- Section 33(8) identifies the purposes of spousal support awards, identifying a number of different purposes; and section 33(9) provides that in determining the amount and duration of such an award, the court must consider "all the circumstances of the parties, including" a list of factors.

• Section 33(10) states that an obligation for spousal support exists "without regard to the conduct of either spouse." However, the section then permits a court, in determining the quantum of support, to "have regard to a course of conduct that is so unconscionable as to constitute an obvious and gross repudiation of the relationship."

Compare these provisions concerning spousal support to those in the *Divorce Act*. To what extent do the provincial statutory provisions differ from those in the federal legislation? Do these differences create advantages or disadvantages for spouses who are seeking spousal support? In practice, there are few differences in spousal support awards pursuant to these different statutes. What explains this level of agreement pursuant to the different statutory regimes? Does your answer suggest that judicial discretion may be beneficial in some cases?

Variation of spousal support awards: A brief note

The *Divorce Act* and Ontario's *Family Law Act* both include provisions that permit courts to order a variation with respect to support orders.

• Section 17(1) of the *Divorce Act* provides authority for a court to vary, rescind or suspend an order for support. Section 17(4.1) further provides that before doing so:

> ... the court shall satisfy itself that a change in the condition, means, needs or other circumstances [of either spouse] has occurred since the making of the spousal support order [and in making the variation order], the court shall take that change into consideration.

• In Ontario's *Family Law Act*, ss 37(1) and (2) authorize a court to vary, discharge or suspend an order, or relieve a spouse's obligation to pay interest or make any other order pursuant to section 34 that "the court considers appropriate." However, section 37(2) provides that such variations or other orders may be made only:

> ... if the court is satisfied that there has been a material change in the dependant's or respondent's circumstances or that evidence not available on the previous hearing has become available.

In the context of these variation provisions, it is important to note that the federal statute requires a "change" in circumstances, while the provincial legislation refers to a "material change" in circumstances. What other differences exist?

In addition, it is significant that these provisions appear to relate to the authority to vary "an order." In this context, of course, it is arguable that a spouse who wishes to set aside the provisions of a separation agreement is not seeking a variation of an "order," and this distinction may result in somewhat different principles in these differing contexts. These issues are discussed again later in this chapter in relation to the decision in *Miglin v Miglin*.

Lump sum support: A brief note

Both the *Divorce Act* and the *Family Law Act* (and other provincial legislation) provide that a court may order spousal support as a periodic payment or a lump sum. The issue of when it is appropriate for a court to order payment by way of a lump sum continues to be litigated, particularly in cases where a payee spouse may fear that a periodic sum will not be paid or that enforcement of such an order may be difficult.

For example, in *Davis v Crawford*, 2011 ONCA 294, the Ontario Court of Appeal reviewed a lump sum spousal support award for a cohabiting spouse whose relationship ended after 23 years. The trial judge had ordered lump sum spousal support for the woman in an amount of $135,000, and the appeal court dismissed the man's appeal.

In doing so, the Ontario Court of Appeal rejected the payor spouse's submission that *Mannerino v Mannerino* (1992), 48 RFL (3d) 237, had narrowly restricted a court's authority to order lump sum support to situations in which there was a risk that support would not be paid or other "unusual" circumstances. As the court stated:

> [58] Had Parliament or the [Ontario] legislature intended that the discretion to make an award of lump sum spousal support to a married or unmarried spouse be as highly constrained as the appellant argues is prescribed by *Mannerino*, those bodies surely would have said so. Moreover, we can find nothing in the legislative history relating to either Act, or to predecessor Acts, suggesting such an intention....

The court suggested that it is necessary to assess the advantages and disadvantages of a lump sum award of spousal support in the circumstances of each case. In *Davis*, the court noted that the trial judge had found (in relation to issues of credibility) that the appellant had greater assets and means than he had acknowledged, and that he was attempting to shelter these assets from the respondent's reach. Thus, in addition to the trial judge's concerns about risk of payment for an award of periodic support, the appellant's failure to make proper disclosure suggested that a "clean break" for the parties was highly desirable. In this context, the appeal court concluded that the advantages of an award of lump sum support outweighed any disadvantages.

For another case involving a complex assessment of the appropriate economic adjustment at marriage breakdown and the role of lump sum support, see *Pollitt v Pollitt*, 2010 ONCA 1617; 2010 ONSC 1186; and Robert Todd, "What is Appropriate Lump-Sum Support?" *Law Times* (20 June 2011) 10.

Additional Resources

American Law Institute, *Principles of the Law of Family Dissolution* (St. Paul, MN: American Law Institute Publishers, 2002) chapter 5.
Brenda Cossman, "A Matter of Difference: Domestic Contracts and Gender Equality" (1990) 28 Osgoode Hall LJ 303.

MJ Mossman, "Family Law and Social Welfare in Canada" in J Bernier &
A Lajoie, eds, *Family Law and Social Welfare Legislation in Canada*
(Toronto: University of Toronto Press, 1986) 43.

Carol Rogerson, "The Canadian Law of Spousal Support" (2004) 38:1 Fam
LQ 69.

Carol Smart, "Feminism and Law: Some Problems of Analysis and
Strategy" (1986) 14 Intl J Soc L 109.

IV.
PRINCIPLES OF SPOUSAL SUPPORT:
JUDICIAL VIEWS OF THE 1985 *DIVORCE ACT*

SPOUSAL SUPPORT AS "COMPENSATION"

Distinguishing agreements (*Pelech*) and orders: The "compensation" principle for spousal support

In *Moge v Moge*, the Supreme Court addressed the issue of variation
of an order for spousal support, a context that differed from the *Pelech*
trilogy where the spouses had signed agreements. Moreover, as noted
earlier, the reasoning in the *Pelech* trilogy seemed to have contributed
to the "feminization of poverty" for many women post-separation and
divorce. In this way, *Moge* presented an opportunity for the Supreme
Court to rethink issues about entitlement to spousal support pursuant to
the *Divorce Act*.

In examining the case, pay special attention to the court's review of
section 15.2(6) and the goals of spousal support awards.

Moge v Moge
[1992] 3 SCR 813

In *Moge v Moge*, the spouses had married in Poland in the mid-1950s and
then decided to emigrate to Canada, moving to Manitoba in 1960. There
were three children. The wife had a grade 7 education and had worked
briefly in Poland as a sales clerk. During the marriage, she was responsible
for child care, laundry, housework, shopping, cooking, etc. She was also
employed in the evenings as a cleaner from 5 to 11 pm. The husband
worked as a welder. Although he claimed to be equally involved in household chores, the Manitoba Court of Appeal found that the husband did not
undertake any chores at home to balance his wife's part-time work and
financial contribution to the family.

The spouses separated in 1973 and the wife obtained an order for custody of the children. Her husband was ordered to pay $150 per month
spousal and child support. Mrs. Moge continued to work as a cleaner and

also took care of the home and the children. Her older children babysat during her hours of work. In 1980, Mr. Moge filed a divorce petition, but continued after the divorce to pay the same amount of spousal and child support. He remarried in 1984. Mrs. Moge was eventually laid off in 1987, when she was earning about $795 per month, and she received unemployment insurance benefits of about $593 per month. She continued to actively seek employment. At this point, Mr. Moge was earning about $2,000 per month (gross) and also had some money from investments. He and his second wife had purchased a home, and his second wife was also employed.

In this context, Mrs. Moge applied to vary the amount of child and spousal support. The Manitoba Court of Queen's Bench ordered a variation in the amount of $200 per month spousal and $200 per month child support, for a total of $400 per month. During the period 1987 to 1989, Mrs. Moge also worked part time when she was able to get work.

In 1989, Mr. Moge applied to vary both orders for support. The court ordered the cessation of child support, and ordered that spousal support would also cease on 1 December 1989. On appeal, however, the Manitoba Court of Appeal allowed Mrs. Moge's appeal in part and ordered spousal support of $150 for an indefinite period.

Mr. Moge then appealed to the Supreme Court of Canada, citing the *Pelech* trilogy. According to his argument, his former wife should have become self-sufficient after so many years, and if she had not achieved self-sufficiency, Mr. Moge argued that no link existed between her lack of self-sufficiency and the marriage (the test established in *Pelech*.)

In the Supreme Court of Canada, L'Heureux-Dubé J expressly rejected the broad view of the trilogy in Mr. Moge's argument, and continued:

[26] A careful reading of the trilogy in general and *Pelech* in particular indicates that the court has not espoused a new model of support under the Act. Rather, the court has shown respect for the wishes of persons who, in the presence of the statutory safeguards, decided to forgo litigation and settled their affairs by agreement under the 1968 *Divorce Act*. In other words, the court is paying deference to the freedom of individuals to contract....

[28] Professor J.D. Payne in my view best identifies the flaws of the early interpretation of the trilogy in "Further Reflections on Spousal and Child Support After Pelech, Caron and Richardson" (1989), 20 RGD 477, when he states at p. 487:

Professor McLeod's proposed extension of *Pelech*, *Caron* and *Richardson* to nonconsensual situations and to provincial statutes as well as the new *Divorce Act, 1985*, virtually eliminates the significance of statutory criteria, whatever their form and substance, and at the same time closes the door to the wise exercise of judicial discretion that can accommodate a diverse range of economic variables on marriage breakdown or divorce.

Notwithstanding the common law's recognition of a spousal agency of necessity, it must not be forgotten that current spousal support laws are of statutory origin. Furthermore, subject to overriding constitutional doctrines, the sovereignty of Parliament ... remains paramount. Judge-made law may explain, but cannot override, statute law.

In addition, there are diverse appellate rulings in Canada that endorse the view that the principles articulated in the trilogy should not be applied to nonconsensual situations....

[29] In light of my reading of *Pelech*, I decline to accede to Mr. Moge's argument that this court has already determined the basis on which entitlement, or continuing entitlement, to spousal support rests in the absence of a settlement agreement intended by the parties to be final under the Act.

[30] Since this case is not one which involves a final agreement entered into between the parties in order to settle the economic consequences of their divorce, I leave for another day the question of causal connection under the Act which was discussed in the trilogy in the particular context of a final settlement under the [1968] *Divorce Act*.

[31] The present appeal not only does not involve a final settlement agreement but deals specifically with a variation application following a support order at the time of divorce, a question to which I will now turn....

L'Heureux-Dubé J made several preliminary observations, including rejecting Mr. Moge's argument that the *Divorce Act* espoused a self-sufficiency model as the only basis for spousal support:

[35] The self-sufficiency model advanced by Mr. Moge has generally been predicated on the dichotomy between "traditional" and "modern" marriage. Often, in order to draw the line after which no more support will be ordered, courts have distinguished between "traditional" marriages in which the wife remains at home and takes responsibility for the domestic aspects of marital life, and "modern" ones where employment outside the home is pursued. Perhaps in recognition that, as Judge Rosalie S. Abella (now J.A.) wrote in "Economic Adjustment On Marriage Breakdown: Support" (1981), 4 *Fam. L. Rev.* 1, at p. 4, "[i]t is hard to be an independent equal when one is not equally able to become independent," courts have frequently been more amenable to finding that "traditional" marriages survive the so-called "causal connection" test than "modern" ones....

[38] There are, however, many cases which do not fall easily into either category. These cases pose difficulties for courts which attempt to make assessments based on two clear stereotypes, especially when determining the question of self-sufficiency....

[41] Given the concerns I harbour about making a spouse's entitlement to support contingent upon the degree to which he or she is able to fit within a mythological stereotype, ... the distinction between "traditional" and "modern" marriages does not seem to me to be as useful as perhaps courts have indicated so far. While it may reflect flexibility on the part of courts and constitute an attempt to achieve fairness, I am of the view that there are much more sophisticated means which may be resorted to in order to achieve the objectives set out in the Act, a matter which I will deal with later in these reasons.

[42] The second observation I wish to make is that, in determining spousal support it is important not to lose sight of the fact that the support provisions of the Act are intended to deal with the *economic* conse-

quences, for both parties, of the marriage or its breakdown. Marriage may unquestionably be a source of benefit to both parties that is not easily quantified in economic terms. Many believe that marriage and the family provide for the emotional, economic, and social well-being of its members. It may be the location of safety and comfort, and may be the place where its members have their most intimate human contact. Marriage and the family act as an emotional and economic support system as well as a forum for intimacy. In this regard, it serves vital personal interests, and may be linked to building a "comprehensive sense of personhood." Marriage and the family are a superb environment for raising and nurturing the young of our society by providing the initial environment for the development of social skills. These institutions also provide a means to pass on the values that we deem to be central to our sense of community.

[43] Conversely, marriage and the family often require the sacrifice of personal priorities by both parties in the interests of shared goals. All of these elements are of undeniable importance in shaping the overall character of a marriage. Spousal support in the context of divorce, however, is not about the emotional and social benefits of marriage. Rather, the purpose of spousal support is to relieve *economic* hardship that results from "marriage or its breakdown." Whatever the respective advantages to the parties of marriage in other areas, the focus of the inquiry when assessing spousal support after the marriage has ended must be the effect of the marriage in either impairing or improving each party's economic prospects.

[44] This approach is consistent with both modern and traditional conceptions of marriage inasmuch as marriage is, among other things, an economic unit which generates financial benefits (see M.A. Glendon, *The New Family and The New Property* (1981)). The Act reflects the fact that in today's marital relationships, partners should expect and are entitled to share those financial benefits.

[45] Equitable distribution can be achieved in many ways: by spousal and child support, by the division of property and assets or by a combination of property and support entitlements. But in many if not most cases, the absence of accumulated assets may require that one spouse pay support to the other in order to effect an equitable distribution of resources. This is precisely the case here, as the parties are not wealthy; for the most part, all they appear to possess are their respective incomes....

[47] A third point worthy of emphasis is that this analysis applies equally to both spouses, depending on how the division of labour is exercised in a particular marriage. What the Act requires is a fair and equitable distribution of resources to alleviate the economic consequences of marriage or marriage breakdown for both spouses, regardless of gender. The reality, however, is that in many if not most marriages, the wife still remains the economically disadvantaged partner. There may be times where the reverse is true and the Act is equally able to accommodate this eventuality.

[48] These caveats having been made, the question of spousal support which lies at the heart of this appeal must be dealt with first by examining the objectives of the Act....

L'Heureux-Dubé J recognized that the interpretation of sections 15 (now s 15.2) and 17 of the *Divorce Act* required a different analysis than the interpretation of sections of the previous divorce legislation, and continued:

> [51] I fully agree with Professor Payne who has commented on these objectives in *Payne on Divorce* (2nd ed., 1988), at p. 101, that:
>
>> Judicial implementation of the newly defined policy objectives should, to some degree, result *in a shift from the narrow perspective of a "needs" and "capacity to pay" approach*, particularly in cases where one of the spouses has substantial means.... In this context, it should be observed that the four policy objectives defined in the *Divorce Act, 1985* are not necessarily independent of each other. They may overlap or they may operate independently, depending upon the circumstances of the particular case. *Legislative endorsement of four policy objectives manifests the realization that the economic variables of marriage breakdown and divorce do not lend themselves to the application of any single objective.* Long-term marriages that ultimately break down often leave in their wake a condition of financial dependence, because the wives have assumed the role of full-time home-makers. The legitimate objective(s) of spousal support in such a case will rarely coincide with the objectives that should be pursued with respect to short-term marriages. Childless marriages cannot be treated in the same way as marriages with dependent children. The two-income family cannot be equated with the one-income family. A "clean break" accommodated by an order for a lump sum in lieu of periodic spousal support can often provide a workable and desirable solution for the wealthy, for the two-income family and for the childless marriages of short duration. Rehabilitative support orders by way of periodic spousal support for a fixed term may be appropriate where there is a present incapacity to pay a lump sum and the dependent spouse can reasonably be expected to enter or re-enter the labour force within the foreseeable future. *Continuing periodic spousal support orders may provide the only practical solution for dependent spouses who cannot be reasonably expected to achieve economic self-sufficiency. There can be no fixed rules,* however, whereby particular types of orders are tied to the specific objective(s) sought to be achieved. In the final analysis, the court must determine the most appropriate kind(s) of order, having regard to the attendant circumstances of the case, including the present and prospective financial well-being of both the spouses and their dependent children.... [Emphasis added.]

L'Heureux-Dubé J then addressed the goal of self-sufficiency:

> [52] All four of the objectives defined in the Act must be taken into account when spousal support is claimed or an order for spousal support is sought to be varied. No single objective is paramount. The fact that one of the objectives, such as economic self-sufficiency, has been attained does not necessarily dispose of the matter.... [T]he Act recognizes that each former spouse shall attain economic self-sufficiency, insofar as practicable, within a reasonable period of time, but it does not say that such economic self-sufficiency is the dominant consideration." ...

> [53] Many proponents of the deemed self-sufficiency model effectively elevate it to the pre-eminent objective in determining the right to quantum and duration of spousal support. In my opinion, this approach is not consonant with proper principles of statutory interpretation. The objective of self-sufficiency is only one of several objectives enumerated in the sec-

tion and, given the manner in which Parliament has set out those objectives, I see no indication that any one is to be given priority. Parliament, in my opinion, intended that support reflect the diverse dynamics of many unique marital relationships....

[54] It is also imperative to realize that the objective of self-sufficiency is tempered by the caveat that it is to be made a goal only "insofar as is practicable." This qualification militates against the kind of "sink or swim" stance upon which the deemed self-sufficiency model is premised.

[55] That Parliament could not have meant to institutionalize the ethos of deemed self-sufficiency is also apparent from an examination of the social context in which support orders are made. In Canada, the feminization of poverty is an entrenched social phenomenon. Between 1971 and 1986 the percentage of poor women found among all women in this country more than doubled. During the same period the percentage of poor among all men climbed by 24 percent. The results were such that by 1986, 16 percent of all women in this country were considered poor: M. Gunderson, L. Muszynski, and J. Keck, *Women and Labour Market Poverty* (1990), at p. 8.

[56] Given the multiplicity of economic barriers women face in society, decline into poverty cannot be attributed entirely to the financial burdens arising from the dissolution of marriage: J.D. Payne, "The Dichotomy Between Family Law and Family Crises on Marriage Breakdown" (1989), 20 RGD 109, at pp. 116–117. However, there is no doubt that divorce and its economic effects are playing a role....

L'Heureux-Dubé J referred to the research of Lenore Weitzman in the United States and then referred to the Department of Justice study that examined the economic impact of divorce, and the 1988 study which showed that two-thirds of divorced women had incomes below the poverty line. In this context, she stated that "It is apparent that support payments, even assuming they are paid, are making only a marginal contribution to reducing economic hardship among women following divorce," and then continued:

[62] As Lamer CJ stated in *Multiform Manufacturing Co. Ltd. et al. v. R et al.*, [1990] 2 SCR 624; 113 NR 373; 32 QAC 241, at p. 630 SCR, "[w]hen the courts are called upon to interpret a statute, their task is to discover the intention of Parliament." ...

[63] It would be perverse in the extreme to assume that Parliament's intention to enacting the Act was to financially penalize women in this country. And, while it would undeniably be simplistic to identify the deemed self-sufficiency model of spousal support as the sole cause of the female decline into poverty, based on the review of the jurisprudence and statistical data set out in these reasons, it is clear that the model has disenfranchised many women in the courtroom and countless others who may simply have decided not to request support in anticipation of their remote chances of success. The theory, therefore, at a minimum, is contributing to the problem....

[64] In the result, I am respectfully of the view that the support model of self-sufficiency which Mr. Moge urges the court to apply, cannot be supported as a matter of statutory interpretation, considering in particular the diversity of objectives set out in the Act....

L'Heureux-Dubé J then examined the concept of compensatory support:

[65] A burgeoning body of doctrine and, to some extent, jurisprudence is developing both abroad as well as in Canada which expresses dissatisfaction with the current norms along which entitlement to spousal support is assessed. This body of doctrine in particular proposes instead a scheme based on principles of compensation....

[67] The theory, however, is not new, as is evident from the Law Reform Commission Working Papers and Report, 1972–1976. Antecedents of the compensatory spousal support model may be found in portions of the Law Reform Commission of Canada's Working Paper 12, *Maintenance on Divorce* (1975). The Commission recommended, inter alia, that the mere fact of marriage not create a right of maintenance and that the economic disabilities incurred due to marriage and the eventuality of children be compensated....

[68] Legislative support for the principles of compensation may be found in ss. 15(7)(a)–(c) and 17(7)(a)–(c) which are extremely broad in scope and which direct the court, in making or varying a support order, to recognize any economic advantages or disadvantages arising from the marriage or its breakdown, to apportion between the spouses any financial consequences arising from the care of children over and above those consequences which have already been made the subject of child support and to relieve economic hardships arising from the marriage. As a matter of statutory interpretation, it is precisely the manner in which compensatory spousal support is able to respond to the diversity of objectives the Act contains that makes it superior to the strict self-sufficiency model.

[69] Although the promotion of self-sufficiency remains relevant under this view of spousal support, it does not deserve unwarranted pre-eminence. After divorce, spouses would still have an obligation to contribute to their own support in a manner commensurate with their abilities.... In cases where relatively few advantages have been conferred or disadvantages incurred, transitional support allowing for full and unimpaired reintegration back into the labour force might be all that is required to afford sufficient compensation. However, in many cases a former spouse will continue to suffer the economic disadvantages of the marriage and its dissolution while the other spouse reaps its economic advantages. In such cases compensatory spousal support would require long-term support or an alternative settlement which provides an equivalent degree of assistance in light of all of the objectives of the Act....

[70] Women have tended to suffer economic disadvantages and hardships from marriage or its breakdown because of the traditional division of labour within that institution. Historically, or at least in recent history, the contributions made by women to the marital partnership were nonmonetary and came in the form of work at home, such as taking care of the household, raising children, and so on. Today, though more and more women are working outside the home, such employment continues to play a secondary role and sacrifices continue to be made for the sake of domestic considerations. These sacrifices often impair the ability of the partner who makes them (usually the wife) to maximize her earning potential because she may tend to forego educational and career advancement opportunities. These same sacrifices may also enhance the earning potential of the other spouse (usually the husband) who, because his wife is tending to such matters, is free to pursue economic goals. This eventually may result in inequities....

[71] The curtailment of outside employment obviously has a significant impact on future earning capacity. According to some studies, the earning capacity of a woman who stays at home atrophies by 1.5 percent for each year she is out of the labour force. ... Labour force interruptions are common and this accentuates the need for compensation. One Statistics Canada report, *Family History Survey: Preliminary Findings* (1985), notes that 64 percent of Canadian women report suffering work interruptions because of parenting or domestic responsibilities. The figure for men was less than one percent (p. 26). The studies, while remaining untested, do illustrate the problems faced by women who re-enter the labour force after a period during which they stay at home to care for the family.

[72] Often difficulties are exacerbated by the enduring responsibility for children of the marriage, [citing statistics about custody for men and women].... The diminished earning capacity with which an ex-wife enters the labour force after years of reduced or nonparticipation will be even more difficult to overcome when economic choice is reduced, unlike that of her ex-husband, due to the necessity of remaining within proximity to schools, not working late, remaining at home when the child is ill, etc. The other spouse encounters none of these impediments and is generally free to live virtually wherever he wants and work whenever he wants.

[73] The doctrine of equitable sharing of the economic consequences of marriage or marriage breakdown upon its dissolution which, in my view, the Act promotes, seeks to recognize and account for both the economic disadvantages incurred by the spouse who makes such sacrifices and the economic advantages conferred upon the other spouse. Significantly, it recognizes that work within the home has undeniable value and transforms the notion of equality from the rhetorical status to which it was relegated under a deemed self-sufficiency model, to a substantive imperative. Insofar as economic circumstances permit, the Act seeks to put the remainder of the family in as close a position as possible to the household before the marriage breakdown. As Judge Abella wrote in *Economic Adjustment On Marriage Breakdown: Support*, supra, at p. 3:

> To recognize that each spouse is an equal economic and social partner in marriage, regardless of function, is a monumental revision of assumptions. It means, among other things, that caring for children is just as valuable as paying for their food and clothing. It means that organizing a household is just as important as the career that subsidizes this domestic enterprise. It means that the economics of marriage must be viewed qualitatively rather than quantitatively.

[74] The equitable sharing of the economic consequences of marriage or marriage breakdown, however, is not a general tool of redistribution which is activated by the mere fact of marriage. Nor ought it to be. It is now uncontentious in our law and accepted by both the majority and the minority in *Messier v. Delage*, supra, at pp. 416–417 SCR, that marriage per se does not automatically entitle a spouse to support....

[75] The Act refers to economic advantages and disadvantages flowing from marriage *or its breakdown*. Sections 15(7)(a) and 17(7)(c) may not be characterized as exclusively compensatory. These latter paragraphs may embrace the notion that the primary burden of spousal support should fall on family members, *not* the state. In my view, an equitable sharing of the economic consequences of divorce does not exclude other considerations, particularly when dealing with sick or disabled spouses. While the losses or disadvantages flowing from the marriage in such cases may seem minimal in the view of some, the effect of its breakdown will not, and support will still be in order in most cases. We must recognize, however, as do

Payne and Eichler, that family law can play only a limited role in alleviating the economic consequences of marriage breakdown....

[76] As economic consequences have to be shared in an equitable manner by both partners, it is my view that the Act, while envisaging compensation for the economic advantages and disadvantages of marriage or marriage breakdown, does not necessarily put the entire burden of such compensation on the shoulders of only one party. I stress here that in the discussion of spousal support one must not lose sight of the fact that the real dilemma in most cases relates to the ability to pay of the debtor spouse and the limits of support orders in achieving fair compensation and alleviating the economic burdens of the disadvantaged spouse. While the disadvantages of the kind I mention hereunder are compensable, though not necessarily automatically or fully compensated in every case, the ultimate goal is to alleviate the disadvantaged spouse's economic losses as completely as possible, taking into account all the circumstances of the parties, including the advantages conferred on the other spouse during the marriage.

[77] The four objectives set out in the Act can be viewed as an attempt to achieve an equitable sharing of the economic consequences of marriage or marriage breakdown. At the end of the day however, courts have an overriding discretion and the exercise of such discretion will depend on the particular facts of each case, having regard to the factors and objectives designated in the Act....

L'Heureux-Dubé J then examined the issue of judicial discretion in ordering spousal support and concluded that it required an examination of all four objectives set out in the Act. She also identified a need to examine the financial consequences of the end of a marriage in broad terms, including issues of loss of seniority, missed promotions, and lack of access to fringe benefits such as pension entitlements and job training programs. In addition, she expressly recognized that the most significant economic consequence of marriage or marriage breakdown arises from the birth of children and it may be necessary to compensate for care of children, both during marriage and after marriage breakdown. Quoting *Brockie v Brockie* (1987), 5 RFL (3d) 440 (Man QB (Fam Div)); aff'd (1987), 8 RFL (3d) 302 (Man CA), she stated:

> To be a custodial parent involves adoption of a lifestyle which, in ensuring the welfare and development of the child, places many limitations and burdens upon that parent. A single person can live in any part of the city, can frequently share accommodation with relatives or friends, can live in a high-rise downtown or a house in the suburbs, can do shift work, can devote spare time as well as normal work days to the development of a career, can attend night school, and in general can live as and where he or she finds convenient. A custodial parent, on the other hand, seldom finds friends or relatives who are anxious to share accommodation, must search long and carefully for accommodation suited to the needs of the young child, including play space, closeness to day care, schools and recreational facilities, if finances do not permit ownership of a motor vehicle, then closeness to public transportation and shopping facilities is important. A custodial parent is seldom free to accept shift work, is restricted in any overtime work by the day care arrangements available, and must be prepared to give priority to the needs of a sick child over the demands of an employer. After a full day's

work, the custodial parent faces a full range of homemaking responsibilities including cooking, cleaning and laundry, as well as the demands of the child himself for the parent's attention. Few indeed are the custodial parents with strength and endurance to meet all of these demands and still find time for night courses, career improvement or even a modest social life. The financial consequences of all of these limitations and demands arising from the custody of the child are in addition to the direct costs of raising the child, and are, I believe, the factors to which the court is to give consideration....

[84] Although the doctrine of spousal support which focuses on equitable sharing does not guarantee to either party the standard of living enjoyed during the marriage, this standard is far from irrelevant to support entitlement.... Furthermore, great disparities in the standard of living that would be experienced by spouses in the absence of support are often a revealing indication of the economic disadvantages inherent in the role assumed by one party. As marriage should be regarded as a joint endeavour, the longer the relationship endures, the closer the economic union, the greater will be the presumptive claim to equal standards of living upon its dissolution....

[85] In short, in the proper exercise of their discretion, courts must be alert to a wide variety of factors and decisions made in the family interest during the marriage which have the effect of disadvantaging one spouse or benefitting the other upon its dissolution. In my view, this is what the Act mandates, no more, no less.

[86] Such determination demands a complex and, in many cases, a difficult analysis. The same, of course, might be said of the evaluation of damages in contract or in tort. However, this complexity does not excuse judges from hearing relevant evidence nor from fully applying the law....

L'Heureux-Dubé J then considered the evidentiary requirements and suggested that the Court could take judicial notice of the economic consequences of marriage breakdown:

[87] Given the principles outlined above, spousal support orders remain essentially a function of the evidence led in each particular case. In some cases, such evidence might come in the form of highly specific expert evidence which enables parties to present an accurate picture of the economic consequences of marriage breakdown in their particular circumstances.... Although of great assistance in assessing the economic consequences of marriage breakdown in a particular marriage, such evidence will not be required nor will it be possible in most cases. For most divorcing couples, both the cost of obtaining such evidence and the amount of assets involved are practical considerations which would prohibit or at least discourage its use. Therefore, to require expert evidence as a sine qua non to the recovery of compensation would not be practical for many parties, not to mention the use of court time which might be involved. It would be my hope, therefore, that different alternatives be examined....

After considering some other possibilities, she stated:

[90] The doctrine [of judicial notice] itself grew from a need to promote efficiency in the litigation process and may very well be applicable to spousal support....

[91] Based upon the studies which I have cited earlier in these reasons, the general economic impact of divorce on women is a phenomenon the existence of which cannot reasonably be questioned and should be amenable to judicial notice. More extensive social science data are also appearing. Such studies are beginning to provide reasonable assessments of some of the disadvantages incurred and advantages conferred post-divorce.... While quantification will remain difficult and fact-related in each particular case, judicial notice should be taken of such studies, subject to other expert evidence which may bear on them, as background information at the very least....

[92] In all events, whether judicial notice of the circumstances generally encountered by spouses at the dissolution of a marriage is to be a formal part of the trial process or whether such circumstances merely provide the necessary background information, it is important that judges be aware of the social reality in which support decisions are experienced when engaging in the examination of the objectives of the Act....

L'Heureux-Dubé J then applied these principles to the facts in *Moge*:

[94] Since this appeal involves an application for a variation order, here an order for the termination of support by Mr. Moge to Mrs. Moge, s. 17(4) of the Act applies.

[95] As a necessary preliminary condition to making such an order, s. 17(4) of the Act requires that the court be satisfied that "there has been a change in the condition, means, needs or other circumstances for either former spouse ... for whom support is or was sought occurring since the making of the support order or the last variation order or the last variation order made in respect of that order."

[96] That there has been a change in the circumstances of the parties since the last support order was not seriously contested and I agree with both the trial judge and the Court of Appeal that the threshold requirements of s. 17(4) of the Act are satisfied.

[97] The sole remaining consideration is whether the application of Mr. Moge to terminate support ought to have been granted in this case. In my view, it should not have, and the majority of the Court of Appeal was right in finding an error of principle on the part of the trial judge....

[98] The four objectives of spousal support orders under s. 17(7) of the Act, as explicated above and applied by the Court of Appeal, are met in this case. For this reason, the following specific findings are in order based on the evidence in the record:
1. Mrs. Moge has sustained a substantial economic disadvantage "from the marriage or its breakdown" within the meaning of s. 17(7)(a) of the Act.
2. Mrs. Moge's long-term responsibility for the upbringing of the children of the marriage after the spousal separation in 1973 has had an impact on her ability to earn an income so as to trigger the application of s. 17(7)(b) of the Act.
3. Mrs. Moge continues to suffer economic hardship as a result of the "breakdown of the marriage" within the meaning of s. 17(7)(c) of the Act.
4. Mrs. Moge has failed to become economically self-sufficient notwithstanding her conscientious efforts.

[99] These findings are irrefutable even in the absence of expert evidence relating to the appropriate quantification of spousal support. It follows that in view of all of the objectives of spousal support orders set out in s. 17(7) of the Act, continuing support is in order in this case. Accordingly, there was no error in the Court of Appeal....

McLachlin J agreed with L'Heureux-Dubé J as to the outcome of the appeal, but commented in some detail on the statutory provisions, emphasizing that the case was "first and last a case of statutory interpretation." Thus, she stated (at 879):

[107] Considering the factors together, the judge's task under s. 17(7) of the statute is to make an order which provides compensation for marital contributions and sacrifices, which takes into account financial consequences of looking after children of the marriage, which relieves against need induced by the separation, and, to the extent it may be "practicable," promotes the economic self-sufficiency of each spouse.... The judge must base her decision on a number of factors: compensation; child-care; post-separation need; and the goal, insofar as practicable, of promoting self-sufficiency.

[108] The need to consider all four factors set out in s. 17(7) rules out the strict self-sufficiency model which Mr. Moge urged upon this court. The trial judge erred, in my respectful opinion, in giving no weight to the first three factors of s. 17(7) and in imposing a categorical requirement of self-sufficiency.

Appeal dismissed.

Notes and Questions

The significance of *Moge* and compensatory support

The decision of the Supreme Court in *Moge v Moge* was recognized as creating a shift in the law of spousal support. For example, one comment stated:

> *Moge* confirms what clients have been telling counsel for years: women remain the more economically disadvantaged partner after marriage breakdown. It thoroughly and accurately discusses the economic impact of marriage and divorce, and why women are plagued by financial difficulties after a separation or divorce.
>
> It would be "perverse in the extreme" to think that seven members of the Supreme Court of Canada would spend eight months writing a unanimous ... decision about a $150 per month support case from Winnipeg if they did not intend to set a new standard of spousal support for the profession and the courts. (Ronald S Foster, "*Moge v. Moge*: What It Means to Family Law Lawyers" (1993) 43 RFL (3d) 465 at 465)

At the same time, some commentators recognized that such decisions about entitlement to spousal support must inevitably focus too narrowly to address many of the issues facing vulnerable spouses post-separation or divorce. In reflecting on this comment, consider the extent to which the absence of state initiatives means that "private" spousal support cannot overcome the feminization of poverty.

Uncomfortable Victories and Unanswered Questions:
Lessons from *Moge*
(1995) 12 Can J Fam L 283 at 328

Colleen Sheppard

The *Moge* case represents an important victory for women to the extent that it acknowledges the actual economic disadvantages created by the gendered division of labour within the family.... To the extent that *Moge* symbolizes recognition by the Supreme Court of Canada of the way in which the unequal division of labour within the family contributes to the feminization of poverty, its impact has extended beyond the domain of spousal support law....

And yet, while responding to some concerns, the Court's analysis generates others.... [A]s the post-*Moge* cases confirm, there remains considerable uncertainty about how to assess fair compensation for the economic consequences of marriage. The dilemma of discretion and malleable legal standards also persists in the legal regulation of spousal support. In addition, *Moge* risks reinforcing the tradition of privatization as the norm of familial economic well-being rather than moving us toward a more public and collective approach to individual economic security.

More troubling than the perhaps inevitable persistence of legal uncertainty, is the silence on the larger context of women's economic vulnerability. The *Moge* case does not address social factors beyond marriage that help to account for Zofia Moge's current economic needs. It does not deal with gender, race, ethnic origin, or language discrimination in the labour force. It does not mention patterns of familial dependence reinforced by immigration law and policy. Nor does it touch upon the absence of affordable and accessible child care or social assistance programs. The litigation model often overlooks the larger systemic dimensions of the issues being adjudicated. But these dimensions matter deeply to anyone concerned about the feminization of poverty and the importance of ensuring that women are provided with fairness, justice, and access to economic security that is not dependent on the resources of individual male spouses. Thus, despite the lengthy discussion of the underlying philosophy of spousal support by L'Heureux-Dubé J., the larger questions of the social context of Zofia Moge's economic insecurity remain beyond the realm of the court debate. Relegated beyond the margins, they should be occupying the centre of public debate about economic rights and family roles.

Spousal support orders in the courts post-*Moge*
Carol Rogerson undertook an assessment of spousal support orders in Canada in the years following the *Moge* decision. According to her analysis, the concept of compensatory spousal support was increasingly embraced in the context of "privatization" policies that shifted primary responsibility for dependency from the state to the family. To what extent does this analysis suggest a need for courts to take account of systemic issues concerning family economies?

Spousal Support After *Moge*
(1997) 14 Can Fam LQ 281 at 385–387

Carol Rogerson

The landscape of spousal support post-*Moge* is both radically transformed and strikingly familiar. *Moge* has clearly reversed the trend toward minimalist spousal support awards that took hold with the first wave of modern family law reform. Spousal support awards post-*Moge* are more generous than they were in the past: more spouses are entitled to support and awards are, in general, for longer periods of time and higher amounts. Women who have remained out of the labour force for significant periods of time during marriage can now expect judicial recognition of the long-term economic consequences they will carry with them after marriage breakdown.

Yet from another perspective the current landscape of spousal support is a familiar one. Despite the gloss of a compensatory analysis, the expanded role of spousal support post-*Moge* appears to be driven, in large part, by a concern with responding to post-divorce need and preventing post-divorce poverty, rather than by principles of providing fair compensation to women for their unpaid labour in the home and providing for the equitable sharing between the spouses of the economic consequences of the marriage. Although there are exceptions, many lawyers and judges continue to feel more comfortable with a traditional understanding of spousal support as a private scheme of income security rather than with a compensatory model, and continue to rely upon the conventional concept of need (and its corollary, self-sufficiency) to structure and give content to the compensatory principle. As a result, it is those spouses who demonstrate the greatest economic need and who will experience the greatest economic hardship after marriage breakdown — whether by reason of age, illness, lack of skills, or a poor economy — who are viewed as the most sympathetic candidates for spousal support, while those who have youth, good health, and employability in their favour are seen as self-sufficient economic actors, despite their past and on-going responsibilities for the care of children. [In this context, the "radical message of *Moge* about women's entitlement to compensation for their work in the home may be diluted....]

From a broad political perspective, it is no surprise that the compensatory message of *Moge* is being subtly reshaped into a message of the obligation of the family members to provide for each other's economic needs. In a period of diminishing public resources and a recessionary economy, the family has re-emerged as a central economic institution and a locus of economic security for vulnerable citizens. Our political language of rights and entitlements is being replaced with the language of obligations and responsibilities, with particular emphasis on the obligations of family members to care for each other. The fact that many citizens in need have no family resources to draw upon is lost from sight, as is the fact that it is women who will assume responsibility for many of the caring functions being delegated to the family, but whose claims of entitlement to compensation for their work are being delegitimated.

Following *Moge*, a number of judicial decisions probed the continued applicability of the principles in *Pelech*. For some examples, see *G(L) v*

B(G) (1995), 15 RFL (4th) 201 (SCC); *Wilkinson v Wilkinson* (1998), 43 RFL (4th) 258 (Alta QB); and *Bailey v Plaxton* (2000), 6 RFL (5th) 29 (Ont Sup Ct). This issue about the role for *Pelech* was finally resolved by the Supreme Court of Canada in *Miglin v Miglin* in 2003, discussed later in this chapter.

Moge and gender equality in spousal support orders

The application of the *Moge* principles was considered in a few cases in which a former husband sought spousal support from his former wife. Consider the application of the *Moge* principles in these cases.

Hough v Hough
(1996), 25 RFL (4th) 319 (Ont Gen Div)

In this case, the parties had married in 1974, each for the second time. At the time of the marriage, Mr. Hough was president of Canadian Sports Network and a vice president for McLaren Advertising. He was prominent in the sports broadcasting industry and had associations with many prominent and wealthy people. At the time of the separation, however, Mr. Hough was retired from the Molson Group of Companies, where he had been employed as a vice president. His retirement income from all sources was approximately $81,000 a year.

At the time of the marriage, Mrs. Hough was a stockbroker and, at separation, she was a commissioned salesperson and a director and vice president of Scotia McLeod. Although she was over 65 at the time of the trial, she did not intend to retire and hoped to work at least two more years. Her commission income from her employment was approximately $510,000, and she received an additional $780 per month in Canada Pension Plan (CPP) and old age security (OAS).

The parties disagreed about a number of matters. For example, Mr. Hough claimed that it was through his contacts with wealthy individuals that Mrs. Hough was able to be so successful and have such a broad clientele. However, Mrs. Hough disputed this, and it was not accepted by the court. The court found that during their 21 years of marriage, the parties had pooled their resources and that, during the last decade, Mrs. Hough had earned substantially more income than Mr. Hough. Mrs. Hough gave evidence that she was in charge of earning income, and that Mr. Hough was in charge of spending it.

At the time of trial, the parties' net family property had been equalized, and each had received assets valued at approximately $1.3 million. The only remaining issue was spousal support.

Mr. Hough was claiming monthly support from Mrs. Hough so that he could meet his proposed budget of $120,000 per year. Mr. Hough asserted that his proposed budget would approximate the standard of living that he had experienced before separation, and that it would be an economic hardship if he were forced to live on his existing income without receiving support from Mrs. Hough. At the time of the trial, Mr. Hough was sharing his home with his 24-year-old grandson who was employed, but did not pay rent. Mr. Hough stated that his grandson lived with him in order to provide him with companionship and to help care for a pet.

Mrs. Hough argued that no spousal support should be paid and that the parties should go their separate ways in every respect.

In deciding to award Mr. Hough time-limited spousal support, Mac-Donald J stated (at 325):

> I was urged during argument to follow *Moge v. Moge*.... One of the results of this decision is that courts have moved away from the clean break model of support which was popular prior to the 1985 amendments to the *Divorce Act*. After *Moge*, support is viewed as essentially compensatory in nature which is awarded to compensate a spouse for economic disadvantage flowing from the roles adopted in the marriage or the breakdown of the marriage. Beyond that, *Moge* is of little assistance to me because the background and circumstances of Mr. and Mrs. Moge are so vastly different from those of Mr. and Mrs. Hough. It is for this reason that the other cases, to which I was referred, are also of little assistance....
>
> It is clear that Mr. Hough suffered no economic disadvantage as a result of the marriage. Now that the marriage is over, the court must look at whether the court should relieve against the economic disadvantage that Mr. Hough faces by reason of the fact that he is now separated from and about to be divorced from Mrs. Hough who earns unusually high income.

Ms. DeMarco referred me to the following extract from *Moge* which appears at p. 490:

> The equitable sharing of the economic consequences of marriage or marriage breakdown, however, is not a general tool of redistribution which is activated by the mere fact of marriage. Nor ought it to be. It is now uncontentious in our law and accepted by both the majority and the minority in *Messier v. Delage*, supra, at pp. 13–14, that marriage *per se* does not automatically entitle a spouse to support. Presumably, there will be the occasional marriage where both spouses maximize their earning potential by working outside the home, pursuing economic and educational opportunities in a similar manner, dividing up the domestic labour identically, and either making no economic sacrifices for the other or, more likely, making them equally. *In such a Utopian scenario there might be no apparent call for compensation. The spouses are able to make a clean break and continue on with their respective lives. Such cases would appear to be rare.* [Emphasis added.]

Ms. DeMarco focused on the emphasized portion above and urged me to consider that while such cases are rare, they are not *non-existent* and that *this case* is one of those rare cases. On this analysis, Ms. DeMarco urged me not to award support to Mr. Hough....

Section 15(7)(d) directs the court to promote the economic self-sufficiency of each spouse within a *reasonable* period of time *insofar as is practicable*. In my view, it is not reasonable for Mr. Hough, given his age, to adhere to the notion that he will not sell his condominium given its large equity. He is, however, at liberty to make these choices but it is not reasonable for him to visit the consequences of these choices upon Mrs. Hough. Similarly, it is not reasonable for him to say that one of the reasons for his investment strategy is that he wishes to preserve an estate for his children from his first marriage. This is, of course, a natural objective of a parent but Mr. Hough cannot visit the consequences of this objective upon Mrs. Hough who is legally entitled to expect that Mr. Hough will maximize his own resources to support himself.

Having made these findings, I return to the lifestyle issue. Although not explicitly expressed in the statute, it is in my view implied in s. 15(5) [now section 15.2(4)] by the words the condition means, and needs "and other circumstances of each spouse." These words give the court a wide discretion under ... the Act....

I am fixing support at $5,000 per month for 2 years; the first payment is to be made on November 1, 1996; thereafter Mrs. Hough's support obligation will be $2,500 for another twelve-month period. I consider that the applicable objectives of [the *Act*] can be met within the 3-year period. At the end of the 3-year period, Mrs. Hough will not have a support obligation.

Is *Hough* consistent with the reasoning in *Moge*, having regard to the differences based on the gender of the payor spouse and the relative wealth of the parties? Why, or why not?

Consider this situation:

The spouses separated after 28 years of marriage. Both had been employed during marriage, but the husband lost his full-time employment after separation. Although he then obtained part-time work, he was not likely to obtain full-time work without retraining. However, he suffered from learning disabilities that made retraining difficult. Is the husband entitled to spousal support?

In *Nock v Nock* (1998), 43 RFL (4th) 110 (Ont Gen Div), the court awarded spousal support of $400 per month for 18 months, relying on the language of *Moge* that

the four objectives set out in the Act can be viewed as an attempt to achieve an equitable sharing of the economic consequences of marriage or marriage breakdown. At the end of the day, however, courts have an overriding discretion and the exercise of such discretion will depend on the particular facts of each case, having regard to the factors and objectives designated in the Act.

In exercising this discretion, the court stated:

[12] It is clear that the court's discretion must be in relation to both the factors and the objectives of section 15.2. It is also clear that the court must be ultimately satisfied that, but for the breakdown of the marriage, the ensuing consequence faced by the claimant spouse would not have occurred. Applying the factors of that section to this case, Mr. and Mrs. Nock were married for twenty eight years, were both fully employed, and performed similar functions within the marriage in respect to both employment and family obligations. Within the context of the objectives of section 15.2, Mr. Nock had a significant disability while he was married, the effects of which caused him no disadvantage as long as he was fully employed. However, it should have been apparent to both parties that should Mr. Nock lose his employment the significant impairment of his learning skills in the job market would present him with a formidable disadvantage in the job market. Had Mr. Nock lost his employment dur-

ing his marriage he would have been able to rely on the income stream of his spouse for his living expenses until he was able to achieve employability with the tutorial assistance that he required. Because he cannot access that financial resource due to his separation from Mrs. Nock, I find that he has sustained an economic hardship which flows directly from the breakdown of the marriage.

To what extent is this decision consistent with *Moge*? Do these cases suggest that, in addition to focusing on compensatory support, *Moge* may also have introduced more gender equality into assessments of the disadvantages of marriage breakdown? To what extent do cases such as *Hough* and *Nock* reflect principles of need or equality, as well as compensation, in relation to spousal support entitlement?

Compensatory support and provincial legislation: *Keast v Keast*

As discussed in Chapter Six, the issue about sharing professional degrees was resolved in a number of cases by means of an award of compensatory support, particularly pursuant to section 33(9)(j) of Ontario's *Family Law Act*.

In an early case about professional degrees, *Keast v Keast* (1986), 1 RFL (3d) 401 (Ont Dist Ct), the wife had worked as a nurse to support her husband when he decided to forgo his job as a secondary school teacher to train as a physician. She had also maintained their family home in London while he attended medical school in Kingston, and she also looked after their two children. A few years later, the couple separated and Mrs. Keast was unemployed and then on welfare by reason of a breakdown in her physical and mental health. By the time of the trial, the judge concluded that Mrs. Keast would be able to work, but probably only on a reduced hours basis and in a less stressful environment than a public hospital.

In this context, Killeen J held:

> I am persuaded that Mrs. Keast should have a support order and one which not only embraces her basic needs, based on her accustomed standard of living before her husband's career change in 1981, but one which recognizes her very real physical, psychological and financial sacrifices and contributions to the realization by her husband of his dream and efforts to become a doctor.

Moreover, having regard to the likelihood that Mrs. Keast would not obtain employment as a nurse for at least a year or so, the fact that she would continue to experience uncertain health, her substantial financial contribution to her husband's career change (during a period of deteriorating health), and the potential for substantial increases in earnings for Dr. Keast, Killeen J ordered support as follows (at 410):

> $600 monthly in permanent support for life; and

> "a quasi-restitutionary or compensatory support sum ... [for] her contributions to Dr. Keast's career potential, fixed at $1,000 monthly but commencing in 1990 and continuing for ten years thereafter."

Killeen J also decided the case of *Linton v Linton* (1988), 11 RFL (3d) 444 (Ont HC), and his approach to professional degrees (using compensatory support rather than property provisions) was subsequently confirmed by the Ontario Court of Appeal in *Linton* and in *Caratun v Caratun*, discussed in Chapter Six.

Additional Resources

Nicholas Bala, "Recognizing Spousal Contributions to the Acquisition of Degrees, Licences, and Other Career Assets: Toward Compensatory Support" (1989) 8 Can J Fam L 23.

Alison Diduck & Helena Orton, "Equality and Support for Spouses" (1994) 57 Mod L Rev 681.

Susan Drummond, "Judicial Notice: The Very Texture of Legal Reasoning" (2000) 15:1 CJLS 1.

Miriam Grassby, "Spousal Support — Assumptions and Myths versus Case Law" (1994–1995) 12 Can Fam LQ 187.

Hon Claire L'Heureux-Dubé, "Re-examining the Doctrine of Judicial Notice in the Family Law Context" (1994) 26 Ottawa L Rev 551.

James McLeod, "Case Comment: *Moge v. Moge*" (1993) 43 RFL (3d) 455.

Julien Payne, "An Overview of Theory and Reality in the Judicial Disposition of Spousal Support Claims Under the Canadian Divorce Act" (2000) 63 Sask L Rev 403.

BEYOND COMPENSATION: EXPANDING THE RATIONALE FOR SPOUSAL SUPPORT OBLIGATIONS

Non-compensatory support: Rethinking responsibilities of families and the state

The objectives for spousal support in section 15.2(6) of the *Divorce Act* identify a variety of circumstances in which such support may be ordered. This breadth of objectives is also coupled with a wide scope for the exercise of judicial discretion, features that were emphasized in *Moge v Moge* and in a number of subsequent lower court decisions.

In this context, the Supreme Court of Canada again considered the basis for entitlement to spousal support pursuant to the *Divorce Act* in *Bracklow v Bracklow* in 1999. In *Bracklow*, there was little basis for awarding compensatory spousal support, but Mrs. Bracklow clearly remained economically vulnerable after her marriage ended. In reviewing the Court's reasoning, consider how the context for Mrs. Bracklow created a need to fashion the principle of "non-compensatory" support, payable by a former spouse. To what extent does *Bracklow* seem to absolve the state of any responsibility for dependency (by contrast with the reasoning in *Messier* and *Pelech*)?

Bracklow v Bracklow
[1999] SCR 420

The parties were married in December 1989 after cohabiting for four years. During the first two years of their relationship, the appellant (Mrs. Bracklow) paid two-thirds of the household expenses because she was earning more money than the respondent, and because her two children from a previous marriage were living with them. After 1987, however, they shared the household expenses equally, a pattern that continued while the appellant was working. However, when Mrs. Bracklow became unemployed, the respondent financed the family's expenses.

The appellant had experienced various health problems from the beginning of the spousal relationship and in 1991, she was admitted to hospital suffering from psychiatric problems. She had not worked since that time, and it seemed unlikely that she would ever work again. Except for periods when the appellant was too ill, the parties divided household chores equally.

The spouses separated in 1992 and were divorced in 1995. The respondent remarried and his new wife was employed. The appellant obtained an interim spousal support order of $275 per month, increasing to $400 per month on 15 May 1994. She also received $787 monthly in disability benefits.

At trial, the judge held that no economic hardship befell the appellant as a consequence of the marriage or its breakdown. Nor were her health problems due to the marriage. He also found that there was no express or implied agreement between the parties that they were responsible for each other's support. Thus, the trial judge concluded that the appellant was not entitled to support from the respondent. However, based on the respondent's offer, he ordered payments of $400 per month to continue until September 1996, "a decision based upon the [respondent's] proposal not upon the necessity of law." The Court of Appeal affirmed the decision.

In the Supreme Court of Canada, the court allowed the appeal and remitted to the trial judge the issue of the amount and duration of support for the wife on the basis that she was legally eligible for post-marital support.

McLACHLIN J (for the court):

[1] What duty does a healthy spouse owe a sick one when the marriage collapses? It is now well-settled law that spouses must compensate each other for forgone careers and missed opportunities during the marriage upon the breakdown of their union. But what happens when a divorce — through no consequence of sacrifices, but simply through economic hardship — leaves one former spouse self-sufficient and the other, perhaps due to the onset of a debilitating illness, incapable of self-support? Must the healthy spouse continue to support the sick spouse? Or can he or she move on, free of obligation? That is the question posed by this appeal. It is a difficult issue. It is also an important issue, given the trend in our society toward shorter marriages and successive relationships....

McLachlin J reviewed the facts in the case and set out the relevant sections of the B.C. legislation and sections 15.2(1), (4), and (6) of the federal *Divorce Act*. She then reported the decisions of the trial judge and the B.C. Court of Appeal, both of which had confirmed that Mr. Bracklow "owed his wife no obligation of support." The Court of Appeal had also confirmed the trial judge's conclusion that there was no "causal connection" between the economic disadvantage and the marriage breakdown, and his finding of fact that the parties had no express or implied agreement that one would be responsible for the other's support. The trial judge also expressly decided that the marriage vow to support one another in sickness or in health carried no legal significance.

McLachlin J stated that the issue was whether a spouse has an obligation to support a former spouse over and above compensation for loss incurred as a result of the marriage and its breakdown (or to fulfill contractual support obligations). She answered "yes" to this question:

> [15] The lower courts implicitly assumed that, absent a contractual agreement for post-marital assistance, entitlement to support could only be founded on compensatory principles, i.e., reimbursement of the spouse for opportunities forgone or hardships accrued as a result of the marriage. I conclude, however, that the law recognizes three conceptual grounds for entitlement to spousal support: (1) compensatory; (2) contractual; and (3) non-compensatory. These three bases of support flow from the controlling statutory provisions and the relevant case law, and are more broadly animated by differing philosophies and theories of marriage and marital breakdown....

McLachlin J reviewed the history of spousal support obligations in Canada, including the trend to equality in marriage obligations, now reflected in both provincial and federal legislation. However, she concluded that the new legislation "did not entirely supplant the traditional obligations to support."

> [18] Legal equality did not translate into actual or substantive equality, and in its absence, one spouse might still be obliged to support the other. Accordingly, the *Divorce Acts* of 1968 and 1986 and provincial family support and property legislation recognized that in many circumstances one spouse might still be required to provide support for the other upon marriage breakup. The new philosophy of spousal equality brought to the fore the idea that parties' agreements on support should influence their rights and obligations during the marriage and upon its breakup, as well as the idea that to compensate a spouse for his or her contributions to the marriage or for sacrifices made or hardships suffered as a result of the marriage. Contractual support obligations, while not new, were given new emphasis by statutory stipulations that the courts take into account support agreements, express or implied, between the parties. The propriety of compensatory support was recognized by this Court in *Moge*, supra, as flowing from the 1986 *Divorce Act*. While a few cases prior to *Moge* had acknowledged that support criteria extended beyond needs and capacity to pay, the reasons of L'Heureux-Dubé J. in *Moge* offered the first comprehensive articulation of the view that when a marriage ends, spouses are entitled to be compensated for contributions to the marriage and for losses sustained as a consequence of the marriage. The same reasons, however, made it clear that compensatory considerations were not the only basis for support. Judges must exercise their discretion in light of the objectives of spousal orders as set out in s. 15.2(6), and after having considered all the factors set out in s. 15.2(4) of the *Divorce Act*. By directing

that the judge consider factors like need and ability to pay (as explored below), the new *Divorce Act* left in place the possibility of non-compensatory, non-contractual support....

[19] In analysing the respective obligations of husbands and wives, it is critical to distinguish between the roles of the spouses during marriage and the different roles that are assumed upon marriage breakdown.

[20] To begin, when two spouses are married, they owe each other a mutual duty of support: 1986 *Divorce Act*. Marriage, as this Court has said, is a joint endeavour: *Moge*, supra, at p. 870. The default presumption of this socio-economic partnership is mutuality and interdependence. This comports with the statutes and with the reasonable expectations of Canadian society. Thus the *Family Relations Act* states: "A spouse is responsible and liable for the support and maintenance of the other spouse ..." (s. 89(1)). Parties, of course (subject to the Act), may alter this expectation, either through explicit contracting (usually before the union is made with a prenuptial agreement), or through the unequivocal structuring of their daily affairs, to show disavowal of financial interweaving. The starting presumption, however, is of mutual support. We need not elevate to contractual status the marital vows of support "in sickness and health, till death do us part" to conclude that, absent indications to the contrary, marriages are generally premised on obligations and expectations of mutual and co-equal support.

[21] When a marriage breaks down, however, the situation changes. The presumption of mutual support that existed during the marriage no longer applies. Such a presumption would be incompatible with the diverse post-marital scenarios that may arise in modern society and the liberty many claim to start their lives anew after marriage breakdown. This is reflected in the *Divorce Act* and the provincial support statutes, which require the court to determine issues of support by reference to a variety of objectives and factors.

[22] The reason that a general presumption of post-marital support would be inappropriate is the presence in the latter half of our century of two "competing" theories of marriage and post-marital obligation [citing Rogerson].

[23] The first theory of marriage and post-marital obligation is the "basic social obligation" model, in which primary responsibility falls on the former spouse to provide for his or her ex-partner, rather than on the government. This model is founded on the historical notion that marriage is a potentially permanent obligation (although it revises the archaic concept of the wife's loss of identity with the voluntary secession of autonomy of two, co-equal actors as the basis for the ongoing duty). The payment corollary of this theory has been referred to as the "income replacement model," because the primary purpose of alimony payments, under the basic social obligation model, is to replace lost income that the spouse used to enjoy as a partner to the marriage union. The advocates of this theory vary in degree of fidelity. For example, some espouse permanent and indefinite support under this model. Others argue that the goal should be not just to meet the dependent spouse's post-marital needs, but to elevate him or her as closely as possible to the standard of living enjoyed during the marriage. Yet others, like Rogerson, contend that the social obligation entitlement to spousal support need not translate into a permanent obligation.

[24] At the other end of the spectrum lies what may be termed the "independent" model of marriage. This model sees each party to a marriage as an autonomous actor who retains his or her economic independence

throughout marriage. The parties, while they "formally" commit to each other for life at the time of their vows, regard themselves as free agents in an enterprise that can terminate on the unilateral action of either party. The theory of spousal support that complements this model is the "clean-break" theory, in which a former spouse, having compensated in a restitutionary sense any economic costs of the marriage on the other spouse, moves on with his or her life, possibly to enter into more such relationships. Again, the proponents vary in their degree of allegiance. Some prefer to characterize the clean-break model as encompassing "transitional support," in addition to straight restitution, due to the general dislocation costs of unwinding the partnership.

[25] The independent, clean-break model of marriage provides the theoretical basis for compensatory spousal support. The basic social obligation model equally undergirds what may be called "non-compensatory" support. Both models of marriage and their corresponding theories of spousal support permit individual variation by contract, and hence provide a third basis for a legal entitlement to support.

[26] These two theories (and I recognize that I paint with broad strokes, creating these two anchors for sake of simplicity) represent markedly divergent philosophies, values, and legal principles.

[27] The mutual obligation model of marriage stresses the interdependence that marriage creates. The clean-break model stresses the independence of each party to the union. The problem with applying either model exclusively and stringently is that marriages may fit neither model (or both models). Many modern marriages are a complex mix of interdependence and independence, and the myriad of legislative provisions and objectives discussed below speak varyingly to both models. As *Payne on Divorce* (4th ed., 1996), at pp. 269–70, puts it, "The economic variables of marriage breakdown and divorce do not lend themselves to the application of any single objective."

[28] The independent, clean-break model of marriage and marriage breakdown reflects a number of important policies. First, it is based on the widely accepted modern value of the equality and independence of both spouses. Second, it encourages rehabilitation and self-maximization of dependent spouses. Third, through its acceptance of a clean break terminating support obligations, it recognizes the social reality of shorter marriages and successive relationships.

[29] These values and policies support the compensatory theory of support (and, to some extent, the contractual theory as well). The basic premise of contractual and compensatory support is that the parties are equal. As such, when the relationship ends, the parties are entitled to what they would receive in the commercial world — what the individuals contracted for and what they have lost due to the marriage, and its breakdown. Insofar as marriage may have created dependencies, it is the duty of dependent spouses to strive to free themselves from their dependencies and to assume full self-sufficiency, thereby mitigating the need for continued compensation.

[30] The mutual obligation theory of marriage and divorce, by contrast, posits marriage as a union that creates interdependencies that cannot be easily unravelled. These interdependencies in turn create expectations and obligations that the law recognizes and enforces. While historically rooted in a concept of marriage that saw one spouse as powerful and the other as dependent, in its modern version the mutual obligation theory of marriage acknowledges the theoretical and legal independence of each spouse, but equally the interdependence of two co-equals. It postulates each of

the parties to the marriage agreeing, as independent individuals, to marriage and all that it entails — including the potential obligation of mutual support. The resultant loss of individual autonomy does not violate the premise of equality, because the autonomy is voluntarily ceded. At the same time, the mutual obligation model recognizes that actual independence may be a different thing from theoretical independence, and that a mutual obligation of support may arise and continue absent contractual or compensatory indicators.

[31] The mutual obligation view of marriage also serves certain policy ends and social values. First, it recognizes the reality that when people cohabit over a period of time in a family relationship, their affairs may become intermingled and impossible to disentangle neatly. When this happens, it is not unfair to ask the partners to continue to support each other (although perhaps not indefinitely). Second, it recognizes the artificiality of assuming that all separating couples can move cleanly from the mutual support status of marriage to the absolute independence status of single life, indicating the potential necessity to continue the primary burden of support for a needy partner who cannot attain post-marital self-sufficiency on the partners to the relationship, rather than on the state, recognizing the potential injustice of foisting a helpless former partner onto the public assistance rolls.

[32] Both the mutual obligation model and the independent, clean-break model represent important realities and address significant policy concerns and social values. The federal and provincial legislatures, through their respective statutes, have acknowledged both models. Neither theory alone is capable of achieving a just law of spousal support. The importance of the policy objectives served by both models is beyond dispute. It is critical to recognize and encourage the self-sufficiency and independence of each spouse. It is equally vital to recognize that divorced people may move on to other relationships and acquire new obligations which they may not be able to meet if they are obliged to maintain full financial burdens from previous relationships. On the other hand, it is also important to recognize that sometimes the goals of actual independence are impeded by patterns of marital dependence, that too often self-sufficiency at the time of marriage termination is an impossible aspiration, and that marriage is an economic partnership that is built upon a premise (albeit rebuttable) of mutual support. The real question in such cases is whether the state should automatically bear the costs of these realities, or whether the family, including former spouses, should be asked to contribute to the need, means permitting. Some suggest it would be better if the state automatically picked up the costs of such cases [citing Rogerson]. However, as will be seen, Parliament and the legislatures have decreed otherwise by requiring courts to consider not only compensatory factors, but the "needs" and "means" of the parties. It is not a question of either one model or the other. It is rather a matter of applying the relevant factors and striking the balance that best achieves justice in the particular case before the court.

[33] With these theories and policy concerns of marriage and marriage breakdown in mind, I turn to the pertinent statutes. They reveal the joint operation, in different provisions, of both legal paradigms, and hence the compensatory, non-compensatory, and contractual foundations for an entitlement to post-marital spousal support....

McLachlin J then turned to an examination of the B.C. *Family Relations Act* and the federal *Divorce Act*, indicating that *Moge* demonstrated the approach to interpreting these provisions. McLachlin J concluded (at para 37) that the legislative provisions "accommodate both models of marriage and marriage breakdown outlined above." She identified the provisions supporting both the compensatory and contractual bases for spousal support and concluded (at para 40) that "they do not confine the obligation to these grounds." She examined the provisions of the *FRA* and then considered the *Divorce Act*:

> [41] Section 15.2(6) of the *Divorce Act*, which sets out the objectives of support orders, also speaks to these non-compensatory factors. The first two objectives — to recognize the economic consequences of the marriage or its breakdown and to apportion between the spouses financial consequences of child care over and above child support payments — are primarily related to compensation. But the third and fourth objectives are difficult to confine to that goal. "[E]conomic hardship ... arising from the breakdown of the marriage" is capable of encompassing not only health or career disadvantages arising from the marriage breakdown properly the subject of compensation (perhaps more directly covered in s. 15.2(6)(a): see *Payne on Divorce*, supra, at pp. 251–53), but the mere fact that a person who formerly enjoyed intra-spousal entitlement to support now finds herself or himself without it. Looking only at compensation, one merely asks what loss the marriage or marriage breakup caused that would not have been suffered but for the marriage. But even where loss in this sense cannot be established, the breakup may cause economic hardship in a larger, non-compensatory sense. Such an interpretation supports the independent inclusion of s. 15.2(6)(c) as a separate consideration from s. 15.2(6)(a). Thus, Rogerson sees s. 15.2(6)(c), "the principle of compensation for the economic disadvantages of the *marriage breakdown* as distinct from the disadvantages of the marriage" as an explicit recognition of "non-compensatory" support [see "Spousal Support After Moge,"emphasis in original].
>
> [42] Similarly, the fourth objective of s. 15.2(6) of the *Divorce Act* — to promote economic self-sufficiency — may or may not be tied to compensation for disadvantages caused by the marriage or its breakup. A spouse's lack of self-sufficiency may be related to forgoing career and educational opportunities because of the marriage. But it may also arise from completely different sources, like the disappearance of the kind of work the spouse was trained to do (a career shift having nothing to do with the marriage or its breakdown) or, as in this case, ill-health.
>
> [43] In summary, nothing in the *Family Relations Act* or the *Divorce Act* suggests that the only foundations for spousal support are compensatory. Indeed, I find it difficult to confine the words of the statutes to this model. It is true that in 1986 the *Divorce Act* was amended to place greater emphasis on compensation. This represented a shift away "to some degree" from the "means and needs" approach of the 1968 Act: *Payne on Divorce*, supra, at p. 267. But while the focus of the Act may have shifted or broadened, it retains the older idea that spouses may have an obligation to meet or contribute to the needs of their former partners where they have the capacity to pay, even in the absence of a contractual or compensatory foundation for the obligation. Need alone may be enough. More broadly, the legislation can be seen as a sensitive compromise of the two competing philosophies of marriage, marriage breakdown, and spousal support....

McLachlin J then considered the jurisprudence, including *Moge* and the cases decided after it, quoting Carol Rogerson (at para 47):

The current approach is typically justified by reference, first, to *Moge*'s rejection of the applicability of the causal connection test, and second, to the fact that the spouse who is ill suffers disadvantage from the breakdown of the marriage and the loss of financial support from the other spouse.

McLachlin J also referred (at para 48) to a report of the Scottish Law Commission, and then concluded:

> **[48]** Divorce ends the marriage. Yet in some circumstances the law may require that a healthy party continue to support a disabled party, absent contractual or compensatory entitlement. Justice and considerations of fairness may demand no less.

> **[49]** In summary, the statutes and the case law suggest three conceptual bases for entitlement to spousal support: (1) compensatory, (2) contractual, and (3) non-compensatory. Marriage, as the Court held in *Moge* (at p. 870), is a "joint endeavour," a socio-economic partnership. That is the starting position. Support agreements are important (although not necessarily decisive), and so is the idea that spouses should be compensated on marriage breakdown for losses and hardships caused by the marriage. Indeed, a review of cases suggests that in most circumstances compensation now serves as the main reason for support. However, contract and compensation are not the only sources of a support obligation. The obligation may alternatively arise out of the marriage relationship itself. Where a spouse achieves economic self-sufficiency on the basis of his or her own efforts, or on an award of compensatory support, the obligation founded on the marriage relationship itself lies dormant. But where need is established that is not met on a compensatory or contractual basis, the fundamental marital obligation may play a vital role. Absent negating factors, it is available, in appropriate circumstances, to provide just support....

In considering the issue of quantum of entitlement, McLachlin J suggested (at para 50) that the issues of eligibility and quantum were connected, in the sense that "the same factors that go to entitlement have an impact on quantum." In this case, Mrs. Bracklow asserted that the court should assess her "needs" to determine quantum and that the only issue was "duration" of the payments. Mr. Bracklow argued that the length of the marital relationship was the only factor relevant to the amount of support (suggesting the length of the marriage as a "proxy" for the extent of interdependency). McLachlin J rejected both approaches:

> **[53]** Both these arguments miss the mark in that they fix on one factor to the exclusion of others. The short answer to Mrs. Bracklow's argument is that need is but one of a number of factors that the judge must consider. Similarly, the short answer to Mr. Bracklow's contention is that the length of the marital relationship is only one of a number of factors that may be relevant. While some factors may be more important than others in particular cases, the judge cannot proceed at the outset by fixing on only one variable. The quantum awarded, in the sense of both amount and duration, will vary with the circumstances and the practical and policy considerations affecting particular cases. Limited means of the supporting spouse may dictate a reduction. So may obligations arising from new relationships insofar as they have an impact on means. Factors within the marriage itself may affect the quantum of a non-compensatory support obligation. For example, it may be difficult to make a case for a full obli-

gation and expectation of mutual support in a very short marriage. (Section 15.2(4)(a) of the *Divorce Act* requires the court to consider the length of time the parties cohabited.) Finally, subject to judicial discretion, the parties by contract or conduct may enhance, diminish or negate the obligation of mutual support. To repeat, it is not the act of saying "I do," but the marital relationship between the parties that may generate the obligation of non-compensatory support pursuant to the Act. It follows that diverse aspects of that marital relationship may be relevant to the quantum of such support. As stated in *Moge*, "[a]t the end of the day…, courts have an overriding discretion and the exercise of such discretion will depend on the particular facts of each case, having regard to the factors and objectives designated in the Act" (p. 866).

[54] Fixing on one factor to the exclusion of others leads Mrs. Bracklow to an artificial distinction between amount and duration. The two interrelate: a modest support order of indefinite duration could be collapsed into a more substantial lump-sum payment. It also leads her to the false premise that if need is the basis of the entitlement to the support award, then the quantum of the award must meet the total amount of the need. It does not follow from the fact that need serves as the predicate for support that the quantum of the support must always equal the amount of the need. Nothing in either the *Family Relations Act* or the *Divorce Act* forecloses an order for support of a portion of the claimant's need, whether viewed in terms of periodic amount or duration. Need is but one factor to be considered. This is consistent with the modern recognition, captured by the statutes, of the variety of marital relationships in modern society. A spouse who becomes disabled toward the end of a very short marriage may well be entitled to support by virtue of her need, but it may be unfair, under the circumstances, to order the full payment of that need by the supporting spouse for the indefinite future.

[55] Mr. Bracklow's fixation on the length of the marital relationship leads to other difficulties. He elevates this Court's observation in *Moge* about general expectations in long-term marriages to an immutable rule constraining the factors applicable to determining quantum of support. And he introduces "morality" into the calculation of quantum. This is unnecessary, because the statutes already state what the judge should consider. It is also unhelpful, because it does not in the end explain why the length of the marital relationship should serve as the sole "moral" determinant of support, to the exclusion of need and other factors. The flexible mandate of the statutes belies such rigidity.

[56] Mr. Bracklow makes a final policy argument. In an age of multiple marriages, he asserts, the law should permit closure on relationships so parties can move on. Why, he asks, should a young person whose marriage lasts less than a year be fixed with a lifelong obligation of support? When can a former spouse finally move on, knowing that he or she cannot be drawn back into the past by an unexpected application for support?

[57] Again the answer is that under the statutes, the desirability of freedom to move on to new relationships is merely one of several objectives that might guide the judge. Since all the objectives must be balanced, it often will not be possible to satisfy one absolutely. The respondent in effect seeks a judicially created "statute of limitations" on marriage. The Court has no power to impose such a limitation, nor should it. It would inject a rigidity into the system that Parliament and the legislatures have rejected. Marriage, while it may not prove to be "till death do us part," is

a serious commitment not to be undertaken lightly. It involves the potential for lifelong obligation. There are no magical cut-off dates....

[58] The trial judge found that this was a modern marriage of two independent people; that the parties did not confirm expressly or by conduct that they owed each other an obligation of support; and that Mrs. Bracklow had suffered no disadvantage as a result of the marriage or its breakdown. There are two ways of interpreting these findings. The first is that the judge held that Mrs. Bracklow was entitled to neither contractual nor compensatory post-marital support. This fails to address the possibility of non-compensatory entitlement to support. Alternatively, the trial judge may be read as holding that because Mr. and Mrs. Bracklow had no express or implied agreement for intra-marital support, no hardship of any kind was experienced by Mrs. Bracklow on divorce, as she would have been no better off had they stayed married. To say this, however, is to deny the presumption of intra-marital support that may fairly be imputed to married couples, absent contrary indications. The trial judge — by holding that absent affirmative, proactive indications, the Bracklows shared no mutual support expectation during their marriage — turned the presumption on its head. This belies the reality that it is artificial to expect spousal couples to expressly "confirm" their mutual obligations and expectations.

[59] Refocusing the facts of this case through the correct juridical lens suggests that while the early years of the Bracklows' union might indicate the atypical partnership of strict independence (rebutting the presumption of intra-marital mutual interdependency), by the end the Bracklows had established a more interdependent relationship. In addition to adjusting their expenses to a more even ratio, it is evident that Mr. Bracklow covered Mrs. Bracklow's needs in the early stages of her illness. Accordingly, it follows that divorce did in fact render Mrs. Bracklow in a state of economic hardship, as contemplated by s. 15.2(6)(c) of the *Divorce Act*.

[60] Bearing in mind the statutory objectives of support and balancing the relevant factors, I conclude that Mrs. Bracklow is eligible for support based on the length of cohabitation, the hardship marriage breakdown imposed on her, her palpable need, and Mr. Bracklow's financial ability to pay. While the combined cohabitation and marriage of seven years were not long, neither were they (by today's standards) very short. Mrs. Bracklow contributed, when possible, as a self-sufficient member of the family, at times shouldering the brunt of the financial obligations. These factors establish that it would be unjust and contrary to the objectives of the statutes for Mrs. Bracklow to be cast aside as ineligible for support, and for Mr. Bracklow to assume none of the state's burden to care for his ex-wife.

[61] I leave the determination of the quantum of support to the trial judge, who is in a better position to address the facts of this case than our appellate tribunal. My only comment on the issue is to reiterate that all the relevant statutory factors, including the length of the marital relationship and the relative independence of the parties throughout that marital relationship, must be considered, together with the amount of support Mr. Bracklow has already paid to Mrs. Bracklow. I therefore do not exclude the possibility that no further support will be required, i.e., that Mr. Bracklow's contributions to date have discharged the just and appropriate quantum. Absent settlement between the parties, these issues are for the trial judge to resolve.

Notes and Questions

The determination of spousal support in *Bracklow*

Although the Supreme Court identified principles applicable to non-compensatory spousal support in *Bracklow*, the court remitted the assessment to a trial court in British Columbia. In the subsequent hearing, [1999] BCJ No 3028 (SC), the husband was ordered to pay $400 per month for five years. In reaching its conclusion, the court took into account Ms. Bracklow's disability and her low income as well as her inability to work, and Mr. Bracklow's improved financial circumstances and his obligations to his second wife.

In this case, the amount of spousal support was the same as that ordered at the initial trial five years earlier, although the duration was for a longer period. Each party was required to meet their own costs.

Assessing *Bracklow*'s approach to spousal support

In a comment about *Bracklow*, Carol Rogerson began by reviewing the stages for spousal support principles in Canada from the 1968 *Divorce Act* to the Supreme Court's decision in *Bracklow*, and then explained how the Supreme Court's approach in *Bracklow* had resulted in a rise in discretionary decision making with respect to spousal support.

Spousal Support Post-Bracklow: The Pendulum Swings Again?
(2001) 19 Can Fam LQ 185

Carol Rogerson

In 1983 there was *Messier v. Delage*, which directed judges to make awards that were "fit and just" on the facts before the court, a test that was generally understood as providing a fairly generous basis for spousal support, and in particular one that precluded the kind of crystal-ball gazing about future potential for self-sufficiency involved in time-limited orders. Then in 1987 there was the *Pelech* trilogy with its test of "causal connection," which narrowed the basis for spousal support and led to an increased emphasis on clean breaks and the widespread use of time-limited support orders. In 1992 the pendulum swung back in the direction of a broader basis for spousal support with the release of *Moge* and its re-conceptualization of spousal support around the idea of compensation. And now, most recently, we have *Bracklow*, with its talk of spousal support as a "basic social obligation." In terms of swings of the spousal support pendulum, *Bracklow* is generally regarded as further broadening the basis of spousal support even beyond what was accomplished by *Moge*, although as I shall argue below, I think it also carries with it some narrowing potential....

Rogerson also noted Justice McLachlin's recognition that there are no simple answers to the question of the appropriate model of spousal support because there are competing and often conflicting policy pulls that must be balanced by both legislatures and courts:

> As her judgment recognizes, on the one hand, marriage is no longer a life-long union; we allow people to divorce fairly easily and to form new relationships and commitments, suggesting that we should place some value on disentangling the spouses and promoting spousal independence after relationship breakdown. As well, we no longer subscribe to the assumption that women are inherently dependent on men for their support. On the other hand, we also know that marriage and cohabitation can create complex interdependencies that are hard to unravel; not every former spouse is going to be able to become economically self-sufficient — and certainly not easily or quickly. How to achieve an appropriate balance of these values is the issue with which the law of spousal support has been struggling for the past several decades....

Rogerson then explained how the recognition in *Bracklow* of multiple bases for spousal support, and the absence of any philosophy to guide decision making tended to discourage clear thinking about why spousal support was being awarded. In this context, she identified a number of problems post-*Bracklow*:

> To my mind, the most significant impact of *Bracklow*, as evidenced by the subsequent case law, is the Supreme Court of Canada's message that there is no one model or philosophy of spousal support and there are no fixed rules or guidelines for determining spousal support. Put simply, the message is "it's all discretion." Spousal support awards are simply the result of the trial judge exercising his or her discretion in determining the appropriate balance between different support objectives and factors in response to the facts of particular cases. This is a message that has been taken to heart by trial judges and reiterated constantly in the post-*Bracklow* case law. There is no doubt that spousal support was a highly discretionary area of law even prior to *Bracklow*. But *Moge* was a noble attempt to achieve some conceptual clarity and coherence in the face of legislation that simply offers a checklist of factors and objectives. What was needed post-*Moge* were more attempts to find patterns in the evolving case law and to work out guidelines for the implementation of amorphous concepts such as compensation and need. *Bracklow*, I fear, may impede these much-needed efforts....
>
> What gets lost when all support claims are lumped together as based on need and dependency is the sense of compensatory support as an earned entitlement, like a share of matrimonial property, based on the economic contributions that women have made to the family through their assumption of responsibility for child rearing, contributions that can be valued not only in terms of wives' foregone opportunities, but also in terms of the economic advantage conferred on husbands who have been able to devote themselves to their employment, while enjoying the benefits of children and family life. When spousal support is conceptualized as grounded only in need and in obligations arising from the fact of marriage, the legitimacy and strength of the support claim is weakened ... [and need] is an easily manipulated concept; it is very easy to find that someone who is able to cover their basic necessities or is employed has no need and is self-sufficient....

Rogerson then noted that spousal support awards were at an "all-time high," especially in Ontario, and then continued:

Even if the regressive potential of the "needs and means" analysis does not appear to be an immediate cause of concern, at least in Ontario, I would argue that *Bracklow* has still had an overall negative impact on the general law of spousal support as it deals with the vast majority of typical spousal support cases involving marriages with children in which the primary caregiver has a compromised earning capacity. This negative impact is due to the extreme emphasis in *Bracklow* on discretion and the absence of rules in determining spousal support, which deflects attention away from the important and necessary goal of trying to develop guidelines and rules to bring predictability and consistency to this area of law....

Rogerson also noted the potential for time-limited support orders post-*Bracklow*, precisely the result of the trial judge's reconsideration after the decision of the Supreme Court of Canada. In conclusion, she suggested that

[s]pousal support post-*Bracklow* is not too different a world from that of spousal support post-*Moge*. The *Bracklow* decision added very little of a concrete nature to the existing structure of spousal support law. The only clear ruling in the case was that spousal support is not exclusively compensatory in nature — a conclusion that seemed obvious and merely endorsed the dominant practice post-*Moge*. The difficult issues in spousal support are those of quantum rather than entitlement — determining the amount and duration of support — both in the atypical cases that raise pure non-compensatory claims, as well as the vast majority of ordinary spousal support cases where the compensatory aspects of spousal support loom large. *Bracklow* offered no specific guidance on these issues, with the Court even refusing to make a ruling on the appropriate quantum on the facts of *Bracklow*, and instead sending the issue back to the trial court for re-determination. The difficult issues that surfaced as the law of spousal support developed post-*Moge* remain largely the same, with *Bracklow* having provided no answers or guidance.

To what extent do you agree with this assessment of *Bracklow*?

Additional Resources

Christine Davies, "The Ever-Changing Picture of Support and Other Developments" (2002–2003) 20 Can Fam LQ 213.

Marie Gordon, "What, Me Biased? Women and Gender Bias in Family Law" (2001–2002) 19 Can Fam LQ 53.

Miriam Grassby, "Two Income Couples: Presumption of Need for the Lower Income Spouse" (2004) 20 Can J Fam L 321.

Carol Rogerson, "The Canadian Law of Spousal Support" (2004–2005) 38 Fam LQ 69.

THE RELEVANCE OF FAULT IN SPOUSAL SUPPORT CLAIMS

Section 15.2(5) of the *Divorce Act* precludes a court from taking into account "any misconduct of a spouse in relation to the marriage."

This section was considered by the Ontario Court of Appeal in *Walsh v Walsh*, 2007 ONCA, a case in which a former wife had become obsessed with her former husband's infidelity and had been engaged in litigation on an ongoing basis. There were indications that she was suffering emotional strain, but she had provided no medical evidence, and the trial judge had concluded that she had in fact chosen not to try to seek employment, characterizing her actions as "flagrant" in the circumstances. Thus, the trial judge had concluded that she had not met the goal of becoming self-sufficient within a reasonable period according to section 15.2(6) of the *Divorce Act*. In this case, leave to appeal to the Supreme Court of Canada was denied.

However, the Supreme Court had considered a case one year earlier, on appeal from British Columbia, with rather similar facts. In examining *Leskun v Leskun*, consider the Court's reasoning in relation to section 15.2(5).

Leskun v Leskun
2006 SCC 25

The spouses were married in 1978 and they divorced in 1999. During their 20-year marriage, the wife worked, contributed financially to her husband's continuing education, and had one child. However, shortly after the separation, the wife became ill with a serious back injury and she also lost her job in a bank when her position was eliminated. At the same time, her husband told her of his wish to divorce in order to marry another woman.

At the time of the divorce in 1999, the court ordered spousal support for the former wife in an amount of $2,250 per month until she was able to return to full-time work. In 2003, the husband's application to terminate support, on the basis that he was then unemployed and in financial difficulty, was rejected by the judge because the former wife was not yet self-sufficient and remained in need of spousal support.

The B.C. Court of Appeal affirmed this decision, stating that the *Divorce Act* did not preclude taking into account that the wife's failure to achieve self-sufficiency was the result, at least in part, of the emotional devastation caused by the former husband's misconduct. The Court of Appeal also noted other factors that indicated that support should continue, including the wife's age (she was nearly 60 years old at separation), and her poor health.

The former husband appealed to the Supreme Court of Canada, which dismissed the appeal in a short judgment:

BINNIE J:

[2] I agree with the appellant and with the concurring opinion of Newbury J.A. in the British Columbia Court of Appeal that the majority judgment wrongly suggests that a court can achieve indirectly what Parliament has said the court is not to do directly. The needs and circumstances of the claimant spouse will of course be relevant to a failure to achieve the objective of self-sufficiency. It is the attribution of fault to the

other spouse that is deemed by Parliament to be irrelevant to the issue of spousal support in a regime designed to deal with the consequences of marital breakdowns on a no-fault basis.

[3] However, there were a number of other factors, unrelated to the observations about misconduct, that led the Court of Appeal unanimously to dismiss the appellant husband's claim for a reduction in support payments. The judgment under appeal can and should be sustained on that basis. I would therefore dismiss the appeal.

The Court reviewed the facts. Both the woman's daughter and her grandchild resided with her. The husband was about 10 years younger than the wife, and he had helped to raise two daughters of the wife from her first marriage. The wife had helped the husband to obtain an MBA and a qualification as a CGA, both of which boosted his income earning capacity. However, the wife had cashed in her RRSPs and her pension contributions to provide this financial assistance to her husband, thus contributing to her financial problems at divorce. The wife was unable to find employment, having worked in banking since the age of 17. In reviewing the decision of the trial judge that the former wife had not achieved self-sufficiency and remained in need, the Court noted that both Southin JA and Newbury JA had agreed to dismiss the appeal.

[13] Southin J.A. noted that while there was agreement that the respondent was not self-sufficient, the chambers judge had made no findings as to why this was so, nor did the chambers judge express a view as to whether the respondent should have or could have become self-sufficient. In Southin J.A.'s view, the *Divorce Act* does not prevent consideration of a failure to achieve self-sufficiency as being the result, at least in part, of the emotional devastation caused by the other spouse's misconduct. Southin J.A. made clear that there were "further factors" supporting the ruling of the chambers judge, including the age of the respondent at the time of the break-up of the marriage, her health problems and unrelated family sorrows (para. 57). Southin J.A. was not prepared to hold that the respondent had conducted herself in such a manner as to be disentitled to support....

[14] Newbury J.A. also dismissed the appeal. She accepted that the respondent remained in need of support and was not self-sufficient. However, she held that the *Divorce Act*'s strictures against considering the misconduct of a spouse in relation to the marriage when considering support orders meant that "bitterness" cannot be an adequate reason for not achieving self-sufficiency (para. 62). Newbury J.A. felt that the respondent ought to have been employable at least on a part-time basis in the banking business. While the respondent had advised the court that she had sought employment unsuccessfully, she failed to file any evidence on this point [she was unrepresented]. On the other hand, Newbury J.A. noted the respondent's age and family and medical difficulties which were exacerbated by the breakdown of the marriage. For those reasons, and not because of any misconduct-related devastation, she "reluctantly" upheld the support order (para. 63).

The Court explained that the appellant's argument did not challenge the evidence about his former wife's failure to become self-sufficient, but he claimed that she *ought* to have moved on emotionally in the five years between the separation and the hearing before the trial judge and become self-sufficient. Although the Court noted that additional documentary evidence of the former wife's efforts to obtain employment would have been useful, the Court did not interfere with the trial judge's finding of fact on this issue, which was upheld in the B.C. Court of Appeal.

[20] I believe that stripped of the rhetoric, the appellant has a valid point of statutory interpretation. Prior to the 1985 Act, s. 11 of the *Divorce Act*, S.C. 1967-68, c. 24, directed the court to have "regard to the conduct of the parties and the condition, means and other circumstances of each of them" in exercising its discretion in making an award of spousal support. The 1985 Act sought to eliminate misconduct, as such, as a relevant consideration. Section 15.2(5) of the *Divorce Act* now provides that in making an interim or final order for spousal support, "the court shall not take into consideration any misconduct of a spouse in relation to the marriage". In addition, s. 17(6) instructs the court not to consider any conduct in a variation application that could not be considered in the making of the initial order. These provisions make it clear that misconduct should not creep back into the court's deliberation as a relevant "condition" or "other circumstance" which the court is to consider in making or varying a spousal support order (s. 15.2(4)). Misconduct, as such, is off the table as a relevant consideration.

[21] There is, of course, a distinction between the emotional *consequences* of misconduct and the misconduct itself. The consequences are not rendered irrelevant because of their genesis in the other spouse's misconduct. If, for example, spousal abuse triggered a depression so serious as to make a claimant spouse unemployable, the consequences of the misconduct would be highly relevant (as here) to the factors which must be considered in determining the right to support, its duration and its amount. The policy of the 1985 Act however, is to focus on the consequences of the spousal misconduct not the attribution of fault.

[22] Certainly, the "condition ... needs and other circumstances" includes the capacity of the respondent to be self-sufficient for whatever reason. Whether or not the claimed inability or incapacity of the claimant spouse is credible is for the trial judge to determine. It is not helpful to cast about to assign blame.

[23] A break-up in the circumstances found here will perhaps inevitably precipitate a period of shock and emotional trauma for the jilted spouse, but Parliament has concluded that the attempt to get to the bottom of all the rights and wrongs that contributed to the break-up is likely impossible and in any event irrelevant to the task of sorting out the financial consequences. As to the "legal tsunami", I agree with the *amicus curiae* that for the most part parties will realize "that the only way out [of the financial difficulties consequent on the break-up] is if they pull themselves up by their own bootstraps".

[24] If the misconduct point were to be viewed in isolation, the appellant is correct, but the point cannot be viewed in isolation. The fact is that both the chambers judge and Newbury J.A., who differed from her colleagues on the relevance of the misconduct, cited numerous other factors (also referenced by the majority judgment) to reject the appellant's attempt to extricate himself from any further financial responsibility for his former wife....

[26] Section 15.2(6)(*d*) of the *Divorce Act* provides that one of the *objectives* of the spousal support order is to, "*in so far as practicable*, promote the economic self-sufficiency of each spouse within a reasonable period of time". This Court has rejected characterizing this objective as a

duty, see *Moge v. Moge* ... and *Bracklow v. Bracklow*.... The respondent advanced a number of reasons why, despite alleged efforts, she had been unable to return to the workforce. She was believed.

[27] Failure to achieve self-sufficiency is not breach of "a duty" and is simply one factor amongst others to be taken into account. As stated in Moge and repeated in Bracklow:

> At the end of the day..., courts have an overriding discretion and the exercise of such discretion will depend on the particular facts of each case, having regard to the factors and objectives designated in the Act.

[28] Clearly where incapacity is alleged some independent evidence, including medical evidence would be highly desirable. But it is not essential....

The Court discussed the distinction between a motion to review and an application to vary. This distinction is important as there is a higher threshold for variation than for review. Section 17(4.1) of the *Divorce Act* requires a court to "satisfy itself that a change in the condition, means, needs or other circumstances of either former spouse has occurred" prior to varying an order for spousal support (variation orders are discussed in the next section of this chapter).

In contrast, section 15.2(3) permits a court to make an order for spousal support "for a definite or indefinite period or until a specified event occurs, and may impose terms, conditions or restrictions in connection with the order as it thinks fit and just." Such orders are known as review orders because they permit a spousal support order to be reviewed when the condition or event in the initial order transpires without the applicant spouse having to meet the section 17 threshold.

In *Leskun*, there was some confusion about whether the husband's application was for a section 15.2 review or a section 17 variation. The Court concluded that resolving this issue would make no difference to the outcome but took the opportunity to clarify the nature and parameters of review orders:

> [36] Review orders under s 15.2 have a useful but very limited role.... one or both parties at the time of trial may not, as yet, have the economic wherewithal even to commence recovering from the disadvantages arising from the marriage and its breakdown. Common examples are the need to establish a new residence, start a program of education, train or upgrade skills, or obtain employment. In such circumstances, judges may be tempted to attach ... a condition pursuant to s. 15.2(3) of the *Divorce Act*, that entitles one or other or both of the parties to return to court for a reconsideration of a specified aspect of the original order. This will properly occur when the judge does not think it appropriate that at the subsequent hearing one or other of the parties need show that a change in the condition, means, needs or other circumstances of either former spouse has occurred, as required by s. 17(4.1) of the *Divorce Act*.

In such circumstances, a judge may properly attach a section 15.2(3) condition to the order which will permit the parties to return to court for a reconsideration of a specific aspect of the order. But review orders should be used only when there is "genuine and material uncertainty" at trial so that the parties should be entitled to alter the support award without meeting the section 17 threshold of demonstrating a material change in circumstances. In *Leskun*, the review order was justified because there was "serious doubt at the time of trial as to the true financial situation and prospects of the wife and what level of support would actually be needed" (at paras 37–38). The Court cautioned that judges should be careful to specify the precise issue that may be reviewed:

> **[39]** ... courts should resolve the controversies before them and make an order which is permanent subject only to change under s. 17 on proof of a change of circumstances. If the s. 15.2 court considers it essential (as here) to identify an issue for future review, the issue should be tightly delimited in the ... order. This is because on a "review" nobody bears an onus to show changed circumstances. Failure to tightly circumscribe the issue will inevitably be seen by one or other of the parties as an invitation simply to reargue their case.

Notes and Questions

The role of fault in "no fault" divorce

Do you agree with the Supreme Court's characterization of the wife's claim in *Leskun*? How significant were the additional factors, such as her age and ill health and her narrow employment experience, in the Court's conclusion? Do you agree with the Court that there is a "distinction between the emotional consequences of misconduct and the misconduct itself"? Does this case mean that it is possible to consider a spouse's conduct *indirectly* in relation to an application for spousal support?

Consider this situation:

> After a marriage of 23 years, the spouses separated and the husband was ordered to pay spousal support. Some years later, he applied to terminate this support on the basis that section 17(6) of the *Divorce Act* prohibited consideration of spousal misconduct during the marriage, but that misconduct occurring after the end of the marriage could be taken into account.
>
> In this case, the husband argued that his former wife had made no effort to become self-sufficient. In addition, she had resisted access arrangements for one of their children for about five years, and had been found in contempt and imprisoned for 21 days. The husband also argued that his former wife had poisoned the daughter's mind in relation to her father and had alienated her affections for him. In addition, the husband asserted that his former spouse had encouraged the daughter to claim (falsely) that her father had molested her, and that the wife had told others that her former husband was suffering from the onset of Alzheimer's disease.
>
> The wife had few marketable skills, having been out of the workforce for 13 years at the date of separation. How should the court respond to this application?

In *Ungerer v Ungerer* (1998), 37 RFL (4th) 41 (BCCA), the court concluded that

> ... I think that the question to be asked where misconduct is alleged as a reason to terminate post-divorce spousal support is whether that misconduct is of such a morally repugnant nature as would cause right-thinking persons to say that the spouse is no longer entitled to the support of her former husband, or to the assistance of the court in compelling the husband to pay....

As a result, the court terminated the spousal support award six years after the date of divorce. See also *Stewart v Stewart* (2000), 12 RFL (5th) 218 (NSSC), where the court concluded that the husband's abusive conduct post-divorce did not constitute "conduct in relation to the marriage" and that it could therefore be included as one of several factors to support the court's decision to deny his claim for spousal support.

FLA provisions about conduct and spousal support

In *Morey v Morey* (1979), 24 OR (2d) 124 (Prov Ct (Fam Div)), the court considered the requirements of Ontario's *FLA*, s 33(10). In that case, the court considered factors relevant to determining that a spouse was disentitled to spousal support on the basis of conduct that constituted unconscionability as an "obvious and gross repudiation of the relationship." According to *Morey*, it is necessary to demonstrate by affirmative evidence that

> a) the conduct must be exceptionally bad;
> b) the conduct must be such as could reasonably be expected to destroy the marriage;
> c) the conduct must have persisted in the face of innocence and virtual blamelessness on the part of the other spouse...;
> d) the commission of a so-called matrimonial offence is not necessarily sufficient...;
> e) the party raising the issue of relevant conduct should be prepared to undertake that there is a *bona fide* belief that the test ... can be satisfied [with risks of punitive costs if the court finds that the issue is frivolous]; and
> f) the pleadings ... should set out a summary of the conduct relied on to meet the test....

To what extent do these requirements limit the availability of section 33(10) to disentitle a spouse to support?

Bruni v Bruni
2010 ONSC 6568

In this case, the spouses were married for 11 years, and after separation, they both repartnered. They signed a separation agreement, providing that the former wife would have sole custody of two children, and that the former husband would have reasonable access. However, the former spouses had an acrimonious relationship and it seemed that the mother had alienated her daughter from her father. The father eventually initiated action to set aside the separation agreement, an issue discussed later in Chapter Eight.

However, in this same action, the former wife had claimed spousal support, and the court assessed her entitlement, including consideration of the Spousal Support Advisory Guidelines. The court then turned to section 33(10) of the *Family Law Act*, and the court's authority to consider "a course of conduct that is so unconscionable as to constitute an obvious and gross repudiation of the relationship."

In considering this section of the *FLA*, the court held that the section could apply post-separation as it did not expressly confine "unconscionable conduct" to the period prior to separation. In addition, the court concluded that the term "relationship" included the relationship of spouses as co-parents. In considering section 33(10), the court stated:

> **[209]** The parental alienation in this case reflects an intent by [the former wife] to destroy the relationship between Taylor and [her father]; it is shocking conduct. It also amounts to a hideous repudiation of the relationship between [the former spouses] as co-parents of Taylor. The harm here probably is irreparable. Certainly, it is extremely serious at best. How could such conduct not satisfy the requirements of s. 33(10), stringent as they are?

> **[210]** While [the father's] access conduct has largely reflected nothing more than inept parenting, [the mother's] behaviour has been evil. Is there a remedy?

> **[211]** Dollars cannot replace the father–daughter relationship that [the mother] has destroyed. However, in the circumstances of this case, justice has only a Hobson's choice. [The mother's] alienation of Taylor and [her father] must be condemned, and an effective method of expressing that condemnation is by way of a reduction in spousal support....

Thus, the court relied on section 33(10) to reduce the wife's entitlement to spousal support to an amount of $1.00 per month.

Do you agree with the court's interpretation of the language of section 33(10)? Is it consistent with the legislative intention? To what extent do the cases suggest different kinds or levels of "misconduct" in relation to spousal support claims pursuant to *FLA*, s 33(10) or the *Divorce Act*, s 15.2(5)? For other examples of "misconduct" cases, see *Smith v Smith*, [2002] Ont Sup Ct J LEXIS 1126; and *Krigstin v Krigstin* (1992), 43 RFL (3d) 334 (Ont Gen Div).

Additional Resources

John-Paul Boyd, "Tsunami in a Teapot: *Leskun v. Leskun*" (2007) 40 UBC L Rev 293.

Susan Engel, "Compensatory Support in *Moge v. Moge* and the Individual Model of Responsibility: Are we Headed in the Right Direction" (1993) 57 Sask L Rev 397.

Miriam Grassby, "Two Income Couples: Presumption of Need for the Lower Income Spouse" (2004) 20 Can J Fam L 321.

Carol Rogerson, "The Canadian Law of Spousal Support' (2004–2005) 38 Fam LQ 69.

V.
RETHINKING *PELECH* AND THE ROLE OF FAMILY AGREEMENTS

BALANCING GOALS OF FAIRNESS VERSUS FINALITY?

As the Supreme Court clearly indicated in *Moge*, that decision was not intended to alter the principles outlined in *Pelech* with respect to the limited role for judicial intervention in separation agreements negotiated by the parties. In *Bracklow*, the Court added a "non-compensatory" basis to the "compensatory" ground established in *Moge*, but also acknowledged a continuing role for a "contractual" basis for spousal support. However, in *Bracklow*, the Court did not address the test for setting aside spousal support provisions in a contract, as set out in *Pelech*.

In 2003, however, the Court considered the "contractual" basis for spousal support again in *Miglin v Miglin*. Unlike the factual situations in *Moge* and *Bracklow*, the spouses in this case had signed a separation agreement that limited the duration of spousal support payable to Mrs. Miglin. Both spouses had received legal and other expert advice prior to signing the agreement, but some years after doing so, Mrs. Miglin filed a claim for ongoing spousal support.

In reviewing the Court's reasoning in *Miglin*, it may be important to recognize that this case was decided in 2003, that is, one year after *Nova Scotia (AG) v Walsh* (2002) and one year prior to *Hartshorne v Harshorne* (2004). In this context, consider again the significance of the Court's interest in preserving individual "choice" and the finality of "family bargains."

Miglin v Miglin
2003 SCC 24

The spouses were married in 1979, and five years later, they purchased a lodge in Northern Ontario as equal shareholders and then proceeded to run it as a family business. In this context, they each drew a salary of approximately $80,000 per annum. They had four children and divided their time together between the lodge and the matrimonial home in Toronto. The parties separated in 1993, when the four children were between 2 and 8 years of age. Both the husband and the wife were then in their early 40s.

Eventually, after more than a year of negotiations, they executed a separation agreement in which it was agreed that the children would reside primarily with the wife and that the husband would pay $60,000 annually in child support. He also agreed to pay the mortgage on the matrimonial home and transferred his one-half interest in the home (valued at $250,000) to the wife. In return, the wife released her interest in the lodge (also valued at $250,000) to the husband. The wife released any interest in an unvalued outfitting business owned by the husband as well. In addition, the parties entered into a consulting agreement in which the wife was entitled to receive an annual salary of $15,000 from the lodge for a period of five years, and this consulting agreement was renewable on consent of the parties. Overall, the parties agreed that the wife would fully and finally release any entitlement to spousal support.

After the divorce, relations between the parties became acrimonious. Just prior to the expiry of the consulting agreement, the wife applied for sole custody, child support, and spousal support under section 15.2 of the *Divorce Act*. In effect, because the parties had made an agreement with respect to spousal support, the wife's application was an "initial" application for spousal support.

The trial judge awarded the wife spousal support in an amount of $4,400 per month for a period of five years, and the Court of Appeal upheld the quantum of this award of support and removed the five-year limit. Thus, the wife succeeded in her application for indefinite support at this rate.

On appeal to the Supreme Court of Canada, however, a majority of seven justices concluded that the appeal should be allowed, LeBel and Deschamps JJ dissenting.

BASTARACHE and ARBOUR JJ:

[1] This appeal concerns the proper approach to determining an application for spousal support pursuant to s. 15.2(1) of the *Divorce Act*, ... where the spouses have executed a final agreement that addresses all matters respecting their separation, including a release of any future claim for spousal support. Accordingly, this appeal presents the Court with an opportunity to address directly the question of the continued application of the *Pelech* trilogy ... in light of the significant legislative and jurisprudential changes that have taken place since its facts arose and since its release.

[2] In broader terms, the appeal raises the question of the proper weight to be given to any type of spousal support agreement that one of the parties subsequently wishes to have modified through an initial application in court for such support. In that sense, the matter is not restricted to spousal support agreements that contain a time-limited support arrangement or to agreements which contain a full and final release from support obligations by one or both parties.

[3] The parties to this appeal, now divorced, entered into a final agreement that sought to settle all of their financial and personal affairs surrounding the breakdown of their marriage. In addition to property

equalization, custody, access and support of their children, and a commercial contract between the respondent and the appellant's company, the parties agreed to release one another from any claims to spousal support. This Court must determine the proper weight to be accorded that agreement where one party subsequently makes an application for spousal support under the *Divorce Act*.

[4] As we explain below, we believe that a fairly negotiated agreement that represents the intentions and expectations of the parties and that complies substantially with the objectives of the *Divorce Act* as a whole should receive considerable weight. In an originating application for spousal support, where the parties have executed a pre-existing agreement, the court should look first to the circumstances of negotiation and execution to determine whether the applicant has established a reason to discount the agreement. The court would inquire whether one party was vulnerable and the other party took advantage of that vulnerability. The court also examines whether the substance of the agreement, at formation, complied substantially with the general objectives of the Act. As we elaborate later, these general objectives include not only an equitable sharing of the consequences of the marriage breakdown under s. 15.2, but also certainty, finality and autonomy. Second, the court would ask whether, viewed from the time the application is made, the applicant has established that the agreement no longer reflects the original intention of the parties and whether the agreement is still in substantial compliance with the objectives of the Act. In contrast, the trial judge's and the Court of Appeal's approaches failed to value a determination by the parties as to what is mutually acceptable to them. We would thus allow this appeal....

[28] As mentioned earlier in these reasons, this appeal is concerned with the continued application of the *Pelech* trilogy. The three cases making up this trilogy were decided immediately after the promulgation of the 1985 Act, but deal with situations governed by the 1968 Act. Those cases establish a change-based test under which a court is permitted to override a final agreement on spousal support only where there has been a significant change in circumstances since the making of the agreement. The test establishes a threshold that is defined as a radical and unforeseen change that is causally connected to the marriage. It does not deal with the fairness of the agreement or its attention to the objectives of the *Divorce Act*. It is designed to promote certainty and to facilitate a clean break in the relationship of the parties, focussing on individual autonomy and respect for contracts. Since the release of the trilogy, the law of spousal support has evolved. A compensatory approach was adopted in *Moge v. Moge*, [1992] 3 SCR 813. A more nuanced approach was developed in *Bracklow v. Bracklow*, [1999] 1 SCR 420. Self-sufficiency, autonomy and finality remain relevant factors in our case law, but many question whether the emphasis put on them by the trilogy remains. The question posed is whether agreements concluded with the intent that they be final can, under the 1985 Act, be overridden on grounds other than those defined in the trilogy....

[29] The issues in the present appeal resemble those facing this Court in the *Pelech* trilogy. Despite significant changes in the intervening years, the basic question remains: What role should a pre-existing agreement play in determining an application for spousal support? ...

[31] The facts and reasoning of the three cases constituting the trilogy have attracted substantial scholarly and judicial commentary. We do not propose to review those decisions in detail again here. Suffice it to say that the *Pelech* trilogy has come to stand for the proposition that a court

will not interfere with a pre-existing agreement that attempts fully and finally to settle the matter of spousal support as between the parties unless the applicant can establish that there has been a radical and unforeseen change in circumstances that is causally connected to the marriage. The trilogy represents an approach to spousal support that has been described as a "clean break," emphasizing finality and the severing of ties between former spouses....

[32] With the coming into force of the 1985 Act and the release of the trilogy the following year, confusion ensued as to whether the trilogy had any continued application. The confusion may stem from two main factors. On the one hand, the 1968 Act, while providing less direction on the issue of support, could be interpreted as not inconsistent with the new, more detailed statute....

[33] On the other hand, some members of the judiciary and several scholars recognized the potential difficulties in applying the *Pelech* trilogy in the new statutory context....

[34] In addition to generating some confusion, the trilogy received no small degree of criticism, from both legal scholars and family law practitioners. The main thrust of the criticism levied at the trilogy was summarized by McLachlin J. (as she then was) in a speech delivered to the National Family Law Program over a decade ago. McLachlin J. suggested that the "joint venture model" of marriage, which viewed married persons as autonomous individuals entering into equal partnerships who should and do take responsibility for themselves, informed the economic self-sufficiency or "clean break" theory of spousal support endorsed by this Court in *Pelech*. Although McLachlin J. fully endorsed the model of equality on which the trilogy was based, she cautioned that that model did not necessarily conform to everyone's reality. This disjuncture, in her view explained much of the criticism to which the trilogy has been subjected (the Honourable Madame Justice B. McLachlin, "Spousal Support: Is It Fair To Apply New-Style Rules to Old-Style Marriages?" (1990), 9 *Can. J. Fam. L.* 131).

[35] Since the trilogy, decisions from this Court have recognized a shift in the normative standards informing spousal support orders. In *Moge, supra,* at p. 849 L'Heureux-Dubé J. held for the majority that the underlying theme of the 1985 Act is the "fair and equitable distribution of resources to alleviate the economic consequences of marriage or marriage breakdown." In making an order for support, she noted that the court must have regard to *all four* of the objectives of spousal support, none of which is paramount. Self-sufficiency is only one of those objectives and an attenuated one at that (to be promoted "insofar as practicable" (p. 852)). L'Heureux-Dubé J. concluded that Parliament appears to have adopted a compensatory model of support, one which attempts to ensure the equitable sharing of the economic consequences of marriage and its breakdown.

[36] Regarding the trilogy specifically, L'Heureux-Dubé J. held that it had no application to the circumstances of that case, where there had been no final agreement between the parties. In her view, the trilogy did not address issues of entitlement to support in the absence of an agreement. Nevertheless, her reasoning with respect to the "compensatory model" of support only served to fuel debate as to whether the *Pelech* trilogy still governed at all....

The majority judges also reviewed the decisions in *G(L) v B(G)*, [1995] 3 SCR 370, and *Willick v Willick*, [1994] 3 SCR 670, and different views in the majority and dissenting opinions in these cases with respect to the continuing applicability of the *Pelech* test.

[40] In light of these developments in the understanding of spousal support, the question "Does the trilogy apply or not?" is perhaps too mechanical, and the answer does not turn solely on the existence of a new Act. Parliament's recognition of competing objectives of spousal support renders the trilogy's privileging of "clean break" principles inappropriate, but this is not to suggest that the policy concerns that drove the trilogy are wholly irrelevant to the new legislative context. On the contrary, the objectives of autonomy and finality, as well as the recognition that the parties may go on to undertake new family obligations, continue to inform the current *Divorce Act* and remain significant today. What has changed is the singular emphasis on self-sufficiency as a policy goal to the virtual exclusion of other objectives that may or may not be equally pressing according to the specific circumstances of the parties. Such an emphasis on self-sufficiency is inconsistent with both the compensatory model of support developed in *Moge*, and the non-compensatory model of support developed in *Bracklow*. It is also inconsistent with the interpretive point made in both cases that no single objective in s. 15.2(6) is paramount: *Bracklow*, at para. 35; *Moge*, at p. 852. Nevertheless, promoting self-sufficiency remains an explicit legislative objective.

[41] In addition to these competing policy goals, we also note that the current statutory language does not support direct incorporation of the trilogy test....

[42] The current statutory context ... is quite different in that Parliament has explicitly directed the court to consider a change in circumstances only where the application is for variation [pursuant to section 17]....

[43] Section 15.2 provides no such similar direction. Rather, the court is explicitly directed to take into account certain non-exhaustive factors, and instructed that a support order should advance certain specified objectives. On a plain reading of the statute, then, there is simply no basis for importing a change threshold, radical, material or otherwise, into the provision. Indeed, on an initial application for support, the very concept of "change of circumstances" has no relevance, except to the limited extent that there might have been a pre-existing order or agreement that needs to be considered.

[44] How, then, should trial judges exercise the discretion vested in them by virtue of the Act where a party who makes an initial application for support has previously entered into an agreement that purports to have settled all matters between the spouses? How should trial judges assess the appropriate weight to be given such an agreement where s. 15.2 of the 1985 Act appears to accord it no greater priority than other factors?

[45] It is helpful initially to identify several inappropriate approaches. In our view, the answer to these questions does not lie in adopting a near-impermeable standard such that a court will endorse any agreement, regardless of the inequities it reveals. Neither, however, does the solution lie in unduly interfering with agreements freely entered into and on which the parties reasonably expected to rely. It is also not helpful to read between the lines in s. 15.2 so as to identify a single implicit overriding legislative objective overshadowing the factors specifically set out. The fact that judicial and societal understandings of spousal support have changed since the release of *Pelech* and the adoption of admittedly competing factors in s. 15.2(6) does not lead to an unfettered discretion on the part of

trial judges to substitute their own view of what is required for what the parties considered mutually acceptable....

[46] Nevertheless, the language and purpose of the 1985 Act militate in favour of a contextual assessment of all the circumstances. This includes the content of the agreement; in order to determine the proper weight it should be accorded in a s. 15.2 application. In exercising their discretion, trial judges must balance Parliament's objective of equitable sharing of the consequences of marriage and its breakdown with the parties' freedom to arrange their affairs as they see fit. Accordingly, a court should be loathe to interfere with a pre-existing agreement unless it is convinced that the agreement does not comply substantially with the overall objectives of the *Divorce Act*. This is particularly so when the pre-existing spousal support agreement is part of a comprehensive settlement of all issues related to the termination of the marriage. Since the issues, as well as their settlement, are likely interrelated, the support part of the agreement would at times be difficult to modify without putting into question the entire arrangements.

[47] Having determined that the narrow test enunciated in the *Pelech* trilogy for interfering with a pre-existing agreement is not appropriate in the current statutory context, we now consider the approaches taken by the courts below in this appeal....

The majority judges considered the "fairness" test applied by the trial judge, who assessed the agreement solely in relation to the spousal support objectives in section 15.2(6). The majority rejected that approach because:

[53] The objectives in s. 15.2(6) do not accommodate within them the compelling objectives of finality, certainty and autonomy that Parliament has also seen fit to endorse in the *Divorce Act*. It should not be overlooked that s. 9(2) of the Act imposes a positive duty on counsel to advise clients of alternatives to litigation ...

[54] Section 9(2) of the 1985 Act clearly indicates Parliament's intention to promote negotiated settlement of all matters corollary to a divorce.... Without some degree of certainty that the agreement will be respected by the court, parties have little incentive to negotiate a settlement and then to comply with the terms of their undertakings. The policy goal underlying s. 9(2) would then be entirely defeated.

The majority also rejected the material change test applied in the Court of Appeal. The court then considered the proper approach to applications under section 15.2:

[64] An initial application for spousal support inconsistent with a pre-existing agreement requires an investigation into all the circumstances surrounding that agreement, first, at the time of its formation, and second, at the time of the application. In our view, this two-stage analysis provides the court with a principled way of balancing the competing objectives underlying the *Divorce Act* and of locating the potentially problematic aspects of spousal support arrangements in their appropriate temporal context. Before doing so, however, it is necessary to discuss some of the interpretive difficulties affecting spousal support.

[65] As a starting point, we endorse the reasoning of this Court in *Moge*, *supra*, where L'Heureux-Dubé J. held that the spousal support objectives of the *Divorce Act* are designed to achieve an equitable sharing of the economic consequences of marriage and marriage breakdown. By explicitly directing the court to consider the objectives listed in s. 15.2(6), the 1985 Act departs significantly from the exclusive "means and needs" approach of the former statute. We note, however, that there is a potential tension between recognizing any economic advantages or disadvantages to the spouses arising from the marriage or its breakdown and promoting, even if only to the extent practicable, the economic self-sufficiency of each spouse (ss. 15.2(6)(a), and (d)). The way to reconcile these competing objectives is to recognize that the meaning of the term "equitable sharing" is not fixed in the Act and will, rather, vary according to the facts of a particular marriage. Parliament, aware of the many ways in which parties structure a marriage and particularly its economic aspects, drafted legislation broad enough that one cannot say that the spousal support provisions have a narrow fixed content. Contrasted with the former Act, then, these objectives expressly direct the court to consider different criteria on which to base entitlement to spousal support, while retaining the objective of fostering the parties' ability to get on with their lives.

[66] The role that these objectives was intended to play, however, must be understood in the proper statutory context. Whether by way of an initial application or an application to vary, the criteria listed in s. 15.2(6) and s. 17(7) pertain to spousal support orders imposed by the court. Nowhere in the *Divorce Act* is it expressed that parties *must* adhere strictly, or at all, to these objectives in reaching a mutually acceptable agreement. Rather, the listed objectives relate only to orders for spousal support, that is, to circumstances where the parties have been unable to reach an agreement. Moreover, the positive obligation that the Act places on counsel to advise their clients of alternatives to litigation, noted above, indicates Parliament's clear conception of the new divorce regime as one that places a high premium on private settlement. Parliament's preference appears to be that parties settle their dispute, without asking a court to apply s. 15.2(6) to make an order. This is not to suggest that the objectives are irrelevant in the context of a negotiated agreement. The parties, or at least their counsel, will be conscious of the likely outcome of litigation in the event that negotiation fails. Consideration of the statutory entitlements will undoubtedly influence negotiations. But the mutually acceptable agreement negotiated by the parties will not necessarily mirror the spousal support that a judge would have awarded. Holding that any agreement that deviates from the objectives listed in s. 15.2(6) be given little or no weight would seriously undermine the significant policy goal of negotiated settlement. It would also undermine the parties' autonomy and freedom to structure their post-divorce lives in a manner that reflects their own objectives and concerns. Such a position would leave little room to recognize the terms that the parties determined were mutually acceptable to them and in substantial compliance with the objectives of the *Divorce Act*.

[67] Having said this, we are of the view that there is nevertheless a significant public interest in ensuring that the goal of negotiated settlements not be pursued, through judicial approbation of agreements, with such a vengeance that individual autonomy becomes a straitjacket. Therefore, assessment of the appropriate weight to be accorded a pre-existing agreement requires a balancing of the parties' interest in determining their own affairs with an appreciation of the peculiar aspects of separation agreements generally and spousal support in particular....

As the majority judges noted, each of the parties suggested a model for the exercise of judicial discretion in the context of a section 15.2 application. The appellant submitted that the proper test for determining how much weight should be accorded to a pre-existing agreement should be similar to that adopted by provincial legislatures, such as section 33(4) of the Ontario *Family Law Act*. This test is one of "unconscionable circumstances." By contrast, the respondent proposed a more searching standard of review to examine the prior agreement as a whole, and having regard to the factors and objectives listed in section 15.2 of the *Divorce Act*. According to the court, both positions had merit, but neither was entirely satisfactory.

[73] In our view, there is merit to each of these positions. Nevertheless, we believe that the approach that will provide both negotiating spouses and, failing agreement, courts with a principled and consistent framework is not that proposed by either party. The test should ultimately recognize the particular ways in which separation agreements generally and spousal support arrangements specifically are vulnerable to a risk of inequitable sharing at the time of negotiation and in the future. At the same time, the test must not undermine the parties' right to decide for themselves what constitutes for them, in the circumstances of their marriage, mutually acceptable equitable sharing. Our approach, for example, takes greater account of the parties' subjective sense of equitable sharing than the objective "unconscionable circumstances" standard proposed by counsel for the appellant.

[74] Negotiations in the family law context of separation or divorce are conducted in a unique environment. Both academics and practitioners have acknowledged that this is a time of intense personal and emotional turmoil, in which one or both of the parties may be particularly vulnerable. Unlike emotionally neutral economic actors negotiating in the commercial context, divorcing couples inevitably bring to the table a host of emotions and concerns that do not obviously accord with the making of rational economic decisions....

[75] Add to this mix the intimate nature of the marital relationship that makes it difficult to overcome potential power imbalances and modes of influence....

[76] We also note that, depending on the circumstances of the parties, a wide array of interrelated elements may make up a global separation agreement. Such a separation agreement may comprise division or equalization of marital property, provision for custody and support of any children, as well as provisions for spousal support, be it in the form of lump sum, periodic payment, time-limited payment or a waiver and release. These matters, with the exception of the property division, are primarily prospective in nature, although compensatory spousal support is retrospective....

[77] In our view, Parliament's recognition of the potential complications in the process of contracting spousal support is reflected in the *Divorce Act* itself. We see this in the direction to the court to consider an agreement as only one factor among others, rather than to treat it as binding, subject merely to remedies in contract law. Accordingly, contract law principles are not only better suited to the commercial context, but it is implicit in s. 15 of the 1985 Act that they were not intended to govern the applicability of private contractual arrangements for spousal support.

[78] Therefore, in searching for a proper balance between consensus and finality on the one hand, and sensitivity to the unique concerns that arise in the post-divorce context on the other, a court should be guided by the objectives of spousal support listed in the Act. In doing so, however, the

court should treat the parties' reasonable best efforts to meet those objectives as presumptively dispositive of the spousal support issue. The court should set aside the wishes of the parties as expressed in a pre-existing agreement only where the applicant shows that the agreement fails to be in substantial compliance with the overall objectives of the Act. These include not only those apparent in s. 15.2 but also, as noted above, certainty, finality and autonomy.

[79] With these broad concerns in mind, we now turn to the specifics of the two-stage approach to the exercise of the court's discretion.

(A) STAGE ONE

[80] In an originating application for spousal support, where the parties have executed a pre-existing agreement, the court should first look to the circumstances in which the agreement was negotiated and executed to determine whether there is any reason to discount it.

(i) The Circumstances of Execution

[81] It is difficult to provide a definitive list of factors to consider in assessing the circumstances of negotiation and execution of an agreement. We simply state that the court should be alive to the conditions of the parties, including whether there were any circumstances of oppression, pressure, or other vulnerabilities, taking into account all of the circumstances, including those set out in s. 15.2(4)(a) and (b) and the conditions under which the negotiations were held, such as their duration and whether there was professional assistance.

[82] We pause here to note three important points. First, we are not suggesting that courts must necessarily look for "unconscionability" as it is understood in the common law of contract. There is a danger in borrowing terminology rooted in other branches of the law and transposing it into what all agree is a unique legal context. There may be persuasive evidence brought before the court that one party took advantage of the vulnerability of the other party in separation or divorce negotiations that would fall short of evidence of the power imbalance necessary to demonstrate unconscionability in a commercial context between, say, a consumer and a large financial institution. Next, the court should not presume an imbalance of power in the relationship or a vulnerability on the part of one party, nor should it presume that the apparently stronger party took advantage of any vulnerability on the part of the other. Rather, there must be evidence to warrant the court's finding that the agreement should not stand on the basis of a fundamental flaw in the negotiation process. Recognition of the emotional stress of separation or divorce should not be taken as giving rise to a presumption that parties in such circumstances are incapable of assenting to a binding agreement. If separating or divorcing parties were generally incapable of making agreements it would be fair to enforce, it would be difficult to see why Parliament included "agreement or arrangement" in s. 15.2(4)(c). Finally, we stress that the mere presence of vulnerabilities will not, in and of itself, justify the court's intervention. The degree of professional assistance received by the parties will often overcome any systemic imbalances between the parties.

[83] Where vulnerabilities are not present, or are effectively compensated by the presence of counsel or other professionals or both, or have not been taken advantage of, the court should consider the agreement as a genuine mutual desire to finalize the terms of the parties' separation and as indicative of their substantive intentions. Accordingly, the court should be loathe to interfere. In contrast, where the power imbalance did vitiate the bargaining process, the agreement should not be read as expressing

the parties' notion of equitable sharing in their circumstances and the agreement will merit little weight.

(ii) The Substance of the Agreement

[84] Where the court is satisfied that the conditions under which the agreement was negotiated are satisfactory, it must then turn its attention to the substance of the agreement. The court must determine the extent to which the agreement takes into account the factors and objectives listed in the Act, thereby reflecting an equitable sharing of the economic consequences of marriage and its breakdown. Only a significant departure from the general objectives of the Act will warrant the court's intervention on the basis that there is not substantial compliance with the Act. The court must not view spousal support arrangements in a vacuum, however; it must look at the agreement or arrangement in its totality, bearing in mind that all aspects of the agreement are inextricably linked and that the parties have a large discretion in establishing priorities and goals for themselves.

[85] When examining the substance of the agreement, the court should ask itself whether the agreement is in substantial compliance with the *Divorce Act*. As just noted, this "substantial compliance" should be determined by considering whether the agreement represents a significant departure from the general objectives of the Act, which necessarily include, as well as the spousal support considerations in s. 15.2, finality, certainty, and the invitation in the Act for parties to determine their own affairs. The greater the vulnerabilities present at the time of formation, the more searching the court's review at this stage.

[86] Two comments are necessary here. First, assessment of an agreement's substantial compliance with the entire Act will necessarily permit a broader gamut of arrangements than would be the case if testing agreements narrowly against the support order objectives in s. 15.2(6). Second, a determination that an agreement fails to comply substantially with the Act does not necessarily mean that the entire agreement must be set aside and ignored. Provided that demonstrated vulnerability and exploitation did not vitiate negotiation, even a negotiated agreement that it would be wrong to enforce in its totality may nevertheless indicate the parties' understanding of their marriage and, at least in a general sense, their intentions for the future. Consideration of such an agreement would continue to be mandatory under s. 15.2(4). For example, if it appeared inappropriate to enforce a time limit in a support agreement, the quantum of support agreed upon might still be appropriate, and the agreement might then simply be extended, indefinitely or for a different fixed term.

(B) STAGE TWO

[87] Where negotiation of the agreement is not impugned on the basis set out above and the agreement was in substantial compliance with the general objectives of the Act at its time of creation, the court should defer to the wishes of the parties and afford the agreement great weight. Nevertheless, the vicissitudes of life mean that, in some circumstances, parties may find themselves down the road of their post-divorce life in circumstances not contemplated. Accordingly, on the bringing of an application under s. 15.2, the court should assess the extent to which enforcement of the agreement still reflects the original intention of the parties and the extent to which it is still in substantial compliance with the objectives of the Act.

[88] The parties' intentions, as reflected by the agreement, are the backdrop against which the court must consider whether the situation of the

parties at the time of the application makes it no longer appropriate to accord the agreement conclusive weight. We note that it is unlikely that the court will be persuaded to disregard the agreement in its entirety but for a significant change in the parties' circumstances from what could reasonably be anticipated at the time of negotiation. Although the change need not be "radically unforeseen," and the applicant need not demonstrate a causal connection to the marriage, the applicant must nevertheless clearly show that, in light of the new circumstances, the terms of the agreement no longer reflect the parties' intentions at the time of execution and the objectives of the Act. Accordingly, it will be necessary to show that these new circumstances were not reasonably anticipated by the parties, and have led to a situation that cannot be condoned.

[89] We stress that a certain degree of change is foreseeable most of the time. The prospective nature of these agreements cannot be lost on the parties and they must be presumed to be aware that the future is, to a greater or lesser extent, uncertain. It will be unconvincing, for example, to tell a judge that an agreement never contemplated that the job market might change, or that parenting responsibilities under an agreement might be somewhat more onerous than imagined, or that a transition into the workforce might be challenging. Negotiating parties should know that each person's health cannot be guaranteed as a constant. An agreement must also contemplate, for example, that the relative values of assets in a property division will not necessarily remain the same. Housing prices may rise or fall. A business may take a downturn or become more profitable. Moreover, some changes may be caused or provoked by the parties themselves. A party may remarry or decide not to work. Where the parties have demonstrated their intention to release one another from all claims to spousal support, changes of this nature are unlikely to be considered sufficient to justify dispensing with that declared intention. That said, we repeat that a judge is not bound by the strict *Pelech* standard to intervene only once a change is shown to be "radical." Likewise, it is unnecessary for the party seeking court-ordered support to demonstrate that the circumstances rendering enforcement of the agreement inappropriate are causally connected to the marriage or its breakdown. The test here is not strict foreseeability; a thorough review of case law leaves virtually no change entirely unforeseeable. The question, rather, is the extent to which the unimpeachably negotiated agreement can be said to have contemplated the situation before the court at the time of the application.

[90] The court's focus should be on the agreement's continued correspondence to the parties' original intentions as to their relative positions and the overall objectives of the Act, not on whether a change occurred *per se*. That is to say, we do not consider "change" of any particular nature to be a threshold requirement which, once established, entitles the court to jettison the agreement entirely. Rather, the court should be persuaded that both the intervention and the degree of intervention are warranted. That is, at this stage, even if unbending enforcement of the agreement is inappropriate, that agreement may still indicate to a trial judge the parties' understanding of their relationship and their intentions. Even an agreement that is not determinative as a result of the parties' circumstances at the time of the application warrants compulsory consideration under s. 15.2(4).

[91] Although we recognize the unique nature of separation agreements and their differences from commercial contracts, they are contracts nonetheless. Parties must take responsibility for the contract they execute as well as for their own lives. It is only where the current circumstances represent a significant departure from the range of reasonable outcomes

anticipated by the parties, in a manner that puts them at odds with the objectives of the Act, that the court may be persuaded to give the agreement little weight. As we noted above, it would be inconsistent if a different test applied to change an agreement in the form of an initial order under s. 15.2 and to variation of an agreement incorporated into an order under s. 17. In our view, the Act does not create such inconsistency. We do not agree with the Ontario Court of Appeal when it suggests at para. 71, that once a material change has been found, a court has "a wide discretion" to determine what amount of support, if any, should be ordered, based solely on the factors set out in s. 17(7). As La Forest J. said in his dissent in *Richardson, supra,* at p. 881, an order made under the Act has already been judicially determined to be fit and just. The objectives of finality and certainty noted above caution against too broad a discretion in varying an order that the parties have been relying on in arranging their affairs. Consideration of the overall objectives of the Act is consistent with the non-exhaustive direction in s. 17(7) that a variation order "should" consider the four objectives listed there. More generally, a contextual approach to interpretation, reading the entire Act, would indicate that the court would apply those objectives in light of the entire statute. Where the order at issue incorporated the mutually acceptable agreement of the parties, that order reflected the parties' understanding of what constituted an equitable sharing of the economic consequences of the marriage. In our view, whether acting under s. 15.2 or under s. 17, the Court should take that into consideration....

[92] In the circumstances of this appeal, we are of the view that the global Separation Agreement should be accorded significant and determinative weight. Looking to the Separation Agreement at the time of its formation, we find nothing to indicate that circumstances surrounding the negotiation and execution of the agreement were fraught with vulnerabilities. On the contrary, the record reveals that these parties underwent extensive negotiation over a substantial time period and engaged the services of several professionals, including experienced and expert counsel. Negotiation of the Separation Agreement lasted some 15 months. Ms. Miglin, in addition to legal advice, received detailed financial advice, both in terms of tax planning and income projections, throughout the negotiation process.

[93] At the trial, Ms. Miglin suggested that she was not content with the Separation Agreement and felt pressured by her husband to agree to the spousal support release. As she phrased it, it was a confusing and emotional time for her. We do not doubt that marital separation is almost inevitably a time of emotional upheaval and confusion. Regardless, in this case there is ample evidence to conclude that any vulnerability experienced by Ms. Miglin was more than adequately compensated by the independent and competent legal counsel representing her interests over a prolonged period, not to mention the services provided to her by other professionals. It is unnecessary, therefore, for us to determine whether Ms. Miglin's evidence relating to her personal feelings would have been sufficient to demonstrate a vulnerability in this case and, if so, whether that vulnerability was exploited. The extent of Ms. Miglin's professional assistance obviously comes at the upper end of the range, and we would not wish to suggest that hers was the minimum required to assure fair negotiation.

[94] Turning to the substance of the Separation Agreement, we also find nothing to demonstrate a significant departure from the overall objectives of the *Divorce Act.* At the time of separation both the Lodge and the matrimonial home had net values of approximately $500,000. The Separa-

tion Agreement provided for Ms. Miglin to transfer to Mr. Miglin her one-half interest in the Lodge in exchange for the transfer to her of his one-half interest in the matrimonial home. Mr. Miglin agreed to assume sole responsibility for the mortgage on the house. We cannot agree with the trial judge's characterization of this arrangement as "not an equal split." He made this assessment on the basis that the business was income-producing and the house was not. Valuation of an asset necessarily takes into account its characteristics, including its potential income, capital appreciation and risks. In the same way that a single asset should not be counted twice (*Boston v. Boston*, [2001] 2 SCR 413, 2001 SCC 43), the factors that went into an asset's valuation should not be considered a second time. Presumably, viewed subjectively, in light of Mr. Miglin's and Ms. Miglin's respective abilities, interests and needs, the business was of greater interest to him and the matrimonial home more attractive to her. That is why they divided the assets as they did. There was no basis for the trial judge to conclude that one asset was worth more than another of identical value. In our view, the division in the Separation Agreement reflects the parties' needs and wishes and fairly distributed the assets acquired and created by them over the course of their marriage.

[95] The Separation Agreement also provided that Ms. Miglin would receive child support in the amount of $1,250 per month, per child, for an annual total of approximately $60,000, taxable in her hands and tax-deductible to Mr. Miglin. The child support arrangement was subject to both an annual cost of living increase and the caveat that it would be revisited, if necessary, once reasons for judgment were released from this Court in *Thibaudeau* ... [[1995] 2 SCR 627], or Parliament enacted legislation that altered the child support tax scheme. The record reveals that the quantum of child support was arrived at in full contemplation of Ms. Miglin's spousal support release. We also note that correspondence between counsel suggests that it was Ms. Miglin's preference to release Mr. Miglin from spousal support on condition that her economic needs were addressed through child support.

[96] The Consulting Agreement, executed between the Lodge and Ms. Miglin, was for a term of five years, with an option to renew on the consent of both parties. Both the trial judge and the Court of Appeal found this arrangement to be "thinly veiled spousal support." If it was, there should be no pejorative sense to the term. If the commercial contract is construed as a form of spousal support, it simply means that the agreement contains a time-limited spousal support agreement with a renewal option, rather than a total waiver of spousal support. Either way, neither is intrinsically unfair nor contrary to the objectives of the Act. There is nothing inherently sinister about a release or a waiver any more than there is about a time-limited arrangement. Any support clause has to be assessed in the full context of the broader agreement, the overall circumstances of the parties, and the degree of compliance with the objectives of the Act. In our view, the Consulting Agreement reflects the parties' intentions to provide Ms. Miglin with a source of employment income for a limited time. That the parties chose such a method to provide the income to Ms. Miglin does not detract from the commercial nature of the contract. Moreover, the vehicle chosen is appropriate to the manner in which the parties structured their economic lives during the marriage.

[97] It is true that Ms. Miglin stopped receiving her salary of $80,500 from the Lodge. The obvious reason, though, is that she had also stopped working more or less full-time for the Lodge. During the marriage she had hired babysitters to permit her to work at the Lodge. After the separation she could hire babysitters so she could work for a new employer.

Or, as in fact she chose, she was free not to seek other employment and to support herself and her children, during the five years of the Consulting Agreement, on the combined income of roughly $75,000 consisting of $60,000 in child support and $15,000 from the Consulting Agreement. Her own financial analyst's tables indicated her choice not to work. Recall too that, since Mr. Miglin had assumed sole responsibility for the mortgage on the matrimonial home, Ms. Miglin's expenses included no rent or mortgage payments.

[98] It is in the context of these arrangements that the final release and waiver of spousal support must be assessed. Overall, the Separation Agreement provided for a certain level of revenue to the wife, in the form of ongoing child support and the consulting fees for a five-year period, with a possibility of renewal. In this way, the Agreement sought to redress any disadvantages arising from the marriage and its breakup in part through the vehicle of the business which was, as it had been throughout the marriage, the parties' major source of income. At the same time, the Separation Agreement sought to facilitate the disentanglement of the parties' economic lives and promote their self-sufficiency. The Separation Agreement advances the 1985 Act's goals of finality and autonomy. During the marriage, Ms. Miglin continued her education (obtaining her BA), earned a salary and obtained work experience; a case was therefore not made out for compensatory support. It is unnecessary, therefore, to determine whether the Separation Agreement would still have complied substantially with the objectives of the Act on facts closer, say, to those in *Moge*.

[99] Accordingly, we find the Separation Agreement at the time of its formation to have been in substantial compliance with the *Divorce Act*.

[100] The Court of Appeal found that, at the time of the support application, the non-renewal of the Consulting Agreement and changes in the child-care arrangements constituted a material change sufficient to justify overriding the spousal support release. As we noted earlier, we do not accept the Court of Appeal's "material change" test as the appropriate basis for dispensing with an otherwise enforceable agreement. Still, with respect to the findings, we believe them to be in error.

[101] With respect to the Consulting Agreement, we note that Ms. Miglin brought her application for corollary relief in June of 1998 — prior to the expiry of the five-year term of the contract. Moreover, the parties agree that Ms. Miglin performed the terms of her contract for a period but performed no work for the Lodge, contrary to the Consulting Agreement, for the last two years of the contract. She did, however, continue to receive payment under that contract until its expiry in December 1998. Needless to say, Mr. Miglin opted not to renew the Consulting Agreement at the end of its term. We fail to see how, at the time of application, the ongoing receipt of payment for services not being performed can constitute a change of any kind.

[102] Regarding the purported changes to the child-care arrangements, the *ad hoc* parenting arrangements that developed during the period of amicable relations between the parties no doubt reflected the changing needs of the growing children. These changes are an ordinary fact of life. We note too that by the time of the trial, the eldest child was residing primarily with Mr. Miglin.

[103] Moreover, even if we accept that the expiry of the Consulting Agreement can be construed as occurring at the time of Ms. Miglin's application, we do not consider its non-renewal to be sufficient to render

continued reliance on the original agreement inappropriate. First, the contract stipulated that renewal required the consent of both parties. Second, the income projections and tax planning advice provided by Ms. Miglin's accountant at the time of negotiation carried that assumption and thus made her fully aware that she would be without that income in five years. Third, there is no evidence of any damaging long-term impact of the marriage on Ms. Miglin's employability or that at the time of negotiation she underestimated how long it would take to become self-sufficient. Ms. Miglin is an educated woman with employable skills who worked in the business throughout the marriage. Although she is no doubt responsible for the day-to-day care of the three children residing with her, she has previously demonstrated her willingness to engage child-care services. The parties dispute whether Ms. Miglin attempted to pursue any employment. What is clear from the correspondence between counsel during negotiation of the agreement, however, is that Ms. Miglin had no intention of working.

[104] The only real changes we see are the variation of the child support award in accordance with the Guidelines and the fact that the eldest child is now residing primarily with Mr. Miglin. The quantum of child support established in the Agreement provided Ms. Miglin with a minimum amount of income in contemplation of her not working. Her lawyer, in a letter to Mr. Miglin's counsel, states: "She is clearly not going to be working. Taking care of the children is a full time job at this time. It does not change the nature of the spousal support release anyway...." Furthermore, the correspondence makes it clear that Ms. Miglin contemplated a reduction in income when the Consulting Agreement ended and was advised by her accountant to plan ahead for this drop in income. In our view, the change to the obligations regarding child care did not take Ms. Miglin's current position outside the reasonable range of circumstances that the parties contemplated in making the Separation Agreement.

[105] At the Court of Appeal, counsel for Ms. Miglin suggested that her financial position deteriorated after the breakdown of the marriage. The record demonstrates (and she concedes), however, that her net worth in fact increased by at least 20 percent. At the time of her support application, a financial statement dated June 2, 1998, filed as part of the record, valued her net worth at $750,000 with essentially no debt. The statement shows that she held $246,000 in RRSPs, $83,000 in cash, and an unencumbered five-bedroom home valued at $395,000. The only debt listed on the statement was an unsubstantial debt for a credit card. By the time of trial, one year later, she valued her home at $400,000. There was no evidence that the terms of the agreement resulted in conditions under which Ms. Miglin could not assure her family's livelihood and had to deplete her assets, thus bringing her outside the range of circumstances in which she pictured herself at the time of executing the Separation Agreement.

[106] The respondent's evidence and argument regarding her circumstances at the time of her support application fail to demonstrate that the agreement fairly negotiated and substantially compliant with the objectives of the 1985 Act at its formation should not continue to govern the parties' post-divorce obligations towards each other....

LEBEL J (dissenting):

The dissenting judges agreed that the *Pelech* trilogy was no longer applicable. LeBel J reviewed the statutory provisions and spousal support cases, including *Pelech*, *Moge*, and *Bracklow*. He identified a "paradigm shift" in the Court's spousal support jurisprudence. *Pelech* emphasized "individual responsibility" and a "clean break" between spouses. In contrast, *Bracklow* took a "contextual approach," holding that "the desirability of freedom to move on to new relationships is merely one of several objectives that might guide the judge" (*Bracklow* at para 57). According to LeBel J, *Bracklow* and *Moge* take a "holistic and fact-based approach to spousal support" that is "in keeping with the diversity of factors and objectives in the 1985 Act" and recognizes that marriage "often creates complicated and gender-based interdependencies that cannot adequately be addressed by stressing formal equality or deemed self-sufficiency." This shift in the Court's jurisprudence "bolsters the conclusion that I reached ... on a plain reading of the statute: the trilogy's radical change and causal connection threshold test for judicial intervention in 'final' agreements can no longer stand" (at paras 203–204).

However, LeBel J concluded that consistency with the contextual approach to spousal support would require that the new test "be one that insists on the substantive equality of the parties during the marriage and at the time of separation, by ensuring that the agreement equitably apportions the economic consequences of the marriage and its breakdown" (at para 205). Further, a contextual approach:

> [207] ... not only respects the diversity of marital relationships, but also recognizes the social and socio-economic realities that shape parties' roles within these relationships and upon marital breakdown. The private contractual model is blind to these realities and is therefore fundamentally incompatible both with the contextual approach to spousal support propounded by this Court and with the language of the 1985 Act.

In paras 208–210, LeBel J differentiated between the two approaches, noting that the private contractual model enforces a high standard for unconscionability before a contract may be set aside. Proof of unconscionability requires "both a substantial inequality of bargaining power between the parties that is exploited by the stronger party who preys upon the weaker and substantial unfairness or improvidence in the terms of the agreement." This test "reflects the strong presumption that individuals act rationally, autonomously and in their own best interests when they form private agreements." Non-enforcement is justified only when that presumption is displaced. Thus, the unconscionability standard is appropriate in commercial settings but not in family law, where its effect "is to preclude any recognition of the unique context in which separation agreements are made and the special circumstances that they are intended to govern." LeBel J noted that separation agreements "are often negotiated in situations that are emotionally charged" and which "may be further complicated by what are typically gender-based inequities in bargaining positions between the parties. In addition, separation agreements are inherently prospective in nature and, as family law experts stress, the parties may have difficulty accurately forecasting how the economic consequences of their marriage and its breakdown will play out over time."

He emphasized the role of continuing gender inequality in respect of "the degree to which social and economic factors may constrain individuals' choices at the bargaining table," noting that "... there continues to be a disjunction between the principle of equality and the lived economic and personal reality of many married women, and the law needs to be able to recognize and to accommodate the situations where this disjunction exists." Further, "it is typically women who come to the bargaining table as the financially dependent spouse, and hence the more vulnerable party in the negotiating process" (at paras 214, 215). As a consequence of these complexities:

> [218] ... the private contractual model — and similarly any model based on the assumptions that underlie it — has limited value in the spousal support context. Even where an agreement is not strictly speaking unconscionable, it may nonetheless be inappropriate for the court to uphold it. While it is important to respect the will of the parties, courts cannot assume that the parties' spousal support agreements necessarily provide a clear and transparent guide to their intentions, which, as in any area of the law, are often difficult to ascertain. In the family law context, the parties' "freedom" to contract may be significantly constrained by social and economic factors, and may be decidedly unequal. An agreement may be a product of many implicit, as well as explicit, compromises. It may reflect fundamentally flawed assumptions about how the consequences of the marriage and its breakdown will affect the parties' post-divorce lives. In light of these factors, I question the desirability of a policy of excessive deference that puts the courts in the position of enforcing support agreements because they are presumed to represent the objective expression of the parties' free will. While representation by competent counsel is advisable, even necessary, in this context and while professional advisors should certainly seek a proper settlement and most do, the presence of counsel will not always be sufficient to redress these problems....

After reviewing the change-based test in the Ontario Court of Appeal, LeBel J set out principles for applications pursuant to section 15.2. In his view, the language in section 15.2 of the *Divorce Act* requires a court faced with an application to override a spousal support agreement to assess "whether the agreement is objectively fair at the time of the application" (at para 227).

> [228] This threshold allows the reviewing court to intervene regardless of whether the unfairness at the time of the application stems from the unfairness of the initial agreement, the parties' failure at the time the agreement was negotiated to accurately predict how the economic consequences of the marriage or its breakdown would play out over time, or changes in the parties' circumstances.... It places the emphasis on whether the support agreement has *in fact* brought about an equitable distribution of the economic consequences of the marriage and its breakdown, the ultimate goal of spousal support embodied in the statute and affirmed by this Court. In contrast, the majority's two-part test creates an artificial distinction between an assessment of the agreement at the time it was signed and an assessment of the agreement at the time of the application. Where an agreement is not voidable for reasons relating to the circumstances of execution and is found to be in substantial compliance with the Act at the first stage, it will be subject to a very strin-

gent test for variation at the second stage. As I noted above, this approach is inadequate to deal with the problems that family law experts identify flowing from the inherently prospective nature of spousal support agreements. Its effect is to penalize parties who do not accurately predict the future by subjecting agreements that may have appeared fair at the outset, but that result in unfair circumstances, to a stricter standard for judicial intervention. In addition, the majority's approach fails to accord appropriate weight to a consideration of whether the agreement is in fact meeting the objectives in s. 15.2(6) at the time of the application. In my view, a single standard is preferable. Courts should not be in the business of enforcing unfair agreements irrespective of whether the unfairness is inherent in the provisions of the initial agreement or manifests itself only as the economic consequences of the marriage and its breakdown play out in the parties' lives over time....

[230] ... [T]his approach reflects what Parliament has determined to be the driving consideration in support awards: achieving an *equitable* disentangling of the parties' economic relationship upon marital breakdown. It is inappropriate to allow parties, by way of private agreements, to subvert this statutory policy ... and to require courts to sanction this subversion by mandating deference to unfair agreements.

LeBel J explained that this assessment would require courts to undertake a "fact and context specific" examination "of all of the parties' circumstances at the time of the application" in order to determine whether "the agreement adequately meets the spousal support objectives in s. 15.2(6)." This examination would include the roles played by the parties during the marriage and the childcare arrangements made at the time of relationship breakdown as well as other factors. Specifically,

[b]ecause parties may attempt to achieve economic equity in a variety of ways (i.e., through property division and spousal support), the *entirety* of the parties' financial arrangement upon marital dissolution and not merely the spousal support provisions in their agreement must be considered. This is precisely the kind of comprehensive inquiry called for under s. 15.2. The inquiry must consider all aspects of the parties' relationship, addressing pure need as well as compensation.... (at para 231)

He also took issue with the majority's emphasis on section 9(2) of the *Divorce Act*:

[238] ... ['W]hile ... settlement is clearly to be encouraged, I do not think that the 1985 Act may properly be understood to privilege settlement *per se*. A general provision such as s. 9(2) cannot be read independently from the very specific legislative objectives for spousal support outlined in s. 15.2(6). Parties, while encouraged by s. 9(2) to settle their affairs privately, are not permitted to contract out of the Act. The 1985 Act requires courts to make spousal support orders that aim as much as possible to comply with the objectives codified in s. 15.2(6). Given this statutory framework, what the 1985 Act may be said to encourage is not settlement in itself but rather settlements that accord with the legislative objectives for spousal support articulated in s. 15.2(6). To conclude otherwise is to fail to conceive of the 1985 Act as an integrated whole. It is also potentially to put courts in the position of enforcing unfair agreements that contradict the objectives of the very Act that empowers them to hear support applications in the first place.

[239] In the spousal support context, then, the legislated policy goal is not negotiated settlement but rather the negotiation of fair settlements, with fairness evaluated according to the objectives of the 1985 Act....

LeBel J therefore concluded that it was not appropriate to defer to the spousal support waiver in the separation agreement. As he suggested (at para 245), the separation agreement and the consulting agreement "failed to realize reasonably the objectives of section 15.2(6) at the time they were negotiated and ... this continued to be the case at the time of Ms. Miglin's application for corollary relief." In particular, he concluded that Ms. Miglin's disposition of the business resulted in significant disadvantages to her, particularly because the exchange of the business and the matrimonial home, while equally valued, did not create equality — Ms. Miglin exchanged an income-producing asset for a non-income-producing asset. She also lost her employment income of approximately $80,000 per annum. Clearly, the fact that the consulting agreement had an open-ended renewal clause also recognized the possibility that she would continue to have need of an income stream. According to LeBel J (at para 246), "the resulting inequity was compounded when Mr. Miglin failed to renew the consulting agreement." In addition to these economic disadvantages arising from the breakdown of the marriage, she also suffered disadvantages from the roles adopted by the parties during their marriage and in the organization of their domestic lives.

[253] For the reasons that I have identified, the parties' financial arrangements manifestly failed to address the fact that Ms. Miglin disproportionately suffered economic disadvantages flowing both from the roles that the parties adopted during their 14-year marriage (and in terms of childcare, after the marriage as well) and from the breakdown of the marriage. This was not a situation in which the parties' financial arrangements upon separation provided for an income stream for the dependent spouse that, although somewhat lower than what a court might have awarded, was nonetheless reasonable in the circumstances. The Separation Agreement provided no spousal support or income stream whatsoever to Ms. Miglin, while the Consulting Agreement allowed for only $15,000 annually, which Mr. Miglin terminated after five years despite Ms. Miglin's ongoing need. While the majority suggests that Ms. Miglin's net worth has increased since the parties' separation, the reality is that Ms. Miglin will have no income stream, other than the support that she receives for her children, for the foreseeable future unless she sells her home or divests herself of her RRSPs, which she requires for her future security.

[254] Considered as a whole, then, the parties' financial arrangements were insufficient to fall within the generous ambit within which reasonable disagreement is possible in terms of realizing the spousal support objectives in s. 15.2(6) at the time of Ms. Miglin's application. It was thus appropriate for the trial judge to intervene and award her corollary relief. As the question of quantum of support was not pleaded before this Court, I assume without deciding that the amount awarded by the trial judge, and upheld by the Court of Appeal, was appropriate.

Appeal allowed.

Notes and Questions

Impact of *Miglin*

The judgment in *Miglin* attracted censure from academics and practising lawyers for its lack of clarity and for appearing to set an unrealistically high threshold for interference with a domestic contract. As James McLeod commented in his Annotation of the case:

> If the majority comments are given full effect, the only change that may cross the new threshold is the unexpected illness of children which interferes with a custodial parent's ability to earn income.... [If this is the new test, it] is higher than that in the trilogy, which is clearly not what the majority intended. The main problem with *Miglin* is that no one understands the new test. [By rejecting the proposals of both counsel, and without the benefit of family law expertise, the] court was on its own and unfortunately did not explain what it was doing very well.... The best advice a lawyer can give a client right now is not to enter into final settlement agreements. By emphasizing the importance of final settlements, the court may have undermined the prospects of such settlements. (James McLeod, "Annotation of *Miglin v Miglin*" (2003) 34 RFL (5th) 263 at 272)

Carol Rogerson shared those concerns. She "predicted that the strongest message taken from *Miglin* would be that agreements should be upheld — that courts should be reluctant to intervene and that parties should be made to live with the terms of the agreements that they had signed." She added that:

> The first year of trial decisions after the release of *Miglin* by and large proved the accuracy of that prediction. In the immediate aftermath of *Miglin* the test for overriding spousal support agreements was generally interpreted as a very strict one. For the most part, the only agreements that courts were willing to override were those that involved such blatant flaws in the negotiation process (*i.e.*, serious vulnerabilities and power imbalances) that the agreements would have been set aside even without *Miglin* on the basis of common law doctrines of duress, undue influence or unconscionability. Absent extremely flawed negotiations, even agreements that departed significantly from statutory entitlements were upheld. (Carol Rogerson, "Spousal Support Agreements and the Legacy of *Miglin*" (2012) 31 Can Fam LQ 13 at 14)

This "strict approach" initially appeared to be confirmed by the Supreme Court's judgment in *Hartshorne v Hartshorne*, 2004 SCC 22 (discussed in Chapter Five). However, this approach has been modified over time. Three years after *Miglin* was released, "there were indications that courts were becoming more reluctant to uphold outcomes that departed significantly from the statutory norms under the *Divorce Act*, at least without clear evidence that both parties had consciously turned their minds to this outcome and had made a fully informed decision to accept it" (Rogerson at 16).

As discussed below, later Supreme Court judgments have further modified the effect of *Miglin*, as have other developments, including widespread acceptance of the Spousal Support Advisory Guidelines. Some aspects of the judgment have been clarified while others remain confused. In her assessment of developments to 2011, Rogerson acknowledged that it is "very difficult to precisely pin down the current meaning of Miglin" due to the "complex and confused nature of [spousal support] law and the fact that the underlying norms are unstable and in flux." As a result,

> The most that can be said is that the threshold for intervention with spousal support agreements under *Miglin* has been lowered to some degree; the patterns that were emerging in the three year reviews of *Miglin* have become clearer and the courts are attempting to achieve a reasonable balance between the values of finality and fairness. There is clearly more aggressive scrutiny for procedural fairness. With respect to substantive fairness, courts are also showing increasing willingness to over-ride agreements that depart *significantly* from the substantive norms of fairness under the *Divorce Act*. At year one the main message that was taken from *Miglin* was that courts should respect final agreements or, put another way, that people should be held to the bargains that they make. Now, at year nine, the message is often slightly modified: that courts should uphold *fairly negotiated* agreements or that courts should uphold *reasonable* agreements. (Rogerson at 20)

More specifically, Rogerson found that although *Miglin* is frequently applied, there are only a small number of what she calls "core" *Miglin* cases, where the test

> is actually applied to the circumstances contemplated in the original deci-sion, *i.e.* to determine whether a court should exercise its statutory discre-tion to award support under the *Divorce Act* contrary to the terms of a final agreement.... The courts are not filled with cases in which spouses are seeking to override their spousal support agreements. (Rogerson at 22)

Many of the challenges to spousal support agreements within those "core" cases have succeeded, often on the basis of flawed negotiations at stage 1, part 1 of the *Miglin* analysis. Further, even in those cases where "the ruling in favour of overriding the agreement is based solely on sub-stantive unfairness" at stage 1, part 2 or stage 2 of the *Miglin* analysis, "a careful reading of many of these cases reveals facts that suggest the pres-ence of procedural flaws, although that was not the basis of the legal rul-ing." This widespread recognition of flawed negotiations and other procedural flaws is related to "[s]hifting norms of fair bargaining ... in the area of domestic contracts generally" (Rogerson at 22) and will be discussed below.

Finally, the threshold for judicial intervention on the basis that the agreement is substantively unfair remains fairly high: "Courts are not easily overriding spousal agreements simply because a spouse might have done better had he or she gone to court." However, widespread acceptance of the Spousal Support Advisory Guidelines (explained in the next section of this chapter), which set out ranges for spousal support quantum and dura-tion based on a formula, has "likely contributed to a clarification of what constitutes a significant departure from the statutory norms." As a result, "courts are willing to override spousal support agreements that depart *sig-nificantly* from the statutory norms ... particularly if they leave a former spouse in a state of financial hardship." Further, "[t]he application of the foreseeability test under *Miglin* stage 2 is often shaped by substantive norms: courts will often find that the parties could not have reasonably contemplated a result dramatically at odds with the spousal support objectives under the *Divorce Act*" (Rogerson at 23).

Miglin, fairness, and gender issues

In a review of *Miglin* after the decision of the Ontario Court of Appeal, Martha Shaffer and Carol Rogerson concluded that striking a balance between fairness on one hand and certainty on the other in family agreements was not an easy task. However, they examined the relationship between family contracts and spousal support provisions to argue that concerns about the finality of contracts may represent "hidden" concerns about the legitimacy of spousal support obligations *per se*. (See Martha Shaffer & Carol Rogerson, "Contracting Spousal Support: Thinking Through *Miglin*" (2003–4) 21 Can Fam LQ 49.)

The authors also examined several reasons for complexity in family contracts concerning spousal support, including

- fairness concerns in relation to spousal support obligations;
- problems of shifting norms so that bargains negotiated in one context may appear unfair when the norms change; and
- the complexity of different statutory thresholds for original applications for spousal support, by contrast with applications for variation.

Do you agree with this assessment?

According to Julien Payne, *Miglin* reflected hidden gender issues:

> The principles formulated by the majority in *Miglin* are conceptually gender neutral and apply equally to payors and payees. In practice, men will fare better than women under *Miglin* because men are typically payors and women are typically payees and finality usually favours the former group. In addition, the principles set out in *Miglin* are inevitably subject to the practicability of the payor's retention of an ability to pay. (Julien Payne, "First Impressions of Miglin in the Supreme Court of Canada" (PPFL/2003-001))

To what extent do you agree with this assessment? How were issues about gender disparities conceptualized in the reasoning of the majority and dissenting judgments? To what extent might gender issues play into concerns regarding fairness and shifting norms? Is there a need to continue to take account of gender disparities in marriage, and at marriage breakdown?

Continuing issues: doctrinal blurring and *Miglin* stage 1

Carol Rogerson identified and analysed a number of continuing problems relating to "pervasive conceptual confusion and the blurring of boundaries" with regard to *Miglin*, in part because the *Miglin* test raises significant difficulties and also because it is frequently applied to domestic contracts that were made in circumstances different from those in *Miglin*. Although "[t]here is an increasing tendency to automatically and unthinkingly resort to *Miglin* any time a case involves a domestic contract," Rogerson cautions that

> It is important to start with a clear understanding of the legal context for which the *Miglin* test was created. The *Miglin* test, as originally articulated, relates to the exercise of a specific statutory power — the power ... to make and vary awards of spousal support under the *Divorce Act*. A spousal support agreement is, by the express terms of the statute, not binding on courts but rather a factor to be considered. Courts under the *Divorce Act* may disregard or override an agreement and make an order for spousal support that is contrary to the terms of a prior agreement. *Miglin* provides a set of guidelines to structure the exercise of the court's discretionary power, specifically to determine the weight to be accorded to a *final* agreement when awarding spousal support under the *Divorce Act*.
>
> Unfortunately, this clear conception of when *Miglin* is applicable is often forgotten.... (Rogerson at 21 and 24)

Rogerson highlights several areas of concern with regard to application of the *Miglin* test to circumstances outside of those for which it was developed. The first set of concerns relate to the doctrinal blurring between the common law standards for unconscionability and stage 1 of the *Miglin* analysis. According to Rogerson,

> ... When dealing with challenges to a spousal support agreement, issues of the validity and enforceability of an agreement (under the common law, and in Ontario under s 56 of the FLA) should logically be dealt with first, followed by a *Miglin* analysis if there is a valid and enforceable agreement. *Miglin* should be used to determine whether *an otherwise valid agreement* should nonetheless be overridden or disregarded in an application for spousal support under the *Divorce Act*.
>
> Such clear distinctions between the validity analysis and the *Miglin* analysis are rarely found in practice however.... In cases where the agreement in issue deals both with property and spousal support, in Ontario the challenge to the property provisions is often analyzed under s 56(4) and the spousal support provisions are analyzed under *Miglin*.... (Rogerson at 25–26)

> [This blurring] was exacerbated by the Supreme Court of Canada's 2009 decision in *Rick v Brandsema* [discussed below]. *Rick* reinterpreted *Miglin*. No longer was *Miglin* stage one seen as adding requirements of procedural fairness beyond those imposed by the common law of unconscionability. Instead, *Miglin* was seen as a direct ruling on and a *reformulation* of the common law test for unconscionability....
>
> As a result of *Rick*, the boundary between unconscionability and *Miglin* stage one has collapsed completely....
>
> When the context is solely an application for spousal support under the *Divorce Act* [this distinction] ... is perhaps not so important at the end of the day.... All of these bodies of law are moving in the same direction with respect to the requirements of fair bargaining in the domestic context and the result under the *Divorce Act* will be the same ... the more problematic consequences of this conceptual confusion and doctrinal blurring arise when the agreements in issue deal with matters other than spousal support and it becomes more important to distinguish between legal doctrines and their effects. (Rogerson at 27–28)

The fact that the *Miglin* test overlaps with other common law and statutory doctrines affecting domestic contracting has led to further blurring due to its application in circumstances that go beyond spousal support, especially with regard to agreements for property division. The Supreme Court added to the confusion with its judgment in *Hartshorne* (see Chapter Five), which "used ideas from *Miglin*, and in particular the ideas of respect for autonomous choice, to constrain the courts' discretion to override property agreements simply because they departed from the statutory norms." This was "a relatively limited extension of *Miglin* principles," and was "confined to B.C. where there was a specific statutory power to override unfair agreements." However, *Hartshorne*'s limited extension of *Miglin* is sometimes misread, with "the idea tak[ing] hold in some quarters that *Miglin*, rather than providing a framework for the interpretation of specific statutory powers, conferred a new set of general powers on courts for setting aside all domestic contracts, including property agreements" (Rogerson at 29).

> This misreading of *Miglin* has now ... been reinforced by the Supreme Court of Canada's 2009 decision in *Rick v Brandesma* [sic]. In *Rick* the court reformulated the common law test for unconscionability in the family law context to incorporate the higher standards for fair negotiations that are part of the *Miglin* stage one analysis, specifically a requirement of full and honest disclosure, and then used that reformulated conception of unconscionability to set aside a property agreement. The most surprising part of the decision ... was that this expanded conception of unconscionability was not presented as a novel extension of the common law, influenced by ideas from *Miglin*. Instead the original *Miglin* decision, which clearly involved the interpretation of a statutory power, was simply read, or more accurately misread, as a reformulation of the law of unconscionability. (Rogerson at 30)

"Unconscionability" and *Rick v Brandsema*

The Supreme Court of Canada also reviewed some aspects of *Miglin* in 2009. In *Rick v Brandsema*, 2009 SCC 10, the spouses had married in 1973 and they separated in 2000. They had five children. The husband and wife operated a dairy farm together.

At separation, they negotiated an agreement, which was achieved with "intermittent representation by lawyers" and by efforts of mediation. One year after signing the agreement, the former wife applied to set it aside on the ground of unconscionability or for an order for reapportionment pursuant to section 65 of the B.C. *Family Relations Act*.

The trial judge held that the agreement was unconscionable because the husband had exploited his wife's mental instability during negotiations, and had deliberately concealed or undervalued some assets. As a result, even though the parties had expressed an intention for an equal division of assets, the wife received significantly less than her entitlement under the Act. The trial judge ordered an award of the difference between the negotiated settlement and the wife's entitlement under the Act.

The B.C. Court of Appeal allowed the husband's appeal, disagreeing about the extent of the wife's vulnerabilities and concluding that they were compensated for by her counsel's representation.

In the Supreme Court of Canada, the appeal was allowed. Abella J held that the "singularly emotional environment" involved in the negotiation of a separation agreement requires special care to ensure a fair distribution of assets and the absence of exploitation. An acceptable settlement depends on both parties providing full and honest disclosure of all relevant financial information. This duty "anchors the ability of separating spouses to genuinely decide for themselves what constitutes an acceptable bargain, it also helps protect the possibility of finality of agreements" (at para 48).

In the end, the Supreme Court concluded that the trial judge was correct to hold that the separation agreement was unconscionable in the circumstances. In relation to *Miglin*, Abella J stated:

> The circumstances of this case move us to consider the implications flowing from *Miglin* for the deliberate failure of a spouse to provide all the relevant financial information in negotiations for the division of assets. In my view, it is a corollary to the realities addressed by this Court in *Miglin*, that there be a duty to make full and honest disclosure of such information when negotiating separation agreements.
>
> The husband's exploitative conduct, both in failing to make full and honest disclosure and in taking advantage of what he knew to be his wife's mental instability, resulted in a finding of unconscionability.... (at paras 5–6)

As Robert Leckey argued, the Supreme Court of Canada introduced some confusion in *Rick* because this case focused on the common law (equitable) doctrine of unconscionability. By contrast, *Miglin* represented an interpretation of statutory provisions in the *Divorce Act* concerning the weight to be attached to a private agreement in the context of an application for spousal support. As Leckey further noted, the majority in *Miglin* had expressly stated that its test was more lenient than common law unconscionability. Moreover, since the remedy for unconscionability involves "equitable compensation," it may not be appropriate in a context in which a court finds a basis for reapportioning assets in accordance with the statutory regime. In addition, since the court in *Rick* was dealing with the property provisions of a separation agreement, by contrast with spousal support in *Miglin*, the court may have failed to take account of the finality of property orders. And finally, since the doctrine of unconscionability is included in family contract legislation in different ways among the provinces (see, for example, Ontario's *FLA*, s 56(4)(c)), the *Rick* decision raises some problems about the relationship of federal and provincial legislation. In particular, the absence of the common law doctrine of unconscionability in Québec law creates uncertainty about the application of this decision there. See Robert Leckey, "A Common Law of the Family? Reflections on *Rick v Brandsema*" (2009) 25 Can J Fam L 257.

After the Supreme Court's decision in *Rick v Brandsema*, how would you characterize the continuing validity of the Supreme Court's test for separation agreements, as set out in *Miglin*?

Recall the Ontario Court of Appeal decision in *LeVan v LeVan*, discussed in Chapter Five, and the authority in the *FLA*, section 56(4)(a) to set aside an agreement where a party fails to disclose assets and debts. In *LeVan*, there was no suggestion that the wife suffered from "mental instability" although she was clearly under pressure from her husband to sign the marriage contract prior to the wedding. If the husband had made full disclosure, would the court have reached the same result? In other words, how significant was the wife's mental situation to the outcome in *Rick*?

Impact of *Rick v Brandsema*

Issues regarding flawed negotiations were examined in *Stevens v Stevens*, 2012 ONSC 706. Pamela and Joel Stevens were married for 16 years and had three children together. They were both university graduates who had good jobs when they married; however Pamela quit her job when Joel was transferred to London, England so that she could travel with him. Joel later started his own company where Pamela worked part-time; she also did volunteer work and raised their children.

In 2006 Joel admitted to having an affair with another woman. He wanted to leave Pamela but would not leave their home until they had a parenting agreement in place. They slept in separate rooms. The couple consulted lawyers. Just three weeks later, they reconciled. Pamela wanted to quickly get a marriage contract together. Pamela and her lawyer's notes are consistent in that they both stated Pamela's intention for the contract was to give Joel one-half of the value of the matrimonial home. However, the final Marriage Contract contained an error: it said that Pamela intended to give Joel the *full* value of the matrimonial home. It was a drafting error that neither Pamela nor her lawyer were aware of. Even the cover letter stated that the intention was to give Joel *one half* the value of the Matrimonial Home. The contract also included a mutual release of spousal support. Both parties signed the erroneous contract. If the contract were implemented, the error would result in Joel receiving $1.5 million more than Pamela had intended. The marriage ended in January 2007 when Pamela found out that Joel went on a vacation with his lover after they had reconciled.

Joel claimed that the contract reflected the agreement between the parties. Pamela disagreed, claiming the intention was to give Joel only half of the value of the matrimonial home, not the full value. The issues were whether the marriage contract should be set aside because:

1. There was a fundamental mistake such that there was no consensus ad idem;
2. The marriage contract was unconscionable;
3. Pamela Stevens lacked the capacity to enter into and/or did not understand the nature and/or the consequences of the marriage contract.

Harper J considered the mistake and whether it was so fundamental as to render the contract void or voidable. He determined that the evidence proffered by Joel and his lawyer, Ms. Klukach, regarding when they knew about the inconsistency between the cover letter and the contract was not credible and accepted the evidence of Pamela's lawyer:

> **[92]** I accept Ms. Tsao's version of the negotiation process. Paragraph 12(1)(a) contains a mistake that was not intended. That mistake was known by Ms. Klukach and her client, Joel. Neither Joel nor Ms. Klukach got any clarification of the mistake. A simple phone call followed by a confirmation in writing is all that was necessary. I find that without that simple clarifying act, Ms. Klukach and her client took advantage of the mistake and allowed the process to conclude, while knowing that there was no meeting of the minds on this very material issue. ...

> **[95]** I find that one of the most fundamental terms of this contract was [para.] 12(1)(b), which provided for the amount to go to Joel and resulted in a mutual release of spousal support obligations. I find that was a term on which there was no consensus ad idem. I find that Joel was aware of this mistake and took advantage of it.

> **[96]** As a result of my findings and application of the law, I find that this contract is void ab initio.

Pamela took anti-depressant medication from 1995 to 2006. She stopped taking the medication abruptly and without consulting a physician when she found out her husband was having an affair. As a result, her behaviour changed and she stopped listening to those who usually gave her advice on legal and financial matters, including her own lawyer (at paras 111–120). It was during this period that the Marriage Contract was signed. Two months after signing Pamela was admitted to hospital with severe depression. She was released a couple of weeks later with new medication. She testified that she hated everything she had done between the early spring of 2006 and her hospital admission. An expert testified regarding Pamela's capacity during the period when the contract was signed (at paras 129–133). The expert concluded that it was "highly probable and in fact virtually certain" that Ms Stevens's mental state was impaired so that she could not understand the nature and consequences of the agreement (at para 134).

Harper J considered this evidence and found that as a result of her mental state, "Pamela was not open to hearing the information that she needed to hear during the crucial Marriage Contract negotiation period (at para 147). He set the Marriage Contract aside "on the basis of Pamela's lack of capacity to understand and appreciate the nature and consequences of the agreement as per section 56(4)(b) of the Family Law Act" (at para 149).

Harper J also reviewed the court's discretion to set aside a domestic contract on the grounds of unconscionability under *FLA*, ss 56(4) and 33(4)(a) (at paras 150–153). He then referred to the formulation of the test in *Miglin*, and its relationship to support:

> **[154]** The Supreme Court of Canada in *Rick v. Brandsema*, [2009] 1 S.C.R. 295, [2009] S.C.J. No. 10, 2009 SCC 10 commented on the unique circumstances in which domestic contracts are negotiated. At paras. 43 and 44 of this judgment, Abella J.A stated:

Miglin represented a reformulation and tailoring of the common law test for unconscionability to reflect the uniqueness of matrimonial bargains:

> [W]e are not suggesting that courts must necessarily look for "unconscionability" as it is understood in the common law of contract. There is a danger in borrowing terminology rooted in other branches of the law and transporting it into what all agree is a unique legal context. There may be persuasive evidence brought before the court that one party took advantage of the vulnerability of the other party in separation or divorce negotiations that would fall short of evidence of the power imbalance necessary to demonstrate unconscionability in a commercial context between, say, a consumer and a large financial institution.

Where, therefore "there are any circumstances of oppression, pressure, or other vulnerabilities", and if one party's exploitation of such vulnerabilities during the negotiation process resulted in a separation agreement that deviated substantially from the legislation, the Court in *Miglin* concluded that the agreement need not be enforced (at paras 81–83).

[155] In *Brandsema*, the Supreme Court of Canada stressed the importance of respecting the "parties" right to decide for themselves what constitutes for them, in the circumstances of their marriage, mutually acceptable and equitable sharing. Abella J. stated, at para. 45, that "[p]arties should generally be free to decide for themselves what bargain they are prepared to make". However, the court also emphasized, at para. 50:

> In other words, the best way to protect the finality of any negotiated agreement in family law, is to ensure both its procedural and substantive integrity in accordance with the relevant legislative scheme.

Harper J acknowledged that the Miglin test was formulated to apply agreements concerning spousal support, but suggested that it was clear in *Brandsema* that "the same approach offers guidance for the conduct of negotiations for agreements generally," including with respect to property entitlement. He found that "Pamela was in a vulnerable state throughout the negotiation process" (at paras 157–158). He considered the couple's cumulative actions in order to determine whether or not Joel took advantage of Pamela's vulnerability (at paras 160–179). Thus, he set aside the Marriage Contract.

After setting aside the agreement, the court proceeded to assess the parties' entitlements to equalization and spousal support. Because the wife had remained at home during the marriage, the court ordered the husband to make a lump sum retroactive compensatory spousal support payment of $136,182.

There was additional litigation with respect to costs: (2012) ONSC 6881. In the end, Pamela was awarded costs:

> [26] It is hard to prioritize the bad conduct on the part of Joel during this whole process as there are so many egregious incidents of Joel taking advantage of Pamela. In my reasons I found that Joel was aware of the mistake in the Marriage Contract and he attempted to take advantage of it. I found that this conduct amounted to equitable fraud and that is yet

another example that could stand alone for a finding of bad faith. I do not need to itemize all of his conduct that I found in my reasons for judgment that amounted to bad faith.

The trial judgment and the costs order were both affirmed on appeal. See *Stevens v Stevens*, 2013 ONCA 267.

Unconscionability pursuant to *FLA*, s 33(4)

The *FLA* provides for the setting aside of a provision for support or a waiver of support in a domestic contract if it results in "unconscionable" circumstances, or if the recipient of support or the person who waived it becomes entitled to social assistance. In addition, a court may set aside such a provision if there is default at the time of an application.

This statutory provision ensures that a person does not become a public charge on a social assistance program as a result of agreeing to waive or to receive insufficient spousal support. In addition, section 33(4) permits a court to take account of "unconscionability."

In *Scheel v Henkelman* (2001), 11 RFL (5th) 376, the Ontario Court of Appeal allowed an appeal from a lower court decision, in which the trial judge had upheld a waiver of spousal support in a cohabitation agreement. In this case, the parties had cohabited for 10 years, although they had known each other for a long period, and the woman worked as an assistant to the man in his real estate and business activities. The resources available to the woman applicant, following separation, were quite low, particularly compared to those of her cohabiting partner. According to the Court of Appeal, the woman's age (65), her inability to work, and her monthly pension of $407, in a context in which the male respondent had assets of $2.5 million, resulted in unconscionable circumstances pursuant to section 33(4). As the court concluded (at para 23), "it would be shocking to the conscience to require the appellant to live on her modest pension." The court thus ordered spousal support in the amount of $3,500 per month.

Continuing issues: Orders, variation, agreements and "final" agreements

Courts have had difficulty determining when to apply section 17 of the *Divorce Act*, which applies to variation of spousal support, and when to apply the *Miglin* test.

These issues arise in part because of some genuinely confusing language in the *Divorce Act*. Section 15.2(1) of the Act authorizes a court to "make an order requiring a spouse" to pay support to the other spouse. In contrast, section 15.2(2) authorizes a court to "make an interim order requiring a spouse" to pay support "pending the determination of the application under subsection (1)." Because of this language, section 15.2(1) orders are often referred to as "final" in order to distinguish them from "interim" orders under section 15.2(2).

However, "final" orders made under section 15.2(1) are not truly final because they may be varied pursuant to section 17 of the *Divorce Act*, which authorizes a court to order variation of a previous spousal support order. Section 17 requires that:

> Before the court makes a variation order in respect of a spousal support
> order, the court shall satisfy itself that a change in the condition, means,
> needs or other circumstances of either former spouse has occurred since
> the making of the spousal support order or the last variation order made
> in respect of that order, and, in making the variation order, the court
> shall take that change into consideration.

The test for application of section 17 requires the party seeking variation to
establish that there has been a "material change of circumstances" since the
last order. A material change of circumstances" is defined as "a change ...
that, if known at the time, would likely have resulted in different terms"
(*Willick v Willick*, [1994] 3 SCR 670 at para 22). The material change of
circumstances test for variation of an *order* is easier to meet than the *Miglin*
test for variation of an *agreement*. However, courts remain confused about
which test to use, in part because of misapplications of *Miglin*, but also
because agreements for spousal support are sometimes incorporated into a
court order.

The *Miglin* case required the Supreme Court to assess the content of a
separation agreement (which provided for a final settlement between the
spouses) in relation to a *subsequent* section 15.2(1) application for spousal
support by Ms. Miglin. Thus, the question was whether the court should
override or set aside the spousal support clauses in the separation *agreement*. By contrast, section 17 of the *Divorce Act* (and similar provincial
statutes) is used where a party applies to vary an existing spousal support
order.

Recall that the agreement between the Miglins was intended as a final
settlement of all issues between the parties. Thus, "[a]s originally articulated, the *Miglin* stage 2 test was understood to be a distinctive test crafted
for final agreements — more stringent than the ordinary material change
test applied in a variation context." According to Rogerson, spousal support
agreements are final in the *Miglin* sense only if they time-limit or waive
spousal support. Such final agreements are relatively unusual:

> Spousal support is by its nature a prospective, on-going obligation. The
> default assumption is that, spousal support is open to modification in
> response to changing circumstances. Thus spousal support orders made by
> courts are subject to variation and often include conditions for review;
> similarly, when parties negotiate their own settlement of spousal support,
> their agreements often make provision for variation or review. (Rogerson
> at 34)

In addition, many agreements for spousal support provide for ongoing support without explicit provision for variation or review (on review orders, see
Leskun v Leskun, 2006 SCC 25, earlier in this chapter).

In Rogerson's view, the *Miglin* test should be applied only to final
agreements. *Miglin* is nevertheless "often misapplied to agreements that
expressly provide for review or variation or that provide for indefinite support where a power to vary might be reasonably implied." The *Miglin* test
should not be applied in these circumstances because it is more stringent
than the material change test that was intended by the parties. Where the
Miglin test is applied, it "is often applied as if it were no different than the

material change test — a move that generates sensible results but produces doctrinal confusion" (Rogerson at 35).

A more serious "source of doctrinal blurring is the on-going confusion regarding how to apply *Miglin* to consent orders given the statutory context of section 17 of the *Divorce Act* which explicitly includes the material change test. The failure to think clearly about the relationship between the material change threshold and the *Miglin* stage 2 test has contributed to the confused merger of the two tests" (Rogerson at 35). The Supreme Court has recently considered this issue in *LMP v LS*, discussed below.

Are there good reasons to continue to recognize this distinction between orders and agreements? In reflecting on this question, consider the views in the majority and dissenting judgments with respect to the context in which separation agreements are negotiated (and the interpretation of section 9 of the *Divorce Act*). What underlying policy goals are promoted by these differing views in *Miglin*?

The impact of *Miglin* and *Rick*: *LMP v LS*

In *LMP v LS*, 2011 SCC 64, the Supreme Court of Canada considered an appeal from Québec concerning a husband's application for variation of spousal support in a separation agreement. The husband was a litigator in Montreal, and the wife (who did not have a high school leaving certificate) had assumed a traditional role in the home. One year after the parties' marriage, the wife had been diagnosed with multiple sclerosis, and she was then assessed by a private disability insurer as permanently disabled and unable to work. Thereafter, she received LTD benefits. The couple had two young children, and they separated after 14 years of marriage.

At the time of their divorce, the spouses agreed to a consent judgment, in which the husband undertook to pay child support as well as spousal support. The agreement did not specify a date for review or termination of these obligations. Nor did the agreement require that the wife seek training or employment.

Four years after the divorce, the wife applied for increased child support because the husband's income had increased. In response, the husband applied to terminate the wife's spousal support, arguing that she had made no effort to look for work. He also produced contested medical evidence to support his assertion that she was capable of working part time. However, he did not claim any change in his wife's medical condition. The trial judge accepted the husband's argument that the passage of time relieved him of his obligation to pay spousal support, based in part on the court's positive assessment of the former wife when she was giving evidence at the trial. The Québec Court of Appeal upheld the trial decision (see 2010 QCCA 793 and 2009 QCCS 3389).

The Supreme Court of Canada was unanimous that no material change had occurred since the agreement was made and incorporated into the initial order. Thus the husband's application for variation was denied and the original spousal support order was restored. However, the court split on the test to be applied. A majority of judges (Abella, Rothstein, Binnie, LeBel, and Deschamps JJ) held that *LMP* represented an application to vary a support order, pursuant to section 17 of the *Divorce Act*. In this context, they held that while *Miglin* applied in relation to an initial application for spousal support (in relation to a private agreement), the case was not so relevant to an application to vary. Because the factors outlined in section 17, by contrast with section 15.2(4), do not refer to an "order, agreement or arrangement relating to support of either spouse," the court suggested that treatment of an agreement must be different in a variation context. In a concurring judgment, two judges (Cromwell J and McLachlin CJ) expressed the view that the general principles of *Miglin* and deference to private agreements should apply to both initial and variation applications.

The majority judges reviewed the law of variation and the material change of circumstances test in section 17(4.1) of the *Divorce Act*:

[29] In determining whether the conditions for variation exist, the threshold that must be met before a court may vary a prior spousal support order is articulated in s. 17(4.1). A court must consider whether there has been a change in the conditions, means, needs or other circumstances of either former spouse since the making of the spousal support order.

[30] In our view, the proper approach under s. 17 to the variation of existing orders is found in *Willick v Willick*, [1994] 3 S.C.R. 670 (S.C.C.), and *B(G.) c G (L)*, [1995] 3 S.C.R. 370 (S.C.C.). Like the order at issue in this case, *Willick* (dealing with child support) and *G. (L.)* (dealing with spousal support) involved court orders which had incorporated provisions of separation agreements....

[31] *Willick* described the proper analysis as requiring a court to "determine first, whether the conditions for variation exist and if they do exist what variation of the existing order ought to be made in light of the change in circumstances".... In determining whether the conditions for variation exist, the court must be satisfied that there has been a change of circumstance since the making of the prior order or variation. The onus is on the party seeking a variation to establish such a change.

[32] That "change of circumstances", the majority of the Court concluded in *Willick*, had to be a "material" one, meaning a change that, "if known at the time, would likely have resulted in different terms".... *G. (L.)* confirmed that this threshold also applied to spousal support variations.

[33] The focus of the analysis is on the prior order and the circumstances in which it was made. *Willick* clarifies that a court ought not to consider the correctness of that order, nor is it to be departed from lightly.... The test is whether any given change "would likely have resulted in different terms" to the order. It is presumed that the judge who granted the initial order knew and applied the law, and that, accordingly, the prior support order met the objectives set out in s. 15.2(6). In this way, the *Willick* approach to variation applications requires appropriate deference to the terms of the prior order, whether or not that order incorporates an agreement.

[35] In general, a material change must have some degree of continuity, and not merely be a temporary set of circumstances.... Certain other factors can assist a court in determining whether a particular change is material. The subsequent conduct of the parties, for example, may provide indications as to whether they considered a particular change to be material....

The majority judges concluded that the material change in circumstances test applies "whether or not a spousal support order incorporates an agreement" (at para 36). However, if an agreement was incorporated into a spousal support order, the substance of that agreement may be relevant to the court's assessment of whether there was material change:

> [38] The agreement may address future circumstances and predetermine who will bear the risk of any changes that might occur. And it may well specifically provide that a contemplated future event will or will not amount to a material change.

> [39] Parties may either contemplate that a specific type of change will or will not give rise to variation.... Even significant changes may not be material for the purposes of s. 17(4.1) if they were actually contemplated by the parties by the terms of the order at the time of the order. The degree of specificity with which the terms of the order provide for a particular change is evidence of whether the parties or court contemplated the situation raised on an application for variation, and whether the order was intended to capture the particular changed circumstances. Courts should give effect to these intentions, bearing in mind that the agreement was incorporated into a court order, and that the terms can therefore be presumed, as of that time, to have been in compliance with the objectives of the *Divorce Act* when the order was made.

However, an agreement incorporated into an order where there was only general language regarding variation in case of material change does not give the court any additional information. Further, even where there is express language of finality in an agreement that was incorporated into an order, the court retains its jurisdiction under section 17:

> [42] Ultimately, courts are tasked with determining if a material change of circumstances has occurred so as to justify a variation of a s. 15.2 order under s. 17. The analysis is always grounded in the actual circumstances of the parties and the terms of the s. 15.2 order; what meaning a court will give any general statement of finality found in an order will be a question to be resolved on that basis. As we have explained, in some situations, the agreement incorporated into the order may help shape what is meant by a "material change of circumstances". Where a s. 15.2 order deals with a specific change, it assists courts by answering the *Willick* inquiry through its terms. Conversely, when the order is general, or simply purports to be final, these less specific terms provide less assistance to courts in answering the *Willick* inquiry. Sometimes, in such cases, the circumstances of the parties may be such that courts will give little weight to a general statement of finality and conclude that a material change exists. However, at other times, in such cases, the circumstances of the parties may also be such that the courts will give effect to a general statement of finality and conclude that a material change does not exist....

> [45] In Justice Cromwell's opinion, however, "the parties' agreement must be accorded significant weight at the variation stage" because it "is critical evidence of what they actually or ought reasonably to be taken to have contemplated at the time" paras. 76 and 83). With respect, the general proposition that spousal support agreements should be accorded "significant weight" in the search for a material change under s. 17 is problematic. As explained earlier, while a term stating that a specific type of change will — or will not — give rise to variation will constitute such "evidence" and will inform the court's application of the *Willick*

test, an agreement containing only general terms, such as a general statement of finality, provides little guidance in practice on whether or not a
particular event or circumstance was contemplated by the parties or on
the consequences the parties would have ascribed to it. The court will of
necessity interpret any such general provision by reference to the parties'
circumstances at the time of the s. 15.2 order. These circumstances may
or may not lead the court to conclude that the parties have contemplated the event and, consequently, whether a material change warranting
a variation has occurred: the court must find a "change, such that, if
known at the time, would likely have resulted in different terms"
(*Willick*, at p. 688).

[46] The examination of the change in circumstances is exactly the same
for an order that does not incorporate a prior spousal support agreement
as for one that does. A general statement that the agreement must be
accorded "significant weight", even though its implications in a concrete
case are unclear, in effect raises the threshold necessary to establish a
"material change" under s. 17 when there is an agreement, and emphasizes legal certainty and finality at the expense of the statutory requirements of s. 17. Such a result is reminiscent of the "clean break" approach
of the *Pelech* trilogy, rejected in *Moge* and *Miglin* because it was held to
be inappropriate in the context of the current *Divorce Act*.

[47] If the s. 17 threshold for variation of a spousal support order has
been met, a court must determine what variation to the order needs to be
made in light of the change in circumstances. The court then takes into
account the material change, and should limit itself to making only the
variation justified by that change. As Justice L'Heureux-Dubé, concurring
in *Willick*, observed: "A variation under the Act is neither an appeal of
the original order nor a de novo hearing" (p. 739). As earlier stated, as
Bastarache and Arbour JJ. said in *Miglin*, "judges making variation orders
under s. 17 limit themselves to making the appropriate variation, but do
not weigh all the factors to make a fresh order unrelated to the existing
one, unless the circumstances require the rescission, rather than a mere
variation of the order" (para. 62).

[48] Variation involves the application of both s. 17(4.1) and s. 17(7) of
the *Divorce Act*. In *Hickey*, L'Heureux-Dubé J. described the interplay
between them as follows:

> On an application for variation of an award of spousal support, the
> court must first find, under s. 17(4), that there has been a material
> change in the conditions, means, needs, or circumstances of either
> spouse.... Once this threshold is passed, the court must consider the
> four objectives of spousal support enumerated in s. 17(7) of the
> *Divorce Act*....

[50] In short, once a material change in circumstances has been established, the variation order should "properly reflect[] the objectives set out
in s. 17(7), ... [take] account of the material changes in circumstances,
[and] consider[] the existence of the separation agreement and its terms
as a relevant factor".... A court should limit itself to making the variation
which is appropriate in light of the change. The task should not be
approached as if it were an initial application for support under s. 15.2 of
the *Divorce Act*.

The majority judges addressed the threshold question of whether a
"material change" had occurred, and concluded that both the trial judge
and the Court of Appeal had erred by conducting a hearing *de novo* on the

issue of the wife's ability to work without determining whether a material change had occurred. For the majority, because no such material change had occurred, there was no basis for variation.

A minority of judges (Cromwell J and McLachlin CJC) agreed with the majority on the outcome of the case. They also agreed that the threshold test for variation is whether there was a material change since the making of the last order and that the fact that the agreement was incorporated into an order indicates that the order was appropriate at the time that it was made.

However, the minority judges differed with the majority on the applicability of *Miglin* and argued that the *Miglin* stage 2 test should be used when a party seeks to vary an agreement that has been incorporated into an order. Specifically, they disagreed with the majority's premise that because the factors outlined in section 17, by contrast with section 15.2(4), do not refer to an "order, agreement or arrangement relating to support of either spouse," then *Miglin* would apply to initial applications under section 15 but not to the assessment of variation applications where an agreement was incorporated into an order. The minority judges argued that the language of sections 15.2 and 17 is similar and that "even without th[e] express inclusion" of agreements in section 15.2(4)(c), the parties' agreement would be a factor for s 17 consideration because it "must fall within the 'condition, means, needs or other circumstances' for the purposes of s 17(4.1)" (at para 83).

Further, although the majority judges were clear that the parties' agreement might be relevant to the material change test depending on the specific terms of the agreement, the minority was of the view that this approach did not place sufficient emphasis on the fact that the parties had come to an agreement and on the objectives of certainty and finality that were emphasized in *Miglin*. For the minority judges:

> [76] ... *Miglin* stands for the proposition that the parties' comprehensive, final agreement must be accorded significant weight at the variation stage, as it is at the initial application stage. In addition, *Miglin* provides considerable guidance about how this ought to be done....

> [84] ... I do not understand how, as a matter of logic, the parties' comprehensive and final agreement could not be central to considering whether there had been a material change. The *Willick* test is applied on the basis that a change is not material if it was known to the parties or must reasonably be taken as having been contemplated by them. The parties' agreement is critical evidence of what they actually or ought reasonably to be taken to have contemplated at the time.

> [85] ... I agree that the Court in *Miglin* was clear that the "material change" threshold applicable on a variation does not apply on an initial application. However ... the Court was also clear that important weight is to be given to the parties' agreement in both situations. The Court noted that it would be inconsistent to do otherwise.... In any event, I do not understand how in logic the Court's analysis in *Miglin* could not be applicable to a s. 17 variation. The very issue discussed in *Miglin*'s second step is how change over time affects the weight to be given to an agreement.... That same consideration is an important issue facing a court on a varia-

tion application in relation to an initial order that was the product of an agreement.

[86] My colleagues take quite a different approach, proposing that only where an agreement specifically provides for a particular matter will it be of much help in answering the *"Willick* question".... As for types of changes other than those specifically addressed in the agreement, the fact of the agreement is likely not to be of much assistance on the material change question. To me, this approach is at odds not only with *Miglin*, but also with one of the basic purposes of agreements, namely to apportion the risks of future uncertain events in order to achieve finality and certainty. Giving considerable weight to the parties' comprehensive, final agreement does not, as my colleagues suggest, bring back the "clean break" approach rejected in *Miglin*; it applies the express holding and underlying principles of *Miglin*.

Despite the minority judges' emphasis on its importance, *Miglin* was not raised at the lower courts in *LMP v LS* (or in its companion case, *RP v RC*, 2011 SCC 65).

To what extent does the majority decision confirm or limit the use of *Miglin* as a precedent?

Contracts, orders, and variation: Academic assessments of *LMP*

In Carol Rogerson's view, the Supreme Court's judgment in *LMP v LS* did little to clarify the uncertain state of post-*Miglin* jurisprudence:

> ... In the courts below, *Miglin* was never raised, and rightly so. The case, involving a non-final agreement for indefinite spousal support that had been incorporated into a consent order was treated as a straightforward variation application governed by the threshold test of a material change in circumstances. However, reflecting the pervasive doctrinal confusion about when the *Miglin* test is applicable, *L.M.P.* was transformed into a potential *Miglin* case before the Supreme Court of Canada. And it was thus in a case in which *Miglin* arguably had no relevance that the Court attempted to deal with, and divided on, the general issue of the applicability of *Miglin* in the context of variation applications under s. 17 of the *Divorce Act*....
>
> *L.M.P.* leaves many questions unanswered about the role of *Miglin* and the treatment of final agreements under [DA, s 17]. On the more "radical" reading of the decision, the majority reasons have completely eliminated the *Miglin* test from the analytic framework that is to be applied when dealing with variation applications in respect of consent orders under s 17, replacing *Miglin* with the test of material change [in s 17]. On this view the threshold for modifying incorporated agreements, even final agreements terminating spousal support, has been lowered, perhaps significantly lowered.... This broad reading of the majority reasons would be consistent with Abella J's reasons in *Miglin* at the Ontario Court of Appeal in which she was of the view that the appropriate threshold for intervention in agreements, whether under s 15.2 or s 17 [of the DA] should be material change. On this reading, *L.M.P.* further confirms some of the general shift of the pendulum over time in this area of law, ... with less weight being given to final agreements and more weight to concerns of fairness, both procedural and substantive.
>
> A more modest reading of *L.M.P.* would confine the decision to its facts [especially because *Miglin* was not argued in the lower courts in this

case].... On this view, the case reflects much of the on-going doctrinal confusion about the applicability of *Miglin*.... (Rogerson at 62, 63, 64)

Technically, *Miglin* did not apply to *LMP v LS* because the agreement between the parties did not time-limit or waive spousal support. It was thus not a final agreement in the *Miglin* sense. Part of the difficulty in this area is that neither the majority nor the minority analyses were clear on the distinction between "final" in the sense of the final agreement in *Miglin* and "final" in the sense of an order as per 15.2(1) of the *Divorce Act*.

What is the solution to this uncertainty about spousal support principles in relation to negotiated agreements? Recall the emphasis in Chapter Five on non-litigation alternatives: is it appropriate to amend legislation to create greater certainty for spouses who reach consensual agreements? Why or why not?

In reflecting on these questions, consider these comments in Rollie Thompson's Annotation of *LMP v LS*:

> ... *Miglin* itself was an initial application for spousal support after the parties had previously concluded a comprehensive final agreement that contained a provision for time-limited spousal support. An agreement for spousal support is ordinarily characterised as a "final agreement", because there is a waiver of spousal support entirely or a time limit upon it. The application of *Miglin* to the variation of spousal support orders based upon "final agreements" has caused difficulties. Some courts have applied *Miglin* to "non-final" agreements, either on initial applications or variations. Some courts have applied *Miglin* to agreements that contain explicit "material change" clauses or review provisions. These two recent appeals do little to resolve these disagreements and confusions, and may have added a few.
>
> Technically, all seven judges agreed on the outcome on the facts in both cases, so that the minority reasons are not a "dissent". But the minority judgment in *L.M.P.* is certainly a dissent on the law, in tone and in content. Writing for himself and the Chief Justice, Cromwell J. says the majority is wrong in holding that *Miglin* "has nothing to do with variation applications" (para. 63). For the minority, the incorporated agreement plays "a central role" on variation and the *Miglin* principles are "highly relevant to this exercise".
>
> Before I delve into this judicial struggle, it is important to note that neither Quebec case raised *Miglin* directly, despite Justice Cromwell's assertion. He repeats the term "comprehensive, final agreement" four times in his reasons, occasionally lapsing back to just the qualifier "comprehensive" (tellingly I would suggest). Cromwell J. then calls the 2003 agreement and order between L.M.P. and L.S. "comprehensive" and "final" (para. 94). Comprehensive it may have been, but it was not "final" in the *Miglin* sense of that word. Spousal support was not waived or time-limited, but was indefinite. The minority uses the word "final", not in its technical *Miglin* sense, but in some generic meaningless way: all non-interim agreements or orders in this sense are "final", that is, until they are varied or reviewed. That is not the meaning of "final" in *Miglin*....
>
> Despite the absence of any "final agreement" in the *Miglin* sense, the minority judges were determined to apply the *Miglin* analysis to these two cases, a disconcerting development, and one rejected by the majority. To apply *Miglin* to the variation of an agreed-upon indefinite order would significantly increase the threshold of "material change", given the demand-

ing stage two test under *Miglin*. That test is impossible to paraphrase, so I'll just quote the court, at para. 91 of *Miglin*:

> It is only where the current circumstances represent a significant departure from the range of reasonable outcomes anticipated by the parties, in a manner that puts them at odds with the objectives of the Act, that the court may be persuaded to give the agreement little weight.

The majority in *L.M.P.* does reject the applicability of the *Miglin* two-step analysis in these variation cases, in favour of the traditional "material change" test under s. 17 of the *Divorce Act*. Much of the majority judgment is a reaffirmation of the well-established law of variation....

... there is more difficulty, where Justices Abella and Rothstein wade into the *Miglin* debate with the minority. Another wobbly definition of "final" creeps into the analysis. The pair treat Justice Cromwell's definition of "final" as a "general" form of finality in an agreement, "a general term providing that it is final, or finality may be necessarily implied" (para. 41). This "general" version "merely states the obvious: the order of the court is final subject to s. 17 of the *Divorce Act*" (para. 41). The next few paragraphs, and especially para. 45, are less than clear about whether some form of more "specific" finality, i.e. a waiver of spousal support or time-limited support, will be treated differently at the variation stage. Like the minority, but with the opposite effect, the majority opinion fails adequately to identify and explain what is a "final agreement".

The majority is clear that *Miglin* does apply to a "final agreement" in the face of an initial application for support under s. 15.2, for those were the *Miglin* facts. The majority is equally clear that the "material change" threshold must apply to all variations under s. 17, including a "final agreement" incorporated into a court order, and that this statutory threshold is lower than that specified in stage two of *Miglin*. How much lower, I will discuss below.

Justice Cromwell calls out the majority on this point, as it was clear in *Miglin* that the court wished to maintain consistency in judicial treatment of "final agreements" under s. 15.2 and under s. 17. Whether an agreement is or is not incorporated into a court order depends upon local rules, local practices and the parties' desire to avoid public support enforcement schemes. The accident of incorporation should not alter the test to be applied to a "final agreement", i.e. one with a waiver or time-limited spousal support....

Neither the majority nor the minority judgment in *L.M.P.* does anything to lessen the current disagreements or confusions about *Miglin*. Had they each defined their terms more carefully and accurately, they could have provided some help. Had the majority directly addressed true "final agreements", those that contain waivers or time limits, then we would not have been left to wonder if a simple "material change" test is all that is required for such agreements. Had the minority restricted its analysis to this narrow class of "final agreements" incorporated into orders, then there is much in their reasons that could have clarified the variation of such orders. Sadly, *L.M.P.* will just perpetuate and add to the *Miglin* controversies....

In conclusion, I can venture one suggestion. After *L.M.P.*, it will likely be easier to vary a spousal support provision based upon an agreement than it was before. The "material change" test applies, without an agreement or with an agreement. The parties will have to be much more specific in their agreement if they wish to limit or control future variations of spousal support. General statements of finality will not be given much weight in the material change analysis. It is not clear whether the court has lowered the threshold for variation of orders based upon truly "final agreements", i.e. agreements that waive or time limit spousal support. But the majority has provided some vague language that will certainly make it easier for recipients to make that argument. (Rollie Thompson, "Annotation: *Droit de la famille — 091889* and *Droit de la famille — 09668* [*LMP v. LS*]" (2012) 6 RFL 7)

Carol Rogerson has observed that although the law in this area remains confusing and uncertain, "the general shift of the pendulum over time" is toward "less weight being given to final agreements and more weight to concerns of fairness, both procedural and substantive" (Rogerson at 64). Do you agree? What effect might *LMP v LS* might have on that process?

The "variation" issue: Section 17 of the *Divorce Act*

In *Bhupal v Bhupal*, 2009 ONCA 521, the Ontario Court of Appeal considered a husband's application to vary his obligation to pay spousal support on the basis that his former wife had remarried and was being supported by her new husband. The parties had entered into minutes of settlement that provided for a review after five years, or on the basis of a "material change in circumstances."

The trial judge dismissed the motion on the basis that the husband knew, at the time of signing the minutes of settlement, that the wife was in a new and serious relationship that would likely result in marriage. On appeal to the Ontario Court of Appeal, the court held that the motion judge's findings were amply supported by the evidence, and that they constituted an "insurmountable" hurdle for the husband. Noting that the new husband was a close friend of the former husband, the court rejected the claim for variation based on a "material change."

Additional Resources

N Bala & S Chapman, "Separation Agreements & Contract Law: From the Trilogy to *Miglin*" in Law Society of Upper Canada, Child & Spousal Support Revisited (Toronto: Law Society of Upper Canada, 2002).

Martin Craig, "Unequal Shadows: Negotiation Theory and Spousal Support under Canadian Divorce Law" (1998) UT Fac L Rev 135.

Christine Davies, "The Ever-Changing Picture of Support and Other Developments" (2002–2003) 20 Can Fam LQ 213.

Andrea Himel, "Bargaining in the Shadow of the 'End of Finality'" (1998) 16 Can Fam LQ 399.

Robert Leckey, "Relational Contract and Other Models of Marriage" (2002) 40 Osgoode Hall LJ 1.

Marcia Neave, "Resolving the Dilemma of Difference: a Critique of 'The Role of Private Ordering in Family Law'" (1994) 44 UTLJ 97.

Rollie Thompson, "To Vary, To Review, Perchance To Change: Changing Spousal Support" (2012) Can Fam LQ 355.

Carol Rose, "Bargaining and Gender" (1995) 18 Harv JL & Pub Pol'y 547.

VI.
A REFORM INITIATIVE: SPOUSAL SUPPORT ADVISORY GUIDELINES (SSAGs)

THE INTRODUCTION OF SSAGs

The background to the SSAGs in 2002

In a Background Paper to begin discussion about Spousal Support Advisory Guidelines in 2002, Carol Rogerson explained that:

> The project is put forward as one that builds on current practice. Yet, current practice is diverse. In order to bring more structure and certainty into the law choices have to be made as to what are "emerging trends" or "best practices" and the law will thus be "re-structured" along those lines. The project thus contemplates a certain degree of change, but change that is consistent with the current legislative structure and basic framework that comes from decisions of the Supreme Court of Canada interpreting those provisions. One way to see the project is as facilitating or "speeding up" the normal common law process for the development of the law whereby the best understandings or interpretations of the current law eventually rise to the surface. The normal process of legal development has fallen apart in this area of law because of an excessive emphasis on discretion and individualized decision-making and a failure to focus on underlying principles and structure. (Carol Rogerson, "Developing Spousal Support Guidelines in Canada: Beginning the Discussion" (Background Paper) (Ottawa: Department of Justice, 2002) at 65)

The SSAGs in 2008

After much discussion and debate, the Spousal Support Advisory Guidelines were introduced. Although their application in practice often depends on the use of computer software, the basic principles reflect two elements:

- the recognition of basic principles about entitlement to spousal support, based on legislative provisions and judicial interpretation of them, especially in the Supreme Court of Canada; and

- efforts to structure discretionary decision making with respect to issues about quantum and duration of spousal support.

Spousal Support Advisory Guidelines
(2008) at 1–156 (excerpts)

Carol Rogerson and Rollie Thompson

INTRODUCTION

In 2001 the federal Department of Justice identified the need for a project to explore the possibility of developing some form of advisory spousal support guidelines. The aim of the project was to bring more certainty and predictability to the determination of spousal support under the

Divorce Act. The project was a response to growing concerns expressed by lawyers, judges, mediators and the public about the lack of certainty and predictability in the current law of spousal support, creating daily dilemmas in advising clients, and negotiating, litigating or — in the case of judges — deciding spousal support issues....

The authors explained that the process of creating the SSAGs involved the release of a draft proposal in January 2005. Pursuant to this proposal, draft SSAGs were in use for three years, as the authors received feedback and comments. In July 2008, the authors released the final version of the SSAGs.

The authors also explained that, by contrast with the Child Support Guidelines that were legislated in 1997, *the SSAGs are intended to be informal guidelines that operate on an advisory basis only within the existing legislative framework.*

[THE STATUS OF THE SSAGS]

The Advisory Guidelines are intended as a practical tool to assist in determinations of spousal support within the current legal framework — to operate primarily as a starting point in negotiations and settlements. The project was not directed at a theoretical reordering of the law of spousal support or at creating a new model of spousal support. The formulas ... are intended as proxies for the spousal support objectives found in the *Divorce Act* as elaborated upon by the Supreme Court of Canada. Our goal was to develop guidelines that would achieve results over a wide range of typical cases.

Given the informal nature of these advisory guidelines, they have been developed with the recognition that they must be broadly consistent with current support outcomes while also providing some much needed structure and consistency to this area of law — a not insignificant challenge. As informal guidelines, they *do not address entitlement*, but deal only with the amount and duration of support *once entitlement has been established*. In the same vein they confer *no power to re-open existing spousal support agreements* beyond what exists under current law.

CONTENT OF THE ADVISORY GUIDELINES

The Advisory Guidelines are based on what is called "income sharing." Contrary to popular conception, income sharing does not necessarily mean equal sharing. It simply means that spousal support is determined as a percentage of spousal incomes. The percentages can vary according to a number of factors. The Advisory Guidelines offer two basic formulas that base spousal support on spousal incomes and other relevant factors such as the presence or absence of dependent children, and the length of the marriage. The formulas deal with the amount (sometimes referred to as quantum) and duration of spousal support once entitlement to support has been established. The formulas generate ranges of outcomes, rather than precise figures for amount and duration, which may be restructured by trading off amount against duration.

The Guidelines are advisory only and thus always allow for departures from the outcomes generated by the formulas on a case-by-case basis where they are not appropriate. While we have tried to specify exceptions to assist the parties and the courts in framing and assessing any departures from the formulas' ranges, they are not exhaustive of the grounds for departure. There is still considerable room for the exercise of discretion under the Advisory Guidelines but it will be exercised within a much more defined structure than existed before — one with clearer starting points. Budgets, which are currently the primary tool in spousal support determinations, increasingly play a reduced and less central role.... (at 1–2)

The authors provided a comprehensive background to the SSAGs, including the legislative directions in sections 15.2(4), (5) and (6) of the *Divorce Act*, and a detailed overview of how these provisions were interpreted in *Moge v Moge* and *Bracklow v Bracklow*. They also addressed the problems created by these decisions (at 9):

> The culture of spousal support after *Bracklow* was one that emphasized individualized decision making and an absence of rules. Multiple theories of spousal support competed with each other while, on the ground, spousal support cases were negotiated and argued under an amorphous needs-and-means framework dominated by budgets. "Need" means many different things to different people and many different theories of spousal support can be couched in the language of need. The guidelines project sprang from the growing concern expressed by lawyers and judges that the highly discretionary nature of the current law of spousal support had created an unacceptable degree of uncertainty and unpredictability.
>
> Similar fact situations could generate a wide variation in results. Individual judges were provided with little concrete guidance in determining spousal support outcomes and their subjective perceptions of fair outcomes played a large role in determining the spousal support ultimately ordered. Appeals were often of little help because appeal courts frequently dispose of appeals with little explanation, deferring to trial judges on issues of quantum and duration. Lawyers in turn had difficulty predicting outcomes, thus impeding their ability to advise clients and to engage in cost-effective settlement negotiations.
>
> And for those without legal representation or in weak bargaining positions, support claims were simply not pursued. Despite a very broad basis for entitlement under the existing law, many spouses did not claim spousal support, being unwilling to engage in the difficult and costly process required.
>
> More generally, the uncertainty and unpredictability that pervaded the law of spousal support was undermining the legitimacy of the spousal support obligation. The widely differing understandings of the nature of the spousal support obligation generated concerns about unfair outcomes at both ends of the spectrum. In some cases, awards were perceived as too low, in others as unjustifiably high.
>
> The Advisory Guidelines were a response to these concerns. They were developed for the purpose of bringing more certainty and predictability to spousal support determinations. They incorporate the basic principles of compensation and need that the Supreme Court of Canada has identified as the bases for spousal support under the *Divorce Act* but provide a more structured way of implementing those principles through formulas based on income sharing, i.e., formulas based on sharing specified percentages of spousal incomes....

The authors identified the need for the SSAGs (at 11) because of the extent to which uncertainty had increased post-*Bracklow* in the judicial development of spousal support principles. In addition, there was a sense that the introduction of child support guidelines in 1997 had demonstrated the advantages of *average* justice, by contrast with individualized justice. Canadian reform proponents also looked to the experience of principles developed by the ALI in the United States. And finally, the availability of sophisticated computer software encouraged the possibility of more effective SSAGs. In embarking on the SSAGs project, the authors identified four objectives (at 11–12):

- reducing conflict and encouraging settlement;
- creating consistency and fairness;
- reducing costs and improving efficiency in the family law system; and
- providing a basic structure for further judicial elaboration.

> The goal of the project was not to raise the current levels of support over the broad run of cases. Greater consistency under a scheme of advisory guidelines would mean that some spouses would see higher support awards and others would see lower awards. We did recognize that a scheme of advisory guidelines would likely lead to more frequent spousal support awards as spouses who previously would have given up on seeking spousal support because of the costs and unpredictable results of the highly discretionary regime would find it easier to claim spousal support....

The authors reviewed the process of defining the SSAGs and the feedback on their Discussion Paper of 2005. They also reviewed the support provided by courts in relation to the SSAGs (at 23–25):

- In *Yemchuk v Yemchuk*, 2005 BCCA 406, the B.C. Court of Appeal approved the SSAGs as "a useful tool to assist judges in assessing quantum and duration of spousal support." This case also clarified the legal status of the SSAGs in the courtroom, concluding that the SSAGs did not constitute evidence, but formed part of legal argument and reasoning, and could thus be cited as any other article, text or government document.

- Subsequently, in *Redpath v Redpath*, 2006 BCCA 338, the B.C. Court of Appeal incorporated the SSAGs into the standard of appellate review. Thus, if an award is substantially above or below the range and there are no exceptional circumstances to explain this divergence, the standard of review may include appellate intervention. In this context, the court noted that *Hickey v Hickey*, [1992] 2 SCR 518, the Supreme Court decision about appellate review, had been decided prior to the SSAGs.

- In *SC v JC*, 2006 NBCA 46, the New Brunswick Court of Appeal similarly approved of the SSAGs as tending to create more consistency and predictability, and fostering settlement. Leave to appeal to the SCC in this case was denied, see [2006] SCCA No 246.

- In 2008, the Ontario Court of Appeal also endorsed the SSAGs in *Fisher v Fisher*, 2008 ONCA 11 (considered later in this chapter).

The authors also noted that even in provinces where there has not been appellate review of the SSAGs, many trial courts had adopted the SSAGs, citing Nova Scotia, Saskatchewan, Alberta, and Newfoundland and Labrador.

According to the authors, it was only the Québec Court of Appeal which offered a more lukewarm acceptance of the SSAGs. See *GV v GC*, [2006] JQ No 5231.

The SSAGs in Practice

The authors reiterated (at 27) the advisory nature of the SSAGs and the intent that they operate within the existing legal framework. Moreover, the SSAGs do not deal with entitlement, and they do not confer any power to reopen or override final agreements on spousal support. The SSAGs do, however, apply to interim orders, and they generally apply to initial determinations of spousal support rather than to reviews or variations (subject to a few exceptions).

The authors then identified two formulas:

- the "without child support formula"; and
- the "with child support" formula.

Both formulas use income sharing as the method for determining the amount of support, and the starting point for the determination of income under both formulas is the definition of income under the federal Child Support Guidelines (to be discussed in Chapter Eight).

The authors then explained the content of these two formulas (at 32–33) as follows:

> #### 3.3.3. The without child support formula [see also 2008 SSAG, chapter 7, for details]
>
> In cases where there are no dependent children, the *without child support* formula applies. This formula relies heavily upon the length of marriage — or more precisely, the length of relationship, including periods of pre-marital cohabitation — to determine both the amount and duration of support. Both amount and duration increase with the length of the relationship. This formula is constructed around the concept of *merger over time* which offers a useful tool for implementing both compensatory and non-compensatory support objectives in cases where there are no dependent children in a way that reflects general patterns in the current law.
>
> Under the basic without child support formula:
>
> > The *amount* of spousal support is 1.5 to 2 percent of the difference between the spouses' gross incomes for each year of marriage, to a maximum range of 37.5 to 50 percent of the gross income difference for marriages of 25 years or more. (The upper end of this maximum range is capped at the amount that would result in equalization of the spouses' net incomes — the net income cap.)
> >
> > *Duration* is .5 to 1 year of support for each year of marriage, with duration becoming indefinite (duration not specified) after 20 years *or*, if the marriage has lasted 5 years or longer, when the years of marriage and age of the support recipient (at separation) added together total 65 or more (the "rule of 65").
>
> #### 3.3.4 The with child support formula [see also 2008 SSAG, chapter 8, for details]
>
> In cases where there are dependent children, the *with child support* formula applies. The distinctive treatment of marriages with dependent children and concurrent child support obligations is justified by both theoretical and practical considerations and is reflected in current case law.
>
> On the theoretical front, marriages with dependent children raise strong compensatory claims based on the economic disadvantages flowing from assumption of primary responsibility for child care, not only during the marriage, *but also after separation.* We have identified this aspect of the compensatory principle as it operates in cases involving dependent

children as the *parental partnership principle*, and have drawn on this concept in structuring the *with child support* formula. For marriages with dependent children, length of marriage is not the most important determinant of support outcomes as compared to post-separation child-care responsibilities.

On the practical front, child support must be calculated first and given priority over spousal support. As well, the differential tax treatment of child and spousal support must be taken into account, complicating the calculations. The *with child support* formula thus works with computer software calculations of net disposable incomes.

Under the basic *with child support* formula:

> Spousal support is an *amount* that will leave the recipient spouse with between 40 and 46 percent of the spouses' net incomes *after child support has been taken out*. (We refer to the spouses' net income after child support has been taken out as Individual Net Disposable Income or INDI.)

> The approach to *duration* under this formula is more complex and flexible than under the *without child support* formula; orders are initially indefinite in form (duration not specified) but the formula also establishes durational ranges which are intended to structure the process of review and variation and which limit the cumulative duration of awards under this formula. These durational limits rely upon both length of marriage and the ages of the children.

> The *with child support* formula is really a cluster of formulas dealing with different custodial arrangements. *Shared and split custody* situations require slight variations in the computation of individual net disposable income, as the backing out of child support obligations is a bit more complicated. There is also a different, hybrid formula for cases where *spousal support is paid to the custodial parent*. Under this formula, the spouses' Guidelines incomes are reduced by the grossed-up amount of child support (actual or notional) and then the *without child support* formula is applied to determine amount and duration. Finally, there is one more hybrid formula for those spousal support cases where the child support for *adult children* is determined under section 3(2)(b) of the *Child Support Guidelines*....

The authors also explained (at 34–35) the use of the ranges for spousal support awards, and the possibility of restructuring such awards (by increasing the amount or shortening duration, by extending duration, or by using the amount and duration to calculate a lump sum award). In addition, they noted (at 35–36) that the SSAGs itemize a series of exceptions to assist in assessing departures from the SSAGs (including compelling financial circumstances in an interim period, debt payments, prior support obligations, illness or disability of a recipient spouse, etc).

Overall, the authors concluded (at 156):

> [I]t now appears that the Spousal Support Advisory Guidelines have become entrenched as a useful tool in the law of spousal support. As such, they have now become part of the everyday analysis employed by spouses, lawyers, mediators and judges.... In only a few short years, the Spousal Support Advisory Guidelines have gone from concept to Draft Proposal to final version, and now belong to all those who operate in the field of family law.

The SSAGs in practice in Ontario

As noted above, the SSAGs have received widespread (but not unanimous) support from courts in Canada. In Ontario, the Court of Appeal confirmed the usefulness of the SSAGs in 2008 in *Fisher v Fisher*.

Fisher v Fisher
2008 ONCA 11

In *Fisher v Fisher*, the Ontario Court of Appeal reviewed a spousal support award and allowed the wife's appeal. The spouses had married in 1985 and they separated 19 years later, when both spouses were in their early 40s. They did not have children.

The wife, along with her husband's parents, supported the husband to complete two degrees, a BA and also a Bachelor of Education. He taught high school for 11 years, and then accepted a job with the Teachers Federation (OSSTF) in 2004 at a salary of $120,000, which subsequently increased to $140,000 in 2006.

The wife earned an average of $30,000 during the marriage in clerical positions, many of which were part-time or seasonal, with periods of absence from the workforce. However, she had begun to take some university courses part time and by the time of the trial, had almost completed a degree in Fine Arts. At the time of trial, she earned $30,000.

On separation, the husband began to live with his new partner and her two children, and although the new partner was a physiotherapist in the United States, she did not attempt to qualify in Ontario. The husband married this new partner, and took responsibility for supporting her and the children, although his new wife also received about US $700 per month in child support from the children's biological father.

The former wife was completely shocked when her husband indicated that he wanted to separate, as she had been planning to leave her employment to move to Toronto to live in the new home that the couple had purchased. She became clinically depressed and was on disability leave for about a year (and in receipt of disability benefits). The parties equalized their assets, which included the matrimonial home and the husband's pension, and the husband paid an equalization payment to his former wife in an amount of approximately $102,000.

With these funds, the former wife purchased a home for $191,000, which the trial judge characterized as a "huge 'step down'" in lifestyle. The husband purchased a home for $328,000 for his new family, and thus had significant expenses.

At trial, the court reviewed the principles of entitlement with respect to spousal support, and concluded that Ms. Fisher had suffered an economic disadvantage as a result of her husband's decision to end the marriage. According to the Court of Appeal, the trial judge had taken account of a number of factors in determining the quantum and duration of the spousal support award:

- The trial judge had determined that it was practicable for the wife to become self-sufficient from her earnings or adjust her standard of living by the end of 2008;

- The trial judge had recognized the former husband's obligations to his new family as significant, so that it was a reality to be taken into account; and

- The trial judge also concluded that indefinite support was not warranted:

> **[69]** [On the basis of Ms. Fisher's] relative youth, her good health, the fact that she has no dependants and has no (significant) debt, and her past and present work record/ethics/opportunities, ... I speculate that over the next few years Ms. Fisher will become entirely self-sufficient and, like Mr. Fisher, perhaps enter into a new relationship (or partnership) whereby her day-to-day expenses can at least be shared....

The wife appealed, in part on the ground that the trial judge had failed to award support based on the SSAGs. The Court of Appeal allowed the appeal.

... STANDARD OF REVIEW

> **[25]** Based on the standard of review of a support order set out by L'Heureux-Dubé J. in *Hickey v. Hickey*, [1999] 2 S.C.R. 518 at paras. 10–11, I am mindful that the discretionary decision of the trial judge, who in any event is very experienced, is entitled to considerable deference and should not be interfered with absent an error in principle, a significant misapprehension of the evidence, or unless the award is clearly wrong....

The Court of Appeal concluded that the trial judge had erred in finding that the wife had worked full time, and that it was not appropriate, in the absence of evidence, to speculate about the wife's potential to enter a new relationship. The court also concluded that the husband's responsibility for his second family warranted consideration on appeal, and that the trial judge's order for review of the spousal support award in future was not appropriate.

APPLICATION OF THE LAW

The Court of Appeal set out the factors in sections 15.2(4) and (6) of the *Divorce Act*. In assessing the means and needs of the parties, the court focused particularly on the husband's new family obligations, stating:

> **[41]** In this case, the respondent voluntarily assumed significant responsibility for his second family when he knew, or should have known, of his pre-existing obligation to his first family. He assumed this obligation even though the second family is capable of contributing to its own support provided the respondent's new partner completed her qualifications to practise as a physiotherapist in Ontario. In addition, the second family receives child support from the children's biological father. This is not a case where the respondent was obliged to support his new family, at least beyond the temporary legal obligation based on their initial immigration status. In any event, there was no evidence that the respondent's obligations to his first family would impoverish his second family. In these circumstances, the respondent's endorsement of his second wife's preference to remain at home cannot be relied upon to reduce his support obligation to his first family....

In considering section 15.2(6), the court concluded that the wife was economically disadvantaged by the breakdown of the marriage:

[47] As the trial judge noted, the appellant's standard of living was significantly reduced when she moved to a small townhouse (a disadvantage also suffered by the respondent in view of his similar loss of the matrimonial home and the diminution in capital). Specifically, the trial judge found that the appellant "lost not only her future dream and the large financial salary increase in which she was led to believe she would share, but she also lost the comfortable middle-class lifestyle to which they both had been accustomed." (para. 60) In addition, the appellant was economically disadvantaged by the reactive depression she suffered after the separation. The resulting interruption to her employment reduced her income, at least in the short term.

[48] It follows that the economic disadvantages from the marriage breakdown were more pronounced for the appellant, particularly regarding the reduction in her standard of living....

In considering economic hardship, the court considered the trial judge's conclusion that the wife did not suffer hardship because she could provide for her basic needs on $30,000 per year. However, the court decided to consider this issue in relation to the objective of promoting self-sufficiency:

[53] Self-sufficiency, with its connotation of economic independence, is a relative concept. It is not achieved simply because a former spouse can meet basic expenses on a particular amount of income; rather, self-sufficiency relates to the ability to support a reasonable standard of living. It is to be assessed in relation to the economic partnership the parties enjoyed and could sustain during cohabitation, and that they can reasonably anticipate after separation. See *Linton v. Linton* (1990), 1 O.R. (3d) 1 (C.A.) at 27–28. Thus, a determination of self-sufficiency requires consideration of the parties' present and potential incomes, their standard of living during marriage, the efficacy of any suggested steps to increase a party's means, the parties' likely post-separation circumstances (including the impact of equalization of their property), the duration of their cohabitation and any other relevant factors.

[54] Self-sufficiency is often more attainable in short-term marriages, particularly ones without children, where the lower-income spouse has not become entrenched in a particular lifestyle, or compromised career aspirations. In such circumstances, the lower-income spouse is expected either to have the tools to become financially independent or to adjust his or her standard of living.

[55] In contrast, in most long-term marriages, particularly in traditional long-term ones, the parties' merger of economic lifestyles creates a joint standard of living that the lower-income spouse cannot hope to replicate, but upon which he or she has become dependent. In such circumstances, the spousal support analysis typically will not give priority to self-sufficiency because it is an objective that simply cannot be attained....

The court quoted from *Moge* and continued:

[57] In this case, I have already noted that the appellant's claim is largely a needs-based one arising from the financial dependence that developed mainly in the latter years of the marriage when the respondent's income began to increase significantly. By the time of separation, the parties anticipated sharing an average <u>joint</u> income of about $125,325.

[58] Yet the respondent submits that the appellant should be considered self-sufficient on the basis of her current $30,000 income. I reject this submission. It is not only obvious that the appellant would need more than her $30,000 income to maintain her pre-separation standard of living, she would still require support even if that income increased to $41,000. Accordingly, the goal of self-sufficiency based on her income-earning capacity is not practicable in a reasonable time. However, that does not end the matter.

[59] The question remains whether it is reasonable to expect the appellant to gradually adjust her standard of living to one commensurate with her own income. The answer depends on a balancing of all the objectives and factors, which I will address under quantum of support.

SUMMARY OF OBJECTIVES

[60] In summary, the appellant suffered no established economic disadvantage arising from the marriage either by the assumption of child care responsibilities or in any other way that compromised her career or educational aspirations. Any minimal disadvantage cannot be compared to that of a long-term traditional spouse who made career sacrifices to the significant advantage of the other spouse. While the appellant's economic assistance at the beginning of the parties' marriage provided an advantage to the respondent, the primary basis for the appellant's support claim is framed as an inability to attain self-sufficiency in light of the marital standard of living....

The court then addressed the issue of the review order granted by the trial judge and decided that it was not appropriate in this situation:

[63] A review allows an application for support without the need to prove the material change in circumstances required in a section 17 variation application. Unless the review is restricted to a specific issue, it is generally equivalent to an initial application for support and necessitates a complete rehearing of every issue from entitlement to quantum. Thus, a review, particularly one relatively proximate to the time of the originating order, causes unnecessary and significant expense for the parties, not only emotionally, but also financially....

[70] Review orders in effect turn an initial order into a long-term interim order made after trial. Accordingly, they should be the exception, not the norm. They are appropriate when a specified uncertainty about a party's circumstances at the time of trial will become certain within an identifiable timeframe. When one is granted, it should include specifics regarding the issue about which there is uncertainty and when and how the trial judge anticipates that uncertainty will be resolved.

[71] In any other case, a trial judge should issue a final order based on a preponderance of the evidence called by the parties. In the family law context, a final order will always be subject to variation, which will suffice to protect against future events. A variation is available not only when there is an unexpected change in circumstances, but also when an anticipated set of specified circumstances fails to materialize. This is particularly the case where an initial order specifies a trial judge's anticipation that the recipient spouse will or should be able to earn a given income within a particular time frame. This flexibility is to be contrasted with a review order, which invariably places the burden on the applicant, albeit in the context of an initial application....

[73] In this case, the trial evidence indicated that the appellant was making reasonable efforts at self-sufficiency. There was little evidence that her financial circumstances would change at an identifiable point in the future, apart from the potential return of her income to pre-separation levels, which would not have rendered her self-sufficient when considered in the context of her marital standard of living. Thus, there was no basis for the review date provided in the trial judgment. As well, the order did not comply with the *Leskun* requirement for a tight delimitation of the facts subject to review.

[74] Accordingly, I conclude that the imposition of the review order constituted an error in principle on the facts of this case....

The court then addressed the commencement date of the support award, and concluded that the trial judge's refusal to order its commencement as of the date of the interim support order was incorrect. The court then turned to the issues of quantum and duration.

[83] This assessment must be completed in the context of the legal principles carefully reviewed by the trial judge, including the factors relevant to whether support should be indefinite or limited-term.

[84] The factors and objectives require a balancing of the parties' circumstances, including the duration of the parties' cohabitation, their ages, their incomes and prospective incomes, the effects of equalization, the stages of their careers, contributions to the marital standard of living, participation in household responsibilities, the absence of child-care obligations, the respondent's increased cost of living arising from his new employment, the parties' reasonable expectations, the respondent's rapid pre- and post-separation increases in income, the appellant's limited claim for compensatory support and her greater need for transitional support.

[85] In reaching his decision to limit the duration of support, the trial judge referred to several authorities and specifically referenced the appellant's "relative youth, her good health, the fact that she has no dependents and has no (significant) debt, and her past and present work record/ethics/opportunities". As I have said, I agree with the trial judge that indefinite support was not indicated on the facts of this case.

[86] In this case, the appellant's dependency on the marital standard of living was not entrenched in the manner it would have been in a traditional marriage where the parties enjoyed a gradually increasing standard of living. The respondent's substantial income increases started in approximately 2002. This provided the parties with a better standard of living during the last years of their marriage than they enjoyed in the many preceding years, a standard of living that would have increased further commensurate with the respondent's 2004 income.

[87] In this circumstance, Professor Rogerson's observation in "Spousal Support Post-*Bracklow*: The Pendulum Swings Again?" is apt:

Such discrete [limited-term] obligations may also arise in longer relationships where both parties have worked throughout the relationship and the lower-income spouse is understood to have only a limited claim to non-compensatory, transitional support to cushion the drop in standard of living occasioned by the marriage breakdown. (p. 259)

[88] To provide the appellant with a reasonable transition following her nineteen-year marriage, it is my view that the appellant will need support for seven years, beginning with the year of separation. In my view, a seven-year order complies with the spousal support objective of recogniz-

ing the appellant's economic disadvantage arising from the marriage and its breakdown, while also encouraging the appellant to complete her transition to self-sufficiency, whether by reason of earning a higher income or, more likely, by adapting her lifestyle to her then income.

[89] To achieve an equitable result regarding the amount of support, I have averaged the parties' incomes for the last years. In the respondent's case, I use his increasing income in the three years prior to separation, as well as his substantially increased income in the year of separation, even though it was largely received post-separation. This results in an average salary for the respondent of $89,825, which allows for the parties' expectation that they would have shared those increases but for the separation.

[90] For the appellant, as with the respondent, I use her income earned in the three years prior to separation and in the year of separation which produces an average income of $35,500.

[91] On the basis of these averages, in my view, the appropriate amount of transitional and compensatory support for the appellant is reflected by an award of $3,000 monthly for a three and a half year period from October 1, 2004, to March 1, 2008, followed by a further three and a half years at $1,500 monthly from April 1, 2008 until September 1, 2011. I would then terminate support. Such an award cushions the appellant's drop in standard of living caused by the marriage breakdown.

[92] While I have assessed the amount and duration of spousal support based on the circumstances involved, it is helpful to consider the reasonableness of this award by reference to the Guidelines. As noted, the trial judge's omission of any reference to the Guidelines in the trial reasons is the final issue raised in this appeal.

SPOUSAL SUPPORT ADVISORY GUIDELINES

[93] Since it is clear that the Guidelines were put to the trial court, the appellant argues that the trial judge erred in failing to take them into account in determining the quantum of support. In fairness to the trial judge, at the time of trial, the Guidelines were released only one year earlier and were not yet the subject of widespread commentary....

The court reviewed the origins of the SSAGs, and the decision of the B.C. Court of Appeal in *Yemchuk v Yemchuk*. The court also reviewed circumstances in which the SSAGs do not apply, and continued:

[97] Accordingly, the Guidelines cannot be used as a software tool or a formula that calculates a specific amount of support for a set period of time. They must be considered in context and applied in their entirety, including the specific consideration of any applicable variables and, where necessary, restructuring.

[98] Importantly, the Guidelines do not impose a radically new approach. Instead, they suggest a range of both amount and duration of support that reflects the current law. Because they purport to represent a distillation of current case law, they are comparable to counsel's submissions about an appropriate range of support based on applicable jurisprudence. However, if the Guidelines suggest a range that conflicts with applicable authorities, the authorities will prevail.

[99] Counsel on this appeal advise that in London, where this support order was made, the Guidelines are widely used by the bar as a starting point for the purpose of assessing an appropriate level of spousal support, or for checking the validity of a proposed settlement....

The court reviewed the ways in which the SSAGs have been used, including the concerns expressed in Québec, and their use in defining a standard of review in *Redpath* in the B.C. Court of Appeal, and continued:

[103] In my view, when counsel fully address the Guidelines in argument, and a trial judge decides to award a quantum of support outside the suggested range, appellate review will be assisted by the inclusion of reasons explaining why the Guidelines do not provide an appropriate result. This is no different than a trial court distinguishing a significant authority relied upon by a party.

[104] I turn to the application of the Guidelines. The "Without Child Support Formula" purports to incorporate both compensatory and non-compensatory support objectives by focusing on a combination of the difference in the parties' gross incomes and the length of their cohabitation. This approach is consistent with a party's needs serving as a proxy for dependency. The formula is set out in section 5.1 of the Guidelines:

Amount ranges from 1.5 to 2 percent of the difference between the spouses' gross incomes (the gross income difference) for each year of marriage, (or, more precisely, years of cohabitation), up to a maximum of 50 percent. The range remains fixed for marriages 25 years or longer at 37.5 to 50 percent of income difference.

Duration ranges from .5 to 1 year for each year of marriage. However support will be indefinite if the marriage is 20 years or longer in duration or, if the marriage has lasted five years or longer, when years of marriage and age of the support recipient (at separation) added together total 65 or more (the "rule of 65").

[105] According to Professors Rogerson and Thompson, trial judges and lawyers often overlook or ignore the integral component of duration of marriage. The Guidelines use duration to categorize cohabitation: a short-term cohabitation is one of less than five years; a medium-term cohabitation is from five to nineteen years and a long-term cohabitation is twenty years or longer.

[106] However, under the Guidelines, a medium-term marriage becomes a long-term one (giving rise to indefinite support) if the partes' years of marriage, plus the age of the support recipient at the date of separation, equals or exceeds sixty-five. This refinement recognizes that an economically-dependent older spouse may have trouble thereafter attaining self-sufficiency.

[107] While the "rule of 65" does not apply in this case, the general principle that it adopts in classifying marriage based on a spouse's age at separation is still relevant. This is because age is a strong indicator of an individual's ability to become self-sufficient.

[108] In circumstances such as these, where the marriage falls just outside of the Guidelines' classification of a "long-term" marriage, a court may still decide that an indefinite support order is appropriate. Similarly, a court may decide that limited-term support is appropriate even though the period of cohabitation is twenty years or more. This is because, as the Guidelines note, while courts should consider the age of the parties and the duration of the marriage, they must also consider all other relevant circumstances.

[109] In recognition of the symbiotic relationship between amount and duration, the Guidelines emphasize:

Amount and duration are interrelated parts of the formula — they are a package deal. Using one part of the formula without the other would undermine its integrity and coherence. As discussed below, *the advisory guidelines provide for restructuring, which allows duration to be extended by lowering the monthly amount of support.* (p. 39) [Emphasis added]

[110] In this case of a medium-term nineteen-year marriage, the Guidelines provide a range of support. At the low end of the range, the appellant would receive 28.5% of the parties' income differential of $54,325, or $1,290 monthly ($15,483 annually). At the high end of the Guidelines' range, the appellant would receive 38% of the differential, or $1,720 monthly ($20,644 annually). In accordance with the formula for duration, support would be payable for a period ranging from 9.5 to nineteen years.

[111] The award I consider appropriate in this case, at least initially, both exceeds this range for amount and falls below the range for duration. Thus, I turn to the provisions for restructuring, which essentially involve converting the specific ranges of support to a lump sum amount (without consideration for present values). In this case, this conversion results in a broad support range from a low of $147,088, to a high of $392,236.

[112] This global range can be compared to the trial award as a "litmus test of reasonableness". The trial award, including interim support, but assuming termination in December 2008, totals a lump sum of $94,200, an amount that falls far below the Guidelines, although I recognize that this does not account for what may have been the final result after a review hearing.

[113] In comparison, the support award that I propose in these reasons would total $189,000. This figure falls within the Guidelines global range, albeit toward the low end of that range.

RESULT

[114] In the result, I would allow the appeal, set aside paragraphs 2 and 3 of the divorce order and substitute an order for spousal support of $3,000 monthly commencing October 1, 2004, and continuing to March 1, 2008. Thereafter I would award support of $1,500 monthly from April 1, 2008, terminating after a final payment on September 1, 2011. I would also vary paragraph 5 of the order to make reciprocal the obligation to disclose annual incomes to the other spouse as long as support is payable.

[115] This termination order is designed to provide the appellant with support to enable her to become financially independent, or adjust to a lower standard of living within seven years. It also assumes that the respondent will maintain his income in a manner consistent with his current employment. The order is, of course, subject to variation by reason of a material change in circumstances.

[116] I would award costs of the appeal to the appellant in the amount of $9,000, inclusive of disbursements and Goods and Services Tax.

Notes and Questions

Assessing *Fisher*

In an assessment of the application of the SSAGs in decided cases, Rogerson and Thompson commented as follows on *Fisher*:

Non-compensatory claims involve claims based on need. Need can mean an inability to meet basic needs, but it has also generally been interpreted to cover, as an aspect of economic hardship, a significant decline in standard of living from the marital standard. Non-compensatory support reflects the economic interdependency that develops as a result of a shared life, including significant elements of reliance and expectation....

In *Fisher v. Fisher* the Ontario Court of Appeal provided some limited sharing of the post-separation income increase, by taking a four-year average income for both spouses, including the year of separation when the husband's income first increased. This partial sharing was not explained further, but it would appear to reflect the length of the marriage (19 years), the immediacy of the increase (the year of separation) and the non-compensatory basis for support (less compelling argument for sharing). (Carol Rogerson & Rollie Thompson, "Spousal Support Advisory Guidelines: A User's Guide to the Final Version" (2009) 28 Can Fam LQ 209 at 211 and 238)

To what extent do you agree that the SSAGs resulted in greater fairness to Ms. Fisher, in terms of the quantum and duration of her spousal support award?

Consider this situation:

The spouses separated after 23 years of marriage. The husband was a tenured professor and his wife taught on a contractual basis in a private school. At separation, the children lived with the father. Two were attending university, while the youngest was in elementary school. The spouses made their own arrangements about financial issues, and the wife did not pay child support while the husband did not pay spousal support. The wife made financial contributions to the children directly. Eventually, however, the husband sought child support and the wife requested spousal support.

In *Cassidy v McNeil*, 2010 ONCA 218, the appeal court allowed the wife's appeal in part.

At trial, the husband's income was $137,000 annually, while the wife was earning $85,000. The trial judge had ordered the wife to pay child support for the daughter, and had ordered the husband to pay spousal support of $1,200 monthly for five years.

The Court of Appeal held that the trial judge had wrongly focused only on the wife's need for spousal support, but examined the evidence and found that the wife had established other bases for entitlement to spousal support. In particular, the court noted that she had made her career secondary to the needs of the family, including three moves to accommodate the husband's education and employment, and a few years out of the workforce to care for the children. The wife also suffered from some health issues relating to pregnancies.

In assessing spousal support, the court concluded that

[69] ... Over the 23 years of their marriage, the parties' expectations and interdependency would have evolved into an economic merger of their interests. That merger, together with the wife's somewhat compromised career path, meets the threshold of entitlement to spousal support.

In this case, the court applied the SSAGs and decided that the trial judge's award of spousal support was at the high end of the range, and that this amount was not appropriate in light of the wife's level of income. Thus, the Court of Appeal varied the spousal support award to $950 monthly, payable indefinitely. In addition, the court awarded costs to the wife in the amount of $15,000, inclusive of disbursements and GST.

To what extent did the application of the SSAGs result in a more appropriate outcome in this case?

The principle of deference to the trial judge

In *Hickey v Hickey*, [1992] 2 SCR 518, the Supreme Court indicated that appellate courts should generally defer to the trial judge in the absence of a significant error. However, the appeal court in *Fisher* revised the decision of the trial judge. Does this suggest that deference to the trial judge may be easily overcome? How should this issue be resolved? Should *Hickey* be reconsidered in light of the SSAGs?

The SSAGs and private agreements

According to Rogerson and Thompson, the SSAGs "confer no power to re-open or override *final* spousal support agreements." This issue is outside the scope of the SSAGs. In this context, the current legal principles about agreements continue in place, including principles of unconscionability, the Supreme Court's decision in *Miglin* and subsequent cases, and some provincial statutory provisions. Thus,

> A final agreement — i.e., one waiving or terminating spousal support or setting a fixed amount with no provision for review or variation — will thus preclude the application of the Advisory Guidelines unless the agreement can be set aside or overridden under existing law. (Rogerson & Thompson, 2008 *SSAG* at 43)

However, as Rogerson and Thompson argue (at 43–44), the SSAGs have an important role to play in the *negotiation* of agreements by "providing a more structured framework for negotiation and some benchmarks of fairness." Some courts have used the SSAGs to identify agreements that are "unfair," and in other cases, it is possible for courts to use the SSAGs to determine the appropriate amount and duration of spousal support. In addition, the SSAGs may have some impact on agreements that are not final agreements. However, as was recognized in *Miglin*, "the parties' intentions, as reflected in their agreement, may still continue to influence the spousal support outcome...."

Spousal support, the SSAGs and social assistance

The SSAGs use the Child Support Guidelines to determine income. Since these Guidelines assume that a payor spouse on social assistance has no income, no spousal support is payable in this situation.

Social assistance may also be relevant for recipient spouses, particularly in a context in which the spouses negotiate a private agreement, rather than seek a court order for spousal support. In this situation, a spouse who is not represented in the negotiation process may abandon a claim to spousal support, and in the absence of other resources, may need social assistance. Recall the provisions of the *FLA*, particularly section 33(4), permitting a court to set aside a contract on the basis of unconscionability if it results in a spouse becoming entitled to social assistance. In this situation, a separating spouse may be compelled to seek support by the state. Although it is beyond the scope of this discussion, it is also important to recognize connections between principles of support in family law and pursuant to social assistance legislation. See MJ Mossman & Morag MacLean, "Family Law and Social Assistance Programs: Rethinking Equality" in PM Evans & GR Wekerle, eds, *Women and the Canadian Welfare State: Challenges and Change* (Toronto: University of Toronto Press, 1997) at 117.

Additional Resources

Scott Booth, "The Spousal Support Advisory Guidelines: Avoiding Errors and Unsophisticated Use" (2009) 28 Can Fam LQ 339.

James McLeod & Alfred Mamo, *Annual Review of Family Law* (Toronto: Carswell, 2009).

Carol Rogerson & Rollie Thompson, "Spousal Support Advisory Guidelines: Report on Revisions" (2009) 28 Can Fam LQ 193; and "Spousal Support Advisory Guidelines" A User's Guide to the Final Version" (2009) 28 Can Fam LQ 209.

Rollie Thompson, "Following *Fisher*: Ontario Spousal Support Trends 2008–2009" (2009) 28 Can Fam LQ 241.

VII.
REFLECTING AGAIN ON THE POLICY CONTEXT OF FAMILY SUPPORT

> In the end, ... the real encouragement for self-sufficiency is not found in spousal support law, or in the Advisory Guidelines, but in the harsh economic reality facing most separated or divorced spouses. In all but the highest income cases, a recipient must find more income in order to avoid a drop in her or his standard of living, as spousal support is limited by the payor's ability to pay.... (Carol Rogerson & Rollie Thompson, *Spousal Support Advisory Guidelines* (Ottawa: Department of Justice, 2008) at 140)

FAMILY RESPONSIBILITIES FOR DEPENDENCY POST-SEPARATION

"Privatizing" responsibilities for dependency

As the judicial decisions about spousal support reveal, current family law principles emphasize the responsibilities of families to provide financial support for their members, even post-separation. In this context, the role of the state in supporting dependency seems to be one of enforcing these private obligations. In this way, the principles of spousal support have evolved in significant ways since the dissent in *Messier v Delage* and the *Pelech* trilogy. In this context, the ability of a former spouse to provide sufficient support to alleviate another spouse's dependency is a significant factor in determining entitlement, as well as quantum and duration.

Thus, the expanded definition of "spouse" to include cohabiting couples, both opposite sex and same sex, not only creates legal recognition for such families, but also reflects governmental policies of expanding the number of family members with responsibilities to provide for those who are vulnerable or dependent. In this way, legal recognition has economic consequences. In relation to same-sex couples, for example, Susan Boyd identified some problems of "privatizing" family responsibilities for dependency:

> For some individuals, ... this option of turning to family is simply not possible — if they have no family or are alienated from family members, as lesbians and gay men all too often are. Moreover, some families do not have the economic capacity to meet the needs of their impoverished members even if they are willing. (Susan B Boyd, "Best Friends or Spouses? Privatization and the Recognition of Lesbian Relationships in *M v. H*" (1996) 13 Can J Fam L 321 at 336)

Even in the context of opposite sexes, the privatization of responsibility for dependency may lead to practices that are not necessarily appropriate. For example, consider comments made by family law solicitors in research undertaken in the United Kingdom about the advice they might give to clients in support of claims to avoid ongoing spousal support obligations.

The Ties That Bind
(1984) at 190–191

Carol Smart

... [There is a] tendency to individualise and decontextualise domestic disputes, [leading] solicitors to individualistic solutions to the problems posed by divorce. The following solicitor expresses this thinking quite clearly.

> It's a funny business our matrimonial law. He's more or less supposed to have taken her on for life, for better or for worse, despite the divorce law, and theoretically the only thing that lets him off the hook is when she remarries. And so I always advise men clients who are in the position to pay more money to the wife ... as a joke I don't mean it seriously because if you give her too much she may think she's on to a good thing and hang on to it. But I always say send her expensive perfumes, offer to babysit for her and get her, you know, send her out to dances, you know send a car for her to take her because the *sooner she's off your hands and into somebody else's the better.* You know I say the last thing you want to do is to be upsetting her all the time so that she is perpetually going around weeping and looking [so] awful

that nobody else will look at her. You know you've got to strike a nice balance so that she's happy and attractive and then somebody else will take her because theoretically she's on his back until she remarries. [Emphasis in original]

This ... quote is an excellent example of a process of depoliticisation. Basically, structural events are interpreted solely as conflicts between individuals where, given enough cunning, one party can rid himself of an unfortunate problem. In this solicitor's account your sympathy is drawn to the poor husband who has this awful problem and the wife is reduced to a burden. Attention is not drawn to her poverty and her inability to survive financially but to the desirability of offloading her (suitably happy and attractive) on to someone else. And then of course the cycle can repeat itself. Whilst she is happily remarried she can repay her keep in kind (i.e. domestic labour and sex), but should this marriage fail as well she becomes a burden again, hopefully to be passed on to another man although she may well be too old to be considered attractive by then.

What is so noticeably absent in the accounts of most of these solicitors is a recognition that the problems of divorce stem from the problems of marriage. Of course these problems are exacerbated by a drop in living standards as well as a great deal of emotional misery, but the issues of conflict that solicitors deal with do not arise on divorce, they arise from the nature of marriage. There is a continuity from marriage to divorce because the sexual division of labour which is celebrated as natural and desirable during marriage is precisely the basis of the main conflict on divorce....

Although these comments occurred in the U.K. context, it is clear from the assessment (above) about the "harsh economic reality" at separation or divorce that similar strategies may be relevant in Canada as well. In this context, recall Margrit Eichler's assessment in Chapter Five that most women are just "one man away" from poverty.

Substantive reform of post-separation dependency?

In this context, while the principles of spousal support and the recent initiatives in relation to SSAGs offer much more certainty and fairness to dependent spouses post-separation, they do not fundamentally confront the underlying problems that create this dependency. In addition, the current principles essentially regard the solution as one that must be provided by family members, with little or no assistance from the state. In thinking about what might be necessary to create more fundamental reform, consider these suggestions:

Critics of divorce reform have long argued that a central problem arises from treating the issue as simply divorce, when in fact the issue is marriage and men's and women's roles within it. We believe that in fact the issue is still broader. It implicates fundamental understandings of private relationships and public responsibilities.... [Our recommendations for reform] imply an expanded concept of responsibility not only for divorcing spouses and parents but also for the state.... We need both special programs for divorced parties and changes in broader welfare and employment policies that affect family life.... Expanded child-care and parental leave provisions, flexible workplace schedules, wider health and pension coverage, counselling services for single parents and children, retraining programs for displaced homemakers, and further social initiatives targeting minority and low-income groups are also crucial to any effective reform strategy. (Deborah Rhode & Martha Minow, "Reforming the Questions: Questioning the Reforms" in SD Sugarman & HH Kay, *Divorce Reform at the Crossroads* (New Haven, CT: Yale University Press, 1990) 191 at 209–210)

Additional Resources

American Law Institute, *Principles of Family Dissolution: Analysis and Recommendations* (St. Paul, MN: American Law Institute Publishers, 2002).

Nicholas Bala, "Entitlement to Spousal Support: Asking the Tough Questions" in Martha Shaffer, ed, *Contemporary Issues in Family Law* (Toronto: Carswell, 2007) 235.

Ruth Deech, "The Principles of Maintenance" (1977) 7 Family Law 229.

John Eekelaar, "Uncovering Social Obligations: Family Law and the Responsible Citizen" in Mavis Maclean, ed, *Making Law for Families* (Oxford & Portland, OR: Hart Publishing, 2000) 9.

Katherine O'Donovan, "Should All Maintenance of Spouses be Abolished?" (1982) 45 Mod L Rev 424.

Susan Moller Okin, *Justice, Gender and the Family* (New York: Basic Books, 1989).

PRIVATIZATION AND CHILDREN'S SUPPORT FOR THEIR PARENTS: THE NEED FOR REFORM BEYOND THE CONTEXT OF SEPARATION AND DIVORCE?

In the early decades of the 20th century, provincial legislation in different parts of Canada was enacted to create obligations for children to support their parents in some circumstances.

For example, section 32 of Ontario's *FLA* creates an obligation on the part of an adult child, who has the ability, to provide support for a needy parent if the parent "cared for or provided support for the child." That is, the child's support obligation depends on the child's resources and the parent's need, but it also limits such support unless the parent had earlier cared for or supported the child. For an example of a mother's successful claim against her four adult children, see *Godwin v Bolsco* (1993), 45 RFL (3d) 310 (Ont Prov Div); affirmed (1996), 20 RFL (4th) 66 (Ont CA).

Similarly, section 90 of the B.C. *FRA* created an obligation for an adult child to support a needy parent (for example, see *Newson v Newson*

(1998), 43 RFL (4th) 221 (BCCA); *Nevill v Nevill*, [1998] BCJ No 2802 (SC) (QL); and *Anderson v Anderson*, [2001] BCJ No 418 (SC) (QL)). In 2007, the British Columbia Law Institute issued a report recommending removal of this parental support obligation, concluding that governments should introduce more systematic policies to support needy seniors, and in 2009, the Ministry of the Attorney General issued a report confirming that many of those surveyed supported the elimination of this obligation. Thus, the *Family Law Act*, SBC 2011, c 25 (in force 2013) eliminated this obligation.

To what extent do provisions such as *FLA*, section 32 (in Ontario) suggest that there may be additional family law obligations to provide financial support for dependent family members, beyond the context of separation and divorce?

In the context of demographic data about the aging of Canada's population, should children bear responsibilities for supporting their parents or should this obligation belong to the state? If children should bear at least part of this obligation, how should the obligation be defined?

In reflecting on these questions, consider the following decision.

Dragulin v Dragulin
(1999), 43 RFL (4th) 55 (Ont Gen Div)

Octavian Dragulin applied for support from his daughter Helen pursuant to section 32 of the *Family Law Act*. Mr. Dragulin was 73 years old and recently unemployed. He was divorced from Helen's mother and had remarried (his second wife was 59 and had emigrated from Romania to Canada in 1997; she had no assets and only a small pension). Mr. Dragulin came to Canada as a refugee in 1951. Helen was 45, a clerk with Canada Post, and lived in a home she co-owned with her mother, and her sister also lived in the home and paid rent.

In late 1996, Helen won a lottery worth $1 million, but she continued to live modestly. She did not wish to support her father.

However, the court held that Helen should pay her father $400 per month. Examine the reasoning in the decision (at 57):

> ... There are three issues to determine in applying s. 32 of the *Family Law Act*: the need of the parent, whether the parent provided care or support for the child, and the capacity of the child to support the parent.
>
> **CAPACITY TO GIVE SUPPORT**
> There is no issue in this case about Helen Dragulin's capacity to support her father. In fact, she provided him with support in the past, when he was in financial difficulties during the period when her parents were in the process of separation and divorce and at a time when her assets were significantly less.
>
> She is employed full time with Canada Post as a clerk, and she still has substantial amounts of her lottery winnings. Her Financial Statement indicates that she has $4,547.24 per month surplus after paying her expenses.

None of the other children were joined in this application. However, the evidence indicates that Helen is the only one with the capacity to provide parental support.

CARE AND SUPPORT FROM THE PARENT

The second issue is whether care or support were provided by the plaintiff to the defendant when she was a child. The defendant argued strenuously that she was not cared for by her father as a child, and that her childhood was unhappy, because her father was verbally abusive. She and her sister Anna expressed great bitterness about their treatment by their father. In Helen's view, she received no emotional support from him, and he called her insulting names while she was growing up. Both also described Mr. Dragulin's beatings of his son, Michael.

It was Helen's evidence that she began to support the family from the time she was ten years old, doing cooking and laundry, while her mother was out at work. As a teenager, she also worked part-time to earn money for necessary personal expenses. However, both in examination for discovery and her testimony at trial, she admitted that her father had provided financial support for the family when she was growing up. He was the primary source of financial support for the family until she was ten years old, when her mother began to work outside the home.

There has been minimal contact between the children and their father since the 1984 divorce, and contact ceased following a letter he wrote, addressed "To whom it may concern," in August, 1994, in which he demanded reconciliation or an explanation of the family's past treatment of him within 30 days. It ended with a curse if they did not respond.

The language of s. 32 of the *Family Law Act* is clear: a parent must have "cared for *or* provided support for the child" (emphasis added). The terms are not conjunctive, and the parent need not show both support *and* care. Moreover, the Act includes no defence of fault or misconduct in the award of parental support (see *Godwin v. Bolcso* (1993), 45 RFL (3d) 310 (Ont. Prov. Div.); affirmed (1996), 20 RFL (4th) 66 (Ont. CA)), nor does it take into consideration the nature and quality of the current interaction between parent and child. In contrast, a child is not entitled to parental support if he or she is sixteen years of age or older and has withdrawn from parental control (s. 31(2)).

The evidence is clear in this case that the plaintiff provided financial support for his family when the defendant was a child, and she conceded that. The standard of living was not a high one, but this was a family in which the parents arrived in Canada in 1951 and had to struggle to establish themselves, learning English, acquiring educational qualifications, and pursuing various employment and business opportunities, some of which proved very poor investments. The children were required to work hard in the home and contribute financially, but this does not detract from the fact that they were provided with financial support by their father when they were children within the meaning of s. 32 of the Act. The family's subsequent estrangement from Mr. Dragulin following the parents' divorce does not undermine the fact that support was received within the meaning of s. 32....

NEED OF THE PARENT

The central issue in this case is the need of the plaintiff. Decided cases provide little guidance with respect to this issue, as the few cases reported have focused on whether there has been past support by the parent or on the relationship between spousal and parental support, concluding that spousal support is the primary obligation (see, for example, *Skrzypacz v. Skrzypacz* (1996), 22 RFL (4th) 450 (Ont. Prov. Div.); *Whiteley v. Brodie* (May 13, 1994), Doc. Kingston 160/93 (Ont. Prov. Div.)). In *Blum v. Blum*

(1982), 132 DLR (3d) 69 (Ont. Fam. Ct.), a son was ordered to pay his mother $270.00 per month, after taking into account her need and the son's obligations to support his wife and children, as well as his father. In *Godwin*, supra, support of $1,000.00 per month was awarded on an interim basis, shared among the four children....

While both Mr. Dragulin and Mrs. Dragulin have improved their standard of living over time, they have continued to live modestly. His proposed budget indicates that he wishes to improve his standard of living now that his daughter has won the lottery. However, ss. 32 and 33(9) of the Act provide that his claim must be based on need, not wants, and he can not seek an increase in his standard of living just because of his daughter's good fortune. These needs must also be his personal needs, not those of his second wife, to whom his daughter Helen owes no support obligation.

In determining his needs, I have not considered his claims for vacation, gifts, the portion of food and expenses for Maria Dragulin, and telephone costs, which include many calls to Rumania. In addition, his claims for drug expenses are excessive, as they take no account of public subsidies for senior citizens.

As well, Helen Dragulin has no obligation to fund the taxes for the Lake Simcoe property. That property could be sold if Mr. Dragulin wished to do so, to pay for vacations or other expenses. If he does not choose to sell the lot, he must bear its carrying costs.

The issue of the condominium is more difficult. While Mr. Dragulin does have an asset here that theoretically could be sold, were he to do so, his living expenses for an equivalent rental apartment would significantly exceed the $371.41 he now pays.

After subtracting items from his current budget which are not necessities for him personally, the plaintiff's personal needs still significantly exceed his income of approximately $1,000.00 per month. Therefore, there will be judgment for the plaintiff, with support of $400.00 per month ordered payable by the defendant, Helen Dragulin, to Octavian Dragulin, commencing October 1, 1998.

Notes and Questions

Family responsibility for dependency?

To what extent does *Dragulin* reveal underlying assumptions about familial obligations for economic support? Is it appropriate for Mr. Dragulin to share in his daughter's good fortune in winning the lottery? To what extent do these cases appear consistent with the Supreme Court's emphasis on individual autonomy in *Miglin*? Could the daughter in *Dragulin* have entered into a contract with her father with respect to limitations on his entitlement to support?

Consider *Skrzypacz v Skrzypacz* (1996), 22 RFL (4th) 450 (Ont Prov Div):

An applicant mother sought interim support from her son who had sponsored her to come to Canada from Poland. The son filed evidence supporting his claim that his mother was never his primary caregiver and had never provided support for him. The applicant failed to file any documentation in support of her claim to entitlement under an immigration sponsorship agreement, nor did she file any evidence to counter her son's allegations. Therefore, the court found that she failed to meet the criteria for entitlement under section 32 of the *Family Law Act*.

In *Ontario (Dir of Family Support Plan) v Burgess* (1994), 5 RFL (4th) 451 (Ont Prov Div), a former husband sought to have a grown son contribute to his former wife's support (although the former wife did not participate in this request). The husband's application was dismissed. See also *Smeland v Smeland* (1997), 29 RFL (4th) 360 (BCSC).

Additional Resources

Christa Bracci, "Ties That Bind: Ontario's Filial Responsibility Law" (2000) 17 Can J Fam L 455.

Tonya L Brito, "The Welfarization of Family Law" (2000) 48 U Kan L Rev 229.

Brenda Cossman & Judy Fudge, eds, *Privatization, Law, and the Challenge to Feminism* (Toronto: University of Toronto Press, 2002).

Shelley AM Gavigan, "Paradise Lost, Paradox Revisited: The Implications of Familial Ideology for Feminist, Lesbian, and Gay Engagement to Law" (1993) 31 Osgoode Hall LJ 589.

MJ Mossman, "Conversations About Families in Canadian Courts and Legislatures: Are There 'Lessons' for the United States?" (2003) 32:1 Hofstra L Rev 171.

Jane E Ursel, *Private Lives and Public Policy* (Toronto: Women's Press, 1992).

8

Children and Family Dissolution: Rights, Relationships, and Economic Support

In child custody law, women, and those men who provide caregiving labour themselves or understand its demands, must continue to point out the day-to-day demands of caring for children in a society that is structured on the privatization of caring labour. Simultaneously, we must struggle for the structural changes that will be more likely to produce a society that will encourage more collective responsibility for children and those who attend to their needs and their welfare. (Susan B Boyd, *Child Custody, Law, and Women's Work* (Toronto: Oxford University Press, 2003) at 226–227)

Fixed schedules or formulae for the determination of child support could promote (i) simple and inexpensive administrative procedures for assessing the amount of child support; (ii) consistency of amounts in comparable family situations; and (iii) higher child support payments that more realistically reflect the actual costs of raising children. They are unlikely, however, to resolve the economic crisis of separation and divorce for women and children. The war on poverty requires more than piecemeal reform of child support. (Julien Payne, "Spousal and Child Support after *Moge*, *Willick* and *Levesque*" (1995) 12 Can Fam LQ 261 at 298)

I.
FAMILY DISSOLUTION:
THE CONTEXT FOR CHILDREN

CHILDREN AND THE SOCIAL CONTEXT OF FAMILY DISSOLUTION

"Family life pathways": Family changes and the context for children

As these quotations suggest, the children of separating or divorcing parents experience many different challenges as a result of these changes in their families, including changes in family economy.

Statistics about families and change indicate that children now experience a variety of family structures, including parents who are cohabiting rather than in a marriage relationship. In addition, rising rates of separation and divorce mean that increasing numbers of children live in one-parent families.

According to the 2006 General Social Survey (Vanier Institute of the Family, *Families Count* (Ottawa: Vanier Institute of the Family, 2010) at 62–65):

• Four out of ten adults involved in separation had dependent children; many of these adults repartner.

• Within three years of separation, one-third of fathers and one-quarter of mothers had remarried or begun to live with a new partner. Ten years later, more than 63 percent of children had seen their mother set up home with a new partner and 67 percent had seen their father do so.

• Children born to cohabiting couples were much more likely to experience significant change than those born to married spouses.

These statistics suggest that separation or divorce are common features of family life in Canada, and it is likely that they will remain common for children born in the 1990s and 2000s. In this context, demographers have argued that

> [t]here are few hard-and-fast rules as to how these transitions should be made, how rights and responsibilities towards children should be divided between parents in different households, and how parents should share resources among children who do not all live in the same household. [This complexity needs to be understood by those involved in assessing the impact of family change on children, or in developing public policies to deal with this complexity.] (*Families Count* at 64, quoting Heather Juby, Céline Le Bourdais and Nicole Marcil-Gratton, *Moving On: The Expansion of the Family Network after Parents Separate* (Ottawa: Department of Justice Canada, 2004) at vii)

This comment clearly suggests a need to focus on the ways in which change that results from family dissolution must take account of *both* the impact on children, and *also* the need for responsive public policies.

Indeed, as *Families Count* noted, the pace of change in family relationships requires new terminology to reflect the fluidity and diversity of family life.

In this context, the term "family life pathways" may be more useful as a way of understanding "the impact of different living arrangements on children and their parents, and [also] how changes in family context impact long-term health and well-being" (see *Families Count* at 62).

Economic issues about children at family dissolution

In addition, economic issues for families have significant consequences for children:

> For children living in poor families, low income simply fails to provide the resources necessary for good health and developmental outcomes. Low income is a significant predicator of low infant birth weight, increased infant mortality, and overall poor child health and development (see *Families Count* at 116).

Although family dissolution is not the only reason for children's poverty, it seems that children living in a one-parent family is a risk factor for, and can exacerbate, poverty.

- About 250,000 children who live in female lone-parent families represent 39 percent of all poor children in Canada (see *Families Count* at 118).

- In this context, a recent study of reported usage at food banks reveals an increase of 9.2 percent, over March 2009 (and these figures track the usage per person without double counting if the person used the food bank more than once in the month). Moreover, the 2009 usage was higher than 2008 by 18 percent. See Roger Sauvé, *The Current State of Canadian Family Finances* (Ottawa: Vanier Institute of the Family, 2011) at 26.

- Even more significantly, it seems that income inequality in Canada has been growing. According to Sauvé, the share of total after-tax incomes shrank for the bottom four-fifths of households, while the top 20 percent of households increased its share of the total income pie from 41.0 percent in 1990 to 44.3 percent in 2008 (Sauvé at 27).

Thus, in taking account of "family life pathways," economic issues require careful attention, especially in relation to their impact on children.

Yet, in spite of the concerns identified in the quotes at the beginning of this chapter, issues about children in post-dissolution families (including issues of caregiving and issues of economic support) have generally been addressed as matters of "private" concern, rather than in terms of "public" policy. In this way, it is families who have continuing responsibility for children post-separation or divorce, a situation sometimes characterized as the "privatization" of responsibility for Canadian children.

Organization of this chapter: Making connections between "care" and "support" for children

Custody and access: This chapter begins by focusing on issues about custody and access. It starts with a brief examination of some research about children's experiences of parental separation or divorce, focusing on the need to examine the variety of ways in which children as individuals respond to family dissolution. This section also provides some information about the public policy context and the history of legal principles concerning children at divorce.

The next section focuses on current legal principles regarding decisions about children at divorce or separation. In general, federal and provincial legislation has adopted the "welfare" principle, that is, that custody and access should be determined in accordance with a child's "best interests." This section focuses on judicial interpretation of these principles in a variety of circumstances, including a brief introduction to the UN *Convention on the Rights of the Child* of 1989 (ratified by Canada in 1991).

The chapter then focuses on processes for decision making and different arrangements for custody and access, including sole and joint custody. In this context, the material takes into account the process issues in Chapter Five as they relate to children, particularly mediation and collaborative law processes, and the role of experts in assessing children and creating parenting plans. This section also considers recent developments, including parallel parenting, to deal with parental conflict and to promote the "best interests" of children at family dissolution. The chapter also provides a brief overview of some reform recommendations and critiques with respect to issues of custody and access.

Child support: The chapter then turns to issues about child support. This section begins by exploring the evolution of child support in Canada, and the increasing emphasis on private family support at separation or divorce. It then provides an overview of legislative definitions of "parent" and "child," and judicial interpretation of these relationships. As will be evident, the courts have tended to adopt expansive interpretations, so that some persons who have no biological or adoptive relationships to children ("social parents") may nonetheless have support obligations in particular circumstances.

The chapter then examines the Child Support Guidelines, introduced throughout Canada in 1997, the result of co-operation among the federal, provincial and territorial governments. In this context, the material provides an overview of the Guidelines and their interpretation by the courts, focusing particularly on sections that may involve judicial discretion (ss 5, 7, 8, 9 and 10).

This section concludes with some recommendations for reform and critiques of current arrangements for child support.

Connecting "care" and "support": Although the legal principles regarding custody and access often appear to be quite distinct from those regarding obligations for child support, the economic impact of family dissolution may provide incentives to contest particular kinds of arrangements for custody and access. In this way, it is sometimes important to connect issues about caregiving arrangements and issues about economic support for children post-family dissolution.

For example, section 9 of the Child Support Guidelines permits a reduction in the amount of child support payable where a parent "has a right of access to or has physical custody of a child" for 40 percent of the time over the course of a year.

As will be discussed later in this chapter, such provisions concerning child support may encourage contested claims for custody or access, as part of the overall economic re-adjustment package for the spouses involved in separation or divorce. In this way, issues about custody or access and issues about child support may become entangled in complicated parental negotiations or litigation.

Thus, although the legal principles are addressed separately in this chapter, it is important to note how they may intersect for families and children at separation or divorce.

Additional Resources

Cynthia Grant Bowman, "The Legal Relationship Between Cohabitants and their Partner's Children" (2012) 13 Theor Inq L 127.

Brenda Cossman & Judy Fudge, eds, *Privatization, Law and the Challenge to Feminism* (Toronto: University of Toronto Press, 2002).

John Eekelaar, "The End of an Era?" in Sanford Katz, John Eekelaar & Mavis Maclean, eds, *Cross Currents: Family Law and Policy in the United States and England* (Oxford: Oxford University Press, 2000) 637.

Lucinda Ferguson, "Family, Social Inequalities, and the Persuasive Force of Interpersonal Obligation" (2008) 22 Intl JL Pol'y & Fam 61.

Shelley AM Gavigan & Dorothy E Chunn, "From Mothers' Allowance to Mothers Need Not Apply: Canadian Welfare Law as Liberal and Neo-Liberal Reforms" (2007) 45 Osgoode Hall LJ 733.

Sheila Kamerman & Alfred Kahn, eds, *Family Change and Family Policies in Great Britain, Canada, New Zealand and the United States* (Oxford: Clarendon Press, 1/997).

Mary Zenorini Silverzweig, "Stepping Through the Quagmire: You're Not My Dad" (2009) 11:2 JL & Fam Stud 497.

Carol Smart & Selma Sevenhuijsen, eds, *Child Custody and the Politics of Gender* (London: Routledge, 1989).

Alison Harvison Young, "The Changing Family: Rights Discourse and the Supreme Court of Canada" (2004) 80 Can Bar Rev 749.

II.
CUSTODY AND CARE: PERSPECTIVES AND POLICIES ABOUT CHILDREN AT FAMILY DISSOLUTION

RESEARCH PERSPECTIVES

Research about post-dissolution families and children

Legal regulation concerning children whose parents separate or divorce involves complex, and sometimes controversial, issues. For most children, family dissolution results in some changes in their lives, and managing these changes may create challenges for children, as well as for their parents. Changes in adult relationships, including economic relationships, often produce stress for parents involved in separation or divorce too. However, as the material about parenting workshops at divorce in Chapter Five suggested, some legal policies have been designed expressly to promote the continuation of healthy parent–child relationships for both parents and their children, and to encourage parents not to involve children in parental disagreements.

In this context, some research emphasizes how separation or divorce often creates serious problems for children:

1. Some psychological research indicates that parents may project on to their children their own feelings about their family dissolution. Thus, a parent who is content with the decision to separate may conclude that the children, who seem content as well, are accepting their parents' decision. By contrast, if the parent is unhappy about the decision to separate, that parent may conclude that the children are unhappy and hiding their feelings. If the parties are not able to reach an agreement about the children, they may become involved in a dispute about custody that appears to focus on the children, but may relate to much more than just the children. (See Robert Emery, *Renegotiating Family Relationships: Divorce, Child Custody, and Mediation* (New York: Guilford Press, 1994); Kathryn Abrams & Hila Keren, "Who's Afraid of Law and the Emotions?" (2010) 94:6 Minn L Rev 1997; and Robert E Emery, "Anger is Not Anger is Not Anger: Different Motivations Behind Anger and Why They Matter for Family Law" (2009) 16:2 Va J Soc Pol'y & L 346.)

2. Other research has documented how children in families disrupted by divorce do worse than children in intact families on a number of measures of well-being, including poverty. For example, see Barbara Dafoe Whitehead, "Dan Quayle was Right", *The Atlantic Monthly*, (April 1993) 47. However, this U.S. research was rebutted in Canada by the suggestion that it is not divorce *per se*, but rather

the economic consequences of family breakdown that create prob-
lems for children. See Leah McLaren, "The Kids (of Divorce) are
All Right", *The Globe and Mail* (11 September 1999), quoting Dr.
Robert Glossop of the VIF.

3. Some researchers have attempted to identify factors that may
    assist children's adjustment to family breakdown. They include
    protecting children from conflict and violence, ensuring adequate
    economic support, developing adults' capacity for parenting after
    family breakdown (by defining clear roles for parents and chil-
    dren), preserving parents' functions in their children's lives, and
    developing a positive environment by responding to children's
    questions and fears. Some researchers also promote the use of
    detailed "parenting plans" (discussed later in this chapter), while
    recognizing that they may not be appropriate in cases of abuse,
    alienation or high conflict. See Rhonda Freeman, "Parenting after
    Divorce: Using Research to Inform Decision-Making about Chil-
    dren" (1998) 15 Can J Fam L 79; Jessica J Sauer, "Mediating Child
    Custody Disputes for High Conflict Couples: Structuring Media-
    tion to Accommodate the Needs & Desires of Litigious Parents"
    (2007) 7:3 Pepperdine Dispute Resolution LJ 501; and Allison M
    Nichols, "Toward a Child-Centered Approach to Evaluating Claims
    of Alienation in High-Conflict Custody Disputes" (2014) 112:4
    Mich L Rev 663.

As these examples of research and perspectives reveal, there are many
complex issues involved for children at separation or divorce, and researchers have recommended processes for resolving custody and access issues in
ways that promote continuing relationships for parents and their children.
Some of these processes are reviewed later in this chapter.

Questioning the concept of "harm-ism" for children at family dissolution

Because of ongoing reform efforts in Canada relating to issues of custody
and access, it may be important to compare some reform efforts in a number of other common law jurisdictions.

For example, legislative reform in the United Kingdom in the 1990s
resulted in the abandonment of legal categories of "custody" and "access."
Instead, the *Children Act* required parents to continue their parental responsibilities post-separation or divorce, although courts could make orders
regarding a child's "residence" or to structure "contact" with a parent.

According to sociological research in the United Kingdom, these
arrangements were introduced in the context of a "'narrative of harm' ...
which suffuse[d] contemporary public debates about divorce." In this
context, some researchers engaged in documenting the empirical experiences
of children, particularly with respect to this pervasive narrative of "harm":

> We wanted to explore how transformations in family life in Britain might be reshaping children's lives and thereby changing the nature of childhood at the turn of the century. More specifically, we wanted to see how children themselves might shape their own childhoods in the face of family change and what this might mean for the way they practised their family lives. In a policy context, too, we wanted to explore how new ideas about childhood might transform how we "see" and respond to children whose parents have separated or divorced.... (Carol Smart, Bren Neale, & Amanda Wade, *The Changing Experience of Childhood: Families and Divorce* (Cambridge: Polity Press, 2001) at 19)

As a result of their research, Smart, Neale and Wade argued that it was not appropriate to assume that all children are alike or want the same things:

> We found brothers were happy with arrangements while their sisters were not, or that a younger sibling might be content with contact while an older sibling was not. It was not uncommon for two children in the same family to have different parenting arrangements in place, depending on how they each got on with their parents. We cannot therefore assume that all children will benefit from the same processes or solutions. The idea of the welfare of "the child" may be unhelpful simply because it implies that general principles can be devised that can be applied in a blanket fashion — a kind of "one size fits all" approach. A more flexible approach which takes into account the individuality of each child in a family might embrace more elements of citizenship, while also attending rather more to the well-being of each child (at 167).

Acting on their research, the authors rejected the focus on "harm-ism" and suggested that some children's participation in family decision making represented a democratization of the family, concluding that

> [t]here is more than one story to be told about children's experiences of their parents' divorce. Not all the stories are happy ones but many are about resilience, transformations, growing self-reflexiveness, and the development of a new set of perspectives on parenting and family practices. The growth in the divorce rate in the second half of the twentieth century dramatically changed children's experiences of childhood. Even those children whose parents stay together will know children whose parents are divorced. This does not make divorce easy for children, but it changes the landscape of childhood into one in which these personal transformations become highly probable. In this context children need to acquire new skills (both practical and emotional) to navigate this new moral terrain (at 173).

In reflecting on the statistics about children at family dissolution and the research conclusions from different perspectives, consider how these perspectives may influence particular legislative choices or judicial views with respect to the experiences of children whose parents separate or divorce. Keep these comments in mind as you review the legislative principles and judicial interpretations about children and care in post-dissolution families in Canada.

The "public" policy context

As Susan Boyd's comment at the beginning of this chapter illustrates, it is also necessary to examine how social policies that assume the primacy of parental care for children may exacerbate the impact of separation or divorce, both for children and their adult caregivers.

That is, while it is clearly important to take account of the needs of children as individuals, the scope for meeting children's needs at family dissolution may be significantly constrained by social and legal policies that emphasize extensive, even exclusive, *parental* responsibility for their children.

If parents are the persons with full legal responsibility for children, concerns will tend to focus on the relative strengths and weaknesses of parents as caregivers. Such analyses all too often fail to examine the role of extended families and communities, as well as public policies that shape the contexts in which children live and the need for public support to ensure their well-being. Although this problem is particularly relevant with respect to issues of financial support for children, especially post-separation or divorce, it also has an impact on decisions about responsibilities for caregiving.

In this way, concerns about children post-family dissolution need to take account of both *private* family relationships as well as *public* policies that provide (or sometimes fail to provide) care and support for families and children when adult relationships break down.

The recent context for legal reform in Canada has often been controversial. A decade ago, after two major reviews by the federal government in the 1990s (see Canada, Department of Justice, *Custody and Access: Public Discussion Paper* (Ottawa: Supply and Services Canada, 1993); and Special Joint Committee on Child Custody and Access, *For the Sake of the Children* (Ottawa: Parliament of Canada, 1998)), the government introduced Bill C-22 in 2002. This Bill, which did not become law in Canada, reflected recommendations of the Joint Committee's Report, *For the Sake of the Children*.

Among other suggestions, Bill C-22 recommended eliminating the legal categories of "custody" and "access," replacing them with obligations for parents to negotiate parenting plans, with the help of mediation, if necessary.

The underlying principle was that just as parents must negotiate about their children's well-being during an intact relationship, they should continue to exercise the same responsibility post-separation or divorce. In this way, the proposed legislation reflected the view that *while marriage or cohabitation may end, parenthood is forever.*

Obviously, this legislation was similar to the U.K. *Children Act*, and it also reflected family law reforms in other jurisdictions such as Australia. A further effort to reform custody and access was initiated in 2009 (see Bill C-422), but it did not become law. However, in the current political context in Canada, such reform initiatives may surface again. Thus, it is important to note how rhetoric about children's needs and experiences at family dissolution may influence legislative choices and judicial decision making. See, for example, the *Family Law Act*, SBC 2011, c 25, Part 4, which prescribes detailed arrangements for guardianship and contact with children.

CHILDREN AND FAMILY DISSOLUTION: THE LEGAL CONTEXT

The history of custody and access in law

According to Boyd, child custody laws in Canada have been altered in significant ways since the 19th century, and the current "best interests" principle is relatively recent:

> The transformation of child custody laws in Canada and most Western countries over the past two centuries has been striking. The broad outline of legal history of child custody laws reveals a more or less complete reversal, and a half-turn again by the 1980s. At the beginning of the nineteenth century, laws in countries such as England and the United States affirmed an almost absolute paternal right to custody of children born within wedlock, reflecting the elevated legal status of the husband/father within the institution of marriage. By the beginning of the twentieth century, this absolute paternal right had begun to wane and to give way to an emphasis on the welfare of children. By the mid-twentieth century, mothers were said to have a presumption in their favour when seeking custody of children "of tender years." By the 1980s, child custody law was pronounced to be a neutral domain, where the "best interests" of children came first, and where mothers and fathers, and potentially other parties connected to the children, had an equal right to legal custody. By the 1990s, reforms of child custody laws in many jurisdictions purported to embody these changes and to deepen them by emphasizing shared parenting. (Boyd at 2)

Boyd's explanation of the evolution of legal principles concerning custody and access (and related issues of child support) demonstrates how legal principles often changed as a result of political, economic and social developments:

- In the early 19th century, for example, Canadian jurisprudence recognized paternal rights to custody and "guardianship" of legitimate children, both during marriage and after separation. However, as a result of lobbying efforts by Lady Caroline Norton in England, the English Parliament enacted *Lord Talfourd's Act*, 2 & 3 Vict, c 54, in 1839, which permitted access, and sometimes physical custody, rights to mothers in relation to children less than seven years old. However, as Boyd noted, a mother's access and custody rights related to physical, not legal custody, and they were contingent on her not engaging in "immoral" conduct. Overriding paternal authority for children remained in place.

- By the early 20th century, the patterns were becoming more uneven. Some legislatures and courts recognized the "tender years" doctrine (which awarded maternal custody in relation to young children), while others were beginning to examine the welfare of children. (See Karina

Winton, "The Spoilt Darling of the Law: Women and Canadian Custody Law in the Postwar Period (1946–1960)" (2002) 19 Can J Fam L 193.) In relation to the tender years doctrine, however, mothers were subjected to considerable scrutiny. As Boyd noted:

> Any notion that mothers were favoured in custody cases under this doctrine must be read in light of the intense scrutiny of maternal and wifely conduct that preceded a finding of all things being equal between the parents. Proper conduct was required of the mother before application of the "presumption". (Boyd at 71)

- In the 1960s and 1970s, when divorce rates began to rise, there were new pressures on child custody principles. In addition, the *Charter* began to influence ideas about parental "equality" in relation to shared parenting in the 1980s. However, according to Boyd, these principles did not diminish the scrutiny of mothers' behaviour, although they tended to enhance the status of fathers in custody disputes:

> [T]he liberal spirit of the time was not evident when [mothers] went to court to seek custody of their children. Their sexual conduct, their lack of fidelity to marriage and to the sexual division of labour, and their economic viability could all generate difficulties for their claims for custody.... The equality rights discourse that emerged during the 1980s accelerated the trends towards enhancing the status of fathers in custody and access claims. (Boyd at 101)

The current principle for determining custody and access pursuant to the *Divorce Act* is the "best interests of the child" (s 16), and this principle is also applicable under Ontario's provincial legislation, the *Children's Law Reform Act*, RSO 1990, c C.12 (s 24). However, since the content of this principle is not fully defined in legislation, the cases may reflect some earlier legal principles and social assumptions about what is in a child's "best interests."

"Mothers" and "fathers": The equality debate

As Boyd's historical review of custody and access arrangements reveals, legal principles have evolved over time as societal views about the respective roles of mothers and fathers have changed. In this context, the gender neutral "best interests" test focuses judicial attention on children rather than their parents.

In practice, however, application of this test may reveal "hidden" assumptions about mothers and fathers. That is, societal expectations about the roles of mothers and fathers may influence perceptions about what is in a child's "best interests."

For example, Boyd suggested that custody and access cases often reflect an ideology of a "good mother":

> [T]he ideology of motherhood reproduced in custody and access law relies on a notion that mothers will assume responsibility for children, that they will put aside their own interests, and often their participation in the so-called "public" sphere, in order to do so, and that they can expect to be

paid nothing for this labour of love.... Mothers whose behaviour or choices depart from these assumptions and expectations can expect to be treated more suspiciously, even negatively, in the legal system as well as in society. (see Boyd at 218)

In addition, as Boyd noted, the *Charter*'s principle of equality has influenced, sometimes quite subtly, the ways in which claims by mothers and fathers with respect to custody and access have been assessed. More specifically, the adoption of Child Support Guidelines, linking payment of child support to a payor's income, seemed to fuel concerns on the part of fathers to be more engaged with their children — in terms of increasing numbers of claims for custody but, more often, in relation to claims for greater access.

Although these claims will be examined in more detail later in this chapter, it is important to note how "fathers' rights" claims have challenged the law of custody and access, not only in Canada but in many other jurisdictions. While these claims are often presented quite simply as a response to feminist demands, the context is arguably much more complicated:

[D]escribing the rise of the [Fathers' Rights Movement] in terms of a "backlash" to increased female power is, at best, a caricature which fails to capture the multifaceted, fast changing, complex realities of men's and women's experiences of family breakdown and shifting gender roles. The greater prominence of the FRM might be better understood as one aspect of a complex renegotiation of understandings of men's roles as parent in the light of shifting gender relations, household forms, discourses about parenting and childhood, legal norms and modes of governance. (Richard Collier & Sally Sheldon, "Fathers' Rights, Fatherhood and Law Reform — International Perspectives" in Collier & Sheldon, eds, *Fathers' Rights Activism and Law Reform in Comparative Perspective* (Oxford & Portland, OR: Hart Publishing, 2006) 1 at 14)

In this context also, there are important connections between issues about care of children and issues about economic support for them. Accordingly, these ideas will be important as you review the cases and discussion about the "best interests" principle in this chapter.

The legislative context for the "best interests" principle

1. The *Divorce Act*
   For a married spouse who has filed an application for divorce, the legal principles for determining applications for custody and access are set out in section 16 of the *Divorce Act*.
   - The basic principle is "the best interests of the child," determined by reference to the condition, means, needs, and other circumstances of the child (see s 16(8));
   - Conduct is irrelevant unless it affects the ability of a person to act as a parent (see s 16(9)); and
   - Courts must give effect to the principle that a child should have as much contact with each spouse as is consistent with the best

interests principle, and thus section 16(10) requires courts to "take into consideration the willingness of each person for whom custody is sought to facilitate such contact" (the friendly parent obligation).

In addition, section 16(4) permits a court to order custody of, or access to, any or all children of the marriage "to any one or more persons." This section provides the authority for an order for "joint" legal or physical custody, discussed later in this chapter.

2. Provincial legislation

For married spouses who have not filed for divorce, and for cohabiting couples who separate, provincial legislation governs applications for custody and access.

In Ontario, the *Children's Law Reform Act* provisions apply. Although the precise legislative language varies somewhat from province to province, the basic principle for custody and access determinations pursuant to provincial legislation is the "best interests" of the child (for example, see *CLRA*, s 24).

In addition, section 28(1) permits orders for shared custody, and authorizes a court to define the incidents of custody or access. Amendments in 2009 define new procedures for custody and access applications (see ss 21.1–21.3).

As discussed in Chapter Five, some issues concerning the constitutional division of powers may arise in relation to custody, access, and child support (see Peter Hogg, *Constitutional Law of Canada* (Toronto: Carswell) (looseleaf) at chapter 27). Note again the recommendations of the Senate Committee to remove legal categories of "custody" and "access" and to provide for mediation and parenting plans (and Bill C-22 (2002), which was not enacted).

ARRANGEMENTS FOR CUSTODY AND CARE: AN INTRODUCTION

"Sole custody" with "access"; and "joint" or "shared custody"

Although the legislation does not address the legal arrangements for custody in detail, there is a wealth of interdisciplinary literature about how parents should structure their post-separation parenting arrangements.

Particularly as a result of the emergence of fathers' rights organization, ideas about shared parenting have become more accepted. Indeed, as was noted above, the United Kingdom abandoned the terminology of "custody" and "access" altogether, and the Senate Committee in Canada made recommendations for a continuation of shared parenting post-family dissolution. Although the Committee's recommendations have not been implemented (since Bill C-22 failed to be enacted), many experts involved with children whose parents are separating or divorcing firmly encourage ideas of shared parenting.

At the outset, therefore, it is important to explain the legal context for custody and access and for joint or shared parenting, and particularly to distinguish between having legal authority for children on one hand and being responsible for physical care of children on the other.

- **"Custody" as legal authority:** When a parent is granted legal "custody" of a child, it means that the custodial parent has legal authority to make decisions concerning the child with respect to health, education, and welfare (usually including the choice of religious faith). In this context, a parent who is granted "access" has the right to spend time with the child, and to receive information about the child's situation, usually in accordance with the terms of a court order or separation agreement.

  By contrast with this arrangement, an award of "joint custody" means that both former spouses have legal authority to make decisions for children in relation to health, education and welfare (including religion).

  A joint (legal) custody arrangement thus means that the parents must find ways to reach agreement on these matters, and this requirement usually means that the parents must interact with each other on a regular basis.

  In this context, courts have expressed different views about whether judges should order joint custody, or whether this option should be available only for parents who negotiate such an arrangement in a separation agreement. The issue is whether the co-operation necessary for joint legal custody can be ordered, or whether it must be negotiated and accepted by willing parties.

- **Physical "custody" and caregiving responsibilities:** However, even where one parent has legal "custody," while the other has legal "access," or where the parents have "joint custody," separate arrangements for physical care of children may be negotiated or ordered.

  Thus, even though one parent has "custody" and the other "access," it is possible for both parents to share equal amounts of time in providing physical and emotional care for children. For example, parents may provide physical care for a child equally even though one parent has legal "custody" and the other has legal "access."

  In a case where the parents continue to take equal responsibility for child care, such an arrangement constitutes "physical joint custody." If the parents also share responsibility for decision making about the child, they have "legal joint custody."

As these possible arrangements reveal, parents may agree to provide physical care for, and to make decisions about, their children in a variety of ways, and courts may issue orders that reflect this range of possibilities.

In recent years, moreover, many parents have been encouraged to agree to detailed "parenting plans" that set out specific arrangements for their children, including where the child will sleep on a weekly basis, how the child will spend holidays, and which parent is entitled to make particular decisions for the child.

In addition, courts have ordered "parallel parenting." Such orders include detailed parenting plans as well as authority for a parent with physical custody to make decisions about the child during the time that the child is in that parent's care. These orders may also require parents to co-operate with respect to decision making about the child.

As will be discussed later in this chapter, some courts require parenting plans in assessing an application for custody, and courts have sometimes engaged in designing very detailed plans for parallel parenting, particularly in cases where the parents are engaged in high conflict. At least to some extent, these issues remain controversial.

However, at this point, it is important to recognize the distinction between joint or shared custody that involves *authority for decision making*, by contrast with an arrangement that provides for *sharing physical care* for children. See also Sheila Holmes, "Imposed Joint Legal Custody: Children's Interests or Parental Rights?" (1987) UT Fac L Rev 300.

Notes and Questions

The principles in practice

In reflecting on the concept of "best interests" as the basic principle for determining custody and access pursuant to both the *Divorce Act* and provincial legislation, consider the following excerpt describing a contested case in Nova Scotia in the 1980s.

Although many courts have now introduced case management and other processes (discussed in Chapter Five) to limit the inappropriate use of the court system, this example reveals how the "best interests" test provides considerable scope for judicial interpretation and ongoing litigation.

"Multiple Meanings of Equality: A Case Study in Custody Litigation"
(1989) 3 CJWL 256

Jane Gordon

In this case, the husband left his pregnant wife and one young child to obtain employment in a distant part of Canada. The husband's decision eventually resulted in the couple's separation, and they then negotiated a separation agreement. However, the husband later challenged aspects of the agreement, as well as the divorce and corollary relief orders, in a series of legal proceedings that included motions and appeals regarding issues of access and financial responsibility in relation to the children. In this case, the wife held a tenured academic appointment and the husband was generally unemployed. The wife described part of the court process as follows:

... The division of children's time is, I think, problematic and complex. The notion that time should be evenly divided between parents seems to me to turn children into commodities, treating them as just another piece of matrimonial property to be evenly divided. It reflects the assumption that children have no particular interest in or choices about the way in which their time is allocated; that the interest of children and their parents are identical; and that no matter what the relative involvement of each parent with the child prior to marital breakup, the children's time should be evenly split between adversarial parents.

Fathers like my ex-husband have argued that equal division of children's time between parents is fair and reflects the [principle] of equality. This simply is not the case. This superficial notion reduces time spent parenting to only one dimension: time spent with children. There are other dimensions to parenting. Time spent "with" children can include a number of hours the child spent with the parent, inclusive or exclusive of the activities of the child which do not involve active interaction with the parent — sleeping, voluntary activities of various sorts such as dancing or swimming lessons, nondiscretionary activities such as medical and dental appointments, school, time spent on homework and other school-related tasks, normal recreational time (regular Cub meetings), and special recreational time (Cub camping trips). Time spent *on* children includes shopping for their clothes and shoes; doing laundry; planning special events; arranging for activities, appointments, babysitters, and so on.

If the issue of access to children's time is to be one of true equality, then all dimensions of responsibility for children should be considered. On the one hand, non-custodial parents have often reported they felt like visitors in the lives of their children. On the other, custodial parents have said they felt like drudges and disciplinarians in comparison. If equality is to be an issue in the allocation of parental time with children, then dimensions other than the bare amount of time "with" the children must be considered....

As you review the material in this chapter, consider whether, and to what extent, these issues have been addressed by legal processes since this case was in the courts in the 1980s.

Hearing children's voices: The research context

Although children are at the centre of disputes regarding custody and access (and child support), they are not parties to proceedings regarding separation and divorce. It is their parents who are the legal parties engaged in negotiations or other methods of dispute resolution, even though it is the children whose "best interests" are under consideration in relation to custody and access determinations.

There are a number of arrangements that are available to permit children's wishes and preferences to be submitted to the court, and these arrangements are discussed later in this chapter (see *Stefureak v Chambers* (2004), 6 RFL (6th) 212 (Ont Sup Ct), including the "Annotation").

Significantly, however, some research suggests that while children want their voices to be heard at family dissolution, they prefer to have their voices heard *within their families* rather than in legal proceedings:

Very few of the children and young people we interviewed were interested in having a voice in legal proceedings unless they felt that they had no voice in their family. Very few wanted the privacy of their families opened up to professional intervention and none spoke in terms of legal rights. But many did want to be able to participate in decisions, they wanted fair and caring arrangements and relationships, they wanted respect and dignity too....

[W]e suggest that [separate representation for children] is too narrow an approach to achieve the rounded complexity of the enlarged notion of citizenship-in-context that the children we interviewed were implicitly articulating. Very often what the children wanted was flexibility in contact arrangements, a degree of autonomy and control in their lives, ways of resolving differences without extinguishing love and affection, ways of maintaining relationships without losing their sense of selfhood.... These important ingredients do not add up to legal rights, yet for many children they were the essence of good family life. (Smart, Neale & Wade at 121–122)

To what extent does this research suggest a different way of balancing the goals of protection for children's interests and ensuring that their voices are heard in disputes about family dissolution? How might the findings of this research be implemented in practice?

As you examine the material in this chapter, consider again the role for law in reorganizing family relationships after separation or divorce.

Additional Resources

Constance Backhouse, "Shifting Patterns in Nineteenth Century Canadian Custody Law" in David Flaherty, ed, *Essays in the History of Canadian Law*, vol 1 (Toronto: The Osgoode Society, 1981) 212.

Nicholas Bala, "A Report from Canada's 'Gender War Zone': Reforming the Child-Related Provisions of the Divorce Act" (1999) 16 Can J Fam L 163.

Dawn Bourque, "Reconstructing the Patriarchal Nuclear Family: Recent Developments in Child Custody and Access in Canada" (1995) 10:1 CJLS 1.

Susan B Boyd, "W(h)ither Feminism? The Department of Justice Public Discussion Paper on Custody and Access" (1995) 12:2 Can J Fam L 331.

Susan B Boyd, "Backlash and the Construction of Legal Knowledge: The Case of Child Custody Law" (2001) 20 Windsor YB Access Just 141.

Maria Coley, "Children's Voices in Access and Custody Decisions: The Need to Reconceptualize Rights and Effect Transformative Change" (2007) 12 Appeal 48.

Richard Collier, "The Fathers' Rights Movement, Law Reform, and the New Politics of Fatherhood: Some Reflections on the UK Experience" (2009) 20 U Fla JL & Pub Pol'y 65.

Brenda Cossman & Roxanne Mykitiuk, "Reforming Child Custody and Access Law in Canada: A Discussion Paper" (1998) 15 Can J Fam L 13.

Linda Elrod & Milfred Dale, "Paradigm Shifts and Pendulum Swings in Child Custody: The Interests of Children in the Balance" (2008) 42:3 Fam LQ 381.

Michael Grossberg, *Governing the Hearth: Law and the Family in Nineteenth-Century America* (Chapel Hill, NC: University of North Carolina Press, 1985).

Daniel L Hatcher, "Don't Forget Dad: Addressing Women's Poverty by Rethinking Forced and Outdated Child Support Policies" (2012) 20:4 Am UJ Gender Soc Pol'y & L 775.

Hon Claire L'Heureux-Dubé, "A Response to Remarks by Dr. Judith Wallerstein on the Long-Term Impact of Divorce on Children" (1998) 36:3 Fam Ct Rev 384.

Mary Ann Mason, *From Father's Property to Children's Rights: The History of Child Custody in the United States* (New York: Columbia University Press, 1994).

Aliamisse O Mundulai, "Stretching the Boundaries in Child Access, Custody and Guardianship in Canada" (2005) 21:2 Can J Fam L 267.

Bren Neale & Carol Smart, "Experiments with Parenthood?" (1997) 31:2 Sociology 201.

Caroline Sawyer, "Conflicting Rights for Children: Implementing Welfare, Autonomy and Justice within Family Proceedings" (1999) 21:2 J Soc Welfare & Fam L 99.

Noel Semple, "The Silent Child: A Quantitative Analysis of Children's Evidence in Canadian Custody and Access Cases" (2010) 29 Can Fam LQ 1.

"Symposium on Fathers and Family Law" (2006) 40:2 Fam LQ.

Mariana Valverde, *The Age of Light, Soap, and Water: Moral Reform in English Canada, 1885–1925* (Toronto: University of Toronto Press, 2008).

III.
CUSTODY AND CARE: DECISION MAKING ABOUT CHILDREN AND THEIR "BEST INTERESTS"

Clearly, there is an inherent indeterminacy and elasticity to the "best interests" test which makes it more useful as a legal aspiration than as legal analysis. It can be no more than an informed opinion made at a moment in the life of a child about what seems likely to prove to be in that child's best interests. Deciding what is in a child's best interests means deciding what, objectively, appears most likely in the circumstances to be conducive to the kind of environment in which a particular child has the best opportunity for receiving the needed care and attention. Because there are stages to childhood, what is in a child's best interests may vary from child to child, from year to year, and possibly from month to month. This unavoidable fluidity makes it important to attempt to minimize the prospects for stress and instability. (Abella JA in *MacGyver v Richards* (1995), 11 RFL (4th) 432 at 443 (Ont CA))

AN INTRODUCTION TO THE "BEST INTERESTS" PRINCIPLE

Contextualizing the "best interests" principle

In reviewing judicial interpretations about children's best interests at separation or divorce, it is necessary to remain aware that the vast majority of cases are negotiated and settled, rather than litigated in the courts. When the best interests test is considered by the courts, however, each party is required to adduce evidence to support their claim for custody or access. In this context, the issue about "best interests" may become linked to issues about whether joint or sole custody is more appropriate, or whether child support payments will be affected by specific types of arrangements.

In addition, issues about "best interests" may be considered in the larger social context of family dissolution. As will be evident, however, the "best interests" principle focuses on a determination by adults with respect to a child's interests, an approach that is quite different from recognizing children's wishes or "rights."

In considering the analysis of "best interests" in the following excerpt, note carefully the concerns identified by the author. Many of these concerns will be more fully illustrated in the cases and discussion that follow this excerpt.

"The Best Interests of the Child"
Spec Lect LSUC 2000 — Family Law (2001) 1 at 1–5

Nicholas Bala

There are few legal doctrines that have come to so completely dominate an area of law as the rule that governs disputes related to children — the best interests of the child principle. Leading Canadian precedents, federal and provincial statutes and international treaties are all premised on the principle that decisions about children should be based on an assessment of their best interests. This is a central concept for those who are involved in making decisions about children, not only for judges and lawyers, but also for assessors and mediators. Even politicians and parents frequently cite the best interests of the child as the touchstone that guides their actions and decisions.

Interestingly when children themselves make claims, either in the courts or social contexts, they are much less likely to use a best interests approach, which from a child's perspective is paternalistic. Rather, children tend to make claims based on their own rights. Sometimes children argue that it is in their own best interests to be able to exercise their rights, or at least to be able to express their views about decisions that affect them.

The popularity of the best interests principle is scarcely surprising. This principle now has great intuitive appeal, though this was not always the case, and in some other countries the best interests principle plays a much smaller role than in Canada. Although the best interests of the child principle has become the dominant principle for dealing with most child related disputes, it is also important to be aware of its limitations. The best interests principle has a paradoxical nature. While focusing *sub-*

stantive decision-making on the best interests of the particular child, it encourages a decision-making *process* that is often harmful to children.

In some of the discussions about the determination of a child's best interests, there are suggestions that this can be an objective and almost scientific inquiry. While the knowledge of child psychologists and other mental health professions can have an important role in best interests decisions, it is also clear that the values, biases, beliefs and experiences of the person making a best interests decision will inevitably affect the decision.

Some academic critics argue that the best interests principle is so vague as to be meaningless, charging: "This standard provides no clues as to how it is to be satisfied. Judges could just as easily have no standard at all." Judges themselves may be less critical, but Justice Southin of the British Columbia Court of Appeal [in *Rockwell v. Rockwell* (1998), 43 RFL (4th) 450, at 460] acknowledged that when making best interests determination "judges are tied by the invisible threads of their own convictions." The noted American legal scholar, Robert Mnookin, observed:

> Deciding what is best for a child poses a question no less ultimate than the purposes and values of life itself. Should the judge be primarily concerned with the child's happiness? Or with the child's spiritual and religious training? Should the judge be concerned with the economic "productivity" of the child when he grows up? Are the primary values in life in warm interpersonal relationships, or in discipline and self-sacrifice? Is stability and security for a child more desirable than intellectual stimulation? These questions could be elaborated endlessly. And yet where is the judge to look for the set of values that should inform the degree of what is best for the child? Normally the custody statutes do not themselves give content or relative weights to the pertinent values. And if the judge looks to society at large he finds neither a clear consensus as to the best child rearing strategies nor an appropriate hierarchy of ultimate values. [See Robert Mnookin, "Child Custody Adjudication: Judicial Functions in the Face of Indeterminacy" (1975) 39 *Law & Contemporary Problems* 226 at 260–261]

The recognition that the values and attitudes of decision-makers play a crucial role in determining outcomes has almost become trite in the postmodern world, whether the decisions are made (or influenced) by judges, lawyers, assessors, mediators, parents, politicians or academics. From an increasingly broad range of critical perspectives come charges that judges making best interests decisions are biased. The best interests principle is a virtual Rorschach inkblot test for critics.

Feminists were among the first critics, arguing that the best interests principle allows judges to hide their biases against women who fail to adopt traditional roles and that the use of the best interests test often masks decisions that are harmful to women. More recently fathers groups have been challenging the family law system for its alleged bias against men, claiming that the Canadian judiciary applies the best interests test in a way that discriminates against fathers. It has also been argued that Canadian judges may sometimes give too little or too much weight to issues of race when making best interests decisions. Gays and lesbians have claimed that best interests decisions have reflected a bias against homosexuals, while more recently some "pro-family" scholars have argued that best interests decisions have failed to give sufficient recognition to the importance of heterosexual marriage.

Beyond concerns about bias are charges that the best interests approach promotes litigation and is therefore harmful to children. The best interests principle requires decision-makers to focus on the individual needs and circumstances of the particular child. This type of factually specific decision-making makes it difficult to predict the outcome of cases, and thus encourages litigation rather than settlement. Almost anything might be relevant to [a] child's best interests, so cases can be complex and costly to litigate. Because the test is vague, the outcome of litigation may seem unpredictable, which may encourage exploitative threats by one parent to litigate about children if the other parent does not offer a favourable settlement on other (usually monetary) claims.

While the best interests test is the dominant test in judicial decision-making, it is clear that individuals and agencies who care for children are not motivated solely by the promotion of a child's best interests when making decisions about them. Resource and institutional constraints play a significant role when state agencies are involved in making decisions about children. In intact families, parents frequently make decisions that take account of their own welfare as adults, as well as the welfare of their children.

Although the welfare of children is sometimes increased if their parents separate, the decision to separate is usually made in the interests of one or both adults, and in some cases the children's best interests might be better served if the parents [did] not separate. However, often it is only after separation that parents start to think about the best interests of their children. A tragic irony is that in cases of high-conflict parental separation, the process of litigation and determination of the child's best interests is itself harmful to the child, despite the claim of each parent to be seeking to promote the child's best interests....

In reflecting on Bala's assessment of the "best interests" test, identify the nature and significance of the concerns noted. To what extent might these concerns be addressed by more detailed legislative language? For example, compare section 16 of the *Divorce Act* with the list of factors in section 24 of Ontario's *Children's Law Reform Act*. To what extent might these legislative provisions offer more direction for judicial decision making? Would more detailed legislation hurt legal and judicial innovation?

The "best interests" test in practice

Consider Bala's concerns in relation to the following trial court decision in which a father claimed custody of his son, Teague, while the father's application was opposed by the child's mother. Although many of the significant legal principles concerning children's "best interests" have been established by appellate courts, it is also important to explore how a trial court assesses evidence and reaches its conclusions.

Examine the reasoning about the evidence carefully in the following case, particularly in relation to the factors used to identify the child's best interests. Reflect also on how the court reached its conclusion having regard to the fact that neither parent was "perfect." How does this conclusion affect your understanding of the principle of "best interests"? Does this case confirm some of the concerns identified by Bala?

Carton v Watts
(1998), 42 RFL (4th) 149 (Alta Prov Ct)

JORDAN J:

This is an application by Byron Carton for custody of his son, Teague Carton. Debbie Watts, Teague's mother, opposes the application. Mr. Carton is one of Teague's legal guardians, Miss Watts having consented to a guardianship order being granted by this Court.

Mr. Carton has applied for sole custody of the child and has offered liberal and generous access to Miss Watts. If he cannot have sole custody, he asks for a joint custody order providing that he is to have day to day care and control of the child, again with liberal and generous access to Miss Watts.

Mr. Carton believes that Miss Watts has a drinking problem and that because she has had difficulties raising a son from a previous relationship, it would be in Teague's best interests for his father to have sole custody, or failing that, day to day care and control of the child in a joint custody regime.

Mr. Carton expressed his concern about Miss Watts' drinking problem on his first day in court on this matter on March 29, 1996. He reiterated that concern during his testimony in the trial of this action in the spring of this year. He offered as proof of his allegations descriptions of a few incidents concerning alcohol use and one incident of alleged illicit drug use. He described Miss Watts' "instability" by referring to her inability to raise her son by a previous relationship. He testified that this young man, Frankie, has been in the care of the Director of Child Welfare for several years. He went on to describe how difficult Frankie had been even when Mr. Carton and Miss Watts took him into their home in an ill-fated attempt to turn him around.

Following Mr. Carton's evidence about Frankie, I required Frankie's Child Welfare worker to attend to give evidence the next day. Her name was Patricia Dennis. Miss Dennis did not paint a glowing picture of this young man, but she certainly did not lay blame at Miss Watts' feet. Frankie is a difficult adolescent. He endured his parents' difficulties, he spent an extremely tumultuous 4 1/2 years with his father but was required by this father to leave. He lived for a time with Mr. Carton and Miss Watts but this too was unsuccessful.

At the time she testified, Miss Dennis planned to transition Frankie to Supported Independent Living (a program offered by Alberta Family and Social Services wherein teenagers between the ages of sixteen and eighteen live independently of group homes or foster settings, but with the continued involvement of their social workers. The children must attend to their own room and board or rent, food, clothing and recreation.

They are given a monthly allowance to pay for these things. It is not an overly generous stipend and many young people in the programme have difficulty making ends meet. In part this is because they do not have adequate budgeting skills, or are impulsive in their spending habits. It is also because the amount of money they receive is not sufficient to allow them to have an adequate standard of living in a city such as Calgary where accommodation is at a premium and consequently very expensive.)

Miss Dennis testified that Frankie would have a difficult time adjusting to the financial constraints of the program and that there are difficulties in finding a placement for him. He has an unhealthy need for the finer things of life. Miss Dennis was not describing a young man who merely needed Hilfiger shirts and Docker pants to fit in with the crowd.

Instead she described him as an adolescent whose precarious identity was tied to his ability to present himself in such expensive attire. He is a young man with significant problems.

In addition to his own evidence Mr. Carton called three witnesses. Their evidence provides no substantial assistance to the court.

When Miss Watts testified she described her relationship with Teague and her young daughter (Teague's nine year old half sister), her relationship with Mr. Carton, Teague's relationship with his father, and her problems with Frankie. She described the incident at a family get together which deteriorated into a physical altercation.

Miss Watts was nervous but thoughtful and deliberate as she gave her evidence. She perceives Mr. Carton to be a very controlling individual and she believes that he has emotionally abused her. Emotional abuse can, of course, only be measured by a subjective analysis. I am satisfied that Miss Watts was telling me the truth about the abuse she believes she has been subjected to. The subjective test is met. Mr. Carton's demeanour in court is corroborative of her description of him as domineering and controlling. When Miss Watts tells me that he controlled her particularly in financial matters and that he called her names, I believe her and find that he continued until recently to try to control her financially. This is apparent from his begging off from child care responsibilities so that he could do such things as go golfing. He required her to pay for the baby sitting on these not infrequent occasions — something she could not afford to do and for which she could not even plan.

Miss Watts testified that it is Mr. Carton's controlling nature which compels her to ask for sole custody. She believes that she must have the sole right to make the major decisions for Teague because nothing else would be tolerable for her. She is convinced that if Mr. Carton has sole custody of Teague he will use this to continue to control her in the same fashion that he has in the past. She is equally clear that a joint custody order cannot work for the same reason. She is eager, however, for Teague to maintain his relationship with his father.

Miss Watts also testified about her use of magic mushrooms, a substance then prohibited under the *Narcotic Control Act*. I am satisfied that she did not know exactly what it was that she was taking, but that she knew that she was doing something improper, if not illegal. I am further satisfied that the use of this illicit drug was the only thing that Miss Watts was not frank about. She was embarrassed and obviously worried about the impact of this information in this proceeding. I am not overly alarmed by either her evidence to the court or her one time use of an illicit substance. As for the unfortunate altercation at the family gathering, I note that no one was hurt and I am satisfied that it was an isolated incident of the sort which happens from time to time when there are large family gatherings and alcohol is consumed.

Lastly, Miss Watts feels that Mr. Carton should not have sole custody or day to day care and control of the child because he is too emotionally rigid in his parenting style, and he is somewhat laissez-faire in the amount of attention he devotes to Teague while the child is in his care.

Mr. Carton's counsel asked me to draw an inference from Miss Watts' slow and deliberate demeanour that she was taking her time so as to be able to formulate deceptive answers, if not outright falsehoods. I totally reject that suggestion. While there was no expert evidence before me to explain the type of demeanour and behaviour one could expect to observe in a person who has been subjected to controlling behaviour from a partner, I do not believe such evidence is necessary to enable me to draw the conclusion that she is such a woman. Expert evidence is only admissible in a jury trial if it is necessary to explain something outside the range of the ordinary man's experience. The behaviour I am commenting on is well within the experience and observation of most adults in our society. Miss Watts' demeanour on the witness stand was that of a person who found the experience very difficult to cope with. She was facing a man who having controlled her for years, was now seeking to control her in an even more dramatic fashion — he was asking the court for sole custody of their child. There was nothing devious or deceptive about her evidence save for the one matter I have already commented on.

As for Mr. Carton, it is very clear to me that his is a very one-sided description of what went on in this relationship. I find Mr. Carton to be a very controlling individual and find that his evidence is as coloured as one might expect from such an individual. I do not accuse him of lying....

It seemed self-evident at first that I could not deny Mr. Carton's application for custody. How can it be in a child's best interests to stay in the care of a parent who has demonstrated her inability to successfully raise a child? By the end of the evidence I had been reminded of how wrong first impressions can be. Miss Dennis did not testify or even attempt to convince me that Miss Watts was an inappropriate parent. She was not able to substantiate Frankie's complaints that his mother drank too much.

I was satisfied at the end of her evidence that many of Frankie's problems were well beyond her control and certainly not caused by her. I am satisfied that Miss Watts' failures with Frankie do not disentitle her to the opportunity to raise her second son. She is a warm and loving parent. No one has offered any criticism of her parenting of her daughter, now age nine. She is undoubtedly high-strung, and may even on occasion drink too much. But I do not find that her lifestyle interferes with her ability to raise Teague.

Yet, we are not dealing with the question of Miss Watts' "fitness" as a parent. The question in a custody case in 1998 is, what is in the child's best interests? I find that it would not be in Teague's best interest to grant sole or even joint custody to Mr. Carton. He would be subjected to a life with a very controlling, rigid individual. I am satisfied that he would observe his father continue and to some extent succeed in controlling Miss Watts. It is not in a child's best interests [to] be raised in such an environment when there is a suitable alternative available.

I am further satisfied that it is [in] Teague's best interest that his mother have sole custody because I am convinced it is Miss Watts who will ensure and facilitate access. I have no such confidence about Mr. Carton's ability to do the same without attaching strings which will perpetuate the emotional abuse she has endured.

Mr. Carton's application for sole custody is denied as is his application for joint custody.

Miss Watts shall have sole custody of the child. Access is to be spoken to at a later date.

Application dismissed.

Notes and Questions

Assessing "best interests" in trial courts

Carton v Watts is an example of a trial court decision concerning custody. What factors were most influential to the outcome of this case? Do you agree with the emphasis placed by the trial judge on the "independent" witness, Patricia Dennis? To what extent did the judge rely on evidence to support his conclusions about Ms. Watts' demeanour? What evidence was relied on to conclude that Mr. Carton was a "controlling" individual? Why was it not in Teague's best interests to be in the custody of a controlling individual?

These questions are not easy to answer, of course.

In this context, it is important to take into account a principle often adopted by appellate courts that they will not intervene in relation to custody and access decisions unless there is an error in principle or a clear factual error in a matter of significance. See *Haider v Malach* (1999), 48 RFL (4th) 314 (Sask CA), leave to appeal to SCC refused.

What is the rationale for such restraint on the part of appellate courts? To what extent is it possible that the combination of discretionary legislative language and this stance on the part of appellate courts may offer too much discretion to trial judges? Is there a solution to this issue? Should the standard of review be different in family law cases from other types of private law?

Although many of the cases about the "best interests" principle in this chapter are decisions of appellate courts, including the Supreme Court of Canada, it is important to understand the highly significant role of trial courts in this context. In reflecting on *Carton v Watts*, consider again how the court reached its conclusion about Teague's "best interests"? Does this case suggest that the principle in practice may require decisions that will result in the "least harm" (rather than the "best interests") for a child?

Consider this situation:

> In this case, the spouses were married in 1999, had a daughter in 2000 and separated in 2001. At the time of the divorce order in 2002, the court awarded custody to the mother, and also made a temporary order for access for the father, pending mediation and a further order. Between 2001 and 2008, eight different judges made at least 25 orders, and the court record consisted of 13 volumes and more than 2000 pages. There were also a number of contempt orders, and by the time the court finally dealt with the issues about custody of this child, she was already 8 years old. How should a trial court assess the child's "best interests" in this case?

In *Geremia v Harb* (2008), 90 OR (3d) 185 (Sup Ct), the court concluded that a revised access arrangement for the father was appropriate, but denied costs to both parties. In addition, the court made this further order:

> [94] ... [N]either party shall be permitted to commence or continue any proceeding in the Superior Court of Justice, directly or indirectly related to their child, without first having obtained leave of the court. I make this order pursuant to s. 140(1) of the *Courts of Justice Act* ... which permits a judge of the Superior Court to do so where satisfied that a person "has persistently and without reasonable grounds ... instituted vexatious proceedings in any court ... or conducted a proceeding in any court in a vexatious manner...." The parties have gorged on court resources as if the legal system were their private banquet table. It must not happen again....

To what extent was the judge's order to preclude further legal proceedings without leave of the court in the child's best interests? Is it possible to distinguish the court's responsibility for the child's best interests from judges' concerns about inappropriate parental behaviour in *Carton v Watts* or in *Geremia v Harb*? Why or why not?

ALI recommendations about custody and access decision making

In its comprehensive review of principles about family dissolution in the United States, the American Law Institute concluded that there were a number of unavoidable tensions in the law's objectives for the allocation of responsibility for children at family breakdown. Specifically, the ALI noted the tension between the goals of predictability on one hand and the fairness of individualized decision making on the other:

> The predictability of outcomes helps to reduce litigation, as well as strategic and manipulative behaviour by parents. Predictable outcomes are insufficient, however, unless they are also sound. And it is difficult to imagine sound outcomes in custody cases unless the diverse range of circumstances in which family breakdown occurs are taken into account. In short, predictability is important, but so is the customization of a result to the individual, sometimes unique, facts of a case. (American Law Institute, *Principles of Family Dissolution: Analysis and Recommendations* (St Paul, MN: American Law Institute Publishers, 2002) at 1)

In this context, the ALI recommended principles designed to improve planning for children's needs at family dissolution, including parental responsibility for creating a parenting plan, "an individualized and customized set of custodial and decision-making arrangements for a child" (ALI at 7). In reflecting on this recommendation, consider the extent to which it might have been helpful in resolving the parental disputes in *Carton v Watts* or in *Geremia v Harb*. Do these cases suggest a need to take account of the "unique" facts of a case?

In the end, the ALI concluded that, in spite of its indeterminacy, it was preferable to retain the "best interests" test. However, the ALI suggested redefining the test (at 104) as follows:

> 1) The primary objective ... is to serve the child's best interests, by facilitating all of the following:
> a) parental planning and agreement about the child's custodial arrangements and upbringing;
> b) continuity of existing parent–child attachments;
> c) meaningful contact between the child and each parent;
> d) caretaking relationships by adults who love the child, know how to provide for the child's needs, and place a high priority on doing so;
> e) security from exposure to conflict and violence;
> f) expeditious, predictable decision making and the avoidance of prolonged uncertainty respecting arrangements for the child's care and control.
>
> 2) A secondary objective ... is to achieve fairness between the parents.

To what extent do these principles provide useful guidance in custody and access decisions? If these principles had been applied in *Carton v Watts*, would the outcome of the case have been different? To what extent are the factors listed in the *CLRA* different from those proposed by the ALI? Is there a need to reform the *Divorce Act* or Ontario's *Children's Law Reform Act*?

The *Convention on the Rights of the Child*

The United Nations General Assembly approved the *Convention on the Rights of the Child* in 1989, and it has been ratified by a large number of countries, including Canada in 1991. Significantly, however, the United States has not yet ratified the Convention.

The *Convention* creates obligations for "states parties" to respect and ensure defined rights for children. Although the *Convention* is not part of Canada's domestic law, courts may use its provisions to interpret domestic laws.

In particular, Article 3 provides that the best interests of the child "shall be *a* primary consideration in all actions concerning children."

Clearly, the wording of Article 3 permits consideration of factors other than best interests, and the *Convention* does not fully define these factors. Thus, there is a similar indeterminacy to the use of the best interests test in the *Convention* as is found in federal and provincial legislation in Canada.

Moreover, one assessment of international protection for children's rights concluded that much work needed to be done to implement the principles of the *Convention* in Canadian law and policy:

> Governments and the courts appear to use the Convention only as a strongly worded guiding principle, rather than acting as if they are bound by it. The [Senate] Committee concluded that "jurisdictional complexities, the absence of effective institutions, an uncertain approach to human rights law, and lack of transparency and political involvement indicate that the [Convention] is being ineffectively applied in the Canadian context." There appears to be a strong disconnect between Canada's international law obligations and domestic law. (Senator Raynell Andreychuk, "The Work of the Standing Senate Committee on Human Rights: An Overview of *Children: The Silenced Citizens*" (2008) 71 Sask L Rev 23 at 28)

The *Convention* has been considered in some litigated cases. For example, in *Baker v Minister of Citizenship and Immigration* (1999), 174 DLR (4th) 193, some members of the Supreme Court of Canada concluded that the principles of the *Convention* might be used as interpretive guides in litigation focused on federal or provincial legislation.

Other international covenants that are relevant both for custody of female children and for custody/access rights for mothers, are the *Universal Declaration of Human Rights* and the *Convention on the Elimination of All Forms of Discrimination Against Women*.

Additional Resources

John Eekelaar, "The Importance of Thinking that Children have Rights" in P Alston, S Parker & J Seymour, eds, *Children's Rights and the Law* (Oxford: Oxford University Press, 1992) 221.

Ann Laquer Estin, "Transjurisdictional Child Welfare: Local Governments and International Law" (2013) 22:3 Transnat'l L & Contemp Probs 595.

R Brian Howe & Katherine Covell, *Empowering Children: Children's Rights Education as a Pathway to Citizenship* (Toronto: University of Toronto Press, 2005).

Paul Millar, *The Best Interests of Children: An Evidence-Based Approach* (Toronto: University of Toronto Press, 2009).

Martha Minow, "Rights for the Next Generation: A Feminist Approach to Children's Rights" (1986) 9 Harv Women's LJ 1.

Stephen Parker, "The Best Interests of the Child — Principles and Problems" (1994) 8 International Journal of Law and the Family 26.

Noel Semple, "Review of Paul Millar, *The Best Interests of Children: An Evidence-Based Approach*" (2010) 48 Osgoode Hall LJ 695.

Suzanne Williams, "Perspective of the Child in Custody and Access Decisions: Implementing a Best Interests and Rights of the Child Test" (2007) 86 Can Bar Rev 633.

Suzanne Williams & Cheryl Heykoop, *Ten tips for legal professionals: meaningful child participation in family justice processes* (Vancouver: International Institute for Child Rights and Development and Law Foundation of British Columbia, 2010).

APPLYING THE BEST INTERESTS PRINCIPLE IN CONTEXT

As this section has already demonstrated, the legal principle of "best interests" in relation to children at family dissolution is clear and apparently quite simple. However, the application of this principle in practice may be much more fraught because the content of the "best interests" test remains highly discretionary.

Thus, even in the context of section 24 of the *Children's Law Reform Act*, which sets out a list of factors, there is no indication as to which factors are entitled to priority, and a court must take account of "all the child's needs and circumstances." The court is also expressly constrained in relation to "past conduct," but it may consider the commission of violence or abuse in some cases. However, section 24 generally provides only a list of factors to be considered within this discretionary decision making.

As a result, to understand how "best interests" may be interpreted in practice, it is necessary to examine how the test has been applied in a variety of contexts. This section reviews a number of circumstances in which courts have assessed the "best interests" to reveal the content of the test in practice.

WORKING MOTHERS AND THE "TENDER YEARS" PRINCIPLE

Young children and mothers' custody: 1950s to 1970s

As explained in the historical overview at the beginning of this chapter, the traditional principles regarding custody permitted mothers to have physical custody of children of "tender years" (under age seven), on the basis that they could better provide care for young children. According to Boyd, this preference that mothers should provide care for young children (in their best interests) implicitly reflected gendered expectations about mothers' primary responsibilities for caregiving (see Boyd at 65–72). Thus, when increasing numbers of mothers began to enter the paid workforce in the 1960s and 1970s, their "abandonment" of their children sometimes affected the best interests principle at separation or divorce. In examining the material about the "tender years" principle and about working mothers, reflect on the relationship between social expectations and judicial interpretation of the "best interests" principle.

The "tender years" principle was reviewed by the Supreme Court of Canada in 1976 in *Talsky v Talsky*, [1976] 2 SCR 292. In *Talsky*, the Court reviewed an earlier Ontario decision, *Bell v Bell*, [1955] OWN 341 (CA), in which the appeal court had stated (at 344):

> There is another circumstance which in my very respectful opinion the learned judge has overlooked, or if it was present to his mind he has not given due weight to it, namely that this infant is a little girl of very tender years. No father, no matter how well-intentioned or how solicitous for the welfare of such a child, can take the full place of the mother. Instinctively, a little child, particularly a little girl, turns to her mother in her troubles, her doubts and her fears. In that respect nature seems to assert itself. The feminine touch means so much to a little girl; the frills and the flounces and the ribbons in the matter of dress; the whispered consultations and confidences on matters which to the child's mind should only be discussed with Mother; the tender care, the soothing voice; all these things have a tremendous effect on the emotions of the child. This is nothing new; it is as old as human nature and has been recognized time after time in the decisions of our Courts....

According to the Supreme Court of Canada in *Talsky*, however, "the rule that children of tender years belong with their mother is ... a principle of common sense. It is simply one of the more important factors which must be considered in the granting of custody...." *Talsky*'s tender years reasoning was relied on as late as *S(BA) v S(MS)* (1991), 35 RFL (3d) 400 (Ont CA), although it was repudiated by the Supreme Court of Canada in *Young v Young*, [1993] 4 SCR 3 and referred to as "stereotypical" in *Van de Perre v Edwards*, 2001 SCC 60 (at para 34).

In reviewing *Talsky*, Boyd argued that judicial comments about Mrs. Talsky's conduct in leaving the marriage very nearly undermined her custody claim. Although she succeeded in gaining custody in the end, the judgments also revealed a deeply divided court (see Boyd at 86–89).

Mothers in the paid workforce, custody, and children's best interests: The 1980s

Recall the statistics in Chapter One about the rise in the number of women, particularly mothers, who began to enter the paid workforce in the second half of the twentieth century. This development challenged courts' traditional views about women as primarily involved in household work and child care. Thus, in a number of cases after *Talsky*, the issue of the continuing application of the tender years doctrine was considered, particularly in the context of custody claims on the part of mothers who were involved in the paid workforce.

R v R

In *R v R* (1983), 34 RFL (2d) 277 (Alta CA), the Alberta Court of Appeal dismissed a mother's appeal from a decision granting custody of a daughter, aged four-and-a-half, to the father, notwithstanding that the mother had had interim custody and that the judge at trial had found her to be a fit parent.

The husband was a rancher, working a property with his father, and the spouses had a homestead near the husband's parents. When the marriage broke down, the wife moved with the daughter to Lethbridge, 50 miles away, closer to the mother's family. She worked in Lethbridge. At the trial, both parents were held to be fit parents, but the father had plans to remarry while the wife did not. The judge found that the husband was preferable as the custodial parent because he could have the child with him during the day, while he did the farm chores, while the wife would have to put the child in care during her hours of work. The father's mother was also readily available for babysitting. The mother was given liberal access on weekends. On appeal, the court considered whether there were any "errors of law," and reviewed the tender years doctrine.

In rejecting the appeal, the majority concluded (at 286) that the view expressed by Roach JA in *Bell* no longer applied:

> This view confuses cultural traditions with human nature; it also traps women in a social role not necessarily of their choosing, while at the same time freeing men: if only a mother can nurture a child of tender years, then it is the clear duty of the mother to do so: because the father *cannot* do it, he is neither obliged nor entitled even to try. Also, it is seen by some as self-perpetuating: by putting the female child in the custody of somebody who accepts the maternal role model so described, the rule ordains that she will have just such a role model at close hand during her most impressionable years. Thus, the "tender years principle," which at first glance seems only innocently sentimental, is seen by many as part of a subtle, systemic sexual subordination....
> In what might be called the supra-modern marriage, strenuous efforts are made to avoid *any* role distinction based upon sex.... Taken in this context, the remarks made by judges in the past about "tender years principle" do not come to much. All that can be said in this age of changing attitudes is that judges must decide each case on its own merits, with due regard to the capacities *and* attitudes of each parent. We should take care not to assign to this idea ... the august status of being the only one consis-

tent with human nature or common sense.... And we must remember that our role is not to reform society; our role is to make the best of a bad deal for the child who comes before us for help.

Thus, the majority concluded that there was no error in the trial judge's conclusion that the child would be better off with the father than in professional daycare (with the mother). Dissenting from this decision, McGillivray CJA found that the trial judge had given insufficient consideration to the tender years principle, and that the husband's ability to spend time with the child should not be determinative because "there must be tens of thousands of children doing very well in daycare centres across the country."

In reviewing these differing views of the majority and dissenting judges, consider the extent to which societal views about working mothers may be reflected in legal analysis about the "best interest" principle. Compare the reasoning in *R v R* with the Manitoba case that follows:

Klachefsky v Brown

In *Klachefsky v Brown* (1988), 12 RFL (3d) 280 (Man CA), the Manitoba Court of Appeal allowed an appeal by a mother who was denied custody of two children, a girl of eight and a boy of five and a half.

At trial, the judge found that the couple had established an excellent arrangement with respect to the children, with each of them spending equal amounts of time with the children. Each parent had established a household in Winnipeg in which the children were nurtured. A few years later, after the father had remarried (a woman with whom the children felt very comfortable), the former wife (the children's mother) was required to move to Vancouver for purposes of her work. The trial judge found that both parents were fit, but that "on balance, if this were a contest between Mr. Klachefsky and Ms. Brown, I would choose Ms. Brown." Nonetheless, the judge decided that it was in the best interests of the children to stay with their father during the school term with generous access to their mother during holidays.

According to the appeal court, the trial judge seemed to have given undue weight to the fact that there would be less (or no) need for child care in Winnipeg because the new Mrs. Klachefsky would be available to them 24 hours a day, as well as having extended family support. The majority decision (Philp JA dissenting) stated (at 282):

> In my opinion, the trial judge committed a palpable error in placing undue emphasis on the fact that the mother in Vancouver will require paid assistance to provide care for her children.... Both children will be returning home from school around 3:30 p.m. but the mother does not arrive home from work until around 5:30 p.m. She has made arrangements for a competent person to be at the home from 3:00 o'clock on until the mother's arrival. Daycare and home care arrangements of this kind are a fact of life which many parents and children face, and there was no evidence before the judge that the children would suffer the least harm from being exposed to a few hours when they are neither at school

nor with their mother. Whether an alternate caregiver is paid or unpaid cannot be decisive of what is in the best interests of the children....

The learned judge also, in my opinion, committed error in this case by failing to take into account the relative stability of the parents' way of life. Since the separation, the mother has maintained a stable family unit consisting of herself and her two children with help from her mother and other people with whom she has had good rapport. There is every indication that she could maintain that stable home in Vancouver. On the other hand, the evidence shows that the home provided by the father, however excellent it has been as found by the learned trial judge, has not been a stable one [the appeal court cited evidence of the father's serial relationships and some uncertainty about the stability of his relationship with his current wife]....

In my opinion, given the judge's conclusions that as between the parents he would prefer Ms Brown, a preference with which I agree, the judge fell into error in failing to take account [of] the father's record of instability in his home life compared with her stability, and in giving far too much weight to the fact that the mother might have to rely on paid daycare for two hours a day while she looks after the children in Vancouver. [Appeal allowed]

Notes and Questions

The continuing impact of "tender years"?

To what extent did the appeal court in *Klachefsky* rely on the tender years doctrine to allow the mother's appeal? In considering this question, reflect on the extent to which societal views about mothers' roles, the appropriateness of child care centres, and the reasons for mothers to engage in employment activity may have influenced judicial reasoning in these cases in the 1980s. How should these factors be taken into account now?

Consider this situation:

The parties were married in 1986, and they separated in January 1987, five months after their child was born. In custody proceedings, the expert evidence suggested that the mother was overly protective, but that it did not pose a risk to the child. The Official Guardian's representative recommended custody to the mother. However, the trial judge interpreted the expert evidence as establishing a risk to the child if she remained in the mother's care and awarded custody to the father. The mother appealed. Is the tender years doctrine relevant here?

In *S(BA) v S(MS)* (1991), 35 RFL (3d) 400, the Ontario Court of Appeal concluded that there was an error of magnitude in the trial judge's decision because the judge had concluded that the expert evidence established a danger to the child from the mother. In addition, the Court of Appeal suggested that the trial judge had overlooked the tender years doctrine and that the mother had cared for the child since the separation quite adequately. The court concluded that the cumulative effect of these errors was sufficient to have affected the outcome of the case and accordingly ordered a new trial. Similarly, in *A(D) v H(EL)* (1990), 28 RFL (3d) 356 (Ont Dist Ct), the court allowed an appeal by a mother who worked part time because the father, who worked full time, would require paid caregivers. More recently, on the issue of work arrangements, *Cox v Harvey*, 2000 NFCA 42, held (at para 17) that being a stay-at-home parent is not determinative for custody.

Note how the appellate courts in these cases also held that there was an error in the trial judge's reasons. Why was such a conclusion relevant?

To what extent is it appropriate to eliminate use of the tender years doctrine? Does it reflect current social expectations about caregiving by mothers and fathers? Even if this "presumption" were eliminated, should facts about caregiving during an intact relationship be relevant to determining what arrangement is in a child's best interests post-separation or divorce? Is there a need for legislative reform? Why or why not?

Mothers as politicians: The 1990s

Boyd examined a highly controversial custody case in British Columbia in 1994 in which Judy Tyabji, a member of the B.C. legislature, unsuccessfully sought custody of her three children after she left her husband and became involved with another male politician, Gordon Wilson, then leader of the B.C. Liberal Party. Although Tyabji had been granted interim custody of the children and two court-appointed experts had recommended that she have primary responsibility for the children because she was the "historical emotional caregiver" for them, the trial judge concluded that her "aggressive, career-oriented lifestyle" made her less attractive than the children's father in terms of custody. The father lived in a more rural setting and worked in a grocery store. Even though Tyabji had frequently made arrangements to stay involved with her children as well as fulfill her political activities, the court expressed concern that the children's needs would be sidetracked by her career. See *Tyabji v Sandana* (1994), 2 RFL (4th) 265 (BCSC).

Does this case suggest that social expectations about mothers and fathers, in relation to their children, continue to be different. For example, one critique of this case referred to the fact that Prime Minister Trudeau received custody of his three sons while holding high political office, suggesting a different standard for politicians who were fathers, by contrast with those who were mothers. See "Was Pierre Trudeau a Busy Guy?" *The Globe and Mail* (5 March 1994).

Additional Resources

Pat Armstrong, *The Double Ghetto: Canadian Women and their Segregated Work* (Toronto: McClelland & Stewart, 1994).

Susan B Boyd, "Child Custody and Working Mothers" in Sheilah Martin & Kathleen Mahoney, eds, *Equality and Judicial Neutrality* (Toronto: Carswell, 1987) 168.

Susan B Boyd, "Looking Beyond *Tyabji*: Employed Mothers, Lifestyles and Child Custody Law" in Susan B Boyd, ed, *Challenging the Public/ Private Divide: Feminism, Law, and Public Policy* (Toronto: University of Toronto Press, 1997) 253.

Angela Campbell, "Proceeding with 'Care': Lessons to be Learned from the Canadian Parental Leave and Quebec Daycare Initiatives in Developing a National Childcare Policy" (2006) 22 Can J Fam L 171.

Elizabeth J Hughes, "Mother's Vicarious Hand: Primary Caregiving Reconceived as Relationship and Responsibility" (2002) 20 Can Fam LQ 467.

Meg Luxton & Harriet Rosenberg, *Through the Kitchen Window: The Politics of Home and Family* (Toronto: Garamond Press, 1986).

MJ Mossman, "Lawyers and Family Life: New Directions for the 1990's" (1994) 2 Fem Leg Stud 61 and 159.

Fiona E Raitt, "The Children's Rights Movement: Infusions of Feminism" (2005) 22 Can J Fam L 11.

Elizabeth Shilton, "Gender Risk and Employment Pension Plans in Canada" (2013) 17 CLELJ 101.

CONDUCT AND THE ABILITY TO PARENT

Recall section 16(9) of the *Divorce Act*, which prohibits consideration of conduct in determining a custody application, unless the conduct is relevant to "the ability of a person to act as a parent." Provincial legislation often includes similar provisions (see *CLRA*, s 24(3)), in addition to express provisions about conduct that is violent or abusive (see *CLRA*, s 24(4)).

In relation to the issue of conduct that relates to a person's "ability to parent," consider the following example. To what extent is this case about conduct relating to parenting? Does this case also suggest a need to consider societal views about "good" parenting, especially on the part of mothers?

Fishback v Fishback
(1985), 46 RFL (2d) 44 (Ont Dist Ct)

In *Fishback v Fishback*, the court considered a custody dispute between a mother and father. In this case, there was evidence that the mother had abandoned her marriage because she was "bored" by her husband. She established a new relationship with a man whom the court found to be somewhat unreliable (although perhaps more exciting). The evidence also revealed that the husband had begun a new relationship with a woman who impressed the court with her good judgment and fondness for the children. In granting custody to Mr. Fishback, Misener DCJ stated in part (at 48):

> ... My concern in deciding who should have custody is confined entirely to the best interests of the children. One conclusion I draw from the facts

that I have so far related is simply that Mrs. Fishback was quite prepared — and I think that she consciously thought about it — to deprive the children of the benefit of the constant presence of a good father, of at least a good husband, if not a totally satisfactory one, and of a reasonably harmonious family relationship for no other reason than to find more excitement in life. I am not suggesting that she does not now genuinely love Mr. Yeoman; perhaps she does. Perhaps she is totally dedicated to him. The fact remains that she deliberately sought that state of affairs, knowing full well that the children could never derive a benefit anything close to the loss that they would suffer from it. This factor is not of great significance in determining what is in the present and future best interests of the children, but it certainly is a factor that is entitled to some weight in determining custody because it indicates, at least to some degree, the importance that each parent attaches to the best interests of the children in determining their own future conduct....

I think that Mr. Fishback's proposal for the care of the children, should he receive custody, is somewhat better than the present arrangements that Mrs. Fishback supplies. Mr. Fishback has become acquainted with Lucinda Tye. She is a married woman, without children, and separated from her husband. Mrs. Tye and Mr. Fishback have been keeping company. There is at least the probability that in due course they will marry, and I hope they do. Mrs. Tye testified. I was most impressed with her. She has become well acquainted with the children. She has for some time helped Mr. Fishback almost continuously in their weekend care. The children like her. Mrs. Tye does not stay overnight. Doubtless, Mr. Fishback would consider that immoral and wrong in the absence of marriage, and I am not able to say that he is wrong in that judgment, or, for that matter, that he is right in that judgment. Regardless, he proposes to have Mrs. Tye look after the children in their home at all times when he is unable to be there because of his employment. Mrs. Tye has undertaken in her testimony to do so, even at the expense of forgoing other employment opportunities. I am satisfied that that arrangement will be put in place immediately.

That is not to say that Mrs. Fishback has not so far fully and properly cared for the children in the last nine months. She has, and I am sure that she has cared for them well. But that care has been built around her relationship with Mr. Yeoman. Mr. Yeoman testified. While I do not wish to be at all unfair, I am obliged to say that neither his past performance nor his demeanour as a witness left me fully confident that his present relationship with Mrs. Fishback will last. They both say that they intend to marry. Needless to say, I hope they do and that it remains a happy one throughout. But I am not as confident of the stability of Mrs. Fishback's life from here on in as I am of the stability of Mr. Fishback's. And I think that Mrs. Tye has more to contribute to the total upbringing of the children in non-economic terms than does Mr. Yeoman....

Notes and Questions

Fishback and the "best interests" principle

What is the basis for the court's conclusion in this case that the mother's conduct is relevant to determining "best interests"? How is her choice of a partner, who may not be as stable as her husband, related to her ability to parent? Should one's choice of associates or partner reflect on a party's ability to parent? Does this decision rely on social expectations about the conduct required of a "good" mother? Is it possible to distinguish conduct that is related to the ability to parent and other kinds of conduct? Is this question different for mothers and for fathers?

Violence and abuse in relation to "best interests"

Recent amendments (ss 24(4) and 24(5)) of the *CLRA* require consideration of violence or abuse towards a spouse, any child, or anyone in the household in assessing a person's "ability to parent." There is no similar express provision in the *Divorce Act*.

The issue of violent conduct had been considered in some cases in the 1980s and 1990s. For example, in *Renaud v Renaud* (1989), 22 RFL (3d) 366, the Ontario District Court held that a spouse's violent conduct was a relevant factor in a custody dispute.

According to the court, the husband had been "abusive, unco-operative and meanspirited," and the court held that it was in the best interests of the children to remain with their mother, who had been the primary caregiver. This case marked a departure from earlier cases, which did not generally consider physical abuse between spouses to be relevant to determining ability to parent in relation to children. *CRL v REL*, [1998] WDFL 328 (Sask QB), held that physical and emotional abuse is relevant to the determination of custody and access.

However, courts may require substantial evidence of violence and its impact.

For example, in *Li Santi v Li Santi* (1990), 24 RFL (3d) 174 (Ont Prov Ct (Fam Div)), the wife left the matrimonial home and went with her children (a boy of four and a girl of nine months) to a transition house in London. At the hearing concerning interim custody, there were disputes about the evidence and the extent to which certain exhibits, not in the form of affidavits, were legally persuasive to justify the wife's allegations. The court granted interim custody to the father, stating:

> In the result there is no clear and cogent evidence which would justify the mother's removal of the children from their accustomed environment. Their best interests, it seems clear to me, can be safeguarded by their father in the former matrimonial home and an interim order will go granting him their custody. The mother should have generous access to the children. If counsel cannot agree to an appropriate schedule, I may be spoken to. The trial of this action will be expedited and the necessity of a pre-trial waived. Costs are reserved to the trial judge.

The decision in *Li Santi* was reviewed in *Howard v Howard* (1999), 1 RFL (5th) 375 (Ont Sup Ct). In *Howard*, the mother left the matrimonial home, taking the children with her. Although the court noted the importance of discouraging self-help without the involvement of the courts in such cases, the judge held that it was in the best interests of the children to return to the matrimonial home, and thus granted the mother interim custody as well as an order for interim exclusive possession of the matrimonial home. In *Batsinda v Batsinda*, 2013 ONSC 7869, a mother refusing to comply with orders while making abuse allegations militated against either party having full custody: the court devised a mixed custody/mixed access regime.

These cases raise difficult issues for courts. Recall the discussion of violence and abuse issues in Chapter Four. How should law respond to issues of family violence in the context of disputes about custody of children? This issue is also reviewed later in this chapter in the context of high conflict family dissolution cases.

Additional Resources

Hilary Astor, "The Weight of Silence: Talking About Violence in Family Mediation" in Margaret Thornton, ed, *Public and Private: Feminist Legal Debates* (Melbourne: Oxford University Press, 1995) 174.

Nicholas Bala, "Spousal Abuse and Children of Divorce: A Differentiated Approach" (1996) 13 Can J Fam L 215.

Nicholas Bala et al, *Spousal Violence in Custody and Access Disputes: Recommendations for Reform* (Ottawa: Status of Women in Canada, 1998).

Jan Jeske, "Custody Mediation within the Context of Domestic Violence" (2010) 31:2 Hamline J Pub L & Pol'y 657.

S Grace Kerr & Peter G Jaffe, "Legal and Clinical Issues in Child Custody Disputes Involving Domestic Violence" (1999) 17:1 Can Fam LQ 1.

Linda C Neilson, *Spousal Abuse, Children and the Legal System* (Fredericton, NB: Muriel McQueen Fergusson Centre for Family Violence Research, UNB, 2001).

Linda C Neilson, "Putting Revisions to the Divorce Act through a Family Violence Research Filter: The Good, the Bad, and the Ugly" (2003) 20 Can J Fam L 11.

Melanie Rosnes, "The Invisibility of Male Violence in Canadian Child Custody and Access Decision-Making" (1997) 14 Can J Fam L 31.

Eleanor M Schnall, "Custody and Access and the Impact of Domestic Violence" (2000) 18 Can Fam LQ 130.

Merle H Weiner, "International Child Abduction and the Escape from Domestic Violence" (2000) 69:2 Fordham L Rev 593.

"BLOOD" TIES AND "BEST INTERESTS"

Blood relationships as merely one factor for consideration

Pursuant to Ontario's *CLRA*, s 24(2), "the relationship by blood" between the child and a person applying for custody is one factor to be considered in determining a child's best interests. However, it is merely one factor to be considered. It is not determinative. How should courts assess a child's best interests in relation to blood ties?

For example, in *KK v GL and BJL* (1984), 44 RFL (2d) 113, the Supreme Court of Canada dismissed an appeal in relation to a decision of a NWT court to award custody of a child to prospective adoptive parents, rather than have a child returned to the biological mother (who had consented to the adoption and then changed her mind). According to the court, the best interest of the child "is the paramount consideration when the court addresses [a custody decision]."

In reaching its decision, the Supreme Court reviewed a decision of the Ontario Court of Appeal in which custody of a child was granted to foster parents rather than to the child's biological mother, in accordance with the court's determination about the child's best interests (see *Re Moores and Feldstein*, [1973] 3 OR 921 (CA)). In addition, the Supreme Court referred to *Racine v Woods* (discussed in Chapter Three) and *Beson v Director of Child Welfare (NFLD)*, [1982] 2 SCR 716.

In the end, the court in *KK v GL and BJL* concluded that the child's best interests mandated custody for the prospective adoptive parents. In part, the court stated (at 126):

> This conclusion is consistent with modern authority in this court and others: see *Racine*, *Beson* and *Re Moores and Feldstein*. I would therefore hold that in the case at bar the dominant consideration to which all other considerations must remain subordinate must be the welfare of the child. This is not to say that the question of custody will be determined by weighing the economic circumstances of the contending parties. The matter will not be determined solely on the basis of the physical comfort and material advantages that may be available in the home of one contender or the other. The welfare of the child must be decided on a consideration of these and all other relevant factors, including the general psychological, spiritual and emotional welfare of the child. It must be the aim of the court, when resolving disputes between rival claimants for the custody of a child, to choose the course which will best provide for the healthy growth, development and education of the child so that he will be equipped to face the problems of life as a mature adult. Parental [biological] claims must not be lightly set aside, and they are entitled to serious consideration in reaching any conclusion. Where it is clear that the welfare of the child requires it, however, they must be set aside.

Consider this situation:

The child's biological mother died. In this situation, the mother's sister and brother-in-law applied for custody, and their application was opposed by the child's biological father. What factors are relevant to the child's best interests in this case?

In *Crocker v Sipus* (1992), 41 RFL (3d) 19, a case complicated by several procedural issues, the Ontario Court of Appeal eventually awarded custody to the child's aunt and uncle. Thus, as these cases confirm, a blood relationship constitutes merely one factor in determining best interests.

"Best interests" in relation to siblings

A number of cases have considered the importance of keeping siblings together. For example, see *White v White* (1994), 7 RFL (4th) 414 (NBQB). *KK v AK*, 2012 NBQB 276, held that sibling cohesiveness also applies to partially-related siblings (in this case, half-brothers) and *MDC v TC*, 2012 NBQB 376, extends that principle to the situation of step-siblings. While keeping siblings together is one consideration, it is not determinative of custody. See *Jones v Jones* (1994), 4 RFL (4th) 293 (Sask QB) at para 23. In this context, some cases have expressly considered the significance of bonding: see *R(M) v H(S)* (1997), 32 RFL (4th) 127 (Ont Prov Div); and *Poole v Poole*, 1999 BCCA 203.

"BEST INTERESTS" AND IDENTITY: THE SIGNIFICANCE OF RACE

Van de Perre v Edwards
2001 SCC 60

In this case, the Supreme Court of Canada considered a custody dispute about a son born to a single Caucasian Canadian woman after her 18-month sexual affair with an African American professional basketball player. The father was married and had twin daughters, and his family was based in North Carolina.

The case was quite controversial. In summary:

• The child's mother brought an action for custody and child support when the son was three months old. After a lengthy trial, the trial judge awarded sole custody to the mother and granted access to the father: see *KV v TE*, [1999] BCJ No 434 (SC) (QL).

• The father appealed the trial decision. At the invitation of the B.C. Court of Appeal, the father's wife applied for status as a party, and requested an order for joint custody with the father. Although joint custody was awarded, this judgment was stayed pending the mother's appeal to the Supreme Court of Canada: see *V(K) v E(T)*, 2000 BCCA 167; 2000 BCCA 236.

• On appeal to the Supreme Court of Canada, the trial decision was restored.

In part, the Supreme Court of Canada was concerned about whether the correct standard of review had been applied by the Court of Appeal. The Supreme Court of Canada concluded that the Court of Appeal had usurped its function in reconsidering evidence submitted at trial, stating (at paras 36ff):

> The Court of Appeal found that the trial judge gave "no consideration" to issues of race and interracial problems that Elijah might face. In fact,

the trial judge noted that there had been some testimony at trial related to the race of Elijah and the importance of being exposed to his heritage and culture as the son of an African-American father. Rather than discussing the child's race in detail, however, the trial judge noted that this child is of mixed race and, as such, his Caucasian Canadian heritage must also be considered.

The interveners, the African Canadian Legal Clinic, the Association of Black Social Workers and the Jamaican Canadian Association, submit that race is a critical factor in custody and access cases. In my view, the importance of this factor will depend greatly on many factual considerations. The interveners state that there are key tools a Canadian biracial child will need in order to foster racial identity and pride: the need to develop a means to deal with racism and the need to develop a positive racial identity. The corollary to these needs is the parental ability to meet them. The interveners do not state that the minority parent should necessarily be granted custody; rather, the question is which parent will best be able to contribute to a healthy racial socialization and overall healthy development of the child. This question is one of fact to be determined by the courts on a case-by-case basis and weighed by the trial judge with other relevant factors.

The interveners submit that, although some studies show that Black parents are more likely to be aware of the need to prepare their children to cope with racism, the main issue is which parent will facilitate contact and the development of racial identity in a manner that avoids conflict, discord and disharmony. But again, this is only one factor to be considered by the trial judge. I would also add that evidence of race relations in the relevant communities may be important to define the context in which the child and his parents will function. It is not always possible to address these sensitive issues by judicial notice, even though some notice of racial facts can be taken; see *R v. Williams*, [1998] 1 SCR 1128 (SCC). The weight to be given to all relevant factors is a matter of discretion, but discretion must be exercised with regard to the evidence. In essence, the interveners argue that race is always a crucial factor and that it should never be ignored, even if not addressed by the parties. They favour forced judicial consideration of race because it is essential in deciding which parent is best able to cope with difficulties biracial children may face. This approach is based on the conclusions reached concerning the present state of race relations in Canada. As I have said, racial identity is but one factor that may be considered in determining personal identity; the relevancy of this factor depends on the context. Other factors are more directly related to primary needs and must be considered in priority (see R.G. McRoy and C.C. Lijima Hall, "Transracial Adoptions: In Whose Best Interest?" in Maria P.P. Root, ed., *The Multicultural Experience* (1996) at pp. 71–73). All factors must be considered pragmatically. Different situations and different philosophies require an individual analysis on the basis of reliable evidence....

Race can be a factor in determining the best interests of the child because it is connected to the culture, identity and emotional well-being of the child. New Brunswick, for example, has adopted legislation prescribing mandatory consideration of "cultural and religious heritage" for all custody determinations (*Family Services Act*, SNB 1980, c. F-2.2, ss. 1 and 129(2)). British Columbia has included similar language in its provisions regarding adoption, but not in those found in the *Family Relations Act* applicable in this case. (*Adoption Act*, RSBC 1996, c. 5, s. 3.) The adoption and custody contexts may differ because the adopted child will generally cease to have contact with the biological parent while custody will generally favour contact with both parents. Nevertheless, it is generally understood that biracial children should be encouraged to positively identify with both racial heritage[s]. This suggests the possibility of a biracial identity (i.e. "forming an identity that incorporates multiple racial heritages," see Pollack ... ["The Role of Race in Child Custody Decisions Between Natural Parents Over Biracial Children" (1997), 23 *NYU Rev. L. & Soc. Change* 603], at p. 619). It is important that the custodial parent recognize the child's need of cultural identity and foster its development accordingly. I would therefore agree that evidence regarding the so-called "cultural dilemma" of biracial children (i.e. the conflict that arises from belonging to two races where one may be dominant for one reason or another) is relevant and should always be accepted. But the significance of evidence relating to race in any given custody case must be carefully considered by the trial judge. Although general public information is useful, it appears to be often contradictory (T.L. Perry, "The Transracial Adoption Controversy: An Analysis of Discourse and Subordination" (1993–94), 21 *NYU Rev. L. & Soc. Change* 33, at p. 59), and may not be sufficient to inform the judge about the current status of race relations in a particular community or the ability of either applicant to deal with these issues.

For the Court of Appeal to intervene, it would have to find a material error. Although Warren J. did not discuss in detail the role that race plays in determining the best interests of the child, he did state that there is an overarching need for the child to be in a stable and loving environment. The limited findings of the trial judge on this issue reflected the minimal weight that the parties themselves placed on the issue at trial. Therefore, notwithstanding the role that race may play in custody determinations, it appears that the trial judge noted that this issue was not determinative and that, in this case, Elijah would be in a more stable and loving environment if custody was granted to the appellant. He clearly considered the mixed race of Elijah and implied that race may impact s. 24(1)(a) in some cases; however, the trial judge obviously was of the view that, even if the biological father provided some benefits as regards fostering a positive racial identity, these benefits did not outweigh the negative findings related to him. By intervening in the consideration of race by the trial judge, the Court of Appeal failed to apply the correct standard of review. It should not have intervened; this issue was given disproportionate emphasis at the initiative of the Court of Appeal....

Notes and Questions

Race and best interests in custody cases

According to Boyd, the Supreme Court clearly rejected the intervenors' argument that race should be a crucial factor in custody determinations, reducing the "question of race to only one of many factors that may be relevant in a given case." As a result, the court's decision provided little guidance on *how much* priority to assign to the issue of race in determining a child's best interests (see Boyd at 180).

In some lower court decisions, courts appear to have been attentive to a child's need to connect to racial heritage, with varying results. For example, in *Ffrench v Ffrench* (1994), 118 DLR (4th) 571 (NSSC), the court awarded custody to a Caucasian mother, rather than to the children's African Canadian father, partly on the ground of the mother's awareness of the children's need for continuing contact with their African Canadian heritage.

By contrast, an African Canadian mother was awarded custody because she was more attentive to the father's French Canadian heritage than he was to her cultural background: see *Camba v Sparks* (1993), 345 APR 321 (NS Fam Ct).

As Boyd noted (at 179), however, some custody disputes involving mixed-race children may employ a rather simplistic analysis. For example, in *Kassel v Louie*, 2000 BCSC 1417, custody was awarded to a Chinese Canadian father, rather than to a Caucasian mother, in part because the judge concluded that the child resembled his father in his looks, and in spite of the fact that the child had lived mainly with his mother. According to Boyd, the judge appeared to place emphasis on the fact that, as the only male heir in the family, the boy was important to the life of the father's extended family.

In the context of these cases, identify the level of priority that should be accorded to race as a factor in determining a child's best interests in custody cases. Recall the discussion in Chapter Three about race in the context of adoption. Are the same considerations appropriate in custody determinations as in the adoption context? Why or why not?

Race as an "environmental" issue?

Consider this comment about the Supreme Court's analysis in *Van de Perre*:

> [There is a tension in this case between a need to reject racial stereotyping on one hand and the necessity on the other to recognize] the reality of racism and the context in which biracial children live, ... a society that often discriminates against those who "look different...." Because the perception of the biracial child is external to the child, it is a factor that is not dependent on the particular child or even on the particular facts. Indeed, as the social science evidence has suggested, the categorization of biracial children ... is a social and psychological phenomenon that permeates most of society. The consequences of being so categorized are also not dependent on the particular circumstances of the child. If the child is categorized as "non-white," the stereotypes and prejudices that go with that categorization will be applied to the child.... Because mixed-race children necessarily embody two or more different races and heritages, such classifications may lead to heightened identity problems because of the disparity between the way in which the child sees him- or herself in relation to the world, and the way in which the world perceives the child.... (Tammy Wing-Yun Law, "The Race Issue in Custody Law: Is *Van de Perre* Right?" (2003) 21 Can Fam LQ 153 at 165–167)

How should this concern be taken into account in relation to the principle of a child's "best interests"?

Additional Resources

Emily Carasco, "Race and Child Custody in Canada: Its Relevance and Role" (1999) 16 Can J Fam L 11.

Hadley Friedland, "Tragic Choices and the Division of Sorrow: Speaking about Race, Culture and Community Traumatisation in the Lives of Children" (2009) 25:2 Can J Fam L 223.

Marlee Kline, "Child Welfare Law, 'Best Interests of the Child' Ideology, and First Nations" (1992) 30:2 Osgoode Hall LJ 375.

Beryl Tsang, *Child Custody and Access: The Experiences of Abused Immigrant and Refugee Women* (Ottawa: Education Wife Assault, 2001).

Tammy Wing-Yun Law, "The Race Issue in Custody Law: Is *Van de Perre* Right?" (2002) 21 Can Fam LQ 153.

Joanna Woolman & Sarah Deer, "Protecting Native Mothers and Their Children: A Feminist Lawyering Approach" (2014) 40:3 Wm Mitchell L Rev 943.

"BEST INTERESTS" AND IDENTITY: THE SIGNIFICANCE OF RELIGION/CULTURE

Issues about identity may also focus on religion in terms of culture and community. To what extent are these issues different from those regarding race and identity? Consider this question in relation to the following decision.

Libbus v Libbus
(2008), 62 RFL (6th) 416 (Ont Sup Ct)

This issue about religious culture and identity was a significant issue in custody litigation between a father who had been raised in the Catholic religion and a mother who was Jewish. In *Libbus v Libbus*, the spouses had been married in a Jewish ceremony, and when their two children were born, the parents agreed that they would be raised in the Jewish religion. The father fully supported his children's Jewish faith and participated in its rituals. The family also celebrated Christian holidays with the father's mother out of respect for her beliefs.

However, after the family had moved to the community of Uxbridge/Sunderland, the wife began to feel increasingly isolated, and eventually the parents separated. The mother then wished for the children to move and attend school in Thornhill, rather than in Uxbridge, so as to foster their identity in a Jewish community. The father preferred that the children remain living in Uxbridge, as it was the only school they had ever attended, and it offered French immersion.

What is in the children's "best interests" in this context?

In assessing the parents' claims, the court considered extensive expert evidence about religion and culture, and specifically, whether it was in the best interests of the children to live in Thornhill or Uxbridge, in terms of enhancing the likelihood of their developing a positive Jewish identity. For example, according to one expert:

[154] Dr. Mock points out that Judaism is not just a religion but also a way of life, and a value system. It has ethnic and cultural elements. It has, unfortunately, become "racialized" as a result of Nazi policy during the 1930s and 1940s. Adopting a Jewish identity is not restricted to a religion only. Many people who are not particularly religious identify themselves as Jews on a cultural level. [The expert report also reviewed the development of ethnic, racial and religious identity, suggesting that it first begins in children at the age of three, and that children thereafter enter a second phase of "identification" when the child recognizes group belonging.]

[157] The identification phase is instilled in children through such things as parochial school and family practices. While children may adopt certain negative or positive feelings during this time, it is more likely that they just accept things as they happen.

[158] [The last phase then involves an understanding that some groups are more valued than others and a desire to become part of the preferred group.] ... When a child is the only child who needs to be away for a religious holiday, that child is likely to feel different and not in a positive way. A child's peer group plays a crucial role during this time. Families that are trying to instil an identity have to work even harder with their child to ensure that the child is receiving positive reinforcement so that the child does not engage in self-hatred. This is almost impossible to do unless the child has a peer group that helps him or her to feel that he or she is not second-class....

[159] A child is likely to feel proud about his or her identity if that identity is reflected in the community and in the school curriculum....

In assessing the issue, including the expert evidence, the court concluded:

[194] The issue that has to be addressed, notwithstanding [the father's] efforts and intentions, is whether the Jewish identity of the children can be better fostered in their present school [in Uxbridge] or at [a school in Thornhill].... In order to successfully raise the children in the Jewish faith and as cultural Jews, something more than strong family values is needed. That value is enhanced, especially as children get older, not only by family, but also from peers and the wider community.

[195] The strain that would likely occur in a setting that offers little accommodation to [the children] to pursue Jewish values is obvious to me. In custody cases and cases involving decisions incidental to custody such as education, the court must often consider plans that are somewhat speculative in that the future care and guidance of children must be considered. Custody decisions are not just "in the moment." In this case, I considered the plans of both parents and found [the mother's] plan the one that would suit the best interests of the children. [The father's] plan for their care is a good plan but the law requires me to determine the best plan, not simply a good plan....

According to the court, the father's plan was not as good because the children "will struggle to maintain their Jewish identity." The court also commented that the father had not converted to Judaism, and that the paternal grandmother was an observant Catholic, so that neither of them would be able to raise the children as Jews in Uxbridge. In the end, the court concluded that the children should attend the new school in

Thornhill, and the parties were required to renegotiate access and care arrangements accordingly.

In *Ignjatov v Di Lauro*, 2014 ONSC 4228, the mother had sole custody but had agreed in Minutes of Settlement not to change the children's Catholic religion and to consent to their participation in religious activities organized by the father. The mother's unilateral cancellation of one daughter's First Communion was described as "shocking conduct" that was devastating to the child and her extended family on the father's side (at para 15). The First Communion was rescheduled and the father was awarded costs associated with the cancelled event.

Notes and Questions

Religious identity, culture and community in relation to "best interests"

To what extent is this case about religious identity? Or is it about culture and community? Do you agree with the expert witness that it may also be about race? Does this case suggest that cultural or religious identity is just one factor for consideration, as suggested in relation to race in *Van de Perre*? How would you describe the court's reasoning with respect to "best interests"?

Identity in relation to "stability": Contexts of custody and adoption

In reflecting on these questions, consider that the father had argued that stability, in terms of the children's home, community and school, as well as the support provided lovingly by their paternal grandmother, were all more significant than their Jewish identity. Indeed, he argued that the children's mother had raised the issue of Jewish identity as a "smokescreen" because she wanted to move (with the children) to a location closer to a Jewish man whom she planned to marry.

Does the outcome in this case, a competition between stability and (religious or cultural) identity, suggest that identity may be more important in custody cases than in adoption cases (such as *ANR and SCR v LJW*, discussed in Chapter Three?) Are there differences in the contexts of custody and adoption that are relevant in comparing issues of stability and identity? Why or why not?

Additional Resources

Rex Ahdar, "Religion as a Factor in Custody and Access Disputes" (1996) 10:2 Intl JL Pol'y & Fam 177.

Claire Archbold, "Family Law-Making and Human Rights in the United Kingdom" in Mavis Maclean, ed, *Making Law for Families* (Oxford & Portland, OR: Hart Publishing, 2000) 185.

Annie Bunting, "Elijah and Ishmael: Assessing Cultural Identity in Canadian Child Custody Decisions" (2004) 42:3 Fam Ct Rev 471.

Hadley Friedland, "Tragic Choices and the Division of Sorrow: Speaking about Race, Culture and Community Traumatisation in the Lives of Children" (2009) 25 Can J Fam L 223.

Alice Hearst, *Children and the Politics of Cultural Belonging* (New York: Cambridge University Press, 2012).

Charlee Lane, "For Heaven's Sake, Give the Child a Voice: An ADR Approach to Interfaith Child Custody Disputes" (2010) 10:3 Pepp Disp Resol LJ 623.

Joseph Mucci, "The Effect of Religious Disputes in Child Custody Disputes" (1986) 5 Can J Fam L 353.

SE Mumford, "The Judicial Resolution of Disputes Involving Children and Religion" (1998) 47 ICLQ 117.

Beryl Tsang, *Child Custody and Access: The Experiences of Abused Immigrant and Refugee Women* (Ottawa: Education Wife Assault, 2001).

Shauna Van Praagh, "Religion, Custody, and a Child's Identity" (1997) 35:2 Osgoode Hall LJ 309.

"BEST INTERESTS" AND IDENTITY: THE SIGNIFICANCE OF LANGUAGE OF SCHOOLING

Like religious considerations, linguistic and cultural issues can also be of significance when determining custody. In *Perron v Perron*, the Father appealed an order granting custody of their three children to the Mother and access to him. The Father's first language was French though he could speak English, and the Mother's first language was English though she could speak French. The Father wanted the children to be enrolled in a homogeneous French-language school. At the time of the appeal, the children were enrolled in a French immersion school where 50% of the courses were taught in English and 50% were taught in French. The Mother wanted the children to remain in French immersion.

The Father claimed that the trial judge should have considered whether it was in the best interests of the children to include, as a condition of granting custody to the Mother, that the children would attend a homogenous French language school.

The trial judge held that the language issue was a distraction from what is in the best interests of the children, and that the French immersion program provided the children with sufficient exposure to the French language. Custody was granted to the Mother without considering an order making homogeneous French-language schooling a condition of custody. Consider the Court of Appeal's decision:

Perron v Perron
2012 ONCA 811

[18] The education offered in a homogeneous French-language school is quite distinct from what is provided in a French immersion program. A homogeneous French-language school responds to the cultural and linguistic needs of the Francophone community. In contrast, the French immersion program is designed for English speakers in an English-language majority environment and provides bilingual instruction — usually 50 per cent in French and 50 per cent in English. See *Solski (Tutor of) v. Quebec (Attorney General)*, 2005 SCC 14, at para. 50. ...

[20] Homogenous French-language education brings many advantages. It promotes full mastery of the French language and the development of the child's cultural identity. This type of instruction also allows the child to become bilingual in French and English, because a homogeneous French-language school helps the child to develop a high level of skill in both French and English: Aménagement Linguistique Policy, at p. 42. In addition, in a social environment dominated by English, a child will generally communicate in English in many aspects of daily life and, as a result, acquire knowledge of the language of the majority: Aménagement Linguistique Policy, at p. 23. It should also be noted that bilingualism provides a number of advantages in terms of employment: Aménagement Linguistique Policy, at p. 42.

[21] Apart from these advantages, where children have one Francophone parent, knowledge and mastery of the language and culture of the linguistic minority promotes and helps maintain the bonds between the children and the Francophone parent.

With respect to whether or not the trial judge erred by failing to consider whether it was in the best interests of the children to make a custody order with a condition about the children's language of education, the court held that the trial judge should have turned his mind to the possibility of a conditional order in these circumstances (para 35).

[36] It may be that the trial judge did not consider the possibility of a conditional order because of the parties' approach during the proceedings. A review of the trial proceedings suggests that the focus at trial was on who would get custody and on terms of access. I have concluded nonetheless that it was an error under the circumstances not to consider the option of ordering French-language schooling as a condition of awarding sole custody to the respondent.

The question therefore becomes whether the court should make the conditional order on appeal.

[42] In my opinion, the court should be particularly sensitive to the language of education in circumstances where there is only one Francophone parent and the English-speaking parent has been granted custody. In such circumstances, there is necessarily less contact with the French-speaking parent and the linguistic and cultural environment of the children is likely to become that of the linguistic majority.

[43] It is true that, in this case, the children would have some exposure to French in the French immersion program. But since French immersion instruction largely reflects the majority culture, the risk of cultural and

linguistic alienation of the children from their father and their father's family is increased.

[44] In a linguistic minority environment, homogeneous French-language schools are generally preferable to French immersion programs for ensuring that both languages, namely French and English, are maintained at the highest level. In a region with a large English-speaking majority, homogeneous instruction in French does not result in losing the language and culture of the linguistic majority. This does not therefore imply a choice of preferring the culture and language of the minority over those of the majority. In a minority setting, homogeneous French-language schools in fact make it possible to maintain cultural and linguistic links with both the French-speaking and English-speaking parents. In accordance with s. 24(2)(d) of the *Children's Law Reform Act*, the children's language of education should therefore be taken into account when determining their best interests.

The Court of Appeal held that the trial judge erred. The language of the children's education was an important consideration. However, two years had passed since the trial. Given the passage of time, it was found to be in the children's best interests to remain in their French immersion schools. The Court unanimously dismissed the appeal. Application for leave to appeal to the SCC was filed, but was dismissed without reasons on June 13, 2013: *Perron v Perron*, [2013] SCCA No 26.

To what extent was this case decided using principles of the best interests of the child?

"BEST INTERESTS" AND IDENTITY: GAY AND LESBIAN PARENTS

Although the status of gay and lesbian families has changed in recent decades, particularly with the recognition of same-sex marriage in Canada, custody cases involving gay and lesbian parents may still be controversial.

To understand this context, consider the decision in *Barkley v Barkley* in Ontario in 1980, and the factors considered by the court at that time. As the more recent decision in *Buist v Greaves* (discussed later in this chapter) demonstrates, these factors are no longer used, at least explicitly. Yet, it may still be important to take account of the all-too-recent vulnerability of gay and lesbian parents involved in custody disputes.

Re Barkley and Barkley (1980)

In *Re Barkley and Barkley* (1980), 28 OR (2d) 136 (Prov Ct (Fam Div)), Nasmith J reviewed several cases (at 139) in the context of a claim to custody of her daughter by a lesbian mother.

In *Case v Case* (1974), 18 RFL 132 (Sask QB), MacPherson J stipulated that homosexuality was *not a bar* to an award of custody and that it was simply a factor to be considered along with others. However, he awarded custody of two young children to the father, perhaps because the court was concerned that the lesbian mother slept in the same bed with her homosexual partner, and because he had not had the benefit of having the partner as a witness. In this case, the court concluded (at 138): "I greatly fear that if these children are raised by the mother, they will be too much in contact with people of abnormal tastes and proclivities."

In *K v K* (1975), 23 RFL 58, [1976] 2 WWR 462, Rowe J, of the Alberta Provincial Court, distinguished the *Case* decision, although agreeing that homosexuality was just one factor for consideration. In awarding custody to a homosexual mother, who also slept in the same bed as her partner, and did not engage in any sexual contact in the presence of the children, the trial Judge was supported by strong evidence from a psychologist who testified that the mother and the child had a close relationship which was one of the best mother–child interactions she had seen in her professional practice. The psychologist noted that the child was happy, well-adjusted and doing very well in school, and concluded (at 61) that "the manner in which one fulfills one's sexual needs does not relate to the abilities of being a good parent." In this case, the mother's lesbian partner was called as a witness and the court found her impressive.

In *D v D* (1978), 20 OR (2d) 722 (Co Ct), Smith J dealt with an application to vary a decree *nisi*. The decree had been silent as to custody and the father later sought custody of two children, aged 13 and 8, who had been in his *de facto* custody since the separation. It was clear that the father was bisexual and that he was involved in a continuing homosexual relationship. The trial Judge (at 726) treated his homosexuality as a possible problem, but awarded the father custody, thus confirming the status quo. In doing so, the judge made the following findings:

(a) the father was bisexual;
(b) the father was discreet;
(c) he was not an exhibitionist;
(d) the public did not know about his sexual orientations;
(e) he did not flaunt his homosexual activities;
(f) he was not a militant homosexual;
(g) the court felt that he could "cope with" the problems;
(h) there was no evidence that the children would become homosexual;
(i) the main homosexual partner made a favourable impression on him.

After reviewing these cases, the court in *Barkley* stated:

... In the present case, a focus on the quality of the parent–child relationship here produces a good case for the mother as the more appropriate person to have custody of Lynn.

As in *D. v. D.* any possible ill effects for Lynn from the mother's sexual orientation have been minimized by the following circumstances:
(1) she is not militant;
(2) she does not flaunt her homosexuality;
(3) she does not seem to be biased about Lynn's orientation and seems to assume that Lynn will be heterosexual;
(4) there is no overt sexual contact apart from sleeping in the same bed;
(5) the sexual partner has a reasonably good relationship with the child.

Whatever significant risks remain in the area of Lynn's necessary adjustments to our "homophobic" society, they are too esoteric and speculative for me to attach much weight to. I think they must give way here to the more concrete *indicia* of "best interests"....

The court thus awarded custody to the mother and access to the father.

Notes and Questions

Appellate court comments: *Bezaire v Bezaire*

Although the outcome in the *Barkley* case was positive for the lesbian mother, the case reveals how societal perceptions influenced the legal reasoning in relation to applying the "best interests" principle. In 1980, another case involving a lesbian mother reached the Ontario Court of Appeal.

In *Bezaire v Bezaire* (1980), 20 RFL (2d) 358 (Ont CA), the wife left her husband in 1974, taking her two children (aged two and three) with her. She alleged that her husband had been violent and physically abusive to her, and she also claimed to have been sexually brutalized by him. Her husband had once pleaded guilty and been convicted of assaulting her. Ms. Bezaire was eventually taken by police to a woman's shelter, and in a court hearing a few weeks later, she was awarded custody and child support.

As a result, Gail Bezaire became a sole parent to her children and her husband exercised some access, although a bit erratically. At the time of their divorce hearing in 1978, however, he again contested custody. Since Ms. Bezaire had come out as a lesbian after leaving her husband, he sued for divorce on the ground that her sexuality had caused the breakdown of the marriage (see the grounds for divorce in the 1968 *Divorce Act*), and he also claimed that her sexuality disqualified her as a fit parent.

The trial court granted the divorce and also awarded custody to Ms. Bezaire. However, the court also imposed conditions, requiring that Ms. Bezaire maintain a stable residence and that she refrain from engaging in homosexual relationships.

Both parents appealed. Mr. Bezaire appealed the custody decision and Ms. Bezaire appealed the conditions.

In the hearing three months later, the court held that Ms. Bezaire had "flagrantly disregarded" the conditions, because she had moved without notifying the court and because she had engaged in a lesbian relationship. As a result, the children went to live with their father.

However, Ms. Bezaire became increasingly concerned that the children were being physically and sexually abused. She asked for the children to be represented and also requested an assessment of the children and the parents. The court-appointed psychiatrist corroborated the allegations about physical and sexual abuse on the part of the father, and recommended (supported by the children's representative) that custody be returned to the mother.

However, based on several procedural issues, the Ontario Court of Appeal confirmed the father's custody. In doing so, however, two Justices addressed the issue of gay and lesbian parenting:

> ARNUP J. (at 365): I would make one comment upon an aspect of the case which gave Judge McMahon a great deal of concern and which has been canvassed at some length before us. That is the question of the effect of and the weight to be given to evidence that the mother not only exhibited homosexual tendencies but clearly lived at various relevant times in a homosexual relationship.... In my view homosexuality, either as a tendency, a proclivity or a practised way of life, is not in itself alone a ground for refusing custody to the parent with respect to whom such evidence is given. The question is and must always be what effect upon the welfare of the children that aspect of the parent's make-up and life-style has, and it will therefore be a question of evidence in that very case as to whether what has been shown to exist has or may tend to have effects adverse to the welfare of the children....

> WILSON J. (dissenting on other grounds) (at 367): I would like to add as an addendum to these reasons that in my view homosexuality is a neutral and not a negative factor as far as parenting skills are concerned. To the extent the learned trial judge proceeded on a different view I would respectfully disagree with him....

Yet, in spite of these supportive comments, Ms. Bezaire lost custody of her children. Eventually, she fled, taking the children with her to a location outside Canada. This action constituted child abduction since her former husband was legally entitled to custody. In 1985, her former husband located her and the children, and she then returned to Canada and surrendered to police.

Ms. Bezaire was tried on a number of related charges and convicted. In the end, she received an absolute discharge on an abduction charge, a three-year suspended sentence on a charge of harbouring, three years' probation, and she was ordered to obtain counselling and do 300 hours of community service.

In the context of widespread publicity about this case, did the views expressed by the judges in the Ontario Court of Appeal concretely address the problems experienced by Ms. Bezaire? In reflecting on this question, consider the following comment about the *Bezaire* case:

> The appellate judges argued, then, that each case must be judged on the basis of its evidence. Even such a fair-minded approach, however, contains within it a pitfall for the lesbian mother. Because of the "rampant heterosexism" of our society, the child of a lesbian might well be the object of abuse and ridicule by neighbourhood children if the mother's lesbianism were discovered or even suspected. Such an experience would, of course, be an unpleasant one for the child. Anticipating such derision, judges in Canada, as in the United States, Britain and elsewhere have opted primarily for paternal custody rights, thereby reflecting and reinforcing the prevailing attitudes toward lesbianism. (Katherine Arnup, " 'Mothers Just Like Others': Lesbians, Divorce, and Child Custody in Canada" (1989) 3 CJWL 18 at 28)

Research about parenting and sexual orientation: The "environmental" challenge

In this context, consider the results of research in the United States, which indicated no significant differences between lesbian and heterosexual mothers, and that the more important indicator of adjustment was stability in the home, not sexual orientation. See Cheryl Meyer, "Legal, Psychological and Medical Considerations in Lesbian Parenting" (1992) 2 Law & Sexuality 237.

Consider this research in relation to *Saunders v Saunders* (1989), 20 RFL (3d) 368 (BC Co Ct).

In *Saunders*, a gay father in British Columbia was denied access to his child on the basis of his homosexual relationship because of "environmental" concerns on the part of the judge (at 370):

> The child has a normal, stable home in which there are only the normal environmental circumstances for maturity to develop. Surely it cannot be argued the exposure of a child to unnatural relationships is in the best interests of that child of tender years. While it is an impossibility to protect a child from many undesirable situations, even when they are very young, the prudent parent does not voluntarily and deliberately expose a child to any environmental influence which might affect normal development....
>
> There can be no doubt that consenting adults may enter into whatever sexual arrangements they wish, for better or worse. I am not convinced ... that the exposure of a child of tender years to an unnatural relationship of a parent to any degree is in the best interests of the development and natural attainment of maturity of that child. That is the issue, not the rights of homosexuals. The courts have on occasion found, in given circumstances, the best interests of the child are served by placing custody with a homosexual father or lesbian mother. In those cases, however, the children have usually been older, but more importantly the parent has exercised great restraint in minimizing the sexual choice of that parent as a role model for the child.

Have these harmful prior precedents influenced today's law, explicitly or implicitly? How are they relevant to the best interests test?

Additional Resources

Katherine Arnup, ed, *Lesbian Parenting* (Charlottetown, PEI: Gynergy Books, 1995).

Nicholas Bala & Christine Ashbourne, "The Widening Concept of Parent in Canada: Step-Parents, Same-Sex Parents, and Parents by ART" (2012) 20:3 Am UJ Gender Soc Pol'y & L 525.

Susan B Boyd, "Lesbian (and Gay) Custody Claims: What Difference Does Difference Make?" (1998) 15 Can J Fam L 131.

Elaine Craig, "Converging Feminist and Queer Legal Theories: Family Feuds and Family Ties" (2010) 28 Windsor YB Access Just 209.

Shelley AM Gavigan, "Mothers, Other Mothers, and Others" in Dorothy Chunn & Dany Lacombe, eds, *Law as a Gendering Practice* (Toronto: Oxford University Press, 2000) 100.

Fiona Kelly, "Multiple-Parent Families under British Columbia's New Family Law Act: A Challenge to the Supremacy of the Nuclear Family or a Method by which to Preserve Biological Ties and Opposite-Sex Parenting?" (2014) 47 UBC L Rev 565.

Fiona Kelly, "Equal Parents, Equal Children: Reforming Canada's Parentage Laws to Recognize the Completeness of Women-led Families" (2013) 64 UNBLJ 253.

Robert Leckey, "Contracting Claims and Family Law Feuds" (2007) 57 UTLJ 1.

Jenni Millbank, "Lesbians, Child Custody, and the Long Lingering Gaze of the Law" in Susan B Boyd, ed, *Challenging the Public/Private Divide: Feminism, Law, and Public Policy* (Toronto: University of Toronto Press, 1997) 280.

Nancy Polikoff, "Lesbian Mothers, Lesbian Families" (1989) 14 NYU Rev L & Soc Change 907.

Nancy D Polikoff, "From Third Parties to Parents: The Case of Lesbian Couples and Their Children" (2014) 77 Law & Contemp Probs 195.

Joanna Radbord, "Same Sex Families and the Law" (2013) 33 Windsor Rev Legal Soc Issues 1.

BEST INTERESTS AND ACCESS: A CHILD'S "RIGHT"

As demonstrated by the examples above, courts determine parental custody on the basis of what is in a child's best interests. However, access for the other parent is not automatic. Indeed, like custody, parental access must also be determined having regard to the principle of a child's best interests.

In examining the case that follows, identify the factors that the court considered relevant to deciding the father's claim to access. Are these factors the same as those used in claims for custody? Should they be the same? Why or why not?

Craig v Antone
(1987), 7 RFL (3d) 409 (Ont Prov Ct (Fam Div))

In this case, the court assessed the test to be applied in relation to an access claim by a parent, and also the onus of proof with respect to such a claim.

Specifically, the father's counsel argued that access is a right of a parent, and that this right can be lost only where the evidence discloses some real apprehension of emotional or physical harm to the child. According to the mother's counsel, the test was simply "best interests."

In addition, the parents disagreed about the onus of proof in an access claim, having regard to the wording of section 20(4) of the *CLRA*. The father's counsel argued that the suspension of custody rights, but not those of access, pursuant to this section, implied a presumption in favour of access.

The court quoted the views of Abbey Prov J in *Trudell v Doolittle*, [1984] WDFL 933 (unreported), stating:

> I am not prepared to take the meaning of s. 20(4) that far. The provision, in my view, although it provides that in the circumstances where parents live separately the entitlement to access, as opposed to the entitlement to custody, is not suspended, does not go so far as to create by statute a presumption in favour of access such that, in the determination of that access by application under the Act, the onus is cast upon the parent resisting the right of the other to access.

With respect to the second point — namely, whether or not a denial of access must be based on apprehended danger to the child — I cannot improve upon the analysis of the trial judge in *Trudell v. Doolittle* in a lengthy passage from his reasons commencing at p. 14 as follows:

> It therefore may be said, I believe, that even prior to the passage of the present s. 24 of the *Children's Law Reform Act*, the paramount principle applicable in the determination of the right of access was the best interests of the child. Although certain other guidelines came to be generally accepted as helpful in the determination of the best interests of the child, those guidelines were secondary to the paramount principle.
>
> As examples of the application of certain of the guidelines and the overriding principle together, the following statements may assist:
>
> (a) Although it may be generally considered as a sound general guideline that access should be granted except where a danger to the child might be apprehended, nevertheless, if upon consideration of the evidence as a whole the granting of access could not be said to be in the child's best interests, it should not be granted even though there be no evidence of apprehended danger.
>
> (b) Although it may be generally presumed that it is in a child's best interests to come to know its biological father, nevertheless, if upon consideration of the evidence as a whole applicable to a particular case it cannot be said that access would be in the best interests of a child, it should not be granted....

In my view, the decisions in *Trudell v. Doolittle* and *Boileau v. Boileau* reflect the law of Ontario on this point....

On the facts before me, there is no evidence of more than a chance, and perhaps reluctant, acquaintance between the respondent and the child. The conduct, generally, of the respondent has been disreputable and his relationship with the applicant even less than tenuous. Although the respondent appeared contrite for his past transgressions, his expressed wishes were purely speculative. I conclude that the lack of real motivation which has been a continuing factor through his unproductive attempts at rehabilitation in the past will, unfortunately, probably continue, and to impose his sudden presence on this child in any form would be completely contrary to her best interests.

The words of the respondent in the witness box convince me of his yearning for an illusory relationship of some importance to him, different from the other liaisons in his life. I cannot ignore the fact, however, that his opportunity to form a substantial bond with the applicant and his child was thrown aside by his commitment to an aberrant lifestyle and his opportunistic and callous behaviour towards the applicant. Although he is now apparently repentant, the evidence is that he threatened to kidnap the child only to cause emotional harm to the applicant. In my view of the law, there is no justification for the father having even supervised access to the child and, accordingly, the relief he seeks is denied and his claim dismissed....

Order accordingly

Notes and Questions

Denial or suspension of access

The court in *Craig v Antone* denied the father's claim to access to his child. Indeed, the court was not even prepared to grant supervised access, that is, access visits that are supervised by a third party.

Although somewhat unusual, there are other cases in which parents (usually, but not always, fathers) have been denied access to children, or where existing access arrangements have been suspended or terminated.

For example, in *Lidkea v Jarrell* (1999), 49 RFL (4th) 324 (Ont CA), the court dismissed an appeal by the father from a decision suspending access to his daughter. According to the court, there was ample evidence to support the view that suspension of access was in the child's best interests.

Similarly, the Saskatchewan Court of Appeal confirmed an order denying a father's access to his son where there was evidence that the son did not wish to have contact with his father after the father exposed the son to his sexual activity in a car. See *Gorgichuk v Gorgichuk* (1999), 50 RFL (4th) 395 (Sask CA). Similarly, in *Doncaster v Field*, 2014 NSCA 39, the father who had ADHD and Asperger's Syndrome, punched his son 4 times in the shoulder. The son did not subsequently want to see the father. The father was acquitted of assault at trial but access was terminated. The Court of Appeal held that although the termination of access appeared "harsh", no errors could be identified to overrule the judge's termination.

Moreover, in *S v S* (1998), 115 BCAC 146, the B.C. Court of Appeal ordered that a father be prohibited from bringing further suits to compel access to two children, after he had failed in a number of such attempts. The children were the result of an incestuous relationship with his daughter, for which he had been convicted and imprisoned. (See also *Abdo v Abdo* (1993), 50 RFL (3d) 171 (NSCA) where an abusive man (to both his ex-partner and his child) was denied access.)

Custody/access claims by grandparents and others

- **Provincial legislation:** Provincial statutes frequently permit custody or access claims by persons other than parents.

    For example, Ontario's *CLRA*, s 21(1), permits "a parent of a child or any other person" to apply for custody.

Amendments to the *CLRA* (SO 2009, c 11) have created new obligations in relation to such claims (see s 21), including the submission of an affidavit containing:

- the person's proposed plan for the child's care and upbringing;
- information about the person's current or previous involvement in family proceedings, including any related to child protection; and
- any other information relevant to considering the factors in *CLRA*, ss 24(2), (3) and (4).

In addition, there are requirements for persons applying for custody to submit to police and CAS record checks (see ss 21.1–21.3).

As may be evident, these amendments were enacted to prevent harm or abuse to children in relation to applications for custody and access, and they apply to parents as well as other persons seeking custody or access.

However, according to a number of family court judges who opposed these amendments, clients without the means to pay for legal representation, custody assessments, or expert evidence may not be able to present applications according to these new provisions. The judges suggested that it would be preferable to request investigations by the Office of the Children's Lawyer to ensure that all relevant facts are before the court in custody and access disputes. See Robert Todd, "Family Court Judges Warn Bill would have 'Unintended Consequences'", *Law Times* (6 April 2009).

Recall the discussion in Chapter Five about legal processes for resolving disputes at separation and divorce. To what extent do the 2009 legislative amendments take account of the context of current legal processes for determining custody and access in the "best interests" of children? Do they encourage other family members (including grandparents) to come forward to apply for custody or access to children?

- **Federal legislation:** The *Divorce Act* permits persons other than parents to apply for standing in proceedings about custody or access of children, but any such application requires leave of the court (see ss 16(2) and (3)). These provisions have been reviewed in a number of cases.

For example, in *Arnink v Arnink* (1999), 2 RFL (5th) 24 (BCSC), the court reviewed the applicable principles and held that the grandparents were appropriate parties (for purposes of custody and access claims only) in divorce proceedings between their son-in-law and daughter. In this case, the grandparents had been primary caregivers of the two children. The children's father, who was the petitioner in the divorce action, opposed their application.

In granting the grandparents' application, the court stated (at 27):

> I am satisfied that the "not frivolous or vexatious" test used by Cummings J. is the appropriate test to use. It should be noted that the sole consideration in a custody dispute is the best interests of the child: s. 16(8) of the *Divorce Act* and s. 24 of the *Family Relations Act*. In order that the best interests of the child or the children can be determined, any individuals who can bring themselves within

the definition of "persons" as set out in the *Family Relations Act* (s. 35(1.1) of the Act) would qualify as persons who should be granted leave to apply for custody. I am satisfied that the onus of showing that the application for leave is frivolous or vexatious lies with the party opposing the application. In the case at bar, the plaintiff has not shown that the request of the Andersens to be at liberty to apply for custody is frivolous and vexatious. The mere fact of them joining with their daughter to add further weight to the application of the defendant for custody and to diminish the ability of the plaintiff to obtain custody can hardly be said to make their application frivolous and vexatious....

There is nothing before me which would suggest that the application of Mr. and Mrs. Andersen is anything but a genuine attempt to apply for custody of their two grandchildren along with their daughter. Whether or not that application will ultimately be granted, I am satisfied that leave should be granted pursuant to s. 16(3) of the *Divorce Act*.

Consider also a number of cases in which applications by grandparents have been denied:

- In *Chapman v Chapman* (2001), 15 RFL (5th) 46, the Ontario Court of Appeal denied a grandmother's application for access when the children's parents (in an intact family situation) had decided to restrict it. According to Abella JA, in the absence of evidence that parents are not acting in children's best interests, their decisions should be respected. Parents are responsible in law for the welfare of their children. See Lorna Yales, "Rights in a Multi-Generational Reality", *The Lawyers Weekly* (17 February 2012) 13.

- In *T v P*, 1999 ABCA 87, the Alberta Court of Appeal denied an access claim presented by grandparents on the ground that their persistent efforts to pursue their claim in the media over a five-year period were not in the children's best interests.

- In *F v S*, 1999 BCCA 398, a grandmother's request for an access order, objected to by the child's mother, was denied.

- In *Hayes v Moyer*, 2011 SKCA 56, the court denied an application for access by grandparents. See also Donalee Moulton, "Sask CA Denies Grandparents Access to Grandchildren", *The Lawyers Weekly* (23 September 2011) 10.

Do these cases suggest that courts are responding to children's best interests? How should courts foster family relationships in relation to children's best interests? For a discussion about recommendations for reforms to include other family members, particularly grandparents, in post-separation relationships with children, see Special Joint Committee on Child Custody and Access, *For the Sake of the Children* (Ottawa: Parliament of Canada, 1998), recommendation 12 and Law Reform Commission of Nova Scotia, *Grandparent–Grandchild: Access* (Halifax: 2007). The Ontario legislature has twice attempted to introduce a bill to amend the *CLRA* with respect to grandparent access. Both attempts failed when Parliament was prorogued in 2012 and an election was called in 2014. Consider, however, a critique of grandparents' "rights" to access, reflecting the idea that most parents permit access to relatives who respect boundaries. See "The Problem with Ontario's Grandparents Rights Bill" at <http://www.on-the-other-hand.com/the-problem-with-ontarios-grandparents-rights-bill/> (29 April 2013).

By contrast with access applications by grandparents, a NWT court upheld an access claim by a stepmother after her relationship with the child's father had ended, concluding that such access was in the child's best interests. See *D(G) v M(G)* (1999), 47 RFL (4th) 16 (NWTSC). Why was this case decided differently than those involving applications for access by grandparents?

Additional Resources

Aliamisse Mundulai, "Stretching the Boundaries in Child Access, Custody and Guardianship in Canada" (2005) 21 Can J Fam L 267.

Martha Shaffer, "To Grandmother's House We Go? An Examination of Grandparent Access" (2003–2004) Can Fam LQ 437.

Special Joint Committee on Child Custody and Access, *For the Sake of the Children* (Ottawa: Parliament of Canada, 1998).

ACCESS, RELIGION, AND BEST INTERESTS

The authority of a parent with legal custody to determine a child's religious upbringing may sometimes conflict with the religious beliefs of an access parent. In this context, issues may arise with respect to the access parent's freedom to express religious beliefs to a child. Such cases involve courts in determining what arrangements are in the best interests of the child.

According to the Alberta Court of Appeal in *Bachor v Lehmann-Bachor*, 2001 ABCA 53, the custodial parent's authority is clear:

> **[34]** It has long been recognized that the custodial parent has the sole and primary responsibility to oversee all aspects of the child's day-to-day life and long-term well-being.... Section 16(5) of the *Divorce Act* gives the access parent a right to be informed of these decisions, but "courts in Canada have never adopted the view that the custodial parent's decisions are subject to the approval of the non-custodial parent" [quoting L'Heureux-Dubé J in *Young v Young*, discussed below]. As Ms. Lehmann-Bachor is Cassandra's custodial parent, it is clear that she is responsible for pivotal decisions respecting Cassandra's religion.

However, it is possible for an access parent to share their religion with a child as well. For example, in *S v G*, 2002 ABPC 88, a lower court in Alberta concluded that it was not contrary to a child's best interests to spend Christmas with her mother, the access parent. In this case, the father, who was the custodial parent, had joined a religious group that considered

Christmas a pagan holiday, and thus did not wish his child to take part in these holiday festivities.

Such cases raise questions about whether, or to what extent, courts must examine religious practices to determine whether they pose concerns with respect to a child's best interests. And it is also clear that courts may not infringe a parent's freedom of religion. All the same, courts may determine that a parent's religious practices are not consistent with a child's best interests. For example, see *Ackie v Ackie* (2004), 5 RFL (6th) 1 (Ont Sup Ct); and *Stubbert v Ferrare* (2002), 25 RFL (5th) 428 (Ont Sup Ct).

Religious practices and best interests: *Young v Young*

In *Young v Young* (1993), 49 RFL (3d) 117, the Supreme Court of Canada reviewed two cases in which access fathers wished to share their Jehovah's Witness faith with their children, even though the children's custodial mothers objected. In fact, there were two cases on appeal.

One case was *Young v Young*, on appeal from British Columbia based on the *Divorce Act*, while the other was *DP v CS*, on appeal from Québec pursuant to the *Civil Code*.

Although the cases were heard and decided together, there were a number of different judgments and the Court was split in its reasoning.

Moreover, the outcomes were not the same. The access father in British Columbia succeeded in his claim, while the custodial mother was successful in the case on appeal from Québec.

Significantly, however, the Court seemed to agree that the test was the "best interests" of the child, although there was some disagreement among the judges about the meaning of this standard.

At the same time, the long and confusing reasons for judgment in these cases mean that the Supreme Court's decision has not provided great clarity in this context. The following comment provides some clarification of the main issues.

Custody, Access and Religion
(1994) 11 Can Fam LQ 317

Martha Bailey

Bailey first considered the constitutional questions, and in particular whether the best interests test violated the guarantee of freedom of religion and expression in the *Charter*. As she noted, this issue required consideration of whether the *Charter* could apply to "private" actions regarding access. All members of the court agreed that if the test were properly interpreted, it did not violate the *Charter*, although they disagreed with respect to how to analyze this relationship. Bailey then addressed the issue of children's rights (at 327–343):

... As L'Heureux-Dubé J. observed, the rights of freedom of expression and religion "are shaped and formed both by the particular context in which they are exercised and the rights of others." The judge considered that

> there are other powerful competing interests which must be recognized, not the least of which, in addition to the best interests of the children are the freedoms of expression and religion of the children themselves. There is cogent, persuasive evidence, found credible by the trial judge, that the children themselves do not want to discuss religion with their father or be subject to his comments about beliefs which are at odds with their own religious upbringing, whether they take the form of indoctrination, instruction or mere observation. Indeed, the letters written to the trial judge disclose that, not only do they not want it, but also that the prospect of such discussions has so profoundly disturbed the children and coloured the periods of access that they no longer wish to continue to see the respondent according to a schedule.

The difficulty with taking into account the rights of children, however, is that children are not parties to the proceeding, and generally are not represented in custody and access hearings. The "rights" of children, particularly a child's right to access, are regularly deployed by judges in their reasons for judgment and by parties in support of their own claims, but children are not given an opportunity to define their interests for themselves.

Even if the parent's rights are not privileged over the interests of the child, it is problematic that a child is not represented in contested proceedings of this kind, but perhaps justifiable within the logic of a welfarist framework, where the child's interests are defined by others but given priority. When the project of protecting the best interests of the child is displaced by that of protecting the *Charter* rights of the parent, however, the child should be permitted representation. Further, as we develop the notion of children as rights-bearing individuals, able, or potentially able, to define their interests for themselves, the opportunities for children to have representation in legal proceedings that profoundly affect their lives must necessarily be expanded....

Bailey then considered the custodial parent's authority and the right to maximum access, identifying the different approaches to this issue for McLachlin J and L'Heureux-Dubé J:

McLachlin J. interpreted the best interests of the child test in light of the policy of favouring extensive access and of allowing the child to know fully both parents, and noted that the policy has been legislatively enshrined in s. 16(10) of the *Divorce Act*. Her Ladyship said, "Parliament has expressed its opinion that contact with each parent is valuable, and that the judge should ensure that this contact is maximized. ... To the extent that contact conflicts with the best interests of the child, it may be restricted. But only to that extent." Sopinka J. made the additional point that the *Charter* rights of the access parent also support an interpretation of the best interests of the child test in light of the policy of extensive access.

Taking the strong policy favouring access as a starting point, McLachlin J. said that "the proposition, put to us in argument, that the custodial parent should have the right to forbid certain types of contact between the access parent and the child, must fail"....

McLachlin J.'s introduction of harm as a factor to consider when determining the best interests of the child shows the power of s. 16(10) of the *Divorce Act*. Though stating that the best interests of the child is the only test, the *Divorce Act*, s. 16(10) apparently privileges one factor, the value of contact with the non-custodial parent, despite the fact that the value of contact is only one of many factors to consider and will not always be the most important or decisive consideration. Section 16(10) led McLachlin J. to interpret the best interests of the child in light of a presumptive benefit of unrestricted access, and to reason that in some cases the presumption may not be displaced unless there is evidence of harm or a risk of harm. This is incorrect. The general value of unrestricted access is widely recognized, but, despite s. 16(10), it has not yet been promoted to a presumptive benefit that should displace the best interests test, and in my view it should not be. If unrestricted access truly is beneficial to a child, then the best interests test will support it. If it is not in the best interests of the child, taking into account the benefits of access and all other factors, but does not reach the harm threshold proposed by McLachlin J., the best interests should govern the outcome.

L'Heureux-Dubé J. disagreed with McLachlin J's approach, objecting to the introduction of a harm test to the interpretation of the best interests of the child. She said, "[t]he best interests of the child is not simply the right to be free of demonstrable harm, it is the positive right to the best possible arrangements in the circumstances of the parties." She stressed the obligation of the legal system to minimize the adverse effects of divorce on children, and said that this "requires a vision of the best interests of the child that is more than neutral to the conditions under which custody and access occur. The harm test clearly cannot meet this objective." Furthermore, she said, the harm test purports to further the best interests of the child by promoting unfettered contact with the non-custodial parent, but "in reality the test subordinates the best interests of children to a presumptive right of the non-custodial parent to unrestricted access."

Also on the issue of the interest of the child in knowing the access parent, L'Heureux-Dubé J. stated that restrictions on access do not necessarily prevent children from knowing the access parent in a meaningful way, and that unrestricted access may lead to the deterioration or even the ultimate destruction of the relationship. While L'Heureux-Dubé J. agreed that "maximum contact between the child and the non-custodial parent is a worthwhile goal," she did not stress this factor in her interpretation of the best interests of the child, as did McLachlin J. Rather L'Heureux-Dubé J. emphasized the importance of minimizing conflict between parents that adversely affects the child, on the grounds that such conflict "is the single factor which has consistently proven to be severely detrimental to children upon separation or divorce"....

L'Heureux-Dubé J. argued against the trend of increasing the authority of the access parent, pointing out that the *Divorce Act* "neither suggests nor requires the division of parental responsibilities between the custodial parent and the access parent." She linked such an increase in authority with joint custody:

> The arguments in favour of increased authority over the child by the access parent are closely related to those which support a presumption in favour of joint custody. ... They rest on the premise that the relationship of authority and obligation that existed between each of the parents and the child during the marriage should and can continue despite the fact that the parents may no longer be willing or able to cooperate on its exercise.

She argued against joint custody orders on the grounds that in the few custody cases that end up in court, parents generally do not have the requisite willingness to cooperate in child-rearing. Further, she noted that in considering joint custody or access orders, courts should be mindful of that gap between the ideals of shared parenting and the reality that "men as a group have not yet embraced responsibility for childcare," and that women most often bear that responsibility before and after divorce, even if joint custody is ordered. This responsibility includes "increased social, economic and emotional burdens that far exceed those of the intact family"....

Even more problematic is the fact that a "vast number of non-custodial parents are in default of their most serious obligations to their children, as is [Mr. Young]: the responsibility to provide economic support." Her Ladyship concluded: "There is a certain irony in the claim to greater contact and control on the part of access parents in the face of such widespread neglect of children's basic needs."

L'Heureux-Dubé J. argued against greater authority for the access parent on the basis of specific problems faced by custodial mothers and their children. It is not clear, however, that maintaining an authoritative role for the custodial parent and a relatively powerless role for the access parent will address the problems identified or lead to more equitable results. The problem of "deadbeat dads" who default on their child support obligations can probably best be solved by better support enforcement. The problem of "disappearing dads" who do not remain emotionally involved with their children is not likely to be changed by maintaining a restricted definition of access, and may be attenuated by a reformulation of the access role. In reformulating Canada's custody and access law, the trend towards providing for continuing equal parental responsibility for both parents following divorce or separation will have to be seriously considered.

Should disappearing and deadbeat dads be wooed with an enhanced legal role when they have not demonstrated commitment to their children? There is certainly an irony here, and it does seem unfair to diminish the authority of the mother who bears the burden of childcare in order to enhance the role of the father who has contributed relatively little. As L'Heureux-Dubé J. pointed out, however, it is not only some access fathers who are seeking a more significant role: many custodial mothers want fathers to be more involved. Rather than massaging the irony of enhancing the role of the access parent, then, it may be more helpful to consider the evidence as to whether an enhanced role for the access parent would alleviate the disappearing dad syndrome without exacerbating other problems....

Regardless of the respective roles of custodial and access parent addressed so extensively by L'Heureux-Dubé J., the current law does allow for challenges by the access parent to decisions taken by the custodial parent, and it allows custodial parents to seek restrictions on access. In both cases, the best interests of the child is the relevant criterion, and the authority of the custodial parent is not the issue. There is a relationship between the child's interests and the custodial parent's authority, because the parent's ability to function effectively may be diminished if the authority of the role is reduced and the access parent is permitted to challenge child-rearing decisions. But this is only one factor to consider in coming to a determination of what is in the best interests of the child. In her consideration of this issue, L'Heureux-Dubé J. perhaps went too far in identifying the best interests of the child with maintenance of the custodial parent's authority....

McLachlin J. interpreted the best interests of the child test in light of a presumptive benefit of unrestricted access; L'Heureux-Dubé J. in light

of a presumptive deference to the custodial parent. The presumptive benefit of access, the more ascendant view, is problematic when it displaces
the best interests of the child with a harm test and leads some courts to
give insufficient consideration to detrimental aspects of access. The presumptive deference to the custodial parent is problematic because it gives
too little weight to concerns of the access parent that may be valid and
may inhibit involvement by the access parent. The best interests of the
child is the sole test and should be addressed directly, taking into consideration all relevant factors, including the benefits of access and the value
of supporting the custodial parent.

Bailey also addressed the problem of parents' conflicting religious
beliefs:

> Significantly, no member of the Supreme Court of Canada took [the] view
> that conflicting religious beliefs between parents are necessarily harmful to
> children or grounds for restricting access. The fact that the parents have
> differing views and that each is teaching the child about his or her reli-
> gion is not necessarily contrary to the best interests of the child. The Jus-
> tices varied, however, in their views on the level of conflict required to
> justify imposing restrictions on the access parent. Sopinka J., on one end
> of the continuum, asserted "conflict between parents on many matters
> including religion is not uncommon, but in itself cannot be assumed to be
> harmful unless it produces a prolonged acrimonious atmosphere."
> McLachlin J. did not go so far, and correctly pointed out [that] "[c]onflict
> between parents is, in and of itself, not a sufficient basis for assuming that
> the child's interests will not be served." Cory and Iacobucci JJ. did not
> refer to "conflict," but said, "[n]either differences of opinions of parents
> regarding religious questions nor the frank discussion of their differing
> religious perceptions by both parents with the children will be automati-
> cally harmful. Indeed it may often be beneficial"....

Notes and Questions

Applying the best interests test in disputes about religion

In *S v S*, [1997] 3 SCR 1003, the Supreme Court of Canada allowed in
part a mother's appeal regarding restrictions relating to custody of her
child. The case reflected differing views in the courts:

* The trial judge in the Québec court had granted custody to the mother,
  but ordered her not to bring the child to religious ceremonies, demon-
  strations, or other reunions of a similar nature. She was also not allowed
  to bring the child with her for the door to door preachings, and was prohibited from indoctrinating the child with the precepts of her faith (Sev-
  enth Day Adventist).

* The Québec Court of Appeal dismissed the appeal by the mother: see
  [1997] RDF 215.

In the Supreme Court of Canada, the Court stated that "we are not
satisfied that the best interest of the child has been compromised by the
practices of the custodial parent." In the circumstances, the Court allowed
the appeal to the extent of "removing the restrictions imposed upon the

appellant as regards the activities which she is entitled to do with or in the presence of her child." Reflect again on *Libbus v Libbus*, discussed earlier. To what extent do courts interpret the best interests principle differently in relation to claims for custody and in relation to issues about access parents' activities?

Consider this situation:

> The father and mother were both Orthodox Jews. Following their separation, the father had begun to live with a non-Jewish woman, who had only recently converted to the Jewish faith. There were two children, and their mother was concerned that the father and his new wife might depart from the restrictions applicable to an Orthodox Jew (such as travel by automobile on the Sabbath). How should this issue be resolved?

In *Fruitman v Fruitman* (1998), 37 RFL (4th) 416 (Ont Gen Div), the court held that no restrictions should be ordered in this case with respect to the religious upbringing of the children. In *Heath v Zdep* (2000), 101 ACWS (3d) 544 (Ont Ct J) at para 31, it was noted that "the best interests of a child usually means that a child's relationship with the other parent is more important than exclusive conformity with the religious practices of one parent." In *Seed v Desai*, 2014 ONSC 3329 at para 50, a Roman Catholic mother was free to serve pork to her children over the objections of their Muslim father, and he was allowed to let the children fast with him.

Additional Resources

Claire Archbold, "Family Law-Making and Human Rights in the United Kingdom" in Mavis Maclean, ed, *Making Law for Families* (Oxford and Portland, OR: Hart Publishing, 2000) 185.

Nicholas Bala, "Developments in Family Law: The 1993–1994 Term" (1995) 6 SCLR (2d) 453.

J Mucci, "The Effect of Religious Disputes in Child Custody Disputes" (1986) 5 Can J Fam L 353.

Shauna Van Praagh, "Religion, Custody, and a Child's Identity" (1997) 35:2 Osgoode Hall LJ 309.

"BEST INTERESTS" AND THE RELOCATION OF CUSTODIAL PARENTS

The legal background regarding relocation

In 1996, the Supreme Court of Canada considered *Gordon v Goertz*, [1996] 2 SCR 27, a case in which an access father wished to prevent or restrict the relocation of a custodial mother and their child from Saskatchewan to Australia. In considering this issue, the Supreme Court was required to review two decisions of the Ontario Court of Appeal, which had adopted different approaches to this issue.

Carter v Brooks

In *Carter v Brooks* (1990), 2 OR (3d) 321 (CA), the Ontario Court of Appeal became the first appellate court in Canada to decisively rule that the custodial parent did not have an inherent "right to move."

In *Carter*, the parties had separated shortly after their son's birth, and the child had remained with the mother with the father's approval. Some years later, the mother informed the father that she planned to move from Ontario to British Columbia with her new partner. The father opposed the move and applied to the court for joint custody and an order restraining the mother from removing the child from his current geographic jurisdiction.

The trial judge awarded custody to the mother, but held that it was in the child's best interests to live in close proximity to the father and thus restrained the mother from removing the child. This decision was upheld on appeal.

Speaking for the court, Morden JA indicated that the sole matter to be considered was the best interests of the child. Morden JA stated that while he was inclined to the view that a "reasonable measure of respect" should be paid to the custodial parent's interests, he was not prepared to formulate a steadfast rule that placed the onus on the non-custodial parent to prove that the move was not in the child's best interests. Instead, he held that each parent bore an "evidential burden" to demonstrate to the court what was in the child's best interests.

In *Carter*, the court held that the mother had not demonstrated that the child's best interests were better served by the move.

MacGyver v Richards

Five years later, a different panel of appellate judges took a different approach. In *MacGyver v Richards* (1995), 22 OR (3d) 481 (CA), Abella JA, writing for the majority of the court, held that courts *must* have deference to the custodial parent's decision to move in all but the most exceptional cases.

Here, the mother wished to move with the parties' child to Washington State for four years while her new fiancé, a master corporal in the armed forces, served a four-year service commitment there. The father opposed the move and applied for joint custody and an order preventing the child's relocation.

At trial, the mother was awarded custody but with the stipulation that the child remain in North Bay, Ontario. On appeal, the custody order was upheld but the restriction was lifted, so that the mother was free to move with the child.

In dismissing the father's appeal from this decision, Abella JA departed from the court's earlier decision in *Carter v Brooks* in several ways.

Significantly, Abella JA noted that the child's relationship with the custodial parent was generally more important to the child than his or her relationship with the non-custodial parent, and that courts should "forcefully acknowledge" that the child's best interests and the custodial parent's interests are "inextricably tied" together.

Abella JA also stated that courts had wrongly been passing judgment on the "necessity" of the custodial parent's move, and that so long as the parent was acting "responsibly," the reason for the move should not be further questioned.

In *MacGyver*, no evidence was presented that the mother was maliciously trying to keep the child from the father and, because the mother was acting responsibly, Abella JA ruled that impairment of the father's relationship with the child was not a sufficient reason to prevent the move. In this case, the Court also noted that there were no restrictions on a move by an access parent, even if the access parent decided to move without consideration of a child's best interests.

Relocation and the Supreme Court of Canada: The principles

The differing approaches in *Carter v Brooks* and in *MacGyver v Richards* created some uncertainty about when a custodial parent's decision to relocate would be successfully opposed by a parent with access. This issue was the subject of an appeal to the Supreme Court of Canada in *Gordon v Goertz* in 1996.

Gordon v Goertz

In 1996, the Supreme Court of Canada considered the relocation issue in *Gordon v Goertz*, [1996] 2 SCR 27, when a custodial mother wanted to relocate to Australia to pursue educational goals, while the child's father (who had been granted access) remained in western Canada.

Writing for the majority, McLachlin J held that it was in the best interest of the child to move to Australia with her mother, but the Supreme Court removed a lower court requirement that the father's access be exercised only in Australia, thus permitting the father to exercise access in Canada as well. For lower court decisions, see (1993), 111 Sask R 1 (Unif Fam Ct) and (1995), 128 Sask R 156 (CA).

In its ruling in *Gordon v Goertz*, the Supreme Court of Canada provided guidelines concerning the principles applicable to relocation by custodial parents in circumstances where such relocation may affect the access parent's contact with the child.

- **Establishing a "material" change**

  Essentially, the Supreme Court held that a parent who applies to the court to change a custody or access order under the *Divorce Act* must first establish a material change in circumstances affecting the child (pursuant to section 17). Only when this threshold is met should the judge embark on a fresh inquiry into the best interests of the child, having regard to all of the relevant circumstances of the case.

- **Determining a child's "best interests"**
The Court also decided that the focus of the inquiry must be the child's interests and not the interests or rights of the parents involved. McLachlin J rejected the approach of Abella JA in *MacGyver*, and instead adopted the approach taken by Morden JA in *Carter*. According to the Court, while the custodial parent's views are entitled to "great respect," the examination of both the initial ruling and any new evidence cannot begin with a presumption in favour of the custodial parent. Instead, both parents bear an evidentiary burden in establishing the child's best interests. In addition, Justice McLachlin noted that the maximum contact principle in sections 16(10) and 17(9) of the *Divorce Act* is not absolute and is subject always to the child's best interests.

- **Defining "best interests" in relocation cases**
McLachlin J set out (at para 49) the Court's views with respect to relocation applications:
  - The parent applying for a change in a custody or access order must meet the threshold requirement of a material change in circumstances;
  - If this threshold is met, a judge must embark on a fresh inquiry with respect to a child's best interests, having regard to all the circumstances of the child's needs and each parent's ability to meet them;
  - The inquiry is based on the findings of the judge who made the initial order and evidence of new circumstances;
  - There is no presumption in favour of the custodial parent, although this parent's views are entitled to great respect;
  - Each case turns on its own circumstances and the focus is on the best interests in the particular circumstances of each case;
  - The focus is on the child's best interests, and not the interests and rights of parents;

  Thus, in assessing the application a judge should consider, *inter alia*:
  - (a) the existing custody relationship and relationship between the child and custodial parent;
  - (b) the existing access arrangement and the relationship between the child and the access parent;
  - (c) the desirability of maximizing contact between the child and both parents;
  - (d) the views of the child;
  - (e) the custodial parent's reason for moving *only* in the exceptional case where it is relevant to that parent's ability to meet the child's needs;
  - (f) disruption to the child of a change in custody;
  - (g) disruption to the child consequent on removal from family, schools and community....

Applying the Test in *Gordon v Goertz*

Applying the test to the facts in *Gordon v Goertz*, the court found that the move to Australia amounted to a material change in circumstances as contemplated by section 17 of the *Divorce Act*.

The court stated that the mother's proposed move to Australia would seriously curtail the frequent and meaningful contact that the father enjoyed with his daughter; and, as the terms of the prior order were premised on the child remaining within a reasonable distance of the father, the move would breach a previous order.

However, the court held that although the trial judge failed to give sufficient weight to these factors, when all the factors were now considered together, the judge was correct in continuing custody with the mother despite the mother's intended move.

At the same time, the court found that there was nothing to justify the lower court's order restricting Goertz's access to be exercised only in Australia, and instead ordered that the access order be varied to allow access to be exercised in Canada also.

Concurring Reasons: "Best Interests" in Relation to the Custodial Parent

Although agreeing with the majority justices' result, L'Heureux-Dubé J disagreed with the court's stance on the rights of a custodial parent.

In her opinion, any restriction on the rights of custodial parents should be the exception, not the rule, and should not be inferred from generous or specified access provisions. Instead, specific stipulations must have been included in the court's initial order.

According to L'Heureux-Dubé J, an assessment of the whole situation is warranted only where the alleged change is of such a nature or magnitude as to make the original order irrelevant or no longer appropriate. In this situation, the non-custodial parent should bear the onus of showing that the proposed change of residence is not in the child's best interests and that the custody should be varied or that the child should remain in his or her current jurisdiction.

In this context, L'Heureux-Dubé J argued that only where there is an agreement or court order that restricts changing the child's residence should the onus shift to the custodial parent to establish that the decision to relocate is not made to undermine access and that he or she is willing to restructure access. She went on to note that the proposed change of residence by a custodial parent will not normally justify a variation in custody. Indeed, a variation of custody should be considered only where the non-custodial parent demonstrates that the best interests of the child will be detrimentally affected by the move, *and* that the quality of the non-custodial parent's relationship with the child is of such importance to the child's best interests that prohibiting the change in residence will not cause detriment to the child that is comparable to or greater than that caused by an order to vary custody.

Notes and Questions

Relocation principles and mobility rates among Canadian families

The Supreme Court's decision in *Gordon v Goertz* identified an approach to relocation applications that is based on considerable judicial discretion. To what extent is such an approach useful in a context in which relocation for Canadian families is often necessary?

According to statistics, for example, more than 50 percent of Canadians aged between 25 and 39 changed their place of residence between 2001 and 2006, and more than one-third of Canadians between the ages of 40 and 49 did so. Moreover, it seems that

> ... mobility is higher among those who are divorced, separated or widowed compared to those who are married or in common-law relationships.... The probability of migrating is closely associated with the events taking place in the lives of individuals. People move to go to school, to look for better jobs, to establish new relationships or to leave old ones, to provide better opportunities for children, to move closer to family, and for a host of other reasons.... (*Families Count* at 24–25).

Consider how these rates of mobility in Canada may require determinations about best interests for children in relocation applications in accordance with the majority's views in *Gordon v Goertz*. To what extent are the majority's views consistent with these rates of mobility?

Problems of judicial discretion in relocation decisions

As a number of critiques have suggested, the views expressed by the Supreme Court in *Gordon v Goertz* require a high degree of discretionary decision making by judges. To what extent do the factors identified by the Court assist in defining such an exercise of discretion, particularly since the Court included these factors *inter alia*? In assessing the Court's views, consider Boyd's critique that *Gordon v Goertz* "reasserted a wide power of judicial decision making in the custody realm, despite the abundant evidence that judicial discretion often leads to contradictory and sometimes highly problematic results because of the indeterminacy of the best interests test" (Boyd at 152). See also Nicholas Bala & Andrea Wheeler, "More Clarity Needed for Relocation Cases", *The Lawyers Weekly* (17 February 2012) 10, online: <http://www.lawyersweekly.ca>.

Commenting on research undertaken by Rollie Thompson on cases concerning relocation decided after *Gordon v Goertz*, Boyd also noted the impact of the Supreme Court's decision:

> Some commentators have pointed out that the practical effect of the Supreme Court of Canada's ruling is unclear.... It may well be that deference to some custodial parents will occur, at least where they appear to have carried out their responsibilities properly.... A few judges have also been able to appreciate that in some instances, such as where a father has abused a mother, frequent contact between father and child is less of a priority. Thompson found that some judges approved moves in cases

where the emotional and financial well-being of the caregiver mother would be enhanced in the new location.... In practice, it appears that in approximately 60 per cent of cases decided since *Goertz*, the move is permitted, returning to the situation after the indeterminate decision in *Carter v. Brooks* and before the deference decision in *MacGyver v. Richards*. However, the moving parent is often required to pick up a proportion of the increased costs of access expenses, either sharing them equally or paying them all; alternatively, the quantum of child or spousal support paid to the custodial parent may be reduced.... As well, moves are more likely to be denied in cases involving some form of shared custody.... Moreover, it seems likely that custodial mothers who are able to obtain good legal advice and representation and who propose a clear plan for contact between children and fathers are more likely to be permitted to move....

If "reasonable" custodial parents are more likely to be permitted to relocate, a potential problem still arises in the ways that reasonableness and responsibility will be interpreted....

Cases decided since *Gordon v. Goertz* also suggest that economic issues and class may influence judicial decision-making. The parties in *Gordon v. Goertz* had sufficient funds to enable contact between father and child despite the considerable geographical distance. The harder question arises when lack of economic resources will inhibit frequent contact with a non-custodial parent.... Also worrisome is that many cases where relocation is disputed likely never make their way to court, particularly if finances are limited. (Boyd at 154–155)

See also DA Rollie Thompson, "Relocation and Relitigation: After *Gordon v. Goertz*" (1999) 16:3 Can Fam LQ 461; and Thompson, "An Addendum: Twenty Months Later" in Harold Niman & Gerald P Sadvari, eds, *Special Lectures of the Law Society of Upper Canada 2000 — Family Law: "Best Interests of the Child"* (Toronto: Law Society of Upper Canada, 2001) at 352.

Do you agree with this assessment? Why or why not?

The impact of *Gordon v Goertz* in Ontario: *Woodhouse* and *Luckhurst*

As noted in Boyd's comment, cases that have applied the *Gordon v Goertz* factors reveal a range of outcomes in different circumstances. Consider, for example, two decisions of the Ontario Court of Appeal, released shortly after the Supreme Court's decision in 1996:

• In *Woodhouse v Woodhouse* (1996), 29 OR (3d) 417, the Ontario Court of Appeal refused to allow the mother to relocate to her new husband's native Scotland with the parties' children. At trial, the court accepted an independent assessor's findings that while the best interests of the mother and her new husband would be to live in Scotland, it was not in the children's best interests because the move would make it impossible for the children to maintain a meaningful relationship with their father. Although the mother proposed a schedule of five yearly visits, including a month in the summer, in Canada, the court held that the scheme did not provide for reasonable, frequent access and could only be implemented at great financial expense to the father.

In applying the test in *Gordon v Goertz*, the Court of Appeal found that the trial judge's findings represented no error to justify overturning the lower court's decision, and in keeping with the Supreme Court's decision, the custodial parent's interests were not given an automatic preference. The appeal court concluded that the proposed move represented a material change in circumstance, but that there was no indication that the children's best interests would be better served by moving to Scotland rather than staying in Ontario. In considering the facts of the case, the court also examined the financial and economic results of the family moving to Scotland versus staying in Ontario, and concluded that the family income would be about the same regardless of residence. With respect to the effect of the move on the children, the court found that to move the children would be more disruptive for them than to remain in Ontario. In coming to its decision, the court also expressed concern about whether the mother would comply with an Ontario order for access, given her previous decision to stay in Scotland with the children beyond an agreed period.

Osbourne JA, dissenting, took the view that the trial judge focused too heavily on the assessor's report and had proceeded on a general assumption that there was a positive correlation between the frequency of access and the best interests of the children in all cases. By doing so, the best interests of the children in *this* case were not fully considered.

The Supreme Court of Canada, L'Heureux-Dubé J dissenting, refused leave to appeal: see (1997), 209 NR 80 (SCC).

Compare the result in *Woodhouse* with the following case:

• In *Luckhurst v Luckhurst* (1996), 20 RFL (4th) 373, which was released concurrently with *Woodhouse*, the Ontario Court of Appeal again applied *Gordon v Goertz*. However, in *Luckhurst*, the Court of Appeal upheld the trial judge's decision allowing the mother to move with the children.

Upon the parties' separation they had agreed that they would share joint custody of their two children although the children's primary residence was with their mother. The mother entered into a new relationship and began cohabiting with her new partner. They later had a child together. The new partner, unable to obtain secure employment in London, found a job in Cobourg, and the mother applied for an order allowing her to move with her children to Cobourg. In her application for relocation, she stated that she was willing to drive the children to a halfway point in order to assist the father's access. In response, the father brought a cross application for custody.

The Court of Appeal upheld the trial judge's decision to award custody to the mother without a limitation on the children's residence. In reaching its decision, the court followed the decision in *Gordon v Goertz*, noting that the children would still be able to see their father regularly and, while access would be exercised at some inconvenience to the father, the mother was willing to make reasonable arrangements to assist in the preservation of the quality of the relationship between the father and the children.

In the context of these decisions, do you agree with the assessment of Thompson and Boyd with respect to the impact of *Gordon v Goertz*? To what extent is there a need for legislative reform? Consider this suggestion:

> Relocation disputes are governed by the best interests of the child test. Some have argued in favour of adopting a presumption that the custodial parent's relocation plans are in the best interests of the child. Any such presumption would undermine the best interests of the child standard and should not be adopted. In determining the best interests of the child, however, careful attention should be given to the potential negative effect on the child should the custodial parent be restricted from relocating. The relative importance of maintaining frequent and continuing contact with both parents should also not be overemphasized in relocation disputes. Social science evidence indicates that other factors — specifically, a well-functioning custodial parent and avoidance of parental conflict — are also linked with positive outcomes for children. There is no evidence to support giving priority to maintaining frequent and continuing contact with both parents in cases of conflict.... (Martha Bailey & Michelle Giroux, *Relocation of Custodial Parents* (Ottawa: Status of Women Canada, 1998) at iii)

The continuing challenge of *Gordon v Goertz*: *Lickfold v Robichaud*

In assessing the test for relocation identified by the Supreme Court, consider this situation:

> A man and woman met in New Brunswick and began to cohabit there. Eventually, after their son was born, the man was transferred and the family moved to Kemptville Ontario. The woman worked as a waitress in Kemptville and the couple organized their work so that they could care for the child together. However, their relationship deteriorated, and the woman (who was Acadienne) left the family home to return to New Brunswick with her son.
>
> After the father obtained an interim order for custody of the child in Ontario (see *CLRA*, s 22), the mother received legal advice to return with the child to Ontario, and she did so. The couple then agreed to care for the child jointly, but this arrangement did not work out satisfactorily.
>
> Thus, in a court action, each party applied for sole custody, and the father also applied for joint custody. The mother applied for permission to relocate to New Brunswick, and the father opposed this application.

How should this case be resolved?

In *Lickfold v Robichaud*, [2008] OJ No 4117 (Sup Ct), the court reviewed the factors for determining "best interests" in *CLRA*, s 24, as well as evidence submitted by the Office of the Children's Lawyer (OCL) who had interviewed the child. The court concluded that it was in the best interests of the child for him to remain in the joint care of his parents, on an alternating week basis, but also addressed the need to avoid parental conflict in these care arrangements. According to the court, it was "certainly worth a try" to realize the best parenting arrangement for their son.

In relation to the relocation application by the mother, the court reiterated the guidelines set out in *Gordon v Goertz*. Although the court noted that the mother had *bona fide* reasons for wanting to move to Tracadie in New Brunswick, any such move would make the parenting arrangement impossible. In addition, the court concluded that the evidence indicated that any substantial separation from his father would be devastating for the child. As a result, the court set out a detailed arrangement for parenting of the child (a "parallel parenting" arrangement, discussed later in this chapter).

To what extent does *Lickfold v Robichaud* reflect the discretionary nature of decision making pursuant to *Gordon v Goertz*? For other examples of rejection of the application to relocate, see *Andrade v Kennelly*, 2007 ONCA 898; and *Young v Young* (2003), 34 RFL (5th) 214 (Ont CA).

The emergence of "virtual" access

Some recent cases in Canada, and in other jurisdictions (including the United States and Australia), have ordered "virtual" access arrangements in relation to relocation applications. For example, in *FJN v JLN* (2004), 9 RFL (6th) 446 (Ont Sup Ct), the court permitted the custodial mother to move to California. However, the court ordered that, in addition to physical visitation by the access father every fourth month, the father was entitled to exercise access through unlimited "telephone, email, webcam and postal communication" at all reasonable hours. The mother was ordered to purchase the necessary equipment and supply it to the father. See also Susan Pigg, "Virtual Visits amid Real Divorces: More Courts allowing Parents to sustain Relationships Online", *Toronto Star* (13 April 2009) A4.

For some assessments of these new developments in relocation decisions, see Andrew Schepard, "Virtual Visitation: Computer Technology Meets Child Custody Law" (2002) 228 NYLJ 3; Sarah Gottfried, "Virtual Visitation: The Wave of the Future in Communication between Children and Non-Custodial Parents in Relocation Cases" (2002–2003) 36 Fam LQ 475; Jason LaMarca, "Virtually Possible: Using the Internet to Facilitate Custody and Parenting Beyond Relocation" (2012) 38 Rutgers Computer & Tech LJ 146; Christine E Doucet, "'See You on Skype!': Relocation, Access, and Virtual Parenting in the Digital Age" (2011) 27:2 Can J Fam L 297; and David Welsh, "Virtual Parents: How Virtual Visitation Legislation is Shaping the Future of Custody Law" (2008) 11 JL & Fam Stud 215.

Reconsidering *Gordon v Goertz*?

According to Thompson, the Supreme Court has shown little interest in reconsidering its decision in *Gordon v Goertz*, and has denied leave to appeal in a number of cases. For example, see *Elliott v Elliott*, 2009 ONCA 240; leave to appeal denied 2009 CarswellOnt 5629 (SCC).

Thus, the current situation with respect to legal principles about relocation of the custodial parent was described (pessimistically) a few years ago as

> ... a world of mobility without presumptions, without burdens, with a "fresh inquiry" into custody with each proposed move, with litigation and relitigation, and with the lack of consistency or predictability that comes with a pure "best interests" test.... One of the most unfortunate effects of *Gordon v. Goertz* has been its demolition of any law at all in this field, to the point that trial and appeal judges are unprepared to develop any working principles or generalizations of any kind.... In Canada, there is little "law" of relocation left. (DA Rollie Thompson, "Movin' On: Parental Relocation in Canada" (2004) 42:3 Fam Ct Rev 398 at 407)

In a recent study of relocation decisions from 2001 to 2011, Nicholas Bala and Andrea Wheeler noted that the number of such decisions increased each year, but that the "success rate" for these applications remained relatively steady at 50 percent. Although 90 percent of the applicants were mothers, the "success rate" for mothers and fathers was almost the same (50 percent). In one-third of cases, the relocating parent cited improved economic prospects, while just under one-third involved a new intimate relationship for the mother. In one-fifth of the cases, the reason for the move related to enhancing the presence of familial support. Significantly, the age of the child and the distance of the move were not statistically significant factors in relation to the outcome of cases. However, parents with sole custody were permitted to move in 64 percent of the cases, compared to 50 percent of cases involving joint legal custody; and moves were permitted in only 30 percent of cases involving joint physical custody. Allegations of violence also affected these decisions, with moves allowed in 81 percent of cases where the allegations were substantiated. Finally, the wishes of children were mentioned in only one-quarter of cases. See Nicholas Bala & Andrea Wheeler, "Use of Guidelines could reduce Legal Costs", *The Lawyers Weekly* (17 February 2012) 10–11.

In the context of these findings, the authors proposed "Relocation Advisory Guidelines," creating a presumption of relocation if

- the parent seeking relocation has legal or *de facto* sole custody;
- the parent opposing relocation has perpetrated acts of familial abuse; or
- the child wishes to move.

They also suggested a presumption against relocation if

- there is shared physical custody;
- the parent seeking relocation has made unfounded allegations of abuse;
- the child does not wish to move; or
- the parent seeking relocation has unilaterally moved the child.

To what extent would these proposed reforms assist in limiting legal costs? Interestingly, British Columbia's new *Family Law Act*, SBC 2011, c 25 (in force 2013), includes express provisions regarding relocation (see Part 4, Division 6), although they do not include presumptions. These provisions continue to use the "best interests of the child" principle, but they also provide that the relocating parent must satisfy the court that the proposed relocation is made "in good faith." Among other factors, good faith includes the reasons for the move, as well as its potential to enhance the life of the child. In the context of these reforms, is there a need to reconsider legal principles about relocation?

Two cases applying B.C.'s new law are *MM v CJ*, 2014 BCSC 6, which allowed the move, and *LS v RS*, 2014 BCSC 1213, which denied the mother's attempt to move from British Columbia to Kent, England. While ss 61–69 of the B.C. *FLA* are quite comprehensive, a parent who has thus far been able to successfully claim that paramountcy requires the application of the relocation test of the federal *Divorce Act*.

Some commentators have also suggested a need to reconceptualize ideas about caregiving, particularly on the part of the parent with primary responsibility. For example, Elizabeth Hughes has argued that "time" is not the fundamental factor for consideration, but rather the assumption of responsibility for overseeing a child's care and development:

> The responsibility function of primary parenting is even more susceptible to being overlooked than the physical care function and in that primary caregiving suffers from a kind of "double invisibility." This tendency results partly from the relatively intangible and abstract nature of the responsibility aspect of primary care, which makes it difficult to identify and to measure from both a conceptual and an evidentiary perspective. In addition, caregiving functions related to decision-making or parental authority have conventionally been associated with fathers. It is clear that the standard by which primary caregiving has traditionally been defined is simply no longer adequate, and that a new understanding of what constitutes primary caregiving is essential in child custody law. (Elizabeth Hughes, "Mother's Vicarious Hand: Primary Caregiving Reconceived as Relationship and Responsibility" (2002) 20 Can Fam LQ 467)

Taking account of such comments, how might issues about "best interests" and relocation be reformulated by reform legislation or reconsideration by the Supreme Court?

Additional Resources

Martha Bailey & Michelle Giroux, *Relocation of Custodial Children* (Ottawa: Status of Women Canada, 1998).

Nicholas Bala & Joanna Harris, "Parental Relocation: Applying the Best Interests of the Child Test in Ontario" (2006) 22 Can J Fam L 127.

Susan B Boyd, "Child Custody, Relocation, and the Post-Divorce Family Unit: *Gordon v. Goertz* at the Supreme Court of Canada" (1997) 9:2 CJWL 447.

Carol Bruch & Janet Bowermaster, "The Relocation of Children and Custodial Parents: Public Policy, Past and Present" (1996) 30 Fam LQ 245.

Jonathan Cohen & Nikki Gershbain, "For the Sake of the Fathers? Child Custody Reform and the Perils of Maximum Contact" (2001) 19 Can Fam LQ 121.

Berend Hovius, "Mobility Issues in Custody and Access Cases" in James McLeod, ed, *Child Custody Law and Practice* (Toronto: Carswell looseleaf) chapter 7.

Patrick Parkinson & Judy Cashmore, "When Mothers Stay: Adjusting to Loss after Relocation Disputes" (2013) 47 Fam LQ 65.

DA Rollie Thompson, "Where is B.C. Law Going? The New Mobility" (2011) 30 Can Fam LQ 235.

DA Rollie Thompson, "Ten Years after *Gordon*: No Law, Nowhere" (2007) 35 RFL (6th) 307.

Judith Wallerstein & Tony Tanke, "Psychological and Legal Considerations in the Relocation of Children Following Divorce" (1996) 30:2 Fam LQ 305.

"BEST INTERESTS" IN RELATION TO ABDUCTION, ABUSE, AND ALIENATION: THE DARK SIDE

Abduction

Abduction and the Hague *Convention*

Parental mobility following separation may create legal issues with respect to the jurisdiction to make orders about custody and access, and in relation to the enforcement of such orders. The *Convention on the Civil Aspects of International Child Abduction* attempts to provide a systematic procedure for dealing with children when their parents separate and one parent (without judicial authorization) removes (abducts) them from their ordinary jurisdiction of residence.

In Ontario, the *Convention* is attached as a schedule to the *Children's Law Reform Act*, and its provisions are reflected in sections 22 and 23 of the statute. Perhaps because of increasing rates of parental mobility post-separation, there have been a number of cases concerning the *Convention* in relation to child abduction in appellate courts:

• In *Thomson v Thomson*, [1994] 3 SCR 551, the Supreme Court of Canada reviewed a complex matter of custody pursuant to the *Convention* and ordered that the mother return the child (from her home in Manitoba) to Scotland, where the father had (before the child's removal to Manitoba) obtained a custody order. See also Vaughan Black & Christopher Jones, "Case Comment on *Thomson v. Thomson*" (1994–95) 9 Can Fam LQ 321.

• In *Kinnersley-Turner v Kinnersley-Turner* (1997), 24 RFL (4th) 252 (Ont CA), the court dismissed the mother's appeal from the trial decision ordering her to return her child to England. Following the mother's and father's divorce, the mother was granted custody and the father was awarded access. The custody order permitted the mother to move to Canada, but it contained an undertaking by the mother to return the child to England if called upon to do so. The mother and child lived off and on between Canada and England for a few years, but during a time in England, the father decided that the mother was unfit and applied for custody. Without notice to the father or to the court, the mother returned to Canada, with the child, stating to her solicitor that she did not wish the father to have further access to the child. Upon the father's application to have the child returned, pursuant to the Hague *Convention*, the English court so ordered. The Ontario court agreed that the mother, pursuant to the *Convention*, was obliged to return the child to England. (See also *Rechsteiner v Kendall* (1999), 1 RFL (5th) 101 (Ont CA); *Finizio v Scoppio-Finizio* (1999), 46 OR (3d) 226 (CA); *Jackson v Graczyk*, 2007 ONCA 388; and *Ellis v Wentzell-Ellis*, 2010 ONCA 347.)

The *Convention* in Relation to Refugee Status: I(AMR) v R(KE)

In *I(AMR) v R(KE)*, 2011 ONCA 417, the Ontario Court of Appeal issued its detailed reasons for allowing an appeal concerning a teenaged girl who had obtained refugee status in Canada, and who had then been returned to her mother's custody in Mexico pursuant to the mother's Hague *Convention* application, even though the girl feared that her mother would further abuse her. (In an earlier decision (see 2011 ONCA 302), the court had allowed the appeal, set aside the order pursuant to the Hague *Convention*, and ordered a new hearing in which the girl, to be returned to Ontario, would be able to participate.)

According to the Court of Appeal's reasons, the judge hearing the mother's application pursuant to the Hague *Convention* had failed to address its exceptions relating to the return of a child. In particular, the court held that the girl's rights pursuant to section 7 of the *Charter* were engaged in circumstances where she would face a risk of persecution if she were returned to her mother in Mexico, so that the judge was required to conduct a risk assessment prior to ordering her return pursuant to the *Convention*. Moreover, because the girl had not received notice of the mother's application, and she had no legal representation and no opportunity to explain her own views, the application hearing infringed her section 7 rights. In the circumstances, the court ordered a new hearing to consider the mother's application pursuant to the Hague *Convention*.

In this case, the court considered arguments about the relationship between section 115 of the *Immigration and Refugee Protection Act* and section 46 of the *Children's Law Reform Act*. In an examination of these arguments, the court held that there was no conflict between these provisions, and that the doctrine of paramountcy was not invoked, because the Hague *Convention* (article 13(b)) permits a court to refuse an application for the return of a child if there is risk that such return would expose a child to physical or psychological harm:

[74] ... [I]n our opinion, when a child has been recognized as a Convention refugee by the [Immigration and Refugee Board], a rebuttable presumption arises that there is a risk of persecution on return of the child to his or her country of habitual residence. A risk of "persecution" in the immigration context clearly implicates the type of harm contemplated by art. 13(b) of the Hague Convention.

[75] This case is a powerful illustration of this point. A mere five months before the hearing of the Hague application, the IRB had concluded that the child was at sufficient risk of persecution, due to harm at the hands of her mother, to warrant recognition of refugee status. In these circumstances, while the IRB ruling granting refugee status to the child was not dispositive of whether the grave risk of harm exception to return under art. 13(b) of the Hague Convention was established, it nonetheless gave rise to a rebuttable presumption that this exception was engaged....

[78] Accordingly, in our view, a determination of refugee status must be treated by a Hague application judge as giving rise to a rebuttable presumption of a risk of harm when determining whether to grant an order of return in respect of a refugee child.... [The court held that this principle was also supported by the *Convention on the Rights of the Child*.]

In addition, the court distinguished *JH v FA*, discussed in Chapter One, because that case held that "family law court orders are not meant to frustrate the deportation of persons ordered removed under immigration legislation" (para 81). Do you agree that these two cases are substantially different?

I(AMR) v R(KE) received a good deal of attention from the media. For example, see Nicholas Keung, "Refugee's Future in Hands of Court", *Toronto Star* (14 April 2011) GT3; Oakland Ross, "Deported teen makes daring return from Mexico; Girl, 14, was wrongly expelled from Canada", *Toronto Star* (5 May 2011).

Additional Resources

Martha Bailey, "The Right of a Non-Custodial Parent to an Order for Return of a Child Under the Hague Convention" (1996) 13 Can J Fam L 287.

Vaughan Black, "Statutory Confusion in International Child Custody Disputes" (1992–93) 10 Can Fam LQ 279.

Robyn Diamond, "Canadian Judicial Initiatives respecting the Handling of Hague Convention Cases" (2008) 50 RFL (6th) 275.

Andrea Himel, "Parents Stealing Kids: Part I — A Canadian Perspective on the Legal and Social Problem of Child Abduction" (2000) 18 Can Fam LQ 225.

Jason Nitz, "Splitting the Baby Internationally: Evaluating the Least Restrictive Conundrum When Protecting Children from International Parental Abduction" (2013) 16:2 Scholar: St Mary's Law Review on Race and Social Justice 417.

Linda J Silberman, "The Hague Convention on Child Abduction and Unilateral Relocations by Custodial Parents: A Perspective from the United States and Europe — Abbott, Neulinger, Zarraga" (2011) 63:4 Okla L Rev 733.

Abuse

Best Interests and Allegations of Child Abuse

Allegations of child abuse, in the context of disputes about custody and access, present difficult issues of proof and judgment for courts. Recall the recent amendments (ss 24(4) and 24(5)) of the *Children's Law Reform Act* concerning "best interests" and violence/abuse. In egregious cases, courts may issue contempt orders against parents who defy orders relating to custody and access, and in some cases, parents may be imprisoned. Such problems sometimes occur in a context in which one parent believes that abuse is occurring but does not have sufficient proof for a court proceeding. However, some experts also believe that claims of abuse are sometimes fabricated.

For example, in 1992, the Ontario Court of Appeal dismissed an appeal (with one dissent) by a father from a trial decision cancelling access to the father, even though the court also found that the mother had not proved her allegations of sex abuse in relation to their daughter. In part, the majority (Abella and Tarnopolsky JJA) reached their conclusion on the ground that there should be a variation of an order only where there has been a material change in circumstances. They concluded that

> ... in the absence of any benefit to the child from continued contact with the father, and based on solid evidence of years of harassment by the father, the judge made no error in terminating the access.... The father's biological relationship should not be allowed to override the child's welfare. (*M(BP) v M(BLDE)* (1992), 42 RFL (3d) 349 (Ont CA); leave to appeal to the SCC refused, (1993), 48 RFL (3d) 232 (SCC)).

In *Armstrong v Kahn* (1998), 33 RFL (4th) 438 (Ont Gen Div), the parties had joint custody of their one child. The child resided with his mother, and his father had unsupervised access to him. Shortly after this custody agreement was reached, the child began complaining that his father was abusing him. Specifically, he complained that his father called him "bad names" and hit him. The boy began to react violently whenever he was scheduled to see his father and his school performance deteriorated. The father had also threatened the mother's life in the child's presence and the child had begun to talk about his own death on a daily basis. The mother applied for sole custody with no access to the father and a restraining order. Both of the mother's requests were granted. The court found that the father physically, verbally, and emotionally abused the child, who was suffering from post-traumatic stress syndrome as a result of the abuse. The court found that the child's behaviour would further deteriorate if even supervised access was allowed to continue.

In *McMillan v McMillan* (1999), 47 RFL (4th) 173 (Ont Gen Div), the court reviewed the circumstances of a mother's ongoing actions interfering with the father's access to two children, aged 12 and 14. The mother had been found in contempt previously, and on this occasion, the court held that imprisonment for five days was appropriate. The mother was also ordered to pay costs of $2,000. The court stated (at 180):

> I am aware that there is a period of time immediately following the separation of spouses when emotions run high and otherwise sensible people are prone to act like vengeful lunatics. A court order deliberately breached during that delicate time frame may attract the compassion of the court. However, a court order which is wilfully, deliberately and repeatedly breached many years after such compassion can reasonably be expected to extend is an entirely different matter. Such is the situation facing this court. I also note that this case is not an instance where the breach of the court order was well motivated; neither is it an example of an isolated or non-continuing contempt.
>
> Our system of justice cannot and should not tolerate the deliberate disobedience or defiance of a court order. The protection of the administration of justice requires that such conduct be dealt with appropriately.

Best Interests and Allegations of Spousal Abuse

In addition to issues about child abuse, custody and access cases may be complicated by issues of spousal abuse:

> Where spousal violence has occurred or is occurring between the separating partners, custody and access issues become more complicated. Abusive partners sometimes use custody or access to children as a means of perpetuating abuse or prolonging control over a former spouse. As well, abused spouses might feel disempowered in their ability to contest the demands of their abusive partners. Some degree of understanding about the dynamics of abusive relationships must inform development and operation of law that will be applied in these circumstances.... Given the link between litigation over child custody/access and spousal abuse, the influence of child custody and access laws on spousal abuse must be considered.... The "best interests of the child" paradigm ... may not be the best for resolving child custody and access disputes where spousal abuse exists between the parents.... (Kathy L Grant, "Deserving of Further Attention: A Case Streaming Approach to Child Custody and Access in the Context of Spousal Violence" (2005) 22 Can J Fam L 57 at 59–60 and 66)

In cases in which a parent alleges spousal abuse, judicial inquiries often require examination of issues about credibility and context. For example, in *Brigante v Brigante* (1991), 32 RFL (3d) 299 (Ont Unif Fam Ct) and in *KAS v DWR*, [1995] OJ No 1711 (Prov Div), judges concluded that mothers had exaggerated incidents of abuse, and refused to terminate access by the children's fathers. Recall also the discussion of cases concerning best interests and (mis)conduct issues, earlier in this chapter.

In a study of spousal violence in the context of custody and access disputes, Bala et al identified both direct and indirect effects of spousal violence on children. Particularly in relation to indirect effects, they noted that

> [t]here is a growing body of research on the negative effects on children of observing or hearing one parent being abused by another. Children

who observe inter-parental abuse are often terrified by the experience, and may not understand it. In some cases witnessing even a single serious incident of abuse can produce post-traumatic stress disorder in children. Even if a child does not directly observe spousal abuse, living in a home where there is spousal abuse can have serious negative effects.... (Nicholas Bala et al, *Spousal Violence in Custody and Access Disputes: Recommendations for Reform* (Ottawa: Status of Women Canada, 1998) at 11–12)

As part of this study, the authors made recommendations for legislative and program reforms (see at 69–75).

Additional Resources

Nicholas Bala, "Abuse and Neglect Allegations in the Context of Parental Separation" in Nicholas Bala et al, eds, *Canadian Child Welfare Law: Children, Families and the State*, 2nd ed (Toronto: Thompson Educational Publishing, 2004) at 291.

Nicholas Bala, Peter Jaffe & Claire Crooks, "Spousal Violence and Child-Related Cases: Challenging Cases Requiring Differentiated Responses" (2009) 27 Can Fam LQ 1.

Joan S Meier, "Domestic Violence, Child Custody, and Child Protection: Understanding Judicial Resistance and Imagining the Solutions" (2002–2003) 11:2 Am UJ Gender Soc Pol'y & L 657.

Linda Neilson, "Assessing Mutual Partner-Abuse Claims in Child Custody and Access Cases" (2004) 42 Fam Ct Rev 411.

Nancy Ver Steegh, "Differentiating Types of Domestic Violence: Implications for Child Custody" (2006) William Mitchell College of Law, Legal Studies Research Paper Series, No. 41.

Nancy Ver Steegh, "Eight Reasons Why Attorneys Representing Parents in Child Protection Proceedings Should Use an Intimate Partner Violence Screening Protocol" (2014) 40:3 Wm Mitchell L Rev 1048.

Nancy Ver Steegh, Gabrielle Davis & Loretta Frederick, "Look Before You Leap: Court System Triage of Family Law Cases Involving Intimate Partner Violence" (2012) 95:3 Marq L Rev 955.

Alienation

Best Interests and Parental "Alienation"

The issue of "alienation" in the context of custody and access disputes is controversial and has become increasingly visible in some recent contested cases. In an assessment of alienation allegations in Canadian cases, a recent study suggested that

[a]lthough there are continuing controversies on some issues, there is now a growing body of research and psychological literature on alienation, and there is a degree of consensus in some areas. It is clear that in high-conflict separations, it is common for one or both parents to express anger and make negative comments to their children about their former partners. While many children are resistant to this parental conduct, it affects

them in a significant portion of cases. Although there is no reliable research on the incidence of alienation, studies suggest that for children experiencing high-conflict separations, 20% to 50% experience some degree of alienation from one parent, at least at some point in time, and for some children alienation persists for many years after separation. [Alienation may occur either directly or indirectly, and may be mild to severe. In addition, it is necessary to distinguish "realistic estrangement" from "pathological alienation".]

...

[I]n determining whether there is alienation in the particular case, Canadian courts analyze the facts and weigh the opinion of experts, especially court-appointed assessors. Reflecting the views of mental health researchers, the courts have generally tried to determine whether a child's refusal to have contact with a parent is justified or is due to inappropriate influences by an alienating parent. For legal purposes, deciding whether alienation has occurred is ultimately not a clinical diagnosis that a mental health professional makes, but a conclusion that a judge must make about a particular state of facts. In many cases, an assessment of the credibility of the parents is central to the decision.... (Nicholas Bala et al, "Alienated Children and Parental Separation: Legal Responses in Canada's Family Courts" (2007) 33 Queen's LJ 79 at 87, 101–102)

Consider these comments in relation to the following cases.

SGB v SJL

In *SGB v SJL*, 2010 ONSC 3717, the spouses had separated in 1998, when one son was 8 years old and the other only 4. Both children lived with their mother, but both eventually moved to live at the home of their father, and both then rejected their mother and refused to see her. The spouses engaged mediators, parent coordinators, lawyers and mental health professionals to assist them, but the sons continued to reject their mother.

There were numerous proceedings, including:

- An arbitrator who was hired to resolve the parenting issues found that the father had deliberately alienated the children against their mother. In this situation, the arbitrator ordered sole custody to the mother and denied access to the father. The arbitrator also permitted the mother to require the children to participate in a therapeutic intervention concerned with alienated parent–child relationships.

- The father successfully appealed the arbitrator's decision. The court held that the finding of deliberate alienation was appropriate, but that there were errors of law in relation to the remedy awarded. In particular, the court expressed concern about the "extremity" of the remedy of change in custody, coupled with participation in the therapeutic workshop. However, the appeal judge held that she did not have sufficient information in the record to determine what was in the best interests of the younger son (the older son had by then turned 18). Thus, she ordered a trial to hear the issue of disposition on the basis of the arbitrator's findings of fact.

- Both spouses sought leave to appeal this order, but leave was denied. The spouses agreed to a further custody and access assessment, which was completed. However, since the father disagreed with the assessor's recommendations, a trial was necessary, and it was conducted to determine custody of the younger son. As the younger son was then 16, he was regarded as a "mature minor," but the court held that he was still a "child of the marriage" pursuant to the *Divorce Act*, and thus the court could determine custody in his best interests.

In assessing the order to participate in the workshop to deal with parental alienation, the court reviewed the evidence regarding Dr. Richard Warshak and his alienation workshop, as well as other expert evidence about parental alienation. In relation to the appropriate remedy, the court then stated:

> [64] First, doing nothing and simply hoping alienated parent and child will reconnect at some time in the future does not work. What this means is that leaving things as they are and letting JB decide cannot be in his best interests. As all agree, it is in JB's interests to have a relationship with his mother.
>
> [65] Second, any remedy must include removing JB from his father and those in his sphere. All the psychiatrists agree that in cases of severe irrational alienation, the alienated child must be removed from the favoured parent for a time.
>
> [66] Third, for intensive therapy to work on its own, both parents must participate in the process. Father was quite clear that he would not do so....
>
> [67] This leaves only the Workshop, coupled with a change in custody as the only potential remedy with any chance of success in this difficult case. I recognize the Workshop does not come with any guarantees. I know there are some who see it an untested therapy. Unquestionably, further empirical research into its efficacy would help. That said, on the basis of the evidence before me, the other potential remedies provide even less of a chance for JB. Of course, none of them is guaranteed either....

The court reviewed concerns about the separation of JB from his older brother, his special needs, and the assessment report, which had recommended a transfer of custody to the mother and JB's participation in the Workshop. Finally, in relation to the custody issue, the court concluded:

> [125] The evidence points overwhelmingly to a change in custody. In cases of severe irrational alienation such as this one, all the experts recommend the child be removed from the care of the alienating parent. The mother has the ability, the strength and the insight to parent JB appropriately. She puts his interests first, not her own. She is more likely to foster a relationship between JB and his father. JB has a chance of developing a healthy relationship with both his parents only if he is in his mother's custody. Mother will therefore have custody of JB.

The court also ordered that JB attend the Workshop.

The father appealed this decision, and sought a stay of the trial judge's order. This motion was dismissed. However, a few days later, JB brought his own stay motion, and this motion was granted pending an appeal of the trial decision. The mother then sought to set aside the stay, and the

Ontario Court of Appeal dismissed her motion. Significantly, however, the appeal court granted JB's motion for leave to intervene pursuant to rule 13.01(1) of the Rules of Civil Procedure. See *SGB v SJL*, 2010 ONCA 578.

Apparently, this case was settled out of court. Assuming it had proceeded to the Court of Appeal, how might it have been resolved? What do you think a fair resolution of the case would be?

Bruni v Bruni

In *Bruni v Bruni*, 2010 ONSC 6568, the spouses were married for 11 years. After separation, both engaged in stable new cohabiting relationships. They also signed a separation agreement, in which the mother received sole custody of two children, and the father became entitled to reasonable access.

However, the former spouses were extremely hostile towards one another, and it seemed that the mother had completely alienated their daughter from her father. Quinn J stated that *Bruni* is "yet another case that reveals the ineffectiveness of Family Court in a bitter custody/access dispute, where the parties require therapeutic intervention rather than legal attention. Here, a husband and wife have been marinating in a mutual hatred so intense as to surely amount to a personality disorder requiring treatment" (para 2).

When the husband applied to set aside the separation agreement, the court denied his application, holding that the husband had waived his entitlement to legal advice prior to signing the agreement. At the same time, the court held that the daughter's alienation from her father was thoroughly entrenched, and that the spouses had neither the financial ability nor the incentive to undertake counselling to overcome this problem:

> [127] Generally, it is unwise to place an immature 13-year-old in charge of her life. Here, however, [the spouses] have engineered an alienation that is so complete as to leave the court with no feasible option.

> [128] I make these findings: 1) The alienation was not present before [the parties] separated; 2) this is not a case where Taylor [the daughter] has weighed the good and bad attributes of her father and found him, on balance, to be parentally deficient: she sees [her father] as all bad — there is no ambivalence to her feelings; she is not disguising her true feelings; 3) [The father,] although well-intentioned, is an inept father, who has not taken steps to identify, and fix, his shortcomings as a parent; nevertheless, the utter rejection of him by Taylor is disproportionate, unfair and unwarranted; 4) as [the OCL representative] observed, Taylor has aligned herself with [her mother], whose hate for [the father] is palpable; the battle lines are clearly drawn and Taylor knows the side that she wants to be on; 5) I am unable to think of anything that [the father] can do to quickly repair the damage in his relationship with Taylor; and, if I could, I have doubts that he has the skill-sets to pull it off; 6) I did not hear evidence of a single instance of Taylor, since separation, expressing love or affection for [her father]; 7) although children are often required by their parents to do things that they do not want to do, obligating Taylor to visit her father or to engage in counselling is considerably more complicated than insisting that she do her homework or go to the dentist; 8) the history of the parties is such that there is no reason to think they would

meaningfully take part in, or benefit from, therapy or counselling; 9) while it is [the mother's] duty to encourage and support a relationship between Taylor and [her father], that duty has been breached too severely to be remedied by the court; 10) it is not realistic to expect that the parties have the incentive and finances to engage in the extensive therapy and counselling that are needed; 11) depriving [the mother] of custody (some-times an appropriate way of dealing with an alienating parent) would not benefit [the daughter] at this point.

[129] It is my view, sadly, that the alienation here is so severe that it is in the best interests of Taylor not to order or enforce access by [her father]; if access happens, fine....

[131] Absent counselling, matters will worsen, not improve. No practical purpose would be served if the court were to decree a schedule of coun-selling for the parties and the children. The hate and psychological dam-age that now prevail would require years of comprehensive counselling to undo. The legal system does not have the resources to monitor a schedule of counselling (nor should it do so). The function of Family Court is not to change people, but to dispose of their disputes at a given point in time. I preside over a court, not a church....

In the circumstances, the court concluded that it was appropriate to vary the terms of the separation agreement, eliminating the father's access to his daughter. (Recall from Chapter Seven, that the court also concluded that the mother's actions in this case constituted "unconscionable conduct" in the period post-separation according to *FLA*, s 33(10), and thus reduced her spousal support to $1.00 per month.)

To what extent does it make a difference whether the alienating parent is the father (as in *SGB v SJL*) or the mother (as in *Bruni*). Do you agree with the conclusion in *Bruni* that counselling would not assist a reconcilia-tion between the daughter and her father? Is there a need for legislative reform or other responses in such cases? For other recent cases concerning parental alienation, see *Rogerson v Tessaro*, [2006] OJ No 1825 (CA); and *AGL v KBD*, [2009] OJ No 180 (Sup Ct).

The court in *Bruni* concluded that it was not possible to overcome the alienation of the daughter from her father, and sanctioned the mother's behaviour by reducing the amount of spousal support. In other alienation cases, courts have used a variety of sanctions. For example, in *De la Sablonniere v Castagner*, 2012 ONSC 176, the court found that the father had intentionally and methodically interfered with the children's relationship with their mother, and that he had alienated them from her. In this case, the court ordered the father to pay $4000. to the mother for contempt.

However, in *A v C*, 2011 ONSC 278, the mother had successfully alien-ated her son from his father and the court wished to sanction her behav-iour. Nonetheless, because the alienation had continued for 7 years, so that the child was a stranger to the father, the court held reluctantly that any further court proceedings or penalties against the mother were not in the child's best interests.

As these and other cases about alienation make clear, such conduct creates significant challenges for courts. How should this problem be addressed?

Additional Resources

Barbara A Atwood, "Representing Children Who Can't or Won't Direct Counsel: Best Interests Lawyering or No Lawyer at All (2011) 53:2 Ariz L Rev 381.

Amy Baker, "The Long-Term Effects of Parental Alienation on Adult Children: A Qualitative Research Study" (2005) 33 American Journal of Family Therapy 289.

Bruce L Beverly, "A Remedy to Fit the Crime: A Call for the Recognition of the Unreasonable Rejection of a Parent by a Child as Tortious Conduct" (2013) 15 JL & Fam Stud 153.

Janet Johnston, "Children of Divorce who Reject a Parent and Refuse Visitation: Recent Research and Social Policy Implications for the Alienated Child" (2005) 38 Fam LQ 757.

Joan Kelly & Janet Johnston, "The Alienated Child: A Reformulation of Parental Alienation Syndrome" (2001) 39 Fam Ct Rev 249.

DA Rollie Thompson, "Annotation of *Young v. Young*" (2003) 34 RFL (5th) 215.

Richard A Warshak, "Bringing Sense to Parental Alienation: A Look at the Disputes and the Evidence" (2003) 37:2 Fam LQ 273.

IV.
CUSTODY AND CARE: PROCESSES FOR DECISION MAKING AND LEGAL ARRANGEMENTS

THE ROLE OF PROFESSIONALS IN CUSTODY AND ACCESS DECISIONS

Assessments pursuant to *CLRA*, s 30

Section 30 of the Ontario *Children's Law Reform Act* provides for the appointment of a person "with technical or professional skill" to provide an assessment with respect to "the needs of the child" and "the ability and willingness of the parties" to satisfy these needs. The parties are required to pay for such an assessment, unless payment would cause serious financial hardship to a party.

Pursuant to *CLRA*, s 30, courts have attempted to define the criteria for requesting an assessment and the role of such assessments in decision making about custody and access:

- In *Levine v Levine* (1993), 50 RFL (3d) 414 (Ont Prov Div), the court confirmed that assessments would not be ordered in every case and that, even if an assessment is ordered, it remains the responsibility of the court to decide what is in a child's best interests.

- In *Linton v Clarke* (1994), 10 RFL (4th) 92 (Ont Div Ct), the court disapproved of a practice of routine orders for assessments, holding a need for a decision on a "clinical issue" to justify appointment of an assessor.

- In *Delisle v Delisle* (1998), 43 RFL (4th) 186 (Ont Prov Div), the court reviewed the role of an assessor, holding that it was beyond the scope of the assessor's role to attempt to mediate disputes between the parties.

Criteria for appointing an assessor: *Marko-Laschowski v Laschowski*

In *Marko-Laschowski v Laschowski*, 1999 ABQB 37, an Alberta court reviewed the applicable legal principles pursuant to its legislation in relation to an order for an assessment, and its conclusions appear consistent with the *CLRA*, s 30. As the court indicated (at para 26):

> While the majority of cases that were cited by counsel are fact-driven, the following principles emerge:
> 1. The court has a discretion to order a custody/access assessment where it appears that one would be materially helpful;
> 2. There must be some evidence upon which to base the exercise of such a discretion. The sole consideration is the best interest of the child;
> 3. The custody/assessment is a factor to be considered together with all of the evidence in making that determination; and
> 4. The court must determine what is in the best interests of the child.

The court confirmed that an assessment should not be ordered automatically and that the applicant has the onus of justifying such a request. In considering the factual situation, however, the court concluded (at paras 25–26) that it was appropriate to order an assessment:

> Mr. St. Jacques and Mrs. Marko-Laschowski have been separated for almost three years. Mr. St. Jacques has remarried and his wife has a child a few years older than Brodie. Mr. St. Jacques and Mrs. Marko-Laschowski are involved in a highly conflicted situation. Her father was placed on a peace bond after threatening to shoot Mr. St. Jacques. Access has been a problem and continues to be a problem. The police have in the past been involved in enforcing access. The child is dropped off and picked up at a neutral location such as a restaurant or the police station. Each of the parties has accused the other of physically abusing Brodie and each is convinced that they are the better parent. Mr. St. Jacques alleges that Mrs. Marko-Laschowski's father has verbally and physically abused the child. Each alleges that the other is mentally unstable. In the past Mrs. Marko-Laschowski has questioned the child concerning physical injuries that he has sustained while in the care of his father. The child is being drawn into the acrimonious situation that exists between his parents. There have been incidents of violence in front of Brodie. The situation does not appear to have resolved or become less incendiary during the three years since these parties have separated. Custody and access are still hotly disputed. There is significant conflict in the affidavits.
> The purpose of an assessment is to identify the needs of the child and to provide information as to which parent is best able to meet those needs. I am satisfied that a home study is required to

allow the parties to understand the needs of the child and the need for cooperation.

Hearing children's wishes and preferences: Process options

In cases about custody and access of children, the parties to litigation are parents. To what extent should children be involved in these proceedings? This question had been addressed in a number of different ways.

For example, in *Stefureak v Chambers* (2004), 6 RFL (6th) 212 (Ont Sup Ct), the court reviewed four different ways by which a child's views and preferences could be submitted to a court:

1. Through an assessor or another mental health professional who had been in contact with the child;
2. Through the parties and their witnesses, who could provide hearsay evidence of a child's statements outside the court;
3. By means of a judge's interview with a child outside the courtroom; or
4. By having a child provide direct evidence to the court as part of the proceeding.

Although the court concluded in *Stefureak* that an assessment should not be ordered, the decision reviewed these options in some detail. In *H v H* (1999), 48 RFL (4th) 305 (Nfld Unif Fam Ct), the court invoked its *parens patriae* jurisdiction to appoint an *amicus curiae* to protect a child's interest.

As is evident, courts must balance the interest in protecting children in family dissolution cases with a need to ensure that their interests are fully represented, and there have been ongoing debates about how best to balance these goals. (For example, see *Strobridge v Strobridge* (1994), 4 RFL (4th) 169 (Ont CA); Carol Huddart and Jeanne Ensminger, "Hearing the Voice of Children" (1992) 8 Can Fam LQ 95; Jennifer Shuber, "The Voice of the Child in Family Court", *The Lawyers Weekly* (23 September 2011) 9; Gretchen Drummie, "Listening to Children's Voices" (March 2012) 36:3 Can Lawyer 37; Rachel Birnbaum, Nicholas Bala & Lorne Bertrand, "Judicial Interviews with Children: Attitudes and Practices of Children's Lawyers in Canada" (2013) 3 NZLR 465; and Renée Joyal & Anne Quéniart, "Enhancing the Child's Point of View in Custody and Access Cases in Québec: Preliminary Results of a Study Conducted in Québec" (2002) 19 Can J Fam L 173.)

Ontario's Office of the Children's Lawyer: Statutory authority

The *Courts of Justice Act* in Ontario provides for the Office of the Children's Lawyer to assist the court in relation to children in two ways:

- Section 89(3.1) permits a court to request the Office of the Children's Lawyer to provide legal representation for a child; and

- Section 112 provides that the Office of the Children's Lawyer may undertake an investigation and report and make recommendations to a court in a custody and access proceeding pursuant to the *Divorce Act* or the *Children's Law Reform Act*.

In relation to the provision of legal representation by the Office of the Children's Lawyer (s 89(3.1)), some courts have tended to limit such requests. For example, one judge suggested that:

> This remedy [of involving the Office of the Children's Lawyer] should not be available only for the asking. Inasmuch as it implicates the children very directly in the entire litigation, it is a very blunt instrument indeed. It can cause untold harm to impressionable children who may feel suddenly inappropriately empowered against their parents in a context where the children should be protected as much as possible from the contest being waged over their future care and custody. All actions involving custody and access over children should be governed by one paramount consideration: no one should be allowed to act in a way that might endanger their well-being. The test of the "best interests of the children" as insipid and fluid as it might be still remains the benchmark against which any person wishing to interfere in their lives should be measured. (*Reynolds v Reynolds* (1996), 7 OTC 389 (Gen Div), cited by the court in dismissing an application for appointment of the Children's Lawyer in *Bazinet v Bazinet* (1998), 42 RFL (4th) 140 (Ont Gen Div) at 142)

The Office of the Children's Lawyer: *Bhajan v Bhajan*

Recently, the Ontario Court of Appeal considered six cases in which a trial judge, exercising the court's *parens patriae* jurisdiction, had ordered the Office of the Children's Lawyer (OCL) to provide representation for a child or to investigate and provide reports to the court relating to disputes about custody and access.

In *Bhajan v Bhajan*, 2010 ONCA 714, the Ontario Court of Appeal recognized the challenges facing the trial court in these cases, but concluded that it was not appropriate for a trial judge to *order* involvement by the OCL, particularly because sections 89(3.1) and 112 of the *Courts of Justice Act* merely provide authority for courts to *request* such involvement.

In its reasons, the Court of Appeal considered evidence indicating that the OCL's resources were not sufficient to accept all requests. Thus (according to the affidavit of the Acting Children's Lawyer), at the time of the court orders for OCL involvement, there were 5548 referrals from judges in Ontario between 1 April 2009 and 25 August 2010, and the OCL accepted 3432 cases during this period. Accordingly, the Acting Children's Lawyer argued on the appeal that the OCL would not be able to function properly if courts were entitled to order, rather than request, its involvement.

In concluding that it was not appropriate for the trial court to exercise its *parens patriae* jurisdiction in this way, the appeal court reviewed the *Convention on the Rights of the Child*, a number of previous decisions confirming that the OCL has discretion to decide whether to respond to a court's request for its involvement, and the existence of other legislative provisions (such as *CLRA*, s 30) to enable children's voices to be heard in custody and access proceedings. On this basis, the court concluded:

> [24] Assuming, without deciding, that absent words clearly ousting the Superior Court's inherent *parens patriae* jurisdiction the Superior Court has the power to order the OCL to act outside the [*Courts of Justice Act*], it is reasonable to assume that the legislature intended that judges would respect the legislative scheme and not create a parallel procedure. To *order* and not *request* the OCL to act ignores the discretion embodied in the wording of the *CJA* and the underlying reason for that discretion. The OCL has limited resources and it, not the court, is in the best position to decide when and how to utilize its limited resources. Failure to respect the legislative scheme by pre-empting the exercise of the OCL's discretion is an error in principle....

The court then turned to each of the six cases in which the trial judge had ordered OCL involvement, and allowed all six appeals.

What is the context for this decision? Recall the discussion in Chapter Five concerning the limited legal aid resources available for family law proceedings. Is it possible that the trial judge's decision to order OCL involvement in these six cases concerning custody and access was an effort to draw attention to the challenges presented by unrepresented litigants in family law courts in making decisions in the best interests of children? Consider, for example, the comments of the trial judge about one of the cases under appeal, *Bhajan v Bhajan* (C51273):

> I don't intend to serve the child of this relationship ill and I do not intend to conclude that this court is hampered in exercising its *parens patriae* jurisdiction to rescue a child in danger. I am satisfied that the child in this case is, in fact, in danger — in danger of parental alienation, in danger of not being able to see his mother in circumstances which, at present, are bordering on the unconscionable albeit, perhaps necessary, on a short term basis. I have no intention of failing to act to help a child who needs the court's protection who cannot speak for himself without the assistance of an independent, objective and expert assistant to assist the court by representing him and I have no intention of letting this matter slide.... What I am ordering them to do is to consider my direction, as provided on the consent of the parties, [to] appear in court from now, and until relieved by the court, to assist the court with respect to every step in this case involving the child.... (cited by the ONCA at para 36).

Was it appropriate in this context for the Ontario Court of Appeal to take note of existing levels of OCL resources in interpreting the language of the *Courts of Justice Act*? In the context of a court's *parens patriae* jurisdiction, is it arguable that the statute creates a "gap" that must be addressed by this principle? Why is OCL involvement preferable to an order for an assessment pursuant to *CLRA*, s 30? Is there a need for legislative reform to address the need for more resources for the OCL?

Access to counselling records

In addition to assessments ordered by a court, or undertaken by the parties in a custody dispute, some claims have been initiated to obtain access to records of treatment by counsellors and health professionals.

For example, in *Smith v Smith* (1997), 32 RFL (4th) 361 (Sask QB), the mother applied for sole custody of the parties' children, claiming that the father was abusive and controlling toward them. The father, in turn, contended that the mother was mentally unstable and had suicidal tendencies. The father applied to the court seeking full disclosure of all clinical notes, results of meetings and attendances, diagnostic services, and consultation and treatment received from all the professionals who had provided counselling to the mother and the parties' children. In his application for the disclosure, the father contended that the disclosure was relevant and necessary for his trial preparations, and that the mother had fabricated allegations of abuse.

The court relied on the decisions in *M(A) v Ryan*, [1997] 1 SCR 157, and *Hill v Church of Scientology of Toronto*, [1995] 2 SCR 1130, in the Supreme Court of Canada to grant the father's application in part.

Specifically, the court ordered that the mother's therapist and the Catholic Family Services disclose all clinical notes and/or a typewritten summary of such notes pertaining to the mother. The disclosure was to include the results of all meetings, attendances, diagnostic services, consultations, and treatments received by the mother, including the findings of tests, if any, and any reports prepared or received in relation to the mother. However, this order was subject to the following four conditions:

(1) that the inspection be confined to the father's lawyers and expert witnesses and that the father himself not see them;
(2) that any person entitled to see the documents not disclose their contents to anyone not entitled to inspect them;
(3) that the documents be used only for the purposes of the custody litigation; and
(4) that only one copy be made by the father's lawyers, which could then be passed on to the father's expert witnesses.

With respect to the children's counselling sessions, however, the court denied the father's request for disclosure, ruling that disclosure would not be in the best interests of the children.

In dismissing the father's application, the court stated that a child is not well-situated to rationalize and comprehend the need for intrusion upon her thoughts and feelings, and that to urge upon children the virtues of counselling only to compel them to divulge their confidences at a later point was a hypocrisy in which the court would not participate.

Did the resolution of this case represent a good balance for the parents in terms of the court's responsibility for deciding on the children's "best interests"? Should parents ever have access to their children's counselling records? Does your answer change if the children are being parented in a joint custody relationship? Why or why not?

PROCESSES FOR RESOLVING CUSTODY AND ACCESS CLAIMS

Policies emphasizing alternatives to litigation

Processes for decision making in family law matters were explored earlier in Chapter Five, including arbitration, mediation, negotiation, and collaborative law. In relation to issues about custody and access, these processes are especially significant since many family experts encourage parents to resolve their disputes concerning their children without the conflict that is assumed to accompany litigation.

Both federal and provincial statutes encourage spouses to settle their affairs at dissolution without resort to litigation.

For example, section 31 of the *CLRA* specifically mandates a court, at the parties' request, to appoint a mediator who is required to confer with the parties and attempt to obtain an agreement. The section also provides protections for admissions made in mediation sessions in the event that a matter cannot be settled and the litigation resumes.

Recall also the provisions in sections 9 and 10 of the *Divorce Act*, which provide encouragement for mediation or other processes of reconciliation and settlement.

In relation to the issues identified earlier with respect to family law bargaining, why are matters of custody and access more appropriate for mediation and other alternative methods of dispute resolution, rather than for litigation?

Limits of alternative processes?

Assuming that alternatives to litigation may protect children from parental conflict, what measures should be required to meet concerns about family law bargaining? For example, recall the limits proposed by some commentators with respect to the use of mediation in the context of abuse or violence. Are there other concerns about the use of mediation in determining custody and access? How should "best interests" be defined in such a context? Is the avoidance of litigation always in a child's "best interests"?

Similar questions may need to be posed with respect to other aspects of family law bargaining, in the context of custody and access issues. For example, to what extent is the "openness" of collaborative law processes a problem in family law bargaining about children? In one case reported by Julie Macfarlane, a collaborative lawyer's encouragement to her client to disclose information about the couple's son's difficulties at school may have created a greater risk of violence on the part of the husband toward his wife and his son. In this case, financial resources dictated that the husband and wife had to live in the same home until they were able to settle their corollary relief issues in the collaborative law process. Are there issues of concern in such a context? In commenting on this case, Macfarlane cautioned:

[P]erhaps [the wife's] lawyer underestimated the extent of the pressure being placed on [the wife]....

As Macfarlane also noted, the husband's anger with the son may have resulted in tension and anxiety for the wife, so that she wanted to achieve a settlement, a precondition for her to require her husband to move out of the home.

> It is unclear whether [the wife] and her lawyer really examined all of the relevant information — including the behaviour of ... the husband ... before [the wife] made her final decision. Unfortunately, these circumstances created a series of inevitable pressures on [the wife] to accept the offer [which met her immediate needs but might prove unsatisfactory in future. As Macfarlane suggested, there might have been some other options available.] For example, perhaps there could have been a short interim agreement in which [the husband] moved out of the house at their shared expense....
>
> [In relation to putting the information about the son on the table in the four way meeting, Macfarlane noted that] this incident demonstrates the risk of applying collaborative principles without regard for context. Disclosing this information compromised the safely and security of [the wife] and her son. A commitment to openness — an important value for collaborative law — cannot be allowed to trump other considerations, especially when the client is vulnerable.... (Julie Macfarlane, *The New Lawyer: How Settlement is Transforming the Practice of Law* (Vancouver: UBC Press, 2008) at 162–163)

Recall the discussion about collaborative law and its limitations in Chapter Five. To what extent should a client such as the wife in this case have been "screened" out of collaborative law processes or mediation because of her vulnerability? Are there additional safeguards that could be introduced to protect vulnerable family members who engage in family bargaining? Is there a need for legislative reform?

Family bargaining and access to legal advice

Recall the discussion in Chapter Five concerning access to lawyers in terms of both representation and legal advice, and the current rates of unrepresented litigants in family courts.

In the context of the principle of best interests for children at family dissolution, is it possible to argue that access to legal advice and representation may be essential to meet this legislative objective?

How should policy makers respond to these needs for legal advice and representation? In this context, Ontario government policy appears designed to stream family law matters to dispute resolution outside the courts. Thus, these current policy initiatives include four components:

- the Family Law Information Centres at courts (which provide basic information and community referrals);

- the Mandatory Information Program (information offered by a lawyer and mental health professional about the process of separation and divorce);
- the two-hour, free, on-site mediation service at courts for litigants on the docket each day (available on a first come-first served basis); and
- off-site mediation, a subsidized service with reduced rates based on a sliding scale.

The mediators, whether lawyers or social workers, and in both the on-site and off-site programs, will all be accredited through the Ontario Association of Family Mediators. See Lorna Yates, "Mediate393: New Family Mediation Program in Toronto", *The Lawyers Weekly* (23 September 2011) 11.

What kinds of concerns may arise in relation to these policy initiatives? In this context, it is noteworthy that some empirical research in Australia suggested that legal aid costs were actually lower when clients had some basic access to legal advice *before* they embarked on mediation or other non-litigation alternatives to dispute resolution. See Rosemary Hunter, "Adversarial Mythologies: Policy Assumptions and Research Evidence in Family Law" (2003) 30 JL & Soc'y 156.

Additional Resources

See also references in Chapter Five.

Becky Batagol & Thea Brown, *Bargaining in the Shadow of the Law: The Case of Family Mediation* (Annandale, NSW: Themis Press, 2011).

Nicholas Bala & Nicole Bailey, "Enforcement of Access & Alienation of Children: Conflict Resolution Strategies & Legal Responses" (2004–2005) 23 Can Fam LQ 1.

Nicholas Bala & Alan Leschied, "Court-Ordered Assessments in Ontario Child Welfare Cases: Review and Recommendations for Reform" (2008) 24 Can J Fam L 11.

Rachel Birnbaum, Barbara Jo Fidler & Katherine Kavassalis, *Child Custody Assessments: A Resource Guide for Legal and Mental Health Professionals* (Toronto: Thomson Carswell, 2008).

Margo Kushner, "A Review of the Empirical Literature about Child Development and Adjustment Post-separation" (2009) 50 Journal of Divorce & Remarriage 496.

Randall Letie & Kathleen Clark, "Participants' Evaluation of Aspects of the Legal Child Custody Process and Preferences for Court Services" (2007) 45:2 Fam Ct Rev 260.

Noel Semple, "Whose Best Interests? Custody and Access Law and Procedure" (2010) 48 Osgoode Hall LJ 287.

Noel Semple, "The Silent Child: A Quantitative Analysis of Children's Evidence in Canadian Custody and Access Cases" (2010) 29 Can Fam LQ 1.

Noel Semple, "Judicial Settlement-Seeking in Parenting Cases: A Mock Trial" (2013) 2 J Dis Resol 301.

Carol Smart & Vanessa May, "Why Can't They Agree? The Underlying Complexity of Contact and Residence Disputes" (2004) 26 J Soc Welfare & Fam L 347.

Jo-Anne Stolz & Tara Ney, "Resistance to Visitation: Rethinking Parental and Child Alienation" (2002) 40 Fam Ct Rev 220.

Matthew Sullivan & Joan Kelly, "Legal and Psychological Management of Cases with an Alienated Child" (2001) 39 Fam Ct Rev 299.

"SHARING" CUSTODY AND CARE: JOINT CUSTODY, PARENTING PLANS, AND "PARALLEL PARENTING"

The history of joint custody: Agreements and orders

Recall that joint legal custody requires parents to co-operate in decision making about their children with respect to issues of health, education and welfare. In practice, there are many cases in which parents negotiate separation agreements, including an agreement for joint custody. The more controversial issue is whether courts should order joint custody where the parents are not in agreement.

It seems that the background to such discussions of joint custody often starts with two cases decided by the Ontario Court of Appeal in 1979: *Baker v Baker* (1979), 23 OR (2d) 391; and *Kruger v Kruger* (1979), 25 OR (2d) 673. In both cases, the appellate court declined to order joint custody.

- In *Baker*, the Court of Appeal indicated that a "realistic and practical" approach was required in the resolution of custody litigation, and that joint custody should be ordered only in "exceptional circumstances which are rarely, if ever, present in cases of disputed custody" (at 396).

- In *Kruger*, a majority of the appellate court confirmed the approach in *Baker*, but there was also a strong dissenting judgment by Wilson JA:

  > In my view, it is the responsibility of the Court on a custody matter to assess, preferably with professional assistance, the ability of the parents to co-operate on the upbringing of their children and in the light of that assessment to choose from the range of options open to it the one which will best serve the children's short and long-term interests. This is of paramount importance in a case where the trial judge finds that both parents exhibit sterling parenting qualities and that the relationship between parents and children discloses a high degree of love and affection on both sides. (at 698)

These differing views about the appropriateness of court orders for joint legal custody, in the absence of parental agreement, continue to resonate in parental negotiations and litigation concerning custody and care.

An introduction to joint custody, parenting plans, and parallel parenting

In this context, it is necessary to consider developments with respect to joint custody, as well as the use of parenting plans and parallel parenting orders. Although this section will examine these concepts in greater detail, it may be useful to explain them briefly at the outset.

- **Joint custody** usually refers to "joint legal custody" in which parents share authority to make decisions about a child in relation to health, education and welfare (including religion). It is also possible for parents to share "joint physical custody" with an arrangement that permits a child to spend substantially equal time in the care of each parent. With an arrangement of "joint physical custody," it is possible that the parents also have "joint legal custody," but it is also possible for one parent to have "custody" and the other parent to have "access," and for these parents to have substantially equal "physical custody." In this context, it is important to note that most litigated disputes are about "joint legal custody," that is, decision-making authority.

- **Parenting plans** are encouraged for separated and divorced parents, whether they have joint custody or custody and access arrangements in law. Parenting plans focus on the precise arrangements for physical care of children post-family dissolution, and may include detailed arrangements for sharing time with a child, holiday arrangements, communication, and connections with extended families of each parent, etc. Such plans generally relate to physical care arrangements rather than decision-making authority, although they may also include such matters in accordance with the legal arrangements for custody and access, or joint custody. The goal of parenting plans is to set out in detail the arrangements for the child at separation or divorce, so as to avoid altercations between the parents in future. In this way, the plans are intended to promote the child's best interests in relation to avoiding parental disputes.

- **Parallel parenting** involves detailed arrangements for decision making by parents, and has been ordered by a number of courts in an attempt to avoid ongoing litigation in high-conflict parental disputes post-dissolution. Although parallel parenting orders may incorporate similar arrangements as are found in parenting plans, they also address parental authority for decision making, in an effort to define which parent may make specific decisions for a child. Such decisions may include both those identified for joint custody (that is, health, education, and welfare), but may also include other kinds of decisions. Sometimes parallel parenting may permit the parent with physical care of the child to make all decisions while the child is in that parent's care, or such an arrangement may divide decision making between parents so that each parent is entitled to make decisions that are most important to that parent in relation to a child.

A number of aspects of these arrangements remain controversial at the present time. Thus, this section provides an overview of current issues and some commentary about them.

JOINT CUSTODY

The rise of joint custody arrangements

> The rising appeal of joint custody during the 1980s is not difficult to understand. Judges became more conscious of the arbitrariness of the adversarial system in divorce.... At the same time professionals in social work and mediation were redefining divorce as an emotional or therapeutic process rather than a legal one.... Judges and lawyers, who find custody cases difficult..., were more than happy to accept guidance from non-legal professionals and to delegate authority to the psy-professions where possible. (Boyd at 120)

Thus, as Boyd reported, by the 1980s, "joint custody seemed to lend itself to social engineering efforts by judges" (Boyd at 121). Coupled with increasing reliance on mediation and counselling, joint custody arrangements (in both negotiated agreements and court orders) became more frequent. Significantly, perhaps, such joint custody orders related to authority for decision making, not physical care for children. Indeed, there is evidence that mothers have continued to have primary responsibility for day-to-day child care (Boyd at 123–124).

In the 1990s, some professionals continued to argue that joint (legal) custody was appropriate only for parents with a deep commitment to the well-being of their children, and respect for the contribution of the other parent to their lives. More specifically, it was suggested that joint (legal) custody should not be used as a bargaining chip in settlement negotiations, and that it was not at all appropriate if parents were engaged in high conflict or where their views about child-rearing were discordant. In addition, some professionals suggested that shared parenting (joint custody) was not appropriate in cases involving hotly contested litigation about custody. For example, see A Leonoff, "Joint Custody and Beyond" (1995) 29:1 L Soc'y Gaz 29.

Lower court decisions in the 1990s:
Opposing views

The controversy about whether joint legal custody should be ordered by courts, particularly where one parent was opposed to it, continued in the 1990s. In the two cases that follow, examine the reasoning for the judges' decisions, either to order or not order joint custody. To what extent do these cases reflect different views about parenting post-separation or divorce? Or do they reflect differing views about the role of courts in encouraging parents to focus on the "best interests" of their children?

Biamonte v Biamonte
(1998), 36 RFL (4th) 349 (Ont Gen Div) at 359

... The central issue in these proceedings was the mother's claim for custody and the father's request for an order for joint custody or in the alternative for sole custody. It is obvious that this couple would never survive any order for joint custody. Because the parties are not in agreement as to joint custody, there is no choice on my part but to dismiss the claim for joint custody. (*Kruger v. Kruger* (1979), 25 OR (2d) 673 (ONCA).) In mid-trial, Mr. Biamonte asked for permission to amend his pleadings to claim sole custody of the two children, notwithstanding that he had just signed an agreement whereby he had granted sole custody to his wife. Which leads me to examine which of these two parties would be the best parent. There is no doubt in my mind that the wife is a much more concerned and appropriate parent. This is even though she may have associated with Mr. Vattovaz whose past performances leave this court with a somewhat acrid taste in its mouth. But as indicated above, there is no claim by Mr. Vattovaz for custody of the children and his past behaviour should not be looked at with a fine-tooth comb especially where there is no allegation that he might ever be a danger to the children themselves. Mr. Biamonte's main concerns for his children's welfare appeared to be centered on his wife's boyfriend. These concerns, I am satisfied, have more to do with Mr. Biamonte's obsession at trying to control his ex-wife than at a genuine concern for the welfare of his children. Therefore, there will be an order that custody of the children be entrusted to Mrs. Biamonte with access to the children as laid out in the minutes of settlement filed at the start of the proceedings....

Mudie v Post
(1998), 40 RFL (4th) 151 (Ont Gen Div) at 159

In *Mudie v Post*, Salhany J awarded joint custody in circumstances where an unmarried couple were the parents of two young boys. The mother was seeking sole custody, but the court concluded that it was appropriate to make an order for joint custody.

... Historically, custody battles have been an all or nothing proposition. Sole custody orders have been the norm with access to the non-custodial parent through visitation rights. Such orders have granted legal responsibility and physical control to a single custodial parent to the exclusion of the other. A sole custodial order has given the custodial parent the right to decide where the child will live, how the child will be educated, what religion, if any, the child will adopt and what medical and dental care will be provided. The result has been that the voice of the non-custodial parent in the upbringing of his or her child has been essentially unheard. Any voice of the non-custodial parent in such important decisions affecting the life of "their" child has only been heard where the custodial parent has cared to listen.

I pause to stress the word "their" in reference to the child. It is often forgotten that the child, whatever result the court reaches, is the product of both parents. No decision of the court, no matter how limiting in the access granted to the non-custodial parent, can ever take away the fact that the non-custodial parent is still the parent of that child. It is for that reason that where a sole custody order has been made, the losing parent leaves the courtroom, feeling not only alienated from "their" child, but also alienated from the justice system which has adopted the winner-take-all approach to a custody dispute.

... One of the main arguments advanced by those who believe that legal custody should not be separated from physical custody is that it does not work. My experience, after trying custody cases for almost 20 years, is that it does work and works far better to reduce post-trial applications than a sole custody order. Indeed, the frequent applications that are brought in this Court in this jurisdiction after a sole custody order has been made to enforce an access order has led me to the conclusion that joint custody orders are less subject to ongoing litigation than sole custody orders....

I have come to the conclusion that it is in the best interests of the children in this case that there be a joint custody order. I say that because I am convinced that if sole custody were granted to the respondent, she would continue to obstruct the applicant's attempts to develop a relationship with the children. As I said earlier, it was my distinct impression from her evidence that she would prefer that the applicant be entirely out of her life and the life of the children. I am satisfied that if I were to grant her sole custody, she would make every effort to limit the applicant's contact with the children. In my view, the only practical solution to prevent this is to ensure that she is not given absolute control of the children. Indeed, this is a case where neither should be in absolute control....

Joint custody and the Ontario Court of Appeal: Recent decisions

In 2005, the Ontario Court of Appeal considered two cases (*Kaplanis* and *Ladisa*, with judgments released on the same day) concerning joint custody and reviewed again the relevant principles. In examining the reasoning, consider whether, or to what extent, they suggest new developments since *Baker* and *Kruger*?

Kaplanis v Kaplanis
(2005), 10 RFL (6th) 373 (Ont CA)

In *Kaplanis v Kaplanis*, the court allowed an appeal by the mother from a trial judge's decision ordering joint legal custody. In this case, the appeal court granted sole custody to the mother and ordered a new trial to define the father's access.

The spouses married in 1998, and their daughter was born in 2001. According to the court, the marriage was "tumultuous" and the spouses separated in 2002 when the father left the matrimonial home after uttering a death threat to the mother. Although the mother provided an affidavit stating that she was not a victim of violence, attempts by the spouses at counselling were unsuccessful.

At trial, the self-represented father sought an order for parallel parenting, but this arrangement was resisted by the mother on the basis that the parties could not communicate without screaming at each other.

Nonetheless, the trial judge concluded that the wife's interest in obtaining sole custody undermined her willingness to communicate, holding that:

> In my view, considerations of the best interests of [the daughter] in the context of her extended familial relationships, must not preclude joint custody, merely because the parties, fresh from the wounds of their failed marriage, find it difficult to be civil to each other....

The trial judge also ordered ongoing counselling for the parents, and if the parents were unable to agree with respect to decisions about their daughter, the counsellor was authorized to make the decisions for them.

In allowing this appeal, the Ontario Court of Appeal stated:

> [10] As in any custody case, the sole issue before the trial judge was the best interests of the child. The fact that both parents acknowledged the other to be "fit" did not mean that it was in the best interests of the child for a joint custody order to be made. [The evidence should have addressed the bonds between the child and each parent and their ability to parent her, the father's plans for caring for the child and the benefits of any such arrangement to the child. The trial judge did not have this evidence.]

> [11] The fact that one parent professes an inability to communicate with the other parent does not, in and of itself, mean that a joint custody order cannot be considered. On the other hand, hoping that communication between the parties will improve once the litigation is over does not provide a sufficient basis for the making of an order of joint custody. There must be some evidence before the court that, despite their differences, the parents are able to communicate effectively with one another. No matter how detailed the custody order that is made, gaps will inevitably occur, unexpected situations arise, and the changing developmental needs of a child must be addressed on an ongoing basis. When, as here, the child is so young that she can hardly communicate her developmental needs, communication is even more important. In this case there was no evidence of effective communication. The evidence was to the contrary.

> [In addition, the trial judge did not have the benefit of expert evidence about the child's needs.]

> [14] It may certainly be desirable for parents to take counselling on how to better parent their child and to hire a counsellor or parenting coach to resolve disputes. The order provided by the trial judge was, however, problematic. The legislation does not specifically authorize the making of an order for parental counselling and, while some judges have held the court has inherent jurisdiction to make a counselling order, carrying out the order requires the co-operation of the parents. There was no evidence that the parties would be able to agree on whom to appoint [and no agreement about a process for resolving this problem.]

> [15] Having regard to the above factors, the trial judge erred in making an order for joint custody of the child [and in ordering the parties to attend counselling and appoint a counsellor to resolve their disputes. In the absence of any plan presented by the father with respect to the care of the child, the Court ordered sole custody to the mother. The Court ordered a new trial to assess the father's access, and indicated a hope for the involvement of the Children's Lawyer.]

Compare this reasoning to *Ladisa v Ladisa* (2005), 11 RFL (6th) 50, in which the Ontario Court of Appeal dismissed the mother's appeal in relation to an order for joint custody. In doing so, the court noted that the order for joint (legal) custody was based on the express wishes of the three children, aged 9 to 16 years old, and that it was also supported by a professional assessment. The oldest child lived with the father, and the two younger children resided with each parent on a rotating weekly basis.

In denying the mother's appeal, the court indicated that the reasons in *Kaplanis* were also relevant to the court's decision in this case.

Notes and Questions

The "communication" requirement for joint custody

In lower court decisions after *Kaplanis* and *Ladisa*, courts were required to assess the ability of the former spouses to communicate about a child, in order to determine whether to make a joint custody order. Indeed, in a subsequent case, *Lawson v Lawson* (2006), 29 RFL (6th) 8, the Ontario Court of Appeal reiterated its position that joint custody was not appropriate if the parties were unable to co-operate or communicate effectively.

How should courts resolve gaps between "parental ability to communicate" on one hand and a "child's best interests" on the other? Does this assessment require reconsideration of the efficacy of joint custody arrangements in the interests of children?

According to Martha Shaffer, a majority of post-*Kaplanis* cases have involved conduct on the part of a parent seeking joint custody that demonstrates an inability to communicate or co-operate with the other parent. Indeed, in many of these cases, the conduct is so egregious that it goes beyond an unwillingness to co-operate with the other parent, and demonstrates an inability to act in a child's best interests. However, post-*Kaplanis*, such conduct is often discussed as revealing problems of parental communication, rather than conduct that *per se* undermines a custody claim. In addition, there is a gendered nature to such cases, which very often involve problematic conduct on the part of men. According to Shaffer,

> ... The post-*Kaplanis* case law revealed two interesting and unanticipated trends. The first of these is the over-use of the *Kaplanis* analysis. *Kaplanis* is used in cases where it is clear that joint custody is not in the children's best interests because of problematic conduct of one of the parents.... In effect, the *Kaplanis* focus on "communication and cooperation" seems to have taken over the analysis of joint custody claims, with the result that courts will deny joint custody on the basis that the parties are incapable of effective communication and co-operation when joint custody should have been denied because of problematic parental conduct.
>
> The second trend concerns the relationship between legal custody — the right to make significant decisions regarding the child — and physical custody — the amount of time each parent spends with the child. Some courts are denying claims for joint custody on the ground that the parents are unable to communicate or co-operate, yet at the same time are order-

ing that the parents have equal time, or nearly equal time, with the children. Orders such as these raise an obvious question — if joint custody is not in the children's best interests because the parents are incapable of civil communication and co-operation, how is it in the children's best interests to spend equal time in households which do not share information, or worse, which are mired in open conflict? ...

The research on the effects of conflict on children's adjustment to divorce is also relevant here. Studies have consistently shown that exposure to parental conflict is harmful to children and a major source of reduced well-being. To the extent that equal time parenting arrangements expose children to conflict they will have a negative impact on children's well-being.... Equal time parenting presents high conflict couples a myriad of opportunities to battle one another. It is hard to see how these arrangements can be in the child's best interests where the parents are too conflicted to exercise joint custody.... ("Joint Custody since *Kaplanis* and *Ladisa*: A Review of Recent Ontario Case Law" in Martha Shaffer, ed, *Contemporary Issues in Family Law* (Toronto: Carswell, 2007) 431 at 464–471)

Joint custody, tender years, and the primary caregiver

To what extent, if at all, should courts consider the tender years principle, or the role of the primary caregiver, in assessing whether an order for joint custody is in a child's "best interests"?

Warcop v Warcop
(2009), 66 RFL (6th) 438 (Ont Sup Ct)

In *Warcop v Warcop*, the court considered the wife's application for sole custody. The spouses had married in 2003 and separated in 2007. They had one son, a happy child who thrived in the company of both parents.

The wife did not claim custody on the basis of the tender years doctrine, but she argued that, as the child's primary caregiver, she was entitled to sole custody. The court considered the tender years doctrine, the significance of the primary caregiver, and the principles concerning sole and joint custody:

> [85] There is some authority at the Superior Court level for the proposition that the primary caregiver should be given preference [citing *Brotherton v. Brotherton*, [2006] OJ No. 2844; and *Spencer v. Spencer*, [2006] OJ No. 4144. There is some danger, in my view, that any such principle could become a proxy for the now-discredited tender years doctrine [although the court had earlier noted the Court of Appeal's acceptance of tender years in *S(BA) v. S(MS)* (1991), 35 RFL (3d) 400 (Ont. C.A.).] At the time of separation, it is quite likely that very young children have been cared for, primarily, by their mothers. [Thus, the court held that any preference for a primary caregiver must be based on evidence, not presumptions.]

The court then reviewed the development of principles concerning joint custody, from *Baker* and *Kruger* to *Kaplanis* and *Ladisa*, and concluded:

> [94] In the final analysis, in my view, an order for joint custody is not to be rejected based on any rigid standard as formerly reflected in *Baker*....

The focus is simply on the best interests of the child. The best interests of the child will obviously not be fostered if the parents are unable to communicate and cooperate in making decisions that affect the child. However, a standard of perfection is not required, and is obviously not achievable. The issue is whether a reasonable measure of communication and cooperation is in place, and is achievable in the future, so that the best interests of the child can be ensured on an ongoing basis. In making this assessment, the Court must be governed by the evidence that has been presented as to the communication and cooperation between the parties to date; the mechanisms [that] are in place to ensure that it will continue; and the assessment of the judge as to the capabilities of the parties to do so in the future....

The court then considered whether there was evidence of sufficient co-operation and communication to order joint custody, and concluded:

[100] ... It is clear ... that these parties have already demonstrated a degree of cooperation and joint decision-making that is commendable. On many issues of importance, they have already agreed. On others, they have set up a mechanism for agreement. Of importance, where impasse develops and it may become necessary to seek court resolution on an issue, the parties have agreed to proceed first to mediation. In other words, every attempt will be made to seek agreement before resorting to third party intervention.

[101] It is also important to note, in my view, that on a day-to-day basis, the parties have been able to communicate. They do so through emails and a log that is passed back and forth. The communications have been informative and respectful. There is no reason to believe that they will not continue to be so in future....

Although the court considered some negative factors, including an incident in which the mother was arrested, as well as one occasion when the father did not return the child on schedule, the court concluded that an order for joint custody was in the child's best interests.

A note on the "primary caregiver presumption" (United States)

In considering the appropriateness of sole custody or joint custody orders, some courts in the United States adopted presumptions as to what arrangement is in a child's best interests. For example, West Virginia adopted a primary caregiver presumption in *Garska v McCoy* 278 SE 2d 357 (W Va 1981). In doing so, the court indicated a goal of creating a legal framework for family law bargaining, particularly in mediation processes, so that the primary caregiver's bargaining position would have greater certainty.

In relation to the primary caregiver presumption, courts were required to determine which parent had primary responsibility for caregiving in the intact family, using a number of defined factors, including (at 363):

1. preparing and planning of meals;
2. bathing, grooming and dressing;

3. purchasing, cleaning and care of clothes;
4. medical care, including nursing and trips to doctors;
5. arranging social interaction among peers after school;
6. arranging alternative care giving (such as day care);
7. putting a child to bed, attending to a child in the night, and waking a child in the morning;
8. disciplining a child, including toilet training and teaching manners;
9. educating a child in religious, cultural and social matters; and
10. teaching elementary skills such as reading.

According to the court, if these responsibilities were shared fully and equally, then no presumption was appropriate. However, if one parent was clearly the primary caregiver, then that parent should be entitled to custody, if fit. *Garska* was not followed in the American cases of *Von Bank v Von Bank*, 443 NW 2d 618 (ND Jul 17, 1989); *Nickerson v Nickerson*, 158 Vt 85, 605 A 2d 1331 (Vt Feb 07, 1992); *Taylor v Taylor*, 849 SW 2d 319 (Tenn Feb 22, 1993); and *Snyder v Snyder*, 1993 WL 240118 (Ark App Jun 30, 1993). It seems that the "primary caregiver presumption" as a legal tool, has not survived intact.

The primary caregiver presumption is not part of the legislative framework in the federal or provincial statutes in Canada. In addition, as noted in the *Warcop* case above, the primary caregiver during an intact relationship is just one factor to be considered in relation to determining a child's best interests. In *Warcop*, the mother's claim for sole custody, on the basis that she had been the primary caregiver for the child, was rejected in favour of an order for joint custody.

To what extent do you agree that this presumption is not appropriate in Canada? For an assessment that revealed how such a presumption may not be appropriate in the absence of structural changes to permit both fathers and mothers to participate meaningfully in paid work and parenting, see Susan B Boyd, "Potentialities and Perils of the Primary Caregiver Presumption" (1990–91) 7 Can Fam LQ 1.

The "no order" order: Reform proposals and
Waugh v Waugh

As noted earlier in this chapter, the federal Joint Committee Report recommending reforms to child custody and access favoured the elimination of these terms and the adoption of parenting orders instead. As the report suggested:

> Parenting plans shift parents' focus away from labels ("I have custody, you just have access") to the schedule, activities and real needs of the child. (Special Joint Committee on Child Custody and Access, *For the Sake of the Children* (Ottawa: Parliament of Canada, 1998) at 31)

For an example of such an arrangement, consider an interim application in *Waugh v Waugh* (1998), 42 RFL (4th) 415 (Ont Gen Div).

In *Waugh*, the father requested an order for interim joint custody of the couple's only child, while the wife asked for interim sole custody. The father claimed a need for joint custody in order to maximize his bonding with the child (a one-year-old) and to allow him to demonstrate his ability to care for the child pending determination of the custody issue. (There was also an issue about whether the husband should have the child every weekend, or only every second weekend.) In assessing the alternatives, the court concluded (at para 6):

> ... The issues then are relatively narrow. The first being whether or not the father will have "joint custody" with the mother pending the trial; and secondly, whether the father will have the child for the entire weekend each weekend or simply on alternate weekends.
>
> The parties have separated. Since then while one can anticipate, given the pleadings filed and affidavits delivered, there is going to be antagonism between them, the fact is that they seem to have worked out between themselves, with the assistance of their counsel, a fairly reasonable sharing of child care obligations. The mother is entitled to some time for herself without having to worry about the child. It is only right that the father assist her in that regard by assuming child care responsibilities. He, for his part, is willing to do this and indeed is willing to do this even more than the mother is requesting.
>
> With respect to the issue of the so called "joint custody" of the child, the fact is that at law at the present time the two parents are equally entitled to share the responsibilities and the benefits of custody. In other words, at law they in fact each have coextensive custody of the child at the present time.
>
> I do not anticipate any major decisions that must be decided between now and the trial. In the pleadings each raises serious allegations about the ability of the other to care for the child over a long period of time.
>
> Quite frankly, I am inclined simply to make no order as to custody thereby leaving the general rule in place. There will be, in the circumstances, an order in the nature of a residential order directing where the child will live but making no other provision with respect to custody.

The court held that the child would reside with her mother and, on alternate weekends, with the father.

Clearly, although this "no order" order occurred in the context of an interim, rather than a final, decision, it is important to recall that such an arrangement was also recommended by the Joint Committee Report in Canada, and that a similar proposal was enacted in the United Kingdom. Is this order similar to joint custody? Why or why not? If this arrangement is different from joint custody, which arrangement is preferable? Should the type of arrangement be fixed or contextual?

A CASE STUDY OF JOINT CUSTODY IN CONTEXT: *BUIST v GREAVES*

In *Buist v Greaves*, [1997] OJ No 2646 (Gen Div), the court considered claims about custody and access in relation to the child's best interests. This case demonstrates the interrelationship of a number of issues about custody and care of children, including the use of expert evidence to assess the appropriateness of joint custody and the court's assessment of a relocation claim.

Although the case involved two women in a lesbian relationship, the court held that the issue of sexual orientation was not relevant to determining the issue of "best interests" for a child. As you examine the reasoning in this case, consider whether, or to what extent, you can nevertheless identify assumptions about "good mothering" in the context of this same-sex relationship.

BENOTTO J:

The plaintiff, Ms. Buist, and the defendant, Ms. Greaves, are very intelligent, successful women who lived together in a same sex relationship in London, Ontario between 1988 and 1995. They are both high profile feminists. While together, Ms. Greaves bore a child Simon who is now 4 1/2 years old. Ms. Buist claims sole or joint custody of Simon and an order that he not be removed from London. This is a significant request because Ms. Greaves has been offered a job in Vancouver and wishes to move there with Simon. Ms. Buist also claims a declaration that she is a "mother" of Simon and compensation for the unjust enrichment she says Ms. Greaves enjoyed as a result of her contributions during their relationship. Ms. Greaves counter-claims for child support.

Ms. Buist is a lawyer. She works primarily in the area of family law with an emphasis in women's issues. She is a politically active feminist. Ms. Greaves is a doctor of sociology, a writer, researcher and consultant. She is widely renowned in feminist circles and the past vice-president of the National Action Committee on the Status of Women. She was, until recently, the director of the Centre for Research on Violence Against Women and Children and a faculty member at Fanshawe College.

The court reviewed how the parties began dating in 1985, when Ms. Buist was at the beginning of her career, while Ms. Greaves (who was 9 years older) was more established in her profession. She had been previously married and had a son Lucas who lived with her. In 1988, Ms. Buist moved into Ms. Greaves' home, which had been the matrimonial home during her marriage, but which she now owned. Ms. Greaves also had a country property in Elora. Ms. Buist had no assets of significance.

Ms. Greaves had wanted for some time to have another child. She unsuccessfully attempted conception through heterosexual intercourse. She and Ms. Buist then went to Boston together to a fertility clinic known to be accepting of lesbians. They planned and discussed the conception. For a while, sperm was delivered by courier from Boston to Toronto. This did not result in a pregnancy. Ms. Greaves requested and received a referral to a fertility clinic in a hospital in Toronto where she attended by herself because she did not wish to disclose that she was in a lesbian relationship. She got pregnant but suffered a miscarriage. After the miscarriage, her relationship with Ms. Buist ran into difficulty because Ms. Buist had an affair with a female law student she had hired. Ms. Greaves still wanted a child and returned to a clinic in London. Ultimately, Simon was conceived.

Ms. Buist and Ms. Greaves planned for Simon's birth together. They retained the services of a mid-wife. Friends had a baby shower for them. Ms. Buist carried a beeper around with her so she would know when Ms. Greaves went into labour. Ms. Buist was with her in the delivery room when Simon was born on December 16, 1992. Together they had a "Mad Hatter" party for Simon to celebrate his birth. Two women friends, also in a same sex relationship, were Simon's "goddess mothers."

Simon was a very loved baby. He lived with his mother, Ms. Greaves, Ms. Buist who also cared for him, and his brother Lucas. Ms. Greaves and Ms. Buist shared in all aspects of his life. They divided their time between the Wellington Street home and the property in Elora. They went on trips together and became close friends with Simon's goddess mothers who had a child of their own a few months later. This child, Avery, became Simon's friend. Although Ms. Buist was publicly recognized as a lesbian, Ms. Greaves did not open her private life to the public to the same degree. It is clear, however, that Ms. Greaves and Ms. Buist were, and considered themselves to be, a family.

Ms. Buist shared greatly in Simon's care. She got up in the night and early in the morning to feed him. She was involved in the choice of nannies, of doctors and of schools. Many of the friends that they shared at the time gave evidence about Ms. Buist's involvement in Simon's life. Clearly she was very involved. She was not however, the primary care giver. I accept the evidence of Ms. Greaves and find that Ms. Greaves was the primary care giver. This became more clear as the years went by as the events unfolded which will be described below.

Simon is a lovely child. Unfortunately, he has a learning disability which requires therapy. He is slow in his speech. He also has behaviour problems. He attends speech therapy, currently three times a week. He has also attended special behavioural and developmental therapy. He has been given an enormous amount of loving care and intense attention by Ms. Greaves. Thus, the prognosis for him looks good. One of his doctors, Dr. Rosenbaum, said in November 1996, that his "long-term outlook is probably much better than was originally thought, and that the more Simon shows us what he knows and can do, the more comfortable [Ms. Greaves] will feel about his long-term future."

In October 1994, when Simon was not quite two, Ms. Buist began having a sexual affair with another law student employed by her named Leslie Reaume. Ms. Reaume was then married to a man. Ms. Greaves suspected something was wrong but Ms. Buist denied the sexual aspect of the relationship. In the spring of 1995, on the 10th anniversary of their relationship, Ms. Buist told Ms. Greaves that she was in love with Ms. Reaume.

Ms. Greaves did not want the relationship to end and was willing to do whatever was necessary to keep the relationship together. She offered to put Ms. Buist on title to her property; they even discussed Ms. Buist adopting Simon. Ms. Greaves was upset by the prospect of separation. She was concerned about the effect of a separation on Simon and also on Lucas who by then was 15. Ms. Buist had developed a close relationship with Lucas. Although Ms. Buist would later give evidence that the worst possible thing for Simon is change, she chose to leave the relationship. She moved out in September 1995. This was the greatest change in Simon's life to that date. He was 2 1/2 years old.

Within eleven days of the separation, Ms. Buist had her counsel write a letter to Ms. Greaves about access to Simon. While the letter itself was written in conciliatory terms, Ms. Greaves did not know that. She was too upset to even open it. It was a letter from a lawyer and she perceived that as a threat.

Access to Simon became a source of great conflict between the parties. Ms. Greaves was busy trying to put her life back together and provide stability for Simon. Ms. Buist wanted to spend as much time with him as she could. Ms. Greaves thought access was disruptive, Ms. Buist wanted as much access as possible. The conflict escalated. In March 1996 this action was started. In May 1996 Madam Justice Chapnick made an interim order for access. It provided more access than Ms. Greaves wanted but she felt relieved that at least there would be some order in her life and Simon's. The order did not provide as much access as Ms. Buist wanted and within a short time she was asking for more and the conflict resumed. When she wanted to keep Simon for a long weekend, Ms. Greaves refused. At one point Ms. Greaves threatened to call the police if Simon was not returned in accordance with the order. Justice Chapnick had made no order as to custody.

In the fall of 1996 Ms. Greaves was recruited by the British Columbia Women's Hospital and Health Centre to be its Executive Director. She was offered the job in December. The job is a significant step up for her both financially and career wise. It represents the chance for Ms. Greaves to move to a larger funding base and out of a very focused area of violence to women's health issues generally. She would be the leader of a major initiative, enjoying a broader scope and larger networks. In many ways, this is the position that her entire career has been directed to. It is clearly a major step up.

It is a credit to Ms. Greaves that Dr. Penny Bellem, a physician and vice-president of the hospital, came to Toronto to give evidence about the position and about how they hope to have her in Vancouver. The job was to start on May 1, but that was postponed because of this litigation to July 15.

The facilities available for Simon in Vancouver are superb. Ms. Greaves will be part of a network of hospitals that will provide for him excellent therapy and care. A letter was filed in evidence from Dr. Robert Armstrong, the head of Developmental Paediatrics at the University of British Columbia. He spoke about the facilities available in British Columbia. Dr. Alexander, who was in Ontario for eleven years, and is a colleague of Dr. Rosenbaum (one of Simon's doctors), said "with full confidence" that the services available to Simon would "equal if not exceed" those in Ontario. Counsel for Ms. Buist initially objected to the admission of Dr. Alexander's letter into evidence. Counsel for Ms. Greaves then undertook to call him as a witness. Ms. Greaves also signed a direction authorizing Ms. Buist and her counsel to speak to Dr. Alexander about his evidence in the expectation that his attendance would not be necessary. I was then advised that Dr. Alexander would not be called. Ms. Buist's counsel told the court that he need not be called on her account. She then, however, took the position that his letter could not be referred to for the truth of its contents. That was the reason that Ms. Greaves' counsel undertook to call him and to thereby have him available for cross-examination. Ms. Buist's counsel said it was not necessary to call him. The implication was that she did not need to cross-examine him. I therefore allow the letter to stand as evidence of its contents. I add, however, that even without the evidence in the letter, my decision would not change. I am satisfied on the evidence of Ms. Greaves and of Dr. Bellem, that Simon, being Ms. Greaves' first priority, will receive the same high level of care in British Columbia as he has received in Ontario.

Ms. Greaves told Ms. Buist of her wish to move to the Vancouver job in January 1997. "Over my dead body," Ms. Buist replied. She threatened to take Simon away from her. Her claim was amended to seek sole custody of him. In submissions, her counsel said this was only to afford the court an option should Ms. Greaves decide to move to Vancouver without Simon. Ms. Greaves, however, stated that she would not move without Simon.

CUSTODY AND RELOCATION

At the heart of the very emotional issues in this case is four year old Simon. I must determine what is in his best interest. The focus of my determination is Simon's interests, not the interests and rights of Ms. Greaves and Ms. Buist.

Ms. Greaves is Simon's biological mother and has been his primary care giver since his birth. When the parties were together, they shared in the decision making process. However, Ms. Greaves was still the primary decision maker and care giver. In April 1994, when Simon was 16 months old, Ms. Buist prepared and commissioned a Statutory Declaration sworn by Ms. Greaves which included the sentence: "There is no other parent of [Simon] who is known to me or who has any legal claim for parental rights including custody."

Ms. Buist and the witnesses called by her agree that Ms. Greaves is an excellent mother. I have no doubt that this is true. Moreover, Ms. Greaves is the centre of Simon's world, and thus of his security. When he was away from her last summer for the court ordered access, Ms Buist brought him home early because he missed his mother so much. When he is with his nanny during the day, he speaks of his mother, not of Ms. Buist. There is absolutely no doubt that Simon must remain with his mother. This is generally acknowledged by Ms. Buist. She states that she does not want to take Simon away from his mother and that her claim for sole custody was simply to provide the court with an option if Ms. Greaves chose to leave for Vancouver without him. As Simon must remain in the care of Ms. Greaves, the issue becomes whether joint custody sought by Ms. Buist is in his best interest.

Dr. Goldstein, a well recognized assessor, conducted an assessment pursuant to the order of Mr. Justice Ferrier. The assessment was ordered only a few weeks before trial. The focus of his assessment was "whether the move [to Vancouver] is in the best interest of Simon." Despite the stated objective of his assessment, and the very short time available to him to complete it, he ventured an opinion on joint custody. He felt that it is the optimum situation for a child where the parents have the child's best interest at heart, are reasonable enough to communicate, and intelligent and sensitive enough to deal properly with other people in the lives of the children. He would recommend joint custody for Simon and would like to see a mechanism (such as mediation) that would allow for it.

While I agree with Dr. Goldstein's general views on joint custody, I do not accept his recommendation. In my view, Dr. Goldstein, in the short time available to him, could not have done the investigation necessary to make a determination on custody. A joint custody order, here, would invite disaster. The level of conflict is simply too high. While Ms. Buist held Ms. Greaves responsible for the animosity that exists between them, I find that, as in most cases, the responsibility is divided. I believe that Ms. Greaves felt hurt and abandoned after the separation. She then felt very threatened by the involvement of a lawyer. Ms. Buist, on the other hand, was intent on pursuing her relationship with Simon. She believes that Simon is her son and that she is unfairly being kept from him. I had the distinct impression that her pursuit of her claims had more to do with her perception of her own rights than they did with the best interests of Simon.

This is not an exceptional case where joint custody should be imposed against the parties' wishes. The parties can scarcely speak to each other. The litigation has driven the parties even farther apart. Moreover, I do not find that both parents are equally suitable to the custodial parent. Ms. Greaves is the sole person who should have custody. Simon cannot be separated from his mother. Even Ms. Buist recognizes that.

The fact that Simon has special needs and requires therapeutic intervention increases the need for the parties to be able to work cooperatively. Even during trial there were problems between the parties in relation to Simon's speech therapy. Ms. Buist went to Thames Valley Centre where he was supposed to be receiving therapy. Instead, she found Simon being looked after by a care giver. The therapist was meeting with

Ms. Greaves. She assumed that a clandestine meeting was taking place and that this was further proof of Ms. Greaves' wish to exclude her from Simon's life. In fact, the triggering even for the meeting was a letter written by Ms. Buist's counsel to the Centre wherein she insisted that Ms. Buist be treated the same as Ms. Greaves. Although leave was granted during trial for Ms. Buist to be recalled to give this evidence, she did not mention the letter until cross-examination. As it became clear, the people at the Centre were seeking clarification about, and trying to comply with, her letter. This is but one example of the level of suspicion, misunderstanding and difficulty that permeates the current relationship of Ms. Greaves and Ms. Buist. It is so pervasive that, in my view, it would not be in Simon's best interest to be placed in the midst of it. I have no doubt that Ms. Greaves will make informed, reasoned, careful and correct decisions for Simon if she is granted sole custody. Furthermore, I believe that she will keep Ms. Buist informed of all matters relating to him. I therefore find that it is in Simon's best interest to be in the sole custody of Ms. Greaves.

The next issue is whether it is in his best interests to move. I am guided by the summary of the law in *Gordon v. Goertz* (1996), 19 RFL (4th) 177. The importance of Simon remaining with Ms. Greaves must be weighed against the continuance of full contact with Ms. Buist, his community in London, and his extended family. The ultimate question is his best interests. In considering Simon's best interest, I have regard to the following factors:

1. The existing custody arrangement and the relationship between Simon and Ms. Greaves: As already stated, I view Simon's continued close relationship with his mother to be crucial to his well being. There is no doubt in my mind that to remove him from Ms. Greaves' care would be disastrous.

2. The existing access arrangement and the relationship between Simon and Ms. Buist: Simon sees Ms. Buist on alternate weekends and one evening during the week. It is clear that he loves Ms. Buist and considers her part of his family. This is not disputed by Ms. Greaves.

3. The desirability of maximizing contact between the child and both Ms. Greaves and Ms. Buist: Maximum contact between Simon and Ms. Buist can only be achieved if they remain in the same city. Simon's difficulty with the language would make it difficult, if not impossible, for him to maintain regular contact with Ms. Buist. She fears that he will be unable to express his feelings about losing her and this will cause him harm. Dr. Goldstein said that it is not in Simon's best interest to be moved. Simon has limited flexibility and limited vocabulary. He worried about a lack of further development or a regression as a consequence of the loss he would suffer.

4. Ms. Greaves' reason for moving is only to be looked at in the exceptional circumstance where it is relevant to her ability to meet Simon's needs: I have no doubts about Ms. Greaves' ability to meet Simon's needs. She is intimately involved in the details of his speech therapy and schooling. She has done an extraordinary amount of research on the therapy and care available to him in Vancouver.

5. Disruption to the child of a change in custody: A change of custody would be devastating to Simon.

6. Disruption to the child consequent on removal from family, schools and the community he has come to know: A move for Simon would involve a change in therapists and schools, friends, and a change in the pattern of contact with people close to him, most importantly,

Ms. Buist. Lucas is going to move and Simon would have him as a constant. Ms. Greaves' parents plan to spend time in Vancouver with him. His close friend David Currah is hoping to move to Vancouver. He has changed schools and nannies in the past. While the transition was not easy, it was done carefully and sensitively and he did adjust. Ms. Buist saw no difficulty in introducing him to her new partner Leslie Reaume, who she says "Simon loves." Simon adjusted to that change as he did to the separation.

Dr. Goldstein was concerned about the many changes Simon would have to face if he moves: a new school, new home, new therapists and, most importantly, a loss of regular contact with Ms. Buist. He said that it would be in Simon's best interest not to have these changes take place and not to experience this loss "if it could be arranged for all of this to take place in an atmosphere of cooperation, and devoid of undue struggle." This assumption that he makes is not consistent with the evidence that I have heard. The ongoing conflict between the parties makes undue struggle a necessary consideration.

Dr. Goldstein was wisely motivated by the desire to eliminate any risk for Simon and viewed the move as a risk. He sought to avoid change without adequate consideration to the fact that this change may be beneficial. He did not have, in my view, the information necessary to adequately weigh the alternatives of life in Vancouver versus life in London. By not speaking to Dr. Penny Bellem, he did not know of the extent of the vast resources available to Simon, or of the policy of Ms. Greaves' prospective employer that encourages mothers in their child raising duties. In Vancouver, Ms. Greaves will have a job which significantly advances her career, Simon will have the advantage of her higher income and the facilities available to him at vastly reduced costs. He will have his brother Lucas with him. In London, Simon will have to move anyway because the Wellington property has been sold, primarily so that his mother could pay her legal fees. His care giver, Jennifer Guay, has gone back to school. His mother, in London, has resigned from her job. Some of Ms. Greaves' previous support network in London has dissipated because many of her former friends gave evidence in the proceedings. (Many of them, who gave evidence at trial, seemed surprised that the effect of their involvement in the case would be to end their relationship with Ms. Greaves. This, notwithstanding the fact that some of the evidence given related to private talks they had with Ms. Greaves when she was in the midst of despair as a result of the separation.) If Ms. Greaves were required to remain in London, she would have an inferior job and a different home. This is not in Simon's best interest.

Dr. Goldstein did not contact any of Simon's doctors or therapists although the basis of his recommendation turns on Simon's special needs. He did not seem to appreciate the unworkable nature of the joint custody agreement he hoped for. He said that moves were always difficult but acknowledged that the main thing for a successful move is that the primary parent will take the child's needs into account. As I have already stated, I have no concerns about Ms. Greaves in this regard.

In weighing all of the pros and cons of a move to Vancouver, I come to the inescapable conclusion that Simon must move with his mother. The losses that will inevitably flow from a less regular schedule of contact with Ms. Buist are more than offset by the benefits of moving with his mother and brother.

Ms. Buist takes the position that it is in Simon's best interest that he not be moved because change is not good for him. She thinks the mother should put her needs secondary to him. I note that, when she made the decision to leave Ms. Greaves, she chose what was best for her, not for Simon. In making her choice, she precipitated the most significant change in his life. I also note that Simon adjusted to that change, as I believe he will to the move.

The sexual orientation of the parties is not relevant to my decision. Families exist in a variety of forms. What is important is the love, nurturing and security in which Simon can continue to grow and prosper. Whenever families separate, upset for the child is inevitable. From the child's perspective, the best solution is an intact family. One of the unhappy by-products of a separation is that all choices, from the child's point of view, are thus second best. Where the courts are called upon to resolve these issues, the choice is often to pick amongst these second best choices. It is somewhat unrealistic for parties to assume a lack of change after separation.

I believe that Simon's best interest is served by being with his mother in Vancouver and by maintaining regular contact with Ms. Buist. I believe Ms. Greaves when she says that she will ensure an ongoing relationship with Ms. Buist. This is demonstrated by the parenting plan she put forth as part of her opening trial statement. It sets out extensive times, including three weeks in the summer, for Ms. Buist to have time with Simon. The proposal and her demeanour in the witness box when she confirmed it, convince me that the ongoing relationship with Ms. Buist will continue. The parenting plan as put forth by Ms. Greaves will form part of the order. As Ms. Buist may not have complied with the May 1 notice requirement for August vacation, I may be spoken to if there are difficulties with this summer or the time for commencement of the parenting plan....

The court also considered Ms. Buist's application for a declaration pursuant to *CLRA*, s 4, that she was a "mother" to Simon. Since this case arose prior to the Court of Appeal's decision in *AA v BB and CC* (see Chapter Three), the court held that a child could have only one mother. In addition, however, the court ruled that it was not in Simon's best interests to declare that Ms. Buist was his mother:

There is no doubt that the relationship between Simon and Ms. Buist is very close; however, Simon does not consider her his mother. Ms. Greaves is his mother. He calls her "mama" while he calls Ms. Buist "gaga" which is short for "Peggy." He was given Ms. Greaves' last name at birth. I accept Ms. Greaves' evidence that Ms. Buist did not start referring to him as her son until after the separation. (She learned about it when she read a magazine article quoting Ms. Buist.) Most significantly, when with Ms. Buist and away from Ms. Greaves for an extended time, he is distraught. Ms. Buist lived with Simon's mother in a relationship that was not committed. She began her second affair of the relationship when Simon was less than 2. She left her home when Simon was 2 1/2. She drafted and commissioned an affidavit confirming that Ms. Greaves (not she) was Simon's parent. Most significantly, from Simon's perspective, Ms. Greaves, not Ms. Buist, is his mother. Thus, even if I had the jurisdiction to declare that a child could have two mothers under section 4, I would not, on the facts of this case, exercise my discretion to do so. Ms. Buist has not, on balance of probabilities established the relationship of mother and child.

Benotto J also considered and rejected Ms. Buist's claim that Ms. Greaves had been unjustly enriched, and that Ms. Buist was therefore entitled to restitution. Although Buist had filed volumes of documentation in support of her claim, the court held that there was no evidence that Ms. Buist's contributions contributed to the increase in value of any of the assets; Ms. Buist did not enhance the earning potential of Ms. Greaves; the parties shared equally in the division of household duties; and there was no evidence that Ms. Buist was financially worse off personally or professionally because of the relationship. In addition, Benotto J ordered that Ms. Buist pay Ms. Greaves $450 per month in child support for Simon, a reduced amount that took into account the costs of exercising access.

Additional Resources

Nicholas Bala & Susan Miklas, *Rethinking Decisions About Children: Is the "Best Interests of the Child" Approach Really in the Best Interests of Children?* (Toronto: Policy Research Centre on Children, Youth, and Families, 1993).

Brenda Cossman & Roxanne Mykitiuk, "Child Custody and Access — Discussion Paper" (1998) 15:1 Can J Fam L 13.

Elizabeth J Hughes, "Mother's Vicarious Hand: Primary Caregiving Reconceived as Relationship and Responsibility" (2002) 20 Can Fam LQ 467.

Nancy Mandell, "The Child Question: Links Between Women and Children in the Family" in Nancy Mandell & Ann Duffy, eds, *Reconstructing the Canadian Family: Feminist Perspectives* (Toronto: Butterworths, 1988) 49.

Paul Millar, *The Best Interests of Children: An Evidence-Based Approach* (Toronto: University of Toronto Press, 2009).

Karen M Munro, "The Inapplicability of Rights Analysis in Post-Divorce Child Custody Decision Making" (1992) 30 Alta L Rev 852.

Noel Semple, "Review of Paul Millar, *The Best Interests of Children: An Evidence-Based Approach*" (2010) 48 Osgoode Hall LJ 695.

Carol Smart, "The Legal and Moral Ordering of Child Custody" (1991) 18:4 JL & Soc'y 485.

Carol Smart & Selma Sevenhuijsen, eds, *Child Custody and the Politics of Gender* (London: Routledge, 1989).

PARENTING PLANS

The Special Joint Committee's recommendation for parenting plans

In its Report about custody and access in 1998, the Special Joint Committee stated that parenting plans should be adopted to replace "custody" and "access" arrangements:

> Parenting plans, especially if negotiated directly between parents or with the help of a mediator, are customized to meet the needs of a particular

child and family and have the added advantage of flexibility. Such plans can account for children's specific needs, in terms of activities and schedules, but can also provide for much-needed review as the child develops and his or her needs and interests change. Other people important to the child can be accommodated in a parenting plan, such as by scheduling time with grandparents or other extended family members, or by specifying that such contact is important and that the parents will facilitate such contact. Of course, such provisions would not apply in a case where such contact was considered contrary to the best interests of the children involved. In addition to establishing a dispute resolution mechanism to which the parents will have recourse should they be unable to settle a disagreement, parenting plans should specify the timing and process by which parents will revisit the plan as necessary as the child matures. [The Report also noted that, where parents were unable to agree, they would be entitled to submit their respective plans to a court, and the court would make a parenting plan order that meets the child's best interests.] (Special Joint Committee on Custody and Access, *For the Sake of the Children* (Ottawa: Parliament of Canada, 1998) at 31–32)

Accordingly, the Report recommended that divorcing parents be encouraged to develop parenting plans, setting out details about each parent's responsibilities for residence, care, decision making and financial security for children, together with a dispute resolution process to be used by the parents. It was also recommended that parenting plans require sharing between parents of health, educational and other information relating to the child's development and social activities (see Recommendation 11). This recommendation has not been adopted at the present time in Canada. However, the United Kingdom announced in February 2012 a plan to introduce a "presumption of shared parenting." See Barbara Kay, "It Takes Two to Raise a Child", *National Post* (15 February 2012).

To implement these recommendations, the Report suggested that the *Divorce Act* be amended to require parents applying for a parenting order to file a proposed parenting plan with the court (see Recommendation 13). This recommendation was not implemented.

However, as noted earlier, 2009 amendments to the *Children's Law Reform Act* in Ontario now require a parent or other person applying for custody or access to a child to provide an affidavit containing the person's proposed plan for the child's care and upbringing, and information about the person's previous involvement with child protection or criminal proceedings (see ss 21(1) and (2), as enacted by SO 2009, c 11). Does the prescribed form of the affidavit in s 21(2) inhibit access to justice for parents with lower socioeconomic status? Why or why not?

Parenting plans and dispute resolution processes

The Special Joint Committee also recommended in 1998 the use of mediation and alternative dispute resolution processes in the preparation of parenting plans. Although lawyers and judges often support the concept of parenting plans, this initiative has been particularly supported by counsellors, social workers and psychologists who are involved with separating and divorcing parents. Thus, not surprisingly, the concept of parenting plans is linked to non-litigation methods of resolving disputes. As the Committee explained (at 32–33):

> Experts in mediation from across Canada testified about the importance of promoting this non-adversarial method of helping families restructure themselves after divorce. The benefits of mediation and other alternative dispute resolution mechanisms include reducing rather than escalating tension and conflict between divorcing parents and reducing expenses; they also have the capacity to include children and other interested parties more easily than would be the case with litigation. The growth of mediation as a forum for making parenting decisions after separation or divorce is a widespread international phenomenon....
>
> Women's advocates and some mediators expressed concern about mediation in situations where there has been abuse. They believe that the abusive partner would use mediation as a forum in which to harass or overpower the other partner. These groups also testified that since violence is a common occurrence in Canadian families, mandated mediation would put many women and children at risk....

In this context, the Report recommended (at 33):

> This Committee recommends that divorcing parents be encouraged to attend at least one mediation session to help them develop a parenting plan for their children. Recognizing the impact of family violence on children, mediation and other non-litigation methods of decision making should be structured to screen for and identify family violence. Where there is a proven history of violence by one parent toward the other or toward the children, alternative forms of dispute resolution should be used to develop parenting plans only when the safety of the person who has been the victim of violence is assured and where the risk of violence has passed. The resulting parenting plan must focus on parental responsibilities for the children and contain measures to ensure safety and security for parents and children (Recommendation 14).

Consider again the issues about family law bargaining, discussed in Chapter Five, in relation to these recommendations for parenting plans and alternative methods of dispute resolution at family dissolution. To what extent do the safeguards suggested by the Committee's Report ensure the safety and security of vulnerable family members?

PARALLEL PARENTING

The context for parallel parenting

Court orders for parallel parenting generally occur in a context in which the parents are unable to communicate effectively or to co-operate in parenting their children. In these cases of "high conflict" between the parents, it has been suggested that while joint custody would be inappropriate, an order for "parallel parenting" within a joint custody order may be useful. This view was explained in *TJM v PGM,* [2002] OJ No 398 (Sup Ct), where the court concluded that

[40] [J]oint custody can be an appropriate disposition even in cases where parents are openly hostile and uncooperative. The key is to set up a joint custody arrangement that involves "parallel parenting" versus "cooperative parenting." Under such an arrangement [parallel parenting], both parents have equal status but exercise their rights and responsibilities associated with custody independently from one another.

In this way, the idea of parallel parenting reserves parenting rights and responsibilities for both parents but does not require them to co-operate with one another. Although some judges and lawyers are enthusiastic about such orders, others remain skeptical about their utility. In examining these differing views in the excepts that follow, identify the rationales for supporting such arrangements and the reasons for opposing them.

Support for parallel parenting orders

In an assessment of judicial management of high conflict family law cases, it was noted that although these cases represent only 2–3 percent of a court's caseload, they consume the vast majority of a court's time. Thus, parallel parenting orders were proposed as a way of dealing with these cases.

Managing High Conflict Family Law Cases
(2007) 86 Can Bar Rev 515 at 520–521

Hon Marguerite Trussler

... The view that joint custody is not appropriate where there is conflict is misguided. There is a significant difference between joint custody and joint parenting. Joint parenting does require cooperation. Where there is conflict and a lack of cooperation, the proper approach is to use parallel parenting, rather than joint parenting, within a joint custody order.

Parallel parenting orders require the courts to make extremely detailed orders that fully set out the roles of the parties.... The parenting plan helps to remove the children from the battle zone. Parenting is shared in a clearly defined and structured manner and responsibilities are clearly delineated.... Some basics of a parallel parenting order are:

- The terms "primary residence" and "access" are avoided wherever possible in favour of the neutral term "parenting time."
- Each parent assumes total responsibility for the children during the time they are in his or her care.
- There can be no expectation of flexibility or negotiation.
- The parent who does not have parenting time has no say or influence over the actions of the other parent while the children are in that parent's care.
- Neither parent may plan activities for the children during the other parent's time.
- Contact should be avoided or minimized [using a neutral place or third party to facilitate the exchange of the children].
- Children are not to deliver messages or written notes.
- A system of communication such as a parenting book, email exchange or a specially designed parenting communication program must be used.

• The parenting arrangements must be extremely detailed including exchange time and mode, vacations, schooling, medical practitioners, and so on....

Parallel parenting orders in Ontario courts

As Justice Trussler noted (at 516–522), the experience with court orders for parallel parenting has been somewhat different among provincial jurisdictions in Canada. In Ontario, however, a number of cases have implemented parallel parenting orders:

• In *Mol v Mol*, [1997] OJ No 4060 (Gen Div), the court reviewed the law on joint custody, starting with Wilson JA's dissent in *Kruger* in 1979, and held that the mother's unwillingness to consider a joint custody arrangement, in a context in which the parents held little respect and trust for each other, did not preclude ordering joint custody with a parallel parenting arrangement. In this case, the court also held that such an arrangement was essential in the best interests of the children.

• In *Dagg v Pereira* (2000), 12 RFL (5th) 325 (Ont Sup Ct), a case involving intense conflict between the parents, including assaults, the judge relied on the dissenting view of Wilson JA to outline detailed arrangements for a parallel parenting arrangement.

• In *Ursic v Ursic* (2006), 32 RFL (6th) 23, the Ontario Court of Appeal upheld a lower court order for parallel parenting. In *Ursic*, there was a lack of communication between the parties and a good deal of conflict, but the child was not exposed to the conflict. In this situation, the trial court had ordered joint custody with a parallel parenting plan, and the appeal court approved of this arrangement.

• Relying on *Ursic*, the trial court in *Moyer v Douglas*, 2006 CarswellOnt 8268 (Sup Ct) ordered a parallel parenting plan, based on an assessment undertaken by a social worker pursuant to section 30 of the *CLRA*. However, the court did not accept the plan submitted by the assessor and designed a different plan that incorporated very detailed arrangements for residence, vacations, holidays, birthdays, etc.

Parallel parenting: Joint custody "with a vengeance"?

By contrast with Justice Trussler's views, above, other commentators reviewed these Ontario cases involving parallel parenting orders, and noted that a central argument in favour of parallel parenting is the model's preservation of parental equality with respect to custodial rights (a principle enshrined in *CLRA*'s recognition that each parent may be entitled to custody).

To what extent do you agree with the following assessment?

Joint Custody with a Vengeance
(2004) 22 Can Fam LQ 1 at 22–27 and 31–32

Philip Epstein and Lene Madsen

Epstein and Madsen first reviewed arguments in favour of, and opposed to, parallel parenting orders noting that:

> ... Thus, some of the most vocal supporters of joint custody and parallel parenting are men's rights groups ... that regard these new custodial orders as equality measures.... The second argument proponents raise is that parallel parenting is simply in the best interests of children.... Related to these two arguments is the practical benefit, from a judicial perspective, of being spared the invariably difficult task of choosing one parent, where evidence suggests that both are capable parents.

The authors noted that some provisions in the federal and provincial legislation promote such arrangements. However, they argued that parallel parenting arrangements may not take into account sufficiently the impact of conflict on children and the social science literature that supports this impact. There is also research which belies the judicial optimism that parallel parenting orders will foster co-operation between high-conflict parents. In addition, "best interests" in this context seems to be focused on the goal of achieving equality between the parents. In this context, the authors suggested:

> These critiques are of course not new. Since the arrival of joint custody, feminists and others have raised concerns regarding the concept of [formal] equality upon which the concept is premised, and the consequences, particularly for women, of assuming formal equality. Early on, commentators expressed concern that "pretending" parents are substantively equal may result in parenting arrangements whereby women undertake most of the daily care of their children, while their former partners retain control over decisions which in the end affect not only their children but women as well. These critiques were raised in the context of simply joint custody in low-conflict situations, but are exponentially more powerful when applied to parallel parenting....
>
> In *Kruger*, Justice Wilson had before her parents described as co-operative, open and honest, with a demonstrated ability to make a joint custodial arrangement work.... Against these facts, she sought to make a "more humane custody order" that in her view would serve both the short- and long-term best interests of the children.
>
> Parallel parenting bears little relation to this vision of joint custody put forward by Justice Wilson and cannot in our view be described as the humane outcome she sought to achieve.... In our view, the judicial optimism about the ability of these orders to foster co-operation is as yet unwarranted, and the version of equality that the orders promote, hollow and barren. In the end, it is our view that when Justice Wilson proposed that courts "do everything possible" to maintain children's relationships with both parents, parallel parenting was far from what she had in mind....

How should courts respond to this critique in relation to possible orders for parallel parenting?

In reflecting on this challenge, consider a comment published in response to Epstein and Madsen by two professionals involved in alternative processes for dispute resolution of custody matters. In this context, they argued that it is important to understand parenting plans and parallel parenting in developmental and psychological terms.

Thus, they argued that although parenting plans and parallel parenting arrangements offer no panacea in the struggles experienced by children and their families at separation or divorce, these arrangements tend to protect children from parental conflict and facilitate relationships with each of a child's parents. In addition, these critics suggested that these arrangements build on parents' strengths rather than focusing on their limitations.

In promoting parenting plans and parallel parenting, these commentators argued that neither "sole custody" nor "joint custody" titles actually define *how* decisions are to be made. More significantly, courts do not generally monitor parents on a day-to-day basis as they implement court orders relating to their children:

> [S]olutions for every day parenting practices that arise post-separation and divorce have little or nothing to do with legal custody. Family law problems are intertwined with human relations and the law. Historically, the law has been inadequate in facilitating and/or monitoring the needs of children and families pre- and post-separation and divorce. Hence, the introduction of parenting plans, parallel parenting, and the proliferation of various alternative dispute-resolution methods (ie information sessions about family law, assessment, mediation, collaborative law services and parenting coordinators).... While the court may suggest to parents how to behave in front of one another when the children are around, the court can not facilitate how the parents can learn to actually do this. Through discussion with a dispute resolution professional a parenting plan can facilitate this process.... (Rachel Birnbaum & Barbara Jo Fidler, "Commentary on Epstein and Madsen" (2005) 24 Can Fam LQ 337 at 343)

To what extent do these comments confirm or refute the arguments of Justice Trussler on one hand, or Epstein and Madsen on the other? Consider how parallel parenting arrangements may be useful in the context of current governmental policies in Ontario that emphasize providing information to parents in custody disputes, along with opportunities for mediation. To what extent may cases requiring parallel parenting orders require judicial oversight rather than mediation?

Additional Resources

Nicholas Bala, Rachel Birnbaum & Hon Donna Martinson, "One Judge for One Family: Differentiated Case Management for Families in Continuing Conflict" (2010) 26:2 Can J Fam L 395.

Jonathan Cohen & Nikki Gershbain, "For the Sake of the Fathers? Child Custody Reform and the Perils of Maximum Contact" (2001) 19 Can Fam LQ 121.

Barbara Jo Fidler, "Developing Parenting Time Schedules: Conundrums and Considerations" in Martha Shaffer, ed, *Contemporary Issues in Family Law* (Toronto: Carswell, 2007) 353.

Raymond Guerette, "Accessing Justice in the Family Courts of New Brunswick" (2012) 63 UNBLJ 49.

Elizabeth Hughes, "The Language and Ideology of Shared Parenting in Family Law Reform: A Critical Analysis" (2003) 21 Can Fam LQ 1.

Martha Shaffer, "Joint Custody, Parental Conflict and Children's Adjustment to Divorce: What the Social Science Literature Does and Does Not Tell Us" (2007) 26 Can Fam LQ 285.

Bren Neale & Carol Smart, "'Good' and 'Bad' Lawyers? Struggling in the Shadow of the New Law" (1997) 19:4 J Soc Welfare & Fam L 377.

Bruce Smyth, ed, *Parent–Child Contact and Post-Separation Parenting Arrangements* (Melbourne, Australian Institute of Family Studies, 2004).

Bruce Smyth et al, "Legislating for Shared-Time Parenting after Parental Separation: Insights from Australia" (2014) 77 Law & Contemp Probs 109.

ASSESSING "SHARED PARENTING" REFORMS

Empirical studies in Australia

As noted, other jurisdictions such as the United Kingdom and Australia abolished formal orders for "custody" and "access" some years ago. However, it seems that these legal changes may not always result in substantive changes for separated or divorced families. For example, Helen Rhoades examined the results of three empirical studies of the impact of such reforms in Australia and concluded that

> ... [t]he findings of the three studies show that the intended results of the reforms have largely failed to materialize. Parents continue to organise their arrangements around a custody and access division of labour, the new terminology remains alien to the bulk of the population (including separated couples), litigation has increased, and judges and practitioners approach final hearings about residence much as they did before.
>
> A range of reasons were given for this failure by respondents to the studies, including the inherent logistical difficulties of co-parenting across two households, and the perceptions of many practitioners that the reforms were no more than "old wine in new bottles." But a dominant theme of the responses was that the separation process is simply not conducive to co-operation between former spouses, particularly among those who use the legal system to resolve their disputes. As one registrar of the Court put it:
>
>> The shared parenting concept is totally at odds with the types of parents who litigate....
>
> (Helen Rhoades, "The Rise and Rise of Shared Parenting Laws: A Critical Reflection" (2002) 19 Can J Fam L 75 at 90–91)

Rhoades's study focused particularly on the relationship between the goals of increased contact with both parents, on the one hand, and protection from violence on the other, concluding that these messages were often contradictory in practice. Although there were a number of problems with the reforms, Rhoades argued that the basic vision of "shared parenting" was fundamentally flawed:

> The shared parenting reforms were based on a vision of the ideal post-separation family. This is not just a matter of marginalising women's (tentatively raised) concerns about violence. It also ignores the diverse reality of families generally. For one thing, it takes no account of the inherent fluidity of family life which affects parenting before and after separation. The reforms created a paradox by encouraging ongoing collaboration while at the same time imposing an enforceable right of contact that assumes a static arrangement.... [M]ore dangerously, the shared parenting regime treats all children alike, as a monolithic group with the same needs. In doing so it marginalises children from violent homes, whose perspective of family is very different to that of children who have not shared their experience. And collaboration between these children's parents is not uppermost in their list of needs....
>
> Perhaps more fundamentally there is a sense that these reforms were a cynical exercise, a sympathetic (empathetic?) response to the complaints of a particular constituency, with little genuine commitment to bringing about cultural change.... (Rhoades at 107–108)

In reflecting on these comments, consider the extent to which legal reforms can succeed in achieving fundamental change for families and the relationships among family members. How does your answer to this question affect your perception of the role for law with respect to arrangements for the children of divorce?

Additional Resources

American Law Institute, *Principles of the Law of Family Dissolution: Analysis and Recommendations* (St Paul, MN: American Law Institute Publishers, 2002).

Susan B Boyd, *Child Custody, Law and Women's Work* (Toronto: Oxford University Press, 2003).

Elizabeth Hughes, "The Language and Ideology of Shared Parenting in Family Law Reform: A Critical Analysis" (2003) 21 Can Fam LQ 1.

Eleanor Maccoby & Robert Mnookin, *Dividing the Child* (Cambridge, MA: Harvard University Press, 1992).

Helen Reece, *Divorcing Responsibly* (Oxford & Portland, OR: Hart Publishing, 2003).

Helen Rhoades, "The Rise and Rise of Shared Parenting Laws: A Critical Reflection" (2002) 19 Can J Fam L 75 at 90–91.

Helen Rhoades, "Contact Enforcement and Parenting Programmes: Policy Aims in Confusion" (2004) 16 Child and Family Law Quarterly 1.

Carol Smart, "The 'New' Parenthood: Fathers and Mothers after Divorce" in Elizabeth Silva & Carol Smart, eds, *The New Family?* (London: Sage Publications, 1999) at 100.

Carol Smart, Bren Neale & Amanda Wade, *The Changing Experience of Childhood: Families and Divorce* (Cambridge: Polity Press, 2001).

Jennifer H Sperling, "Reframing the Work–Family Conflict by Rejecting the Ideal Parent Norm" (2013) 22 Am UJ Gender Soc Pol'y & L 47.

V.
CHILD SUPPORT: "PUBLIC" AND "PRIVATE" RESPONSIBILITIES?

Child support enforcement is part of a wholesale shift in the legal regulation of the family and the balance of relationships between mothers and fathers. Child support starts from the need to insure that a larger percentage of the nation's resources are linked to children, but ... child support in itself is unlikely to solve the problem of child poverty. Rather, its greatest impact is likely to be on the middle class and on the conduct of relationships that never become the subject of court orders. Like many exercises in setting norms, the most visible aspects of the process may well be the sanctions against those who fail to comply. The success of the endeavour, however, is more likely to lie with the creation of a new ethic of parenthood. (June Carbone, "Child Support Comes of Age: An Introduction to the Law of Child Support" in J Thomas Oldham & Marygold Melli, eds, *Child Support: The Next Frontier* (Ann Arbor, MI: University of Michigan Press, 2000) 3 at 11)

THE EVOLUTION OF CHILD SUPPORT OBLIGATIONS

The context for child support in Canada

Although child poverty remains an issue for many children in Canada, it seems that issues about financial security and uncertainty are often experienced by children in post-dissolution families:

The experience of divorce and separation is a profound life transition for most children.... What is harmful to children is ... the decline in financial security and parental resources that too often accompanies divorce or separation.

Redefining family relationship post-divorce can be often as challenging. "There are no social rules or conventions governing how divorced families should behave, nor are there conventions governing how divorced or blended families fit into society." Children are in the position of navigating not one but two or more new family situations. From this perspective, an exclusive focus on "family breakdown" can serve to impede constructive legislative and policy changes that could cushion the problems that children and families can experience when forging new family relationships. (*Families Count* at 66, citing Zheng Wu & Christoph Schimmele, "Divorce and Repartnering" in Maureen Baker, ed, *Families: Changing Trends in Canada*, 6th ed (Toronto: McGraw-Hill Ryerson, 2009) at 177)

Since separation and divorce usually involve the creation of two households, rather than just one, and since repartnering may bring additional financial obligations, issues about financial security for children at family dissolution are complex. Moreover, for families with limited financial resources, the challenge of providing adequate support for children is often significant. And, as will be discussed later in this chapter, levels of child support are usually based on income received by a payor parent in the previous year, so that increases or decreases in income may not be immediately reflected in child support obligations. All these factors make arrangements for child support payments complicated.

The evolution of legal principles concerning child support

Judicial principles for determining child support awards after the enactment of the *Divorce Act* in 1968 were highly discretionary.

In Ontario, for example, the decision in *Paras v Paras* (1970), 2 RFL 328 (Ont CA) established that

- child support should be set at a level that would maintain the child at the pre-divorce standard of living; and that
- the costs of achieving that standard be apportioned between the parents in proportion to their respective incomes.

As is apparent, the *Paras* principle requires considerable discretion to determine the amount payable in each particular case. More significantly, the principle assumes the continued existence of sufficient resources to enable children to have the same standard of living post-divorce (in spite of the need to support two households) as they had enjoyed in the intact family. Clearly, there will be many situations in which family resources are insufficient to meet this standard.

Moreover, the variability of child support awards, partly as a result of the wide scope for discretionary decision making by judges, increasingly created concerns about fairness and consistency. In one assessment, for example, Carol Rogerson concluded that

> [p]roblems begin to appear ... when one examines more closely the way in which the costs associated with children are calculated, the way in which they are apportioned between the parents, and finally, the quantum of child support awarded. As in the spousal support cases..., there is often an obvious disjuncture between the principles articulated and the actual outcomes in terms of quantum of support. The end result is that in the majority of child support cases awards are not set at levels which will meet the *Paras* standard or even at levels which would guarantee an equal standard of living between the children's household and that of the non-custodial parent. Typically the household of the custodial parent (usually the mother) and children is left with an income between 40 and 80 per cent of that enjoyed by the non-custodial parent. Thus what is typically a three-person household subsists on less than what is typically, until the husband remarries, a one-person household. (Carol Rogerson, "Judicial

Interpretation of the Spousal and Child Support Provisions of the Divorce Act, 1985 (Part II)" (1991) 7 Can Fam LQ 271 at 274)

In addition to these problems, other commentators identified problems with the tax treatment of child support, and recommended reforms. For example, see Nerys Blown & Susan Milliken, "The Failure of the Legal System to Protect the Economic Rights of Children" (1989) 7 Can J Fam L 366.

In the 1990s, several courts tried to define more precisely how to determine the obligations of parents for child support.

For example, in *Levesque v Levesque* (1994), 4 RFL (4th) 375, the Alberta Court of Appeal set out a list of factors to be considered in determining the amount of child support; and the *Levesque* analysis was substantially accepted by the Supreme Court of Canada in *Willick v Willick*, [1994] 3 SCR 670. See Christine Davies, "The Emergence of Judicial Child Support Guidelines" (1995) 13 Can Fam LQ 89.

In the context of these developments, however, the Supreme Court of Canada considered an appeal from Québec concerning the treatment of child support in relation to income tax. In particular, Suzanne Thibaudeau argued (in part) that the inclusion/deduction provisions of section 56 of the *Income Tax Act*, RSC 1985, c 1 (5th Supp), pursuant to which her former husband (the payor) could deduct the amount of his child support payments, while she (as the payee custodial parent) had to include them in the calculation of her income, violated the equality guarantee in section 15 of the *Charter*.

In *Thibaudeau v Canada*, [1995] 2 SCR 627, a majority of the Supreme Court of Canada concluded that the inclusion/deduction provisions did not infringe the equality rights guaranteed by section 15(1) of the *Charter*. Two justices, the only two women members of the court, dissented, adding to the controversy about the need for reform of child support arrangements in Canada.

In this context, national Child Support Guidelines were enacted through the co-operation of federal, provincial, and territorial governments in Canada in 1997. (See Nicholas Bala, "Ottawa's New Child-Support Regime: A Guide to the Guidelines" (1999), 21 RFL (4th) 301; Lisa Philipps & Margot Young, "Sex, Tax and the *Charter*: A Review of *Thibaudeau v. Canada*" (1995) 2 Rev Const Stud 221; and Faye Woodman, "The *Charter* and the Taxation of Women" (1990) 22 Ottawa L Rev 625.)

"Public" and "private": Child support and economic re-adjustment at separation

As June Carbone's comment above suggested, legal obligations of child support reflect a societal commitment to the economic well-being of children, particularly in the context of separation and divorce. However, her comment argued that legal principles also reveal an emphasis on privatized family support for dependency, reinforcing how the well-being of children is the primary responsibility of the family rather than the state.

According to Carbone, concerns about child poverty as a result of rising divorce rates and single-parent families became intertwined in the 1990s with broader fiscal policies that emphasized the need to conserve governmental resources. Thus, in a number of jurisdictions, including Canada, there were major efforts to reform the legal obligations of parents for child support, both to increase the levels of support for children and also to ensure better enforcement of these obligations. As Carbone explained (at 3), principles concerning child support obligations have increasingly become more significant in the modern effort to define and enforce family obligation.

As these comments suggest, child support obligations need to be examined not only in relation to obligations between former spouses but also within a larger context of public policies about responsibility for dependency at family dissolution. In this way, child support is also part of the package of economic re-adjustment for families at separation or divorce.

In addition, however, Carbone argued (at 3) that child support obligations represent "a critical element in a larger shift from the husband–wife relationship to parent–child ties as the defining element of family obligation." Moreover, she suggested that this change has been accomplished without addressing a number of fundamental questions:

> This legal shift is problematic at least in part because it proceeds from a public-policy consensus on the need for greater financial contributions to children without clearly addressing the relationship between fathers and mothers necessary to bring about such contributions. Reform supporters, an otherwise unlikely alliance of women's groups committed to greater equality and conservatives eager to protect the public fisc, agree only on a starting point — the principle that all parents should support their children. The almost universal support for the governing principle, however, begs the difficult questions of implementation: How does "natural" obligation translate into dollar amounts? Is it independent of the parents' relationship to each other? Of the circumstances of the child's conception and birth? Of obligation toward other children? Of ideas of equality and fairness between the parents?

Some of these questions continue to be addressed in Canada with respect to our national Child Support Guidelines. Thus, as you review the materials that follow, consider the extent to which the Guidelines have privatized responsibility for supporting children at family dissolution, and the extent to which they have redefined parent–child relationships. In addition, it is important to explore the extent to which judicial discretion is necessary in the implementation of the Guidelines. To what extent have they achieved their stated goals of fairness and consistency?

Additional Resources

Vicky Barham, Rose Anne Devlin & Jie Yang, "Public Policies and Private Decisions: The Effect of Child Support Measures on Marriage and Divorce" (2006) 35:2 J Leg Stud 441.

Vicky Barham, Rose Anne Devlin & Chantale LaCasse, "Are the New
  Child-Support Guidelines 'Adequate' or 'Reasonable'?" (2000) 26:1
  Can Pub Pol'y 1.

Ross Finnie, "The Government's Child Support Package" (1997) 15 Can
  Fam LQ 79.

Tina Maisonneuve, "Child Support Under the Federal and Quebec Guidelines: A Step Forward or Behind?" (1999) 16 Can J Fam L 284.

Paul Miller & Anne Gauthier, "What Were They Thinking? The Development of Child Support Guidelines in Canada" (2002) 17 CJLS 139.

Laura W Morgan, "Family Law at 2000: Private and Public Support of the
  Family — From Welfare State to Poor Law" (1999) 33:3 Fam LQ
  705.

MJ Mossman, "Child Support or Support for Children? Re-Thinking the
  'Public' and 'Private' in Family Law" (1997) 46 UNBLJ 63.

VI.
CHILD SUPPORT: DEFINING PARENT–CHILD RELATIONSHIPS

> When is a person obligated to support his or her partner's children and
> how should a court determine the amount and duration of support assum-
> ing a person has assumed the role of a parent? There aren't many cases
> where Judges answer either question very well. (James McLeod, *Family
> Law Newsletter*, 2001 at 34, cited in R James Williams, "No Silk Purse
> from this Sow's Ear: Social Parents and Child Support" in Martha
> Shaffer, ed, *Contemporary Issues in Family Law* (Toronto: Carswell, 2007)
> at 259)

DEFINING "PARENT–CHILD RELATIONSHIPS": LEGISLATIVE DEFINITIONS

The federal *Divorce Act* and Ontario's *Family Law Act*

Recall that the scope of federal legislation applies to married spouses who
are seeking divorce, while provincial legislation is applicable to spouses who
are married and separated but have not applied for divorce, and to cohabiting spouses who separate. In addition, there may be issues about conflicts
of laws in the context of applications for child support. For example, see
Sun v Guilfoile, 2011 ONSC 1685, where an Ontario court declined jurisdiction to hear an application where a Japanese court had made an earlier
order for child support.

Both the federal and provincial statutes include definitions of parent–
child relationships, although these definitions are not exactly the same.
In addition, definitions of parent–child relationships often differ from province to province in Canada, and many of these definitions also offer oppor-

tunities for judicial discretion in interpreting them. As a result, there is not always consistency in determinations about the meaning of parent–child relationships in Canada. (In addition to these definitions of parent–child relationships, it is now necessary to consider the definitions contained in the Child Support Guidelines, as will be discussed later in this chapter.)

Definitions for Biological and Adoptive Parent–Child Relationships

Pursuant to section 2(1) of the *Divorce Act*, the definition of "child of the marriage" includes two groups of children:

- Children under the age of majority who have not withdrawn from parental charge; and

- Children who have reached the age of majority or older, who are under parental charge, but are "unable, by reason of illness, disability or other cause, to withdraw from their charge or to obtain the necessaries of life."

In Ontario, section 31(1) of the *Family Law Act* creates obligations of parents to provide support for an unmarried child who is a minor, or is enrolled in a full-time program of education, to the extent that the parent is capable of doing so. Section 31(2) eliminates a parental obligation to support a child who is 16 years of age or older, if the child has withdrawn from parental control.

These definitions appear to create obligations for parents who are biological or adoptive parents, but both statutes also include "expanded" definitions that must be considered.

Expanded Definitions of Parent–Child Relationships: "Social Parents"

In addition to the above definitions, both federal and provincial statutes provide "expanded" definitions of parent–child relationships:

- Section 2(2) of the *Divorce Act* states that included in the definition of "child of the marriage" is a child of two spouses or former spouses if a) they both stand in the place of parents; and b) if one is a parent and the other stands in the place of a parent. The meaning of "in the place of a parent" was analyzed by the Supreme Court of Canada in *Chartier v Chartier* in 1999, discussed later in this section.

- Section 1(1) of Ontario's *Family Law Act* states that a "parent" includes a person who has demonstrated a settled intention to treat a child as a child of his or her family; and "child" is similarly defined. As will be discussed, the language of Ontario's statute about "settled intent" parents is slightly different from that in the federal statute ("standing in the place of a parent"), and these differences are also discussed later in this section.

Consider the legislative language in the federal and provincial statutes. To what extent do these provisions create opportunities for judicial discretion? What policy goals might encourage an expansive interpretation of these statutory definitions? Particularly in a context in which family members have the primary responsibility for supporting children's financial well-being, how should courts interpret these provisions? How do you think differing interpretations will affect family formation and behaviour of social parents?

PARENT–CHILD RELATIONSHIPS: BIOLOGICAL RELATIONSHIPS AND *CLRA* PRESUMPTIONS OF PATERNITY

Ontario's *Children's Law Reform Act* provides that "for all purposes of the law," a person is the child of his or her natural or adoptive parents (see ss 1(1) and 1(2)). In addition, section 1(4) expressly abolished the status of illegitimacy when the statute was first enacted in 1978.

In addition, section 8 of the *CLRA* provides presumptions of paternity, "unless the contrary is proven on a balance of probabilities."

For example, where a person is married to the mother of a child at the time of the child's birth, that person is considered to be the child's father (s 8, #1).

Section 5 permits an application for a declaration of paternity where no presumption is applicable. In addition, section 4 permits an application for a declaration that a person is "the father" or "the mother" of a child. Recall that the limitation in this language was extended by the use of the *parens patriae* jurisdiction in *AA v BB and CC*, discussed in Chapter Three.

Examine the list of circumstances in which presumptions are available in section 8. Is there a need for legislative reform of the *CLRA* more generally? For example, the B.C. *Family Law Act*, SBC 2011, c 25, Part 3 includes detailed provisions for defining "parentage," including in circumstances of assisted reproduction.

Consider the decision in *Low v Low*, regarding the use of assisted reproduction by an opposite-sex couple, who then separated. To what extent does this case confirm the need for legislative reform of the *CLRA*?

Low v Low
(1994), 4 RFL (4th) 103 (Ont Gen Div)

In *Low v Low*, a married couple decided, because of the husband's low sperm count and inability to conceive, to arrange for artificial insemination of the wife by an anonymous donor. The child, Karen, was born and the husband certified the child's birth as her father under the *Vital Statistics Act*, RSO 1990, c V.4. By the time of the child's birth, however, the parties' relationship had so deteriorated that the wife demanded that the husband leave the home. He did so 10 days later. Eventually the husband sought and obtained a divorce.

The wife sought a declaration that the husband was not the father of the child, and the husband sought a declaration that he was the father. In reviewing the applications, the court stated (at 111):

... PATERNITY DECLARATIONS

As indicated, the husband seeks a declaration under ss. 5(1) and (3) of the *Children's Law Reform Act*, RSO 1990, c. C.12 ("CLRA"), that he is Karen's father. The wife seeks a declaration pursuant to the CLRA that he is not Karen's father....

Ferrier J considered sections 1, 4, 5, and 8 of the *CLRA* and continued (at 113):

The words "natural," "natural parent," "parent," "father," and "natural father," appearing in these sections, are not defined in the legislation. In s. 1(1), the word "natural" appears before the word "parents." In s. 8(1)3, the word "natural" appears before the word "father." The omission of the word "natural" as an adjective in describing "father" in other sections suggests the intention of a meaning broader than mere "biological" father, in those sections.

I note also that the declaration authorized in s. 4(1) is *not* that a male person is the "natural father," rather that he is "recognized in law" to be the "father" of the child. This also suggests an intention of a meaning broader than merely the "biological" father.

As well, where a presumption does not arise under s. 8, a person may apply under s. 5(1) for a declaration that a person is his "child" (not "his natural child" or his "biological" child). The declaration is permitted when "the relationship of father and child has been established" (s. 5(3)). This subsection does not use the expression "natural father."

Section 4 provides the remedy of a declaration to those who are able to rely on the presumptions in s. 8. In the case at bar, the presumption has been raised by ss. 8(1) and 8(1)5. Is such presumption rebutted by the fact of artificial insemination? It is not necessary to decide this question, because, in my view, a declaration can be made under s. 5.

Nowhere in s. 5 is there any suggestion that "the relationship of father and child" must have a biological or genetic character. As above noted, this section does not use the word "natural" in describing "father" or "relationship." Why was the expression "relationship of father and child" used in s. 5(3)? I conclude that this expression must mean something broader than a mere biological relationship.

In coming to this conclusion, I am guided by s. 10 of the *Interpretation Act*, RSO 1990, c. I.11:

10. Every Act shall be deemed to be remedial, whether its immediate purport is to direct the doing of anything that the Legislature deems to be for the public good or to prevent or punish the doing of anything that it deems to be contrary to the public good, and shall accordingly receive such fair, large and liberal construction and interpretation as will best ensure the attainment of the object of the Act according to its true intent, meaning and spirit.

In *Bagaric v. Juric* (1984), 44 OR (2d) 638, the Court of Appeal made the following observations about the CLRA, at p. 647:

The Act, being solely concerned with the status of children, does not deal with the consequences which might flow from the declaration of that status as a result of other legislation. The importance and significance of a declaration of parentage by itself is emphasized in that: "any person having an interest" may apply under s. 4(1) for such a declaration where s. 8(1) is applicable; the child may apply for a declaration that a female person is the mother; the child may apply for a declaration of paternity where no presumption under s. 8(1) applies; a male person may apply to have a child declared to be his child. There is no time limitation on these applications except that under a s. 5 application both persons to the relationship must be living. Finally, there is no necessity for corroboration, although the Act introduces the right to secure blood tests, the results of which might, under particular circumstances, be considered to be corroborative of the mother's evidence.

At p. 648, it was further stated:

The fact that the Legislature severed from the declaration of parentage any issue as to expenses and maintenance, placing them in new and different statutes, is of significance. It is also of significance that the right was greatly widened involving all children and both mothers and fathers. The Legislature recognized by this legislation present social conditions and attitudes as well as recognizing that such declarations have significance beyond material ones. It must be remembered that the Act itself is entitled *"Children's Law Reform Act."* (Emphasis added.) [Emphasis in original.]

Apparently there is no previous decision interpreting this legislation where a declaration is sought in a case of artificial insemination by an anonymous donor. Counsel were unable to refer me to any Canadian case involving similar legislation, but courts in the United States have dealt with similar issues. While recognizing that the legislation being considered was, in each case, different from that being considered here, I note that in most cases the United States courts have found "the husband" to be the lawful father of the child for virtually all purposes. Although not binding on this court, the American case law is instructive, and of assistance. I make particular reference to two US decisions.

In *S. v. S.*, 440 A2d 64 (1981), the Superior Court of New Jersey held that a husband in Mr. Low's position is the lawful father of a child conceived via artificial insemination. At p. 68 of that decision, the court looks at the issue in the context of public policy:

Insofar as this is the case, the best interests of the child, the mother, the family unit and society are served by recognizing that the law surrounding AID insemination *deals with the creation of a family unit and more particularly with the creation of parent–child relationships*. Thus viewed, the public policy objectives served by legitimacy laws should similarly and consistently be applied in dealing with closely related problems presented by the use of AID techniques. [Emphasis added.]

In *Brooks v. Fair*, 532 NE 2d 208 (1988), the mother of the child asked the court to determine the non-existence of the parent–child relationship between her child, who was conceived via artificial insemination, and the man who was her husband at the time of the birth. The Court of Appeals of Ohio agreed with the lower court's determination that there existed a parent–child relationship.

Considering the language of the CLRA, the *Interpretation Act* and the observations of the Court of Appeal in *Bagaric v. Juric*, I conclude that Mr. Low is entitled to the declaration he seeks under s. 5 of the *Children's Law Reform Act*. Accordingly, a declaration shall issue that

Timothy David Low is the father of Karen Elizabeth Low, born April 10, 1990.

The court ordered custody to the mother, with liberal access to the father.

Notes and Questions

Parentage and biological connections

Recall the cases discussed in Chapter Three in relation to the court's analysis in *Low v Low*. Is *Low* consistent with judicial conclusions about parental status in the absence of biological connection? Consider also recent developments with respect to "openness" in adoption and with respect to sperm donors. How should courts reconcile parental status in these cases? Is the best interests of the child principle of assistance? Do such cases encourage the recognition of more than two parents? See Yehezkel Margalit, Orrie Levy & John Loike, "The New Frontier of Advanced Reproductive Technology: Reevaluating Modern Legal Parenthood" (2014) 37 Harv Women's LJ 107.

Is it relevant that in *Low v Low*, the claims were asserted in order to obtain legal recognition of the parent–child relationship? Should the same principles be used to determine liability for child support? You may wish to reconsider this question after reviewing definitions in the Child Support Guidelines later in this section. See for example, June Carbone & Naomi Cahn, "Marriage, Parentage, and Child Support" (2011) 45:2 Fam LQ 219.

Proving paternity: *Re Rhan and Pinsonneault*

In some cases, it may be necessary for parties to litigate the issue of parentage.

Section 10 of Ontario's *Children's Law Reform Act* permits a court to grant leave for blood tests or DNA tests, but there is no legal requirement for a person to undergo such tests.

However, section 10(3) appears to create some risk for a person who chooses not to take blood tests after leave has been given. What factors should be considered by a court in granting leave for blood tests pursuant to section 10?

In *Re Rhan and Pinsonneault* (1979), 27 OR (2d) 210 (Co Ct) the mother of a 22-month-old child brought an application for blood tests (prior to the availability of DNA tests) to determine parentage, apparently because she was required to do so to retain entitlement to social assistance. In a review of the principles applicable to such an application, the court suggested a number of factors for consideration:

1. Were the applicant and respondent married at the time the child or children were born? This is the situation in *Re H. and H.* referred to above, where the husband was seeking divorce on grounds of living separate and apart from his wife since 1958 and the wife alleged that five children of the marriage resulted from the husband's access dur-

ing separation. Here, clearly, there is a presumption that the husband is the father of the children born during marriage and the order was granted.

2. Did the parties cohabit in a common law relationship of some duration during which time or shortly thereafter a child was born?

3. Did the respondent admit sexual intercourse with the applicant at or near the time calculated to be the point of conception but now denies that he is the actual father of the child but alleges another is?
   ...

4. Although there was not a common law union, did the respondent admit to an extramarital relationship with the applicant wherein sexual intercourse occurred from time to time thus making it possible that he is the putative father?

5. Was the applicant able, through affidavit and other evidence, to establish a *prima facie* case of putative fatherhood notwithstanding the denial of the respondent as to fatherhood and/or ever having sexual intercourse with the applicant?

On the facts in *Re Rhan and Pinsonneault*, the court concluded that it was not appropriate to make an order for blood tests because the applicant's evidence revealed a one-night stand at a motel with the respondent almost two years earlier, and because her application was filed only to meet the requirements of the welfare authorities. In this situation, the court exercised its discretion to deny the claim, noting that although there was a duty to protect the interests of the child, there was also an obligation not to infringe the personal rights of the respondent:

> On the facts of this case, to make such an order bearing in mind that approximately 22 months went by before notice was given to the respondent of his alleged fatherhood, on the basis of an accusation stale with age arising out of an alleged experience of two-hour duration between parties who had no previous or subsequent relationship, platonic or otherwise, and brought into Court on the heels of the demands of the welfare officials for action would not be in keeping with the spirit of the section and the spirit of justice as this Court understands it....

For other cases in which applications for blood tests were denied, see *L(FA) v B(AB)* (1995), 15 RFL (4th) 107 (Man CA); and *M v S* (1999), 48 RFL (4th) 145 (NS Fam Ct).

Constitutional challenges to *CLRA*, s 10

There have been a number of challenges to the constitutionality of provisions such as section 10. In *P(K) v N(P)* (1988), 15 RFL (3d) 110 (Ont HC), the applicant challenged the validity of this section pursuant to section 7 of the *Charter*, but the court held that there was no constitutional infringement, stating (at 111):

> ... I do not find that the impugned provision interferes with the physical or mental integrity of the individual. It does not authorize the forcible taking of blood. The impugned provision requires that the party seeking a blood test must apply to court for leave to obtain the tests and to then submit the results in evidence. If the court grants leave to obtain blood tests, the

individual is nonetheless entitled to refuse to submit to the tests pursuant to s. 10(3) of the Act. The result of such a refusal is to provide the court with the power to "draw such inferences as it thinks appropriate."

The drawing of an inference against a party who does not provide relevant evidence in a court proceeding, when that evidence is within the exclusive control of that party, does not constitute compulsion or coercion. It is an evidentiary matter to be considered in the context of a civil proceeding in which paternity is an issue.

If there is no compulsion or coercion involved in an order made under s. 10 of the Act, the provision constitutes neither a denial nor an infringement of the rights guaranteed by s. 7 of the Charter....

The constitutionality of section 10 was reviewed and upheld in *Silber v Fenske* (1995), 11 RFL (4th) 145 (Ont Gen Div). See also *Rath v Kemp* (1997), 26 RFL (4th) 152 (Alta CA); and *D(JS) v V(WL)* (1995), 11 RFL (4th) 409 (BCCA). Should privacy rights relating to blood testing trump effective processes to determine paternity? Why or why not?

PARENT–CHILD RELATIONSHIPS: THE CHALLENGE OF "ADULT" CHILDREN

Withdrawing from parental charge: *Seabrook v Major*

According to section 2(1) of the *Divorce Act*, a parent has no obligation for a child under the age of majority who has withdrawn from parental charge. Similarly, pursuant to section 31(2) of Ontario's *Family Law Act*, a parent has no obligation for a child who is 16 years or older who has withdrawn from parental charge.

In *Seabrook v Major* (2005), 79 OR (3d) 528 (Div Ct), the court considered an appeal from an order granting an increase in child support to the mother of two sons, born in 1988 and 1989. The parties divorced in 1995, and the mother obtained custody of the two sons.

The spouses' younger son suffered from severe developmental and behavioural disorders together with a type of attention deficit hyperactivity disorder. He was temporarily in care in 1996 and 1997, and a Crown wardship order was granted in 1998. According to this order, the mother was obliged to pay $80 per month to the Children's Aid Society to assist in caring for her son, although the order terminated her parental status. Eventually, it seems that the son was assigned to a group home where he was able to receive treatment, but his mother also remained actively involved in his care and contributed to his financial support.

The father resisted the mother's application for additional support in relation to the younger son, arguing that he was no longer a child of the marriage pursuant to section 2(1) of the *Divorce Act*.

The trial judge concluded that the mother's continuing involvement with her younger son, including with respect to medical and other consultations and her physical care and financial contributions to his support, resulted in the son being a "child of the marriage," even though he was a Crown ward.

On appeal, a majority reversed the trial judge's decision, but all three judges wrote opinions.

- According to Meehan J, the provisions of the *Child and Family Services Act* clearly removed the care and control of a child from parents "once a finding has been made that the child is a child in need of protection" (at para 24).

- According to Swinton J, the definition in the *Child and Family Services Act* means that "a Crown ward is no longer in the charge of his or her parents, even though he remains their child in law. Therefore, he is not a "child of the marriage...." (at para 30).

- According to Molloy J (dissenting), the fact that a child has been found to be in need of protection and is therefore in the care of a Children's Aid Society does not necessarily mean that the child is no longer a "child of the marriage":

    On the contrary, ... the particular circumstances of the child must be looked at in context to determine if the parent seeking support may still be regarded as having "charge" of the child to a sufficient degree to be eligible to receive support for the child (at para 37).

    On the facts in this case, Molloy J held that the younger son remained a child of the marriage, in spite of the protection order, and thus it was appropriate to vary the child support order accordingly.

What are the consequences of this decision for the "child" in this case?

Although the issue in the case turned on the relationship between the definition of a "child of the marriage" in the *Divorce Act* and provisions regarding Crown wardship in Ontario's *Child and Family Services Act*, are there larger policy issues in such cases as well? For example, how should support issues about children with disabilities who are above the age of majority be resolved? What difference does it make whether the child with such disabilities is in an intact family, or in a family in which the spouses have divorced? Does the outcome in this case assign responsibilities for caring for a dependent family member between parents and the state appropriately?

"Adult" children and ongoing child support: The legislative context

Both the *Divorce Act* and the *Family Law Act* create ongoing financial obligations for parents of children who are over the age of majority in some circumstances. The continuation of financial obligations for these "adult" children has resulted in a good deal of litigation.

For example, in *Sullivan v Sullivan* (1999), 50 RFL (4th) 326 (Ont Div Ct), a woman aged 22 succeeded in obtaining interim child support, payable by her father, because she attended school, but only part time as a result of illness. In commenting on this case, decided pursuant to section 31(1) of the *FLA* (which requires full-time attendance at school), James McLeod critiqued the courts' discretionary decision making pursuant to statutory language, and provided an overview of how courts have interpreted the relevant provisions. In examining his comments, consider whether, or to what extent, there is a need for reform to create similar definitions in federal and provincial legislation?

Annotation of *Sullivan*
(1999) 50 RFL (4th) 326 at 327–328

James McLeod

... Over the past few years, it has become increasingly clear that courts are not particularly troubled by the words of the relevant legislation in child-support cases. However, this appears to be the first time that an appeal court has simply ignored the words of the legislation and the existing case law to reach what it considers a fair result.

An adult child has a more limited right to support under the *Family Law Act* than under the *Divorce Act*. Under the *Divorce Act*, s. 2(1) "child of the marriage," a spouse must pay child support for his or her adult children who are under parental charge and unable to withdraw from parental charge or maintain themselves for a legally acceptable reason: see *Welsh v. Welsh* (November 3, 1998), Doc. St. Catharines 35,110/ 95 (Ont. Gen. Div.), where Quinn J. reviewed in detail the circumstances when an adult child was entitled to support under the *Divorce Act*. According to the definition of "child of the marriage" in s. 2(1) of the *Divorce Act*, a court cannot order child support for an adult child who has withdrawn from parental charge. In many cases, courts ignore the requirement that an adult child is entitled to support only if he or she is still under parental charge and extend support to any child who is unable to maintain himself or herself for a legally acceptable reason. This interpretation ignores that, grammatically, the statutory requirement that an adult child must be under parental charge applies to both children who are unable to withdraw from parental charge and children who are unable to obtain necessaries for themselves. The courts have extended child support under the *Divorce Act* to adult children in school who no longer live with a parent at any point in the school year. One of the more extreme examples of the current overinterpretation of s. 2(1) of the *Divorce Act* is *Colonval v. Munson* (May 5, 1998), Doc. Victoria 5939/ 26455 (BCSC), where Cowan J. held that an adult child continued to be entitled to support as long as he remained in school, notwithstanding the fact that he cohabited with his girlfriend; see also *Collins v. Collins* (1998), 221 AR 111 (QB) (no need for child to live at home to receive support).

The court had less discretion as to whether to award child support under the *Family Law Act* in *Sullivan* than if the claim had been brought under the *Divorce Act*. Pursuant to s. 31 of the *Family Law Act*, an adult child is entitled to support only if he or she has not voluntarily withdrawn from parental control and is enrolled in a full-time program of education. The onus is on a person claiming child support to prove that an adult child is entitled to support: *Keighley v. Keighley* (December 30, 1997), Doc. New Westminster DO 16392 (BCSC), except that a court will not presume voluntary withdrawal from parental control under s. 31(2) of the *Family Law Act*: *Giess v. Upper* (1996), 28 RFL (4th) 460 (Ont. Gen. Div.); *Zedner v. Zedner* (1989), 22 RFL (3d) 207 (Ont. Prov. Ct.). In *Sullivan*, the mother alleged that the child still lived at home and was under her control. At least at an interim stage, this should be sufficient to overcome the proviso in s. 31(2) of the *Family Law Act* (voluntary withdrawal from parental control)....

The problem in *Sullivan* is that even if the adult daughter is under parental control, she is not enrolled in a full-time educational program. The undisputed evidence is that the daughter attended university only part time. It is interesting to note that s. 31(1) of the *Family Law Act* does not state that the child must attend school full time, just that she must be enrolled in a full-time program of education. Arguably, if a child is enrolled full time but attends school only part time, she may still be entitled to support: *Copeland v. Copeland* (December 9, 1992), Doc. Newmarket 24698/92 (Ont. Gen. Div.), [1993] WDFL 122, TLW 1236-023 (court not to impose a standard of devotion, priority and effort on a child as a condition of continuing a claim for support). However, in *Geiss v. Upper* ... [(1996), 28 RFL (4th) 460 (Ont. Gen. Div.)], the court held that a child's participation in an educational program must be meaningful and of such a nature and quality as to be consistent with the program's purposes and objectives.... Although courts tend to grant support to children in need, especially children making a reasonable effort to pursue an education within their limitations, a court cannot grant support to a child who is not entitled to support under the relevant legislation. It is submitted that Walsh J. erred in granting support under the *Family Law Act* to an adult child who was not enrolled in a full-time program of education and the Divisional Court erred in upholding the daughter's support entitlement, albeit in a reduced amount. The court's refusal to award the daughter any of her costs of the proceedings suggests that the court recognized that its conclusion was questionable, to say the least. The father had more resources than the daughter, did not succeed in extinguishing support and could better afford the costs of the litigation. In most cases, it is submitted that the daughter would have received at least part of her costs.

What is the explanation for the court's expansive interpretation in *Sullivan*? To what extent do you agree with McLeod's critique that the decision was not in accordance with the statutory definition in section 31 of the *Family Law Act*? To what extent does the court's interpretation in *Sullivan* seem to reflect decisions pursuant to the *Divorce Act*? Is it relevant that governmental support for students was declining at the time of this decision? Does this case reflect a shift in state responsibility for dependent "adult" children to their families? Reflect on these questions in relation to the discussion that follows about responsibilities for post-dissolution families to support children in relation to the expenses of post-secondary education, a responsibility that is not legally assigned to parents in intact families. Is it discriminatory that non-students do not get this support? Should parents be required to fund advanced (Masters and Doctoral) post-secondary degrees?

Adult children and post-secondary education

Section 2(1) of the *Divorce Act* provides for payment of support for a child who is over the age of majority but unable, by reason of "illness, disability or other cause," to withdraw from parental charge or obtain the necessaries of life. As a number of commentators have indicated, courts tend to regard a child's pursuit of post-secondary education as worthy of support, and some have applied a "presumptive approach".

For example, in *McConnell v McConnell*, 2002 SKQB 72, a Saskatchewan court stated that the presumption of entitlement to further education or training nonetheless did not entirely discharge the onus of establishing that, by reason of the educational pursuit, the child is unable to withdraw from parental charge or obtain the necessaries of life.

Moreover, in *Farden v Farden* (1993), 48 RFL (3d) 60, a B.C. Master identified eight factors for consideration in the exercise of discretion in cases involving adult children pursuing post-secondary education. Although some of these issues need to be taken into account in relation to the Child Support Guidelines, discussed later in this chapter, the "*Farden* factors" remain substantially valid.

In this context, section 2(1) of the *Divorce Act* appears to create obligations on the part of divorced parents to provide financial support for the post-secondary education of their adult children, a legal obligation that is not required of parents in an intact family. As the cost of post-secondary education has risen, moreover, while the extent of governmental support has somewhat declined, a number of *Charter* challenges have been launched pursuant to section 15 equality. However, courts have tended to deny such challenges. See Nicholas Bala & David Faour, "When Does Childhood End?: Canada's Lengthening Obligation to Support Adult Children" (2014) 33 Can Fam LQ 69.

For example, in *Beutler v Maki*, 2005 SKQB 393, the court stated in part (at paras 35–36):

> It must be borne in mind that the *Divorce Act*, the Guidelines and their judicial interpretation, have created an anomaly. An intact family has the ability to require of their child that he or she pay 100% of post-secondary education. There is no appeal from that decision. No variance can be sought. If that is the decision of the parents, that is the hurdle the child faces.
>
> The situation for a broken family is radically different. The payor, regardless of his or her consent, may be obligated to contribute for post-secondary education. The case law is relatively consistent in requiring that contribution be for the first degree. There are cases where it has been extended beyond that.
>
> As a result, you have like-situated individuals (parents of adult children in university) being treated radically differently, solely by reason of their marital status. For devotees of arguments under the *Charter* of Rights and Freedoms, that type of condition typically engages *Charter* remedy. However, there are a number of decisions that have determined that the anomaly is not an affront to the *Charter*....

For other cases denying that the *Charter*'s equality guarantee was infringed, see *Souliere v Leclair* (1998), 38 RFL (4th) 68 (Ont Gen Div); and *Rebenchuk v Rebenchuk*, 2007 MBCA 22.

Notes and Questions

The impact of agreements: *Hyde v Lang* and
Louie v Lastman

There are some cases in which courts have granted entitlement to support for adult children, even though their parents had agreed that no such support would be payable.

Consider this situation:

> The parents separated and entered into an agreement, which was sanctioned by the court. The agreement specified that the father would not see the couple's child and that he would not pay child support. The mother supported the child financially and emotionally and neither the parents nor the child attempted to reestablish the father's relationship with the child.
>
> However, after completing one year of university education, the child applied for support pursuant to section 31 of the *FLA*. The father argued that the agreement signed at separation with the child's mother resulted in the child's lack of entitlement to such support. How should this argument be resolved by the court?

In *Hyde v Lange* (1996), 22 RFL (4th) 317 (Ont Gen Div), the court granted support on the basis that the child was entitled to support pursuant to section 31(1). Stating that the *Family Law Act* was rooted in dependency, the court held that the child's right to support should not be affected by the fact that a parent did not exercise access, nor from any arrangement entered into by her parents that compromised her right to support.

Do you agree that this decision is correct, that is, that agreements entered into by parents should not preclude subsequent applications for child support, at least in relation to children attending post-secondary educational institutions?

Compare *Hyde v Lange* to *Louie v Lastman (No 1)* (2002), 61 OR (3d) 449 (CA).

In *Louie*, two brothers, born in 1958 and 1962 respectively, claimed retroactive child support when they discovered that a man who had been known to them in childhood as a friend of their mother was in fact their biological father.

The boys had been raised by their mother and her husband until the spouses' separation in 1969. Thereafter, their mother received social assistance and some small monthly payments from the boys' biological father. However, the mother eventually signed an agreement, releasing all claims against the biological father in 1974, in return for a lump sum of $25,000 and payment of her legal fees. The biological father was a wealthy merchant, and later mayor of Toronto, and the boys wished to establish that he had a fiduciary obligation to them because they had been raised in poverty, while the father's two sons with his wife had experienced "wealth and privilege."

According to the Ontario Court of Appeal (at 454), the claim was not entitled to succeed:

> No matter how the appellants attempt to frame their action, in the end it is nothing more than a claim for retroactive child support and, as such, it cannot succeed. I would not foreclose the possibility that a fiduciary claim for child support outside the legislative scheme where the child is in need and there is a gap in the legislative scheme. That, however, is not this case. The appellants concede that had their mother made a claim for child support under the legislation in force while they were children, the court could have made an order for support. It is not open to the appellants to come forward and make a support claim decades after they are no longer dependent....

In *Louie v Lastman*, would the mother's agreement with the biological father have precluded an order for child support during the years when the boys were dependent and under the age of majority? Is this case really about a lack of "need" and dependency? (See also *S(L) v P(E)*, 1999 BCCA 393, where the court similarly refused to make an order for retroactive child support on the basis that the parties had made an agreement to this effect in 1984.) The issue of retroactive child support is also considered later in this chapter.

The relevance of a parent–child relationship: *Parsons v Parsons*

In some cases, courts have ordered payment of child support by a parent, even when the child does not co-operate in maintaining any relationship with the payor parent.

For example, in *Parsons v Parsons* (1996), 17 RFL (4th) 267 (Ont Gen Div), the father was ordered to pay child support to his wife in an amount of $400 for one year in relation to his daughter, aged 24, who was a medical student. The daughter had no ongoing relationship with her father, but the court held that she was a "child of the marriage" pursuant to section 2(1) of the *Divorce Act*, and that she had not disentitled herself from assistance. In doing so, however, the court advised the father that he could apply for a review of the support after one year, if no parent–child relationship had been established by that time.

According to Marie Gordon, *Parsons* is probably typical of such situations:

> There seems to be a consensus that the quality of a child's relationship with his or her parent is but one of a number of considerations in a determination [pursuant to section 2(1) of the *Divorce Act, 1985*]. The older cases read a little sternly, implying a filial duty and the requirement of a connection between support and an ongoing relationship.... Most judges, however, are loath to disentitle a child from support simply because of an unhappy or non-existent parent/child relationship....

Judges seem sensitive to the fact that the deterioration of a parent/
child relationship is seldom a simple, unilateral, inexplicable act of
a child.... Rather than terminating support, judges are more likely to
use their powers to impose conditions, require reporting and "check-
ins," hold children responsible for some expenses, take a "wait-and-see"
approach, or to allow a parent to re-apply if there is no effort at
communication.... (Marie Gordon, "'Making the Break': Support for Adult
Children in 2006" in Martha Shaffer, ed, *Contemporary Issues in Family
Law* (Toronto: Carswell, 2007) 299 at 320)

Is this an appropriate resolution of cases such as *Parsons*?

Additional Resources

Hon David Corbett & Claudia Schmeing, "Child Support for Estranged
  Adult Children: 'Parent as Wallet' or 'Can't Buy me Love'" (2011) 30
  Can Fam LQ 165.
Philip Epstein & Ilana Zylberman, "Support for Adult Children in Cases of
  Estrangement: The Parent as Wallet" in *Special Lectures of the Law
  Society of Upper Canada, 2006* (Toronto: Irwin Law, 2007).
Aaron Franks, "Post-Secondary Education and the 'Twixters'" (2006) 24
  Can Fam LQ 55.
Marie Gordon, "'Making the Break': Support for Adult Children in 2006"
  in Martha Shaffer, ed, *Contemporary Issues in Family Law* (Toronto:
  Carswell, 2007) 299.
Terry Hainsworth, "Support for Adult Children" (1999) 17 Can Fam LQ 39.
Jeffery Wilson, "The Forgotten Child: Children who have Withdrawn from
  Parental Control" (LSUC-OBA Continuing Education Program,
  Toronto, 2 and 3 May 2002).

PARENT–CHILD RELATIONSHIPS: "STANDING IN THE PLACE OF A PARENT" OR "SETTLED INTENT" PARENTS

"Step" or "blended" families: Rising numbers

While stepfamilies were most often created in the past after the death of a
parent, they are now more commonly formed after the dissolution of a
marriage or a cohabiting relationship. Such families are often referred to as
"blended families":

A blended family is one with at least one child from a previous relationship of the mother or father or both, plus one created in the current relationship. About eight out of ten blended families have had at least one
child together....
    Second and third unions experience higher rates of dissolution than
first-time unions, [but] stepfamily couples who decided to have a child
together stay together longer than those who do not....

> Policy-makers and courts have only just begun to grapple with the complexities that stepfamilies present, particularly around issues such as the rights and responsibilities of step-parents. For example, stepparents have been ordered to pay child support for stepchildren where there is a longstanding relationship.... [C]ourts are taking the lead in setting out the parameters of caring relationships — and the benefits and duties that flow from them.... (*Families Count* at 68)

These comments suggest that repartnering is frequently part of the process of family dissolution, and that this development means that adults, other than biological and adoptive parents, will be involved with children in many blended families. How should these adult and child relationships be treated in law?

"Expanding" parent–child relationships in law

In the context of the dissolution of adult relationships through separation or divorce, and adult repartnering, both federal and provincial legislation indicate that adults in such relationships may be regarded as "parents" in some cases. For example, as noted earlier:

- Section 2(2) of the *Divorce Act* provides that a "child of the marriage" may include children for whom one or both of the spouses "stand in the place of a parent."

- Similarly, section 1(1) of Ontario's *Family Law Act* includes as parents persons who have demonstrated a "settled intention" to treat a child as "a child of his or her family."

However, the legislation does not provide definitions for this terminology about "standing in the place of a parent" or demonstrating a "settled intent" to treat a child as a child of the family. As a result, judges have been required to exercise discretion to determine when such relationships have been established. Sometimes, these relationships are referred to as "social parent" relationships, thus distinguishing them from biological or adoptive relationships.

However, problems may arise in circumstances where a social parent's relationship with a child's parent terminates. And, as noted above, such subsequent repartnering relationships seem to be somewhat more fragile than first unions.

In this context, one significant question addressed by the courts was whether a social parent could terminate a parent–child relationship when the intimate relationship with the child's biological parent ended.

This question was answered in different ways by courts in different provinces. See especially *Carignan v Carignan* (1989), 22 RFL (3d) 376 (Man CA); and *Theriault v Theriault* (1994), 149 AR 210 (CA). In 1999, the Supreme Court of Canada addressed this issue and considered these differing approaches in appellate courts in *Chartier v Chartier*.

Chartier v Chartier
[1999] 1 SCR 242

In *Chartier v Chartier*, the parties were married for one year and had one biological child. However, the wife had a child from a previous relationship, for whom the husband stood "in place of a parent" in accordance with section 2(2) of the *Divorce Act*. When the marriage ended, the wife applied for support for both children.

The trial judge held that the husband had terminated the relationship with the wife's child and so ordered no support for her: see (1996), 111 Man R (2d) 27 (QB (Fam Div)). Relying on its earlier decision in *Carignan v Carignan*, the Manitoba Court of Appeal dismissed the appeal: see (1997), 29 RFL (4th) 96.

On appeal to the Supreme Court of Canada, the wife's appeal was allowed. In part, Bastarache J stated (at para 17):

> ... There is one body of case law, exemplified by *Carignan*, *supra*, that states that a person standing in the place of a parent is entitled to make a unilateral withdrawal from the parental relationship. The other body of case law is typified by *Theriault v. Theriault* (1994), 149 AR 210 (Alta. CA); it states that a person cannot unilaterally withdraw from a relationship in which he or she stands in the place of a parent and that the court must look to the nature of the relationship to determine if a person in fact does stand in the place of a parent to a child.
>
> Before considering these two lines of authority, I would note that in both cases the courts have engaged upon a historical review of the doctrine of *loco parentis* and taken the view that the words "in the place of a parent" used in the *Divorce Act* were intended to have the same meaning. The doctrine of *loco parentis* was developed in diverse contexts, trust law, tort law, master–apprentice relationships, schoolmaster–pupil relationships, wills and gifts..., at another time. Alison Diduck, in "*Carignan v. Carignan*: When Is a Father Not a Father? Another Historical Perspective" (1990), 19 *Man. LJ* 580, explains how this common law doctrine was applied in family matters, over the years, in various jurisdictions. She concludes, at pp. 601–602, by saying:
>
> > The *in loco parentis* doctrine is a creature of 19th century patriarchy. It evolved during a time when it was a morally offensive notion for a man to be held responsible for another man's child. As Mendes de Costa UFJ stated in a 1987 decision, it has "its roots deep in history" and "carries with it connotations of times past" (*Re Spring and Spring* (1987), 61 OR (2d) 743 at 748). Notwithstanding Parliament's choice of similar wording in the *Divorce Act, 1985*, it is arguably open to counsel (or to courts) to suggest that Parliament deliberately chose to reject the common law notion of *in loco parentis*, and that the current statute should be interpreted "free from the shadow of earlier authorities." (*Ibid.*, at 749.)
>
> I agree that the policies and values reflected in the *Divorce Act* must relate to contemporary Canadian society and that the general principles of statutory interpretation support a modern understanding of the words "stands in the place of a parent." ...
>
> This being said, it is my opinion that the decision in *Theriault*, *supra*, provides the proper approach to this issue as it recognizes that the provisions of the *Divorce Act* dealing with children focus on what is in the best

interests of the children of the marriage, not on biological parenthood or legal status of children. *Theriault* was an appeal from an interim maintenance award made to the mother and primary care-giver of two children made against the husband in a pending divorce suit. The children were not the husband's biological children. The husband gave advice and supervision to the two children from infancy but, at the hearing for interim support, he argued that his commitment to the children arose from the marriage and was conditional on the continuation of that relationship.

Kerans J.A. rejected the approach in *Carignan*, *supra*, and held, at p. 213, that once someone "has made at least a permanent or indefinite unconditional commitment to stand in the place of a parent," the jurisdiction of the courts to award support under the *Divorce Act* is triggered and that jurisdiction is not lost by a subsequent disavowal of the child by the parent. Underlying Kerans J.A.'s decision is the best interests of the child. At p. 213, Kerans J.A. held:

> Our society values parenthood as a vital adjunct to the upbringing of children. Adequate performance of that office is a duty imposed by law whenever our society judges that it is fair to impose it. In the case of the natural parent, the biological contribution towards the new life warrants the imposition of the duty. In the case of a step-parent, it is the voluntary assumption of that role. It is not in the best interests of children that step-parents or natural parents be permitted to abandon their children, and it is their best interests that should govern. Financial responsibility is simply one of the many aspects of the office of parent. A parent, or step-parent, who refuses or avoids this obligation neglects or abandons the child. The abandonment or neglect is as real as would be a refusal of medical care, or affection, or comfort, or any other need of a child....

Whether a person stands in the place of a parent must take into account all factors relevant to that determination, viewed objectively. What must be determined is the nature of the relationship. The *Divorce Act* makes no mention of formal expressions of intent. The focus on voluntariness and intention in *Carignan*, *supra*, was dependent on the common law approach discussed earlier. It was wrong. The Court must determine the nature of the relationship by looking at a number of factors, among which is intention. Intention will not only be expressed formally. The court must also infer intention from actions, and take into consideration that even expressed intentions may sometimes change. The actual fact of forming a new family is a key factor in drawing an inference that the step-parent treats the child as a member of his or her family, i.e., a child of the marriage. The relevant factors in defining the parental relationship include, but are not limited to, whether the child participates in the extended family in the same way as would a biological child; whether the person provides financially for the child (depending on ability to pay); whether the person disciplines the child as a parent; whether the person represents to the child, the family, the world, either explicitly or implicitly, that he or she is responsible as a parent to the child; the nature or existence of the child's relationship with the absent biological parent. The manifestation of the intention of the step-parent cannot be qualified as to duration, or be otherwise made conditional or qualified, even if this intention is manifested expressly. Once it is shown that the child is to be considered, in fact, a "child of the marriage," the obligations of the step-parent towards him or her are the same as those relative to a child born of the marriage with regard to the application of the *Divorce Act*. The step-parent, at this point, does not only incur obligations. He or she also acquires certain rights, such as the right to apply eventually for custody or access under s. 16(1) of the *Divorce Act*.

Nevertheless, not every adult–child relationship will be determined to be one where the adult stands in the place of a parent. Every case must be determined on its own facts and it must be established from the evidence that the adult acted so as to stand in the place of a parent to the child.

Huband J.A., in *Carignan, supra*, expressed the concern that individuals may be reluctant to be generous toward children for fear that their generosity will give rise to parental obligations. I do not share those concerns. The nature of a parental relationship is complex and includes more than financial support. People do not enter into parental relationships with the view that they will be terminated.

Notes and Questions

Social parents and child support

Do you agree that informed adults may choose not to enter new relationships because of the potential consequences of child support obligations if the spousal relationship ends? Should such "parents" be automatically assigned support obligations if they were not aware of them when they decided to enter a relationship with a child's parent? In reflecting on this question, consider the following critique:

Bastarache J's reasons are consistent with the weight of recent authority. An adult should not be allowed to terminate his or her relationship with a child. It is not in a child's best interests to have parent figures passing through his or her life. With respect, holding that a step-parent incurs a long-term child-support obligation does not prevent that from happening. The Supreme Court of Canada seems to assume that a person will continue his or her relationship with a child if he or she has to pay support. The court ignores the fact that, in many cases, denying or terminating support merely makes the law reflect the reality of the post-separation relationship between step-parent and child.

The fact that adults live together does not amount to a commitment that they will remain together. Many relationships are of short duration. Many people are not inclined to make the accommodations necessary to ensure that their relationship will continue. In light of this, should the courts impose a long-term financial commitment on a person who was pleasant to a partner's child for a short time? The Supreme Court of Canada apparently believes that it should. It is surprising that a short-term spousal relationship that is insufficient to give rise to a spousal support claim may be sufficient to give rise to a child-support claim where the adult–child relationship was incidental to the spousal relationship.

The Supreme Court of Canada rejected the suggestion that a person may not be as inclined to interact with a child if he or she will incur a long-term financial relationship. Bastarache J. does not explain how he decided what effect his decision would have on peoples' actions. With respect, people are more aware of the legal consequences of their actions in a family law context than they were a few years ago. The increase in the use of the remedial constructive trust to share property and the extension of rights to less traditional family units has led to a greater awareness that personal relations carry legal consequences. It will not be surprising if men, in particular, seek contractual protection from child support or attempt to minimize their interaction with a partner's child. While it may not speak well of many men, it also would not be surprising if women with children had an even more difficult time forming family relationships after *Chartier.*

In *Chartier*, the parties cohabited, married, separated, reconciled and separated again, all within three years. As a result, Mr. Chartier acquires a long-term child-support obligation. Whether that is reasonable is not the question. The Supreme Court of Canada has decided that it is the law. The task facing many lawyers will be to advise their clients on how to prevent that from happening to them. It appears that the only way to prevent a long-term child-support commitment is never to establish a parent–child relationship with a partner's child. Social scientists will have to decide whether that is a good way to force people to interact. (James McLeod, "Annotation of *Chartier v. Chartier*" (1999) 43 RFL (4th) 2 at 4)

Applying *Chartier*: *Gardiner v Gardiner*

Notwithstanding the Supreme Court's decision in *Chartier*, some courts have distinguished it.

For example, in *Gardiner v Gardiner*, 2001 NSSF 20, the Nova Scotia Supreme Court (Family Division), considered a father's application for a declaration that his wife stood *in loco parentis* to his two sons (from a previous relationship). The parties had cohabited for two years and been married for three. There was evidence that the children's biological mother had remained in contact with the children, and that their father and a nanny had provided most of their day-to-day care. In addition, the evidence showed that the wife had not expended money to support the children nor had she provided primary care for them because she worked outside the home. In this case both sons were experiencing some difficulties: the older son had behaviour problems while the younger one, Nicky, had cerebral palsy.

In concluding that the wife should not be held to be *in loco parentis* pursuant to section 2(2) of the *Divorce Act*, the court stated (at 244):

> ... Therefore, should Cheryl Gardiner be found to be *in loco parentis* to Nicky, she will carry with her the financial obligation to contribute to the support of that child for so long as he continues to be dependent, which will be for the rest of his natural life.
>
> Does a relationship of five years with Nicky's father warrant this life-long responsibility to her husband's son? According to *Chartier*, it does. *Chartier* stands for the proposition that once *in loco parentis* is established, the child must be treated in the same manner as one's biological or adopted child.

In the end, although the court found that the wife had taken on some responsibilities as a parent or caregiver, the relationship did not establish the foundation for the long-term implications attached to a finding of *in loco parentis*. Was it the nature of the relationship, or the extent of the support obligation, that was most significant in this case? To what extent should this case be regarded as exceptional? Do you agree with the outcome in *Gardiner*? What additional facts do you think would be required for a finding that an *in loco parentis* relationship was established? See Christine Dobby, "Whose Responsibility? Disabled Adult 'Children of the Marriage' Under the *Divorce Act* and the Canadian Social Welfare State" (2005) 20 Windsor Rev Legal Soc Issues 41.

More recently, in *NP v IV*, 2013 BCSC 1323, the court stated at para 49 that:

> a finding that a stepparent who has given a child no affection, no comfort, nor met some other of their needs since their first having assumed the office of a parent, cannot debar the Court from a determination that they are a person standing in the office of parent. In other words, the parent–child relationship need not be a model one. Otherwise, every person in such office who neglected their duties could rely on that very neglect to dodge the obligations flowing from standing in the place of a parent ... As Kerans J.A. also pointed out ... "Financial responsibility is simply one of the many aspects of the office of parent."

The statutory language and cohabiting relationships

In *Chartier*, the Supreme Court of Canada decided that a married spouse stood "in the place of a parent" to the other spouse's child, and thus was required to pay child support for this child. To what extent should the *Chartier* principles apply in situations involving cohabitation only?

In reflecting on this question, recall the Supreme Court's decision in *Nova Scotia (AG) v Walsh*, discussed in Chapter Six, and the court's conclusion that marriage constitutes a choice about rights and responsibilities that do not necessarily apply to cohabiting couples. Should this argument apply with respect to the issue of whether a person who cohabits with a parent becomes a social parent to his or her child? Recall also *Jane Doe v Alberta* (Chapter One) and the court's conclusion that intention is just one factor. The overriding principle is always "best interests" in relation to children.

Consider these issues in relation to *Monkman v Beaulieu*, a Manitoba decision about the application of *Chartier* to cohabiting couples. Note also the court's reasoning about the different statutory language with respect to a person who "stands in place of parent" and one who demonstrates a "settled intent" to treat a child as the person's family. Do you agree that this language is appropriately interpreted to create the same obligations? Why or why not?

Monkman v Beaulieu
2003 MBCA 17

In *Monkman v Beaulieu*, a majority of the Manitoba Court of Appeal held that the *Chartier* principles apply to cohabiting couples as well as to those who are married. In this case, the parties began to cohabit in August 1988 and separated in January 1992. They had one child together, but the mother had four other children, one of whom was the focus of this case. She was one month old when the adults' relationship had begun, and she had called the respondent "Dad" from about the age of two. The affidavit evidence demonstrated that the respondent had accepted her as his stepchild, and the child had no connections with her biological father. Thus, according to Steel JA, the evidence supported an inference that the respondent stood in the place of a parent to this child.

The court then considered provisions of the *Family Maintenance Act*, RSM 1987, c F20, and its wording about a parent who acts *in loco parentis*. This wording was translated in the *Divorce Act* as "standing in the place of a parent." However, in interpreting this language, the appeal court did not draw any distinctions between these different forms of wording, and also focused on the requirement in section 2(1) that the best interests of a child "shall be the paramount consideration of the court." In exploring this requirement, Steel JA stated (at paras 30–31):

> Unilateral severance focuses on the interests of the adult who assumed the *in loco parentis* relationship. A court should instead give the provisions an interpretation which protects the interests of the dependent child. The interpretation that best serves children is one that recognizes that when adults intentionally take on the role and responsibilities of a parent, then the children can depend on the continuation of that role.
>
> An interpretation that adopts unilateral severance disregards any notions of bonding and attachment between the child and a psychological parent. Family law affecting children has moved from preserving parental rights over children to decisions identifying the best interests of children and promoting children's welfare. Those, I believe, are the objectives of the Acts, and *in loco parentis* should be interpreted harmoniously with those objectives.

In addition, Steel JA considered the relevance of the fact that the parties in *Monkman* had cohabited, rather than married, noting the rising numbers of cohabiting relationships in Canada and the trend in family law to extend legal obligations to children regardless of the legal status of adult relationships. She also examined the wording of section 36 of the statute, and concluded (at paras 46 and 48) that:

> in situations dealing with children, where the best interests test prevails, there should be no distinction in the application of the *in loco parentis* test between children living in a relationship where the parties are married and children living in a relationship where the parties are not married. This general conclusion does not preclude the possibility that in a particular case, the evidence may be that the parties did not marry specifically because of a hesitancy on the part of the non-parent in assuming the role of a parent towards a child. Such evidence might tend to negate the existence of a deliberate intention to enter into a parental role and would be relevant to the factual determination of whether an alternative parenting relationship had been established in that particular case....
>
> In summary, the crucial element in all of this should be the relationship between the child and the adult and not the relationship between the adults.

In reaching this conclusion, Steel JA acknowledged (at para 47) that her approach created uniformity between the federal and provincial statutes, a result that she approved for family law matters. Recall *Walsh v Bona* and *Québec (AG) v A*. Consider if Steel JA's approach is consistent with dicta from the Supreme Court of Canada regarding the fundamental difference between marriage and cohabitation.

By contrast with the majority's approach, Huband JA dissented, in part relying on the present tense in section 36(4). For him, there were clear distinctions between the purposes of the divorce legislation (for married spouses), by contrast with the *Family Maintenance Act* (applicable to cohabiting couples). In addition, however, Huband JA expressed concern that the motions judge had only affidavit evidence on which to base the fundamental conclusion that the respondent stood *in loco parentis*.

What are the implications of the majority decision in *Monkman*? To what extent does the majority approach tend to further expand the potential for identifying parents to whom child support obligations may attach? What policies are thereby furthered?

Statutory language and cases in other provinces

In *Monkman v Beaulieu*, the court focused on the language in the Manitoba statute which used the Latin phrase *in loco parentis*, concluding that this phrase was substantially the same as the language of the *Divorce Act*, interpreted in *Chartier*.

Several provinces, including Ontario, use the language of demonstrating "a settled intent" to treat a child as part of the person's family. To what extent should the decision in *Monkman v Beaulieu* be applied in other provinces, such as Ontario?

While there is not always uniformity with respect to decisions about the support obligations of social parents, the language of "settled intent" parents has been interpreted quite broadly.

For example, in *Cheng v Cheng* (1996), 21 RFL (4th) 58 (Ont CA), a mother brought a motion to amend her statement of claim to proceed against her father in law and mother in law to claim support for herself and her children. The claim for child support was said to be based on the provisions of the *Family Law Act*, particularly asserting that the grandparents had "demonstrated a settled intention" to treat the children as children of their family. The Ontario Court of Appeal allowed the mother's appeal from a trial decision dismissing her motion. The appellate court held that the Act did not exclude grandparents as persons who might be responsible for the support of children, assuming that they had been significantly involved with them. (Note that the actual claim for support in this case was to be decided in a later trial of the action.)

To what extent might an ongoing relationship between adult partners create a "settled intent" parent in relation to one of their children? See, for example, *Do Carmo v Etzkorn* (1995), 16 RFL (4th) 341 (Ont Gen Div), where the court held that the existence of an ongoing relationship, but without cohabitation, did not create a "settled intention" parent.

Chartier and the Child Support Guidelines

Some commentators have argued that, because *Chartier* related to obligations created prior to the introduction of the Child Support Guidelines, the revised provisions of the *Divorce Act* and section 5 of the Guidelines create a different context for assessing the obligations for child support for social parents.

In particular, section 5 of the Guidelines, discussed later in this chapter, focuses on the apportioning of support obligations between a social parent and "any other parent". See *MacArthur v Demers* (1998), 166 DLR (4th) 172 (Ont Gen Div).

In addition, *Chartier* relied on the best interests of the child test, while this test is not included in the Guidelines.

Consider this argument about limiting the impact of *Chartier*, particularly in relation to the Child Support Guidelines:

> We rely too heavily on, and over-interpret, *Chartier*. It involved a narrow issue. It was based on legislation that has changed. The current legislation is clear in saying that step-parents are to be treated differently than biological parents and that the financial obligations of the biological parents are a factor in determining the child support obligation of a social parent. *Chartier* was based on a radically different Child Support regime than what we now have.... (R James Williams, "No Silk Purse from this Sow's Ear: Social Parents and Child Support" in Martha Shaffer, ed, *Contemporary Issues in Family Law* (Toronto: Carswell, 2007) 259 at 293)

The relationship between child support obligations for biological and social parents is addressed again in the context of the Child Support Guidelines later in this chapter. Although courts have tended to apply *Chartier* in cases after the introduction of the Child Support Guidelines in 1997, you may wish to reconsider this critique again in relation to the discussion of the Guidelines.

Additional Resources

Alison Diduck, "*Carignan v. Carignan*: When Is a Father Not a Father? Another Historical Perspective" (1990) 19 Man LJ 580.

Keith B Farquhar, "Termination of the in Loco Parentis Obligation of Child Support" (1990) 9 Can J Fam L 99.

Marie Gordon, "Third Party Child Support: A Post-*Chartier* Review" (2001) 18 Can J Fam L 327.

Alison Harvison Young, "This Child Does Have Two (or More) Fathers ...: Step-Parents and Support Obligations" (2000) 45 McGill LJ 107.

James McLeod, "Annotation of *Monkman v. Beaulieu*" (2003) 33 RFL (5th) 169.

Carol Rogerson, "The Child Support Obligations of Step-Parents" (2001) 18 Can J Fam L 9.

VII.
CHILD SUPPORT:
THE CHILD SUPPORT GUIDELINES

After almost a decade of study and controversy, ... Canada's federal government introduced legislation to provide for child support Guidelines....

The Guidelines adopt a model which usually determines the amount of child support by reference to the payer's income and the number of children, and came into force on May 1, 1997. At the same time, Canada moved from a tax regime that allowed payers to deduct child support and required recipients to include child support in income to one that is based on "no deduction and no inclusion" for child support.

The changes to child support laws are part of a response to the problem of impoverishment of single parents, especially mothers, and their children following separation.... (Martha Bailey & Nicholas Bala, "Child Support Guidelines, Parental Mobility and Redefining Familial Relationships" in A Bainham, ed, *The International Survey of Family Law, 1996* (The Netherlands: The International Survey of Family Law, 1998) at 69)

THE CHILD SUPPORT GUIDELINES: AN INTRODUCTION

The legislative context

The Child Support Guidelines were promulgated, as of 1 May 1997, as Regulations pursuant to amendments to the *Divorce Act* (see SC 1997, c 1 and SOR/97-175). The basic principles of the *Child Support Guidelines* were developed as part of the consultation process among the federal, provincial, and territorial governments (for example, see Federal/Provincial/Territorial Family Law Committee, *Child Support: Public Discussion Paper* (Ottawa: Department of Justice, 1991).

Although these amendments were directly applicable only in divorce proceedings, negotiations among the federal, provincial and territorial governments resulted in identical or very similar Guidelines for child support applications by cohabiting spouses or by married spouses who are not seeking divorce (Bailey & Bala at 71). The Guidelines for Ontario are appended to the *FLA*: see Ont Reg 463/11 (December 2011).

In addition, the Guidelines introduced a number of new arrangements:

Under the ... Guidelines payments are based on Tables which establish a monthly amount of child support by reference to the payer's income, with the percentage increased for the number of children and modified slightly by income levels. There is a different table for each Canadian jurisdiction, reflecting different tax rates, but Table amounts are about 8–10% of the payer's gross income for one child, 12–17% for two children, and rising to 24–43% for 6 or more children. (Bailey & Bala at 71)

In conjunction with the Guidelines, a number of additional changes took place:

• The former tax inclusion and deduction system was abolished, and the Guidelines now reflect tax rates applicable in each province or territory.

• Enforcement measures were strengthened in relation to child support orders and agreements, including provision for loss of licences for defaulting payors.

- Although the Guidelines must be considered in court orders for child support, they are not mandated in separation agreements negotiated by the parties. However, the Guidelines create a framework for such negotiations, and (as discussed in Chapter Five), courts may also review agreements in the context of divorce pursuant to section 11(1)(b) of the *Divorce Act* (and refuse to grant the divorce in the absence of "reasonable arrangements for the children").

An overview of the Guidelines

The framework for Canada's Child Support Guidelines includes the following:

- A list of objectives (s 1);

- A presumptive rule that child support is to be paid according to tables for each province, based on the payor's income and having regard to the number(s) of children (s 3).
  - There are special rules applicable to payors whose income exceeds $150,000 (s 4); and
  - There are provisions for determining income, including imputed income (ss 17–19);

- A list of "special or extraordinary expenses" (s 7(1) and s 7(1.1)), the cost of which is to be added to the table amounts, pursuant to section 3;

- Adjustments to the amount of child support payable, based on
  - Sharing of child expenses by biological and other parents (s 5);
  - Split custody (s 8);
  - Shared custody (s 9); and
  - Undue hardship (s 10 and schedule II).

(Note also the amendment to the *Family Law Act*, s 39.1, which provides for recalculation of child support awards. Recalculation arrangements are discussed later in this chapter.)

As will be evident, the existence of table amounts for child support provides greater certainty in determining child support awards. However, some provisions of the Guidelines continue to require discretionary decision making by judges. For an early example, see *Middleton v MacPherson* (1997), 29 RFL (4th) 334 (Alta QB).

As Bailey and Bala concluded (at 73–74):

> In adopting child support Guidelines, Canada has joined many other countries. Guidelines are generally more efficient and reduce the financial and emotional costs of resolving family disputes. For many couples, especially those with relatively simple economic affairs, it will be possible to use expeditiously the Tables to determine the amount of child support. Those with more complex affairs and greater resources will still have scope for argument and negotiation though there is likely to be substantially less variation in child support awards than before the Guidelines were introduced.

An introductory example: The table amount and the need for discretion

Using the Ontario tables for child support, consider a situation in which a mother has custody of three children and the father's income in the previous year was $68,500.

> Pursuant to the tables, based on his income at $68,000, the father would pay a basic monthly amount of $1,320 for the three children; plus 1.80 percent of $500, the amount of the additional income over $68,000.

Clearly, the tables make the initial calculation of the basic amount of child support very simple.

However, section 3 provides that a child support payment includes *both* the table amount and any expenses payable pursuant to section 7 (special or extraordinary expenses). In addition, discretion may be involved:

- If the father's income is uncertain or if the court must impute income (ss 17–19);
- If there is a "social parent" with an obligation to provide support (s 5);
- If there are adjustments for split or shared custody (ss 8 and 9) or undue hardship (s 10); and
- If the father's income was higher than $150,000 (s 4).

In all these cases, there may be variables that require negotiation by the spouses or the exercise of judicial discretion by the courts.

THE CHILD SUPPORT GUIDELINES: OBJECTIVES (SECTION 1)

Examine the objectives of the Child Support Guidelines in section 1. To what extent can all four objectives be achieved?

For example, are goals of fairness always consistent with improved efficiency?

Which of these objectives is more likely to be achieved by clear rules, or by the exercise of judicial discretion?

In reflecting on these questions, consider the following comments, based on an assessment four years after the Guidelines were implemented.

Who Wants To Avoid the Guidelines?
(2001) 19 Can Fam LQ 1 at 2–3

DA Rollie Thompson

My early impression of the Guidelines has been the alacrity, the cheerful willingness, with which lawyers and judges have embraced only two of the objectives of the Guidelines, clauses (b) and (d) of section 1 — "certainty" and "consistency." As contestants, most of us have narrowed the answers to just (b) and (d), to improve our chances of getting the right answer. Lost in the shuffle have been "adequacy" and "efficiency": "a fair standard of support" in clause (a) and improving efficiency of the process by giving guidance and encouraging settlement in clause (c).

Let us call these two approaches the "BD" and "AC" approaches.

A large number of BD lawyers and judges are just happy to have tables and formulas, whatever the consequences. The majority of the Nova Scotia Court of Appeal in *Raftus* [(1998), 37 RFL (4th) 59 (NSCA)] leaps to mind here. Another segment of the BD camp believes that certainty and consistency will lead to adequacy and efficiency, or at least that the losses in individual cases are outweighed by the systemic gains.

To date, the AC camp have appeared to be traditionalists, those lawyers and judges unwilling to give up their old individualistic ways, a minority resisting the rules of the new regime. Another growing segment have been hard-headed practical types, who see the impact of the Guidelines and tax changes in individual cases, like the BC Court of Appeal in *Wang v. Wang* [(1998), 39 RFL (4th) 426 (BCCA)].

In the Supreme Court of Canada's only decision on the Guidelines *Francis v. Baker* [(1999), 50 RFL (4th) 228 (SCC)], there are some broad remarks that lend support to the AC camp, or at least suggest that there must be some softening of the BD approach....

Thompson's comments were made in the context of an examination of the scope for agreements by parents, "contracting around" the Child Support Guidelines. After reviewing a number of appellate court decisions in different provinces, particularly with respect to the requirement to apply the Child Support Guidelines to applications for variation, Thompson suggested (at 19):

The Child Support Guidelines constitute a clear statement of public policy, prescribing in minute detail the determination of child support amounts. To be effective public policy, there must be limits upon the parties' ability to "contract out," otherwise the benefits of certainty and consistency will be lost. Inevitably, to make that policy effective, the courts now play an expanded role in approving and monitoring agreements and orders.

The more intrusive judicial role flows from three characteristics of the Guidelines. First, the tables provide a clear "floor" or minimum against which child support can be tested. Under the "old" system, there was no "objective" minimum, only a subjective, individualized, flexible minimum. Second, the Guidelines provide formulas and rules for many variations up, down and around the table amounts. Formulas and rules reduce the range of "reasonable arrangements" and force explanations, from lawyers and from courts. Third, more detailed financial disclosure is required by the Guidelines and related provincial rules, allowing judges to better assess the adequacy and Guidelines compliance of child support....

Thompson provided an analysis of a number of cases in which parties attempted to make agreements that reflected their needs and circumstances and the extent to which courts accepted departures from the Guidelines. Noting that courts are unlikely to recognize the appropriateness of child support amounts that are lower than the Guidelines amount, he also explored the relationship between child support and the disposition of property, tax implications, spousal support awards, and social assistance. He concluded (at 51):

> [T]here must be regular, ongoing dialogue between local Bench and Bar over their respective views on the balance between judicial scrutiny and parental autonomy, between the Guidelines policy of disclosure and the realities of available information, and between enforcing Guidelines compliance and encouraging individualized settlements.

Reflect on this assessment in examining the materials concerning the Guidelines in practice in this section. To what extent is there evidence of some continuing distinctions between AC and BD approaches to the interpretation of the Guidelines?

THE TABLE AMOUNT AND THE PAYOR'S INCOME

Determining a payor's income: Financial disclosure and judicial discretion

Because table amounts in the Guidelines are applied to the payor's income, it is necessary to obtain disclosure of all information relevant to income. In many cases, this issue will not be complicated — income tax and pay statements will provide financial information on which to calculate the payor's income.

However, determining a payor's income for purposes of applying the Child Support Guidelines may involve some discretionary decision making.

For example, in *Middleton v MacPherson* (1997), 29 RFL (4th) 334 (Alta QB), the court attempted to determine the wife's income in a context in which she was involved in upgrading her educational qualifications. As the court stated (at 337):

> In the case of the wife, she testified that if she was permitted to complete her internship in Calgary while finishing her Masters degree, she would expect to earn approximately $200 per week. This could result in the wife's earnings dropping from her earnings in 1996. I prefer to base the wife's present income on the total income reflected in her 1996 income tax return, as urged upon me by her counsel. Although the wife worked part-time as a teacher while taking course work to permit her to obtain a massage therapist's license, then worked as a massage therapist for a period of time, I am of the view that to impute income to her, as urged by counsel for the husband, equal to that of the husband would not be equitable. As a result of taking up a course of study, the wife was able to take on more daytime weekday child care responsibilities. I accept her testimony that her course work will be heavy until she completes her degree [in] the spring of 1998. Her internship should be concurrently undertaken so that she can start to build up a private practice. I therefore find that her income for purpose of the table calculation is $14,563 per year (based on her 1996 tax return). This figure should of course change

> when the wife receives her Masters degree in the spring of 1998 and is eligible for full-time employment as the child will be in grade one. ...

(Note that the court also addressed the issue of increased income in 1998. This issue relates to the problems of arrangements for recalculations of child support, discussed later in this chapter.)

The Guidelines expressly permit a court to determine income pursuant to sections 17–19.

For example, if a payor's income has fluctuated in recent years, the Guidelines permit the court to find that the amount of the payor's income is the average amount. See *Adams v Adams* (2001), 15 RFL (5th) 1 (Ont CA), where the court relied on section 17(1)(b) to apply a three-year average to determine the payor's income.

Imputing income

Section 19 also permits the exercise of judicial discretion to impute income to a payor of child support.

For example, where a parent is "intentionally under employed or unemployed," section 19(1)(a) permits a court to impute an appropriate income to the parent.

In *Drygala v Pauli* (2002), 61 OR (3d) 711 (CA), the court reviewed two lines of cases that had interpreted the intention requirement in section 19(1)(a): one line of cases required evidence of a bad faith intention to undermine or avoid a child support obligation, while the other group of cases held that there was no need to find a specific intent to evade child support obligations before finding such an intention. According to the court (at 718):

> Read in context and given its ordinary meaning, "intentionally" means a voluntary act. The parent required to pay is intentionally underemployed if that parent chooses to earn less than he or she is capable of earning. That parent is intentionally unemployed when he or she chooses not to work when capable of earning an income. The word "intentionally" makes it clear that the section does not apply to situations in which, through no fault or act of their own, spouses are laid off, terminated or given reduced hours of work.
>
> I note that there is no requirement of bad faith in the provision itself, nor is there language suggestive of such a requirement.

In *Drygala*, the Ontario Court of Appeal concluded that the father had failed to recognize his child support obligation, and that it was appropriate to impute income to him on the basis of half-time employment.

Consider these examples:

- The Ontario Court of Appeal applied *Drygala* in *Riel v Holland* (2003), 67 OR (3d) 417, when a payor chose to cease working as an independent electrical contractor and take a salaried position instead. Although his income was significantly reduced by this change in employment, the appeal court confirmed the trial judge's determination to impute the previous higher income to him for purposes of determining his child support obligation.

- Where the payor won $1 million in the lottery and ceased to work and earn income, an Alberta court imputed both employment and investment income to him: see *A v A*, 1999 ABQB 221.

- Where the payor had ceased working overtime at separation, an Ontario court imputed shiftwork income to him in determining the table amount: see *Odendahl v Burle* (1999), 45 RFL (4th) 37 (Ont Gen Div).

- Where a payor was dismissed from his employment for cause, a B.C. court imputed his employment income to him: see *Baldini v Baldini* (1999), 46 RFL (4th) 407 (BCSC).

See DA Rollie Thompson, "Slackers, Shirkers and Career-Changers: Imputing Income for Under/Unemployment" (2007) 26 Can Fam LQ 135.

In the context of these decisions, consider the following assessment of judicial interpretation of the Child Support Guidelines:

> Courts have been given broad discretion when it comes to determining income. A review of the case law has confirmed that the court will impute income if doing so is reasonable in the circumstances and would benefit the children....
>
> Numerous cases illustrate that the court will not tolerate parents who arrange their affairs so as to avoid paying child support. Neither will they trust a parent who has not presented adequate financial information. It is a lawyer's job to advise clients accordingly. (Nathalet Boutet & Christine Kish, "Income Determinations Under the Child Support Guidelines: A Case Law Review" (2000–1) 19 Can Fam LQ 283 at 301–302)

In *Senos v Karcz*, 2014 ONCA 459, a child of the marriage who was over the age of majority, began receiving ODSP (Ontario Disability Support Program) payments totalling approximately $10,000 for his disability. The father, who was paying child support, applied for a reduction in the amount of support. The Court of Appeal held:

> [64] ODSP reflects society's commitment to sharing financial responsibility for adults with disabilities. It makes little sense to calculate child support on the basis that this responsibility falls only on the parents. In my view, the assumption of some responsibility by the state and Antoni's receipt of income support for his board and lodging make the Table approach inappropriate. These circumstances change the equation and call for a bespoke calculation based on Antoni's unique condition, means, needs and other circumstances, including his receipt of ODSP, and the ability of his parents to contribute to his support.
>
> [65] It is useful to analogize to the cases involving adult children attending university, living away from home and earning an income, thereby contributing to their own education and support. There are numerous cases in which courts have concluded that these circumstances make the usual *Guidelines* approach "inappropriate" because the assumptions underlying the approach are not present ...
>
> [67] The Table amount is predicated on the parents alone sharing responsibility for the financial support of their child. In the case of adult chil-

dren with disabilities, the *ODSPA* commits society to sharing some responsibility for support. In my view, this makes the s. 3(2)(a) approach inappropriate, and s. 3(2)(b) should be applied to achieve an equitable balancing of responsibility between Antoni, his parents and society.

The court allowed the father's appeal, but due to insufficient evidence remitted the matter for trial to determine the appropriate amount of support under s 3(2)(b) of the *Guidelines*. The court noted that a complete record would include updated financial information from both parties, a child support budget, and a personal budget for Antoni (including a description of the mother's use of the ODSP payments on Antoni's behalf, her use of the support payments from the father, and her proposed use of any additional payments). See also Marta Siemiarczuk, "Evidence Key in Support Variations for Adult Children", *Law Times* (9 July 2012) 7.

For an argument about "chalimony", child support that takes account of a child's disability, see Karen Czapanskiy, "Chalimony: Seeking Equity between Parents of Children with Disabilities and Chronic Illnesses" (2010) 34 NYU Rev L & Soc Change 253. Czapanskiy argues (at 254–55):

> Parents of children with disabilities or chronic illnesses are often particularly needy of support because of the dramatic impact of a child's condition on a parent's family stability and financial capacity. The role of family law in this area should be to support the caregiver ... and to encourage the people and practices that help them thrive.

Payors with income over $150,000

The Child Support Guidelines tables apply to payors with incomes up to $150,000. For incomes over that amount, section 4 of the Guidelines authorizes a court to determine the appropriate amount payable, if the table amount is considered inappropriate. In a number of cases involving payors with high incomes, courts have interpreted this statutory language. What are the underlying issues in such cases?

Francis v Baker
[1999] 3 SCR 250

Section 4 was considered in *Francis v Baker*, in the Supreme Court of Canada in 1999. The custodial mother of two girls requested child support in accordance with the Guidelines. The payor father had left her five days after their second daughter was born in 1985. In 1997, she was earning $63,000 per year and receiving $30,000 annually in child support. In the same year, the father earned $945,538 and his net worth was $78 million.

The trial judge awarded the mother child support based on the table and the payor's income (see (1997), 150 DLR (4th) 547 (Ont Gen Div)), and the Ontario Court of Appeal dismissed the appeal (see (1998), 38 OR (3d) 481). In the appellate court, Abella JA held that the word "inappropriate" in section 4(b) should be interpreted as "inadequate" so that no downward variation was permissible.

On appeal to the Supreme Court of Canada, Bastarache J reviewed the appeal court's interpretation of section 4 and stated (at paras 39–41):

> Based on the wording of s. 1 and the legislative history, a fair description of the purpose of the Guidelines is to establish fair levels of support for children from both parents upon marriage breakdown, in a predictable and consistent manner. They are designed to ensure, as I said in a different context in *Chartier*, supra, at p. 257, "that a divorce will affect the children as little as possible," or as the Minister said, "to put children first." Indeed, s. 4(b)(ii) itself emphasizes the centrality of the actual situation of the children by expressly requiring that the "condition, means, needs and other circumstances of the children" be considered in the assessment of an appropriate amount of support payable in respect of income over $150,000. In my opinion, it is not at all clear from the statute or the words of the Minister that any single element of this general legislative purpose is to be given more weight than any other, and certainly not more weight than the actual circumstances in which the children find themselves. While Abella J.A. is correct to point out that predictability, consistency and efficiency are among the Guidelines' objectives, these are not the only considerations. I thus respectfully disagree with the Court of Appeal's suggestion that these legislative objectives dictate that child support awards can never be reduced under s. 4.
>
> A proper construction of s. 4 requires that the objectives of predictability, consistency and efficiency on the one hand, be balanced with those of fairness, flexibility and recognition of the actual "condition, means, needs and other circumstances of the children" on the other. Furthermore, this balancing must take into account the ordinary meaning of the word "inappropriate," as well as its use elsewhere in the statute. In my opinion, the plain language of s. 4 is consistent with such an interpretation. Accordingly, the word "inappropriate" in this section must be broadly defined to mean "unsuitable" rather than merely "inadequate." Courts thus have the discretion to both increase and reduce the amount of child support prescribed by the strict application of the Guidelines in cases where the paying parent has an annual income exceeding $150,000. I would note that the respondent did not take issue with this interpretation in either her written or oral submissions.
>
> I add one final comment. As noted above, Abella J.A. was concerned with the differential treatment of children. In my respectful opinion, a broad interpretation of the word "inappropriate" in s. 4 does not deny children of high income parents any of the intended benefits of the Guidelines.... In my opinion, child support undeniably involves some form of wealth transfer to the children and will often produce an indirect benefit to the custodial parent. However, even though the Guidelines have their own stated objectives, they have not displaced the *Divorce Act*, which clearly dictates that maintenance of the children, rather than household equalization or spousal support, is the objective of child support payments.

In *Francis v Baker*, the Supreme Court cast doubt on the interpretation of the Court of Appeal, but concluded that the appellant had failed to demonstrate that the trial judge had erred in exercising discretion pursuant to section 4. As a result, the trial judge's award of $10,034 monthly for the two children was upheld.

R v R
(2002), 58 OR (3d) 656 (CA)

Consider also the Ontario Court of Appeal decision in *R v R*, confirming that the trial judge was correct to take account of the modest lifestyle of a family, even though the payor's annual income was $1.4 million. However, the appeal court also concluded that the trial judge had erred in not giving weight to the increased income of $4.1 million of the payor after separation, particularly having regard to the increased expenses after separation. The trial judge had awarded $16,000 per month for four children.

As Laskin JA stated (at 664), this amount represented errors in two respects:

> First, [the trial judge] based his order entirely on the parties' lifestyle and pattern of expenditure while they lived together. By doing so, the trial judge failed to adequately take into account the large increase in Mr. R.'s income after he and his wife separated. Second, the trial judge erred in failing to consider whether the options proposed by Mrs. R. in her April 2000 budget were reasonable in the light of the increase in Mr. R.'s income.

Significantly, the Ontario Court of Appeal decided that it was appropriate to (re)assess the amount of child support, rather than to order a new trial for this purpose. After reviewing the budget submitted by Mrs. R., the court decided that it was appropriate to award discretionary expenses of $20,000 monthly as well as the basic expenses of $12,000 monthly and $4,000 under section 7 for a total monthly child support payment of $36,000 for the children.

Consider this situation:

> The payor gave evidence of his financial support for seven children (born to four different women) in Canada and the United States. He explained that he provided CAD $3,000 monthly to the Canadian children and US $3,000 to the American children and that he also paid school fees, as required. According to the payor's evidence, he had contributed $216,000 in 2000 in relation to child support, and he argued that he had treated his children fairly and equally.
>
> However, the payments to the Canadian children did not meet the requirements of the Guidelines. How should this case be resolved?

In *Pakka v Nygard* (2002), 61 OR (3d) 328 (Sup Ct) (publication of decision deferred: [2002] OJ No 3859 (Sup Ct) (QL)), Kiteley J rejected Mr. Nygard's argument, stating (at 342):

> I reject the "fairness and equality" argument. It is predicated on the ability of a parent to decide what in his/her mind is a "fair and equal" treatment of the children. That has not been the law for decades. I do not reject the defendant's assertion that he is acting in what he considers to be good faith and that, as a result of having children in different relationships, he has tried to ensure that he has treated them all similarly. That may be a sound approach morally. But it has nothing to do with the state of the law in Ontario today. One need only look at the consequences of applying such a position in our society today: it would allow payors to be virtually uninhibited in imposing what they consider to be a sound moral approach; it would victimize payees who would be subjected to the application of a subjective standard by the payor; and it would make a mockery of the *Child Support Guidelines* and in particular the first objective.... It would be inconsistent with the principles adopted by the Supreme Court of Canada and the Ontario Court of Appeal that the emphasis must be on the actual situation of the child, not the wishes and subjective perspective of the payor.... It would allow the payor to make the rules.

In the result, the court considered (at 348–50) the principles articulated in *Francis v Baker* and other decisions of the Ontario Court of Appeal, and concluded that the payor had not provided "clear and compelling evidence" that the table amount was inappropriate or unsuitable. In addition, the court awarded arrears to July 2001. The court also established 27 June 2002 as the date for a settlement conference. However, according to press reports, the parties reached an undisclosed settlement on 19 March 2004. See Gay Abbate, "Nygard Support Case Ends with Settlement", *The Globe and Mail* (19 March 2004) A11; Kai Falkenberg, "Peter Nygard Answers to No One" *Forbes* 186:10 (6 December 2010) 82, detailing accusations of abusive business practices, sexual harassment and assault, and his claims that his child support would give his child "affluenza." See also *Ewing v Ewing*, 2009 ABCA 227.

CHILD SUPPORT AND "SPECIAL OR EXTRAORDINARY" EXPENSES (SECTION 7)

Statutory provisions for table amounts and section 7

According to section 3 of the Child Support Guidelines, the "presumptive" amount of child support includes the amount defined in the applicable table as well as "the amount, if any, determined under section 7."

As originally enacted, section 7(1) included as "special or extraordinary expenses":

(a) child care;
(b) premiums for medical and dental care;
(c) health-related expenses not covered by insurance; and
(e) post-secondary education.

In addition, section 7(1) included "extraordinary expenses" for

(d)   primary or secondary school education or any educational programs that meet the child's particular needs; and

(f)   extracurricular activities.

In 2006, section 7(1.1) was added to define "extraordinary expenses" more precisely (see O Reg 102/06, s 1). For cases decided before 2006, see *Andrews v Andrews* (1999), 50 RFL (4th) 1 (Ont CA); *McLaughlin v McLaughlin* (1998), 44 RFL (4th) 148 (BCCA); and *Andries v Andries* (1998), 36 RFL (4th) 175 (Man CA).

Examine the wording of sections 7(1) and 7(1.1).

For example, note that section 7(1) provides that a court may include in a child support order an additional expense:

> ... taking into account the necessity of the expense in relation to the child's best interests and the reasonableness of the expense in relation to the means of the parents or spouses and those of the child and to the spending pattern of the parents of spouses in respect of the child during cohabitation.

In addition, note the statutory language in section 7(1.1), particularly in part (b).

Although this statutory language provides factors for consideration by a judge in making such an award, the language clearly provides some scope for discretionary decision making. In this context, therefore, it is important to take account of the requirement in section 3 to include both the table amount as well as any (discretionary) amount payable pursuant to section 7.

The onus falls on the party claiming extraordinary expenses to demonstrate that it falls into a stated category, and that they are reasonable and necessary: *Park v Thompson* (2005), 77 OR (3d) 601 (CA).

"Special and extraordinary" expenses in practice

In 1999, a pilot study of child support awards examined section 7 awards, reporting that

> [t]he most commonly awarded type of expense was medical or dental insurance premiums (9.7 percent of total cases). This was followed by extracurricular activities at 9.3 percent, and child care or day care at 8.5 percent. The least frequently awarded expenses were primary/secondary education (4.7 percent) and post-secondary education (6.9 percent)....
>
> [In addition, the report indicated that there] was a consistent increase in the proportion of cases with special or extraordinary expenses awarded as income level increased. At the lowest income level, only 11.5 percent of cases had special expenses awarded; this proportion increased to 59.5 percent at the highest income level. (Joseph P Hornick, Lorne D Bertrand & Nicholas M Bala, *The Survey of Child Support Awards: Final Analysis of Pilot Data and Recommendations for Continued Data Collection* (Ottawa: Minister of Justice 1999) at 28–29)

According to a subsequent follow-up report for cases between 1998 and 2002, the most common section 7 expenses awarded were for child care. See *The Survey of Child Support Awards: Analysis of Phase 2* (Ottawa: Minister of Justice, 2003). In this context, recall the discussion about child care as primarily a "family" responsibility (Chapter Four). Clearly, this responsibility may continue post-divorce or separation.

Section 7 and post-secondary education

Issues about section 7 and the expenses of post-secondary education have been frequently litigated.

Recall that the definition in section 2(1) of the *Divorce Act* includes as a "child of the marriage" a child who is over the age of majority but unable to withdraw from parental charge. As noted earlier in this chapter, courts concluded that a child who was attending a post-secondary educational institution could qualify as a "child of the marriage," thus requiring payment of educational expenses.

After the introduction of the Child Support Guidelines, however, payment of child support in relation to a "child of the marriage" who was over the age of majority and attending a post-secondary educational institution required, in addition, consideration of two provisions of the Child Support Guidelines:

- First, section 7(1)(e) provides that expenses of post-secondary education may be included as child support if they meet the tests in this section of "necessary" and "reasonable" expenses. Note also section 7(2), which provides for parents to share such expenses in proportion to their incomes, after "deducting the contribution, if any, from the child."

- In addition, it is important to note section 3(2), which permits a court to use the same Guidelines for a child over the age of majority that would apply to a child under this age (that is, the table amount plus section 7 expenses). Alternatively, if the court finds this approach "inappropriate," the court may order an amount it considers appropriate, having regard to the "condition, means, needs and other circumstances of the child and the financial ability of each parent to contribute."

In a 2006 decision, the Ontario Court of Appeal considered these sections in *Lewi v Lewi*.

Lewi v Lewi
(2006), 80 OR (3d) 321 (CA)

In *Lewi v Lewi*, Gillese JA (dissenting) posed the question in this case, as follows:

> To what extent are adult children required to use their own funds to pay for post-secondary education expenses? This question lies at the heart of this appeal.

In *Lewi*, the spouses married in 1983 and separated in 1996. At the time of their appeal, their older son was 20 and the younger one 18 years old. The parties signed a consent order in 2002, pursuant to which the father paid monthly child support based on the table amount for his income, and special expenses of $200 per month for computer related expenses and car insurance for the older son. The order did not address post-secondary education expenses, but the father paid $1,500 for these costs for two years of his older son's university expenses. Both sons planned to continue university studies, with the younger son living away from home to attend university. Their father was a senior executive at IBM and he had remarried; his new wife worked in the paid workforce. The boys' mother was constructively dismissed from her employment at IBM in 1999 and had not worked since then as a result of health problems. She was in receipt of spousal support from her former husband and had sold the matrimonial home to buy a less expensive home for herself and the two sons.

In 2004, the mother brought a motion to increase the father's contribution to child support, pursuant to section 7(1)(e). The father resisted the motion on the basis that both sons had substantial funds of their own, arguing that these funds should be used before any parental contribution. The funds available to the boys were accumulated as a result of gifts to them, particularly from their grandfather. In 2003, the older son's car and investments were valued at about $41,000, while the investments of the younger son were also about $41,000. There was also an RESP in the boys' joint names, valued at about $7000.

The motions judge decided that each of the boys should contribute to their university education, using either summer employment income or their own funds, on a graduated scale. For example, in relation to their fourth year of university, the order required each of them to contribute the greater of actual earnings minus $2,000, or $4,000. The judge then ordered the parents to pay the remaining costs, with the father contributing 77 percent and the mother 23 percent.

On appeal, there were a number of issues for consideration. A major issue was the extent to which, if at all, an adult child with some financial resources should be expected to contribute to post-secondary educational expenses.

In this context, the majority reasons focused on the relationship between section 3(1) and the requirement to take account of the table amount and section 7 expenses on one hand, and section 3(2) with respect to child support determinations for children over the age of majority.

In the end, the majority concluded that the case raised issues about children's contribution to post-secondary education expenses under section 7 in relation to the younger son, and under section 3(2)(b) in relation to the older son. However, the majority also concluded that both sections require the court to consider a child's contribution to these expenses. In assessing the appropriate contribution, the majority indicated that:

> **[157]** It seems to me that the court, in order to exercise its discretion properly under either s. 3(2)(b) or s. 7, when parties dispute the amount of contribution expected of a child, requires the same kind of information regarding the needs of the child and the means of the child and the parents. Nor would the contribution the child is expected to make and the support the parent is obliged to provide necessarily be different under the two provisions. In my view, in fashioning an order applying the broad criteria in s. 3(2)(b), the court may well draw upon the principles of the Guidelines and its experience in applying them. [For example, it would be appropriate for the court to adopt the approach of section 7(2).] The evidence upon which the court might conclude it was just and appropriate that the parents should share the expenses in some other proportion would, I think, be the same under both provisions....

The majority agreed with the dissenting opinion that neither the father's view that the children should contribute all their funds, nor the mother's view that they should not be required to make any contribution, was appropriate.

> **[159]** Both s. 3(2)(b) and s. 7 of the Guidelines require that the means of the child must be considered along with the means of the parents. Section 7, in addition, refers to the contribution of the child, if any. I do not understand this to indicate a greater expectation for the child's contribution under s. 7 compared to s. 3(2)(b). The court has the discretion under both provisions to decide the amount the child should be expected to contribute. In my view, the amount of child support that a parent is ordered to pay should be determined, as a general rule, on the expectation that a child with means, in this case independent assets, will contribute something from those means towards his or her post-secondary school education. The extent of the contribution expected depends on the circumstances of the case. There is no standard formula under either s. 7 or s. 3(2)(b)....

In the end, the court assessed the contributions of the two sons, on the basis of these two different provisions, in the same way. The court concluded that the grandfather's gifts were intended for educational purposes, and that the situation of the parents had changed post-divorce, so that the two boys should be expected to make significant contributions to their university educations. Thus, the court's assessment resulted in each son having some assets at the end of their university programs (about $30,000 for the older son and about $22,000 for the younger son, whose program was more expensive).

In *Lewi*, although the dissenting judge disagreed about the relationship between section 3(2)(b) and section 7, she concluded that the information required for applications pursuant to these sections is the same:

> **[97]** ... [In relation to section 3(2)(b),] the court is to follow the table approach to setting child support for living expenses of an adult child of the marriage unless that approach is inappropriate. If it is, the court may order the amount it considers appropriate based on a consideration of the "condition, means, needs and other circumstances of the child" and the

financial ability of each parent to contribute to the child's support. Similarly, the court is to follow the approach to special or extraordinary expenses provided by s. 7 unless that approach is inappropriate. Only if the approach mandated by s. 7 is inappropriate is the court to set an appropriate amount for such expenses, for an adult child of the marriage, based on s. 3(2)(b)....

[101] Not only is the inquiry under s. 7 more limited in nature than is that under s. 3(2)(b), the discretionary nature of the amount of support ordered under s. 7 is far more restricted than the discretion conferred under s. 3(2)(b). Thus, amounts ordered pursuant to s. 7 are more predictable as they are largely a function of the parties' respective incomes. Not so child support pursuant to s. 3(2)(b) where there are no criteria circumscribing the expense and there is no guiding principle on the allocation of expenses between the parents.... [In the end, the judge concluded that the motions judge proceeded on the basis of s. 3(2)(a), and accepted the conclusion that the son attending university away from home should contribute to this additional cost.]

As this case seems to suggest, both section 7 and section 3(2)(b) permit the exercise of discretion by the court. Does this conclusion suggest that the issue of a child's contribution to post-secondary educational expenses is fact-driven in all cases?

Consider also *Cassidy v McNeil*, 2010 ONCA 218, where the Ontario Court of Appeal upheld a wife's contributions to educational expenses that were paid directly to her two sons who were attending university and living with their father. The court accepted that the parties had an informal arrangement, and that the wife's intention was that her contributions would offset any claim by her former husband pursuant to sections 3 and 7 of the Guidelines. Are there advantages to paying contributions directly to adult children, rather than by way of an agreement or order that usually directs payments to a former spouse?

For financial support of adult children in the American context, see Sally F Goldfarb, "Who Pays for the Boomerang Generation?: A Legal Perspective on Financial Support for Young Adults" (2014) 37 Harv JL & Gender 45; and Abraham Kuhl, "Post-Majority Educational Support for Children in the 21st Century" (2008) 21:2 Journal of the American Academy of Matrimonial Lawyers 763.

"SOCIAL PARENTS" AND CHILD SUPPORT OBLIGATIONS (SECTION 5)

Section 5 and obligations of biological parents

Section 5 authorizes a court to determine an "appropriate" amount of child support payable by a spouse who stands "in the place of a parent," having regard to the Guidelines and "any other parent's legal duty to support the child."

In this context, repartnering by a spouse may often mean that both a biological and a social parent have support obligations to a child. Yet, while section 5 is clear about the obligation, it provides little guidance to judges with respect to the calculation of the respective amounts of child support payable by these different parents.

However, the Ontario Court of Appeal confirmed in *Wright v Zaver* that biological parents and adoptive parents may not rely on section 5 to reduce their child support obligations, even though there is a "social parent" as a result of repartnering.

Wright v Zaver
(2002), 59 OR (3d) 26 (CA)

In *Wright v Zaver*, Ms. Wright and Mr. Zaver were unmarried parents of a son born in 1985. They had engaged in an intimate relationship for about three years, but it deteriorated shortly after the child's birth. The parties signed minutes of settlement a few months later, granting custody to Ms. Wright, denying access to Mr. Zaver, and providing that he would provide a lump sum child support payment of $4,000 but without further ongoing obligation.

In 1990, Ms. Wright married, and she and her husband had a child together. Throughout the marriage, Ms. Wright's husband treated her first son as his own, and when the Wrights separated in 1999, Mr. Wright was ordered to pay child support for both children.

In the context of some financial hardship, Ms. Wright filed an application for child support against Mr. Zaver, who was financially well-off, in relation to his son. Mr. Zaver resisted this application, arguing that there should be apportionment of child support payable for his son in accordance with section 5.

However, the trial judge held that neither a natural nor an adoptive parent can rely on section 5. See *Wright v Zaver* (2000), 49 OR (3d) 629 (Sup Ct) at 638–639:

> [T]he unique circumstances of this case do not fit into any exceptions to the presumptive rule that the biological father should pay child support at the Table amount specified in the Guidelines. That result is perhaps troubling from the perspective that it might seem unfair now to require a father who has been shut out of his child's life for 15 years to commence paying support. The apparent unfairness stems, I think, from the expectation by an access parent that he is entitled to exercise a parental role in exchange for support payments. That, however, has never been the law. The obligation for support is entirely independent of the rights of access. In any event, who is to say that the father might not be able to establish a relationship with the child. It may not be too late and court sanctioned support may very well be a catalyst for such a relationship.
>
> With respect to the issue of double dipping, I can see no authority in the Act to order anything other than Table support for the child. If that means that the mother is able to provide her son with a standard of living

that is slightly better than their basic needs require, so be it. The biological father is extremely well off. It will not be a hardship for him to share some of his wealth with his child. One of the objectives of the Guidelines was to ensure that children "benefit from the financial means of their parents." One might even suggest that the biological father has had a 15-year holiday from support obligations and it is now proper that he honour his moral and legal obligation to his child....

The Ontario Court of Appeal unanimously confirmed the trial judgment in *Wright v Zaver*.

Two of the five appellate judges wrote opinions, but they mainly focused on the contested issue at that time about whether the coming into force of the Child Support Guidelines constituted (automatically) a change in circumstances entitling an applicant to a variation of a pre-existing order.

As Simmons JA noted (at para 35), courts across Canada had taken different views, and the Ontario Court of Appeal had initially decided that the enactment of the Guidelines did not create an automatic right to variation. (See *Sherman v Sherman* (1999), 44 OR (3d) 411 (CA).) Then, in *obiter* comments, the Court of Appeal had suggested that *Sherman* was incorrect on this point. (See Laskin JA in *Bates v Bates* (2000), 49 OR (3d) 1 (CA).)

In *Wright v Zaver*, the Ontario Court of Appeal followed the views expressed in *Bates*, thus deciding that the enactment of the Guidelines created such a right to variation. In addition, the appeal court also upheld the trial judge's reasoning with respect to the order for child support payable by Mr. Zaver.

Consider the implications of this decision about the obligation of a biological parent to provide child support, particularly in the context of rates of repartnering. How significant to this decision was the fact that Mr. Zaver was well able to provide support to his son? And what impact should this decision have on Mr. Wright's obligation, as a person "standing in the place of a parent" to provide support?

Section 5 and "social parents"

Recall the Supreme Court's decision in *Chartier* and its expansive interpretation of the definition of a person "standing in the place of a parent" pursuant to the *Divorce Act*. Recall also that this interpretation was extended to cohabiting spouses in Manitoba in *Monkman v Beaulieu*. These decisions may continue to be relevant in the context of the wording of section 5 of the Guidelines, which also includes the language of "standing in the place of a parent". However, section 5 appears to create significant opportunities for judicial discretion in its application to "social parents."

In reflecting on the discretionary language in section 5, consider this assessment of 120 cases about step-parent support between 1997 and 2000:

What has struck me most forcefully after reviewing this entire body of law is that we do not have a very clear idea of why we are imposing support obligations on step-parents. Our current approach ... has been adopted in the absence of a clear articulation of the basis on which such support obligations are being imposed — is the law primarily concerned with psychological attachment, intention to assume the role and responsibilities of a parent, or the protection of reliance (and if so what sorts of reliance — economic or also psychological)? The law has also developed without reference to the social science literature on the nature and functioning of step-families. That literature, which shows the complexity, diversity and potential instability of step-family relationships, raises both questions about the reasonable social expectations that attach to these relationships and concerns about the appropriateness of imposing long-term support obligations when these relationships break down after a relatively short period of time. (Carol Rogerson, "The Child Support Obligations of Step-Parents" (2001), 18:1 Can J Fam L 9 at 152–53)

In spite of such uncertainties, section 5 obligations have been imposed on social parents. In some cases, the result is that children receive additional economic support. For examples, see *Kobe v Kobe* (2002), 30 RFL (5th) 135 (Ont Sup Ct); *Nelson v Nelson* (1999), 44 RFL (4th) 365 (Alta QB); and *C(K) v B(S)* (2003), 36 RFL (5th) 22 (Ont Sup Ct).

Does this outcome reinforce policies of privatization of support for children? To what extent might the potential liability for child support on the part of social parents limit repartnering arrangements, as was suggested in critiques of *Chartier*?

"Social parents" and mistakes about biological parenthood

How should section 5 be interpreted in a situation where a spouse has stood in the place of a parent unknowingly — that is, in a situation in which a spouse believes himself to be a biological father but is not?

If the focus is on a child's "best interest," is the parent's (incorrect) belief relevant? What constitutes a "fair result" for the non-biological "parent"?

Cornelio v Cornelio
(2008), 94 OR (3d) 213 (Sup Ct)

In *Cornelio v Cornelio*, a former husband brought a motion to terminate his child support obligations for 16-year-old twins (and for repayment of some of the support paid for them) after DNA testing revealed that he was not the biological father of these children. The marriage had ended with separation in 1998 and the parties had agreed to a consent order in 2002 for joint custody and child support.

In support of the motion, the former husband contended that his former wife had failed to disclose an extramarital affair preceding the twins' birth, and that the consent order in 2002 was obtained by misrepresentation and fraud. Thus, he argued that in the absence of all the information required to make an informed decision, he could not have formed the intention to treat the twins as his own children, so that he did not "stand in the place of a parent."

The former wife claimed not to remember the affair, as a result of medication she was taking at the time. In any event, she argued that Mr. Cornelio's conduct toward the children during the marriage should determine whether he "stood in the place of a parent."

The court reviewed a number of cases, including *LS v CS*, [2002] OJ No 1890 (Ct J), which reflected "a traditional approach to the concept of *in loco parentis*, one that depends on the actual intention of the putative parent and the voluntary assumption of a parental role". In these cases, as the court noted, the focus is on the dealings and communications between the spouses, and they do not consider the length, character and importance of the relationship between the child and the "parent" (para 9).

The court then referred to *Chartier* and its emphasis on the best interests of a child, rather than the intention of the putative parent. The court also examined *B(B) v B(CP)*, 2005 ONCJ 101, in which the court had examined circumstances similar to those in *Cornelio* with respect to the "settled intent" required pursuant to the *Family Law Act*:

> ... The appropriate question to ask is whether the relationship that existed at the time that the family was functioning as a unit, up until separation, was one in which the father treated the child as his own. To permit a father, in a sense, to "backdate" his decision to parent the children ignores completely the reality of the children's lives. Although the father may have made a different decision had he been advised of the facts at the time of the child's birth, the fact is that he was a parent to the child for many years. The emotional bonding, shared memories and trust that [were] built up over time cannot be wiped out with the stroke of a pen. For better or for worse, with intention or without it [the respondent] is the [children's father in all the ways that fatherhood matters — love, guidance, pride, nurturing, role modeling, connection — [the respondent] is a father to these [children]. It is their concept of him as father that was — and continues to be — important. This was not a relationship entered into by either child or parent in a tentative or temporary fashion. It has been, since the children's birth, the only paternal relationship that either the [children] or [the respondent] has known.
>
> Modern society has moved away from a rigid definition of the family.... There has been a recognition both by society at large and our legal system that it is the relationship that matters, not the legality. It is the sense of family and bonding between parent and child that is important, not whose DNA is lodged in the child's cells.... If we are to be sensitive to the realities of these [children's] experience and to act in their best interests, the court must acknowledge the fact that [the respondent] has demonstrated a settled intention to treat them as his own children (*Cornelio* at para 12, quoting *B(B) v B(CP)* at paras 20–21).

In *Cornelio*, the court also reviewed cases in which a "social parent's" support obligation might be reduced from the table amount, and cases confirming the absence of obligation on the part of a spouse to disclose infidelity. In addition, the court referred to *Doe v Alberta* (discussed in Chapter One) and concluded that:

This case recognizes that a spouse with no biological connection to a child, who has agreed with the child's mother at or subsequent to the child's birth that he will assume no obligation for child support, may nevertheless by his conduct stand in the place of the child's parent and accordingly owe child support at some time in the future. Put another way, the child's right to future child support cannot be excluded by the present conduct of the mother and her spouse. An "intention"-based focus would have led to a different result....

The right to child support is the right of a child and is independent of a parent's own conduct, whether it be delay in pursuing support, an attempt to contract out of support or the failure to disclose an extramarital affair that may have led to the conception of the child ... (at paras 21 and 23).

By contrast, in *Collis v Wilson*, (2003) 49 RFL (5th) 11 (Ont Sup Ct), a case also decided under Ontario's *FLA*, the court held that there must be a conscious decision based on knowledge of the child's paternity in order for there to be a settled intention to treat the child as a child of his family. Thus, no settled intention could be formed where the mother had concealed from her husband the true situation of the child's parentage.

Should the different wording in the *FLA* and the *Divorce Act* make any difference? Do you prefer *Cornelio* or *Collis v Wilson's* interpretation of "settled intention" in the *FLA*?

Note that the court in *Cornelio* accepted the applicability of the reasoning in *Chartier* in its interpretation of section 5 of the Guidelines. See also *Peters v Graham*, 2001 NSSC 165. To what extent is there a need for reform to identify the scope of a support obligation on the part of a social parent? Or is this more appropriately a matter for continuing judicial discretion? See Wanda Wiegers, "Fatherhood and Misattributed Genetic Paternity in Family Law" (2011) 36:2 Queen's LJ 623.

SPLIT AND SHARED CUSTODY (SECTIONS 8 AND 9)

Section 8 and split custody

Section 8 of the Child Support Guidelines requires a "set-off" with respect to the obligations of parents to pay child support, when the custodial arrangements involves split custody.

For example, if there are two children of the marriage, and one lives with the former wife and the other with the former husband, section 8 requires a calculation of the support that would be payable by each former spouse, having regard to that parent's income, with the difference between these amounts payable by the spouse owing the larger amount of child support.

In practice, it seems that section 8 has not created significant problems:

The cases involving split custody are relatively straightforward, and any complexity is the result of the complexity built into the Guidelines calculations themselves. Because two support obligations are being calculated rather than one, that complexity is potentially doubled. In the simplest cases there is simply an offset of the two table amounts, subject of course to any issues regarding the determination of income. In other cases the calculation of the two child support obligations is complicated by additional factors built into the Guidelines calculation such as section 7 add-ons claimed by one or both parents; the fact that one or more of the children is over the age of majority allowing a departure from the table amount; the fact that one or more of the children for whom support is claimed are step-children to whom other persons also owe support obligations; or the combination of split and shared custody arrangements with respect to different children in the family. (Carol Rogerson, "Child Support Under the Guidelines in Cases of Split and Shared Custody" (1998) 15 Can J Fam L 11 at 15)

The apparent ease of calculating child support in cases of split custody is not reflected in shared custody situations pursuant to section 9. In some cases, however, section 8 calculations have been invoked with respect to section 9, so that section 8 may provide both a contrast and an analogy to section 9 decisions.

Section 9 and shared custody: The context

Section 9 of the Child Support Guidelines reflects the controversy about shared parenting arrangements in Canada in the late 1990s. As Bailey and Bala explained:

As a result of intense lobbying of sympathetic Conservative Senators, "fathers' rights advocates" were able to secure a few changes before the enabling legislation was finally approved in February 1997. The only significant change in the Guidelines was with regard to situations of "shared" (or joint) custody. The original proposal would have taken account only of situations where "both spouses share physical custody in a substantially equal way." The final Guidelines give a court discretion to set the amount of child support to take account of the "increased costs of shared custody arrangements" if a payer spouse "exercises a right of access to, or has physical custody of, a child for not less than 40% of the time over the course of the year." (Bailey & Bala at 73)

As the authors noted, the language of 40 percent of the "time" was designed to give payors as much scope as possible for claiming the benefit of section 9, but it also created arguments about how to calculate "time" when a child is in school or at camp, etc.

In practice, section 9 requires a court to first calculate the time spent with the child for each parent to determine whether they meet the 40 percent threshold. However, assuming that the threshold has been met, section 9 then permits the court to determine the amount of support payable, having regard to the tables, the increased costs of shared custody arrangements, and the "condition, means, needs and other circumstances" of the child and each parent or spouse. See Merle H Weiner, "Caregiver Payments and the Obligation to Give Care or Share" (2014) 59 Vill L Rev 135; and

Brian Burke & Stephanie Chipeur, "The More the Merrier? Multiple Parents and Child Support" (2010) 29:2 Can Fam LQ 185.

Section 9 and the 40 percent threshold

Issues about the 40 percent threshold in section 9 were raised often in the early years of the Guidelines.

For example, some courts accepted the approach adopted in *Meloche v Kales* (1997), 35 RFL (4th) 297 (Ont Gen Div), that the calculation of time proceeds from the assumption that the custodial time is initially 100 percent of the child's time (including school time) and that the non-custodial parent's access or physical custody of the child must amount to at least 40 percent of that time over a year.

Other cases, such as *Cross v Cross* (1998), 40 RFL (4th) 242 (BCSC) and *Billark v Billark* (1998), 36 RFL (4th) 361 (Ont Gen Div), discussed the possibility of excluding school and sleep time from the calculation.

Many courts have approached the 40 percent threshold as a fairly strict mathematical calculation, though a few cases suggest a preference for considering the nature and quality of the time spent by each parent with the child. For example, see *Rosati v Dellapenta* (1997), 35 RFL (4th) 102 (Ont Gen Div); and *Dennett v Dennett* (1998), 225 AR 50 (QB).

In this context, consider this situation:

> The father's employment required him to leave home around 7 am and not return until about 7 pm, and so he employed a nanny to care for the children while he was working. Does the father have custody of the children, for purposes of section 9, if the children are being cared for by a nanny?

According to *Sirdevan v Sirdevan*, 2010 ONSC 2375, the five children were in the father's care when they were in the care of a nanny, employed by the father. However, in *Rush v Rush*, 2002 PESCTD 22, the father's time on the road as a truck-driver pushed him below the 40 percent threshold. The court held that the father was not to be given credit for the time that he was not physically present with the children (para 14). Which approach do you prefer?

In *Froom v Froom* (2005), 11 RFL (6th) 254, the Ontario Court of Appeal held that there is no universally accepted method of deciding the 40 percent threshold issue, and that rigid calculations of time are not necessarily appropriate. Instead, courts should focus on determining whether physical custody is truly shared by the parents.

In both *LL v MC*, 2013 ONSC 1801, and *Gilby v Goddard*, 2014 ONSC 1363, the courts concluded that the 40 percent rule was not met, relying on *Froom* for flexibility. In *LL v MC*, where both parents provided calculations supporting their positions (the father used days as a basis for the calculation, while the mother used hours), Czutrin J stated: "the parties are very focused on the number 40 per cent" (at para 11), suggesting that a strict numerical approach is imprecise, tedious, and deleterious to the dual relationships with the child.

Section 9 and the quantum of support

Section 9 provides considerable scope for discretion in assessing the quantum of support in cases of shared custody. In this context, courts initially adopted a variety of methods:

- Some courts, for example, adopted the set-off approach, similar to the approach for split custody pursuant to section 8. See *Middleton v MacPherson*, discussed earlier in this section.

- In assessing the increased costs of shared custody in section 9(b), some courts adopted the "Colorado method" of assuming roughly 50 percent of a custodial parent's costs are fixed costs, and then grossing up the set-off amount by 50 percent to reflect the increased costs of shared custody. See *Hunter v Hunter* (1998), 37 RFL (4th) 260 (Ont Gen Div)); but other courts declined to assume the appropriateness of this 50 percent gross up without evidence of actual increased costs (see *Burns v Burns* (1998), 40 RFL (4th) 32 (Ont Gen Div).

- Some courts simply calculated the payor parent's obligation as a proportion of the Guidelines table amount that reflected the amount of time the child was in the care of the custodial parent. See *Spanier v Spanier* (1998), 40 RFL (4th) 329 (BCSC); and *Penner v Penner* (1999), 44 RFL (4th) 294 (Man CA).

The issue of how to assess section 9 support obligations was eventually considered by the Supreme Court of Canada in *Leonelli-Contino v Contino*. The Supreme Court differed from all the approaches taken in this case in the lower courts, and its conclusion leaves a good deal of discretion in determinations pursuant to section 9. Examine the summary of these lower court decisions that follows, and the explanation and critique of the decision in the Supreme Court of Canada. To what extent is there a need for reform of section 9?

Leonelli-Contino v Contino
2005 SCC 63

In *Leonelli-Contino v Contino*, the parents of a child agreed at separation to a joint custody arrangement. The child resided with the mother on a daily basis with generous access by the father, and the father agreed to pay $500 of child support monthly. This amount was increased in minutes of settlement to $563 per month.

Some time later, the mother enrolled in a night course, and requested the father to care for the child for an additional night each week. The father agreed to do so, but also applied to vary his support obligation pursuant to section 9 because the extra night at the father's home meant that the child was with his father for 50 percent of the time.

The legal proceedings in the case were quite protracted. First, the motions judge granted the father's motion, reducing the amount of monthly child support by adopting the formula of section 8 and setting off the father's and mother's table amounts. As a result, the father's child support payments were reduced to $100 per month.

The mother appealed to the Divisional Court, which held that the table amount is to be determined in the best interest of a child (relying on *Francis v Baker*), and that unless the father could provide clear and convincing evidence to rebut the presumptive table amount, he was obliged to pay it. As a result, the Divisional Court ordered that the father pay the table amount of $688, subject to annual adjustments according to his income.

In the father's appeal to the Ontario Court of Appeal, the court reviewed the "formulaic" approach of the motions judge and found that it encouraged predictability but failed to take account of the discretionary requirements of section 9(c). In addition, however, the court suggested that the discretionary approach of the Divisional Court lacked predictability. The Court of Appeal concluded that it was appropriate to use an approach of "structured discretion." (This complex assessment began with the section 8 set-off approach, and then included a 67.6 percent multiplier, as well as taking into account the actual spending patterns of each parent and factoring them into the calculation on the basis of the ratio of parental incomes.) Using this calculation, the appeal court held that the child support payable by the father was $399.61 monthly.

In the Supreme Court of Canada, the mother's appeal was allowed (Fish J dissenting). The Supreme Court concluded that a discretionary approach was appropriate, having regard to the language of section 9 of the Guidelines. Noting that the objectives of the Guidelines create a "palpable tension," the Court suggested that:

> [39] The specific language of s. 9 warrants emphasis on flexibility and fairness. The discretion bestowed on courts to determine the child support amount in shared custody arrangement calls for the acknowledgment of the overall situation of the parents (conditions and means) and the needs of the children. The weight of each factor under s. 9 will vary according to the particular facts of each case....

In applying the three factors in section 9, the Court concluded that the father's child support payment should be $500 per month.

Section 9 and the application of *Contino* principles

The Supreme Court's approach to section 9 was quite complex. In an "Annotation" to this case, Rollie Thompson identified the issues and suggested how the principles of *Contino* should be applied.

"Annotation" of *Contino*
(2005) 19 RFL (6th) 272

DA Rollie Thompson

... Section 9 of the Federal Child Support Guidelines is an awkwardly-worded provision, one which raises difficult questions of policy but decides none of them. To make matters worse, section 9 has been the focus of wider ideological battles over the virtues and vices of "shared parenting." In this dangerous and disputed terrain, it is no mean feat that the Supreme Court of Canada got most of the policy questions "right" in *Contino*, while avoiding the traps and mistakes tripped over by some lower courts....

Thompson noted approvingly the Court's discussion and rejection of a number of propositions about section 9, and then explained the decision as follows:

[T]he Court gave clear direction on a general method for calculating child support under section 9. The Court set out a discretionary rather than a "formulaic" approach and emphasised the need to consider all three factors listed in s. 9 before reaching a result.

Thompson also suggested that *Contino* does not represent a return to *Paras*, even though *Contino*'s focus on budgets provides the basis for adjustments in section 9(a).

Here's the step-by-step method for quantum laid out by Justice Bastarache:
(1) Determine the Simple Set-Off Amount. The starting point under s. 9(a) is the simple or straight set-off of each parent's table amount for the number of children involved in the shared custody arrangement. No pro-rating, no multiplier (paras. 40–51).
(2) Review the Child Expense Budgets. A court must look at the parents' actual spending patterns, based upon child expense budgets, and not just make assumptions about spending. [Specifically, a court must examine *all* the expenses of *both* parents, not just additional expenses relating to increased access. In doing so, a court needs to take account of the overall increased total costs of the child for both parents, including duplicated costs; and any disproportionate assumption of spending by either parent.] (paras 52–53)

These expenses should be "apportioned between the parents in accordance with their respective incomes" (at para 53), to "verify" the set-off (at para 77) and to determine "the need for significant readjustments to the set-off amounts" (at para 78).

(3) Consider the Ability of Each Parent to Bear the Increased Costs of Shared Custody and the Standard of Living for the Children in Each Household. The consideration of these two factors lies at the heart of the s. 9(c) analysis, set out at paras. 54–72, especially paras. 69–70. In assessing each parent's ability to bear the increased costs of shared custody, a court should look at the income levels of each par-

ent, the disparity in incomes, and the assets and liabilities of each. [And a child should not experience a significant variation in the standard of living in each household.] As the term "household" is used, the incomes and resources of new partners in each household would presumably be relevant.

(4) Distinguish Between Initial Orders or Agreements and Variations. [According to *Contino*, such a distinction may be necessary because a recipient parent] "may have validly incurred expenses based on legitimate expectations about how much child support would be provided," especially for fixed costs (para 55)....

Critiquing *Contino*

In spite of the Supreme Court's careful analysis of section 9 of the Guidelines, Thompson also noted some ongoing issues.

First, Thompson concluded that there was no substantial explanation for the award of $500 per month. As the Court stated, it was the appropriate amount in light of the factors considered. As Thompson argued, it seems that decisions pursuant to section 9 remain highly discretionary after *Contino*.

Thompson also noted the problem in this case relating to the wife's decision to purchase a larger home in reliance on the child support initially agreed to. As well, according to Thompson's calculations, the wife's monthly income was slightly higher than the husband's. In this way, *Contino* may be quite fact specific, in spite of the Court's effort to establish appropriate principles for section 9.

Finally, Thompson pointed to the Court's expectations with respect to financial information about the parties' circumstances in order to take account of all relevant factors in the application of section 9. In reflecting on this point, Thompson argued that such obligations might be too onerous:

> [T]hese are family litigants, real parents, not cost accountants. Most have limited resources, more limited than the Continos. Many will not have lawyers or will have limited legal advice [and in any event, a good deal of the cost accounting remains somewhat indeterminate]....

To what extent does *Contino* also demonstrate the tension between the four objectives of the Child Support Guidelines? Although some sections of the Guidelines may provide greater certainty and predictability, section 9 seems to be inherently discretionary.

Recall the issues discussed earlier in this chapter about shared parenting. Does *Contino* suggest that even though shared parenting may avoid difficult decisions about custody and access, it may raise even more challenging issues with respect to child support? Is it also possible that arguments about shared parenting (especially the 40% rule) may reflect litigants' concerns about paying child support more than their interest in caring for children? In reflecting on these questions, consider this suggestion:

... I would favour an approach that allowed a degree of judicial discretion to adjust the Guideline amounts to recognize the financial realities of the parties — the parties' actual expenditures on the children and any significant income disparities between the parties which reflected on their respective abilities to bear the costs of a shared custody arrangement. While I believe it is helpful to see what the Guideline amounts on each parent's income are — in part to provide a comparison point for the numbers which are generated in a *Paras*, budget-based analysis — some discretion to depart from a strict offset of the amounts is necessary in order to ensure that one of the parents is not being deprived of adequate support to meet the children's needs. One must recall that what is often (although not always) at issue in these cases is a reduction from the basic table amount to be paid by the higher income parent. One of the stated objectives of the Guidelines, after all, is to establish a fair standard of support for children. (Carol Rogerson, "Child Support Under the Guidelines in Cases of Split and Shared Custody" (1998) 15 Can J Fam L 11 at 94)

UNDUE HARDSHIP (SECTION 10)

The undue hardship test

Section 10 of the Child Support Guidelines permits some variation up or down with respect to the amount of a support obligation, based on undue hardship. However, any such variation will be denied if the household claiming undue hardship would have a higher standard of living than the other household (see also Schedule II).

According to section 10, it is the relative *standard of living in each household*, not the *incomes of individual payors or recipients* of child support, that must be compared. Schedule II provides guidance with respect to the comparison of household standards of living.

In addition, section 10 preserves judicial discretion with respect to such claims. In providing an overall assessment of the meaning of the statutory language in section 10, Thompson focused on the words in the section:

What takes a circumstance of "potential hardship" into the sphere of "undue hardship" has sent judges to the dictionary and the thesaurus: "excessive, extreme, improper, unreasonable, unjustified," "hard to bear ... and ... inappropriate, unwarranted and excessive," or "excessively hard living conditions." Section 10 creates "a tough threshold to meet," requiring "cogent evidence." In the words of Julien Payne, repeated in various cases, "the hardship must be exceptional or excessive, rather than the inevitable consequence of dividing limited resources between two households." (DA Rollie Thompson, "The Second Family Conundrum in Child Support" (2001) 18 Can J Fam L 227 at 230, citing Julien Payne, "Child Support Under the Federal Child Support Guidelines" (QL DB PDCS) at G10)

Consider this comment in relation to an early case, *Schmid v Smith*. Does this case confirm that section 10 provides a "tough threshold to meet"?

Schmid v Smith
(1999), 1 RFL (5th) 447 (Ont Sup Ct)

... Under the provisions of section 10 of the *Guidelines* counsel for the husband asks the court to award an amount of child support that is different from the amount determined under section 4 on the basis that the husband would otherwise suffer undue hardship. Clause 10(2)(b) sets out a number of circumstances that may cause undue hardship. It is not an exhaustive list. The husband claims that there are three circumstances that cause him undue hardship.

First, the husband claims that he has unusually high expenses in relation to exercising access to the children, a circumstance of potential undue hardship set out in clause 10(2)(b). This relates to the husband's cost of travelling between Canada and the UK to see the children. I understand that the cost is approximately $6,000 per year. I accept the cost as accurate. I find that this is a circumstance of undue hardship.

Secondly, the husband claims that his legal duty to support Alison is a circumstance that causes undue hardship. Clause 10(2)(d) of the *Guidelines* provides that a circumstance that may cause undue hardship is the legal duty to support a child, other than a child of the marriage. Since Alison is a child of the marriage the duty to support her is not an undue hardship.

Thirdly, the husband claims that the higher cost of living in the UK compared with that in Canada is an undue hardship. He deposed his own experience, that the cost of goods and services in the UK is approximately 50% greater. He appended to his affidavit OECD data for February 1999 showing that the same "basket of goods and services" costs approximately 45% more in the UK than in Canada. This data is of little assistance. Expert evidence would be required to interpret it. In any event, to succeed in proving that he suffers undue hardship because of an increased cost of living, it is incumbent on the husband to identify and quantify how he personally has been affected. He has failed to do so.

I have found that the husband's unusually high access costs are an undue hardship. Subsection 10(3) of the *Guidelines* requires me to compare the standard of living of the husband's household with the standard of living of the wife's household. Subsection 10(4) provides that to do so I may use the comparison of household standards of living test set out in Schedule II of the *Guidelines*. I have done this. I have found that after taking support and the husband's access costs into account his household income ratio is approximately 1.25 higher than the wife's household income ratio. In using this comparison I am aware that it is based on "low-income measures amounts for households" based on Canadian economic studies. The husband's household is in the UK and the wife's is in Canada. However there is no other way in which I can make an objective comparison on the evidence before me. Subjectively, the husband is left with approximately $8,500.00 more in net income (after support and access costs) to support himself and one child, than the wife will have to support herself and two children. In addition, the husband has a vehicle supplied to him by his employer, which was not included in his income. Consequently, I find that the standard of living of the husband's household exceeds the standard of living of the wife's household. As a result, I am compelled to dismiss the husband's request under subsection 10(3)....

Notes and Questions

Reassessing the objectives of the Child Support Guidelines

Examine the objectives of the Guidelines again. Which provisions seem to encourage certainty and predictability? Which provisions seem to require more judicial discretion to achieve fairness? Do the Guidelines achieve a reasonable balance between these goals? To what extent do you agree with the following comment about the Guidelines?

> Contrary to popular impressions, the Guidelines lack any real intellectual coherence. The Guidelines can't quite make up their minds what they really want to be, partaking a little bit of every conceivable child support model: percentage-of-income (the tables), *Paras*-style cost-sharing (section 7 expenses), household income equalization (undue hardship) and individualized budgets [several provisions permitting exceptions]. (DA Rollie Thompson, "Who Wants to Avoid the Guidelines? Contracting Out and Around" (2001) 19 Can Fam LQ 1 at 20)

Is it inappropriate for different aspects of the Guidelines to use these differing approaches? Why or why not?

Enforcement of child support

The problem of enforcement of child support obligations has been consistently identified as serious and widespread. For example, a study of support orders at the Family Court in Toronto in 1986 found that 82 percent of the orders were in some degree of default. Such statistics have repeatedly fuelled waves of legislative initiatives, by the federal government as well as provincial legislatures, to ensure that orders are enforced.

Statutes have provided for increasingly serious sanctions — for example, Ontario's *Family Responsibility and Support Arrears Enforcement Act, 1996*, SO 1996, c 31 provides that where no support payments have been received for a period of three months and the arrears are more than $300, the payor will be reported to credit bureaus.

There are also provisions in several statutes that permit the denial of licences, including drivers' licences, where child support obligations have been ignored. For example, see *Mainwaring v Alberta* (1998), 48 RFL (4th) 171 (Alta QB). The Ontario Ministry of Community and Social Services website includes information about "deadbeat dads" who are registered with the Family Responsibility Office (FRO), have not made their court-ordered support payments and cannot be found. The posting of these payors' names and photographs are in an effort to shame them and to seek "the public's help in locating missing defaulting payors." See Good Parents Pay, online: Ontario Ministry of Community and Social Services <http://www.mcss.gov.on.ca/en/goodparentspay/gpp_index.aspx>.

Overall, it appears that governments have determined that the financial well-being of children is the responsibility of the post-divorce family and that the role of the state is to enforce these obligations. (See also *Interjurisdictional Support Orders Act, 2002*, SO 2002, c 13.)

However, enforcement issues remain challenging in family law matters. In *Dickie v Dickie*, 2007 SCC 8, the Supreme Court considered a case concerning a husband who had been ordered to pay about $9,000 monthly in child support as well as spousal support. However, Dr. Dickie moved (along with most of his assets) to the Bahamas, where he remarried and lived a luxurious life style. By the time the case reached the Supreme Court of Canada, he was in arrears of about $700,000.

In 2004, Dr. Dickie had returned to Canada and was cited for contempt for his failure to comply with the court order. In this situation, a majority of the Ontario Court of Appeal (Laskin JA dissenting) exercised discretion to hear Dr. Dickie's appeal from an order requiring him to post security for arrears of child and spousal support in spite of the contempt order. Ms. Dickie appealed this decision of the Ontario Court of Appeal.

The Supreme Court's decision confirmed the dissenting opinion of Laskin JA, and allowed Ms. Dickie's appeal with costs. As a result, the Supreme Court confirmed that courts can exercise discretion to refuse to hear an appeal from a party who has not complied with outstanding family law orders. LEAF intervened in this case to argue that such discretion is necessary to prevent the perpetuation of court actions in the face of non-compliance with orders. Unfortunately, however, Dr. Dickie's residence in the Bahamas meant that his former wife and children might not receive the support owing to them. See also Kirk Makin, "Deadbeat Ex-Spouses Can be Jailed, Court Says", *The Globe and Mail* (10 February 2007) A11.

Recalculating child support

The table amounts in the Child Support Guidelines focus on the income of the payor parent. However, incomes may either rise or fall over time, resulting in a need to alter the amount of child support payable. In addition, other factors in the life of a child may change, necessitating a reconsideration of section 7 expenses, the extent of a new partner's obligation if the relationship ends (s 5), or changes that result in split or shared custody (ss 8 and 9) or undue hardship (s 10).

When the Guidelines were introduced in 1997, the legislation required the provinces to enter into agreements with the federal government to implement a system for recalculating child support. Such arrangements have not yet been fully implemented.

In Ontario, the *Family Statute Law Amendment Act, 2009* amended the *Family Law Act* by adding section 39.1, which provides for recalculation of child support in accordance with regulations made under the Act to reflect updated income information.

This amendment thus provides for the creation of a scheme for recalculating child support in Ontario on an ongoing basis. Other provinces have also adopted recalculation schemes:

• Newfoundland and Labrador, for example, enacted the first recalculation scheme, a mandatory administrative model that requires all child support payors to submit copies of income tax returns on an annual basis. If the income reported would increase or decrease child support payments by more than $5, the parties are notified of a change in the quantum of child support payable, and it takes effect within 31 days. If the payor fails to provide income tax returns, child support is recalculated using the consumer price index for the previous year. See *Western Child Support Service Regulations*, NLR 9/02; and *Family Justice Services Western Final Evaluation* (Ottawa: Department of Justice, 2004).

• By contrast, Manitoba adopted a recalculation scheme based on a formal application process. It requires an individual recipient or payor to apply to the court for recalculation of child support. After an application is received by the court, a Support Determination Officer is appointed to seek financial disclosure from each parent and to determine an appropriate variation. If either party objects, a mediator can be appointed to assist the parties to reach agreement about the recalculated amount. See *Child Support Guidelines Regulation*, Man Reg 58/98.

In reflecting on these different models for recalculating child support, which model appears to offer more efficiency? Which may be better able to achieve fairness in relation to particular circumstances? Is it possible to create a scheme for recalculation that combines both efficiency and fairness?

Retroactive child support: The *DBS* cases

The introduction of recalculation schemes represents a response in part to problems created by the absence of regular arrangements for updating child support awards. In 2006, the Supreme Court heard four appeals from Alberta involving claims for retroactive child support, based on changes in the financial circumstances of the parents.

The Court's decision in *DBS v SRG et al*, 2006 SCC 37, examined the factual circumstances in which claims had been presented for retroactive support pursuant to the *Divorce Act* and Alberta's (now repealed) *Parentage and Maintenance Act*. In *DBS* in particular, the Alberta Court of Appeal set out a list of factors for consideration in claims for retroactive support, but then sent the matter back to the chambers judge for determination. Similarly, the appeal court returned *LJW v TAR* for consideration by the chambers judge. In two other cases, in which lower courts had upheld retroactive awards, *Henry v Henry* and *Hiemstra v Hiemstra*, the Alberta Court of Appeal dismissed appeals.

The Supreme Court allowed appeals in *DBS* and *TAR*, thus restoring the decisions of the chambers judges in these cases. The Court then confirmed the decisions of the Alberta Court of Appeal to uphold the decisions of chambers judges in *Henry* and *Hiemstra*.

• For the majority in the Supreme Court of Canada, Bastarache J held that an award of retroactive child support is permissible pursuant to the *Divorce Act* and the child support guidelines, up to three years in the past, where the recipient parent gives effective notice to the payor whose income has changed. The onus is on the recipient parent to seek out the payor and determine if income has changed. The date of change is not the change in income of the payor parent, but when the recipient effectively gives notice to the payor parent. Unreasonable delay by the recipient parent will militate against a retroactive award; blameworthy conduct by the payor will militate in favour of a retroactive award and may result in the presumptive starting date for the calculation as the material time of the change. Retroactive child support may not be awarded where a child enjoyed a high standard of living despite the absence of chid support or where claims of undue hardship are made. Although creative crafting of retroactive awards may minimize hardship.

- In a concurring judgment, Abella J emphasized child support as a right of the child and a joint obligation of a child's parents. According to this view, entitlement begins when income increases and not when it was disclosed or discovered. Moreover, there is no role for blameworthy conduct as the child support obligation fluctuates with parental income, not parental misconduct. Similarly, there is no necessity for the recipient parent to demonstrate hardship. Finally, she disagreed with an arbitrary three-year judicial limitation period on the amount of child support that can be recovered.

Notwithstanding these differing approaches, the Court was in agreement with the disposition of these cases. To what extent do these cases provide helpful guidelines for recipient parents who wish to increase child support? Does the majority's approach place too heavy a burden on recipient parents to ascertain information that the payor has in his possession? Why might recipient parents (who are typically women) not wish to stay in direct contact with their former partners? Recall also *Louie v Lastman*, discussed earlier in this chapter, and the court's decision to deny retroactive support to two sons in their 40s.

Additional Resources

Justice David Aston, "An Update of Case Law Under the Child Support Guidelines" (1998) 16 Can Fam LQ 261.

Natasha Bakht et al, "D.B.S. v. S.R.G.: Promoting Women's Equality through the Automatic Recalculation of Child Support" (2006) 18:2 CJWL 535.

Nicholas Bala, "Ottawa's New Child-Support Regime: A Guide to the Guidelines" (1999) 21 RFL (4th) 301.

Barbara R Bergmann & Sherry Wetchler, "Child Support Awards: State Guidelines versus Public Opinion" (1995) 29:3 Fam LQ 483.

Dena Bonnet, "Recalculating *DBS*: Envisioning a Child Support Recalculation Scheme for Ontario" (2007) 23 Can J Fam L 115.

G Feltham & A Macnaughton, "Predicting the Popularity of Child Support Strategies" (1997) 30 RFL (4th) 428.

Lucinda Ferguson, "Retroactivity, Social Obligation and Child Support" (2006) 43 Alta L Rev 1049.

Laura Morgan, "Child Support and the Anomalous Cases of the High-Income and Low-Income Parent" (1996) 13 Can J Fam L 161.

Krista Robson, "Unfair Guidelines: A Critical Analysis of the Federal Child Support Guidelines" (2004) 6 Journal of the Association for Research on Mothering 93.

D Smith, "Retroactive Child Support — An Update" (2007) 26 Can Fam LQ 209.

Barry M Tobin, "Enforcement of Support Orders in Ontario" (1998) 15 Can Fam LQ 317.

VIII.
CHILD SUPPORT: THE NEED FOR REFORM?

CHILD SUPPORT AND THE "PRIVATE" FAMILY: THE GUIDELINES IN PRACTICE

Significantly, the Special Joint Committee on Child Custody and Access in the 1990s focused its attention on the ways in which the Child Support Guidelines negatively affected parental negotiations about their children at family dissolution.

In reflecting on their concerns, consider two issues:

• The connection between legal issues about care and custody of children on one hand, and the arrangements for their economic support: To what extent does the separation of these legal issues create problems for parents and their children at family dissolution?

• The fundamental assumption in the Special Joint Committee's report that economic support for children post-family dissolution must be addressed by parents, with little or no assistance from the state.

Examine the Special Joint Committee's concerns in relation to these two issues. To what extent do you agree with the formulation of the problems, and the suggested solutions? What biases or preconceptions do you think the Committee brought to their research and analysis?

Child Custody and Access
For the Sake of the Children (1998) at 47–51

Special Joint Committee on Child Custody and Access

... One of the most frequently mentioned sources of dissatisfaction with the legal mechanism for dividing financial and other responsibilities between parents after separation and divorce was the Federal Child Support Guidelines.... The guidelines came into force at the same time as the tax treatment of child support was changed so that child support payments are no longer taxable in the hands of the recipient, usually the custodial parent, or deductible by the payor, usually the non-custodial parent....

The Federal Child Support Guidelines are generally recognized as having contributed in a positive way to improving predictability with regard to the amount (or "quantum") of child support and to reducing the incentive to argue or litigate over the issue of quantum. However, this was seen as inadequate justification for the extent to which they have increased the conflict between divorcing couples in a number of ways. One of the contentious issues (which was not the direct result of changes stemming from Bill C-41, but was nevertheless part of the controversy around that bill and remains unchanged) relates to the definition of "child of the marriage" in the *Divorce Act*, which has been interpreted judicially to include children over the age of majority (sometimes into their 20s) if they are engaged in post-secondary education. The effect of this judicially established rule has often been to compel non-custodial parents to pay for their children to attend post-secondary institutions, even though parents in intact families obviously are not required to do so....

Another of the concerns raised with respect to the Federal Child Support Guidelines is the so-called 40% rule: the section of the Guidelines that provides that where the payor exercises rights of access to, or has custody of, the child for at least 40% of the time in a given year, the quantum of child support is not determined solely on the basis of the amount set out in the table. In such cases, the court will have regard to the table amount, the increased costs associated with the shared custody arrangement, and the conditions, means and other circumstances of the parents and the child. This very contentious provision was intended to give legal recognition to the increased costs borne by a non-residential parent who spends a large amount of time caring for the child. As a number of witnesses said, the rule has had the unfortunate effect of encouraging parents, who might otherwise have agreed, to fight over the residential schedule for the child....

Many witnesses agreed that the 40% figure was too arbitrary, citing cases where fathers spending as much as 38% of the time with children were still required to pay the full amount under the guidelines. Most of these witnesses argued that recognition of non-residential parents' expenses should be based on a range of 20 to 40% of the time, provided there are proven significant expenses. The expenses of these parents when living a significant distance from their children can be particularly burdensome and should not be ignored. For reasons of fairness, the Committee is concerned about the 40% rule and the guidelines' failure to take into account significant parenting expenses. Members are even more disconcerted by the negative impact of the 40% rule on parenting negotiation and decision making. Witnesses asked the Committee to recommend that the Government investigate further how these aspects of the guidelines should be altered.

This Committee, along with the Senate Social Affairs Committee, heard a number of witnesses object strongly to the perceived unfairness of basing child support solely on the income of the payor, without taking the recipient parent's income into account. The pre-guidelines test for the amount of child support to be paid by the non-custodial parent — the apportionment of the costs of raising the child between the parents according to their relative ability to pay — seems to many to be intuitively more reasonable and palatable. Similarly, the guidelines' financial disclosure provisions, which require regular disclosure by the payor to the recipient, apply only to the payor. This apparent inequity rankles nonresidential parents, who feel that the concerns of custodial or primary residential parents are being attended to without any government action on non-custodial parents' access enforcement problems....

Two other related matters came to the attention of the Committee. One is the mandatory, non-discretionary nature of the guidelines. Even if they wish to, parents are not free to agree to opt out of the support tables or other provisions. Judges will sign child support orders or judgements only if they are satisfied that the requirements of the guidelines have been met. This limit on parents' freedom to settle their affairs by agreement was seen by some as an unreasonable restriction on their ability to make post-separation arrangements for their family as they see fit.

The Committee is also concerned about the impact of the guidelines on parties receiving public assistance. The concern, Members were told, is that in some parts of Canada a recipient parent could be deemed to be in receipt of the amount of child support that had been ordered under the guidelines, even if the support order was in default. The result would be that the support amount would automatically be deducted from that parent's public assistance benefits, potentially leaving the family without adequate funds in the event of non-payment of support. Although the administration of public assistance programs is not within federal legislative jurisdiction, Members of the Committee thought it important that the impact of the guidelines on that type of income be examined carefully.

As consideration of the Federal Child Support Guidelines did not fall strictly within the Committee's mandate, and as the Committee had not actively sought evidence on this topic, most Members of the Committee felt that it would not be appropriate to recommend to the Minister of Justice just how the problems with the guidelines should be corrected.... However, given the volume of evidence dealing with concerns related to the guidelines, the Committee felt that our witnesses' objections should be reviewed by the Minister of Justice....

The recommendations of the Joint Committee were included in the federal Bill in 2002, which was not enacted. In addition, these concerns about child support, addressed by the Committee in relation to its review of custody and access, have not resulted in reforms. All the same, the Committee's report seems to confirm the close connection in practice between these legal issues and their separate treatment. How might these practical connections between issues about custody and access on one hand, and child support on the other, be encouraged in legal principles?

CHILD SUPPORT, POVERTY, AND "PUBLIC" POLICY

A number of proponents of the Child Support Guidelines argued that they would alleviate child poverty. Consider the following comment:

At present, the Guidelines are being applied in a conservative manner, despite the judges' discretion to vary the table amounts upward and requests from parents to do so. For instance, the government's own commissioned research reveals that child support orders higher than the table amounts are rare, leaving the "basic" child support amounts established by the tables as the rule, rather than the exception. This is disconcerting in light of concerns raised by the custodial parents that the amounts stipulated in the tables are not adequate to meet the basic needs of children. Critics of the law reforms have noted that the data used to devise the child support tables did not include the non-monetary costs that are borne by the custodial parent. Household tasks, child care tasks, the need to be near schools, and constraints placed on the custodial parent's employment availability may be not be issues when the family is intact, but they have significant financial impact for the custodial parent following divorce or separation. While there is general support for the bolstered legal principle that child support is the "joint financial obligation" of parents, on an everyday level parents are not feeling the material effects of this idea (i.e., adequate child support gets paid). Shared experiences of "fighting" for child support, for instance, indicate that at least two of the promises of the reforms (efficiency and reduction of conflict and tension) have not been met. At the same time, parents lose control over how their own cases proceed through the legal system. This can significantly impact a parent's ability to act in the "child-focused" way the law requires. (Krista Robson, "'Wrapped in the Flag of the Child': Divorced Parents' Perceptions of and Experiences with the *Federal Child Support Guidelines*"(2008) 24 Can J Fam L 283 at 314–315)

A child whose payor parent is of only modest means, or who is unemployed, ill, or disabled, will be entitled to much less support than one whose payor parent is a high income hockey player or lawyer. Thus, the inequities in the financial well-being of intact families are substantially reproduced for the children of divorce, undoubtedly exacerbated by the need to provide for two households, not just one.

Thus, critiques have also focused on the ways in which the Child Support Guidelines have reprivatized economic support for families and children. To what extent can family law principles respond to such critiques?

What Were They Thinking?
(2002) 17:1 CJLS 139 at 157–158

Paul Millar and Anne H Gauthier

Although child poverty is a major social problem, it is unlikely that child support will play a major role in the solution to that problem. Child poverty exists among poor families. Fathers of the children of poor never-married mothers are also likely to be from a similar social background. When a poor family breaks up, there are extra costs because of the existence of two households instead of one. This is especially true when both parents want to remain active in their children's lives and need accommodation for themselves and their children. Thus the reliance on child support to reduce child poverty puts a large amount of financial strain on one of two poor parents. So while child and spousal support is useful to share financial difficulties pursuant to divorce, it is unlikely to bring a large proportion of divorced custodial parents out of poverty....

Child support collected may not even benefit the other parent, but may instead go to replace social benefits that have been accessed by the recipient parent. In this way, child support represents a major initiative to privatize social benefits. This is likely to increase economic stratification, not reduce it. To put it another way, this is a method of circumventing the progressive taxation system by taxing those who can least afford it. Child support, appropriately implemented, may be useful for reducing inequities after divorce among middle and upper class families, where the children are not poor, but unreasonably large amounts and severe enforcement measures may be detrimental to economic stratification for the poor and working classes. One study of low income non-custodial parents who were behind in their support payments found that while these low income parents were desperately looking for opportunities to work, they suffered from feelings of powerlessness and social and economic isolation. The vast majority had extremely tenuous living arrangements. [See ES Johnson and F Doolittle, "Low-Income Parents and the Parent's Fair Share Program," in I Garfinkel et al, eds, *Fathers Under Fire: The Revolution in Child Support Enforcement* (New York: Russell Sage, 1998) 253 at 274–275.] ... Child support regimes must be carefully implemented in light of these limitations, or the results may be harmful, rather than beneficial to children of poor parents. Child poverty needs a predominantly public approach to be effective — heavy reliance on private support will not produce the desired results.

The insidious aspect of using child support to deal with child poverty is that government and society are now off the hook, since the cause of poverty no longer appears to lie with government or social policy. Rather, a parent's poverty is the fault of a former spouse, someone he or she is no doubt already disposed to blame. Claiming lack of child support as the cause, and increased child support as the cure, of child poverty in Canada will most likely increase hostility between divorced spouses, while removing the impetus for society to assist with the problem. Poor families, by themselves, are not likely to pull themselves out of poverty. To insist otherwise only makes poverty increase.

In reflecting on this critique, consider this comment about the larger context in which Child Support Guidelines were adopted. Is there a need for policy reform with respect to no fault divorce and its consequences?

The privatization of obligations for ongoing financial support for children after divorce contrasts with public policies permitting freely accessible divorce to adults in Canadian society. In this context, there appears to be public support for private decisions to separate and divorce, thus ending the family unit. At the same time, the continuation of significant private familial responsibilities for child support to ensure children's well-being shows how "the family" continues to exist post-divorce, as well as the limited extent of public support for the consequences of state policies ensuring accessible divorce. The [governmental] strategy of defining the problem as one of deadbeat dads ensures the continuation of post-divorce "private" families and distances the state from any [major] "public" responsibility to respond to the problem [of child poverty]. (MJ Mossman, "Child Support or Support for Children? Re-Thinking the 'Public' and 'Private' in Family Law" (1997) 46 UNBLJ 63 at 83–84)

Additional Resources

Shelley AM Gavigan, "Something Old, Something New? Re-Theorizing Patriarchal Relations and Privatization from the Outskirts of Family Law" (2012) 13 Theor Inq L 271.

Margaret Harrison, "The Australian Child Support Scheme" in John Eekelaar & Petar Sarcevic, eds, *Parenthood in Modern Society: Legal and Social Issues for the Twenty-First Century* (Dordrecht and Boston: Martinus Nijhoff, 1993).

Tina Maisonneuve, "Child Support under the Federal and Québec Guidelines: A Step Forward or Behind?" (1999) 16 Can J Fam L 284.

MJ Mossman, "Conversations about Families in Canadian Courts and Legislatures: Are there 'Lessons' for the United States?" (2003) 32:1 Hofstra L Rev 171.

J Thomas Oldham & Marygold Melli, eds, *Child Support: The Next Frontier* (Ann Arbor, MI: University of Michigan Press, 2000).

Courtney Palmer, "Child Support and Shared Parenting in Canada: A Reality Cheque" (2013) 22 Dal J Leg Stud 101.

Paula Roberts, "Child Support Enforcement for Low-Income Children: Part of the Solution or Part of the Problem?" (1992) 1 DCL Rev 143.

Richard Shillington, "Child Poverty and the Benefit of an Illusion" (1999) Canadian Perspectives 14.

Faye L Woodman, "Tax Aspects of the New Child Support Guidelines: One Year Later" (1998) 15 Can J Fam L 221.

Lucie White, "Calling the State to Answer for Child Poverty: 'What Then?'" (1997) 46 UNBLJ 99.

EPILOGUE:
Families and the Need for Law

FAMILIES AND THE LAW

As the discussion of cases and commentaries in this book makes clear, the relationship between law and families is always evolving and often contested.

- In relation to family formation, law may not always recognize units that are regarded by their members as families, but it may also extend familial obligations to persons who do not think of themselves as "family" members.

- In relation to intact families, law has historically regarded these units as "private" and eschewed intervention, but these principles have increasingly evolved so that legal intervention in families may occur to protect vulnerable family members, including children, spouses (usually women) and frail elderly persons.

- More significantly, in relation to divorce and separation, law has increasingly regarded the spouses' decision to separate as "private," while at the same time regulating the post-dissolution relationships with ever increasing legislation. In this way, while there is minimal regulation of spouses' access to divorce, there is substantial (and increasing) legal intervention with respect to issues about corollary relief: care and custody of children as well as financial obligations relating to property and both spousal and child support. Paradoxically, the state has also been (re)defining as "private" the financial well-being of post-dissolution families, thereby shifting these financial obligations from the state to family members, even after their "family" has dissolved.

These legal developments have occurred in a societal context in which no fault divorce is broadly accepted and in which there are relatively high rates of divorce and separation in Canada. Thus, as in other similar jurisdictions, there are mounting pressures in the work of family law courts, and increased needs for legal advice and representation among family law litigants. These pressures and needs have increased at a time when there are also shrinking state resources, a situation that has resulted in policy makers and governments seeking ways to promote alternatives to litigation and to the use of courts for the resolution of family law matters. They have also resulted in diminished access to legal aid services in most parts of Canada. Thus, as noted, recent governmental initiatives in Ontario are intended to stream cases away from courts to alternative methods of dispute resolution, particularly in relation to legal advice and mediation.

In this context, it is important to revisit the fundamental relationship between "families and the law." In reflecting on your conclusions, consider the following comments, written in the context of developments in the United Kingdom but perhaps equally applicable to the future for family law in Canada.

"Family Law and its Discontents"
(2000) 14 Intl JL Pol'y & Fam 59

John Dewar

... There are few areas of law that generate as much controversy and disagreement as family law. It's something potentially that affects us all, in which we all feel we have a stake and of which some of us have had direct experience. Indeed, there are probably few areas of law that affect so many people so directly in their every day lives. Yet it is probably also true that nowhere is the authority or legitimacy of law more often called into question....

I want to offer a defence of the role of law in family matters. I use the word 'defence' deliberately, because the role of law in family matters, and the institutions of law, have come under sustained attack in recent times — a climate that governments concerned to reduce the costs of running a family justice system have been keen to promote. It is suggested that family disputes are only exacerbated by law's involvement, and that the legal system consistently fails to deliver 'justice' to the parties who pass through it. These arguments are heard more and more frequently, and I suspect that they have yet to reach the peak of their intensity. Yet it is not often that one hears the case in reply — the case, that is, for law, and for the values of procedural fairness and legality, that go with it....

I have identified four ways in which the assumptions, objectives or techniques of family law have been modified or displaced since the 1970s. These are:

- [T]he displacement of marriage as the central concept linking law to families, and the growth in the importance of other concepts such as cohabitation or parenthood;
- [A] reduced reliance on discretionary decision-making to more rule-like statutory provisions;

- [A] diversification in the sources of family law norms [including private ordering and human rights]; and
- [T]he fragmentation of the family law system itself.

After reviewing these developments in detail, Dewar concluded:

> [F]amily law should become, and should be celebrated as, what Marc Galanter has called 'a second form of politics,' which 'provides resources and opportunities for the pursuit of our compelling commitments.'
>
> But the form of politics offered by law, and by family law, is distinctive, and here we come to why I think family law, and family lawyers, have a major role to play in debates around the family.... As already noted, family issues are perhaps the ones that generate more passion, intensity of feeling and disagreement than any other. It is a realm in which big ideas are at play, where the passions are engaged and in which the stakes are high for us all. One of the virtues of legal debate is that it calls us back to the level of practicality or functionality — the question, in other words, of what will work. Law's uniqueness, and perhaps its great achievement, lies in its ability to provide a context for what Cass Sunstein calls 'incompletely theorized agreements.' This is what happens when 'people diverge on some (relatively) high-level proposition, [but] might be able to agree when they lower the level of abstraction.'
>
> ... [T]his 'lowering of the level of abstraction' is the very stuff of legal reasoning, and plays a vital role in securing the legitimacy of a political system against a background of a radical division of opinion. By providing a bridge between the world of ideas and large scale social projects on one hand, and the world of strategies and practices on the other, law opens up space for agreement where none might have existed before. This, I suggest, is the distinctive contribution of lawyers to family disputes, at both an individual and collective level. By shifting the focus to the practical or the functional, legal discourse helps us to find common ground. Indeed, given the level and intensity of disagreement about family issues, it may be our only hope.

References

Marc Galanter, "Law Abounding: Legalisation around the North Atlantic" (1992) 55 *Modern Law Review* 1.

Cass Sunstein, *Legal Reasoning and Political Conflict* (Oxford: Oxford University Press, 1996).

Additional Resources

Alison Dicluck, "What is Family Law For?" (2011) 64:1 Current Leg Probs 287.

John Eekelaar, "'Not of the Highest Importance': Family Justice under Threat" (2011) 33:4 J Soc Welfare & Fam L 311.

Case Index

This index includes only cases the author considers significant.